ORGANIZATION AND PATHOLOGY OF THOUGHT

Austen Riggs Foundation Monograph

Number One

ORGANIZATION AND PATHOLOGY OF THOUGHT

Selected Sources

TRANSLATION AND COMMENTARY BY

DAVID RAPAPORT

COLUMBIA UNIVERSITY PRESS

New York and London

Copyright 1951 Columbia University Press

First printing 1951
Fourth printing 1965

Printed in the United States of America

To My Parents

PREFACE

THE KNOWLEDGE that thinking has conquered for humanity is vast, yet our knowledge of thinking is scant. It might seem that thinking eludes its own searching eye. But this may be an illusion, and the eye is perhaps not searching but only staring, or is even blind, as legend has the divining Homer and Ossian; perhaps thinking is reverie, and it is luck that rewards the richly dreaming mind. But the truth would seem to lie somewhere in the middle, between a continuous searching and the blind abandon of dreams, between disciplined quest and the lucky find. Heraclitus said: "If you do not expect the unexpected, you will not find it." Pasteur said: "Luck rewards only the prepared mind." Whatever its nature, thinking comes to the point of invention, discovery, and creation only in some human beings; it serves most of us merely to the point of—at best—understanding what the few have created. And yet the dream-stuff out of which world-changing thought is made is present in all of us, in the sentence-fragments of the brain-injured, in the delusions of the schizophrenic, and in the babbling of the child. This is its enigma.

Repeated experiences of this enigma seem to have set me to thinking about thinking. One is particularly clear in my memory: an algebra class in high school; the Professor is at the blackboard, deducing a theorem; he pauses before the next step and I try to anticipate it—unsuccessfully; he continues, and I understand. Disappointed and puzzled, I ask myself why I cannot foretell the step, when it is so self-evident after I see it done. I must have asked this question in a dim way countless times before, when impressed and hurt in pride by adult omniscience. But I have asked it continuously ever since: the attendant shame and bitterness may have faded; the curiosity and puzzlement have not.

This compilation of papers may or may not seem justified by the Introduction. Its subjective justification is that these papers, when I encountered them, seemed to explain part of the enigma, and so I became fond of them. To me they still seem like gems, even if some are "in the rough." To my mind they grasp and convey something about thinking, even if often what they grasp and how they convey it does not constitute scientific, tested knowledge, and if often we do not yet possess even the methods to test them. The determined effort of our time to produce unassailably tested knowledge—an effort which is the midwife to a majority of the papers that fill our literature—too often ties us to piecemeal pursuits. In their freedom of speculation and breadth of vision, these papers are a refreshing release from such standards for "tested knowledge," however important.

But not only *what* these papers taught seemed important to me. Most of them have a human touch which gives a particular validity to thought, often in abeyance where rigorous scientific proof holds sway. Some of these papers, or at least their concepts, are often quoted but rarely read; thus the true nature of their concepts and the very flavor of their thoughts are lost. None of this may be important where concepts have reached a final definiteness, and science the formula-certainty of tested knowledge, but it seems all-important in a phase where neither of these has been achieved. Silberer referred to science in this phase as "the mythological form of knowledge," and it does not seem yet that psychology in general has outgrown it.

The desire to rescue some of these papers from oblivion has prompted me to assume the slow labors of translation.

The papers originally in German were translated by me; Claparède's paper was translated by my wife, Elvira Rapaport; for the first draft of the translation of Piaget's chapter, I am indebted to Mr. Walter Kass. Both translations and comments owe their final form to my wife, and to my friends, William Gibson and Merton Gill, who have thought through and recast every sentence; my wife in addition checked all the translations against the originals. Where the text still remains unsatisfactory, it is because of my insistences. My friends, Margaret Brenman and Roy Schafer, who read parts of the manuscript, helped me with their suggestions.

I wish to acknowledge here the devoted help of Mrs. Ruth Shippey, my secretary, in completing the manuscript, as well as the aid of Miss Alice F. Raymond, librarian, Miss Martha Sloane, assistant librarian, Mrs. Frances Marias, Mrs. Helen Henderson, Mrs. Marjorie Reder, and Mrs. Dorothy Bergen, secretaries of the Riggs Foundation.

To the Menninger Foundation, and particularly to Dr. Karl A. Menninger, Dr. William C. Menninger, and the late John R. Stone, I am indebted for many years of stimulating work; to the Macy Foundation and its Medical Director, Dr. Frank Fremont-Smith, for aid in two previous studies of which this is an organic outgrowth; to the Riggs Foundation and its directors, Dr. Robert P.

Knight and Dr. Edgerton McC. Howard, for the leisure and facilities which permitted its preparation.

I had hoped that this volume would be published simultaneously with that of my teacher, Paul von Schiller, which was to rescue from oblivion some little-known European studies in the instinctual behavior of animals. But Paul von Schiller is dead, and I can only acknowledge again my indebtedness to him.

D. RAPAPORT

ACKNOWLEDGMENTS

GRATEFUL ACKNOWLEDGMENT is made to the following individuals and publishers for permission to include in this volume papers of which they control the copyright: Dr. Lauretta Bender, for *On the Development of Thoughts*, and *Studies Concerning the Psychology and Symptomatology of General Paresis*, by Paul Schilder; Dr. Karl Buehler, for *On Thought Connections*; Mrs. Otto Fenichel, for *On the Psychology of Boredom*, by Otto Fenichel; Dr. Anna Freud, and Mr. Ernst Freud, for *Formulations Regarding the Two Principles in Mental Functioning, A Note upon the "Mystic Writing-Pad,"* and *Negation*, by Sigmund Freud; Dr. Heinz Hartmann, for *Ego Psychology and the Problem of Adaptation*, and *On Parapraxes in the Korsakow Psychosis*; Dr. Ernst Kris, and *The Psychoanalytic Quarterly*, for *On Preconscious Mental Processes*; Mrs. Kurt Lewin, for *Comments Concerning Psychological Forces and Energies, and the Structure of the Psyche*, and *Intention, Will and Need*, by Kurt Lewin; Harvard University Press, for *Principal Factors Determining Intellectual Evolution from Childhood to Adult Life*, by Jean Piaget; International Universities Press for excerpts from Eugen Bleuler, *Dementia Praecox or the Group of Schizophrenias*; The Macmillan Company, for *The Psychology of Daydreams*, by J. Varendonck.

I am indebted to Dr. Buehler, to Dr. Kris, and to Dr. Hartmann, for reading and giving helpful advice concerning my translation and commentary of their papers. I am also indebted to Mrs. Lewin and to Dr. Fritz Heider for the advice they have given me on the translations of Kurt Lewin's papers.

D. R.

CONTENTS

PART ONE

INTRODUCTION

INTRODUCTION

I

THIS SOURCEBOOK attempts to bring together material on comparatively neglected aspects of the organization and pathology of thinking. For the most part it is limited to writings which are at present not readily accessible to the English-speaking, professional public concerned with the theory of thinking.

The selections were drawn from three different sources: psychology, psychiatry, and psychoanalysis. Most of them are not in the focus of attention, even in their own field. I hope that the volume may contribute to bringing the thinking of these three disciplines closer to each other.

The conception of thought-process which this selection of papers and my comments imply is an extremely—though, I hope, not meaninglessly—broad one. It considers thought-processes primarily from the point of view of their motivation; it broadens the customary concept of thought to include other processes, conscious and unconscious, which occur as integral parts of the process by which motivation finds its outlet in action; it assumes that thought-processes are an aspect of most psychological processes. It is possible that such a concept of thought-processes is too general and therefore might not be tenable in the long run because it would come to include all of psychology. Nevertheless it seems desirable at this time to collect some of the material concerning normal and pathological phenomena of thought which would, without such a broad motivational concept, remain outside the structure of psychological theory. Psychoanalysis appears to contain the outlines of such a broad motivational theory of thinking.

Such a theory would encompass in a unitary framework all forms of consciousness, remembering and forgetting, perceiving (in so far as it is not limited to sensory physiology), unconscious thought-processes (such as those underlying the dream, symbolism, and so on), fantasy-thinking (such as that seen in daydreams, in the thinking of preliterates and children), imagery, hypnagogic hallucinations, ordered everyday thinking, logical thinking, exact scientific thinking, productive and creative thinking both in the sciences and the arts, as well as the pathological variants of each. In one way or another, most of these are touched on in the papers and comments of this volume.

II

A sketch of some aspects of the development of psychology, psychiatry, and psychoanalysis may make clear the need which I hope this volume will help fill.

In the past few decades, *psychology* has become much concerned with motivation and personality. Nevertheless, it has paid little attention to the mediation-processes through which "personality structure" and "motivation" translate themselves into action or, more broadly, behavior. Thought-processes, in the wider sense, have been little studied. Even in the field of memory, where, following Lewin's and Zeigarnik's lead, the role of motivation and personality has been more consistently studied than in other fields of thought-organization, the investigations did not persist to the point of conclusive results. The reasons for this lie partly in the subtlety of the processes in question, which defy the methods of exploration used, and partly in the lack of a comprehensive theoretical framework, however speculative. In the last few years, the relation of perception to motivation and personality has been shifting closer to the center of attention. Here too the mediation-processes have so far been little regarded.

In the *psychiatry* of Kraepelin and Bleuler, thought-disorders were carefully considered—even though only phenomenologically. With the advent of dynamic psychiatry the focus of attention shifted to thought-content, and interest in the formal characteristics of thought-processes faded. Freud, whose influence effected this change, did not intend it. Chapter VII of *The Interpretation of Dreams* and his papers on metapsychology stand as landmarks of his continuing interest in thought-organization. In a footnote to the eighth edition of the former he commented: "Formerly I found it extraordinarily difficult to accustom my readers to the distinction between the manifest dream-content and the latent dream-thoughts. Over and over again arguments and objections were adduced from the uninterpreted dream as it was retained in the memory, and the necessity of interpreting the dream was ignored. But now, when the analysts have at least become reconciled to substituting for the manifest dream its meaning as found by interpretations, many of them are guilty of another mistake, to which they adhere just as stubbornly. They look for the essence of the dream in this latent content, and thereby overlook the distinction between latent dream-thoughts and the dream-work. The dream is fundamentally nothing more than a special *form* of thinking, which is made possible by the conditions of the sleeping state. It is the dream-work which produces this form, and it alone is the essence of dreaming—the only explanation of its singularity." In clinical psychological testing, which obviously deals with thought-*products*, the interest in the thought-*processes* underlying them was, until recently, minimal. On the one hand, mechanical conclusions from scores as to nosological categories and traits and types of personality, and on the other, inferences from *thought-contents* as to "dynamics," were and are still accepted practice, in disregard of the thought-processes mediating these connections. The same problem holds in the work of the clinical psychiatrist. The psychiatric examination and case history are admirable tools in the hand of the experienced clinician. But their limitations are also admittedly great: they use general characteristics of life history, thought-contents, and empathic observations as the basis for judging pathology and personality. Yet between the processes termed personality and its disorders on the one hand, and observational data on the other, there are mediating thought-processes. The responsibility for the expression of the personality in observational and test data is not equally shared by all those processes which are subsumed under the construct, personality; the thought-processes bear a greater and more direct share. These thought-processes do not always reveal themselves in contents, nor are the contents communicated by the subject individually characteristic outside of a certain range. There is accumulating evidence, some of which is discussed in this volume, that to know more about the individuality of thought we must better understand the *formal characteristics* of thought-processes.

The last few decades in *psychoanalysis* have been marked by a growth of interest in defenses and ego-functions, in addition to the previously paramount interest in id-contents and id-mechanisms. Besides the drive-motivations which proved so revealing in the study of forgetting, slips, and so on, ego-motivations have been studied. This has opened the way for the study of ordered thinking (secondary process), in addition to the previous exclusive concern with the primary process. Hartmann and Kris, who were outstanding among the pioneers of these developments, realized and stressed that much of the study necessary for the understanding of these processes would have to take place outside the psychoanalyst's office, in developmental, other observational, and experimental investigations. The theory of thought-processes is a crucial segment of ego-psychology, and the growth of ego-psychology depends in part therefore on their exploration.

This sketch of the conditions in the three disciplines concerned with thinking may serve as background to appraise the need for a broad theory of thinking. Such a theory is necessary for both the clinician and the experimental investigator. The clinician needs it because once a theory is available, however tentative and vague, he will find it easier to capture and communicate the wealth of observations concerning thought-processes which he makes every day; and he needs all the theory he can get to make sense of the material he obtains from his patients. The experimenter needs it to have meaningful and relevant hypotheses which he can test. In the absence of a systematized theory, such concepts as repression, regression, projection, are now taken out of their context and treated piecemeal. It is therefore not surprising if the experimental results are entirely irrelevant to whatever theory we have, or their relevance remains unclear. Since theories grow only in interaction with relevant new data, the prevailing situation also hampers the development of the theory. There is an urgent need to break this vicious circle.

III

This volume attempts to call attention to some little-used methods of investigation important in studying thought-processes.

The psychology of thinking at present not only fails to encompass the entire range of phenomena of thinking and lacks an integrated theory; it also is wanting in the variety of methods of investigation it uses. The prevalent methods are problem-solving and concept-formation, supplemented by a small assortment of test studies. Studies following Piaget's methods, or novel ones like those which approach thinking from the viewpoint of language, are rare. It is interesting to note that of the more than 5,000 entries in the 1948 *Psychological Abstracts*, only about 50 are classified under thinking, and of these a considerable part are concept-formation and test studies.

In this volume a variety of methods is represented; they vary both in the state of consciousness used for the study and in the technique applied. The states of consciousness include dream states (Nachmansohn), hypnotic states (Ach, Schroetter, Roffenstein, Nachmansohn), hypnagogic states (Silberer,

Varendonck), the great variety of states observed in paretic and amnesic syndrome cases (Betlheim and Hartmann, Schilder, Buerger-Prinz and Kaila), and others. The techniques applied include comparison of behavior and introspection (Ach), introspection in the performance of tasks (Buehler, Silberer), free association (Fenichel), self-recording of daydreams (Varendonck), dream suggestion (Schroetter, Roffenstein, Nachmansohn), story-recall (Schilder, Betlheim and Hartmann), recognition (Claparède), analysis of spontaneous productions (Claparède, Buehler, Schilder), Piaget's methods of exploration by controlled conversation, and Lewin's methods, such as resumption and recall of interrupted tasks, substitution, satiation, and isolation. My comments in the footnotes contain references to many others. The application of Egon Brunswik's systematic sampling of design to the problems of thinking, would require a far greater awareness of the techniques available than is the case at present.

The material which would fit into the stated purpose of this volume is so extensive that it was difficult to make a selection, and much has been omitted. I should like to list those omissions which I regret most: (a) Chapter VII of Freud's *The Interpretation of Dreams*, the richest source of the psychoanalytic theory of thinking, which I omitted because of its availability in English; (b) parts of Selz's (679) * volumes, containing discussions of "anticipations" in thinking, because they would have required selections so extensive as to exceed their usefulness; (c) Lewin's (460) fundamental study of the role of "readiness" in thought-organization, because of difficulties both of terminology and extent; (d) Poetzl's (573) study of repression in the course of tachistoscopic perception, because of the difficulty of rendering the associative connections in English; (e) Allers and Teller's (21) study on the recapture of lost memories in the intervals between stimulus and reaction on an association test, because of similar difficulties; (f) parts of Bartlett's (37) penetrating study of the role of attitudes in memory-organization, because of its availability. My regrets are the greater because these six studies represent six different methods (clinical, concept-forming and problem-solving experimental, association-experimental, tachistoscopic-perceptual, testing, and various memory-experimental) of studying thought-organization.

No classic associationist, conditioned-reflex, or conditioned-response contribution is included. They are seldom referred to even in my comments. The

* Numbers in parentheses refer to the Bibliography, throughout.

reasons for this are: (a) my bias that these learning theories contribute little to a theory of thinking; (b) they are readily available, and my purpose was to gather those contributions which have received little attention; (c) I wished to avoid polemics in my comments. I did not include any Gestalt-literature, but it is referred to extensively in my comments.

IV

My original purpose in making comments on these papers was to set them into their historical context and relate them to present-day theories and observations. I also hoped to illumine the importance these papers seem to me to have. A subsidiary purpose was to clarify implications which a true translation cannot make explicit. The wish to translate the author's thought unchanged often led to a struggle between fidelity to letter and to spirit; where I could not serve the latter without violating the former, I commented. As I went along, I found it necessary to comment where I did not understand or saw the point differently from the author. I also found myself increasingly inclined to relate the various papers to each other and particularly to the framework of the psychoanalytic theory of thinking, as I understand it. Finally, the more involved I became in the work, the less I found it possible to exclude those concepts which to my mind seem particularly important for a future theory of thinking: such as states of consciousness, hierarchy of motivating forces, autonomy of the levels of thought-organization, anticipations, and channels of communication. I attempted, particularly in the last chapter, to extract the common theoretical implications of the material contained in the papers collected here. I believe these papers contain fragments of a theory to come, in the center of which will stand the psychoanalytic theory of thinking. I tried to cull these fragments from the papers, speculating freely, attempting not to impose a scheme on the material, and trying to indicate the areas awaiting empirical investigation.

The overlapping of ideas in the various papers and my effort to point out connections between them made some repetitiousness unavoidable, though I have tried to minimize it. I can only hope that, instead of being wasteful and tedious, the repetitiousness will emphasize the connections.

At times, the comments are not directly relevant to the theory of thought-organization. I made such comments when I felt that to enlarge on the context and give a number of pertinent references would be helpful to those readers particularly interested in a specific point.

One of the main difficulties in these comments arose from the fact that the material is divided among psychological, psychiatric, and psychoanalytic sources. I made an attempt to facilitate the reading of each kind for those accustomed to the terminology and thinking prevailing in the other two. I fear that many comments will be restatements of common knowledge to those versed in the topic, while they remain insufficiently explanatory to others.

v

The papers of this volume are organized into five groups: Directed Thinking, Symbolism, Motivation of Thinking, Fantasy Thinking, and Pathology of Thinking. This division was not preconceived, but rather indicates how "the chips have fallen."

The papers grouped under Directed Thinking—a title borrowed from Humphrey's inspiring book—originate in academic psychology. They are not a homogeneous group; the distance between Lewin on the one hand, and Ach and Buehler on the other, is as great as that between either of them and Claparède or Piaget, who are closer to clinical thinking than to experiment. Furthermore, one of Piaget's and much of Lewin's two papers are theoretical; the others report observations and experiments. Piaget's other paper has already appeared in English, but is little-known and seems important enough to reprint. The omission of Gestalt-psychological material (Wertheimer, Duncker, Maier, Katona, Harrower) makes a definite gap, as does that of Tolman's three recent papers. Some will miss material on the relation of language and thought, such as that by Delacroix and others.

The papers on Symbolism came to fill up a section, perhaps disproportionately large. The topic has aroused more experimental interest than any other problem raised by the psychoanalytic theory of thinking, except repression. (I have included no paper on repression. In my *Emotions and Memory* I culled the material on it published up to 1940. Though I now consider the treatment I then presented unsatisfactory, since it generally disregards considerations of ego-psychology, I did not feel that I could devote space to repression in this volume. It is touched on repeatedly in the next section, Motivation of Thinking, and I have referred in my comments to the reviews of the experimental work published since 1940.) These papers on symbolism are in a sense experimental. I regret that I could not include a selection from Cassirer's penetrating "Philosophie der Symbolischen Formen," but it was too difficult to find a self-contained selection which did not include excessive philosophical discussion.

Selecting the papers grouped under Motivation of Thought, representing the psychoanalytic theory of thinking, was the most difficult. Without Freud's, it would have been without foundation. I decided to reprint three selections by him even though they are available in English, and to use the footnotes to gather the other important statements of his theory of thinking. Stekel's paper is included to give a sense of the nature of thought as the average practicing analyst, without psychological-theoretical sophistication, observes it. Including this paper was a concession to my own feelings, in a way against my better judgment: many years ago some of its ideas opened new vistas for me. In this section more than in any other I felt compelled to elaborate on the concepts and theory, because it seemed that, without a general theoretical background, these papers would be harder to master than any of the others. Hartmann's paper was a matter of special concern. It both deals directly with problems of thinking and sets them in the framework of ego-psychology. This material is, however, embedded in an embarrassing wealth of other considerations. I am indebted to Dr. Hartmann for his consent to make a selection. Even so, much which may not seem immediately pertinent was retained, both as important background material and to maintain the paper's continuity. Kris's paper in the next section would have been just as relevant in this one, so an arbitrary placement had to be made.

The section on Fantasy-Thinking includes papers on preconscious thinking, autism, and the daydream. The term "fantasy-thinking" is taken from Freud's introduction to Varendonck's *The Psychology of Daydreams:* "I think it is advisable, when establishing a distinction between the different modes of thought-activity, not to utilize the relation to consciousness in the first instance, and to designate the daydream, as well as the chains of thought studied by Varendonck, as freely wandering or fantastic thinking [Varendonck's translation of "phantasierendes Denken," which I prefer to translate as "fantasy-thinking"] in opposition to intentionally directed reflection. At the same time it should be taken into consideration that even fantastic thinking is not invariably in want of an aim and end-representations" (p. 10). The Bleuler papers, though the source of the widely used concept of autism, are seldom read. The Varendonck selection is taken from a volume which, though published in English, has long been out of print; it is included here not so much for its intrinsic value, but rather as the only study of the daydream as a thought-process. Kris's paper presents the psychoanalytic theory of preconscious mental processes, and thereby gives a theoretical background to the other papers in the section. I regret that I could not include his papers on art, which are important contributions to our field. I have referred to them in the footnotes to his paper.

The section on the Pathology of Thinking is perhaps the least satisfactory. Many other papers in this volume bear on it. The extensive, though rarely searching, studies in the pathology of thinking by tests and experiments, reported in the last two decades, have been disregarded except for footnote comments and references. A rather extensive survey of such test studies by Mr. Martin Mayman will be found in our *Diagnostic Psychological Testing*. The extensive literature on thought-disorders due to brain lesions (Pick, Goldstein, Gelb, Poppelreuter, Schilder) is represented only by Schilder and by Buerger-Prinz and Kaila. The whole literature on language and its disturbances was disregarded, mainly because of my lack of knowledge in this field. The thought-disorders of the functional psychoses, though in many ways quite familiar to present-day psychopathology, are nowhere systematically treated in the literature. Even in Bleuler's classic monograph on schizophrenia, I had difficulty in selecting a section purely on thought-disorder, though it was his declared purpose to treat of it; Storch's important paper on archaic thinking in schizophrenia concerns itself exclusively with the thought-content. I do not know a single paper in which the manic's flight of ideas is systematically treated as a thought-process, except Liepmann's *Ueber Ideenflucht*—a not very satisfactory study. I could have used Stransky's *Ueber Sprachverwirrtheit*, on producing flight of ideas in normal people by distraction, but my attempt to translate it met prohibitive language difficulties. The thought-disorders in neuroses are not represented. I have discussed the amnesias and related phenomena in *Emotions and Memory*, and therefore reluctantly forego dealing with them here. The clinical material on obsessions and phobias has not been systematically treated in terms of the theory of thinking, though psychoanalysis has dealt with it in terms of content and dynamics. The thought-disorders in other neuroses are discussed frequently, if indirectly, in the psychoanalytic selections and my comments.

VI

The job of translation itself was a problem. At times insurmountable difficulties were encountered in translating into English, which favors terse directness, the sensitive or circumstantial language of the German psychologies of the early part of the century, which aimed at nuance of meaning, fine shades of certainty, and a wealth of multi-layered connotations. Those who helped me with the language of the final text sided, in general, with the English; they strove to break down involved sentences, eliminate differences in shading that made no difference in English, express directly what was implied, and avoid those ambiguities which the English ear hears as vagueness rather than richness. I found myself, in general, siding with the author, his connotations, style, and diction. The result is an uneven compromise, in which the central meaning of the authors came out best, and the English second-best; where these considerations tolerated it, the style and connotations of the authors were preserved, but by no means as often as I wished. I believe this to be a definite loss.

A word about the omissions from the selections seems necessary. Considerations both of space and of pertinence to the topic of the volume played a role. I often retained sections not directly pertinent, when they seemed particularly characteristic of the author's thinking, or when their omission would have broken up the continuity of the paper. I have summarized all the more extensive or more interesting omissions in the footnotes.

The authors' own footnotes appear among mine, marked by asterisks alongside the numbers. The use of reduced type and of italics in the original papers was not followed. The authors' paragraphing was for the most part adhered to, though at times with misgivings.

PART TWO

DIRECTED THINKING

CHAPTER I

DETERMINING TENDENCIES; AWARENESS [1]

By Narciss Ach

I. THE EFFECTS OF POST-HYPNOTIC SUGGESTION

THE EXPERIMENTAL FINDINGS of G. E. Mueller and A. Pilzecker were the first to shatter the view of association-psychology that the train of ideas is governed solely by associative reproduction-tendencies. They have shown that perseverating reproduction-tendencies also may determine the contents of consciousness, and may under certain conditions even become dominant.

1. This is a part of the fourth chapter of Ach's (15) monograph. It contains most (pp. 187–239) of the first three sections of that chapter.

The first chapter, on "Method," deals with the problems of the experimental investigation of acts of will, the method of systematic experimental self-observation, and the experimental setup Ach used. The experiments reported in the monograph were undertaken to shed light on the relation of acts of will to thinking. They use the method of reaction-experiment; the subject is exposed to discrete stimuli, is instructed to react to these, and his reaction time is measured. In these experiments Ach obtained systematic records of his subjects' introspections in the preparatory period (between the instruction and the stimulus), in the main period (between the stimulus and the reaction), and in the after-period (following the reaction). Of the method of systematic self-observation—indispensable for any psychology of thinking—Ach writes:

Systematic experimental self-observation has however no value if one does not succeed in inducing, by means of alterations of the experimental set-up and instructions, a change of subjective experience corresponding to the purpose of the experiment. By means of varying the external conditions, control of the data obtained in self-observation must be achieved. Therefore the choice both of experimental set-up and of self-observations is of crucial significance for the results (p. 25).

On systematic self-observation, cf. Ziehen (787); also Lewin (460), and Lewin, Chap. 4, note 49*, below.

The second chapter reports experiments in which the instructions unequivocally define what the reaction of the subject should be ("unequivocally coordinated reactions"—or, in the terminology of Postman, 579 and 582, "single set reactions"). Ach used simple, multiple, and conditional coordinations (Postman's "multiple set reactions"), as well as associative reactions.

The third chapter reports experiments

The investigations reported in this volume indicate that, besides these associative and perseverative reproduction-tendencies, there is yet another factor of decisive influence on the emerging state of consciousness:[2] the determining tendency. Determining tendencies arise from the specific content of the goal-presentation, and define the state of consciousness so that it accords with the meaning of the goal-presentation.[3] These determining tendencies are the basis

---

in which coordination of stimulus and reaction was not unequivocally defined by the instructions. Ach used two setups. In the first, the subject was presented simultaneously with more than one stimulus, to each of which a specific reaction was coordinated; but he was instructed to give only one reaction. Thus the subject had to choose the stimulus to which to react ("reactions without coordinated stimuli"). In the second setup, numbers were presented as stimuli and the subject was to choose whether to add, subtract, multiply or divide them ("reactions without coordination of activity"). The experiments of this chapter involve choices, and provide therefore more explicit opportunity to study acts of will than those in the second chapter.

The fourth chapter, selections from which are translated here, reports some experiments using post-hypnotic suggestions, but is in the main devoted to drawing theoretical inferences. Though the concepts which Ach uses here—"awareness," "determining tendency," "intention," and *Einstellung*—are abundantly referred to in the English literature, the source-material has not been translated and has been little read. For detailed discussions of Ach's experiments, see Titchener (730), Koffka (406), and Boring (83).

2. Ach actually means, "another factor which has a determining influence on what will come to consciousness." He

uses the term "state of consciousness" to avoid speaking of "ideas," since the content of consciousness may be an "awareness" also. Therefore the term is used here in another sense than in our comments.

3. Clearly, the goal-presentation— that is, the task (*Aufgabe*)—is considered here as the source of the "determining tendency" and of its representation in consciousness: the "state of consciousness" or "awareness." "Determining tendency" (a specific form of the *Einstellungen* of the Wuerzburg school) may be considered either a regulative directional principle or a dynamic organizing force. The "set"—its equivalent in American psychology—has been considered variously in either role. Gibson's (269) thorough review of the concept amply demonstrates this. Lewin's intention—quasi-need—tension-system theory is of the dynamic variety. (See Chap. 5, note 30, below.) It is clear that Lewin does not derive the dynamic directive solely from the goal-presentation or goal-intention. He coordinates with it a tension-system and a quasi-need, which he in turn relates to a "genuine" stable need. It is difficult to conceive how a goal-idea could give rise to a force, unless in arising it "triggers" a force, or the formulation is meant only as a paraphrase of "the goal-idea arises as a conscious representative of a force." (Cf. Freud, Chap. 15, notes 14 and 29, below.) In the

of psychological phenomena long described as will-activity.[4] The psychological processes that occur in the wake of suggestions are the most striking examples of these. Suggestions may become effective in the hypnotic state, or in a subsequent state of consciousness, either normal or hypnotic.[5]

The literature reports many post-hypnotic suggestions demonstrating the existence of determining tendencies.[6]* Since they were given mostly for therapeutic reasons, I reinvestigated them in a fashion similar to my other experiments, carefully considering the psychological situation of the subject. The procedure was unknown to the subject.

The following suggestion was given to Subject G. in deep hypnosis: "Later on I will show you two cards with two numbers on each. To the first card you will react with the sum, to the second with the difference of the numbers. When the card appears you will immediately, and of your own will, say the correct number, without thinking of what I have now told you." [7] This suggestion was

post-hypnotic suggestions reported here by Ach, in the operation of sets in everyday life, and in experiments on sets operating in incidental learning (Postman, 582), the goal-idea may be entirely absent from consciousness while the set operates. Gibson (269) comments: ". . . [the set] cannot even be assumed to be aroused by self-instructions, since it may be unverbalized and may even be unconscious" (p. 813).

Gibson (269) traces meticulously the contradictions and confusions surrounding the use of the "set" concept. For a dynamic theory of thinking and personality, the problem of set presents itself primarily under two headings: (a) Supposing the set is a dynamic determiner of thought and behavior—what then are its sources of energy and the conditions under which these energies become structured to yield quasi-permanent sets? (b) Supposing the set is a form in which motivation becomes effective—what then is its place in the hierarchy of motivations and motivation-effecting quasi-

permanent mechanisms (such as interests, attitudes, values)? It seems that the concept of set lies near the point in this hierarchy where the gap between psychoanalytic and academic psychology may some day be bridged.

4. This is the old teleological conception of will. Cf. Knight (390) for a deterministic dynamic conception.

5. Erickson and Erickson (163) have offered evidence that the state in which post-hypnotic suggestions are carried out is always attended by a reestablishment of the trance state. In Ach's experiments the goal-suggestion appears to establish the determining tendency. What lends such hypnotic goal-suggestions their dynamic effectiveness is still not well understood; otherwise we should be nearer to understanding the dynamics of determining tendencies and sets. Concerning a motivational theory of hypnosis, see White (767), Brenman and Gill (88), Rapaport (591, pp. 172 ff.).

6.* Cf. Forel (192, pp. 91 ff.).

7. In Ach's terminology these are un-

repeated and, on request of the subject, its content retold. Thereupon G. was awakened from hypnosis. In order to make the procedure appear as natural as possible and to avoid the appearance of suggestion, I had already shown the cards to G. before the hypnosis, "incidentally" explaining, as it were, their use. Having terminated the hypnosis we went to another room, and after a few minutes of indifferent conversation I showed G. a card with the numbers 6/2. G. immediately said, "8." To the second card, 4/2, he immediately said, "2." The suggestion was, surprisingly, realized. I asked G.—showing him the first card—"Why did you say 8?" "Just happened to say it." "Did you not think at the moment that this is the sum?" "No. I had the need to say 8." "How about this one?" (showing the second card). "It was just accidental that I said 2." "But this is not accidental!" "I had to say that." "Didn't you think that $4 - 2 = 2$?" "No." [8]

In order to allay the suspicion that a suggested amnesia might play a role here, I repeated this experiment, adding the following suggestion: "When questioned, you will be able to describe the experience exactly." The determination by the hypnotic suggestion was again manifest. The suggestion was to give the difference on the first card and the sum on the second. After hypnosis, the instant reaction to card 6/3 was "3"; to card 4/1, "5." Again the subject realized only later that the numbers he spoke were the difference and the sum. The experiment misfired only once: before reacting, the subject repeated the instruction itself. That is, to card 6/3 the subject said, "The sum is 9"; to card 4/1, "The difference is 3." The explanation is that in this case the suggestion was given not in precise form, but as follows: "Upon seeing the first card you will give the sum, upon seeing the second the difference." Indeed, this instruction was followed. A further experiment, using the precisely worded suggestion, yielded the usual results. . . .[9]

The results are similar in the case of the following suggestion: "I will show you some numbers. To the first one, you will say the number that comes before it in the number-continuum, to the second the number that follows it.

---

equivocally coordinated reactions; in that of Postman (579 and 582) they are two isolated simultaneous single sets.

8. This is a simple demonstration that ordered thought-processes may take place without attendant consciousness.

Cf. Kris (429), Chap. 23, this volume, on preconscious thinking; see also M. Prince (584) on co-conscious ideation.

9. Such literalness of hypnotic behavior is commonly seen. M. Erickson has called particular attention to it.

When you see the number, you will utter the correct number, of your own free will and without delay." G. repeats the instructions. A few minutes after hypnosis is terminated, he is shown the number 6 and answers immediately, "5." Now 6 is shown again and he answers immediately, "7." "What did you say after the first number?" "5." "Why?" "I don't know, it just came to my mind." "When I showed it to you the second time you said 7, why?" "I felt the need to say it, but I don't know why." Here, again, the idea corresponding to the meaning of the suggestion becomes directly over-valent. Executing a suggestion does not imply a mediation-process in which the number presented elicits the memory of the suggestion, due to which in turn the correct answer associatively arises. Rather, the determining tendency arising from the suggestion raises above the threshold of consciousness the idea which corresponds to the meaning of the suggestion.[10]

This also explains the effects of negative suggestion. In another experiment I added the suggestion: "You will be shown a third card, but that one you won't be able to see." When shown this third card, G. was silent, moved his head to and fro, trying to look at my hand more closely. "What do you see?" "It looks like you want to show me something." "What do I have in my hand?" "Nothing." G. saw my hand, but not the card it held. . . .

It would be desirable to conduct experiments with time measurements on post-hypnotic suggestions. So far I have not been in a position to do that. My previous reaction-experiments with time measurements, in hypnosis or in a state of systematically narrowed consciousness, led to no results.[11]*

10. This argument directed against association psychology is rather weak. It assumes that all associative mediation processes are conscious. There was no reason for association psychology to make such an assumption. It is not the absence from consciousness, but the directional character of the mediation, which associationism cannot account for. The next experiment with negative suggestions offers a clearer argument against association psychology, since its directional character cannot be disputed nor the result be attributed to association frequencies alone.

11.* See Ach (13).
[Of the authors in this volume, Schroetter (674), Roffenstein (614), and Nachmansohn (537) used hypnosis as their experimental tool. Other outstanding hypnotic experiments of significance for the dynamic psychology of thinking are Erickson's (161) on the psychopathology of everyday life, and Brenman's (88) on "tension-systems." The most sophisticated experimentation using hypnosis in perceptual problems was that of Benussi (44).]

II. CONCERNING DETERMINING TENDENCIES

The influence of determining tendencies has been demonstrated in striking and extreme form by post-hypnotic suggestions, but it can also be demonstrated in reaction-experiments, particularly in those without coordination of activity.[12] This reaction-form is quite variable. In these reaction-experiments there are five different ways in which the determining tendency arising from the goal-presentation manifests itself. The presentation to which the intention refers—in our case, the card with numbers—will henceforth be called referent-presentation.

(a) The goal-presentation was rarely reproduced at the time the referent-presentation appeared. When this happened, it was due to associative or perseverative reproduction-tendencies, and the goal-presentation had been in consciousness even in the preparatory period. With Subject B. this happened altogether three times, with C. only once. On these occasions . . . attention in the preparatory period was below its usual intensity.[13] (b) Besides its reappearance due to perseverative or associative reproduction, the goal-presentation became noticeable when it entered an *apperceptive fusion* with the appearing stimulus. The subject visualized a plus sign, and fitted the stimulus-numbers into the thus prepared schema.[14] The result issued associatively from this apperceptive

12. For the description of such experiments, see note 1, above.

13. The implication seems to be that the task—to add or to subtract—becomes explicitly conscious only when attention is poor, that is, when the subject is not entirely alert. It is a common experience that when tired or anxious, we bridle our wandering attention by focusing on the task with conscious effort (concentration). Gibson (269) has shown that intention and expectation (pp. 803–7) on the one hand, and attention (p. 793) on the other, are closely related to the problem of set. Rapaport *et al.* (602, 597) suggested that attention, concentration, and anticipation are various aspects of the preparation for the emergence and identifiability of an idea in consciousness

(602, I, 385 ff.) Concerning the concept of attention (that is, the relation of attention, hypercathexis, and consciousness), see Chap. 15, note 21, and Chap. 16, note 14, below.

14. Such "fusion" phenomena had already been reported by G. E. Mueller (526) and other association psychologists. Closer study of such phenomena may demonstrate them to belong to one continuum with the Freudian mechanism of "condensation." Cf. Postman and Bruner (578, p. 90) and Rapaport (591, pp. 237 ff.). The fusion-type (c) discussed by Ach is particularly interesting in this respect. Unlike the fusion with the "logical" addition-schema of the present example, it consists of a fusion with a "non-logical" pattern (the pulling to-

fusion. (c) The intention can be realized also by an apperceptive fusion between a presentation readied by it [15] and the referent-presentation. In Subject C., for instance, we note a spatial displacement of the two numbers that correspond to the intention. When the intention is to add, the two numbers pull closer together; when it is to subtract, the smaller number appears to sidle toward the larger. When the result coincides with one of the two numbers presented, it issues from this apperceptive fusion, either associatively or directly. (d) In a fourth set of experiments, we again encounter an apperceptive fusion. Upon perceiving the stimuli, presentations readied by the goal-presentation fuse with those associatively reproduced. This was characteristic of the behavior of Subject A. throughout. When this subject intended to add upon the appearance of 5/2, his intention manifested itself by the internal utterance, "5 and 2 make 7." This occurred repeatedly with C. and once with B. (e) Finally, determination arising from the intention may become effective, so that tendencies readied by the goal-presentation reinforce the reproduction-tendencies which issue from the referent-presentation and correspond to the meaning of the goal-presentation. In these cases, the correct presentation appears in consciousness *immediately* upon the apprehension of the stimuli (referent-presentations). This was the usual procedure of B., and occurred with C. on the last two experimental days. . . . It is characteristic of all forms of determination that their realization is in accord with the meaning of the goal-presentation, whether or not their means be apperceptive fusion or the raising of the intended result over the threshold of consciousness directly through the referent-presentation. Only a few experiments were exceptions to this. The results so far available suggest that in these cases the necessary intensity of intention was not present.[16] As already mentioned, the direct realization of the in-

---

gether of two numbers to be added, and the sidling of a smaller number to a larger from which it is to be subtracted): this pattern somehow represents the subject's internal (affective?) experience of addition and subtraction. Such image patterns, so frequent in thinking, may be the missing links between the formal-logical and the motivational structure of thought.

15. The "presentation readied" by the

intention is, in this example, the spatial displacement pattern. Ach interchanges here the terms "goal-presentation" and "intention."

16. K. Lewin's experiments (Chap. 5, below) indicate that conditions other than insufficient intensity of intention (for example, presence of contrary intentions) may also be responsible for the exceptions Ach found.

tention was most striking in post-hypnotic suggestions. But even in simple experiments without coordination of activity, it was usual with Subjects D. and E. that the number corresponding to the intention came directly to consciousness.

Thus the stimulus alone does not determine the content of consciousness that follows its appearance: the same numbers may be followed at various times by different ones, depending upon the intention. For example, 6/2 may be followed by 8, 4, or 3, according to whether the intention was to add, subtract, or divide.[17] *The same stimulus may lead to the reproduction of different presentations; in each case it is the presentation corresponding to the meaning of the intention which becomes over-valent.* It is due to determining tendencies that, of all the tendencies readied by the perception of the stimulus, those will become reinforced to over-valence which are associatively coordinated with a presentation corresponding to the given intention. . . .

There are yet other observations which indicate the decisive influence of determining tendencies arising from goal-presentations. When an intention to divide was followed by two numbers that would yield a fraction, the perception was accompanied by a state of surprise and an awareness of difficulty, connected with displeasure or with the immediate consciousness, "This doesn't work." No acoustic, kinesthetic, or other presentations occurred in these experiences. When, however, the calculation was easy, no awareness of difficulty or surprise was present. Such experiences were rather frequent. . . .

These observations indicate that the apperception and elaboration of the stimulus (referent-presentation) occur under influences corresponding to the meaning of the goal-presentation.[18] If we do not assume that from the goal-

17. This argument is most convincing where no coordination of activity was implied in the instructions. Concerning the possible argument of "self-instruction," see the reference to Gibson in note 3, above.

18. Ach demonstrated his point on successfully carried-out intentions arising in the course of the performance of simple tasks. Bruner demonstrated it in making successful performance difficult by tachistoscopic exposition of stimuli (578) and by pitting two intentions (sets) against each other (98). In his tachistoscopic experiment, latent, quasi-constant, subjective intentions—that is, values, attitudes—became manifest both in the content of the reactions and in the reaction times. In his other experiment, the interference of the two sets was clearly demonstrated. This method of pitting intentions against each other experimentally is one of the important techniques for the study of determination in thought-processes. See also Postman's (579) experiments on the role of

presentation specific influences arise which are directed toward the apperception of the referent-presentation, then we find no content in the preparatory
period of the examples here given which could explain this behavior upon perceiving the stimulus. Influences, arising from the goal-presentation and directed
toward the referent-presentation, which determine the course of events so as to
accord with the goal-presentation, are called determining tendencies. This term
does not imply anything as to the nature of these curious effects, and expresses
only the fact that mental happening is regulated by intentions, that is, goal-
presentations. The distinction of these tendencies from associative and perseverative reproduction-tendencies will be discussed later on.

*Thus, the ordered and goal-directed course of mental happening is the effect
of determining tendencies.* The independence of goal-directed mental happening from incidental external stimuli, and from the customary associative course
of presentations, is due to the influence of these determining tendencies. We
refer here to the fact of this independence, without discussing its limits. These
determining tendencies may issue not only from existing intentions but from
suggestive influences, from commands, and from tasks. Here we are concerned
only with the effect and not with the origin of these determining tendencies.[19]

The determining tendencies do more than merely establish an ordered goal-
directed course of mental happening. They insure a certain independence [for
the thought-process] by making possible the formation of new associations.
Even though we are bound to the perceived presentation-material, the determining tendencies enable us to bring it into new, previously non-existent, associative connections.

[Passage omitted.] [20]

---

sets in learning. The phenomena of parapraxes are also pertinent here. The latent
intentions (strivings) which come to the
fore in the parapraxes studied by Freud
(210) and elicited hypnotically by
Erickson (161) arise over contrary overt
intentions.

19. Ach conceived of "determining
tendencies" arising only from external
stimulation and instruction (*Aufgabe*).
Intrapsychic determining tendencies (attitudes, interests, sets) were outside of

his realm of observation and interest.
Therein lie the limitations of Ach's investigations. The "determining tendencies" can become a significant subject
matter in dynamic psychology only
when their intrapsychic roots are
studied. Cf. note 18, above; see also
Lewin, Chap. 5, notes 43 and 61, below.

20. The omitted section is devoted to
experiments with nonsense syllables designed to demonstrate the role of deter-

When the stimulus-syllable "mef" has elicited the reaction-syllable "lef," then these two syllables, never before associatively connected, have now acquired an associative bond. . . .[21]

In order to gain a better understanding of the effects of determining tendencies, it is important to analyze the concept of awareness. . . .

III. AWARENESS

Analyses of the contents of consciousness obtained by means of systematic experimental self-observation have shown a variety of experiences in which all of a complex content is simultaneously present in the form of a "knowledge." This knowledge exists in an imageless form, that is, no phenomenological components are demonstrable—neither visual, acoustic, nor kinesthetic sensations, nor their memory images—which would qualitatively define the content of this knowledge. We encountered such experiences in every subject in these experiments. *It is the presence of such imageless knowledge which we designate as awareness.*[22]

The content of such knowledge is given unequivocally and definitively, even though the manner in which it is given is not amenable to analysis. Immediately after the experience of this knowledge, the subject can state what he was aware of concerning it. Such awareness, therefore, is characterized by the knowledge it implies.[23] In our experiments, such experiences were most obvious in the content of expectation at the end of the preparatory period, and in the persev-

---

mining tendencies in the formation of new associations. The instructions used required the subject to form rhymes or alliterations to the nonsense syllables presented as stimuli.

21. According to Ach, the determining tendency responsible for this new association arises from the instruction to rhyme, and the subject's corresponding goal and intention. Just as in the drive-organization of memories (cf. Chap. 15, note 31, below), ideas are connected with each other in terms of a common motivational factor. The two differ in the nature of the motivational factors involved, and in the fact that the "determining tendencies" imply also a formal

link (in this case a rhyme) coupling the two ideas.

22. "Thought," in Buehler's terminology. See Chap. 2, below.

23. The "awarenesses" which Ach observed were apparently of a "knowledge" character; those which Buehler observed often involved "feeling" as well. It seems likely that here the preponderant "knowledge" character of "awareness" is related to the experimental setting and the material used. In everyday life, such "awarenesses" may be also of an abstract-directional or pure-feeling character; though never yet explored, these promise exciting adventures and rewards for their investigators.

erating contents of consciousness in the period following the experiment. Because we can direct our attention to this perseverating content as though it were a perceptual content, we can use it to obtain self-observations. In these, the process just experienced is present all at once—*in nuce*, as it were—without details or images. For example, in a none-too-habituated state of expectation,[24] one of the following complex contents is often simultaneously present as awareness: (a) The stimulus with its spatial determination; that is, the subject knows that an unequivocally determined change (the appearance of a white card) will occur at the spot he fixates on. (b) The subject is aware that this must be followed by a known and unequivocally determined change on his part (the reaction-movement). Also, a relationship between these two unequivocally determined changes is given, in the awareness that as soon as the stimulus appears the reaction-movement must follow. (d) The awareness has a temporal component, in the knowledge that the stimulus will appear within a certain known time-span. . . . Besides these directly given contents of the expectation, and the visual percept (in our case, the screen of the card-changer), the usual phenomena accompanying sensory attention are also present—such as tension-experiences in the upper half of the body and in the optical sense-organ. Occasionally some of these elements of the awareness-complex may appear in the form of images, particularly at the beginning of the preparatory period or in the first experiments of a day.[25] In this respect there are great individual differences, which are rooted in individual endowment. Yet in the majority of the experiments the whole expectation-content, excepting the accompanying phenomena,[26] is present only as imageless knowledge, which we call awareness.

24. It is characteristic of expectations (anticipations) and awarenesses to drop out as soon as the task which evokes them becomes habituated. Cf. Kris, Chap. 23, note 48, below. The process by which this happens is not yet understood. On its clarification hinges the understanding of the relationship of dynamic and static sets. Cf. Gibson's (269) discussion of sets vs. associative habits (pp. 788–89). If it could be demonstrated that habits arise by sets becoming specific, simplified, and autonomous, and that sets as well as attitudes arise similarly from more fundamental motivating forces and their controls, much of the confusion and vexing contradictions in this field would be settled.

25. Thus it appears that, as habituation increases, the reaction, which originally had been preceded by intervening images *and* awareness, changes; first into a reaction preceded by intervening awareness alone, and then into an instantaneous reaction without intervening image *or* awareness.

26. That is, the bodily tension-experiences mentioned. It is worth noting that Muensterberg (532) and Washburn (750) considered these tension-experi-

Should such experiences occur frequently, the simultaneously given constituents of the awareness-content usually begin to fade: the intensity of awareness abates. The knowledge-content remains clear and unequivocal, but it is no longer experienced in its original intensity. This process may also be characterized as the decrease of attention-concentration.[27] Besides these changes in the intensity of a total awareness, there are also intensity differences in the awareness of the various simultaneously given part-contents; in other words, attention is directed more to some than to other constituents of the simultaneously experienced complex content. Meanwhile, the entire content is present as awareness. Thus, for instance, in states of expectancy it frequently happens that the awareness of the reaction to be made—described under (b) above—recedes, relative to that of an unequivocally defined change—described under (a) above. . . . With some subjects—for example, Subject L.—this was more the rule than the exception, in the beginning. L. was unable to maintain simultaneously an equally great intensity of the two part-contents. . . . With much experience, the intensity of awareness—of the whole or part-content—may so recede that its presence as awareness is no longer demonstrable. This was the case with Subject J.: when fixating on the screen, besides weak intentional sensations in the reactor organ, there was only a vague awareness that he must

---

ences ("implicit motor attitudes") identical with the "determining tendencies."

27. The term "attention-concentration" may be misleading. Concentration usually connotes voluntary, effortful turning toward the object of external or internal perception. Attention in turn usually connotes effortless automatic perception. Here we encounter again the relation between attention on the one hand, and determining tendency and awareness on the other. Cf. note 13, above. This relationship is complex. Ach has already commented that when attention is initially poor, the task becomes explicitly conscious. When attention is vigilant, the task is only implicitly conscious in the form of awareness of considerable intensity. When the reaction and thus the whole experience becomes automatized (habituated), the intensity of awareness as well as of attention abates. Woodrow's work (777) also shows the relatedness of set and attention. The interest in and exploration of attention has been waning in academic psychology ever since Titchener (730). Experimental investigations have hardly ever taken into consideration Freud's concept of attention (see notes 13, above, and 31, below). Cf. Bleuler's concept, Chap. 26, below. There is a revival of the concept of attention in Bruner's (578) "vigilance." It is to be hoped that a new effort at exploration of the phenomena of attention is in the making.

react. We designate this recession of the content of awareness as the *automatiza-tion* of the process. In contrast to this, in other instances an increase in the intensity of awareness is demonstrable. Such intensification may occur, for instance, because of repeated internal utterances and continuous concentration of attention.[28] Therefore, we are justified in distinguishing degrees of intensity of awareness in simultaneously given complex contents, as well as in consecutive experiences. . . .[29]

When a content is only an imageless knowledge, immediately preceding or simultaneous with the meaning-awareness, there exists in consciousness a visual, acoustic, or kinesthetic sensation (tension-sensation), or a memory image of the content. These sensations are image-representations in consciousness of the imageless knowledge. They are indicators of the meaning-content. The sensations may, of course, come without such meaning-content, as pure sensory qualities. Thus it happened repeatedly in our experiments that, after the appearance of a colored card, the sensation "yellow" was present solely in its optical quality. Only afterwards did the knowledge arise, "This is yellow," as an independent thought. It could be said that only this thought identified the sensation as the familiar yellow color. Somehow a link to *previous experience* became effective and found expression in this knowledge. This is the process known as *apperception,* which always implies the presence or appearance of the knowledge of a meaning. When a complex content, the part-contents of which show varying degrees of awareness-intensity, is present simultaneously, then that part of the conscious complex which is momentarily in the foreground of awareness may be designated as the apperceived part.[30] It is, as Wundt puts it, in the

28. This point is unclear. The "internal utterance" presumably pertains to the instructions (that is, the task). If, however, the task itself is conscious in a verbal form, it is hard to see how an "awareness" of it also would be present.

29. "Consecutive experiences" refers to the process of automatization of reactions, and to the corresponding decrease in the intensity of attention; "simultaneously given contents" refers to selective perception, which structures experience into foreground and background. Cf. Gibson (269) on selective

perception (p. 793), and on selection in problem-solving (p. 799). See also Tolman (733) on field expectancies (pp. 150–52), and Rapaport *et al.* (602, I, 215–20) on planning ability.

30. In Ach's day, apperception was considered the process of integration, or assimilation, of the perceived stimulus-configuration into the rest of the mental context—a process resulting in the discovery of the "meaning" of the percept. Currently, no perception is considered a photographic reception; since the discovery by Gestalt psychology of the

focus of consciousness. Because of their continuous change of intensity, it is often difficult to judge the degree of awareness of simultaneously given part-contents. As systematic experimental self-observation plainly indicates, attention may be evenly distributed and the simultaneously present part-contents may momentarily show no differences of awareness intensity; therefore, the here-described appearance of the meaning-content must be considered the crucial characteristic of apperception. Herbart gave most careful attention to this phenomenon. These considerations are supported by my previous demonstration that, when a stimulus is apperceived, from the moment of its appearance maximal attention is directed toward a single conscious content (on the basis of a previous *Einstellung*).[31] Thus, the developing stimulus-impression is in the

---

laws of sensory organization, all perception is conceived as a process of integration of the same order as apperception had been. Ach's point is that the distribution of attention over the parts of a percept or other conscious content, and the resulting figure-background articulation, are the essence of the apperception process.

31. Note that here again a relationship is hypothesized between *Einstellung* (attitude, set) and attention. There is a parallel between this and the relationship Freud hypothesizes between drive and attention. Freud (209) wrote:

The sensory excitation performs what is in fact its function; namely, it directs a part of the cathectic energy available in the Preconscious to the cause of the excitation in the form of attention (pp. 515–16).

The act of becoming conscious depends upon a definite psychic function—attention —being brought to bear. This seems to be available only in a determinate quantity, which may have been diverted from the train of thought in question by other aims. Another way in which such trains of thought may be withheld from consciousness is the following: From our conscious reflection we know that, when applying our attention, we follow a particular course. But if that course leads us to an idea which cannot withstand criticism, we break off and allow the cathexis of attention to drop. Now, it would seem that the train of thought thus started and abandoned may continue to develop without our attention returning to it, unless at some point it attains a specially high intensity which compels attention (p. 529).

Clearly, the "specially high intensity" refers to drive-cathexes. The relationship between *Einstellung* and "drive" is still unclear. Cf. note 3, above, and Chap. 15, note 31, below. Allport contributed much to the clarification of the problem.

He concluded (24, pp. 818–19):

It seems necessary to distinguish two types of attitudes: one which is so organized and energized that it actually *drives*, and the other which merely *directs*. Both of these types are conditions of readiness-for-response, both are in a sense dynamic, for both enter into the determination of conduct. The first, however, is specifically *motivational*, the second (which includes besides the *Aufgabe* such "postures of consciousness" as are involved in skills and in the manner and modes of response) are

focus of consciousness; yet in this phase we cannot speak of [complete] apperception. Rather, what takes place is the development of the stimulus-apperception; the apprehension of the stimulus-impression in accordance with the preceding *Einstellung* takes time. Thus a content may be in the focus of consciousness, in the center of attention, without having been apperceived.[32]

---

merely *instrumental.* The true motive underlying an instrumental or directive attitude is often some other driving attitude, or sometimes it is of so primitive and unorganized a nature that it may be called instinctive.

Chein, criticizing Doob's views on attitudes, also contributed measurably, even on points where Gibson (269) failed. Chein wrote (129, p. 186):

... there is an intellectual trap in the commonly accepted principle that if some psychological process is not learned, then it must be innate and, if it is not innate, then it must be learned.

That is: an interlocking between the organization of innate drive-forces under the influence of experience, and the organization of experience under the influence of innate drive-forces, may be the genetic background of attitudes.

32. The observation is not entirely clear. It seems, however, that it is of this sort: I am trying to solve a geometric problem analytically; I complete a calculation and write out the algebraic result; now I first perceive the result—it is in the center of my attention, but it is as yet meaningless to me; then a feeling of familiarity and a vague impression of its relationship to my geometric problem arises, but I do not yet know what it is; next the familiarity becomes clear, but not yet the meaning of my problem; then a vague pattern emerges which links the result to my problem, and while it increases in clarity, no verbal expression of

it is yet available; finally, a word or a phrase expressing the *meaning* of the result arises. If this is the phenomenon Ach observed in a rudimentary form, determined by the restricted experimental situation, then his formulation may be made the point of departure for a more general one: (a) A content may be in the focus of attention (consciousness) without being *fully* apperceived. (b) Apperception is relative and context-determined, and so for that matter are "contents." In one context an experience of a content may amount to full apperception, while in another the same experience is merely a step toward full apperception. For instance, $a^2 - b^2 = (a + b)(a - b)$ may be fully apperceived in an algebraic context; in a geometric context its apperception will require that the relationships between a, b, a + b, a − b become conscious, as also the corresponding geometrical entities. (c) Since apprehension of the meaning of a content in increasingly broader contexts requires reflectiveness of increasingly higher orders, the degree of apperception is correlated with the degree of reflectiveness. (d) Daydreams and similar subjective experiences may also be considered as contents in the center of attention without full apperception. Freud's contention that preconscious material may attain full consciousness by becoming connected with verbal images (Chap. 15, note 32, below) sheds light on one aspect of the process of apperception.

In analyzing their experience, subjects often find it difficult to describe an imageless awareness-content. Part of the experience is at times indicated phenomenologically: by internal utterances such as "must come," or "edge, edge," or word fragments like "add," "before," "after." [33] Such kinesthetic or acoustic-kinesthetic images may well be the basis for the widespread assumption that our thinking occurs always by means of internal speech or adequate visual, acoustic, and other memory images. It must be pointed out, however, that there are very complex contents of which only part-contents and their mutual relationships are present in consciousness, whereas the contents themselves are not or even cannot be represented by adequate verbal designation or by anything like it. When a phenomenological constituent [of such a complex content] is present, it refers only to a corresponding [partial] meaning-content; for instance, "edge" refers to the expectation of the upper edge of the card. At the same time, other simultaneous expectation-contents do not have such phenomenological representation, and are present within the total tension-state only as

---

The relations between apperception, reflectiveness, and relativity of content-meaning to context have so far been little studied. The decades of "behaviorism" placed these beyond the pale of respectable subject-matter for exploration.

33. Apparently the experimental conditions were so restrictive that the imageless awarenesses, and their observed "phenomenological" correlates, pertained directly to the tasks. Imageless awarenesses and their image-correlates are observed in everyday thinking also. There, however, they do not always *directly* and *discernibly* pertain to the task at hand. First of all, it is difficult to discern their pertinence, because the tasks and intentions in everyday thought, in productive thinking, and in problem solving are not as clearly delineated as in Ach's experiments. Secondly, the awarenesses and their concomitants may pertain to latent tasks (aims, wishes) as well as to overt ones; to external interferences and intentions related to them, as well as to task-intentions proper; to concomitant needs and corresponding intentions, as well as to intellectual tasks.

The difficulty of exploring the matrix from which purposive thought arises is therefore threefold: (a) if the task of purposive thinking is restricted—as in Ach's experiments—only some aspects of the matrix become obvious; (b) if the task is not restricted, the intentions are manifold and the coordination of awareness and intention becomes unclear; (c) the very intention of self-observation and the corresponding reflective attitude may alter the matrix.

Dreams, reveries, and other states characterized by limited reflectiveness provide a favorable setting for the study of those aspects of the matrix which cannot be reached by Ach's or even by less rigorously controlled experiments. But these states in turn present other difficulties. Cf. Chap. 22, below.

awareness. Furthermore, it happens at times that complex contents, the verbal expression of which would take several sentences, appear momentarily, like a flash of lightning. Therefore, in their brief existence they could not be given in internal speech. Their meaning-content is unequivocal, and their memory clear and definite, though we cannot demonstrate the presence of any sensory qualities.[34] Thus, for instance, in the preparatory period of an experiment with optical reactions of twofold coordination,[35] Subject C. had a visual memory picture of "O," and with it a lightning thought that it would be most practical to be prepared only for "O"; beside this, there was the awareness that perhaps there would be only "E." . . . In view of the clear and unequivocal content of such awareness, it seems incorrect to assume that these are "obscure sensations" or memory images, too weak to be demonstrable as single contents, but which when taken together result in a realization of the meaning-content.[36]

Experiences such as the following speak against such an assumption: when an awareness without demonstrable imagery is in the focus of consciousness, together with it a reproduced sensation—for example, a white card—appears as a part-content, with a lesser degree of awareness intensity. . . . Often we first observe the presence of an image representation of a meaning-content (for instance, in the form of internal speech, "as fast as possible"), and only then the corresponding meaning-content as an awareness without phenomenological representation. There are, however, instances in which awareness is followed by an image. Thus, in an experiment with numbers, after the intention "subsequent," the number 9 was presented . . . first came the awareness, "I know it," and only then the visual image of zero.

Even though the experience we call awareness was demonstrable in all subjects, there were great individual differences. Many people are given to immediate visual or acoustic-kinesthetic imaging of meaning-contents. The author himself, having neither strong motor nor visual bent, has a definite inclination

34. Though it may seem at first far-fetched, the phenomenon of *déjà vu* may be conceived of as similar to this. (See Chap. 3, note 9, below.) In *déjà vu* a new situation is felt as "experienced once before." This feeling is unequivocal and of great complexity, though it is lacking sensory qualities. Whether besides this superficial similarity there is an intrinsic relationship between the two is so far not known.

35. See note 1, above.

36. In Ach's time, this was the most common argument against the "imageless thoughts" of the Wuerzburg school.

to think in awarenesses; [37] this circumstance may well have contributed to his interest in the analysis of imageless thinking. One area where imageless conceptual thinking is most obvious is the quick and understanding reading of a text. When, for instance, the written sign of the word "bell" is before me, I apperceive the sign and know what it means. The awareness of the meaning is then present in me. According to the *theory of awareness*, it is not necessary that presentations—apperceiving presentation-masses—arise to assimilate the impression, for example, the sound or visual image of a bell. According to this theory, the realization of the meaning-content occurs in a different fashion. It is well-known that every presentation in consciousness—for example, the stimulus-impression "bell"—puts many associated presentations into readiness. This readiness of presentations—that is, their reproduction tendencies—suffices for a conscious representation of what we call their meaning, without their having to enter consciousness. The reproduction is not yet complete, it has only been initiated by, we might say, a stimulation of reproduction tendencies. This stimulation suffices to create an unequivocal relationship in the direction of the "stimulated" reproduction tendencies. These unequivocal relationships are experienced as knowledge, that is, meaning. . . . One of the reproduction tendencies corresponding to it may then become over-valent; that is to say, one of the associated presentations enters consciousness and appears as the conceptual sign of that knowledge. . . .[38]

37. The relationship between personality structure and the individual differences Ach refers to has so far not been exploited, either for heuristic or diagnostic purposes, though Jaensch (352) came close to it.

38. The "associated presentation" in question will be selected by the context. ("Those evening bells, those evening bells" or "bell-bottom trousers"). The context in question is not so much the actual perceptual one, but rather any context which is psychologically relevant; it may imply much or little that is perceptual, or totally disregard it in favor of an intrapsychic context. This selective process implies "anticipations," and consequently a definite distribution of "attention" (cf. note 27, above). If "distraction" (latent or interfering intentions) prohibits the rise of anticipations from the context, perception of the words read in the text will lead to no apperception. This is the case when, arriving at the end of a page, we find we do not know what we have read. The nature of imageless knowledge is clearly illustrated in those cases where the context and the anticipations arising from it lead to an apperception and apprehension which is then contradicted or greatly expanded by the subsequent context. The restructuring that takes place, accompanied by experiences of surprise and amusement (Freud, 214; Schiller, 670) or "aha" experiences (Maier, 498; Duncker,

According to the laws of association and of reproduction of ideas, the more often the associated ideas have been in consciousness (other factors remaining constant), the stronger the reproduction tendency. If the meaningful word "bell" is given, ideas most frequently associated with this sign will be put into the highest degree of readiness. Thus, the stronger the reproduction-tendencies, the greater the state of excitation. On the basis of our previous discussion, we are entitled to speak about differences in awareness-intensity within a simultaneously given complex. Nothing seems to be in the way of assuming that the greater the excitation of readied presentations, and the greater the intensity of reproduction-tendencies, the more intensive the awareness. Therefore, we may describe awareness as an increasing function of excitations of reproduction-tendencies. It follows that of all the reproduction-tendencies stimulated by the word "bell," the awareness of those most frequently experienced will be most intensive. In contrast to these, the other readied presentations, being only occasional and incidental, are of a lesser awareness-intensity. The meaning-content of a given word implies a knowledge in which regularly recurring associative connections have far greater awareness-intensity than those occasionally and incidentally formed. The latter will be neglected and not become effective as awarenesses. Here we encounter an experience-determined process of *associative abstraction*, in that only those presentations become consciously effective in a given meaning-content which have recurred regularly as its constituents. This abstraction process, through the continuous assimilation of presentations in their varying connections, occurs entirely automatically.[39]

---

151), makes manifest those aspects of the imageless-knowledge-matrix which did not previously come to consciousness.

39. It seems plausible that something like this "associative abstraction" does occur in the development of realistic thinking. It seems, however, questionable whether it is due solely to frequency-determined associative reproduction-tendencies. Hence the description of awareness-intensity as an increasing function of reproduction-tendencies is doubtful.

If determining tendencies (sets, *Ein-* stellungen) may be considered as attitudes arising from organization of innate drive-forces under the influence of experience (note 31, above), then the very frequency of occurrence of associative connections may gain a new aspect.

Ach has shown that determining tendencies create new associations (see p. 24, above). If such tendencies represent derivatives of drive-forces organized in terms of experience and social agreement, their regular recurrence should be no surprise. In that case, not the frequency of contiguous occurrence, but the stability of the link to such a common dy-

Since associated presentations which recur regularly represent the constant characteristics of a given concept, associative abstraction determines *the kind of awareness in which a concept is psychologically present in an individual.* This shows that there is no general psychological representation of a concept which is valid for all individuals. Awareness of a concept depends on the association of ideas corresponding to experiences, which again greatly vary with people. Even in the same individual, awareness of a concept does not remain constant.[40] The factors determining the intensity of reproduction-tendencies, that is, of the readiness of a presentation, are also decisive for awareness-intensity. (Such factors are: the frequency of the attention-deployment which brought about the association; the feeling-tone; the time lapse since the association was formed; the generative, effectual, and retroactive inhibitions; the perseverating reproduction-tendencies; the determining tendencies.) [41] For example, if one of these factors reinforces the excitation of one of the readied presentations, the conceptual awareness changes. The mental constellation is subject to constant change, and so is awareness. Herein lies the developmental

---

namic factor would be the basis of the associative bond. Thus "associative abstraction" would occur and would derive its validity (reality-relevance) from the fact that it was originated by determining tendencies and anticipations which themselves were organized in accord with experience.

The problem of the ontogenesis of abstractions is usually overlooked, and consequently they are still often dealt with as a matter of "logic." Logic in turn is still treated "a-genetically." The investigations of concept-formation (see Chap. 26, and its notes, below), Werner's (755) treatment of the genetic psychology of concepts, and Piaget's (557, 558) studies of the development of abstractions have made only the first inroads into this field. Ach's concept of "associative abstraction" seems to imply patterns like those of the addition and multiplication in Boolian algebra. It is possible that

the latter may be usefully applied to the study of concept-formation.

40. The individual variability of concepts Ach describes is a fact attested to by studies both in concept-formation, in which he (12) pioneered, and in association-tests. Cf. Rapaport *et al.* (602, II, 20–22). This variability is dependent not so much on "association of ideas corresponding to experiences which . . . vary with people," but rather on that corresponding to the *organization* of experiences according to dynamic (motivational) principles.

41. We have no systematic theory which would enable us to complement or provide substitutes for Ach's factors according to our present understanding of memory and concept-formation Some of the relevant material, however, has been summarized in these pages. Cf. particularly Chap. 3, notes 18, 19, and Chap. 15, note 31.

potentiality of mental processes. As apperceptive masses are progressively replaced through new associations of ideas, there is a constant change of conceptual awareness; at the same time the excitation of now one, now another,
readied presentation is increased by a previous determination. Therefore, even
identical stimulations, following each other at brief intervals, may result in differing conceptual awarenesses. The psychological representation of a concept
by an awareness is thus not identical with the logical characteristics in its definition. This incongruity of the logical and the psychological contents of concepts is most obvious in children. On the one hand, they lack the broad experience and varied associative connections necessary for the process of associative
abstraction, that is, for the differentiation of the regular from the incidental;
on the other hand, their attention often turns to striking but not regular contents of consciousness. Therefore, often the child does not differentiate between essential and unessential characteristics. For him, any incidental accompanying phenomenon may appear the major characteristic of a concept. A
child's drawings offer a very instructive opportunity to observe his thinking.
They express what he knows about an object rather than what he has perceived
of it: the drawing is objectified awareness.[42]

These considerations suggest that presentations are abstract, or rather, that
all conscious content given as awareness is abstract. The reason is that the incidental associations which are the overtones of every awareness do not attain
appreciable conscious influence as compared with the regular associations.

The discussion of the concept of awareness has bearing on the role of determining tendencies. We have seen that these tendencies determine the course
of mental happening so as to accord with the goal-presentation. In the preparatory period of the experiment, when the intention is formed, reproduction-
tendencies corresponding to the meaning of the goal-presentation achieve a
high degree of excitation, by means of the heightened concentration of attention and the perseverance of the goal-presentation in consciousness. These
reproduction-tendencies, accompanied by meaning-awareness, are brought
simultaneously into relationship with the referent-presentation, influencing it
in accordance with the goal-presentation. Such relationships between goal-
presentations and referent-presentations we call intentions.[43] In contrast to the

42. Cf. Piaget (557) and Heinz Werner (755).

43. Gibson (269) has shown that intention and anticipation are often un-

referent-presentation implied in the intention-awareness, the one on which the determination actually takes effect we call "concrete referent-presentation" (for example, when the intention is to calculate, the number 2 that appears as stimulus is the "concrete referent-presentation"). If the intention is accompanied by a good concentration of attention, it also implies a reference to the future in that it is directed toward a concrete referent-presentation to appear subsequently.

The influence of determining tendencies appears in simplest form in the varieties of apperceptive fusion. To this category belong even those forms of apperception in which the meaning-content may be considered an after-effect of a preceding "Einstellung"; for example, the recognition-reaction in which a yellow or red card is apperceived as colored, in accord with the instructions, or the apperception of its color with the awareness of consent or affirmation, "Yes, this is red." These forms of apperception, therefore, may be designated as *determined apperceptions.*[44] Such is the case also when a white or colored card is apperceived as "something to react to," since this apperception complies with a preceding determination. There is an apperceptive fusion here between the stimulus-impression and the readied reproduction-tendencies, so that comprehension is directly connected with the corresponding meaning. . . .

In contrast to this, in those experiments in which *Einstellung* is poor, the insufficient determination is noticeable already in the apperception. In cases where the preparation has been insufficient, we observe a state of disorientation upon the appearance of the stimulus: the subject does not know what to do.

Besides these described forms, determination may manifest itself in what is known as *specific apperceptive fusion.* Such are particularly frequent and various in reactions without coordination of activity. For example, in the preparatory period Subject B. had a visual image of the plus-sign, representing the intention to "add"; when the stimulus appeared, an apperceptive fusion took place in that the appearing numbers fell into the prepared scheme. The de-

justifiably equated. This seems to be the case here. The intention to perform gives rise to an anticipation of the stimulus, which then influences the perception of it, and to an intention to react, which is then triggered into action by the appearance of the stimulus.

44. "Determined apperceptions" are those which have occurred under the selective influence of a determining tendency, implicit to the intention arising from the task-instruction.

termined presentation [45] followed associatively from this apperceptive fusion. Subject C. experienced a spatial displacement of the two numbers which corresponded to the intention: in adding they pulled together, in subtracting the smaller figure sidled to the larger. . . .[46]

A middle position between special apperceptive fusion and determined apperceptions is occupied by the cases where the apperception of the concrete referent-presentation (for example, of a number) is followed by an imageless meaning-awareness, and where, after that apperception but before the appearance of the result (that is, the determined presentation), knowledge of what will appear is present.[47]

Another form of apperceptive fusion is *apperceptive substitution*, in which a preceding *Einstellung* comes to expression. In the simplest cases, a presentation is given as a part-content of the intention of the preparatory period. This is the case, for example, in our rhyming experiments: the letter "b" appears [as a part content of the intention] and replaces the initial letter of the concrete referent-presentation (stimulus-syllable). The determined presentation may be considered the product of an apperceptive substitution, effected by the determination.[48] . . .

The list, apperceptive fusion, determined apperception, specific apperceptive fusion, apperceptive substitution, does not exhaust the varieties of the effects of determining tendencies. Some of these are transitions to those forms in which determination finds its most striking expression. In these cases, the determined presentation, the end-product of the determination, appears in consciousness

45. That is, the sum.

46. Cf. pp. 20–21 and note 14, above.

47. In determined apperceptions, determination is merely selectiveness of apperception. In specific apperceptive fusion, the determination manifests itself in a schematic, analogical, symbol-like experience. In the cases here discussed, there is an imageless meaning-awareness; in determined apperceptions it is rudimentary or missing; in apperceptive fusion, imagery either accompanies or replaces it.

48. In this case, the "b" plays the same role as the image-schema of addition or subtraction in apperceptive fusion. However, in the latter, the schema (though not necessarily its individual form) seems to be directly given by the instructions; in the former the "b" is patently of subjective origin. The difference is not great: the schema of apperceptive fusion is also individual and subjectively determined, though directly related to the task-instruction and intention; the "b" of apperceptive substitution, in spite of its subjective determination, is also related to the task and intention.

immediately in conjunction with the concrete referent-presentation; and neither the goal-presentation itself, from which the determination arises, nor any part-content of it is demonstrable in consciousness after the appearance of the concrete referent-presentation. The selfsame concrete referent-presentation, once given, may be followed by a variety of determined presentations, selected by the determining tendencies. It is characteristic that even though the appearance of the determined presentation is precipitated by the concrete referent-presentation, its quality depends on the goal-presentation, though the latter is not demonstrable in consciousness. The qualitative characteristics of the determined presentation are beyond doubt due to unconscious (meaning simply not conscious) effects. Thus we define determining tendencies as *unconsciously acting* Einstellungen *which arise from the meaning of the goal-presentation and, directed toward the coming referent-presentation, result in the spontaneous appearance of the determined presentation.*

[Passage omitted.] [49]

49. The fourth section of this chapter, omitted here, deals with *determined abstraction* and *attention*. The former is implicit in Ach's *associative abstraction*. The latter is interwoven with the concept of abstraction: of the simultaneous constituents of a meaning, only those emphasized by abstractions are attended to. The distinction between abstraction and attention is that, in successive experiences, abstraction neglects and tends to eliminate the part-contents, while attention causes them to come to the fore and be observed.

CHAPTER 2

ON THOUGHT CONNECTIONS [1]

By Karl Buehler [2]

I. ON CONSCIOUS THOUGHT RELATIONSHIPS

THE ANALYSIS of the content of a train of thought is not completed by the description of the thoughts [3] contained in it. . . . Besides thoughts, yet other knowledge [4] is present in our thinking. For instance, we know whether or not we are on the right track; whether or not we are approaching our goal; whether the thought occurs to us for the first time or derives from our memory; we may

---

1. K. Buehler (111).

2. This is the second of three consecutive studies. Its method is the same as that of the first study "On Thoughts" (111, I), namely: the subjects (Professors Kuelpe and Duerr and four other psychologists) were presented sentences of complex meaning; they were instructed to indicate understanding by "yes," a lack of it by "no"; thereafter the subjects were asked to report the experiences that preceded their response. The reports were recorded.

Buehler introduced the report of the first study as follows:

There is probably no other specific scientific question to which so many different answers are given as, What is thinking? Thinking is connecting; thinking is analyzing; thinking is judging; thinking is apperceiving; the essence of thinking is abstraction, thinking is relating; thinking is activity—a voluntary process. If, however, the query concerns the specific content of the thought-experience, the answer is unanimous: There is no such thing. Few investigators would take issue with this

3. "Thought" here translates *Gedanke;* it is not used in the special sense explained in note 2 above.

4. "Knowledge" translates *Wissen.* The term is used by Buehler in a special sense: "Knowledge" is related to the contents of "thought" in the same way as "the experience of having a sensation" is to sensations.

---

thesis. The present investigation is designed to contest this very thesis on which most agree, while admitting that each investigator may be right where he differs from the others (p. 237).

Summarizing his observations, Buehler describes the internal dialectics and the task-determined teleological character of thinking, and then poses the question, *"What are the constituents of the experience of thinking?"* (pp. 314–15). In the answer he enumerates the varieties of sensory-, object-, and word-presentations, and concludes: "Something as fragmentary, sporadic, and as accidental in consciousness as the presentations in our experience of thinking cannot be the

know even where we have picked it up; we know how it is related to the one preceding. This knowledge only rarely becomes an independent psychic act [5]; we do not specifically focus on its content. It lies, so to say, in between thoughts. Subjects will actually report: "In the meanwhile I was also aware of this and that." [6]

---

carriers of solid and continuous thought-contents" (p. 317).

Then he enumerates the consciousness of space and of its symbolic direction-changes, and the feelings and experiences which Marbe (499) labeled "positions of consciousness" (*Bewusstseinslagen*), such as doubt, surprise, suspense, pondering, staring into empty space, etc. Buehler concludes:

The most important constituents of experience are not subsumed in these categories (if for the moment we except "positions of consciousness"); though they have no sensory quality or intensity, they do have clarity, certainty, and vividness, commanding psychic interest. Their content differs radically from anything that in final analysis can be reduced to sensations. . . . My subjects have designated these constituents as "awareness," the term Ach used, or simply as "the consciousness that . . . ," or most frequently and correctly as "thoughts." The term "thought" was suggested for these by Binet (62), and we shall adopt it as the one most natural and telling" (pp. 315–16).

Buehler then distinguishes between three kinds of such "thoughts":

(a) *Rule Consciousness:* " . . . it is consciousness of the method of solving a task. In typical cases the experience implies not only the knowledge of how to solve the given task, but also the knowledge of how to solve *such* tasks. . . ." (p. 335).
   Example: "Do you know what Eucken means when he speaks of world-historical

apperception?"—"At first I was inclined to say no, since I have not yet encountered this concept in Eucken. Then it occurred to me: one can determine its meaning without knowing Eucken's, etc." (p. 334).
(b) *Relationship Consciousness:* This form of "thought" is considered in detail in Buehler's second study, translated here. (pp. 343–46)
(c) *Intentions:* "In these the act of meaning itself comes to the fore and not what is meant: as though this *what* were already given and the 'thought' were but a pointing to it" (pp. 346–49).
   Example: "I thought of the skepticism of antiquity (this was spoken internally); this included much: for a moment all three phases of its development were present [in my consciousness]."

Here the relationship to Brentano, Husserl, and Meinong is clear. See Schilder, Chap. 25, notes 6 and 8, below.
5. "Psychic act" is used here as a technical term in Brentano's sense; see note 2, above.
6. The subtlety of the introspective observations and their analysis so characteristic of this paper is shared by the other Wuerzburg studies, and rivals that of Brentano, Meinong, and Husserl. Though such observations have rather narrow limits, their results pose problems for, and offer points of departure and orientation to, a dynamic (motivational) theory of thinking. So far these have not been exploited.

Let us take an experimental record for an example:

"What view did Herbart share with Hume?"—Yes (23").[7]—"First I thought of the association theory ('association' spoken internally). Then I searched for further commonalities. The thought 'presentations are the carriers of psychological life' ('presentations' spoken internally) came. But I thought immediately—this does not fit. What impressed itself on me then was: reference to the psychologically real. But with it there was in my consciousness: that is precisely in what they differ. Then I gave up. (The subject adds:) *I was conscious throughout that each thought had a relationship to the task.* These relationships unified it all, so that my thinking was directed by the idea of finding common characteristics, an idea which then found expression in these relationships."

(Do you understand?) "We depreciate everything that can be explained."— Yes (5")—"Immediately upon hearing it, I thought of a fanatical realist. Then I thought of certain esthetics and immediately said, 'Yes.' It would be difficult to reproduce the thought exactly. . . . The connection of these thoughts to the task was clearly conscious. (Still under the impression of this experience:) It is marvelous, *how we can know something without actually thinking it; I mean that there are in our knowledge conscious relationships which have no objects of their own.*"

In both of these records, thoughts and their relationships to the task were simultaneously conscious. What is a task? Watt [8] used this term for a real factor in thought-processes which must be taken into consideration, along with the associations, in explaining the course of presentations or thoughts. To designate a similar state of affairs in acts-of-will, Ach [9] coined the term "determining tendencies." Both deal with a process. The relationships we have observed are content-correlates of this real factor, and in them the effect of the task comes to consciousness. Throughout, the task itself is usually not represented in consciousness by specific contents, and appears merely as the second reference-point of these relationships. . . .

Thoughts in consciousness are often related to each other, or to psychological contents extraneous to the current process, in the same way as they are re-

7. 23 seconds, reaction time. 9. Ach (14) and (15), Chap. 1, above.
8. Watt (751).

lated to the task. Often a thought brings to consciousness indications of its origin.[10] Thus, for instance, our subjects often reported they immediately knew that the thought was such-and-such a writer's. Aphorisms were attributed mainly to Nietzsche; statements like "I knew immediately: it was Nietzsche" were frequent. This consciousness may have varying degrees of definiteness. We find every hue, from "It sounds as though it would belong there" to the clear consciousness of its role or place in a system. . . ."[11]

Other conscious contents posit relationships to preceding tasks of the experimental session: "I was aware that today there were already several sentences about lying. . . . Besides, there was the consciousness that this task was different from the previous ones; it was something situational and I had to reorient myself. . . ."

Often there is a silent critique of the sentence or the task: "Apparently this is a deliberately far-fetched question"; "How can they ask such a question?" . . . At times such knowledge appears as an affect: "The incompleteness of the sentence disturbed me"; "It was accompanied by the pleasant consciousness that it was more familiar than the preceding one. . . ."

This is merely a small selection from many data on inter-thought knowledge.[12] To round out the picture it should be added that, according to Ach's [13] and Messer's [14] findings, the most frequent content of such knowledge is the ease or difficulty of the task, the possibilities of solution, and similar things.[15] A few examples will show that these observations on reaction- and simple thought-experiments also hold for more complicated thought-processes:

"Do you know how many steps there are to the stairs of the main entrance

10. Cf. Gillespie (275), who summarizes the literature on amnesia and memory-organization. He shows that remembered material carries indices of time, of affective character, of personal relevance, etc. Various memory-disorders are characterized by the loss of some of these indices, and it seems that in their absence remembering suffers (pp. 750 ff.).

11. The omitted part contains further illustrations.

12. "Inter-thought" translates *zwi-*schengedanklich. It implies that the knowledge in question concerns relationships of two or more thoughts.

13. Ach (14) and (15), Chap. 1, above.

14. Messer (516).

15. It is more than mere coincidence that these are the experiences symbolized in the so-called "functional phenomena" of hypnagogic hallucinations. Cf. Silberer, Chap. 8, below, and Chap. 1, note 14, above.

of this university?"—No (6″).—"I thought very quickly of the steps of some philosophical systems and concurrently knew that I wouldn't solve it. . . ."

. . . Contents of consciousness which justify an affirmative answer also belong to this category: "With that, I knew it had a deeper meaning too, but I was to answer the obvious one"; "I knew that my 'No' did not do justice to the sentence, but I was already set to it and left it that way." . . . These are not really explanations of the answers, and if they were, would belong in another context; rather they are indications of how one would defend the answer if one had to.

The forms of inter-thought knowledge discussed so far do not pertain to or connect the actual thoughts; they state something about them as experiences, and connect them as such. They are not conscious connections between two meanings, but rather between two experiences of meaning—a present and a past. Although these are not the actual contents that lead to thought-progression, they have an important function in our thinking. They guarantee the unity of the thought-process and are expressions of the control exerted by the thinker over what goes on in him.[16] When these are altogether absent, the thinker has lost his orientation: he faces individual ideas without knowing what he is to do with them. "What is this to me?" "How does it come?" These are questions that occur not only in the thoughts of a distracted speaker, but even in relatively brief thought-processes; they indicate that the thread has been lost. This "thread" is but the totality of these conscious contents, which safeguard the unity and goal-directedness of thought-processes.[17] They are, however, not

16. Cf. note 4, above. The distinction between knowledge and thought-content there, and "actual content" and "inter-thought knowledge" here, is that between content and awareness of experience. It goes without saying that an awareness of this "awareness" is both feasible and useful in surveying and systematizing experience. This potentiality of the psychological organization is not identical with reflection (see p. 45, below), but underlies it; it allows a hierarchic series of forms to arise within consciousness. Levels of this hierarchic series are characterized by increasing abstractness, and it is possible that the very ability to create abstractions is tied up with the existence and function of these levels. Finally, it seems likely that they play a considerable role in what is called "insight."

17. The more usual assumption is that this goal-directedness is safeguarded by anticipations. The relationship of "the totality of these conscious contents" to "anticipations" is problematic. It is conceivable that this relationship will prove a closer one than it may seem. See Chap. 27, below.

specific to thought-processes; they may connect also presentations or feelings. They are common features of thought-processes and of some acts-of-will; therefore thought-processes whose goal is to solve a problem may be considered conscious acts-of-will.[18]*

How are we to designate these contents of consciousness? Some of the more complex ones will have to be considered thoughts which are independent of but concurrent with the dominant thought.[19] It is incorrect to assume that at one time only a single idea can be present in consciousness; the expression "train of thought" is misleading. Frequently, several simultaneous thoughts are present in consciousness; some of these are knowledge of the sort described above. Most of these contents are so simple and of so little independence that we should, with Ach,[20] call them relationships. We shall designate them *inter-thought relationships*, but to distinguish them from another group of inter-thought relationships to be discussed below, we shall call them *inter-experience relationships*.

Inter-experience relationships—as already mentioned—inform the thinker of what is going on in him. The question immediately arises: does this imply

18.* Cf. Ach (15), pp. 191 ff.
[The relationship of the concept of will, as here used, to motivation and impulse dynamics has never been clarified. The subsumption of thought-processes under "acts-of-will," on the one hand, and the relatedness of will-processes to motivations and to the anticipations arising from them, on the other, are suggestive of a hierarchic connection in the series of impulse, will, anticipation, inter-thought relationships, and thoughts.]

19. The implication seems to be that while thoughts and inter-thought relationships can and should be distinguished from each other as experiences of a different hierarchic order (see note 16, above), the distinction is fluid rather than categorical. There is a transition between thoughts and inter-thought relationships: the more complex the latter become, the more they take on the appearance of the former. The further inference may be drawn that when an inter-thought relationship existing between two thoughts becomes complex, it takes on the appearance of a thought linked to the original two thoughts by other less complex inter-thought relationships.

20. See Ach (15), pp. 235–36. Note Ach's distinction there between "awareness of meaning" and "awareness of relationship." Buehler's distinctions here are somewhat more differentiated. In one respect, however, Buehler's theory is no match for Ach's. For both Ach and Buehler, thinking is organized in a task-directed fashion. To account for the process, Ach introduces a dynamic factor, the "determining tendency," established by the task; in Buehler there is hardly a trace of such a dynamic organizing process.

reflection? Must our experiences become objects of observation before we can know anything about them? If reflection is a specific act of reflecting upon one's thought, the answer is, No. The subject has no consciousness of such an act; the inter-experience relationships appear to him directly together with the thought. This leads to the age-old question of whether, besides its content, the act itself is conscious too. The contribution of our findings to the answer is: at least the relationships between acts [21]* may be conscious without reflection. One may be tempted to conclude that when relationships are conscious, their reference-points—that is to say, the acts themselves—must also be conscious. We shall not discuss here whether this conclusion is justified.[22]

But these inter-experience relationships may be *artifacts of experimentation.* It is conceivable that the situation of being a subject, with the consciousness of having to report one's thoughts, will put one in a reflective frame of mind, conducive to such inter-experience relationships.

This possibility cannot be discounted. Some of these relationships may arise from the conditions of the experiment. Yet I do not believe they all do, since our memory experiments show that they occur even when the subject knows he will not have to report his thoughts.[23] I believe that not all such relationships

21.* Stumpf (724) and Kuelpe (439) would speak of functions rather than acts in this connection.

[It is not clear what the difference is between "the consciousness of relationships" and "reflection." It would seem that they are both parts of a continuum of reflective awareness, the totality of which we call consciousness. Cf. Chap. 13, note 56, below.]

22. Selz's (679) experiments have shown that those anticipations which are conscious do not presuppose the consciousness of both referent ideas, but are rather instruments in, and even prerequisite to, making conscious the second referent of the relationship.

23. Concerning this point, compare Wundt's (779) critique and the answer by Buehler (104), in which he confines himself to his experimental material.

Other considerations may also be brought to bear: (a) In everyday experience too, we encounter reflection upon the content of a thought, upon the experience of a thought, upon the experience of reflection, etc. Buehler's argument has the limitation that it shows only the existence, but not the universality, of this facet of thought-processes. (b) The argument concerning artifacts has been raised not only against Buehler's experiment, but generally—for instance, against the psychoanalytic method. Buehler is right in saying that this argument cannot be summarily dismissed. Yet its limitations must be considered. The heuristic assumption that whatever is elicited as an artifact has a natural counterpart in the process in question has proven a useful deterministic postulate. Phrased in another way: the ex-

experienced are reported. My reasons for this are twofold: first, any of them may be easily overlooked, belonging as they do to our most intimate possessions, which we take for granted; secondly, they are remembered less well than other relationships,[24] as our memory experiments show.

. . . The second group of inter-thought relationships consists of *logical relationships* proper, which make us conscious of how the contents of thought are related to one another—as opposites, as cause and effect, as contradictory, and so forth. These relationships, too, are conscious, often without our paying attention to them. Since they connect the contents of thought, we will call them *inter-object relationships*. We will meet these in abundance when investigating the apprehension of thoughts.[25] Here we give only a few orienting examples:

"Is monism really a negation of personality?"—"Nonsense" (50″)—". . . Between the thoughts on monism and on personality, there was a consciousness *that they are not related at all; it was a consciousness of logical impossibility*."

Other records report, "This is just the opposite of what was said before," or "This agrees with what I often thought," and so forth. It frequently happens that such a logical inter-object relationship attracts attention and becomes the

---

tremes are varieties and exaggerations of normally existing forms, and therefore provide avenues for their exploration. Therefore only a naive disregard for the possible presence of artifacts should be contested, lest it construe extreme cases as representing usual conditions.

It is not certain that Buehler fully avoided this fallacy. The actual frequency and role in thinking of the phenomena and processes he described are still to be established. But this does not decrease the value of his observations. The methodological problems of introspective observation (an indispensable tool for the psychology of thinking) are in urgent need of exploration.

24. In this respect, these relationships share the characteristics of two ex-

tremely different phenomena, daydreams and not yet ingrained abstractions, which are also poorly remembered. We know little about the dynamic conditions that make for these memory difficulties. The fleeting elusive character is not the only common feature of these phenomena: in all three, schematic and anticipation-like patterns play a prominent role. These patterns appear to be fundamental to ordered thinking also, though usually latent in it. A promising field of exploration is open here. The concept of "hypercathexis" may be a means to a systematic ordering of these phenomena. (See Chap. 15, notes 21 and 32, and Chap. 23, note 47, below.)

25. See pp. 48 ff., below.

subject-matter of an independent thought. In such cases inter-thought relationships turn into intra-thought relationships.[26*]

At times, the incorporation of a thought or a presentation into the thought-context will occur only through the addition of such a relationship. A characteristic example:

"Do you know where our other stop-watch is now?" —Yes (5")—". . . I immediately had an image of the rooms of our institute and of the big chest in the middle room. I looked it over quickly. Then I thought: presumably there (spoken internally). An image appeared immediately, like an automatic reaction. *Only after this 'presumably there' did thinking start.* It was as though only this gave meaning to the image." [27*] [Passage omitted.] [28]

Inter-object relationships appear also with the "yes" and "no" answers, containing either their justification or a knowledge of their range of validity (extension or limitation).

"Is straight association psychology represented on this side of the channel?" —Yes (7")—"On a surface in front of me I had something like a map, and it was as though my glance swept over it. In this there was a search after a place; I stopped at X (university city) and said, 'Yes'—*in reference to X and others, which however were not represented in my consciousness.*"

[Passage omitted.] [29]

The conscious grammatical relationships of our verbally formulated thinking probably occupy a unique middle position. Though logical relationships, their function is similar to that of inter-experience relationships. My observations of them are neither extensive nor varied enough for definitive conclusions.

No claim of finality is made for this classification; the present attempt is but to group the manifold of actually encountered conscious relationships. Since it is based on limited material, there is no guarantee of completeness. I believe, however, that the point of view of this classification will be fruitful for future investigation.

26.* Cf. Buehler (111, I, 345).

27.* In the first part of this investigation [Buehler (111, I)] we concluded that images cannot be the building-stones of our thought-experiences (p. 317). Here we encounter the positive aspect of that conclusion: when images enter thinking, they do so via specific mediating relationships. Cf. also 111, I, D, C3, p. 353.

28. An additional example is omitted here.

29. Two further examples are omitted here.

[Passage omitted.] [30]

No investigator in touch with the facts has ever doubted the importance of conscious relationships in thinking. They are rather inclined to overestimate their significance, to view thinking altogether as a relationship-positing activity, and to consider conscious relationships the only conscious contents of thinking. I believe that this goes too far; it would be difficult to maintain that, except for presentation elements, all that becomes conscious—as, for example, the meaning of a word or a group of words—can be reduced to relationships. On the other hand, it must be admitted that the content of many of our most important activities is characterized by certain conscious relationships.

Now we should like to follow up one of these thought activities: comprehension.

II. THE APPREHENSION OF THOUGHTS (THE COMPREHENSION OF SENTENCES) [31]

What is the process of comprehending words or sentences? It is obvious and undisputed that something in the subject meets halfway [32] whatever is to be comprehended, and enters some kind of connection with it. Herbart and his school were particularly interested in this process, and gave the precious name apperception precisely to that variety of apprehension phenomena which includes comprehension. There is agreement concerning the general nature of the apprehension process, but the details are controversial and unclear. What is it that the subject brings halfway toward whatever is to be comprehended, and what connection is made between them? Logic has an easy answer for most cases: the new thought (or whatever else it is) is subsumed under an older and

30. The omitted section deals with the classification of relationships, which Meinong (512) proposed, to replace the theories of Locke, Hume, Mill, and Spencer. Buehler analyzes the commonalities and divergences of Meinong's classification and his own.

31. "Apprehension" translates *Auffassen;* "comprehension" translates *Verstehen.* It seems that *Auffassen* (grasp) refers here to the formal process, and is

actually identical with "apperception"; *Verstehen* refers to the content, and could have been translated as "understanding."

32. "Something in the subject meets halfway" translates "vom Subjekt aus entgegengebracht." This is a description of the process of apperception. Its formulation suggests the role played by anticipation. Cf. Chap. 15, note 22, below.

more general one.[33] But how are we to describe this psychologically? Our records throw at least some light on the nature of these connections: *the relation between the thought to be comprehended and a familiar thought is brought to consciousness by a conscious logical relationship.* The thought presented is in many cases actually met by a more general one; the experience of comprehension lies in the subject's knowing that the more specific is connected with, and how it can be derived from, the more general one. A few examples will demonstrate this: . . . [34]

(Do you understand?) "The most glowing colors in which the virtues shine are the inventions of those who lack them."—Yes (21").—"First, again helplessness; I was unable to bring the possession and lack of virtues into the required contrast. There was a search connected with this (perceptually represented only by eye movements, as though shifting back and forth on a surface), interrupted by occasional reverberations of the words, now of the first, now of the second part of the sentence. Then comprehension came suddenly with an affect like 'Aha!' [35] (not spoken); *the basis of comprehension was the farfetched analogy*, or as I would prefer to put it, a superordinate relationship: one prizes most highly what one lacks. Comprehension was tied in with this, and I said yes."

(Do you understand?) "You ask how the apples got onto the tree; but meanwhile somebody else has silently picked them."—Yes (10").—"After some thinking (in it a word fragment, something like: difference), I had the thought of theoretical and practical behavior ('theoretical' and 'practical' came as words): *and with that I knew I understood.* In the thought there was something implied about the practical man taking advantage of the theoretical man."

[Passage omitted.] [36]

It is obvious that these descriptions are typical of many instances of everyday thinking. On encountering a difficult and strange thought, one halts, and then —suddenly comprehension comes like a revelation. This experience does not

33. Psychology attempted to emulate logic; hence the vogue of studies in concept-formation. But even these, when perspicacious, pointed beyond logical subsumption. Cf. Chap. 26, notes 148–61, below.

34. An example is omitted here.

35. To my knowledge, this is the first mention of the often-quoted aha-phenomenon.

36. An example is omitted here.

consist merely in the presence of a more general thought; the "new light," the "special color," often reported by subjects as distinguishing the comprehended sentence from the uncomprehended one, arises only when the more general thought is brought into relation with the one to be comprehended. When for any reason the process is prolonged, this relationship comes to consciousness as a specific act: "I knew that from this I could derive it," or "I could prove it by this . . . ," or ". . . then suddenly there came the concept 'one-sided truth' (spoken internally), and I knew that with it I could prove the proposition."

[Passage omitted.] [37]

In these examples, the familiar thought brought halfway by the subject was a general one, from which the one to be comprehended could be derived. Comprehension may be based on a reversed relationship, where the thought presented can be comprehended by testing it on a familiar but specific thought.

(Do you understand?) "When the mind begins to moralize, the devils are set loose"—Yes (9").—". . . comprehension came with the word: Nietzsche. This stood for the thought: Nietzsche is an example that if one wants both to be witty and treat of ethics, one is shadow-boxing. . . ." [38]

So far, all our examples imply a subsumption relationship of the two thoughts. The following examples are psychologically equivalent to them, yet the logician will not find it easy to press them into this formula. In these, thoughts are comprehended by fitting them into a thought context: "I understood the thought by becoming conscious that it was Nietzsche." . . . In some cases, we may speak of a labeling of thoughts. "The understanding came with the label 'divine mania' (in a euphemistic sense)." This brings to mind the significance for knowledge of name-giving, known of old.

The relationship of the two thoughts may be objective identity. The experience is then: "That is the same as," or "That is the well-known view." Then, the thoughts differ only in formulation; they are different pictures expressing the same thing. Thus, for instance, the subject comprehends "to look through the last veil—that would be the great tiredness, the end of all creation," by thinking of "The Veiled Picture of Sais." [39] "The worse the student, the more pious the priest" is comprehended by: "This is the same as the familiar simile

37. Two examples are omitted here.   39. F. Schiller (669).
38. An example is omitted here.

of the fermenting must and the good wine." The thought mediating the comprehension may appear as a translation into prose (that is, commonly understandable form) of that which is to be comprehended: "That means then the same as."

(Do you understand?) "Where is an ocean one still can drown in?—that is the slogan of our times"—Yes (11").—"First, reverberation of the words, then a pause. Then a thought emerged linked to the internally spoken word 'depth'; something, a great powerful idea to which one can give one's whole soul, and with that I understood it (the words are explications of originally wordless thoughts.)"

Finally, the relationship may be an explanatory one between the thought presented and the thought mediating comprehension. . . .[40]

(Do you understand?) "It is good to row under a sail"—Yes (7").—"First I thought of the shadow of the sail. But no: the sail itself does part of the work. With that I comprehended. . . ." [41]

However, closer inspection of these explanatory relationships arouses doubts. Do the explanatory thoughts, with which the subject meets the thoughts to be comprehended, originate in his memory? Often this seems to be the case, but at times another conception is possible. At such times the explanatory thought appears as a completion of the thought to be comprehended and is implied, though not directly expressed, in the sentence presented. In this case the subject thinks the sentence to its end, and the completion-thought illuminates the thought presented. The following records illustrate this:

(Do you understand?) "Because you lie about what exists, no thirst arises in you for what is to come."—Yes (9").—". . . the full comprehension came with the word optimism (first came the concept and only then the word). . . ."

(Do you understand?) "Thoughts shrink like raw linen"—Yes (22").— "The thought of elaboration (the word came in acoustic-motor form) came to me immediately, implying that one gets more ideas than one can make use of. With that, I comprehended it. . . ." [42]

. . . Here we come to the question, What actually precedes the characteristic "aha" experience that completes comprehension?

This much, I believe, is clearly shown by our records: *the characteristic ex-*

40. Two examples are omitted here.   42. An example, with Buehler's com-
41. An example is omitted here.   mentary, is omitted here.

perience of comprehension takes place between wholes. It follows that what is
to be comprehended must first become a whole.[43]

How should we conceive of the forming of this tentative whole which is to
be comprehended? This is the reverse of the problem met in the psychology of
language: how does the unitary thought differentiate into the meanings of the
words whereby it is expressed? Our question is: how do word-meanings build
up the thought to be comprehended? Regrettably, our records contain only
two hints for a tentative conception of these processes. The first is that at times
one speaks of varying depths of comprehension. "I grasped the obvious meaning, but the deeper one, the actual meaning of the sentence, I could not find."
It is clear that our "aha" experience leads always to the deeper meaning; one
could assume that a deeper comprehension is always preceded by a more superficial one, by the comprehension of the verbal meaning of the sentence; this
would be the whole mentioned. But this would only postpone the answer, since
the whole of the verbal meaning also would have to be built; yet it solves the
problem of deeper comprehension, since it affords the whole on which it takes
place.[44]

The other hint refers to self-activity and construction, and may prove more
fruitful than the first. Let us consider what happens with a grammatically correct sentence the meaning of which cannot be followed. We know what the
sentence demands of us, and also that we cannot fulfill the demand. If we may
generalize this observation, our tentative whole may be considered a task which
has been comprehended as a whole. Then, the instructions implied by the grammatical structure of the sentence, perhaps with the meaning of one of its dominant concepts as subject-matter, constitute this tentative whole.[45] Our memory

43. The examples in which there is a "rounding out," "thinking to the end," or "completing" of the thought pre- sented, are used by Buehler as an occasion for the generalization that neither thought-fragments nor words, but only complete thoughts will interact in that form of the thought-process which we call comprehension. It seems to be im- plied in what follows that this inference, though derived from this special group of examples, has more general validity.

44. This raises the question of the genesis of a Gestalt, so curiously by- passed by Gestalt-psychology itself. See, however, Sanders (629).

45. The grammatical structure of the sentence usually arouses anticipations, which the meaning of the sentence then fulfills. Thus the "tentative wholes" here in question seem to be related to anticipa- tions. Cf. Chap. 25, notes 185 and 201, Chap. 26, notes 22 and 31, and Chap. 27, notes 58 and 76, below.

experiments make it possible to analyze these processes, and yield some observations supporting this conception. . . .[46]

As we have seen, a logical relationship found between a thought presented and a thought of one's own is a relationship-experience. We can agree with Herbart that a thought to be apperceived is fitted in, by the comprehension-

46. Buehler's (111, III) "On the Remembering of Thoughts," the third study of this series, has three aspects: (a) it explores the role of "thoughts" in remembering; (b) it gives data on the remembering of "thoughts"; (c) it sheds further light on the nature of "thoughts" by means of memory experiments.

In the first two studies, remembering of and referring back to past thoughts are encountered at every step. Buehler writes: "Falling back upon what is familiar is probably the most frequent procedure in all thinking." (111, III, p. 25). The obstacle to studying this was that the original form of the remembered "thought" and the conditions of its acquisition were unknown. Buehler's third study is aimed at exploring the remembering of "thoughts" under controlled conditions, attained by presenting "thoughts" and asking the subjects to recall them.

For this purpose, Buehler conducted four types of experiments (111, III, p. 29):

(a) *Paired Thoughts:* 20 pairs of thoughts, in terse headline form, were presented pair by pair. The instruction given implied only that the task was to comprehend them. Time was given after each pair. The pairs were such that a meaningful relationship between the two thoughts was possible, but not obvious. After one reading, the first thought of each pair was presented again, in random order, and the subject was asked to give the second thought and to describe his experience of the procedure.

Examples: Czar and people; The Chinese Wall; The point of Archimedes; The egg of Columbus; The ennobling power of thought; The picture of Kant.

Results and Inferences: The average number of correct recalls, after one reading, was 17-to-18 of the 20. The introspective reports showed the agents of recall to be the thought-relationships established in the process of comprehension. Buehler concluded: "It was the pure thought-relationships between the members which were registered with such striking ease and speed. They again became conscious when the first thought was re-presented, and aided in the reconstruction of the second."

(b) *Completion Experiments:* These were designed to test the explanation that the results of the first experiment were due to associations by contiguity, and to demonstrate further the role of "thoughts" in remembering. First, 15 simple sentences or sentence-fragments were read to the subjects, with the instruction to comprehend them. Then, sentences of incomplete meaning were read, with the instruction to complete them with one of the items of the first series. Finally, the subject's experience of this procedure was recorded.

Examples:
Flower-wreaths are carried away by the mildest west-wind . . .
Pray once if you go to war, twice if you go to sea . . .
. . . not even the wildest storm takes away a thorn crown.
. . . thrice if you go to marry.

Results and Inferences: Though no contiguity was effective, recall was good (exact data not given). Thoughts pre-

process, among the thoughts we already possess. . . . Whether the comprehended thought becomes our own, whether we retain it, and whether we can
use it, does not depend on comprehension as such. The process of "fitting in"
only defines more closely the meaning. To comprehend a sentence is . . . to
know what is meant by it; and this "what" is determined in the way described.
In terms of the results of our analyses of thought, we might say: *the experiences
of comprehension here investigated are specific cases of indirect meaning;* they
imply the knowledge that the meaning of the sentence is connected with the
comprehending thought brought by the subject halfway; and that this connection is defined in terms of the relationship that has come to consciousness
with it.

This formulation naturally raises the question, Can a sentence be directly
comprehended? My answer is affirmative, based on such frequent statements
in our records as, "This simple thought I understood immediately. . . . My
only experience was that I knew what the sentence wanted to express." [47] To
me, Messer's [48] investigations suggest that direct comprehension is probably the
rule in the case of isolated words. But even there, as Messer has neatly demon-

---

cisely remembered were independent of
the words used. The remembering occurred by means of logical constructions
using "thought-relationships."

(c) *Analogy-experiments:* Two series, each
of 20 proverbs, were presented. In the first
series, the instruction was to comprehend
the proverb; in the second, to state for each
proverb whether there had been one like it
in the first series, and which. Several proverbs which had no analogues in the first
series were included as controls. A subjective experience record was obtained.

Examples: Cobblers wear torn shoes;
Teachers have ill-mannered children,
Sharpening his sickle does not hold up the
reaper;
The feeding of live-stock is no waste of
time.

Results and Inferences: "Thought relationships" are agents of recall: where
they are absent, no turning back to the
first series occurs; where they are present, remembering is nearly perfect and
remains good for days. Where items

without analogues are massed, turning
back to the first series ceases, but occurs
again immediately when an item that has
an analogue appears.

(d) *Password-experiments:* A series of
sentences is presented, then a series of words
from each of the sentences. For the sentences, the instruction was to comprehend;
for the words, to recall the corresponding
sentence.

Examples: The forest has ears, the field
has eyes;
The forest. . .

Results and Inferences: 27 out of 30 items
more or less completely remembered.
Remembering fails if the sentences are
not conducive to thinking, or if the subject is not ready to think or work at
comprehending.

47. Here we see the limitations of
Buehler's findings; cf. notes 6 and 23,
above.

48. Messer (516).

strated, indirect meaning is not infrequent, and a consciousness of the sphere of superordinate, coordinate, and other concepts often plays a role.[49]*

[Passage omitted.] [50]

There is one point in our analysis which is still left in the dark. We have spoken throughout about thoughts brought halfway by the subject to meet the one to be comprehended. One might say that the latter arouses the former by reminding the subject of them; the question is how that occurs. We postponed the query about these real thought-relationships, and took the comprehending thought for granted; this isolation served our purpose of simple presentation.[51] Now we can turn to a few interesting peculiarities of the comprehending experience.

One of the striking phenomena, already observed by Messer [52]* in word comprehension, is the *shift in comprehension*. The unique pleasure accompanying a sudden shift in the comprehension of a sentence is familiar to all; this is the effect used in countless variations by printed and spoken jokes.[53] This shift can be exploited by the psychology of thinking, since it represents the varying of comprehension while the stimulation is kept constant. After some incidental observations of this sort, I decided to make use of this opportunity and collected many promising experimental tasks of this kind. . . . However, the ambiguous sentences I collected offered little difficulty to trained thinkers, and even the few I could use failed to yield satisfactory results. Possibly this effect does not come about unless unexpected. I shall therefore offer only a few occasional observations.

[Passage omitted.] [54]

(Do you understand?) "Want may peek in at the window of diligence, but dare not step through its door?"—Yes (19″). ". . . first I thought that want is a stimulus for diligence (without words); but then—with an aha!—this is

---

49.* Messer (516, pp. 71 ff.).

50. In the omitted section, Buehler takes issue with another aspect of Messer's views.

51. "Real thought relationships" apparently refers to the actual process of apperception. No concept such as "determining tendencies" and/or "anticipations" was introduced by Buehler to account for the actual process. The "iso-

lation for the purpose of simple presentation" which Buehler speaks of, resulted in the construct: "the thought brought halfway." It is probable that in the process of apperception there is no such meeting of two fully developed thoughts; see Chap. 24.

52.* Cf. Messer (516), pp. 89 ff.

53. See Freud (214), Schiller (670).

54. An example is omitted here.

meant differently: want here is something that can be driven away by diligence. This thought was quite general without sensory representation, I derived from the sentence only an optical image like a house with windows. . . ."

(Do you understand?) "One hammers in the nail and the other hangs his hat on it."—Yes (8″)—"First I thought: one supports the other. But then, no, one does the work, the other enjoys the result. The shift came quite suddenly, I don't know why and how. . . ."

What happens in such cases? . . . Often, the shift issues from a single word. The word is ambiguous and by chance its two meanings, together with the other words of the sentence, make two different thoughts. This is seen clearly in the following:

". . . I asked her about the purpose of her 'Dasein' " [55]—Yes.—"First I conceived of this philosophically. Then, after a brief pause, I became conscious that 'Dasein' has yet another meaning. The word seemed suddenly changed, having taken on a spatial significance. With that I knew that there was another meaning to the sentence, I knew approximately what it was but didn't think it through."

The motive for the shift lies mostly in a dissatisfaction with the first comprehension:

(Do you understand?) "We despise everything that can be explained."—Yes (6″).—"The slogan, 'the charm of the mysterious' (internally spoken), came immediately. I knew that this can eliminate the paradox. Yet a residue of dissatisfaction remained. Then I remembered the period of Enlightenment and my attitude toward it (I find it bad taste to want to explain everything). But there still remained a discomfort. Then suddenly came the shift: to explain means to master, what is explained is mastered and thereby settled. Only this gave a satisfying comprehension."

[Passage omitted.] [56]

The study of inter-thought relationships leads us to the characteristic experience of sentence comprehension. The emergence of conscious relationships

55. *Dasein* means both "presence" and "existence."

56. The omitted section contains examples in which (a) the two meanings of the ambiguous sentence are simultaneously in consciousness; (b) the consciousness of ambiguity precedes comprehension; (c) the ambiguity and the meaning of the whole sentence hinge on the same word.

completes the process of comprehension. It was not our intention to delve here into the antecedents of this consummatory act. The entirety of the problem I shall endeavor to treat elsewhere.[57]

57. Buehler elaborated on these explorations (111) in specific chapters of his later writings (105, 106, 108, 110).

CHAPTER 3

RECOGNITION AND "ME-NESS" [1]

By E. Claparède

KATZAROFF [2] has outlined a conception of recognition very close to the one I arrived at in the wake of some experiments with a hypnotic subject and a case of Korsakow syndrome. I should like to say a few words of this "theory of me-ness," which is similar to James's [3] conception, and a more or less clear formulation of which we both arrived at independently. Let us first recall—as does Katzaroff—that the psychological problem of recognition does not imply a consciousness of the past. For the logician, for the common man, and for the psychologist who regards mental activity from an objective point of view, recognition doubtless means that the object one recognizes is *already* known to him. But is that consciousness of repetition—or more exactly, of the *déjà* ("already before")—really contained in what is immediately given subjectively in recognition, that is, in the *feeling of familiarity?* [4] It does not seem so: when

1. Claparède (133). "Me-ness" here translates *moïté*.
2. Katzaroff (378).
3. James (353, I, 650) wrote:

. . . So that if we wish to think of a particular past epoch, we must think of a name or other symbol, or else of certain concrete events, associated therewith. Both must be thought of, to think the past epoch adequately. And to "refer" any special fact to the past epoch is to think that fact *with* the names and events which characterize its date, to think it, in short, with a lot of contiguous associates.
But even this would not be memory. Memory requires more than mere dating of a fact in the past. It must be dated in *my* past. In other words, I must think that I directly experienced its occurrence. It must have that "warmth and intimacy" which were so often spoken of in the chapter on

the Self, as characterizing all experiences "appropriated" by the thinker as his own.

James here refers to Chap. V in his Vol. I, which is still rewarding reading. His keen analysis of self-experience and of the role of the self in psychological processes in general, and thought-processes in particular, poses many questions still unanswered. His section on multiple personalities (pp. 379 ff.) makes particularly fortunate use of clinical material to explore the role of the self in memory and thought-processes.

4. Unlike Claparède, James (353) maintained that memory implies "dating of a fact in the past"; but like Claparède, he realized that it involves another component: "the object of memory is only an object imagined in the past to which

we are shown a design which has been presented to us before, the impression of familiarity, known-ness, like-ness, emerges before the impression of *déjà*, and may even stand alone. Introspection shows this.[5] It is true that in the usual circumstances of life we are prone to localize in the past the impressions we recognize, and this localization can be so rapid that it seems to be an integral part of the immediate recognition process. But this is just an illusion.[6*] If we consider the genesis of the mind, we find that recognition appeared much earlier than any localization. Animals show implicit recognition (of certain prey, of their domicile, and so on), though nothing in their behavior indicates that they apprehend the past and keep count of the dates of events. In children, recognition appears long before any notion of the past.[7]

---

the emotion of belief adheres" (353, I, 652).

5. This use of introspective evidence is questionable (a) unlike Lewin (460, 783), Claparède adduces introspective data as direct evidence, and not to complement and interpret behavioral data; (b) the subject-matter of these introspections is subtly elusive, being the distinction between experiences of "past-ness" and "familiarity" which are not well-defined, and the finer shadings of which particularly are little known. This reservation does not question the common impression that—within limits —the less well-known an object, the more a feeling of familiarity precedes the experience of "déjà" and localization in the past. It merely questions how reliable this "impression" is, and what exactly it means. For example, in encountering objects which are extremely well-known our experience is neither one of recognition, nor of familiarity, nor of past-ness.

The experiments Claparède reports below may be so adapted as to provide behavior-data to complement and interpret introspections.

6.* The theory which accounts for recognition by a localization in the past has hardly any advocates now. It is evident that localization in the past cannot explain—because it implies—recognition: to know whether one has localized correctly, to find the right one in a series of past events and the place where the memory-image is to be inserted, one must first recognize both the series and its diverse elements. Further, to affirm that an event has *already* been experienced, one must refer to a series of past events; but the utilization of that series presupposes what we have come to call recognition.

7. This argument may seem questionable, particularly since we have no evidence that recognition in animal and child is the same process as recognition in the adult human. For example, Lorenz (484) reports that unless the mother stork approaches the nest in a certain rigidly defined manner, the baby storks do not take food from her; neither does the mother stork feed its young unless they open and shut their beaks in a similarly well-defined manner. If a process of recognition is implied here, it would seem to be different from that in grown-up humans, being far more rigidly tied

Furthermore, we have cases where a feeling of familiarity accompanies the perceptions which the person is certain he has never had before: thus for instance it is characteristic of *paramnesia* that in it a feeling of familiarity is accompanied by that of *non-déjà vu* [8]* ("not having seen before").[9] The same

---

to certain "signs" and "valences." It is possible, however, that we take an exaggerated view of this difference. Should not the Zeigarnik (783) experiments warn us that memory (and recognition?) are more dependent on valences than learning experiments would have us believe? Cf. also Rapaport (591).

Elsewhere in my comments (Chap. 15, note 31, below) I have cited evidence for two kinds of organization of memory: the drive (motivational), and the conceptual. The distinction was not meant as a dichotomy, and the transition between the two was conceived to be fluid. Localization in the past and the experience of "déjà" are frames of reference within the conceptual organization of memory. Claparède's, Katzaroff's, and James's views concerning the role of "me-ness" in recognition may be considered early realizations of the existence of an organization of memories other than associative-conceptual. In fact, the "me-ness" of memories could be viewed as an indication that the "motivational organization" participates even in memory phenomena which are regulated by the associative-conceptual memory organization.

The relation between recognition in children and animals, and their notion of a past, bears only distantly on this central issue.

8.* I know full well that in paramnesias this impression is described as one of *déjà vu*. But I believe the *déjà* to be a secondary interpretation of the impression of familiarity. As far as I can judge by my own experience, the immediate impression of paramnesia is that of familiarity; it is exactly because this impression evokes nothing from the past that it seems bizarre and paradoxical, and that the subjects have the definite feeling of having seen it "in another life."

[Cf. Plato's "anamnesis" theory (570, pp. 365–66). The "not learned" (non empirical) knowledge which man discovers by deduction (ratio) is attributed by Plato to learning which has taken place "in another life." Whether subjective experiences of the sort here described could underlie such philosophical speculation is an intriguing, and for the psychology of invention, relevant problem. Cf. Freud (230, p. 366)].

9. Concerning *déjà vu*, cf. Chap. 25, p. 573 and note 274, below. The only psychological explanation so far of *déjà vu* ("fausse reconnaissance") is Freud's (210, pp. 168–71, 230). An example will illustrate his explanation (230, p. 337):

The patient, who was at that time a twelve-year-old child, was visiting a family in which there was a brother who was seriously ill and at the point of death; while her own brother had been in a similarly dangerous condition a few months earlier. But with the earlier of these two similar events there had been associated a fantasy that was incapable of entering consciousness—namely, a wish that her brother should die. Consequently, the analogy between the two cases could not become conscious. And the perception of it was replaced by the phenomenon of "having been through it all be-

holds for phenomena of *premonition* or *prévision immédiate*. For example, a lady hears for the first time a lecturer on a topic unknown to her; it seems to her that the moment he speaks she knows what he will say.[10*] This is a feeling of familiarity which has nothing to do with the past because it applies to the future.[11]

There are other feelings of this sort, more or less similar to that of familiarity, and like it they refer to past events yet do not themselves imply the notion of past: such, for instance, is the *feeling of the usual*. We have this because we repeatedly encounter identical circumstances, and our body, our reflexes, our very senses are so accustomed to these that our consciousness does not perceive them. This feeling of the usual is more subjective, more corporeal, than that of familiarity.

According to our theory, an object is recognized because it evokes a feeling

---

fore," the identity being displaced from the really common element on to the locality.

Cf. also Poetzl (574). More recently Bergler (47, p. 166) summarizing the psychoanalytic literature of *déjà vu* wrote:

Déjà vu is a response to an Id wish which, provoked by a real situation, emerges and causes the unconscious Ego to defend itself against it. In place of the repetition of an unconscious fantasy appears the sensation of *déjà vu*. The identity of two repressed fantasied experiences is replaced in consciousness by the identity of two apparently real situations. The Id impulse is primary; in Freud's example it is an aggressive Id wish, in Ferenczi's a libidinous one. Reality plays only the role of agent provocateur; the Id makes use of a favorable opportunity offered by the outer world to attempt to reel off an instinctual impulse.

Bergler adds his own observations in which the repressed is not an id-wish but a superego reproach. It may be surmised that other repressed and suppressed impulses (such as affects, ego interest, etc.) will also prove capable of producing *déjà vu* phenomena.

These psychoanalytic inferences shed light on the nature of "me-ness," which Claparède holds responsible when events are experienced, whether correctly or not, as though encountered before. The phenomenon is similar to slips of the tongue. But while in the latter the repressed impulse encroaches on the content of the reality-adequate thought, in the former it affects the manner of perceiving reality. That which is familiar to the subject is his previous self-experience of defense against the repressed impulse. It is indeed a "me-ness" experience, but a very specific one: the "me-ness" of a defensive position of the ego.

10.* Fairbanks (169).

11. These phenomena—like the *déjà entendu, déjà raconté, déjà eprouvé*, and *déjà senti* described by Freud—are varieties of *déjà vu*. See also Chap. 13, notes 25, and 29, below.

Claparède's argument that these apply to the *future* fastens on their manner of appearance. Like *déjà vu* phenomena, these too probably have their roots in repressed *past* experiences.

of "me-ness" to which it is tied by virtue of its previous presentations to the subject's consciousness.[12]

Does this approach differ from those which make recognition a consciousness of habit, or of associations which surround all repeated impressions? Could it not be maintained that the difference is but verbal, and that basically this "me-ness," characteristic of perceptions previously "experienced," rests only on the associations of these perceptions with other ideas (the woof of which is the *me*), and is but a name for the feeling which sets the associative chain in motion? No, because innumerable associative chains are stimulated or substimulated in one's life without giving a feeling of familiarity.[13] We can have entirely different feelings when a group of associations is suddenly evoked, such as, "That's it" or "That fits." It happens to me sometimes that I walk up to a shelf in my library to get a certain volume, but as I reach out I do not know which I am looking for. Then I begin to regard the books on the shelf to which my legs have automatically carried me, and when my eyes fall upon the title of the book I need, I have the impression "That's the one," an impression certainly akin to that of familiarity yet different from it. There is no doubt that the impression of "That's it" has a physiological substratum in that a perception stimulates a group of associations or momentarily suspended reactions. It is said that recognition consists in the unlatching of a suitable attitude: to recognize an object is to relate adequately to it. This is true to a great extent. Yet, if that adequate attitude is not accompanied by a feeling that the attitude or its object is familiar, we cannot properly speak of recognition but of *comprehension*. . . . However close this phenomenon is to recognition, it is clearly not the same.[14]

We shall soon see, in connection with a case of Korsakow syndrome, that a

12. In terms of the psychoanalytic theory, we would express this as, "by virtue of the identical striving it aroused"; and in Lewin's, "by virtue of the identical need it had a valence for."

13. This speculative argument is indirectly reinforced by recent experimental evidence, most of which regrettably pertains to recall and perception phenomena. The only study which deals directly with recognition, that of Tresselt and Levy (734), is no more than suggestive, because of an unfortunate choice of the material to be recognized. The study concludes that ego-involvement (presumably related to "me-ness") enhances recognition. Concerning ego-involvement, see Sherif and Cantril (686). For a critique of associative-learning theory from the point of view of ego-involvement, see Alper (29). On the role of ego-involvement in reminiscence, see Alper (28).

14. If we assume that for something to be "familiar" implies an experience of "me-ness," then we must conclude that Claparède's "attitude" concept was quite different from the current one.

chain of fitting associations does not suffice to produce recognition. Yet those associations which do play a role are not just any kind, but those *between the perception and the feeling of me-ness*.[15]

But what is this feeling of "me-ness"? What are its physiological bases? It matters little. I take it to be a fact of observation. If I have experienced a thing, I have the feeling that it is mine, belongs to my experience. This feeling manifests itself even after a few moments of observing a new object: as the object is considered and (ap)perceived, it becomes progressively familiar, appears more and more intimate, and attains finally the character of being "my object." It is not surprising then if on reappearing,[16*] after some time has elapsed, it again evokes that feeling.[17]

An attitude now by definition implies "me-ness." Compare our discussion of attitudes, in Chap. 1, notes 3 and 31. Actually, both in Bartlett's (37) and Koffka's (406) theory, it is the attitudes operating in recognition that confer "me-ness" on it. This also is the core of the psychoanalytic theory of *déjà vu:* the rousing of a definite (repressed) striving confers upon the experience the character of "me-ness" and "already seen." It might be concluded that an abstract "me-ness" does not exist, and that only concrete conditions of the ego (attitudes, etc.) arouse specific and qualitatively varied experiences of "me-ness."

15. Barlett (37), summarizing his experiments on perceiving and recognizing, comes to a similar conclusion. His distinction between hearing and listening parallels Claparède's between "just any" association and that with "the feeling of 'me-ness.'" Bartlett wrote:

Under no circumstances whatever does hearing without listening provide a sufficient basis for recognition. Listening, like hearing, is selective, but here the characteristics of the stimulus play a secondary part. Selective listening is determined mainly by the qualitative differences of stimuli in relation to predispositions—cognitive, affec-

tive, and motor—of the listener (p. 190).

It appears that hearing, though necessary for recognition, by itself gave no sufficient basis for recognition, and that recognition became possible when the hearing reactions were supplemented by an attitude, an orientation, a preferential response on the boy's part toward certain specific auditory situations (pp. 190–91).

In all cases recognizing is rendered possible by the carrying over of orientation, or attitude, from the original presentation to the re-presentation (p. 193).

16.* Cf. James, *Psychology* (354). "Whatever object possesses them [ardour and intimacy] in penetrating consciousness, its representation will partake of an ardour and intimacy analogous to those attaching to the present me." In his recent work "Erkenntnisstheorie," Duerr (150, p. 44) explained recognition similarly: every event of consciousness associates itself with the act of experiencing; when the event again presents itself, that act of experiencing is reproduced. Then the subject is conscious of "having been through it" in the past.

17. Neither the lack of surprise, nor James's and Duerr's similar pronouncements, explain the phenomenon. Clapa-

Thus the theory of "me-ness" differs from those of associative stimulation and habit in assuming that it is not the aura of associations (of any sort) which makes for recognition, but the feeling of "me-ness." [18]

---

rède's observation that "me-ness" is already present in perception is more to the point. Bartlett has experimentally shown that the attitudes responsible for recognition (and its distortions) are responsible for the organization of perception also. He realized that "me-ness" is not an undifferentiated feeling experience, but a matter of specific *selective* attitudes. The concept of selectiveness is crucial: if attitudes select in perception objects which have valences for them, then the same objects having valences will, on representation, arouse the very attitudes which originally selected them. This also is the core of Freud's cathectic theory of perception and memory. (Cf. Chap. 15, notes 21 and 22, below. See also Rapaport, 596.) Recently Tolman (733) found it necessary to introduce similar concepts into his theory of learning.

18. A concrete analysis of the role of "me-ness," which clarifies its relationship to the "aura of associations" and to "habits," was put forth by Koffka (406). Koffka's memory theory, which leans heavily on Koehler's (401) findings, is built on the assumption of the existence of "memory traces" and the dynamics of "trace fields." Koffka's theory also assumes that the trace field contains a relatively well-segregated part—the ego-system. (This ego-concept differs radically from that of psychoanalysis.) Koffka wrote (406):

Our theory of the Ego . . . allows us to accept Claparède's theory, freeing it from those aspects which are the outcome of the period at which he worked, and to incorporate it without any new hypothesis into our own system (p. 594).

In our theory the trace retained the dynamics of the process in a latent form. We also know that our environmental field does not consist of a number of "dead" or "indifferent" things, but that these things possess dynamic characters, such as physiognomic, functional, and demand characters [valences]. All these characters imply an object-Ego relationship, that is, an interplay of forces between the Ego and the environmental objects. Therefore, the trace of an object is, as a rule, part of a larger trace of which the object is but one subsystem, while a part of the Ego is another, these two sub-systems being connected by forces corresponding to the forces obtaining in the process of perception. Communication of the trace with a new object-process means, therefore, at least potentially, communication of this whole trace with the new process. And according to Claparède's theory, recognition can take place only when the whole trace becomes involved and not merely the object subsystem (pp. 594-95).

This theory allows certain deductions about the conditions under which recognition is more or less likely to occur. Since it depends upon the participation of the Ego-part in the particular trace systems, the structure of this system will be of great importance. The closer the dynamic intercourse between the Ego and the object part, the more likely, ceteris paribus, will recognition be. Now in the structure of the behavioral environment there are things close to and remote from the Ego and even some that have practically no Ego-connection. According to the theory, and to all appearances in conformity with the facts, the former are better recognized than the

But does not this theory merely postpone the problem to be solved? It tells us that the objects touching upon our consciousness are characteristically tainted by it, somewhat as a painted bench would leave a mark on those who sat on it—so that consciousness [on meeting these objects again], recognizes

latter. *In many cases the Ego-object relationship will be, at least partly, due to the interests and attitudes of the Ego.* Thus whatever has interested us, attracted our attention, is relatively easily recognized (pp. 595–96).

Koffka describes the role of the ego and attitudes in the trace field and their effect in recognition as follows:

We must remember the trace column with its preservation of the Ego-environment organization, and we must also remember the continuity of the Ego, which gives a special kind of structure to the Ego part of the column. Inasmuch as the Ego is, as a rule, more or less in the center of its environment, we can picture the Ego part of the trace column as its core and the environmental part as a shaft, keeping in mind that core and shaft support each other. We know that the shaft is full of strains and stresses which produce aggregation and other unifications of traces at various levels. But we also know that the core, despite its great internal complexity, has, as a whole, a much stronger unity than the shaft as a whole. If then an attitude arises, what will happen? To follow up our example: if I want to link up figures shown to me now with figures presented yesterday, what is my attitude, and how does it become effective? In the first place this attitude has the character of a quasi-need, it corresponds to a tension in the Ego part at the tip of the column. This tension can be relieved only through that part of the trace column which contains yesterday's figures, since a linking up of today's with yesterday's is possible only if these traces influence the new process. In other words, the attitude requires the creation of a field which includes these particular traces (p. 609).

Koffka, however, doubts whether "me-ness" and "attitudes" are *always* indispensably necessary conditions for the communication with each other of traces, or traces and processes (hypothetical concomitants of past and present stimulations):

It is possible to interpret both Lewin and Bartlett as asserting that communication between process and trace as an event entirely within the shaft of the trace column does not occur. Whether such a claim is true or not, experiments will have to decide. Personally I do not believe it. Again I hold that dynamic relations within the shaft, that is, within the environmental field, and between core and shaft, may be effective, and not only dynamic relations within the core, the Ego system. Despite this belief, which, as I just said, will have to be tested by experiments, I recognize the enormous importance of attitudinal factors. As I envisage the problem, the alternative, either spontaneous recognition or recognition always mediated by attitude, does not exist. That intra-shaft forces are necessary even where an attitude made communication possible, we have seen above. Thus a frank acceptance of the effectiveness of all the forces that may come into play seems the safest position to adopt before new experimental evidence is adduced (p. 611).

The relationship of Koffka's theory to the psychoanalytic theory of memory and thinking, and to the recent experiments on the effect of motivational, set-like, and personality factors, is still unclear; so is the relationship of these factors to Lewin's and Bartlett's findings and theories. Yet it is quite clear that, as soon as we transcend the limitations

them because they bear its stamp, so to speak. But how does it "recognize" this stamp, this characteristic mark, as its own? How does the *me* recognize itself? Does one not reintroduce here the entire problem of recognition?

No; I believe that this new manner of posing the question is a step forward, for it eliminates one unknown: the past. It is no longer a matter of finding out by what mystery an impression can be known as the repetition of one in the past, but merely of finding in an image reappearing in consciousness those characteristics which make for its "me-ness." [19]

Do these characteristics reside in an ease of the motor or intellectual reaction which elicits that perception of "familiarity"? No; because, as we have seen, habit is different from recognition, the habitual is different from the familiar.[20] Besides, if recognition were explained by habit, it should also be explained how

---

of purely associationist theory, the various findings and theories begin to converge. For instance, the problem of trace communications "within the environmental field" (that is, the direct communication of "shafts") shows some similarity to the psychoanalytic problem of relative "functional autonomy" of ego-processes, particularly thought-processes. See Chap. 19, below.

19. Bartlett's application of Head's (314) schema concept may shed further light on Claparède's comment that the concept "me-ness" eliminates one unknown—the past—from the theory of recognition. According to Head, "every postural change enters consciousness already charged with its relation to something that has gone before" (37, p. 199). In other words, it enters consciousness already integrated into the postural-model created by past changes. Every new change in turn alters the model in relation to which the next change will be experienced. These "organized models of ourselves" Head called "schemata" (37, p. 200). Bartlett generalized Head's "postural schema," applying it to memory-organization. The schemata are con-

tinuously changing with new experience. They are organized by attitudes, and it is by means of these attitudes (once they are re-aroused) that the organism "turns round upon its own 'schemata,'" recognizes and remembers. Bartlett concludes: "Remembering is a constructive justification of this attitude" (37, p. 200).

We thus see how the "past" is implicit to the memory schemata, and how it is eliminated by them as an unknown in recognition. Whether or not a memory can become conscious, or an experience recognized, depends upon the attitude which prevailed in the original perception; whether or not its "pastness" also will become conscious depends upon the attitude which determines the recall or the recognition. With the too-well-known, the prevailing attitudes can be justified in recall and recognition without a localization in the past. In *déjà vu*, the attitude and the experience of "pastness" together do not suffice to "justify" the attitude.

20. Cf. MacCurdy (488, p. 113) and Koffka (406, pp. 591 ff., particularly p. 596).

it follows from it. It would have to be explained how a process, merely by being repeated, can give us the impression that it belongs to us, that it is *mine*—that is to say, how can that consciousness of belonging to me, which is the basis of the feeling of familiarity, spring from an impression of an ease of reaction which is qualitatively quite different from it!

We touch here upon a very obscure and surely insoluble question. The continuity and personal character of consciousness are primitive facts for the psychologist, and must be taken for granted. The fact that consciousness regards the objects it perceives as its very own, as belonging to its experiences, and that they evoke, when they present themselves again, the same impression of "me-ness" which they bore before, is no doubt the manifestation of a primitive function which must be so taken for granted, because otherwise mental life would be inconceivable and psychology have no field.

The propensity of states of consciousness to cluster around a *me* which persists and remains the same in the course of time, is a postulate of psychology, as space is a postulate of geometry.[21]

But does this remark not render an explanation of "familiarity" illusory?

No. The unity, continuity, and personal character of consciousness are a *conditio sine qua non* of recognition; it is quite certain that for the psychologist they are given as a primitive datum. But does recognition spring directly from that continuity and that fundamental unity of consciousness? or is it the other way around, that there is an articulation between that fundamental unity and the feeling of familiarity, a link that can be found by empirical science? This is the problem.

If one considers cases of abnormality of or failure of recognition, the answer is clearly positive: the mechanism of the experience of familiarity is accessible

21. Claparède's presentation of "me-ness" and consciousness as postulates must be understood to be a product of his struggle against the prevailing psychology of his time, which was one without "me-ness" and consciousness. The position of Rogers's (617) concept of the "self" in our time is similar. Note W. Hunter's (345) critique of the treatment of "consciousness" in the new Boring-Langfeld-Weld textbook (84), which is illuminating in this respect. Psychoanalysis, however, has succeeded in building a theory which—whatever its other shortcomings—demonstrates that a psychology which does not disregard self and consciousness need not introduce them as postulates, but rather as phenomenal data amenable to theoretical and experimental analysis. See Chap. 16, note 14, below.

to empirical science, and the proof is that it can be destroyed in isolation, while
the other parts of the mental apparatus continue to function more or less normally.[22]

The states in which such isolated destruction or change can be seen are those
to which Katzaroff [23] has already referred: Korsakow syndrome [24] and the
post-hypnotic state.[25] I should like to dwell at some length on the memory function of a Korsakow case which I examined on various occasions:

The patient was a woman hospitalized at Asile de Bel-Air. She was 47 at the
time of the first experiment, 1906. Her illness had started around 1900. Her old
memories remained intact: she could correctly name the capitals of Europe,
make mental calculations, and so on. But she did not know where she was,
though she had been at the asylum five years. She did not recognize the doctors
whom she saw every day, nor her nurse who had been with her for six months.[26]
When the latter asked the patient whether she knew her, the patient said: "No,
Madame, with whom have I the honor of speaking?" She forgot from one minute to the next what she was told, or the events that took place. She did not
know what year, month, and day it was, though she was being told constantly.
She did not know her age, but could figure it out if told the date.

I was able to show, by means of learning experiments done by the saving

22. A pathological condition in which
a certain function (in this case recognition) is particularly impaired offers
exceptional opportunity to study the
function in question. But Claparède's
"destroyed in isolation" implies more.
The more carefully we study the conditions under which a certain function is
"destroyed in isolation," the clearer it
becomes that no such "isolation" actually
exists. (See Chap. 27, below.) Our present theoretical view of the psychic apparatus makes it difficult in any case to
conceive of such isolated destruction.
Cf. our considerations on varying states
of consciousness, Chap. 9, notes 25 and
55, and Chap. 13, notes 21, 22, 50, and
56, below.

23. Katzaroff (378).

24. See Chaps. 13 and 27; cf. also

Rapaport (591, pp. 223 ff.), for evidence
that the disorder in the Korsakow syndrome is by no means an isolated memory disorder.

25. Erickson and Erickson (163) have
adduced evidence that post-hypnotic
memory phenomena are not isolated
memory changes. Post-hypnotic behavior, according to them, is always embedded in a spontaneously renewed
trance state, as indicated by observable
features besides the execution of the
post-hypnotic suggestion.

26. This is the memory disorder usually described as anterograde amnesia.
See Rapaport (591, pp. 218 ff.). For the
description of the most extreme case of
this sort reported, see Stoerring (715).
Cf. also Krauss (418), and Chaps. 13 and
27, below.

method, that not all ability of mnemonic registration was lost in this person.[27*] What is worthy of our attention here was her inability to evoke recent memories voluntarily, while they did arise automatically, by chance, as recognitions.[28]

When one told her a little story, read to her various items of a newspaper, three minutes later she remembered nothing, not even the fact that someone had read to her; but with certain questions one could elicit in a reflex fashion some of the details of those items.[29*] But when she found these details in her consciousness, she did not recognize them as memories but believed them to be something "that went through her mind" by chance, an idea she had "without knowing why," a product of her imagination of the moment, or even the result of reflection.[30]

I carried out the following curious experiment on her: to see whether she would better retain an intense impression involving affectivity, I stuck her hand with a pin hidden between my fingers. The light pain was as quickly forgotten as indifferent perceptions; a few minutes later she no longer remembered it. But when I again reached out for her hand, she pulled it back in a reflex fashion, not knowing why. When I asked for the reason, she said in a flurry, "Doesn't one have the right to withdraw her hand?" and when I insisted, she said, "Is there perhaps a pin hidden in your hand?" To the question, "What makes you suspect me of wanting to stick you?" she would repeat her old statement, "That

27.* Cf. my note (131) and the thesis of Mrs. Bergmann (50), also similar experiments by Brodmann (95) and Gregor (287).

[Prior to these experiments it was assumed that such anterograde amnesias were due to loss of registration ability. See Stoerring (715); compare also Kohnstamm (410).]

28. It is characteristic of what Freud calls the secondary process that in it ideas can be evoked voluntarily, while in the primary process they always rise automatically. It should be noted, however, that at times even in ordered thinking voluntary effort does not avail. The dividing lines are not sharp here. Cf.

Rapaport et al. (602, I, 167–69, 176–79, 195–200, 323–29).

29.* See Katzaroff's (378, p. 25) examples.

30. The inability for voluntary recall and the lack of "me-ness" may both be related to the absence of the necessary "attitude," "motivational set." Cf. Chap. 27, notes 27, 28, 38, 43, 46, below. They report cases in which, instead of lack of "me-ness" of a memory, "me-ness" attended even suggested ideas and raised them to the status of memories. Both observations indicate an impairment of the reflective awareness characteristic of normal states of consciousness.

was an idea that went through my mind," or she would explain, "Sometimes pins are hidden in people's hands." But never would she recognize the idea of sticking as a "memory." [31]

What does a case like this teach us about recognition?

It is clear from these experiments (which I repeated a number of times and in various ways) that if the patient did not recognize the memories or the objects, it was not because the objects evoked no associations or adaptive reactions in her. On the contrary: in the very halls of the institution which she claimed not to recognize (though she had now been there six years), she walked around without getting lost; she knew how to find the toilet without being able to say where it was, describe it, or have a conscious memory of it. When the nurse came she did not know who she was ("With whom have I the honor of talking?"), but soon after would ask her whether dinner time was near, or some other domestic question. These facts prove that her habits were very well re-

---

31. This observation may at first appear strikingly unique. It is so in the sense that the experience implied in the *cognized* thought is not *recognized* even though it is recent. Closer scrutiny shows that the striking uniqueness lies only in the *recency* and *concreteness* of the experience not recognized. A great variety of other cognitions without recognitions is familiar to us in psychopathology and psychotherapy. Obsessions, for instance, are "ego-alien" ideas, that is, we do not recognize them as our own. They are devoid of the direct experience of "me-ness" (even though the attendant anxiety may indirectly indicate "me-ness"). True, in these cases it is not a concrete experience—that is, one in which an external event played a paramount role—which remains unrecognized. Let us consider, however, a delusion; for instance, a simple delusional variant of the obsession, "I may kill my sister": namely, "I *have* killed my sister." Here an internal experience is recognized, correctly in so far as "me-ness" is concerned, incor-

rectly as a concrete external experience. Further examples of cognition without recognition are seen in the course of psychoanalytic (and other) therapy, when memories of concrete events, internal experiences, and relationships emerge in the form of dreams, hypnagogic experiences, daydreams, associations, direct representations amidst vehement denials, direct representations with some "me-ness" but devoid of corresponding emotions, etc. Cf. Freud (248, and 209, pp. 546–47), and Chap. 23, III, below.

The only attempt to systematize form variants of conscious experience, both those here discussed and others, was undertaken by the phenomenological school of philosophy and psychology: Husserl (346), Meinong (511), and Brentano (90). See also Binswanger (63), and for a recent popularizing account, Sartre (631); on Sartre, cf. also Rapaport (598), also Chap. 25, note 6, and Chap. 26, note 128, below.

tained and active, and if she did not recognize her room, her nurse, or the man who had just stuck her with a pin, it was not because these objects were not tied up with associations or adaptive reactions.

If one examines the behavior of such a patient, one finds that everything happens as though the various events of life, however well associated with *each other* in the mind, were incapable of integration with the *me* itself. The patient is alive and conscious. But the images which he perceives in the course of that life, which penetrate and become more or less fixated in his organic memory, lodge there like strange bodies; and if by chance they cross the threshold of consciousness, they do not evoke the feeling of "me-ness" which alone can turn them into "memories." [32]

We can distinguish between two sorts of mental connections: those established *mutually between representations*, and those established between *representations* and *the me*, the personality. In the case of purely passive associations or idea-reflexes, solely the first kind of connection operates; in the case of voluntary recall and recognition, where the *me* plays a role, the second kind of connection enters. [33]

In relation to the *me* as center, the connections of the second kind may be called *egocentric functions*, those of the first *marginal*. In recognition, the action of these egocentric connections is centripetal—that is, the perception or representation given evokes a feeling of "me-ess." In voluntary recall, the action of the egocentric connections is centrifugal. "Voluntary" here means only that the *me* is involved in determining the phenomenon; the manner of its intervention is not stated.

This hypothesis concerning the intervention of the *me*—which by the way

---

32. The phrases "lodge there like strange bodies" and "by chance cross the threshold of consciousness" fail to do justice to the phenomenon. It appears rather that these memories come to consciousness quite appropriately and not "by chance," though they cannot be voluntarily evoked. Therefore we must assume that they *are* integrated with memory- and thought-organization, though in such fashion that "me-ness" does not accompany their conscious experience. The nature of habits and automatisms implies a similar problem for the theory of memory- and thought-organization. Cf. Hartmann on ego-apparatuses, Chap. 19, VIII, below.

33. This is the problem which Koffka has formulated in terms of interactions between trace-core and trace-shaft, vs. those between two trace-shafts. See note 18, above.

merely describes the facts of observation in the form of a mechanism—accounts for the fact that loss of recognition is generally accompanied by loss of voluntary recall.[34]

Similarly, we may assume that hypnosis, or rather the post-hypnotic state, is a suspending of the activity of egocentric associations, which at once blocks recognition as well as voluntary recall; meanwhile marginal associations continue in the form of automatisms, automatic writing, or automatic recall. These the subject does not recognize as memories, but takes to be "inspirations" or casts into an hallucinatory form.[35*]

The difference between the post-hypnotic state and the Korsakow syndrome is that in the latter there is a pathological disorder of the egocentric connections; in hypnosis and post-hypnotic states there is only an inhibitory suspension of them. This hypothesis is in accord with the lack of initiative characteristic of hypnotic subjects.[36*] In the wake of that inhibition, the images presented in hypnosis do not unite with the normal *me*, and when they emerge later, they appear to the *me* as something foreign, never before experienced.[37]

Thus we understand the nature of the relation between feelings of familiarity

34. The relationship of the loss of recognition to the loss of voluntary recall —though by no means proven to be general—is an important and unclear issue. The prerequisite for its clarification is a dynamic theory of the will, which we do not have as yet. It may be assumed that the subjective experience of will, and the motivational conditions to which it corresponds, both depend upon the distribution of cathectic energies at the disposal of the ego, and on their relationship to the cathectic energies of the id. The specific cathectic conditions corresponding to the form-variants of will experience have not been explored as yet. Nor has the relationship been clarified between the motivating attitudes of recognition and recall on the one hand, and the distribution of cathectic energies underlying volition, on the other.

35.* Compare our work on *hypnosis* (132).

[This description of hypnosis accounts only for hypnotic automatisms, and conceives of hypnosis as a state of dissociation. Even so, it is paradoxical to designate automatic writing as a marginal function: usually it embodies material of central importance. It would seem Claparède refers primarily to post-hypnotic suggestions. The ego-syntonic hypnotic phenomena (emotional reexperiencing, catharsis, etc.) are disregarded. See Brenman and Gill (88). Cf. also Rapaport (591, pp. 172 ff.).]

36.* Claparède (132, p. 392).

[The lack of initiative is by no means a general characteristic of the hypnotic and post-hypnotic states. Cf. for instance, Erickson (163, 161).]

37. The fact that there are hypnotic states without post-hypnotic amnesia is disregarded here. See, however, Brenman and Gill (273).

and voluntary recall: both imply the existence of "me-ness." Voluntary acts imply processes which we call "me." If for one reason or another some presentations are not associated with a feeling of "me-ness," the subject does not have the impression of possessing them and thus cannot recall them—as one cannot at will move his ears unless the muscles have first revealed their existence through certain inner sensations. The first prerequisite of recalling a memory is the impression that we possess it. It is thus understandable that if the impression of "me-ness" is destroyed, the absence of recognition which follows is coupled with an absence of voluntary recall.

The feeling of "me-ness" is, so to speak, the tie that binds the memory-image to our *me*, by which we hold on to it and by virtue of which we can summon it from the depths of the subconscious.[38] If that tie is severed, we lose the ability of voluntary recall.[39]

This relation between recognition and voluntary recall seems to me to be corroborated by the examination of the *biological significance of the feeling of familiarity*. What purpose is served by this feeling of familiarity as a distinct conscious phenomenon? The lower animals behave as though they recognized their food, their enemies, etc. But this is a matter of implicit mechanical and reflex recognition, explainable entirely by the existence of innate or acquired

38. In psychoanalytic terms, this would read "preconscious." French psychology and psychiatry used the term "subconscious" for both the preconscious and the unconscious.

39. The relation of recognition to preconscious thought-processes is treated extensively by Kris, Chap. 23, below. The voluntary vs. involuntary character of subjective experience appears to be dependent (as in attention vs. concentration) on the availability and distribution of energy-cathexes at the disposal of the ego (cf. Chap. 15, note 21, below).

The experience of "me-ness" appears to be dependent on the prevailing state of consciousness, which in turn is also dependent on the distribution of attention cathexes (see Chap. 16, note 14,

this volume). In dreams, for instance, though the totality of the dream is built of the dreamer's wishes and experiences, only part of them has a "me-ness." The situation is similar for the loss of "me-ness" in cases of fugue and multiple personality. In recording various thought-formations of my own, ranging from those in hypnagogic to those in dream states, I obtained material suggesting that the closer the state approximates that of the dream the more "me-ness" recedes, self-reflective awareness is in abeyance, voluntary effort (or its effectiveness) becomes sparse, involuntarily rising ideas lacking "me-ness" become more frequent, and thought-formations resembling those of multiple personality begin to occur.

connections between certain impressions and certain adequate reactions.[40] A feeling of familiarity is of no use here. Why did the process of implicit recognition become explicit, that is, mental? For the very reason other physiological processes became so: our processes become conscious (or, if you please, cortical) when they must master new reactions or are sufficiently tied to impressions met before; and they fall back into the subconscious when the habit is sufficiently established. The feeling of familiarity thus appears where its presence, as a mental phenomenon, becomes necessary for an adequate reaction—that is, where the recognized object does not immediately evoke such a reaction.[41] When we meet a friend in the street we greet him without a conscious feeling of familiarity; in this case, implicit reflex recognition suffices. But when someone looks familiar and we cannot at once tell when and where we met him, whether or not we have been introduced and consequently should greet him—there the feeling of familiarity is useful to prod our attention into *searching* our memory (voluntary recall), in order to form an adequate reaction. . . .[42]

These pages do not claim to have greatly illumined the problem of the feeling of familiarity! They are meant to show that the problem is easily accessible to psychological investigation, which is denied by that discouraging and sterile opinion which considers it an irreducible and unanalyzable faculty of consciousness. The feeling of familiarity implies the intervention of the *me*, that is, those factors that constitute the personality; therefore the analysis of its conditions of existence is obscured by the fact that we are still unclear as to the nature and function of these factors. It may well be the most fruitful result of the study of recognition is that it gives us a new angle from which to regard the problems of the *me* and the mechanisms of "me-ness." [43]

APPENDIX

Recognition in spite of distortion of mental images. Those who have conducted experiments requiring a subject to describe the memory of a picture

40. Cf. Lewin, on the valences of genuine-needs, Chap. 5, II, 1 (c), below.

41. Cf. Hartmann, Chap. 19, VIII, and Kris, Chap. 23, note 48, below.

42. Cf. MacCurdy (488).

43. Herein lies the main merit of Claparède's paper. The role of personality factors in such basic processes as learning, memory, recognition, and perception, has been too long disregarded. Claparède elucidated an important facet of this role. Even though recently many experimenters have tackled this issue, few have seen the general problem in such broad terms as Claparède. Cf., however, Alper (28).

observed for a certain time, must have noticed his astonishment when he is again confronted with the original. Though recognizing it at once, he will say, "I didn't imagine it that way." He thought that "this person was turned the other way," "that object was bigger" or "another color"; but all this does not prevent him from being certain that it is the picture he had seen. Recognition does not imply the presence of a memory-image which compares with the original or fuses with the perception.[44] If this were the case, a deformation of the memory-image would block recognition.

I shall present some minor experiments conducted with students—quoting but a few, since they are easily repeated—which clearly show that the recognition process is independent of a memory-image:

A series of eight pictures (colored vignettes) is presented for thirty seconds; immediately afterwards the subject describes them in writing. Then the pictures are again shown, but this time interspersed among other similar ones. The subject is to state which ones he recognizes and what impressions they make on him. The experiments always yielded correct results, that is, the pictures actually seen before were always recognized.

On examining the descriptions and remarks of the subjects, we find that they show little correspondence to the real pictures. For example:

Picture 1. A BASKET FULL OF FRUIT. *Written description:* "A large basket full of flowers." *Verbal remark* upon seeing the picture again: "I thought it was flowers but I see it is fruit; I thought the basket was square and lighter in color. Now I remember having seen the apples and pears."

2. A PARROT ON ITS PERCH. *Description:* "A reddish parrot on a lamp rod." *Verbal remark:* "That is no lamp rod."

3. A WOMAN HOLDING A WATERING POT. *Verbal remark:* "She seems bigger than I thought. I imagine she was watering flowers." (The absence of flowers did not prevent definite recognition.)

4. TWO URCHINS SITTING ON A SLED. *Verbal remark:* "I didn't represent them in that pose; I thought they were sitting astride the sled." The subject then added: "It is not by the memory-image that I recognize it; that came afterwards, I am quite sure."

These few examples—I do not find it necessary to give more—support some of Mr. Katzaroff's conclusions; that is why I mention them here.

44. Cf. Bartlett (37, p. 194).

CHAPTER 4

COMMENTS CONCERNING PSYCHOLOGICAL FORCES AND ENERGIES, AND THE STRUCTURE OF THE PSYCHE [1]

By Kurt Lewin

THUS FAR experimental psychology could rarely take a well-founded stand in the controversy on the theory of human drives and affects, that is, on the theory of central psychic layers. It has concerned itself mainly with the psychology of the sensorium (perception), with imagery (as related to perception), and with the related experimental problems of intellection and memory. The recent advances in these fields and particularly in the psychology of perception were fruitful and sweeping. In contrast to these advances, experimental psychology failed to find an avenue to the exploration of drives and the deeper psychic layers, even though historically there do exist significant points of departure for such explorations in the psychology of will. The reasons for this failure are varied and many.

Externally the difficulty may seem to be merely one of experimental *technique;* for example, that the subject's social milieu cannot be controlled, or that the apparatus is inadequate to measure exactly the time relationships of the fleeting processes involved.

It seems, however, that fundamentally these are not technical difficulties, either here or elsewhere in psychology. The developmental history of sciences shows that the victory of young sciences over such apparently external difficulties is closely related to the development of their theory.[2]

1. Lewin (463). A translation of the second part of this paper was published in Lewin (467, pp. 43 ff.) under the title "On the Structure of the Mind." Here I present only the first part, not previously published in English.
2. The theory of thought-organization is a "young science" indeed. The importance of Lewin's paper for this young discipline is twofold: first, it needs keen awareness of the methodological and epistemological issues Lewin treats of here; second, Lewin's considerations grew from experiments related to and even belonging within the realm of thought organization (460, 783, 65).

[Passage omitted.] [3]

The investigator is subject to a paradoxical, and in the final analysis, unsolvable tension.[4] The fruitfulness of this tension depends on the degree to which he experiences it in the form of a real, concrete, here-and-now approachable and solvable task.

On the one hand, he follows a theory without which his experiments would be blind and senseless, and on the scope and force of which the significance of his experiments depends. The crucial direction here is toward ever more deep and central points, from which it is possible to encompass the totality of the psyche; it is here that the investigator creates a new world. From this vantage point, every concrete instance which the investigator encounters plays merely the role of *an example,* whose theoretical implication is in final analysis always an open question.[5]

On the other hand, the experimental investigator wants to prove his theory by an experiment—that is to say, on a concrete psychological event occurring at a given time, in a certain human being, and in a definite environment. He must build a bridge from the theory to the full reality of the individual case, which is always a historically singular, never-recurring fact with a lively fill of propensities and relationships. He must build such a bridge even if theoretically he is concerned only with one specific aspect of the event. The concrete conditions the investigator accepts as an experiment do not face him as something ambiguous, problematic, and indefinite in their theoretical implication, but rather as inexorable judges of what is true and false. They are the judgment-seat which determines whether his theoretical assumptions are mere fantasies, like so many others', or can claim to be a documented theory. Besides the experimental facts, many of the small and great psychic events of the everyday

3. The omitted part compares the experimenter's position to that of Kierkegaard's "religious man."

4. This tension between fancy, hunch, theory on the one hand, and empirical facts on the other, is a cardinal point for success in experimental science; the subjective experience of this tension in the investigator is a cardinal subject-matter in the psychology of research and discovery, which is a part of the broad field of psychology of thought-organization. Cf. Wertheimer (763), Hadamard (298), Wallas (749), Rapaport and Frank (601), Rapaport (599).

5. This view of the role of theory in experimentation is in its spirit identical with that of Newton's hypothetico-deductive method. The struggle between adherence to the letter and adherence to the spirit of this method characterizes the history of psychology in the last few

partake in this judging role, since every theory must account for them also.

The investigator must be convinced in a very definite, tangible way of the knowability and rationality of the countless facts, inconsequential and shaking, ludicrous and grandiose, with the intangibility and inexhaustibility of which it is his daily sustenance to struggle. The investigator must steadily face the facts . . . with open eyes, and unburdened by any theory; and just because he is an experimental investigator, he must know that only the surface of the mass of so-called facts is clear and unequivocal, and even that only to a limited degree, while its depth is mostly unclear and ambiguous. He must know also that, leaning on a few experimentally established facts, he is entitled to face often a whole array of everyday "facts" with supreme disbelief and knowing-better, even if the everyday facts seem to speak a language entirely different from that of his theory. Finally, he must know that every step of his progress depends on his advances in the sphere of *theory*, and on the conceptual consistency, breadth, and depth reached therein.[6]

The abyss between the apparently abstract theory and the earthbound reality of the experimental procedure—an abyss reflected in the paradoxical position of this reality just described—creates a continuous and great tension in the investigator, which he must use to bridge the gap by tightly knit relationships. He must be able to formulate his theory so as to point up decisive differences between his and other theories, and to give it concrete experimental form so that he may expect certain processes to take one or the other course, depending on whether his theory or another one is correct. From these theoretically predicted *typical* processes he must advance to definite concrete cases, to examples which are not merely imaginary but can be also actually realized; these living examples, though they will always possess propensities which are not implied by the theory must, nevertheless, retain a quite unequivocal relationship to

decades. The issue was rarely formulated as forcefully as it is here by Lewin. Recently Cantril *et al.* (123) formulated it for psychology and Rich (610) for geology.

6. In the field of experimentation concerning thought-processes, this attitude requires developing experiments which will help to encompass, within one theoretical framework, such diverse phe-nomena as memory for nonsense and meaningful material, breadth of general information available for recall and use, repression, reminiscence, amnesia, obliviscence, Korsakow memory-disorder, concept-formation, syncretistic disorders of conceptual thinking, planning, disorders of anticipation and time-sense, etc. Cf. Rapaport (590).

the theoretically essential facts. Finally, the investigator must be able to bring about such concrete cases in the face of objective, technical—and often quite extraneous—difficulties without interfering with or altering what is theoretically essential.

[Passage omitted.] [7]

The bridge between the theoretical, abstract assumptions and the concrete reality of the single experimental case cannot be built by means of well-circumscribed isolated logical operations. We are not dealing here with syllogisms which, somehow pre-formed, must be correctly repeated. The work begins rather from both ends at once, and indeed frequently from many points simultaneously in fits and starts, and the new bricks are added, now here, now there. At times a long shot is taken to push the theory a long stretch forward in the direction of concrete facts, risking the danger that the bridge will be insufficiently arched and that incomplete parts of it will be left precariously dangling up in the air.[8] Then again at other times the progress is left to the driving-force of the experimental facts alone. In final analysis, however, the task is to maintain at every step of the experiment the tension directed toward theory forma-

7. In the omitted section Lewin stresses that the technical arrangements of experiments may be just as important for the subject as the stimulus proper.

8. Lewin's point is that without bold theoretical hunches neither plain deduction from existing theory nor plain induction from experimentally gathered material alone leads to the development of a vigorous experimental science. This point is well elucidated from another angle by Cantril et al. (123, Part III). In early developmental phases of all sciences, such "hunches" become abundant and pave the way for the selection of those few hunches which are amenable to experimental verification. Compare this with Silberer's "mythological forms of knowledge," Chap. 9, pp. 210 ff., below. It is more than a bare possibility that the impatience of our time against hunches, theoretical speculations, or "mythological forms of knowledge" in general, is a handicap rather than a prod for the development of psychology as a science.

It is probable that much unbridled speculation will still be necessary in the field of psychology before we acquire a set of hunches amenable to experimental exploration and broad enough to serve as a base on which an experimental science replacing present-day "dynamic psychology" can be erected. In the field of the psychology of thought-organization, at any rate, facts and knowledge are so fragmentary and scattered that only the most general hunches—rarely amenable to direct experimental test—can capture the field in a synoptic fashion.

Hunches are, however, also forms of thought. Though to a greater or lesser degree they do take the real nature of the subject-matter into consideration, essentially they are fashioned by those fun-

tion and theoretical advance, to eliminate circumstances which weaken the purity of experimental decision, and to make use of every fact that promises to document, disprove, or develop the theory beyond its present form. The fruitfulness and significance of an investigation depends usually on the breadth and intensity of the tension that it has bridged. Experiment and theory are poles of the *same* dynamic whole.

Therefore, even the theoretical assumptions of the experimental investigator must be earthbound and of intuitive certainty. Whatever he undertakes in his concrete research must be determined from both the theoretical and the concrete-experimental end, but not because of his weakness in one or the other. Neither his lack of experimental ability to follow the sway of his ideas, nor the obdurate, inert, or fleeting character of the subject-matter, resisting scientific penetration and formulation, should determine the experiment; rather it should be determined by theory and concrete psychological fact together, because in final analysis recourse to the full concrete reality is the touchstone of the internal validity and depth of a theory.

To my mind, the fundamental phenomenon of scientific life—or at least of experimental investigation—both in theorizing and experimenting, is the sustained dynamic tension between the striving toward ever broader theoretical assumptions and the encompassing of concrete events in all their important and trivial aspects.

Therefore, insufficiencies and difficulties of experimentation are not a matter technical improvements can cope with. They are usually, at least in young sciences, indications that the theory itself is false or, even worse, not sufficiently concrete, live and broad—in other words, not sufficiently mature, or finally is not taken seriously enough. In addition—and this is certainly true for the psychology of affect and will—certain false general views of philosophy, epistemology, and theory of science are often insisted upon, with greater or less conscious awareness, as *methodological* principles; or contrariwise, correct general views of this sort are not followed radically enough in the actual investigations.

---

damental, in many respects primitive, and idiosyncratic patterns of thought which grow from the creative individual's intra-personal dynamics. The problems here touched on are therefore cardinal issues not only for the development of psychology as a science, but also for the development of the psychology of creative thinking. It seems that Lewin meant to speak here of both.

Some of these views, and some objective theoretical problems of general nature, will therefore be profitably discussed before entering upon special problems.

I. THE LAWS OF THE PSYCHE

The thesis that psychic processes follow definite laws is a postulate of psychology, at any rate, of experimental scientific psychology.

The thesis of rigorous lawfulness of the objects of a science asserts itself usually only step by step in the course of rather typical phases of development.[9]* This holds for pyschology, too. The issue is not that the thesis of lawfulness needs to be defended against extraneous philosophical objections, but rather that even when the psychologist-investigator accepts it "in principle" his actual procedures may still not be in accord with it.

Both quantitative and qualitative limitations may be imposed on the validity of the thesis of lawfulness. For instance, it may be considered valid for sensory-perception and memory, but not for the so-called "higher" psychic functions, such as feelings, decisions of will, or at least not for vitally important decisions.[10] Or the lawfulness can be reduced to a mere regularity which is invalid when one has a headache. This attitude toward lawfulness has had far-reaching, methodological consequences; for instance, it is responsible for the unduly great role which purely statistical thinking gained even in the realm of the strictly experimental method.

9.* Lewin (462, pp. 68 ff.).

10. This assertion certainly holds for thought-processes. It is only recently that causal-dynamic—that is, motivational—investigations of thought-processes have begun to spread to psychological laboratories from the therapists' offices and mental hospitals. Compare the reviews of Rapaport (591) and Murphy (533, pp. 362–413). Even at present, some of the most exacting experimental work on thinking still disregards motivational determination (316), and our most recent textbooks have little to say about the causal determiners of thinking (84).

The limitations of lawfulness in the area of the psychology of thinking may take several forms: (a) the problem of thinking may be relegated to the science of logic; (b) the lawfulness may be limited to the direct dependence of thinking upon stimulation, including exteroception and interoception but excluding intrapsychic (motivational) stimulation; (c) the lawfulness may be limited to motivations sharable and shared by groups of individuals, excluding the fundamental motivations which are idiosyncratic to the individual and not sharable with others (such as those which shape the thought-organization of dreams).

These tendencies to the contrary notwithstanding, the task is to facilitate the penetration of research by the thesis of absolutely rigorous and *exceptionless validity of psychological laws*. For research proper it may at first seem irrelevant how vigorously this thesis is insisted upon, since it is a mere prerequisite of experimental investigation and cannot be proven in the same sense as a single psychological proposition can. However, taking this thesis seriously results in a respect for theories which do not recognize barriers between normal and abnormal psychic life, and do not tolerate recourse to exceptions, the easy way of all theories lacking rigor. Psychological laws, once demonstrated, must be assumed to hold absolutely, always, and everywhere, in all their consequences.

[Passage omitted.] [11]

Similarly with the problem of *quantities*. To arrive conceptually at general laws in any field requires the consideration of the *full reality*, including the quantitative—that is, intensity—relationships. One cannot disregard this aspect of reality without the risk of arriving at empty anemic schemes. This is particularly true for the field of "higher" psychic life, where usually quantities and qualities are closely linked to each other. This, however, is not a plea for a blind quest for numbers, nor should it weaken the thesis that qualitative investigation must in a sense precede quantitative, and that in the field of will- and affect-psychology qualitative investigations must have primacy for some time.

This thesis of lawfulness demands considering contradictory examples from the whole field of psychic life [12] . . . thus strengthening the self-critique of theories, which is so needed, particularly in the field of will- and affect-psychology.

In turn, as we soon shall see, the rigorous view of psychic lawfulness broadens the methodological basis of research, by the very position it lends to experiment.

11. The omitted section stresses that the finest nuances of phenomena are just as much subject to thoroughgoing lawfulness as their grossest characteristics.

12. This requirement points up the fact that psychological theories and experiments tended (and still tend) to be so construed as to explain little of our actual experience, which therefore could hardly be used to question or corroborate them. This certainly is not the case for the relation of physical or chemical theory and everyday experience. The requirement will not be misunderstood to be a plea for a commonsense, phenomenological psychology, if it is noted that Lewin wrote: "[The experimenter] is entitled to face often a whole array of everyday 'facts' with supreme disbelief and knowing-better, even if the everyday facts seem to speak a language entirely different from that of his theory "

2. THE EXPERIMENT

The expectation of mere regularities to be demonstrated *statistically* was probably the main source of the view that *repeatability* is the basic requirement of an experiment. This requirement, however, automatically limits the possibility of experimental exploration of processes, such as affects, which are changed by each experiment.[13]

The thesis of rigorous lawfulness of the psyche does away with such limitations. A *single individual case* is sufficient in principle to prove or refute a proposition, provided that the structure of the conditions of the case in question is sufficiently well-established.[14*] Consequently, repeatability instead of being a necessary condition becomes essentially a technical amenity. Analysis by variations, the comparison of planfully produced differences, takes the place of repetition of the identical.[15]

Now the argument that one cannot attain experimentally lifelike conditions, leveled against will- and affect-psychology, is changed in significance. The demand for life-likeness, for the study of vitally important processes and central layers of psychic life, coincides with the thesis of the rigorous psychic lawfulness which also demands that the whole of psychic life be taken into consideration.

The demand of life-likeness, however, must not be misunderstood. For instance, it is argued against the possibility of experimental will-psychology that no important decisions of will can be produced experimentally, because that requires power to interfere decisively with the occupational and family life of man; this would be like having argued against the first experiments in electricity that they would not succeed in creating a real storm, and that the weak laboratory phenomena would be no substitutes. This, however, is a complete misconception of what an experiment is. Experiments do not aim at recreating our natural world. (What knowledge would that yield anyway?)

The quantitative level most propitious for experimental analysis varies from case to case, and the laws themselves shift but little as a function of this level.

13. For a detailed exposition of these ideas, see Lewin (465), Brenman and Gill (272, 89).

14.* Cassirer (127).

15. For more recent statements of this crucial issue of experimental methodology, cf. Klein (386), Schafer (633), and Brunswik (102). The experimental studies of Lewin (460) and his collaborators (783, 370, 337, 140) are masterful examples of the application of this methodological principle.

The only requirement is that the processes to be investigated be actually relevant.

We do not minimize or disregard the fact that, particularly in life phenomena, quantitative change—to use Hegel's formulation—easily results in qualitative shift. Degrees of intensity, however, must not be equated with the depth of the psychic level in question, and the belief that central layers of the psyche cannot be experimentally investigated should more and more prove erroneous.[16]

[Passage omitted.] [17]

Emphasis on the particularly intensive or the extraordinary misconstrues the central tasks of psychological investigation. The *everyday* cases rather than the *unusual ones* are the particularly important and particularly difficult subject-matter of scientific investigation. Just as in physics and economics, the most essential and difficult problems lie in everyday occurrences, and it is they that reveal the laws of the striking, extraordinary, and singular phenomena. The over-emphasis on the extraordinary is, in psychology as in some other nomothetic

16. The core of Lewin's thesis is that many psychological phenomena which were deemed unamenable to experimental analysis can be and were attacked experimentally.

Lewin discusses two different obstacles facing experimentation, the insurmountability of which he disclaims: (a) the necessity to manipulate real life conditions; (b) the difficulty of approaching central layers of the psyche. He argues that these are not real obstacles since —as in physics—*relevant* laboratory processes can be used to by-pass them. Several reservations may be made to this argument: (a) in later years Lewin and his collaborators, in their studies of group dynamics, introduced the concepts of "action research" and "participant observation," both of which, being departures from laboratory procedure, seem to indicate limitations of Lewin's thesis; (b) to investigate nuclear processes, physics had to go to appropriate energy levels and could not study these

phenomena on "relevant" processes of lower intensity; (c) the Lewinian experiments studied successfully certain layers of thought-organization (460, 783, 65, 370, 337) and thought-pathology (278, 418), and opened broad fields of investigation within the ego-psychology of thought-organization (see the reviews of Rapaport, 591, pp. 94–99, and Alper, 27), but did not tackle most of those levels of thought-organization discussed in this volume. It is not that these experiments, and Dembo's (140) experiment on affects and the Barker-Dembo-Lewin (36) experiment on regression do not shed some light on these levels of thought-organization; but apparently these levels must be approached also on their own hunting grounds: in hypnosis, in dream, in pathological states, etc.

17. In the omitted section Lewin reminds us that in 1889 Muensterberg (531) believed that changes of habits cannot be observed in the laboratory but only in everyday life.

sciences, a residue of a developmental phase in which collecting of rarities prevailed over systematic investigation.[18]

3. THE PSYCHOLOGY OF ELEMENTS AND PROCESSES AS GESTALTS

The quest after the elements of which the psyche is composed has long been prevalent in psychological disquisitions; this reflected the developmental state of psychology and was in keeping with the trend of the time. This quest may be considered now—at least in principle—a matter of the past in the fields of perception and intellectual processes. Yet in will- and affect-psychology it has played a paramount role until most recently.

The view that the "higher" psychic processes are also the most complex and most compound ones is erroneous. This error discouraged the investigators from studying experimentally the higher processes, and made such studies appear less worthwhile than the direct exploration of psychic elements. If we disregard this erroneous view, the following considerations gain importance.

The quest was after the *independent* elements composing the psyche. For instance, it sought to find those feeling factors which compose the minimum [to which all others can be reduced] and to learn whether the will is a specific, independent, irreducible element, a "sui generis" experience. Even in the experiments of Ach, and Michotte and Pruem, which initiated the modern, experimental psychology of will, the paramount questions concern the specific nature and independence of will as an experience-element.[19]*

The other chief characteristic of the study of elements is that it attempts to elicit them in utmost purity and independence, and treats them in an *isolated* piecemeal fashion. Though relationships are noted, they are treated as and-sums of their parts, and not adequately as wholes which determine the fate of their quasi-parts.[20]* This insight is fundamental for all psychological processes. It *does not* imply, however, that the *totality* of psychic processes forms *a single* closed unit.[21]* It must be demonstrated for each instance whether or not we deal with a unitary whole-Gestalt, and whether it is a "strong" or "weak" [22]*

18. Though the task of psychology is certainly to attain the level of systematic investigation, it is doubtful whether it has reached that level now and can totally dispense with the methods of the previous phase. Cf. notes 8 and 16, above.

19.* Ach (15, 14), Michotte and Pruem (519).

20.* See Wertheimer (762, 764).

21.* See Lewin (467, pp. 52–62).

22.* See Koehler (399, 396) and Krueger (436).

one. Such a conception, however, demands that we abandon the microscopic attitude typical for the study of elements.

The turn toward the *macroscopic* must occur on various lines. An "action," for instance writing, as a *motor process* has already certain Gestalt qualities, in the structure of its lines, in its general order, and in the rhythm of its course.[23]* Even in such motor processes as halving a line, hitting a point with a hammer, or throwing a ball toward a goal, the structure of the total *external surrounding field*, or at least of a relatively great region of it, plays a decisive role. This circumstance is often disregarded—for instance in psychotechnics. (In halving lines, it matters whether there are other lines on the same sheet, what their relative position is to each other and to the edges of the sheet, etc.) [24]

The *"internal"* surrounding field is not less important than the "external" field. The two together comprise the structure of the *total psychological field*. Over and above the purely motor process, the action of writing is psychologically fundamentally different in calligraphing a sentence and in writing a letter for the purpose of communication. In the former, the intention of the action is directed at the writing itself, while letter-writing is not writing in the same sense at all. In letter-writing the character of the writing movements is as a rule merely accessory, just as mouth movements are in speech. In both of these, the motor action is embedded in a process of an entirely different character—for instance, in a consideration, in a choice of arguments, or in specific formulations—and usually plays a *subordinate role*. The relative significance of this role in the total process varies in drafting an official application, a business communication, or a love letter, and depends also upon whether the writer is a vain or a factual man.[25] The crucial point is that since the motor action is embedded into a broader process-whole, it is senseless to attempt to understand the writing in question as an isolated process. It becomes a subordinate part in a process and can be understood only through that. In fact, the writing becomes

23.* Cf. Werner (758) and Werner and Lagerkrantz (760).

24. These Gestalt-principles concerning the surrounding psychological field are crucial for any study of thought-organization, whether it is carried out by psychological testing or by a more directly experimental method. Cf. Rapa-port (600). It must also be kept in mind that in Lewin's conception this "surrounding field" is part of the *psychological field* and not a reality independent of the subject.

25. Compare note 34, below, concerning the different levels of embeddedness and motivational dynamics.

often a mere "expression" of the specific psychic processes which impose structure on it in writing a letter.

From this vantage point the attempt of psychotechnics to reduce actions to a definite number of movement-elements appears completely misdirected.[26]

Psychic processes in turn are themselves *wholes extending in time*. In our example they are process-Gestalts whose *structure-types* have so far been barely studied. They may be "continuous" or may tend to a definite goal.[27] They may circle around the goal (as pondering does), or come to it always from new approaches, or have the structure of step-by-step approximation, and so forth. Finally, they often have typical "initial" and "closing" phases (for instance, putting on the last dot, heaving a sigh, putting down emphatically the finished work) which stand out as segregated wholes from their temporal context.[28]

It seems to me that even in perception- and imagery-processes studied by sensory psychology, their embeddedness in broader psychic happenings—that is to say, in the general psychological field—is of crucial significance. For instance, they may be embedded in "general contemplation," or in a "search after something definite," or again in a "dreaming with open eyes." [29*] Just as important as the structure of temporal succession are those action-types in which simultaneous processes are structured in varying depth and weight.[30*] Here again certain processes are closely linked in one Gestalt, while others are not.

26. These considerations also have significant implication for the "rationale" of psychodiagnostic tests, which is an integral part of the psychology of thought-organization. Cf. Rapaport (600).

27. Threading beads is a "continuous," drawing a man a "goal" activity. Cf. Chap. 5, note 20, below.

28. The types of time-structures which Lewin describes here are potentially significant forms of thought-organization. Yet, to my knowledge, neither before Lewin's writing nor in the two decades since has their role in thought-organization been systematically studied. Their significance may be better appreciated by collating them with the considerations advanced by Fenichel, Chap. 18, p. 360, note 32, below. Psychoanalytic literature has described other phenomena closely related to time-structure types: thinking and other activities regulated by even routine, or occurring in intermittent spurts, or starting with a spurt only to be abandoned, or delayed until the last moment only to be accomplished in a feverish and uninterruptable spurt. Cf. Fenichel (176, pp. 282–86) and Abraham (4, pp. 372 and 380–81); concerning time-experience in general, see also Harnik (300) and Hollos (335).

29.* Cf. von Allesch (22) and Lewin (461).

30.* Westphal (765).

It is obvious then that in all experiments the specific *situation* attains the role and significance which the surrounding field has in optical and acoustic experiments. Consequently single experiments cannot usually be considered isolated structures. Single concrete experiments, which statistical treatment considers identical, must be treated not statistically, but as full realities. Their *position in the time sequence* of experiments must be regarded,[31]* and in fact the individual experimental sessions may have to be so designed as to form unified wholes.[32]* Instead of the massing of *identical* cases, the concrete specificity of the single experiment should be taken into consideration, even in forming theories. The single case should not be regarded as an isolated fact, however, but rather within the relevant total process and within the entire *psychological* field.[33]

The connection [of a piece of behavior] to *definite sources of psychic energy*, and to definite tensions, is just as important as the embeddedness in unified action-wholes. These connections are a core issue of the process-Gestalts, and are mentioned here because, belonging to a deeper layer of the psychic structure, they are easily overlooked.[34]

For instance, if, after a subject has repeated some such action as writing a word to the point of being "fed up" with it, the action is then embedded differ-

---

31.* See "The method of the 'temporal series,'" in Lewin (460, Part I, p. 236), and Lindworsky (476).

32.* Cf. Lewin (460).
[Actually, in testing, which is experimentation of a sort, breaking up a test into several sessions is avoided.]

33. Cf. pp. 82–83, above.

34. Lewin describes here a threefold embeddedness of behavior and stimulation: (a) embeddedness in that part of the psychological field which corresponds to the external surroundings; (b) embeddedness in the "internal" surrounding psychological field; (c) connection to sources of psychic energy. The various "action-structures" he calls attention to, and the differentiation between "definite sources of psychic energy" which he implies, indicate that this tri-division is but a gross systematization, within each division of which there are yet other subdivisions. Thus embeddedness of behavior is multiple and overlapping. Since behavior depends on the laws of the whole it is embedded in, Lewin's statement expresses the same state of affairs which is conceptualized by psychoanalysis as overdetermination. The distinction made between source of energy and tension may be illustrated by hunger: the energy source is the food-need (or drive); the experience or behavior itself depends not only on the "quality" or intensity of this energy source, but on many other overdetermining factors such as social situation and other needs; all of these together are conceptualized as the actual tension underlying the behavior.

ently, he will resume it without reluctance. This will occur, for example, if the subject is asked to write the word on the back of the page to mark it for the experimenter.[35*]

Similar instances play an extraordinarily great role in education; for instance, in inducing a small child to certain actions it dislikes (eating, taking medicine), and in arousing his interest for, or distracting it from, certain things.

The crucial point here is not the degree to which an altered embedding changes the structure of the action-course; the meaning of an action may change fundamentally even without any significant alteration of the process-Gestalt, *once its psychic energy source has changed*. Writing a word ceases to be "over-satiated" when its source is no longer the subject's intention "to carry out the experimental instructions" but rather to show personal courtesy toward the experimenter. Similarly, with some children at a certain age, simply to forbid something they were reluctant to do will get them to do it.[36*] This works probably because it establishes communication with certain energies of the child, connected with his self-respect. It is of general importance whether a subject feels himself entirely an "experimental subject," so that his actions are in the main directed by the will of the experimenter and by the intention to carry out instructions, or whether he faces the experiment in his usual natural manner— that is to say with his "private-ego." [37]

Our considerations hold for feeling and affect processes also. . . .

Before I tackle the question of the sources and energy reservoirs of psychic processes, I should like first to discuss a few important special problems and concepts.

3a. *The Achievement Concepts*

The use of *achievement concepts* is one of the essential obstacles in the way of discovering the concretely existing Gestalt relations. Not that the task is to

35.* Compare Karsten (370).

36.* Buehler (103).

37. These issues of embeddedness, and through them the issues of communication with various sources of energy, play an obviously great role in thought-organization. "Meanings" depend on embeddedness, and the multiplicity of embeddedness makes for multiple meanings, on various "levels of discourse." The thought-processes of learning vary greatly in their immediate and long-range effects, course, and subjective experience, according to the sources of energy and tensions involved. Incidental learning, rote-learning on instruction, "task-involved" learning, "ego-involved" learning, are some of these forms. The

subsume everything in any remotely possible relationship, but rather to establish whether and where actual Gestalt relations do or do not exist in a given case.

Popular psychological language uses such achievement concepts overwhelmingly (typewriting, inventing, swearing, loving, planning, eating, entertaining, questioning). These concepts . . . are justifiable in such sciences as the law, economics, epistemology, and so forth. Biological psychology, however, will combat them for several reasons, of which only a few shall be discussed here (compare Section 3b on conditional-genetic concepts).[38*]

Let us take a training process, for example, the learning of typewriting. The learning curve rises at first quite steeply to level off later on. In time, a more or less jump-like transition from that level to a higher level takes place, and so forth. The achievement concept "typewriting" lumps all these processes together, as if they were a single action.[39]

In reality, however, a trained typist's work is not the same process as that of the beginner; it differs not merely in quantity of training but in its fundamental psychological character. The typing of the beginner is essentially a search for single letters. The implied process of orientation [on the keyboard] can be practiced, and people can become efficient in this search. But it would be a mistake to describe the work of a trained typist as a well-practiced search of this sort: she knows her machine so that she need not search. . . . The entire process is no more a search than is the beginner's typing a lifting of fingers.[40*]

The discrepancy between those types established according to "achievements" and those according to "actual psychic processes" plays a role not only in the theory of habits or the concept of practice (both of which must be basically revised) [41*]: it is present in all psychological fields. Thus we must give up in principle the attempt to subsume, under unitary psychological laws, processes defined by "achievements."

---

sources of energy and tensions involved in turn are evoked by the relation of the subject-matter to the internal and external "sets." Cf. Alper (28), also Katona (374).

38.* See Lindworsky (476), Lewin (460, Part II, pp. 82 ff.), Peters (552), and Blumenfeld (78).

39. Cf., for example, the analysis of the Babcock Symbol-Digit Test in Rapaport et al. (602), which shows that significant group differences emerge if the total performance time is replaced by timing five subsections of the test (pp. 377–78).

40.* Cf. Blumenfeld (78).

41.* In regard to intellectual processes, cf. Koehler (398).

Traces of this insight are apparent even in applied psychology, which deals usually with pure achievement concepts.[42]

Instead of dealing with achievement-defined "kinds of action," we must start out from *concrete individual instances* to subsume them under types or general laws according to the kind and structure of their actual course.[43*]

The dangers of using achievement concepts cannot be overestimated. Even investigators who are well aware of these have a struggle in almost every experiment to free themselves from misleading relationships and aspects suggested by achievement concepts.

3b. *Phenomenological and Conditional-Genetic Concepts of External and Internal Behavior*

The quest after psychic elements resulted also in an overemphasis on certain *phenomenological* questions, which no doubt have considerable significance, but must not lead us astray by concealing deeper *causal-dynamic* problems.

The quest after independent and irreducible experience elements led to attributing a preferred causal-dynamic position to those experiences which seemed to be particularly pure and striking cases of an experience-type: for instance, in the field of the psychology of will, "primary acts of will."

In this connection some principles reaching beyond the field of the psychology of will, and even psychology in general, must be remembered. (a) The various pure phenomenological types are always linked by transition types. (b) Phenotypically similar structures and processes cannot be expected to show *causal-dynamic* equivalence also—that is, they need not be equivalent as to their causes and effects. Physics and recently biology have amply demonstrated that phenotypic similarity and lack of causal-dynamic equivalence, as well as

42. Scatter analysis, item analysis, and analysis of verbalization, as described for example by Rapaport *et al.* (602), are attempts to get away from achievement concepts usually considered fundamental to all intelligence testing. Introducing such methods of analysis leads away from treating test performance as achievement alone, and centers attention on the thought-processes which underlie achievement. This emphasis culminates in the development of a "rationale" of these processes. Such rationales are contributions toward a general theory of thought-organization.

43.* Cf., for instance, the concept of "consummatory action" and the significance of process-wholes in habit errors. Lewin (460, Part II, pp. 82 ff.).

striking phenotypical differences and close causal-dynamic relatedness, may go together.

Early botanics arranged the plants in groups according to the form of their leaves, blossoms, and so forth—that is to say, according to their phenotypic similarities. It turned out, however, that the same plant may look quite different in the lowland and in the mountains. In the various branches of biology, the often extreme differences in the appearance of "genotypically" identical organisms, due to their sex, developmental stage, and environment, resulted recently in an intensive development of a new set of concepts, which in contrast to the phenomenologic concepts may be designated as conditional-genetic.[44*] Accordingly, the single structure is no longer defined by its appearance but rather as a totality of behavior forms. It is conceived as a realm of potentialities, so that its phenotype is defined only after a specific set of conditions—that is, a situation—is stated.

This [conditional-genetic] concept formation did not issue solely from developmental problems. Adopting such concepts is prerequisite for the investigation of causal problems and actual relationships of all kinds, not only in biology, but in physics, in mathematics, and even in the sciences of history and economics.[45*]

The thesis holds for psychology also: the actual relationships of psychological complexes and happenings, their rise and passing, their causes and conditions, are not sufficiently defined by their phenomenal characteristics. Here too, structures of great phenomenal similarity may issue from very different foundations, according to quite different laws.

Thus strong acts of intending may have much less causal-dynamic weight than others which as experiences are weak or even appear phenomenologically as "mere thoughts" rather than intentions.[46*]

This holds for *feelings* and affects also. A pleasurable feeling and a friendly mood, for instance, may derive dynamically from entirely different processes, in spite of their phenomenological similarity.

An *affect*, though it be very superficial and of little energy, may result in vehement external action and in an internal experience of great excitement. In turn, however, one may appear internally and externally relatively calm, while the underlying affective tension is of incomparable depth and intensity.

44.* Lewin (466).   46.* Michotte et Pruem (519).
45.* Cassirer (127).

Similarly, *behavior forms* may have very different dynamic meanings, though to (external) observation they appear phenomenologically closely related. For instance, an action may appear at two different times equally calm and purposeful, yet the first time be really a calm action within everyday work, and the second time be an externally well-controlled affective outburst. (That some minute indicators often reveal the difference, at least to the trained observer, does not change this state of affairs essentially, nor is it always true even for the best observers.) In such cases introspection is revealing. But in final analysis, not even the arrangement of subjectively experienced structures according to their phenomenal characteristics need coincide with dynamically related types or with analogous genetic-causal relationships.

Generally, in issues of causality and development, that is, in issues of real relationships, we cannot be guided by phenomenal facts, not even when dealing with so-called "pure types." Rather we must attempt to develop conditional-genetic concepts. This, however, does not exclude the most careful observation and exact exploration of phenomenological facts,[47] but in a sense presupposes them.[48*]

By no means should this be considered a stand against the broadest possible application of the phenomenology of external behavior and experience, nor against the use of self-observation.[49*] The latter is an important and indeed generally indispensable tool, particularly for investigations in will- and affect-psychology. The observation of external behavior may yield valuable information concerning the specific structure of psychic events, but decisive information concerning the actual processes often comes only from self-observation.

---

47. Lewin stresses that the ultimate aim of all sciences is to find the "genotypes" of the observed "phenotypes." Indeed, psychology generally had disregarded this principle. He implies, however, that in many fields of psychology much work on a purely phenomenological level is still ahead of us.

We may point out, for instance, that many phenotypes of thought-processes have scarcely been described. The form-varieties of attention, concentration, planning, inductive and deductive reasoning, daydreaming, creative thinking, humor—all are still in need of thorough descriptive exploration. A one-sided emphasis on genotypes may divert attention prematurely from a thorough exploration of phenotypes. Actually, the impact of the dynamics of Freudian as well as Lewinian vintage did have this effect.

48.* Compare Koffka's (407) discussion of "descriptive" and "functional" concepts. See also Buehler (107).

49.* See, for instance, Ach's (15) "systematic experimental self-observation."

The emphasis on psychologically real relationships does not limit us to the externally observable processes, behaviorism to the contrary notwithstanding. From our point of view, the concrete "internal" and "external" *course of events*, as well as the behavior forms described by *self-observation* and *external observation*, all pertain equally to *phenomenological concept-formation*. Conditional-genetic concepts must be developed both for experiences and *external* behavior.[50]

50. The crucial role of self-observation was discussed by Lewin extensively in the report of his first major experimental study (460). Hardly any other principle of method is more important for the exploration of thought-processes. The studies of Lewin (460) and his collaborators (783, 370, 337) made most successful use of it. The procedure of inquiry in diagnostic testing is also one of the applications of this principle. Cf. Rapaport (600).

CHAPTER 5

INTENTION, WILL AND NEED [1]

By Kurt Lewin

I. A FEW FACTS [2*]

1. The Influence of Time on the Effect of the Intention; the Immediate Cessation of the Effect after Consummatory Action

INTENTIONAL ACTIONS are usually considered the prototype of all acts of will. Theoretically a complete intentional action is conceived of as follows: its first phase is a *motivation process*, either a brief or a protracted vigorous struggle of motives; the second phase is an act of choice, decision, or intention, terminating this struggle; the third phase is the consummatory intentional action itself, fol-

---

1. Lewin (464). This paper, though it is *the* representative broad statement of Lewin's initial theory which preceded the presentation of his topological and vector psychology (468), has not previously been translated into English. Its ideas were reflected only in Lewin (467), Ellis (154), and Koffka (406). It is true that there is a fundamental continuity between the four phases of Lewin's work: the first, the experiments on will-measurement and the laws of association (458, 460); the second, the period of affect and action psychology (550, 783, 337, 370, 140, etc.), which was introduced by this paper and the one preceding it in this volume; the third, the period of topological and vector psychology; the fourth, the period of group dynamics. Yet in some respects the later writings do not give the same understanding of Lewin's conception of dynamics as this early paper, which still bears the freshness and the earmarks of

its origins. Moreover, no later papers of Lewin are as closely related to the theory of thought-organization as are the present one, that on the laws of association (460), and some by Lewin's collaborators of the affect and action-psychology period (783, 337, 370). Regrettably none of these has ever been translated.

In some respects, the concepts of dynamics which Lewin presents are related to and may even derive from psychoanalysis. They serve as a bridge between dynamic and experimental thinking. Disregarding all other values of this presentation, this alone would make it a milestone in the development of present-day psychology. For the psychology of thinking it is perhaps so far our only safe, dynamic, and yet experimental point of departure.

2.* For a detailed survey and discussion of the available experimental investigations into the psychology of will, see Lindworsky (476).

lowing either immediately or after an interval, short or long. The second phase, the act of intending, is considered the central phenomenon of the psychology of will. The problem is: how does the act of intending bring about the subsequent action, particularly in those cases in which the consummatory action does not follow immediately the act of intending? It has been demonstrated that in such cases the act of intending need not be repeated before the action.

Indeed, Ach's [3*] experiments have shown that an instruction given in hypnosis is carried out upon a post-hypnotic signal without the subject's knowledge of the instruction. When the occasion (Ach's "referent-presentation") implied in the act of intending occurs, it suffices to initiate the intended consummatory action (Ach's "goal-presentation"). For instance, an optic signal will initiate the pressing of a lever. The question is: what are the further characteristics of this after-effect of the act of intending?

According to prevailing theory,[4] the act of intending creates such a relationship between the "referent-presentation" and "goal-presentation" that the appearance of the former results in an action consistent with the latter. According to the association theory,[5*] an association of the referent- and goal-presentations is the cause of this process. Even the theory of the determining tendency,[6] which denies the associative character of this relationship, assumes that a coupling created by the act of intending between the referent- and goal-presentations is the cause of the intentional action.

The origin of such theories becomes clear if it is remembered that the experimental analysis started with so-called reaction experiments, in which the intention was to carry out certain actions upon arbitrarily chosen signals, which had nothing or very little to do with the actions themselves.[7]

Let us open up the problem by raising an apparently extraneous question: what role is played by the length of time elapsing between the act of intending and the consummatory action? Does the after-effect of the intention decrease progressively as associations do, according to the so-called curve of forgetting? It must be said right away that this after-effect persists over astonishingly long time-spans, even for relatively unimportant and outright nonsensical intentions.

Students were instructed: "Coming to the next laboratory hour (8 days hence), you will twice go up and down the stairs leading to the Psychological

3.* Ach (15). [See also Chap. 1, above.]

4. That is, Ach's theory.

5.* G. Mueller (526).

6. See Ach, Chap. 1, II, above.

7. Cf. Koehler (397, pp. 248 ff.).

Institute." An astonishingly high percentage of the students carried out the instruction, even though they did not renew the intention in the intervening period.

Following certain processes, however, this after-effect ceases in a typical and abrupt fashion. For instance, someone intends to drop a letter into a mailbox. The first mailbox he passes serves as a signal and reminds him of the action. He drops the letter. The mailboxes he passes thereafter leave him altogether cold. In general, the *occurrence of the occasion* (referent-presentation) as a rule *has no effect once the intentional action has been "consummated."* [8]

The apparent obviousness of this statement makes it especially necessary that its theoretical implications be made explicit. According to the laws of association, dropping the letter into the first mailbox should create an association between the mailbox and the dropping of the letter; the forces, whether associative or any other kind, which lead to dropping the letter, should also be reinforced by it. This is a stumbling block for association psychology; moreover it casts doubt on whether the coupling between occasion and consummation

8. Though Lewin's discussion is couched in terms of *actions*, clearly the appearance in consciousness and the effect of *thoughts* are the subject-matter of this discussion.

Cf. Freud (210, pp. 106-7):

We are naturally not in the habit of explaining the forgetting of intentions which we daily experience in every possible situation as being due to a recent change in the adjustment of motives. We generally leave it unexplained, or we seek a psychologic explanation in the assumption that at the time of execution, the required attention for the action, which was an indispensable condition for the occurrence of the intention, and was then at the disposal of the same action, no longer exists. Observation of our normal behavior towards intentions urges us to reject this tentative explanation as arbitrary. If I resolve in the morning to carry out a certain intention in the evening, I may be reminded of it several times in the course of the day, but it is not at all necessary that it should become conscious throughout the day. As the time for its execution approaches, it suddenly occurs to me and induces me to make the necessary preparation for the intended action. If I go walking and take a letter with me to be posted, it is not at all necessary that I, as a normal, not nervous individual, should carry it in my hand and continually look for a letter-box. As a matter of fact, I am accustomed to put it in my pocket and give my thoughts free rein on my way, feeling confident that the first letter-box will attract my attention and cause me to put my hand in my pocket and draw out the letter.

This normal behavior in a formed intention corresponds perfectly with the experimentally produced conduct of persons who are under a so-called "post-hypnotic suggestion" to perform something after a certain time. We are accustomed to describe the phenomenon in the following manner: the suggested intention slumbers in the person concerned until the time for its execution approaches. Then it awakes and excites the action.

(referent- and goal-presentations) plays really the essential role here. If the effect of the act of intending is that a tendency toward consummation arises when the occasion implied in the act of intending occurs, then it is hard to see why on a second occasion this tendency should not appear to the same and even to a greater degree. (The actual absence of the letter, after it was mailed, would prevent full consummation; yet the inhibitory effect of this failure would be expected only at the third mailbox, unless very complex auxiliary hypotheses were employed.) To explain the phenomenon we cannot fall back on a time-decrement of the intention-effect, since when repetitive action *is* intended (for example, to paste an announcement on each mailbox) the intention becomes effective on each occasion. In the case of the intention to mail a letter, however, the forces directed toward action seem suddenly exhausted once the letter is mailed. Thus, the cause of the process does not seem to be simply that the coupling between the referent- and goal-presentations drives toward action when the occasion arises.

A mailbox may elicit the tendency to drop the letter—or at least to check whether or not it has been dropped—even after it has been mailed. This happens mainly with important letters.[9] Such cases are amenable to experimental study.

In studies using reaction experiments for this purpose, the following considerations must be kept in mind. If the subject is instructed, "You will press the lever when you see this signal," the signal will not play the role which a meaningful occasion, objectively connected with the action, would. It will play the role of a "signal" which may acquire the meaning of "command," and may therefore have repeated effects. The repetition of the signal then amounts to the verbal instruction: "Repeat the task again." (For instance, the policeman's raised hand amounts to a direct command.) We shall discuss such cases

9. Lewin's assumption that this happens mainly with important letters is questionable. Since Lewin, as we shall see, explains the intention-effect by tension systems, he must explain this phenomenon by an incomplete discharge of tension. He apparently reasons: if the tension system was unusually "loaded" (important letter), the incomplete discharge becomes plausible. Clinical experience shows that many other conditions may have such an effect, as for instance when doubt (presence of contrary intentions) centers in an action. There is a similarity between the phenomenon here described and *déjà vu*. Cf. Chap. 3, particularly note 9, above. Ovsiankina's (550) study on the resumption of interrupted activities investigated some effects of intentions on actions. Yet the field is still wide open for the study of those variants of the phenomenon here discussed.

again. If the subject is given the task to nail together a frame, and the occasion for this is so chosen that it fits meaningfully into the process-whole—that is, it becomes an occasion and not a command—typically no tendency to repeat the completed task appears. For instance, if the occasion for this frame to be nailed together is when Mr. X. brings in a nail box, there will be no tendency to repeat nailing the frame if Mr. X. brings in the nail box again.

2. The Effect of Intentions when Occasion and Consummatory Action Are Not Predetermined, or when the Occasion Fails to Appear

It is usually assumed that, in the prototype of intentional action, the act of intending defines a *quite specific* occasion and a *specific* consummatory action. The reaction experiments, which were the point of departure for the experimental investigation of will, may serve as a useful paradigm. The referent-presentation may, for instance, be an optical signal and the goal-presentation the pressing of a lever.

Not in every act of intending are occasion and consummatory action so specifically defined.

First of all, *the consummatory action may remain quite indeterminate*. For instance, a person may intend to talk someone into doing a certain thing; the act of intending may leave it entirely open what words and arguments he will use, whether he will first go for a walk with him to make friends without even mentioning the matter, and so forth. The intention to avoid a ball *may* contain the provision that one will veer left; but it may leave it entirely open whether one will veer right or left, jump, or duck.

Such general intentions are more the rule than the exception, and they are not less effective than specific intentions. On the contrary, it is usually more purposeful to let the mode of consummation grow from the total *concrete consummatory situation* than to define it beforehand unequivocally. . . .[10]

10. Indeed problem-solving and other thought-processes also often show this pattern: a very general and non-specific direction is followed, and is made progressively more concrete as it encounters the specific features of the problem or situation in question. Cf. for example, Duncker (151). But there are also many cases in which intentions (to act, to solve a problem, to meet a situation), though highly specific from their inception, are nevertheless purposeful and effective. The degree to which intentions must be general or specific varies both with situations and individual personalities. Both aspects of this variability are salient problems of the psychology of thinking. How the situation determines what de-

The same holds for the precise definition of the occasion in the act of intending. Actually, vitally important and far-reaching intentions, like the decision to pursue an occupational goal or to be a well-behaved child, are extraordinarily indefinite on this point. The actions to be executed and the occasions therefore are left wide open. Indeed, *the very same intention* may give rise, according to the conditions, *to quite contrary actions.* "Good behavior" requires now action, now foregoing of action.[11]

But even where the act of intending predetermines definite occasion and consummatory action, we often encounter the astounding phenomenon that the intention takes effect all of a sudden *in response to quite other occasions and by different consummatory actions.*[12]* This, however, is rare where there is no meaningful objective relationship between occasion and consummatory action, as in the so-called reaction-experiments. But it is frequent where, as in everyday life, there is an *objective* connection between the occasion and the consummatory action implied.[13]

Somebody resolves to write a postal card to an acquaintance soon after returning home in the evening. In the afternoon he gets to a telephone, it reminds him to communicate with the acquaintance, and he does. Or: I resolve to drop a letter in the mailbox when I leave. A friend comes to see me, and I ask him to take care of the letter.

Two points in these examples seem important. In the first case an experience

---

gree of generality of intention is required, is amenable to experimental exploration by Lewin's or even Duncker's methods; the study of its dependence upon individual personality organization may require developing new methods. Psychoanalytic and other clinical experience has made us familiar both with obsessional forms of over-general intentions which resist narrowing and breaking down to concrete and specific moves, and with personalities (for example, hysteriform, passive-narcissistic) who can form, sustain, and act on only the most concrete intentions.

11. This flexibility of intentions used to be considered the characteristic which distinguishes human behavior from that of animals. Fabre's sand-wasp was the favored example for the rigidity of the behavior-organization of animals. Cf. Werner (755, p. 201). The grain of truth in this distinction was beclouded by the generality claimed for it.

12.* Concerning the range and displacement of such actualizing-stimuli, see Lewin (460).

13. Straus (721) in his sweeping critique of conditioning, as a tool of psychological exploration, made this issue of meaningful objective relationships one of the centers of his argument: the animal tied to the Pavlov-frame cannot use those meaningful cues his natural environment would offer him, by which to orient his learning and behavior.

(seeing the telephone) very different from the occasion implied by the act of intending (the return home) actualizes the forces emanating from or connected with the intention. This experience assumes the role of the intended occasion: it initiates a consummatory action, though another than that implied in the act of intending. It is an action which from the vantage point of the act of intending is a *substitute action* or, more correctly, an equivalent action "appropriate to the situation."

In order to maintain the view that the forces striving toward the intentional action derive from a coupling between the occasion and the consummation created by the act of intending, and that these forces are released by the occurrence of the occasion, one might attempt to explain the effectiveness of the "substitute occasion" and the occurrence of the substitute action by assuming that they are special cases of the same "general idea" to which both the intended occasion and consummatory action belong. It has been demonstrated, however, by the psychology of thinking that such a theory of general ideas is in contradiction to concrete psychological facts.[14*]

The main objection to the concept of coupling is that it leaves unexplained why, after such *substitute actions*, the later actual occurrence of the intended occasion generally *no longer arouses a tendency* to consummate the intended action. Why is it that once the letter is entrusted to a friend the mailbox no longer challenges one, though a hundred different interpolated actions will not destroy the effects of the intention? There is no doubt that it is a salient characteristic of intention-effects that they usually cease, once the intended action or its equivalent is consummated. This, however, is not understandable once the forces driving toward the intentional action are conceived of as arising from couplings either of an associative or a non-associative sort.

The following example demonstrates the difficulties of this conception even more clearly. Somebody resolves to tell something to an acquaintance who is about to visit; but the visit is canceled. When *the occasion* fails to occur, the intention-effect is not simply canceled, instead new occasions are sought. This shows directly that *here a state of tension is pressing toward discharge by means of a specifically directed action.*

The objection does not hold that in such cases the original intention is general (to communicate something to the acquaintance) and not specific (to communicate on a certain occasion). There are such general intentions, but cer-

14.* Selz (679).

tainly there are specific ones also. Occasionally, the intentional action will not take place after the intended occasion has failed to occur: in such cases the intended action is "forgotten." Such exceptions will be discussed later on.

The internal tensions may initiate the consummatory action when the expected occasion is delayed too long. For instance, in a race there is a strong tendency *to start prematurely*. Reaction experiments show similar phenomena. In political life also we observe *premature* acting before the intended occasion had occurred.

The effect of intentions in which both occasion and consummatory action are left indeterminate; the effect of occasions different from those implied by the act of intending (substitute occasions appropriate to the situation); the occurrence of objectively equivalent actions; the search for new occasions and the premature actions when the expected occasion fails to occur; the cessation of the intention-effect once the intended action or its substitute has been consummated—all indicate that it is unsatisfactory to describe the causes of intentional actions as forces which on definite occasions drive to definite actions connected with them by a *coupling*.

3. *The Resumption of Interrupted Activities*

Another group of related phenomena should be discussed in greater detail.[15]*

The consummation of an intended action is [initiated but] interrupted. Were the coupling between occasion and consummation decisive, nothing would happen without a repeated occurrence of the occasion, provided that the initiation of the consummatory action creates no new forces. The experimental setting used makes it possible to compare the results with those cases in which the effect of the intention is exhausted by the response to the first occasion. I shall mention only a few of Ovsiankina's results which are relevant to our present subject.

The activities used in the experiment were in general *not* particularly *interesting:* [16] for example, reproduction of a figure by colored building-stones, copying a rank-order correlation table, threading beads, making an animal from plasticine.

In the moment the activity is interrupted, a strong, *acute* effect is observed.

15.* These phenomena have been studied by Miss Ovsiankina [550] at the   Berlin Psychological Institute.
16. See note 26, below.

Subjects *resist* interruption even of not particularly agreeable activities. This assumes occasionally quite stubborn forms. The forces opposing interruption appear to be closely connected with, among other things, the course, structure, and whole-quality of the activity.

In our present context it is of particular interest what happens when the subject, following instructions, interrupts one activity to start and *complete another*. In brief, a *strong tendency to resume the first activity is observed*.

The experiments used two kinds of interruption. First, *incidental interruptions:* the lights go out, presumably due to power failure; the experimenter drops a box of small objects and the polite subject helps to pick them up, and so on. Second, interruptions by direct instruction to start *another activity*.

Though often the incidental interruptions took as much as twenty minutes, the original activity was resumed without exception. After the interruptions by other tasks, resumption was frequent, at times even after a full hour.[17] The subjects knew that the experimenter did not expect resumption; indeed, in some cases the experimenter actually *prohibited it*.

The *act of resumption* is of particular interest to us. The resumption tendency is reinforced when the subject catches sight of the material of the interrupted first activity, for instance, of the piece of paper on which he began to draw. *But even when there is no such external stimulus, the tendency to resumption is present.* The behavior observations and the subjects' self-observations indicate that a few seconds after the interrupting activity is finished, there appears an urge to resume the first activity, even if the subject did not think of it while engaged in the other. This urge appears first in an indefinite form, "There is still something to be done," without the subject's knowing what it actually is.[18]

17. The finding that an activity is more likely to be resumed if interrupted by an "accident" than by instruction to start a new activity can be explained. There is some evidence to show that since the tension-system pertaining to the original activity was established by the intention to carry out the instructions, the new instructions may be taken as a signal of completion, particularly in continuous activities; or they may lead the subject to experience the new activity as a substitute activity; or the new activity itself may be so related to the original that it becomes by its very nature a substitute for it.

18. This experience of "something still to be done" is a frequent concomitant of *forgotten* intentions also. Clinical data seem to indicate that the affect-tone of such experiences is often akin to anxiety. In turn, in some anxiety-states the anxiety experience takes the conscious form: "I should be doing some-

This is usually not a *persistence* of activity, such as occurs in continuous rhyming of nonsense syllables,[19] but rather a typical tendency toward the consummation of an action, that is, toward the equilibration of an inner tension. Accordingly, the resumption tendency is more often absent if the interrupted activity is a continuous, rather than an end-activity.[20]

. . . The intensity of the resumption tendency does not depend directly upon the intensity of the intention which preceded the activity [21]* but rather upon *the subject's internal attitude toward that activity*. "Pure experimental subjects"—that is, subjects who "do everything the experimenter wants," subordinating their will to his—show little or no resumption tendency. The subject must actually have the will to carry out the specific activity.[22]

The *central goals of will* which prompt the subject to accept the instructions of the experimenter are also important here. If the subject is asked to do some work because the experimenter needs it in other experiments, then the subject accepts this work not as a "subject" but as a person who wants to do a favor for the experimenter—that is, as a professional colleague or a social being. This is then a "serious activity," and the resumption tendency is much stronger in it than in a mere "experimental activity." [23]

We are faced with the following facts: a force is demonstrated which drives, even after relatively long intervals, toward the completion of interrupted activity. The manifestation of the force does not require an external stimulus to prompt resumption of the task; frequently the resumption occurs spontaneously.

------

thing, but I don't know what." Cf. also Chap. 18, below, on similar experiences in "boredom."

19. See Lewin (460).

20. Stringing beads is a continuous activity: it is uniform and without structure, even when it has a well-defined end-point. Drawing a man or constructing a figure from blocks is an end-activity. They have a definite structure which sets their end-point.

21.* This finding agrees with the results of many other investigations. Cf. Lindworsky (476), Lewin (458), Boumann (85), Sigmar (688).

22. Cf. note 17, above.

23. The varieties of motivations to which Lewin here points, and particularly the issue of "central goals of will," open up important matters of theory: (a) we seem to be dealing with a hierarchy of motivations, though Lewin's method of treating tension-systems tends to disregard rather than to make this explicit; (b) we are dealing with phenomena in which there is a broad range of

Further examples: Questions discussed but not settled in a meeting, usually continue to preoccupy us and may lead to long soliloquies, particularly if the questions are personally important.[24] If we are interrupted in helping a school-child with a mathematical problem, it may recur to us for a long while even if quite uninteresting. If we slip into reading some stupid fiction but do not finish it, it may pursue us for years.[25] The important experimental finding is that "interest" is not the decisive factor in such cases.[26]

Finally, a few words about those theoretically important cases in which, because of a specific objective relationship between the original activity and the interrupting activity, no resumption tendency appears. A child telling a story is interrupted and told to draw the content of the story. No resumption tendency appears, obviously because the drawing somehow completed the interrupted storytelling. This is a substitute consummation. Such cases seem to be particularly revealing of the forces active in the execution of intentions. Even in real resumption the completing activity need not be the missing part of the original activity. It may be a quite differently structured activity directed

---

individual differences: the wish to do a favor, the wish to comply with instructions, the wish to be done with a set of disagreeable experimental tasks.

24. It is a common experience that bad defeats and great successes also pursue us in this fashion. The catharsis or abreaction theory of psychotherapy took its point of departure in related observations. Cf. Freud and Breuer (91). It is clear also that the symptoms of "traumatic war neuroses" show, in their repetitiveness, some relation to the phenomena here discussed. Cf. Freud (241), Kardiner (369), and Grinker-Spiegel (292). See also Chap. 22, note 30, below.

25. Cf. Freud's enumeration of those unsettled activities which as day-residues play a role in dream formation. See Freud (209), also Chap. 12, note 23, below.

26. Interest here apparently means interest in the content of the activity, but not in "performing well," in "doing the experimenter's bidding," etc. In fact, even interest in the content may be of a great variety; it may refer to the type of activity (building), to the particular task (tower), to the material used (shiny smooth blocks), etc. Once it is realized that all these are interests—that is, motivations—of various sorts, the exploration of their relationships will begin. At present we have only fragmentary information about most of them. Their systematic exploration is the study of the hierarchy of motivations in thought-processes. Lewin here distinguishes between the effects of two different interests: those in the content which influence resumption, and those in the task which do not. For other varieties of interest, see Alper's (27) distinction between ego-involvement and task-involvement.

"toward" the goal, or only playful handling of the material of the original activity.[27]

4. *The Forgetting of Intentions* [28]

An obvious, and in one sense, direct approach to the study of intention-effects is the investigation of the forgetting of intentions.

Two concepts of forgetting must be carefully distinguished. The first pertains to the usual conception of *memory:* the ability to reproduce knowledge once possessed. The ability to repeat an action once performed we will also consider reproduction, though in some respects it is an essentially different process.[29*]

The second concept of forgetting pertains to *intentions which are not carried out.* In everyday life we call it "forgetfulness." It is obvious that we usually remember the content of the intention, even though we have forgotten to carry it out. In such cases the memory-knowledge of the act of intending is extant. A good memory, ability to reproduce knowledge and actions, need not be accompanied by the virtue of not being "forgetful" in carrying out intentions —though some connections between the two may exist.[30]

27. Symptomatic actions (210, pp. 129 ff.) and the exchange of one neurotic symptom for another (252, pp. 11–23, and 217, p. 55) occur in the manner of such substitution.

28. For Freud's discussion, see (210) and note 8, above.

29.* Lewin (460), Part II, pp. 125 ff.

30. In this paper Lewin discusses the motivation of only the second of these two types of forgetting. His study of associations (460) shows, however, that he considered the first type also motivated. Lewin's motivational view of memory and forgetting is so general that, in Gibson's (269) opinion, he converted the whole problem of "habits" into one of "attitudes." Indeed, "readiness," Lewin's dynamic-motivational factor in associations, does not differ in its roots, but only in appearance and effect, from the intentions he discusses here. Both derive from attitudes mobilized by experimental instructions, both are activated—though perhaps to different degrees—by the "intended occasions," and their activation depends on the embeddedness (see below) of the "occasion."

The fact Lewin mentions—that "good memory" and "forgetfulness for intentions" may coexist in a person—would seem to indicate that "readiness" and "intention" either differ in their position in the hierarchy of motivations, or are disparate forms on the same hierarchical level. Clinically we are familiar with those general motivations (intellectualizing, rationalizing) which favor good memory; we know also that these are often related to certain personality structures (usually labeled obsessional) which are prone to ambivalence and doubt in regard to intentions and actions. These relationships are not hard and

[Passage omitted.] [31]

Our concern here is the second concept of forgetting, the *failing to carry out an intention*.

We will disregard those cases where forgetting of intentions is due to momentary strong preoccupation with other matters.[32] The remaining cases promise immediate insight into the conditions under which intentions fail.

As mentioned, intention effects do not seem to show a time-decrement. *The passage of time can no more be considered the cause of real happening in psychology than in physics.*[33] Progressive time-decrements are usually referable to normal life processes. But even then the question remains: what in the whole life process is the *concrete cause*, for instance, of the forgetting of a given intention.

In an experimental investigation of the forgetting of intentions [34*] the subject was to do a number of tasks and, at the end (or at another definite point) of each, sign and date the paper used. After the completion of each task the sheet was handed over to the experimenter.

---

fast. This is a broad field open to systematic investigation. It may hold the key to the relation between those memory phenomena which classical memory investigations dealt with, and those which Lewin, clinical observation, and psychoanalysis tackled.

It is possible that the differences between various forms of memory—such as rote, meaningful, generally relevant (task-involved), personally relevant (ego-involved), and vitally important (subject to "censorship")—are rooted in underlying, different, relatively autonomous levels of motivation, operating with correspondingly different mechanisms. Cf. Tolman (733).

31. In the omitted section Lewin discusses "forgiving" (the opposite of "holding things against people" tenaciously) as a kind of "forgetting." Clinically, both the relation of such tenacity to suspicion and other paranoid traits, and the relation to denial of an extreme

tendency to forgive, are familiar. Lewin's reminder holds out the hope that these clinically familiar relationships may be approached some day from a new angle permitting systematic treatment of their "formal characteristics."

32. Lewin is entitled to exclude these cases from his treatment for the purpose of simplifying the issue at hand. Yet it must not be forgotten that a "momentary strong preoccupation" taking precedence over the intention is in itself a phenomenon causally determined. In fact, it seems justified to suggest that intention-dynamics is subordinate to a more fundamental and overriding motivational dynamics, which determines whether a given intention or a strong preoccupation shall have preference in consciousness and/or action.

33. Cf. Freud (234, p. 119) on the "timelessness" of unconscious processes.

34.* These experiments were conducted by Mrs. Birenbaum at the Berlin

The following results were obtained:

a. Generally, an intention is not an isolated fact in the psyche, but *belongs*, rather, *to a definite action-whole*, to a definite *region of the personality*. Thus, for instance, the signature is usually not embedded in the "objective work" of the task, but rather in that "personal" region which is involved in "handing the work over" to the experimenter.

Thus the transition from the action-region in which the intention is *embedded* to another may bring about the forgetting of the intention. An example from these experiments: the signature is often forgotten when six *similar* activities are followed by a seventh which is different.[35]

A region of intention-effects may be sealed off simply by a pause of a few minutes. After the pause the signature is often forgotten. It is clear that we are not dealing here with a time-decrement of the intention since, even without renewal of the intention, the signing is usually not forgotten when the subject works on ever-new tasks without pauses, and, since the signature is usually still affixed, even when the "pause" lasts not five minutes but a whole day.

The apparent reason for this paradox is that, in a continuous series of experiments, a pause of five minutes is a very considerable interruption; after it, the subject enters a new region, as it were, in which the previous intentions hold little or not at all. If, however, a second group of the experiments takes place

---

Psychological Institute [see Birenbaum (65)].

35. Concerning "embeddedness," see Chap. 4, notes 34 and 37, above. Note that Lewin's discussion in points 1–3 centers in the formal aspects of the embeddedness of the intention, and says little on the corresponding relations to sources of psychic energy. Here Lewin's geometric (topological) conception of psychological happening is forecast. While Lewin's clear view of multiple "embeddedness" amounted to a recognition of overdetermination, the exploitation of this insight was hampered by the geometric conception, which made the "central regions of personality" a subordinate part of the psychological field. This development is, at least in part, the basis of the criticism that topological psychology is formalistic. Such criticism often overlooks the advantages of formal treatment. When formal treatment will have been so extended as to account for overdetermination, and particularly for the happenings in the "central regions," the crucial problem of psychology will have been solved. But even as is, Lewin's consistent application of the geometric conception to one layer of embeddedness has written an important chapter on one level of ego-dynamics. The results of Birenbaum's (65), Zeigarnik's (783), and others' experiments are an important bit of ego-psychology, even though the task of establishing their place within the whole of ego-dynamics still lies ahead of us.

the next day, then for the subject it is a "resumption of yesterday's experiments," and not, as in the first case, a "proceeding to new experiments." Therefore, the subject reenters the situation of the preceding day without difficulty. In fact, it is not necessary to repeat the experimental instructions on the second day in other experiments either: in preparing himself subjectively for the experiment, the subject again accepts the previous instructions.

Such embedded intentions are not forgotten if—but only if—the action-region to which they belong is alive. This is true for everyday life also. Forgetting of an intention, or rather unresponsiveness of an intention to the intended occasion or another proper one, is observed when the occasion presents itself at a time or in a situation where those psychic complexes in which the intention is embedded are not alive.[36] The most frequent cases of forgetting, which we usually attribute to being preoccupied with something else, are probably not solely due to the *intensity of the other experience*. If these intensive experiences belong to the *same* psychic complex, they may even reinforce the intention. Furthermore, forgetting may occur without intensive preoccupation if the momentarily prevailing psychological region is sufficiently distant from the intention. Yet pure intensity-relationships do seem to play some role.

b. The *occasion*, also, is of significance for the problem of forgetting. For instance, the subject will forget to sign his name, quite regularly, if he must change to signing on a larger paper or on one of a different color. Obviously, the paper reminds the subject of the intention, as does the mailbox of the letter to be mailed, or the knot in the handkerchief of something not to be forgotten; they have what I would like to call a *valence*.[37] We have discussed cases in which, though the intentions were quite specific, a whole varied series of events and objects had valences (mailbox-friend). The valence may be fixated, however, as in the example of the paper, to a very specific object. . . .

36. "Alive" here apparently means "still connected with the source of psychic energy, which brought it about or set it into action." Thus, so far, Lewin has demonstrated that forgetting of an intention depends on (a) its embeddedness in an action-region; (b) the articulation of the action-whole; (c) the "aliveness" of the action-region. All three of these are ego-psychological findings concerning the motivational dynamics of thought and action. It is clear, however, that this descending sequence of motivations does not end at this point, and continues into motivations underlying these.

37. The relation of intentions to occasions which have a valence for them is analogous to that of drives to their objects.

c. One of the tasks in the experiments mentioned was the drawing of the subject's own monogram. In this task the subjects regularly forget to sign their names. Association theory would have us expect the opposite: due to the strong coupling between the monogram and the signature, forgetting of the intention to sign should be particularly rare on this task.

Detailed analysis indicates, however, that this is a kind of *substitute consummation*.[38] In view of the whole situation, the subject could hardly have assumed that the monogram would sufficiently identify his work for the experimenter. Actually the signature is "forgotten" without further consideration. The need to sign, established by the act of intending, is apparently somehow satisfied by this monogram signature (though other factors are also at play here). It is significant that monogram writing done as "craft work," and not as "writing one's own monogram," does not have the effect of substitute consummation.[39]

Such substitute- or even part-consummations are frequent causes of forgetting in everyday life also. I shall mention two examples that actually occurred. A man wishes to buy collar buttons. He forgets it repeatedly. Now he makes a detour, to go by a street in which there certainly are men's stores. He is satisfied and happy that he did "not forget his shopping." He arrives at the library and notices that he did not buy the buttons.

A teacher resolves to ask her pupil about a certain matter. About the middle of the study hour she remembers it, and is glad that "she remembered it just

38. Cf. Mahler (497), Lissner (480), and Lewin (467, pp. 247–50). Cf. also note 27, above.

39. The execution of hypnotic and post-hypnotic suggestions provides a broad field for the study of substitute consummations. Suggestions which leave open the occasion and/or the mode of execution show that in a broad sense substitute consummations are a special case of such open-ended intentions. An interesting array of hypnotic phenomena of both types will be found in Erickson (161), Erickson and Kubie (164, 165). These phenomena build a bridge to those conceptualized by psychoanalysis as substitute formations (Freud, 233, pp. 92, 93) and substitute gratifications (Freud, 240, p. 397).

The concept of Lewin, however, pertains to ego-psychology, while the psychoanalytic concepts in their major aspects refer to the primary process. The relationships between the two sets of concepts are yet to be explored, and the occasional similarity of the processes they denote must be handled with skeptical alertness. Only too often have ego-psychological phenomena been taken as identical with id processes. See, for instance, Rosenzweig (620) and Sears (676).

in time." She ends up without having carried out the intention. (In these cases, as in those of everyday life in general, there is naturally no unequivocal proof that going through the street or the mere remembering of the intention, as substitute consummations, were really the causes of forgetting.) [40]

It is often observed that even making a written note of an intention is conducive to forgetting it, though according to the association theory it should reinforce the coupling between the referent- and the goal-presentation. Making a note is somehow a consummation, a discharge. We rely on the note to remind us in due time and weaken thereby the inner need not to forget. This case is similar to the one where remembering the intention to ask something acts as a fulfilment, so that the question is never actually asked.[41]

There are, however, cases where taking notes, even if they are never seen again, facilitates remembering. In these cases the note-taking may, for instance, connect the intended action with a certain personality region (such as the region of occupation) or a certain style of living (such as orderliness), so that the total energy of this region partakes in carrying out the intention.

d. When not a result of substitute consummation, forgetting can often be traced to natural *counter-needs*. The intention to write an unpleasant letter often remains ineffective even if repeated: we forget it whenever we have leisure for it. Freud has called attention to these hidden resistances. Even though not all forgetting can be traced to such natural—and certainly not always to sexual—needs, nevertheless it is of central significance for our problem that *the after-effect of an intention proves to be a force,[42] which may clash with and be made ineffective by needs.*[43]

40. The clinician cannot help but raise the question whether these everyday life examples are merely substitute consummations and nothing more. He will wonder whether there were no strong personal motivations underlying this "not shopping" and "not asking." He will not, we hope, question the ego-psychological lawfulness of substitute consummation, but will rather ask whether in these cases it was not used by deeper-lying motives. Here again we are faced with the relationship of various levels of motivation, that is, overdetermination.

41. Cf. Freud's comments (226) on the psychoanalyst's method of remembering the information given to him by the patient.

42. By after-effect Lewin here means the tension-system set up by intention.

43. Cf. note 8, above. See Freud's (210) "Psychopathology of Everyday Life," particularly the section on "Forgetting of Intentions" (pp. 106–12). Freud wrote (210, p. 108):

We have already discussed the positive relation of intention effects to the needs from which the intention itself arose. (See, for instance, the resumption of "serious" activities.) The ease of forgetting depends upon the intensity of the genuine-need underlying the intention. Signatures were much less frequently forgotten in mass experiments than in experiments with individual subjects. The need to distinguish one's work (other factors being equal) is much greater in a mass experiment.

Whether or not an intention is carried out in the face of obstacles *depends not on the intensity of the act of intending, but rather on the broader goals of will, or natural needs, on which the intention rests.* The study of forgetting has

---

. . . I have found that they could invariably be traced to some interference of unknown and unadmitted motives—or, as may be said, they were due to a *counter-will*. In a number of these cases I found myself in a position similar to that of being in some distasteful service: I was under a constraint to which I had not entirely resigned myself, so that I showed my protest in the form of forgetting.

Apparently it is Freud's adverb "invariably" to which Lewin takes exception. The issue is again the question of overdetermination: Lewin sees one, Freud another, level of it. If the various levels of motivation have a definite functional autonomy, then Lewin's assertion is right; if there is no such autonomy and even the minutest psychic event is overdetermined—that is, determined ultimately by drive-dynamics—then Lewin's contention is incorrect. A third solution would allow Lewin's and Freud's assertions to stand as partial, but correct, representations of the situation. This third solution would assume that in the course of development a hierarchy of new motivational forms (for instance, quasi-needs) develops from the fundamental drive-motivations. Each of these hierarchic levels presumably would have

its autonomy; the underlying motivational levels would persist simultaneously. Specific environmental conditions (occasions—that is, objects of valence—for the basic motivations) and specific internal conditions (for instance, pathological reinforcement of drive motivations or weakening of the autonomy of higher-order motivations) may alter the division of labor implicit in this hierarchy. In such cases, a more basic motivation will take over and use the function usually performed by a higher-order motive. At present our systematically gathered empirical material is so scant that this third solution remains speculative, though it is consonant with present-day psychoanalytic ego-psychology (Hartmann, Chap. 19, I and II, below) and has the advantage over the other two that it is not in outright contradiction of facts.

Lewin's point concerning sexual needs hammers at an open door. It disregards the broad conception of sexuality in psychoanalysis; besides, Freud (210, p. 109) was explicit about the frequent role of aggression in the forgetting of intentions: ". . . here the motive is an unusually large amount of unavowed disregard for others. . . ."

also shown that calm, affect-free acts of intending are usually more effective than those of particularly great or vehement intensity. This may be related to the fact that affective and vehement actions—in general, but with certain exceptions—have less achievement-effect than calm actions.[44]

Under what conditions does an act of intending, and particularly an intensive act of intending, occur? An instructive though exaggerated adage says: "What one intends, one forgets." This means that only *when there is no natural need for an action*, or when there is a natural counter-need, *is it necessary to form an intention*. If the act of intending is not based on a genuine-need, it promises little success. It is precisely when there is no genuine-need that we attempt to substitute for it an "intensive act of intending." (To put it paradoxically: either there is no need to make a certain intention, or it promises little success.)

Wilde (*Dorian Gray*) is acute when he says, "Good intentions are useless attempts to meddle with the laws of nature. Their origin is mere vanity and their results are absolute zero." [45]

II. THE THEORY OF INTENTIONAL ACTION

1. *The Effect of the Act of Intending Is a Quasi-Need*

The experiments on forgetting of intentions, and even more those on resumption of interrupted activities, prove that the [after-effect of] intention is a force.[46] To take effect, this force does not require the actual occurrence of

44. We might speculate, and it may become a subject-matter of experimental exploration, whether calmness and freedom from affects are indicators of the autonomy of the motivational level from which the intention arises, and intensity and vehemence indicators of the weakening or absence of its autonomy. Cf. note 114, below. Lewin's next discussion would seem to support such speculation.

45. Cf. the proverb Freud quotes: "What one forgets once, he will often forget again" (210, p. 112) and the familiar proverb "The road to hell is paved with good intentions."

46. The sense in which the concept "force" is used here is discussed by Lewin in his *The Conceptual Representation and the Measurement of Psychological Forces* (469, p. 17), particularly on pp. 11–19. Lewin wrote: "One can say that psychology derives changes from constructs (dynamic factors) which are of vectorial nature. We call these dynamic facts 'psychological forces.' " Lewin also stresses that all psychological theories imply some such concept and that his effort is to make it more explicit. Theories involving a force-concept as a rule involve an energy-concept also. It would seem that the relation of this force-concept to the

the occasion anticipated in the act of intending in order to elicit the intentional action as its consequence.

There exists rather an internal pressure of a definite direction, an internal tension-state which presses to carry out the intention even if no predetermined occasion invites the action.[47]

The clearest subjective experience of this state of affairs occurs in the resumption of interrupted tasks, when after completion of the interrupting activity a general pressure—that "there is still something I want to do"—appears. In this case, which is frequent in everyday life also, the content of the intention is not yet clear and only the internal tension as such is perceived. Only later does the goal, that is, what one wants to do, become conscious. Indeed, it happens in everyday life that, in spite of searching for it, one cannot remember what he really wanted. (Such indeterminate tensions occur sometimes even where a predetermined occasion by itself reminds one of the intentional activity.) [48]* But in such cases consummatory activities often occur under internal pressure without the stimulation of specific occasions.[49]

---

energy-concepts used (for instance, tension-systems) also needs to be made more explicit. Lewin (469) in his systematic theoretical work did not deal with this problem. The failure to do so became a source of difficulties. For instance, the psychoanalytic as well as the Lewinian theory of affect seems to labor under precisely such difficulties. Cf. Rapaport (591).

47. Here it seems clear that the "tension-state" is an energy-concept and the "intention" a force-concept.

48.* Compare Ach (14).

49. The state of affairs here discussed by Lewin seems to be of fundamental importance for the psychology of thinking. Let us for the moment disregard that, if the concept of "thought-processes" were defined broadly, the processes underlying "resumption" and the phenomena of intention-forgetting themselves would be considered

"thought-processes." Thinking as we usually conceive of it has at times well-defined goals and specified means for reaching them; this is the case, for instance, when we know the sides of a rectangle and want to know its area. Here the goal is the area, the specified means to attain the goal is multiplication. At other times thinking has an unequivocally defined goal, but the means to reach it are not specified; this is the case, for instance, when a well-defined mathematical problem can be solved geometrically, or analytically, or algebraically. Finally, thinking may have a very general and non-specific goal and simultaneously the means to reach it may also be non-specific. This is the case, for instance, where the goal is to establish the length of a distance. It may be a matter of direct or indirect measurement, of pure calculation, or of various combinations of measurement and calcu-

It could be argued that in the experiments mentioned the fact that there is nothing definite to do at the completion of the interrupting activity serves as the "proper occasion." . . . Indeed the "completion of a certain activity" *may* actually acquire the genuine valence of an occasion, for instance, if the intention is to do a certain thing at the completion of an activity.

As a rule, however, "not having anything to do" cannot be considered as an occasion with a definite valence, as is the mailbox for mailing a letter. The effect of momentarily "not being particularly occupied" is only that certain

---

lation. The general goal differentiates into many possible concrete goals, and each of these into a series of sub-goals. The distinction between "means" and "sub-goals" blurs.

There obviously exist all the transitional forms between, and combinations of, these three arbitrarily sketched "types" of thinking. Productive thinking usually is akin to the third type: in it—to put it in Lewin's language—means, occasions, and goals remain indeterminate, and the subjective experience of the goal is often simply an "indeterminate tension" and/or one of a vague direction.

This intrinsic similarity, between the intention effects investigated by Lewin and thinking in general, indicates that thinking, too, is organized by intentions. We are so accustomed to these intentions that we are prone not to notice them unless we encounter difficulty in carrying them out.

The intention-organization of thinking has been clearly recognized and demonstrated by Bartlett (37) and Humphrey (344). Yet Lewin's treatment of intention effects remains so far the most concrete experimental grasp of this issue. Maier (498), Duncker (151), Wertheimer (763), and Koffka (406), with their interest centered in the prob-

lem-structure and the "requiredness" arising from it, underplayed the role of intention-organization of thought in problem-solving.

Psychoanalysis distinguishes two kinds of thought-processes, primary and secondary. (Cf. Chap. 15, particularly note 12, below.) While a great variety of the mechanisms of the primary process has been studied by psychoanalysis, the secondary process, which belongs entirely to the domain of ego-psychology, has been seldom tackled by it. Freud maintained that secondary-process thinking is a detour on the path toward gratification, that is, on the path toward that goal-object which permits discharge of drive tension (209, pp. 525 ff., particularly p. 535). The specific rules that operate on this detour have not been explored. It seems that the laws of intention-effects demonstrated by Lewin could be considered pertinent to the "secondary process." If this assumption is made, then it would follow that, in the course of the "detour," tension-systems derived from the original drive-tension arise and serve as the sources of energy underlying the motivating forces of the detour. Indeed, such considerations are put forth by Lewin below in his discussion of the relation of quasi-needs to genuine-needs.

inner tensions pressing toward the motor region penetrate more easily when the motor region is not otherwise heavily taxed. (The conditions are naturally quite different in the case of real boredom.) [50]

The state of tension arising from the act of intending need not be continuously expressed in conscious tension-experiences. As a rule, it exists over long periods of time, only in latent form, as during the interrupting activity, but that does not make it less real. These facts are related to the psychic function of the motor-region and of consciousness, as well as to the structuring of the psyche into relatively segregated complexes. These latent tension-states may break through momentarily into consciousness even during the interrupting activity, as an experience of pressure toward the original activity.[51]

(A) MISSING AND UNFORESEEN OCCASIONS. The recognition that the driving-force of intentional activity is not an associative coupling but an internal tension-state—that is, a directed internal pressure—makes it possible to explain the various phenomena we described.[52]

Now it becomes understandable why, when the occasion fails to occur, another is sought out, and why, when one keeps waiting too long for the occasion and the internal pressure is too great, premature action results.

We also understand now why the intention is responsive not only to the intended occasions, but also to entirely different objects and events (mailbox and friend). The internal state of tension breaks through as soon as there is a possibility to eliminate or at least decrease the tension, that is to say, as soon as a situation appears to permit activity in the direction of the goal.

50. Fenichel's (179) study on boredom bears out Lewin's conjecture. In boredom the inner tensions, which in the case of "not being particularly occupied" would penetrate more easily, correspond to "prohibited" strivings and are thus blocked to begin with. See Chap. 18, below.

51. Thus the states of tension corresponding to intentions, precisely like those states of tension which arise from drives, can exist for prolonged periods in latent forms, without conscious tension-experiences. The differences between the two are, however, obvious in the symptoms, anxieties, and progressive generalization of inhibition, resulting from drive-tensions being forced into latency for prolonged periods.

52. Lewin here undertakes to demonstrate that the force (intention) and energy (tension) concepts which he has adopted can account for all the varieties of intention-effects. In a broader sense, he attempts to demonstrate that psychological processes can be encompassed by the concept-patterns of energy-dynamics which have been found to apply to physical, chemical, and other processes. For a similar attempt at presenting the psychoanalytic theory of cathexes, see Rapaport (596, 595).

(B) THE CESSATION OF PSYCHOLOGICAL FORCES FOLLOWING CONSUMMATION
OR SUBSTITUTE CONSUMMATION. As soon as the presence of internal tension, and
not an associative coupling, is considered the decisive cause of the consummatory action, the disappearance of the valence of the intended occasion after
consummation can also be deduced. In the extreme case, the effect of the intended occasion fails to occur altogether, because the internal tension is discharged in a "substitute consummation." [53]

Clearly, the forces arising from acts of intending are closely related in type
to those psychological forces which we usually called *needs*, and these in turn
derive either from drives or from central goals of will, such as the will to pursue a vocation.

(C) PARALLEL PHENOMENA IN GENUINE- AND IN QUASI-NEEDS. (*1*) *Genuine-
Needs and Natural Valences. Drive-needs*, such as hunger, are internal tensions,
directed pressures, driving toward so-called "satisfying actions." For drive-
needs also, certain "occasions" play an essential role; they too respond to certain alluring objects and events which have a *valence* for them.[54]

Our psychologically given environment does not consist of a sum of optical,
acoustic, and tactile sensations, but of objects and events.[55*] The recognition
of this has slowly established itself in psychology. It is traditional to attribute
certain feeling-tones to these objects and events; they are pleasant or unpleasant, pleasurable or painful.[56]

Furthermore, it is common knowledge that the objects and events of the environment are not neutral toward us in our role of *acting* beings. Not only does
their very nature facilitate or obstruct our actions to varying degrees, but we
also encounter many objects and events which face us with a will of their own:
they challenge us to certain activities. Good weather and certain landscapes

53. Cf. p. 110 and note 38, above.

54. In the psychoanalytic theory, the
objects which have a valence for a drive-
need are called drive- or instinct-objects,
and are conceived of as cathected
(charged with energy) by the drive. Cf.
Chap. 15, note 29, below. For a rather
original view of genuine-needs, see Maslow (503, 502).

55.* For a detailed discussion of this
issue, see Katz (375).

56. These attributes of objects and
events are also valences, but of a different order from those which challenge us
to definite activities (door—to open,
dog—to pet), which Lewin discusses below. The former were called by Werner
(755, pp. 67 ff.) "physiognomic" attributes. These are non-specific in their
challenge, archaic, idiosyncratic, and related to drive- and affect-tensions; the
valences of doors, dogs, etc., tend to be
more specific and socially shared.

entice one to a walk. A stairway stimulates the two-year-old child to climb it and jump down; doors, to open and to close them; small crumbs, to pick them up; dogs, to pet them; building stones, to play with them; the chocolate and a piece of cake want to be eaten. This is not the place to discuss in detail the nature, kinds, and functions of these "objects and events" which have valences. We will refer here only to a few of their basic characteristics, and will avoid discussing the role which experience and habit play in establishing them.[57]

The intensity with which objects and events challenge us varies greatly. The shadings of such challenge range from "irresistible temptations," to which child as well as adult yields unthinkingly and against which self-control helps little if at all, to those which have the character of "command," to the weaker "urgings" and "attractions," which can be easily resisted and become noticeable only when the person tries to find something to do. The term "valence" comprises all these shadings.[58]

We distinguish positive and negative valences, according to whether we are attracted by something (a good concert, an interesting man, a beautiful woman) or repelled by it (a discomfort, a danger). This dichotomy is correct in that the valences of the first group all press us to *approach* the objects and events in question, while those of the second press us to *retreat* from them. It would be, however, a mistake to assume that this is the crucial feature of valences. It is much more characteristic for valences that they press toward definite *actions*, the range of which may be narrow or broad, and that these actions may be of a great variety even within the group of positive valences. The book entices to reading, the cake to eating, the ocean to swimming, the mirror to looking, a confused situation to decisive action.

The valence of a structure is usually not constant, but depends greatly—in its kind and degree—on the internal and external situation of the person. The study of the vicissitudes of valences reveals their nature.[59]

57. The role of habit and experience on the one hand, and that of drive-needs on the other, in establishing the various kinds of valences open up the whole issue of the hierarchy of motivations. Cf. note 43 above, and Chap. 17, note 13, below.

58. The parsimoniousness of conceptualization in terms of energy-dynamics

here becomes evident. The concept "valence"—defined as the characteristic of objects, action on which discharges tension—serves as explanatory concept for the whole continuum of experiences ranging from "irresistible temptations" to "attractions."

59. There is a parallel between the following discussion of the vicissitudes

The meaning of a structure having a valence is transparent enough in certain basic cases: in these the objects which have the valence are *direct means of need satisfaction* (the cake, the concert if one goes to listen and not to be seen, etc.). In such cases we speak of *independent valences*.[60]

There are, besides, objects and events which have valences due to their relation to the direct means of need satisfaction in the given situation; for instance, they can facilitate satisfaction. They are means to an end and have only a momentary significance. Other such *derivative valences* arise from a space or time extension of structures which have original valences. The house, the street, and even the city in which the beloved lives, may each acquire a valence. The transition between these two kinds of valences is naturally fluid, and the concept of independent valence is also relative.[61]

A valence may undergo great changes, depending on the action-whole in which the object or event in question appears: the mirror which has just enticed the subject to take a look at her hair-do and dress becomes a neutral "instrument" as soon as she is given a task involving the use of the mirror. Similar changes of a most extreme sort occur with the objects of a landscape in war at

---

of valences and the one given by Freud concerning the vicissitudes of drive-valences in his papers "Instincts and Their Vicissitudes" (232), "The Unconscious" (234), and "Repression" (233).

60. Cf. Freud (232, pp. 65–66), concerning the relation of the instinct and its object.

61. Cf. Freud (233, pp. 87–91), concerning instinct-presentations and -derivatives (derivative valences), as well as their relation to cathexes (instinctual energies) and repression. From the point of view of psychoanalysis, Lewin is mainly concerned with derivatives. From Lewin's point of view, much that psychoanalysis would consider derivatives will appear as independent valences, particularly since he considers these concepts relative: that is, derivative valences may give rise to further derivatives, in relation to which they may appear as independent valences. The occupational choice of a medical career will appear to psychoanalysis to have a derivative valence (deriving from the valence which "helping people" has for the person, though this will still not be its ultimate root). To Lewin this occupational choice will appear as an "overriding goal of will," an independent valence; the person's interest in studying he will consider as a derivative valence arising from it. The valence of a boring book will be therefore a second-order derived valence; that is, the act of intending to read it will be founded on the valence which studying has for him.

From the point of view of the theory of thinking, we are again faced with the issue of the hierarchy of motivations, and with their mutual dependence on and independence from each other.

the time of battle.[62]* Besides their dependence upon the momentarily prevailing action, valences have other vicissitudes: greatly tempting delicacies become
uninteresting as soon as one is *satiated*.[63] In fact, *oversatiation* typically changes
the sign of the valence: what was attractive prior to it, repels after it. Oversatiation may even lead to a lasting fixation of a negative valence. (Now and
then it happens that for years one will avoid a favorite dish after once getting
sick on it.) In general, however, a rhythmic rise and fall, following the perio-
dicity of the corresponding needs, is typical for valences.

The vicissitudes of certain valences may be followed over long periods of
time, for instance, those which accompany the development of the individual
from infancy, through childhood and adolescence into adulthood, and old age.
Their course corresponds to the changes in needs and interests, and plays a
fundamental role in development. The development of the achievement-
abilities of an individual does not depend only on the potentialities of "endowment." For instance, the development of speech or of intellectual achievements
is basically influenced by the degree and direction of such "inclinations," which
are the motors of psychic processes.[64]

These vicissitudes, the exploration [65]*of which has only begun, seem to be
similar to the vicissitudes of valences which accompany changes in the general
goals of will that govern the individual. The will to follow an occupation is
an example of such general goals of will. Once a choice of an occupation is
made, certain things which have until then been neutral obtain a positive or a
negative valence.[66]* Much that at first would seem "natural" inborn inclination or disinclination—preference for a certain kind of work, tendency to
cleanliness and meticulousness—can be derived from the occupational goal of
the individual.[67]

62.* See Lewin (459). Cf. also Giese
(270).

63. Cf. Karsten (370).

64. Here Lewin links the developmental vicissitudes of needs, which are
the overriding concern of psychoanalysis
(see Freud, 232), the dependence of intellectual development on "inclinations,"
which plays such an important role in
Piaget's genetic psychology (563, and
Chaps. 6 and 7, below), and the dependence of intellectual achievement on fac-

tors other than endowment, which is the
fundamental thesis of the rationale of
scatter-analysis of intelligence tests (see
Rapaport *et al.*, 602, I, 38–43, 129–31).

65.* Spranger (701), Charlotte Buehler (103), Lau (445).

66.* Cf. Lau (445).

67. From the point of view of classical
psychoanalytic theory, one would have
to argue that though cleanliness or punctuality may be consistent with and even
appear to derive from the occupational

A man's world changes fundamentally when his fundamental goals of will change. This holds not only for the great upheavals which follow a decision to take one's life or change one's occupation, but even for those temporary suspensions of the usual goals of will which occur when one is on vacation. Familiar things may then suddenly acquire a new look; those which went unnoticed a hundred times become interesting, and important occupational matters turn indifferent.

This change of strong positive or negative valences to complete indifference is often astonishing even to the person concerned, and has frequently been described in poetry, particularly in relation to the erotic sphere. Such change of valence is often the first indication of a change in one's internal situation, and may even precede awareness of change in inclinations. The occurrence or absence of a change of valence is frequently the actual criterion of whether a decision—for instance, "to begin a new life in some way"—is apparent or *real;* that is, whether the decision occurred only in subjective experience or is a psychologically effective dynamic change.[68] Conversions are particularly far-reaching and abrupt changes of this sort: "persecute what you have worshipped and worship what you have persecuted."

The structure of the relation between valences and these general goals of will is thus basically the same as that between valences and the goals of single activities.

---

goal, say that of physician, in final analysis cleanliness and punctuality are character traits originating in the resolution of the anal phase of character development. Cf. Freud (215), Abraham (4, 7, 3). Present-day psychoanalytic theory would be more subtle on this point. It would point out that the choice of occupational goal and the specific traits of cleanliness and punctuality must have their origin in common determiners. It would stress that the anal phase itself may have many kinds of resolutions, and the resolution process may be so prolonged that it will be capped only by the actual occupational choice, facilitating the resolution by reaction-formation, which cleanliness and punctuality indeed are. When the argument reaches this point, the contradictory views concerning the determiners of these "inclinations" are resolved to another case of overdetermination.

68. Like psychoanalysis, Lewin is sharply opposed to those behavioristic views which consider conscious experience a mere epiphenomenon, but regards contents of consciousness as phenotypes of those psychologically effective dynamic changes which are the genotypes underlying them. Conscious experiences are indicators of effective dynamic changes; their contents however, as a rule, reveal only indirectly the nature of the change.

These brief considerations show that the natural valences are most closely related to certain inclinations and needs, some of which derive from the so-called "drives," and others from central goals of will of varying degrees of generality. Indeed, since a change of valence corresponds to every change of need, *the proposition that "such-and-such a need exists" is to a certain extent equivalent to the proposition that "such-and-such a region of structures has a valence for such-and-such actions."*

2) *The Effects of Quasi-Needs and Genuine-Needs.*[69] The relation of genuine needs and natural valences, however, is not such that to each need there always belongs a definite structure with a corresponding valence. It is typical for new needs which have not yet been frequently satisfied, and thus particularly for needs previous to their first real gratification, that they have a broad range of possible valences. For instance, for the purpose of systematic study the prototype of sexual and erotic inclinations is not that stage at which a firm fixation on one or more definite people and a specialization of satisfying action has already taken place, but one at which the inclination is diffuse and the region of valences is broad and indefinite.[70]* Yet development does not always proceed from a diffuse to a differentiated and specialized stage. There are processes in which an inclination, at first specific, diversifies. For instance, a child of a year and a half likes at first to "open and close" only a certain clock-case, and only gradually takes to opening and closing of doors, closets and chests of drawers. A diffuse phase followed by gradual specialization and consolidation may also be the course of needs related to general goals of will—for instance, occupational will. (Yet a highly specialized goal may be present from the beginning.) [71]

In the case of such diffuse drive- or central-needs, the *situation* to a great ex-

---

69. The discussion of the relationship of genuine- and quasi-needs presented here by Lewin fits in well with the discussions concerning the hierarchy of motives in our earlier footnotes. It will be noted that Lewin stresses the commonalities of these needs but has little to say about their differences.

70.* von Allesch (23).
[Cf. Freud, 213.]

71. Though the psychoanalytic the-ory of psycho-sexual development has studied such processes of generalization and specification of need-object relations, the major part of this field is still uncharted territory. Lorenz's (484) ornithological studies concerning inborn and acquired parent and companion "images," and sensitive periods in which such acquisition can take place, are an important pioneering step. Cf. note 89, below.

tent determines the valence which will have an effect and the actions which will be carried out.[72] The need to "get ahead in an occupation" implies little or nothing for or against any specific kind of consummatory action. It remains quite indefinite whether one should write or telephone, do activity A or a quite different activity B. Even jobs considered typically "beneath the dignity of one's occupation" and therefore usually avoided (for instance, letter-filing by a bookkeeper), may be considered an honor and done with delight in certain situations (for instance, when a bookkeeper is entrusted to file particularly confidential documents). Thus activities of identical achievement may appear now highly desirable and now taboo, depending on their occupational significance. Even for quite specialized and fixated needs there usually exists a certain, and mostly not even a narrow, range of valences, the actual evocation of which depends only on the concrete situation.[73]

The situation is quite similar to that which obtains for intentions, where occasion and consummatory action are often quite indeterminate. There, too, exists a certain latitude of valences eliciting the intention effects, even when the act of intending has established definite occasions.

This parallel between the effect of a genuine-need and the effect of an intention extends also to many other essential points which will be discussed below. Because of this parallel, whenever an intention is extant we will assume that a quasi-need is present.[74]

Both for genuine-needs and intention-effects there exist certain objects or events of valence, which when encountered arouse a tendency to definite actions. In neither case is valence and action so related that an associative coupling between the two is the cause of the action. The action-energy of drive-needs also originates essentially in certain *internal tensions*, the significance of

72. Beach's (39) studies on the sexual behavior of the rat shed considerable light on this situational factor.

73. Bettelheim's (60, 59) concentration-camp studies contain many examples of this.

74. Lewin here implies a definition of quasi-needs as tendencies directing action and thought which, though they are not commonly classified as needs, behave as forces arising from energy-systems "under tension." It should be noted that not only intentions, but interests, attitudes, preferences, biases, all may behave in this manner. The concept of quasi-need thus is amenable to generalization as well as to differentiation. Such a generalized concept of quasi-needs may well subsume all those factors which psychoanalysis labels "ego-interests" or "ego-motivations."

external drive-stimuli notwithstanding. Where occasions and means of drive satisfaction do not appear from the outside they are *actively sought out*, just as in the case of intention effects.[75]

As an argument against this conception, the so-called *habits* could be marshaled. In fact, popular psychology, and until recently scientific psychology also, considered habits as couplings between certain occasions and actions, and these couplings as the energy source of habit actions.[76] The examples marshaled to support the theory were of this sort: we are not always hungry when we take our meal at set hours. According to recent experimental results,[77*] such cases can be understood if we assume that the action in question is embedded, as a dependent part, in a broader action-complex—for instance, in the "daily routine" or "style of life"—so that its energy, the motor of the action, derives from other need sources.[78] It seems to me that even in such habit actions and special fixations, the structure of the driving forces is still rather clearly discernible: *the significance of external drive-stimuli notwithstanding, needs imply states of tension which press toward satisfaction.* Satisfaction eliminates the tension-state and may, therefore, be described as psychological "satiation." [79]

The valences which a region of structures and events has before satisfaction (in the "hunger state") are eliminated by satiation. The region becomes neutral. Needs and intentions are analogous in this respect also; we have described the

75. Cf. Fenichel, on "stimulus hunger," Chap. 18, particularly note 4, below.

76. Cf. note 30, above.

77.* Lewin (460), Sigmar (688).

78. This explanation is enlightening, but opens further problems of investigation and theorizing; how the embeddedness came about genetically and what kinds of embeddedness are feasible are questions which must be answered sooner or later. The problem may be sharpened by a variation of the example: we work in order to secure food even when we are not hungry. In this example, the need-gratification as the goal of the activity is implied, just as in activities directed at immediate gratification. But gratification is actually delayed, and the need works by anticipation; the activity occurs on a detour, as it were, from the direct path toward gratification. The purpose of the detour is to make eventual gratification certain. Cf. Freud, Chap. 15 and Chap. 17, note 20, below. It could be conjectured that, in the course of such detours, broader embedding activity-complexes are built up which perhaps have quasi-autonomus energy supplies of their own, derived from the energies of that need whose gratification the detour subserves. If this be the case, then we have yet to explore how all this comes about genetically and what structural consequences it has for psychological happening.

79. Cf. Karsten (370).

sudden neutralization of the valence of a structure by the "consummation" of the intentional action. This basic phenomenon of the intention-effect, which a theory of associative couplings can hardly explain without complex auxiliary hypotheses, becomes understandable if the intention-effect is considered to be the arising of a quasi-need and *the consummation of the intention to be its "satisfaction," that is, satiation.*

In fact, *satisfaction experiences* occur very frequently at the end of consummatory actions, even in experimental investigations.

Over and above the phenomenal relationship of consummation and satisfaction experience, the thesis concerning quasi-needs gains support by affording a dynamic explanation and derivation of the characteristics of intention-effects.[80]

If a latent tension-state pressing toward equilibrium (satisfaction) [81] plays the primary role here, then the intention effect should be elicited *by every objectively relevant occasion* and not only by that implied in the act of intending—provided that these occasions exist psychologically and are not paralyzed by counter-forces. If the occasion fails to occur, it is—as a result of the latent state of tension—*actively sought out*, just as in the case of drive-needs and other genuine-needs. If the tension-state is too intensive, then here also inexpedient actions akin to "premature start" come about.

Genuine-needs and quasi-needs show a great deal of agreement also in their special relations to valences. (Since the following data derive only from observations of everyday life, they are in urgent need of experimental exploration, for which they should be considered only as points of departure.)

Increase in the intensity of the genuine-need usually broadens the region of valences also. In states of extraordinary hunger, objects which are otherwise unpalatable and disgust-arousing may attain positive valence. In extremes, earth is eaten and anthropophagy becomes frequent. (In such cases people partly obey the need with inner disgust, but partly the phenomenal valences are changed.) Even in less extreme instances, increasing need-intensity results in a noticeable spread of valences.[82*] The same holds for the so-called intellectual needs. . . . There are similar observations concerning quasi-needs also. The

80. Cf. note 52, above.

81. In psychoanalytic theory also, the concepts of gratification and pleasure-principle are equivalent to equilibration and tendency to equilibration. Cf. Rapaport (596).

82.* Cf. Katz and Toll (377).

region of occasions other than the intended one to which the intention also re-- sponds, usually spreads as the tension resulting from the intention increases.[83] For dispatching an important letter urgently, the visit of a friend or any other occasion is more likely to be utilized than when the letter is an indifferent one. (Later on I shall discuss exceptions related to the nature of vehement activity.)

3) *Fixation in Genuine-Needs and Quasi-Needs. Fixation* is one of the crucial phenomena pertaining to the relation between valences and genuine-needs. It denotes the occasional narrowness of the region of valences in comparison to the region of objects or events which "per se" would seem relevant.[84]

For instance, a child who has several dolls will play always with one and the same doll, or give it disproportionate preference. The child will maintain that the doll "is always well behaved," or "she never lies." Even when the child is out of sorts and pays little attention to the other dolls, she will still love this one. . . .

The fixation on *certain* valences and on *certain* modes of satisfaction plays a great and significant role in psychic life. It is known how extraordinarily intense the fixation of any genuine-need can be, to a human being, or an occupation, or a certain work, and how exclusive a role that fixation may play, and how difficult it often is to resolve.[85]

83. Cf. note 73, above. By his reference to Katz's work Lewin indicates that the whole issue of hunger and appetite is germane to the topic discussed. Indeed, the recent work of Richter (611) and Young (782) sheds considerable light on the need-valence relationship and its ramifications.

84. Cf. pp. 122–123, above.

85. The reference is apparently to those phenomena which psychoanalysis also conceptualizes as fixation. Freud (213, p. 628) in "Three Contributions to the Theory of Sex" wrote:

The significance of all premature sexual manifestations is enhanced by a psychic factor of unknown origin, which at present can be put down only as a psychological preliminary. I believe that it is the *heightened adhesion* or *fixedness* of these impressions of the sexual life which in later neurotics, as well as in perverts, must be added as a supplement to the existing facts. For the same premature sexual manifestations in other persons cannot impress themselves deeply enough to act compulsively on repetition, and to lay out the path of the sexual instinct for the whole future. A partial explanation for this adhesion is perhaps found in another psychic factor which we cannot miss in the causation of the neuroses, namely, in the preponderance which in the psychic life falls to the share of memory traces in comparison to those of recent impressions. This factor apparently depends on intellectual development and grows with the height of personal culture.

In " 'Civilized' Sexual Morality and Nervousness," Freud (216, p. 84) wrote:

[In] the different varieties of perverts . . . an infantile fixation on a preliminary sexual

Such fixations result apparently in an unusually strong valence of the structure in question and have a certain *exclusive function:* other structures lose their valence, entirely or partly. Similarly with the fixation to certain modifications of the satisfying *activity*.

Something quite analogous may be observed in quasi-needs also. An occasion implied by the act of intending may have a fixating effect, narrowing the range

---

aim has impeded the establishing of the primacy of the reproductive function. . . .

In "Predisposition to Obsessional Neurosis," Freud (228, p. 123) wrote:

We must . . . assume that these developments are not always carried out without a hitch, so that the function as a whole is not always subjected to progressive modification. Should any component of it remain arrested at an earlier phase there results what is known as a "fixation-point," to which the function can regress if external hardships give rise to illness.

In "Instincts and Their Vicissitudes," Freud (232, pp. 65–66) wrote:

A particularly close attachment of the instinct to its object is distinguished by the term *fixation:* this frequently occurs in very early stages of the instinct's development and so puts an end to its mobility, through the vigorous resistance it sets up against detachment.

In "Repression," Freud (233, p. 86) wrote:

[Primal repression] is accompanied by *fixation;* the ideational presentation persists unaltered from then onwards and the instinct remains attached to it.

Cf. also Freud (235, pp. 236 ff. and 294 ff.). The experiences favoring the development of fixation were summarized by Fenichel (176) as follows:

a. The consequence of experiencing excessive satisfactions at a given level is that this level is renounced only with reluctance; if, later, misfortunes occur, there is always a yearning for the satisfaction formerly enjoyed.

b. A similar effect is wrought by excessive *frustrations* at a given level. One gets the impression that at developmental levels that do not afford enough satisfaction the organism refuses to go further, demanding the withheld satisfactions. If the frustration has led to repression, the drives in question are thus cut off from the rest of the personality; they do not participate in further maturation and send up their disturbing derivatives from the unconscious into the conscious. The result is that these drives remain in the unconscious unchanged, constantly demanding the same sort of satisfaction; thus they also constantly provoke the same defensive attitudes on the part of the defending ego. This is one source of neurotic "repetitions."

c. One frequently finds that excessive satisfactions as well as excessive frustrations underlie a given fixation; previous overindulgence had made the person unable to bear later frustrations; little frustrations, which a less spoiled individual could tolerate, then have the same effect that a severe frustration ordinarily has.

d. It is understandable, therefore, that abrupt changes from excessive satisfactions to excessive frustrations have an especially fixating effect.

e. Most frequently, however, fixations are rooted in experiences of instinctual satisfaction which simultaneously gave reassurance in the face of some anxiety or aided in repressing some other feared impulse. Such simultaneous satisfaction of drive and of security is the most common cause of fixations.

of the objectively relevant occasions to which less specific intentions might
have been responsive. This holds for consummatory actions too: for instance,
without the specific intention to bring up certain arguments, one would argue
in a discussion appropriately to the situation and therefore purposively; but
specific fixation of the arguments by a preceding act of intending often results
in statements inappropriate to the situation.[86] But, as a rule, fixation does not
have an entirely exclusive effect, either for genuine- or for quasi-needs. In spite
of the fixation a certain range of other valences usually persists, particularly if
the pressure of the genuine- or quasi-need is strong.[87]

With genuine-needs, the occasion and kind of the *first satisfaction* has a particularly fixating effect (first love). This is also true for those intentions which
press toward repetitive action. If several occasions are possible before the first
consummation, then later this first occasion will stand out from the others. This
holds for the first satisfying consummatory action too,[88*] and plays therefore
a considerable role in the so-called training process.[89] In this, which is by no

86. Such phenomena, and their conceptualization by Lewin as "fixations,"
may prove to be of significance for the
psychopathology of thought-processes.
The concreteness or literalness of the
concepts of feeble-minded and of many
brain-injured persons (see Werner, 755),
and the concrete and literal aspects of
schizophrenic thinking (see Benjamin
43, and Chap. 26, note 32, below), show
similarities to these phenomena.

It will clarify the point to keep in mind
that the personality of the subject will
affect the degree to which an occasion
implied in an act of intending will narrow the range of relevant occasions.
Some subjects will always take experimental instructions more literally and
concretely than others. Test investigations reveal an unbroken continuum
from these individual differences to pathological literalness. Thus we may be
faced with a new aspect of the thought-
disorders usually described as those of
concept-formation: it seems possible to

conceptualize them as disorders of need-
tension dynamics. Cf. Kounin (414); see
also the relation of literalness to "attitude-disturbances," Chap. 27, notes 22,
39, 76, below.

87. Indeed this is the case even for
those fixations that psychoanalysis deals
with. The object on which an instinct
fixates will continue to produce new
derivatives and representations, though
of relatively little adaptation value. This
is the case with symptoms, whose adaptation value should not be altogether disregarded.

88.* This may be the origin of "latent
attitudes" and "activity readinesses." See
Koffka (408).

89. The role of primacy in fixation,
though asserted both by Lewin and
Freud, is still quite unclear. An ornithological example may illustrate the point.
Lorenz's studies show that wild birds
have inborn "knowledge" of perceptual
characteristics of their parents, which
therefore have valences for them elicit-

means a uniform process psychologically, valences and their vicissitudes are of great significance.[90]* In learning any activity (for example, turning a lathe) many things lose their natural valences: large wheels or sudden events which are at first frightening become neutral. In turn, other structures and events, at first unnoticed, obtain definite and clear valences when embedded in the new total context.

[Passage omitted.]

In repeating intentional actions, usually certain modes of consummation crystallize. In this crystallization process, frequently called "automatization," the course of activity becomes rigid and lifeless.[91] The quasi-need in early repetitions compares to that in later ones, as a young organism does to an old one. All the potentialities which together provide the conditional-genetic definition of the quasi-need actually exist in the beginning: the need is responsive to a variety of occasions and its form of consummation readily *adapts to the situations*. In later repetitions, however, the *form of consummation* becomes *relatively rigid*: historical factors limit the range of possible modes of behavior. (In some cases, as mentioned, fixation seems to exist from the beginning on.)

As a rule, a *growing independence* of the need- or quasi-need action accompanies, and may even be the prerequisite of, this ossification. A relatively independent specific organism comes about, which acts without requiring the control of the total personality and whose communication with other needs and quasi-needs is limited.[92]

The experiments on the measurement of will may serve as an example.[93]* In these experiments the process—for instance, the occurrence of intended errors

---

ing their "behavior toward the parents." Some wild birds never adopt substitute parents, while domesticated ones are prone to adopt birds of other species and even men as substitutes. The valences of the former are fixed, those of the latter are not. Of special interest here are those autophagous birds which will adopt substitute parents, provided that they encounter them in a "sensitive period" specific to them. These sensitive periods occur soon after hatching and are of very brief duration.

90.* See Lewin (460, Part II, p. 124), and Blumenfeld (78).

91. Cf. Hartmann, Chap. 19, VIII, below.

92. Here Lewin puts forth developmental considerations in some respects similar to those we have touched on in note 43, above. His terms "ossification" and "limited communications" seem to refer to the state of affairs to which we referred as "autonomy." Cf. also Allport (25) on functional autonomy.

93.* Ach (15) and Lewin (460).

(habit-errors)—depends only indirectly on the underlying needs, but directly on the specific form of consummation: a definite "activity-readiness" [94*]—implying a definite form of consummation—and not the presence of a definite quasi-need, decides whether or not a habit-error will occur.

But even in such ossified quasi-needs the energy-source remains the quasi-need itself, that is, in final analysis, the genuine-need underlying it.[95]

Whether it is the act of intending or the course of the first consummations which *establishes* the valences and consummatory actions, the process establishing them is closely related to that of fixation of genuine-needs. It differs in essential points from *associations* as encountered in learning syllables by rote or in any other "change of the stock of knowledge." [96*]

It makes no difference whether the association is conceived as one between occasion and consummation, or one between the occasion and its valence accrued from the intention. The valence of an object, just like its figural Gestalt (though the former varies more than the latter), is not independent of it as a second psychic structure. The valence of an object is as much a part of its essence as its figural Gestalt. In order to avoid misunderstandings, it would be better to speak not of changes in the valence of the object, but of *different* structures which are only figurally and externally identical. A structure whose valence has changed with the change in situation—for example, the mailbox before and after mailing the letter—*is* psychologically a different structure.

[Passage omitted.] [97]

The following consideration appears at first contrary to our conception. We saw that consummation of the intended action—satiation of the quasi-need—as a rule eliminates the valence, since it leaves no real tension driving toward consummation. Everyday observations, however, seem to indicate that such valences can persist for a while even after consummation. It does happen that, though the letter has been mailed, a mailbox subsequently passed again reminds us to mail it.

94.* Lewin (460).

95. Lewin's concept "activity-readiness" denotes a directional determinant in associative learning. Here he implies that it is an "ossified" factor, deriving its energy from a quasi-need. Thus we see again that Lewin's theory implies a hierarchy of motivations.

96.* Selz (679, 680) and Lewin (460). [Cf. also note 89, above.]

97. In the omitted section Lewin again stresses that an association theory based on repetition frequencies cannot explain the disappearance, after consummation, of valences once created.

It is conceivable that this is the inverse of those cases discussed below, in which a *substitute satisfaction* causes the forgetting of the intended action. Here mailing the letter, while objectively achieving the desired result, did not have the *psychic* effect of satisfaction; at any rate, it did not completely eliminate the tension of the quasi-need. Our concern is not with the external activity as such, but with the elimination of tensions.

The same question arises for valences related to genuine-needs:

When a small child refuses some food, bringing the spoon to his mouth is often enough to make him start eating. The older child displays greater control over the direct valence to which the younger yields as to a drive: he shuts his mouth tight, turns his head, and so on. Yet the same result can be attained by distracting the older child's attention. (Above a certain age, not even distraction avails.)

Two factors are essential to this phenomenon. First, the valence has a *stronger effect* if it is not "attended to." Increased "attention" prevents the direct effect of this "stimulus" (valence). We explain this seemingly paradoxical state of affairs by assuming that the field-forces exert their effect more directly when distraction weakens the controls.[98]

The case of distraction is complicated by the negative valence of the food.

Secondly, the full spoon near the mouth has a valence for the child even if he dislikes the food. Popular psychology would explain this as a "habit," a frequent label, anyway, for fixation effects. Since there is no need present for the food in question, the valence must be that of the spoon or that of the spoon's being brought near the mouth in this situation. It appears that the valence has an effect here, even in the absence of a momentary need. Similarly, in everyday life we often do with reluctance things which on other occasions we have done with pleasure.

It is justifiable to ask: is there some genuine- or quasi-need for the activity in these cases even if the major need is absent? It is possible that here we have tensions which are intermediary forms between genuine- and quasi-needs and are related to those general goals of will which shape our everyday life: arising, dressing, taking meals, going to sleep.[99] This assumption is supported by the

98. The problem of the dynamic effect of attention arises here. It is doubtful whether describing attention as control over the effects of field-forces is an advancement. Freud's attempt to con- ceptualize attention as a manifestation of energies at the disposal of the ego seems more consistent with a dynamic theory. Cf. Chap. 15, note 21, below.

99. Here again we are faced with in-

observation that such valences will persist as a rule only for a short while in the face of contrary needs, which in the long run will change the "style of life."

Only experimental analysis can answer the question whether these explanations hold for all cases, or whether under certain conditions—as in fixations—valences persist in spite of the satiation of the quasi-need.

Fixations play an important role in psychic life and our discussion of them in genuine- and quasi-needs is not meant to be a systematic theory.[100] Nor do we assert here that genuine associative couplings have no role in fixation.

We advance only a few fundamental propositions: the restriction of a valence to a definite occasion and the fixation of a specific mode of consummation are extremes in a continuum in which broad regions of events and structures have valences. The theory of quasi-needs, in contrast to the customary conception, considers that the pure and fundamental form of intention processes is found in those cases which are free of specializing fixations limiting the effect of other objectively feasible occasions. The energy sources of these processes are the genuine- or quasi-needs underlying them, and the fixated valences are also mainly related to these. The fixation is not itself the source of the action, but only the determiner of its form or occasion. Even if the relation of occasion and consummatory action were actually an associative coupling, this relation would not be analogous to the association of syllables or other kinds of knowledge, but rather to the fixation of a valence to a definite occasion.

[Passage omitted.] [101]

4) *Substitute Consummation.*[102] If a quasi-need and not an associative coupling between occasion and consummation is the source of intentional action, then some basic problems of *substitute consummation* are also easily clarified.

Genuine-needs too have substitute satisfactions.[103] Genuine-needs and quasi-needs both have a whole variety of substitute consummations. The differences

---

dications suggesting a hierarchy of motivations. Cf. notes 43 and 78, above.

100. It is conceivable that once we understand how fixations come about, that process will prove to be the prototype of the processes by which new hierarchic levels of motivation arise.

101. In the omitted section Lewin demonstrates, by means of data taken from his association studies (460), that fixated valences also weaken by repeated consummation. His point is that habit-strength need not correlate positively with repetition-frequency, and under certain conditions correlates with it negatively.

102. Cf. p. 110, particularly note 38, and p. 117, above.

103. Concerning certain substitute gratifications—symptoms—of drive-

between these varieties are in part fundamental, but it is not easy to define them conceptually because of the transitions between them, and the mixed types among them. We will use the term *substitute consummation* for all of them, and will refer only to a few main variants, without discussing the important questions they raise.

(a) *Consummation appropriate to the situation* is objectively equivalent to the intended consummation and is adapted to the situation. Example: instead of mailing the letter as originally intended, we ask a friend to take care of it. This is not really a substitute consummation; the course of the consummatory action alone is different from that which was anticipated. We know that this is actually the common form of intentional acts, since genuine- as well as quasi-needs usually leave the mode of consummation wide open. The theory of quasi-needs (in contrast to that of associative couplings) has no difficulties with this kind of substitute consummation, in which the goal of the original need is actually reached. The consummatory action eliminates the tension (satiates the quasi-need) and causes the valences to disappear. This holds, we repeat, for genuine needs also.[104]

(b) "Pars pro toto" *consummation*. Example: instead of buying an object, we go through the street where we can buy it; instead of actually carrying out an intention, we record it in a notebook. The consummatory action goes "in the direction of" the original goal, but apparently halts somewhere along the line. Yet the typical dynamic effects of incomplete consummation do not ap-

---

needs, see Fenichel (176, pp. 556 ff.) and Freud (252). Freud wrote (252, pp. 21–22):

Symptoms result from the injuring of the instinctual impulse through repression. If . . . the Ego attains its object of completely suppressing the instinctual impulse, we have no intimation as to how it happens. We learn something about it only from the cases in which repression is more or less unsuccessful. Then it appears in general that the instinctual impulse, despite repression, has found a substitute satisfaction, but one which is greatly crippled, displaced, or inhibited. It is not even any longer recognizable as a gratification. If a substitute satisfaction is achieved, pleasure is not experienced, but instead the achieving of this substitute satisfaction has acquired the character of compulsion.

It must be kept in mind that some substitute gratifications of drive-needs—"reaction formations," "sublimations," etc.—need not be symptoms. In fact, no sharp line can be drawn between neurosis and character-formation; many a substitute gratification may be pathological (symptom) in one personality and characterological (trait) in another.

It is clear that Lewin's "genuine-needs" include more than the drive-needs which we have discussed.

104. In such cases, as Freud would put it, gratification is reached by detour. Cf. note 49, above.

pear and the need-tensions are rather well equilibrated, though the consummation proper did not take place and may, for instance, have been forgotten.
Specific satisfaction experiences following partial consummation seem to contribute to the failure of the consummation proper to occur. . . .

(c) *Unreal consummation, apparent consummation, shadow consummation,*
and the closely related *surrogate consummation.* Example (from Miss Dembo's
experiments): [105] failing to throw a ring over a certain bottle, one throws it
over another more easily reached, or over any near-by hook. There is no action
toward the real goal here. The goal itself is not brought nearer, but the consummatory action resembles somehow that of the genuine consummation.
Usually a certain momentary satisfaction results, which however soon yields
to the original need. It is relatively easy to produce such cases experimentally
—for instance, as "avoidance actions" in difficult tasks.[106]

How can need-tensions press to actions which are not even in the direction
of eliminating the need? This important question will not be discussed here in
detail. The assumption that we have here a tendency "just to do something"
(as in affective restless-activity) would be an insufficient explanation. Various
assumptions are possible, such as "spread" of the original need to actions of
identical type, or actual satisfaction of the original need by the substitute action
(based on the identity of the consummatory action). In the latter case, the
occasional perseverance of the need would be explained as its revival due to
recurring stimulation (valence). (This does not exhaust the possible theories:
for example, there is a clear relation here to the easily misunderstood Freudian
"symbol" concept).[107]

Surrogate satisfactions occur even with drive-needs or central goals of will,
when the satisfying-action proper encounters obstacles: we are "satisfied with

---

105. Dembo (140).

106. The "pars pro toto," "apparent,"
"shadow," "surrogate," and "hidden"
consummations contrast with the "situa-
tion-appropriate" consummations; the
latter follows a *logical* course, while that
of the former is familiar from "pre-
logical" thinking and the "primary
process." Cf. Werner (755) and Freud
(209). Apparently the expression of
tension-system dynamics may follow
either our usual logic or pre-logical pat-

terns. It is likely that thorough study of
substitute gratifications will bring to the
fore varieties corresponding to all forms
of "syncretic," "participatory," "trans-
ductive," and "primary" thought-patterns.

107. The relation of the symbol to
what it symbolizes indeed resembles that
of the substitute consummations to genuine consummation; it too is a pre-
logical relationship. Cf. Silberer, Chap.
9, pp. 211 ff., below.

less," and reduce our aspirations. There exist all degrees of such surrogates, from satisfactions which are not quite complete to those which are mere sham or shadow. Someone who likes to give commands but has no authority will often want to "have his say" at least or even just "be in on it." The youngster who cannot signal the train will shout "Ready, Go" after the station-master. A child who would like to escape from an orphanage has instead a burning desire for a traveling bag. A student who cannot afford to buy a piano collects piano catalogs instead.

In cases like the last, the action may attain independence, giving rise to "substitute needs." (The concept of sublimation is relevant to this point.) [108]

(d) *Hidden apparent consummations.* The second bottle mentioned in (c) may be replaced by a Teddy-bear or something similar, and the type of action itself may "change" until it is hardly recognizable. This may occur when the situation demands that the substitute consummation be concealed, for instance when it is embarrassing.

Besides the intensity of the tension underlying the need in question, *the general level of satisfaction or frustration of the subject* is also crucial in evoking substitute consummations. The experiments on forgetting already mentioned have demonstrated this. The signature is more readily forgotten when the subject is particularly satisfied with his other achievements. . . .

(D) THE REAL RELATIONS BETWEEN QUASI-NEEDS AND GENUINE-NEEDS.

1) *Quasi-Needs and Counter-Needs.* To consider the intention-effect a

---

108. Cf. note 103, above. Freud (235, pp. 299–300) wrote:

The component impulses of sexuality as well as the total sexual desire, which represents their aggregate, show a marked ability to change their object, to exchange it, for instance, for one more easily attainable. This displacement and the readiness to accept substitutes must exert powerful influences in opposition to the pathological effect of abstinence. Among these processes which resist the ill effects of abstinence, one in particular has won cultural significance. Sexual desire relinquishes either its goal of partial gratification of desire, or the goal of desire toward reproduction, and adopts another aim, genetically related to the abandoned one, save that it is no longer sexual but must be termed social. This process is called "sublimation," and in adopting this process we subscribe to the general standard which places social aims above selfish sexual desires. Sublimation is, as a matter of fact, only a special case of the relation of sexual to non-sexual desires.

In his last monograph Freud (257, p. 114) wrote:

The instinctual demands, being forced aside from direct satisfaction, are compelled to take new directions which lead to substitutive satisfaction, and in the course of these *detours* they may become desexualized and their connection with their original instinctual aims may become looser.

quasi-need amounts to more than creating a formal analogue to genuine-needs: *it makes a real relationship between intention-effect and genuine-need demonstrable.*

The various natural needs may conflict with each other: their tension-systems are not completely isolated. In part they are subordinate factors of a general tension-state, and in part there is some real communication between them, corresponding to the connections of the spheres and complexes in question within the psyche as a whole. (This has often been disregarded in the treatment of drives.) [109]

Similar considerations hold for the real relations of quasi-needs to each other and to genuine-needs. This explains the ready "forgetting of intentions" when pitted against a strong genuine *counter-need.*[110*]

The relation and the clashing of quasi-needs and genuine-needs lead us to the problem of *"freedom" of intentions.* The extraordinary liberty which man has to intend any, even nonsensical actions—that is, his freedom to create in himself quasi-needs—is amazing. This is characteristic of civilized man. Children, and probably also preliterates, have it to an incomparably lesser degree. It is likely that this freedom distinguishes man from kindred animals more than does his higher intelligence. (This distinction is obviously related to the problem of "control.") [111]

Yet, one cannot arbitrarily intend "just anything" if the criterion of intending is the formation of an actual quasi-need. Without a real need one cannot resolve to kill oneself or an acquaintance, or even to do something serious against one's true interests. Not even under the pressure of hypnosis are such intentions carried out.[112] These examples make the real relations between quasi-needs and genuine-needs particularly clear.

In children the range of the apparent arbitrariness of intentions is even narrower. Often they cannot endow even relatively neutral objects or events with

109. Whether this issue was actually disregarded is hard to say, since the relation of drives to each other is one of the very obscure problems of psychoanalysis. Cf. Fenichel (176, pp. 129–30), concerning the conflict of instincts, and Freud (255, pp. 142 ff.), concerning the "fusion" of instincts.

110.* See p. 106 ff., above.

111. This is again the issue of the relative autonomy of various levels of motivation, which in present-day psychoanalysis appears as the problem of the relative autonomy of the ego. Cf. notes 43 and 61, above.

112. Cf. P. C. Young's (780) review of the pertinent literature and the papers of Brenman (87) and Erickson (162).

positive valence by means of a quasi-need. The actions they want to intend must arise in part at least from natural valences. (These issues play a great role in the education of the small child.) [113]

2) *Quasi-Needs and Genuine-Needs of Identical Direction.* The real relation between quasi-needs and genuine-needs explains the unanimous result, at first paradoxical, of various experimental investigations, *that the intensity of the act of intending does not decide the effectiveness of the intention.*

The fact that particularly intensive acts of intending are often less effective than weaker ones is, as said before, in part due to the general ineffectiveness of *vehement* as compared to controlled activity.[114] Here the act of intending itself is considered as an action.

More important is the following consideration. The tensions and valences to which the act of intending gives rise are not primary. They derive from some genuine-needs, which in turn arise from drives or general goals of will. After a *quasi-need* arises from a genuine-need, it still remains *in communication with the complex of tensions implicit in the genuine-need.* Even if the intentions to drop a letter in the mailbox, to visit an acquaintance, yes, even to learn a series of nonsense syllables as an experimental subject, are relatively closed and segregated activities, the forces underlying them are not isolated, but arise from general needs, such as the will to do one's occupational work, to get ahead in one's studies, or to help a friend. The effectiveness of the intention does not depend on the intensity of the act of intending but, other factors being equal, rather on the *intensity* (vital nature) and *depth* of the genuine-need, in which the quasi-need is embedded.[115]

---

113. The difference in freedom to create intentions found between adults of our civilization on the one hand, and children and preliterates on the other, parallels the difference in flexibility between secondary-process and primary-process thinking. Though the latter are both directed at gratification, according to Freud, the primary-process insists on immediate *perception* of the gratifying object, while the secondary-process accepts delay of gratification and a detour to it by substitute *thoughts* which somehow share the identity of the gratifying

object. See Freud (223) and (209, p. 535). Cf. also note 11, above, and Chap. 17, note 20, below.

114. Cf. note 44, above. If it were demonstrated that vehement activity is always affect-laden, assuming a conflict theory of affects (see Rapaport, 591), its relative ineffectiveness would be explained.

115. Here Lewin stresses the quasi-need's dependence on and derivation from hierarchically more fundamental needs; below he will emphasize their autonomous and segregated character-

The *genuine-needs* in question are those which give rise to the intention, that is, those which lead one to decide for the action. In the intention to mail a letter, the decisive need is to inform somebody, and this in turn arises from a more general goal of will.

In the course of the consummatory action, however, tensions and forces become frequently manifest which had little or no role in forming the intention. Once an intention is set up or an action is initiated, often the "whole person" becomes immediately engaged in it; thus communication is established with tensions related to "self-esteem" and "fear of insufficiency." There are great individual differences in the ease with which such auxiliary forces connect with intentional actions, and become at times their sole driving force: for instance, to persist as far as possible with a decision once made, is the corollary of a certain life-ideal. The *situation* too has a significant influence in determining the role of these auxiliary forces. For instance, Mrs. Birenbaum's finding, that the signature is less easily forgotten in *mass experiments* than in individual ones, is probably to be explained as the effect of such forces.[116]

The communication with various genuine-needs may be extant from the beginning on, as in the case of the mass experiments. Frequently, however, it is not yet present at the act of intending, and arises only subsequently. This relation of needs is not merely theoretical, like that which obtains between different

istics. Compare our previous discussions of this issue, in notes 43, 49, and 61, above.

In earlier phases of psychoanalytic theory, the sole emphasis may have been on the dependence of all motivation on drives and defenses against them. With the present-day development of psychoanalytic ego-psychology, the interest in the relative autonomy of ego-motivations has increased. The relationship between derivation from drives and relative autonomy is the focus of interest.

116. Lewin rightly stresses here the significance of individual differences; clinical experience fully supports his observation. Indeed, the ease with which "the whole person becomes immediately engaged" is a clinically crucial datum.

A certain degree of engagement in most activities, and the ability to become fully engaged under appropriate conditions, are important landmarks of adjustment; the inclination to become fully engaged on any and all occasions, and the inability ever to become engaged, are usually indicators of pathology. The issues here involved are discussed in psychoanalytic literature under the terms "ego-strength" and "normality." See Hartmann, Chap. 19, below, Glover (276), Jones (359), Hartmann (307), Hacker (296), Nunberg (543). Cf. also Alper's (27) review of the experimental literature on ego-involvement that grew out of Lewin's and Zeigarnik's (783) work; and Sherif and Cantril (686).

yet conceptually comparable types of needs. It is a *real communication* between concrete tension-systems.[117] One can establish only from case to case, but not in general, when communication between systems is extant or absent. Such communication of systems comes about at a definite time, by a real process, which may progress slowly or break through suddenly.

Whether or not, besides these genuine-needs, there is an individually variable *reservoir of active energy*, used by intentional action not based on genuine-needs, is an open question awaiting experimental exploration. Some observations on encephalitics (their quick transition to micrography, their "getting stuck" after a brief spurt) are conducive to such explanation.[118]

The idea that the effectiveness of intentions depends not on their intensity, but rather on the depths of the underlying genuine-need, is in agreement with Lindworsky's repeatedly quoted studies. He too rejects the idea that the repetition of an act necessarily strengthens its driving force.[119]* To him, the decisive factor is the relation of the intention to certain values of the individual.

[Passage omitted.].[120]

An individual's valuation of an object or event undoubtedly exerts crucial influence on his motivation processes and total behavior. But we will have to keep in mind that it is not an objective scale of values which is relevant to our problem, but rather the subjective momentary valuations like those which a child has for a pet dog or a piece of chocolate. These valuations always vary with the changing situation and with the person's "degree of satiation" at the moment. Two facts, however, must be stressed: a) The value of an object is not simply identical with its valence. (A sum of gold somewhere may represent a great value for one person without tempting him to steal it, while for another person it may have a strong valence prompting to steal.) Naturally,

117. The distinction between real and theoretical relations, in Lewin's terms, is that the latter are conceived by the observer, while the former are operant in the subject. The fact that both are ultimately conceived by the observer raises complex problems which cannot be discussed further here.

118. This issue appears in psychoanalytic literature under the following terms: "the sources of ego-energies" (Hartmann, this volume, pp. 392 ff.);

"energies at the disposal of the ego" (Rapaport, 597); "de-libidinized and sublimated energies," or "attention cathexes" (Chap. 16, note 14, Chap. 19, notes 41 and 62, Chap. 23, IV, below).

Recent psychoanalytic theory is inclined to assume the existence of relatively autonomous ego-energies.

119.* Lindworsky (476, p. 242).

120. In the omitted section Lewin discusses the dangers inherent in the historical load of the concept "value."

valuations and valences can be related; at times, however, they are independent.
b) Not values, *but definite, real psychic tensions, psychic systems, are the energy-sources of processes.* These energy systems are the *dynamic* facts which determine the course of processes.[121]

[Passage omitted.] [122]

The experimental subject's "acceptance of an instruction" implies dynamically an intention which is hardly distinguishable phenomenally from mere understanding. Often the mere "thought," that "this could be done in such a way" or "it would be nice if this would happen," fulfills the function of an intention.[123]

Dostoevski [124]* describes an extreme case of this kind in which, though there is no act of intending and a decision is impossible, suddenly the *dynamically real* psychic factors lie exactly as they would subsequent to a decision: "He felt it distinctly and suddenly, he knew it with full clarity, that he would flee, yes, that he really would flee, but he knew also that he was now completely unable to answer the question whether he should flee *before* or *after* [murdering] Shatoff. And he felt that he would surely not flee '*before* Shatoff,' but rather absolutely only '*after* Shatoff,' and that it was so decided, signed and sealed." . . .

121. This is a bare beginning of the clarification of the value-valence relationship, which is of great importance for all branches of psychology. There can be little doubt that, under certain conditions, values do seem to play the motivating role in psychic processes. There are at least three alternative hypotheses by which this observation can be accounted for. (a) Values are expressions of psychic energy-systems; while these systems usually provide only value-signs to objects and events, they will sometimes motivate actions, as needs and quasi-needs do. (b) Values are stationary (ossified) forms of valences, segregated from those tension-systems which originally gave rise to them; but at times they again communicate with these, and then take on a valence quality. (c) Values correspond to quasi-stationary (high potential, low intensity) tension-systems; these, arising originally from fundamental needs, take on the role of controlling structures which regulate the dynamics of those needs.

The last hypothesis is consonant with the psychoanalytic conception of over-determination, and has been gaining increased support by observations made in the recent development of psychoanalytic ego-psychology.

122. The omitted section restates the dependence of quasi-need effects on genuine-needs, and their relative independence from the intensity of the act of intending.

123. Here—by implication—Lewin carries the psychology of intentions into the field of the psychology of thinking.

124.* Dostoevski (149).

In other cases, which are—at least phenotypically—very similar, no such effect occurs. It seems to make a great deal of difference whether a need remains at the stage of mere *wish* or crystallizes into a definite quasi-need. The crucial difference seems to be that crystallization of a quasi-need creates, in principle, an avenue to the motor-region which did not exist before. But not even here is the clear experience of "I really want it" crucial, but rather whether or not a real avenue to the motor-region is created.[125]

3) *The Dynamic Independence (Segregation) of Quasi-Needs.* The degree to which other needs influence a quasi-need in the course of the consummatory action varies greatly.

A subject is instructed to touch two copper cords with two fingers of one hand and to press with the other a lever which closes the circuit. The subject suffers a strong electric shock. There are subjects who, having once decided to do this task, give one a particularly "factual" impression. The course of action becomes very direct (some observers say it becomes "soldierly"). The subjects' introspections corroborate these observations. For example, one subject's experience was that she acted "as in a dream," and had strikingly little more to report.

Other subjects' behavior follows a much less direct course. The internal vacillation and contradictory tensions preceding the decision continue even *after* the decision to accept the instructions. Here the decision does not set a sharp dividing line after the preceding processes, as in the subjects of the "factual" type. Paradoxically, however, it is not the subjects of the "factual" type who have little anxiety about the electrical shock; their fear of pain is considerably greater than that of the more "subjective" type.[126]

The difference illustrated by this example always plays an important role in the consummation of intentions, and is related to general and fundamental problems of psychic structure which can be merely touched upon here. The psyche of an individual is not a homogeneous unity in which every structure and event

125. Though in psychoanalytic theory one of the crucial functions of the systems Preconscious and Conscious is the control of the sluices of motility (cf. Chap. 23, note 3, below), the specific mechanics of this process have never been worked out. Lewin's formulation seems to afford an avenue for ex-perimental exploration of these mechanics. Cf. pp. 151 ff., below. Cartwright *et al.* (124, 125) made some initial steps in this direction.

126. This observation may be related to what Fenichel (174) calls "counterphobic attitude."

is equally related to every other; nor does the mutual influence of these psychic structures and processes depend solely on their intensity, power, or significance. There are psychic regions and complexes which are most closely related to each other, while they are segregated in various degrees from other psychic complexes. The extent to which a psychic event or force influences other psychic structures depends on whether they are embedded in the same or in different complexes.[127]

The independence and segregation of a complex varies from case to case. An example from the motor sphere: a beginner in moving-picture photography stops involuntarily on any sudden and unexpected happening in the field of the picture, and is influenced even by events outside of it, such as every movement of his own head and other hand, all of which prevent his turning the handle of his machine evenly. The experienced operator is undisturbed by all these influences. He has segregated the movement of his arm, the procedure of turning the handle, from his other hand movements and impressions, and has developed it into *a relatively independent action organism*. . . .[128]

Such cases are usually described as "mechanical" action. In the present context, however, it is not the *reflex character* or *stereotypy* of the action which is essential. Even in activities of irregular course, for instance, in catching irregularly thrown balls, or in turning a handle the friction of which is changing, a correction may "quite mechanically" take place by changes in the catching movement or in muscle tension. The mechanism often works like a real organism in which "perceptual basis" and "motor sphere" are tuned together. (Naturally, as with any other organism under given conditions a mechanism too may change from a natural flexibility to rigid automatism.)

The crucial fact here is that an *independent "action-organism"* came about, not that it is mechanical. With a beginner, the turning of the handle is a sub-

127. The internal logic of this example and of Lewin's discussion point to the need for the exploration of individual differences in embeddedness; such studies might prove to be important methods for the investigation of personality-organization. Experimentation with the various forms of stress tests (see, for example, Freeman and Rodnick, 196), which could have given us considerable pertinent information, has missed this opportunity.

128. Lewin's discussion of "automatization," in connection with "fixation" is pertinent to this point. Cf. p. 129 and the corresponding footnotes. See also Hartmann's discussion of apparatuses, automatisms and habits, Chap. 19, VIII, below.

ordinate part of the motor-region as a whole (which is tuned to the perception-basis as a whole); with the experienced moving-picture photographer, the turning of the handle is an independent partial motor-region, which is segregated from the rest of the motor-region and tuned together with a previously subordinate part of the perception-basis into an independent action-organism. The kind and intensity of Gestalt-ties, of system-relations, undergoes a dynamic change: old bonds are dissolved and a new, relatively closed structure is formed.

The previous example of the decision-effect implies an analogous process. In the subject to whom the task was especially painful, and whose consummatory activity was nevertheless particularly factual and direct, the tensions of the quasi-need arising from the act of decision are far more strongly *segregated from the rest of the ego* than in the other subjects. The boundary created between this quasi-need and the other psychic complexes has a double effect. It renders the consummatory action more independent from the other psychic tensions (therefore its directness), and it also affords the individual greater protection against the painfulness of the process (therefore, its dream-character). Thus it becomes understandable that the objectification and isolation of this specific psychic complex occurred precisely in those subjects who were particularly afraid of the pain.

In war, in the course of battle, there often is opportunity to make such observations on the so-called "plucky" soldier.

The degree of independence of the quasi-need from other need tensions thus shows great situational and individual variability.[129]

(E) REMEMBERING FINISHED AND UNFINISHED ACTIVITIES. The effects of tension-states may be observed not only in the intentional actions to which they give rise, but also indirectly in facts of memory-psychology. We may ask, for instance, which is remembered better—an intentional action that is completed, or one that is not completed. At first one would assume that the completed ones will be remembered better, because the subject was longer at them.

The experiment [130]* shows something quite different. The subject is given twenty tasks to do in an experimental hour. The experimenter interrupts part

129. Cf. note 116, above.

130.* These experiments were carried out by Mrs. Zeigarnik at the Berlin Psychological Institute.

[See Zeigarnik, 783; cf. also the reviews of the experimental literature which followed Zeigarnik, in Rapaport, 591, and Alper, 27.]

of these before their completion. Shortly after the subject has done the last of the tasks, he is tested to see which of them he remembers.

The results show that *the interrupted tasks are remembered, on an average, 50 percent better than the completed ones.* There are characteristic differences for various kinds of activities (end-activity versus continuous activity, interesting activity versus indifferent activity), and for various types of subjects. In the present context we must remain quite general, and state only that the *tension-state* which persists after the interruption of the intentional action expresses itself not only in a tendency to resume the action, but also in memory.[131]

These tensions do not always, or for all subjects, cause a better remembering; they may also result in *repression phenomena.*[132] However, particularly in subjects of a certain childish type, these tensions favor remembering.

2. The Conditions of Intention-Formation; Intentional Action, "Will Action" (Controlled Action), and "Drive-" (Field-) Action

If we make a gross estimate of the frequency of intentions in everyday life, considering at first only those intentions which are attended by an experience of a specific act of intending, we find to our surprise that *acts of intending are not very frequent.* True, the day often begins with an act of intending. Usually about 50 percent of students state that their rising that morning was preceded by the specific intention to get up. But throughout the rest of the day, while dressing, breakfasting, going to work, acts of intending are rare.

This scarcity of intending is not explained alone by the assumption that habits or generalized intentions determine the daily routine. Children at play in new situations do not give the impression of frequent acts of intending, not

131. Here Lewin clearly asserts that the findings of his "affect and action psychology" have direct application to the psychology of thought-processes.

132. Zeigarnik (783) and later others, particularly Rosenzweig (620), demonstrated forgetting as a result of undischarged tension-systems. They referred to this phenomenon as "repression." Since the concept repression has been specifically defined (cf. Freud, 233; see also Rapaport, 591, pp. 166–68), their use of the term for this phenomenon was not quite justified. But repression proper is a highly variable process, which does extend to all ideas that come into close relation with any derivative of a prohibited impulse; therefore, it is quite possible that the Zeigarnik-Rosenzweig phenomenon will prove a special form of repression once its nature is clarified. So far this has not been accomplished.

even when they play roughly or fight. Not even the changes which occur when something new attracts them, or when they want something the other child has, are mediated by acts of intending; instead we observe immediate responses, usually described as "drive-like" or "involuntary." *In cases where genuine-needs are directly in play, it is typical that no acts of intending preceded the action.*[133] (Under such conditions, in terms of the theory of quasi-needs, an act of intending would make no sense.)

But not all actions which are not preceded by an act of intending are drive-like. In a conversation, for instance, the answers and the exchanges in general are rarely preceded by specific acts of intending, which occur mainly when one is about to lie or to conceal something. Yet we must realize that such talk—questions and answers without preceding acts of intending—is not all drive-like, but mostly of a volitional character. There are many other everyday actions, for instance occupational, which, though not preceded by specific acts of intending, are neither automatized nor uncontrolled and drive-like. These and other facts, a discussion of which would lead us too far afield, contradict the view that intentional action is the prototype of will action. To establish the action-type to which a psychological event belongs, we will have to regard the character of its course, rather than whether it has been preceded by another act.[134]

133. Clinical thinking would be inclined to distinguish Lewin's "drive-like" and "involuntary" behavior from what it usually considers impulsive and drive-like. It seems that at present we do not have the information to decide whether the clinician's inclination is correct. The situation is further complicated by the fact that clinically much involuntary behavior is considered compulsive rather than impulsive, though the difference between the two is not always defined clearly. To consider impulsive acts as drive-determined, and compulsive ones as determined by a specific form of defense, would not do justice to the complexity of the actual state of affairs. The concept of repetition-compulsion (Freud, 241, Kubie, 437, and Fenichel, 176, pp. 541 ff.) further complicates this issue. It would be perhaps best to conclude that "involuntariness" is a phenotypic characteristic of behavior, which may originate from a great variety of genotypes.

The question also arises whether some of these involuntary, immediate responses are not like those intentions which appear in consciousness only as thoughts: "could be done," "would be nice," "I really want it." For Lewin's discussion of these, see pp. 140–141, above.

134. Lewin here sets out to demonstrate the ambiguities of "will" and "drive" activities. He presently finds it necessary to discard both concepts in order to avoid a contradiction in terms.

Accordingly, the following cases are typically not "drive-actions" but "will-actions": when one does not shun menacing danger or pain, but faces or even goes forth to meet it; when one takes an insult calmly; when one is cool and unfriendly toward a friendly person. This type of action, on which our attention now centers, is *controlled action*.[135]*

If we disregard the *automatized* and—in the strict sense of the term—*reflex-like* actions, the use of the term "drive" proves equivocal. By *drive-action* we mean first of all an "involuntary action, directed by forces *not under the control* of the individual." [136]

Such action is not always an instant effect of a stimulus-constellation and may be preceded by delay, yet sudden response to a stimulus-constellation is indeed often the sign of an uncontrolled reaction. Thus the second meaning of the concepts "drive-like, involuntary, impulsive" is, that the action they qualify is the *opposite* of those *preceded by a specific act of intending*.

It must be stressed that genuine intentional action, preceded by a specific act of intending, is not always of that controlled character which would be

---

135.* Cf. A. Klages (383).
[Other than citing these examples, and stating that they are the prototypes of will-activities, Lewin does not analyze the nature of these "controlled activities." His attention is centered on "un-controlled" or "field activities." F. Heider has called attention, in personal discussion, to this stress on tension-systems and field activities; he doubts that psychological processes are explainable in terms of tension-concepts alone, without invoking structural concepts. It is possible that Lewin did not analyze the nature of controlled activity because of a hesitance to invoke structural concepts. It should be noted, however, that his discussion of general goals of will, daily routine, and automatized apparatuses do suggest that at this time he was working toward structural concepts. Of similar portent may be the question concerning the existence of a "reservoir of active energy" other than need-tensions (p. 139, above). Without having restud-

ied the later phases of Lewin's work with this point solely in mind, I am under the impression that his interest in structure rather decreased, while that in tensions and forces increased, as he went along.

It is worth noting that the development of psychoanalysis took a diametrically opposite course. Note the introduction of the concepts ego, id, and superego in the early twenties (Freud, 243); the restatement of the issue of defenses in the late twenties (Freud, 252); the further development of the psychology of the defenses and the ego in the early thirties (A. Freud, 201); and the more recent studies of the structure of the ego (Nunberg, 543; Hartmann, 305; Kris, Hartmann, and Loewenstein, 309, 310, 311; Hartmann, 303; Kris, 429; Rapaport, 596).]

136. Lewin here apparently means "not under conscious control." Cf. Knight (390) and Waelder (746) on "will" and "freedom."

the opposite of drive-action in the first sense. Naturally an intentional action may take the form of controlled action. When a child decides to go past a dog of which he is afraid, the walking past is occasionally a controlled action; then the child passes the dog with a controlled and calm, though cautious, bearing. *The intentional action is, however, often not a controlled action,* or may show only little control. For instance, in the example given, the intention is often carried out in the form of entirely uncontrolled running past the dog.

In this case, the course of events is as though the intention were a force simply added to the others of the situation (the psychological field), and as though the action ensued in accordance with the force-distribution so created in an altogether drive-like, uncontrolled fashion.

Such uncontrolled or little controlled consummatory action is frequent in intentional actions, and is—in some respects—more characteristic of them than is controlled consummation. The common, simple reaction experiment—certainly a genuine intentional action, based solely on the preceding intention of the subject—is usually, to judge by the consummation and the events following the signal, the pure type of an uncontrolled activity. (Only failures tend to change it into controlled action.) We find it particularly in successful intentions that the action following the appearance of the occasion (dropping the letter into the mailbox) is involuntary, that is, closer to uncontrolled than to controlled actions. Like the term "drive action," its opposite term "voluntary action" has two meanings. It may refer to intentional as well as to controlled action. Thus it will be desirable, for the sake of conceptual clarity, to avoid using the terms "will" and "drive" wherever there is the slightest chance for misunderstanding. Instead of these terms one might use: (a) *controlled action,* and its counterpart "uncontrolled" or "field action," as I prefer to call it (action directly determined by the field forces) [137*]; (b) *intentional action,* which

137.* Naturally, controlled activity, too, is subject to the forces of the total field. However, it is characteristic of controlled activity that the whole person does not enter the field; he maintains a certain degree of reserve and perspective, and therefore has the activity in hand. In other words, the demarcation of the psychic systems differs here from that in uncontrolled activity: the "ego systems" have either a greater independence, or their dominance is firmer.

[Cf. note 135, above. Here Lewin explains field- vs. controlled-activity by embeddedness vs. segregation. Though these considerations seem to have structural implications, they may lead either to concepts of quasi-enduring structures, or merely to concepts of *momentary* embeddedness and segregation in a given situation. In topological psychology they usually have led to the latter. Studies

does not imply any definite type of consummatory action, but only a preceding act of intending, that is, its origin in a quasi-need.[138]

We can be certain of the following. The character of the consummatory action is not determined by the fact that it originated in an intention. The consummation *may* take the form of controlled action, but it is the relatively uncontrolled forms which are characteristic and theoretically essential, since in many respects the intention-effects become particularly clear in these. Objects and events, to which otherwise the person would have remained indifferent, attain a valence due to the intention, and directly initiate uncontrolled pure field-actions. (The theory of determining tendencies, also, emphasizes particularly these cases.)

Now it is clear the essential achievement of the intention is one of preparation.[139]* Due to the act of intending, at some subsequent time a psychological field appears which otherwise would not have existed, or at least not in the same form. *Forming an intention creates conditions which allow us later simply to abandon ourselves to the effects of the field* (letter and mailbox), or permit a [psychological] field to be so transformed, or so supplied with additional forces, that a controlled action becomes feasible or easier.[140]

---

centering on individual differences of inclination to controlled or uncontrolled activity are likely to lead to structural concepts; those centering on inter-individually consistent characteristics of locomotion, in a given psychological field, are not.]

138. To summarize Lewin's argument: By *drive-action*, we usually mean either uncontrolled or non-intentional action; by *will-action*, either controlled or intentional action. Contrary to usual assumption, these are not exclusive but overlapping categories, since intentional-actions too are often uncontrolled. Lewin proposes to avoid the concepts "will" and "drive," and to use the pairs "controlled–uncontrolled" and "intentional–non-intentional." The merit of this proposal, as I see it, is that while "will" speciously appears to be the oppo-

site of "drive," the other pairs are not opposites.

139.* This is also G. E. Mueller's (526) view of intentions, though his theory is fundamentally different from that presented here.

140. We have already stated (note 49, above) that psychoanalytic theory considers secondary-process thinking (and action directed by it) a detour on the path toward gratification. The conception of this path and detour implies an anticipation of the goal, and of the sub-goals governing the detour. The goal—in Lewinian terms—would have a natural, the sub-goals a derivative, valence. This distinction of valences does not explain, however, the difference between "controlled" and "field-directed" forms of consummation. It seems that, while the latter are fully apprehended by the

Now we can state the conditions under which intentions arise. The intention is not characteristic of will-action in its sense of controlled action. An intention, in the narrower sense, arises only where there is a certain *foresight* (which need not imply a precise picture of the future), and the situation as foreseen does not include those valences which by themselves would bring about the desired actions in the form of pure field-actions. An intention also arises when the foreseen situation by itself would lead to field-actions contrary to the desired action.[141]

A typical example, from experiments Miss Dembo undertook for another purpose, follows. The subject was forbidden to leave a certain place, yet would like to; she does not dare to, that is, cannot carry out her leaving in the form of a controlled action. Her way out is to form the intention: "I will go as soon as the clock gets into this or that position." (Similar occurrences are frequent in everyday life.) Thus she creates valences for the future, which will then directly press her to leave, and bring about or facilitate the intended action. (It is an interesting question why, when it is impossible to leave immediately, it is possible to form such an intention. We cannot enter this problem here.)

The following cases are also related to the fact that intentions aim at influencing future situations. It does happen that, in fear of certain anticipated events and situations, we "armor ourselves with firm intentions." If the actual situation proves harmless, we then get the feeling of having hammered at an open door. The relation between intention and foresight becomes particularly clear in such cases, where the *knowledge* of the future was erroneous, and the actual situation does not have the counterforces expected. . . .

---

concept of derivative-valences, the "controlled" activities may necessitate introducing a new distinction of valences. It is possible that the attempt to account for these prompted Lewin to raise the question of a "reservoir of active energies" independent of need-tensions. See p. 139, above; cf. also note 135, above. Clearly, from the point of view of psychoanalytic theory, we are dealing with the issue of the dynamic independence of the ego, ego-energies, and "will." Cf. note 136.

141. The relationship between the motivational dynamics of anticipation as we encounter it in thought-processes (see Rapaport *et al.*, 602, I, 215–20, 254–59; II, 22–24), and the genesis of intentions as described by Lewin, is as yet entirely unclear. It is possible that clarification of this relationship will contribute to understanding "field-directed" and "controlled" activities. Concerning anticipations, cf. also Chap. 27, notes 26 and 58, below.

Concomitant to the intention is usually another process, which is called *decision*. The main functional effect of this process is that it opens or facilitates for the internal tension an access to activity, to motility, either momentarily or in principle (that is, for a future situation). Thus, decision does not create new psychic tensions (if they accompany it, they are not its essence); rather, it creates for an already existing tension a new *access*, in a form previously not extant, *to the* motor-region.[142] The pure phenomenological expression of this dynamic fact of decision is the experience, "I really want it," [143*], "fiat!" [144*] meaning "this is how I will do it." When in a person there are several simultaneous tension-systems of opposing directions, a decision often amounts to the effecting of some kind of equilibrium among them, or to isolating some of them.[145*] At any rate, the internal situation created is one in which a more or less unitary tension-system controls the action. Occasionally in such cases, an internal vacillation is observed before the decision (the so-called struggle of motives).

In this connection it is customary to speak of choice, the implication of which is that in the interest of clear-cut action it is often necessary to suppress some of the tension-systems competing for the access to the motor region. This is not always completely successful, however; then, in spite of the choice, the tensions originating from the suppressed systems will make themselves mildly noticeable in the action. Thus unpurposeful mixed actions may come about, resulting in an inhibition or weakening of the activity.

Decisions as here functionally defined, like intentions, have no unequivocal indicators in [subjective] experience. The firmness of a decision and the intensity of the act of decision are not directly related, and even functionally essential decisions may occur without clear-cut decision-experiences.

Intentions in the functional sense (formation of quasi-needs), and decisions in the functional sense (the suppression or equilibration of simultaneous internal tensions in their claims for control of action), appear at times as closely related, and only conceptually separable, functional components of a [psychic] process; at other times they appear separately in relatively pure forms. The internal decision, the choice of a certain direction, may result in a specific intention for a certain form of consummation. But the intention, the arising quasi-

142. Cf. note 125, above.
143.* Ach (15), Michotte and Pruem (519).
144.* W. James (354).
145.* Cf. Koffka (407) and Claparède (130).

need, usually implies in principle an access of its own to the motor-region, and unless there are internal counter-tensions, requires no specific act of decision for this purpose.

[Passage omitted.] [146]

III. SUMMARY

Intentional action is not the prototype of will-action. It occurs in all forms of transition from controlled action to uncontrolled, drive-like, field-action. . . . All in all, intentional actions belong more to the field-actions than to the controlled actions.

Accordingly, the majority of controlled (will) actions are not preceded by an act of intending. Intentional actions are relatively rare. They are prepared actions, where the act of intending, which is as a rule controlled, prepares an *uncontrolled field-action*.

The effects of intentions are twofold. One of these effects is the *creation* or transformation of certain *future psychic fields;* the other, the creation of immediate or future access to the motor-region for certain psychic tensions. These effects appear frequently together, but at times also separately.

The first of these effects, as a functional factor, may be designated as "intention" in the strict sense, the second as "decision" in the strict sense.

The *decision* equalizes tensions of differing directions which already exist in the total person, or at least changes the internal situation so that the action will be controlled by relatively homogeneous tensions.

Another effect of the intention is that occasions which would have remained neutral without the act of intending acquire valence and issue in certain consummatory actions. In individual cases, the *occasions* as well as the *consummatory actions* may be unequivocally established and limited by the act of intending. But these cases are not the prototype of intention; and even in them, the forces underlying the intentional action cannot be considered associative

146. The omitted part applies to quasi-needs the considerations pertaining to conditional-genetic concepts (Chap. 4, sec. 3b, above). Its salient statement is:

In contrast to the usual procedure, we want to stress that similar concepts will have to be applied to drives and other genuine-needs, also. The pressure of needs always leaves open a certain region of concrete consummatory activities and possible occasions (excepting the cases of pronounced fixation), and *only need and situation* (where the latter is not considered as momentary in time) *together determine unequivocally the phenotypical aspect of the concrete process.*

couplings, established by the act of intending, between the idea of the occasion and the idea of consummation.

The act of intending often leaves the consummatory action, as well as the occasions to which it is to respond, indeterminate. In these cases, and as a rule even where the act of intending implies a definite occasion, the intention may respond to various occasions not foreseen, which have certain objective relations to the intention, or rather to the need underlying it. The same holds for consummatory actions.

Dynamically the intention is defined as the formation of a quasi-need, of a tension-state, which is very similar to and has real relationships with genuine-needs.

(a) To each quasi-need (just as to each genuine-need) there corresponds a certain region of objects and events which have a valence that entices to actions (satisfying actions of the need, which satiate the quasi-need, that is, discharge the tension).

The consummatory actions of a quasi-need vary with the concrete consummatory situation. The quasi-need may press to a single or to repetitive action.

(b) The extent of the region of structures which have a valence depends, among other things, on the strength of the quasi-need. Where this region is unnaturally narrow, the situation is similar to that where genuine-needs are fixated on certain occasions and satisfactions. Fixation may come about by the act of intending or by the (first) consummation, but is not always reinforced by repetition.

(c) The *need-tension* is the primary fact: if sufficiently intensive, and the occasion is delayed, it leads to premature beginning of the consummatory action; when the occasion fails to appear, to actively seeking it out; and when the action is interrupted, to resume it or better retain it in memory.

(d) When the quasi-need is satiated, the valences in general disappear, even in cases of fixation. The valences of the occasion implied by the act of intending usually disappear, even if the consummation occurs in a form or on an occasion not foreseen in the act.

(e) Genuine consummation may be replaced by various forms of substitute consummation. To some extent these have the same effects as consummation proper, and thus may lead to forgetting an intention and failure to resume an interrupted activity.

(f) The quasi-need, created by the act of intending, is not an isolated structure in the whole psyche, but is usually embedded in a *certain* psychic complex or region of the personality. It is in communication with other quasi-needs and genuine-needs derived from certain general goals of will, or drives. The intensity of the intention-effect depends on the intensity and centrality of these needs. The needs to which the quasi-need has real relationships are not necessarily those which have led to the act of intending. The effect of a quasi-need may be inhibited by contrary genuine-needs.

(g) The phenomenal intensity of the act of intending and its other phenomenal characteristics have no decisive significance [for the occurrence and manner of consummation].

CHAPTER 6

PRINCIPAL FACTORS DETERMINING INTELLECTUAL EVOLUTION FROM CHILDHOOD TO ADULT LIFE [1]

By Jean Piaget

I. INTRODUCTION

THE SUBJECT of our investigations is intellectual evolution—that is, the development of knowledge and of its different modes, the genesis of the forms of thought, of their adaptation to experience, and the rules which they obey.[2]

In its point of departure this evolution raises a problem which is essentially biological; the relationship between understanding [3] or perception and its objects is a particular case of adaptation—that is, a combination of assimilation

1. Piaget (564). This English text is that of the Harvard Tercentenary Volume.

2. The investigations to which Piaget refers are his own on language and thought (561), judgment and reasoning (560), conception of the world (559), conception of causality (558), moral judgment (562), and particularly those in his untranslated *La Naissance de l'intelligence* (553).

Piaget's investigations of intelligence —unlike the normative and factorial studies which surrounded the growth of intelligence-testing—are explorations into the nature and development of thought-organization. Indeed, Piaget's genetic method of investigation was for a long time the sole tool for the exploration of intellectual functions as thought-organizations. The clinical psychoanalytic method, though it yielded fundamental theoretical knowledge and observa-

tions concerning the intellectual functions and the thought-organization underlying them (Freud, 209, 223, 234, 248), is not the method of choice for a systematic investigation of this area. The recent method of scatter (pattern) analysis of intelligence tests (Rapaport, Schafer, Gill, 602; Schafer, 636, 632; Rapaport, 597, 592, 593; Mayman, 509) appears to promise a new avenue; this method approaches the thought-process from the individual differences in the level of development of the different thought-functions underlying the various achievements on intelligence tests. By contrast Piaget's method centers on the stages of development which the various aspects of the thought-process pass through, and the forms they assume in each.

3. "Understanding" is used throughout in the sense of "knowledge."

and accommodation—which unites the organism with its external environment.[4] The first question which the theory of the development of . . . understanding must investigate is how this relationship results from biological organization and adaptation. For example, it is impossible to determine how the elementary forms of spatial perception are evolved without seeing how they are related to the mode of inheritance of the organs of perception and of equilibrium, and to the different modes of organic adaptation.[5]

But in the last analysis the evolution of individual thought is closely enmeshed in collective systems of knowledge, especially in those great systems of rational collaboration which deductive and experimental science has produced.[6] The genetic theory of knowledge must therefore reach out into an historico-critical analysis of scientific thought, and also into genetic logic.[7-8] For instance,

4. See Piaget (556), particularly Chap. 7, below. Cf. also Hartmann, Chap. 19, below.

5. Cf. Piaget Chap. 7, pp. 180 ff., below. Piaget—like Hartmann (Chap. 19, p. 384, below)—assumes that the organism is born with certain hereditary adaptations to the environment. He maintains that intelligence is an adaptation, and that to understand it fully we must explore the inherited organic adaptation upon which it is built. This problem involves facts and theories of genetics and evolution. It seems that Piaget's (556) considerations touching on genetics are dated by advances in that field; see Simpson (695, 696).

6. Piaget's writings leave little doubt that, when he says "individual thought is closely enmeshed in collective systems of knowledge," he does not mean only that sciences are such systems and serve as the frame of reference for "socialization" of individual thought. He means also that in the sciences the implications of the individual thought are realized; it is the potentialities of the latter which are the achievements of the former. Hence Piaget assumes a close relationship between the genetic history of knowledge and thought in the child, and the history (particularly pre-history) of science. Cf. p. 170, below.

7-8. Piaget, the philosopher-epistemologist and student of science, was struck by the similarity of the child's conception of physical phenomena to that of pre-Socratic, peripatetic, and Aristotelian physics. See Piaget (558, pp. 20 ff.); cf. also Zeller (784), Windelband (773), Gomperz (285), and Bakewell (34). Indeed, the struggle of the Milesians, Eleatics, Heraclitus, the Sophists, and Socrates-Plato to distinguish "appearance" and "truth" is in essence similar both to the development of reasoning, of the world picture, of causality, etc., in the child described by Piaget and to the development of "reality testing" described by psychoanalysis. The thought-products of these philosophies are often astoundingly similar to those of our children. In their "autistic" fashion, without conclusive—often without any—empirical foundation, their thinking anticipates ideas which subsequently became cornerstones of science: the spherical shape of the earth,

to understand the evolution of the idea of space in the mind of a child, it is not enough to know how this idea is first born. One must also determine how the so-called "displacement groups" which form it follow one another in succession from the motor level to that of the most abstract conceptions; [9] one must establish the respective parts of the scheme of logic and of the intuition [10] in this formation; one must define exactly the relationship between the ideas of space and those of time, object, number, movement, speed, etc. In short, truly to understand the psychological aspect of the development of space, one must attack all the problems which this idea and related ideas suggest in the realm of mathematics and physics; but not from a point of view which is purely reflective and abstract, rather from one which is genetic and experimental. A comparative analysis must intervene between the psychological development of thought and the history of science.[11]

The psychology of intellectual evolution leans therefore upon the biological

---

the evolution theory, the atom theory, etc. Hence, Piaget considered his investigations to be not only *genetic psychology*, but also *empirical*, that is, experimental, *epistemology*. Cf. p. 170, below. Compare also Silberer on the relation of symbolic thinking to pre-scientific forms of thought, Chap. 9, pp. 226, 230, below. See Piaget (560, 558, 556). See also Heinz Werner's (755) admirable analysis of developmental and regressive forms of logic, particularly of space (pp. 167 ff.), time (pp. 182 ff.), and concepts (pp. 213 ff.).

9. The concept of "displacement groups" is discussed by Piaget in greater detail on pp. 164 ff., below; see also note 36, below. His intention is to describe invariants of the space concept, which are inherent to it throughout its development. The concept itself derives from the algebra of "groups"; cf. Felix Klein (385, p. 132). The "displacement groups" mentioned refer apparently to the "group" of displacements in the Euclidian space. The invariants present

throughout development are properties of this "group." Both are givens of physical reality. Corresponding to them there develop, in the infant, organizations of sensory-motor relations to objects; these organizations re-represent psychologically the invariants. Once this development has taken place it permits the identification of objects under changing conditions. In other words, the psychological representation of "displacement groups" is made up of "operations" of sensory-motor intelligence which predicate the invariants by which the infant organism maintains the identity and continuity of objects even when their form of appearance varies. According to Piaget these "displacement groups" (particularly their invariants) are the fundament of the space concept, and that they carry over into all developmental levels of intelligence subsequent to sensory-motor intelligence.

10. See pp. 168–69, and note 38, below.

11. Cf. note 6, above.

theories of adaptation, the psychological theories of understanding,[12] the sociological theories of signs and norms (the rules of socialized thought),[13] the history of science,[14] and upon comparative logic.[15] One can then consider this special branch of psychology as a genetic theory of knowledge, a broad theory which must borrow its elements from a very great number of fields of research, thus partially synthesizing them, but withal an exact and well-defined theory, which has its own method, namely, the envisaging of intellectual realities only from the point of view of their development and genetic construction.

In fact, the best method for the psychological theory of the development of . . . understanding will always be the analysis of the intellectual evolution of the child. The thought of the child alone constitutes a continuous process which by a normal evolution links the initial sensory-motor adaptations to the socialized and scientific forms of understanding. In so far as the development of individual thought from birth to adult life can be observed directly and by experiment, and in so far as it is also open to the influences which various adult social groups have on the formation of the reason, this development forms an ideal field on which to set up all the biological, psychological, sociological, and logical problems of understanding in order to examine their genetic construction. A genetic and experimental epistemology is thus conceivable as a special branch of psychology.

We should like in what follows to give an example of this method and its results in studying—on the three planes of sensory-motor activity, egocentric thought, and rational thought [16]—the genesis of some of those ideas of con-

12. Cf. note 3, above.

13. See G. Mead (510).

14. Mach in his *Mechanics* (496) made an attempt to look upon the history of mechanics as a process of growth of understanding.

15. See Werner (755).

16. For Piaget, these are the three major steps in the development of intelligence. In his "La Naissance" (556, also Chap. 7, below), he considers sensory-motor intelligence the cradle of intelligence development. Egocentric thought is a transitory form between autistic and rational thought. He describes the relation to each other of autistic, egocentric and rational (directed) thought as follows (561, pp. 43–47):

Directed thought, as it develops, is controlled more and more by the laws of experience and of logic in the stricter sense. Autistic thought, on the other hand, obeys a whole system of special laws (laws of symbolism and of immediate satisfaction) which we need not elaborate here. Let us consider, for instance, the completely different lines of thought pursued from the

servation (continuity) which play such a great role in scientific thought.[17] As we trace this growth we shall also have the opportunity of following, on these three successive levels, the steps of one of the most important processes

---

point of view of intelligence and from that of autism when we think of such an object as, say, water.

To intelligence, water is a natural substance whose origin we know, or whose formation we can at least empirically observe; its behavior and motions are subject to certain laws which can be studied, and it has from the dawn of history been the object of technical experiment (for purposes of irrigation, etc.). To the autistic attitude, on the other hand, water is interesting only in connection with the satisfaction of organic wants. It can be drunk. But as such, as well as simply in virtue of its external appearance, it has come to represent in folk and child fantasies, and in those of adult subconsciousness, themes of a purely organic character. It has in fact been identified with the liquid substances which issue from the human body, and has come, in this way, to symbolize birth itself, as is proved by so many myths (birth of Aphrodite, etc.), rites (baptism the symbol of a new birth), dreams, and stories told by children. Thus in the one case thought adapts itself to water as part of the external world, in the other, thought uses the idea of water not in order to adapt itself to it, but in order to assimilate it to those more or less conscious images connected with fecundation and the idea of birth.

Now these two forms of thought, whose characteristics diverge so profoundly, differ chiefly as to their origin, the one being socialized and guided by the increasing adaptation of individuals one to another, whereas the other remains individual and uncommunicated. . . . Intelligence, just because it undergoes a gradual process of socialization, is enabled through the bond established by language between thoughts and words to make an increasing use of concepts; whereas autism, just because it

17. Presumably, this refers to the parallel between (a) the child's discovery, in the course of his development, of enduring objects (conservation of objects) in the confusing manifold of his sensory impressions, and (b) the discovery by science of the conservation of matter, energy, angular momentum, etc., as reliable orienting points in the midst of the continuously changing physical world. Cf. note 9, above.

---

remains individual, is still tied to imagery, to organic activity, and even to organic movements. The mere fact, then, of telling one's thought, of telling it to others, or of keeping silence and telling it only to oneself must be of enormous importance to the fundamental structure and functioning of thought in general, and of child logic in particular. Now between autism and intelligence there are many degrees, varying with their capacity for being communicated. These intermediate varieties must therefore be subject to a special logic, intermediate too between the logic of autism and that of intelligence. The chief of those intermediate forms, that is, the type of thought which like that exhibited by our children seeks to adapt itself to reality, but does not communicate itself as such, we propose to call *Ego-centric thought*. This gives us the following table:

	Non-communicable thought	Communicable thought
Undirected thought	*Autistic thought*	(*Mythological thought*)
Directed thought	*Ego-centric thought*	*Communicated intelligence*

in the development of thought, namely, the passage from egocentric perception and thought to objective reasoning.

For the following hypotheses may be made in this matter. At the beginning of mental life, the world appears to the child as a series of pictures which are

---

We shall quickly realize the full importance of Ego-centrism if we consider a certain familiar experience of daily life. We are looking, say, for the solution of some problem, when suddenly everything seems quite clear; we have understood, and we experience that *sui generis* feeling of intellectual satisfaction. But as soon as we try to explain to others what it is we have understood, difficulties come thick and fast. These difficulties do not arise merely because of the effort of attention needed to hold in a single grasp the links in the chain of argument; they are attributable also to our judging faculty itself. Conclusions which we deemed positive no longer seem so; between certain propositions whole series of intermediate links are now seen to be lacking in order to fill the gaps of which we were previously not even conscious; arguments which seemed convincing because they were connected with some schema of visual imagery or based on some sort of analogy, lose all their potency from the moment we feel the need to appeal to these schemas, and find that they are incommunicable; doubt is cast on propositions connected with judgments of value, as soon as we realize the personal nature of such judgments. If such, then, is the difference between personal understanding and spoken explanation, how much more marked will be the characteristics of personal understanding when the individual has for a long time been bottling up his own thoughts, when he has not even formed the habit of thinking in terms of other people, and of communicating his thoughts to them. We need only recall the inextricable chaos of adolescent thought to realize the truth of this distinction.

Ego-centric thought and intelligence therefore represent two different forms of reasoning, and we may even say, without paradox, two different logics. By logic is meant here the sum of the habits which the mind adopts in the general conduct of its operations—in the general conduct of a game of chess, in contrast, as Poincaré says, to the special rules which govern each separate proposition, each particular move in the game. Ego-centric logic and communicable logic will therefore differ less in their conclusions (except with the child where Ego-centric logic often functions) than in the way they work. The points of divergence are as follows: a) Ego-centric logic is more intuitive, more "syncretistic" than deductive, that is, its reasoning is not made explicit. The mind leaps from premise to conclusion at a single bound, without stopping on the way. b) Little value is attached to proving, or even checking propositions. The vision of the whole brings about a state of belief and a feeling of security far more rapidly than if each step in the argument were made explicit. c) Personal schemas of analogy are made use of, likewise memories of earlier reasoning, which control the present course of reasoning without openly manifesting their influence. d) Visual schemas also play an important part, and can even take the place of proof in supporting the deduction that is made. e) Finally, judgments of value have far more influence on Ego-centric than on communicable thought.

In communicated intelligence, on the other hand, we find: a) Far more deduction, more of an attempt to render explicit the relations between propositions by such expressions as *therefore, if . . . then*, etc. b) Greater emphasis is laid on proof. Indeed, the whole exposition is framed in view of the proof, that is, in view of the necessity of convincing someone else, and

centered about activity and lack any intrinsic stability.[18] The absence of permanent objects and of the objective organization of space seems thus to go hand in hand with a radical and unconscious egocentricity, so that the subject does not consider himself as one thing among many, but only conceives of things in relation to his own actions.[19] Yet at the other extremity of the development the universe is considered as being formed of permanent objects whose movements take place in a space independent of us, and whose many relationships form a series of invariables which prolong the conservation of the object itself; invariables of number, quantity, matter, weight, etc.[20]

(as a corollary) of convincing oneself whenever one's personal certainty may have been shaken by the process of deductive reasoning. c) Schemas of analogy tend to be eliminated, and to be replaced by deduction proper. d) Visual schemas are also done away with, first as incommunicable, and later as useless for purposes of demonstration. e) Finally, personal judgments of value are eliminated in favor of collective judgments of value, these being more in keeping with ordinary reason.

(Cf. also Piaget), 558, pp. 301–3.)

---

18. The psychoanalytic proposition which parallels this maintains that at the beginning of psychic development objects and ideas of objects are merely instinct-representations, lacking stability, and depending on the fluctuating satiation of the instinctual drive. The mechanisms of the unconscious (primary process) are assumed to be surviving witnesses to this initial lack of stable objects. Analysis of these mechanisms shows that the memory (idea) of impressions which were in any way connected with the experience of instinctual tension or its "gratification-discharge" will serve as a full equivalent of the "need-satisfying object" in the primary process. Partial impressions of a gratifying ob-

ject, any other object that shares with it a partial impression (*pars pro toto*), antecedents of the tension- and/or gratification-experience and of any equivalents of it (*post hoc ergo propter hoc*), impressions simultaneous with experiences of tension or tension-discharge (participation)—all may become equivalents of the need-satisfying object, that is, become instinct-representations. Cf. Freud, Chap. 15, notes 12, 29 and 31, below; see also Rapaport (596).

19. H. Werner (755, pp. 59–67) has gathered experimental material showing that in species other than man, and in certain pathological conditions of man, objects are experienced in the fashion Piaget observed in the young child. These objects Werner designated as "things-of-action."

19. This state of affairs is related to the phenomena which psychoanalysis describes as infantile narcissism, implying that no differentiation of "me" and "not-me" has been reached as yet, and that the so-called "omnipotence of ideas" prevails. Cf. Freud (237, pp. 148–49; and 227, pp. 873–77).

20. "Prolong the conservation" refers to the achievements of science, which by creating abstractions extended the developmental achievement which had

One may therefore say then that, in so far as egocentricity is reduced by the co-ordination of the individual point of view with other possible ones, the co-ordination which explains this reduction explains also the formation of logical instruments of conservation (ideas of "groups," systems of relations, etc.) and the formation of invariables in the world of reality (ideas of the permanence of the object, of quantities, weights, etc.).[21]

---

changed mere snatches of fleeting sense-impressions into the constant realities of objects. The abstractions of physics, which capture what is invariable amidst change, extended this constancy (conservation) enormously. Cf. note 17, above. It may be worth noting that perceptual constancies, which are time-honored subject-matters of experimental psychology, may also be profitably viewed in the context of conservation. See Koffka (406, pp. 211 ff.).

21. Piaget asserts here—as previously elsewhere (561, pp. 37–49; and 558, pp. 301–2)—the central role of socialization in the development of intelligence. Though this general idea has been often expressed (G. Mead, 516), its concrete statement that communication is both the cardinal means and the index of socialization of thought-organization, appears to be original and important. The significance of communication in particular, and interpersonal relationships in general, for the development of human thinking, has been little appreciated and less explored. To my knowledge, besides Piaget only Sullivan (726, 725) and Bernfeld (54) had a clear perception of this significance. Sullivan and Bernfeld both expressed their insight as theoretical inference from experience, rather than as empirical finding. Sullivan coined the concept of "consensual validation" (726, pp. 13–14) to say that concepts and thinking become reality-adequate only

by being tested in interpersonal communication. Bernfeld approached the problem from the reverse side, showing the effect of "secrets" on communication and consciousness. My own sporadic observations suggest that a relation between "open channels of communication" and "prevailing state of consciousness" is probably demonstrable. Such a demonstration, however, would require precise definitions of both terms.

The unexplored state of this field is surprising, for two reasons. First, the influence of interpersonal relations on mental development is one of the fundamental implications of psychoanalytic theory. Secondly, the problems of interpersonal and group relationships have been, for the last decade one of the foci of psychological interests. It is puzzling that these two powerful streams of interest did not suffice to prompt a systematic exploration of the role of interpersonal relations in the development of thinking.

Particularly unique to Piaget is the stress of the present passage on the idea that the invariants of groups (note 9), and the systems of relationships, are formed "by the coordination of the individual point of view with other possible ones." Presumably, the groups and relation-systems are so formed as to guarantee conservation of objects not only in time, but also from individual to individual.

II. SENSORY-MOTOR INTELLIGENCE

Even in the most elementary sensory-motor activities with which the intellectual development of the child begins, it is possible to discern certain of the processes of conservation. Because of the final richness of these processes, as well as their initial limitation, it is necessary to analyze them in detail.

It is evident that the reflex mechanisms (for example, sucking), the habits grafted on these reflexes (thumb sucking, etc.), or the more complex "circular reactions" which tend to reproduce an interesting result (to swing suspended toys, etc.) all lead essentially to repetition, and consequently imply a tendency toward persistence. On the one side these factors assume that movements are so organized that they are always capable of returning to their point of departure.[22] From the point of view of space, these motor units form what the geometricians call "displacement groups," closed systems of operations which tend to continuance.[23] On the other side, the elementary psychological activity which is characteristic of them is essentially an "assimilation" [24] of external realities, so that these realities are not considered as entities in themselves, but only as functional elements (things are conceived merely as something to be sucked, something to be swung or handled, etc.).[25] Now this assimilation is also a factor in conservation, since it implies a certain practical recognition and a certain identifying generalization based on habitual repetition. Thus, when the baby of five or six months sees his usual rattle, or even a new plaything, dangling before him, he will swing it at once, assimilating it (by an assimilation which reproduces, recognizes, and generalizes) into the scheme of objects to be swung.[26]

But, if these elementary sensory-motor organizations thus introduce from the very start a certain permanence into the primitive universe by constructing space in practical "groups" and by an assimilation of the things perceived into schemes of action, this conservation and this permanence emanate from

22. Cf. Chap. 7, notes 28, 29, below.
23. See note 9, above.
24. See Chap. 7, below.
25. Cf. note 18, above.
26. This concept of assimilation elucidates the complexity of the process underlying habitual repetition, which has so often been treated perfunctorily by association psychology and its surviving heirs. Cf. however, Schwartz (675).

the subject himself, and hence begin by presenting a purely egocentric character. In other words, there is not yet any conservation of objects as such, nor any permanence in the external world, not even in the space which forms its framework.[27]

First of all, as far as objects are concerned, it is easy to establish the fact that, although the baby is capable of recognizing differences in things at a very early age, almost to the end of his first year he behaves as if the objects which disappeared from his field of perception momentarily ceased to exist.[28] For instance, between the ages of five and eight months, when the child already knows enough to seize any solid objects which he sees, one has only to cover them with a cloth, or place a screen in front of them at the moment

27. Cf. note 18, above. The infant's world, organized around actions dependent on impulses—Piaget's "desirability" (Chap. 7, pp. 189–90, below)—has no permanence. This finding has many parallels—for example, in early Greek thought, and in the behavior of animals. Windelband (773, pp. 31–32) wrote of early Greek thought:

The fact that things of experience change . . . was the stimulus to the first philosophical reflections . . . science asked for the abiding ground of all these changes.

Werner (755, p. 63) wrote of the instability of the animal's world, organized around actions:

Fabre tells that he cut the feelers from a grasshopper paralyzed by a wasp, whereupon the wasp responded by grasping the prey by its palpi. But if these were removed the wasp was helpless. Contrary to what one might expect, the grasshopper's legs did not exist as signal-qualities in the whole continuum of the event of seizing and dragging off the prey . . . the effectiveness of the signal-qualities may depend not only on certain biologically relevant objective characteristics, but also on the readiness for action, a motive which will bring to life an otherwise mute, inoperative signal-quality.

28. This state of affairs may play a great role in the developmental history of those processes described by psychoanalysis as defenses. Flight and denial are considered the predecessors and prototypes of all defenses; and the non-existence in the child's world of what is not-present may well lay the foundation for both of these.

Freud (233, p. 84) wrote of the relation of flight to "repression":

If it were a question of an external stimulus, obviously flight would be the appropriate remedy; with an instinct, flight is of no avail. . . . Repression is a preliminary phase of condemnation, something between flight and condemnation. . . .

Fenichel (176, p. 144) describes denial as follows:

The tendency to deny painful sensations and facts is as old as the feeling of pain itself. In little children a wishfulfilling denial of unpleasant realities is a very common thing . . . the counterpart of the "hallucinatory wishfulfillment." Anna Freud has called this type of refusal to acknowledge displeasure . . . "pre-stages of defense." The gradual development of reality-testing makes such wholesale falsification of reality impossible. However, these tendencies toward denial try to remain operative.

when the baby's hand is directed towards them, and he will give up looking for them and immediately lose his interest.[29] I have even observed this in systematically hiding the bottle when my six-months-old son was about to take it. But one can see a still more curious reaction around nine or ten months, when the child is capable of seeking the object behind the screen and the notion of real exterior permanence begins to put in an appearance. For example, when the baby is placed between two pillows and he has succeeded in finding an object hidden under the right one, the object can be taken from his hands and placed under the left pillow before his very eyes, but he will look for it under the right pillow where he has already found it once before, as if the permanence of the objective were connected with the success of the former action, and not with a system of external displacements in space.[30]

In short, the primitive world is not made up of permanent objects with autonomous trajectories, but of moving perceptive pictures which return periodically into non-existence and come back again as the functional result of the proper action. It is easy to prove still more clearly that this world is centered in the activity of the self by an analysis of the egocentric character of space which determines its configuration.

If the movements of the child are immediately capable of organization into "groups," closed and reversible systems, those "groups" are in the beginning centered entirely on the subject himself, and afford no room for any objective spatial construction. The clearest example of these egocentric "groups" is seen in the way in which a baby, before nine or ten months, rotates objects, a movement which finally forms the idea of the "wrong side" of objects. Everyone has observed a child handling things and turning them over and

---

Fenichel adds: "repression . . . [is] certainly a derivation of . . . 'denial.'"

29. This is the absence of what Piaget—and earlier Brentano and the phenomenologists—called "intentionality" (561, pp. 232 ff.). From the point of view of psychoanalytic theory, the drive is directed toward the concrete need-satisfying object as a means of tension-release. When the object is absent, the tension-release is attempted by hallucinatory wishfulfillment and affect-

discharge. Cf. Freud, Chap. 15, pp. 318–19, 323, this volume.

30. This seems to lend support to the drive-organization conception of primitive experience (see notes 18 and 29, above) rather than to the associationist. We must forego demonstrating here why the Hull theory, which attempts to unite a drive- and association-theory, cannot give a satisfactory account of such observations.

over to explore their various sides. Now do these rotary movements give way immediately to the formation of objective groups? A very simple experiment shows us that this is not so. One has only to give a five- or six-months-old baby his bottle with the nipple away from him, and turn it around slowly before his very eyes. If the child can see a bit of the rubber nipple at the other end of the bottle, he immediately turns the object around, but if he doesn't see the nipple, he doesn't even attempt to turn it, but sucks the wrong end! A series of other experiments with other "displacement groups" has shown the same centering on the subject and not on the object.

How then is the baby going to construct a world of permanent objects situated in a real space, and thus escape from his primitive egocentric universe? It is the work of the sensory-motor or practical intelligence, which precedes language, to set up a system of relations to co-ordinate the series of various perspectives which the baby has and thus cause him to locate himself among objects instead of illusively bringing them to him.[31]

In other words, as the activity of the baby develops and the casual, temporal, and spatial sequences which this activity creates become more complex, objects are detached more and more from the action itself, and the body of the subject becomes one element among others in an ordered ensemble.[32] Thus a total reversal of perspective takes place, which marks the beginning of the objectification of the external world, and of the idea of its permanence. The interplay of practical relationships in the world of reality teaches the child to shift the center of space and its objects from his action to himself, and thus locate himself at the middle point of this world which is being born. In this way the permanence of objects appears as the product of this formation of objective

---

31. "Illusively bringing them to him" apparently describes the same set of phenomena to which the psychoanalyst refers by the term "omnipotence of thought"; the corollary of this is that the sole characteristic of the drive-object is its need-gratifying function. Cf. Freud (227).

32. Compare Freud (232, p. 62):

[The] organism will soon become capable of making the first discrimination and a first orientation. On the one hand, it will detect certain stimuli which can be avoided by an action of the muscles (flight)—these it ascribes to the outside world; on the other hand, it will also be aware of stimuli against which such action is of no avail.

Also Freud (237, p. 148):

. . . motor innervation . . . determines whether the perception can be made to disappear or whether it proves persistent. The capacity of testing reality need be nothing more than this function.

"groups" of displacements, and these groups themselves depend for their creation upon the way in which the sensory-motor or practical intelligence allows
the child to free himself from his initial egocentricity and gives him power
to act on things, thanks to a system of co-ordinated relationships.

But, if the co-ordination of practical relationships leads to a first victory over
egocentricity and to the beginning of the objective idea of conservation, this
external permanence remains limited to the plane of action and immediate perception, and cannot extend at once to the level of conceptual representation
in general. In fact, it is in a sense an "ontological egocentricity" from which
the practical intelligence delivers the individual, and not social and representative egocentricity, which will remain very important even after the appearance
of language, and all through infancy.[33] In other words, the co-ordination of
practical relationships teaches the child that his body is one thing among
many, and that he is thus part of a world of stable objects, whereas at the beginning the baby saw only a world of inconsistent pictures gravitating about
his own activity. But the sensory-motor intelligence is not enough to teach the
child that the perspective he has of this world is not absolute but relative, and
must be co-ordinated with the perspectives of other people to attain a general
and truly objective picture of reality.[34]

III. EGOCENTRIC THOUGHT [35]

Just at the moment when the practical world of which we have been speaking has been created, the child comes into possession of language, and henceforth is called upon to adapt himself to the thoughts of others as well as to
the external material world. Now on this new plane of thought which the
social world creates, the child finds difficulties similar to those he has already
overcome on the plane of the practical universe, and so he passes through
stages similar to those of his escape from initial egocentricity and his progressive
co-ordination. Hence the principles of conservation remain unchanged, only
this time they are on the plane of abstract concepts. Although the child admits

33. Ontology is that branch of metaphysics which deals with the ultimate
nature of existence. The egocentricity
that is overcome by sensory-motor intelligence is egocentricity in regard to
the existence of the world of objects.

Concerning the later course of egocentricity, see Piaget (561, pp. 43 ff.; 558,
pp. 237 ff.).

34. Cf. Ferenczi (180), and note 21,
above.

35. See note 16, above.

the permanence of concrete objects in the world of immediate experience, he really has no idea of the conservation of matter, weight, or movement, nor even any conception of logical or numerical groups. If he fails, it is because he lacks the intellectual instrument with which to construct the "invariables of groups" which are formed by physical realities.[36] This instrument is called "the logic of relations" by the logicians, and is really the tool of co-ordination par excellence, both from the social and from the rational point of view.[37] It is created only as it succeeds in stemming the egocentricity which constantly opposes it.

In order to make the link between the ontological egocentricity of the first sensory-motor stage and the social and logical egocentricity of the beginnings of conceptual thought perfectly clear, let us briefly turn again to the example of space. We have already seen that on the practical plane the child of two

36. Concerning the "invariables of groups," see note 9, above. The algebraic group is a system of operations on a set of elements; the study of such groups is in the main that of their invariants. Piaget—having observed what seemed to him the emergence in the course of development of concepts of invariants of sensory-motor operations —apparently assumes that the latter are a group, in the same sense as the group of displacements in the Euclidian space to which they correspond. Whether he means this as an analogy or in a strict sense, remains unclear. Algebraic groups are a postulational system (see F. Klein, 385, p. 132); if Piaget has adduced proof that his "displacement groups" meet their postulates, I did not succeed in finding it. As an analogy, however, the concept is most fortunate and clarifying. In the long run it may pave the way for psychology to add, beside topology (Lewin, 469, 468), another non-metric mathematical method to its conceptual tools.

37. Cf. Piaget (556), Chap. 7, particularly notes 28, 29, and 47, below. See Russell (624) for a relatively non-technical discussion of "the logic of relationships." This logic, unlike classical logic, treats of abstract relations, rather than of classes of objects and ideas as represented by corresponding concepts. The subject-matter of the logic of relationships consists of the combinations and interrelations of such propensities as symmetry, transitiveness, etc. For example, "sibling of" is a symmetrical relation: if A is a sibling of B, B too is a sibling of A. "Descendant of" is a transitive relation: if B is a descendant of A, and C a descendant of B, C is also a descendant of A. Spatial and other relations of objects too have such propensities, and it is to these that Piaget refers. Needless to say, he does not refer to an awareness of, but only to operations with, such relations in the child.

The logic of relationships is another non-metric mathematical tool which might prove useful in psychology. F. Heider (317) has made an important attempt to apply it to interpersonal relations.

or three years is capable of using a certain number of "groups" of displacements: he knows how to turn an object over, to hide it behind one screen, or a series of two, and find it in the right place, etc. But what will happen when it is a question not only of acting upon the object, but of imagining distant objects, and of co-ordinating the perspective of different observers?

One of our assistants, Mlle. E. Meyer, has investigated this in the following experiment: the child is placed opposite a small model of three mountains, and given a certain number of colored pictures of these mountains; he is then asked which of the pictures show the mountains from the positions occupied successively by a doll on the mountains in the model. The function of age in the development of these reactions is very clear. The little ones do not understand that the observer sees the same mountains quite differently from various points of view, and hence they consider their own perspective absolute. But the older ones gradually discover the relativity necessary to objectivity, after a number of systematic errors due to the difficulty of co-ordinating the relationships in question. Here then on this social and logical plane of the co-ordination of perspectives we have a passing from egocentricity to an objective "group" of changes, exactly parallel to the passage one has observed on the sensory-motor level in the relationships between the baby and the objects handled, only this time the necessity of considering the point of view of other people has created a new difficulty.

Now this process also influences very closely the idea of the conservation or continuity of the mechanical and physical characteristics of objects as well as of their spatial peculiarities. In fact, since the child considers a mountain as being just what it appears to be in his own perspective, it could not possibly have either form or stable dimensions—that is, no "invariables of groups" are constructed. That is actually what observation shows to be true. I have been able to determine in experimenting on my own children, by going about real mountains with them, that at about four or five years of age they still considered the apparent changes due to our own changes of position as quite real. For every mountain they admitted the existence of changes of form and dimensions absolutely contrary to the idea of the permanence of objects. It would be easy to generalize these results for all objects in distant space (stars, clouds, etc.).

But we must show how this preoccupation with the problem of the proper perspective—that is to say, of "immediate experience" as opposed to experience based on rational deduction—hinders the mind from co-ordinating relationships, and finally forming ideas of the permanence of matter, weight, movement, etc. It is clear that every principle of conservation implies a system of relationships which explains real permanence through apparent change. Now in so far as the mind is dominated by "immediate experience," it is not capable of recognizing this relativity, nor the "invariables" which it implies.[38]

Here is an example dealing with the ideas of the conservation of matter and weight. We show children of different ages two paste balls of the same dimensions and weight. Then we change the shape of one of them to a cylinder (a sausage), and we ask if the two objects still have the same weight. Now the little ones think that the weight of the cylinder is less than that of the ball (because a ball appears to concentrate more matter in itself than an elongated cylinder), and they even state that the quantity of paste has diminished because of the change in form! But the older ones believe in the conservation of weight and matter; and between the two one finds a stage at which children think that weight alone varies with form, matter remaining constant.

In the same way, one of our pupils, Mlle. B. Inhelder, has shown that sugar dissolved in a glass of water is not conserved, in the minds of young children: the level which rises at the immersion of the sugar is considered as being

38. Compare Piaget (558, pp. 237 ff., particularly p. 241). The role of "immediate experience" Piaget (558, p. 247) describes as follows:

All the younger children take their immediate perceptions as true and then proceed to interpret them according to their egocentric pre-relations, instead of making allowance for their own perspective. The most striking example we have found is that of the clouds and the heavenly bodies, of which children believe that they follow us.

Also (p. 281):

On the one hand, the universe of the child is close to immediate perceptions, closer to external things than the universe of the adult. On the other hand, it is more subjective, more permeated with characters that are, in fact, taken from internal experience . . . pre-causality which goes with them is marked by a confusion of motivation with physical connections.

Concerning relativity Piaget wrote:

. . . the progress from childish transduction to adult deduction presupposes three complementary processes: a) a progressive relativity of ideas, arising from the fact that the self gradually becomes conscious of the personal character of its own point of view and of the reciprocity between this point of view and other possible ones; b) a progressive transformation of primitive mental experiments into constructions carried out by means of the logic of relations; c) a progressive generalization, resulting from the fact that classes become rigid and well defined in the measure that they are conditioned by a substructure of relations (p. 300).

lowered as before, after the sugar is dissolved; the sugar is conceived of as gradually vanishing, and even the sweet taste, which is all that remains of the dissolved piece, is supposed to disappear after several hours. But older children, by a series of steps it is useless to describe here, succeed in attaining the idea of the conservation of the sugar, its weight, and even the volume it occupied in the liquid.[39] Some even go so far as to construct a kind of crude atomic theory, like that which the pre-Socratic physicists had, to account for these phenomena.[40]

It is the same *a fortiori* [41] in the case of more subtle ideas, such as that of the conservation of movement, or the principle of inertia. It is, indeed, easy to show that the physics of the child begins by being impregnated with an animistic dynamism, which is the direct opposite of the idea of inertia. Things are endowed with active forces, spontaneous and untransmittable, formed on the model of voluntary muscular activity.[42] Later, before arriving at more mechanistic ideas, the child passes through an intermediate period which recalls in many respects the physics of Aristotle. Thus the trajectory of a projectile is explained, not by the conservation of the impulse received, but by an ἀντιπερίστασις in the real sense of the word, the projectile being pushed by the air it displaces in its progress. The clouds move in the same way, by the wind which their displacement arouses, etc.[43]

It seems to us easy to show that all these ideas which are so contrary to the ideas of conservation are explained by the same causes, by an egocentric relationship, not yet reciprocal or rational, between the subject and the objects of the external world. On the one hand, objects are assimilated to the Ego, and conceived on the model of its own activity. Hence the anthropocentric ideas of force, weight, etc., which are common in the physics of the little ones. On the other hand, experience remains "immediate," dominated by a series of successive impressions which have not yet been co-ordinated. It is not formed by that logic of relationships which alone will impress upon it an objective form by co-ordinating the many relationships which are perceived or con-

39. Cf. also Piaget (558, pp. 250–51) and Werner (755, pp. 319–26).

40. Cf. Piaget (558, pp. 23, 24, 57, 58, 119, 161, 263, 265).

41. "A fortiori," like "pars pro toto" and "post hoc propter hoc," is a form of

pre-logical thinking. Its Hebrew equivalent, so common in Talmudic literature, is "al achat khamo v'chamo."

42. Cf. Piaget (558, pp. 123 ff., 262; also 559, III).

43. Cf. Piaget (558, pp. 20, 23–24, 70).

ceived. Thus, in the case of the pellets which change their form, the child does not succeed in freeing his judgment from the illusions caused by habitual perceptions (we know the point at which the evaluations of weight are dependent on factors of form), [in order] that he may co-ordinate the relationships into a coherent ensemble which can support the deduction of real permanence. In short, the absence of permanence is the result of the pre-eminence of immediate experience over rational deduction, and immediate experience is the ensemble of subjective impressions, successively registered and not yet co-ordinated into a system of relationships which encloses the subject in an objective world.

IV. RATIONAL CO-ORDINATION

We saw first of all how the sensory-motor co-ordinations led the child from an unstable world centered about his own activity to an idea of the permanence of objects, based on the formation of "displacement groups" which ordered space into an objective practical universe. On the other hand, we have just established the fact that when thought and abstract concepts are imposed on this sensory-motor world, egocentricity reappears on this new plane, and the world of concepts also begins to be centered in the Ego, and is thus stripped of the basic permanence which reason demands. How is the child to surmount this second group of obstacles and reach the idea of rational permanence?

The process of reasoning on this plane of conceptual thought is exactly the same as on the sensory-motor level, with this difference, that it is a question henceforth of the co-ordination of the perspectives of different individuals, as well as the co-ordination of the different aspects of individual experience.[44] This social co-ordination, which adds a new dimension to those which are already a part of rational co-ordination, creates in the intellectual realm what one might call "logic," in contrast to the sensory-motor or practical intelligence, which makes only perceptions and motions into systems. Logic is then the "group" of operations which co-ordinates the inter-individual relationships with the intra-individual ones into a system capable of assuring the permanence which is necessary to the invariables of experience.[45]

The essence of rational co-ordination is then to be sought in the "logic of

44. Cf. note 21, above.   45. Cf. notes 9 and 36, above.

relations"—that is, in this fundamental group of operations which assures the reciprocity of individual perspectives and the relativity of the facts of experience. To refer again to the example of space, on which we have already insisted, it is the logic of relations which makes the child come gradually to understand, between seven and eleven years, that the left and the right are not absolute, but that his own left corresponds to the right of an individual opposite him, and that an object between two others is at one and the same time at the left of the first and the right of the third. It is then the logic of relationships which permits the formation of the idea of a conceptual space by the co-ordination of the different perspectives possible, and which also allows the imposition of this upon practical space, whose relationships, however well co-ordinated they may be among themselves, are always limited to one's own perspective.[46]

Now this logic of relations, which thus maintains on the level of thought the "groups" of operations outlined by sensory-motor intelligence, and which gradually eliminates intellectual egocentricity, finally succeeds, in the realm we are trying to analyze here, in forming invariables which represent for the reasoning mind so many principles of permanence applicable to the physical world.

In the field of the permanence of quantity, for instance, it is easy to show how the grouping of relationships involves in each case the construction of formal invariables, which, when applied to reality, correct the illusions of non-permanence which we have just described in the "immediate experience" of infancy. In her investigations into the genesis of the ideas of quantity and number, our assistant, Mlle. A. Szeminska, brought to light a number of facts which made this change clear. Here are some of them.

When one fills a large glass with some continuous substance, such as colored water, or a discontinuous one, such as beads, and then separates these into two or four small glasses, or into some narrow and elongated or short and fat ones, etc., the quantities appear to increase or diminish for the child below seven years of age according to whether the subject considers the level of the substance in the receptacles, their size, or their number. Moreover, when one

46. The logic of relationships, according to Piaget (Chap. 7, p. 191, and note 47*, below), is a late developing structure in which that "category of reason" which he calls "quantitative rapport" and the "functional invariant" of the "implicative function" find their expression.

makes two groups correspond piece by piece (for example, the beads in two rectilinear rows), the child considers at first that the two quantities are equal; but this is only an illusion, because one has only to place the elements in one of these groups nearer or farther apart (to put the beads in a heap, or make one row longer and more widely spaced than the other) and the two quantities are no longer considered as equal; a row of ten beads is conceived as increasing in number if they are spaced more widely, and a pile is considered as containing more or fewer beads according to whether one heaps it up or spreads it out before the eyes of the child, etc.

In short, before the age of six or seven there is no idea of the permanence of continuous quantities, nor of discontinuous groups, nor any necessary equivalence between two groups which correspond piece by piece, etc., whatever the active operations may be which the subject himself performs in the course of the experiments. For this reason up to this age the child has not yet formed any idea of cardinal or ordinal numbers which are capable of indefinite extension; nor has he yet elaborated any idea of classes of things in extension, which depends upon the inclusion of parts in a permanent whole.[47] The essential forms which number and logical class give to the mind are thus, after all, bound up closely with the processes of conservation, and one might say in general that if the thought of the child remains prelogical during infancy, it is because of the lack of these very principles of permanence.[48]

Now how does the child proceed from this pre-logical state to the discovery of the permanence of groups and quantities? By the co-ordination of the relationships involved; that is, by those operations of "multiplication of relations"[49] which are essential to the logic of relationships. As soon as he ceases to envisage as separate unities the level, size, and number of the columns

47. Cf. Montessori's (524) teaching methods for numbers, which are designed to foster development of such classes.

48. It seems that the reverse formulation—"the child lacks these principles, because it remains pre-logical during infancy"—would be closer to the facts.

49. Presumably Piaget refers to the "logical multiplication" and perhaps also the "logical addition" of Boolean algebra, in which the product consists of what is common to the multiplicands, and the sum is the totality of all the different elements in the members to be added (elements common to several members appear only once). If we represent two *multiplicands* by two circles which intersect, then the product is the area common to both (intersect). If we represent two members to be *added* by two circles which intersect, the logical sum is the total area enclosed, the overlapping part counting only once. It is to

of liquid, the length of the rows, and the space between the objects, etc., the child succeeds in co-ordinating these relationships, in understanding their relative positions in a system of independent variables, and thus he forms units which are capable of permanence. It is therefore the logic of relationships which transforms immediate experience, with its illusions of perception, into a rational system, the changes of which depend on necessary invariables. It would be easy to show that the idea of the permanence of matter, weight, and movement, which we were speaking of above, is the result of similar processes. In the thought of the child, as in the evolution of the sciences, rational permanence always results from the union of a deduction based on the co-ordination of relationships with an experience similarly formed; and every invariable implies a "group" which creates it—that is, a system of related and reversible changes.[50]

But you will say that the problem is not yet solved, that there still remains the question of how this "logic of relations" which explains the genesis of the principles of conservation and of the "invariables of groups" is itself originated.[51] Now it is first necessary to understand the epistemological character of what we call the egocentricity of the child (that is, a quite unconscious and natural illusion of perspective, which precedes moral egoism and conscious egocentricity).[52] Then one will understand that this process of co-ordination, at once social and intellectual, by which the child escapes from his self-centered point of view to find his place among other people, is actually the rational instrument which makes up this logic of relations. For, in any field, the faculty of knowing is a process of co-ordination in which the ego is subordinated to

---

be noted that: a) the *contents* of concepts are logical products, since they contain only those characteristics common to all elements which the concept subsumes; b) the *realms* of concepts are logical sums, since they comprise all the elements the concept subsumes. Cf. Rapaport *et al.* (602, I, 389–91).

Piaget apparently implies that the development of the form in which functional invariants appear on each mental level is in its pattern akin to that of logical multiplication: it is an extraction of

the common and invariable from changing settings.

50. Piaget apparently means by this that the groups in question are sets of operations (changes) which, in certain respects, return the elements on which they operate into their original position. Cf. pp. 162, 164–65, 172, above.

51. Cf. Piaget, Chap. 7, below.

52. Note the parallel with the psychoanalytic concept "primary narcissism." Cf. Freud (231) and Piaget (561, cited in note 16, above).

some objective system of references, and the logic of relationships is nothing but a tool and a result of this co-ordination; a tool in that it guides the ego in its escape from itself, and a result since it is a grouping of systematic operations and an ensemble of successive invariables.[53]

In conclusion, one sees how the genetic analysis of any aspect of the thought of a child necessarily corresponds to the analysis of scientific thought. Indeed, the effort by which the child, by means of that social and rational instrument which the logic of relationships gives him, escapes from his egocentricity and creates a universe is the very beginning of that ever-present gigantic effort of science to free man from himself by putting him within the relativity of the objective world.

53. The relation of Piaget's "ego" concept to that of psychoanalysis cannot be clarified here. It is clear that Piaget's "knowing," in which the ego "is *subordinated* to some objective system of references," is akin to the subordination of the primary process to the secondary process, in psychoanalysis. In the latter, the acquisition of an "objective system of references" is one aspect of ego-development. Cf. Freud, Chap. 15, particularly notes 30 and 31, below.

CHAPTER 7

THE BIOLOGICAL PROBLEM OF INTELLIGENCE [1]
By Jean Piaget

AN INVESTIGATION of the origin of intelligence must necessarily face the relationship between the mind and the biological organization.[2] No [speculative] discussion of this relationship can lead to a tenable positive conclusion. Yet it is preferable to clarify in advance the postulates with which the investigation begins, rather than to succumb unwittingly to the influence of one of the many possible views concerning this relationship.[3]

Verbal or reflective intelligence rests on practical or sensory-motor intelligence, which in turn is supported by acquired and recombined habits and associations. Habits and associations presuppose the system of reflexes rooted in the anatomic and morphological structure of the organism.[4] Consequently, there is a certain continuity between intelligence and the purely biological processes of morphogenesis and adaptation to the environment. What is the meaning of this continuity?

Clearly, intellectual development is determined by certain hereditary factors. There are two groups of such factors which differ from each other biologically. The classical issue of the relationship of innate ideas [5] to epistemological *a*

1. Piaget (556). This is a translation of the introductory chapter of Piaget's *La Naissance de l'intelligence*. The considerations here may seem abstract and speculative to the reader, but they are founded on Piaget's earlier empirical studies (cf. particularly 558, pp. 237 ff., and 561, pp. 217 ff.) and further studies reported in the volume to which this is an introduction. Some empirical data will also be found in Piaget's other paper included in this volume (Chap. 6).

2. Cf. Hartmann, Chap. 19, II, particularly notes 37, 38, 39, below.

3. By these "views" Piaget refers to the various philosophical solutions of the body-mind problem, and to the various corresponding answers to the basic question of epistemology: "How is knowledge possible?"

4. Piaget's conception of acquired habits and associations "supporting" sensory-motor intelligence remains unclear. Cf. Buehler (109, pp. 2–10).

5. The conception of "innate ideas" assumes that we are born with certain ideas, the existence of which explains how it is that we have general concepts even though the sources of our knowledge—sensory impressions—are con-

priorism [6] was obscured by the failure to distinguish between these two groups.

The first group of these hereditary factors is structural, rooted in the constitution of our nervous system and our sense organs. For instance, we perceive only certain physical radiations, and matter only if it is of a certain size, and so on.

Such structural factors influence the formation of our most fundamental concepts. For example: our intuition of space is certainly determined by them, even though our thinking can develop trans-intuitive [7] and purely deductive spaces.[8]

Though this first group of factors furnishes intelligence with useful structures, its role—in contrast to that of the second group—is essentially a limiting one. Our perceptions are only one set among all those conceivable. The Euclidian space, bound to our organs, is only one of those which fit physical experience. In contrast, the deductive and organizing activities of the mind are limitless and lead, particularly in regard to space, to generalizations surpassing all intuition. This activity of the mind, to the extent to which it is hereditary, is so in a quite different sense from the first group: it is a matter of heredity of function and not of the transmission of a certain structure. It is in this latter sense that H. Poincaré could consider the concept of spatial

---

crete. This is the diametrical opposite of the "tabula rasa" conception, according to which the mind is a *clean slate* at birth and all mental contents are acquired by experience. Descartes (142, pp. 115–32) assumed that the idea of God, as well as the ideas of all universally valid and necessary truths, are innate, and that sensory impressions do not create concepts but only provide the occasion for concepts to become conscious in us.

6. *A priorism* is a specific form of the conception of innate ideas. Its most systematic presentation is Kant's *The Critique of Pure Reason* (367). Cf. also Kant (368) and Poincaré (575). Kant maintained that the validity of a priori synthetic propositions (as for instance Euclid's postulates) cannot derive from experience. To explain the origin of their validity he asserted that the mind synthesizes all experiences in terms of the a priori forms of sensibility, that is, space and time; and in terms of the categories of pure reason, which he classified as categories of quantity, quality, relation, and modification. The validity of synthetic (a priori) propositions derives from the fact that all impingements of the environment are synthesized by the pure mind in terms of these forms and categories, and this synthesis lends them validity.

7. The terms "intuition" and "intuitive" are used by Piaget in the sense of "perception" and "perceptual."

8. Examples are the non-Euclidian spaces, the abstract spaces of modern algebra, and the phase-space of corpuscular physics.

"group" a priori,[9] since it is connected with the very function of intelligence.

The same distinction obtains in the inheritance of intelligence proper.[10] As for structural inheritance: there is the "specific heredity" of the human species and of the particular lineage which admits of certain levels of intelligence, superior to that of the apes, and so on. As for the inheritance of the functions of the mind (the *ipse intellectus* which does not derive from experience): it is evidently connected with the "general heredity of the living organism itself." [11] Just as the organism would be unable to adapt to the variations of the environment, were it not itself organized, so intelligence could not apprehend the givens of the external world, were it not for certain synthetic functions [12] of its own (the ultimate expression of which is the principle of absence of contradictions) [13] and for functions positing relationships, etc. All these functions are common to all intellectual organizations.

This second type of inherited psychological reality is of primary importance for the development of intelligence. Clearly, if there exists, in fact, a functional nucleus of the intellectual organization which arises from the general character of the biological organization, this invariant will determine the direction of all the successive structures [14] that the mind will develop in the course

---

9. See Poincaré (575, pp. 66–91).

10. Up to now the discussion has dealt only with perception.

11. That is, the functions common to all living organisms as against the structures specific to the human species.

12. "Synthetic functions" here translates *fonctions de coherence*. This translation was chosen to point up that Piaget's concept is related to the psychoanalytic concept of the "synthetic function of the ego." Compare Nunberg (543), cited in Chap. 21, notes 2, 10, 20; and discussed in Chap. 19, V, particularly notes 71, 90, below.

13. This refers to one of the three fundamental principles of classical logic: *Identity:* A is A; *Contradiction:* A is not non-A; *Excluded third:* Something is either A or non-A. Freud (209) in distinguishing the primary (unconscious) and secondary (conscious) thought-

processes used this principle as one of his criteria. The principle of absence of contradictions does not hold in the primary process, while one of the salient characteristics of the secondary process is this very principle. Nunberg (543) shows that this principle is the core of the synthetic function of the ego. Cf. also Hermann (327, pp. 24 ff.). By "ultimate expression" Piaget presumably means "expression on the highest level of mental development."

14. This expression is grossly equivalent to Hartmann's (Chap. 19, VIII) "ego-apparatuses" and to Rapaport's (593) "quasi-stationary functions," although Piaget's "structure" concept appears to be broader than the corresponding concepts of Hartmann and Rapaport. Piaget's boundary line between structure and function is different.

of its contact with reality.[15] This invariant will therefore play the role of the a priori of the philosophers: it will impose upon structures certain necessary and irreducible conditions. In contrast to the a priori which has been at times mistakenly construed as structure existing from the very beginning of development, the functional invariant of thought, though it is already at work in the earliest stages of development, impresses itself on consciousness [16] only gradually by developing structures increasingly adapted to functioning. This a priori presents itself in the form of necessary structures only at the completion of the evolution of concepts and not at their beginning. This a priori, although hereditary, is nevertheless the diametrical opposite of the "innate ideas."

The inherited structures, however, *are* like the classic innate ideas and therefore they permit the argument of innateness to be revived for the space perception and "well-structured" perceptions of Gestalt psychology.[17] How-

15. It is probable that when a student develops his knowledge of calculus to the point that it becomes as stable a working organization as is elementary arithmetic to most of us, Piaget would consider this stable organization a structure. In this sense the acquisition of any new system of abstractions amounts to structure building. In psychoanalytic terms such an organization is equivalent to a cathectic organization on a level of heightened potential. Cf. Freud, Chap. 15, pp. 324–25, and notes 30 and 31; also Chap. 23, note 20, below.

16. The phrase "impresses itself upon consciousness" is not fortunate since the fundamental functions of thought find expression through the formal characteristics of structures—which are as a rule not conscious—rather than in the conscious content of these structures. This holds not only for those formal characteristics of thought-structures which we describe as repressive, intellectualizing, isolating, etc., but also for the "categories of reason." We rarely become aware of the formal character-istics of these structures of thinking except through the concentrated reflection of scientific analysis.

17. This assertion is debatable. The space concept and the "well-structured perceptions" (*Praegnanz*) of Gestalt-psychology are to Koehler (399, 400) and Koffka (406) based on hypothetical, functional invariants—of brain-physiology. The trace-theory, on which all Gestalt-psychology is built, is a theory of the dynamics of hypothetical electrochemical potentials. If, for the sake of this argument, this Gestalt-psychological conception is accepted in its full scope, then its space concept and its "well-structured perceptions" are more like Piaget's second than his first group of "hereditary" factors. It is important to clarify this point because it bears not only on Koehler's conception but also on the related concepts of Lewin's tension systems (467, 464, and Chap. 5, above; also Koffka, 406, pp. 333 ff.) and the theory of cathexes of psychoanalysis (cf. Rapaport, 596).

ever, in contrast to the functional invariants, these [inherited] structures imply nothing essential from the point of view of the mind: they are simply limited and delimiting internal givens continuously transcended by external experience and particularly by intellectual activity. They are innate but not in the sense of the a priori of epistemology. . . .

1. THE FUNCTIONAL INVARIANTS OF INTELLIGENCE AND THE BIOLOGICAL ORGANIZATION

Intelligence is an adaptation. In order to grasp its relation to life in general, we must first define the relationship between the organism and its environment. Life is a continuous creation of ever more complex forms, and a progressive equilibrating of these with the environment. To say that intelligence is a particular case of biological adaptation implies, therefore, that it is essentially an organization, the function of which is to structure the universe just as the organism structures its immediate environment.[18] In order to describe the functional mechanism of thought in true biological terms, it would suffice to determine the invariants of all structuring of which the living organism is capable.[19] What we must translate into terms of adaptation [20] are not the earliest specific objectives of practical [21] intelligence (these objectives broaden [in the course of development] to the point where they encompass all knowledge), but rather the fundamental relationship implicit to knowledge itself: the relation between thoughts and objects.[22] In adapting, the organism constructs new material forms, while intelligence broadens this construction by creating mental structures which can be applied to the forms of the environment. At the beginning of mental evolution, intellectual adaptation is in

18. The distinction between "structuring the immediate environment" and "structuring the universe" is not a matter of a dichotomy but one of a hierarchy of techniques of mastery ranging from the ingestion and digestion of food to the development of a theory of nuclear physics.

19. Clearly, Piaget implies here that the cardinal characteristics of each structuring process (function) of the living organism will be the same on the various levels of mental development in forms appropriate to the respective level. It is these unchanging characteristics of the structuring processes which he labels "functional invariants."

20. Presumably "terms of adaptation" here means "biological terms."

21. "Practical" here means sensory-motor.

22. The subject-matter of epistemology is this very relationship.

a sense more restricted than biological adaptation, but later on it broadens and infinitely surpasses the latter. From the biological point of view, intelligence is a particular instance of organic activity and the objects perceived and known are a segment of the environment to which the organism seeks to adapt; therefore, the original organism-environment adaptation is disturbed [by intellectual adaptation]. This does not preclude, however, the search for functional invariants.[23]

Actually mental development implies both variable and invariant elements. Failure to understand this fact led to psychological views, some of which tended to attribute superior qualities to primitive [developmental] stages, others tended to disregard stages and operations: it is, however, preferable to avoid both the pre-formism of intellectualistic psychology and the hypothesis of mental heterogeneities. The difficulties implicit in these theories are resolved by the distinction between variable structures and invariant functions.[24] Just as the major vital functions are identical in all organisms, though the organs differ from group to group, so do we find a continuous series of varying structures in the course of development from infancy to adulthood, while the major thought-functions remain invariant.[25]

23. Piaget means apparently that the adaptation characterized by the biological equilibrium of organism and environment is disrupted and replaced by the new adaptations summarily described as intellectual adaptations. In contrast to this we usually assume that intellectual adaptation comes into play only after the disruption of biological adaptation. Empirical study would probably reveal that these views are complementary rather than contradictory.

Piaget maintains that the fundamental patterns of the superseded adaptations are carried over into the new ones: they are the functional invariants. Cf. Hartmann, Chap. 19, p. 384 and note 68.

24. Pieget refers to two conceptions of mental life. One assumes that even the highest intellectual functions exist from the beginning of development. The other disclaims all connection between primitive forms of mental activity and the later appearing higher functions. Piaget resolves this dichotomy by showing that the invariant functions do indeed exist from the very beginning, but that the structures they create are variant and appear successively in the course of development.

25. For example, in tracing the development of the child's concept of causality, Piaget (558) describes three phases: in the first, causality has an egomorphic and antropomorphic, in the second a naive-dynamic, in the third a realistic structure. But throughout these phases of structure-variance the basic pattern of causality remains the same; it is a functional invariant. Cf. Piaget, Chap. 6, note 9, above.

These invariant functions exist within the framework of the two most general biological functions: *organization* and *adaptation*. Let us begin with the clarification of the latter for while it is generally recognized that intellectual development is but an adaptation, the concept of adaptation remains deplorably vague.

Certain biologists define *adaptation* simply as conservation and survival, that is to say, an equilibrium between the organism and the environment.[26] So defined, however, the concept becomes identical with that of life itself and therefore meaningless. Survival has degrees and adaptation implies precisely such degrees. Consequently, we must distinguish states of adaptation from processes of adaptation.[27] The states of adaptation are unrevealing. Studying the processes of adaptation, however, we learn that adaptation occurs when the organism is so changed by the environment that its integration with the environment increases and its conservation is thereby promoted.

Let us express this in a precise and formal statement. The organism is a cycle of physical, chemical, and kinetic processes which induce each other in constant interaction with the environment. Let a, b, c, etc., be the elements of this organized totality [of processes], and let x, y, z, etc., be the corresponding elements of the surrounding environment. The formula of the organization is then the following:

$$\text{(A)} \quad a + x \rightarrow b,$$
$$\text{(B)} \quad b + y \rightarrow c,$$
$$\text{(C)} \quad c + z \rightarrow a, \text{ etc.}[28]$$

26. Cf. Hartmann, Chap. 19, III, below.

27. Cf. Hartmann, Chap. 19, II, below.

28. The actual meaning of this formula is that environmental influences alter a state or a process of the organism; but the organization of these processes and states is such that once one of them is changed, it initiates others which in interaction with further environmental influences restore the original state. This conception is obviously only a model. The significance of this model is that it corresponds closely both to the psycho-analytic (tension-level lowering and stimulus-removing) conception (595) and the feed-back conception of the psychic apparatus (770, 195).

This formula is one of the several hints suggesting that it is Piaget's hope that his subject-matter is amenable to precise treatment in terms of the algebraic theory of groups and/or the general theory of the logic of relationships. See Piaget, Chap. 6, particularly notes 9 and 36, above. Cf. Russell (624) and Russell and Whitehead (626).

The processes (A), (B), etc., may consist either of chemical reactions (as when the organism ingests substances x which it transforms into substances b which are part of its structure), or some kind of physical transformation, or finally, and particularly, sensory-motor behavior (as when a cycle of body movements a combined with external movements x result in b which enters the cycle of organization).[29]

The relationship which unites the organized elements a, b, c, etc., with the x, y, z, etc., elements of the environment is called assimilation;[30] in other words, the functioning of the organism does not destroy, but rather preserves, the cycle of its organization and co-ordinates the givens of the environment so as to incorporate them into this cycle. Let us assume now that a change occurs in the environment which transforms x into x'. This may have two consequences. Either the organism does not adapt and the cycle breaks down; or the organized cycle is so changed that it again becomes a closed cycle and adaptation thereby occurs:

(A)　$a + x' \rightarrow b'$,[31]

(B)　$b' + y \rightarrow c$,

(C)　$c + z \rightarrow a$.

If we call this result of environmental pressures (the transformation of b into b') accommodation,[32] we may say that adaptation *is an equilibrium between assimilation and accommodation.*

29. It is clear that Piaget's model holds for metabolic and electrochemical processes which, by and large, cyclically restore the organismal equilibrium. The restorative, closed cycle character of sensory-motor organization may become clearer if we call to mind the self-regulating, feed-back character of sensory-motor co-ordination. For instance, in the case of visual-motor co-ordination: a is a visually guided motor action initiated to act on O (object), and x is a change arising either from the initiation of a and/or from O itself; b is the modified visually guided motor action and y is again a change arising either from the initiation of b and/or from O itself; etc. . . . Ideally, whatever b, c, d, etc., de-tour has been made, the process ends in the execution of action a on O. (Cf. Rapaport et al., 602, I, 249–53, 254–59, 271–75, 288–90). The model holds for *action* in general, if action is defined as the means of lowering the tension level of the organism. See Freud (209), pp. 533–34, 535–36. Cf. also Lewin (467, 464, and Chap. 5, above).

30. Cf. Piaget (558, pp. 281 ff.).

31. In Hartmann's (305) terms, x would be an event (element) of the "average expectable environment," while x' would be an event to which the organism has yet to learn to adapt (Chap. 19, note 37, below).

32. Cf. Piaget (561, pp. 227 ff).

This definition of adaptation also applies to intelligence. Actually, intelligence is *assimilation* in so far as it incorporates into its framework all the givens of experience. Intellectual adaptation always involves assimilation whether it is on the level of [conceptual] thinking which introduces the new into the known by means of judgment, thereby reducing the universe to its own terms, or on the level of sensory-motor intelligence which structures the things perceived by bringing them into its schema.[33] There are great differences between organic life (which develops material forms and assimilates the substances and energies of the environment into them), practical or sensory-motor intelligence (which organizes behavior and assimilates the diverse situations offered by the environment into the schemata of motor behavior), and reflective or gnostic intelligence (which merely thinks the forms or constructs them internally [34] in order to assimilate into them the contents of experience); yet all three are similar in that they adapt by assimilating the objects to the subject.

Intelligence is also *accommodation* to the environment, inasmuch as no pure assimilation ever occurs, since the existing schemata of intelligence are constantly modified in order to adjust them to the incorporated new elements. Conversely, objects are never known by themselves since the process of accommodation is always tied up with the inverse process of assimilation.[35] It follows that the concept of an object, far from being innate, is always a product of both assimilation and accommodation.

33. Piaget's term "sensory-motor schema" is related both to Murphy's (533, pp. 161–91) "canalization" concept and Bartlett's (37, pp. 199 ff.) schema, yet it stands in contrast to conceptual organization of contents on the level of thinking. Piaget stresses the commonality of schema and conceptual organization: both are assimilation processes.

34. "To think the forms" apparently refers to objects of experience, and "to construct them" to relations inherent to experience.

35. Piaget probably means that our knowledge of objects could be completely accurate only if we perceived them purely by accommodation, that is, if our nature could change to the nature of the object. This, however, is a contradiction in terms since the change would be—in any case—*our* change; therefore, no accommodation without assimilation. In our knowledge the nature of the object appears only in terms of our own schemata. Here one aspect of Piaget's epistemological stand becomes entirely clear. The object for him is just as unknowable (or knowable only in assymptotic approximation?) as was for Kant (367) the "Ding an sich" ("the thing by itself").

In brief, intellectual adaptation, like any other adaptation, is a succession of equilibria between the complementary mechanisms of assimilation and accommodation. The mind is adapted to reality only if accommodation is complete, that is, if no further change occurs in reality that would necessitate an alteration of the subject's schemata.[36] Conversely, there is no adaptation when a new reality imposes [on the organism] mental and motor attitudes contrary to those adopted through the contact with the givens of a previous reality: there is no adaptation without synthesis, that is to say, assimilation. There are many kinds of possible syntheses and the structure of the synthesis on the motor level is certainly entirely different from that on the reflective or the organic level.[37] But adaptation on any of these levels is an equilibrium of accommodation and assimilation: a stable system.

This brings us to the function of *organization*. From the biological point of view, organization is inseparable from adaptation. They are two complementary processes of the same mechanism, the first its internal, the second its external aspect.[38] We encounter this dual phenomenon, the functional totality and interdependence of organization and adaptation, in the reflective as well as in the practical forms of intelligence. We know full well that an organization is defined by the relationships between its parts and its whole, and similarly each element of an intellectual operation is relative to the others and so is each intellectual operation relative to other such operations.[39] Thus, each scheme is co-ordinated with all the others and is itself a totality of differentiated parts. Every act of intelligence presupposes a system of mutual implications and interconnected meanings. Thus the relationships between intellectual organization and adaptation are the same as those which obtain on the organic level: the principal "categories" intelligence uses in adapting to the external world—space and time, causality and substance, classification, number, and so on—correspond to aspects of reality just as each of the organs of the body

36. Presumably no such ideal state ever exists.

37. This is the counterpart in Piaget's genetic psychology of the synthetic function of the ego, described in psychoanalytic literature. Cf. note 12, above.

38. Piaget here means that organic existence has two aspects: (a) the organism is so organized internally as to perpetuate itself; (b) it is so organized that it can perpetuate itself in its given environment (that is, it is adapted to this environment).

39. This is merely a broad statement of the Gestalt principle. Cf. Wertheimer (762).

corresponds to a special characteristic of the environment.[40] These categories besides being adaptations to objects also imply each other to such an extent that it is impossible to isolate them logically.[41] The dual functional invariant of adaptation and organization expresses itself in the "accord of thoughts and objects" and in the "accord of thought with itself." These two aspects of thought are inseparable: thought organizes itself in adapting to objects, and thought structures objects in organizing itself.[42]

2. THE FUNCTIONAL INVARIANTS AND THE CATEGORIES OF REASON

Our task is now to discover the categories of reason which derive from the functional invariants, that is, those major forms of intellectual activity which are present at all stages of mental development. It is the first crystallization of their structure on the level of sensory-motor intelligence which we will describe in this volume.

Our investigation [of these categories of reason] will not reduce the higher levels of development to the lower. The history of science shows that attempts at establishing continuity between two disciplines does not result in a reduction of the higher levels of organization to the lower ones, but rather in establishing the interrelationships between the two without destroying the originality of the higher level of organization. The functional relationships which obtain between intellectual and biological organization do not diminish the value of reason, but rather extend the concept of vital adaptation.[43] It goes without saying, however, that though the categories of reason are in a sense

40. Piaget attempts here to systematize the most general forms of thought into a set of categories, as did Aristotle in his "Categories" (31) and Kant (367) in his "Critique." Piaget's categories originate in the mind as syntheses of the nature of the organism (organization) and of the influence of its environment (adaptation). This is a new solution of the ancient and vexing epistemological problem. Piaget conceived of his investigations not only as studies in human development but also as a genetic and empirical approach to the problems of epistemology. For a discussion of some of the speculative and deductive ap-

proaches to epistemology, see notes 5 and 6, above; also Chap. 6, pp. 154–55, and notes 6 and 7.

41. "Logically" here presumably means "deductively"; according to Piaget only genetic investigation can demonstrate that these are relatively independent fundamental categories, though they appear to imply each other mutually.

42. This is the genetic equivalent of Hegel's (315) crucial sociological dictum: "Man, in acting on nature to change it, changes his own nature."

43. The issue touched upon here is a cardinal one for all genetic investiga-

pre-formed in biological functioning, they are not contained in it either in the form of conscious or even unconscious structures.[44] Considering biological adaptation as a kind of material knowledge of the environment, we have to assume that a whole series of subsequent structures must be formed before a conscious and gnostic image can arise from this material knowledge which is actually no more than an action mechanism.[45] As already stated, the initial structures mediate between the organism and the immediate environment and express only their superficial relationships, while rational concepts which express functioning as such arise only at the completion of intellectual evolution. The analysis of the lower levels [of mental development] which we attempt in the present investigation is facilitated by the fact that the biological invariants just referred to do give rise to a sort of a priori functioning of reason, once they are reflected upon and elaborated by consciousness in the course of mental development.[46]

The following table summarizes our considerations:

Biological Functions		Intellectual Functions	Categories
Organization		Regulative Function	A. Totality × Relationship (reciprocity)
			B. Ideal (goal) × Value (means)
Adaptation	Assimilation	Implicative Function	A. Quality × Class
			B. Quantitative [47]* Rapport × Number
	Accommodation	Explicative Function	A. Object × Space
			B. Causality × Time

tions. The theories of "emergence," Gestalt-psychology, and Allport's (25) concept of "functional autonomy" are some of the attempts to meet this issue. The slow development of ego-psychology in psychoanalysis well illustrates that the "reductionist" daydream fades slowly in any given new field of investigation. The recognition of the relative independence of ego-organization and ego forces arose only slowly, hampered by exclusive concentration of interest on the dynamics of id forces. (Cf. Hartmann, Chap. 19, I, below.)

44. Piaget's point is that the categories of reason are pre-formed in biological functioning in the sense that the func-

tional invariants inherent to them are those already present in biological functioning. This "pre-formation" is "potential" rather than "actual," and refers, therefore, neither to conscious, nor to unconscious structures.

45. Piaget does not mean a conscious image of the category itself. See note 16, above.

46. The phrases "rational concepts which express functioning as such" and "once [biological invariants] are reflected upon and elaborated by consciousness" may give rise to the same misunderstanding commented on in notes 44 and 45, above.

47.* We distinguish here between re-

The categories of reason related to the biological function of organization are, to use Hoeffding's [48] term, "fundamental or regulative categories," that is to say, they combine with all the other categories and are present in all psychic operations. It seems to me that these categories can be described from the static point of view by the concepts *totality* and *relationship*, and from the dynamic point of view by the concepts *ideal* and *value*.

The concept of totality expresses the interdependence inherent to all organization, intellectual as well as biological. Even though in the first few weeks of existence, behavior and consciousness seem to emerge in the most incoordinate fashion, they do derive from and are continuations of a physiological organization that preceded them, and they do crystallize little by little into more precise systems of synthesis. For instance, the concept of "displacement groups," [49] which is essential to the development of space, is but a manifestation of the organized totality in the form of movement. Similarly, all the other

---

lationships, in the most general sense of the word, and "quantitative rapport," which corresponds on the level of thought to the "logic of relations." In contrast to the logic of classes, the relationships encompassed by the "logic of relations" are always quantitative, whether they represent a comparison of "more" or "less" (as for instance in "darker" and "lighter," etc.) or express ideas of order or series (as for instance in kinship relations, like "brother of," etc.). Unlike both of these, those relationships which are on the same level as the idea of totality imply only general relatedness in the broadest sense of the term (for instance, interrelatedness among the elements of a totality) but no quantitative relations.

[Concerning Piaget's ideas on the "logic of classes" and "logic of relations," see (558, pp. 294–300), and Chap. 6, note 37, above. Piaget's distinction of the three kinds of relations is clear: (a) the

most general relations are those applying to totalities; they express mutual interdependence and are non-specific (a probable example are the relations obtaining within the totality of the restless movements of the infant); (b) the qualitative relations defining classes, which are the subject-matter of classical logic, are more specific, but not amenable to general and formalized (algebraic) treatment; (c) the relations treated by the logic of relations are indeed the most specific and amenable to exact formal treatment. Yet it is hard to see in what sense—except for the purpose of contrasting them with classes—Piaget considers them quantitative, since their main virtue in mathematical logic is that they permit exact treatment of non-quantitative terms.]

48. See Hoeffding (332).

49. See Piaget, Chap. 6, particularly notes 9 and 36, above. Cf. also pp. 162–63, above.

patterns of sensory-motor intelligence are ruled from their inception, both in their relation to each other and in their internal organization, by the law of totality. The same law operates when a causal relationship transforms an inco-ordinated given of the external world into organized environment, and so on.[50]

Hoeffding demonstrated conclusively that the idea of relationship is the correlate of the idea of totality.[51] Actually relationship is also a fundamental category since it is implied in all psychic activities and thus combines with all other concepts. This is so because every totality is a system of relationships and relationships in turn are segments of a totality. It is thus that relationships are already present in the strictly physiological activities and recur at all later levels of development. Primitive perceptions are relative to each other and form organic totalities. (Koehler has demonstrated this for the color perception of chickens.) [52] To list analogous facts on the level of reflective thought would be superfluous.

The categories of *ideal* and *value* represent the dynamic aspect of the [organization] function. By the term "ideal" we designate every system of values which constitutes a whole, hence the final goals of actions; and by the term "value" we designate the specific values related to these wholes, hence the means leading to these goals. Ideal and value are related in the same way as are totality and relation. Ideals and values are totalities in the making, values being merely the expression of desirability on the various levels [of organization]. Actually, desirability is an index showing that an equilibrium has been disrupted or a totality [in the making] has not yet been consummated.[53] It is an indicator that a missing element is sought or is to be created in order that

50. In what sense the categories "totality" and "relationship" are static is not clear unless the term is equivalent here to "formal." Indeed these categories say merely that intelligence is an organization and therefore anything that becomes its subject-matter is incorporated into its totality, becoming related to all its other elements. This in essence is also the pattern underlying the "synthetic function of the ego" although in that function it takes a far more specific (and little explored) form.

51. See Hoeffding (332).

52. See Koehler (395).

53. These categories refer to that realm of behavior in which dynamic psychology (psychoanalysis, Lewinian psychology, etc.) centered: motives—means—goals. The correspondence of Piaget's concepts of "desirability" and "ideals" to the psychoanalytic concepts "drives"

equilibrium be attained. Since ideals are merely as yet unattained equilibria of real totalities, and values but the relations of the means subserving these, the relationship of ideals to values is of the same order as those of totalities to relations. Finality is therefore not a special category but only the subjective representation of the tendency toward equilibrium. A process tending toward equilibrium does not imply finality but only a distinction between a real and an ideal equilibrium.[54] Good examples of this point are the norms of synthesis and unity of logical thought. They represent a perpetual tendency of intellectual totalities toward equilibrium and define the ideal equilibrium, which though never attained by intelligence, nevertheless regulates the values implied in judgment. The operations related to totality and values we will therefore call "regulative functions," in contrast to the explicative and implicative functions.[55*]

---

and "satisfying objects," or to the Lewinian concepts "needs" and "goal (valence) objects" is not altogether clear. However, the fact that Piaget considers "desirability" an index of disequilibrium seems to correspond closely to Lewin's conceptualization of needs as "psychic-tension systems" (Chap. 5, above), and to the psychoanalytic conceptualization of drive regulation by the pleasure-principle (Chap. 15, above), according to which psychological processes tend toward a reduction of tension.

It is noteworthy that Piaget speaks of "desirability on the various levels." One of the main deficiencies of topological (Lewinian) psychology is that—excepting for the early distinction (Chap. 5, above) between needs and quasi-needs —it does not account for the hierarchy of various motivating forces. The recent developments in psychoanalytic ego-psychology seem to point toward an increasing recognition of the hierarchy of observed motivations. Cf. Chap. 23, IV, below; see also Rapaport (591, pp. 78–79, 100–1, 269–70).

54. "Finality" here means "teleology," the determination of processes by the goals they subserve, rather than by causes. Piaget indicates that though values and ideals may appear in subjective experience to be the *determining goals* of actions, the actual *determining cause* is the disrupted equilibrium which (like all energy distributions) tends toward a reestablishment of the equilibrium. For a discussion of causality vs. teleology in the structure of psychoanalytic concepts, see Chap. 15, notes 2 and 9, below.

55.* In "The Language and Thought of the Child," [561, p. 237], we designated the synthesis of implication and explication as "mixed function." Here we have associated this synthesis with the concept of organization. These amount to the same thing: organization implies a synthesis of assimilation and accommodation.

[The concepts of the explicative and the implicative functions are further discussed below. Piaget (561, p. 234) defines them as follows:

What is our conception of the categories related to adaptation, that is to say, assimilation and accommodation? According to Hoeffding [56] there are among the categories of thought some which are more "real" and others, more "formal." The more real ones imply, in addition to the activity of reason a *here* and a *now* inherent to experience; such are, for instance, causality, substance or object, space and time, each of which is a synthesis of [external] givens and deduction. The more formal ones, though not any less adapted [to reality], can give rise to unlimited deductive elaborations, as, for example, logical relations and mathematics. The more real ones represent the more centrifugal processes of accommodation and explication; the more formal ones make possible the assimilation of objects into the intellectual organization and the construction of implications.

The implicative function comprises two functional invariants present at all stages [of mental development]. One of these functional invariants corresponds to the synthesis of *qualities*, that is to say, *classes* (concepts or schemata); the other to that of *quantitative relations* or *numbers*.[57] Actually these elementary tools of intelligence already reveal their mutual dependence in the sensory-motor schemata. The explicative function comprises those operations which permit us to deduce what is real, that is to say, those which guarantee a certain permanence [of reality] and [yet, at the same time] provide reasons for its changes. Consequently, every explication has two complementary aspects. One of these is related to the elaboration of *objects* and the other to *causality;* the former is a product of the latter and of its developmental stage. Thus we arrive at the categories: object x space and causality x time, in which the interdependence of functions is complicated by the reciprocal relation of matter to form.

We see that the functional categories of knowledge form a genuine whole which follows the pattern of the functions of intelligence. This correspondence between the categories of knowledge and the functions of intelligence becomes even more clear in the analysis of the relations of organization to adaptation on the one hand, and assimilation to accommodation on the other.

Considering the interdependence of elements already adapted rather than

---

The explicatory function is the centrifugal moment, in which the mind turns to the external world; the implicatory function is the centripetal, in which the mind turns inwards to the analysis of intentions and of their relations.

56. Hoeffding (332).
57. Cf. note 47*, above.

the adaptation process itself, we have seen that organization is actually the internal aspect of adaptation. Seen from another vantage point, adaptation is simply organization at grips with environmental occurrences. This interdependence recurs on the level of intelligence not only in the interaction of rational activity (organization) with experience (adaptation), which have proved inseparable throughout the history of scientific thought, but also in the interdependence of the functional categories. Actually no objective, causal, spatial-temporal structure is feasible without logical-mathematical deduction; these two kinds of realities constitute mutually interrelated systems of totalities and relations.[58] The interdependence of assimilation and accommodation, that is to say, of explication and implication, is [also] well illustrated by Hume's way of posing the problem of causality: how can the concept of cause be simultaneously rational and experimental? If causality becomes a purely formal category, it fails to take account of reality (E. Meyerson has admirably demonstrated this), while if causality is reduced to a mere empirical sequence, it becomes superfluous. Therefore, the Kantian solution, adopted also by Brunschvicg: [59] causality is an "analogy of experience," that is to say, an irreducible interaction between the relation of implication and the spatial-temporal givens. About the other "real" categories, only this much: they all assume implication of and are accommodations to external givens. Conversely, classes and numbers could not be constructed without the spatial-temporal series inherent in objects and their causal relations. In conclusion, it remains to be noted that just as every organ of the living body is itself organized, so is every element of an intellectual organization itself an organization. Since the functional categories of intelligence develop along the major lines of the essential mechanisms of organization, assimilation and accommodation, they have aspects corresponding to these three functions. . . . How the functions characteristic of the principal categories of the mind crystallize into structures [which despite a relative permanence, ceaselessly change in specific form] and create their own organs is the subject-matter of this entire investigation.

58. This formulation may suggest that genetically the concepts of object, cause, space, time, do not arise without the development of logic and mathematics. This is most certainly not what Piaget meant; he argues here merely the interdependence of the explicative and implicative functions and of the categories corresponding to them. See his table of categories above.

59. Brunschvicg (101).

PART THREE

SYMBOLISM

REPORT ON A METHOD OF ELICITING AND OBSERVING CERTAIN SYMBOLIC HALLUCINATION-PHENOMENA [1]

By Herbert Silberer

THE FOLLOWING is a discussion of an experimental approach to the explanation of dreams. This method has scarcely been used, though the experiments of A. Maury [2] and G. Trumball Ladd [3] appear to imply it. I came upon these phenomena in self-observation quite by accident and was led thus to this experimental method. The findings it yields do not uncover anything that could not be derived theoretically from the psychology of dreams of Professor S. Freud; since they so admirably fit the relationships Freud discovered, they may be taken as striking demonstrations of them (particularly of that "third" factor in dream work which Freud calls "regard for representability" which he treats in Section VI D of "The Interpretation of Dreams").[4]

The origin of my observations can be briefly told. One afternoon (after lunch) I was lying on my couch. Though extremely sleepy, I forced myself to think through a problem of philosophy, which was to compare the views of Kant and Schopenhauer concerning time. In my drowsiness I was unable to sus-

1. Silberer (689).
2. Maury (505, 506, 507). See Freud (208, pp. 17–18); in the translation incorporated in *The Basic Writings of Sigmund Freud* (209) the chapter dealing with this material was omitted.
3. Ladd (440). See Freud (208, p. 23).
4. Freud (209, pp. 514 ff.). The issue of "regard for representability" is: (a) dreams have a perceptual, mostly visual, character; (b) thus the dream-work, the process of dream-formation, among other tasks must represent perceptually

the latent dream-thought; (c) Freud (209, p. 361) wrote:

Whatever is pictorial *is capable of representation* in dreams and can be fitted into a situation in which abstract expression would confront the dream-representation with difficulties not unlike those which would arise if a political leading article had to be represented in an illustrated journal;

(d) in this connection see 209, pp. 492–93, noting particularly the conclusion: "In [dream-] regression the structure of the dream-thought breaks up into its raw material." See also *ibid.*, pp. 485–86.

tain their ideas side by side. After several unsuccessful attempts, I once more fixed Kant's argument in my mind as firmly as I could and turned my attention to Schopenhauer's. But when I tried to reach back to Kant, his argument was gone again, and beyond recovery. The futile effort to find the Kant record which was somehow misplaced in my mind suddenly represented itself to me— as I was lying there with my eyes closed, as in a dream—as a perceptual symbol: I am asking a morose secretary for some information; he is leaning over his desk and disregards me entirely; he straightens up for a moment to give me an unfriendly and rejecting look.

The vividness of the unexpected phenomenon surprised, indeed almost frightened me. I was impressed by the appropriateness of this unconsciously selected symbol. I sensed what might be the conditions for the occurrence of such phenomena, and decided to be on the lookout for them and even to attempt to elicit them. In the beginning I hoped that this would yield a key to "natural symbolism." [5] From its relation to art-symbolism I expected and still expect the clarification of many psychological, characterological, and aesthetic issues.

My intuitive impression as to the conditions for the phenomenon proved true. Experience showed they were two: (a) drowsiness, (b) an effort to think. The former is a passive condition not subject to will, the latter an active one manipulatable by the will. It is the struggle of these two antagonistic elements that elicits the experience which I call the "autosymbolic" phenomenon.

It can be described as an hallucinatory experience which puts forth "automatically," as it were, an adequate symbol for what is thought (or felt) at a given instant. It is essential that neither of the two conditions outweigh the other; their struggle should remain unsettled so that the scales which were to measure their relative weight would oscillate indecisively.

The prevailing of the first condition would lead to sleep, the prevailing of the second one to ordered normal thinking. The "autosymbolic" phenomenon comes about only in a transitional state between sleep and waking, that is, in the hypnagogic state, the twilight between sleep and waking.

It is not maintained here that a translation of thoughts into pictures occurs

5. The exploration of "natural symbolism" is the search for the laws determining the images that may be co-ordinated with given ideas as their symbols. See in this connection Freud (209, pp. 368–96), and E. Jones (360, pp. 154–211).

only in the hypnagogic state. Freud's "The Interpretation of Dreams" [6] shows clearly that it is one of the essential features of dream-formation. We maintain only that translation of thoughts into pictures in the hypnagogic state occurs in relative isolation from the other dream-forming factors. This offers three distinct heuristic advantages: first, experimental analysis of a complex function (which Freud showed dreams to be) which may yield a verification of theoretical deductions; secondly, observation of the factors of dream-work in an isolated and "relatively pure" form, which may shed light upon the interrelation of the dream-factors; [7] thirdly—and this seems to me the most important advantage—a direct and exact observation of one dream-factor which is not feasible with dreams. Before I discuss this point I should like to dwell on the autosymbolic phenomenon itself.

This phenomenon must be considered a "regression process" [8] as hypothesized by Freud in terms of the ψ-systems [9] and their "directions." [10] My experience so far suggests that autosymbolic phenomena can be classified into three groups. These groups are not proposed as genetic differentiations, but merely as a useful classification. These groups are not based on the form of appearance

6. Freud, S. (209).

7. These dream factors are described by Freud (209, pp. 485–86), as follows:

The dream is a psychic act full of import; its motive power is invariably a wish-craving fulfilment; the fact that it is unrecognizable as a wish, and its many peculiarities and absurdities are due to the influence of psychic censorship to which it has been subjected during its formation. Besides the necessity of evading the censorship, the following factors have played a part in its formation: first, a necessity for condensing the psychic material; second, regard for representability in sensory images; and third (though not constantly) regard for a rational and intelligible exterior of the dream structure. From each of these propositions a path leads onward to psychological postulates and assumptions. Thus the reciprocal relation of the wish-motives, and the four conditions [censorship and the enumerated three] as well as the mutual relations of these conditions must now be investigated; the dream must be inserted in the context of psychic life.

Cf. (209, p. 467). For a detailed discussion see *ibid.*, Chap. VII.

8. It seems obvious that Silberer meant here "result of a regression process" and not "a regression process."

9. For a discussion of the ψ-systems see Freud (209, pp. 488 ff.); note particularly middle of p. 492; also Chap. 16, note 6, below.

10. The word *Stroemungen* has been varyingly translated in *The Basic Writings* as "stream" and "current." Freud uses the word to describe the flow of waking excitation from the receptors to motility, as well as the course excitation takes in dreams, which he demonstrates follows the opposite direction. In Silberer's context *Stroemungen* refers only to the direction. Cf., however, Freud (209, pp. 492 and 493).

of the phenomenon, but on the content symbolized in them. They are: I. Material (or content) phenomena; II. Functional (or effort) phenomena; and III. Somatic phenomena.

I. *Material (content) phenomena* are those which consist of autosymbolic representations of thought-contents, that is, of contents dealt with in a thought-process. These may be mere ideas, groups of ideas, concepts used in comparisons or in definition procedures, or they may be judgments and conclusions, subserving analytic or synthetic operations, and so on.

In a state of drowsiness I contemplate an abstract topic such as the nature of transsubjectively (for all people) valid judgments. A struggle between active thinking and drowsiness sets in. The latter becomes strong enough to disrupt normal thinking and to allow—in the twilight-state so produced—the appearance of an autosymbolic phenomenon. The content of my thought presents itself to me immediately in the form of a perceptual (for an instant apparently real) picture: I see a big circle (or transparent sphere) in the air with people around it whose heads reach into the circle. This symbol expresses practically everything I was thinking of. The transsubjective judgment is valid for all people without exception: the circle includes all the heads. The validity must have its grounds in a commonality: the heads belong all in the same homogeneous sphere. Not all judgments are transsubjective: the body and limbs of the people are outside (below) the sphere as they stand on the ground as independent individuals. In the next instant [11]* I realize that it is a dream-picture; the thought that gave rise to it, which I had forgotten for the moment, now comes back and I recognize the experience as an "autosymbolic" phenomenon.

What had happened? In my drowsiness my abstract ideas were, without my conscious interference, replaced by a perceptual picture—by a symbol.

My abstract chain of thoughts was hampered; I was too tired to go on thinking in that form; the perceptual picture emerged as an "easier" form of thought. It afforded an appreciable relief, comparable to the one experienced when sitting down after a strenuous walk. It appears to follow—as a corollary—that such "picture-thinking" requires less effort than the usual kind.[12] The tired consciousness, not having at its disposal the energy necessary for normal think-

11.* I did not go to sleep.

12. Cf. Freud on the role of hyper-cathexis (209, pp. 535–36 and 546); also

Chap. 15, notes 21 and 30, and Chap. 23, note 20*, below.

ing, switches to an easier form of functioning.[13] According to Freud's considerations in "The Psychology of the Dream Process" (the last chapter of "The
Interpretation of Dreams") [14] this is in many respects a primitive form of thinking.[15]

This typical example of the "material" phenomenon shows with what clarity
and certainty the relationship between thought-content and the picture symbolizing it can be demonstrated. The manner in which these "autosymbolic"
phenomena come about gives a clue to their systematic exploration: the
thought-content [16] can be varied at will. The difficulty lies in enforcing certain
thought activities to occur under the most unsuitable conditions. The maintenance of the desirable labile condition [17] requires some training.

II. *Functional (effort) phenomena* are those autosymbolic experiences
which represent the condition of the subject experiencing them or the effectiveness of his consciousness. They are here called "functional phenomena" because they have to do with the mode of functioning of consciousness (quick,
slow, easy, difficult, relaxed, gay, successful, fruitless, strained, and so on) and
not with the content of the thought-act.

This second group of autosymbolic phenomena demonstrates that the symbolizing function of consciousness [18] deals not only with the content of thought;

13. Cf. Freud on consciousnes: (209,
pp. 544 ff.), also Chap. 16, note 14, below.

14. Freud (209, Chap. VII, pp.
468 ff.).

15. See particularly *ibid.*, pp. 493–94,
495, 497.

16. Namely, the content of that
thought on which the subject concentrates.

17. "Labile condition" refers to the
state in which drowsiness does neither
change into sleep nor allow for ordered
normal thinking.

18. The verbatim translation is "the
symbolizing power of consciousness."
But since Silberer appears to conceive of
symbolization as thinking on an energy
level lower than that prevailing in
ordered normal thinking, it was deemed
advisable to translate it as "function." It
may even be questioned whether it is
permissible to attribute this symbolizing
function to "consciousness." It could be
argued that the concept consciousness
becomes too broad if it includes two so
widely differing states as waking and
drowsiness. If its realm is to be broadened
beyond that of waking consciousness
then its definition must be narrowed to
the characteristics which are common to
all states. But what is to prevent us then
from here classing together the states of
consciousness of dreams, fugues, twilight
states, loss of personal identity, and considering the state of consciousness of
each of these a form-variant of "consciousness"? We should, however, first
establish the characteristics common to
all these states of consciousness. These

often it is the mode of functioning of the thought-process that is symbolically represented. One of the most preferred themes of the symbolizing function is the struggle between the two antagonists: the will to think and the resistance of drowsiness. The latter is usually personified, while the will remains the "I." [19]

The feelings [20] which accompany, with greater or lesser clarity, the thought-processes in the hypnagogic state are the preferred subject-matter of functional symbolization. These feelings are most characteristically expressed in those phenomena which represent tiredness or the struggle against it. Because of this preferred theme the functional phenomenon serves as the transition to a third group, the somatic phenomena. As we shall try to show, this third group must be—in a certain sense—separated from the other two.

III. *Somatic phenomena* are those autosymbolic phenomena which reflect *somatic* conditions of any kind: external or internal sensations, such as pressure, tension, temperature, external pain and position sensations, sensations of the joints and muscles, coenesthesias,[21] acoustic, optic, chemical, and mechanical

---

common characteristics would then constitute the new definition of consciousness. It goes without saying that "the symbolizing function" here discussed will *not* be one of these common *general* characteristics: it is not the work of a "power of consciousness"; rather it emerges where abstractive generalization—a distinguishing specific characteristic of waking consciousness—is conspicuous by its absence. Cf. Chap. 13, notes 21, 22, 30, 47, 50, below.

19. One of the outstanding characteristics of the consciousness of the normal waking-state is the sharp distinction made between I and not-I. It distinguishes the "self" from external impressions and from internal—unconscious—impulses. It prevents our mistaking our "empathy" with other people for a "reading-their-minds." It prevents our fear "lest others know our thoughts" from turning into the delusional experience of "our mind is being read." Per-

sonification of the drowsiness, while the "will" remains the "I," appears to indicate that distinguishing between I and not-I is preserved to some extent even in the hypnagogic states Silberer observed. In other states of consciousness parts of the self may not be so perceived. Multiple personalities, and some schizophrenic states, are commonly known examples. My observations show that such states of consciousness occur in the hypnagogic condition also, when drowsiness gains the upper hand. It is conceivable that Silberer observed only one of many possible hypnagogic states of consciousness.

20. The German *Gefuehl* is a much more ambiguous word than the English "feeling" which here translates it. It can be rendered as feeling, emotion, or affect.

21. *Gemeinempfindungen* is the German word. It refers to undifferentiated general feeling-tone of self-experience. The term "coenesthesia," as used by

stimulations,[22] and sensation complexes. For example: pressure of a blanket on the foot, itching of the nose, rheumatic pains in the joints, a breeze touching the cheek, palpitation, noise, the scent of flowers, anxiety, apnoeia, and so forth.

These are the most common dream-producing stimuli. As they have been extensively studied [23] our hypnagogic experiences can make here but few contributions.

The somatic autosymbolic phenomena differ from those of the two previous groups. For them the conditions described—drowsiness and effort to think—undergo certain modifications. The "effort to think" is irrelevant in the genesis of the phenomena of this group, and in the struggle against drowsiness the "will" is replaced by sensations or feelings. To bring about and maintain the twilight state favorable for these autosymbolic phenomena, it is sufficient that the tendency of drowsiness to fade into sleep be hampered to just the right degree. Here I should like to point out that the somatic phenomenon may be the hypnagogic variant of those dreams which serve to awaken us.[24*]

We are now justified in generalizing the scheme of our two antagonistic conditions and in broadening them to (a) drowsiness, and (b) interference with falling asleep.

I shall now offer some examples for my three groups of phenomena. The majority of the examples I observed on myself. I must add that the three types of phenomena are often tangled so that the groups cannot always be sharply separated.

My observations show that the material for symbols is taken mostly from recent experiences.[25*]

That relationship which allows a content to be represented by a symbol I shall call the "symbol-basis" for short. The "symbol-basis," then, is the *tertium comparationis* [26] of symbolism.

Ribot, is the only term known to the translator which approximates this meaning and has gained some acceptance in psychological literature. See Ribot (608, p. 108). See also Hinsie and Schatsky (330), *Psychiatric Dictionary:* "Coenesthetic, from the Greek Koenos: common, and Aisthesis: sensibility."

22. The word "stimulation" stands here for the cumbersome expression "impressions and nerve-stimulations."

23. See pp. 15–28 in Freud (208). The corresponding chapter is omitted in *The Basic Writings.*

24.* Freud (208, p. 337).

25.* Freud (208, Section V).

26. *Tertium comparationis* = the third term of the comparison

GROUP I (MATERIAL PHENOMENA)

EXAMPLE I. My thought is: I am to improve a halting passage in an essay.

Symbol: I see myself planing a piece of wood.

EXAMPLE 2. I think of human understanding probing into the foggy and diffi-cult problem of the "Mothers" (Faust, Part II).[27]

Symbol: I stand alone on a stone jetty extending out far into a dark sea. The waters of the ocean and the dark and mysteriously heavy air unite at the hori-zon.

Interpretation: The jetty in the dark sea corresponds to the probing into the difficult problem. The uniting of air and water, the elimination of the distinction between above and below, should symbolize that, with the Mothers, as Mephistopheles describes it,[28] all times and places shade into each other so that there are no boundaries between "here" and "there," "above" and "below." It is in this sense that Mephistopheles says to Faust: "Now you may sink!—I could just as well say: rise."

EXAMPLE 3. My thoughts center around a dramatic scene, where one actor indicates to the other, without saying so outright, that he knows about a certain state of affairs.

Symbol: I see the scene (unclearly) as one actor is putting a hot metal beaker into the hand of the other. I feel the heat of it myself. (Apparently I have put myself—for the moment—in the place of the second actor.)

27. See Goethe's *Faust* (277, pp. 219-20). Faust promised the king to show him Helena and Paris. He asks Mephis-topheles to arrange this. Mephistopheles balks: one would have to turn to the *Mothers*, the highest goddesses of crea-tion, to achieve this feat. The passage reads as follows:

Mephistopheles:
   Loth am I higher secrets to unfold.
   In solitude, where reigns nor space nor time,
   Are goddesses enthroned from early prime;

'Tis hard to speak of beings so sublime—
   The Mothers are they.
Faust (terrified):
   Mothers!
Mephistopheles:
   Tremblest thou?
Faust:
   The Mothers! Mothers! strange it sounds,
                                    I trow!
Mephistopheles:
   And is so: Goddesses, to men unknown,
   And by us named unwillingly, I own.

28. Goethe's *Faust* (277, p. 210), Part II, Act 1, line 1663.

Interpretation: The actor expresses something without words: the beaker is in a state that does not show in its form.

EXAMPLE 4. I decide to dissuade someone from carrying out a dangerous resolution. I want to tell him: "If you do that, grave misfortune will befall you."

Symbol: I see three gruesome-looking riders on black horses storming by over a dusky field under leaden skies.

EXAMPLE 5. I am trying to think of [29] the purpose of the metaphysical studies I am about to undertake. That purpose is—I reflect—to work my way through ever higher forms of consciousness, that is, levels of existence, in my quest after the basis [30] of existence.

Symbol: I run a long knife under a cake as though to take a slice out of it.

Interpretation: My movement with the knife represents "working my way through." To clarify this apparently silly symbol I must give a detailed explanation. The symbol-basis, that is, the relationship which makes the picture here chosen usable for autosymbolic representation, is the following. At the dining-table it is at times my chore to cut and distribute the cake. I do this with a long and flexible knife, necessitating considerable care. It is particularly difficult to lift the slices; the knife must be carefully pushed *under* the slice (this is the slow "working my way through" to arrive at the "basis"). There is yet more symbolism in the picture. The symbol is a layer-cake, so that the knife cutting it penetrates several layers [31] (levels of consciousness and existence).

EXAMPLE 6. My thought is: I do not need to get the theater tickets anymore, I have them already.

Symbol: For once, this thought-content is represented by both an acoustic and a visual phenomenon. I hear a melody in which syncopation occurs repeatedly. Simultaneously I see the notes of the music.

29. There is no direct English equivalent for the German word *vergegenwaertigen*. To "visualize" is a close approximation. Its use would be, however, confusing in the present context which deals with visual representations.

30. The German expression *Daseins-gruende* has a causal connotation which is lost in this translation.

31. The German noun *Schichte* means "layer," yet is often used in contexts where our term would be "level." This ambiguous use of the noun facilitates the understanding of the symbol in German, but hampers its rendering in English.

Symbol-basis: "Syncopated notes" continue into the new beat; they have already been "taken care of" (in the previous beat).[32]

Symbol-source: A few days earlier I had heard the melody used in the symbol. The player, yielding to his primitive sense of rhythm, sounded every one of the syncopated notes in the new beat.[32]

EXAMPLE 7. In opposition to the Kantian view, I am attempting to conceive of time as a "concept." Thus the individual time-span should be related to the totality-of-time as a particular mass of matter to the total-mass of matter of the same category. This attempt to force a problem into a preconceived scheme results in the following symbol:

Symbol: I am pressing a Jack-in-the-Box into the box. But every time I take my hand away it bounces out gaily on its spiral spring.

Comment: This example already bears the earmarks of the next group.

GROUP II (FUNCTIONAL PHENOMENA)

EXAMPLE 8. Before falling asleep I want to review an idea in order not to forget it.

Symbol: Suddenly a lackey in livery stands before me as though waiting for my orders. This is analogous to the symbol of the "morose secretary."[33] This time, however, I experience no difficulty in thinking and expect to carry out my task, which this time is less difficult. Hence the symbol of the helpful rather than of the angry assistant.

EXAMPLE 9. I lose the thread of my thought. I make an effort to pick it up again, but must admit that I have lost the connecting link.

Symbol: A piece of type-setting with the last few lines gone.

EXAMPLE 10. I am thinking about something. Pursuing a subsidiary consideration, I depart from my original theme. When I attempt to return to it, an autosymbolic phenomenon occurs.

Symbol: I am out mountain climbing. The mountains near me conceal the farther ones from which I came and to which I want to return.

---

32. The definition of syncopation, and therefore the explanation of the symbol, seems less than adequate.

33. See p. 196, above.

EXAMPLE 11. I am considering how I should have a certain person act in a scene (of a play I was writing). It becomes difficult to keep the problem sharply in the center of my consciousness. Before long I hardly know what it was I wanted. (I have reached the characteristic state which gives rise to symbols.) Now I perceive a visual image: I am peeling an apple. The arrival of this symbol interests me and wakes me up. I am thinking of the apple and cannot explain its significance. So I try to pick up my original trend of thought—concerning the scene. Lo and behold, I continue peeling where I left off. The meaning of this peeling suddenly becomes clear. To understand it one must know the symbol-basis. In peeling apples I sometimes attempt to get the peel off in one continuous, not spiral but rather serpentine, strip. I succeed only if I don't lose the connection at the curvatures. In this instance there was such a curvature between the first and the second step of peeling (as the changed position of the apple in my hand clearly showed). The symbol thus represents my effort to secure a connecting link which threatens to break.

This *functional* explanation of the phenomenon seems more convincing than the *material* one, though both are feasible. My task was to have that person act in the play so that his acting would yield *a formally consistent transition* (*continuous* peel) between his previous behavior and the ending of the play, already determined.

It is, however, not out of the question that both relationships, the functional as well as the material, partook in the symbol-formation (overdetermination).

EXAMPLE 12. (Situation): Slumber after the morning alarm went off. I remained in my bed for a little while with the dim wish not to oversleep. Thus my sleep was superficial.

Symbol: An "automatic thermo-clock." (A clock driven by a swinging horizontal bar. The up and down movements of the bar are effected by the intermittent heating of a ball on one end of the bar. Under the ball an alcohol lamp flames up as soon as bar and ball descend to it. When warmed, the bar ascends again. Obviously, there is a liquid of low boiling point in the ball—though one cannot see it externally—which evaporates into the hollow bar, and then, when cooled and condensed, flows back into the ball.)

Symbol-basis: The horizontal bar (state of consciousness) cannot sink deep (into sleep): as soon as it starts sinking, the little flame (attention) sends it upwards (into waking).

Symbol-source: A few days before I had seen a drawing of such a clock in a science review.

GROUP III (SOMATIC PHENOMENA)

EXAMPLE 13. I take a deep breath, my chest expands.

Symbol: With the help of someone, I lift a table high.

EXAMPLE 14. My blanket rests so heavily on one of my toes that it makes me nervous.

Symbol: The top of a decorated canopied carriage scrapes against the branches of trees. A lady hits her hat against the top of her compartment.

Symbol-source: I had attended a flower parade that day. The high decorations of the carriages often reached to the branches of the trees.

EXAMPLE 15. I have a rhinolaringitis with a painful irritation which forces me to swallow saliva steadily. Fever.

Symbol: Each time I am about to swallow I have a picture of a water bottle which I am supposed to swallow; after each swallow another one takes its place.

Comment on somatic phenomena: Somatic components are frequent symbol-sources of Groups I and II. Thus in Example 1 (for material phenomena) the position of the piece of wood I am planing is that of my lower arm; I really feel that my lower arm represents this piece of wood.[34] Here a most recent sensation [35] serves as a symbol-source.

MIXED PHENOMENA

EXAMPLE 16. In conclusion I shall describe a complicated phenomenon, interesting because of a remarkable concentration of the various symbol-forming processes.

I am in a train and very tired. With my eyes closed, I am leaning against the corner of the compartment. Time and again the setting sun shines into my face. It disturbs me but I am too tired to get up and draw the shade. So I let it shine

34. This is a literal translation of Silberer's phrase. I assume that he means "this piece of wood represents my lower arm."

35. Presumably this refers to the postural sensation of the lower arm.

on me and watch the visual impressions that come as the sunshine hits my eye-lids. Remarkably enough, the figures are different each time, but each time uniform. This is apparently a specific apperception-phenomenon.[36]* I see first a mosaic of triangles, then one of squares, and so on. Then I have the impression that I myself am putting together the mosaic figures in rhythmical movements. Soon I find that the rhythm is that of the axles of the train, which I hear con-tinuously. This suggests the idea that autosymbolic pictures can be influenced by acoustic perceptions; thus a person talking to someone who is in a hypna-gogic state could direct his imagery.[37]

All of a sudden the following autosymbolic phenomenon occurs: I see an old lady, to the right, setting a table with a checkered table-cloth, each square of which encloses a figure resembling one of the sun-mosaics previously men-tioned; the figures are all different.

The person setting the table of my imagination with a variety of pictures represents my idea of the possibility of influencing autosymbolic phenomena from the outside.

Another symbol-source must also be mentioned here: the previous evening I had a talk with an elderly lady who told me a medley of tales of her life. It was late and I was already tired. I sat at a table with the lady on my right.

36.* All I mean is that the uniting of light-impressions into various geometri-cal figures is not in the sensory-impres-sions but in their apperception.

[The distinction between sensory-impression and apperception can be con-sidered dated. The hope to isolate "pure sensations" is all but given up. H. Head (314), W. Koehler (397), Schilder (Chap. 25, pp. 519–20, below), and others showed that perception (sensa-tion) is always an integration of the new stimulation with previous similar stimu-lations, as well as with the prevailing state of the organism. The selective, elaborative, integrative, and interpreta-tive role once attributed exclusively to apperception was demonstrated by Gestalt-psychology to take place also in what was previously considered pure perception.]

37. The relationship of this observa-tion to synesthesias (755, pp. 86 ff.), and intersensory effects in general (338) is obvious. Silberer's formulation suggests new experimental possibilities.

CHAPTER 9

ON SYMBOL-FORMATION [1]

By Herbert Silberer

WITH THE PASSAGE OF TIME it has become increasingly clear that the psycho-analytic method, developed by S. Freud, can be applied to many and varied fields of study. Having originated in an ingenious conception of certain phenomena of neuroses, it grew beyond these and, steadily increasing in stature, found application in realms undreamed of in the beginning. . . .[2] The method is proving itself as fruitful in the psychology of healthy persons as in that of sick, in that of groups as in that of individuals.

Whatever issue the psychoanalyst may tackle, one of his main tasks is to decipher symbols. We constantly encounter phenomena which must not be taken at face value; they must be considered symbolic representations of something which hides behind them, which underlies them. They must be considered the manifest expression of something latent.[3] This relationship of manifest and latent meaning will certainly be familiar to those who have read "The Interpretation of Dreams,"[4] where it obtains between the manifest dream content and latent dream thought. A survey of such phenomena shows that this mode of representation follows definite laws. It is characterized by a tendency to replace the abstract by the concrete,[5] and by the choice of representations [6] which have, so to speak, a vital connection with what is to be represented. A vital connection exists, for instance, between the plant and the soil in which

1. Silberer (694).
2. The omitted section gives further appraisal of psychoanalysis.
3. Silberer's description of all relationships between manifest and latent as symbolic implies an extremely broadened concept of symbolism. For a discussion of this point, see Jones (360, particularly pp. 184 ff.), This paper by Jones is the only extensive discussion of Silberer's work. Jones, however, underestimates

Silberer's contribution and fails to recognize that its value is independent of the implied definition of symbolism.
4. Freud (209).
5. The German term here is *das Anschauliche*. The translation "concrete," though not incorrect, underplays that connotation of the term which could be expressed as "visually perceptible."
6. The German term here is *Bilder* = "pictures."

its roots branch out to give it support and nourishment. However, the simile of the plant expresses but one characteristic of the symbol: its intrinsic connection with the meaning.[7] It should be added that the symbol appears to be more or less of the same nature as that which it symbolizes.

A symbol may remain uncomprehended for a long time; however, once it is interpreted, the enlightened observer will readily see the relatedness of the symbol and what it symbolizes. In fact, this relatedness is so stringent that the observer will be amazed that he could have overlooked it and considered the symbol incomprehensible. (This does not preclude—as we shall see—that a symbol may have several "meanings.") This experience of sudden understanding, this feeling of close relatedness of meaning and symbol, is not specific to the application of psychoanalysis.[8] It is common wherever meaning-laden symbols are at first overlooked or misunderstood and then laboriously deciphered—whether by one's own effort or with the help of others. Life is full of such symbols, and nobody can discover all of them. This is best illustrated by religious symbolism. The history of the interpretation of myths [9] is in this respect just as instructive as the subjective experience of individuals who in their youth consider dogmatic teachings to be the truth itself, and learn only later to regard them as symbolic. The symbol—seen from this vantage point— is an adequate form of "the truth" for a given level of mental development. A form [10] approximating "the truth" more closely and on a higher level [11] would exceed the mental capacity of the recipient and be therefore uncomprehended and rejected. The cause of rejection, however, need not be purely intellectual,[12] but may also be affective. The difference between conventional and deeper symbolic connections can perhaps be best illustrated by con-

7. The term "meaning" (of the symbol) stands here for either "that which is symbolized," or "that which is its referent."

8. Note, however, Jones (360, p. 207): "When the meaning of the symbol is disclosed, the conscious attitude is characteristically one of surprise, incredulity and often of repugnance."

9. An excellent modern treatment of myths as symbolism is found in E. Cassirer (126, Vol. II).

10. The term "form" here apparently stands for "form of thought."

11. "Higher level" here apparently stands for "higher level of abstraction."

12. Whether the description of the "mental level" in question as "purely intellectual" is correct can be seriously debated. It is quite safe to assume that to each "mental level" corresponds—or even underlies—a specific organization of impulses and affectivity. Yet Silberer may be justified in distinguishing "men-

trasting the common trademark Δ with the Pythagorean Hygieia-symbol.
. . .[13] In the first the sign is arbitrarily chosen and could be just as well replaced by any other geometric figure, that is, it is a symbol only in a *diluted*
sense. In the second, it is what I would call an *"essential"* symbol,[14]* that is, a
sign which has a close relationship to its meaning or meanings so that it cannot
be changed without seriously interfering with this relationship.[15] Such symbols
imply necessity. . . .[16]

The symbolism psychoanalysts deal with is broadly conceived, though not
diluted like that of trademarks. The symbols they deal with imply necessity.
Being products of nature and not artifacts of agreement, they obey stringent
laws. These psychological laws may be intricate and hard to discern, yet they
are rigorous and clear. . . .[17]

The symbols the psychoanalyst encounters in his work are always found
to be related to those met with in mythological forms of knowledge.[18] This

---

tal level" and "affectivity" as different
causes for rejecting symbols. It seems
that "mental level" here refers to the prevailing general impulse-affect-thought
organization; while "affectivity" refers
to a specific affect interfering with the
prevailing organization. Cf. Chap. 26,
notes 40 and 49, below.

13. In the omitted part Silberer dwells
on the various meanings of the concept
"symbol." He shows that the use of the
concept is superficial when it denotes
things, such as trademarks, which do not
presuppose an intrinsic connection between the symbol and that which it
symbolizes.

14.* This is to say, a relationship
which, once understood, appears inevitable.

15. Silberer does not give a stringent
exposition of the concept "close relationship." There is reason to believe that
such an exposition would have to use the
psychoanalytic concept overdetermination; that is, it would have to introduce
the assumption that the connections
between an "essential" symbol and its

"meaning" are manifold. Later on Silberer discusses the issue of overdetermination but does not come to the
conclusion here suggested. In fact, he is
inclined to exempt hypnagogic symbols
from the requirement of "overdetermination."

16. The omitted part subsumes symbolism under what Silberer calls "mythological forms of knowledge." For the
explanation of this concept he refers to
his *Phantasie und Mythos* (690).

17. In the omitted part Silberer indicates that besides symbols proper, the
psychoanalysts' conception of symbolism includes metaphors and related
phenomena. Note, however, Jones's
(360) discussion which demonstrates
conclusively that it is Silberer's symbol
concept that includes metaphors, while
the psychoanalytic conception of symbolism does not. Jones's concept seems
to be too narrow. Silberer's merit was
that he did not stick to a narrowly defined concept of symbol.

18. "Knowledge" here translates
Erkennen. This concept implies that

should be no surprise: they are branches of the same tree. It is human nature, psychic lawfulness, that creates symbols, pictorial signs representing something which at a given time, for some reason, cannot manifest itself in consciousness in its "true" form.

The genuine symbol is the form of appearance of the underlying idea. It is the stringent psychological laws governing this form of appearance which lend symbols a character of inevitability. Dreams, acts of compulsion neurotics, religious ceremonies (when divested of purely historical elements), the cosmogonic myths of the ancients, are pictorial images determined by inner [19] necessity and not by arbitrary agreement. Though the symbol is the *necessary* form of appearance of a group of ideas under given conditions, it cannot be cognized [20] as a mere symbol by the one in whose mind [21] it came into existence. If it could be so cognized, and one could state that "this idea A of mine is merely an image, or a symbol, of idea B," the group of ideas underlying the symbol could appear to the mind's eye in form B also.

If, however, we concede that for each given stage of mental [22] development and each given state of mind [23] there is only one possible form of manifestation of an idea, then form B cannot yet be clearly in consciousness when it is form A that corresponds [24] to that stage or state.[25] One could have, at best, a feeling,

---

mythological ideas are attempts at coming to terms with, or at explaining, nature in general and human nature in particular. In this sense, then, mythological ideas serve the same purpose as the ideas of modern science; both belong in the class, "knowledge." The German terms *Erkennen* and *Erkenntnis* and the equivalent Greek term *episteme* have broader connotations than the term "knowledge." They tolerate, as well as express, the heterogeneity of scientific and mythological ideas better than the concept "knowledge" does.

19. "Inner" here stands for "intrapsychic."

20. The word "cognized" is used here to translate *erkannt werden*. The common connotation of the verb *erkennen* is "to recognize."

21. "Mind" here translates the nebulous German term *Geist* (Spirit).

22. Again "mental" stands here for *geistig*.

23. "State of mind" translates *psychische Verfassung*. The end of the sentence indicates that by *psychische Verfassung* Silberer means "state of consciousness." It seems to be implied throughout this article that consciousness has many states corresponding to the phylogenetic status and the condition of the individual (tiredness, sleepiness, confusion, intoxication, etc.).

24. The phrase "corresponds to a mental state" expresses the same idea as the term "adequate to," used previously.

25. This formulation seems oversimplified and may, therefore, cloud an important issue. There seem to exist

a vague foreboding, that the idea which one has in mind [26] is merely a pictorial transcription of a thought which may later on be recaptured in a purer form (or which had been grasped earlier and lost); a close comparison,[27] however, is not possible under such conditions.

Actually, modern ethnological and linguistic research contends that myths are not metaphoric expressions, allegory-like pictures deliberately invented by primitive people, but rather the only possible expression of their conception of nature, at the time, and for their mental development, adequate.[28]* A people which speaks in metaphors does not experience what it says as metaphoric; the symbols it uses are regarded by it not as symbols but rather as realities; though a few exceptional individuals, ahead of their times, may know or sense that besides the current conceptions there are others which come nearer to the

states of consciousness in which form A and form B coexist; the states of artistic "inspiration" and "scientific" invention may be conceived as such. In these states "feelings" unite with "form," and "hunches" with "empirical material"; thus form A and form B appear in them together, with a fluid transition from one to the other. However, a reservation must be made: it is possible that instead of coexistence and fluid transition, we are faced here with rapidly alternating states of consciousness. It is conceivable that inspiration on the one hand and its creative artistic elaboration on the other occur in two distinct states of consciousness. (Cf. Kris, 421, and Chap. 23, IV, below.) So far empirical evidence is insufficient for a decision between these two alternatives. This issue has similarities to the one Freud (234) deals with in "The Unconscious" (p. 108). It may be similar even to the issue of the relation between historico-political awareness and the socio-economic process. If so, then Kant's distinction of *an sich* and *fuer sich* experience also becomes relevant here. The *an sich* action is one which is simply caused and acted; the *fuer sich* action is one where the individual has advance awareness of purpose and cause.

26. The German expression *vorschwebt* expresses the vagueness of such ideas. This nuance, however, is lost in the translation.

27. The comparison referred to is that of the symbol with the thought underlying it. Comparison (that is, conceptual evaluation) emerges here as the criterion of clear presence in consciousness. See Rapaport *et al.* (602, I, 385 ff.).

28.* This point of view, however, must not be pushed so far as to disregard the metaphoric expressions of language. Much of the image-expression of knowledge in a period must be attributed to the tendency of language to fall behind and limp after the development [of thought]. Language always refers back to an earlier phase of conceptual development, without thereby giving up its close connection with subsequent development. There is only a temporal lag here.

truth.[29] To the dreamer, too, his dream-images appear not as mere symbols, but rather as the real relations of things.[30]* The compulsion neurotic has no notion, unless apprised, that his obsessive ideas and compulsive actions are mere symbols, circumscriptions of something underlying them, substitute formations for something which can present itself to him only in such forms. Let us recapitulate: no one whose apperception is symbolic can at the time be clearly aware of the fact or of its extent.

To recognize a symbol—or in general, any picturing [31]—as such, presupposes the achievement of a more advanced level of psychological development than that on which the symbol was created.[32] Mythological conceptions had to be outgrown before they could be recognized for what they were. To use the previous example: one must be familiar with the more abstract and intellectually more refined B-form of a cognition in order to identify as provisional

29. Here, as well as earlier in this article, higher levels of abstraction are identified with "truth." This is an indicator of Silberer's devotion to the epistemology of philosophical idealism.

30.* I should like to remind the reader that Abraham (5) considered the myth as the dream of a people; and that Nietzsche (538) commented that dream-thinking is identical with the causal-thinking of times past.

31. "Picturing" here translates *das Bildliche*. The English term, being more concrete than the German, misses some of its connotations. *Das Bildliche* is not "picturing" in the visual sense alone, but also in that of imagery and allegory.

32. For Silberer psychological development here apparently connotes both historical and individual development. Even so, the formulation oversimplifies the situation. Later on Silberer offers a more adequate formulation. Yet it may not be superfluous to discuss here the weaknesses of the present one. It is more the rule than the exception that forms of thought adequate to an earlier level of psychological development survive and coexist with thought formations of the highest subsequent level. For instance, dream-thinking coexists with waking thinking. Silberer's formulation seems inadequate for such cases; an added assumption is necessary. One possible assumption would be that dream-thinking and waking-thinking take place in two distinct forms of consciousness. With this added assumption, Silberer's formulation would read: the recognition of a symbol presupposes the achievement of a more advanced development than the one which created it. The symbol character of thought will be recognizable where the state of consciousness to which such symbols or thoughts belong is no longer experienced (as in myths), or where the state of consciousness which created the symbol reemerges only as an island within the state of consciousness characteristic of the highest subsequent level (as in dreams).

its archaic-symbolic A-form. It is thus that later periods can see the symbolic and mythical in the conceptions of past periods.[33]* The mythological does not cease to exist: its creation and subsequent recognition will presumably continue for all time. The state of affairs in the psychology of the individual is analogous. Here, too, a higher vantage-point must be reached before a symbol can be recognized as such. In the case of the psychopath [34] such a higher vantage-point is taken by the doctor; in the case of the dreamer, by himself—as soon as he awakens. The doctor who treats the neurotic by the psychoanalytic method endeavors to lead him back to that higher vantage-point which his illness caused him to abandon: when the patient understands the symbols of his psyche, as a rule he abandons the symbol. . . .[35]

We have described—if only sketchily—our point of view, and should now consider the main object of our interest, the psychological process of symbol-formation. . . .[36]

Here three problems are outstanding: (a) what is the process of symbol-formation? (b) what conditions bring it about? (c) what is its purpose? The latter two questions deal with the same issue, one from the causal, the other from the teleological point of view. Before we can concern ourselves with cause and purpose, we must first have a secure hold on the subject-matter. Therefore, we must first clarify what takes place in symbol-formation. . . . We have dwelt on it in our introduction and shall now add a few points. . . .

When searching for the underlying basis of a symbol of any kind, we are bound to arrive at a series of things, rather than at a single thing. The symbol never hangs by a single thread, rather it is part of the weave of a whole fabric. We can follow the chain of ideas which give the symbol its significance; we can see them radiate from the symbol as a hub, in many directions. The symbol,

---

33.* It is thus also that exceptional men who are ahead of their times see it and are, therefore, understood only by later generations.

34. The word "psychopath" is used here in its original sense, as in "psycho-pathic hospital" or "psychopathology." The connotation "antisocial character" is a more recent acquisition.

35. In the omitted section Silberer deals with the relation of symptom and symbol. He asserts that though symboliz-ing processes are often involved in symptom formation, by no means are all symptoms symbols.

36. Here Silberer states that he will first give a general discussion and then some examples. The latter will be omit-ted here, and the reader is referred to Silberer's other paper appearing in this volume, Chap. 8, above.

then, is said to have "Praegnanz." [37] The convergence of many association-chains in one point may be observed in myth-symbols of folk-fantasy, as well as in symbols experienced by the individual. . . . The latter type is too well known to psychoanalysts to need documentation: it is the well-known phenomenon of *overdetermination*,[38] which from another point of view appears as *condensation*. . . .[39]

We observe overdetermination even in symbols that occur in autosymbolic hallucinations, though these are poor in "multiple meaning" since they adhere closely to the psychological experience which precipitated them.[40] Here the threads of significance [41] emanating from the symbol fasten upon closely neighboring ideas. Consequently, the symbolic relationship (between the symbol and its object or, for caution's sake, its chief object) becomes tighter, more obvious, and more definitive. . . .[42]

37. The word *Praegnanz* is a technical psychological term in Gestalt-psychology. But even prior to this, the German language used it essentially, though not technically, in the same sense.

38. It seems probable that all thinking is characterized by overdetermination, and that in this respect there is no categorical difference between symbolic and logical thinking. The main question, which so far has not been satisfactorily answered, is: *how* does overdetermination vary in different forms of thinking?

39. In the omitted section Silberer puts forth an argument against the view of some psychoanalysts that relatedness to sexual matters is a necessary condition of all symbol-formation (note 12, above, and 78, below). He offers the "autosymbolic phenomena" as evidence to the contrary. Whether or not Silberer's contention is correct, his argument would be questionable if sexuality were broadly conceived by his opponents. Furthermore, if "sexuality" were replaced by the concept "wishfulfillment" Silberer's argument would be further weakened. Not even the refer-

ence to "autosymbolic phenomena" would support his argument, since many of these "functional" or "autosymbolic" phenomena may be wishfulfillments as well as symbolic translations into dream pictures of the functional state of mind, etc. Silberer's argument is cogent against a narrow conception of wishfulfillment and sexuality. His "autosymbolic phenomena" show that a study of symbolism must break through these narrow conceptions. If, however, sexuality and wishfulfillment are conceived broadly as "impulse dynamics" and "tendency to decrease psychic tension," his argument becomes a demonstration rather than a refutation of his opponents' argument.

40. In note 39 above, I have questioned the general validity of this thesis. My own hypnagogic autosymbolic hallucinations do not seem to bear out the simplicity claimed by Silberer.

41. This refers to chains of associations.

42. In the omitted part Silberer deals with Camilla Lucerna's (486) "*Das Maerchen*": Goethe's *Naturphilosophie als Kunstwork*. Lucerna realized that

Another characteristic of symbol-formation which deserves special attention is the tendency to picturing.[43] When a psychological entity [44] undergoes
symbolic substitution it takes on a sensory form, though otherwise it is usually
more abstract. Thus we may speak of the direction of the symbolizing-process,
and in so doing we arrive—at least for the psychology of the individual—at the
Freudian concept of "regression." Freud [45] says:

The hallucinatory dream we can describe only by saying that the excitation follows
a retrogressive course. It communicates itself not to the motor end of the apparatus,
but to the sensory end, and finally reaches the system of perception. If we call the
direction which the psychic process follows from the unconscious into the waking
state *progressive*, we may then speak of the dream as having a *regressive* character.

Assuming that the concept "regression" is used in the broadest sense, we too
can use it for our purposes. This will soon be supported by considerations of
developmental history.[46]

Let us not forget that there are two avenues open for the exploration of
symbols. One of them leads through dreams, neuroses, autosymbolic hallucinations, and the like. To me it seems that in these the symbol appears as a substitute for something that I could under normal conditions clearly grasp, think, or
feel: a thought which in daytime—assuming an intact psychic apparatus—
would be entirely clear, presents itself in my dream, etc., symbolically.[47] Here
the symbol appears when I am *no longer in command* of the idea underlying it.
If we now consider the developmental history of human knowledge, if we

---

symbolism implies overdetermination,
which allowed her to demonstrate that
the figures in Goethe's "Maerchen" are
not allegorical but symbols which are
the hub of association chains along political, esthetic, philosophical, scientific
lines. She further demonstrated Goethe's
awareness of this.

43. Cf. note 31.

44. "Entity" here translates *Wesen-
heit*. Whether it is conceptually correct
to refer to what is symbolized as an "entity," rather than function, process, or
even "content" of a process (against its
"formal characteristics"), cannot be discussed here.

45. Freud (209, p. 492). Cf. also Kris,
Chap. 23, IV, below.

46. The history referred to is the
history of human thinking as reflected in
myth.

47. This statement contains the kernel
of a contradiction in terms. What presents itself, for example, in the dream
is—according to psychoanalysis—a
thought that could *not* be thought in the
waking state: it is always unacceptable
and intolerable to consciousness. In his
subsequent sentence Silberer does indicate his cognizance of this state of affairs.

remember how, generation after generation, man pursues knowledge [48] through series of images and mythologies—then the symbol appears as a substitute for ideas of which humanity has *no command as yet*. The conditions favorable to symbol-formation may be reached either by advancing toward or by receding from the idea represented by the symbol. Some curious misunderstandings in the literature of the history of culture can be traced to—among other factors —the neglect of the first of these possibilities. The disregard for the second proved a hindrance to the development of psychology and psychotherapy. . . .[49]

If we follow the formation of symbols in the course of evolution, we find that they appear when man's mind reaches out for something which he cannot as yet grasp. Symbols come about also when a once greater power to grasp is decreased as in the dream or in mental disorder. The attempt to grasp the idea underlying a symbol fails in both cases, and a more primitive [50] conception is resorted to than the one aimed at by evolution. In such cases—as we already know—the symbol is not experienced as such until the prevailing frame of mind [51] is superseded. In both cases, then, symbol-formation appears as a falling-short-of-the-idea, as a regression to a *previous* and inadequate mental level.[52] In dream regression, and in neurotic regression, we fall back not only upon our childhood, but also upon the analogous developmental stages of mankind.

Unwittingly we have now approached that point of view which studies "conditions" and "causes." It goes without saying that the best material for

48. "Knowledge" here translates *Erkenntnis* (*episteme*).

49. In the omitted section Silberer quotes extensively from F. W. J. von Schelling (638). The quotation shows that Schelling understood the epistemological and psycho-historical status of symbolism in early myth, legend, and philosophy. Plato's mythical representation of the psyche in Phaedrus, and Hesiod's explanation of human misery in the Pandora myth, are used as examples.

50. "More primitive" here means: inadequate at the given level of mental development, or adequate only at an earlier level.

51. Silberer apparently meant state of consciousness.

52. It may seem that the term regression is misapplied to symbolism as a falling-short-of-the-idea because one is *not yet in command* of it. We must remember, however, that Plato used symbolic myths whenever he was not yet sufficiently in command of the idea to give it a discursive-logical form. In the rest of his writings, however, he was a master of inference and logical proof. Thus, his myths *in relation* to his other creative products may be justifiably labeled as regressive.

such study is a pure form of the phenomenon in question, freed of all side issues. . . .[53]

To my mind, the hallucination phenomena I have described [54] present the picturing-process which produces symbols in its purest form and in strictest isolation from side issues. In these, which are in part deliberately elicited, thought contents, prevailing psychologic-functional states, and to a lesser degree somatic states, are translated into images. These images carry not only unmistakable earmarks of their origin, but give one the indescribable conviction that they are only a translation into a pictorial symbol of the thought, feeling, and so on.[55]

In the report cited I suggested that this translation is a fatigue-phenomenon, the prerequisite for its occurrence being drowsiness counteracted either by

53. Silberer comments here on the fact that symbol-formation, far from being easily observed in pure form, is encountered in the most varied uses and applications.

54. See Chap. 8, above.

55. My self-observations do not corroborate Silberer's experience. Compare also Stekel (705) and Jones (360) on this point. Silberer conceives of symbol-formation as a function of the prevailing state of consciousness (sleepiness, tiredness, primitivity) and not primarily as a function of motivational (or wish) dynamics. Freud championed the latter view. His presentation of it in Chap. VII of "The Interpretation of Dreams" (209) is consistent with the theoretical structure of psychoanalysis. Silberer does not discuss the relation of these states of consciousness to unconscious motivation, censorship, and repression, and treats such states of consciousness as if they were not generally dependent on motivational dynamics. Direct evidence to decide this controversy has not been so far proffered. The motivational determinants of various states of consciousness (sleep, half-sleep, drug and intoxication states, confusion, delirium, monoideic-somnambulism, states of fugue, states of loss of personal identity, etc.) and of the formal characteristics of the thought-processes which occur in them have not been systematically explored. Hypnagogic hallucination is an example showing that organization of thought-processes varies according to states of consciousness; the state in question is that preceding full sleep, and the hallucinations are the thought-processes whose formal characteristics Silberer seeks to determine. He claims that their outstanding formal characteristic is the perceptual translation of the idea or of the subjective state experienced. Freud, however, maintained that such translations characteristically express unacceptable impulses. The subjective experience, which is for Silberer the crucial material, is for Freud like day-residues in dreams, only the occasion and the means to express fundamental "wishes." For Freud's views on Silberer, see (209, p. 479; 237, p. 144; 255, pp. 37–38).

a strong will to think or by a somatic stimulation. Later on [56] I generalized this view [57] of the conditions for symbol-formation by assuming that "regression" will take place "whenever a thought or idea proves too difficult to be supported by a given state of consciousness." According to this view, the thought will then be represented by a picture. This interpretation is in harmony with the role of symbolization in ethnopsychology. But the adjective "difficult" is not quite appropriate, at least not sufficiently revealing. It may be adequate without amplification when regression, disregarding its other aspects,[58] can be considered a reverting from apperceptive to associative [59] thought-processes. But in neuroses, and generally wherever affects come into play, it does not fully describe the state of affairs and leaves a gap. Before attempting to fill this gap, I want to review the theoretical discussions of some renowned authors in the field of psychopathology, which are relevant to our topic and agree with the views I derived from my observations on hallucinations and dreams.

First, it needs to be demonstrated (in order to make my view concerning "difficulty" plausible) that the associative thought-process is "easier" than the apperceptive; that is to say, it is a mode of thought which can operate at a lower level of the energy which is available for thinking. This comparatively primitive mode of thought takes over when normal thought fails. Everyday experience demonstrates this. When we are tired and do not feel like thinking, and sit distracted, leafing through illustrated magazines in a café, we do enjoy looking at the pictures "thoughtlessly" but find it difficult to decide to read the text.

56. Silberer (690). See also (694) and (691).

57. For autosymbolic hallucinations Silberer sustained this view in its original form.

58. The "other aspects" are the distortion and wishfulfillment, which Silberer considers absent in hypnagogic hallucinations. Cf. pp. 229–30, and note 98, below.

59. *Apperceptive* here designates thought-processes of a higher, *associative* those of a lower, abstraction level. In apperceptive thinking, external stimulations are integrated according to principles inherent in the organism, as well as according to present context and past experience. In associative thinking the reality referent of the stimulus, and the effort at integrating external and intrapsychic reality, are given up, and intrapsychic connections of ideas prevail over reality-adequate conceptual connections. This distinction parallels that between secondary and primary processes (Chap. 17, note 20). Whether in view of all this the adjective "difficult" can still be considered adequate, even in Silberer's limited use, is questionable.

In such moments we prefer (many people always do) the pictorial to the abstract. It requires less effort. . . .[60]

Jung [61] offers some considerations which are important for the causal interpretation of our material. In connection with the analysis of a dream, after commenting on the characteristics of mythological thinking, he states:

I want to emphasize that the multiple meaning of the individual dream pictures (Freud's "overdetermination") is in itself an indicator of the indefiniteness and lack of clarity of dream thinking. One dream picture may pertain to two different com-

60. In the omitted section Silberer summarizes the views of Schelling and Pelletier concerning symbolism. They closely resemble his own. He quotes Jung's (363) summary of Pelletier's views: Pelletier considers the symbolism of catatonics to be related to their attention-disturbance and to the consequent "apperceptive weakness." Silberer comments: "These do allow one to understand why symbolization should occur, but rarely explain why one and not another symbol is formed. In dreams, underlying these processes there are certain directing tendencies which we first learned about from Freud's investigations." Thus here—concerning dreams—Silberer concurs with Freud. He acknowledges that motivational dynamics play a role in symbol-formation. However, in his view this role is limited to the choice of symbol and does not give rise to symbolizing. The conditions responsible for symbolization are, according to him, (a) lowered level of the energy available for thinking; (b) attention-disturbance; (c) apperceptive weakness.

Some indirect evidence that attention-disturbance is an expression of conditions prevailing in motivational dynamics, and not a final and irreducible condition characteristic of the organism,

is offered by Rapaport, Schafer and Gill (602, pp. 166–72, 176–79, 195–200). Cf. also Freud's theory of attention: (223, p. 15), (209, pp. 515–16, 545); also Chap. 15, notes 20 and 21, below.

Concerning the argument on the role of fatigue and lowered energy, Freud wrote (210, p. 50):

Let us assume that I was so reckless as to take a walk at night in an uninhabited neighborhood of a big city and was attacked and robbed of my watch and purse. At the nearest police station I report the matter in the following words: "I was in this or that street, and was there robbed of my watch and purse by *lonesomeness* and *darkness*". . . . To be correct, the state of affairs could only be described by saying that, *favored* by the lonesomeness of the place and under *cover* of darkness, I was robbed of my valuables by *unknown malefactors*.

Now, then, the state of affairs in forgetting names need not be different. Favored by exhaustion, circulatory disturbances and intoxication, I am robbed by an unknown psychic force of the control over the proper names belonging to my memory; it is the same force which in other cases may bring about the same failure of memory during perfect health and mental capacity.

61. C. G. Jung (363). The page references are to the English edition, though the translation here offered is my own.

plexes [62*] of waking life, even when they are sharply distinguished in the waking state. The two complex-contents merge, at least in their symbolic form, because of the decreased sensitiveness to distinctions which prevails in dreams. . . . Experimental evidence appears to indicate that voluntary motor activity is demonstrably influenced by simultaneous autonomic activity (breathing). Complexes are—from all we know about them—continuous autonomic excitations or activities. Each not only influences conscious activity, but shapes other complexes. Consequently, complexes include elements of each other—a state of affairs that may be labeled as a fusion. Freud designates this, from a somewhat different point of view, as "overdetermination" (p. 56).[63]

Thus Jung proposed here a causal explanation of the condensation occurring in symbols. He goes even further, attempting to shed light upon the superficial associative links of dream-thinking, by drawing upon the results of association-experiments.[64] The superficial associations of dream-thinking are similar to those found in distraction-experiments.[65] This supports the assumption that

when attention is decreased, thinking runs along quite superficial connections. A state of decreased attention finds expression also in decreased clarity of presentations.[66] When the presentations become unclear, so do the differences between them, hence our sensitiveness to these differences will also suffer, being merely a function

---

62.* I am assuming here that the reader is familiar with the theory of complexes and the concepts of dissociation, repression, etc., current in psychoanalytical circles.

[The concept of complexes never reached full clarity and was soon abandoned by psychoanalysts. A complex was conceived as a set of ideas grouped around an affect or conflict. Mental life was considered to be an aggregate of such complexes. See Rivers, et al. (613). The concept dissociation was a precursor of the concept repression. It denoted that independence of functioning by which one complex, at the expense of the others, gained a governing role over the behavior of the organism. Observations on multiple personalities contributed considerably to the crystallization of the concept. See Rapaport (591, pp. 206–14). The concept played a considerable

role in the psychology of Janet, Morton Prince, etc. For a discussion of the concept see W. McDougall (494). For a brief treatment of the repression concept, see Rapaport (591, pp. 166–68); for a systematic treatment see Freud (233). Cf. also Chap. 15, note 21, below.]

63. Jung is somewhat inexact here. The specific phenomenon in question is designated by Freud as "condensation." "Overdetermination" is a far more general concept, applicable to all psychological causality.

64. See Jung (365).

65. These are association experiments complicated by interfering external stimuli. Cf. Jung (365).

66. "Presentations" here translates *Vorstellungen*. Other possible translations: "images," "ideas."

of attention and clarity.[67] Therefore, nothing prevents the merging of otherwise distinct presentations ("psychological molecules") (pp. 57–58).

Such is the origin of the "mediate" associations in the distraction-experiment.

We can easily conceive of replacing the external distractions of our experiment by a complex exerting its autonomous influence alongside that of the ego-complex. . . . (p. 57).

I want to call your special attention to these last statements and to those which follow, as I intend to return to them later. . . .

When the complex is stimulated,[68] conscious association is disturbed and superficial associations [69] appear, because the attention is turned to [or inhibited by] the autonomous complex.[70] Normal function of the ego-complex implies the inhibition of other complexes, otherwise conscious, directed associative function would be impossible.[71] Thus it is obvious that a complex can manifest itself only indirectly: through unclear, symptomatic associative-actions of a more or less symbolic character. . . . In general the manifestations of complexes must be weak and unclear, because they lack full attention-cathexis, which is engaged by the ego-complex. . . . [72] It is for this reason that an autonomous complex can think [73] only super-

67. Jung's emphasis on the role of attention is of interest. Otherwise his discussion is partly on the level of the philosopher-psychologist dealing with the indistinct concept "clarity," and partly on the level of mechanistic association psychology.

68. It is here assumed that the appearance in consciousness of an idea or percept related to a complex will stimulate (excite, activate) that complex.

69. These form a category in Jung's (365) classification of associations. It includes punning and rhyming associations, in contrast to conceptual associations. Freud (209, pp. 484–85) dealt extensively with these "superficial" associations. It should be pointed out that they are superficial only in respect to formal logic. The relationships they express are likely to be fundamental in regard to emotional and impulse dynamics.

70. It is clear that Jung's conception of "attention" here is one of "energy dynamics." Freud (209, pp. 516–29, 545)

had already set the pattern for such a treatment of attention. For a more recent treatment of this sort, see Rapaport, Gill and Schafer (602, I, 166 ff.) The uncertainty expressed in the alternate conceptions, "turned to autonomous complexes" and "inhibited," receives some clarification by the concept "counter-cathexis" introduced by Freud (209, p. 537) and (233, p. 90).

71. That is, directed, ordered thinking would be disrupted in an uncontrolled and haphazard fashion by the appearance in consciousness of ideas pertaining to autonomous complexes.

72. In Rapaport, et al. (602) the subjective experience of attention and attention-performance appear as indicators of the energy freely available to the ego. The concept cathexis as now used in psychoanalysis was not fully crystallized at the time of Jung's writing: "cathexis" here translates Besetzung, literally "charge."

73. The notion that complexes can

ficially and unclearly, that is to say, symbolically. Consequently, the automatisms [74] and constellations, the end-products of this thinking which are injected by the complex into the activity of the ego-complex, that is, into consciousness, must also be symbolic (pp. 57–58).

During sleep the ego-complex yields to the imperative, "You will sleep and nothing will disturb you."

Thus, time and again, the complexes succeed in presenting their pale and apparently senseless tangential associations to the sleep-ego, just as they do in waking life. It is not the complex-thoughts proper that present themselves, since it is primarily against them that the sleep-suggestion is directed. . . . To suppress a complex means to deprive it of its attention-cathexis, its clarity. Therefore, the complexes must get along in their thinking with just a fraction of clarity. This allows only for vague and symbolic expressions, which consequently lack distinction and merge easily. A specific censorship for dream thoughts (in Freud's sense) need not be postulated: The inhibition issuing from the sleep-suggestion provides the necessary explanation (p. 59).[75]

Freud had shown that those connections within the dream which cannot be explained by mere "apperceptive weakness" are brought about by complexes of great affect-intensity. Stekel expressed this tersely: [76*] "The dream is essen-

---

"think" derives from observations of hysterical dissociations: fugues, monoideic somnambulism, etc. Such a view would be untenable today. The thought-process is now conceived as integral and indivisible; but its manifest forms may show continuity (as in normal thought) or discontinuity (as in fugues), logical orderedness (as in normal thought) or symbolical orderedness (as in dreams, reveries, delusional states). The specific manifest form of the thought-process always expresses the degree of completeness of its preparatory process. Preparatory processes are manifest where the final product is symbolic, but complete ones are usually latent where the final product is deductive logical reasoning. Cf. Schilder (Chap. 24, particularly pp. 507–8, below).

74. Here automatisms are actions of an individual of which he is not aware and which he may not even understand when he is confronted with them. Automatic writing, fugues, posthypnotic suggestions are examples. Cf., however, Hartmann, Chap. 19, VIII, particularly note 106, below.

75. This assertion fails to indicate the source of the effectiveness of the "sleep-suggestion." The Freudian concept of dream-censorship was little more to begin with than the conceptualization of the source and mode of effectiveness of the "sleep-suggestion." Jung's attempt to explain condensation as a fusion due to lack of clarity is a more anthropomorphic and less dynamic attempt than even this original conception of dream-censorship.

76.* Stekel (707). This rich study stresses abundantly and trenchantly the role of affects.

tially a play of presentations in the service of affects." Verily, the lowering of
the mental level and the weakening of apperception lead to a picturing of
thought which, in turn, serves the affects.[77] Such service, however, presupposes
a preexisting relationship. This is given in the fact that affects do play more or
less of a role in symbol-formation in regard both to the material (content) and
the picturing process. Later on we shall hear further about the elasticity of this
"more or less." [78] We have just quoted Jung on the extent to which the ego-
complex and the other complexes interfere with each other. Theodor Lipps
would have put it this way: the interference consists in a partial deflection of
attention (due to a deflection of "psychic force" [79*] in the course of a competi-

77. The use of the concept "affect" in
early psychoanalytic literature is most
ambiguous. See Rapaport (591, p. 28). It
is used very concretely to denote observed affect-manifestations, and also
very abstractly to denote psychic energy
in general. It could be asserted that in
early psychoanalytic literature "affect"
was the precursor of the "libido" and/or
"drive" concepts.

78. This statement might well be the
theoretical crux of Silberer's treatise. So
far in this paper he has asserted a dualistic
theory of symbol formation: apperceptive weakness, with or without the effect
of complexes, leads to symbol-formation.
(Cf. notes 12 and 55, above). In his
earlier paper (689) he asserted that in
autosymbolic phenomena, "apperceptive
weakness" alone will lead to the translation of thought into symbolic form.
Here, however, he seems to be forced by
his own logic to assert a diametrically
opposite principle: "Such service presupposes a preexisting relationship."
(The exact logical status and the validity
of this requirement has not, to my
knowledge, been clarified. Yet it seems
that its validity is often tacitly assumed
in good clinical research. It is possible
that future study will establish it as an
axiom of any treatment of psychological

phenomena in terms of energy-distributions.) This assertion implies that symbolization referable alone to "apperceptive weakness" does not exist. Silberer's
way out of this contradiction is to assume
"more or less" affect participation,
which—considering the difficulty of
quantification—is a rather dangerous expedient. We can avoid Silberer's dilemma
if we assume: (a) that "affects" always
play a role in symbol-formation as well
as in other thought formations; (b) that
this role of "affects" may be one of interference with a certain form of thought-
organization (for example, blocking due
to a "complex"); or (c) one of establishing a certain state of consciousness and a
corresponding form of thought-organization: for example, hypnagogic state,
sleep-dream state, fugue-state. (Cf. note
93, below.) This formulation does away
with the non-affective hypnagogic phenomena. It should be kept in mind that in
this formulation the term "affect" is used
in Silberer's sense and is thus an equivalent of drive-motivation.

79.* This is equivalent to what we referred to above as "energy."
[Psychoanalytic language would have
used here the term "libido," or more recently the term "cathexis."]

tive struggle). The conditions of the ego-complex favorable for symbol-formation are tiredness and apperceptive weakness. These are referable to a diversion of attention caused by complexes interfering with each other in much the same way as did the tendency to sleep and its adversary, the tendency to think (or whatever can replace it), in my experiments on hypnagogic hallu-cinations.

I am not departing from the prevailing view—taking into account both nor-mal and psychological phenomena in individual and ethnopsychology—when I consider the *insufficiency of apperception*, relative to the demands of its subject-matter, the most important and most general condition of symbol-formation. The term "insufficiency," in contrast to "weakness," emphasizes that the effectiveness of the apperceptive ability depends on the subject-matter.[80] In regard to our topic, the merit of Freud, Jung, and their followers lies mainly in that they have *indicated the role of affects and complexes in caus-ing such insufficiency, and analyzed the role of complex-content as the subject-matter of symbolism*. These two are by no means the same thing. Besides the psychological state of insufficiency, which is the general condition for the appearance of picturing, there must also be a subject-matter to be pictured.[81] A symbol without subject-matter to which it refers would be no symbol. Finally—as I hasten to add—one must consider the pictures chosen as the means of symbolic expression: we must note not only the subject-matter that the symbol expresses, but also the sources from which it draws its pictures or their elements. In regard to the relationship of these factors there is a trenchant formulation in "The Interpretation of Dreams," which I believe has eluded the attention of many readers. . . .[82]

80. The assumption of such relativity, in and of itself, transgresses the bounds of a dualistic theory, though it alone does not lay the foundation for a monistic theory.

81. This distinction between psycho-logical state and content clearly shows the dualistic nature of the theory. A mo-nistic theory would not disclaim this distinction: it would consider both phenomena dependent on the same fun-damental variables. For example, these fundamental variables may be conceived as drives. In that case, these drives and their prevailing mode of control would determine both the character of the state of consciousness and the content as well as form of the ideas entering conscious-ness.

82. In the omitted part Silberer quotes a passage of Schelling which he believes to resemble closely Freud's passage quoted below.

In discussing the "transformation of presentation contents into sensory pictures" Freud [83] writes:

Wherever such regression occurred, we regarded it as an effect of resistance opposing the normal progress of thought into consciousness,[84] and of the simultaneous attraction exerted upon it by memories of sensory vividness. The regression in dreams is perhaps facilitated by the cessation of the progressive stream flowing from the sense-organs during the day. In the other forms of regression [85] the motives of regression must be strengthened in order to compensate for the absence of this auxiliary factor. We must also bear in mind that in pathological cases of regression, just as in dreams, the process of energy-transfer must be different from that occurring in the regressions of normal psychic life, since the former renders possible a full hallucinatory cathexis of the perceptive system. What we have described in the analysis of the dream-work as "regard for representability" may be attributed to the *selective attraction* of visually remembered scenes touched by the dream-thoughts.

The most important point here is "resistance opposing the normal progress of thought into consciousness." This resistance is the counterpart of the "insufficiency" we have referred to. What is meant by the "normal" progress? It is that manner of apperception of the "progressing" thought which corresponds to the mental level of the healthy man of our time when awake:[86] it is the full mastery of common, as well as of all possible, thoughts. It is a mastery which considers all inferior apperceptions of the same thought as mere preparatory phases, slips, myth formations, and—if they involve picturing—symbols. Thus, from the point of view of the "normal man," Schelling's "childish man" experiences resistances—due to insufficient apperceptive training [87]—to the

83. "The Interpretation of Dreams" (209, p. 496). The translation of this quotation is Brill's, but I have corrected certain of its inadequacies.

84. The "normal progress to consciousness" Freud has discussed in detail (209, pp. 488 ff.). The "normal" progress is considered to begin at the perceptual system, to take its course through memory systems to unconscious directing ideas, through censorship to preconscious verbal ideas, to consciousness, and then to the motor system. This course is important for Freud mainly as a *direction*, and it is not implied that all thoughts or actions pass through the *full* course:

some may originate or may appear to originate at a middle point. It goes beyond the scope of this commentary to discuss the implications and the later modifications of this conception. See Chap. 16, note 6, below.

85. For instance, in schizophrenic hallucinations.

86. It may be questioned whether this is not an intellectualist's overestimation of the intellect of the healthy man of our time. Freud certainly had many doubts on just this point. See (209, p. 536).

87. To equate resistance with "insufficient apperceptive training" is to draw an unwarranted parallel between indi-

"normal" conscious forms of an idea, to him still unknown and of which he has only vague notions. . . .[88]

The next important point is what Freud calls "motives" of regression. This concept, used in the plural, conveys that *apperceptive insufficiency* (the prerequisite for the transition from the apperceptive to the associative form of thought-process, often but not always implying picturing and symbolization) can have various causes. This is the key to a unitary conception of all symbol-formation. The essential differences between various symbol-phenomena seem to me to lie not in the process itself, . . .[89] but, rather, primarily in the conditions resulting in apperceptive insufficiency.

Anticipating this point, I have already mentioned [90] that the rejection of one form of an idea due to the inadequacy of the mental apparatus to receive it in that form may occur for purely intellectual as well as for affective reasons.[91] The "capacity of the mental apparatus" depends not solely on intellectual but also on affective factors. Psychoanalysts who deal with the psychology of neuroses and dreams, know that such rejection or non-admittance of ideas is frequently determined by affects.

According to these considerations, the apperceptive ability to cope with an idea in consciousness can suffer limitation or disturbance from two sides. *First,*

---

vidual-psychological and ethnopsychological conditions. The technical concept "resistance" as coined by Freud seems to be equated here with resistance in a far more general and non-technical sense. Even though a "resistance to the new and/or unknown" can be resistance in the more technical sense in a given patient, it is undemonstrated that this holds for all resistance against "the new" in history.

88. In the omitted part Silberer carries further the analogy with Schelling's assertions.

89. The omitted part designates the manifest differences between symbol-phenomena as secondary and independent of symbol-formation.

90. See p. 209, above.

91. The sharp categorical distinction between "affective" and "intellectual" is related to what we have considered a dualistic theory (note 78, above). The normative attitude to "normality" just expressed by Silberer seems fashioned after the same pattern. A monistic theory would not disclaim that preparatory phases of thought-processes are discernible, nor would it deny the validity of a distinction between "intellectual" and "affective"; it would however recognize that in everyday thinking, preparatory phases and final products of thought co-exist, and that as far as the thought-process is concerned, "affective" and "intellectual" are two ways of looking *at it* rather than two divisible parts *of it.*

the insufficiency can be a want of development (as in childhood and/or in preliterates), or a temporary weakening of the apperceptive ability due to a general decrease in energy available for thinking (as in sleep). *Secondly*, it may be due to the intervention of affects which by a pleasure-mechanism make the progress of the idea difficult,[92]* or else divert attention-energy to the autonomous complexes (see Jung, above).

The influence of affects, however, does not consist alone in their interference with the apperceptive function. Besides this negative effect, they have the positive one that, with the attention-energy they attract, they tend to make effective the complexes to which they pertain. Strictly speaking, in this role the affects are not disturbing but, rather, positive factors in symbol-formation. Every idea, thought, and affect-toned complex which strives to reach consciousness is such a positive factor.[93]

In a general condition of apperceptive weakness, this positive factor—namely, a subject-matter which strives to become conscious, and in relation to which the apperceptive weakness turns into apperceptive insufficiency—is transformed into a symbol, the "meaning" of which will be the subject-matter in question. . . .[94]

92.* What is "made difficult" is the clear apperception of the content of presentations and ideas. Here, then, the theory concerning the "difficulty" (pp. 219 ff., above), which must have appeared at first quite unsatisfactory, may gain more meaning.

[This role of the pain-pleasure mechanism is treated in the theory of repression and its fine points may be found in (209, pp. 535 ff.), also Chap. 15, note 20, below.]

93. Actually, more recent psychoanalytic and psychological theorizing would probably represent this state of affairs as follows: (a) it would replace "affects" by "drives" or "motivating forces"; (b) it would maintain that ideas, thoughts, complexes, do not strive to reach consciousness but that only drives (wishes, impulses) do so, "pushing" ideas and thoughts into consciousness as their "representatives"; (c) it would consider the "apperceptive sufficiency or insufficiency" a function of drive-control and of ability to delay; (d) it would distinguish not only apperceptive and associative forms of thought, but many varieties, combinations, and transitions of these; (e) it would account for these varieties by reconstructing the underlying varieties of drive control. It would thus distinguish periodic changes in drive control (for example, sleep), breakdown of control of a specific drive (for example, symptoms which are symbolic), breakdown of control of drive-systems (for example, fugues and somnambulisms), and more or less generalized breakdown of control (for example, psychoses); (f) it would defer accounting for ethnological symbolism until more empirical material is available.

94. In the omitted part Silberer first

Among symbols, two types can be distinguished.

The *first type* of symbol originates in an "apperceptive insufficiency" that comes about on an intellectual basis. In symbols of this type, disturbing competitive ideas (competing affect-toned complexes) play no role.

The *second type* of symbol arises in the wake of an "apperceptive insufficiency" that comes about on an affective basis: an idea is translated into a picture in a competitive struggle with other complexes. This amounts to a sidetracking of the idea as it strives toward consciousness.

I hasten to add that there will probably never be encountered a phenomenon which is a pure case of either type. We deal always with mixed cases; in some the characteristics of the first, in some those of the second, are outstanding.[95]

The *first type* is based on a more or less evenly distributed (relative) weakness of apperception, so that, though the idea striving to become conscious does not emerge in a clear form, it remains *undistorted*. It is as though an object were observed through a uniformly woven veil.

------

summarizes Bleuler's (75) critique of Freud's "censorship" concept. According to Bleuler, the censorship concept "could well be replaced by a more general one, namely that of inhibition by contrary affective needs." Then Silberer proceeds to adopt Bleuler's view and to apply it to symbol-formation. Quoting a dream from Ferenczi, he attempts to demonstrate that the competition of affects leads to a loss of clarity and merging of presentations: that is, to apperceptive insufficiency.

The censorship concept and Bleuler's critique of it cannot be discussed here in detail. It should be pointed out, however, that more recent developments in psychoanalysis, which did modify the "censorship" concept considerably, moved not closer to but further from Bleuler's views. I have in mind the development of psychoanalytic ego-psychology. The concept of the ego arose because clinical data necessitated the postulation of an emergent new structure which is, among other things, the embodiment of controls over affects and impulses; Bleuler's assumption of the mutual control of contrary affects and impulses could not account for the data in question. This turn of the theory will not surprise students of energy distributions. It is rather the rule than the exception that clashing energy distributions come to a dynamic equilibrium, and that such equilibria tend to structuralize and to crystallize relatively stable characteristics. Without attempting to follow Bleuler's theory further, I should like to invite the reader to visualize the chaos of a theory in which every observational datum would be referred to the seething cauldron of an infinite combination of competing tendencies. Concerning Bleuler's theory see Chap. 20, pp. 404–8, and Chap. 26, notes 137, 138, below.

95. Here Silberer approaches but does not achieve statement of a monistic theory. He falls short of it because he fails to reconcile this formulation with his earlier formulations which contradict it.

The *second type* is based on a *one-sided* (one might even say, tendentious) disturbance of apperception, so that the idea striving to become conscious emerges unclear and displaced.[96] It is as though an object were observed through a spotted veil or through optically distorting glasses.

Both types obey an inherent subjective necessity. The first type may in addition have objective necessity; it yields symbols which appear valid and successful even to an outsider. Mythological knowledge with which ethnopsychology is concerned is grossly of the first type, although it is not entirely free of the second. The intensity of the influence of the second type is most clearly seen in people of different racial [97] characteristics. In people who have the same characteristics, the rules of affect-interference are the same, so that to them these rules appear to have general validity. Then "interference" becomes the "norm," and will not strike the observer who belongs to the same group. . . .[98]

I have stated above that thinking in symbols, and the change from apperceptive to associative thought-processes, correspond to a regression to primitive forms of thought.[99] Symbol-formation itself falls back upon visual perception,

96. Instead of "displaced" it would be more meaningful to say "distorted."

97. The use here of the term "racial" —judged by the context—is probably not strict. It may be assumed that Silberer had in mind culturally differing, and geographically or otherwise isolated, groups.

98. In the omitted part, Silberer quotes his hypnagogic hallucination concerning the essence of transsubjectively valid judgments as an example of the first type of symbolism. (See Chap. 8, p. 198, above). It may be open to question whether all that occurs in this example is merely a symbolic translation of an abstract idea, due to apperceptive weakness concomitant with tiredness and sleepiness. His conception of the example implies no overdetermination of its elements, and consequently no explanation of why precisely this and not another

symbol arose. In my experience even such obvious symbolizations have meanings in terms of personal dynamics; moreover, so does the thought which initiates the process of falling asleep.

Silberer next refers to the dream he quoted from Ferenczi as an example of the second type of symbolism. The dream itself was omitted in this translation for reasons of space. Any analyzed dream (see Freud, 209; Sharpe, 682; or Stekel, 707) will provide examples of condensations, displacements, distortions, etc., attributed by Silberer to affect-interference.

99. Apperceptive thinking is apparently defined as thinking based on abstract-conceptual connections and subsumptions. Associative thinking is, in turn, defined as thinking based on contiguity, concreteness, and on similarity not of objective attributes but of the

gestures, and sign-language. In dreams and neuroses, thinking in concepts and talking in words change into visual perception (hallucinations) and sign-language (symptomatic actions). It is as if the advance made, and stored in the association-system,[100] by the apperceptive work of culture since the time of such primitive thought-forms, should of a sudden disappear in part or whole. One may conceive the development from associative-perceptual to appercep-tive-conceptual thinking as continuous as one wishes; yet somewhere there must be a jump in this progress. A continuous transition from the associative to the apperceptive is conceivable; but one from the *perceptual* to the *conceptual* would pose the same difficulties as that from sensation-bound perception to discursive [101] intelligence.[102]

---

feelings and strivings represented. See in this respect H. Werner (755, pp. 67 ff., 232), on "physiognomic" percepts and concepts.

100. Silberer's conception of "associa-tion-systems" was probably much like Bleuler's: one not merely concerned with memory-organization, but also re-sponsible for ordered and goal-directed thinking in general. See Chap. 26, pp. 587–88, below. Thus, "associative sys-tems" here correspond roughly to what Freud conceptualized as the "secondary process." (See Freud, 209, pp. 525 ff.) Bleuler's influence is apparent in Sil-berer's wording, and there is no trace of evidence that, like Freud (209, pp. 488 ff.), he was familiar with Henry Head's (314) schema concept later elaborated by Bartlett (37) into the con-cept of memory schemata. (See, in this respect, also Rapaport, Gill and Schafer, 602, pp. 129–31.) Bleuler's influence must not be underestimated; neither Jung, Rorschach, nor many other con-temporaries escaped it. Through Ror-schach (618) much of his thinking seeped into American clinical psychol-ogy in the form of implicit assumptions

concerning the relation of "association-systems" and "thought-organization."

101. The term "discursive" is used here in the philosophical sense: "able to draw inferences."

102. It seems likely that Silberer was overimpressed with concepts as logic conceives of them. Psychological in-vestigations of concepts (see H. Werner, 755; Weigl, 753; Hanfmann and Kasanin, 299; Goldstein and Scheerer, 284; Rapa-port, Gill and Schafer, 602) considerably undermine the pride logic takes in them. These investigations show a continuous transition from the primitive concrete-perceptual to the abstract forms of con-cepts. Nor would the gap of sensation-bound perception and discursive intelli-gence appear so unbridgeable to the present-day psychologist. The awe of discursive intelligence which Silberer shows is disappearing in our time: we have learned that even those who are capable of displaying such intelligence do so only occasionally. Such psycho-logical discoveries do not invalidate the science of logic as a "psychologistic" view of logic might claim; however, they limit its range of application, and

Since symbols are rooted in sensuality,[103] it is unsatisfactory to consider them merely a transition from the apperceptive to the associative form of the thought-process. Waking thinking and dream-thinking (and whatever is analogous to it) constitute a dichotomy. Thus, the old dichotomy, intellect vs. sensuality, seems neither philosophically nor psychologically the mere fancy it has sometimes been considered in the Modern Age.[104]

We have discussed the first two questions, what symbol-formation consists of and what its conditions are, as best we could; now we shall deal briefly with the third question, its purpose.

When dealing with manifestations of life, it always makes good sense to search systematically for purposes. Such procedure leads to a finalistic (teleological) point of view, which is the counterpart of the causal point of view. . . .[105]

Our task here is to find out in what sense symbol-formation might be purposive. A real answer requires knowledge of what would happen if symbol-

---

shake the fallacious pride of man as master of the powerful tool of logic.

103. Sensuality here translates *Sinn-lichheit*, which denotes the sensorium and connotes everything connected with the "senses" and not with the "psyche," as philosophy of an idealistic vintage conceived of them.

104. Silberer's view here reflects Freud's first impact on many of his philosophically inclined followers, and on philosophical thinking in general. Freud's findings, demonstrating that "the psychological" appears as the determining cause of behavior, and even of some physiological processes, were hailed by many as a new mine of evidence for idealism, vitalism, spiritualism, etc. The *fin de siècle* reaction against "materialism" is the proper background against which Silberer's views should be appraised, to see what must be discounted as temporal in them. After such a discounting, there still remains a host of sharp observations

and colorful original thoughts. Freud himself never made any concessions to philosophical idealism.

105. In the omitted section Silberer outlines and discusses the teleological aspects of Freud's theory. Indeed, Freud abundantly used concepts of teleological character: instincts have aims and objects; illness yields primary and secondary gains; pleasure is sought, etc. In contrast to vitalistic teleology, there is no trace in Freud of postulating a "plan" which the goals express. Consequently all of Freud's teleological formulations are, in the long run, amenable to causal formulation. Many of these teleological concepts still remain the most parsimonious ones at our disposal with which to order the phenomena in question. It would not be far-fetched to say that with Freud the choice of teleological formulations is always a matter of parsimony. Cf. Chap. 15, notes 2 and 9, below.

formation did not occur, and for that our knowledge of the mechanics of this process is insufficient. At least, then, let us see what follows from what has been said so far.

If the intelligence [106] aspect of the psychic apparatus is rated by its useful function of gaining knowledge, then symbol-thinking certainly appears to be purposive. In the course of the development of intelligence, the mechanism of symbol-formation effects an understanding of that which is as yet not understandable. Thus are gathered the threads of knowledge out of which man weaves his concepts. In cases of later apperceptive insufficiency, due to tiredness and other disturbances, symbol-formation serves as a substitute mechanism, which enables ideas and complexes to manifest themselves in spite of the disturbed condition of apperception. It is as though a provident housewife kept candles and oil lamps in an electrically illuminated house in case the current should fail. . . .[107]

106. The term "intelligence" here translates *intellektual*. The latter concept is more general, implying all of the rational aspects of the human individual. The former mainly connotes "capacity."

107. In the omitted section Silberer first compares Bleuler's causal theory with Freud's teleological point of view, in an attempt to reconcile them.

This is followed by a classification of hypnagogic hallucinations, with rich illustrative material. Since Silberer's other paper (Chap. 8, above), contains ample illustrations, we omit them here.

CHAPTER 10

EXPERIMENTAL DREAMS [1]

By Karl Schroetter

THIS IS THE FIRST REPORT on a series of dream experiments I have conducted. I shall present a few samples of the experiments but no theoretical conclusions, since these will be incorporated in a future publication in book form.[2]

In these experiments the subjects were put into deep hypnotic sleep which is, as we know, characterized by unconsciousness and followed by amnesia.[3] In this hypnotic state I gave them dream suggestions; 4–5 minutes after this they would spontaneously begin to dream.[4] According to my instructions, the subjects indicated the beginning and the end of the dream by signs; thus the duration of the dream could be exactly measured. After awakening they reported to me the content of the dream. In another series of experiments the dream took place during the night that followed the suggestion.[5] In these cases the subjects were given the post-hypnotic suggestion to write down the dream for me the next morning.

The experiments fall into two groups.[6]

1. Schroetter (674).

2. This book was never published. Schroetter died soon after the present paper appeared.

3. Hypnosis is a powerful tool in the exploration of thought-processes. But this description of hypnosis is sweeping and inexact. The nature of hypnotic "unconsciousness" and "amnesia" have been in many ways redefined by recent investigation. See Schilder and Kauders (667), Brenman and Gill (88).

4. For material concerning suggested dreams see: Roffenstein (614), Nachmansohn (537), Fervers (188), Farber and Fisher (170), Brenman and Gill (88, pp. 162–68), McDowell (495), McCord (491), Brenman (86), Wolberg (776, 775). For another type of hypnotic experiments on dreams, see Farber and Fisher (170). For dream experiments not using hypnosis, see Maury (507), Vold (744), Ladd (440), Vaschide (741), Straecke (717), Poetzl (573), Klein (384), Cubberley (135).

5. Note the parallel procedure in Brenman and Gill (88, p. 162), and Nachmansohn (Chap. 12, below).

6. In evaluating the bearing of these experiments on thought-organization and more particularly on its symbolic forms, their relationship to Silberer's experiments (Chap. 8, above) may be profitably kept in mind: (a) In both Schroet-

GROUP I

The subjects were given 3–7 stimulus words and instructed to dream about them. Furthermore, these stimuli were combined with real or suggested bodily stimuli. This series of experiments was inspired by Prof. Hermann Swoboda of the University of Vienna who had, three years before, stimulated the dentist Edward Wolf (at present in Zabern, Elsass) to conduct such experiments. This first group is of only limited interest to psychoanalysts: what follows is a selection made accordingly.

EXPERIMENT 1. Here, an actual complex (wish-fantasy) is seen with great clarity.

Subject: Mr. F., student of philosophy, age 22.

Suggestion: You will dream of: the Nobel prize, Mr. Mayer, Lieutenant H., Stalehner, the picture: "Schwind's Honeymoon," and the house on Michael Square (built by the architect Loos).

Bodily stimulus: The left hand of the subject is put under his buttocks so that the arm is turned inward and obliquely set.

Dream duration 3'16" (in hypnosis): I stand before a marble house with green marble slabs on it. I want to get in. The door-man demands a ticket; it seems to me a railroad ticket. I have none. Mayer comes and says he will take me along; he is going to fetch the Nobel prize in chemistry for his brother. The situation changes. I stand in a triangular place where a military funeral is taking place. I am again facing a marble house. At a glass window [7] I see Miss E.,

---

ter's and Silberer's work, experience is translated into symbol-language. (b) In Silberer's work the symbolic translation is ascribed to the state of consciousness characteristic of the hypnagogic condition; in Schroetter's work it is referable either to the hypnotic state alone (for example, Experiment 1) or to both the hypnotic state and the direct suggestion to disguise the content (for example, Experiment 10). Cf. Roffenstein (614), who failed to obtain symbolization without specific suggestion to that effect, and Farber and Fisher (170),

who succeeded in doing so. (c) In Silberer's work abstract thoughts, states of consciousness, and body-experiences were symbolized; in Schroetter's, the symbolization is of isolated ideas, bodily stimulations, or of wishes and activities, some of which are considered taboo. (d) In Silberer's material the experience symbolized occurred spontaneously, while in Schroetter's it was suggested or stimulated.

7. See below Schroetter's explanation of this redundant expression.

dressed in a black harlequin costume, cleaning the glass panes. She does the cleaning with her left hand in that position (you know!), oblique and turned inward, the way she always does. I turn into a side street and meet you. You carry a large picture and are saying: "This is Schwind's Honeymoon."

Analysis: (necessarily incomplete as I am not yet in full command of the technique of dream-analysis): Mr. F. is entirely under the sway of the complex of his love for Miss E. But she is the lover of Lieutenant H., mentioned to F. [in the dream suggestion]. F.'s revenge on his rival is to let the latter die—to wit, in place of Lt. H., he dreams of a military funeral. Miss E. is near by in a black harlequin costume. Black means mourning. The harlequin costume is partly due to the Stalehner suggestion—the place where masked balls are held and which F. had visited. Moreover, her paradoxical clothing expresses the glimmer of hope still left to F. after he had done away with his opponent. This is also why "The Honeymoon" comes at the end. At the beginning of the dream F. could not travel, since he had no ticket. Note further the debasement expressed in Miss E.'s role as a maid, and the clever use of the body-stimulus to the same end (the "oblique position").[8] The cleaning of the panes is also meaningful. Some time before the dream took place, Lt. H. was treated for syphilis. Later the diagnosis was proven erroneous. But F. doubted this correction and once said jokingly: "When he sits down on a glass pane, it turns into a (mercury) mirror." Now, E. must clean that off. Hence the redundancy: glass window.[9]

8. This phrase "oblique position" is idiomatically used in German to mean inappropriately low status. It is worth noting that the bodily stimulus appears in the dream without specific suggestion to that effect.

9. If Schroetter's interpretation of this dream is correct, we have here an experimental dream in which a wish of the subject is expressed. How basic is the wish disclosed by Schroetter's reconstruction cannot be decided, nor even whether there is an additional, more fundamental wish implied. The crucial experimental finding is not the presence of this wish, but rather that experimen-tally suggested elements do appear in the dream and are treated as "day-residues" by the dream mechanisms. See Freud (209, pp. 500–506), particularly:

To put it figuratively [in the dream] a day-thought plays the part of the *entrepreneur* . . . but the *entrepreneur*, who we say has the idea and feels impelled to realize it, can do nothing without *capital*; he needs a *capitalist* who will defray the expense, and this capitalist who contributes the psychic expenditure for the dream, is invariably and indisputably, whatever the nature of the waking thoughts, *a wish from the unconscious.*

In other cases the capitalist himself is the *entrepreneur;* this, indeed, seems to be the

[Passage omitted.] [10]

EXPERIMENT 3. To show the effect of clang associations.

Subject: Miss B., medical student, age 20.

Suggestion: You will dream of: Miss Vlasta Mach, the medical student, Zanker, the singer from the Institute of Anatomy (also a medical student, whose name I did not know, but—as it turns out later—the subject did). All three

---

more usual case. An unconscious wish is excited by the day's work, and this now creates the dream. And the dream-processes provide a parallel for all the other possibilities of the economic relationship here used as an illustration. Thus the *entrepreneur* may himself contribute a little of the capital, or several *entrepreneurs* may seek the aid of the same capitalist, or several capitalists may jointly supply the capital required by the *entrepreneurs*. Thus there are dreams sustained by more than one dream-wish and many similar variations which may be readily imagined, and which are of no further interest to us (p. 506).

It is noteworthy that of the elements suggested, the Nobel prize, Mr. Mayer and "Schwind's Honeymoon" appear unchanged in the dream. Whether or not this is true of "the house on Michael Square" is unclear. Stalehner and Lt. H. are indirectly represented by the harlequin costume and by the military funeral respectively. These differences, in the way the suggested elements are treated, bespeak—as Roffenstein (Chap. 11, below) has pointed out—the genuineness of the experimental result, but the disguised elements are indirectly represented rather than symbolized. For this distinction between "indirect representation" and "symbolization," see Jones (360). He adopts the view of Rank and Sachs (589): the characteristics of symbols that distinguish them from other indirect representations are

representation of unconscious material, constant meaning, independence of individual conditioning factors, evolutionary bases, linguistic connections, and phylogenetic parallels in myths, cults, religion, etc. (360, p. 164).

He adds: "All symbols represent ideas of the self and the immediate blood relatives, or of the phenomena of birth, love and death" (360, p. 170).

Whether or not this formulation is too rigid, and the actual transition between indirect representation and symbolization is a more continuous one, is beside the point here. The fact remains that in this sense Stalehner is not symbolized but indirectly represented. The indirect representation uses here the dream mechanisms of "pars pro toto" (representing the masked-ball establishment by a costume), of displacement (namely onto Miss E.), and condensation (the harlequin costume, its black color, and the window cleaner). As for Lt. H., he too is only indirectly represented. The expression of the dreamer's death-wishes by the funeral comes near to symbolism. It may be that the most genuine symbol in the dream, the marble house for the inaccessible woman, is overlooked by Schroetter.

10. Experiment 2 is omitted here since it adds nothing to Experiment 1, neither in the kind of suggestions made, nor in their execution.

persons will turn into something in keeping with the clang-associations to their names. You won't know this in your dream. Then I explained to her what clang-associations were.

Dream (the following night): You wanted to give a musical soiree and promised me lots of fun. I came. Dr. P., Miss M., Vlasta Mach, Werner Seifert (the singing student), the medical student Zanker, were present. W. Seifert sang beautifully from "Siegfried." Then suddenly soap bubbles started to come out of his mouth. Zanker grabbed them away from him and played tennis with them; meanwhile he turned into a certain Zamirowitz, a tennis court acquaintance. By and by Seifert went up entirely in soapbubbles. Then I said to you: "As a chemist you must know how that is done." You answered: "You have to ask a druggist about that." Where am I to get the druggist? Suddenly I see that in place of Vlasta Mach, that is, in her blue blouse, there sits the druggist I patronize: it seemed to me that his name was Wlastl Mladenov. . . .

Remarks: [11] The situation is similar to that of a recent evening when all those

11. The dream actually fulfills the suggestion: Seifert, Zanker, and Mach all turn into someone (or something) else related to their names by clang association. It is further noteworthy that Schroetter has chosen names which have a meaning: *Mach* = do, *Zanker* = querulent, *Seifert* (the singer) = *Seife* = soap. In the dream the things into which these people turn are related to their names, not only by clang association but also by these meanings.

Though it is generally believed that all dreams are wishfulfilling, Schroetter makes no effort to find the wish here. But this experimental dream does demonstrate with great clarity a fundamental psychological characteristic of dreams as thought processes. Schroetter's dream suggestion contains isolated ideas and a task (*Aufgabe*). The dream does not only fulfill the task, using the suggested ideas, but welds them all into one continuous—even though apparently absurd—thought. Psychoanalysis described this process as "regard for intelligibility"

(Freud, 209, pp. 455 ff. and 486), which is a function of the awakening consciousness, and which effects an intelligible synthesis of the dream elements.

General psychology (Watt, 751; Buehler, 111; Ach, 15; etc.) would describe this thought-process of the dream in terms of the concepts, tasks (*Aufgaben*) and determining tendencies, which have been demonstrated to be the unifying agents of the heterogeneous elements of trains of thought. Cf. Chap. 1, above.

Schroetter's experiment appears to be closely related to Erickson's (161) experiments on the psychopathology of everyday life. Erickson also suggested tasks to his subjects. In the post-hypnotic state the subjects creatively integrated many incidental facets of the reality situation (not included in the suggestion) into the execution of these tasks, just as Schroetter's subject in the dream-state creatively united not only the isolated suggested elements, but additional mental content (for example, Seifert) as well.

named, excepting Werner Seifert and the medical student Zanker, were present. I had introduced the latter to the subject on the same day. She had seen the opera *Siegfried* three days before. *"You must ask a druggist about that"* is a nearly verbatim quotation from a certain professor. Finally, it is a characteristic trait of suggested dreams that the hypnotist plays a role in them.[12] *I am the chemist:* I actually have a pharmacist's degree.

EXPERIMENT 4. Miss B. The following night.

Suggestion: In the first part of the dream everything will be abnormally small, and in the second part abnormally large.

Dream: We (you, F., and I) are sitting at Wimbergers. You are hypnotizing me. I go under. When I awake a priest stands before me and says: "The soul belongs to heaven and must be saved from you," and such like. I say nothing. You answer: "But this is my wife!" The priest: "Sooner will a camel go through the eye of a needle than she be your wife." I say: "Oh, to crawl through the eye of a needle—that I can." I pull out a large needle and crawl through. In the meantime I become as small as my little finger. Then you say to me: "You must be able to do that, you glacier-flea."

Then we all leave. We walk arm in arm; we are very small and put a magnifying glass between our shoulders, so that we can see each other. Then I ask you for a cigarette. You take one out, a tremendously big one, and a box of matches—the size of a house. We go to Stephen Square. There is a poster with three words on it—Gessler, Altvater, Jaegerdorf. I say: "Let's go up Bisamberg." We reach it in three steps (one over the Danube), since we have become monstrously big through the magnifying glass.

12. It is not clear whether Schroetter means a role in the manifest content or in the latent dream-thought. If the former, then neither some of his other experiments (Numbers 6, 7, 8, 9, 10) nor those of other investigators bear him out. If he means the latter, he fails to offer evidence for this statement. It may be asked whether the role of the hypnotist in the suggested dream parallels that of the therapist in a spontaneous dream occurring in therapy. Against such a parallel is the evidence showing that hypnotically suggested dreams cannot be equated with spontaneous dreams. Brenman (86) describes a most instructive series of hypnotically induced dreams with characteristic differences in their thought-organization and demonstrates that there is a fluid transition between them. She concludes that hypnotic dreams are "forced fantasies" (see Ferenczi, 181) and range from "embellished reminiscences" and "static pictorial images," through "quasi allegories of contrived flavor," to "quasi dreams," and "dreams" that can hardly be distinguished from the usual ones.

Remarks: The night before we were in the Wimberger Restaurant, where I was careless enough to hypnotize the lady in public. This upset two gentlemen, to whom I then replied: "But Miss B. is my wife." Thus, here again we have a verbatim repetition. Also: *"You glacier-flea"* comes from the previous night: a gay fellow called her that jokingly. She is very small. *Arm in arm:* we walked home that way. The gay fellow spoke of a magnifying glass. She was on *Bisamberg* that same day. There she met a *priest*. The *poster* is also a day-residue.[13]

GROUP 2

The second group of experiments I undertook on my own initiative. It is based on the Freudian theory. A latent dream content [14]—like those Freud and

13. This experiment reveals little that is new; moreover, Schroetter does not reconstruct the wish implied. Our reasons for including it: (a) It shows clearly how this very general suggestion is realized by using day-residues. Schroetter's remarks on this experiment suggest that these day-residues must have been accompanied by intense feelings. Feelings, however, are always related to impulses and wishes. Therefore, we may infer that the suggestion mobilized a wish, which in turn made use of day-residues; (b) It shows Schroetter's relationship to this subject and an indiscretion of his. This may explain why Roffenstein, (Chap. 11, p. 252, below) questions Schroetter's statement that his subjects were unfamiliar with psychoanalysis; (c) It shows that, though the dream is replete with indirect representations and symbols, the suggestion itself is carried out without disguise.

14. Schroetter's claim that in the following experiments his suggestions were "latent dream contents" cannot be accepted. The contents of his suggestions do occur frequently in latent dream-thoughts. But whether the personality organization of any particular subject is such that a given suggested content will be the equivalent of the latent wish of a spontaneous dream cannot be prejudged.

Schroetter's experiments fall into several groups according to the type of suggestion given. In Experiments 11, 12, and 14, sensations are suggested; in Experiments 1, 2, and 3, isolated ideas. The suggestions in Experiments 8 and 13 are fulfillments of *conscious* wishes of the subject. The suggestions in Experiments 5, 6, 7 and 10, refer to the fulfillment of probably tabooed ideas; it is these Schroetter labels "latent dream contents." These suggest sexual activities, but as indicated, are wishfulfillments by assumption and implication only. A latent dream-content cannot be suggested in this fashion. A latent dream-content either emerges spontaneously as in Schroetter's first experiment, in which case the experimenter has no control over it; or a very general suggestion may be given which indicates the type of wish sought for, leaving it to the subject to mobilize an actual wish of his, falling into the desired category. A suggestion of this kind would read: you will have

his school have discovered with their method of dream analysis—is used as the dream suggestion. The experimental method is the same as in Group 1. It is important that the subjects were not familiar with Freud's work, nor did they suspect the meaning of their dreams.[15]

EXPERIMENT 5. *Subject:* Miss B.

Suggestion: You will dream of sexual intercourse with your friend B, first in a normal, then in an abnormal fashion. You are to *forget* the suggestion and then to dream of it symbolically.[16] *No further explanation was given.*

Dream (in hypnosis): Sunday afternoon. I am expecting my friend B. We want to celebrate his name-day. He brings a bottle of wine wrapped in a coat. Upon his request I take a glass from the cupboard and hold it up to him; he

---

a dream about incestuous wishes. Dream suggestions in the course of hypnotherapy may approximate this form. The therapist sees that the patient is struggling with a conflict. He wants to bring it into the open and suggests: you will have a dream that will clarify this problem. See Brenman (86). For the study of thought-organization all four types of Schroetter's experiments (suggestions of isolated ideas used by the dream as day-residues, of sensations used in the same way, of conscious wishes, and of tabooed ideas) are important since each elucidates one phase of thought-formation.

15. Compare Roffenstein (Chap. 11, p. 252, below).

16. In the absence of further information about Miss B. one cannot say whether this wish would be normally repressed by her. Thus there is some doubt whether this suggestion is a "latent dream content." (See note 14, above.) The instruction to forget the suggestion may have been designed by Schroetter to bring about repression: to render this an unconscious wish. It is noteworthy that symbolization is also specifically suggested. In Experiment 1, dream-

mechanisms are at work without specific suggestion (the representation of the rival as dead; the cleaning of the glass window, etc.). One may wonder why it is necessary to give a specific suggestion to obtain symbolization, which is after all a dream mechanism. In hypnotherapy such suggestion seems unnecessary. Farber and Fisher (170) too found it unnecessary for their experiments. They describe their procedure as follows (170, pp. 209–10):

Under deep hypnosis the subject is told, "I am going to recall an experience that happened to you some time ago. You have probably forgotten it, but as I describe it, you will remember it in all its details." The experience is then described and the subject is told: "A dream will come to you. Raise your right hand when the dream begins and lower it when the dream is finished. . . ." It should be noted that the subject is not instructed to dream about the suggested situation, but merely told that a dream will come to him. We have been more successful in eliciting dreams with this method, probably because it permits greater freedom of fantasy on the part of the subject.

pours out some wine. I am frightened by that, cry out and drop the glass. It breaks and the wine spills over the floor. I am very angry with B. for ruining the rug. He consoles me: "I'll make up for that. Give me another glass for the wine." I bring another one. He wants to pour out the rest of the wine carefully into the glass. But after pouring a few drops, he snatches away the bottle.[17]

Remark: The peculiar sensuous movements of the subject—which defy description—obviously pertained to the latent content.

EXPERIMENT 6. *Subject:* Miss B.

Suggestion: You will dream that you have intercourse with a man, French fashion. (The experimenter knew that this kind of intercourse was known to her by that name.) [18]

Dream (in hypnosis): I feel as if a mass is descending upon me from the upper edge of my eye, preventing me from seeing, and settles on my shoulders like heavy wings. I wrap myself up in it entirely as if it were a hooded cape and go to a masked ball to look for B. I enter. A multitude of people running around, noise, stench, candles burning. Then I see—in fact I saw nothing—B in a corner with a wench. "Oh, you are here, I knew you'd come." Then he wants to shake hands with me, but pulls back his hand and searches his pockets for his gloves. He doesn't find them. Then he takes out a cigarette and puts it in his mouth. I want to snatch it away from him and burn myself badly. He says: "What are you doing?"

17. The symbols "bottle" and "pouring" are clear. The duplication of the act is also represented. The meaning of the further details of the dream, however, can only be speculated about because the subject's wishes, fears, and experience that could elucidate them are unknown. In Experiment 1, Schroetter saw that the dream elements he suggested were tied together in the dream by a wish of the subject. With the exception of Experiments 8 and 13 we hardly hear from Schroetter of the subject's wishes, but only of the wishes suggested by him. Yet the subject's wishes, conflicts, and experiences patently appear in Experiments 4 and 5 as well as in the subsequent ones. The hypnotic subject is not a symbolizing automaton and his wishes are not in abeyance even if the superimposed suggested wish clouds them and the lack of associative material prevents reconstruction on any but a purely speculative basis. Cf. Chap. 12, note 21, below.

18. Since in the next experiment (No. 7) it is stated that no suggestion for symbolization was given, one wonders whether such was the case here, too, or whether the lack of comment is a deficiency of the record.

Dream duration: 4 minutes, 5 seconds.

Remark: The lady explained the first sentence of the dream spontaneously by a severe headache she had before the hypnosis. This is certainly used, but the symbolization of the position in the act is very clear. (Wings over the shoulders = legs; mass = foreign body, also the "inability to see.") [19] It is to be noted that multitude of people = secret, according to Freud; the burning candles suggest the same. Another fact should be mentioned: on the night of the experiment her friend B. visited a tavern and she expressed the wish to surprise him there.

EXPERIMENT 7. *Subject:* Miss E., pharmacist, age 24.

Suggestion: You will dream that you have homosexual intercourse with your girl friend L. You will forget the suggestion and then dream. (No suggestion to symbolize.) [20]

Dream (the following night): I sit in a small dirty café holding a tremendous French newspaper. There is hardly anyone there, except a few peddlers. A woman with a strong Yiddish accent asks me twice: "Don't you need anything?" I don't answer, burying myself in the paper. She comes a third time. I angrily put down the newspaper and recognize in her my acquaintance L. She holds a threadbare suitcase with a sticker on it that reads: "For ladies only!" She is dressed like an old woman, in dirty rags, with a kerchief on her head. "Don't you want to come with me, I am on my way home." I leave the café with her and we go through an unfamiliar street, but soon find ourselves in Mariahilf, where she lives. On the way she hangs onto me; I find this unpleasant but suffer it in order not to offend. Before her house she pulls an enormous bunch of keys out of a rag, selects a key and gives it to me: "I trust only you with it; it is the key to this case. You might like to use it. Just watch that my husband doesn't get hold of it; I couldn't stand that. He is so indiscreet, always wanting to prowl

19. Whether this is symbolization or indirect representation is hard to decide. The cigarette, however, and the episode built around it are clear symbolizations of the penis and of "French fashion" intercourse.

The representation of the headache by a heavy mass is an interesting example of the way in which the dream-work weaves day-residues and sensory stimuli into the manifest dream content in order to express the latent dream thought (here the "French fashion" intercourse).

20. Cf. note 16 above. This example supports to some extent the experience of Farber and Fisher (170).

around among my things; I can't stand that." "I don't get a word of what you are saying." "Just don't give me away, my husband must not find out." She goes into the house, leaving me with the key.[21]

Remarks: Miss L., the friend, is Jewish, while the dreamer is of Aryan origin.

EXPERIMENT 8. *Subject:* Miss E.

Suggestion: You will dream of the fulfillment of your most ardent wish.

Body stimulus: 1. The experimenter twice strokes the middle of the lady's underarm. 2. He twice pinches a bone of the left foot while she is dreaming.

Preliminary remarks: I knew the subject's greatest wish. She is the lady who plays a role in Mr. F.'s dream (Experiment 1). She loves a lieutenant, but, for external reasons, it is difficult to consider engagment.[22]

Dream (in hypnosis): I am traveling to Dalmatia. My mother and Lt. H. come to Gravos to meet me. From the pier we walk in a rapid brook (which is actually in Lastua, Campagna); since the road is very bad I hang onto the lieutenant. With the words: "So that you don't go arm in arm with anyone else," he cuts up my left arm lengthwise with his sword. It starts to rain hard. We should be going home. Then my left foot is caught in a crevice; my mother goes on to get an umbrella, while H. wraps me in his raincoat; we remain alone waiting for mother.[23]

Remarks: The trip to Dalmatia already contains the wishfulfillment, as Lt. H. is stationed there.[24] The mother fosters the relationship, but in her presence the

21. This is the most frequently quoted Schroetter experiment. See Freud (209, p. 386; 255, p. 36). It contains—to one familiar with dream-work—strikingly clear examples of dream-mechanisms, and a collection of classic symbols: "suitcase" = woman; "housekey" = penis; "house" = woman; etc.

22. Schroetter's "Preliminary remarks" make it clear that he had in mind a conscious wish of Miss E. It seems evident that the dream obtained deals with much more than this simple conscious wish.

23. The contents of the dream referring to arm and foot seem to be related to the bodily stimuli applied by Schroetter. Cf. note 8, above.

24. This is, according to Schroetter, the fulfillment of Miss E.'s conscious wish. It appears undisguised in the manifest content and gives the impression that the suggestion was used by the dreamwork like a day-residue. The dangerous and gruesome parts of the dream content are, however, suggestive of an unconscious wish.

pair is never *per tu.*[25] The words "So that you . . ." are an important link in connection with the transference, but more of this later.[26]

EXPERIMENT 9. *Subject:* Miss E.

Suggestion: Dream something that symbolizes your present psychic state.[27]

Dream: (in hypnosis): I go through a forest that is in autumn colors. The road rises steeply; it is cold and icy. Beside me walks someone I do not see; I only feel a hand pressing mine; then I get very thirsty. A spring gurgles nearby. I want to drink but there is a sign by the spring like on a vial of poison—skull and crossbones.

Remarks: The dream reflects the unhappy mood of the subject upon hearing of Lt. H.'s syphilis.[28]

EXPERIMENT 10. *Subject:* Mr. F.

Suggestion: Dream that you have sexual intercourse with your stepmother. Dream it in disguised form.[29]

Dream duration: 2 minutes.

Dream (in hypnosis): My father is dead and lies on a bier in a large coffin. A young girl enters whom I do not know. I trifle with her and begin to pat her. She resists and says she is my sister. Suddenly my father stands behind me and tells me something I don't understand. My little brother comes in through the door.

Remarks: Mr. F. lost his mother in early childhood. He has had a stepmother for ten years; she has but one child, the little brother, as he calls him. F. has no

25. "Per tu" = addressing one familiarly in the second person.

26. To this suggestive point concerning Miss E., Schroetter never does come back. There is various evidence, such as his remark at the end of Experiment 13, of his reluctance to discuss transference material.

27. This suggestion concerning the subject's frame of mind renders the experiment very similar to those of Silberer; note particularly Chap. 8, Example 2, above.

28. The dream not only reflects an unhappy mood but it also deals with the specific problem leading to the unhappiness. Assuming that Schroetter is correct about what was uppermost in the subject's mind, one might speculate that it represents the danger of sexual relations with Lt. H.

29. Note again the suggestion to disguise.

sister. It is remarkable, though, that he addressed the poems of his adolescence to his "sister." [30]

In the following experiments I investigated also the symbolization of bodily processes.[31]

EXPERIMENT 11. *Subject:* Miss B.

Preliminary remark: The lady suffered from a stubborn headache, of which I freed her by hypnosis.

Suggestion: You will dream of your headache vanishing.

Dream: I stroll on the Ring [32] with a giant hat on; the wind flutters it, threatening to carry it off. I hold it, but it flies off and everyone stares at me. Then I get into an automobile that goes by; but there must be horse hair in the upholstery for it scratches my hands.

Remark: The last element is due to a bodily stimulus: I tickled the back of the sleeper's hands.

EXPERIMENT 12. *Subject:* Mr. F.

Suggestion: You have a toothache and a mild urge to urinate. In the course of the next five minutes you will dream something.[33]

Dream: We were in the Prater at the Watschenmann.[34] I slapped him so long

---

30. Schroetter gives pertinent data about Mr. F. but he does not clarify the connection between the data and the dream. At first sight, the dream seems to be a mildly disguised representation of the suggestion: incestuous activity takes place in the manifest content. Closer inspection, however, suggests that more elaborate dream-work may have taken place: the death of the father, the father's revival, the little brother coming in through a door.

31. The rest of the experiments (excepting No. 13) actually form a third group. This group using suggestions of bodily stimuli is related to those experiments Nos. 2 and 8, which use bodily stimulations. The difference is that there

the stimulation took place, while here it was suggested. The very fact of stimulation in the hypnotic state may be conceived as a suggestion to include it in the dream. Cf. notes 8 and 23, above. It must be remembered, however, that ordinary dreams utilize such stimulations spontaneously. See Maury's (507), Ladd's (440), Vold's (744) Straecke's (717), and Klein's (384) experiments, as well as Scherner's (639) obervations.

32. "Ring" is the main avenue of Vienna.

33. The suggestion here is quite like that of Farber and Fisher (170); see note 16, above.

34. "Prater" is Vienna's amusement park; the "Watschenman" is one of its

that his face got bigger and bigger. Then we took a boat to an inn, and drank a lot of beer.

Dream duration: 1 minute, 20 seconds.

Remark: The symbolism of the boat-ride is clear and contains the motivation of the urge to urinate.[35]

I have already indicated that I observed the phenomenon of "transference" (of the hypnotic subject to the hypnotist). The following case is an illustration.

EXPERIMENT 13. *Subject:* Miss B.

Preliminary remark: Miss B. was supposed to leave for her vacation, but she wanted to stay in Vienna.

Suggestion: You will dream of the fulfillment of your wish to remain here.[36]

Dream: (the following night). I pack my suitcase for the trip. Among the linens I find a peculiarly folded towel. I try to play it, accordion fashion. Being unsuccessful, I throw it on the floor in rage, sit down at the desk and write on legal-size paper page after page of one single word. I do it with the impression that I am acting under a compulsion. That makes me think I am crazy and so I want to kill myself. I attempt to cut my wrists with a nail-file, but soon stop, for this craziness of mine isn't really so bad. But I write a telegram: "Cannot come home. Am paralytic. Discretion. Matter of honor." The main thing is that no one should notice my state. I must be especially careful about Dr. Schroetter, as he is a psychologist. It would be best that he not know about my decision to stay in Vienna. Then I get a letter from you: "It would give me pleasure to go on a hike with you Easter Monday, perhaps to Steinhof. At 8 at the University." I think you want to take me to an insane asylum. You are after me. I don't dare go out into the street. But I must send the wire. I leave the house, full of anxiety, find a carriage at the door with you in it waiting for me. You force me into the carriage, hold my hand in a tight grip and stare at

---

features, a dummy whose face is slapped. There is a spring indicator to measure the strength of the slap.

35. Schroetter's remark is rather unclear. The water and the beer drinking indirectly represent the urge to urinate. Cf. Straecke (717). The swelling face of

the dummy indirectly represents the toothache.

36. The suggestion is similar to that of Experiment 8. Cf. note 14, above. Neither in Experiment 8 nor here was amnesia suggested.

me strangely—like in hypnosis. This stare makes me frightfully uncomfortable, my anxiety keeps mounting, I extricate myself, tear the door open and jump out of the running carriage. An acquaintance, a regimental surgeon, catches me as I fall.

Remarks: The dream is directed entirely at me. The lady herself offers the following details: the previous day she had been sorting linens, heard accordion music in a nightclub, and overheard a conversation at the table next to her concerning various forms of insanity. She had drawn in playful distraction some figures on a piece of paper, and when she noticed what she was doing, said: "crazy." The meaning of the dream is clearly this: If I go crazy, I can stay here.[37] Insanity is brought into close relationship to hypnosis. (The popular conception: hypnosis drives one crazy). A pregnancy fantasy (not rare in this subject) shows up clearly: "Discretion. Matter of honor" and "that no one notice my state."

Certain considerations prevent me from elaborating further on this rather easily understood dream.[38]

37. The correctness of Schroetter's interpretation of this dream may be questioned. "If I go crazy I can stay here" fits the first part of the dream. That it is consonant with the second part also, should have been demonstrated: it appears on superficial inspection unlikely. It seems that the subject's dream went beyond what was suggested, just as in Experiments 1 and 8. The suggested wish in Experiment 8 and the suggested isolated details in Experiment 1 were used by the dream to represent spontaneous wishes. This phenomenon is noteworthy since it shows characteristics of the experimental dream that have a bearing on thought-organization. All dreams, spontaneous and hypnotic, are organized by unconscious wishes. These wishes may play two somewhat differing roles in relation to the suggested contents, depending on the quality of the latter: (a) When the suggestions are isolated elements or generalized conscious wishes the task is too ill-defined, and the dream formation will be determined by an unconscious wish of the subject which has some affinity to the suggested material; (b) When the suggestion is a concrete wish, as in Experiments 5, 6, 7, and 10, then the dream-forming unconscious wish will tend to coincide with the suggested one, and the experimental demonstration of symbolization is likely to be direct.

38. The conscious wish used as a suggestion is directly fulfilled here, not symbolized or indirectly represented. The dream-work and symbolism deal with more fundamental wishes and fears; Schroetter refers to these by stating that "the dream is directed entirely at me." (Cf. the end of Experiment 8, and note 13.)

CHAPTER II

EXPERIMENTS ON SYMBOLIZATION IN DREAMS [1]
By Gaston Roffenstein

[Passage omitted.] [2]

PROMPTED BY Hermann Swoboda, Schroetter attempted by a very simple experimental procedure to prove the validity of the Freudian symbolic interpretation of dreams.[3] The subject is given the hypnotic suggestion to dream of a sexual activity with amnesia for the suggestion. The post-hypnotic dream then contains the sexual activity not in explicit but in symbolic form.[4] The symbols are in general the ones familiar to us through Freud's "The Interpretation of Dreams."

There is an important difference between an experimental and a spontaneous dream: in the former the intended meaning of the dream is known in advance—it is suggested hypnotically, while in the latter it has to be *inferred*.[5] The similarity that obtains between the translation into dream-symbols of the hypnotic suggestion and Freudian interpretation of dream-symbols is obviously a tentative verification of that interpretation.[6] This holds even in the face of the nec-

1. Roffenstein (614).

2. The introductory part of this paper is omitted since it deals with the general problem of the validity of psychoanalytic theory. In it Roffenstein refutes Allers' (20, 19) "immanent" critique of psychoanalysis, which maintains that the psychoanalytic method is worthless and all that it "discovers" is either postulated a priori by the method or arrived at by intuition independent of the method. Roffenstein's own methodological critique of psychoanalysis is sharp and thoughtful, though not always well informed. For this critique see also Roffenstein (616, 615). The methodological discussion outlines the role and emphasizes the significance of the experiments reported.

3. See Schroetter (Chap. 10, above); reproduced partly in Silberer (692).

4. For reservations on this point, see Chap. 10, notes 16, 17, 18, 19, above.

5. For other differences, see Brenman (86).

6. Both Roffenstein and Schroetter were satisfied with this form of verification, but by not obtaining (or at least not reporting) their subjects' associations to the experimentally produced dreams, they missed an important opportunity to further verify the method. The study of these dreams (particularly of those reported by Schroetter)—

essary reservations which I shall make. Some of Schroetter's results are striking and enlightening. . . .[7]

In Schroetter's Experiment 9 symbolization is suggested. In his Experiment 7 the subject dreams in symbols without direct suggestion to this effect; she seems to know what the experimenter is after.[8]

---

as our footnotes show—leaves many doubtful points. These cannot be cleared up, and the potentialities of the experiments cannot be fully exploited, since the associations of the subjects are not available. Though Nachmansohn (Chap. 12, below) made a very thoughtful attempt in this direction, this is a broad field still open to exploration.

7. Here Roffenstein quotes Schroetter's Experiments 7 and 9, Chap. 10, above.

8. Cf. Chap. 10, notes 13 and 18, above. The explanation "she seems to know what the experimenter is after" is either ambiguous or too facile. The reasons for a subject's symbolizing without any specific suggestion to this effect may be varied: (a) There is a general tendency in all experimental work for the subject to discover the experimenter's wishes and to comply with them. (b) This tendency to comply is usually heightened in the hypnotic state. (c) The hypnotic state of consciousness tends to facilitate indirect representation and symbolization. Silberer (Chap. 8 and 9, above) also claimed such a propensity for hypnagogic states. In contrast to Silberer, psychoanalysts (for example, Jones, 360; see also Chap. 9, notes 55, 60, above) have assumed that this propensity of the hypnagogic state becomes operative only when it is triggered by repressed affects, impulses, or wishes. It may be that the mechanism by which the hypnotic state tends to facilitate the expression of un-

conscious wishes in indirect and symbolic forms is a similar one. (d) Repression and censorship play a crucial role in all symbolization: only what must not become directly expressed is symbolized. (See Jones, 360, p. 183; also Nachmansohn, Chap. 12, note 81, below.) The inter-individual and intra-individual variability of what is or is not symbolized would then be explained by the personality structure of the subject, including both the general intensity of censorship and the selective consorship of the specific contents which are repressed.

The role of the hypnotic, hypnagogic, and dream-states would be then the weakening of the censorship to the point where, by the use of symbolization, otherwise censored material may be indirectly expressed. This assumption is supported in part by Nachmansohn's study (Chap. 12, below). Note that Freud's views were by no means as rigidly held as Jones's (Chap. 12, note 81, below) and that Fenichel's (176) viewpoint synthesizes those expressed by Silberer and Jones. Fenichel's views are also consistent with the pertinent material summarized by H. Werner (755). Fenichel wrote (176, p. 48):

Silberer explained symbolism as an "apperceptive insufficiency of the ego." He certainly was right, although his superficial classification of symbols according to the cause of this insufficiency cannot be accepted. Jones is not convincing in his statement that retracing symbolism to insuffi-

These experiments, simply and ingeniously conceived, would be an important support for the theory of symbolic translation. However, it has so far been impossible to repeat them. Orthodox psychoanalysis, being unconcerned with the problem, has shown no interest in doing so; [9] Schroetter died very soon after the publication of his experiments. Dattner, Schilder, and the author failed in their attempts to repeat these hypnotic experiments: the subject either did not dream at all (in spite of good hypnotic and post-hypnotic suggestibility), or the dream was reproduced *tel quel* without distortion or change,[10] frankly sexual activities being expressed in unembellished form even when symbolic representation was definitely suggested. In the suggestions the word "symbolic"

---

cient apperception is like retracing slips of the tongue to fatigue. Slips of the tongue are not an essential part of the state of fatigue (they are only precipitated by this state), whereas it is an essential part of archaic thinking with insufficient apperception to experience the world in symbols.

9. Without belittling the significance of *experimental verification* of psychoanalytic findings it may be pointed out that: (a) This formulation disregards the fact that it takes certain kinds of people to do clinical investigations and certain others to experiment. Though this is not a hard and fast dichotomy, it becomes very marked in both very undeveloped and highly specialized periods of a science. Cf. Rapaport (599). (b) Experiment is not the only method of verification. The methodology of systematic observation (cf. Hartmann and Kris, 309) as a verification procedure is not radically different from modern experimental methodology (see Lewin, 465; Brenman and Gill, 272, 89; Brunswik, 102; Schafer, 633; Klein, 386). (c) There are complex and overdetermined psychological phenomena in which experimental study may be entirely inapplicable or may yield much less than is

derived from systematic observation of the phenomena.

10. This may seem very surprising after a casual reading of Schroetter's report. Detailed study of that report reveals, however (see the footnotes to Schroetter's paper in this volume), that some suggestions *did* appear in the dreams without distortion, disguise, or change. Moreover, Schroetter's report does not state how many subjects he used altogether, how many of these yielded "poor" results, what the total number of experiments was, nor the percentage of "negative" results with those subjects whose experiments he did report. Many variables seem to interact in the results of such experiments: the type of hypnotic state created by the experimenter, the personality of the subject, the type of suggestion given, the type of content suggested. Any particular combination of these may be "unfavorable" and bring negative results. Actually, negative results are important data for a psychology of thinking, since their investigation may reveal those conditions unfavorable for symbolization and indirect representation just as the varieties of positive results will reveal the favorable conditions.

naturally had to be replaced by more colloquial German words, such as "dressed up," "hidden," "hinted," "distorted," "disguised," and so on. In several cases resistance was expressed to crudely sexual, and particularly to perverse, dream contents: "I would not dream such a thing." This corresponds well with our present knowledge concerning the limits set by personality make-up to hypnotic and post-hypnotic suggestibility.[11]

The suspicion remained that Schroetter's subjects were familiar with the Freudian theory. This [explanation of Schroetter's results] would rob the experiments of any validity.

But finally, after several failures, the present author did succeed in obtaining *complete proof*.

The subject is a 28-year-old totally uneducated nursemaid of sub-average intelligence, who grew up and still lives in an entirely uneducated milieu untouched by scientific aspirations; she is mentally healthy; the dreams she communicated and occasional statements she made indicate unmistakable though mild homosexual coloring.[12]

Here, too, there were at first only failures: in the dreams resulting from the suggestion to dream about crudely sexual activities, the suggestions were reproduced verbatim and undisguised. To have talked to the subject about symbolization would have been useless, but even words of similar meaning were not too well understood. Finally the suggestion was worded as follows:

You will dream of—here followed the assigned dream—but you must dream this so, distort the dream so, hide its contents so, that the dream will seem entirely innocuous; nobody must recognize what you actually dream. You must so dream that you could tell this dream to any stranger without embarrassment. Only you and I will know the real meaning of the dream; only we will know that you dreamt ac-

11. Cf. note 10 above. Erickson (161, 162), Wolberg (776), P. C. Young (780) and others in recent studies show that the quality of the hypnotic state depends, among other things, upon the personality of the subject, as do the content that can be elicited and the suggestions that can "take" in the hypnotic state. The work of Finzer, Kaywin, and Hilger (379) is a striking demonstration of this. In collaboration with Gill, they repeated Farber and Fisher's (170) work. They asked naive subjects to interpret in hypnosis dreams of other subjects. Their results do not seem to corroborate the findings of Farber and Fisher; on the contrary, they found that the "interpretations" bring out the interpreting subject's own problems and wishes. Cf. Chap. 10, note 9, above, and Chap. 12, below.

12. Apparently latent homosexual trends are meant and not mild overt homosexuality.

tually of—here again followed a statement of the suggested dream meaning. For all other people the dream must look entirely innocent. You will tell me the dream as soon as you awake, immediately on my asking you whether you have dreamt much recently. You will remember with certainty that you dreamt this dream last night.

The wording of the suggestion was repeated in various ways. Naturally, complete amnesia was suggested for these instructions. It goes without saying that giving examples, such as analogies from other dreams, and so on, was strictly avoided. It can be asserted with full confidence that this uneducated person had never in any form been exposed to *Freudian* psychoanalysis. She never saw any of Freud's writings, or the popular books and papers of his students or those of the leaders and followers of similar movements. Not even in social contact did she learn anything about these matters. The author did not tell her the purpose of the sessions at any time, not even in the form of a hint; nor has the amnesia for the dream suggestions ever been lifted.

Under these conditions the experiments were successful. The symbolizations are given below. Most of them correspond to Freud's scheme. Some are atypical, but in our opinion these deviations increase the value of the experiment. As in hypnotic research generally perfect results lead one to suspect dissimulation, while occasional false performances demonstrate the genuineness of hypnosis (see in this respect Troemner [13] and others), so do these occasional atypical results in our series of experiments bespeak their genuineness; they refute the possibility that the subject has knowledge of common symbolism.

Now for the experimental results. In the experiment technical words were, of course, replaced by commonly understood expressions. The duration of each dream, determined by agreed upon signs, was about three-fourths of a minute. A more exact determination of the duration was not intended.

EXPERIMENT 1. *Dream Suggestion:* Fellatio with your previous employer, Mr. X. At first she resisted, saying, "I would not have such a dream; certainly not with Mr. X!" The suggestion was repeated, stressing that nobody would understand the real meaning of the dream. *Dream:* "I sit in the kitchen. Suddenly the bell rings; the master calls me. I go to his room. He asks me to sit down on a chair. On the table I see many bananas. The master tells me to eat. I take one and peel it. It tastes fine."

The analogy with Freudian sexual symbolism is striking. The banana is

13. Troemner (735), Moll (523).

probably overdetermined. The use of this symbol is remarkable. It is unmistakable though, so far as I know, none too frequent.[14]

EXPERIMENT 2. *Dream Suggestion:* Masturbation in bed. *Dream:* "I lie in bed. The blanket is so heavy on me. I open the covering to see what is inside; instead of feathers there are bonbons. I eat them, they are tasty."

The dream is not as transparent as that of Experiment 1; nevertheless, "to eat bonbons" is a not infrequent picture in psychoanalysis for sexual pleasure.[15]

EXPERIMENT 3. *Dream Suggestion:* Homosexual intercourse with your sister. *Dream:* "I am up in a cherry tree with my sister. We are small children. Instead of picking the cherries we sit so that we can bite them off and consume them that way." [16]

EXPERIMENT 4. *Dream Suggestion:* You are raped by Mr. Y. (According to the subject, Mr. Y. has a venereal disease.) *Dream:* "I am asleep in the grass. Suddenly I am attacked by a big dog, a Dobbermann; it tears at my throat; I am trying with all my might to push him away with my hands. I shout. It relents and I see blood flowing down from my throat and say to myself: *now I must die.*"

The fact of suspected venereal disease does not come to clear expression, certainly not in its classical form as in Schroetter's experiment,[17] but the rape is well represented; the probable analogy of death and orgasm is worth under-

14. The symbolization both of the penis and the fellatio are clear here. It is also striking that material which would directly indicate the subject's own (not suggested) wishes and conflicts (so abundant in Schroetter's experiments and also present in the fellatio dream he reported) is absent here. Perhaps this can be explained by the suggested content being syntonic with the subject's wishes ("It tastes fine").

15. This appears to be indirect representation rather than symbolization. Moreover, one suggested element, "bed," is directly represented.

16. The symbolization is clear. Cf.

Jones's (360) observation on the linguistic connections of genuine symbols (Chap. 10, note 9, above) and the American slang meaning of "cherry." There is, in addition, an individual accent in the expressions, "bite them off" and "consume them."

17. The reference is apparently to Miss E.'s cleaning the window in Experiment 1 or to Lt. H.'s cutting up Miss E.'s hand in Experiment 8. But the dire consequences in the present dream may be *indirect representations* of the fear of syphilis. At any rate, the symbolization of rape is clear.

scoring.[18] Weininger[19] regards the dog as a symbol of a criminal.

EXPERIMENT 5. *Dream Suggestion:* Intercourse with the father. *Dream:* "I dreamt about my father, as if he had presented me with a great bag, a traveling bag, and with it he gave me a large key. It was a very large key. It looked like a key to a house. *I had a sad feeling,* and I wondered about its being so big; it couldn't possibly fit. Then I opened the bag. A snake jumped out right against my mouth. I shrieked aloud and then I awoke."

Here, too, the suggestion met with intense inhibition and resistance; only upon energetic repetition and the reiterated explanation that it would be distorted in the dream, was it carried out.

The results of Experiment 5 are actually the most striking: the key, the snake, the bag, the large key and small keyhole. It should also be noted that key and bag are used the same way as by Schroetter's dreamers.[20]

Since the conditions of this experimental series fulfill the criteria of validity, even when judged with due skepticism towards far-reaching conclusions, the results are noteworthy. To be sure, *only* the problem of symbolization is clarified, while everything else [about psychoanalysis] remains untouched and controversial for the time being. We do not want to overestimate the value of the experiment. The sexual symbolism of dreams has already found partial support in the symbolism of myths, folk-lore, and schizophrenia. . . .[21] Thus we do not lack independent evidence for individual symbol interpretations but only for their relationship to the experience of the analysand whose unconscious ideas are inferred by interpreting symbols without subjecting the interpretation to any further verifying control. This is the point of departure of the charge of circular reasoning.[22]

Even though symbolization in general, and certain symbol relationships of content in particular, have been made plausible to some degree, the parallel between folk-lore, myths, and so on, on the one hand, and the dream on the other,

---

18. Without further evidence this is at best speculation, particularly in view of Mr. Y.'s syphilis.

19. Weininger (754).

20. The reference is to Schroetter's Experiment 7. The personal coloring in "right against my mouth" is again noteworthy.

21. See Rank (587); Freud (227); Jung (364); Roffenstein implies that these other lines of evidence are independent of psychoanalysis.

22. This argument disregards the verification obtained by free association.

has not escaped justified doubts. *Our experiment, however, proves symbol-formation in dreams.*

[Passage omitted.] [23]

23. In the omitted concluding section Roffenstein asserts that the experimental method used attests not only to the validity of dream symbolism, but also to the usefulness of the psychoanalytic method. Having drawn this positive conclusion, in contradiction to Allers, he proceeds—now in accord with Allers— to question the role of repressed ideas in dream-formation. He ends up with the statement: "The role and meaning of symbolization are still fully open to discussion. The present communication should serve only toward the clarification of this small segment of the problem [of psychoanalysis]."

CHAPTER 12

CONCERNING EXPERIMENTALLY PRODUCED DREAMS [1]

By M. Nachmansohn

THIS INVESTIGATION originated when I set myself the task of combatting a patient's sleeplessness due to headaches of organic origin. . . . The patient readily accepted the [hypnotic] suggestion of sleep and analgesia. However, after a few hours she awoke with a most intense headache and was unable to sleep again.[2]

1. Nachmansohn (537). This is an abbreviation of the full title: "Concerning Experimentally Produced Dreams with Critical Comments on the Psychoanalytic method (Preliminary Communication)." The critical section is omitted here.

Of the three papers on dreams translated in this volume, this is the least known, though most thoughtful. Schroetter's and Roffenstein's papers were in the main concerned with isolated wishes and their symbolization, that is, with the co-ordination of drive and its ideational representation in that form of thinking which we call dream; but Nachmansohn goes further and gropes after the integration of this co-ordination within the personality structure of the dreamer.

These three experiments may be looked upon as a step toward translating into conceptual-scientific terms the ancient knowledge that the individual's thinking reveals his character. What concepts will translate this knowledge into science? Since logical thinking has the semblance of commonality for all people,

its concepts were not very promising for this purpose. In fact, they made thinking appear solely dependent on external conditions and their changes. The discovery of the role in thought-processes of wishes and drives, that is, of motivations, made it feasible to conceive of thinking as having its roots in the individual. But there is a fly in this ointment: drives and wishes, too, prove to have a high degree of commonality; their symbolic representation seems even to have some degree of universality. Thus, while the concepts drive and wish find the roots of thought in the individual, they do not encompass individual specificity of thinking expressive of the individual's character. The search for the sources of individual specificity is the unique feature of Nachmansohn's study. These sources constitute one of the central problems of the ego-psychology of thinking, the fundamental elements of which are treated in the three Freud selections (Chap. 15, 16, and 17) in this volume.

2. Cf. Schroetter's Experiment 11. The comparison sheds light on the degree of penetration and sophistication of

1. AN EXPERIMENT ON THE SLEEP-PROTECTING ROLE OF THE DREAM

This gave me the opportunity to test Freud's hypothesis, which Kuelpe [3] and his school also accept, that dreams protect sleep.[4] I gave the hypnotic suggestion that if the headache returned she should dream about it without awakening. Simultaneously I suggested to her to dream at night that she had left the hospital, was at work as a teacher and the children were very much attached to her. I gave this suggestion with the idea that an agreeable dream which corresponded to her innermost wishes—for the fulfillment of which she could not even hope because of her severe organic brain disease—might have some reassuring and comforting significance for her. . . .[5]

Dream 1: "I was teaching in a home for children. There were boys and girls in the class. I used the first hour for arithmetic. I do not know what exercises I gave them. My head was buzzing and I didn't even know whether the answers were correct. Then, suddenly, I was in the middle of a forest with the children; we had nature-study. The buzzing in my head did not stop. I told the children that I was going to Wil where there is a doctor who might help me. In that moment I heard the nurse talk. It was already after the morning bell." [6]

The patient slept through that night, for the first time in several months.

---

the two authors. Schroetter's question about headache was, "How is it symbolized?"; Nachmansohn's, "How can it be used to test a fundamental Freudian hypothesis?" The role of proprioceptive stimulation in dreams has been observed by many investigators. See Freud's (208) and Straecke's (717) reviews of these investigations; cf. also Chap. 10, note 4, above. The most extensive experiments using such stimulation were Straecke's (717).

3. Kuelpe (439).

4. See Freud (209, pp. 209–11, 287, 468–69, 512–13, 514–25, particularly pp. 518, 519).

5. Apart from corresponding to the content of the patient's wishes, the suggested dream-content appears—according to the dream reported below—suitable to support also the sleep-wish by

turning the rousing stimulus into a part of the wishfulfillment and thus postponing awakening. Nachmansohn says that teaching children was the "innermost wish" of the patient. Since it was a conscious wish, it would be more exact to say that it was a form in which some of her innermost wishes found expression. What these wishes were should not be conjectured here. Conscious occupational choice is usually an overdetermined product of drives, as well as of defenses and other adaptive means at the disposal of the ego.

6. The struggle of the wish (whatever its latent content) with the rousing proprioceptive stimulus is rather clear in the dream, as is the progressively increasing preponderance of the stimulus. Thus this dream may be considered to support the Freudian formulation: the

These hypnotic sleep suggestions were successful for several weeks. Then they failed and a depression developed. . . . At any rate, for a while the patient did succeed in disposing of the pain by a dream, apparently in the same fashion as that in which bladder stimulations are disposed of.[7]

[Passage omitted.] [8]

The ready post-hypnotic execution of dream-suggestions prompted me to the following dream experiments, carried out on this patient and two others who were in hypnotic treatment with me for psychological disorders. . . . I had nearly completed these experiments, and had already mentally digested my material, when I heard of Roffenstein's [9*] and Schroetter's [10*] similar experiments. Their results and mine are similar and thus support each other. I found it feasible to investigate so-called dream-distortions, the symbolic and other indirect representations of "latent dream thoughts."

Before presenting the results I shall give a brief description of the subjects and a precise statement of the procedure. This will allow the testing of the results *under exactly identical conditions.*[11]

---

dream is a guardian of the sleep. A scrutiny of the suggestion shows, however, that it commanded that "if the headache returned she should dream about it without awakening." The evidence would be conclusive only if two other experiments had also been carried out: (a) Suggestion: "If the headache returned she should dream about it." Expected result: dream and no awakening. (b) Suggestion: "If the headache returned she should not awaken." Expected result: either failure by awakening, or spontaneous dream.

In a footnote Nachmansohn comments:

In cases of nervous [psychogenic] sleeplessness, sleep-suggestion supported by suggestion to have a pleasant dream was every time successful and without deleterious sequelae, though in certain cases it proved best to suggest dreamless sleep.

Though this experiment is not without value, opportunities for further experimentation are clearly open.

7. Cf. Straecke (717).

8. The omitted section contains two dreams (Nos. 2 and 3) similar to Dream 1.

9.* Schroetter (674), also Chapter 10, above.

10.* Roffenstein (614), also Chapter 11, above.

11. Nachmansohn's meticulous and thoughtful procedure is in line with one of the prime requirements of clinical research. These requirements, however, do not include repeatability "under exactly identical conditions"—such conditions simply do not exist in human beings. The requirement Nachmansohn's study meets is that of exact recording of varying conditions in order to allow theoretical accounting for the results corresponding to them. Cf. Lewin (465), Brenman and Gill (272).

Subject 1, age 24, very intelligent, laborer parentage; grade school education; after school active in the socialist youth movement; very enthusiastic though not very deep; very "flowery" style. . . . At 18, organic brain disease followed by many epileptiform attacks. Between attacks, when headache is absent, a somewhat naive honest character. . . . A year earlier she embraced Catholicism, allegedly because social democracy had completely failed in the war and had no backbone; influenced by Catholic Sisters in this. She heard about psychoanalysis when studying to become a children's nurse. She is positive that she never heard about dream interpretation. She knows the word *symbol* from the Catholic church but cannot define its meaning for everyday life; therefore I avoided it in my suggestions, using rather the expressions "indirect," "disguised," and the like.

Subject 2, age 45. Catholic peasant parentage. Excepting affect-lability, no demonstrable mental disorder. Grade-school education, poor orthography, altogether unread. An able and thorough seamstress. Psychoanalysis is unknown to her, she can hardly pronounce the word. Very dry, without any fantasy; subjectively honest.

Subject 3, age 36. Child of well-endowed people; attended high school for girls. At times intense and uncontrolled affectivity; honest, noble character; intelligent. She heard about psychoanalysis, but not about dream interpretation or any specific symbol interpretation. Scientific interpretation of dreams seems to her improbable; it sounds to her like occultism, about which she has heard. A while back she began "psychoanalysis" in another institution, but it was broken off after two sessions because she neither associated nor brought ideas: "It just did not work."

One can say with a good conscience that none of the subjects was familiar with dream interpretation.

II. [EXPERIMENTS ON SYMBOLIZATION]

Now for the experiment. The dream-suggestion was a post-hypnotic suggestion put into writing and read to the subjects in deep hypnosis. An additional suggestion was given: to write down the dream in the morning immediately after awakening. When this suggestion was omitted, usually nothing was written down. . . . Finally, I always suggested amnesia for the dream-suggestion, and in early experiments I added: "It is up to you whether or not you will know the content of the suggestion; the fact that I gave it to you as a suggestion in hypnosis should remain unknown to you." [12] I added this for the sake of my follow-up of the dream record two hours later with an analytic investigation. I wanted to avoid suppressing free associations by an addition to the usual "censorship" of a hypnotic suggestion for amnesia. The results of the "dream interpretation" did not seem to be influenced by this suggestion; accordingly later on I omitted it.

a. Representation of Sexual Intercourse and Pregnancy

Dream 4: (a) Suggestion: "You are a nurse (for Subject 2: "a seamstress") in Amsterdam in the house of a widower. You have an affair with him and you become pregnant. You expect a child." (No suggestion to symbolize).[13]

---

12. The meaning of this suggestion is: Nachmansohn tells the subject that he has no objection to her understanding the dream she will have, or to her being able, either spontaneously or with the help of free associations, to translate the manifest dream into its latent dream-thought. Nachmansohn's assumption was that the latent thought of the dream would be identical with the content of his dream-suggestion, and he wished not to prevent the patient's discovery of this latent thought. Nachmansohn's conception shows an insufficient appreciation that, from the point of view of the dream-work, the suggestion contains two kinds of elements: (a) those which will be treated by the dream-work as innocuous day-residues (as in Schroetter's Experiment 1, Chap. 10, note 9, above; see also Freud, 209, p. 507), and; (b) those which contain the wish implied in the suggestion. It is this wish on which the dream will center, and which in the successful experiments will be treated as day-residues of uncompleted task character (cf. note 23, below).

Yet the careful distinction Nachman-sohn makes between the fact of suggestion and the content suggested, his care that the subject should not take the suggestion as prohibiting knowledge of its content, which would thereby become unamenable to reconstruction by free association, are good indicators of his psychological sensitivity and thoughtfulness. This, coupled with the absence of magical omniscience—so frequent in hypnotic investigators—increases the intrinsic reliability of this report.

13. Nachmansohn's suggestions link into a continuous story the action and/or person he wants symbolized. The story —as will be seen below—is adapted to some extent to the subject; more so as a rule than Schroetter's or Roffenstein's suggestions, though they also tried to include in their suggestions employers, lovers, known wishes of their subjects, etc. The details of Nachmansohn's suggestions make them a combination of those of Schroetter's experiments which suggested dream elements and those which suggested tabooed actions. (Cf. Schroetter, Chap. 10, note 14, above.)

(b) Solution by Subject 1: "Last night I was a nurse in Amsterdam. The father of the child was a widower of about 40. The man beat me with a piece of wood.[14] I had strong anxiety. I knew in the dream that I had sexual intercourse with him." (On questioning:) "I did not experience that; I knew I was pregnant; I beat my abdomen and wanted to jump out the window, but suddenly Dr. B. of S. held me back. I awakened bathed in sweat and excited—but not sexually."

The masochistic tendency, of which the patient is aware even when awake but without yielding to it, is expressed clearly. I shall not attempt to decide whether this dream is an expression of the alleged childish concept of sexual intercourse as self-castigation, or whether the masochistic tendencies of the patient suffice to explain it; however, I am inclined to the latter assumption. Though the suggestion concerned sexual intercourse, she only "knew" [15]* of it in her dream, but had clear dream hallucinations of the beating.[16] The idea struck me that, by diminishing "censorship," dream-suggestion may bring within reach of diagnosis matters hardly amenable in common dreams. (Though such a procedure has many sources of error, misleading suggestions can be avoided by careful technique.) . . .

Subject 1 was an "obedient" dreamer. Unless I gave explicit suggestion for indirect representation, she *nearly* always dreamt as suggested, with no more distortion than in this dream. The distortions reflected the innermost tend-

---

14. "Piece of wood" is a relatively common male sex symbol. Cf. Freud (235, p. 128).

15.* Concerning this "knowing" in dreams, see P. Koehler (394) and Hacker (297).

[Cf. also note 54, below.]

16. Nachmansohn's comments on this dream seem somewhat confusing. Whether due to "childish conception" or "masochistic tendencies," the phrase "the man beat me with a piece of wood" is an indirect representation of intercourse. That the subject in addition "knew" that she had intercourse with the man may be due to (a) the additional suggestion leaving it to the subject whether or not she will know the content of the dream suggestion; (b) the absence of suggestion for symbolization; (c) the "obedient" character of the subject (see the following paragraph); or any combination of these. It is clear, however, that Nachmansohn is intent on establishing that in dream-thinking the expression of the suggested thought is shaped by the personality of the subject. Whether or not the term masochism correctly expresses the predominant personality characteristic in question, Nachmansohn's point is sufficiently well supported.

encies of the subject.[17] Subject 3 carried out suggestions only in strongly disguised form, even when there was no suggestion for indirect representation.[18]

(c) Solution by Subject 3: "I am on a small steamship going from E. to Z. Suddenly we are in high seas; I become terribly seasick; a sailor who looks like the waiter comes and says I should call Dr. Sch. I get up and go down some stairs, then I am in the office of Attorney H. in St. Gallen. He asks me whether W. actually had seven years ago committed the lowly political crime he is accused of. He adds: you will not incriminate W., the statutory limit has passed. I was about to speak when Attorney H. turned into W. and I awoke."

Pregnancy is rather transparently represented by seasickness. The rest of the dream underscores the bad traits of W. as a substitute for something else.[19]

17. Compare with the naïveté and suggestibility reported in the personality sketch (p. 260, above).

18. Compare with the inability to associate freely, high intelligence, and complexity reported in the personality sketch (p. 260, above).

19. Nachmansohn seems to imply: W.'s bad traits appear as substitutes (indirect representations) for his having had intercourse with the subject and having made her pregnant. The associations Nachmansohn reports provide the basis for the inference: W.'s bad traits can serve as indirect representations of intercourse resulting in pregnancy because they came into sharp relief precisely in "irresponsible behavior when faced with the subject's pregnancy." This example illustrates one of the crucial characteristics of the thought-processes called dream-work and free association; though they differ radically from conscious logical thought, their similarities to it are also striking. Our use, in an abstract sense, of words which usually denote something concrete is the paradigm of all abstracting and conceptualizing. For instance, we use the adjective *hard* for a difficult task; it is the quality of materials which we find it difficult to work on, to break, etc. This pattern is common to waking- and dream-thinking. That crucial characteristic of learning which modern psychology has come to refer to as "transfer of learning" (see Katona, 374, pp. 108 ff.; Koffka, 406, pp. 430, 546–47) implies the same pattern. One of the crucial differences between the thought-processes compared here lies in the fact that the common element which makes the abstract use of concrete words and "transfer of learning" possible is public, regularly recurring, agreed upon, familiar, and therefore apparently "predictable"; while the common element which links the thought with the image in dreams is private, unique to individual experience (save for a minimal number of symbols for which universality is claimed), unconscious, and therefore uncanny rather than familiar. In fact, in dream-work, free association, *déjà vu*, etc., the common element is often an affect or drive. This specific difference between the two types of thinking I state here in terms not far removed from the observational level;

W. actually committed the crime, and owes his freedom and honor to the discretion of the subject. She never took this very tragically. The interview showed that she twice thought she was pregnant by W., and each time she had an "insane" rage when he made light of it and would not consider marrying her. Later on this man shamelessly abandoned her. "Deep down" her disappointment and need for revenge were still not assuaged, even though externally she made her peace with him, and at the time of the dream she was still strongly fixated on him. She still hoped to "save him." The dream initiated a change in this unhappy relationship of twelve years' duration which she blames for her drinking, and so on. In the interview she said spontaneously: "You know, Doctor, this dream shook me up this morning. I suddenly felt anger with W., an anger which you so far haven't seen in me, and one which I never felt before. You know—it was quite the other way around." (Continues seriously:) "He took everything for granted; he would have, even if I hanged myself for him. He is responsible—for all of it. People told me a dozen times. I believed it inside —but you know—I still defended him." (She struggled with tears.)

It is interesting that the suggestion to be in the house of a widower is apparently [20] not carried out. The explanation is that at the time of the dream she still hoped W. would divorce his wife, whom he preferred to the subject, and marry the latter as he sometimes said he would. Both the facts and the subject's account shows W.'s wife to be a bad person. About the death of this woman she would feel accordingly. Thus it is no accident that the suggestion, "You will have an affair with a widower" activates the whole "W. complex" and brings it to a transparent representation. Hate, revenge, disappointed love—all partly repressed—break through in this dream with elementary force. She is amazed that only yesterday she could defend W. so warmly, while now she harbors such anger toward him. . . .[21]

---

on an explanatory level the difference would be stated in terms of two different conditions of energy (cathexis) economy. Cf. Chap. 15, notes 29 and 30, below.

20. The emphasis is on the word *apparently*. Nachmansohn proceeds to demonstrate the subject's death wishes against W.'s wife. Since dreams represent wishes, by fulfillment W. is dreamed of as a widower.

21. That the suggested content is dreamed of symbolically is again achieved by mobilizing fundamental personal wishes to which it corresponds. Symbolization in dream is not a mere one-to-one translation of a suggested content, it is a process by which the con-

Compare the solution of the dream suggestion by Subject 2:

Solution: "I live in a beautiful house in Amsterdam. Several of my former seamstresses are working in my sewing room, among them H.H. I am cutting out the linen, but as soon as it is cut, it is already sewn (like in a fairy story). A man lives with us; I am married to him and I *know* that I am pregnant. I notice with sudden fright that I am far away from my homeland.[22] Then you come (the author) and we go to the railroad station at R. (her hometown in Switzerland). Then we are in the hospital in your room, your wife is there too. I wake up happy." While giving me the dream, the subject said half in anger: "I shall not write down any more dreams. All stupid stuff. I can't understand what you want with it."

It is interesting to compare the ways the three subjects comprehend and represent the suggestion to have an affair with a widower. Subject 1, an outspoken masochist, has herself beaten; Subject 2, who had a strict Catholic upbringing, is married outright; Subject 3 dreams in a symbolic way of being pregnant which twice before she had thought was the case.[23]

---

tent of the suggestion is integrated into the context and dynamics of the thought-formation called dream. This context, however, is always highly idiosyncratic, drive-determined, and personality-integrated.

This dream, though hypnotically suggested, is quite like a common dream. Cf. Brenman (86), or Schroetter, Chap. 10, note 12, above. It is noteworthy that as a rule Nachmansohn obtained night-dreams by hypnotic suggestion, while Schroetter, Roffenstein, Farber, and Fisher (170) used, in the main, dreams produced in hypnotic sleep. It is quite possible that this method was one of the factors that allowed Nachmansohn to notice individual differences, and yielded some dreams not appreciably distinguishable from common dreams.

22. It is possible that the second part of the dream is a restatement and more indirect representation of the suggestion.

This would indicate that indirect representations are here organized around drives and attitudes involved in the transference to the experimenter. The complete material necessary for a conclusive demonstration of this is not available; but note the affect-reaction at the end of the dream, and compare note 24, below.

23. Cf. note 1, above. Nachmansohn aptly illustrates the personality-syntonic character of the symbolic and/or indirect representation of an idea. Concerning the three dreams in question, as well as Nachmansohn's comments below, the following observations are offered. Such hypnotically suggested dreams unite several elements: (a) the content of the suggestion, which is objected to by the censorship with a severity that varies with the individual; (b) the intention of the subject to carry out the suggestion [cf. Ach in Chap. 1, and Lewin in Chap.

The dream of Subject 2 is undisguised wishfulfillment and corresponds entirely to her uncomplicated peasant psyche. But even her elaboration of the suggestion expressed inner tendencies. At first, the suggestion to be in Amsterdam was fulfilled verbatim. But this did not correspond to her wishes: she wanted to stay in Switzerland. So she dreamed she was in her home town, but did not like it there, either, because of her relatives. She preferred to stay near the hospital to have the support of the doctor.[24] The dream has a "prospective character" and shows that only those hypnotic suggestions are accepted which

---

5, above, also Brenman's (88) hypnotic experiments, particularly pp. 195 ff.] which depends on the relationship to the hypnotist and on the form of the suggestion, hence ultimately on personality characteristics determining both; (c) a wish of the subject, mobilized by the suggestion or prevailing in the subject generally or temporarily, which in either case depends on the control of wishes (drives) characteristic of the subject's personality. It is likely that (a) and (b) together are related to (c) as day-residues are to the dream-wish. On the latter, see Schroetter, Chap. 10, note 9, above, and Freud (209, pp. 497–508).

Freud (209) wrote:

Unsolved problems, harassing cares, overwhelming impressions, continue the activity of our thought even during sleep, maintaining psychic processes in the system which we have termed the preconscious. The thought-impulses continued into sleep may be divided into the following groups:

1. Those which have not been completed during the day, owing to some accidental cause.

2. Those which have been left uncompleted because our mental powers have failed us, that is, unsolved problems.

3. Those which have been turned back and suppressed during the day. This is reinforced by a powerful fourth group:

4. Those which have been excited in our unconscious during the day by the work-

ings of the preconscious; and finally we may add a fifth, consisting of:

5. The indifferent impressions of the day, which have therefore been left unsettled.

We need not underrate the psychic intensities introduced into sleep by these residues of the day's waking life, especially those emanating from the group of the unsolved issues. It is certain that these excitations continue to strive for expression during the night, and we may assume with equal certainty that the state of sleep renders impossible the usual continuance of the process of excitation in the preconscious and its termination in becoming conscious (p. 501).

. . . [for] the nocturnal excitations in the preconscious there remains no other path than that taken by the wish-excitations from the unconscious; they must seek reinforcement from the unconscious, and follow the detours of the unconscious excitations. But what is the relation of the preconscious day-residues to the dream? There is no doubt that they penetrate abundantly into the dream; that they utilize the dream-content to obtrude themselves upon consciousness even during the night, indeed, they sometimes even dominate the dream-content, and impel it to continue the work of the day; it is also certain that the day-residues may just as well have any other character as that of wishes (pp. 501–2).

24. There is more to this point and to the fright reported in the dream than meets the eye. Note the patient's reluc-

agree with the personality of the subject. Everything else is rejected, at times even on pain of anxiety. . . .

Since an experience can be symbolically represented in various ways, I suggested the same content in various forms.[25]

Dream 5: (a) Suggestion (given only to Subject 1): "You are attacked and raped by a stranger. You expect a child. You represent all this indirectly. You will dream about the headaches." (Otherwise the instructions are the same as those initially described.)

(b) Solution by Subject 1: "In my dream I was taking a walk. I had a beautiful view of all of S. Suddenly a huge snake curled around me.[26] (In the discussion she is somewhat abashed and naive: "I dream all the time about snakes, though I never saw one.") I defended myself but it was useless. I was completely exhausted. I saw a small child near by; he tried to come to me. Finally, the monster yielded its strangle-hold and I crushed its head with my shoes.[27] I looked for the child but he wasn't there. Throughout the dream I felt the top of my head rising and sinking.[28] The sleep was good but I *must* have had anxiety: when I awoke tears were still rolling down my cheeks."

---

tance to record future dreams and compare the material on transference in Nachmansohn's commentary. There may be some doubt whether the dream "is undisguised wishfulfillment and corresponds entirely to her uncomplicated peasant psyche." It is noteworthy that the suggestion is first directly fulfilled and with but one change (marriage instead of an affair), and only then follows the segment which is the subject's own creation. A consideration of her rigidity (see personality sketch) and of the transference situation may give a more adequate explanation than Nachmansohn's. The wishfulfillment would then by no means be so transparent; nor would the suggested content be identical with it. Nachmansohn's interpretation of anxiety would also be rendered inadequate by these considerations. The scant material as well as our aims here do not allow us to pursue this point further.

25. The goal was to obtain a variety of symbolic and indirect representations of an idea, action, or wish. There is no theoretical reason to expect that varying the forms of the suggestion would vary the symbolization correspondingly, since no regularity governing choice of symbols has so far been discovered. There is reason, however, to expect that varying the form of the suggestion would influence the use of other indirect representations (condensation, displacement, etc.) See note 23, above.

26. Common male symbol. Cf. Freud (235, p. 128), and Roffenstein, Experiment 5.

27. Crushing the snake's head and the disappearance of the child go beyond the suggestion and reflect specifically personal impulses or inclinations.

28. A not uncommon indirect representation of intercourse. Compare this representation with that of Dream 4 and

The patient knew that the snake is supposed to represent sexual drive. But since she had no awareness of the suggestion to dream symbolically of sexual intercourse, and since fifteen hours had passed between the suggestion and the dream, her knowledge of the sexual meaning of the snake should not devaluate this typical symbolization of the sexual act. . . .[29] The child, his disappearance, and the search for him represent in a rather transparent way the anxiety of illicit pregnancy and probably also the impulse to get rid of the foetus.[30] In general, even those dreams of this subject which followed a suggestion to symbolize were far more transparent than those dreams of Subject 3 not preceded by such suggestion. In the course of these investigations I gained the impression that the extent of distortion is proportional to the complexity of the personality.[31]

Dream 6. (a) Suggestion (given only to Subject 3:) "You have founded a hotel, are married to a doctor, have sexual intercourse with him and become pregnant. You represent all this indirectly, etc."

(b) Solution by Subject 3: "In the barn in R. I clean the horses myself; the hired man comes and says: 'The leather strapping of the horse is torn.' I say: 'Well, then we won't drive out.' I go to Doctor N.'s wife (the author's) and say that we can't drive out. We sit in a kiosk and eat lunch. Big travel bags [32] are brought out. Mrs. N. says they belong to us. We remain there the whole summer. I tell the chambermaid to change our rooms, to put the things in the quietest room, and to put a child's bed [33] from Room 27 into Dr. N.'s room.

---

with the discussion of "masochism" and "headache."

29. This argument is obviously weak; it does not hold up against Roffenstein's thesis (Chap. 11, pp. 252–53, above) that such experiments have validity only if the subjects are unfamiliar with dream symbolism.

30. The transparency of the child motif is doubtful; without further supporting evidence this interpretation is no more convincing than several other feasible ones.

31. This is another attempt to encompass and express the impression that the

dream-thought is characteristically personality-bound. But note its inadequacy and vagueness. Cf. notes 1 and 23, above.

32. Common female symbol. Cf. Freud (235, p. 128), Schroetter, Experiment 7, and Roffenstein, Experiment 5.

33. This and the small child motif in Dream 5 are rather obvious indirect representations of pregnancy. It is somewhat questionable whether they are standard symbols, since they are too transparent. See Freud (235, p. 125), and Jones (360) but cf. Chap. 10, note 9, above, and note 81, below.

I go with Dr. N. to the Rhine and want to tell him something but instead I say, 'It is too beautiful here to talk, I would like to live here forever.' "

In discussing the dream the patient admits a strong transference to the author, but rejects the idea that she would like to take Mrs. N.'s place.[34] In the dream she is clearly unmarried.[35] She has no associations to "traveling bag." That it might mean pregnancy [36] she finds a comical idea, even after her attention is called to the "child's bed," so out of place in the dream: "The purest riddle," she says, almost angrily. She would rather assume that the trip to the Rhine, where it is too beautiful to talk and where she would like to live forever, is an indirect representation of a love relationship. But she comments repeatedly: "But I can't fathom this at all."

Dream 7: (a) Suggestion (given only to Subject 1:) "You are with a mission in Africa. You get married and become pregnant. You will represent all this indirectly."

(b) Solution (excerpt of a very extensive dream): "I am in Africa." [Where?] [37]* "Yes, in Africa and I teach black Negro children. There is a young man there, too. He reminds me of a friend of my youth, Wilhelm; he looks just like him. I saw many little snakes [38] and I was afraid of them—but Wilhelm knew what to do. We were married. There were beautiful palm trees where we lived. I am sitting under a palm tree and I see two flames rising; they were woven into each other.[39] Then they divided and I saw a little creature (animal or man?) now glowing and now fading out." [40]

34. In the dream she obviously does: the travel bags are hers, she has the baby bed put into Dr. N.'s room, and she goes with him to the Rhine where she finds something better to do than talk. This threefold restatement appears stringent even if we make allowance for the fact that the suggestion contains the phrase "married to a doctor."

35. Obviously, this pertains to the manifest content. Whether she is married in the latent dream-thought cannot be decided, though her taking Mrs. N.'s place and putting the child's bed into Dr. N.'s room may well imply that she is.

36. Traveling bag per se need not mean pregnancy. It is a symbol for the female sex organ and the female body.

37.* Interjected question of the investigator.

38. Cf. note 26. It is worth noting that, though both the suggestions and manifest contents of Dream 5 and Dream 7 are different, the crucial symbol used remains the same.

39. Clear indirect representation of intercourse. Flame is so frequent a representative of passion, excitement, love, that it may be considered a symbol in the strict sense.

40. Compare with the appearance and

No associations. Then she talks of the brief affair with her lover, W., who had fallen in battle. No associations concerning the flames. On my asking whether she believes that the flames represent intercourse and the "creature" pregnancy,[41] she answers, somewhat tortured and somewhat embarrassed, "How do I come to such ideas? I am not concerned with such things. I can admit easily that it is my greatest wish to have a child, but with my illness. . . ."

b. Symbolization of Birth

I have only one birth-dream, of Subject 2, at my disposal. The other two subjects did not dream about it, even on repeated suggestion.[42]

Dream 8: (a) Suggestion: "You are no longer in the hospital; you are married and give birth to two children. You are dreaming of the birth of one of them." (No suggestion to symbolize.)

(b) Solution: "Dr. K. took my handkerchief, led me into the garden, and I opened my mouth. He got hold of my tooth with the kerchief and pulled out two teeth. Then comes Dr. N. (the author), he takes me by the hand, he consoles me warmly and all my pains are gone. I go to bed and we talk to each other and the good Mrs. N. is there, too, and gently strokes my face. I am pregnant. My little Pauli (six-year-old daughter by her divorced husband) is in the crib exactly, but quite exactly, as when she was born. Dr. N. comes and asks: 'Now, do you still have your toothache?' . . ."

The context of the dream shows beyond doubt that the pulling of the two teeth represents the birth of two children (the formulation of the dream-task was perhaps not quite apt [43]). The hypocrisy [44] towards Mrs. N. (whom she

---

disappearance of the child in Dream 5, and with note 27, above.

41. The description gives the impression that the inquiry was crude and suggestive. It is hard to see what can be gained by such bald directness. It is possible that the description is worse than the procedure. Yet such reports are prone to give an alarming and actually misleading impression of the clinical method of handling dreams.

42. This is striking in subjects who dream so readily; yet no explanation of

this is given in terms of their personalities.

43. The reference is to the phrasing of the suggestion: "You give birth to *two* children. You are dreaming of the birth of *one* of them." (Italics mine.)

44. The term "hypocrisy" seems poorly chosen to indicate the ambivalence and the defense against impulses that probably determine the presence and behavior of "good Mrs. N." in the dream.

drowned at the time in a spontaneous dream), and the transference come strikingly to expression. She admits this: "Your wife need have no worry because of a sick 45-year-old woman. After all one just must love somebody. . . ." [45]

Symbolization of children was obtained only from Subject 1: the others dreamed about them directly. The suggestion to represent them indirectly was simply not accepted. Is this because these two older people have no "censorship" against the idea of having children, and the 25-year-old unmarried Catholic girl is horrified at the idea? These questions will be left open. [46]

Dream 9: (a) Suggestion: "You are with a mission in Africa. There you meet a strong young man. With him you have four children and are expecting another. You are pregnant. You will dream all this indirectly so that no one can know what the dream means."

(b) Solution (only Subject 1): "I was in a mission garden. There stood a strong young date tree. I had the feeling that I had been in Africa for a very long time. I took care of this tree and of four other little trees. The last of these was small, I believe one year old. I loved this place very much and I planted a new seed." [47]

In the discussion she relates that in the dream she did not feel that the trees were children, but felt strongly that she must take care of them. [48]

45. In the omitted section Nachmansohn refers to Freud's view of tooth-pulling as a "castration symbol" (see Freud, 235, p. 129) and to his quoting Jung that it may be a "birth symbol" also (see Freud, 209, p. 388). Freud regards the two interpretations compatible; the tooth-pulling symbol may be overdetermined in any given case, condensing and thus expressing two trends, that is, castration and birth.

46. Cf. note 31, above.

47. Symbols such as the trees in this dream reopen the problem: how sharply can symbols be distinguished from other indirect representations? Comparison with the established symbol "seed" brings the issue into sharp relief. Cf. Chap. 10, note 9, above.

48. This is one of the really remarkable observations in Nachmansohn's material. The idea "children" changes its form and is indirectly represented by trees. There is no conscious awareness of the identity of the "trees" and "children." The affect-core of the idea, is, however, unchanged. It must have been such observations that led Mueller-Freienfels (529), Abramowsky (11), and Stekel (Chap. 14, below) to the view that ideas are appearance-forms of affects. Though their concept of affect and its relation to motivation is unclear, they attempted to conceptualize an important observation. Cf. Silberer, Chap. 9, notes 77, 78, 93, above; Schilder, Chap. 25, notes 79, 195, 210, below, and Rapaport (591, pp. 28 ff.). Similar phenomena are

[Passage omitted.] [49]

(In spite of repeated suggestions, a symbolic representation of the death of near relatives could not be obtained from any of the subjects. The suggestion was either directly fulfilled or the subject dreamt about the death of a distant unknown relative or even that of a stranger.) [50]

Rebirth, however, was symbolically represented by Subjects 1 and 3; Subject 2 did not accept the suggestion.

Dream 11: (a) Suggestion: "You will dream of a fresh start of your messed-up life. You will dream of your rebirth." (No suggestion for symbolization.)

(b) Solution by Subject 3: (Having written no record, she reports verbally): "I don't know any longer what I dreamt last night. I know only that there was an infant and—you know—babies under two are a horror to me." Then the following dream-fragment occurs to her: "I was here in the dining room of the hospital and the Dutch woman came in. I was amazed at how she got here. She said: 'You know that you have to leave on Wednesday.' 'Well, I have no idea about that. What should I do on the outside?' said I. 'But,' said she, 'you must go to A. Mrs. X. got sick.' "

The discussion reveals that this Dutch woman had helped her to "escape" to Holland, where she had gone in order . . . to begin a new life.[51] The idea

---

rather abundant in dreams I have recently recorded. It is revealing to compare Nachmansohn's observation with Freud's (209, p. 434) statement: "Analysis tells us that *the ideational contents have undergone displacements and substitutions* [in dreams] *while the affects remained unchanged.*" Cf. also Freud's observations in his note to this point (*ibid.*, pp. 434–35).

49. The omitted section contains Dream 10, which is similar to Dream 9.

50. Such substitutions of important figures by unimportant ones is a standard form of indirect representation in the dream. Cf. Freud (209, p. 507).

51. Thus the idea of rebirth is indirectly represented through the Dutch woman who once in the past helped her

to start life anew. This is a paradigm of one of the fundamental characteristics of dream-thinking, that is primary-process thinking (cf. note 19, above). Any memory image of an idea or experience which once expressed an impulse, or was related in any way to its expression, may be used by dream-thinking to express it again. It is on this characteristic of primary-process thinking that psychoanalysis based its technique of free association. Since drive impulses will push into consciousness ideas and memories that once expressed them, it is possible to infer from these ideas and memories the character and fate of the drives. To facilitate such manifestation in consciousness of drive-impulses, psychoanalysis adopted a "fundamental rule."

of leaving the hospital frightened her because at first she would have to go to relatives whom she could not stand. Whether Mrs. X.'s sickness implied unconscious death wishes against certain people it was impossible to learn.

The concept of rebirth is altogether strange to this very wordly lady (just as to Subject 2): she said, "That is just hifalutin nonsense. . . ."

About this rule Fenichel (176, p. 23) wrote:

The patient is requested to say everything that enters his mind, without selection.

To understand the meaning of this rule, we should recall how a person acts in everyday life who does not follow the rule. His impulses toward actions or words are determined by: (a) external stimuli of any kind to which he reacts; (b) his physical state which gives him internal stimuli and determines the intensity and mode of the impressions by external stimuli; (c) certain conceptual goals, the thought of what he wants to do or say, which makes him suppress that which does not belong to the subject; and (d) the derivatives of all the warded-off impulses that try to find discharge.

The counterpart of the "fundamental rule" is the psychoanalyst's method of remembering the material related by his patients, which is based on the same assumption. Freud (226, pp. 324–25) describes it as follows:

Curiosity is inevitably aroused about the technique which makes it possible to deal with such abundance of material, and the expectation is that some special means are required for the purpose.

The technique . . . disclaims the use of any special aids, even of note-taking . . . and simply consists in making no effort to concentrate the attention on anything in particular, and in maintaining in regard to all that one hears the same measure of calm, quiet attentiveness—of "evenly hovering attention." . . . In this way a strain which

could not be kept up for several hours daily and a danger inseparable from deliberate attentiveness are avoided. For as soon as attention is deliberately concentrated . . . one begins to select from the material before one; . . . and in this selection one's expectations or one's inclinations will be followed. This is just what must not be done, however; if one's expectations are followed in this selection there is the danger of never finding anything but what is already known, and if one follows one's inclinations anything which is to be perceived will most certainly be falsified. It must not be forgotten that the meaning of the things one hears is, at all events for the most part, only recognizable later on.

It will be seen, therefore, that the principle of evenly distributed attention is the necessary corollary to the demand on the patient to communicate everything that occurs to him without criticism or selection. If the physician behaves otherwise he is throwing aside most of the advantage to be gained by the patient's obedience to the "fundamental rule of psychoanalysis." . . .

What one achieves in this way will be sufficient for all requirements during the treatment. Those elements of the material which have a connection with one another will be at the conscious disposal of the physician; the rest, as yet unconnected, chaotic and indistinguishable, seems at first to disappear, but rises steadily into recollection as soon as the patient brings something further to which it is related, and by which it can be developed.

The psychoanalytic theory of thinking, which underlies both the "fundamental rule" and the psychoanalyst's at-

The reaction of Subject 1, who is very concerned with religious matters, is quite different.

Solution by Subject 1: "I dreamt that I walked through the fields toward D. (a Catholic church near the institution). I came to a small body of water surrounded by rattan and many waterplants. In the middle of it I saw beautiful sea-roses. I wanted to get to the other shore but did not find the way. I went through the water; it was not deep but creeping plants hindered me. I picked the sea-roses and took them to my room. One bud grew particularly; it blossomed out and became a beautiful flower before my very eyes. I took care of it; I was happy. When the bell rang I awoke very refreshed." [52]

When I asked her whether or not she felt in the dream that the flower might mean a child,[53] she said: "I have seen only a flower, but now and then I thought it was a child." Such "thoughts," also described in real dreams, were dealt with extensively by Hacker.[54] She added, "While awake and writing down the dream, I kept thinking that if I were healthy I would accept a child."

---

titude of "evenly hovering attention," was put forth only in an implicit form by Freud. See Freud (209, Chap. VII, 223, and 248); also Chaps. 15, 16, 17, below, and the corresponding footnote commentary. See also Rapaport (596). This theory of thinking is in harmony with developmental psychological findings as presented, for instance, by Werner (755) and Piaget (557).

52. Rather clear symbolization of birth. Cf. Freud (235, p. 132).

53. Again, the questioning appears too direct and suggestive. If such inquiry should prove inevitable, it would be more expeditious and interesting to carry it out by the multiple-choice method which MacCurdy used in investigating retention (memory) in a case of Korsakow syndrome. See Katzaroff (378), Claparède (133), Koffka (406, pp. 592–94), and MacCurdy (488).

54. Cf. Hacker (297, p. 57): "In my dream I spoke to an acquaintance and there were several others there. If I were asked how the others looked, I should have to say: 'I don't know, I didn't see them, I only *know* that they were there.'" I have encountered such "thoughts" abundantly in my own dream records. These "thoughts" seem to be characteristic of dreams, setting them apart from reveries (dream-like formations in states of consciousness more "awake" than dreaming proper). I find them, for example, in my records in the following form: "I see my father and I know that he approves of me now. But I do not know how I know that—he does not speak to me nor does he smile." I have used the phrase "the implicative character of dreams" to describe such observations. I find little if any of this in my records of reveries. This observation is tentative and in need of verification. The term "thought," which Hacker adopted from Buehler, is not altogether fortunate here, as it may be confused

When asked whether or not she had the feeling that the flower (child) represented herself, she answered: "No, surely not—that would not be possible." She also stated that she was not aware in her dream that the water might mean rebirth.

At this point I must state that by means of "free associations" alone, without knowledge of the dream-suggestion, I would have discovered no rebirth-wish in this dream. It may be that others would have been more adroit than I.[55]

This selection from a material of 65 experiments leaves no doubt that the dream works with symbols and indirect representations, and that typical symbols exist. All this was long ago established by Freud and other investigators of dreams; the credit for scientific and therapeutic evaluation of these findings certainly goes to Freud.

Were those findings derived by the psychoanalytic method of free association? Can the present experiments be used to justify and support that method (as Roffenstein believes they can)? These are independent questions to be discussed in detail later on.[56]

---

with the "latent dream-thought" and with thoughts (in the usual sense of the word) explicit in the manifest dream-content. Yet this term has the merit of stressing the commonality of this dream phenomenon with what Buehler (111) calls "thought." See Chap. 2, note 2, above.

55. Nachmansohn's otherwise detailed knowledge of psychoanalytic theory shows a gap at this point. Freud observed that to symbols proper usually no free associations are obtained (Cf. Freud, 235, pp. 122, and 124–25.) This does not preclude the inferring of a dream-symbol from the dream-context (that is, in this case it may be inferred from the flower-child "thought" that coming out of the water symbolizes birth). Nor does it make symbols undecipherable, since it is claimed they always have analogies in myth, folklore, or language. Actually, the water motif (see note 52, above) was recorded by Freud as a birth symbol. As to rebirth, Freud clearly stated (235, p. 125) that the dream does not symbolize any and all ideas:

The nature of the symbol relationship is a comparison, but not any desired comparison. One suspects a special prerequisite for this comparison, but is unable to say what it is. Not everything to which we are able to compare an object or an occurrence appears in the dream as its symbol; on the other hand, the dream does not symbolize anything we may choose, but only specific elements of dream thoughts.

Whether or not rebirth is indirectly represented in this dream, and whether it can be deciphered, once the water-birth symbolism is taken for granted, cannot be established in the absence of associations.

56. Here the question of the validity of the psychoanalytic method of free as-

III. [AN EXPERIMENT ON THE ROLE OF CENSORSHIP]

The experiments clearly prove the existence of the so-called "censorship," [57] even though hypnotic suggestion can counteract its effect in persons as accommodating as Subject 1: where the suggestion did not require symbolization, she dreamt "verbatim"; yet she too used distortion—without my suggestion—when the content of the suggested dream clashed too much with her sensitivities. [58]

---

sociation is tied in with the problem of symbolism and the lack of free associations concerning symbols. Nachmansohn disregards the considerations summarized in note 55, above.

57. For the description of censorship, see Freud (235, pp. 110–20; 209, pp. 223–24, 510–11, 546; and 234, pp. 124–25). To avoid an anthropomorphic misunderstanding of the censorship concept, it is important to remember that Freud (235, p. 114) wrote:

I hope you will not consider the expression too anthropomorphically, and picture the dream censor as a severe little manikin who lives in a little brain chamber and there performs his duties; nor should you attempt to localize him too much, to think of a brain center from which his censoring influence emanates, and which would cease with the injury or extirpation of this censor. For the present, the term "dream censor" is no more than a very convenient phrase for a dynamic relationship. This phrase does not prevent us from asking by what tendencies such influence is exerted and upon which tendencies it works; nor will we be surprised to discover that we have already encountered the dream censor before, perhaps without recognizing him.

For such was actually the case. You will remember that we had a surprising experience when we began to apply our technique of free association. We then began to feel that some sort of a resistance blocked our efforts to proceed from the dream ele-

ment to the unconscious element for which the former is the substitute. This resistance, we said, may be of varying strength, enormous at one time, quite negligible at another. In the latter case we need cross only a few intermediate steps in our work of interpretation. But when the resistance is strong, then we must go through a long chain of associations, are taken far afield and must overcome all the difficulties which present themselves as critical objections to the association technique. What we met with in the work of interpretation, we must now bring into the dream work as the dream censor. The resistance to interpretation is nothing but the objectivation of the dream censor. The latter proves to us that the force of the censor has not spent itself in causing the dream distortion, has not since been extinguished, but that this censorship continues as a permanent institution with the purpose of preserving the distortion.

58. In the form of a new experimental attack, Nachmansohn again picks up the thread of the relationship of dream-organization and personality-structure. Cf. notes 1, and 23, above. In order to test the effectiveness of the censorship, Nachmansohn suggests dream-contents for direct undisguised representation; for comparison, he gives the same subject the same content with suggestions for both direct and disguised dream-representation.

Dream 12: (a) Suggestion: "You are maltreated by your foster-mother (much hated by the subject). You say bad words to her. She forces you to apologize and to kiss her hand. Dream all this directly."

(b) Solution [59] (not put down in writing): "I know only that there was a big fight, I don't remember anything else, it was horrible. I awoke with a terrible anxiety and my night-gown was drenched with sweat."

Masochistic tendencies force "entrance into consciousness" of the fight, but the apology is entirely suppressed.[60] I succeeded in eliminating this suppression when, a few days later, I gave her a similar suggestion and again explicitly instructed her to represent it directly in her dream.

I never succeeded in obtaining a direct representation from Subject 3. "Censorship" was unusually severe in her,[61] so much so that her conscious associations contributed nothing to the interpretation of her dreams; indeed they were often outright misleading.[62]

Subject 2, the simplest personality of the three, dreamt in the least disguised manner. Hers were always transparent wishfulfillment-dreams. Even when the suggestion was to symbolize, her representations remained rather transparent. Her dreams resemble the type seen in children.[63]

---

59. By Subject 1, as inferred from the context.

60. The relationship of the "big fight" to masochistic tendencies is very questionable, yet Nachmansohn's general conception is of great interest. He apparently implies that dream-suggestions corresponding to tendencies syntonic with the personality come to more or less direct expression in the manifest dream-content, while those corresponding to non-syntonic (repressed) tendencies or clashing with syntonic ones are altogether eliminated (repressed). It is not clear whether the apology corresponds to a non-syntonic trend or to one clashing with a syntonic trend. It may be assumed that while the idea of "apology" was eliminated, the affect reported by the subject corresponds to it.

61. It is implied that the censorship in Subject 3 remained in effect in every dream, in spite of hypnotic suggestions to the contrary. Cf., however, note 72, below.

62. As this statement is not documented, its exact meaning cannot be assessed. If it were to imply that free associations lead to false conclusions as to the meaning of the dream, it would disavow the thesis of thoroughgoing psychic determinism. If it were to imply that the free associations proved unproductive, it would only mean that resistance (the waking-state equivalent of censorship, see note 57, above) was encountered.

63. It may well be questioned whether the relationship between personality-structure and dream-distortion is so simple. Cf. note 72, below.

In Subject 1 and Subject 2 the solution of the suggestions often engendered anxiety. (See Dreams 4, 5, 12, and so on.)

A comparison of the suggestions of direct representation with those of indirect representation shows that anxiety appeared much more frequently in the former.[64] The assumption offered itself that suggestion suspends "censorship" and that dreaming of painful experiences is accompanied by anxiety, just as other hallucinations [65] are usually followed by corresponding affects. This led me to experiments in which I suggested the same content twice, with a suggestion first for indirect and then for direct representation.

Dream 13: (a) Suggestion: [66] "You are accused of gossiping and threatened with spanking. First you defend yourself, later you yield and are publicly spanked."

(b) Solution 1 (indirect) [67]: "I was in a big white room. Many people were going in and out. On the table I saw a crucifix. There was a book too, it was open, I never saw one like it; on one side the letters were in fine writing in gold and on the other the Ten Commandments. I was very curious what was going on and hid behind a bench. I saw an endless line of people big and small marching past the table. They looked dead. Then I saw a girl, hardly more than a child. In her hands she carried a branch of thorns. Her eyes were big and wide open, her mouth tight shut. The writing in the book became bigger and bigger. I saw the girl bend as though under a heavy weight. Her facial expression became more vivid. Soon she bent her head forward. A tremor went all over her body and her hands rose. She followed the others silent and resigned. I was very excited, had anxiety but did not wake up."

Solution 2 (direct) [68]: "A great mass of people in front of the town hall in

64. Apparently indirect and/or symbolic representation thus prevents anxiety development: the prohibited idea passes censorship in disguise. When, however, a direct representation is demanded and produced, censorship is rendered partially ineffective: unable to prevent prohibited impulse-representations from entering consciousness, it spends itself in issuing the danger signal of anxiety. See Freud (252, p. 109).

65. The word "other" indicates that Nachmansohn, in keeping with Freud's views, subsumes dreams under hallucination phenomena. Cf. Freud, Chap. 15, pp. 318–19, below, and notes 12, 14, 15.

66. The subject is not named; it can only be conjectured, from the anxiety development, that it was Subject 1.

67. That is, the suggestion given required indirect representation.

68. That is, the suggestion given required direct (undisguised) representation.

Sch. I am accused but I don't know of what. Suddenly I am running through town, looking for someone (I don't know whom). I feel I should apologize. I wake up with great anxiety much before the morning bell and cannot sleep again."

Anxiety was engendered in both cases; in the first it did not lead to awakening; in the second it did. In the first case distortion (projection onto another person, religious disguise, absence of actual accusation, and so forth) sufficiently lessened anxiety so that sleep did not have to be interrupted. The second case being a more direct representation, the distortion apparently did not manage to bind anxiety even to the extent of allowing sleep to continue. Taking into consideration all the anxiety dreams quoted here, we can assert that the censorship, with the aid of distortions, endeavors to maintain sleep, though in people strongly inclined to anxiety, such as Subject 1, it has little or no success. In Subject 3, no anxiety dream could be elicited by any method; in Subject 2, because of the lightness of her sleep, the provocation of anxiety dreams was deliberately avoided.

Solution 1 by Subject 3: [69] "I was in the workshop of the hospital. I wanted to go into the garden and asked the attendant to open the door. She said: 'Don't go that way, you will catch a cold.' I answered: 'If you don't open right away, I will break down the door.' I get into a rage and I run against the door with a chair. You come in and are not angry at all. I go away from the door and sit down at a machine. You ask me what I wanted to do. I say: 'Frieda (the attendant) has prevented me without any reason from going out. She must be punished.' When you came in I felt guilty but not anxious."

Solution 2 (direct representation): "I was with my mother. My father came in (both long dead). He said to my mother: 'Prepare a meal for *my wife.*' I look at mother; she says: 'You didn't even know that we were divorced five years ago.' I get very angry and shout: 'And you want to take care of *my* household. First the boy must be taken care of' (I never had a brother). Suddenly House 13 of the hospital. Sch. (an attendant) came and said I had a visitor. My father was there. 'You alone,' said he, 'are to be blamed for it all because you made such fuss. Now your mother is dead and I am as poor as a beggar. Now you must take care of us.' I shouted wildly: 'If you would only let your wife go to the theater again, you could live.' He went away angry. Then came Sch.

69. Apparently the suggestion was for indirect representation.

and said: 'Up there at the new building your father lies, shot dead.' I said: 'I don't care, have him taken away.' No anxiety, no awakening. . . ."

It is important for us here that the suggestion [70] did not succeed in suspending the "censorship." The censorship worked with its full arsenal of distortions, reversals, projections, displacements, and condensations. Instead of dreaming that she is accused of gossiping, she gossips about the innocent Frieda who is always friendly and correct toward her patient.[71] . . . Twenty years after the death of her father she heard from her aunt about his Don Juan life; in her first rage she called it "miserable ornery gossip," and is still angry with the aunt for this revelation. In the meantime many other things about her mother had become clear to her, and she came to hate her dead father deeply. Here again we see how a dream-suggestion may unearth a carefully hidden "complex" and thereby expedite analysis.[72] The absence of anxiety no longer surprises us. It was either overshadowed by the anger or not engendered at all.

Not even painful sexual ideas elicited anxiety in Subject 3. Subject 1, however, always experienced strong anxiety even in her well-disguised sexual dreams. Yet I could not maintain that her libido repression was more intense than that of Subject 3.[73]

70. Namely, the suggestion for direct representation.

71. There is some confusion here: for the dream in which Frieda occurs, *indirect* representation was suggested, so that dream distortions should not come as a surprise. What is surprising is Solution 2: a suggestion for *direct* representation results in a most complex indirect representation.

72. This effect of dream-suggestions is due to their role as day-residues of incompleted task character; unconscious impulses make contact with and express themselves through them. Cf. note 23 above, and Freud (237, pp. 139-42). The more obvious the contact, the greater the dream-distortion of censorship. Successful suggestions for direct representation may be prohibitive of such contact. For this reason, Nachmansohn's inference—that censorship in Subject 3 was highly developed since she never followed suggestions for direct representation (p. 277) while in Subject 2 it was weak since she always did—may be questioned. The following, diametrically opposite, assumption is just as plausible: the rigidity of Subject 2 (p. 260) amounts to extremely rigorous censorship, which allows no unconscious impulse to connect with the unfinished task set up by the dream suggestion (Cf. note 23); in Subject 3, who is intense and uncontrolled (p. 260), censorship was so flexible or weak that even suggestion for direct representation did not insulate the suggested dream-content from unconscious impulses, the infiltration of which resulted in dream-distortions.

73. In view of note 72 above, a different explanation may seem feasible.

Dream 14: (a) Suggestion: "In your dream you will have sexual intercourse with a big strong man. You will get hold of his organ and kiss it. All this you dream so indirectly that the uninitiated will not understand it. When you awake you will not understand the meaning of the dream." (On my suggestion she had this dream immediately, while in hypnosis. All other dreams reported here were dreamt in the night following the hypnosis.) [74]

Solution by Subject 1: "I dreamt that I took a big hike from S. toward F. There were ruins on the sunny side. I was very tired and lay down on the grass amongst the ruins. Near me stood a *big elm tree in full bloom.* In my dream I fell asleep but was soon awakened by a disagreeable wetness. A small *serpent,* grey like a little *snake,* moved on my body back and forth. My anxiety and excitement were very great. *I felt disgust.*"

Solution by Subject 3: "Mrs. Sch. and I take a walk. We come to *a beautiful cherry tree.*[75] I lay down under the *cherry tree.* Mrs. Sch. ran away. I put into my mouth a cherry that hung low. It tasted very good. Suddenly I noticed that I bit into a big worm.[76] I felt such disgust I had to vomit. Upon this I awoke, very disappointed that I was not under the cherry tree. No anxiety."

Subject 3 dreamt this in a far less disguised form [77] than Subject 1; considering their personalities, this is well understandable. Yet, the latter did not succeed in suppressing anxiety. Such complexities have so far made it impossible for me to quite clarify the etiology of anxiety in dreams.

Both anxiety dreams (the gossip- and the sex-dream) clearly indicate that anxiety in dreams is not solely due to repressed sexuality. Though in our case the accusation of gossiping was implanted by suggestion, life creates similar situations in abundance; we can and do have dreams about these, and they are attended by anxiety.[78]

74. Cf. note 21, above.

75. Cf. Dreams 7 and 9, as well as the solution of Dream 14 by Subject 1.

76. More commonly, "worm" is a symbol for child. See Freud (235, p. 131). But the worm = penis symbolism is also frequent. The common child = penis equation may be the connecting link between the two. See Freud (235, p. 129).

77. This statement is not altogether convincing. Both dreams symbolize intercourse. But only the dream of Subject 3 symbolizes the kissing of the penis, while that of Subject 1 suppresses it and develops anxiety. Thus it seems questionable that Subject 3 disguised less than Subject 1, particularly if averting anxiety-development is taken as a criterion of successful disguise.

78. Nachmansohn's critique is justified, though weakened by the juxtaposi-

The presence here of dream distortions other than symbolization, such as "condensation" and "displacement," is too obvious to need demonstration. It may be stressed with Allers [79] that the realm of validity of these concepts is broader than Freud seemed to assume. These psychological processes are demonstrable at every step of our daily life, but condensation is usually clumsier in the dream and therefore easier to demonstrate. For instance, the writing and speech of educated people are a condensation in comparison to those of uneducated people. Let us take any sentence at random: "One-sided endowment is usually accompanied at least by partial diligence." Everybody will understand this sentence without explanation, though it is a condensation of at least two trains of thought: people of one-sided endowment may lack diligence, but if the endowment is strong it will insure that at least in its realm they will be diligent. The condensation came about by means of the words "at least" and "partial diligence." The phrase "partial diligence" is actually nonsensical. If one is diligent one is entirely so, if only in a special field. The word "partial" does not pertain to diligence, but rather to the totality of the demands of life, of which a one-sided endowment, plus the necessary diligence, fulfills only a part. Thus here, just as in dreams, we encounter a coupling of two constituents which do not belong together. The difference is that conscious waking thoughts work with abstractions, while dream-thought works with visual representations. In principle the condensation is the same in both. That "displacements" are encountered at every step of waking life would probably not be questioned by Freud; they are easily demonstrable.[80] Condensation and displacement are

---

tion on the same conceptual level of repressed sexuality and of life situations. Freud's (252) reformulation of the theory of anxiety meets the point Nachmansohn raises.

79. Allers (20).

80. Nachmansohn's comparison is somewhat forced and overlooks those distinctions quoted below from Freud and those discussed in note 19, above. Nevertheless, there is no doubt that phenomena analogous to dream-mechanisms occur in waking thought. The term "wishful thinking" was coined to express

this fact. Schilder's concept "sphere" (Chap. 24, pp. 502, 515 f., below) and Bleuler's concept "autistic thinking" (Chaps. 20 and 21, below), were born of an effort to account, within a unitary frame of reference, for dream mechanisms and forms of waking thought (pathological and normal) similar to them. Their attempts may be considered unsuccessful. So far we have no satisfactory investigation of this aspect of waking thought. Freud was aware of the problem and sketched a framework for such investigation in his "Two Prin-

partly functions of the censorship and partly expressions of a highly complicated psychological structure.[81] Since these propensities of our psyche are more
pronounced in waking life, it may be asserted that censorship is more active in

ciples" (223) and "Negation" (248),
Chaps. 15 and 17, below. The lack of
systematic investigation of preconscious
thought as a preparation to conscious
thought—Varendonck's (739, 740) attempt notwithstanding—has left this
framework empty at crucial points.
Compare, however, Kris, Chap. 23, below.

Freud (235, pp. 144–45) wrote:

Substitution by allusion is known to our
conscious thinking also, but with a difference. In conscious thinking the allusion
must be easily intelligible, and the substitute must bear a relation to the actual content. Jokes, too, often make use of allusion;
they let the condition of content associations slide and replace it by unusual external associations, such as resemblances in
sound, ambiguity of words, etc. They retain, however, the condition of intelligibility; the joke would lose all its effect if
the allusion could not be traced back to the
actual without any effort whatsoever. The
allusion of displacement has freed itself of
both these limitations. Its connection with
the element which it replaces is most external and remote, is unintelligible for this
reason, and if it is retraced, its interpretation gives the impression of an unsuccessful
joke or of a forced, far-fetched explanation. For the dream censor has only then
accomplished its purpose, when it has
made the path of return from the allusion
to the original undiscoverable.

81. This has an important implication:
condensation and displacement, though
used by the censorship, are anchored in
our complex psychological structure.
This point is parallel to Silberer's assertion that symbolization is used to express
conflictful material but is also the usual

form of experiencing and expression in
states of consciousness characterized by
"apperceptive insufficiency." Cf. Silberer, Chap. 9, pp. 225 ff., above. The
unsettled question is whether these two
aspects of our psyche can thus be separated. The answer depends on whether
there is for every state of consciousness
an underlying specific drive- or affect-
organization, implying both conflict and
censorship. In final analysis, the question
boils down to which manner of description is more economical. How unsettled
these questions are, becomes clear when
one considers that Jones's (360, p. 183)
view is diametrically opposed to Silberer's:

Only what is repressed is symbolized; only
what is repressed needs to be symbolized.
This conclusion is the touchstone of the
psychoanalytic theory of symbolism.

He also maintains that

. . . true symbolism, in the strict sense, is
to be distinguished from other forms of
indirect representation (ibid., p. 157).

Freud (235, p. 125) in turn wrote:

It must be admitted that the idea of symbol
cannot be sharply delimited at all times—
it mingles with the substitution, dramatiza-
tion, etc., even approaches allusion.

Freud also recognized that the "regressive" course of excitation, the prerequisite for the operation of all dream-
mechanisms, is by no means limited to
dream-states, but occurs in the waking
state also (209, pp. 492–93):

What takes place in the hallucinatory
dream we can describe in no other way
than by saying that the excitation follows

waking life than in the dream.[82] These assertions do not diminish Freud's merit: he was the one to call attention to and emphasize the significance of these processes.

---

a retrogressive course. It communicates itself not to the motor end of the apparatus, but to the sensory end, and finally reaches the system of perception. If we call the direction which the psychic process follows from the unconscious into the waking state *progressive*, we may then speak of the dream as having a *regressive* character.

This *regression* is therefore assuredly one of the most important psychological peculiarities of the dream-process; but we must not forget that it is not characteristic of the dream alone. Intentional recollection and other component processes of our normal thinking likewise necessitate a retrogression in the psychic apparatus from some complex act of ideation to the raw material of the memory-traces which underlie it. But during the waking state this turning backwards does not reach beyond the memory-images; it is incapable of producing the hallucinatory revival of the perceptual images. Why is it otherwise in dreams? When we spoke of the condensation-work of the dream we could not avoid the assumption that by the dream-work the intensities adhering to the ideas are completely transferred from one to another. It is probably this modification of the usual psychic process which makes possible the cathexis of the System P [perception] to its full sensory vividness in the reverse direction to thinking.

82. Nachmansohn presents this as a new finding, whereas it is a commonly accepted thesis of psychoanalysis. In the following quotation the equivalence of the concepts "censorship" and "resistance" should be kept in mind. Cf. note 57, above, and Freud (209, p. 473). Freud (209, p. 480) wrote:

Let us now return to the facts of dream-forgetting. So far, of course, we have failed to draw any important conclusions from them. When our waking life shows an unmistakable intention to forget the dream which has been formed during the night, either as a whole, immediately after waking, or little by little in the course of the day, and when we recognize as the chief factor in this process of forgetting the psychic resistance against the dream which has already done its best to oppose the dream at night, the question then arises: what actually has made the dream-formation possible against this resistance? Let us consider the most striking case, in which the waking life has thrust the dream aside as though it had never happened. If we take into consideration the play of the psychic forces, we are compelled to assert that the dream would never have come into existence had the resistance prevailed at night as it did by day. We conclude then, that the resistance loses some part of its force during the night; we know that it has not been discontinued, as we have demonstrated its share in the formation of dreams—namely, the work of distortion. We have therefore to consider the possibility that at night the resistance is merely diminished, and that dream-formation becomes possible because of this slackening of the resistance; and we shall readily understand that as it regains its full power on waking it immediately thrusts aside what it was forced to admit while it was feeble. Descriptive psychology teaches us that the chief determinant of dream-formation is the dormant state of the psyche; and we may now add the following explanation: *the state of sleep makes dream-formation possible by reducing the endopsychic censorship.*

IV. [AN EXPERIMENT ON DREAM PRODUCTION IN THE WAKING STATE]

It attracted my attention that my subjects produced not only dreams of real dream-character—disregarding space, time, and so forth—but also others which were strikingly correct.[83] One encounters these among common dreams too, though not frequently. This posed two questions: could the subject invent dreams of suggested contents in the waking state; and would the basic propensities of the invented dreams be identical with those of sleep-dreams? To answer these questions I undertook a special series of experiments: I read the suggestion to subjects in the waking state and asked them to make up a dream then and there. I gave them all the time they wanted.

Dream 15: Suggestion: "Your aunt and uncle died. You got the inheritance and it is greater than you thought it would be. You endow a hospital or some other such institution, you marry and get pregnant. You dream of sexual intercourse. You will represent all this so that only the initiated can understand it, since it makes a bad impression to dream of the death of relatives."

Solution in the waking state by Subject 1. Beginning exactly at 8:59 A.M.: "I can't begin" (interrupts herself). "I am far away, I get a letter from my neighbors (I can read the writing clearly), I should come home right away. When I get home I find the doors closed; knocking about in the city I come to the graveyard and see two newly made graves, and have the feeling that they are those of my uncle and aunt. No, this is too transparent." After six minutes the subject quits. She has the feeling that this "inventing" is silly. At 9:07 A.M. hypnosis is induced.

At 9:10 A.M. the dream suggestion is read with the addition: "When you finish dreaming you will wake up immediately and tell your dream. You will not know that I suggested the dream in hypnosis."

In the hypnotic sleep: restless movements and signs of excitement. At 9:15 the patient wakes up, is drowsy, but gives the following record: "I dreamt that I am in Bern" (obviously the dream is more concrete). "I get a telegram that I must go right away to Zurich. My girl friend was waiting for me at the railroad station and asked whether I would come with her to Sch. She was very interested in the new buildings at the mouth of the Rhine and in the experiments to

83. Here Nachmansohn, as Freud often did, labels logically ordered thinking "correct" and dream-thinking "incorrect."

make the Rhine navigable. I suggested we go first to M. and see the old cloister crypts where they are excavating. She agreed. On our way we passed the Town Hall; there was a great mass of people there and they carried red flags covered with black veils" (the uncle of the subject is a Socialist). "We stood there for a while and heard that the great leader of the party died, no name, nothing. We walked on. I asked my friend: 'Who died?'—since I knew most of them quite well. No answer. We came to the Rhine and were in the cloister. I invited her to come to us. The house was closed but I felt I knew how to get in and went into the garden. We got into the house; it was empty and quiet. I was surprised. In the garden I saw a St. John's tree which stood quite askew and I thought that an animal had undermined it. Then I saw an iron box. We could not open it. We called the neighbors and they broke the box; we found jewelry, money, and a letter. The letter was the will of the uncle and a letter from my father was with it. The letter said that the money belonged to him and he gave it to his brother for safekeeping. I cried in the dream that I won't be able to talk any more to my uncle. I said, 'Now I want to serve humanity.' We traveled back to Zurich, I entered the Socialist school for women. There I learned how to draw blueprints for houses but I don't know any longer what sort of houses. Suddenly I was in W. There I had trees removed and asked somebody's advice; he looked like Wilhelm, he was not a teacher but somehow a doctor. We hit a swamp. He said: 'This can be bridged.' But we both sank into the swamp. There were creepers and moss, and it was impossible to get out. I sank and sank and awoke with a cry."

This production, which has all the characteristics of a dream, was dreamt within five minutes; a world of experience is contained in it. A comparison with the invention made in the waking state gives the impression that this may be a possible method of exploring poetic production.[84]

Solution 1 of the same dream-suggestion by Subject 3 in the waking state. She immediately declares: "I have no imagination." She is talked into trying it. She interjects a comment like that of Subject 1: "The task disturbs me, it becomes too transparent." At 10:58 A.M. hypnosis is induced. At 11:01 A.M. the dream suggestion is read. At 11:03 A.M. the subject awakes:

"I dreamt that I was in A. in a very beautiful place in a big rest hall. First I was in W. There was an old lady, a distant relative of my father, whom I did

84. Cf. Kris (421, 422) and Housman (342).

not know. One of her nieces asked me whether I would want any of the furniture the aunt left behind. I said I would like to have the Neuenberg clock. 'Very well, I will have it packed for you.' Then came a man with a big box and packed the clock. I traveled to A. The box came along as baggage. When I wanted to get it in A. it was not to be found. Now I stand in the railroad station of A. There comes Dr. L. of Zurich. 'What are you looking for that you tarry so long?' says he. I tell him that I brought along such a beautiful clock and now it disappeared. 'Let me have the check and please go up; I will get it for you.' I went away happy. When I got to the house there was a great disorder. I went to the kitchen just as I was and put the soup on the stove. Then came Dr. L. and said: 'Here is the box, but let me open it right away or it may again disappear.' He comes back and says: 'If you knew what I know, you wouldn't have let me unpack the clock.' 'What is that?' said I. 'I won't tell you'—said Dr. L. 'You should come and see for yourself. . . .' *A long, long corridor and terrible disorder*. Near a small room there stood the clock. The hands were of diamonds and so were the numbers on the clock face. Then I awoke." [85]

The patient needed only two minutes to compose this. She dictated very quickly, and when I asked her to slow down so that I might record it, she said: "But then I will forget three-fourths of it. I have the feeling that I have already forgotten a lot of it. I dreamt much more than that. I must have slept for a long while." Schopenhauer's saying proves true: "Our capacity of representation in dreams far outstrips our power of imagination." [86] But this ability is present in all inspirational creation.[87]*

[Passage omitted.] [88]

85. Corridor, box, jewels, and even clock, are fairly common female symbols; cf. Freud (235, p. 128, and 229).

86. Cf. Kris (421), and Chap. 23, below. The study of artistic creation, and scientific invention and discovery, is actually one of the promising avenues for the exploration of thought-processes. See Hadamard (298), Rapaport and Frank (601), Levey (450, 451, 452), Ribot (609), Wallas (749), Sharpe (683), Wertheimer (763), Waelder (747).

87.* Nachmansohn (536).

88. The remaining twelve pages of the paper are devoted to the discussion of psychoanalysis as a method and its sources of error. This discussion, fundamentally sympathetic to psychoanalysis and in some of its points constructively critical, is laden with misunderstandings and lack of information; its inclusion would go beyond the scope of this volume.

CHAPTER 13

ON PARAPRAXES IN THE KORSAKOW PSYCHOSIS [1]

By Stefan Betlheim and Heinz Hartmann

IF WE START OUT from the general view that there is a close relationship between organic-cerebral and psychic mechanisms,[2] it seems justified to raise the question whether the psychologically well-described and well-known processes of repression, displacement, and condensation have their counterpart in the realm of organic disorders. There have been attempts to clarify problems of organic brain-disorders from the psychological point of view; we will refer

1. Betlheim and Hartmann (58).

2. The point of view referred to is probably specifically that of Schilder and his collaborators. Some aspects of it are touched upon in Schilder (655, and Chap. 25, below). The most extensive discussion of this view in English is probably Schilder's (642, particularly pp. 65 ff.); see also (648, 658, 643). To characterize Schilder's position, we might say that there have been two dominant positions in psychiatry: one assumed that mental illness is organic in origin, implying that the organic cause was of the same order as that of neurological and/or glandular disorders (perhaps slightly more subtle and hidden); the other assumed that mental disorders are of psychological origin and it is this we must discover (even if everything psychological must have a physiological substratum). Schilder saw in neurological disorders psychological concomitants and their sequelae, and in psychological disorders organic concomitants and their sequelae. To him the gap between neurological process and neurological disorder versus fundamental psychological process and psychological disorder did not seem as wide as it does to most investigators, nor as narrow as it seems to those who would derive mental disorder directly from gross physiological change, or vice versa. This fundamental orientation made him more interested than any other investigator in the processes that occur in this "gap": in the neurological basis of psychological manifestations and in the use of neurological mechanisms by psychological changes. His point of view thus implies a greater unity of the psycho-physical organism than does any other view, particularly since he did not let his view remain a program but proceeded to fill it with empirical observations. Whatever the final verdict may be on Schilder's achievement, it will recognize that, among other things, he and his associates made more concrete observations on the so-called body-mind interaction in "borderline" conditions—general paresis, encephalitis, brain injuries, epilepsy, schizophrenic motor phenomena, toxic amentia, etc.—than any other group of investigators.

here only to the studies of Pick,[3]* Poetzl,[4]* and Schilder.[5]* The latter two, bringing psychoanalytic considerations to bear on their data, were able to demonstrate mechanisms in aphasia that may be considered related to repression. We have set ourselves the task of testing, by means of learning experiments, the efficacy of this approach on those parapraxes (that is substitute-formations) which are part of the memory-disorder of the Korsakow psychosis.[6]

The psychological studies of the Korsakow syndrome have set themselves the task of analyzing its most striking symptom, namely, the impaired registration [7] of recent impressions. They did so by experiments, which in the negative sense established and circumscribed the defect, and in the positive sense demonstrated whatever traces such recent impressions left. We are indebted to Brodmann [8]* and Gregor [9]* for the experimental proof that the learned material is not lost in the Korsakow psychosis but, as Gregor puts it, is demonstrable by means of Ebbinghaus's saving procedure. Several observers before him had already been impressed by the fact that experiences during the psychosis which were apparently forgotten would occasionally reemerge even after surprisingly long time intervals.

3.* Pick (565).

4.* Poetzl (573).

5.* Schilder (641).

6. For a description of the psychosis see Jelliffe and White (358) and for a summary of the literature of its memory disorder see Rapaport (591, pp. 226–29). The Korsakow psychosis is at times referred to as the "amnesic syndrome" or, incorrectly, as the psychosis of alcoholic polyneuritis.

7. "Registration" here translates *Merkfaehigkeit*, often used in the German literature in contrast to *Erinnerungsfaehigkeit* ("recall-ability"); cf., for example, Kohnstamm (410).

Merkfaehigkeit has been variously translated as "impressibility" or "notation"; it implies either the ability to notice, or the ability to make a record, or both. If it is considered, however, that much may be noticed that is not noted (registered) for future recall (as in rote testing of Digit Span; cf. Rapaport *et al.*, 602, I, 176–79), and much may be noticed and noted without becoming available for recall (spotted only by saving procedures or in indirect representations), then the concept of *Merkfaehigkeit* proves ambiguous. It is possible that this ambiguity will be cleared up only after Freud's cathectic (energy) concepts of consciousness, attention, recall, and repression have been systematically applied to it. Cf. Rapaport *et al.* (602), on attention and concentration, I, 167 ff., 176–79, 195–200; on information pp. 129–31, on learning, pp. 323 ff.; and see also Chap. 15, pp. 320–21, and notes 19, 20, 21, below. Cf. also Poetzl (573).

8.* Brodmann (95).

9.* Gregor (287, 288).

We can therefore assume that even in this very severe organic disorder experience is not annihilated, but only its reproduction is inhibited in a manner so far unknown. Schilder [10]* demonstrated the same for the epileptic twilight state. But we do not know how the traces of these experiences are represented; nor do we have thorough investigations of the relationship between the content of the patient's impressions and his distorted reproductions.[11] There are only a few hints to the answer to this question: Gregor observed that in learning a series of words, any word learned may be replaced by one related to it by content or by clang association [12] and that occasionally associative fusions (Mueller and Pilzecker) [13]*occur.[14] He also observed that the distortion often reveals a "tendency to the trivial." Not infrequently one encounters the view that the missing memory is replaced by "any" other at "random." According to some investigators (Moenckemoeller [15]* Gruenthal [16]* and others), the content of confabulations is taken from the everyday life of the patient; other investigators emphasized the fantastic character of these confabulations. How much and what form of recent experience and recent learning can be demonstrated in confabulations has been little explored.[17] It is known that delirious experiences frequently reemerge in the form of confabulations.

We started out by comparing material learned with its distorted reproduc-

10.* Schilder (666).

11. Cf., however, Hartmann's later papers (304, 308).

12. Association by content may be either conceptual or analogical. Replacement of ideas by others associated to them by analogy or clang is a common method of operation of the primary process. Cf. Freud (235, 209).

13.* Mueller and Pilzecker (527). The phenomenon described as "associative fusion" is analogous to the Freudian concept of condensation.

14. See Ach, Chap. 1, pp. 20–21, above. This phenomenon is related to the primary-process mechanism of condensation.

15.* Moenckemoeller (522).

16.* Gruenthal (294).

17. This obviously implies the question whether or not confabulations may contain distorted reproductions of experiences acquired after the onset of the illness.

The observation of the "tendency to the trivial" and the observation that the content of confabulations, even though fantastic, seems to be taken from the everyday life of the patient, are in agreement with Schilder's observations on paretics. Comparing paretics and schizophrenics, Schilder asserted that while the thoughts of the latter are archaic, those of the former are trite and even "silly." (Cf. Schilder, 655, 641, and particularly Chap. 25, II c, below.) It is an open question whether or not this distinction holds between schizophrenia and all organic psychoses.

For a thoughtful discussion of con-

tion. Besides some neutral bits of prose and a poem, we had the patients learn brief stories of crudely sexual content. Since the distortion by psychic influences of objectionable and particularly of sexual imagery and thoughts has been particularly well investigated in the analysis of dreams and neurotic symptoms (Freud), we expected to get an answer to some of our questions by using such short stories as learning material.

It goes without saying that only meaningful material could be used for our purpose. We chose the following bits of prose:

I. Rabbi Moir, the great teacher, sat on the Sabbath in the school instructing the people, while at his home his two sons were struck by lightning and died.

II. (a) A young girl went for a walk in the fields all alone. A young man came, attacked her and threw her to the ground. The girl struggled, but it was no use. The man pulled up her skirts and pushed his stiff organ into her sheath.[18] After the intercourse he fled, leaving the crying girl lying on the ground.

II. (b) A young man attacked a young girl, pulled up her skirt and pushed his stiff organ into her sheath.

III. When the mother left the house, the father locked himself up in a room with his daughter, threw her on the bed, and raped his own child.

These stories were read to the patients who were then asked to reproduce them. Help was given when needed. Even though we were of the opinion that those mechanisms which we will demonstrate in the reproduction of learned material are also demonstrable in spontaneous confabulations, we chose not to investigate the latter because it seemed hardly feasible to establish the exact relationships between experiences and their elaborations in spontaneous confabulations.[19]

---

fabulation see Korner (411) and Williams and Rupp (771).

18. "Sheath" translates the word *Scheide*, which means both the sheath of a sword and the vagina. There is no exact English equivalent.

19. The last three paragraphs contain the central idea of this investigation. Freud (209) in his dream analyses, Jung (365) in his association experiments, Bleuler (71) and Schilder (652) in their schizophrenia studies—using the material of dreams, associations, and psychotic productions, respectively—reconstructed the latent meaning conveyed by these thought-products and the processes which translated the latent meaning into these manifest forms. In studying confabulations, Betlheim and Hartmann did not follow these investigators' procedure burdened by its twofold task of reconstructing both the underlying meaning and of inferring the mechanisms that bring about the manifest thought-form. They fixed the experience and obtained the recall, so that they could

To avoid tiresome repetitions, we will use a few easily understandable signs. For instance: "IIb 3 times +" means that the story IIb was reproduced after three presentations without error. "+ 1 time" means that the story in question was read once again.

A complete publication of the very extensive case histories does not seem feasible. We will give here only extracts.

CASE NO. 1. M.R., a divorced woman, age 27, was admitted to the psychiatric clinic on February 16, 1924, with the following information. On February 8 she was delivered after a pregnancy of normal length. In the last few days before delivery her orientation became impaired and she did not remember the

---

center solely on the mechanisms that transformed the former into the latter.

This method, not radically different from the dream-experiments of Schroetter, Roffenstein, and Nachmansohn (Chaps. 10, 11, 12, above) is essentially identical with Schilder's (Chap. 25, below) and is similar in externals to Koeppen and Kutzinsky's (402) experiments. For a review of other similar experiments, see Rapaport (591, pp. 250 ff.). The hypnotic state in the dream experiments and the Korsakow patients' state of consciousness productive of confabulations—the former deliberately produced, the latter a spontaneously occurring pathological condition—guarantee the presence of the translating mechanisms these investigations aimed to study. Freud, Jung, Bleuler, and Schilder studied these mechanisms where they could find them, covering a wide variety of these phenomena, but sacrificing prior knowledge of the underlying experiences. The hypnotic-dream experimenters as well as Betlheim and Hartmann prescribed to their subjects what to reproduce and were thus in possession of the underlying experiences, but were wanting on another score. As indicated

in our footnotes to Schroetter, Roffenstein, and Nachmansohn, hypnotic dreams are often more meager in the variety of mechanisms than are natural dreams. The present experiment of Betlheim and Hartmann is also relatively meager in the mechanisms revealed: symbolism is the main mechanism seen. The material presented to the subject has a very different relation to psychic life from that of real experiences, dreams, spontaneous associations, confabulations, and schizophrenic products. Even though Schilder's (655) paresis study and Hartmann's later investigations (304 and 308) of the Korsakow psychosis revealed further varieties of the mechanisms in question, it remains true that the more the original experience is experimentally controlled, and thereby restricted, the less rich the phenomenon elicited is likely to become. Cf. Chap. 27, note 80, below. Both clinical and controlled experimental studies will be needed to clarify more fully the role of these mechanisms. Other experimentally promising spontaneous states, such as mild schizophrenic hallucinoses, fugues, etc., have yet to be tried out as means of such exploration.

delivery itself. According to a close girl-friend, the patient had been drinking for many years, mainly brandy, and especially heavily in the last few months. Allegedly, she had never before become psychologically conspicuous.

On admission the patient was restless, fearful, and poorly oriented. She showed a marked disturbance of registration (a test-word and a 3-digit number were forgotten within one minute) [20] and a definite tendency to confabulate. A superficial intelligence test showed no disturbance of comprehension and judgment. Somatic findings: Pupils normal, nystagmus on fixating in every direction. Tremor of the upper extremities, patellar-reflex absent on both sides. Achilles-reflex weak on both sides. Paresis of all extremities, severe in the lower and milder in the upper. No signs of nerve degeneration. Musculature and nerve trunks of all extremities painful on pressure. Dulled cutaneous sensitivity, lowering of tactile, pain, and temperature sensitivity, particularly in the lower extremities. Spinal fluid: Pandy, Nonne-Apelt, Goldsol, Wassermann, Meinecke negative. Serum Wassermann negative.

In the next few days the patient showed signs of mild delirium, a slight clouding of consciousness, mild motor restlessness and primarily optic, occasionally acoustic, and perhaps even tactile hallucinations. At times she was anxious, saw frogs and snakes in her bed, a child between her thighs and was afraid that she would crush it. Memory of the delivery could not be elicited. These states of delirious excitement repeated themselves with the same content through several days and then abated completely.[21]

The patient then became lucid. Her mood was at first very labile, and the registration defect striking. In her spontaneous confabulations her family played an important role. She had no awareness of or insight into either her psychological or her somatic condition. At times the patient put forth her confabulations with great certainty—indeed, the doubting listener was met by a supercilious smile; at other times, often soon afterward and for the same confabulations, the patient assumed the attitude healthy people take toward their

20. Cf. note 7, above.

21. Note that "mild delirium," "slight clouding," and "excitement" describe a state of consciousness in which a hallucinatory form of thought-processes prevails, with sexual contents and the otherwise amnesic experiences of delivery breaking through in disguised form. This state of consciousness is followed by one which is still quite outside of the range of waking states of consciousness of normal and neurotic people. It is this latter state of consciousness in which the experiment takes place.

daydreams, that is, she did not seem to take them seriously. [At this point] learning experiments were initiated, using both neutral and crudely sexual material. The patient's attention and will to learn were highly variable.[22]

February 28. After seven repetitions, Story I was reproduced correctly except for minor errors.

February 29. I, 4 times + .

March 3. On being asked for the story, she related: "Two daughters of the Rabbi died, namely, their heads were chopped off." [23] She said she had read this story at home.

March 8. (What was the story you were told?) "About Abraham and Isaac and Abraham's sons." (Anything else?) "The two sons of Abraham died and Isaac was very sick." On repeated questioning: "About Nathan the Wise, he was deported from the country, and then he taught the people." [24]

22. Fluctuating attention and will to learn (concentration) are essential characteristics of this state of consciousness indicating the available cathetic energies of the ego and their manner of deployment. Cf. Rapaport *et al.* (602, I, 167 ff.; cf. also Chap. 9, pp. 218–19, and notes 55, 93, above, and Chap. 26, notes 40, 39, below.

The state of consciousness used in this learning experiment as an experimental tool was thus characterized by lucidity (no clouding), labile mood, variable will and attention, inclination to confabulations, lack of insight and of awareness of illness and fluctuation of attitude toward confabulations on the scale "ego-syntonic—ego-alien." It should be noted that an attempted repetition of this experiment could not take the "Korsakow-syndrome" as such for the experimental condition; to obtain comparable experimental conditions one would have to use as subjects patients in the described state of consciousness. For this reason these experimental conditions may *never* be duplicated, though variants of it may occur. Lewin (465) has shown that this is true for all psychological experimenta-

tion, even if it is not equally obvious in all situations.

The study of the subject's state of consciousness thus becomes a major prerequisite for many experiments in psychopathology. In the case under consideration the experiment started only when the mechanisms at work were no longer concealed by the effects of "delirium" and "clouding."

23. "Daughters" for "sons" and "chopped-off heads" for "struck by lightning" are the distortions that come about by the substitution of associated ideas, which Gregor refers to (p. 290 above) and which led Schilder (Chap. 24, pp. 517–18, below) to the concept of the "sphere" within which related ideas are associated and become replaceable by each other when pathology sets in, and within which the preparatory phases of thought-development occur. The relationship of the concept "sphere" to Freud's primary process has been repeatedly discussed in these pages (see, for example, Chap. 24, note 17).

24. Note the series of associative substitutions: Rabbi—Abraham and Isaac —Nathan the Wise.

After three presentations the meaning of IIa was reproduced in abbreviated form, but it was clear that the patient fully understood its content. A few minutes later, but without a new presentation of IIa: "A young gentleman found a young girl lying in the field. He pulled up her skirts and misused her and pushed the knife into her sheath." When asked why she was talking about a knife, she said: "You said that he had a knife!" After three more readings: "On the edge of a field a young girl knelt and cried. . . . (What else?) About a young hunter. She ended up in a cloister." + 1 time: "On the edge of a field a young gentleman found a young girl. He pulled up her skirts and wanted to misuse her. But she struggled and he didn't succeed. My cousin also told me about it." [25] After one reading of IIb: "A youngster saw a young girl lying down and pushed the sheath-knife into her shear." [26] When the sex stories were read, the patient was by no means bashfully defensive, but on the contrary, showed a certain pleasure in the content.[27]

March 9. (The first story?) "Something about Isaac, I don't know any more." Later: "I have read myself about Sabbath in the Bible."

March 10. (Story?) "That about Nathan I have written down once before.[28] About Isaac, how was that . . . just suddenly. . . ."

March 11. IIb, 1 time +.

March 12. When asked about the story read the day before: "Don't know. . . . It comes to my mind in bits. . . . (Young man?) He knifed her. It was

25. This is an example of reduplicating paramnesia so characteristic of the Korsakow syndrome. It was first described by Korsakow (413) and Pick (566). The pertinent literature was reviewed by Westphal (766). Cf. also Schilder, Chap. 25, pp. 571–73, below.

In these patients the experiences are tied to an affect or impulse so closely but to memory-frames-of-reference so loosely (see Chap. 15, note 28, and Chap. 26, note 21, below) that a past experience of that affect or impulse connected with partly or entirely different contexts, suffices to make the present experience appear as one that has been repeatedly experienced. The primary process (the impulse-organization of memory) prevails over the secondary process (the organization in memory-frames-of-reference).

26. The translation does not convey the distortions so striking in the original German. The story phrase was: "sein steifes Glied in ihre Scheide"; the word *Glied* ("organ") was symbolically replaced by *Messer* ("knife"). Then, we may speculate, the adjective *steif* ("stiff") did not fit and was replaced by *schneidend* ("cutting"). Finally interchanging *Scheide* and *schneidend* resulted in: "Scheidemesser in die Schneide," which seems to change the vagina into a cutting instrument.

27. Apparently the implication is that there was no conscious suppression.

28. See note 25, above.

her brother. (Knifed whom?) The sister. (What else?) The brother, the other Abraham was his name. . . . Mother said I should tell the Catechist not to question me so much!" [29] During these days the patient addressed one of us constantly as teacher or Catechist, and the other as a merchant from her neighborhood and thought that she was being taught religion.[30] On the same afternoon: (The story?) "I don't know." (Young man and young girl?) "They get married in the end."

March 13. IIb, 1 time: "He pulled up her stiff [31] skirt. . . . (What else?) I can't." IIb, 1 time. Suddenly very anxious: "Doctor, could you not look out the window, my sister-in-law got wounded! (Where?) On the head! (How?) They shot at her. . . . A soldier went after her, he jumped on a train and wanted to knife me." [32]

March 14. She claimed to be 14 years old, in the 6th grade, and considered the investigator her teacher. After one reading, III is repeated correctly but not verbatim. After the second and third readings it was strongly distorted (in spite

29. The patient's wish not to be questioned is displaced to her mother and related as the mother's instruction. It is possible to describe this, too, as a paramnesia, but it is actually simpler to describe it as a displacement common in the primary process. Both descriptions fit. If this were a dream, we would be likely to call it a displacement, but in waking thought it impresses us as a memory-disorder.

Note also the interweaving of elements of two different stories, resembling the mechanism of condensation. Cf. Schilder, Chap. 25, below.

30. This point allows a glimpse into the deviant state of consciousness in which the experiments took place. Knowledge of the prevalent affects and defenses which the patient brought into her interpersonal relationship with the investigators would probably explain the origin of the patient's frame of reference of "being taught religion." Compare Gill and Rapaport (274) on a specifically cir-cumscribed state of consciousness in a case of loss of personal identity, which similarly found expression in an altered frame of reference. Cf. also notes 21, 22, above.

31. An example of both condensation and displacement.

32. The reduplication in symbolic form of the rape motif (shooting, knifing) deserves attention. This is also a good example of both confabulation and the fluidity of the temporal frame of reference. First the rape is translated symbolically into shooting; then this is displaced onto the sister-in-law and into the present, and perhaps by way of association with shooting, the soldier is added. Disturbances of the temporal frame of reference are so frequent in Korsakow psychoses that Van der Horst (340) attempted to explain the whole psychological texture of the syndrome as the loss of "temporal signs" of experiences.

of help) and the objectionable parts disappeared completely. After the 4th reading: (as the mother left the house . . .) "The father locked himself in with the daughter. (What then?) Then he broke the dishes." + 1 time. (About whom is this story?) "About the Holy Mary." [33]

March 15. (Tell the story! As the mother left the house . . .) "The doctor locked himself up with the younger sister. (She laughs. What else?) The teacher locked himself up with the daughter. . . . (Go on!) Next time." [34]

March 17. III was correctly reproduced after three presentations; then it was read again: (What did I tell you?) "I heard that they brought the cows and tied the bull up with a velvet ribbon." [35] When asked to tell it again: "When the mother left the house she took the rope and wanted to hang the servant. A father drowned and then they found him alive." [36]

March 24. Story I was slowly read to her; she recognized it only upon hearing the words "by lightning" and then finished it correctly.

March 28. (Told you about a Rabbi?) I, +.

April 28. The patient was mostly in a good mood, humorous and jocular. The somatic status was by and large unchanged. When asked whether she was told about a rape, the patient answered in the affirmative and reproduced the story correctly with some help. I + III, 1 time +.

May 5. Only mild disturbance of registration. No confabulation. The patient was oriented in space and time. She was amnesic for the entire time of her pregnancy, for the delivery and for her first four weeks at the clinic.[37]

33. "Breaking the dish" is a not un-common symbol for defloration in par-ticular and intercourse in general. Note, for example, the Jewish marriage ritual of "breaking the dish"; see Reik (607). The phrase about the "Holy Mary" is probably both denial and wishfulfill-ment, like the phrase, "they got mar-ried in the end," in the recall of March 12.

34. "The doctor," "the teacher," have several interesting implications: (a) they indicate how the patient experiences her relationship with the doctor-investigator (teacher and raping father); (b) they indicate how the strivings experienced toward the doctor-teacher-father deter-mine recall, or rather distortion of re-call; (c) they illustrate again the disre-gard for temporal frames-of-reference.

35. The cow and the bull tied with a velvet ribbon are again symbolic rep-resentations of the story. It is remark-able that the state of consciousness is so fluid that directly after a correct repro-duction comes this completely symbolic version.

36. This is again a confabulation. This time the theme is punishment.

37. Amnesia for such special states of consciousness is the rule rather than the exception. Compare Abeles and Schilder

July 19. The symptoms of polyneuritis had considerably receded. Psychologically the patient was entirely lucid, but had an amnesia for her pregnancy and delivery which could not be lifted even by narco-hypnosis (Dr. Schilder). I, 1 time +. IIb, 1 time +.[38]

CASE NO. 2. A woman, age 48, was transferred on April 7, 1924, from the medical department to the psychiatric clinic. Two months previously she had collapsed in the street and had had a mild paresis of the left upper and lower extremities ever since. On admission to the clinic the patient was restless and showed a marked impairment of registration and a pronounced inclination to confabulation. Signs of delirium became prominent in the first few days.

Neurological findings: Pupils enlarged, react sluggishly to light and convergence. Motor cranial nerves normal. No nystagmus. Mild paresis in the left upper extremity. No spasms. In the lower extremities no paresis, no spasms. Deep reflexes present, evidence of nerve degeneration on both left and right. Left ankle clonus. No Babinski. Parkinson-like tremor in the left leg. On attempting to walk or stand the patient immediately fell backward. Sensation undisturbed. Fundi normal. Spinal fluid: Nonne-Apelt, Pandy, Goldsol, and Wassermann negative. Cell count 5. Serum Wassermann negative. The right hand grasped constantly toward objects held out to the patient.[39]* No aphasic or apraxic disorder.

Learning experiments similar to those with Case No. 1 were begun.

April 11. I was reproduced after three presentations meaningfully but not verbatim. The patient confabulated about every element of the story.

April 14. IIa, 1 time: "A young girl went across the field, a young man went down the stairs.[40] He let the young girl fall down [41] and pulled up her skirts

---

(2); Rapaport (591, pp. 197 ff.); Gill and Rapaport (274).

38. These final correct recalls upon a single re-presentation, indicating a saving in relearning, further demonstrate that the patient did not fail to register the stories but that her prevailing states of consciousness allowed only for such recalls as were obtained. The fluctuation in the quality of recall suggests that the patient's state of consciousness also showed considerable fluctuation in those characteristics in terms of which it was described. See note 22, above.

39.* Concerning this phenomenon one of us (Betlheim) will report elsewhere.

40. Going up stairs is a common symbol of intercourse.

41. In dreams, "to fall" is a common representation of intercourse; compare also the phrase "fallen woman." Note the reduplication of the motif in the

and stuck his slanted knee,[42] where did he stick it?" + 1 time: "A young girl went over a road, there came a young man, the girl stumbled, he let the girl stand there crying and shouting (Why did she cry?) I told you she fell down the stairs." + 1 time: "A young girl went on a stairway, she slipped and stumbled." IIb, 2 times: "A young man ran down the stairs and the girl fell and broke her knee." IIb, + 1 time. The contents were fully comprehended.

April 15. (The story I told you?) "Two girls went up a stairway, two boys went after them, they married the two girls, because one was pregnant and the other went home." [43] IIb, 3 times: "Now I will tell it exactly. Two girls went across a field, one of them was pregnant, then they went up the stairway, then the young doctor threw one of the girls down, pulled up her skirt and examined her." [44]

April 16. (The story?) "Two young men and two young ladies ran up the stairs. When the two men ran up they stopped and stuck their slanted knees into the sheath." [45]

April 17. IIb, 1 time: "Two girls who hopped over a stairway, jumped off the stairway, and the two boys jumped up again, the girl has fallen and he pulled up her little skirt. When he saw that she was pregnant, he married her. What I am afraid of is only to be looked at from the side. When the man hears me say that, he will say: That's what you do while I am in the insane asylum. I have never been stuck in such a sickness. (What kind?) Well, clap! They can threaten me as long as they want to that they will cut off my tongue and dig out my eyes! I have done nothing wrong." [46] Pictures presented to her were

patient's rendering of the story. Cf. Schilder, Chap. 25, pp. 541 and 571 below.

42. Some of the instructiveness of the German version is lost in the translation. *Steifes Glied* ("stiff organ") is transformed by substituting *Knie* ("knee") for *Glied* and replacing *steif* by *schief*, meaning "skewed," "slanted," etc. *Schief* replacing *steif*, however, has also the connotations of crooked, unfair, crippled.

43. This is the most widely known of these reproductions, having been quoted by both Freud (255) and Schilder (647).

It is noteworthy that the intercourse motif appears in three different representations: stair-walking, marriage, pregnancy. Cf. note 41, above.

44. Cf. note 34, above.

45. Note again the coexistence of a symbolic and a but slightly disguised representation.

46. Note the confusion, the referring of the recalled story to herself, and the experience of the organic illness in terms of the "dismemberment motif" and the "punishment for sex-sins." Schilder (655) called attention to the frequency of these motifs in organic psychoses.

well apperceived in whole and in detail. The patient talked much, joked readily, and made a show of superiority.

April 19. The patient was completely lucid. "People think perhaps I want to be Empress, out of envy . . . but I could become one. (Emperor?) Well, I think Wilhelm the 28th." [47]

April 28. IIb, 1 time +. Shortly after, she was requested to repeat it. "A man meets a young girl in the field, he attacked her and stuck his crooked [48] finger into her sheath. When he saw that the girl became a mother, he married her." Somatic status unchanged.

May 5. The patient stated that she did not want to drink coffee because there was poison in it. Her statements on the events of the last few days and hours and on the duration of her stay at the clinic were completely false, and were elaborated in the manner of confabulations. When asked about the stories she had been told: "They were innocuous, about two girls and a boy. (What else?) Two girls hopped down a stairway and the boys."

May 8. Death. Autopsy (May 9): Old mitral endocarditis with insufficiency and some stenosis. Cystitis and pyelitis calculosa. High-grade oedema of the leptomeninges and of the brain. Chronic internal hydrocephalus. Microscopic study not yet available.

CASE NO. 3. M.P., a woman, age 49, admitted to the psychiatric clinic on June 25, 1924.[49] Patient had been drinking heavily for 15 to 20 years, allegedly up to 1½ liters of rum daily. She had been bedridden for a week. She was disoriented and asserted she had lunched the day before with Chancellor Seipel, and expressed similar other ideas.

On admission the patient was disoriented as to time and place. She was in a good mood and jocular. Questions put to her as well as perceptions were completely forgotten in a few minutes; confabulatory activity was very rich. Somatic status: tremor of tongue and fingers, pupils react poorly to light. Paresis of the upper and lower extremities; could neither stand nor walk. The

47. Here "lucidity" designates a state of consciousness free of confusional clouding which, however, does not exclude confabulations or delusions.

48. "Crooked" translates *krumm;* cf. note 42, above.

49. In view of the subsequent dates this must be a misprint. It should probably have read May 25 or June 5; compare p. 302, below: "Cases No. 2 and No. 3 died after a few weeks of observation."

muscles and nerve trunks of all extremities painful on pressure. Patellar and Achilles reflexes absent on both sides. No pyramidal signs. No nerve degeneration phenomena.

June 13. The patient was very distracted and at first rejected the learning experiment. Every statement of hers was embellished with confabulations.[50] IIb, 8 times. She did not reproduce it correctly even once and the distortions were extreme. Yet the numerous reproductions showed that the patient did comprehend the meaning of the material. Her comprehension (upon superficial examination) seemed generally good.

June 14. IIb, 1 time: "A young man and a young girl are together . . . the need . . . the organ in Number 4 (Number 4?) Well, that I do not know." [51] After repeated reading: "A young man has an affair with a young girl and stuck therefore organ Number 4. . . . (Number 4?) That's what I would say." After yet another repetition: "A young man gave me four cigarettes and I will take the four cigarettes; it is hidden as soon as I got it." [52]

June 20. Death.

The cardinal symptoms of the Korsakow psychosis are demonstrable in all these cases. The first two cases also showed initially signs of delirious confu-

---

50. The patient's state of consciousness is characterized by disorientation, extreme distractibility, extremely quick loss of recent impressions, and incessant confabulation. Thus it appears that of the three cases this is the one in which the learning experiment took place in a state of consciousness nearest to what is usually described as confusion. Lucidity, present to some degree in the other cases at the time of the experiment, is lacking here.

51. Note the fragmentation of the sentence. The German *Glied* has a more direct reference to the male sex organ than the English "organ." "The need" is perhaps an indirect representation of an implication of the story. "Number 4" may be an indirect representation; it resembles the use of "Number 1" and

"Number 2" of child language for urination and defecation and the corresponding organs.

52. "Cigarette" is a common male sex symbol. Cf. Schroetter Chap. 10, above, Experiments 4 and 6. "Four cigarettes" and "hidden as soon as I got it" suggest a more far-reaching condensation than that seen in the other two patients' recalls. Yet here, too, the coexistence of a barely disguised expression ("affair") and a symbolic representation ("cigarette") is striking. As would be expected from the patient's state of consciousness (see note 50, above), the mechanisms of Korsakow confabulations are mixed with confusional forms of thought in the patient's reproductions. The material is too meager to yield differential characteristics of the formal properties of thought

sion.[53] Cases No. 2 and No. 3 died after a few weeks of observation without the psychosis having subsided, whereas the first patient has already been at the clinic for five months, and for the past few weeks has neither confabulated nor shown disturbances of registration. However, her amnesia for her pregnancy and delivery, as well as for the first weeks of her stay in the hospital has persisted. It is not without interest that the child, for whose birth the patient is amnesic and whose existence she denies even when she is directly told of it, appeared as an hallucination in the delirious phase—the child in the bed between the thighs. (Cf. Bonhoeffer.) [54*] In Cases No. 1 and No. 3 the etiological factor appears to be chronic alcoholism, which expresses itself neurologically in the polyneuritis. In Case No. 2 neither the anamnesis nor the clinical picture nor even the autopsy gives definite information as to etiology; the internists suspected uremia as the etiological factor.

Upon superficial examination comprehension seemed undisturbed in all three cases. (Compare, however, Gregor.) [55*] The attitude toward confabulations was variable: at times they were put forth with great seriousness and deep conviction, and at other times in a playful and detached way, or even in the manner normals look upon their daydreams.[56] It seems to be significant that we found no correlation between registration disturbance and confabulatory tendency. It is justifiable to assume that impairment of registration tends to facilitate the emergence of subjective material, which in turn may render the retention of

---

in these states of consciousness. Here is a broad and important field open to empirical study.

53. The delirium of the first two cases had subsided by the time the experiments were begun. Though it is implied that the third case was not delirious, she was obviously confused at the time of the experiment.

54.* Bonhoeffer (82).

55.* Gregor (287, 288).

56. What is called here "attitude" is actually "reflective awareness." It seems to be a sub-species of the function that distinguishes imagery from hallucination and percept, thought from reality. The following are some form-variants

of reflective awareness: ideation without specific awareness, ideation with awareness, awareness with awareness that one is aware, etc. Though the role in reality testing of some forms of reflective awareness is well known, neither its phenomenology nor its dynamic role have so far been systematically studied. Ego-syntonic and ego-alien obsessional ideas provide an opportunity for such study. It seems probable that differences in the quality (and intensity?) of such reflective awareness will prove crucial in differentiating between various states of consciousness. Cf. Chap. 25, pp. 532 ff., and Chap. 27, notes 27, 28, 32, 43, 45, below.

external impressions difficult; nevertheless, these disorders seem to run two rather independent courses. Episodes of humorous criticism intermingled with phases of depression were common to all three cases and were very clear even in the case whose anamnesis offers no clue of an alcoholic etiology. Case No. 2 showed fleeting megalomanic ideas. The perseveration of parapraxes, noted by several authors, was particularly striking in Cases No. 1 and No. 2. To these we shall return later on. We can also corroborate Pick's [57]* observations regarding the unfaltering insistence upon obviously contradictory statements. Self-references became strikingly prominent in these patients so that even experiences of others communicated to them were immediatly treated as belonging to their own person.

Our experiments encountered the same difficulties, rooted in the nature of the Korsakow psychosis, which have been observed by previous investigators: fluctuation of attention, little inclination to learn the material offered, even to the point of refusal, and finally a peculiarly irregular alternation between remembering and forgetting so that a memory apparently lost suddenly appears, while one that was just there disappears.[58] In our first two cases, traces of the learned material were demonstrable by means of Ebbinghaus's saving procedure. In the third case a systematic learning of bits of prose, however, short, could not be accomplished.[59] We found no significant difference between innocuous and objectionable material in the number of repetitions necessary for learning. The following are examples of distorted reproductions of an innocuous story. (Case No. 1. I, March 8): "About Abraham and about Isaac and about Abraham's sons," and on the same day: "About Nathan the Wise, he was expelled from the country and then taught the people." [60] Here a word of the story, "Rabbi Moir," is replaced by one which is associatively related to it and belongs to the same sphere. We must remember that the mechanism is the same here as in "physiological" [61] forgetting, with the exception that

57.* Pick (566).

58. These memory phenomena appear to be related to reminiscence and obliviscence. Buxton (116) called attention to the "*now* you see it *now* you don't" character of reminiscence. Alper (28) offers the most recent discussion of the pertinent literature and an interesting and suggestive experiment showing the dependence of reminiscence upon ego-attitudes.

59. Cf. note 50, above.

60. The translation falls short of the perseverative word-play of the original: "expelled" translates *aus dem Lande gewiesen,* and "taught" translates *unterwies.*

61. In German, "physiological" is

we can demonstrate—as Freud has shown [62]—that in most of these cases there is a psychological motivation underlying the distortion. Our findings on the reproduction of objectionable material were similar except that substitute formations [63] also occurred; for example: (Case No. 2, IIa, April 15) "The two girls went up a stairway, two boys went after them, they married the two girls, because one was pregnant and the other went home." Similarly, Case No. 1 (IIa, March 8) replaces the words: ". . . stuck his stiff organ into her sheath" by ". . . pushed the knife into her sheath." When asked why she talked about a knife, the patient said: "You said that he had a knife." The rape scene several days later: "He knifed her"; and at another time: "They shot at her." Another example: (Case No. 3, IIb, June 14) the words, "stiff organ," are replaced by "cigarette," etc. Here the parapraxes are related to the learned material as a symbol is to what it symbolizes. Therefore, objectionable phrases are replaced by words familiar to us as typical symbols from dream analysis and other sources. (To climb stairs, to knife, to shoot, are symbols for intercourse: knife and cigarette are penis symbols.) Our conclusions are based on typical ubiquitous symbols, of which there are but few, and not on those symbolizations [64] in which there is a broader range of individual variability, because the latter cannot be evaluated without thorough analytic study of the life-history of the

used to mean "normal," as the antonym of "pathological."

62. The reference is to Freud (210). The authors' assertion is questionable. Schilder (Chap. 25, II c, below) has shown that in thought disorders of organic origin this type of memory disorder—replacement of "Rabbi Moir" by "Nathan the Wise"—need not be directly related to a specific repressed striving. Silberer (Chap. 9, notes 55 and 59, above) asserted that certain states of consciousness are in themselves conducive to the use of indirect representation and symbolism. In our discussion of Bleuler's (71) work on schizophrenia we were forced to conjecture that, unlike parapraxes in which a specific drive-representation breaks through, many schizophrenic symptoms can be understood only if we assume that they are not referable to a specific drive or affect but rather to a state of consciousness created by the prevailing condition of drives and affects. See Chap. 26, notes 40, 49, below. The situation under discussion appears to be similar.

63. The meaning of "substitute formations" is not very clear. It seems from the following discussion that the authors mean by this phrase symbols and symbolizations. The transition between these and the "associative replacements" in innocuous stories seems fluid. In any case, the material presented seems too meager to elucidate this problem.

64. In this volume we have referred to these phenomena as "indirect representations" and not as "symbols."

patient. By this procedure we also hope to forestall the objection—rooted in a misunderstanding of the theory of symbolism—that since in psychoanalysis every idea of an object may be interpreted as a symbol, the demonstration of symbols in our cases has no value as proof. Climbing stairs as a symbol seems especially significant to us because it is clearly unexplainable by a conscious wish for distortion. Significantly, the symbolic distortions occurred frequently just before or just after a correct reproduction (without further readings).[65]

Distorting in order to rob the story of its objectionable character and render it harmless is present not only in the symbol formations but also in additions and substitute formations.[66] In reproducing IIa (March 8) patient No. 1 said: "But she struggled and he didn't succeed"; or patient No. 2 gave a happy ending to the story: "They married the girls, because one was pregnant." A greater resistance to learning crudely sexual stories than to learning harmless ones was found only in patient No. 3 and even there only in the beginning when it took the form of bashful rejection. We want to add that even when the distorted reproduction contained apparently random actual percepts there was often a deeper relationship determining the choice of that perception material.[67] It has already been emphasized that parapraxes often stubbornly perseverate. To us it seems that this was true of symbolizations to an even greater extent.[68]* The stair-climbing in Case No. 2 may serve as an example because it was retained in nearly every reproduction while other elements of the reproductions varied. We find this somewhat analogous to the stubborn persistence of neurotic symptoms due, according to Freud's conception, to the circumstance that they are sustained by both the repressing and the repressed tendencies—from both sides, as it were. Thus we have demonstrated that in learning experiments the un-

65. The implication is that we are not dealing here with conscious suppression due to shame and embarrassment. In our footnotes we have consistently indicated the many places where in one and the same sentence direct expression of sexual material appears together with disguised substitutes. Such phenomena, and the intermittent correct recalls to which Betlheim and Hartmann point, show that it is not shame or embarrassment that suppresses the sexual material, but the prevailing (highly fluctuating) state of consciousness makes for these substitutions.

66. Here "substitute formations" is used in the sense of denial. Cf. note 63, above.

67. By "perception material" the authors probably mean memories of past percepts. Abraham, Nathan the Wise, Holy Mary, and the like are examples in point.

68.* This is in good harmony with

doubtedly organically anchored registration disorder of the Korsakow psychosis leads to substitute formations. Some of these are the result of displacement onto associatively related ideas within the same sphere and others are related to the idea learned in the same fashion as is a symbol to what it symbolizes. This relationship is familiar from the analysis of parapraxes, dreams, neurotic symptoms, and schizophrenic thinking. We cannot further discuss here the characteristics which distinguish the two kinds of distortion process described. But we want to emphasize that in our experiments only the crudely sexual material underwent a symbolic disguising process. This observation is in keeping with the teachings of psychoanalysis concerning the close relationship of drive life and symbolic thinking and with the considerations that lead psychoanalysis to call symbolic thinking "the language of the unconscious," as well as with Schilder's theory in which symbols are considered preparatory stages of thought development.[69] The process which in our cases led to symbolic distortions we must consider organically founded, but its effects must be described as analogous to repression, though the nature of this process is unknown.[70]

As an aside we should like to mention that since our findings are derived from experiments, the method of which is independent of psychoanalytic postulates, they may be considered experimental verifications of the validity of certain Freudian symbol interpretations. In this respect they are related to investigations on the mode of representation of sexual material presented to hypnotic subjects in post-hypnotic dream suggestions. Schroetter [71*] and Roffenstein [72*] reported positive results [derived from such investigations] confirming Freud's interpretation of dream symbols.

We have already indicated that in the Korsakow psychosis and in epileptic twilight states the memory-traces are retained; however, their reproduction must be considered hampered by an organic process. Apparently, the difference between such amnesias and the so-called "functional" ones is that the

---

Kogerer's (409) finding that in the Korsakow psychosis dreams are often better retained than real experiences.

69. See Schilder "On Thought Development," Chap. 24, below.

70. In our comments we advanced the hypothesis that an organically founded specific state of consciousness can account for distortions and symbolizations in a manner analogous to that of the hypnagogic state of consciousness in Silberer's experiments (Chaps. 1 and 2, above). Concerning the sharp distinction made by the present authors between sexual symbolism and other distortions and substitutions, see Chap. 12, note 81, above.

71.* Schroetter [Chap. 10, above].

72.* Roffenstein [Chap. 11, above].

psychological genesis of the latter is demonstrable, while in the former an unknown organic factor takes its place.[73] Whether or not the "registration" of the memory-trace takes the same course in both cases cannot be decided with certainty. Schilder's [74*] work undoubtedly supports this assumption.[75] He has shown that in several important types of organic amnesias impressions apparently forgotten may be brought to consciousness in deep hypnosis in the very form in which they were experienced. He studied amnesias following epileptic twilight-states and attempts at suicide by hanging. The amnesias following the latter were convincingly shown by Wagner-Jauregg [76*] to be organically determined.

This brings us to the question: how are we to conceive of the representation of memory-traces in our cases? The most obvious assumption would be that the original impressions are retained undistorted and their emergence in symbolic disguise is to be ascribed to an organic reproduction-inhibiting factor. But there is another assumption that cannot be lightly dismissed, namely that in certain cases and for certain contents even the registration of the memories may take place in symbolic form.[77] Again we must recall the theories of Freud who was the first to assert that on early levels of development the symbol and what it symbolizes are identical.

That the memory disorder of the Korsakow syndrome is organically founded is conceded by all investigators (excepting only Moebius). But one can assume, as Bonhoeffer [78] did long ago, that there is also a functional factor and that only its interaction with the organic-cerebral factor yields the total psychological picture of the Korsakow syndrome. The functional factor of the memory disorder seems clearest in post-traumatic cases. Even if we consider the functional factor secondary, it is permissible to assume that in our cases too, psychologically demonstrable tendencies make use of organically pre-formed distortion mechanisms. The aim of our investigation was to demonstrate through the study of symbolic distortions how the deliberate application of psychological insight affords a partial glimpse into the operation of these organic mechanisms.

---

73. Cf. Rapaport (591, pp. 214 ff.). The authors discuss here only the amnestic aspect of the disorder, but it is apparent that they would apply the same considerations to its paramnestic aspects (distortions, symbolizations, etc.).

74.* Schilder (664).

75. The assumption in question is that in organic amnesia there operates a mechanism analogous to repression.

76.* Wagner-Jauregg (748).

77. Compare Poetzl (573).

78. Bonnhoeffer (82).

PART FOUR

MOTIVATION OF THINKING

CHAPTER 14

THE POLYPHONY OF THOUGHT [1]

By Wilhelm Stekel

IT MAY SEEM UNBELIEVABLE that "flight of ideas" [2] is more the rule than the exception with us all. Psychoanalytic observation shows that there are two kinds of thought: one is first thought out and then put into words; the other escapes observation before being verbalized. A question arises here: Can the latter kind be experienced as thought? They are thoughts in *status nascendi.* . . . We conclude that there is a thinking without words. . . . But is this not contrary to experience? We are wont to regard thought as something words can express.

. . . Under certain conditions this kind of thinking is actually observable. It turns out to be a thinking in pictures. When asked to associate freely, some patients at once produce a string of pictures that obviously represent preliminary stages of thought. Only analysis can discover the symbolic meaning of these pictures; they are important affects [3] hiding in a simile. . . .

1. W. Stekel (706). This fragment of Stekel's paper is included here because it presents—in a literary and allegoric fashion—that one-sided view of the psychoanalytic theory of thinking to which clinicians are particularly prone, and which therefore is incorrectly considered by many to be an accurate representation of the psychoanalytic theory of thinking. The view is one-sided in that it underemphasizes the structuralized and relatively autonomously functioning equilibria reached in psychic development as a result of the struggle among intrapsychic forces as well as between these forces and reality; at the same time it overemphasizes the role played in normal thinking and action by the struggle of motivational forces. It is understandable that the clinician makes this error because in the associations of his patients he is daily faced with a continuous struggle of such forces. While Freud's "Psychopathology of Everyday Life" (210) might suggest such a view, Chap. VII of his "The Interpretation of Dreams" (209) and his "Two Principles" are its best antidote. Modern psychoanalytic ego-psychology, and particularly the conception of the conflict-free ego-sphere (Hartmann, Chap. 19, below) show how far we have advanced beyond such a conception.

2. "Flight of ideas" is the term usually used for the most common symptom of manic patients. Stekel here uses it to mean the substratum of thought from which ordered thinking emerges and of which we are generally unaware. Cf. Schilder, "Thought Development," Chap. 24, below.

3. The term "affect" is here used by

The process of verbalizing our thoughts is certainly more complicated than we had imagined. We often search for the proper term to express a situation or feeling, make an unconscious choice of many possible words, and by our choice betray the presence of deeper complexes [4] that are left unverbalized.

Words are compromises. Idea and word are best matched if they relate to concrete objects. . . . A symbolic use of concrete objects permits . . . a cathecting by affects [5] of . . . [the objects]. For example, the expression, "separated from bed and table" [6] shows that the word "table" can obtain a sexual connotation. . . .

The process of verbalization of feelings, moods, affects, and abstract concepts is much more difficult; there the words truly represent compromises, since they have different meanings in different situations, and for different people. If we consider for a moment the complex meaning of the word "love," we shall see how rarely word and feeling can match.

The thought-process preceding verbalization must be conceived of as a struggle between opposing impulses. In his volume on slips of the tongue, Freud [7] demonstrated that repressed strivings often manage to gain expression against the speaker's will. To us slips of the tongue prove only that there is a permanent struggle afoot between strong opposing strivings.[8]

Stekel in the sense of "motivating force" or "drive." We have pointed out that Bleuler, Chap. 20, notes 15 to 20, below, Schilder, Chap. 25, notes 79 and 195, below, and Silberer, Chap. 9, notes 77 and 93, above, used the term similarly.

4. For the definition of the term "complex" see Chap. 9, note 62*, above. The term was already outdated in psychoanalytic literature at the time this paper was published. Actually, it never was a concept in the main stream of psychoanalytic theory. As used in this article, it was introduced into the literature by Jung, while Freud used it only in the limited contexts of the castration- and Oedipus-complex.

5. Here the term "affect" is used as "psychic energy." Cf. M. Prince (583).

6. This is the verbatim translation of

a German phrase referring to the separation of husband and wife (the equivalent of "has left my bed and board"; *a mensa et thoro*).

7. Freud (210).

8. It is implied that the striving to express logical, ordered thought and the strivings which come to expression in slips of the tongue are in continuous struggle even when no slips occur. This, in turn, implies that the strivings underlying logical and ordered thinking are usually victorious in this struggle. As we stated in note 1, above, the psychoanalytic theory of thinking differs from Stekel's view of thinking as a continuous battle of titans, in that it has demonstrated that a dynamic equilibrium of these two kinds of striving has long since been superimposed upon the original

All energy originates in the drive-life. Both speech and the thought-process which precedes it, draw their energy from this source. One of Nietzsche's most penetrating insights was: "Thinking is but the expression of how the drives mutually relate to each other." . . .[9]

Thinking obeys two principles: the pleasure-principle and the reality-principle (Freud). Most of a normal person's thinking obeys the reality-principle. But the question arises: Can the pleasure-principle actually be held in temporary abeyance? So far it has been maintained, also by Freud, that pleasure- and reality-principle alternate.[10]

Actually there is no separating them! There is a constant struggle between them. This struggle can be interpreted to mean that our reality appraisal must be wrung from the pleasure-principle. . . .

While we attend to reality, still another tendency is active in us, the striving for pleasure, which remains largely unconscious. . . . Man, therefore, has a hidden world of thoughts, which cannot be expressed by language. . . .

This discrepancy between speech and thought, or rather between what we want to say and what we can say, is due mainly to the fact that we never have single thoughts but always many, an entire polyphony, of which speech expresses but one melody; the other voices and the counterpoint remain hidden.

---

basic struggle and that slips of the tongue are disturbances of this equilibrium. Nevertheless, Stekel's view does express an important aspect of the development of thought, an aspect which once again comes to the surface in varying degrees in psychopathology (cf. Schilder, Chap. 24, below) and in the progressive uncovering of primitive thought-processes in psychoanalytic therapy.

9. That all energy "originates in the drive life" was not questioned by psychoanalysts until recently, when concern with inborn ego-apparatuses suggested that these may also be sources of energy (Hartmann, Chap. 19, below). Furthermore, the concepts of "desexualized libido," "delibidinized cathexes," and "bound cathexes" of the secondary proc-ess (as contrasted with the "free cathexes" of the primary process) indicate that there is a qualitative change in the organization of these drive energies in the course of individual development. There are reasons to assume that the energies available to the ego, which play a role in thinking, though they originate in drives may have a new emergent organization different from that of drives. (Cf. Freud on attention-cathexes, Chap. 15, pp. 320–21, and note 21, below.)

10. A comparison with Freud's "Two Principles" (Chap. 15, particularly pp. 318–26, and note 29, below) shows that this is a gross oversimplification both of the problem and of Freud's views concerning it.

The notion of thinking in a single direction is no longer tenable. I maintain that the thought-process shows a remarkable condensation.[11] Verbalization is preceded by a struggle which usually ends with the victory of the reality-principle.

I picture thinking as a stream of which only the surface is visible; orchestral music of which only the melody is audible. Obviously, differing tones in the various voices create dissonance. But one must bear in mind that the law of bipolarity [12] also holds for thinking. The anti-polar voice dies out, or else expresses itself as a symptom or symptomatic action. Contrary impulses come to the fore simultaneously. . . .

These inner voices often do not reach consciousness. . . . Some patients, who are given to daydreaming and fantasying, do not remember their daydreams. The daydreamer looks inward, thinks without words, listening for the overtones without grasping the melody. He hears only chords or single tones. Perhaps he thinks without verbal-images, perhaps only in symbolic pictures that hide the thoughts.

Once it is recognized that thinking is a polyphony and not one voice, the difficulties of psychoanalytic treatment are easily appreciated. What we are after lies in the middle voices or even in the counterpoint. Under certain conditions, the leading voice may be useless for our purpose. I have in mind patients who always recount the events of the previous day and talk weeks on end, never running out of important up-to-date topics. . . .

11. It is implied that the final thought-product is a compromise which condenses the representations of the various strivings struggling for expression. Stekel considers that secondary-process thinking is just as much a product of condensation as is primary-process thinking.

12. By this term Stekel apparently means "ambivalence."

CHAPTER 15

FORMULATIONS REGARDING THE TWO PRINCIPLES IN MENTAL FUNCTIONING [1]

By Sigmund Freud

WE HAVE LONG OBSERVED that every neurosis has the result, and therefore probably the purpose,[2] of forcing the patient out of real life, of alienating him from actuality. Nor could a fact such as this escape the observation of Pierre Janet; [3*] he spoke of a loss of *"la fonction du réel"* as being a special characteristic of the neurotic, but without discovering the connection of this disturbance with the fundamental conditions of neurosis. By introducing the concept of repres-

1. This selection is made from the translation published in the *Collected Papers* (223). For the original, see Freud (222).

2. The reader accustomed to causal explanations may be taken aback by the use of the concept "purpose." Indeed Freud has often been accused of having created a vitalistic-teleological theory of psychic life. Yet Freud's "purposivism" is neither vitalistic nor teleological. It is a heuristic method. Self-regulating dynamic systems may always be described in terms of both cause and purpose. The less we know about such a system the more will we be forced to use purposive concepts for its adequate description, since premature causal explanations will of necessity disregard some of its crucial characteristics. Tolman's "Purposive Behaviorism" (732) sheds light on this problem. The "closure" and "Praegnanz" concepts of Gestalt-psychology could be called teleological in the same sense as the Freudian theory.

The problem of purpose is of particu-

lar significance for the theory of thinking. The Wuerzburg school of psychology, the one which devoted the most interest to thought-processes (cf. Ach and Buehler, Chaps. 1 and 2, above), introduced the concepts *task* and *anticipation*. These were also teleological in the sense described above. If thinking was to be encompassed conceptually such concepts were at first inevitable, since thinking is a process by which behavior is directed toward a future event or, put in another way, in which behavior is directed by a future event. The crucial task of the science of thinking is to discover how in the present, which is a product of the past, this directedness by and orientation toward the future are effected. Freud's present essay sheds light on this issue; it deals with the question of how behavior and thought, while causally determined by drives (the pleasure-principle), also subserve the adaptation to reality (reality-principle).

3.* Janet (355).

sion into the genesis of the neuroses we have been able to gain some insight into this connection.[4] The neurotic turns away from reality because he finds it unbearable—either the whole or parts of it. The most extreme type of this alienation from reality is shown in certain cases of hallucinatory psychosis which aim at denying the existence of the particular event that occasioned the outbreak of insanity.[5*] But actually every neurotic does the same with some fragment of reality. And now we are confronted with the task of investigating the development of the relation of the neurotic and of mankind in general to reality, and of so bringing the psychological significance of the real outer world into the structure of our theory.[6]

In the psychology which is founded on psychoanalysis we have accustomed

4. It may at first glance seem obscure that Freud invokes the concept of repression to gain insight into alienation from reality. When we speak of repression, we usually think of the elimination from consciousness of an affect or idea pertaining to a drive (Freud, 233, p. 86). But repression has other aspects, also, one of which Anna Freud (201, pp. 100 ff.) called "restriction of the ego." This restriction comes about as follows: when a drive and its ideational representatives are barred from consciousness, much that is related to them is also barred; interests corresponding to the drive are barred; the range of experiencing is narrowed and the accumulation of experiences hindered; since past experiences are not available to consciousness, new relationships among experiences do not develop; the scarcity of such relationships limits apperception, and a vicious circle is set up. This process is so far-reaching that it becomes apparent even on intelligence tests in the gross limitations of information and vocabulary. See Rapaport et al. (602, I, 129–32).

5.* Griesinger (291, pp. 168–70).

6. It may seem surprising that Freud was this tardy in "bringing the psycho-logical significance of the real outer world into the structure of . . . [his] theory." Therefore, it will be important to remind ourselves of some historical relationships. Philosophical psychology, the ancestor of scientific psychology, was a subsidiary of epistemology. Its major query was: How do we acquire our knowledge of the world of reality? It studied psychic functions mainly in their relation to the acquisition of knowledge of reality. Though there were exceptions to this, the milestones of psychology—Bacon's Novum Organon (33), Descartes's Passions de l'ame (143), Hobbes's De Homine (331), Locke's An Essay Concerning Human Understanding (481), Hume's Inquiry Concerning the Human Understanding (343), Leibnitz's New Essays on the Human Understanding (446)—were written in the service of epistemology. In its beginning, scientific psychology did not radically change this focus of interest. It was centered in stimulus and reaction, that is, in the evaluation by the psychic apparatus of the impingements of external reality, though some studies employing introspection were already concerned with intrapsychic reality.

ourselves to take as our starting-point the unconscious mental processes, with the peculiarities of which we have become acquainted through analysis. These we consider to be the older primary processes,[7] the residues of a phase of development in which they were the only kind of mental processes.[8] The sovereign tendency obeyed by these primary processes is easy of recognition; it is called the pleasure-pain (*Lust-Unlust*) principle, or more shortly the pleasure-principle.[9] These processes strive towards gaining pleasure; from any operation

---

Freud's point of departure was different: he was concerned with the evaluation by the psychic apparatus of *internal stimuli* (drives, needs) rather than *external stimuli*. In the "Interpretation of Dreams" (209, p. 542) he wrote:

The unconscious is the true psychic reality; in its inner nature it is just as much unknown to us as the reality of the external world, and it is just as imperfectly communicated to us by the data of consciousness as is the external world by the reports of our sense organs.

Thus it occurred that only after considerable exploration of psychic reality and in the wake of observations concerning maladaptations to external reality did Freud have to face the problem of reality adaptation. However, it should be noted that in Chap. VII of "The Interpretation of Dreams" he tackled this problem repeatedly.

For the theory of thinking, it may be of some advantage to note that his manner of facing the problem in the present essay shows some similarity to Leibnitz's formulation of the problem of epistemology. Leibnitz asked: How is it possible that reasoning arrives at conclusions which coincide with the outcome of processes occuring in reality? or in his own words: How can there be a correspondence between "verité de fait" and "verité de raison"? Freud's problem was: How can the apparatus regulated by

the pleasure-principle (drives) be also adapted to reality? This parallel indicates the significance of Freud's problem for the psychology of thinking as well as for epistemology.

7. See Chap. VII of "The Interpretation of Dreams" (209), particularly pp. 533–36.

8. For evidence in ethnological, pathological, and developmental data see H. Werner (755). Whether these primary processes, as we know them, were ever "the only kind of mental processes" and, if so, how in that "phase of development" reality-adaptation was achieved, is an insufficiently studied question. For its discussion see H. Hartmann, Chap. 19, particularly notes 39 and 43, below.

9. The "pleasure-principle" may appear to be a teleological concept, and indeed it is, but only in the sense discussed in note 2, above. If we consider Freud's formulation of the pleasure-principle, the nature of this "teleology" becomes clearer (209, p. 533):

We . . . discussed the psychic results of experiences of gratification, and were able . . . to introduce a second assumption, namely, that the accumulation of excitation is felt as pain, and sets the apparatus in operation in order to bring about again a state of gratification, in which the diminution of excitation is perceived as pleasure. Such a current in the apparatus, issuing

which might arouse unpleasantness ("pain") mental activity draws back (repression).[10] Our nocturnal dreams,[11] our waking tendency to shut out painful impressions, are remnants of the supremacy of this principle and proofs of its power.

In presupposing that the state of mental equilibrium was originally disturbed by the peremptory demands of inner needs, I am returning to lines of thought which I have developed in another place.[12] In the situation I am considering,

---

from pain and striving for pleasure, we call "wish."

Here the concepts pleasure, pain, wish, are divested of their subjective, phenomenological, anthropomorphic, and teleological character. They are terms designating energy distribution: pain = increasing disequilibrium of energy; wish = the process aimed at restoring equilibrium; pleasure = decreasing disequilibrium of energy.

It becomes clear here that: (a) Freudian psychology, including the psychology of thinking, is a conceptual structure framed in terms of energy distribution; (b) there is no necessary correspondence between the subjective experiences of pain, pleasure, and wish and the concepts represented by these terms. Under specific conditions, increasing disequilibrium may be experienced as pleasure and decreasing disequilibrium as pain. See Fenichel, Chap. 18, pp. 350–51, below.

See Freud (209, p. 537; 233, p. 85; and 241, p. 6). Cf. also Freud (232, particularly pp. 61–64).

10. See Freud (233).

11. The reference is to the wishfulfillment character of dreams; see Freud (209, pp. 497–514).

12. Freud wrote (209, pp. 508–9):

. . . first the apparatus strove to keep itself as free from stimulation as possible, and therefore, in its early structure, adopted the arrangement of a reflex apparatus which enabled it promptly to discharge by motor paths any sensory excitation reaching it from without. But this simple function was disturbed by the exigencies of life . . . which . . . first confronted it in the form of the great physical needs. The excitation aroused by the inner need seeks an outlet in motility, which we may describe as "internal change" or "expression of emotions." The hungry child cries or struggles helplessly. But its situation remains unchanged; for the excitation proceeding from the inner need has not the character of a momentary impact, but of a continuing pressure. [Cf. Freud, 232, particularly pp. 61–64.] A change can occur only if in some way there is an *experience of satisfaction*, which puts an end to the internal excitation. An essential constituent of this experience is the appearance of a certain percept (of food in our example) the memory image of which is henceforth associated with the memory trace of the excitation arising from the need.

From the point of view of the psychology of thinking, this postulates a specific relationship between the excitation and the memory image, the need and the idea of the need-satisfying object; or in K. Lewin's (Chap. 5, above) terms, the need and the object which has valence for the need; or in the usual psychoanalytic terms, the instinctual drive and its object or ideational representation. It is indispensable for a dynamic, that is, motivational theory of the thought-process, to hypothesize some such relationship. If

whatever was thought of (desired) simply took an hallucinatory form,[13] as still happens today with our dream-thoughts every night.[14]* This attempt at satisfaction by means of hallucination was abandoned only in consequence of the absence of the expected gratification, because of the disappointment experienced.[15] Instead, the mental apparatus had to decide to form a conception of the real circumstances in the outer world and to exert itself to alter them.[16] A new principle of mental functioning was thus introduced; what was conceived of was no longer that which was pleasant, but that which was real, even

---

thought is determined (motivated), like any other form of behavior, it must rise to consciousness as an expression of forces. Just as action is in the final analysis propelled by drives, so must thought also be. Just as drive-compelled action is partly supplemented and partly supplanted by reality-adapted action when drive controls are established, so is drive-compelled thought (ideation, drive representation, primary process) partly supplanted by reality-testing thinking (ordered, goal-directed thought, secondary-process). It is irrelevant whether or not the particular infantile situation Freud describes as the origin of thought-processes is demonstrable by direct observation. It is a postulated model from which concepts may be derived applicable to available empirical material.

The direct relationships between needs and appetites demonstrated by Katz (376), Richter (611), P. T. Young (781, 782), and others, provide indirect support for Freud's theory of the relationship between drive and object.

13. Freud wrote (209, p. 509):

Thanks to the established connection [between the trace of excitation and the memory trace of the object affording gratification] there results, at the next occurrence of this need a psychic impulse which seeks to revive the memory image of the former percept, and to reevoke the former percept itself; that is, it actually seeks to reestablish the situation of the first satisfaction. Such an impulse is what we call a wish; the reappearance of the percept constitutes the wishfulfilment, and the full cathexis of the percept by the excitation springing from the need, constitutes the shortest path to the wishfulfilment. We may assume a primitive state of the psychic apparatus in which this path is actually followed, that is, in which the wish ends in hallucination. This first psychic activity, therefore, aims at an identity of perception: that is, at a repetition of that perception which is connected with the satisfaction of the need.

14.* The state of sleep can recover the likeness of mental life as it was before the recognition of reality, because a prerequisite of sleep is the deliberate rejection of reality (the wish to sleep). [Compare Freud 209, pp. 512–20.]

15. Freud wrote (209, p. 533):

But this hallucination unless it could be maintained to the point of exhaustion, proved incapable of bringing about a cessation of the need, and consequently of securing the pleasure connected with gratification.

16. The terms "to decide" and "to exert itself" are anthropomorphic and seem to be strikingly out of context. Cf. Freud (209, p. 533); see also Chap. 12, note 57, above.

if it should be unpleasant.[17]* This institution of the reality-principle proved **a** momentous step.[18]

a. In the first place the new demands made a succession of adaptations necessary in the mental apparatus, which, on account of insufficient or uncertain knowledge, we can only detail very cursorily.

The increased significance of external reality heightened the significance also of the sense-organs directed towards that outer world, and of the *consciousness* [19] attached to them; the latter now learned to comprehend the qualities of sense in addition to the qualities of pleasure and pain which hitherto had alone been of interest to it.[20] A special function was instituted which had periodically

17.* I will attempt to amplify the above schematic presentation with some further details. It will rightly be objected that an organization which is a slave to the pleasure-principle and neglects the reality of the outer world could not maintain itself alive for the shortest time, so that it could not have come into being at all. The use of a fiction of this kind is, however, vindicated by the consideration that the infant, if one only includes the maternal care, does almost realize such a state of mental life. Probably it hallucinates the fulfilment of its inner needs; it betrays its pain due to increased stimulation and delay of satisfaction by the motor discharge of crying and struggling and then experiences the hallucinated satisfaction. Later, as a child, it learns to employ intentionally these modes of discharge as means of expression. Since the care of the infant is the prototype of the later care of the child, the supremacy of the pleasure-principle can end in actuality only with complete psychic detachment from the parents. . . .

18. For one of the aspects of reality-testing, not discussed in this paper, see Chap. 17, below, and Ferenczi (183). Cf. also Freud (237, p. 147).

19. For a discussion of the relation between the sense-organs and consciousness, see "Note upon the Mystic Writing-Pad," Chap. 16, particularly notes 6, 7, and 8, below.

An earlier statement of Freud's (209, pp. 544–45) conception of consciousness is as follows:

What role is now left, in our representation of things, to the phenomenon of consciousness, once so all-powerful and overshadowing all else? None other than *that of a sense-organ for the perception of psychic qualities.* According to the fundamental idea of our schematic attempt we can regard conscious perception only as the function proper to a special system for which the abbreviated designation *Cs* commends itself. This system we conceive to be similar in its mechanical characteristics to the perception-system and hence excitable by qualities, and incapable of retaining the trace of changes: that is, devoid of memory. The psychic apparatus which, with the sense-organ of the perception-systems, is turned to the outer world, is itself the outer world for the sense-organ of *Cs*, whose teleological justification depends on this relationship. We are here once more confronted with the principle of the succession of instances which seems to dominate the structure of the apparatus.

20. Freud (209, p. 515) wrote:

For consciousness . . . can be excited in waking life from two sources: firstly from the periphery of the whole apparatus, the

to search the outer world, in order that its data might be already familiar if an urgent need should arise; this function was *attention*.[21] Its activity meets the

perceptive system; and secondly, from the excitations of pleasure and pain which emerge as the sole psychic qualities yielded by the transpositions of energy in the interior of the apparatus. All other processes in the ψ-systems, even those in the preconscious, are devoid of all psychic quality, and are therefore not objects of consciousness, inasmuch as they do not provide either pleasure or pain for its perception. We shall have to assume that *these releases of pleasure and pain automatically regulate the course of the cathectic processes*. But in order to make possible more delicate performances, it subsequently proved necessary to render the flow of ideas more independent of pain-signals.

Freud seems to imply that to begin with, excitations from the perceptive system arouse only qualities of pleasure and pain. "Quality" here means "quality perceptible to consciousness." The distinction between "possessing quality" and "not-possessing quality" seems analogous to the Gestalt-psychologists' distinction between "loud" and "silent" processes. See Koffka (405).

21. Freud (209, p. 529) discussed attention earlier as follows:

The act of becoming conscious depends upon a definite psychic function—attention—being brought to bear. This seems to be available only in a determinate quantity, which may have been diverted from the train of thought in question by other aims [that is, other trains of thought]. Another way in which such trains of thought may be withheld from consciousness is the following: from our conscious reflection we know that, when applying our attention, we follow a particular course. But if that course leads us to an idea which cannot withstand criticism, we break off and allow the cathexis of attention to drop. Now, it would seem that the train of thought thus started and abandoned may continue to develop without our attention returning to it [that is, without becoming conscious] unless at some point it attains a specially high intensity which compels attention. . . . The train of thought cathected by some aim becomes able under certain conditions to attract the attention of consciousness, and by the mediation of consciousness it then receives "hypercathexis."

Attention is thus the function of the system Conscious: to obtain attention-cathexis, that is, hypercathexis, and to become conscious are synonymous. When the unconscious (drive) cathexis of a train of ideas becomes high, it attracts attention-cathexis—the thought becomes conscious, unless it is counter-cathected (anti-cathected), that is, repressed.

Freud's theory of attention is based on the dynamics of energic cathexes. It seems useful to present here further material concerning cathectic dynamics. This purpose is well served by Freud's discussion of repression, especially since it is also an integral part of the psychoanalytic theory of thinking (234, pp. 112–14):

. . . repression is essentially a process affecting ideas, on the border between the Systems Ucs and Pcs (Cs). . . . It must be a matter of withdrawal of cathexis; but the question is, in what system does the withdrawal take place and to which system does the cathexis withdrawn belong?

In the Ucs the repressed idea remains capable of action and must therefore have retained its cathexis. So it must be something else which has been withdrawn. Let

sense-impressions halfway, instead of awaiting their appearance.[22] At the same
time there was probably introduced a system of *notation*,[23] whose task was to

us take the case of repression proper ("after-expulsion"), as it affects an idea which
is preconscious or even has already entered
consciousness. Repression can consist here
only in the withdrawal from the idea of
the (pre)conscious cathexis which belongs
to the system Pcs. The idea then remains
without cathexis, or receives cathexis from
the Ucs, or retains the unconscious cathexis
which it previously had. We have, therefore, withdrawal of the preconscious, retention of the unconscious, or substitution
of an unconscious for a preconscious
cathexis. . . .

But this process of withdrawal of libido
does not suffice to make comprehensible to
us another characteristic of repression. It
is not clear why the idea which has retained its cathexis or has received cathexis
from the Ucs should not, in virtue of its
cathexis, renew the attempt to penetrate
into the system Pcs. The withdrawal of
libido would then have to be repeated, and
the same performance would recur inter-
minably, but the result would not be repression. In the same way the mechanism
just discussed of withdrawal of preconscious cathexis would fail to explain the
process of primal repression; for here we
have to consider an unconscious idea
which as yet has received no cathexis from
the Pcs and therefore cannot be deprived
of it.

What we are looking for, therefore, is
another process which maintains the repression in the first case and, in the second,
ensures its being established and continued; and this other process we can only
find in the assumption of an *anti-cathexis*
by means of which the system Pcs guards
itself against the intrusion of the unconscious idea. We shall see from clinical examples how such an anti-cathexis established in the system Pcs manifests itself.
This it is which represents the continuous
effort demanded by a primal repression but

also guarantees its persistence. The anti-
cathexis is the sole mechanism of primal
repression; in the case of repression proper
("after-expulsion") there is in addition
withdrawal of the preconscious cathexis. It
is quite possible that the cathexis withdrawn from the idea is the very one used
for anti-cathexis.

For further discussions of "attention"
see "Note upon the Mystic Writing-
Pad," Chap. 16, note 14, below, and
Freud (209, pp. 515-16, 535-36, 546).

22. The idea of "meeting the sense-
impressions halfway" was also expressed
by Freud as a "groping in many directions, tentatively sending forth cathexes." Unlike attention, drive cathexes
do not meet the sense-impressions "halfway." Prior to the functioning of attention, if the sense-impression does not im-
pinge upon the apparatus, affect discharge and hallucinatory image of the
need-satisfying object arise, but there is
no search for the need-satisfying object
in reality. Meeting the sense-impressions
halfway is the attentive-purposive activity by which the organism, even when
not in need, notices and organizes its
world to provide for the time when the
need will arise. It is the activity by which
the human perceptual world acquires its
richness as compared with the worlds
of animals, in which the few relevant objects are those which directly gratify instincts or are closely related to such objects.

23. "Notation" translates *Merken*.
The word has two connotations: "to
notice" and "to make a note." It is clear
that "notation" is here closely linked to
attention cathexis, though the formulation is somewhat ambiguous. Freud ap-

deposit the results of this periodical activity of consciousness—a part of that which we call memory.[24]

In place of repression, which excluded from cathexis as productive of "pain" some of the emerging ideas, there developed an impartial *passing of judgment*,[25] which had to decide whether a particular idea was true or false, that is, was in agreement with reality or not; decision was determined by comparison with the memory-traces of reality.

A new function was now entrusted to motor discharge, which under the supremacy of the pleasure-principle had served to unburden the psychic apparatus of accretions of stimuli, and carried out this task by sending innervations into the interior of the body (mien, expressions of affect);[26] it was now employed for the purposive alteration of reality. It was converted into *action*.[27]

---

parently has reference only to those memory systems which record the results of the "periodic searching of the outer world," as against those which record the experiences of gratification. Compare the digit-span and attention studies of Rapaport *et al.* (602, pp. 166–79).

24. Concerning memory Freud (209, p. 533) wrote:

To change the outer world appropriately by means of motility requires the accumulation of a large total of experiences in the memory systems [compare Freud, 209, pp. 488 ff.], as well as a manifold consolidation of the relations which are evoked in this memory-material by various directing ideas. . . . The activity of the second system [the one regulated by the reality principle], groping in many directions, tentatively sending forth cathexes and retracting them, needs . . . full command over all memory material.

Compare this formulation with Freud (248 and 234, particularly p. 121); see also "Note upon the Mystic Writing-Pad," Chap. 16, pp. 335–36, below.

25. Cf. Freud (Chap. 17, below), Schilder (Chap. 25, pp. 532 ff. and 558–62, below) and Ferenczi (183).

26. In an earlier formulation of affect Freud (209, p. 521) wrote:

We here take as our basis a quite definite assumption as to the nature of the development of affect. This is regarded as a motor or secretory function, the key to the innervation of which is to be found in the ideas of the Ucs.

Later Freud (234, p. 111) wrote:

. . . ideas are cathexes—ultimately of memory-traces—whilst affects and emotions correspond with processes of discharge, the final expression of which is perceived as feeling. In the present state of our knowledge of affects and emotions we cannot express this difference more clearly. . . . Affectivity manifests itself essentially in motor (that is, secretory and circulatory) discharge resulting in an (internal) alteration of the subject's own body without reference to the outer world; motility does so in actions designed to effect changes in the outer world.

Cf. also Brierley (92) and Rapaport (591, pp. 24–34).

27. See Hartmann (306); cf. Freud (237, pp. 148–49):

In an earlier passage [see Freud, 232] we claimed that the still helpless organism had the capacity for making a first orientation

Restraint of motor discharge (of action) had now become necessary, and was provided by means of the process of thought, which developed from ideation.[28] Thought was endowed with qualities which made it possible for the mental apparatus to support increased tension during a delay in the process of discharge.[29] It is essentially an experimental way of acting, accompanied by

in the world by means of its perceptions, distinguishing both "outer" and "inner" according to their relation to actions of the muscles. A perception which is made to disappear by motor activity is recognized as external, as reality; where such activity makes no difference, the perception originates within the subject's own body—it is not real. To be thus able not only to recognize, but at the same time to rid himself of, reality is of great value to the individual, and he would wish to be equipped with a similar weapon against the often merciless claims of his instincts. That is why he takes such pains to *project*, that is, to transfer outwards, all that becomes troublesome to him from within.

This function of orienting the individual in the world by discrimination between inner and outer must now, after detailed dissection of the mental apparatus, be ascribed to the system Cs (Pcpt) alone. Cs must have at its command motor innervation which determines whether the perception can be made to disappear or whether it proves persistent. The capacity for testing reality need be nothing more than this function. We can say nothing more precise on this point, for we know as yet too little of the nature and mode of operation of the system Cs. We shall place the testing of reality, as one of the great *institutions of the Ego*, alongside the *censorships* which we have come to recognize between the psychic systems, and we shall expect that analysis of the narcissistic affections will help to reveal other similar institutions.

In summary, motility first serves as the channel of discharge for tensions due to needs of drive origin; later it becomes

the tool of primordial reality-testing by distinguishing between inner and outer sources of stimuli, that is to say, between the "I" and "not I"; finally, it assumes the character of action, altering the external world for the purpose of gratification. Freud (243, p. 30), described this last phase by stating that at this point of development the control of the sluices of motility becomes the function of the ego. See also Ferenczi (186, particularly pp. 230–32).

28. In this statement Freud contrasts the terms "ideation" and "thinking." The implication is that ideation pertains to drive-representations, thinking to reality-representations; these terms express the difference between the id- and the ego-organization of thought.

29. This statement comprises the essence of Freud's theory of thought-processes, in the center of which stands the concept of delay: (a) Since internal (drive) stimuli constitute a continuous pressure (see note 12, above), their excitation cannot be completely discharged. (b) Immediate discharge of need-tension is dependent upon the presence (perception) of a satisfying object (see note 12, above). (c) The memory trace of the excitation and that of the need-satisfying object become associated and, when the need again arises, the memory of the need-satisfying object emerges with hallucinatory vividness. This memory image becomes the ideational representation of the drive underlying the need (that is, energy disequilib-

displacement of smaller quantities of cathexis together with less expenditure (discharge) of them.[30] For this purpose conversion of free cathexes into "bound" cathexes was imperative, and this was brought about by means of raising the level of the whole cathectic process.[31] It is probable that thinking

---

rium; see note 13, above). (d) Ideation is the process by which a need causes the memory image of the need-satisfying object to appear in consciousness. This hallucinatory experience and the accompanying affect-discharge (see note 26, above) do not bring lasting gratification (see note 15, above). (e) Therefore the expenditure of cathexis in affect-discharge and in making the memory-image hallucinatorily vivid has to be prevented, that is, discharge must be delayed. Small amounts of the energy saved by this delay will be used by the thought-process to prepare for finding the need-satisfying object in reality. Cf. Freud (209, p. 533). (f) The major part of this saving will be used to find the need-satisfying object and in action upon it. (See note 30, below). (g) Ideation yields its place in the course of development to the process of thought in which all ideas related to the need-satisfying objects are so organized as to enable a planful search for the need-satisfying object in reality.

30. Freud's earlier and more detailed statement of the cathectic dynamics of thought as experimental action reads (209, pp. 533–34):

The activity of the second system [that of the secondary-process, conscious, goal-directed thinking], groping in many directions, tentatively sending forth cathexes and retracting them, needs on the one hand full command over all memory-material, but on the other hand it would be a superfluous expenditure of energy were it to send along the individual thought-paths

large quantities of cathexis, which would then flow away to no purpose and thus diminish the quantity needed for changing the outside world. Out of regard for purposiveness, therefore, I postulate that the second system succeeds in maintaining the greater part of the energy cathexes in a state of rest, and in using only a small portion for its operations of displacement. The mechanics of these processes is entirely unknown to me; anyone who seriously wishes to follow up these ideas must address himself to the physical analogies, and find some way of picturing the sequence of motions which ensues on the excitation of the neurones. Here I do no more than hold fast to the idea that the activity of the first ψ-system aims at *the free outflow of the quantities of excitation* [pleasure-principle], and that the second system, by means of the cathexes emanating from it, effects an *inhibition* of this outflow [delay], a transformation into dormant cathexis, probably with a rise of potential. [Breuer and Freud, 91, pp. 139–48; and Freud, 209, pp. 536, 546.] I therefore assume that the course taken by any excitation under the control of the second system is bound to quite different mechanical conditions from those which obtain under the control of the first system. After the second system has completed its work of experimental thought, it removes the inhibition and damming up of the excitations and allows them to flow off into motility.

31. Cf. Chap. 23, notes 11, 20, and 39, Chap. 22, note 30, below, and Freud (209, pp. 534, 536, and 546). The cathexes of drives are referred to as "free" cathexes, they shift freely from

was originally unconscious, in so far as it rose above mere ideation and turned to the relations between the object-impressions, and that it became endowed with further qualities which were perceptible to consciousness only through its connection with the memory-traces of words.[32]

---

one idea to another (see, for example, Freud, 209, p. 531). Their mobility is inferred from the observation of displacement, condensation, etc., in dreamwork, symbol-formation, etc. This free mobility can be more readily understood by taking into consideration developmental conditions. Since the infant's perception is global, diffuse, and undifferentiated, so is its percept and memory of the need-satisfying object. This memory arises when the need mounts; therefore the two may be considered associated. The memories which arise in this way are termed ideation, and this relation between need and memory is the drive-organization of memory. In the course of development, differentiation takes place, and discrete partial aspects of the need-satisfying object crystallize. These are at first within the framework of the drive-organization of memory: they all become ideational representations of the drive. Any one of these or any combination of them may appear in consciousness when the need arises. In other words: any of them may be cathected by the emerging need, even those which were originally only incidental to the undifferentiated experience of the need-satisfying object. This is the meaning of free cathexes from the point of view of thought-organization. Ethnological, pathological, and developmental parallels of the processes here described may be found in abundance in H. Werner's (755) treatment of perception and concepts. In the course of development a memory-organization determined by ex-

perience and realistic logic is superimposed upon this drive-organization of memory. This transition is synonymous with the development of the secondary process out of the primary (see Freud, 209, pp. 525 ff.), and is one aspect of the development of reality testing and the ego. Memory-frames of reference (see Rapaport et al. 602, I, 29–32; II, 16–20) and schemata (see Bartlett, 37) develop, in which memories are no longer organized around drives as their interchangeable representations, but rather in logical (spatial, temporal, etc.) frames of reference which correspond to experienced reality. Their emergence in consciousness is no longer dependent upon drive-cathexes. Along with the development of these frames of reference the ego develops as an emergent organization with cathectic energy of its own: attention-cathexis (see note 21, above). This cathexis, however, is not freely transferable from one representation of a drive to another; it is bound in that it is transferable only to ideas with identical objective meaning, and even then, in amounts incomparably smaller than those involved in the displacements of free cathexes. Cf. Ferenczi (184, p. 382); see also Chap. 17, note 20, below.

32. Concerning verbal traces Freud (234, pp. 133–34) wrote:

What we could permissibly call the conscious idea of the object can now be split up into the *idea of the word* (verbal idea) and the *idea of the thing* (concrete idea); the latter consists in the cathexis, if not of the direct memory images of the thing, at

b. There is a general tendency of our mental apparatus which we can trace back to the economic principle of saving in expenditure; it seems to find expression in the tenacity with which we hold on to the sources of pleasure at our disposal, and in the difficulty with which we renounce them. With the introduction of the reality-principle one mode of thought-activity was split off; it was kept free from reality-testing and remained subordinated to the pleasure-principle alone. This is the act of *fantasying*, which begins already in the play of children, and later, continued as *daydreaming*, abandons its dependence on real objects.[33]

c. The supersession of the pleasure-principle by the reality-principle with all the mental consequences of this, here schematically condensed in a single sentence, is not accomplished in reality all at once; nor does it take place simultaneously along the whole line.

[Passage omitted.] [34]

---

least of remoter memory-traces derived from these. It strikes us all at once that now we know the difference between a conscious and an unconscious idea. The two are not, as we supposed, different records of the same content situated in different parts of the psyche, nor yet different functional states of cathexis in the same part; but the conscious idea comprises the concrete idea plus the verbal idea corresponding to it, whilst the unconscious idea is that of the thing alone. The system Ucs contains the thing-cathexes of the objects, the first and true object-cathexes; the system Pcs originates in a hypercathexis of this concrete idea by a linking up of it with the verbal ideas corresponding to it. It is such hypercathexes, we may suppose, that bring about a higher organization in the mind and make it possible for the primary process to be succeeded by the secondary process which dominates the Pcs. Now, too, we are in a position to state precisely what it is that repression denies to the rejected idea in the transference neuroses—namely, translation into words which are to remain attached to the object. The idea which is not put into words or the psychic act which has not re-

ceived hypercathexis then remains in the unconscious in a state of repression.

Cf. also Freud (209, p. 546), and Freud (243, pp. 21–26). For further discussion of this point see Chap. 26, note 107, below. For Freud's revision of these views, see Chap. 23, p. 477, particularly notes 9 and 10, below.

33. Cf. Varendonck (740), and Freud (243, p. 23).

Here it again becomes clear that Freud's theory is a psychology in terms of energy distribution, the basic tendency of which is to eliminate states of disequilibrium, that is, to equalize potentials. Since, for various reasons, no stable equilibrium can be established, new controlling energy distributions are superimposed upon the original and fundamental ones surviving beneath.

34. The omitted section deals with the relation between the sexual instincts and fantasy, and the ego-instincts and consciousness. [The distinction ego vs. sexual instincts has become outdated by the later development of psychoanalytic

d. Just as the pleasure-Ego can do nothing but wish, work towards gaining pleasure and avoid "pain," so the reality-Ego need do nothing but strive for what is *useful* and guard itself against damage.[35] Actually, the substitution of the reality-principle for the pleasure-principle denotes no dethronement of the pleasure-principle, but only a safeguarding of it. A momentary pleasure, uncertain in its results, is given up, but only in order to gain in the new way an assured pleasure coming later.

[Passage omitted.] [36]

The deficiencies of this short paper, which is rather introductory than expository, are perhaps only to a slight extent excused if I acknowledge them to be unavoidable. In the meager sentences on the mental consequences of adaptation to the reality-principle I was obliged to intimate opinions which I should have preferred to withhold, the vindication of which will certainly require no small exertion. But I hope that benevolent readers will not fail to observe where even in this work the sway of the reality-principle begins.

-----

theory, and the translation of this discussion into the language of the present theory would be cumbersome and beyond the scope of this volume.]

35. The expression "pleasure-ego" and "reality-ego" are of the period of theory formation (preceding *The Ego and the Id*, Freud, 243) to which note 34, above, refers.

36. The omitted sections illustrate in brief the bearing of the concept "reality-principle" on various areas of human activity.

CHAPTER 16

A NOTE UPON THE "MYSTIC WRITING-PAD" [1]
By Sigmund Freud

[Passage omitted.] [2]

ALL THE FORMS of auxiliary apparatus which we have invented for the improvement or intensification of our sensory functions are built like the sensory organs themselves or portions of them: for instance, spectacles, photographic cameras, ear-trumpets. Measured by this standard, devices to aid our memory seem particularly imperfect, since our mental apparatus accomplishes precisely what they cannot: it has an unlimited receptive capacity for new perceptions and nevertheless lays down permanent—even though not unalterable—memory-traces of them. As long ago as in 1900 I gave expression in "The Interpretation of Dreams" [3]* to a suspicion that this unusual capacity was to be divided between two different systems or organs of the mental apparatus. According to this view, we possess a system Pcpt-Cs [perception-conscious], [4] which receives perceptions but retains no permanent trace of them, so that it can react like a

1. Freud (250).

2. In the omitted introductory section Freud reviews our usual mnemonic aids and finds that there are two kinds: the paper-pen type which gives permanent records but is usable only once, and the slate-chalk type, which can be used over and over again but only after the previous record is destroyed. In the rest of the paper Freud restates some of the assumptions concerning perception and memory which he derived from clinical investigations. The reader may ask, Why perception and memory in a volume on thought-organization? The answer is that dynamic psychology finds it increasingly difficult to differentiate thought-processes from perception and memory-processes, or to reach an under-

standing of the former without the latter.

3.* The translation [209, p. 490] of the decisive sentence, however, is misleading: "for consciousness memory and quality are mutually exclusive in the ψ-systems" should read "memory and the quality of being conscious are mutually exclusive in the ψ-systems." (Ed.)

[The passage referred to is quoted below in note 6. The quotation follows the English translation (209) yet corrects its gross shortcomings.]

4. Perception-Conscious (Pcpt-Cs) was conceived as a psychological system alongside the systems Unconscious (Ucs) and Preconscious (Pcs). For Freud's modification of this conception, see Chap. 23, p. 477, particularly notes 3*, 9 and 10, below.

clean sheet to every new perception; while the permanent traces of the excitations which have been received are preserved in "mnemonic systems" lying behind [5] the perceptual system.[6] Later, in "Beyond the Pleasure Principle," [7*]

5. The phrase "lying behind" has here a temporal connotation: in the course of the process of perception, the mnemonic systems are reached by the excitation later than the system perception-conscious:

. . . there is no need to assume an actual spatial arrangement of the psychic system. It will be enough for our purpose if a definite sequence is established, so that in certain psychic events the system will be traversed by the excitation in a definite temporal order. (Freud, 209, p. 488).

6. It seems useful to present here Freud's earlier and fuller discussion of this point. He wrote (209, pp. 488–90):

All our psychic activities proceed from (inner or outer) stimuli and terminate in innervations. We thus ascribe to the apparatus a sensory and a motor end; at the sensory end we find a system which receives the perceptions, and at the motor end another which opens the sluices of motility. The psychic process generally runs from the perceptive end to the motor end. The most general scheme of the psychic apparatus has therefore the following appearance:

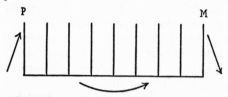

But this is only in compliance with the requirement, long familiar to us, that the psychic apparatus must be constructed like a reflex apparatus. The reflex act remains the type of every psychic activity as well. We now have reason to admit a first differentiation at the sensory end. The per-

7.* Page 28 of the English translation (241) where, once more, the original meaning is unfortunately missed: "consciousness arises *in the place of* the memory trace" should read *"instead of."* The same mistake is repeated, in a more marked form, in the translation of an additional footnote in "The Interpretation of Dreams" [209, p. 490]: "consciousness occurs actually *in the locality* of the memory-trace," which should read, once again, *"instead of* the memory-trace." This characteristic detail of Freud's theory of the dynamics of consciousness does not appear to have been mentioned elsewhere in his writings: it seems likely, therefore, that it has hitherto escaped presentation in English. (Ed.)

cepts that come to us leave in our psychic apparatus a trace, which we may call a *memory-trace*. The function related to this memory-trace we call "the memory." If we hold seriously to our resolution to connect the psychic processes into systems, the memory-trace can consist only of lasting changes in the elements of the systems. But, as has already been shown elsewhere, obvious difficulties arise when one and the same system is faithfully to preserve changes in its elements and still to remain fresh and receptive in respect of new occasions of change. In accordance with the principle which is directing our attempt, we shall therefore ascribe these two functions to two different systems. We assumed that an initial system of this apparatus receives the stimuli of perception but retains nothing of them—that is, it has no memory; and that behind this there lies a second system, which transforms the momentary excitation of the first into lasting traces. The following

I added a remark to the effect that the inexplicable phenomenon of conscious-ness arises in the perceptual system *instead of* the permanent traces.[8]

Some time ago there came upon the market, under the name of the Mystic Writing-Pad, a small contrivance that promises to perform more than the sheet of paper or the slate. It claims to be nothing more than a writing tablet from

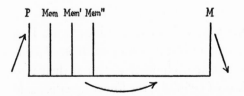

would then be the diagram of our psychic apparatus:

We know that of the percepts which act upon the ψ-system, we retain perma-nently something else as well as the con-tent itself. Our percepts prove also to be connected with one another in the mem-ory, and this is especially so if they origi-nally occurred simultaneously. We call this the fact of *association*. It is now clear that, if the ψ-system is entirely lacking in memory, it certainly cannot preserve traces of associations; the individual ψ-ele-ments would be intolerably hindered in their functioning if a residue of a former connection should make its influence felt against a new perception. Hence we must rather assume that the memory-system is the basis of association. The fact of associa-tion, then, consists in this—that in conse-quence of a lessening of resistance and canalization the excitation transmits itself from one of the *mem*-elements to a second rather than to a third *mem*-element.

On further investigation we find it nec-essary to assume not one but many such *mem*-systems, in which the same excita-tion transmitted by the ψ-elements under-goes a diversified fixation. The first of these *mem*-systems will in any case con-tain the fixation of the association through simultaneity, while in those lying farther away the same material of excitation will be arranged according to other forms of combination; so that relationships of simi-larity, etc., might perhaps be represented by these later systems. . . .

The ψ-system, which possesses no ca-pacity for preserving changes, and hence no memory, furnishes to consciousness the complexity and variety of the sensory qualities. Our memories, on the other hand, are unconscious in themselves; the most deeply impressed form no exception. They can be made conscious, but there is no doubt that they unfold all their activi-ties in the unconscious state. . . . But when memories become conscious again they have no sensory quality, or a very negligible one in comparison with the per-ceptions. If, now, it could be confirmed *that memory and the quality of being con-scious are mutually exclusive in the ψ-sys-tems*, we would here gain a most promising insight into the nature of the neuron-excitations.

8. This refers to Freud's (241, pp. 27–29) statement as follows:

Consciousness is not the only peculiar feature that we ascribe to the processes in this system. Our impressions gained by psychoanalytic experience lead us to the supposition that all excitation processes in the other systems leave in them permanent traces forming the foundations of mem-ory-records which have nothing to do with the process of becoming conscious. . . . But we find it difficult to believe that such lasting traces of excitation are formed also in the system Pcpt-Cs itself. If they re-mained permanently in consciousness they would very soon limit the fitness of the system for registration of new excitations (here I follow throughout J. Breuer's [91]

which notes can be erased by an easy movement of the hand. But if it is examined more closely it will be found that its construction shows a remarkable agreement with my hypothetical structure of our perceptual apparatus and that it can in fact provide both an ever-ready receptive surface and permanent traces of the notes that have been made upon it.

The Mystic Pad is a slab of dark brown resin or wax with a paper edging; over the slab is laid a thin transparent sheet the top end of which is firmly secured to the slab while its bottom end rests upon it without being fixed to it. This transparent sheet is the more interesting part of the little device. It itself consists of two layers, which can be detached from each other except at their two ends. The upper layer is a transparent piece of celluloid; the lower layer is made of thin translucent waxed paper. When the apparatus is not in use, the lower surface of the waxed paper adheres lightly to the upper surface of the wax slab.

To make use of the Mystic Pad, one writes upon the celluloid portion of the covering sheet which rests upon the wax slab. For this purpose no pencil or chalk is necessary, since the writing does not depend on material being deposited upon the receptive surface. It is a return to the ancient method of writing upon tablets of clay or wax: a pointed stylus scratches the surface, the depressions upon which constitute the "writing." In the case of the Mystic Pad this scratching is not effected directly, but through the medium of the covering sheet. At the points which the stylus touches, it presses the lower surface of the waxed paper on to the wax slab, and the grooves are visible as dark writing upon the

---

exposition in the theoretical section of the "Studien ueber Hysterie," 1895); on the other hand, if they became unconscious we should be confronted with the task of explaining the existence of unconscious processes in a system whose functioning is otherwise accompanied by the phenomenon of consciousness. . . . Though this may not be an absolutely binding consideration, it may at any rate lead us to conjecture that becoming conscious and leaving behind a memory-trace are processes incompatible with each other in the same system. . . . If one reflects how little we know from other sources about the origin of consciousness the pronouncement that

consciousness arises instead of the memory-trace must be conceded at least the importance of a statement which is to some extent definite.

The system Cs would thus be characterized by the peculiarity that the excitation process does not leave in it, as it does in all other psychic systems, a permanent alteration of its elements, but is as it were discharged in the phenomenon of becoming conscious.

[The quotation follows the English translation, yet corrects several inadequacies.]

otherwise smooth whitish-grey surface of the celluloid. If one wishes to destroy what has been written, all that is necessary is to raise the double covering sheet from the wax slab by a light pull, starting from the free lower end. The close contact between the waxed paper and the wax slab at the places which have been scratched, upon which the visibility of the writing depended, is thus brought to an end and it does not recur when the two surfaces come together once more. The Mystic Pad is now clear of writing and ready to receive fresh notes.

The small imperfections of the contrivance have, of course, no importance for us, since we are only concerned with its approximations to the structure of the perceptive apparatus of the mind.[9]

If, while the Mystic Pad has writing upon it, we cautiously raise the celluloid from the waxed paper, we can see the writing just as clearly on the surface of the latter, and the question may arise of why there should be any necessity for the celluloid portion of the cover. Experiment will then show that the thin paper would be very easily crumpled or torn if one were to write directly upon it with the stylus. The layer of celluloid thus acts as a protective sheath for the waxed paper, to keep off injurious effects from without. The celluloid is a "protective barrier against stimuli"; the layer which actually receives the stimuli is the paper. I may at this point recall that in "Beyond the Pleasure Principle" [10*] I showed that the perceptive apparatus of our mind consists of two layers, of an external protective barrier against stimuli whose task it is to diminish the strength of excitations coming in, and of a surface behind it which receives the stimuli, namely, the system Pcpt-Cs.[11]

9. It will be interesting to note Plato's conception (571, p. 195) of memory which, like Freud in this paper, compares the nature of the mnemonic function to a mnemonic aid used in his time:

Socrates: I would have you imagine, then, that there exists in the mind of man a block of wax, which is of different sizes in different men; harder, moister, and having more or less of purity in one than another, and in some of an intermediate quality.

Theaitetos: I see.

Socrates: Let us say that this tablet is a gift of Memory, the mother of the Muses; and that when we wish to remember anything which we have seen, or heard, or thought in our own minds, we hold the wax to the perceptions and thoughts, and in that material receive the impression of them as from the seal of a ring; and that we remember and know what is imprinted as long as the image lasts; but when the image is effaced, or cannot be taken, then we forget and do not know.

10.* (241, pp. 30 ff.)

11. The reference is to Freud's passage (241, pp. 30-32):

The analogy would not be of much value if it could not be pursued further than this. If we lift the entire covering sheet—both the celluloid and the waxed paper—of the wax slab, the writing vanishes and, as I have already remarked, does not reappear again. The surface of the Mystic Pad is clear of writing and once more capable of receiving impressions. But it is easy to discover that the permanent trace of what was written is retained upon the wax slab itself and is legible in suitable lights. Thus the Pad provides not only a receptive surface that can be used over and over again, like a slate, but also permanent traces of what has been written, like an ordinary paper pad: it solves the problem of combining the two functions *by dividing them between two separate but interrelated component parts or systems*. But this is precisely the way in which, according to the hypothesis which I mentioned just now, our mental apparatus performs its perceptual function. The layer which receives the stimuli—the system Pcpt-Cs—forms no permanent traces; the foundations of memory come about in other, adjoining systems.[12]

. . . [the] outer world . . . is charged with the most potent energies, and . . . [the primitive organism] would be destroyed by the operation of the stimuli proceeding from this world if it were not furnished with a protection against stimulation (Reizschutz). It acquires this through its outermost layer . . . that keeps off the stimuli, that is, makes it impossible for the energies of the outer world to act with more than a fragment of their intensity on the living layers immediately beneath. These are now able under cover of the protecting layer to devote themselves to the reception of those stimulus masses that have been let through. . . . For the living organism protection against stimuli is almost a more important task than reception of stimuli; the protective barrier is equipped with its own store of energy and must above all endeavor to protect the special forms of energy-transformations going on within itself from the equalizing and therefore destructive influence of the enormous energies at work in the outer world. The reception of stimuli serves above all the purposes of collecting information about the direction and nature of the external stimuli, and for that it must

suffice to take little samples of the outer world, to taste it, so to speak, in small quantities. In highly developed organisms . . . the sense organs, which essentially comprise arrangements for the reception of specific stimuli, . . . also possess special arrangements adapted for a fresh protection against an overwhelmingly intense stimulus and for warding off unsuitable kinds of stimuli.

[The quotation follows the English translation, but corrects some inadequacies.]

In this connection see Bergman and Escalona (52) on cases of childhood schizophrenia. They found the concept of "protective barrier" a useful explanatory construct. Their cases seemed to show a correlation between weakness of the "stimulus barrier" as shown by unusual sensitivities and a precocious, though fragmentary, development of the ego and particularly of the intellect. Cf. also Chap. 27, pp. 655–56, particularly notes 21 and 22, below.

12. In an earlier writing, Freud (209), discussing memory, perception, and con-

We need not be disturbed by the fact that in the Mystic Pad no use is made of the permanent traces of the notes that have been received; it is enough that they are present. There must come a point at which the analogy between an auxiliary apparatus of this kind and the organ which is its prototype will cease to apply. It is true, too, that once the writing has been erased, the Mystic Pad cannot "reproduce" it from within; it would indeed be a mystic pad if, like our memory, it could accomplish that.[13] None the less, I do not think it is too far-fetched to compare the celluloid and waxed paper cover with the system Pcpt-Cs and its protective barrier, the wax slab with the unconscious behind them, and the appearance and disappearance of the writing with the flickering-up and passing of consciousness in the process of perception.[14]

But I must admit that I am inclined to press the comparison still further. On the Mystic Pad the writing vanishes every time the close contact is broken between the paper which receives the stimulus and the wax slab which preserves the impression. This agrees with a notion which I have long had about the method in which the perceptual apparatus of our mind functions, but which

---

sciousness, commented: "We are here once more confronted with the principle of the succession of instances which seems to dominate the structure of the apparatus" (p. 545). This principle which permeates his conception of the psychic apparatus (note 5, above) reflects Freud's view that a division of labor between structural systems organized in a succession of hierarchic controls is the prerequisite for the complex functioning of the psyche.

13. The "reproduction from within" in the psychic apparatus is the effect of the motivating forces working in remembering and thought-organization. See Lewy and Rapaport (603), and Rapaport (591).

14. Freud's views on consciousness may be summarized as follows: (a) it is the sense organ for the perception of psychic qualities, the objects of which are the excitations of the extero- and interoceptors (209, p. 544); (b) it is a sense organ "excitable" by psychic qualities but devoid of memory (pp. 544–45); (c) it is the effect of a specific cathexis—called "attention-cathexis"—of ideas (pp. 516, 529, 545) and this attention-cathexis is energy at the disposal of the ego (cf. Rapaport et al., 602, pp. 167–69); (d) early in development the distribution of attention-cathexes is regulated by the pleasure-pain principle, later by the reality-principle (209, pp. 536, 544–45); (e) the cathexis at the disposal of the ego may be utilized either as countercathexis for the establishment and maintenance of repression (Freud, 234, pp. 112–14), or as hypercathexis for raising ideas to the level of consciousness (Freud, 209, p. 536; and 243, pp. 19–26, particularly p. 26).

The periodic "flickering-up" Freud mentions above is discussed in "The Two Principles" (Chap. 15, notes 22 and 23, above) as due to fluctuations in the distribution of attention-cathexis.

I have hitherto kept to myself. I have supposed that cathectic innervations [15] are sent out and withdrawn in rapid periodic impulses from within into the completely pervious system Pcpt-Cs. So long as that system is cathected in this manner, it receives the perceptions (which are accompanied by consciousness) [16] and passes the excitation on to the unconscious mnemonic systems; but as soon as the cathexis is withdrawn, consciousness is extinguished and the functioning of the system ceases. It would be as though the unconscious stretches out feelers, through the medium of the system Pcpt-Cs, towards the external world, and these are hastily withdrawn as soon as they have sampled the excitations coming from it.[17] Thus I attributed the interruptions, which with the Mystic Pad have an external origin, to the discontinuity in the current of innervation; and the place of an actual breaking of contact was taken in my hypothesis by the periodic non-excitability of the perceptual system. I further suspected that this discontinuous method of functioning of the system Pcpt-Cs lies at the bottom of the origin of the concept of time.[18*]

15. The term "innervations" may sound strange in dynamic psychology. It will be remembered, however, that Freud's conceptualization leaned on neurology for a considerable period. This is obvious in the quotation in note 6, above, where he leans on the reflex model even in developing his theory of thought, which is to date the only consistent antagonist of the theory of conditioned reflex and response, notwithstanding the efforts of French (197) and of Mowrer and Kluckhohn (525) to reconcile the two. Freud's correspondence with Fliess (according to a verbal communication of E. Kris) shows that as late as 1898 Freud was working on a neurological theory of the psyche and the thought-process. The manuscript of this theory, contained in the Fliess correspondence (207a), is the neurological counterpart of what Freud presented in Chap. VII of "The Interpretation of Dreams" (209).

16. The expression "accompanied by consciousness" does not seem consonant with Freud's theory of consciousness (see note 14 above). The percepts become conscious *when* and *because* they are cathected in the Pcpt-Cs system by attention-cathexis.

17. See Freud: "Two Principles" (Chap. 15, above) and "The Interpretation of Dreams" (209, p. 535). In the "Two Principles" this process was attributed to the function of attention which seemed to be conceived of as autonomous. The reference here to the "unconscious" seems to be inconsistent with this other formulation. Cf., however, Chap. 15, note 21, above.

18.* An elaboration of Freud's views on this subject (also touched on in *Beyond the Pleasure Principle* [241], p. 32) will be found reported in the last pages of Marie Bonaparte's paper on "Time and the Unconscious" [81] of this *Journal*, pp. 466–67, and footnote 18.— Ed.

[The evidence on which this last con-

If we imagine one hand writing upon the surface of the Mystic Pad while another periodically raises its covering sheet from the wax slab, we shall have a concrete representation of the way in which I tried to picture the functioning of the perceptual apparatus of our mind.[19]

---

sideration is based is not presented, nor is it obvious. The relation of time experience to the control of impulses, and to the related ability to delay action in favor of thought, would seem more obvious and for it evidence can be marshaled from psychopathology and child psychology.]

19. Organizing theoretical considerations around something as apparently extraneous as this mnemonic gadget may seem strange to academic psychologists. It will be noted, however, that; a) Freud uses this gadget as an analogy and aid in systematizing and amplifying his previous theoretical inferences drawn from clinical observations (the theories cited from "The Interpretation of Dreams" are based mainly on observations on dreams, those from *Beyond the Pleasure Principle* mainly on traumatic neuroses); b) the observations and the inferences all refer to a psychological "no-man's land" into which this was the first pioneering attempt. Pioneering requires new concepts and models and it is not rare that, at first, these take the form of analogies. Freud outlines here the cathectic theory of perception, consciousness and memory, or more generally of thought-organization. Tolman's (733) recent paper, Murphy's (533), Bruner's (96, 97, 100), Bergman's (52), and Klein's (387) observational studies and Rapaport's survey (591) of others, show that this theorizing fructified experimental and theoretical thinking.

CHAPTER 17

NEGATION [1]

By Sigmund Freud

THE MANNER in which our patients bring forward their associations during the work of analysis gives us an opportunity for making some interesting observations. "Now you'll think I mean to say something insulting, but really I've no such intention." We see at once that this is a repudiation, by means of projection,[2] of an association that has just emerged. Or again: "You ask who this per-

1. Freud (248). The concept "negation" appears first in Freud's "The Unconscious" (234, p. 119):

There is in this system no negation, no dubiety, no varying degree of certainty: all this is only imparted by the work of the censorship which exists between the Ucs and Pcs. Negation is, at a high level, a substitute for repression. In the Ucs there are only contents more or less strongly cathected.

Cf. also Freud "From the History of an Infantile Neurosis" (239, p. 559).

In a footnote Freud (212, p. 70) added in 1923 to his "Fragment of an Analysis of a Case of Hysteria," we also read:

There is another very remarkable and entirely trustworthy form of confirmation from the Unconscious, which I had not recognized at the time this was written: namely, an exclamation on the part of the patient of, "I didn't think that," or "I didn't think of that." This can be translated point-blank into: "Yes, I was unconscious of that."

2. The expression "projection" refers here to the phrase: "You'll think." The implication of the concept projection is that such reactions express an unconscious idea or impulse of the subject.

The concept "projection" has been extensively used in psychoanalytic literature and more recently also in clinical psychology. (In the latter it was introduced by L. Frank; see 194 and 193.)

The clinical psychological use of the term in the expression "projective techniques" dilutes the original concept considerably. Since various products (handwriting, painting, fingerpainting, play constructions, etc.) and reactions (Rorschach, Thematic Apperception, Association Tests) are characteristic for the individual, it was formulated that the individual projects his "private world" into the external reality. (See Frank, 194, and Rapaport, 594, 593). Projection in this latter sense is the structuring of behavior and experience by the subject's unique structuring-principles. This conception of projection is broad indeed, since with the exception of highly stereotyped behaviors established by social consensus all behavior and experience may be expected to be syntonic with and bear the imprint of the organizing and structuring principles of the individual personality. Recently Bruner (96) and earlier Poetzl (573) offered evidence

son in the dream can have been. It was *not* my mother." We emend this: so it was his mother.[3] In our interpretation we take the liberty of disregarding the negation and of simply picking out the subject-matter of the association. It is just as though the patient had said: "It is true that I thought of my mother in connection with this person, but I don't feel at all inclined to allow the association to count." [4]

There is a most convenient method by which one can sometimes obtain a necessary light upon a piece of unconscious and repressed material. "What," one asks, "would you consider was about the most unlikely thing in the world in this situation? What do you think was furthest from your mind at the time?" [5] If the patient falls into the trap and names what he thinks most in-

---

that this holds even for perception of structured reality-material. Study of the Bellevue Scale and other non-projective tests has shown that even material for which high social agreement exists is invested with the individual's organizing principles in the process of organization into broader units (see Rapaport, 593). Projection in the more limited sense is of course observed in psychological tests, as for example in the externalization of unacceptable ideas and feelings in the Thematic Apperception and Rorschach Tests.

But the psychoanalytic use of the term is also quite variable. Schilder (Chap. 25, pp. 520–21, note 8, below) protested against the inclination of some psychoanalysts to consider all object-perception to imply projection. The concept projection is used in significantly different senses in phobic projection (Fenichel, 176, pp. 203–5), paranoid projection (Freud, 224, pp. 448–53, and Fenichel, 176, p. 428), the simple projection, "You will think," that implicit to all dreams (Freud, 237, p. 139) and that observed in transference phenomena (Freud, 224 a).

From the point of view of psychoanal-ysis, projection is first of all a defense-mechanism; from the point of view of the theory of thinking, it is one of the mechanisms of thought-organization. While projection as a defense-mechanism is fairly well understood, as a mechanism of thought-organization which has many variants suggesting a hierarchic layering it has not yet been systematically explored.

3. The mechanism Freud describes is the same as Shakespeare's: "Methinks the Lady doth protest too much."

4. The justification of Freud's interpretation is based on the fact that the language of drives (that of the dream proper) cannot say "no." It can only point to its object and its gratification. The "no" is the function of the ego (censorship, waking consciousness) and the superego ("thou shalt not"). See Freud (209, pp. 345–46). K. Abel (1), and Freud's review of the latter (221, pp. 184–91), indicate that this holds for the oldest languages also, in that the same words are used for the expression of opposites. Cf. also Varendonck, Chap. 22, notes 26 and 35, below.

5. The aim of this question is to create the same psychological situation as the

credible, he almost invariably in so doing makes the correct admission. A nice counterpart of this experiment is often met with in obsessional neurotics who have been initiated into the meaning of their symptoms. "A new obsessive idea came over me; and it immediately occurred to me that it might mean so and so. But of course that can't be true, or it couldn't have occurred to me." The explanation of the new obsessive idea, which he rejects in this way upon grounds picked up from the treatment, is of course the right one.[6]

Thus the subject-matter of a repressed image or thought can make its way into consciousness on condition that it is *denied*.[7] Negation is a way of taking account of what is repressed; indeed, it is actually a removal of the repression, though not, of course, an acceptance of what is repressed. It is to be seen how the intellectual function is here distinct from the affective process.[8] Negation

one which prevails when a "negation" spontaneously arises. It attempts to arouse forces that would "negate" the drive-representation as soon as it rises to consciousness, and thereby to obviate the danger of its being acted on, which is the reason for repressing it. This example clearly illustrates that negation is a significant aspect of the thought-process. It shows how communication can play a dynamic role in thought-organization: the question permits a loosening of repression by preparing the ground for negation.

6. The implication here is that patients learn in the course of the psychoanalytic treatment that the "censorship" prevents unacceptable ideas from coming to consciousness. Obsessional patients are able, however, by the mechanism of isolation to bring to consciousness ideational representations of unacceptable impulses divorced from their corresponding affect (see Fenichel, 176, pp. 287–88). In this instance Freud refers to the patient's claim that the idea so brought to consciousness cannot be true, because otherwise it could not have passed censorship. Thus the thought-process *negation* here

uses in part the patient's knowledge of "censorship" and in part the defense-mechanism of *isolation* to bring the representation of a repressed drive to consciousness.

7. The translation is not accurate. It should read "on condition that it is negated." The term "denied" would refer to the defense-mechanism of denial. Fenichel (176, p. 144) describes *denial* and differentiates it from *negation* as follows:

The ability to deny unpleasant parts of reality is the counterpart of the "hallucinatory wishfulfilment." Anna Freud has called this type of refusal to acknowledge displeasure in general "pre-stages of defense." The gradual development of reality-testing makes such wholesale falsification of reality impossible. However, these tendencies toward denial try to remain operative. They succeed best against certain single internal perceptions of a painful nature. Freud explained that the "negation" of such a perception may be a compromise between becoming conscious of the data given by the perception and the tendency to deny.

8. The reference here is again to the process of isolation and to the related

only assists in undoing [9] *one* of the consequences of repression—namely, the fact that the subject-matter of the image in question is unable to enter consciousness. The result is a kind of intellectual acceptance of what is repressed, though

---

processes of intellectualization and rationalization. Empirical evidence led Freud (233, p. 91), to theorize that instinct representations have two aspects, an ideational and an affective, which may have two independent fates:

In our discussion hitherto we have dealt with the repression of an instinct-presentation, and by that we understood an idea or group of ideas which is cathected with a definite amount of the mental energy (libido, interest) pertaining to an instinct. Now clinical observation forces us further to dissect something that hitherto we have conceived of as a single entity, for it shows us that beside the idea there is something else, another presentation of the instinct to be considered, and that this other element undergoes a repression which may be quite different from that of the idea. We have adopted the term *charge of affect* for this other element in the mental presentation; it represents that part of the instinct which has become detached from the idea, and finds proportionate expression, according to its quantity, in processes which become observable to perception as affects. From this point on, in describing a case of repression, we must follow up the fate of the idea which undergoes repression separately from that of the instinctual energy attached to the idea.

This formulation is significant for several aspects of the psychoanalytic theory of thinking. It elucidates the conditions of the defense-mechanism of isolation; see Fenichel (176, p. 155 ff.), Freud (252, pp. 55–57); and cf. Anna Freud (201, pp. 37–38). It is fundamental for the understanding of the defense-mechanism of intellectualization (A.

Freud 201, pp. 177–78) and for that of the conditions of the development of the secondary process and intellect (Freud, 209, pp. 533–36 and Fenichel, 176, p. 159). It refers to the observation which is the cornerstone of the psychoanalytic theory of affects; see Freud (209, p. 521, and 234, p. 111), Brierley (92), and for a summary, Rapaport (591, pp. 28–33).

The concept of isolation as a defense-mechanism was formulated by Freud relatively late in his *The Problem of Anxiety* (252) and even then very tentatively. Fenichel (176, pp. 155–56) describes it as follows:

Here the patient has not forgotten his pathogenic traumata, but has lost trace of their connections and their emotional significance. He shows the same resistance to a demonstration of the true connections that a hysteric shows to the reawakening of his repressed memories. Thus here again counter-cathexis is operative; its operation consists in keeping apart that which actually belongs together. . . . The most important special case of this defense-mechanism is the isolation of an idea from the emotional cathexis that originally was connected with it.

It seems that the thought-process *negation* implies the defense of *isolation*, particularly that special form of it to which Fenichel refers.

9. The translation is not accurate. *Rueckgaengig machen* means to controvert, to cancel. The translation "undoing" would refer to the defense-mechanism *undoing* (*Ungeschehen machen*). For the concept of *undoing* see Freud (252, pp. 53–55). Fenichel (176, p. 153) wrote:

in all essentials the repression persists.[10]* In the course of analytic work we often bring about a further very important and somewhat bewildering change in the same situation. We succeed in also defeating the negation and in establishing a complete intellectual acceptance of what is repressed—but the repression itself is still not removed.[11]

Since it is the business of the function of intellectual judgment [12] to affirm or deny the subject-matter of thoughts, we have been led by the foregoing remarks to the psychological origin of that function. To deny something in one's judgment is at bottom the same thing as to say: "That is something that I

There are no sharp lines of demarcation between the various forms of defense mechanisms. Reaction formation was related to repression, and undoing is related to reaction formation. In reaction formation, an attitude is taken that contradicts the original one; in undoing one more step is taken. Something positive is done which, actually or magically, is the opposite of something which—again actually or in imagination—was done before.

This mechanism can be most clearly observed in certain compulsive symptoms that are made up of two actions, the second of which is a direct reversal of the first. For example, the patient must first turn on the gas-jet and then turn it off again.

10.* The same process is at the root of the familiar superstition that boasting is dangerous. "How lovely that I've not had one of my headaches for such a long time." But this is in fact the first announcement of a new attack, of whose approach the patient is already aware, though he is as yet unwilling to believe it.

11. See Freud (234, pp. 108–9, and 233, particularly pp. 85–87).

It becomes here quite clear that the thought-process conceptualized as repression is more basic than those described as isolation and negation. Com-

pare Anna Freud (201, pp. 45 ff., particularly p. 52).

For a discussion of a mechanism by which the unpleasant is affectively accepted see Ferenczi (183, particularly p. 369). He believes that the unpleasant is accepted, in accordance with the pleasure-principle, to ward off an even greater unpleasantness. Cf. Chap. 15, p. 328, above.

12. Concerning the concept of judgment see Chap. 15, note 25, above, and Freud (233, p. 84). The psychoanalytic concept of judgment is closely linked with the "reality principle" and the function of "reality testing." Fenichel (176, p. 39) wrote:

A more objective perception presupposes a certain psychological distance of the perceiving Ego from the data of perception, a judgment about the sources of the experienced sensations and, more than that, a *correct* judgment, an ability for differential learning, whereas the primitive experiences are felt as still undifferentiated wholes which make their appearance repeatedly. The pleasure-principle, that is, the need for immediate discharge, is incompatible with correct judgment, which is based on consideration and postponement of the reaction. The time and energy saved by this postponement are used in the function of judgment. In the early states the weak Ego has not yet learned to postpone anything.

would rather repress." A negative judgment is the intellectual substitute for repression: [13] the "No" in which it is expressed is the hallmark of repression, a certificate of origin, as it were, like "Made in Germany." By the help of the symbol of negation,[14] the thinking-process frees itself from the limitations of repression and enriches itself with the subject-matter without which it could not work efficiently.[15]

The function of judgment is concerned ultimately with two sorts of decision. It may assert or deny that a thing has a particular property; or it may affirm or dispute that a particular image (*Vorstellung*) exists in reality. Originally the property to be decided about might be either good or bad, useful or harmful. Expressed in the language of the oldest, that is, of the oral, instinctual

13. The phrase "intellectual substitute" in a sense conveys the major implication of this paper. Negation appears to be a re-representation of repression on a higher level of integration. This appearance of a defense-mechanism in an altered form on a higher level of integration is not singular. The many variants of "projection" discussed in note 2, above, also seem to constitute a hierarchy of re-representations. Nor is this limited to defenses alone. Mechanisms like those of the primary process (displacement, condensation, etc.) also seem to work on various levels of organization; cf. Chap. 12, note 80, above.

Even affects seem to have "intellectual" (Landauer, 442) and "cold" (E. Lewy, personal communication) counterparts. The systematic exploration of the hierarchic levels of representation of impulses, affects, and defenses within the ego-organization is one of the important tasks of psychoanalytic ego-psychology in general and of a systematic dynamic theory of thought-processes in particular. One of the important pertinent problems is the nature and energy source of strivings, attitudes, interests, etc., which seem to play the role of motivating forces in the secondary-process, that is, in goal-directed purposive thinking. Cf. Chap. 5, notes 43, 61, 78, 121, above.

14. The term symbol is not used here in its technical sense but rather as a synonym for "hallmark."

15. The need of the thought-process for abundant information was discussed by Freud (209, p. 533) as follows:

To change the outer world appropriately by means of motility requires the accumulation of a large total of experiences in the memory systems, as well as a manifold consolidation of the relations which are evoked in this memory-material by various directing ideas. . . . The activity of the second system, groping in many directions, tentatively sending forth cathexes and retracting them needs . . . full command over all memory-material. . . .

Repression, however, interferes with the availability of memories to the thought-process. Negation permits memories and relationships to enter consciousness and to serve reality orientation and thinking without lifting the repression of the drives whose representations they are, that is, without giving the drives access to motility.

impulses, the alternative runs thus: "I should like to eat that, or I should like to spit it out"; or, carried a stage further: "I should like to take this into me and keep that out of me." That is to say: it is to be either *inside me* or *outside me.* As I have shown elsewhere, the original pleasure-Ego tries to introject into itself everything that is good and to reject from itself everything that is bad.[16] From this point of view what is bad, what is alien to the Ego, and what is external are, to begin with, identical.[17]*

The other sort of decision made by the function of judgment, namely, as to the real existence of something imagined, is a concern of the final reality-Ego, which develops out of the previous pleasure-Ego (a concern, that is, of the faculty that tests the reality of things).[18] It is now no longer a question of whether something perceived (a thing) shall be taken into the Ego or not, but of whether something which is present in the Ego [19] as an image can also be rediscovered in perception (that is, in reality). Once more, it will be seen, the question is one of *external* and *internal*. What is not real, what is merely im-

16. For Freud's more detailed discussion of the conditions he describes here as predecessors of judgment, see Chap. 15, note 27, above. For the definition of the "pleasure-ego," see Freud (232, pp. 78–79).

17.* "Instincts and Their Vicissitudes" [232, pp. 62–63].

18. Freud's discussion may be summarized as follows: The most primitive predecessor of judgment attempted to decide by motor action what is "me" and what is not "me," that is, what is internal and what is external. The second, still primitive predecessor of judgment, attempted to accept (introject) only pleasurable and to reject (project) painful excitations, both of internal and external origin; later on it repressed both kinds if they aroused dangerous tension. The judgmental function Freud discusses here deals with ideas already accepted, already internal; the function of judgment here is to discern whether they are *merely* internal or whether there is in reality a counterpart to them. The further development of judgment is a differentiation which comes to expression in the many form-varieties of conscious experience: we can experience ideas as dreams, possibilities, percepts, assumptions, memories, etc., and true, false, certain, uncertain, etc. Cf. Chap. 26, note 128, and Schilder, Chap. 25, pp. 532 ff., 558–62, and note 86, and Kris, Chap. 23, note 30, below. See also Freud (223, p. 18; 232, particularly pp. 62–63 and 78–79; and 237, particularly pp. 147–49).

19. The phrases "taken into the Ego" and "present in the Ego" appear to reify the relationships in question. The Ego being a concept, the referent of which is a "cohesive organization of mental processes" (Freud, 243, p. 15), nothing can be "taken into" or be "present in" it. The phrases are apparently meant as shorthand for "is or should become a subject-matter of one or the other Ego function or process."

agined or subjective, is only *internal;* while on the other hand what is real is also present *externally.* When this stage is reached, the pleasure-principle is no longer taken into account.[20] Experience has taught that it is important not only whether a thing (an object from which satisfaction is sought) possesses the "good" property, that is, whether it deserves to be taken into the Ego, but also whether it is there in the external world, ready to be seized when it is wanted. In order to understand this step forward we must recollect that all images originate from perceptions and are repetitions of them. So that originally the

20. The pleasure-principle is replaced by the reality-principle and correspondingly the primary process by the secondary process of thought. Compare Freud (209, pp. 535–36), concerning these processes:

The psychic process which is alone tolerated by the first system I shall now call the *primary process;* and that which results under the inhibiting action of the second system I shall call the *secondary process.* I can also show . . . for what purpose the second system is obliged to correct the primary process. The primary process strives for discharge of the excitation in order to establish with the quantity of excitation thus collected *an identity of perception;* the secondary process has abandoned this intention, and has adopted instead the aim of an *identity of thought.* All thinking is merely a detour from the memory of gratification (taken as a purposive idea) to the identical cathexis of the same memory, which is to be reached once more by the path of motor experiences. Thought must concern itself with the connecting-paths between ideas without allowing itself to be misled by their intensities. But it is obvious that condensations of ideas and intermediate or compromise-formations are obstacles to the attainment of the identity which is aimed at; by substituting one idea for another they swerve away from the path which would have led onward from the first idea. Such procedures are, therefore, carefully

avoided in our secondary thinking. It will readily be seen, moreover, that the pain-principle, although at other times it provides the thought-process with its most important clues, may also put difficulties in its way in the pursuit of identity of thought. Hence, the tendency of the thinking process must always be to free itself more and more from exclusive regulation by the pain-principle, and to restrict the development of affect through the work of thought to the very minimum which remains effective as a signal. This refinement in functioning is to be achieved by a fresh hypercathexis, effected with the help of consciousness. But we are aware that this refinement is seldom completely successful, even in normal psychic life, and that our thinking always remains liable to falsification by the intervention of the pain-principle.

Concerning the cathectic process involved and the role of consciousness in it, compare Freud (209, p. 545):

It is probable that the pain-principle first of all regulates the displacements of cathexis automatically, but it is quite possible that the consciousness contributes a second and more subtle regulation of these qualities, which may even oppose the first, and perfect the functional capacity of the apparatus, by placing it in a position contrary to its original design, subjecting even that which induces pain to cathexis and to elaboration.

mere existence of the images serves as a guarantee of the reality of what is imagined. The contrast between what is subjective and what is objective does not exist from the first. It only arises from the faculty which thought possesses for reviving a thing that has once been perceived, by reproducing it as an image, without its being necessary for the external object still to be present. Thus the first and immediate aim of the process of testing reality is not to discover an object in real perception corresponding to what is imagined, but to *rediscover* such an object, to convince oneself that it is still there.[21] The differentiation between what is subjective and what is objective is further assisted by another faculty of the power of thought. The reproduction of a perception as an image is not always a faithful one; it can be modified by omissions or by the fusion of a number of elements. The process for testing the thing's reality must then investigate the extent of these distortions.[22] But it is evident that an essential precondition for the institutions of the function for testing reality is that objects shall have been lost [23] which have formerly afforded real satisfaction.

Judging is the intellectual action which decides the choice of motor action, which puts an end to the procrastination of thinking, and which leads over from thinking to acting. This procrastinating character of thought, too, has been discussed by me elsewhere.[24]* Thought is to be regarded as an experi-

21. Freud apparently refers to the distinction between verification of the existence of the referent of a memory image in reality (rediscovery) and the successful search for a reality referent of an invention of creative imagination (discovery).

22. The distortions referred to may be of two major classes: (a) structural changes of the memory occurring with the passage of time such as are extensively dwelt on by Gestalt-psychology (Rapaport, 591, pp. 124–25); (b) distortions referable to psychological dynamics, such as those subserving wishfulfillment, self-esteem, etc. (Rapaport, 591, pp. 167–72).

23. "Lost" apparently here means "absent" or delayed in appearance. The de-

lay in the appearance of the need-satisfying object, according to Freud, originally gives rise to a hallucinatory experience of the object, and this in turn becomes the point of departure for the arising of memory images and their organization. The search in reality, for the need-satisfying object, with the help of these images, is the prototype of the thought-process. Cf. Freud, Chap. 15, above.

24.* *Collected Papers*, in the work cited.

[I can find in the cited paper, "Instincts and Their Vicissitudes," no discussion of the "procrastinating character of thought." The reference may be to the "Two Principles" (223, p. 16):

mental action, a kind of groping forward, involving only a small expenditure of energy in the way of discharge.[25] Let us consider where the Ego can have made a previous use of this kind of groping forward, where it can have learned the technique which it now employs in thought-processes. It was at the sensory end of the mental apparatus, in connection with sensory perceptions. For upon our hypothesis perception is not a merely passive process; we believe rather that the Ego periodically sends out small amounts of cathectic energy into the perceptual system and by their means samples the external stimuli, and after every such groping advance draws back again.[26]

The study of judgment affords us, perhaps for the first time, an insight into the derivation of an intellectual function from the interplay of the primary instinctual impulses. Judging has been systematically developed out of what was in the first instance introduction into the Ego or expulsion from the Ego carried out according to the pleasure-principle. Its polarity appears to correspond to the opposition between the two groups of instincts which we have assumed to exist.[27] Affirmation, as being a substitute for union, belongs to Eros; while negation, the derivative of expulsion, belongs to the instinct of destruction.[28] The passion for universal negation, the "negativism," displayed

---

Restraint of motor discharge (of action) had now become necessary, and was provided by means of the process of *thought*, which was developed from ideation. Thought was endowed with facilities which made it possible for the mental apparatus to support increased tension during a delay in the process of discharge.

25. For a more detailed discussion of thought as "experimental action," see Chap. 15, note 30, above.

26. See Freud, "Note upon the Mystic Writing-Pad," Chap. 16, particularly notes 14 and 17, above.

27. The reference is here to the *Beyond the Pleasure Principle* and to the assumption of the two groups of instincts: life and death instincts. These assumptions and their consequences have not been shared by many psychoanalysts; see, for example, Fenichel (176, pp. 59–61).

28. It is noteworthy that Freud, in laying the groundwork here for the understanding of the relation of judgment to introjection and projection, and of negation to repression, in terms which suggest reappearance of these functions in changed forms on higher hierarchic levels of integration, persists in relating these functions to specific drives. This is the procedure Hermann (329, 327) followed in studying logic, and Nunberg (543) in describing the synthetic function of the ego. It would seem that such formulations underestimate the autonomy of ego functions, that is, the autonomous laws of the emergent higher levels of integration. These seem to have motivations of their own which, though they derive from drives, are changed in

by many psychotics, is probably to be regarded as a sign of a "defusion" of instincts due to the withdrawal of the libidinal components. The achievements of the function of judgment only become feasible, however, after the creation of the symbol of negation has endowed thought with a first degree of independence [29] from the results of repression and at the same time from the sway of the pleasure-principle.

This view of negation harmonizes very well with the fact that in analysis we never discover a "No" in the unconscious, and that a recognition of the unconscious on the part of the Ego is expressed in a negative formula. There is no stronger evidence that we have been successful in uncovering the unconscious than when the patient reacts with the words: "I didn't think that," or "I never thought of that." [30]

---

character and have a relative independence from the drives. Nevertheless, Freud does speak below of an "independence of the thought-process." For a discussion of the autonomy of ego-functions, see Hartmann, Chap. 19, I and II, particularly note 41, below.

29. General considerations on the nature of this "independence" may be found in Knight (390), and Hartmann, Chap. 19, VIII, below.

30. Cf. Freud (212, p. 70); see also Varendonck, Chap. 22, notes 26 and 35, below.

CHAPTER 18

ON THE PSYCHOLOGY OF BOREDOM [1]

By Otto Fenichel

[Passage omitted.] [2]

IT IS PROBABLE that the conditions and forms of behavior called "boredom" are psychologically quite heterogeneous. . . . Here we will attempt to characterize only a certain type.

Let us take our point of departure from Lipps's [3]* definition. . . . Boredom "is a feeling of displeasure due to a conflict between a need for intensive psychological activity and lack of stimulation or inability to be stimulated thereto." Let us add that, besides the need for, there is simultaneously an inhibition of, intensive psychological activity; the inhibition is experienced as such—one does not know *how* one should or could be active; and as a result of this conflict, stimulation by the outside world is sought. Let us add further that "the lack of stimulation" often does not correspond to an external reality; this is indicated in the addition of "inability to be stimulated." Boredom is characterized by the coexistence of a need for activity and activity-inhibition, as well as by stimulus-hunger and dissatisfaction with the available stimuli. Thus the central problem of the psychology of boredom is the *inhibition* of both the drive to activity and the readiness to accept the craved-for stimuli.[4]

1. Fenichel (179), also in "The Selected Papers of Otto Fenichel" (in press, Norton, 1951). The reasons for including this paper here are: (a) its consistent application of the psychoanalytic conception of the drive-thought relationship is unique in the psychoanalytic literature; (b) it is an unusually felicitous example of the investigative method combining clinical observation, clinical experiment, and theoretical inference, characteristic of psychoanalysis; (c) it touches also on the issue of time-experience, which is a significant and very obscure area of the psychology of thinking.

2. In the omitted section Fenichel refers to the only previous psychoanalytic study of boredom, by Winterstein (774).

3.* Lipps (477).

4. The "pleasure-principle," the fundamental and most familiar explanatory concept of psychoanalysis for drive-processes, demands that existing drive-tensions be reduced by gratification. See Chap. 15, note 9, above. The re-

Phenomenologically, the psychological state of boredom is best described as "the displeasurable experience of a lack of impulse." This formula poses a problem which must first be solved: we assume that the tension-state of the psychic apparatus is heightened by internal and external stimuli, and that this increased tension elicits impulses, that is tendencies, aiming at reestablishing the tension-free state.[5] Thus we ought to expect displeasurable drive-tensions and pleasurable drive-gratifications, that is to say, displeasurable impulses and pleasurable lack of impulses. The problem that pleasurable impulses nevertheless exist has often been discussed.[6*] The corresponding problem of a displeasurable lack of impulses is that of boredom. But boredom, the definition shows, is not just a lack of impulses, but also a "need for intensive psychic activity"; "lack of impulses" and "freedom from tension" by no means coincide here. Rather, we are faced with the problem: why does this tension not result in impulses, why does it—instead of manifesting itself as drive-impulse—require a stimulation from the outside world to indicate what the person should do to decrease his tension?

Naturally, "stimulus hunger" that turns toward the outside world is also encountered outside the realm of boredom. It arises the moment the small child recognizes that stimuli arising in the outside world can be used for drive-gratification. Pleasurable stimuli, once experienced, give rise to a craving for

---

lation of "stimulus-hunger" to "pleasure-principle" is stated by Fenichel (176, p. 35) as follows:

The first acceptance of reality is only an intermediary step on the road to getting rid of it. This is the point at which a contradiction of basic importance in human life arises, the contradiction between longing for complete relaxation and longing for objects (stimulus-hunger). The striving for discharge and relaxation, the direct expression of the constancy principle, is necessarily the older mechanism. The fact that external objects brought about the desired state of relaxed satisfaction introduced the complication that objects became longed for; in the beginning, it is true, they were sought only as instruments which made themselves disappear again. The longing for objects thus began as a de-

tour on the way to the goal of being rid of objects (of stimuli).

Compare Lewin's (464) comment on boredom, Chap. 5, pp. 115–16, above. Translated into Lewin's terms, Fenichel's formulation would read as follows: In boredom counter-needs isolate the tension-systems of the drives from the motor sphere, and these counter-needs also embed them in such a manner that the objects which are their intended occasions are not experienced as such, that is, as objects having a valence for the drive-tension.

5. See note 4, above.

6.* See Freud [213, pp. 605–8, particularly the footnote on p. 607; and 244, p. 256. Cf. also 241].

them in states of drive-tension.[7] These cravings are accompanied by a rejection of available objects and stimuli unsuited to bring about discharge, and when more suitable ones are unavailable they lead to introversion, fantasy-activity, and in final analysis to actual-neurotic phenomena due to a damming-up of libido.[8] Can such a state of craving for adequate objects, and the displeasure at available inadequate ones, be called "boredom"? Correctly speaking it cannot; yet at times it is that. Of objects and stimuli which do not give us the "aid to discharge" we legitimately expect, we are accustomed to say that they "bore" us.[9] We shall come back to this point. But the person who "is bored," in the strict sense of the word, is searching for an object, not in order to act on it with his drive-impulses, but rather to be helped by it to find a drive-aim which he is missing.[10]

The drive-tension is present, the drive-aim is missing. Boredom appears to be a state of drive-tension in which the drive-aims are repressed; yet the tension as such is experienced, and therefore one turns to the external world for help in the struggle against repression. The person who is bored can be therefore compared to one who has forgotten a name and inquires about it from others.

This formula, which is correct but not specific, makes the "inability to become stimulated" somewhat more comprehensible. When a bored person is looking for stimulation because he has lost his drive-aims to repression, it is understandable that, to stimulations which could bring about the desired discharge, he will offer the same resistance which resulted in the repression of the drive-aims; and that if the "stimulation" offered by the external world is too distantly related to the original drive-aim, there cannot occur displacement of the cathectic-energy onto the activity suggested by the stimulation.[11]

7. See note 4, above.

8. The conception of actual neuroses originated early in the development of psychoanalysis, and though it still survives (176, pp. 185–88) it is something of a foreign body in the present-day structure of psychoanalytic and psychiatric theory. For the original statements of the conception see Freud (207, p. 240, and 203).

9. Compare Fenichel's phrase "legitimately expect" with Hartmann's conception of the individual's adaptation to his "average expectable environment," Chap. 19, notes 37 and 72, below.

10. For the definition of drive-aim, drive-object, drive-impetus, see Freud (232, p. 65): "The *aim* of an instinct is in every instance satisfaction, which can only be obtained by abolishing the condition of stimulation in the source of the instinct." Cf. also Chap. 27, notes 13, 21, and 89, below.

11. Here Fenichel implicitly states the psychoanalytic conception of the relation of thought to drive. It is the direct

He who wards off a drive-demand is in conflict; the Id wants drive-action, the Ego does not. The same conflict repeats itself in relation to the stimuli of the external world. The Id takes hold of them as "drive substitutes," while the Ego —even though it would discharge its tensions—does not wish to be reminded of the original drive-aim, and seeks therefore "diversion" or "distraction" of its energies which are fixated on the unconscious drive-goal. Thus if the original drive persists, one resists diversion and distraction; but one also resists substitutes too closely related to the original aim.[12]

We know of various conditions of high tension accompanying repressed drive-aims. We expect in such cases a condition which differs very considerably from boredom. Everybody knows the general "jitteriness," inner and/or motor restlessness, seen in such cases. Though this state of restlessness is very different from the manifest quiet of boredom, we recognize that the two conditions have an inner relationship. *The difference between states of boredom and motor restlessness is that in the former the cathexes are tonically bound, while in the latter their binding is clonic.* We are left with the question, what condi-

---

relation of these which Fenichel is concerned with here. Thus he can disregard the ego aspects of thought-organization which have been repeatedly discussed in this volume.

The conception may be sketched as follows: Stimuli and/or ideas are, from the point of view of the drive, representations of the drive-satisfying object. Their appearance serves as a signpost on the way toward tension-discharge, that is, gratification. These representations may be closely or distantly related to the drive-object. If the drive is repressed, the close representatives of the drive-objects are also repressed, and the stimulus even if objectively present is not experienced as a drive-representative; while the distant representatives of the drive-object, though not necessarily repressed, are not experienced as such either. For instance, if one represses a drive which is consciously experienced as a wish for suc-

cess in a profession, the major opportunities for success will be tabooed and shunned, and the everyday inconspicuous drudgeries which are prerequisite to any success will not be recognized as a means to the end, will offer no attraction, and yield no pleasure. This is the point at which interpersonal communication can attain catalytic role in drive-dynamics.

12. Substitute formation is one kind of drive-derivative or -representation. Cf. Freud (234, p. 123):

Substitute formations are . . . highly organized derivatives of the unconscious; . . . these succeed in breaking through into consciousness, thanks to some favorable relation, as, for example, when they coincide with a preconscious anticathexis.

See also Freud (234, pp. 116–17; and 233, pp. 92–93). Cf. Lewin (464) on substitute consummation (Chap. 5, II, 1, c4), above.

tions will give rise to such tonic cathexes and when do they take the typical form of boredom? Obviously tonic-forms of acute drive-tensions with repressed drive-aims have yet other alternative manifestations.[13]

13. The conception of "bound cathexes," though it is central to the cathectic theory of psychoanalysis, refers to one of the least understood psychoanalytic observations. The concept was advanced by Breuer (259, pp. 139 ff.) in 1895, and Freud retained it throughout the changes of his theoretical conceptions, stressing that the process to which it refers is still little understood. In 1915 Freud (234, pp. 120–21) stated the concept, and the observations it refers to, as follows:

The processes of the system [preconscious] display, no matter whether they are already conscious or only capable of becoming conscious, an inhibition of the tendency of cathected ideas towards discharge. When a process moves over from one idea to another, the first retains a part of its cathexis and only a small part undergoes displacement. Displacement and condensation after the mode of the primary process are excluded or very much restricted. This circumstance caused Breuer to assume the existence of two different stages of cathectic energy in mental life: one in which that energy is tonically "bound" and the other in which it moves freely and presses towards discharge. I think that this discrimination represents the deepest insight we have gained up to the present into the nature of nervous energy, and I do not see how we are to evade such a conclusion. A metapsychological presentation most urgently calls for further discussion at this point, though perhaps that would still be too daring an undertaking.

Cf. also Freud (209, pp. 533–34, 535–36; and 241, pp. 35–36, 41–42).

The drive cathexes of the id and the primary thought-process are characterized as mobile, striving for discharge in keeping with the pleasure-principle; and the cathexes of the secondary thought-process are characterized as "bound," their discharge delayed in keeping with the reality-principle. The process of "binding" thus provides the crucial distinction between the id and the ego organization of thought-processes. For attempts to clarify the concept of "binding," see Hartmann (303), Rapaport (596), and Chap. 22, note 30, and Chap. 23, pp. 477–78, 485, particularly note 11, p. 478.

The usual concept (Breuer's) is that of tonic binding, modeled after the tonus of the muscle, independent of voluntary innervation. Tonic binding of cathexes transforms them into energies not striving toward discharge. Fenichel's "clonic binding" is to my knowledge a new term in the literature. As I understand it, the term expresses that while in the states of motor restlessness under discussion, the drive-cathexes are bound, their binding is such that it allows for some spasmodic discharge. The cathectic conditions of such motor restlessness may prove similar to those of affect-discharge and -expression. Cf. Chap. 15, note 26, and Chap. 17, note 8, above.

Fenichel's conceptualization here is in harmony with accumulating evidence that there is no categorical difference between mobile and bound cathexes, but rather a continuum of cathexes bound in various degrees. The process of binding also divests the cathexes of the hallmarks of their specific drive-origin: it neutral-

The question of whether these considerations are valid for all forms of boredom will be left open. They are certainly so for a certain pathological type of boredom which can be clinically investigated. . . .[14]

In such boredom, while subjectively the intensive conflictful excitation seems to have disappeared, there are signs to show it is actually there. In this respect, boredom is a variant or sub-division of "depersonalization," where the libido is usually by no means withdrawn from internal perception; rather, it is countercathected, as the increased self-observation indicates.[15]*

Boredom makes some children cry. Such crying and restlessness break the tonic binding of cathexes, and then what these children call boredom is hardly distinguishable from manifest restlessness and jitteriness. That children call it boredom shows the relatedness of these conditions. Thus, the meaning of this boredom may be schematically formulated as follows: "I am excited. If I allow this excitation to continue I shall get anxious. Therefore I tell myself, I am not at all excited, I don't want to do anything. Simultaneously, however, I feel I do want to do something; but I have forgotten my original goal and do

---

izes them. See Hartmann (303) concerning the various degrees of neutralization of energies.

14. In the omitted section Fenichel discusses the relation of monotony to boredom: (a) monotony, with its lack of new stimulation, usually leads to withdrawal of cathexes and ultimately to sleep; (b) however, rhythmic monotony (such as that of primitive dance) may lead to excitement; in the course of psychoanalytic treatment, rhythmic equilibrium-experiences are often traces of infantile sexual excitements; (c) monotony-excitations may become intensely displeasurable, for instance in persons who can tolerate only a degree of sexual excitement without anxiety, or under conditions which do not provide a climax; (d) boredom, excitation, anxiety, and interruption-displeasure are closely related, and seem to differ from each other only quantitatively.

15.* Cf. Fenichel (177).

[The relationship between the dynamic conditions underlying boredom and depersonalization links the problem of boredom in yet another significant way with the theory of thought-processes. In our comments we have attempted to point up consistently the relationship between states of consciousness and form of thought-organization. We have had the opportunity to discuss repeatedly the problem of awareness (Chap. 13, note 56, and Chap. 17, note 18, above). States of depersonalization are characterized by a lack of "me-ness" in experience (Chap. 3); in a sense they are the opposite of certain states of consciousness observed in Korsakow patients (Chap. 27, note 43, below) characterized by a proneness to endow suggested contents with "me-ness" and to attribute reality to them. Concerning depersonalization states, see also Schilder, 653; and Oberndorf, 545, 546, 547, 548.]

not know what I want to do. The external world must do something to relieve me of my tension without making me anxious. It must make me do something, but so that I shall not be responsible for it. It must divert me, distract me, so that what I do will be sufficiently remote from my original goal. It should accomplish the impossible, afford a discharge without drive-action." [16]

This meaning of boredom became particularly clear in a patient whose analysis was dominated by intense transference-resistance. The resistance manifested itself either in continuous motor restlessness or in boredom. The analysis indicated that both conditions, apparently so different, were expressions of the same latent psychic situation. The patient called his motor restlessness "being angry." He was continually angry, at times in a rage with the doctor; but all he had against him was that he had not miraculously cured him overnight. His associations were completely inhibited, and he raged that the analyst did not change this by a magic word. This "being angry" was accompanied by phenomena seen in acute libido-disturbances: general restlessness and the torturing subjective feeling that the psychic situation was unbearable. The sexual life of the patient revealed the meaning of this behavior. He suffered from an acute libido disturbance: when with a woman, he entered the situation in normal fashion; he experienced normal pleasure until the excitation reached a certain degree; then—often before, and at times even after, the penis was inserted—came a sudden change. He experienced intense displeasure of a general sort, did not know what to do next and became "angry" with the woman because, he felt, she should do something to free him of this disagreeable situation. In matters other than sexual he also displayed a masochistic character, con-

16. Under usual conditions, too, there are repressed drives and drive-aims; yet the struggle of repression is apparently less intensive than in boredom. It leaves a great variety of stimuli which are neither so close to the drive-aim that they must be repressed, nor so far from it that they are of no "interest." It is within this range that the autonomous interest- and attention-cathexes of the ego determine the course of thought and action. Cf. Freud, Chaps. 15 and 17, above, and Hartmann, Chap. 19, below. The width and variety of this range of sustained interests is therefore one of the gauges of ego-strength. In other words, the amount of energy which the person can dispose of by investing it in objects, by becoming interested in activities, even when essential drive-aims and drive-objects are in abeyance, is an indicator of ego-autonomy and ego-strength. These interests, and the organization of thinking which corresponds to them, constitute one of the major areas of the ego-psychology of thinking. Cf. Lewin, Chap. 5, pp. 138–39.

tinuously demonstrating his unhappiness, and being "angry" at those present because they were not overcome by sympathy and did not perform some miracle to liberate him. Analysis showed that this general, but in the sexual sphere exacerbated, excitation repeated the infantile situation of lying in bed with his mother. Having repressed his active phallic wishes towards his mother, he expected her to intervene and give him both guiltless sexual gratification and diversion from his sexual thoughts. Characteristically, this action which he expected from his mother, and later from everybody, was conceived of as an oral gratification.[17] On certain days his masochistically-colored excitement was replaced by a state of "boredom." Though he could not associate on these days either, his feeling was quite different. He experienced no intolerable tension; allegedly he experienced "nothing at all," but continuously asserted that analysis and everything in it was so boring that he did not feel like saying anything, or even know what he should say, and would soon give up the analysis. The manner in which this state alternated with the one described above left no doubt that it was primarily a successful defense against the *expectation-excitement* with which the patient otherwise awaited the craved-for magic (oral) intervention of the analyst. I shall communicate here a small association experiment carried out on such a day to demonstrate that the —other times manifest—excitation was present, but in tonic binding. When the patient declared he was bored, he was asked to follow with particular conscientiousness the fundamental rule of psychoanalysis, and to be sure not to suppress any idea as "too boring." [18] The patient began by relating that he was

17. Concerning the relationships of masochism, orality, and passivity, see for instance Bergler's (45) one-sided, yet challenging, presentation.

18. For the "fundamental rule," see Chap. 12, note 51, above. It appears that the patient's inability to associate usually kept him from following the "fundamental rule." What in this case appears as an isolated experiment is the usual procedure of psychoanalysis, which may be therefore viewed as a continuous series of such clinical experiments. The general theory of psychoanalysis provides the theoretical framework, the pa-

tient's general situation and the theory together provide the assumptions to be tested, and the concrete momentary situation provides the experimental conditions. It is true that, in the clinical-therapeutic setting, the assumptions and concrete situation are rarely discerned as sharply as in the example Fenichel presents here. But they are more often so discerned and discernible than the non-clinical experimenter would suppose. Such opportunities for clinical experimentation could be exploited more systematically. The reason they are not is that the therapeutic interest and setting

looking into the corner of the room and thinking, What if a cobweb were there? One could take a broom and brush *up and down* the wall, *always up and down*. Besides, he had a toothache; he had come directly from the dentist, who had run his drill *up and down* his teeth. His attention was called to the fact that the dimensions of sensations in the mouth are often misrecognized; therefore the idea of brushing off the wall showed that psychologically he was still at the dentist's, not at the analyst's, and that in his fantasy the analyst was doing something exciting in his mouth. "Now only nonsense comes to my mind," the patient continued; "I could say any random word, for instance, 'light switch' or 'chamber pot.'" "Light switch" and "chamber pot" are means by which adults attempt to quiet an anxious child at night. Thus the patient's state could be interpreted as follows: "I have anxiety, do something quieting (or disquieting) in my mouth!" The boredom which the patient experienced denied his excitation in the same fashion that depersonalization would have. . . .[19]

We cannot deny that all this does not solve the question we have raised: what makes "tonic binding" possible, and how is the tonic binding of "boredom" distinguished from that of other states? When does motor restlessness arise, and when a feeling of lack of impulses with a craving for diversion?

We cannot offer a final answer to this question. One thing must be kept in mind: tonic binding, hence also boredom, fends off *more* than motor restlessness does—it fends off the motor impulses themselves.[20] But this again is no

---

is not conducive to experimental thinking, rather than that the principal difficulties are too great. We discuss this method here because it seems that many problems of thought-organization will have to be studied first—if not altogether —in their natural setting rather than in laboratory experiment.

19. The omitted section deals with the nature of those drives whose goal is passive.

20. Restless motor-activity may be regarded as affect-expression. The question Fenichel raises pertains therefore to the theory of affects. In psychoanalytic theory, affect-charge and idea—the matrix from which affect-expression and thought arise in the course of ego development—are considered partly indicators and partly safety valves of drive-tension. Compare Chap. 15, note 26, and Chap. 17, note 8, above, also Brierley (92), and Rapaport (596). The problem of the process whereby cathexes become bound is closely connected with the control of drive-tension, and therefore also with the indicators of drive-tension, that is, affect-charge and idea. Affect and thought develop only after the development of the control of drive-discharge has begun. To what extent and under what conditions affect-expression (for example, restlessness) and thought-organization (for example, bored lack of

answer in principle, because, on the one hand, there are states of dammed-up libido, of complete motor calm, which cannot be characterized as boredom; and on the other hand, there are states of boredom accompanied by all kinds of restless activity. "Blasé" people are noted for more or less nonsensical activities due to "boredom." . . . This is a variant of boredom in which the bored ego does not wait for the stimuli of the external world, but thinks up its own "substitute actions" to release the tension, that is, to replace drive-action, to "divert" itself from it, and to deny it. The paralysis of the motor system is thus neither the sole nor the essential characteristic of boredom. It may be absent in boredom, and at any rate something must be added to it, namely, that mechanism which we consider related to depersonalization, whereby a person can manage completely to conceal from himself the presence of extremely high inner tension.[21] It is well known that people endowed with fantasy are rarely bored, and those given to boredom produce no daydreams, because of inability or inhibition. (The patient I quoted had no fantasy life at all.) Apparently, rich fantasy makes for a certain amount of unburdening in daydreams, whereas its lack requires a massive countercathexis to block internal perceptions.[22]

Is the internal perception of one's own excitation lacking, in such a state? We mentioned the outbursts of crying in boredom, and had to add that we cannot consider it characteristic. Apparently the transition from "jitteriness" to boredom is fluid; but extreme cases are characterized by feeling a certain degree of lack of excitation, which is what they call "being bored."

[Passage omitted.] [23]

The relationship between boredom and lonesomeness is now easily under-

---

thoughts) complement or supplant each other, is as yet an unsolved problem of the theory of affects and thinking.

21. Fenichel seems to imply that the defense-mechanism of isolation, which appears to be the one involved here, is sufficent to account for these phenomena.

22. Concerning the role of fantasy in defense-processes, see Anna Freud (201). Cf. also Chap. 22, note 30, below.

23. The omitted section may be summarized as follows: (a) Fenichel raises the question of whether any specific drives can be found, the repression of which leads to boredom. He concludes that drives whose goals are passive are not specific to it. (b) He stresses the relationship of boredom to mood-swings, and particularly to depressions coupled with such means of diversion as addictions or *Wanderlust*. He concludes, however, that narcissistic and oral-sadistic needs central to these disorders are not the only ones which when dammed up can lead to boredom.

stood. If the situation of a bored person is correctly described as a state of drive-tension which is not conscious to him, but represents dangers, to cope with which he expects help from external stimuli, then it is clear that the etiological conditions of boredom and lonesomeness must be identical. Their relationship to masturbation, like that of neurotics with an anxiety of being closeted, is of two kinds: the bored person, like the lonesome one, may fear actually the temptation to masturbate and combat it by becoming conscious of a craving for diversion rather than of masturbatory impulses; or else in an attempt to escape burdensome drive-tension, the aim of which is completely unconscious to him, he may resort to repeated acts of masturbation. There are many threads connecting boredom and compulsive masturbation.[24]*

Let us recall in this connection Ferenczi's "Sunday neuroses." [25]* There are Sunday neurotics whose symptom is merely that on Sundays, or during vacations, they *are bored*. While at work, these people succeed in what the bored person strives for in vain, namely "to divert themselves" while in a state of pent-up drives. When the diversion is unavailable, the tension is noted and the hitherto latent "boredom" becomes manifest. As a rule, memories of the Sundays of childhood play a role here; the damming-up of drives was artificially increased then, the great drive-hunger of children being particularly prevented from drive-manifestations.

Now that we have sketched the mechanisms of a pathological form of boredom, the question is: are these the essential mechanisms of all boredom? How does a differently structured "normal" boredom look? It arises when we must not do what we want to do, or must do what we do not want to do. This "harmless" boredom appears at first to be entirely different from that so far described, but the common features of the two are easily recognized: *something expected does not occur*. Here it fails to occur because the structure of the real situation does not allow the expected discharge; there it fails to occur because one represses the drive-action to prevent anxiety. (Similarly, in a state of ungratifiable tiredness, the sleep-hindering external world is experienced as boring.) It is difficult to predict, however, when a frustrating external world will mobilize aggressions and when it will be merely experienced as "boring." One should not forget that we have *the right to expect* some "aid in discharge" from

24.* See Fenichel (175 pp. 290–91,   25.* See Ferenczi (185).
301–3).

the external world. If this is not forthcoming, we are, so to speak, justifiably bored.[26] To characterize this situation, Winterstein [27]* quotes Field Marshal Ligne: "I am not bored,[28]* it is the others who bore me." This is why an "affect-inhibited" person, one equipped with strong characterologically-anchored countercathexes—as for instance a particularly correct or otherwise rigid person—is so boring. His emotional aloofness does not correspond to people's drive-expectations of each other. Often such people are anxious lest they prove boring, and we must say that their anxiety is well-founded. Analysis of this anxiety shows that this quality of boring people, so feared by the patient himself, may harbor a great deal of sadism.

One other aspect of boredom, which clearly bears upon its nature, is its relationship to *time*. The German word "Langeweile" itself . . . indicates a change in subjective time-experience.[29] When we experience many stimulations from the outside world, the time—as we know—appears to pass quickly. Should the external world bring only monotonous stimuli, or should subjective conditions prevent their being experienced as tension-releasing, then the "while is long." This basic propensity of subjective time-experience, which gave the phenomenon of "Langeweile" its name, seems to be but a secondary consequence of the mechanisms described. However, the possibility cannot be rejected that a primary disturbance of the subjective time-experience facilitates the emergence and play of these mechanisms. Precisely this is the case with people who have sexualized their time-experience, a particularly frequent occurrence in certain types of anal character.[30]* In this light we can agree with Winterstein's [31]* description of certain anal characters as particularly disposed to boredom, and his relating the phenomenon of boredom in general to that of "stinting with time." [32]

26. Cf. note 9 above.

27.* Winterstein (774).

28. The German for "to bore" is a reflexive verb.

29. *Langeweile*, German for "boredom," literally means "longwhile."

30.* Cf. Harnik (300).

31.* Winterstein (774).

32. For other psychoanalytic considerations concerning time, see Spielrein (700), Hollos (335), Ferenczi and Hollos (187), Bonaparte (81), Schilder (651), Dooley (148).

The issue of time-experience seems connected by many threads with those observations to which the concept of "delay" refers. For the concept of "delay," see Freud, Chap. 15, particularly note 29, above. Poor tolerance for "waiting" (and exaggerated punctuality) attended by mounting tension, exaggerated adolescent impatience to grow up

The rest of Winterstein's remarks on the disposition to boredom is also in agreement with our considerations. He writes: "Two types may be distinguished here: the blasé, who becomes callous through overstimulation, who craves for pleasure but is unable to enjoy it (such boredom may have a physiological foundation); and the one who escapes painful boredom by working, because he finds everything boring which is not fulfilment of a duty." These two types appear to us essentially as two variants of a chronic damming-up of libido, taking the form of tension with the drive-goal repressed. The first type is orgastically impotent, "craving" because unable to enjoy pleasure. (We do not believe that his "callousness" is due to "overstimulation." We would rather assume that the psychogenic damming-up of libido is the cause of both his craving after stimuli and his becoming callous.) The second is the "Sunday neurotic" mentioned above. We believe that in both cases boredom has a physiological foundation, namely that of the damming-up of libido.[33]

(with the later experience of never having grown up), fantasies implying a short life-span, impatient urge to complete some work, overintense wishes for a pleasant situation never to end, are significant time-experiences of great individual variability. A preliminary collation of data concerning such experiences, with life-histories of the subjects collected by Dr. Alfred Gross and myself, suggests a relation between "ability to delay"—that is, quality of "drive control"—and time-experiences of this sort, including boredom.

33. It seems that libido is used here in the broadest sense as "drive-energy" in general.

Since the delay of drive-discharge is the cradle of thought (Chap. 15, note 29, above), time-experiences, normal and pathological, are significant subject-matter for the psychology of thinking.

CHAPTER 19

EGO PSYCHOLOGY AND THE PROBLEM OF ADAPTATION [1]

By *Heinz Hartmann*

1. [THE CONFLICT-FREE EGO-SPHERE]

WE ENCOUNTER the issue of adaptation in psychoanalysis in three contexts: first and mainly as a problem of ego-theory, then as one of the therapeutic aims, and lastly as a pedagogical consideration. It is striking that while it is more or less clear what we mean by "ego-syntonic," experience shows that the concept "reality-syntonic" [2] seems to be made of rubber, so that the most diverse and even partly contradictory views can hide behind it.

The problem of adaptation is certainly one which cannot be solved by psychoanalysis alone. Biology and sociology also have justified claims to this subject-matter of research. . . . This problem is in the center of our interest mainly because of those developments in psychoanalysis which have brought into focus the investigation of ego-functions. . . .

[Passage omitted.] [3]

. . . Psychoanalysis set out from the study of pathological phenomena and

1. Hartmann (305). I present here a translation only of selections from Hartmann's extensive paper. The sections presented are those which are related to the psychology of thought-processes. Though the paper is not concerned primarily with thought-processes as such, it is of considerable importance to our topic for two reasons. Since it treats of adaptation, the problem of intellectual development is one of its foci; consequently it contains much that applies to thought-processes. Furthermore, since its aim is to stake out the field of ego-psychology in the broadest sense, it sets the framework for the psychoanalytic theory of the secondary thought-process, the development of which has thus far been limited both within id-psychology and ego-psychology in the narrower sense.

2. "Reality-syntonic" refers here to the adaptive aspects of ego-function and thought-content.

3. In the omitted section Hartmann states that his aim is to carry over the concepts which psychoanalysis has developed in the study of the "central sphere of personality" (that of the drives, and their control) to other realms of psychic life, which have so far not been studied by psychoanalysis.

of conditions that form a bridge between normal psychology and psychopathology. At first its focal working ground was the id and the drives. But soon, new problems, concepts, formulations, and demands for explanation arose, reaching out beyond this narrower field and pointing toward an all-embracing theory of psychic life. A decisive and perhaps the most clearly delineated move in this direction is the recently developed ego-psychology. . . .[4]

The goal of psychoanalysis—as formulated by Anna Freud [5]—is to attain the broadest possible knowledge of the three psychic institutions. . . . All psychological investigations share some partial goals with psychoanalysis. It is this partial commonality of subject-matter which brings into sharp relief the distinctive characteristics of psychoanalytic thinking. . . . The recent developments in psychoanalysis have not changed in the least its crucial characteristics, namely its basically biological orientation, its genetic, dynamic, economic, and topographic points of view, and the explanatory [rather than descriptive] character of its concepts. Therefore psychoanalytic and non-analytic psychology tackling the same subject-matter will, of necessity, arrive at different results. . . . Psychoanalysis . . . contains potentially a theory of psychic development. . . . This, however, makes it necessary to review, with the eyes of psychoanalysis, those psychological phenomena which were the subject-matter of psychology before psychoanalysis and which are now outside of psychoanalysis, and to encompass them within our knowledge.[6]

It has often been said that while the psychology of the id is a "preserve" of psychoanalysis, ego-psychology is the broadest meeting ground of psychoanalysis with non-analytic psychological knowledge. . . . Though psychoanalytic ego-psychology shows and will show even increased concern for the details of behavior and for the shadings of conscious experience, it is not merely a "surface" psychology. . . . Examples in which ego-psychology goes considerably below the "surface" are the rarely treated problem of the laws of preconscious processes [7] and the relationships between the unconscious, pre-

4. Freud (243, 252, 257); A. Freud (201).

5. A. Freud (201).

6. Here Hartmann indicates that he considers psychoanalysis a psychology which is capable of integrating within its theoretical framework *all* psychological phenomena. In this paper he places within the framework of psychoanalytic psychology in general, and psychoanalytic ego-psychology in particular, the phenomena studied by various branches of psychology.

7. The only study which treats this problem systematically is Kris's recent paper, Chap. 23, below.

conscious and conscious parts of the ego.[8] The dynamic-economic point of view which applies to all psychic life, has so far been little applied to these problems. It follows from the development of psychoanalytic psychology—as here described—that we understand as yet relatively little about those processes and working methods of the psychic apparatus which lead to adaptive achievements. . . . The purely descriptive, phenomenological aspects [of psychological investigation] have a special importance in ego-psychology. Details of the psychological superficies, which could have been disregarded before, gain great importance in it. . . .[9]

The close connection between theory and therapeutic goals, so characteristic for psychoanalysis, makes it understandable that certain ego-functions commanded our interest earlier than others. These functions were the ones directly related to *conflicts* between the psychic institutions. Consequently, we have not studied until recently the process of coming to terms with the environment and other ego-functions, except for the few which began to play a role early in psychoanalysis. . . . We must recognize that though the ego does grow on conflicts, these conflicts are not the only sources of ego-development. . . .[10]

8. Freud's (233, 234) investigations which laid the groundwork for the study of these relationships preceded the formulation of the structural concepts of ego, id, superego. Even so, his later studies (243; 255, pp. 82–112; and 257, pp. 33 ff.) of these relationships were built on these earlier investigations. Cf. Chap. 23, I, below.

9. Before the advent of its ego-psychology, psychoanalysis considered the "details of the psychological superficies," with which the various branches of psychology concerned themselves, as physics does "sensory qualities": they were to be reduced to the unconscious drive and defense processes underlying them, just as physics reduces sensory qualities to quantitative relationships. Ego-psychology, however, has to recognize and study the autonomous relationships that

obtain within the "psychological superficies," that is, within the various areas of ego-structure and ego-function.

10. The extent of the step Hartmann takes here will be more fully realized if it is compared with Freud's description of the origin of the reality-principle. See Freud, Chap. 15, and Chap. 17, note 28, above. Freud attributed the origin of the process of reality-testing, of the function of delay of discharge, and of notation, attention, judgment, and action, all to the conflict between instinctual-drive and reality. The scope of Hartmann's view becomes even clearer if it is compared with Freud's view of the role of conflict in ego-formation. See Freud (243, 246, 245).

Freud (243, p. 36) wrote:

When it happens that a person has to give up a sexual object, there quite often ensues

Not every adaptation to the environment, not every learning and maturation process arises from a conflict. I refer to the *conflict-free* development of perception, intention,[11] object-comprehension, thinking, language, recall phenomena, and productivity; to that of the well-known phases of motor development, grasping, crawling, and walking; and to the maturation and learning processes implicit in all these and many others. . . . I am certainly not implying that these and other pertinent childhood activities remain untouched by psychic conflicts; nor do I imply that disturbances in their development do not give rise to conflicts, or are not woven into other conflicts. On the contrary, I want to emphasize that their vicissitudes play a great role in the well-known typical and individual instinctual developments and conflicts, in that they may facili-

---

a modification in his ego which can only be described as a reinstatement of the object within the Ego, as it occurs in melancholia; the exact nature of this substitution is as yet unknown to us. It may be that, by undertaking this introjection, which is a kind of regression to the mechanism of the oral phase, the Ego makes it easier for an object to be given up or renders that process possible. It may even be that this identification is the sole condition under which the Id can give up its objects. At any rate the process, especially in the early phases of development, is a very frequent one, and it points to the conclusion that the character of the Ego is a precipitate of abandoned object-cathexes and that it contains a record of past object-choices.

The following passage from Freud's "Analysis Terminable and Interminable" (256, pp. 394–95) demonstrates, however, that later on he too assumed the existence of sources of ego-formation other than conflictual:

Our next question will be whether all Ego-modification (in the sense in which we are using the term) is acquired during the defensive conflicts of early childhood. There can be no doubt about the answer. We have no reason to dispute the existence and importance of primal, congenital Ego-variations. The single fact is decisive that

every individual selects only certain of the possible defense-mechanisms and invariably employs those which he has selected. This suggests that each individual Ego is endowed from the beginning with its own peculiar dispositions and tendencies, though we cannot predicate their nature and conditioning factors. Moreover, we know that we must not exaggerate the difference between inherited and acquired characteristics into an antithesis; that which has been acquired by our ancestors is certainly an important part of what we inherit. When we speak of "archaic inheritance" we are generally thinking only of the Id and apparently we assume that an Ego was non-existent at the beginning of the individual's life. But we must not overlook the fact that Id and Ego are originally one, and it does not imply a mystical overestimation of heredity if we think it credible that, even before the Ego exists, its subsequent lines of development, tendencies and reactions are already determined.

11. It is clear from the context that "intention" is used here in the sense of "intentionality" as Brentano (90) and Piaget (556) use it, and not as Ach and Lewin do in their papers included in this volume. "Intentionality" designates the directedness implicit in all mental activity. See Chap. 25, note 6, below.

tate or inhibit the individual's ability to master such conflicts. I propose that we adopt the provisional concept of *conflict-free ego-sphere* for functions, in a given individual or in general, *in so far* as they exert their actual effect outside of the realm of psychic conflicts. . . . The conflict-free sphere is not a province of the psyche, the development of which must by principle remain immune to conflicts, but rather processes *in so far* as they remain in the individual empirically outside of the sphere of psychic conflict. It is quite possible to delimit for both the cross-sectional and the longitudinal aspects of the individual psychic life, what lies within this conflict-free sphere. Thus far we do not have systematic psychoanalytic knowledge of this sphere. We have only partial knowledge of the reality-fears and defense-processes resulting in "normal" development, and of the contribution of the conflict-free sphere to the form varieties and results of defense (and resistance) and to the displacement of drive-aims, and so on. We do not need to prove that investigations *limited* to this sphere, as they in general are in academic psychology, must overlook fundamental psychological constellations.[12]

12. The concept of "conflict-free ego-sphere" is perhaps Hartmann's most important single contribution among the many in this rich and sweeping paper. This concept actually condenses two ideas: (a) ego-development has conflict-free as well as conflictual sources; (b) though any of these conflict-free sources, and any of their maturational products, may at various times become involved in conflict, they form the nucleus of that group of structures and functions within the ego which is at any given time "conflict-free."

Elaborating a further point pertinent here, and discussed by him below (pp. 374–75, and notes 40 and 69), in a later paper Hartmann (303) wrote:

Through what one could call a "change of function," what started in a situation of conflict may secondarily become part of the "conflict-free sphere." Many aims, attitudes, interests, structures of the ego have originated in this way. What devel-

oped as an outcome of defense against an instinctual drive *may* grow into a more or less independent and more or less structured function.

The significance of the concept of "conflict-free ego-sphere" can be best appraised if the past attitude of psychoanalysis toward the secondary-process thought is recalled (cf. Stekel, Chap. 14, above). Such thought, in so far as it was treated by psychoanalysis, was considered either rationalization, projection, displacement substitute, or product of "isolation" from affects, etc. This attitude was so pervasive that Hermann (328, 329, 327) who, more than any other psychoanalytic investigator, was involved in the study of thinking and logic, centered mainly in primary-process mechanisms in seeking the psychological roots of the laws of logic and thinking (329, 327). This is the more striking since he *did* conceive of relationship-experiencing as a specific ego-

. . . If we take seriously the claim of psychoanalysis to be a general theory of psychic development, we must study this area of psychology too, both in the course of analyses and in direct observation of infant development. At present the situation is the same for the conflict-free ego-sphere as it once was for the entire psychology of the ego. Ego-psychology used to be for psychoanalysis "that other realm" which, though one had to enter it at every turn, was not encompassed theoretically. This is still the case for the conflict-free ego-sphere. This boundary, too, will soon fall.

In dealing with the problem of adaptation we are concerned both with processes related to conflict situations and processes pertaining to the conflict-free sphere. . . . For instance, the study of the influence of special endowments on the distribution of narcissistic, object-libidinous, and aggressive energies, on the facilitation of certain forms of conflict-solution, and on the preferential choice of certain defense-processes is a clinically important and thus far insufficiently studied problem. . . .[13] The concrete study of many ego-disturbances in psychoses and of many psycho-physical interrelations must also take account of this conflict-free sphere. These problems cannot be completely resolved if only their drive and conflict aspects are considered.

Our knowledge of the ego began with the study of its defensive activities. . . .[14] However, psychoanalysis encountered problems which necessitated the study of other ego-functions and other aspects of ego-activity. . . .[15]

---

formation (328). Hartmann's concept has opened an avenue for psychoanalytic thinking to deal with thought-processes in terms other than rationalization, projection, etc. Thus he opened to psychoanalysis the realm of phenomena so far studied only by academic psychologists. He stressed, however, that the psychoanalytic study of these phenomena will include their overdetermination and their potentiality of becoming involved in conflict.

13. Concerning these "special endowments" (artistic, mechanical, and other gifts) cf. the passage from Freud (256) quoted above in note 10. See also the study by Bergman and Escalona (52)

which suggests innate differences in the strength of the "stimulus barrier" (see Chap. 16, note 11, above) and links the early development of "special gifts" and the precocity of ego-development to these differences.

14. See Anna Freud's (201) *The Ego and the Mechanisms of Defence*. Cf. also Freud's two early papers (202, 206), in which the concept of defense and several specific defense-mechanisms are already described.

15. Note, however, that even in his last major writing Freud (257, pp. 46–47) maintained:

An investigation of normal, stable states, in which the frontiers of the Ego are safe-

To use a simile: the description of a country, a nation, a state, includes besides its involvements in wars with the neighboring nations or states . . . its boundaries, the peacetime traffic across the borders, the development of the populace, the economy, the social structure, the administration, etc. A state may also be considered a system of institutions, whose effectiveness is expressed in legislation and jurisdiction, etc. . . . Our task would be to investigate how psychological conflict and "peaceful" internal development mutually facilitate and hamper each other. Similarly, the interplay between conflict and external development, such as that in various forms of "apperception" must also be studied.[16] Thus, to take a quite simple example, learning to walk upright com-

---

guarded against the Id by resistances (or anti-cathexes) and have held firm, and in which the Superego is not distinguished from the Ego because they work together harmoniously—an investigation of this kind would teach us little. The only things that can help us are states of conflict and rebellion, in which the material in the unconscious Id has a prospect of forcing its way into the Ego and into consciousness and in which the Ego arms itself afresh against the invasion. Only under such conditions can we make observations which will confirm or correct our views upon the two partners.

Yet Freud was also quite aware of these other aspects of ego-activity. He wrote (257, pp. 15-16):

Under the influence of the real external world which surrounds us, one portion of the Id has undergone a special development. From what was originally a cortical layer, provided with organs for receiving stimuli and with apparatus for protection against excessive stimulation, a special organization has arisen which henceforward acts as an intermediary between the Id and the external world. This region of our mental life has been given the name of *Ego*.

The principal characteristics of the Ego are these. In consequence of the relation which was already established between sensory perception and muscular action,

the Ego is in control of voluntary movement. It has the task of self-preservation. As regards *external* events, it performs that task by becoming aware of the stimuli from without, by storing up experiences of them (in the memory), by avoiding excessive stimuli (through flight), by dealing with moderate stimuli (through adaptation) and, finally, by learning to bring about appropriate modifications in the external world to its own advantage (through activity). As regards *internal* events, in relation to the Id, it performs that task by gaining control over the demands of the instincts, by deciding whether they shall be allowed to obtain satisfaction, by postponing that satisfaction to times and circumstances favorable in the external world or by suppressing their excitations completely.

16. It is noteworthy that Hartmann includes "apperception" under *peaceful* "external development." In earlier psychoanalytic theory the apperception and distortion of external reality was chiefly considered in terms of drives and conflicts. Thus, for example, Poetzl's (573) tachistoscopic experiments, demonstrating repression even in apperception, aroused widespread interest. Cf. also Rapaport (591, pp. 237 ff., particularly pp. 244-45).

bines two groups of processes. The first group comprises constitution, practice, maturation of the apparatus subserving walking, and learning processes. The second group includes libidinous processes, identifications, and drive and environmental factors, both endogenous and exogenous, which may lead to conflicts and to disturbances of function.[17]* None of these processes can alone explain this important step in development. It would, however, be an error to assume that the contrast of conflict-situation and peaceful development corresponds directly to the antithesis of pathological and normal. The normal human being is free neither of problems nor of conflicts. Conflicts are inherent to human existence. Naturally, the area and degree of influence of conflicts differ in pathological and normal cases. . . .[18] The most fruitful avenue to the problems of conflict was unquestionably (and for obvious reasons) the study of disturbed functions; but the exploration of the conflict-free sphere may use primarily the (direct and indirect) observation of undisturbed development.

[Passage omitted.] [19]

Some of the relationships between the drives and mental development are well known. We know that drive-conflicts and drive-taboos may hamper intellectual development temporarily or permanently. Yet Anna Freud [20] has also shown that intellectualization, representing an attempt to master the drive by indirect means, may serve as a defense against instinctual danger in puberty. The relation of this process to reality shows that this mechanism of defense has an aspect which may justifiably be considered an adaptation process. It is in this sense that Anna Freud says that instinctual danger may make a man wise. We are entitled to ask: what determines the choice of this path of drive-mastery? and what determines the degree to which any particular person will use intellectualization? [21] . . . It could scarcely be a mistake to assume the

17.* See Schmiedeberg (671).

18. Hartmann discusses the problem of normality more extensively in this paper than the present selection indicates. The concept of normality involves cardinal problems of ego-psychology and the theory of thinking. See particularly Jones (359), Glover (276), Hartmann (307) and Hacker (296); compare also Waelder (746) and Knight (390) on a specific aspect of the problem.

19. The omitted section discusses the change brought about by ego-psychology in the attitude of psychoanalysis toward education.

20. Anna Freud (201).

21. The application of the psychoanalytic findings and theories here referred to serves as the basis for the use of scatter-analysis (pattern-analysis) in psychodiagnostic intelligence testing. Cf. Rapaport (597) and Rapaport et al. (602, I, 37–43, 87–90, 129–31).

existence of an intelligence factor codetermining—as an independent variable
—the choice and success of this defensive process. Though we have some
understanding of these issues, our knowledge of them is certainly not systematic. Learning to think and learning in general are independent biological
functions which exist beside, and in part independently of, drives and defenses.

Ordered thinking is directly or indirectly reality-oriented.[22] Those typical
forms of defense against drives which result in heightened intellectual achievements, indicate that certain forms of conflict-solution are accompanied by a
biological guarantee of adaptation to external reality. This, naturally, does not
hold for all defense-processes. It holds for intellectualization generally and is
not restricted to puberty.

The intellectualization of drive life, the attempt to master drive processes by connecting them to ideas which can be handled in consciousness, belongs to the most
general, earliest and most necessary achievements of the human ego. It is an indispensable constituent of the ego, rather than merely one of its activities.[23*]

The description of this phenomenon as a defense does not fully define it; its
reality-oriented and adaptation-facilitating characteristics and regularities must
also be included.[24] The manner and extent of indirect regulation of defenses by

22. "Ordered thinking" here refers
clearly to the "secondary process." See
Freud (209, pp. 525 ff.) and Chap. 17,
note 20, above.

23.* Anna Freud (201) p. 178.

[Cf. also (201, pp. 172–80), devoted
to a discussion of intellectualization in
puberty. Anna Freud's formulation is
noteworthy since it suggests that connecting drives with thoughts "neutralizes" or "binds" the drive-energies and
that this process is not simply one of the
activities of the ego, but somehow its
essence. This touches on the obscure
issue of sublimation. Concerning "binding of energies" by the secondary process, see Rapaport (596), and Chap. 18,
note 13, above. Concerning "neutralization," see Hartmann, Kris and Loewenstein (311), and Hartmann (303).]

24. Cf. note 12, above. In a later paper
Hartmann (303) summarized evidence

(indicated also on p. 384, below) suggesting that the defense-mechanisms do
not make their first appearance as such,
but rather seem to arise from and be
modeled after some forms of instinctual
behavior (for instance, introjection), or
after reflexes, which he considers fore-
stages of autonomous ego-function (for
instance, closure of the eyelids on light
stimulation). He considers this formulation tentative and leaves open whether
we are dealing here with genetic connections or mere analogies.

He (303) concludes:

. . . It might well be that the ways in
which infants deal with stimuli—also the
functions of delaying, of postponing discharge . . . —are later used by the ego in
an active way. This active use for its own
purposes of primordial forms of reaction
we consider . . . a rather general characteristic of the developed ego.

ego-functions not related to conflicts will also be of interest. Mental development is not solely a result of the struggle with drives, with love-objects, with the superego, and so on. For one thing, we have reason to assume that there are preexisting apparatuses which serve this development; but about this, more later on. For another, memory, associations, and so on, are functions which cannot possibly be derived from the relationships of the ego to the drives or the love-objects; but rather are taken for granted in our conception of these relationships and their development.[25]

[Passage omitted.] [26]

In our clinical work we observe every day the effects of the differences in intellectual development, in motor development, and so on, on the child's manner of coping with conflicts and we note also how this in turn influences intellectual and motor development. Through such observations we establish descriptively the interaction of the conflict-sphere with other ego-functions. . . .[27]

. . . I need not remind you of the role of fantasy-formation, in the strict sense of the word, in the psychology of neuroses. In her recent volume Anna Freud [28] discusses the function of fantasy in the development of the child. She investigates the denial of reality by fantasy and shows that the child, refusing to accept a disagreeable bit of reality may, under certain conditions, deny its existence and replace it by fantasy-formations. This is a process well within the limits of normal ego-development. Anna Freud asks what determines whether this process becomes pathological. Presumably this depends on a number of factors. Among these, the degree of maturity of those ego-apparatuses of perception, of thinking, and particularly of causal thinking, and so on, which vouchsafe the relationship of the human being to his environment, certainly

25. The framework Hartmann creates here may be filled in partly by Piaget's considerations (Chaps. 6 and 7, above), in which the biological roots of intellectual functions are stressed. Cf. also Freud (Chap. 15, above), where he hints at the partial independence of memory from conflict: "At the same time there was probably introduced a system of *notation* . . . a part of that which we call *memory*."

26. In the omitted section Hartmann indicates that a thorough knowledge of the conflict-free sphere will enable one to judge ego-strength and ego-weakness independently from the outcome of conflicts. In his discussion he refers to Hendrick (321).

27. The omitted section stresses that the very same phenomena may be studied both as to their role in conflict and their adaptation value.

28. Anna Freud (201, pp. 73–88).

plays an outstanding role. Anna Freud said: "Perhaps it is generally true that the more mature the ego the stronger are its ties to reality." . . .[29]

. . . What are the adaptive elements of fantasy life? In answering this question we must keep in mind the fundamental biological significance of reality-testing, and particularly the distinction between fantasy and reality. Varendonck [30*] . . . is of the opinion that the biological significance of fantasy-thinking, in sharp contrast to dream-work, lies in its attempts to solve problems of waking life. . . . It is generally known that fantasy can be fruitful even in scientific thinking, which is the undisputed domain of rational thinking. Moreover it uses fantasy not merely as a combining agent but also as allegory-like, pictorial thinking. . . .[31] Not even the psychic life of healthy adults is ever free of some denial of reality, the denied reality being replaced by fantasy-formations. Consider, for example, religious ideas and the view people take of infantile sexuality.[32]

It is possible, and indeed probable, that the relationship to reality is learned by way of detours. There are reality-adaptations which at first certainly lead away from the real situation. The function of play is an example. . . .[33] Another example in point is the auxiliary function of fantasy in the learning

29. In the omitted section Hartmann stresses that without the study of the nature of the apparatuses mentioned it is not possible to gain an understanding of the role of fantasy. He refers to Jaensch's (352) studies on the relation of eidetic imagery and fantasy.

In discussing the nature of fantasy and its role in adaptation, Kris (Chap. 23, below) suggests that differences in cathexes are responsible for the difference between the two roles of fantasy, the one being reflecting, planning, and the fostering of reality-adaptation, and the other the expressing of id-wishes. The former uses neutralized energic-cathexes, while those of the latter are libidinous or aggressive cathexes, little or not at all neutralized. It may be conjectured that the maturity of the ego and the strength of its tie to reality are reflected in the kind and amount of energic-cathexes that the ego has available for use.

30.* Varendonck (740).
[Cf. also Varendonck, Chap. 22, and Kris, Chap. 23, below.]

31. In his paper "On Preconscious Mental Processes," Kris (Chap. 23, below) dwells on the role of fantasy in creative, artistic and scientific thinking. He describes the appearance of fantasy in these processes as a regressive phenomenon and concludes:

. . . many types of productive processes, from wit to art, and many other phenomena of inventiveness can be fully explained only if we assume that the ego regulates its own capacity to regression, that its organizing functions include the function of voluntarily and temporarily withdrawing cathexis from one area or the other, in order later to regain improved control.

32. Cf. Freud (223, pp. 17 ff.; and 218).

33. See the psychoanalytic symposium on play (173). In a personal communi-

process. Though fantasy always implies an initial turning away from a real situation, it can also be a preparation for the reality. . . . It may fulfill a synthetic function by provisionally connecting our needs and goals with possibilities of their realization. Those fantasies which separate the human being from external reality, but open internal reality to him are well known. . . . The primary function of these fantasies is autoplastic and not alloplastic; but we would be the last to deny the general importance of increased insight into intrapsychic life, and its particular importance in the mastery of the external world.

. . . Taking our point of departure from pathology, from the psychology of neuroses and psychoses, we have come to overestimate the positive developmental significance of the shortest pathways to reality, and it is only when we set out from the problem of reality-adaptation that we recognize the positive value of fantasy. . . .[34]

Denial is based on flight, and *avoidance* even more clearly so; Anna Freud has shown us how they both result in ego-limitation. But avoidance of the environment in which difficulties are encountered—and its positive correlate, the search for one offering easier and better possibilities for action—is also a most effective adaptation process. . . .[35]

[Passage omitted.] [36]

---

cation, Hartmann suggests that thinking, the outstanding example of detour-activity, might well have been discussed here. For Hartmann's discussion of this point in a later paper see note 71, below.

34. Hartmann means that psychoanalysis, impressed by loss of reality-testing in the neuroses and psychoses, came to overvalue realistic and rational thinking, while the study of reality-adaptation has demonstrated that not only realistic thinking, but fantasy—and, we may add, other forms of non-rational thought such as wishful thinking and empathy, as well as emotions—also play a crucial role in adaptation. Cf. Kris in note 31, above. The issue touched on here is a broad and important one. Shallow rationalism and pragmatism in philosophy also overestimate both the significance and the possibility of direct paths toward human goals, failing to recognize where such paths do not exist. Reason, like the cortex, does not always control all functions of the organism, and often resigns its controlling function in the interest of the whole organism.

35. Hartmann shows that the defense-mechanisms of denial and avoidance may have positive significance for adaptation. The adventurer-explorer, the pioneer settler, and the man of the frontier, are extreme but good examples of men maladjusted to their homeland who went out to find a new environment to which they could adjust. The socio-psychological and mental-health significance of this method of adaptation and the effects of the decreasing mobility of man in the world have so far been insufficiently appreciated.

36. The omitted section deals with the relation of rational and affective action, and with the relation of social science

II. [ADAPTATION]

[Passage omitted.]

Our considerations—particularly of the conflict-free ego-sphere—led us to those functions more or less closely related to the tasks of reality-mastery, that is to say *adaptation*. . . .

[Passage omitted.] [37]

. . . Adaptation, thus, is primarily a relationship, a reciprocal relationship of the organism and its environment. . . . It would be feasible to distinguish between a state of adaptation of organism and environment, and the *process of adaptation* which brings that state about. . . .[38]

Psychoanalysis is a tool by which we can discern those processes which bring about a state of adaptation between the individual and his environment through direct and active changes either of the environment or the person. We may also investigate the relationship between the adaptation processes and the pre-formed tools of human adaptation. These issues become more clear if we assume that adaptation (speaking mainly about man) is guaranteed both in its grosser and finer aspects, on the one hand, by the primary equipment of man and the maturation of the apparatuses, and on the other, by those actions directed by the ego which (using this equipment) actively improve the individual's relationship to the environment and balance the disturbances of this relationship. . . .[39]

---

and psychoanalysis. It suggests that the extension of the psychoanalytic theory to the conflict-free sphere will facilitate the coordination of the points of view of these two sciences. Cf. Hartmann (306).

37. The omitted section stresses that though adaptation has always been a central concept of psychoanalysis, it has so far been applied only to disorders of adaptation, while the mechanisms leading to successful adaptation were taken for granted. Hartmann points out that adaptation is a relation of *average expectable environment* and personality, and thus cannot be studied merely as a matter of the internal balance of the individual. He also maintains that the con-

cept of adaptation is modeled on the manner in which animals "fit in" with their environment. (This relationship of animal and environment was the center of interest of Uexkuell, 738, 737, and his school.)

38. In the omitted section Hartmann associates his views concerning "fitting in" in particular and adaptation in general with those of A. E. Parr (551) and dissociates them in some respects from those of Uexkuell (737).

39. Here Hartmann's previous assertion that the ego does not arise solely from the id and does not grow solely on the conflicts is given further content. The core of what is later "the conflict-

I have already shown that familiar processes considered from the point of view of adaptation often, but not always, appear in a new light. . . .[40]

A behavior which arose originally in the service of defense against a drive may in the course of time become an independently working structure. The drive then plays a triggering role in this automatized apparatus. . . . As long as this automatization is not suspended, the drive does not determine the course of events in detail. . . . Such an automatized apparatus may . . . by virtue of an alteration in function . . . change from being a means into a goal in its own right. . . .[41]

[Passage omitted.] [42]

---

free sphere" are the pre-formed tools of adaptation, the human equivalents of those mechanisms which guarantee "fitting-in" in animals. It follows that human adaptation has two facets: pre-formed tools (endowment, special talents, general apparatuses, such as memory, perception, etc.) and actions directed by the ego (such as defenses, syntheses, problem solving, etc.).

40. The omitted section deals with the concept of "functional change": "It is a familiar psychoanalytic conception that a form of behavior originating in a certain realm of life may in the course of development find application in a different realm and in an entirely different function."

41. In his later paper, "Ego Psychology," Hartmann (303) designates the independence of these automatized apparatuses as *secondary autonomy*, in contradistinction to the *primary autonomy* of inborn ego dispositions and apparatuses and their development.

Concerning automatization see further, Section VIII, below. Lewin (Chap. 5, p. 129 and pp. 141–42, above), also treats of such "automatizations." For both Hartmann and Lewin the explanation of habits is related to this concept

of "automatization." Hartmann implies that such automatized, independent, and conflict-free structures may be reabsorbed into the conflict-sphere: their automatization may be suspended. In other connections Hartmann indicates that some such automatizations may be irreversible. The issue is far from closed and requires study.

It seems that in Hartmann's conception such automatized apparatuses may be "triggered" by the drive, may subserve other functions, or may become goals in their own right. In the latter case, we may assume, they will be triggered by ego-regulations or reality-stimuli and will use ego-energies which are neutralized to various degrees. See notes 23, 29, above. In my commentary on Lewin's paper I have pointed out that automatization seems to be linked with the development of the hierarchy of ego-motivations; see Chap. 5, notes 92, 100, 42, above.

42. Part of the omitted section deals first with three methods of adaptation —autoplastic, alloplastic and the finding of new appropriate environments; and then with the contradictions between the adaptation of the individual and the species.

. . . The far-reaching possibility of putting drives, once they have been in-hibited, into the service of adaptation may be also considered pertinent here. . . . The long period of helplessness of the human child and the rela-tion of this period to the fact that in man a very essential part of the adapta-tion processes is acquired by learning, is of particular import in this connection. But the newborn human child is not devoid of all "instinctual equipment" (sucking, swallowing, eye-closure on light stimulation, crying), nor of much additional inborn equipment the greater part of which matures only later on (drives and ego-apparatuses). Yet the decisive fact remains that the "instinctual equipment" the newborn has ready for use is comparatively meager. . . .[43]

43. Hartmann compares here the in-stinctual equipment of human beings and animals. Below (Section IV) he makes the further point that the id and its drives do not correspond directly to the in-stincts of animals. In his paper "Com-ments on the Psychoanalytic Theory of Instinctual Drives" (301, p. 376), he en-larges on this point, quoting the biologist Myers (535):

What in a man can be compared to "in-stincts" one author states consists . . . far less essentially in the release of appropri-ate, inborn, mechanized reflexes, far less essentially in any stereotyped means of achieving certain "ends" than in the aware-ness . . . of those "ends," in the interests in and the desires . . . for them, in the "innate determining tendencies" evoked . . . and in the use of intelligence brought to bear in their achievement. . . . In man, indeed, intelligence has largely usurped the functions of specific inherited be-havior.

Hartmann comments (*ibid.*):

Some of the characteristics of human be-havior, which are often difficult to account for by the biological concept of instincts, coincide rather neatly with those phenom-ena which the analytic theory of drives was developed to cover: the relative inde-pendence from outer stimuli which makes

for a greater plasticity of adaptive be-havior; the greater variability of responses to inner stimuli; the continuity of the driv-ing forces; the fact that there is constant transformation of the energies we relate to the drives—therefore the relaxation of tension in one system has always to be considered in connection with the tensions in other systems, etc.

In the last passages of the present paper Hartmann advances the view that the ego does not arise from the id, the usual conception, but both are the result of a process of differentiation. Finally, jointly with Kris and Loewenstein (310, p. 19) he introduces the concept of the "undifferentiated phase," the common matrix of inborn endowment from which both id and ego arise, and develops further his concept of human instinct:

In introducing his concepts of psychic structure, Freud speaks of a gradual differ-entiation of the ego from the id; as an end result of this process of differentiation the ego, as a highly structured organization, is opposed to the id. Freud's formulation has obvious disadvantages. It implies that the infant's equipment existing at birth is part of the id. It seems however that the innate apparatus and reflexes cannot all be part of the id, in the sense generally accepted in psychoanalysis. We suggest a different as-

[Passage omitted.] [44]

. . . I would like to contrast here only two forms of adaptation, which differ widely in their prerequisites and consequences under certain conditions, but not always. I am referring to the *progressive* and *regressive* adaptations. The

sumption, namely that of an undifferentiated phase during which both the id and the ego gradually are formed. The difference is not merely one of words. The new formulation permits a better explanation of some of the basic properties of both id and ego. During the undifferentiated phase there is maturation of apparatuses that later will come under the control of the ego, and that serve motility, perception, and certain thought-processes. Maturation in these areas proceeds without the total organization we call ego; only after ego-formation will these functions be fully integrated. To the degree to which differentiation takes place man is equipped with a specialized organ of adaptation, that is, with the ego. This does not mean that there do not remain in the id certain elements that further the "maintenance" or preservation of the individual (Loewenstein, 482). However, the differentiation accounts for the nature of the instinctual drives of man, sharply distinguished as they are from animal instincts. One gains the impression that many manifestations of the id are further removed from reality than any comparable behavior of animals. The instincts of the animal (Lashley, 444) mediate its adjustment to the reality in which it lives and their properties determine the extent of the possible adaptation. With man, adjustment is mainly entrusted to an independent organization. One may raise the question whether, early in the infant's life, a residual equipment of "instincts" exists, that later loses its function of adjusting to the environment.

44. An outline of the final part of the omitted section is: (a) the theories concerning the role in adaptation of the prolonged helplessness of the human child; (b) the role of tradition and identification in adaptation; (c) the environment to which man adapts is society, in the building of which he himself partakes; (d) the individual's ego-development is controlled in part by the structure of society, which determines the adaptation-probabilities of various behavior-forms; (e) propensities which lead to difficulties in adaptation in one social group may fulfill socially essential tasks in another; (f) the mechanisms of human adaptation are multi-layered, ranging from regulations biologically pre-formed, to those effected by the organization of society; (g) it is spurious to contrast the biological and environmental factors in adaptation, since the biological factors also imply reference to and close coordination with the environment; (h) the distinction between the id and the ego as the biological and non-biological parts of the organism is spurious, since biology and psychology are merely two different methods of investigation, using two different sets of concepts; (i) the problem is not to distinguish the "biological" and "psychological" in development, but rather the congenital, maturational, and environmentally determined; (j) the issue of the exogenous or endogenous origin of changes in adaptation may be reduced to the question of whether the external events to which the organism responds are within the range of average expectation, that is whether the organism has already developed methods of adaptation for coping with them.

term progressive adaptation is self-explanatory; it is an adaptation in the direction of development. Yet there are adaptations—successful, and not mere attempts at adaptation—which use the pathways of regression. . . . Even certain purposeful achievements of healthy people on a high level of adaptation may require a detour through regression. This is possible because the functioning of the most highly differentiated organ of reality-adaptation cannot alone guarantee an optimal total adaptation of the organism. . . .[45] [For example] fantasy is always rooted in the past, but by connecting past and future, it becomes under certain conditions the basis for setting realistic goals. Other examples are the picture-like symbolic elements familiar in productive scientific thinking and poetry as well as any other form of artistic activity and experience. . . . Kris speaks of "regression in the service of the ego." [46]

III. [ADAPTATION AND EGO-APPARATUSES]

The relationship of the individual to his environment is "disturbed" from moment to moment and must again and again be returned to an equilibrium. An "equilibrium" is not necessarily normal; it may also be pathological.[47] (It

45. See note 34. Compare also the related conclusion of comparative developmental psychology. H. Werner (755, p. 39) wrote:

. . . It is quite misleading to define the difference between the man of lower and the one of higher civilization by contending that the one exhibits a primitive behavior and the other does not. The distinguishing mark of the advanced type is that an activity at a higher level is at his disposal which includes, rather than excludes, primitive activity.

46. Hartmann's bibliographic reference is to Kris's (431) paper on the psychology of caricature. Cf. also note 31 above. Kris, returning to this problem in his various papers, goes so far as to consider the ego's ability to suspend its usual function and to give way to more primitive, regressive forms of function —as it does in dreams, sexual intercourse, creative inspiration, and daydreams—an

important indication of ego-strength. Cf. Kris (428), Kris and Pappenheim (434). These considerations are of importance for the psychology of creative thinking and may even point to methods for the exploration of the relation between primary- and secondary-process thinking.

47. These statements are generalizations of the psychoanalytic view of psychodynamics. Freud, like Fechner, considered the psychic apparatus a system of energy-distributions tending toward equilibrium on the level of the lowest potential possible under the given conditions. Stimulations (internal and external) cause "tension," that is disequilibrium, which in turn initiates a process directed toward restoring the equilibrium (wish, wishfulfillment). (Cf. Freud, 209, pp. 503, 533; Freud, 241; and Rapaport, 595.) Hartmann here generalizes this equilibrium-theory to the in-

would obviously be meaningless to label every disturbance of equilibrium a conflict. This would rob the concept of any precision. Every stimulus disturbs the equilibrium, but not every stimulus causes conflict.[48] These processes therefore occur partly in the conflict-free sphere.) Apparently there are in every organism mechanisms for maintaining or reestablishing equilibrium. . . . Of course, tensions arise within the organism also, and not only in its relations to the outside world. I will assume that the relationships of these tensions to the Freudian regulation principles (pleasure-principle, reality-principle, nirvana-principle), and the relationship of repetition-compulsion to instinct and to the ability to regenerate, and so forth are well known.[49] I need not mention here how the repetition-compulsion may serve adaptation, as for instance, in traumatic neuroses. . . .[50] Psychoanalytic experience has also taught us, however,

---

dividual-environment relation conceived as an organic whole. This generalized view, however, is transparently analogous with Lewin's tension-system dynamics and his thesis that behavior always is determined by both personality and environment, though the tensions of which Lewin speaks are on a different level of motivational dynamics and the observations he interprets are also different from those of psychoanalysis.

Hartmann's point, that an equilibrium may be pathological as well as normal, opens up an important issue. The psychological equilibria with which we are concerned do not constitute complete discharges of tension. They are but equilibria on the lowest possible tension-level (potential) attainable under the given psychological conditions. The very existence of psychic structure implies the maintenance of a basic tension-level by virtue of continuous delay of discharge, ego-control by means of defenses, and elaboration of the products of the primary by the secondary process. Pathological conditions contribute to the maintenance and heightening of the basic tension-level by preventing

tension-discharge which would be otherwise possible. Indeed the necessity in psychology for structural concepts, in addition to those of energy-dynamics, arises from the fact that tensions cannot be completely discharged but can only reach equilibrium on various levels. This point is well illustrated by Freud's (209) description of the secondary process: "It effects an *inhibition* of this outflow [of excitation], a transformation into dormant cathexis, probably with a rise of potential" (p. 534). It seems possible that the considerations on "bound" cathexes can be related to recent speculations of physicists concerning the role of "negative entropy" in life phenomena. Compare Schroedinger (673) and Brillouin (94).

48. Lewin would put it thus: the tension systems (disequilibria) created by stimuli are relatively segregated from the tension systems of basic needs (drives). Cf. Lewin, Chap. 5, II, 1, D 3), above.

49. For a systematic discussion of these concepts see Bibring (61).

50. See the symposium on war neuroses (260) and Freud (241).

that, because of the complex structure of the psychic apparatus, internal disturbances lead very easily to disturbances in reality-relationships.[51] Besides the equilibrium between individual and environment, our knowledge of the psychological apparatus permits us to discern two additional relatively well defined states of equilibrium. . . . These are the equilibrium between drives (vital equilibrium) and the equilibrium between psychological institutions (structural equilibrium). . . . Actually, yet a fourth equilibrium should be added: that between the synthetic function and the rest of the ego, since the ego is not merely a resultant and its synthetic function is, so to speak, a specific organ of equilibrium at the disposal of the person. . . .[52]

[Passage omitted.] [53]

Let us now return to the principles of regulation. Our intention is to demonstrate the relative independence of ego development. . . . There are undoubtedly reactions in which the pleasure-principle serves self-preservation. . . . Yet, as Freud puts it, "it is a long way from the pleasure-principle to the drive of self-preservation." [54] Psychoanalysis has impressed upon us the extent to which the pleasure-principle disturbs adaptation.[55] This may easily

51. See Freud (246 and 245).

52. A more recent paper by Hartmann (303) seems to suggest that this fourth equilibrium may be conceived more broadly than one between the synthetic function (Nunberg, 543) and the rest of the ego. Hartmann wrote (303):

So far we have come to see ego development as a result of three sets of factors: inherited ego characteristics, influences of the instinctual drives, and influences of external reality; to these we have to add as a fourth factor the influences different functions of the ego exert on each other.

Thus it may not be incorrect to formulate that the fourth equilibrium is one between the various ego-functions.

53. In the omitted section Hartmann shows that "fitting-in" and "adaptation" (cf. note 39, above) are mutually dependent on each other. He finds that the synthetic function represents this relationship on the ego level. In this connection Hartmann notes that adaptation-failures due to primary (congenital and maturational) disorders of the ego-apparatuses have as yet been scarcely studied. (We may add that the most extensive studies of the secondary—acquired—disorders of these apparatuses are those of Schilder, noteworthy among which are his studies in general paresis, included in this volume. Freud considered that war-neuroses arise as a result of a secondary disorder of such an ego-apparatus, namely of the "stimulus barrier." See Freud, 241 and 250. Bergman and Escalona, 52, described childhood schizophrenias which seemed to suggest an explanation in terms of a primary disorder of the "stimulus barrier." Study of congenital cases of deafness, blindness and muteness may shed light on these problems.)

54. The role of instincts in adaptation is discussed more fully in a later paper by Hartmann (301).

55. Cf. Freud (241, pp. 5 and 67).

seduce us to underestimate its significance in the mastery of the external world. Since Freud's "Two Principles" [56] we know the extent to which the reality-principle replaces or modifies the pleasure-principle in man. In another, and not less fundamental paper, "Negation," [57] Freud continues with these considerations and discusses the essentials of reality-testing and the relationship of thinking to perception (compare also Ferenczi,[58]). How this modification into the reality-principle could, so to speak, be foisted upon the pleasure-principle has still not been answered unequivocally.[59] We understand that the psychic apparatus must search the external world for pleasure possibilities as soon as its needs exceed a certain measure and can no longer be satisfied by fantasy. The turn toward reality may also be a defense against anxieties aroused by fantasies and may serve to control anxiety. In both cases the turn to the external world and the compulsion to recognize it are still under the auspices of the pleasure-principle. The individual trades pleasure for displeasure or a greater pleasure for a lesser one. However, the reality-principle has an essential implication besides the increased regard for the external world. "A momentary pleasure of doubtful consequences is given up, but only to gain thereby a later, secure pleasure." . . .[60] We know that the reality-principle is, in a sense, a pursuit of the pleasure-principle by other means. But this step—the ability to renounce immediate pleasure-gain in order to secure a greater one in the future—cannot be derived from the pleasure-principle alone; not even memories of pain experiences suffice to explain it. . . .[61]

We are, however, familiar with the function of anticipating the future and orienting our actions according to it (and with the function of relating means

56. Freud (223), Chap. 15, above.

57. Freud (248), Chap. 17, above.

58. Ferenczi (183).

59. From the point of view of cathectic dynamics we have a slender thread of evidence which may contribute to the understanding of the establishment of the reality-principle. Freud refers to this when he conjectures (234, p. 114) that in repression the cathexis withdrawn from the instinct-derivative is used as the counter-cathexis to keep it out of consciousness. This would suggest that, when reality prevents discharge, the undischarged tension is turned into a controlling energy-distribution, which becomes a representation of reality. Hartmann (303) and Rapaport (596, 595), discuss this issue in some detail.

60. See Freud, Chap. 15, p. 328, above. Cf. also Freud (209, pp. 533–34 and 535–36).

61. In the omitted section Hartmann discusses attempts to explain the origin of the reality principle. He points up the weaknesses of both French's (198) attempt to explain it invoking the repetition-compulsion and Ferenczi's (183) attempt to explain it by the role of masochism.

and ends correctly to each other). It is a function of the ego and certainly an adaptation-process of the highest significance. We are entitled to assume that ego-development enters this process [of accepting the reality-principle] as an independent variable, though naturally the ego-function in question here may secondarily yield pleasure.[62]

[Passage omitted.] [63]

We saw that the modification of the pleasure-principle into the reality-principle . . . does not come about by itself but rather presupposes a certain level of [independent] development of the ego. . . .

. . . There are no drives in man which would in and of themselves guarantee

---

62. In dynamic terms this means that while the ego controls the discharge of drive-energies (superimposing the reality-principle upon the pleasure-principle), its own activity also amounts to the discharge of energy at its disposal (pleasure). Summarizing Freud's views, Hartmann (303) wrote in a later paper:

In the development toward reality, the pleasure possibilities offered by the developing ego functions, love and other rewards gained from the object, and at a later stage the gratification arising from the renunciation of instinctual satisfaction are all essential.

Freud (214) in his "Wit and Its Relation to the Unconscious" wrote specifically:

When our psychic apparatus does not actually act in search of some urgently needed gratifications, we let this apparatus itself work for pleasure gain. We attempt to gain pleasure from its very activity.

These considerations show that though the ego controls the drive-energies and prevents or delays their regulation by the pleasure-principle, the ego's energies themselves (or at least part of them) abide by that same principle. Some light is shed on this point by Hartmann (303) when he writes:

Aggressive as well as sexual energy may

be neutralized. . . . Theoretical as well as clinical considerations speak in favor of assuming that there are gradations in the neutralization of these energies, that not all of them are "indifferent" to the same degree.

All these conclusions, inferences, and speculations are of import for the psychology of thinking, since the motivations of thought-processes range from drives to routine "interests" and the dependence of thought-organization on the kind of motivation underlying it is still entirely unexplored.

63. In the omitted section Hartmann introduces a broader concept of reality-testing, which relates to the familiar narrow one as adaptation does to "fitting-in." See notes 39 and 53, above. "Fitting-in" and reality-testing in the broader sense are conceived as biological givens coordinating the organism with its environment; adaptation and reality-testing in the narrower sense are acquired. Hartmann apparently implies that reality-testing cannot be understood without taking into consideration its broader (biological) aspect. This is the implication of his statement that ego-development enters the process of accepting the reality-principle as an independent variable.

adaptation, yet on the average the whole ensemble of drives, ego-functions, ego-apparatuses, and the principles of regulation, as they meet the average expectable environmental conditions, do have survival value. Of these elements, the function of the ego-apparatuses—is "objectively" the most purposeful. . . .

Secondarily the functions of all these psychological and physical ego-apparatuses do become points of departure for the pleasure-principle. . . . The pleasure possibilities of the apparatuses of the conflict-free ego-sphere seem to play a very significant role in the adaptation to the external world. (The opening of such new pleasure sources furthers ego-development.) . . . Let us consider somatic processes of maturation: just as the phases of libido-development depend upon somatic maturation processes, for instance the sadistic and anal impulses develop "certainly in relation to the appearance of teeth, growth of musculature and control of sphincters," [64] so too is ego-development dependent on the somatic maturation of certain apparatuses. . . . In the course of ego-development there occur changes in the sources and character of pleasure. The pleasure-potentialities afforded at the various levels of development by the ego, its functions, and apparatuses are of great significance for the stability of ego-organization, its effectiveness, and the kind and extent of its functions (synthesis, defense, assimilation, learning ability, etc.). . . . [65]

IV. [DEVELOPMENT AND ADAPTATION]

. . . We cannot speak about a differentiation of an ego and an id in animals in the same sense as we do in human adults. . . . The more precise division of labor between the ego and the id in adult man . . . *increases the alienation of the id from reality*. In animals these two institutions, ego and id, would be closer to a middle position in regard to reality. . . . Reality relationships pre-form the aims and means of gaining pleasure in lower animals to a greater extent than

64. Freud (255).
65. Cf. note 62, above.
The omitted section indicates that while the ego is strengthened by the pleasure-gain from its own activities, the sexualization (libidinization) of these activities may lead to their inhibition. In terms of cathectic-dynamics we would say: ego-functions which are invested with drive-cathexes instead of cathexes of various degrees of neutralization leave the conflict-free sphere and become involved in conflict. In the field of the psychology of thinking, obsessional rumination and other forms of excessive intellectualizing are examples. Cf. Fenichel (176, pp. 179–84, 295–300, 311–15), also Chap. 26, notes 60 and 107, below.

in man. Therefore, one must be particularly cautious in drawing phylogenetic inferences from observations made on the human child.[66]

Besides, the newborn infant is not wholly a creature of drives; he has inborn apparatuses (perceptual and protective mechanisms) which function purposively and perform a part of those functions which, after the differentiation of ego and id, belong to the ego. A state of adaptation exists before processes of adaptation begin to function. . . . Defenses also already exist on the instinctual level though not in their common and narrower sense.[67] Ego-development is a differentiation, in which these primitive regulating factors are increasingly replaced or supplemented by more effective regulating factors. . . . Differentiation progresses not only through the mastery of new demands and tasks by creating new apparatuses, but mainly by the latter taking over, on a higher level, functions which were originally carried out by more primitive regulations. . . .[68]

[Passage omitted.] [69] Moreover, the human individual possesses at his birth an inventory of psychic dispositions as yet unexplored in detail. These are con-

66. Cf. note 43, above, for references to Hartmann's later elaboration of this point.

67. Cf. note 24, above.

68. Hartmann's persistent effort to broaden the framework of psychoanalytic psychology so as to coordinate it with biology becomes most clear at this point. (His efforts to coordinate it with general psychology and sociology we have already seen above.) The clarification of the relation between drive and instinct, the conception of inborn apparatuses which are the precursors of the concept "undifferentiated phase," the description of the development of ego-regulations in a manner analogous to the "progressive cerebralization" of functions, all serve to establish the continuity with biology. The collation of these conceptions with those of Piaget (Chaps. 6 and 7, above) will show the perspicacity of Hartmann's theorizing. In the relation between drive-dynamics and the specifics of the inborn apparatus it is Hartmann who emphasizes the former and Piaget the latter, while the continuity with biology is stressed by the concepts of both.

The conceptual patterns Hartmann uses here are not dissimilar from those used in recent biological writing on the integration of the theories of genetics and evolution. See Simpson (696, 695).

69. The omitted section states that the ego-functions come about: (a) as functional changes of more primitive regulations; (b) as new regulations arising in the course of development; (c) as the maturation of apparatuses which, together with the drive-constitution, are ontogenetic givens. Hartmann refers to Bally's (35) and Loewy's (483) studies on the role of the motor-apparatus in ego-development.

stitutional factors of importance in ego-development; for instance, according to Brierley [70] there is a constitutional factor in the individual differences of anxiety-tolerance. . . . I want to stress . . . that defense-processes may *simultaneously* serve both drive-control and adjustment to the external world. . . . The ego serves adaptation, inhibition and synthesis. . . .[71]

[Passage omitted.] [72]

It is known that the development of the psychic structure also serves adapta-

70. See Brierley (93).

71. In a later paper Hartmann (303, pp. 2–4) summarized the functions of the ego as follows:

Which functions do we attribute to the ego? The catalog would be a long one, longer than the catalog of functions of either the id or the superego. No analyst has ever endeavored to give a complete listing of ego-functions, nor is it among the aims of my presentation to give one. Here I shall mention only some of the most important ones. You know that among them Freud has always emphasized those which center around the relation to reality: "the relation to the external world is decisive for the ego" (Freud). The ego organizes and controls motility and perception—perception of the outer world but probably also of the self (we think that self-criticism, though based on self-perception, is a separate function which we attribute to the superego). The ego tests reality. Action, also, in contradistinction to mere motor discharge, and thinking, which is according to Freud trial action with small quantities of psychic energy, are functions of the ego. Both imply an element of inhibition, of delay of discharge. In this sense many aspects of the ego can be described as detour activities; they promote a more specific and safer form of adjustment by introducing a factor of growing independence from the immediate impact of present stimuli. In this trend toward what we may call internalization, the danger signal is also in-

cluded, besides other functions that can be described as anticipatory. I also want to remind you here of what Freud thought about the relation of the ego to time perception. From what I just said it already appears that a large sector of the ego's functions can also be described from the angle of its inhibiting nature. You know that A. Freud speaks of a primary enmity of the ego vis-à-vis the instinctual drives; and the ego function most extensively and intensively studied in analysis, that is, defense, is a specific expression of its inhibiting nature. Another set of functions we attribute to the ego is what we call a person's character. And still another one that we can conceptually distinguish from those mentioned so far are the coordinating or integrating tendencies known as the synthetic function. These, together with the differentiating factors, we can comprise in the concept of an organizing function; they represent one level (not the only or the earliest one) of self-regulation in man. While speaking of the reality aspect of the ego, or of its inhibiting, or its organizing nature, etc., we are of course aware of the fact that its specific activities may and actually do express many of these characteristics at the same time.

72. The omitted section discusses that the newborn infant is adapted to its environment, but shows no adaptation processes in the usual sense; it would perish under other than average expectable conditions.

tion. This is true by definition for the differentiation of the ego and the id, but it also holds for the identifications which build the superego. . . .[73] Thinking, and particularly causal thinking, implies not only synthesis and fitting-in, but also differentiation. We are dealing here with the coexistence of differentiation and integration (see, for example, Werner,[74]) so familiar in biology. The formation of the psychic institutions is not the only psychological expression of the development of this function of differentiation; it also expresses itself in reality-testing, judgment, the broadening of the perceptual- and action-world, the separation of perception from imagery, of cognition from affect, and so on. Precocity of differentiation or relative retardation of synthesis may disrupt the balance of these two functions. When we speak of the precocity of ego-development, we often mean the precocity of these differentiation-processes.[75] Together with the synthetic function this differentiation-function must also be recognized as an important achievement of the ego. . . .

[Passage omitted.] [76]

v. [THOUGHT-PROCESSES AND ADAPTATION]

The development of organisms, described here as a process of progressively increasing "internalization," results in the formation of a central regulating factor which is usually referred to as the "inner world." [77] This internal world is interpolated between the receptors and the effectors. We are familiar with

73. See Freud (243, pp. 34–53; 255, pp. 82–112; and 257, pp. 16–17).
In the omitted section Hartmann refers to the views of Rado (586) and Nunberg (543) concerning this point. He also demonstrates the significance of differentiation processes in ego-development (Cf. note 71, above.)

74. Werner (755).

75. Bergman and Escalona (52) felt that in the cases of infantile schizophrenia which they studied as well as those described by Kanner (366), the special sensitivity and precocity was a compensation by differentiation for the weakness of the "stimulus barrier." Cf. notes 13 and 53, above.

76. The omitted section may be out-lined as follows: (a) Neurotic disturbances of adaptation are in essence also adaptations and may or may not have survival value. (b) Ego-functions have a rank-order of biological purposiveness. Ego-strength depends on this rank-order as much as on the customary criteria of the ego's relation to the plasticity of drives and its tolerance for tensions. (c) The understanding of both adaptation disturbances and ego-function rank-orders depends on the thorough exploration of the conflict-free ego-sphere.

77. The concept "inner world" (analogous to K. Lewin's "private world") may seem to be merely a new term for familiar facts. Actually it is a predecessor of the concept of "self" Hartmann (303)

it in human adults as a regulating factor in the ego. The width of the subjective world, the degree of sensitivity to experiences, and many other differentiation products show inter-individual differences. . . .[78]

[Passage omitted.] [79]

The biological utility of the internal world is obvious in adaptation, in differentiation, and in synthesis. We shall discuss this utility, but first let us cast a cursory glance at the biological meaning of thought-processes, the relevant elements in this connection being perception, reproduction, imagery, thinking and action. . . . The inner world and its processes together create a bipolar adaptation-relation: withdrawal from the external world is for the purpose of better mastery over it. The fact that goals are not directly attacked but that detours (means) are interpolated, is a decisive step in development. . . . The development of consciousness does not completely coincide with the development of the inner world. Freud has stressed the social significance of consciousness. Perhaps W. Stern is right in considering consciousness the expression of conflict. . . .[80]

The world of thought and the world of perception are two factors in ego-regulation which need not coincide at every point. Perception and ideas orient us in a world of spatial-temporal images. Thinking frees man from the immediate perceptual situation. Reproduction and imagery are of course preparations for this process.[81] Exact science, the highest form of thinking, attempts to exclude all images and qualities from this world of thought. Psychoanalysis was the first psychology to make a serious attempt to exclude conscious qualities.[82] Nevertheless, in many situations images do play a regulative role in human action. Both these worlds have a specific relation to action, since both thought . . . and image . . . carry a tendency to action.[83]

---

defined in a later paper. It is used here to give body to the result of the process of internalization.

78. On "internalization," see also note 71, above.

79. The omitted section discusses the "stimulus barrier" and the fact that there is no such barrier in relation to drives. See Freud (250), also Chap. 16, note 11, above.

80. For Freud's theory of conscious-ness, see Chap. 16, note 14, above. For the social nature of consciousness see Sullivan (725, 726), also Piaget, Chap. 6, notes 21 and 16, above.

81. For Freud's theory of thinking see his "Two Principles," Chap. 15, particularly note 29, above. Cf. also Freud (209, Chapter VII); Freud (248), this volume, and Rapaport (596).

82. Cf. note 9, above.

83. Cf. Schilder, Chap. 25, I, c, below.

Let us consider more closely the relation of the thought function to the tasks of adaptation, synthesis, and differentiation. . . . In these considerations we will have to disregard much that we know about thinking—for instance, its use of desexualized libido, its conjectured relation to the death-instinct, its role as helper (rationalization) or opponent of the id, its dependence on cathectic-energy, its facilitation or inhibition by processes of drive and affect and by the superego, and so on. . . .

Freud states that the ego achieves a delay of motor-discharge by interpolating thought-processes.[84] This process is obviously one aspect of the more general development we have already described, namely that by differentiation organisms become more independent of immediate environmental stimulations. Thinking was also described by Freud as experimental action using small quantities of energy.[85] This description elucidates both the biological function of thinking and its relation to action. It appears that in organisms of higher order, trial-activity is increasingly displaced into the interior of the organism; the preparatory trials no longer appear in the form of motor-actions toward the external world. . . .

The intellect implies an enormous extension and differentiation of reaction-possibilities; it subjects the reactions to its selective control; it creates and utilizes means-end relationships. By means of causal thinking connected with space- and time-perception, and particularly by turning his thinking back upon the self, the individual liberates himself from his slavery to the stimulus-reaction compulsion of the immediate here and now.[86] The intellect understands and invents; according to some views its function is more to pose than to solve problems; [87] it decides whether the individual is to accept the reality of an event or is to change it by his intervention (alloplastic adaptation); it seeks to control and to steer the repetitive character of instincts and drives. The intellect creates derivative needs; it turns means into ends and ends into means. . . .[88]

[Passage omitted.] [89]

---

84. See Freud, Chap. 15, particularly note 29, above.

85. See Freud, Chap. 15, pp. 324–25, above; and Freud (209, pp. 533–34).

86. See Hartmann (303) concerning the concept of self and its differentiation from the concept of the ego.

87. Delacroix (139).

88. Cf. Lewin, Chap. 5, note 49, above.

89. In the final part of the omitted section Hartmann reviews various theories concerning the nature and biological significance of intelligence. He stresses that while all intellectual func-

. . . We consider that the typical and individual vicissitudes of drives determine the possibilities and limitations of knowledge; we consider intellectual achievements as the means for solving conflicts as well as for rationalizing; we consider these intellectual achievements in relation to the demands of the external world and the superego—and in their interaction with other ego-functions.[90] In analyzing inhibitions, neuroses, and particularly psychoses, we became familiar with all degrees of disorder of various intellectual functions. While it is true that severe disorders of intellection occur only in psychoses, milder, mostly temporary and reversible disorders frequently occur in other forms of psychological illnesses. Each one of the intellectual functions we enumerated may be disturbed: selective control, thinking in terms of time, reality-testing, objectivation, abstraction, ability to delay,[91] and so on. A specific failure of adaptation corresponds to the disturbance of each of these functions.[92]

I would like to digress to discuss the nature of the thought-process in the course of psychoanalytic treatment, in which the object of thinking is the subject himself in a specific sense. Since, even when it is the object of action, the person is always the means of action, the function of thought is here fundamentally the same as when the external world is its object. Psychoanalytic work shows that insight into one's own behavior depends on the assimilation of

---

tions are ego-functions, the intellect is not identical with the ego. He maintains with Hermann (326) that a person's adaptivity is not proportionate to his intelligence. He points out with McDougall (492) that no sharp dividing line can be drawn between instinct (drive) and intellect.

90. This is Hartmann's most important single statement concerning the place of thought-processes in the psychic apparatus. It states that, in final analysis, drives are limiting principles of thought: where there are no drives, drive-derivatives, or neutralized drive-energies, there are no thoughts; that thoughts subserve the ego by solving conflicts and the id by rationalizations; that they serve to meet the demands of reality and the superego; and that they interact with the other ego-

functions, such as defenses, synthetic and differentiating regulations, and ego-interests, and are motivated and limited, or at least tagged and colored by them.

91. Straecke (718).

92. Our knowledge concerning these thought-disorders in neuroses derives from clinical observations, which are of necessity fragmentary. In fact, so far no attempt has been made to collate the recorded clinical observations on these thought-disorders. But psychodiagnostic testing has gathered some systematic pertinent material. See, for example, Rapaport et al. (602). In fact not even the disorders of thought in psychoses have been systematically explored. See our comments on Bleuler, Chap. 26, below.

unconscious tendencies both of the ego and the id.[93] Nunberg [94] has shown particularly convincingly that the synthetic function of the ego directs these assimilation-processes. Defenses not only keep thoughts, images, and drive-impulses out of consciousness, but also prevent their assimilation by the thought-organization.[95] When the defensive processes are eliminated, the psychic ele-

---

93. Concerning the unconscious parts of the ego, see Freud (243) and (255). It is not clear why Hartmann does not include here the superego.

94. Nunberg (540).

95. Defenses either render thoughts unconscious (repression), whereupon they become subject to the laws governing the primary process, or by displacement, denial, or isolation, subject them to vicissitudes akin to those of the primary process, without necessarily rendering them unconscious. All these processes transform thoughts so that they take the form of isolated, concrete memories and lose their relationships to other thoughts. Freud (243, p. 23) wrote:

The study of dreams and of preconscious fantasies on the lines of J. Varendonck's observations gives us an idea of the special character of this visual thinking. We learn that what becomes conscious is as a rule only the concrete subject-matter of the thought, and that the relations between the various elements of this subject-matter, which is what specially characterizes thought, cannot be given visual expression. Thinking in pictures is, therefore, only a very incomplete form of becoming conscious.

Cf. also Freud (209, p. 493):

If we look upon the dream as a process of regression within the hypothetical psychic apparatus, we have at once an explanation of the empirically proven fact that all thought-relations of the dream-thoughts are either lost in the dream-work or have

difficulty in achieving expression. According to our scheme, these thought-relations are contained not in the first memory-systems, but in those lying farther to the front, and in the regression to the perceptual images they must forfeit expression. *In regression the structure of the dream-thoughts breaks up into its raw material.*

It is obvious that without relationships to other thoughts no assimilation and integration with the contents of the systems Preconscious and Conscious can take place. Hermann (328), under the influence of the Wuerzburg School and its "imageless thought relationships" (compare Chaps. 1 and 2, above), was so impressed by the loss of relationships in primary-process thinking that he hypothesized a special "relationship-system," within the System Perception-Preconscious–Conscious posited by psychoanalysis. Hermann (328, p. 5) wrote:

The conclusion of *The Interpretation of Dreams*, that in the manifest dream the judgments and relationships of thinking are contained only in so far as they are perceptually represented, shows that this relationship-system can be without cathexis even when the perception system is well cathected. Ideas of reference and the strongly formal nature of schizophrenic thinking suggest that this relationship-system can also become independently hypercathected. Certain special talents, such as logical and mathematical, could be conceived of as intensive cathexis and higher organization of this relationship-system.

ments and connections which they had warded off become amenable to memory and reconstruction. Interpretation helps us not only to regain hidden material but must also reconstruct the correct causal relations of the elements of this material—their causes, forces, and range of influence on other elements of experience. . . .[96]

. . . In the course of the psychoanalytic process one learns to face one's own psychic contents as objects of experience and thought and to consider them as parts of a causal network. Thus, psychoanalysis proves to be the highest development of thinking directed toward the inner life, in that it changes and regulates both adaptation and fitting-in.

[Passage omitted.] [97]

VI

[Section omitted.] [98]

96. In the omitted section Hartmann shows that psychoanalytic therapy does not only *recover*, but also *discovers* relationships. (Cf. Bergman, 51.) The discovery of relationships implies not only the re-discovery of the repressed relationships that existed in childhood, but also the discovery of relationships which the recovered material should have within the system of relationships of the grown-up individual. He also points out that repression is present in normal adults and that such repression is not necessarily pathological. Lack of self-perception is not self-deception, except where the self is the object of the intended knowledge. Self-deception is always accompanied by a misunderstanding of the external world. (Cf. Sullivan, 725).

97. The omitted section discusses the problems of "rational action." For an extended discussion of this issue see Hartmann (306).

98. Section VI of Hartmann's paper may be outlined as follows: (a) The concern of psychoanalysis with the steering role of drives resulted in centering its attention in the dependence of will and ego-interests on needs, and diverted it from their autonomous role. [Cf. Hartmann, 303, on ego-interests, a concept which overlaps if it is not identical with that of "attitudes" (24, 129) and "ego-involvements" (686) of academic psychology, and which is fundamental to the study of the hierarchy of motivations of thought-processes. Cf. our comments on Lewin (Chap. 5, notes 43, 49, 135, 140, above), and Buerger-Prinz and Kaila, Chap. 27, note 31, below.] (b) The hierarchy of values belongs in part to the conflict-free sphere. While values are derived from social value-hierarchies, their selection and development have their own genetic history in the individual. They are synthetic achievements of and play a role in mastering anxiety. They may or may not be such as to gain social rewards or be in harmony with the interests of society [Miller and Dollard, 521, and Mowrer and Kluckhohn, 525, and other theories of the conditioned-

VII

[Section omitted.] [99]

VIII. [AUTOMATIZATION, AUTONOMY AND EGO-APPARATUSES]

[Passage omitted.] [100]

. . . In action the ego uses somatic apparatuses. I will first discuss the motor-apparatuses. In adults these are organized for certain achievements. If these are well-established achievements, the motor-apparatus functions automatically, and the coordination of both the somatic systems and the specific psychic acts involved in the action is automatized. With increasing exercise of the action, the mediating links disappear from consciousness.[101] Observation of such phenomena led Kretschmer [102] to postulate a law of "formular abbreviation." . . .[103]

Not only the motor-apparatus, but also perception and thinking show *automatization*. Exercise automatizes methods of problem-solving just as much as it does walking, speech, or writing. . . . The idea of a thoroughly flexible ego is a grossly idealized conception; yet normally even well-established actions and methods of thought are not completely rigid. . . .

[Passage omitted.] [104]

---

response variety notwithstanding. Cf. also Chap. 5, note 121, above.] (c) Art and religion are also synthetic achievements. Both the creation of works of art and their appreciation come about through "regressive adaptations." Religion, which is, among other things, an objectivation of a scale of values, is a method of synthesis accessible to many people because it satisfies the demands of all three psychic institutions.

99. Section VII of Hartmann's paper deals with the problem of normality, that is, mental health. He discusses values and education in relation to normality. For an extensive discussion of these issues see Hartmann (307); cf. also note 18, above.

100. In the section here omitted Hart-

mann again discusses the psychology of action, this time centering in the criteria of "realistic action."

101. Concerning automatisms, see Section II and particularly note 41, above.

102. Kretschmer (419).

103. "Formular abbreviation" means replacement of an action by an automatization, in which the action is only schematically performed.

The omitted section points to the possibility of studying these automatizations in cases in which they are affected by organic disorder. (Cf. Schilder, 650, 654, 661, 662.)

104. In the omitted section Hartmann shows that the habit-training or canalization theories of psychic life are an at-

The logical place of these automatisms in the psychic topography is the pre-conscious. In his "Wit and the Unconscious" Freud expressed this as follows: "These processes which take place in the preconscious and lack the attention-cathexis which is the prerequisite of consciousness, are appropriately termed 'automatic.' " It is certain, however, that not all the preconscious processes are automatic and that rather extensive recombination of elements also takes place in the preconscious. . . .[105]

[Passage omitted.] [106]

. . . It cannot be a matter of "chance" that automatisms play so great a role among those processes which are either directly adaptive or are used by adaptation-processes. It is obvious that automatization may have economic advantages, by saving attention-cathexes in particular and conscious-cathexes in general. In using automatisms we apply already existing means, the structure of which we need not create anew at every occasion, and consequently some of the means-end relations can be, so to speak, taken for granted. . . .[107] These apparatuses achieve what we expect of any apparatus: they facilitate the trans-

---

tempt to account for the phenomena of automatization. He also shows that automatization and habit formation may arise from many sources. (In Lewin's terms, habits and automatisms are pheno-types of a great variety of genotypes.)

Though Lewin's and Hartmann's discussion of the relation of habits and automatisms, and to some extent Murphy's (533) discussion of canalization, do form points of departure for a dynamic psychological treatment of the problem of habits, this is still an obscure field for dynamic psychology. Its inherent difficulties, which were well described by Gibson (269) have so far been hardly touched.

105. Cf. Kris (Chap. 23, below). See also Freud (209, pp. 528-29).

106. In the omitted section Hartmann stresses that while he uses the term au-tomatism only for the somatic and pre-conscious ego-apparatuses, Janet uses it to characterize id-processes. He quotes Freud (252, p. 55), Landauer (443), Fenichel (177), Reich (604), and Alex-ander (17, 18) to indicate some of the ways in which automatisms may be changed in pathological processes. Ex-amples are: de-automatization, libidini-zation, and the use of automatisms as defenses against drives or anxieties. Hart-mann stresses that while all these authors emphasize the regressive and flight char-acter of automatization, he views them as purposive achievements of importance for adaptation.

107. Schilder, in his Brain and Per-sonality (642) wrote: "We deal with general tendencies in the psychic life. We wish to mechanize what once had a meaning. . . . The organism produces tools in order not to be compelled again and again to a psychic effort. What once had been an expression becomes finally an automatic movement, a mannerism, a stereotyped movement." Cf. note 103, above.

formation and the saving of energy.[108] There are many complicated central psychic achievements whose successful performance presupposes automatization.[109] [Passage omitted.] [110]

. . . Flexibility and automatization are both necessary and characteristic hallmarks of the ego; in purposive achievements some functions will take a flexible, and some an automatized form, while in others the two will mix in various proportions. . . .

[Passage omitted.] [111]

. . . In action the ego uses both somatic and psychic apparatuses. . . . Thus far investigators have paid little attention to the role of these apparatuses in the possibility, direction, development, and success of action.[112] However, if we take the conflict-free ego-sphere into account and if we want to achieve a general psychology of action, the study of these apparatuses becomes indispensable, because otherwise all our statements about action will include an unknown; knowledge of these apparatuses is a prerequisite for the predictability

108. It should be noted that this formulation is akin to Freud's description of the secondary process. Cf. Freud (209, pp. 533–34 and 535–36); see also Chap. 15, note 30, above.

109. We have suggested elsewhere (Chap. 27, notes 39 and 76, below) that every abstraction, and system of abstractions, may be considered such a means of saving energy, such an automatized apparatus.

110. The omitted section deals with the advantages of automatization for psychic economy: "Under certain conditions a behavior formula is a better guarantee of coping with the environment than is adapting anew to every occasion." While it is a goal of therapy to transform ego-rigidities which result in difficulties of adaptation, into mobile ego-achievements, this does not hold for automatisms in general because of their intrinsic adaptation value.

111. Part of the omitted section discusses the relationship of the "musts" implied in automatisms to the "freedom"

of autonomous ego-functioning, with the conclusion that

the normal ego should be able to exert control, but should also be able to accept a "must"; this, far from vitiating normality, is one of its prerequisites. . . . The ego should not be equated with flexible thinking and acting, which is only one of its functions; . . . it does think and act flexibly but not exclusively so.

The rest of this section dwells on the relation of the automatisms to the pleasure-principle and the repetition compulsion.

112. Certain aspects of the function of these apparatuses have been extensively studied by academic psychology. What Hartmann means is that they have been little studied by psychoanalysis, and that even in academic psychology they have not been investigated in relation to goal-directed integrated behavior. Some of the studies of Lewin and his collaborators (550, 370, 337) and some of Luria's (487) studies have, however, made a beginning in this direction.

of actions. . . . These apparatuses, somatic and psychic, influence the development and the functions of the ego which uses them; we maintain that the ego has one of its roots in such apparatuses. A particularly clear example of this was offered by Schilder [113] who showed how a disorder of the central equilibrium-apparatus may influence object-relations. An example of more general significance is the effect of language-development on thinking. It is obvious that the apparatuses, both congenital and acquired, need a driving force in order to function; therefore the psychology of action cannot be understood without a drive-psychology.

Not all the apparatuses which are put into the service of the ego in the course of development are acquired by the individual. It is more than probable that perception, motility, intelligence, etc., are built on constitutional endowments.[114] [Passage omitted.] [115]

. . . In some cases it will be expedient to assume that both the drive-processes and the ego-mechanism arise from a common root at the time of the ego-id

---

113. Schilder (642).

114. Cf. Section I, above. If one were to choose perception as an example, the meaning of this statement placed into its historical context is about as follows. Academic psychology dealt with perception by and large as a function independent of the individual personality, stressing its uniform inter-individual lawfulness. Psychoanalysis has thus far been interested in perception only as it subserves drives and defenses. Now psychoanalysis is beginning to take into consideration the fact that perception is built on constitutional endowments and is one of the preexisting apparatuses which, once the ego and id have arisen from the original undifferentiated phase, become ego-apparatuses. It would be a mistake, however, if one were to conclude that at this point psychoanalytic theory simply adopts the view of perception which used to be held by academic psychology.

First of all this ego-psychological view raises the questions of inter-individual

115. In the omitted section, to document the autonomy of motility and perception Hartmann discusses ego-functions which emulate patterns of drive-functions (as "giving" and "taking" emulate "projection" and "introjection"), and maintains that it is improbable that perception and motility would do so. He stresses that *ego*-constitution deserves just as much attention as does drive-constitution—thus far the main concern of psychoanalysis.

---

differences in constitutional endowment, and of intra-individual differences between the perceptual, motor, and other aspects of constitutional endowment. Hartmann and Kris (309) have made this clear in their stress on the need to study the earliest phases of individual development. Cf. Leitch (447) and Bergman and Escalona (52).

Secondly, the integration into the ego of the perception-apparatus, as hypothesized by Hartmann's view, reintroduces the problem of individual differences on

differentiation; but secondarily, after the period of structuralization, the two may enter into the most varied connections with each other.

. . . Strictly speaking, there is no ego before the differentiation of ego and id, but in the same sense the id does not yet exist either. Both are products of a differentiation process. Those apparatuses which, after this differentiation, are unequivocally in the service of the ego we will consider inborn ego-apparatuses. . . .[116]

[Passage omitted.] [117]

Now it becomes clear why psychoanalytic ego-psychology must of necessity come to grips with these problems. Our first considerations demonstrated that autonomous ego-development is one of the prerequisites of all reality-relations. Our further considerations made it probable that this is also the case for many other ego-functions. This made it necessary for us to enter upon a detailed discussion of the ego-apparatuses. I may be permitted to stress here again that no satisfactory definition of the concepts ego-strength and ego-weakness are feasible without taking into account the specificity and developmental level of the ego-apparatuses which underlie intellect, will, and action. . . .

a higher level. The problem may be formulated as follows: does the individual's developing ego-structure, as it integrates the perception-apparatus, imprint its characteristics upon it? Klein (387, 386) seems to have found some evidence to support this assumption.

Thirdly, Hartmann's theory assumes that the perception-apparatus (and kindred apparatuses) may have various vicissitudes. It may remain within the conflict-free sphere or it may become involved in conflict. Once it is involved in conflict, it may be used either in symptoms or in defenses. Both of these uses may either enhance or hamper the perceptual function, not only by quantitative differences in its cathexis but also by qualitative changes in its role.

Fourthly, Hartmann assumes that by a change of function defenses and symptoms may acquire new roles in adaptation. It is conceivable, therefore, that when perception is once involved in conflict, it may emerge with a changed role in the economy of the psychic apparatus.

Although these speculations are tenuous, they show the vast difference between the problems of academic perception-theory, and those of psychoanalytic ego-psychology. It may be that the exploration of these problems will require methods of sampling which will reach beyond the customary ones, and even beyond the ecological method proposed by Brunswik (102). While Brunswik sampled experimental designs, the new methods may have to sample aspects of individual differences.

116. For an elaboration of this hypothesized ego-id relationship see Section IV, and note 43, above.

117. The omitted section deals with the process of maturation. It dwells on the fixed and the flexible aspects of endowment and sketches the corresponding interrelations of environment and endowment.

PART FIVE

FANTASY-THINKING

CHAPTER 20

AUTISTIC THINKING [1]

By Eugen Bleuler

ONE OF THE MOST IMPORTANT SYMPTOMS of schizophrenia is the preponderance of inner life with an active turning-away from the external world. The most severe cases withdraw completely and live in a dream world; the milder cases withdraw to a lesser degree.[2] I call this symptom *autism*.[3*]

The present paper was written before the publication of Jung's study, "On

1. Bleuler (68). The only relatively extensive discussion in English of Bleuler's (69) ideas on autism is the publication of a lecture he delivered in this country. Compare Bleuler (76, pp. 45–47), where the term "autistic thinking" is replaced by "dereistic thinking." Bleuler (73, p. 144) wrote:

I have called it autistic thinking, since it was encountered first and in clearest form in the autism of schizophrenics. This name, however, was misunderstood (even in Jasper's "Psychopathology"). Thus I was constrained to rename it. *Dereistic* derives from reor, ratus sum (ratio, res, real), to think logically, that is, in a fashion corresponding to reality. Thus *dereistic thinking* is a thinking that disregards reality.

2. The most extensive theoretical and experimental use of the concept autism is found in Gardner Murphy's work. See Murphy (533, pp. 362–90), for a summary of the experimental work on autism carried out with his collaborators, R. Levine (454), Proshansky (585), Schafer (635), J. Levine (453), Seelemann (677), Postman (581). Murphy (533, p. 365) defines autism as: ". . . movement of cognitive processes in the direc-

tion of need satisfaction. . . ." The shortcoming of the definition is that in the long run all human behavior and thought subserves and is directed toward satisfaction, and the distinctive character of autistic thinking is probably its short-circuit course toward satisfaction. Ordered i.e., goal-directed, thinking—as Freud put it—is a detour on the path toward gratification. Murphy must be credited with stimulating and sustaining interest in this aspect of thought-organization when the unsatisfactory results of experimentation in this field caused interest to wane; compare Rapaport (591). Following Murphy's work, interest in the problem is again spreading, as indicated by the studies of Postman and Bruner (96, 97, 99, 98, 577, 578), McClelland (490, 32), Klein (386, 387), and others.

3.* The concept autism and Jung's concept introversion greatly overlap, the latter denoting the turning inward of libido which normally should seek its objects in reality. However, autistic strivings may also be directed outward, as for instance in the schizophrenic world-reformer who wants to remold

the Two Kinds of Thinking." [4] What I call logical or realistic thinking was termed by this author *directed thinking;* what I call autistic thinking, he called *dreaming* or *fantasying.*

The former uses verbal material as its means of communication and is effortful and exhausting; the latter works with reminiscences and is effortless and, as it were, spontaneous.[5] The former creates new acquisitions and adaptations, imitates reality, and aims to alter it. The latter turns away from reality, liberates subjective wishes, but does not further adaptation.[6]

society and is constantly active in the outside world, or in the little girl in whose fantasy a piece of wood is a child, or in those who animate objects or create a god out of an abstract concept or force.

[The concepts autism and introversion both derive from Freud's conception that withdrawal of libidinous cathexes from objects is the prerequisite of repression and that repression results in a luxuriant fantasy elaboration of the repressed material. See Freud and Breuer (259), Freud (207, pp. 276–77; 217, pp. 51 ff., and 218, pp. 176 and 178). Freud (223, 225, 231, 232, 233, 234, 237, 238) developed this conception further. Jung (362) used this conception of the withdrawal of libidinous cathexes and the resulting fantasy-elaboration as the basis of his typology. For him it became a category of psychic functioning and a basis for classifying character-structure; for Freud it was but one aspect of psychic energy-dynamics. When Jung wrote his *Psychology of the Unconscious* (364) he had not yet thus broadened the concept. In the footnote here discussed Bleuler assumes that Jung's "introversion" (turning inward of libido) implies total disregard of reality. To this Bleuler objects, citing examples of autistic actions on objects of the outside world. It is questionable whether Jung actually took the view cogently attacked here by

Bleuler. It seems rather that he disregarded the problem. Bleuler's objection also applies to Freud's theory. Freud (224), however, saw the problem and suggested that what Bleuler calls here "outward directed autistic strivings" are "restitution" phenomena. Freud showed that schizophrenic delusions are not only wishfulfillments but also attempts at recapturing objects lost by the withdrawal of object cathexes.]

4. This paper is Chap. I of Jung's *Psychology of the Unconscious* (364). His description of the "two kinds of thinking" (pp. 14, 21–22, 36) closely follows Freud's formulations, but lacks both the theoretical concern with thought-processes characteristic of Freud's (209) Chapter VII and the rich observational material of Bleuler's present paper.

5. The distinction between directed thinking and fantasying as effortful vs. effortless is not further elaborated by Jung; while not entirely correct (directed thinking may or may not be effortful), the observation is original and important. Cf. Rapaport *et al.* (602, I, 166 ff.) on effortless attention and effortful concentration.

6. This statement is questionable: autistic fantasying may in the long run facilitate adaptation by abreaction and there is some evidence to suggest that it also serves to bind mobile cathexes. Cf. Chap. 23, and Chap. 22, note 30, below.

His essential points agree with mine. I want to mention only a few differences between us: In my opinion autistic thinking can also be directed, and thinking proper can be directed and realistic (logical) without putting concepts into words; in fact, words and their associations often play a crucial role in autistic thinking.[7]

The thinking of schizophrenics—which is much like that of dreams—is insufficiently known, but I am tempted to say that it has laws of its own, the deviations of which from the usual laws of thinking explain most schizophrenic thought-disorders, especially delusions. We find the same mechanisms in dreams, in the daydreams of normals and hysterics, in mythology, in superstition, as well as in other deviations of thought from reality.[8] There are essen-

7. It is unclear whether Jung claimed that fantasies are not directed. Freud (209), however, clearly insisted that when conscious directing ideas are abandoned, new unconscious directing ideas take over (pp. 482–83). The difference between the two kinds of thinking lies not in the presence or absence of direction but rather in the different character of their directedness: one leading to immediate tension-discharge or revival of the image of past gratification, the other leading to a delay of tension-discharge and finding again in reality a situation affording gratification. Freud described these directions (209, pp. 535–36) as aiming for "identity of perception" and "identity of thought" (meaning), respectively. Bleuler points to an important observation: daydreams and fantasies often do show direction of the second type, in that they at times become preparatory phases of action; see Varendonck (Chap. 22, below). The borderline between thinking and daydreaming is actually fluid; see Kris (Chap. 23, IV, below). Kris (421, 422, 423, 431) has shown how in artistic creation and humor the ego may make use of mechanisms of the primary process. In turn, dreams (in the form of second-

ary elaboration) and daydreams (in the form of anticipatory planning) both become elaborated by the secondary process.

As regards the role of words in autism: Jung, and even Freud, overstressed the relation between the secondary process and words; cf. Freud (243, pp. 21 ff.; 234, p. 133; and 209, p. 546). Freud even assumed that verbal material in dreams is limited to reproduction of actual fragments of perceptions (237, p. 143; and 209, pp. 335–36). Yet Freud saw clearly that non-verbal material has an important role in the secondary process (209, p. 492) and, like Bleuler, recognized the important role of verbal material in schizophrenic thinking ruled by primary-process mechanisms (234, pp. 133 ff.). In his last writing Freud (257) recognized that there is no necessary relation between verbalization and secondary process; cf. Chap. 23, p. 477, and notes 9* and 10*, below.

8. It is historically interesting to note that the present paper, unlike Bleuler's *Dementia Praecox* (71), actually equates the laws of schizophrenic and dream thinking. We shall encounter in the present paper only two points at which his later views on the organic basis of the

tially only quantitative differences between the dream of the youngster who plays general on his hobby-horse,[9] the poet whose poem abreacts his unhappy love or transforms it into a happy one,[10] the twilight state of the hysteric,[11] and the hallucinations of the schizophrenic in which his most impossible wishes appear fulfilled. All these are but points along the same scale.

---

schizophrenic association-disorder are foreshadowed (notes 38 and 39*, below).

9. Bleuler correctly perceived that there is a common core in these phenomena but oversimplified the issue by assuming merely quantitative differences. The following footnotes show some of the actual complexities and suggest that there are here qualitative differences in reality appraisal and state of consciousness.

Among these phenomena the quotations from Freud and Markuszewicz indicate qualitative varieties of consciousness in the play of children. Freud (218, p. 174) wrote:

The opposite of play is not serious occupation but reality. Notwithstanding the large affective cathexis of his play-world, the child distinguishes it perfectly from reality; only he likes to borrow the objects and circumstances that he imagines from the tangible and visible things of the real world. It is only this linking of it to reality that still distinguishes a child's "play" from "daydreaming."

But compare Markuszewicz's (500) description of a child of four who, after his parents took away his pet kitten, himself behaves like a kitten and can hardly be moved to eat except under the table. Here the identification with the kitten amounts to a loss of reality:

He created an idea that had more reality, for the moment, than the surrounding objects . . . in it his wish to have the kitten

back was realized . . . and the parents who took it away were defied (p. 249).

According to Freud, identification with objects, animals, and people, does occur in play but breaks down when the presence of adults reminds the child of reality. In Markuszewicz's case the identification persisted *in spite* of the adults present: the play and its daydream content were conflict-laden and encroached upon reality. It might be argued that this child went beyond what can be called "play," but if so, there is clearly a continuum between his activity and "play."

10. Freud (218, p. 180) has shown that, in poetic imaginative creation, daydreams undergo far-reaching and varied elaboration:

We do not in any way fail to recognize that many imaginative productions have traveled far from the original naive daydream, but I cannot suppress the surmise that even the most extreme variations could be brought into relationship with this model by an uninterrupted series of transitions.

On the other hand, compare Kris (428) who showed that the source of art creation may reach beyond the daydream and be experienced as inspiration in a fashion analogous to mystical visions and hallucinations. Cf. also Housman (342).

11. See Freud (217), and Abraham (6) on the altered states of consciousness in hysteria.

The paranoid patient B.S. in Jung's *Dementia Praecox* [12]* is Switzerland and also the herons of Ibycus; she is the possessor of the whole world and of a money-factory seven stories high; she is a double-school-of-technology and a representation of Socrates. I have again and again explained to a patient that I consider him mentally ill and have so testified in the probate court; yet he is convinced that I testified to his health and have told him so every time we have met, and insists therefore that he be discharged. A barber apprentice discovered the telephone, the telegraph, the steam engine, and many other things that existed even before he was born. A woman is visited by her bridegroom Jesus Christ and is at the same time the Good Lord.

At first all this may appear sheer nonsense, and from the point of view of logic it is. But on closer scrutiny we find an understandable connection in every one of these cases: the essential ideas correspond to affective needs, that is, to wishes, and occasionally to fears. For instance, the patient is the *Herons of Ibycus* so as to feel free of guilt and blemish; she is Switzerland because she wants to be as free as that country. The ideas of the litigant, the inventor, the bride of Christ, all express directly fulfilled wishes. The delusions of the paranoiac form a logical structure with only a few false premises and inferences in its foundation or among its building stones; the delusions of schizophrenics are not as systematic, yet they are not the chance heap of an unruly chaos of delusions which they seem on superficial observation. Rather, every single one is the expression of one or more complexes which thus find fulfillment or attempt to come to terms with the contradictions of the environment. Nevertheless, in their details we find many illogical connections which are not, or at least not directly, determined by complexes; they are trains of thought which, though emulating forms of logical development, are held together by entirely incidental clang associations, by equating differing concepts, by symbols, and so forth.[13] Contradictions of reality are not sensed. No attempts are made to alter the external world in terms of these ideas.[14] Beyond the simplest

12.* Jung (363).

13. Bleuler thus attempts to account for the fact that not all delusions are transparent wishfulfillments. The distorting influences listed are characteristics of the primary process and account for part of the lack of transparency. A part of the obscurity is probably due to the altered state of consciousness and corresponding forms of thought (see Chap. 25, note 40, below), and a part to the fact that the wishes themselves are of an obscure, infantile character. Cf. Nunberg (541, 542).

14. This contradicts what was said in note 3*, above.

functions, like eating and sleeping, such patients live only in the world of their ideas, and at times this makes them quite happy.

Thus autistic thinking has its own direction. It mirrors the fulfillment of wishes and strivings, thinks away obstacles, conceives of impossibilities as possible, and of goals as attained. It does so by facilitating those associations which correspond to the striving, and by inhibiting those which contradict it, that is by *mechanisms familiar to us as influences of affects*. To explain autistic trains of thought no new principles are needed.[15] It goes without saying that what we see here is affects at work, since a striving is but the centrifugal aspect of that process the central aspect of which we call affect.[16]

This is the reason why there is no sharp borderline between autistic and ordinary thinking: autistic, that is affective, tendencies easily penetrate the latter.[17]

15. Here, as in his *Dementia Praecox*, it is clear that Bleuler regarded autism (which for him accounted for primary-process phenomena) as consisting merely of the facilitating and inhibiting mechanism of affects. Memory experiments with affect-toned material showed that such a simple mechanism does not exist (Rapaport, 591) and that the explanation of unrealistic thinking is not this simple. Bleuler's concept of "affect" (Chap. 26, notes 137, 138, below) is indistinct and ill-defined. The explanation of autism requires the concepts of the primary and secondary process, the mechanisms operating in them, censorship, repression, and state of consciousness. As we shall see, not even these suffice to explain all of the phenomena of autism Bleuler discerningly described.

16. At this point it becomes clear how Bleuler subsumes strivings, interests, etc., that is, all directional or motivating forces, under affects. In his view affect is the subjective experience (central aspect) of motivation. Such a conception of affects can hardly account for the somatic processes of emotional expression. The conception is rendered untenable if those observations are taken into consideration which indicate that affects arise only where drive discharge has been blocked; cf. Rapaport (591, pp. 24–26 and 33); MacCurdy (489, pp. 87–88).

17. Though this explanation seems unsatisfactory, the fluid transition between autistic (primary process) and ordinary (secondary process) thinking seems to be a fact. Bleuler here again proves himself a good observer. Freud (209, p. 536) too had an inkling of this fact but gave no systematic explanation:

Hence, the tendency of the thinking process must always be to free itself more and more from exclusive regulation by the pain-principle, and to restrict the development of affect through the work of thought to the very minimum which remains effective as a signal. This refinement in functioning is to be achieved by a fresh hypercathexis, effected with the help of consciousness. But we are aware that this refinement is seldom completely successful even in normal psychic life, and that

The manic overestimates himself because of his pathologically exaggerated euphoria and the melancholic has ideas of insufficiency because of his depression, but even normal persons will only too often draw false conclusions to suit their mood and inclination. . . . Even in science, what one would like to believe is readily proven and contradictory facts are easily ignored. . . . All the objections raised by bright people in good faith against railroads, hypnosis, suggestion, abstinence, Freudian theories, are interesting contributions to the tragicomedy of human mental life. . . .

---

our thinking always remains liable to falsification by the intervention of the pain-principle.

To obtain a clearer picture of this state of affairs let us consider one of Bruner's (96, 578) experiments. He rated his subjects on the Allport-Vernon scale of values and tachistoscopically presented to them words pertaining to these values. The misreadings displayed condensations, displacements, and distortions, much like those familiar from psychoanalytic studies. The direction of these, however, correlated highly with the subjects' rated "values." Clearly, these are "autistic" phenomena. Yet they occur in a setting where ordinary thinking or perception is expected to prevail. The explanation that here drives have broken through their controls as in slips of the tongue would disregard the relative autonomy of the value systems of the ego. An explanation in terms of Bleuler's concept of affect would disregard the fact that the phenomena Bruner observed are more complex than a facilitation or inhibition of perceptual processes. Indeed Bruner's results show that *autism*, possibly a good label, is no explanation without a set of specific mechanisms and principles. It is possible that the explanation of the irrational (autistic) phenomena of ordinary thinking will necessitate an extension of the psychoanalytic theory of cathectic dynamics. (See Rapaport, 596.) The present psychoanalytic theory assumes that the secondary process arises when the drive cathexes of the primary process become "bound": when they do not tend to immediate discharge but admit of delay. It also assumes that this process of "binding" furnishes the ego its "sublimated" energies. A possible extension of this theory would be that the "binding" process creates a new distribution of cathectic energies superimposed upon that of drive-cathexes. This new energy-distribution would result in new directed forces within the ego (values, attitudes, interests, etc.). These forces in turn would evince tendencies toward discharge similar to those of "mobile" drive cathexes. Controlling and delaying (that is, binding) energy-distributions would again build up over these, resulting in a new set of derivative forces. Thus a hierarchy of progressively more and more "bound" energy-distributions would characterize the psychic structure. The "values" and "interests" of Bruner would be considered as belonging in this hierarchy. To the degree that they strove for direct discharge, they would cause phenomena resembling those of the primary process. Cf. Hartmann (303), Rapaport (596); and Kris and Varendonck (Chaps. 22, 23, below).

Though any tendency may find expression in autism, there is a great difference between positive and negative strivings. This difference becomes clear if
we consider the corresponding affects. Negative affects also have the tendency
to assert themselves, to facilitate the emergence of kindred ideas, and to inhibit contradictory ones; a deprived person may get so involved in his pain
that he will seek more pain. Nevertheless the general tendency is to strive for
as much pleasure as feasible, to get rid of pain as soon as possible, and first of
all—as a rule—to seek not painful but pleasurable experiences. A healthy person
in a normal mood will not be prone to think up a sad story and to empathize
with its hero.[18]

Thus autistic thinking is actually a search for pleasurable and avoidance of
painful ideas; this sheds light on Freud's similar though somewhat more narrow
concept of *pleasure-mechanisms*.[19]*

Autistic thinking is governed by two principles; these contradict each other
for negative but coincide for positive affects:

18. Bleuler attempts here to account
within his frame of reference for what
he considers to be the infrequency with
which facilitation by negative affects is
observed. In effect he disposes of it as
"just not healthy." It seems that here the
"affect facilitation" theory of autism
founders. Without the theory of repression (233), and the theory of anxiety
(252), there seems to be at present no
way to explain the role of "negative affects" in autism.

19.* "Formulierungen ueber die zwei
Prinzipien des Psychischen Geschehens"
[(222) and Chap. 15, above]. . . . I
don't want to accept the expression
"pleasure-mechanisms" because action
and thinking in accordance with reality
are also expressions of pleasure-mechanisms. Freud's pleasure-mechanisms (and
our autistic thinking) differ from reality-functions in that the former produce pleasure by *ideas* rather than by
affect-toned experiences.

[Bleuler considers the "pleasure-
mechanism" (pleasure-principle) too

narrow, because according to him it
neglects the "facilitation" by negative
affects; but he also considers it too broad,
because according to him it is present in
reality-functions as well as in autism.
Freud (209) realized that action and
thinking according to reality are aimed
at pleasure-gain. Unlike Bleuler, however, he realized that it is characteristic
for such thinking and action that pleasure-gain can be delayed and a detour toward safe and secure gratification can be
made (209, p. 535). It is characteristic
for autistic thinking (primary process)
that delay of pleasure-gain is not possible, and therefore in it instant hallucinatory or dangerous actual gratification is
preferred to delayed and safe gratification. Bleuler's distinction between
"pleasure by ideas" and "pleasure by affect-toned experiences" differentiates
realistic and autistic thinking only very
loosely. In realistic functioning there is
"pleasure by ideas" and in autistic functioning there is "pleasure by affect-toned
experiences."]

1. Every affect strives to sustain itself; it facilitates those ideas which are in accord with it, lending them exaggerated logical weight, and inhibits those which contradict it, decreasing their significance. Thus gay people assimilate gay ideas more easily than sad ideas, while the reverse is true for sad people.

2. We are so built that we strive to acquire and hold onto what is pleasant, and to avoid what is unpleasant. Painful ideas and experiences are met by a defense which may repress them *in statu nascendi,* or even after they have entered consciousness.[20] A strong affect-tone makes an idea, among other things, more memorable and more accessible to consciousness (the two are not quite the same thing); nevertheless many strongly unpleasant ideas, just because they are unpleasant, are forgotten or suppressed through the operation of this second mechanism.[21]*

20. In the first principle Bleuler restates the "affect-facilitation" theory of autism; in the second he introduces the pleasure-principle and the mechanism of repression. No reconciliation of the two is, however, offered (see note 15, above) and the difficulties mentioned in note 18, above, still stand.

21.* This pertains only to certain classes of such experiences which I would not like to characterize just yet. Simple unpleasant experiences, such as a broken leg, do not succumb so easily to repression. But ambivalent experiences, those damaging to one's self-esteem or pride, and those creating conflicts of conscience and so forth, do belong to this class.

[The observation and distinction are astute. They were encountered anew in relation to the Zeigarnik-effect. Zeigarnik (783), working with Lewin, found that interrupted tasks are remembered better than completed ones. The theory accounting for this effect assumed that the intention to perform the tasks creates a tension-system (quasi-need), which is discharged when the task is completed. The undischarged tension-systems of the interrupted tasks were held responsible for their superior recall. See Chap. 5, II, 1E, above. The experiments proceeded from Freud's assumptions, and even though they deal only with conscious material, the theory arrived at assumes a process which closely parallels that described by the pleasure-principle. Rosenzweig (620, 621) repeated these experiments but he connected interruption with failure. The results did not show the Zeigarnik-effect: the successes (completed tasks) were remembered better than the failures (interrupted tasks). Rosenzweig considered his results an experimental demonstration of repression. Like Bleuler, he spoke of "damage to self-esteem," the awareness of which had to be repressed. Bleuler's experience and Zeigarnik's and Rosenzweig's experiments show that the determinants and mechanisms of memory and thought are multiple. Whether or not we subsume all these determinants under the heading of autistic motives, it remains true that there probably is a whole hierarchy of motivating forces and a corresponding hierarchy of mechanisms productive of autistic phenomena. For a review of the

Freud considered only the latter mechanism. I believe, however, that the concept forms a genetic whole only in terms of my broader formulation. All affects function just like the pleasure-mechanisms. Depression creates delusions of unworthiness just as euphoria creates delusions of grandeur. The depressive schizophrenic is no longer the inventor of all things, but rather the cause of all misfortune, a shark who kills everyone; he is not elevated but rather thrown to the other patients to be dismembered. In sleep and fever an anxiety, somehow somatically rooted, leads to terror-laden hallucinations. A delusion of persecution creates negative feelings, but it is built with the aid of already existing ones, as will be further discussed below. All these processes can be derived only through tortuous hypothetical byways from the pleasure-principle but easily and directly from affect-function.[22] Thus the contrast remains incomplete if only the pleasure-pain principle and not all autistic thinking is counterposed to the reality-principle.[23]

Autistic thinking need not consider reality since it brings to consciousness ideas corresponding to an internal tendency, a momentary mood, or some striving; whether or not something is real, possible, or thinkable, is of no concern to it. Reality enters only in that it has supplied and still supplies the presentation-

---

literature of pertinent experiments, see Rapaport (591, pp. 94–99) and Alper (27). For similar relationships in experiments on reminiscence see Alper (28).]

22. Here Bleuler again uses the term affect in the sense in which psychoanalysis uses the term drive. The complicated derivation and role of affects (see Chap. 15, note 26, and Chap. 17, note 8, above) is not considered, and the role of affect in his conception is simple facilitation or inhibition of ideas. Bleuler is right in asserting that the derivation of ideas from the pleasure-principle is often tortuous; it has to invoke repression, projection, and other defense-mechanisms. The derivations from affect-facilitation, however, are glib and fall short of being explanations. Bleuler's assertion that "all affects function just like the pleasure-mechanisms" is incorrect. Affects, as

Bleuler conceives of them, have merely a general facilitating or inhibiting effect; pleasure-mechanisms are specific: they condense, displace, substitute, symbolize, turn ideas into their opposite, repress, isolate, project, introject, negate, etc. The depressive idea, "I am the cause of all misfortune" is, according to Bleuler, simply brought about by affect-facilitation, but this does not explain why just this and not any other idea which is in keeping with the depressive affect is facilitated. The derivation of the depressive idea from pleasure-mechanisms (tension-reduction) is tortuous: the cathexis of love-objects, ambivalence, loss of objects, introjection, projection, etc., all enter the arena. The result, however, is specific.

23. Here Bleuler is probably right. Cf. note 17, above.

material which the autistic mechanisms use either as their point of departure or as their subject-matter.

Thus autistic thinking can express all kinds of tendencies and strivings of the human being.[24] Since it disregards reality and logic, it can harbor the most diverse wishes even if they are mutually incompatible or unacceptable to consciousness. In realistic thinking, in our life and actions, many drives and wishes are ignored and suppressed in favor of those subjectively [25] important; many of these hardly ever come to consciousness. In autistic thought any of the following contradictions may be expressed simultaneously: to be a child again, capable of artless joy, and a mature man effective, powerful, and in high position; to live forever, and to give up this burdensome existence for the Nirvana; to possess the beloved, and to preserve one's freedom; to be active heterosexually and homosexually, etc.[26]

Unseemly strivings do come to consciousness in one form or another, even in the most righteous man. Upon seeing a heap of money the idea of appropriating it may come to him, even if only as a joke. Criminal ideas, for instance the wish that somebody who is in our way suffer a mishap, are probably present in everyone, though they do not always come directly to consciousness. Actually it seems that suppressed drives are particularly prone to come to the fore in autistic thinking. It is therefore no surprise nor an indicator of immorality in the analyst or analysand that sexuality and its perversities are regularly encountered in autistic thinking.[27]

In autistic thinking—in contrast to realistic thinking—ideas do not submit to or suppress each other: therefore, several different strivings may easily converge in a single autistic idea. Thus many dream pictures and delusions are mixed compositions, not only because of the number and variety of their elements (condensation) but also because they express different complexes simultaneously. This *overdetermination*, to use Freud's term, is self-explanatory.[28] But overdetermination is not specific to autistic thinking. Realistic thinking is

24. Cf. again note 17, above.

25. The expression "subjectively" is somewhat confusing. It seems that Bleuler meant: "In favor of drives and wishes more important to the realistic ego."

26. This is the suspension of the rule of absence of contradictions. It is characteristically suspended in the primary process. See Freud (234, p. 120).

27. Cf. Freud on daydreams (218, pp. 176–77), and on their relation to sexuality (223, pp. 17 ff.).

28. This introduces new points not implied in Bleuler's two principles of autism, but clearly part of the primary-process mechanisms.

also far more complicated than the textbooks of psychology would have it, and association is dependent upon a small number of determinants only when we arbitrarily restrict the possibilities, for instance, by posing a mathematical task. But it is well known that even then deviant associations are more frequent than we expect.[29]

The second consequence of disregarding reality is that the laws of logic become effective in thought-material only in so far as they can subserve the purpose of representing unfulfilled wishes as fulfilled.

Thus autism may use any available thought-material, however incorrect. It operates with incompletely thought-out concepts and equates concepts which have but a very unimportant objective component in common. It expresses ideas by most far-fetched *symbols,* which are then often misrecognized and conceived of in their concrete sense, so that one thing will stand for another, giving rise to real displacements.[30]* A jealous patient wishes that his father would die; through the idea "creator" he identifies father and mother and now sees the mother dead. Fire is a common symbol of love; the schizophrenic takes this for reality and translates it into hallucinations—that is, into real sensations —of being burned.[31]

It is also noteworthy how autism disregards time-relationships. It mixes present, past, and future without any concern. Strivings, which from the point of view of consciousness have long been settled, are still alive in it; memories long inaccessible to realistic thinking are fresh in it, and even preferred, for they clash little with actualities. In relation to reality, that is, for realistic thinking, many experiences are settled; there is no logical reason to consider them in our actions or thinking.[32] Memories have a feeling-tone, which is often even increased by the contrast with reality. This feeling-tone can easily change the

29. Bleuler is correct that both primary- and secondary-process products show overdetermination. In fact the latter are often overdetermined in a more complex way than the former, inasmuch as they are determined by reality considerations as well. Concerning overdetermination, see Waelder (745), and Freud (204, p. 117; 205, p. 213; and 212, pp. 40, 73).

30.* Realistic thinking also uses symbols but as a rule is continuously aware that they are used to represent another concept. [The concepts of symbolism and displacement, though not quite accurately used, are again additions to Bleuler's catalog of autistic mechanisms.]

31. Here again a new aspect of autism is touched upon, familiar both from hypochondriac and schizophrenic cases. Freud (234, p. 130) labeled it "organ-speech."

32. Compare Freud (234, pp. 119–20) and (218, pp. 177–78).

idea "if my father were alive" quite imperceptibly into "my father is alive." I do not agree with Freud when he says that the unconscious is timeless; but this holds for autistic thinking in so far as autism may, but need not completely, ignore time relationships.[33]

Even here, the contrast between the two functions is not absolute. Autism does not altogether scorn concepts and relationships derived from experience; it uses them only if they do not contradict its purposes and ignores or blocks them if they do (the dead lover is imagined as he was in reality, but that he died is not envisaged). Autistic mechanisms influence not only reality-appraisal but also drives, for example, the drive for survival; the goals of our actions are determined by anticipated pleasure and pain, that is, by the pleasure- and pain-tone of goal presentations: we strive for what seems pleasant, useful, or good.[34]

My description of autistic thinking has been one-sided. I gave the impression that direction by strivings is its essential characteristic; in pathological cases this is indeed the rule. This directedness by strivings, however, may recede. When the sun is represented with wings because it moves in the sky or with feet like most creatures that we see move, we can deduce that an affective need to explain the movement or the representation is at play . . . yet it seems forced to assume that these are affective directions of the kind so far described. Not wishes or fears, but only momentary strivings, that could just as well be given up, underlie the train of thought here. No specific affective direction can be assumed to play a role when a child, who has heard that the stomach is the

33. The difference between "if my father were alive" and "my father is alive" does not depend on the feeling tone. This state of affairs is known as the "omnipotence of thought" (see Freud, 227, pp. 865 ff.). Everything represented by the primary process *is* psychological reality; therefore anything that is thus "thought" is *made to be*. This aspect of primitive thought was clear to Levy-Bruehl (455) and to Werner (755). It is the relation to impulse dynamics and not to feeling tone that gives "thought" this magic power. For another aspect of this issue, see Chap. 22, notes 25 and 35, below.

34. Here it becomes clear that Bleuler conceives of autism fundamentally as a certain form of *organization* of percepts, ideas, drives, and behavior in general. He does not consider it a *drive-organization* of percepts, ideas, and behavior. This is implied in his statement that "autistic mechanisms influence not only reality-appraisal but drives also." In the psychoanalytic conception reality-appraisal (secondary process) is influenced by autistic mechanisms precisely because the latter are drive-mechanisms (primary process); drives are *not influenced* by autistic mechanisms, but rather the autistic mechanisms are their mode of operation.

kitchen of the body, imagines that in the body there is a kitchen, like that of her doll, with a cook in a white hat and a gray apron. Such ideas may be *used* by pathology but can never *themselves* produce pathological symptoms. In the mythology of the individual and of peoples, however, such modes of thinking play a great role. *This purely intellectual aspect of autistic thinking has scarcely been studied. My presentation has an important gap in this respect which I cannot fill at this time.* Only Jung has discussed this theme in a paper, "Concerning the Two Kinds of Thinking." [35]

Autistic thinking may be of two different degrees of deviation from reality. Though not sharply distinct, these two degrees differ rather significantly. *The difference lies in that stable concepts are dissociated and then arbitrarily rebuilt in one, but not in the other.* Furthermore, the number of autistic operations is much greater in one than in the other. The autism of waking normal people ties in with reality and operates as a rule with normally formed stable concepts. Only mythology, the essence of which is to reach out beyond time and space, deals with concepts arbitrarily. The dream and the frank autism of schizophrenia are completely independent of reality; they create and use concepts composed of arbitrarily assembled propensities and may change them at any moment. This explains how sleep and schizophrenia may compose otherwise quite unthinkable nonsense, while other autistic products are readily understood by normals.[36]

35. Jung described these phenomena, but he did not attempt to explain them. It was Silberer (Chap. 9, pp. 209 ff., above) who asserted that mythological thinking and other forms of autism may be due either to affects or to apperceptive insufficiency. He claimed that mythologies arose at a time in the development of mankind when apperceptive capacities had not yet reached their present level and therefore the natural phenomena which became the subject-matter of mythology could be conceived of only in the symbolic or indirect form of the myth. Apperceptive capacity is obviously directly related to abstractive ability. It should be stressed that a people who did not achieve our level of abstraction (apperceptive capacity) in regard to certain natural phenomena may have reached and even surpassed our capacity of apperception in regard to others, for example, ethics. That affects (drives) have no role in myth-formation is questionable. Certainly this is not generally true of the autistic fantasy of children; compare Markuszewicz's (500) paper. It is, however, likely that thought-formations which are "autistic" for our level of apperception are proper to other "levels of apperception," that is, to other forms of conscious experience.

36. Even if this is not a satisfactory explanation it poses clearly the unsolved problem of form-varieties of autism (note 17, above). It is possible that the

Instead of total concepts or objects the dream often presents only those of their elements which it needs. Often not even one's own person is thought of in detail: we may not know whether our position was standing or prone; our dream may not make clothes for us even if it does not think of us as naked. Dream-figures are usually composites of various people. A schizophrenic may think of the doctor as his doctor, and simultaneously as the priest N., the shoe-maker M., and in addition his lover. The same holds for objects, object-presen-tations, and even abstract concepts. Concepts may replace each other by virtue of a common—often subsidiary—component, resulting in a confused symbol-formation. The representation of love, or even the lover, by visible scorching fire can still be understood by normals; some symbols are much harder to under-stand.

The connection of ideas in a dream or schizophrenic delirium can be com-pletely nonsensical and full of the grossest contradictions, while the autistic fantasies of hysterics, pseudologia patients, and normal people are, with the exception of a few isolated logical gaps, perfectly understandable.[37]

The distortion of reality by the autism of the dream and schizophrenia is due to a disruption of associations in these conditions. The nature of this disruption cannot be discussed here.[38]

It should be noted, however, that states of great distraction may bring about disruption indistinguishable from that of dreams and schizophrenia, and that mythology . . . also operates with the queerest symbols and fragmented con-cepts.[39]*

---

striking differences between various forms of autistic thought are due to the different states of consciousness in which they occur. Cf. Chap. 9, notes 32, 78, 93, and Chap. 13, note 62, above.

37. Bleuler argued above for a con-tinuous transition between various forms of autism. Here he seems to contradict his own assertion. Compare Freud (209), on "fantasies during sleep," which speak for such a continuous transition (p. 355, particularly the footnote).

38. At this point Bleuler hints at his later ideas (see Chap. 26, note 2) on the organic origin of "schizophrenic dis-sociation." See also note 39*, below.

39.* Jung and Freud are inclined to ascribe even such disruption of associa-tions—in both schizophrenia and dreams —to affects. [At the time Bleuler wrote this, Freud occasionally still spoke of af-fects in this connection. Yet "The Inter-pretation of Dreams" (209), already well known, spoke of drives and contained the theory of the primary process and its cathectic dynamics.] They would as-sume either that the incorrect thought-material is already present in the waking normal person and is used preferentially by the autistic mechanism, or that it is

The delusional formations of *mental disorders of organic origin* occupy a special position. They show excessive affect-function, in that in manic conditions [of organic origin] definite delusions of grandeur are created, while in depressive ones they are of inferiority. The decrease in the number of simultaneously possible ideas and associations (which is at times misleadingly called dissociation) makes these delusions, in contrast to those of manic-depressives, nonsensical, and thus similar to schizophrenic delusions. But these delusions have distinctive characteristics which readily identify the usual case. It is, however, very difficult to characterize this distinction in a general way. For us it is important to note that in organic disorders true autism is rare, since no essential dissolution of concepts, no splitting of the personality, nor seclusion from the outside world takes place in them.[40]

In the various forms of idiocy autism plays no important role. Here we have the same variations as in normal people, but on a lower intellectual level. Difficulties in differential diagnosis occur only with the high-grade defective, whose unclear concepts may appear similar to the fragmented concepts of the

---

created by the needs of autism. [The two alternatives which Bleuler allows Freud are irrelevant to the latter's theory. In this theory the primary process—the matrix of autistic phenomena—is continuously working, and the "incorrect thought-material" it produces can be classed neither as already present in the waking state nor as created *ad hoc*.] I prefer to assume that a primary dissociation in sleep and schizophrenia makes for this abnormally strong autistic effect. The presence of far-reaching dissociations in normal persons, in myth-formations, and in distracted attention would speak for the views of Freud and Jung; in support of my views, it can be argued that the disorders in dementia praecox and in dreams are much more far-reaching than in distraction, and that association-disturbances in schizophrenia are demonstrable even where no affect-interference or distraction is observed. [It is here that Bleuler explicitly postulates a

"primary dissociation" in sleep and schizophrenia. Cf. notes 8 and 38 above. The later organic explanation of this dissociation is, however, not yet introduced. How Bleuler intended to solve the problem of dissociation in dream-thought when he introduced his organic assumption for dissociation in schizophrenia does not become clear from those writings of Bleuler which were available to me.]

40. Mental disorders of organic origin do show predominant affect lability and irritability. Indeed their delusions appeared to Schilder (Chap. 25, IIc, below) distinctively pedestrian and trivial in comparison to the "archaic" schizophrenic delusions. In actuality, however, the distinction is not as sharp between organics and schizophrenics as Bleuler asserted and as Schilder described, nor is it true that organic cases may not show a "dissolution of concepts."

schizophrenic, since both allow entirely unrelated things to be equated.

I do not have sufficient experience to describe the autism of various *epileptic conditions*.

Autistic thinking may be a fleeting episode of a few seconds' duration, or it may fill a life and entirely replace reality, as in demented schizophrenics who live in their dreams, allowing themselves to be dressed and fed. Between these two extremes we find all shades of transition. The autistic world may be a continuous whole or may consist only of isolated and fleeting thoughts, illusions, or delusions that interrupt realistic thinking from time to time.[41] In either case, for the consciousness of the patient, it is a *reality*, the relationship of which to actual reality cannot be described in general terms. In hysterical twilight-states the direct perception of the external world is usually quite consistently remolded in the sense of autism: the patient is in heaven socializing with saints, and all sensory impressions that would contradict this undergo either illusionary transformation to suit the basic idea or are not apperceived. In general the schizophrenic confounds the two worlds; should he become aware of contradictions, the world of delusions proves dominant and of greater reality, and he will act according to it. But when his energy abates, the continuous and consistent influences of the environment attain objective, though not subjective, prevalence: the patient adapts himself in many ways to the institution, puts up with reality, with the third-class care [if this is all he can afford] and with the menial work,[42] but within he remains the Emperor of Europe around whom the whole world revolves, and in contrast to whose imperial dignity the humiliations of institutional life do not even count. In many respects, even if not for every (internal and external) experience, the boundaries of the real and the autistic world become so fluid in schizophrenia that such a distinction seems no longer to exist for the patient. The schizophrenic prefers the autistic world affectively, but logically he does not sense the difference any more: for example, many schizophrenics take their night-dreams for reality even if they know them to be dream-experiences.[43]

41. Cf. note 36, above.

42. Note that here abating energy is made responsible for the absence of autistic action, while previously "introversion" and "autistic fantasying" were made to account for it.

43. It is hard to see what Bleuler means, even if we set aside for the moment the criticism leveled against his "affect" concept. What could be the meaning of an "affective preference" for the autistic world if it is no longer dis-

In conditions other than schizophrenia the relationship of autism to reality is quite different. The patient suffering from *pseudologia phantastica* [44] will also think up a more or less arbitrary story and then communicate it, usually when stimulated by a definite external situation. He does it for instance to embezzle money. He thinks himself into his own tale, so that "he believes his own lies" and is often for considerable periods unaware of playing a false role. But if he wants to, or if circumstances force him, as when investigated, he is able to fully realize the situation.

Most normal people have, particularly in their youth, spun some kind of yarn, but they always knew how to distinguish it from reality, even if the dreamt-up situation was so vivid that they experienced appropriate affects. This is *normal autism*.[45] The play of fantasy in itself may be autistic or realistic. Recombination—along lines analogous to reality-connections—of ideas corresponding to reality leads to new insights; if these insights have a certain [objective] significance, they are called discoveries or inventions; [46] this process is not autistic. What is usually called fantasy disregards one or more aspects of reality, replacing them by arbitrary presuppositions; it is autistic. The greater

---

tinguishable from the world of reality? Bleuler's use of the term "logically" appears to betray the source of the difficulty. The nature of schizophrenic autism can be clarified only by genetic psychological considerations not by those of logic. The essence of autism is that intrapsychic reality assumes in thought and/or action the role which properly belongs only to external reality.

44. See Fenichel (176, p. 529).

45. Bleuler's observation is correct: though daydreams occur in what appears to be a special state of consciousness, we always know that they are "autisms." "Wishful thoughts," superstitions, prejudices, biases, and other autisms that slip into our everyday thought we usually do not recognize as autistic. Our theoretical understanding of autism within "the normal range" is extremely limited. Part of our ignorance is due to our inade-

quate knowledge of preconscious processes. Cf., however, Kris and Varendonck, Chaps. 23 and 22, below.

46. Kris (421, 422, 428) has shown that in poetic and artistic invention, autistic (primary) processes are utilized by the ego. The same seems to hold for scientific discovery and invention. Cf. Hadamard (298), Poincaré (575), Rapaport and Frank (601). The dynamic conditions under which the ego makes use of such primary processes for creative activity is described by Freud (234, p. 127); his description is quoted in Chap. 23, notes 37 and 41, below. Cf. Bergler's (46, 49) elaboration of this conception.

In scientific invention and discovery probably something else also has to be present: a set of quasi-stationary abstract thought-patterns into which patterns of instinctual conflict have been sublimated and crystallized. Cf. Rapaport (599).

the number of presuppositions and connections which do not correspond to reality, the more autistic the train of thought. *Thus there are degrees in autistic thinking and in their transitions to realistic thinking, but only in the sense that the proportion of autistic to realistic concepts and associations is variable.*[47] An altogether autistic thinking consisting only of concepts rebuilt in an autistic fashion and nowhere connected by the laws of logic naturally does not exist.

Hysterics may at times—like pseudologia patients—believe their tales even when not in a twilight-state; but in contrast to pseudologia phantastica, they usually separate reality from autistic imagination quite sharply. Hysterical autism shades into normal daydreaming on the one side and into hysterical twilight-states on the other.

The poet, if he be genuine, does the same. He abreacts his complexes, his affective needs, more or less consciously into an artistic creation.

Autism enters the *play* of *children* much as it enters the creations of poets. For the little girl a few rags are a child; a boy with his hobbyhorse and wooden sword acts out his power- and fighting-instincts, and so on.[48] As a rule, the poet and the child put more reality into their fantasy creations than one is at first inclined to believe. The little girl loves the rags as if they were the child they represent; Kleist was in tears after he allowed his Penthesileia to die.[49]

47. It is hard to see why Bleuler insisted that the differences are merely quantitative, while at the same time he strongly emphasized the difference between daydream and schizophrenic autism. Nor is it clear why the reveries that culminate in invention are not considered autistic, when otherwise only quantitative differences in the mixing proportion of autistic and realistic thought are admitted. As far as I can see there are both qualitative and quantitative differences.

Some inventions—certainly not all—begin with a daydream pattern, in a search in reality for something that conforms to that pattern, and once the autistic pattern and the matching segment of reality meet, they culminate in invention. The difference between a barren daydream and one culminating in invention is in the urge that drives from the one but not from the other to verification present only in the latter. It is one aspect of reality-testing and of the action of sublimated drive pertaining to the daydream pattern. Reality is relative (cf. Laforgue, 441); the conquest of autism and its transforming into reality is the perpetual struggle of humanity.

48. See "Spielen und Spiele" (173).

49. The autistic (egocentric) thinking of children has been penetratingly studied by Piaget. He too found it necessary to differentiate many facets of autism. Piaget (557, p. 546) wrote:

The first stage is characterized by a sort of reasoning by participation, akin to the manner of the primitives. The child declares, for example, that the shadow produced on the table comes from under the

Autism and autistic thinking are most familiar to normal people from their night-dreams; these too lack all connection with reality and all intellectual consideration of what is or is not possible.

Mythological reality is remarkable. Even those of its ideas which from the point of logic seem utter nonsense, are really believed by many people; indeed,

---

trees or from the sky, that is to say, from night, or from the depths of the room. In other words, for him there is not only identity of substance between the shadow produced and all the other shadows in the universe, but also direct action one with the others. It is sufficient to put a book above the table for a piece of the sky or a fragment of shadow hanging under the trees to rush to take up a place under the book.

During the second stage, the child renounces those participations, but, for all that, does not abandon the idea that shadow is a substance and that this substance moves about by itself. For the child the shadow comes from the hand, or from the book, and it can take its place on either side, no matter which. The relation between the shadow and the source of light is not understood at all.

During the third stage, this relation is, on the contrary, distinctly perceived. The child realizes that the shade is always on the side away from the window or the lamp. But the child still continues to believe that the shadow is a substance issuing from the book or from the hand. If this substance makes for the side away from the daylight it is because the shadow is black and flees from the day.

It is only during the fourth stage, that is to say about nine to ten years, that the shadow is clearly understood as absence of light, and that the object, the cause of the shadow, is considered as a simple screen. We thus see how these various actions converge to show the progressive abandonment of dynamism in favor of rational and mechanical explanation.

In *The Language and Thought of the Child* (561) Piaget discussed the rela-

tionship of Bleuler's "autism" to his "egocentric thought" (pp. 43 ff.) and the relation of his syncretism concept (p. 132) to the concept of autism (pp. 157 ff.). In *The Child's Conception of Physical Causality*, Piaget (558, pp. 202–3) wrote:

Now, if we examine these parallel evolutions, logical and ontological, in greater detail, we shall distinguish three main stages in each. The first is that which precedes any clear consciousness of the self, and may be arbitrarily set down as lasting till the age of two to three, that is, till the appearance of the first "why," which symbolizes in a way the first awareness of resistance in the external world. As far as we can conjecture, two phenomena characterize the first stage. From the point of view of logic, it is pure *autism*, or thought akin to dreams or daydreams, thought in which truth is confused with desire. To every desire corresponds immediately an image or illusion which transforms this desire into reality, thanks to a sort of pseudo-hallucination or play. No objective observation or reasoning is possible: there is only a perpetual play which transforms perceptions and creates situations in accordance with the subject's pleasure. From the ontological viewpoint, what corresponds to this manner of thinking is primitive *psychological causality*, probably in a form that implies *magic* proper: the belief that any desire whatsoever can influence objects, the belief in the obedience of external things. Magic and autism are therefore two different sides of one and the same phenomenon—that confusion between the self and the world which destroys both logical truth and objective existence.

even outstanding minds have placed their reality above that of the sensory world when the two clashed. We can find every transition from this stand, from viewing mythology as symbolic with more or less reality underlying it, through viewing it merely as poetic truth, to totally rejecting it.

Autistic *withdrawal from reality* is often of an active nature. This is true of the dream and is due to the sleep-mechanisms themselves. In schizophrenia and hysterical twilight-states active withdrawal is one of the forms in which the autistic mechanism may appear. In addition to wanting to believe what corresponds to his wishes, the schizophrenic also wants to withdraw actively from the reality which angers and irritates him. This striving finds expression in the negativism and seclusion from the environment which is so striking in many severe schizophrenics. Because of the revulsion against the outside world and external stimuli, the patient's thoughts are turned away from ideas of reality and at times even from external impressions, and the psyche turns toward the pleasure in certain unreal ideas.

The conscious strivings of many of those schizophrenics who are not negativistic turn toward reality, but the claim of the autistic world of thought intrudes in the form of hallucinations, delusions, automatisms, and similar symptoms rising from the unconscious.

Naturally some withdrawal from reality is implicit in the wishful thinking of normal people who "build castles in Spain." Here, however, it is mainly an act of will by which they surrender themselves to a fantasy. They know that it is just a fantasy, and they banish it as soon as reality so demands.

I would not call the effects of these mechanisms "autism" unless they are coupled with a definite withdrawal from the external world. The delusions of a manic-depressive fit his mood and are due to a pathological exaggeration of affects; their formation is analogous to the affective thinking of normals: this is not autism in our sense.[50] Whether all affective thinking should be labeled autistic is a question I want to leave open. A positive answer to this question would imply that the concept of autistic thinking is broader than that of autism.[51]

---

50. Cf. MacCurdy (489). Bleuler implies that withdrawal is not present in manic-depressive psychoses. Psychoanalytic theory would not concur with his view, though it would recognize significant differences between the schizophrenic and circular psychoses in the distribution of cathexes (particularly as regards the superego).

51. Bleuler seems to indicate that for him autism consists not merely in autistic thought but also in withdrawal and that

The relationship between autistic and realistic thinking is in many respects that of opposition.

Realistic thinking represents reality; autistic thinking imagines what corresponds to an affect, which is as a rule something pleasant. The purpose of realistic functions is to reach a correct understanding of the environment, to find the truth. Autistic functions aim to evoke ideas [of similar] affect-tone (mostly pleasure-toned) and to suppress those of a contrary affect. The realistic mechanisms regulate our relationship to the outside world and subserve survival, nourishment, attack, and defense; the autistic ones create direct pleasure by eliciting pleasure-toned ideas and suppress displeasure by blocking related ideas. Thus there are autistic as well as realistic need-gratifications. When satisfaction is gained autistically there is less reason and force to act; the normal dreamer and the schizophrenic are well-known examples. A person completely immersed in autistic thinking appears apathetic and stuporous. The opposition of these two functions comes to particularly clear expression in their mutually inhibiting effects. When affects have the upper hand, either momentarily, or as a matter of disposition, logical thinking is suppressed and autistically falsified. In turn, realistic considerations in normal people prohibit the luxurious growth of autism. When autistic ideas are present in normal people, they are rather clearly kept apart and their influence on action is restricted or entirely suppressed.

When logical thinking is weakened for some reason, autistic thinking will prevail either relatively or absolutely.[52] Such conditions may be divided into four groups:

1) *The child* lacks the experience necessary to handle the logical forms of

---

therefore the presence of autistic thinking alone without the other signs of autism does not amount to autism. It seems that here again Bleuler is struggling with those still unsolved problems to which note 15, above, referred.

52. This in essence expresses the idea which Silberer formulated as "apperceptive weakness." Cf. Chap. 9, pp. 216 ff., above. Some transient conditions in which "apperceptive weakness" may occur and which have been used for the experimental exploration of autism may be profitably listed: extremely brief (tachistoscopic) presentation of stimuli, indistinct or unstructured stimuli (darkness, inkblot-like material), hypnosis, states of increased needs or interests (hunger, self-esteem in test situations), drug-intoxication (alcohol, barbiturates, scopolamine, morphine, ether, mescal, hashish, etc.), drowsiness, distraction, and fatigue.

thinking and to know the potentialities of the outside world. If the child is an imaginative one, his thinking may easily become autistic.[53]

2) In the areas which are insufficiently or not at all amenable to *our understanding and logic* and in those which are ruled by affectivity, logic must naturally recede: thus, for instance, in the questions of *Weltanschauung*, religion, love, and eschatology.[54]

3) *When for one reason or another feelings gain undue significance*, logic will relatively recede; this occurs in strong affects, neurotic dispositions, and neuroses proper.[55]

4) When associative connections are loosened, their significance decreases, as in the dreams of normals and in schizophrenia.[56]

[Passage omitted.] [57]

In certain respects the two functions complement each other. When reality does not fulfill our wishes, autism represents them as fulfilled or capable of fulfillment. In social ethics, man has of necessity created the concept of justice, [because of] the need to feel that pleasure and pain are distributed according to merit; [in actuality, however,] we see nothing of this justice in nature, in fate, and in all that does not depend on our human order. This gap is filled by religion, which distributes reward and punishment according to our principles of justice, but it does so in the hereafter which realistic thinking with its critical faculty cannot reach.

Because man thinks of the future, the individual drive for survival necessarily arouses a fear of death, or to put it positively, the wish for a life without death; this wish too is fulfilled by religion. The need for causality, one of the important stimuli to realistic thinking, cannot be satisfied on many important points; the gap is filled by mythology.[58]

---

53. Cf. note 49, above. See also Werner (755, pp. 312–30, and 213 ff.).

54. Clearly myths and their symbols also belong in this category. Eschatology is the doctrine of the last or final things, such as death, resurrection, immortality, judgment.

55. Strivings which have succumbed to repression or other defenses belong in this category.

56. Here again, as in Bleuler's *Demen-tia Praecox*, the term "association" denotes logical associative connections.

57. In the omitted section Bleuler discusses the importance of sexual drives in the content of autistic thinking. Cf. Freud (223, p. 17).

58. Cf. Nunberg (543, p. 127). His conclusions shed some light on the psychodynamic conditions responsible for man's creation of myths to fill the gaps in his knowledge.

When concepts are inadequate our need for logic leads to our complementing them autistically: the sun is a man driving a wagon across the sky, illness is a creature that responds to certain kinds of magic, and so forth. On higher levels of culture, thinking becomes sharper, and, because these pictures and symbols are all too often thought of concretely and easily mistaken for realities, they are replaced by ideas conforming more closely to reality. For Freud autistic thinking is so closely related to the *unconscious* that for the uninitiated the two concepts shade into each other. If, however, one considers the unconscious—as I do—to consist of all those activities which are in every respect identical with ordinary psychological functioning except that they do not become conscious, one will have to keep these two concepts apart. *In principle, autistic thinking can be either conscious or unconscious.* The dream and the illogical disquisitions of schizophrenics are forms of conscious autistic thinking. In the symptom-formation of neuroses and in many schizophrenic processes the work of autism is completely unconscious. In neuroses its results manifest themselves in varied neurotic symptoms, while in schizophrenia they are seen in primordial delusional ideas, hallucinations, memory falsifications, compulsions, and so forth. As a rule, autistic thinking is more often unconscious and realistic thinking more often conscious, because the essence of conscious thinking is to regulate our relationship to the external world.[59]

59. It is not difficult to understand how Bleuler arrived at these conclusions: on the one hand he regarded daydreams and wishful thinking as conscious autistic phenomena; on the other hand he saw realistic, fully formed, and elaborate ideas appear in rich completeness in consciousness and had no conception of a preconscious to account for their genesis. So he concluded that both realistic and autistic thoughts may be conscious or unconscious. The error of this reasoning is best seen in his regarding dreams and schizophrenic delusions as conscious autistic thoughts. These are of course conscious in their manifest form, but their latent thought-content usually remains unconscious. However, there are schizophrenics who are at times aware of the real meaning of their delusions and there are introspective and intuitive people who can at times become aware of the meaning of their dreams. Indeed in dream formation the ego makes use of the primary process to gain its end: fulfillment of its wish to sleep. That is how in the dream a primary (autistic) process becomes conscious. It is however a "censored" product, and it expresses the latent dream-thought not directly but in disguise. Notwithstanding Bleuler's assertion, unconscious (not preconscious!) ideas are always autistic, and non-conscious realistic ideas always preconscious. Conscious autistic ideas do exist, but their genesis and dynamics are little understood (see note 17, above).

Autistic thinking does not always reach its goal. It often has internal contradictions. Some of our ideas, particularly those strongly feeling-toned and thus most prone to elicit autistic thinking, are ambivalent, that is, accompanied by both positive and negative feelings. What one strives for has its disagreeable sides. The beloved has shortcomings; he may have every desirable personal characteristic but not the wealth one would want or vice versa. . . . Conflicts of conscience seem to be the kind of internal contradiction which have the most damaging effect. . . . While realistic thinking leads to self-reproach and regret over something bad *actually done*, autistic thinking leads to the same agony over something bad that was *only imagined;* these "imagined" sufferings are all the worse because they are unapproachable by logic, in part because autistic functions are independent of logic, and in part because their origin is unknown to the subject.[60] When a patient does not know why he is anxious he cannot prove to himself that he has no reason to be anxious.

Since autism represents our wishes as fulfilled, it naturally leads to *conflicts with the environment*. One may ignore reality but it will again and again make itself felt. Under conditions which cannot be called pathological, where the wish is not realized in hallucinations and delusions, the autistic person disregards the obstacles to the fulfillment of his wishes; he thinks too optimistically, as it were, and will therefore fail in life, or if life does not offer him what he most desires will feel rebuffed and withdraw into himself.[61] In pathological cases, the obstacle—when it cannot be fully ignored—must be transformed by

60. The internal contradictions of autism are more of the nature of "conflicts of conscience" rather than of "what one strives for has its disagreeable sides." Actually, undisguised wishfulfillment is rarely encountered except in the dreams of children and the daydreams of some adults. Dreams and even schizophrenic thought are subject to censorship and secondary elaboration (in dreams) or rationalization (in delusions).

61. It is well worth noting that this concept of normality is far broader than the current one. Though the gullible optimist who is a failure and the disappointed misanthrope are autistic, they are but variants within the normal range. Our intolerance for "non-conformists," "failures," "eccentrics," "introverts" and our inclination to consider them "mental cases" may be a sign of our superior insight and diagnostic skill. But it is equally possible that it is a sign of the change in the outlook of humanity which has occurred in the last forty years or of the difference between the civilization to which Bleuler belonged and the one in which we live. This determination of thought by the culture of the place and time is an important aspect of the organization of thinking—not dealt with in this volume. It should be stressed

autistic thinking. While autism leads primarily to the fulfillment of wishes and thereby to expansive illusions, the perception of the obstacles produces delusions of persecution. . . .[62]

Autism is itself often the carrier of the conflicts which affects create in us. Let us assume that an event is painful for a normal person. Pain, like any other affect, has a tendency to persist, to survive the event, and to radiate onto other experiences, in brief to create a lasting painful mood. This is overcome—apart from the usual effect of time—by new experiences bringing new affects. Joy, while it lasts, overshadows pain or at least attenuates it. But the painful event has access to memory, just like any other experience. The situation is different when autistic defenses come into play, because they keep the pain and the painful idea out of consciousness. Whether or not an affect can be thus completely abolished, I do not know. At any rate, both in normal and particularly in pathological conditions, we see many such blocked affects reappear and can observe their effect (in the form of expressive movements and pathological symptoms) even though the affects themselves do not become conscious. This shows that the affect in question was dissociated from consciousness and not abolished. At least this is true of many cases.[63] It goes without saying that the

---

that the difference between Bleuler's view and the current one is not merely in content but rather in the method of establishing categories (conceptualization).

62. We now know that the delusions of persecution can be understood only in terms of the mechanism of projection; and the obstacles that play a role in bringing about projection are—contrary to Bleuler's view—intrapsychic. See Freud (224) and Fenichel (175, pp. 324 ff.).

63. The problem touched on here is that of "unconscious emotions." Freud (234) insisted that: "It is surely of the essence of an emotion that we should feel it, that is, that it should enter consciousness" (pp. 109-10). He says further that when we talk of an unconscious affect we usually mean either one which is iso-

lated from the idea corresponding to it and is displaced to another idea, or one which has been repressed and is a potential disposition in the unconscious. He wrote (234, p. 111):

. . . a comparison of the unconscious affect with the unconscious idea reveals the significant difference that the unconscious idea continues, after repression, as an actual formation in the system unconscious, whilst to the unconscious affect there corresponds in the same system only a potential disposition which is prevented from developing further. So that, strictly speaking, although no fault be found with the mode of expression in question, there are no unconscious affects in the sense in which there are unconscious ideas. But there may very well be in the system unconscious affect-formations which, like others, come into consciousness. The whole difference arises from the fact that

tendency inherent in all affects to gain mastery over the whole psyche is present here too. "Repression" must therefore (always?) be sustained by autistic mechanisms, and, in turn, repressed affects or their consequences must manifest themselves in autistic phenomena. A schizophrenic and even a dreaming normal person may falsely believe that someone close to him has just died, and be heartbroken. At one time or another the idea of that person's death occurred to him as a wish but, being too painful, was suppressed before becoming conscious. Now, in autism, it reemerges as a fulfilled wish, causing the pain the person wanted to avoid.[64]

By fulfilling a wish, autistic thinking may create a symptom complex that we call illness. The loss of the beloved is repressed and instead the patient hallucinates that he is living with her. A *Ganser delirium* . . . that is to say, unconscious simulation, may come about either autistically or through realistic thinking. Yet conscious will could hardly so long and so consistently sustain such a complex pathological picture as the *Ganser syndrome* often is, without making use of affect-mechanisms which, once unleashed, continue their activities spontaneously. The onset of such a delirium often does not correspond to the intentions of the psyche as a whole, but rather only to a more or less suppressed partial striving, the realization of which may bring more harm than good.[65]

There are other cases, too, in which autism leads to illness. It may, for in-

---

ideas are cathexes—ultimately of memory-traces—whilst affects and emotions correspond with processes of discharge, the final expression of which is perceived as feeling. In the present state of our knowledge of affects and emotions we cannot express this difference more clearly.

It will be remembered (Rapaport, 591, pp. 24–34) that affect-charge and ideas arise when drive-discharge is delayed. Discharge of the affect-charge gives rise to emotional expression and emotion felt. It is, however, a fact of observation that emotional expression may be suppressed while emotions (or at least some feelings derived from them) are still felt. Since they are discharges of drive-cathexes, affects once repressed probably differ from other cathexes of repressed drives only in that they exist as "potentialities," which, when repression lifts, become affects and are discharged as such, rather than as "formations" which undergo elaboration in the unconscious and produce derivatives which may escape censorship and appear in consciousness.

64. The "pain" Bleuler speaks of is either anxiety (252), or guilt (238). The reemergence of such ideas, however, occurs as a rule only if their appearance can serve to forestall even more painful and less tolerable ideas. Cf. Bergler (46).

65. Cf. note 60, above.

stance, allow the patient to withdraw from the demands of reality which are too difficult for him (flight into illness).[66] At times such autistic needs prevail against the conscious tendencies of the patient, who can be actually severely damaged by the illness. When deviation from normality is not that far-reaching, autism may allow a person to be lost in speculations instead of acting, become involved in useless things, make plans that cannot and hence need not be carried out, or pursue insoluble problems where a decision is either irrelevant or impossible.

If an already existing illness, such as a latent schizophrenia, makes normal contact with reality impossible, similar ways out will be found. It is quite clear to me that part of the symptoms of schizophrenia are attempts to come to terms with the illness and with reality; Freud called them unsuccessful "attempts at restitution." [67] From the point of view of the patient some of these attempts do reach their goal, in that he withdraws from the outside world and enjoys the hallucinatory fulfillment of his wishes.

Since realistic thinking, the *fonction du réel*, the coming-to-terms with the complex demands of reality, is so much more easily disrupted by illness than is autistic thinking, which is actually reinforced by pathological processes, French psychologists led by Janet assume that the "function of reality" is the highest and most complex [mental process].

Only Freud takes a clear stand on this matter. He insists that in the developmental series the pleasure-mechanisms are primary. In his conception, the infant whose real needs are completely fulfilled by his mother without any contribution from him, and the developing chick shielded by the eggshell from the outside world, live completely autistically. He assumes that the infant probably "hallucinates" the fulfillment of his inner needs, expresses his displeasure, when stimulation mounts and gratification is absent, by the motor-discharge of crying and kicking, and thereupon hallucinates the gratification.[68] There I cannot follow him. I do not see any hallucinatory gratification in the infant, but only a gratification by actual food intake. A chick in the egg grows up on physically

---

66. For a discussion of "flight into illness," or "paranosic gain," see Freud (219, p. 102; and 220, p. 336).

67. Cf. Freud (224, p. 463).

68. Cf. Chap. 15, pp. 318–19, particularly note 14*, above. These assumptions of Freud are theoretical reconstructions for which much indirect evidence is now available, both in psychoanalytic material and the observations of general developmental psychology. See Rapaport (596).

and chemically tangible food and not on ideas of eating. I do not see that older children prefer an imagined apple to a real one; the imbecile and the primitive are veritable realists and the latter commits his autistic stupidities—exactly as do we who have attained the pinnacle of human thinking—only when his understanding and experiences are insufficient, as in thinking about the cosmos, natural phenomena, illnesses, and other blows of fate and methods of defending against them, all of which are too complicated relationships for him.[69] The autistic thinking of the imbecile is just as simplified as his realistic thinking. I cannot find a creature, or even conceive of one capable of survival, who does not react first of all to reality and who does not act, however low a creature it be; nor can I conceive of autistic functions below a certain complexity of organization. Autism requires a complex memory. Thus, for instance, animal psychology (excepting a few observations on higher animals) knows only the reality-function.[70]

This contradiction can be easily resolved: *The autistic function is not as primitive as the simple forms of reality-function, but—in a certain sense—more primitive than the highest forms of the latter observed in man.* Lower animals possess only the reality-function and no creature thinks exclusively autistically. At a certain level of development, the autistic function is added to the reality-function and develops with it from there on.[71]

69. The child's growth on actual food saves him from autism—hallucinatory gratification—just as little as the primitive is saved by his "veritable realism" from magic and mythical thinking. In both the child and the primitive, the unknown and the forbidden are huge areas filled in by autism, magic, and myth.

70. Surely Bleuler would admit that the "reality-function" of the animal is different from that of the human being. The coordination of instinctual impulse and object is one of the guarantees of survival of the animal (cf. Fabre, 168; Uexkuell, 738; Lorenz, 484; Schneirla, 672). Even where such coordination is not the sole guarantee, the mechanism of delay and the "secondary process" play a limited role in comparison to man.

In man the latter is far-reachingly superimposed over the impulse-object coordination. Cf. Chaps. 15 and 17, above.

71. Realistic thinking (secondary process) results in an organization which controls that other thought-organization called autistic thinking (primary process). In this sense there is justification in considering—as Freud did—that autistic thinking is primary to realistic.

It is important to note that in a sense Bleuler is right: in part the bases of realistic thinking preexist and mature in relative independence of autism and conflict. Hartmann (Chap. 19, I, and note 43, above) discusses this issue as that of the "conflict-free ego sphere," pointing out that "fitting-in" is prior to conflict and reality-testing.

We can discern a few phases of the phylogenetic development, though naturally there are no sharp delimitations: [72]

I. Simple external situations are apprehended and acted upon: grasping food, attacking or taking flight, and so forth. These are hardly more than reflexes capable of but limited differentiation and complexity. Though these are accompanied by feelings of pleasure and displeasure, affectivity plays no special role in them, because it amounts merely to those changes in the general condition of the organism which are indivisibly connected with the specific processes in question (grabbing of food, flight).

II. Memory images are created and used by later emerging functions, but only in relation to external stimulation and to subserve realistic functions. Independent thinking solely in terms of memory-pictures is as yet impossible. The best-developed memory-pictures seen on earlier levels are apparently those subserving spatial orientation; we must not assume however that they are the only ones.

It is possible at this point for affects connected with memories to exert a certain influence upon the selection of the engrams that are to be used. The ant will choose the path which led to its prey before, not because it "thinks" that there is more that can be gotten there, but rather because the corresponding series of engrams implies positive feelings or drives.

III. In time more complicated and more sharply delineated concepts are created, and their use becomes increasingly more independent of external stimulation.

IV. Without external prompting, concepts are combined in accordance with experience into logical functions, that is, into inferences from things known to those unknown, and from the past to the future. There becomes possible not only a weighing of various alternatives, that is, choice of action, but also cohesive thinking exclusively in terms of memory-pictures and hence without reference to sensory stimuli and needs.

It is only at this point that the autistic function can emerge.[73]* *Only at this point can there be ideas accompanied by the vivid feeling of pleasure, only now*

72. I will not comment on Bleuler's outline of the phylogenetic development, both because from our present vantage point it seems quite sketchy and because we have so little reliable knowl- edge or even reasonable speculation with which to replace it.

73.* When a female dog raised in isolation (Gerard-Varet, 267, p. 485) imitates warming and suckling a piece of

can wishes be formed and bliss attained by their fantasied fulfillment, and only now can the environment be transformed in thought by not thinking (dissociating) of what is painful about it and by adding self-invented pleasurable ideas. The unreality-function thus cannot be more primitive than the beginnings of real thinking, and the former must develop parallel with the latter. The more complex and differentiated concept-formation and logical thinking become, the more exact is their adaptation to reality and the greater the *possibility* of their independence from the influence of affects. On the other hand, there is a proportionate increase in the possibility that feeling-toned engrams of the past and feeling-toned ideas about the future may become influential. The large number of thought-combinations permits an infinite manifold of fantasies, while the existence of innumerable feeling-toned memories of the past and affective ideas concerning the future gives a direct impetus to fantasying. In the course of this development the differences between the two kinds of thinking become steadily sharper until they develop into actual opposites which can bring about conflicts of increasing severity. A lack of balance between these two extremes in an individual may produce either dreamers who only concoct combinations without regard for reality and do not act, or else sober realists who are so filled with realistic thinking that they live only for the moment, anticipating nothing.[74]

There are several reasons why in spite of this parallel phylogenetic develop-

---

bread as if it were a pup, she only carries out an instinct-function lacking its proper object, as does a room-bred squirrel going through the motions of burying nuts into the floor. To a child, however, who handles a piece of wood as if it were a baby, the idea of a baby is already known.

74. As is generally true in psychological matters the optimum is neither the maximum nor the minimum. A type of drive-control conducive to daydreaming but prohibitive of action is just as unfavorable for adjustment as is a type of drive-control which permits action but is prohibitive of fantasy and freedom of thought. So far Bleuler's observation is accurate. There are, however, types of impulse-control which are more difficult to derive from Bleuler's conception of the relationship of autism to realism. Drive-controls influence not only fantasy and action but also emotion. There are forms of drive-control which are generally inhibitory, prohibitive of action, emotion, and fantasy. A theory in which affect-mechanism is the mainspring of autism encounters serious difficulties in attempting to explain obsessional forms of drive-control in which affects are suppressed or displaced, obsessive fantasies are luxuriant, and action is paralyzed by doubt.

ment, realistic thinking appears to be the higher and is the one more affected by mental disorder.

We are not born with the essential features of the reality-function; most of them must be acquired in the individual's lifetime. Endowment with the capacity to form many sharply defined concepts is an empty potentiality in the absence of rich experience to supply the material for the concepts and their delineation; logical combinations must also be acquired by experience, and even the broadest minds cannot encompass every factor of a complex state of affairs without experience as to what elements need to be taken into consideration. Thus reality-thinking works not only with inborn ability ("intelligence") but also with functions which can be acquired only by experience and specific exercise. We know, however, that such functions are infinitely more vulnerable than those rooted in the organism.

The situation is quite different with the mechanisms used by autism. They are inborn. Affects and strivings have always been exerting on our mental life the same influences which direct autistic thinking; they facilitate or inhibit thoughts to suit their own direction and choose without further consideration between various reaction possibilities. Much before his first year of life is over the child exhibits apparently complex affect-reactions. Not only does he react to love with love and expressions of love, and to threats with anxiety and crying, but also with rebuff to rebuff, which often finds a strikingly shrewd expression—and indeed it would be shrewd if it had been found by logical means. Even without understanding words, the child reacts to the affect-expressions of others; his own affects tell him, without consideration or experience, that love is to be answered by love, threats by defiance or anxious submission. Not only does he bring inborn reactions (smiling, hitting, and so forth) automatically into action but he also organizes his meager supply of ideas to suit his goals.[75]

The lying of very small children is such an affect-reaction. Peculiarly enough, there are educators who are not only morally outraged at such occurrences but are amazed that the simple childish soul can bring them about. But if a child

75. Apparently Bleuler also acknowledges the priority of autistic over realistic thinking, but he disguises it as "affective" thinking. From the point of view of psychoanalysis there is no difference between affective and autistic influences; both are subsumed under the concept primary process. Note, however, the difficulties this conception has yet to cope with; see note 17, above.

who is asked whether she took the apple knows she will be spanked for a yes, she has two forms of possible reaction. One is the consideration that she did eat the apple and must admit it; the other is the simple affect-reaction that one avoids unpleasantness. . . .

Excuses are to be similarly understood. They follow affect-impulses and therefore present themselves much more readily than does the truth, and occasionally attain remarkable complexity even in small children.

This behavior becomes more understandable if it is realized that simple nature never manifests itself without affective reasons. For simple nature language is but the handmaiden of wishes. It is quite foreign to it to state facts objectively in words.[76] A small child speaks only about what is of interest to him, what is of positive or negative feeling-tone. If he is expected to make a statement without relationship to feeling, he fails. Questioning children and primitives often fails because what they say does not correspond to the facts but rather to what they understand the questioner to expect of them. The tone of the question rather than its content determines the answer. . . . Such reactions are present in schizophrenics but are foreign to normal adults.

The inborn nature of autistic forms of thought is particularly obvious in *symbolism*. It shows a most unbelievable uniformity from person to person, period to period, race to race, dream to mental disorder and mythology. A very few motifs underlie hundreds of myths. The occasion for symbolism is always the same few complexes, and its means of expression also remain the same. The bird, ship, or casket that brings the newborn and carries the dying back to their secret place of origin, the bad (step-) mother, and so forth, are repeated constantly and mean always the same things. The conception of a circular course of life, the return of the aged . . . into the uterus or some other place where children come from, is still part of the self-created *Weltanschauung* of children between two and four, and is much the same as the mythologies and sagas of early millennia. The quite different conceptions transmitted by the parents are not assimilated and remain ineffective in the face of the autistic fabulations; indeed the little ones hold on to these and may even develop them further in conscious contradiction to parental authority.

Symbols familiar from religions of the distant past reappear in the delusional formations of schizophrenics who have no connection to that vanished world.

76. Cf. Mueller-Freienfels (529).

It would not be correct to speak here of inborn ideas, but when one is concerned with these matters similar conceptions come to mind; at any rate we have to assume that autistic symbolism contains an inborn *direction of ideas* inherent in every human being. . . .[77]

Autistic thinking also needs experiential material: in order to dream that one is a prince one must know that princes can have everything, including the most beautiful princess, and that their destiny is to live the carefree life of a king. In order to dream oneself rich, one must know that money can buy many good things. Such concepts can be so easily acquired that they are already present in earliest childhood and may even weather the most severe generalized brain disease. Clear concepts and compelling connections are obviously deleterious to fantasy. The child still enjoys the idea that he will be a prince some day; the grown-up remains aware of the impossibility of fulfillment of this wish, and at most he may occasionally say: "If I were a prince. . . ." It is also important that while for the realistic function there is only *one* correct result, autism has "endless possibilities" (Jung) and its goals can be reached in the most varied ways. Thus the differences between good and poor functioning of the latter do not appear great even when they are most extreme. While there is a difference in principle between correct and false inferences or arithmetic calculations, the tale of a child and that of a genius are equivalent as far as autistic purpose and subjective fulfillment are concerned.[78] When concepts grow vague and the logical function is inadequate, realistic thinking can lead only to incorrect results; autistic thinking, however, is not only undisturbed by such failures but is directly fostered by them in that they permit greater freedom of thought. . . .[79] Thus the *correct* combination in reality is a much higher

77. The material on symbolism in myths, fairy tales, and dreams has been assiduously gathered by psychoanalysts. Some of the outstanding contributions are: Jung (364), Abraham (5), Riklin (612), Rank and Sachs (589), Ferenczi (182), Rank (587), Silberer (690). Cf. also Cassirer (126). Jung uses the concepts of inborn symbolism and "racial memory" extensively, while Freud speaks of them only occasionally (the most clearly in 258).

78. It would seem that there is a radical difference between the tale of the child and the genius. The latter, besides being subjective fulfillment, is deliberate action, planful in character and communicative in aim. The role which the ego plays in bringing it about and in shaping it from an impulse or inspiration is different from that in the child's tale. See Chap. 23, IV, below.

79. Actually autistic thinking appears not only when realistic thinking is not yet or no longer effective (that is, when the ego does not have the strength re-

achievement than a combination corresponding to a wish. The latter is just like shooting a salvo—it has only to make a big noise; the former has a definite target to hit.[80]

If autistic thinking appears to be a kind of detrimental rambling, why is this phylogenetically young function of such extent and power that it already rules most psychological functions at the age of two (playing and daydreaming), that it becomes easily dominant in adults, is able to pit people and classes against each other in gruesome wars of annihilation, and gains mastery over the entire psyche in many pathological disorders of the reality-function?

First of all, it must be emphasized that the whole [phylogenetic series of the] animal kingdom is oriented to seeking pleasure and avoiding pain and that subjectively the quest for pleasure has come to be a goal in itself. That which is pleasure-toned is more or less useful to the individual and the species, while that which is painful is also harmful.[81] The principle upon which the existence of animals and the organization of their psyche are built cannot be suddenly abandoned just because on a certain level of development a danger emerges in the application of a new principle. The higher organism has to overcome the danger or perish. It is also possible that there is an apparatus inhibitory to autism; at any rate the pressing need of normal creatures to survive creates a powerful counterweight to it. In the final analysis, however, the species has to come to terms with the existence of autism. A certain amount can be easily borne; only in excess does it become deleterious. The delineation between moderation and excess is again difficult to find; therefore autism will never be quite conquered even in its deleterious forms. . . .

---

quired for synthesis), but also when the ego is strong and rich in synthetic power and can allow unconscious strivings to come to the fore in the form of inspirations. See Chap. 23, V, below.

80. To use Bleuler's manner of expression, the highest achievement is the correct combination of reality and wish. Humor, artistic creation, wisdom, a flexible manner of living, are various aspects of such an achievement.

81. In its literal sense, this statement is certainly not a tenet of psychoanalysis, nor is it correct. It is bald hedonism. The psychoanalytic view equates pain with tension and pleasure with tension-reduction. Cf. Freud (241). Whether in and of itself either is useful or harmful to a given individual or a species is questionable. What is useful or harmful to a species is a matter of natural selection in evolution and can hardly be predicted, since the process of evolution is slow and environmental changes occurring in its course may change what seems at one time useful into something harmful or vice versa; cf. Simpson (695).

It cannot be assumed that natural selection will ever do away with this new and limitless field of affective activity, especially since autism, even as it is now, has a positive value. The anticipated pleasure enforces consideration and preparation prior to an endeavor and enhances the energy of the striving.[82] Animals, and particularly lower ones, with their limited capacity for imagination and rudimentary memory often show remarkably little perseverance in following a goal, but man can become enthusiastic about the hunt while still in his cave and can make plans and weapons in advance. This kind of activity shades imperceptibly into autistic thinking proper. There must already have been people on earlier levels of development who, lacking in energy, satisfied their thirst for action by mere plan-making. If the hunting scenes of the artist of the paleolithic cave or the war songs of Tyrtaeus stimulated their fellows, there must already then have been human beings who could be satisfied with autistic hunting and warring, whether because they were themselves artists, or because they enjoyed the art of others.[83] I believe that this is the best example of where the borderline lies between harmful and useful autism and how indefinite it is. Art is useful when it stimulates and heightens vital energy, but harmful when it supplants action and when esthetic needs become so overwhelming that one cannot exist without an artistic environment.

Autistic thinking is also useful as an abreaction. In many cases it is not possible to abreact disagreeable experiences in a proper fashion. It may not be possible to win back the lost beloved who turned to another man, or to slay the slanderer, as one should, and so forth. But since our organism is so built that it must discharge such excitations, abreaction in fantasy, dream, or work of art is useful.

82. More than that: (a) the pleasure and pain signals remain important clues even for normal thinking; (b) as long as these signals are not inhibited and done away with, autism (primary-process thinking) will also obtrude into consciousness; (c) the root of such autistic thinking is in the same instinctual drives which motivate our actions, so that without paralyzing ourselves we shall never completely banish the primary process; (d) the obsessive-compulsive neurosis is a gigantic experiment of nature which attempts to banish impulses, affects, and primary-process thinking, and in his "logical" efforts at banishing these the compulsion neurotic falls a victim to their magic. (See Freud, 220.)

83. It would seem that Bleuler misinterpreted the significance of primitive cave-dweller art. According to our present understanding it served as a magic ritual guaranteeing success in battle and hunting. The Navajo sand-paintings and the many magic-ritual artifacts of surviving preliterates (see Werner, 755) seem to bear this out.

However, the danger of exaggeration is great, and the number of those who withdraw from life after a disappointment and whose internal abreaction never ends is none too small.

A further usefulness of autism is that it broadens the opportunity for the *exercise of thinking-ability*. The child is even less able than the adult to judge what is possible and what is not. But fantasies increase his combining capacity, as does motor-play his bodily skills. When playing soldier or mother, he exercises necessary idea- and feeling-complexes [84] in the same sense as the playing kitten prepares to catch living creatures. But there is the danger that one may not at the right moment be able to tear oneself away from the dream to make the jump to reality. On this point patients with pseudologia phantastica fail consistently.

A small degree of autism carried into life may be of some use. What is true of affects in general is true of this special application of their mechanisms. A degree of one-sidedness is indispensable in pursuing certain goals. One must overestimate the value of the goal in order to increase one's desire for it; one must not imagine all the difficulties and the methods of surmounting them, for this would prevent action and decrease one's energy. Real enthusiasm is unthinkable without autism, partly as an accompanying phenomenon and partly as a reinforcing cause. He who wants to influence the masses must feel no reservations, let alone think or express them.

Thus it is likely that in the future, too, autistic thinking will develop parallel with realistic thinking and will help to create cultural values as well as superstitions, delusions, and psychoneurotic symptoms.[85]

SUMMARY

Autistic thinking is independent of logical rules; it is directed by affective needs.

It is most obvious in dementia praecox and in the dream, next in mythology and superstition, and finally in the daydreams of hysterics and normals and in poetry.

Autistic thinking can use entirely illogical material; clang associations and incidental connections of any percepts or ideas may replace logical associations. Concepts incompletely thought through, false identifications, condensations,

84. Cf. Hendricks (322, 323).   85. Cf. note 82, above.

displacements, symbols treated as realities, and other similar abnormal thoughts constitute part of the material which it uses. Normal material and trains of thought are by no means shunned but used side by side with the abnormal.

Logical thinking which corresponds to reality is a reproduction in thought of the connections which reality offers.

Autistic thinking is directed by strivings which disregard logic and reality. The affects that underlie strivings, facilitate associations that favor them and inhibit opposing ones according to well-known laws.

It is our tendency to avoid pain not only when inflicted from without but also when elicited by mere ideas. The success of autistic thinking consists mainly in the creation of pleasant ideas and in the suppression of unpleasant ones. To think of wishes as fulfilled is one of the main activities of autism.

When a negative mood prevails, negative autistic-strivings may ensue. This occurs in depression and when conflict is experienced between autistic ideas and reality. . . .

Autistic thinking, just like logical thinking, can be either conscious or un-conscious. In dementia praecox the results of autistic thinking appear in con-sciousness as hallucinations, primordial delusional ideas, pseudo-memories. . . .

There may be a kind of thinking that could be called autistic which fulfills logical needs in an illogical fashion (as do certain elements of mythology and symbolism), and in which affective direction plays a subordinate role.

Autistic thinking is not a primitive form of thinking. It could be developed only after thinking in pure memory-pictures had become dominant, as against instantaneous psychic reactions to actual external situations.

Ordinary thinking, *fonction du réel*, is primary and cannot be dispensed with any more than can reality-directed action by any creature viable and with a psyche.

That the weakening of logical thinking leads to autistic thinking is under-standable, because logical thinking in terms of memory-pictures must be learned from experience, while autistic thinking follows inborn mechanisms. These mechanisms can utilize any idea-material according to laws inherent to all creatures.

That autistic thinking plays such an important role and is not eliminated by natural selection is rooted partly in that the finite mind is unable to draw a line between reality and autistic fantasy, and partly in that even pure autism has its usefulness as a thought exercise, just as bodily play is an exercise of bodily skills.

Nevertheless its phylogenetic significance is in many respects still unclear to us, as for example, the significance of its role in the arts.

CHAPTER 21

AUTISTIC-UNDISCIPLINED THINKING [1]
By Eugen Bleuler

EVER SINCE ANCIENT TIMES man's drive for knowledge and understanding has created theories about the origin of the world, the purpose of human existence, the origin of cosmic phenomena, the meaning of the Bad, and thousands of other things important for him. These theories had no reality value. Humanity attempted to change fate by magic and prayer. It fought illness with ineffectual means, and in other ways, too, used its energies uselessly, and even harmfully. Primitives created taboo systems, which in our eyes amount to an imposition of unbearable demands on their mental and physical energy, time, and comfort, and which are not only useless but often directly harmful.[2]

This was the result of a thinking unmindful of the limits of experience, a thinking that did not insist upon testing its conclusions by realistic and logical

1. Bleuler (70). I present one long and four briefer excerpts from this monograph. The first section is Bleuler's introduction.

2. Cf. Silberer (693) and Nunberg (543). Silberer shows that magic and myth are forms of thought which attempt to capture the meaning of the surrounding world. They differ from "logical" and "scientific" thought as we conceive of the latter, in that they correspond to a more primitive form of consciousness, to a state of "apperceptive weakness." (See Chap. 9, pp. 216 ff., above.) Nunberg (543) shows that the synthetic ego-function operates in all psychic productions, and is a derivative in the ego of the libidinous (uniting) forces of the id: "In the genesis of delusions rationalization seems to play the same part as that played in other preconscious thought-processes [and dreams] by secondary elaboration, which reconciles such antitheses as are too abrupt and fills up gaps in our thinking" (p. 122). Silberer's and Nunberg's studies provide a first orientation to the genesis of the autistic phenomena which Bleuler describes.

Bleuler's valuations, such as "no reality value," "useless," and "harmful," may well be questioned. Practices and taboos of preliterates which appear so nonsensical in our frame of reference have a definite place in the dynamic equilibrium of their lives. The impression of uselessness and harmfulness is often due to the fact that they are observed after Western civilization has already disrupted the dynamic equilibrium of which they were an organic part. Cf. Erickson (156, 159, 160, 157).

criteria. Such thinking is analogous to and in a sense even identical with dream-thinking and the thinking of the autistic schizophrenic who disregards reality, fulfills his wishes by grandiose delusions, and projects his impotence in delusions of persecution. Hence the name *autistic thinking*.[3] It has its own laws, and these deviate from those of (realistic) logic. It is not after truths, but after the fulfillment of wishes; it does not operate with the experientially established associations of strict, realistic-logical thinking, but with incidental associations of ideas, vague analogies, and above all, affective needs.[4]

As our knowledge broadens, the realm of autistic thinking automatically shrinks. Our conception of the history and organization of the universe, though in many respects hypothetical, is no longer autistic: we draw our conclusions in a logical fashion and only from what is observed, and know which of these conclusions are only probable.[5] But concerning our conception of the purpose

3. Cf. Bleuler (68; also Chap. 20, above). It must be kept in mind that insistence on testing conclusions by realistic and logical criteria does not replace the productive and creative impulse: discovery, invention, and creation, in science as well as in art, will always be based on the creative impulse, which is unique, individual, and autistic. Cf. Hadamard (298), Poincaré (575), Lowes (485), and Kris (421). Validity is provided for scientific inventions by empirical and logical criteria, and in artistic inventions by concern for communication. The roots of invention will, however, always be autistic. The unique quality of the creative man is that he is both sufficiently free and strong to allow his impulses and their ideational representations to come to consciousness and sufficiently controlled to be able to delay and hold these in order to validate them by empirical or logical criteria (science) or communicability (art). Creation and invention are autistic products, but they are so constructed as to reveal a segment of nature or to communicate a segment

of experience. Compare Rapaport (559, pp. 256–57).

In psychology and psychiatry there are, and will be for some time to come, many inventions which we have as yet no means to test empirically. Nevertheless we need these inventions, because out of them will grow the methods which will enable us to put them to empirical and logical tests.

4. Concerning Bleuler's views of realistic-logical thinking as originating in experientially established associations, see note 18, below, and Chap. 26, note 5, below.

5. It is probably not unfair to regard this conclusion as the wishful thinking of Bleuler, the rationalist. Actually, Bleuler acknowledges in the next sentence that in the realm of thinking about values no diminution of autism takes place. Our understanding of dreams has not diminished their autism. Hartmann (303), speaking of the clash of ego-interests with superego demands, points out that constant sources of conflict are inherent in the psychic structure itself.

of humanity and our existence, I have not yet heard anything but autistic mythology (because this question implies a false premise and cannot be realistically answered). . . .[6]

In medicine, the drive to help is still too quick and uninhibited, deliberation as to how and where to help too slow and halting. . . . Hence, the many mistakes and the zealous medical activity in maladies which get better by themselves as well as in those which are incurable.[7]

The drive, the instinct to help is the main prerequisite [in medical work] and, from the ethical standpoint, the highest. Yet it cannot in its present form (if at all) cope with the complicated task of conquering sickness, pain, and death. *The drive to heal can only be the spring and driving power of our actions; its direction, the where and how, is entirely a matter of the intellect.* To improve matters we must, first of all, become conscious of this new division of labor.[8]

The drive-character of autistic thinking distinguishes it from simple careless

---

Where there is conflict there is repression, and where there is repression there is primary process, that is, autism. Hartmann wrote:

This is particularly addressed to those more sanguine among our analytical colleagues who, in applying analysis to social and political problems, picture a world near to perfection, as to mental health or to social moral behavior, once the utilitarian ego-interests have taken over control.

In fact the realm of values and their influence appears broader today than Bleuler could possibly have conceived. Cf. Bruner (97, 98), Sherif (684), Bartlett (37), Murray (534), Murphy (533, pp. 362 ff.).

6. The section which follows is an excerpt from (70, pp. 79–81).

7. This is a point which might well be remembered in judging the present vogue of shock and lobotomy in the treatment of the mentally ill.

8. Bleuler's dichotomy of the drive to heal and the methods of healing points up that in "the upper reaches of the mind" we see repeated the same struggle with which we are familiar as that between the primary and the secondary process. The pleasure-principle implies that the drive-tension seeks discharge; the reality-principle postpones the discharge until safe and adequate conditions for discharge are found or created. The "drive to heal" is not one of the fundamental drives; it is a partial and derived motivation, originating from the control and concatenation of various partial drives. (See Rapaport, 596; Hartmann, 303; and Kris, 429.) Yet the same rules hold for it as for the primary drives.

Apparently there is a multilayered hierarchy of drives and their derivatives —the various motivating forces; and there is a multilayering of controls postponing their discharge. Whenever there is an insufficiency of such controls, direct discharge and autism come about. An example of this latter in medicine is here described by Bleuler.

thinking. If after treating a hundred cases of influenza with aspirin and observing a favorable course, I drew the conclusion that aspirin cures influenza, I
would merely have indulged in careless thinking. I would have disregarded the
fact that most cases of influenza spontaneously take a favorable course. But, if
I reject hypnosis with the argument that it weakens the will, my thinking is
autistic, since I advance this imaginary argument only because the power of
hypnosis over the intimate ego happens not to suit me; in other words, my
argument is purely affective, and this autistic logic is merely a means to an end.[9]
When the primitive builds for himself a conception of the origin of the world,
he is thinking autistically. He is out to satisfy his need for causal explanation [10]
and is unconcerned about experienced reality, about what is possible and what
is not. When the dreamer or schizophrenic considers himself the happy lover
of the beauty who in reality is inaccessible to him he is thinking autistically;
both disregard the impossibility and substitute something that does not correspond to reality. To flatter a patient, ascribe his nervousness to overwork; to
give him a blow, ascribe it to masturbation. Both explanations issue from autistic
thinking. Careless thinking does attempt to account for reality, but in an inadequate fashion; autistic thinking is concerned with reality only in so far as
it can use it and actively excludes it wherever it appears to hinder its purposes.
Careless thinking is oligophrenic and leads to error; autistic thinking is paranoid
and leads to delusions.[11] [Passage omitted.] [12]

9. Bleuler, in trying to distinguish between careless and autistic thinking,
raises an important problem. The "drive-
character" of autistic thinking is a fact
of observation, but a haphazard, un-
determined, careless thinking would not
fit into the fabric of dynamic psychology. Careless thinking too would have
to be strictly determined. How its determination (motivation) differs from
the drive-determination of autistic thinking is an as yet unanswered question. It
is possible that the explanation to be
found will parallel Schilder's comparison
of aphasic and common parapraxes
(Chap. 25, p. 566, below) and the complex vs. state of consciousness determina-

tion of schizophrenic thought (Chap.
26, note 40, below).

10. This need for causal explanation
is shown by Nunberg (543, pp. 123-24)
to be the core of the synthetic function
of the ego:

The compulsion which man is under to
inquire into the first cause of the world
of phenomena—the need for causality—is
accordingly the sublimated expression of
the reproductive instinct of Eros. That
which in the id appears as a tendency to
unite and bind together two living beings
manifests itself in the ego also as a tendency to unite and to bind—not objects,
however, but thoughts, ideas and experiences. Thus, in the need for causality the

The concept of drive is used here in the broadest sense, not only for the complex, instinct-like drives. The influence of affects is similar: they direct thinking into certain channels without regard to whether these channels are true and real. Every affect tends to facilitate what is syntonic with it and to inhibit what is in contradiction to it.[13] The lover sees only the good side of the beloved and suppresses ideas concerning the bad; the hater does the reverse. . . .[14]

The clear and affect-independent statement, "This I do not know," requires a high level of relationship to reality.[15] [Passage omitted.] [16]

A consideration of the *development of thinking* will clarify the reasons why normal civilized human beings, and even those academically educated, have not as yet been able to surpass autistic thinking. . . . Experiences become effective through their memory-engrams. He who was burned bewares the fire; *a previous experience, an engram, acquires the effect of the actual stimulus.* Engrams which have something in common are—psychologically speaking—combined into ideas which reproduce reality more or less faithfully and, like perceptions, they too serve as the basis of action. Association of ideas is analogous with experiences and thus creates connections similar to those existing in reality: this is [the basis of] logical thinking.[17] Again, the results of thinking, the recognition of logical and other connections, are pictures of reality, just as are directly perceived connections; thus they too serve as the basis of action. The remembering animal need not wait for a thing to happen; it can "foretell" by associating the outcome to the premise. Having made an associative bond

---

binding (synthetic) tendency of Eros reveals itself in a sublimated form in the ego. It would seem that this need represents a very important principle—that of connection—in the psychic realm as a whole.

11. This further distinction between a "careless" and an "autistic" thinking, though useful, does not settle the problem discussed in note 9, above.

12. The passage following is an excerpt from (70, p. 81).

13. See Bleuler's theory of affects, Chap. 20, note 22, above.

14. The passage following is an excerpt from p. 82.

15. It is true that the drives (the unconscious, the dream) know no negation; they can only posit their object. It is only the reality-testing ego which negates. Yet, as Freud's paper "Negation" (Chap. 17, above) shows, the statement "this I do not know" is not always "affect-independent." Often it is merely the obverse side of affect-dependence.

16. The remaining part of this section is the translation of (70, pp. 89 ff.).

17. Cf. note 4, above.

between cause and effect, it can, by acting on the cause, bring about the desirable effects and avoid the undesirable ones. . . .[18]

The combinations of ideas are, however, innumerable, particularly in the human brain with its infinite possibilities of connections. The closer the ideas stick to experience, the smaller the possibility of adaptation to unusual events; the less they stick to it, the greater the danger of creating false analogies. The more broadly the analogies are conceived, the less similarity there is between the situations which are treated as equivalents by the associations, and thus the greater the danger that incidental similarity will seem essential, and thinking and action be misguided. Thus, the relative liberation of thinking from reality is a prerequisite for new combinations, adaptation, and discovery on the one hand, and a source of errors on the other.[19] Therefore, thinking must always be measured against and corrected by reality.

At first all thinking is groping, alternately overshooting and withdrawing. In our immediate environment in everyday life, that is, in most of our functions, we follow old and familiar pathways. Where new tasks are faced, to which past experience has no strict analogies, we use more far-fetched similarities and more often stray from the desired goal, because the false pathways are infinitely many at every point, while the correct ones but few at best.[20]

18. It is noteworthy that reality-adequate thinking (experientially established association) is dealt with by Bleuler as purely a matter of logical (associative) prediction, with total disregard for the motivation involved. The epistemological difficulty (cf. Chap. 15, note 6, above) posed by ordered thinking in that it is both *intrapsychically motivated* and *reality-adequate* was not squarely faced by Bleuler. He avoided it by disregarding the role of motivation in logical thinking. This procedure is rather characteristic of the academic theories of thinking, including Gestalt-psychology. See, however, Tolman (733).

19. Here again we find one of those astute and subtle observations which make Bleuler's paper worthy of study despite the fact that it is theoretically loose and sometimes rambling. Effective concept-formation, productive thinking, and creative imagination are described here as existing only within the narrow range where thought is neither concretely reality-bound (compare Goldstein, 284) nor purely fanciful or over-abstracted to the point where it loses its connection to reality (cf. Freud, 234, also Chap. 26, note 107, below).

20. These considerations are related to the selective function of the anticipations (*Einstellungen*, see Chap. 25, notes 106 and 185, below) issuing from the prevailing motivations, memories, percepts, and their combinations, which are one aspect of the synthetic function of the ego. Compare Nunberg (543, p. 121):

. . . The thirst for understanding seeks explanations, and where our knowledge is sufficient, we advance; but where the prerequisites are insufficient, it
results in useless work and error. The need to avert the blows of fate prompts
us to act where our ignorance of the causal relationships precludes our choos-
ing the correct means, or even where there is nothing we can possibly change.
It is only the thinking of civilized man which attempts systematically to reduce
to a minimum the expenditure of action and thought, and to replace chance and
blind trial by reckoning, or at least to limit their extent.[21] But even civilized
man has not reached the heights of which he dreams; in many respects his
thinking is just as wanting in discipline as that of primitives.

. . . We communicate our thoughts and ideas in the form of information,
suggestion, request, and command, to influence and direct our environment.
But we do the same where it is of no use, as in wishes, prayers, and magic phrases,
and we treat fate and forces of nature as if they were human beings. Like the
bowler who twists his body to direct, as it were, the ball he has already let go,
we expect our blessings and curses to take effect; this kind of thinking takes
the pathological form of "omnipotence of thought" in compulsion neurotics.[22]
When a primitive is unable to kill his enemy with a weapon, he will destroy
his picture and expect to hurt him thereby; through a far-fetched analogy, the
picture takes the place of the person. In modern people symbolic action, though
in itself impotent, may indirectly reach the desired effect by arousing in oneself
and others a fanatic conviction that the hated person is a disgrace to humanity
and should be exterminated; when this spreads and is reinforced, it may even
lead into action.[23]

. . . [When] the superego is fully developed the task becomes more complicated, for the ego is called into action on
several fronts at once. (1) It reconciles the
conflicting elements in the autonomous instincts within the id and allies them one
with another so that there is unanimity of
feeling, action and will. (The ego tolerates
no contradiction). (2) It brings the instinctual trends of the id into harmony
with the requirements of reality. (3) It
strikes a balance between the claims of the
superego and of reality on the one hand,
and of the id on the other.
. . . this new creation is a product of

the ego and arises out of the assimilation
of insupportable inner and outer stimulation. It is in this process of assimilation
that we have the first and plainest manifestation of the ego's influence as an intermediary and binding force, that is, of its
synthetic function.

21. Cf. Freud (209, pp. 533–34).
22. Cf. Freud (227) and Kris (421).
23. Cf. recent literature on propaganda and psychological warfare: Kris
(433), Erickson (158), and Bettelheim
(59, 60).

Since there is no dividing line between correct and far-fetched thinking, the correctness of thinking must be newly established for each case. . . . If a desired goal cannot be achieved in reality, it will be represented in fantasy as somehow accomplished. The creation of magic formulae, the belief in their effectiveness, and dreaming oneself into situations which are unreal also satisfy such a need. Though the phrase "the wish is father to the thought" has acquired a connotation of censure, we must not forget that it can also have a positive significance: if we want to approach a goal we must conceive of it as reachable even if it cannot be achieved by the means available at the time.[24]

One of the important stimuli to autistic thinking is this: when in a critical moment the human being makes the transition from instinctive action to conscious deliberate action, without having as yet accumulated sufficient knowledge, he will be particularly helpless for some time after.[25] The man who in the mountains or at sea relies on map and compass, very quickly loses the natural orientation which has for generations enabled, for example, the traffic to Iceland over the foggy North Sea. . . . A deep graphological intuition deteriorates easily if one begins to search consciously for graphological indicators by which to go. This phenomenon is most startlingly seen in psychological endowments inborn in nearly everyone, such as, for instance, the ability to orient oneself among people by most minute affective nuances and to tell an imbecile from a normal person with ease. The same people who ten years before did these things instinctively with playful ease, without realizing that it is not a matter of direct perception, are altogether helpless in the psychiatric clinic. If they actually became specialists in psychiatry, they find it altogether "unscientific" to pay attention to affects. With such premises it will be no surprise that their assertions about the finer connections of affectivity with the rest of our psychological life will turn out to be quite autistic. . . .[26]

24. Bleuler touches here on the dynamics of action, a field still quite unexplored on the map of psychological knowledge. An approach to this problem has been made by the studies on the "level of aspiration." For surveys of this literature see Escalona (166a), and Lewin (467).

25. Cf. Chap. 19, III, above, on the guarantees of survival through instinct-ual action as compared with those through action regulated by the secondary process. Cf. Thorpe (729) on instinctive behavior and note his bibliography of the pertinent literature.

26. Bleuler's point is well illustrated by the stories of the blacksmith who was marvelously skillful in removing cataracts with his pocket knife and who never dared to touch another one after

Over and above the genetic necessity of autistic thinking and its useful pioneering for new knowledge, it has considerable value as *thought exercise*. Just
as a kitten's play prepares it for catching a mouse, so does a child who spins a
yarn in which he is the hero exercise his combinatory endowment and enrich
his ideas about the world and his ability to set realistic goals and to act on them.[27]
For adults too, autistic thinking enlarges the realm of thinking and research
beyond what is actually known. It stimulates us to attack problems which cannot be exactly answered with available knowledge, persistent inquiry into
which, however, may lead to scientific knowledge. Meynert's brain mythology
had an extremely fructifying effect, astronomy grew out of astrology, chemistry out of alchemy. . . .[28]

So far we have contrasted autistic thinking to "ordinary" thinking. But this
formulation is not exact: "ordinary" thinking does not exclude autistic thinking; rather is it a mixture of realistic and autistic thinking in which the former
is usually preponderant.[29] In some situations, however, autism prevails: for ex-

------

admiring surgeons explained to him the
remarkable precision of his procedure,
and of the centipede who could not
move after an ant expressed his astonishment about how he could keep so many
legs in order. Hartmann (Chap. 19,
above), and Kris (Chap. 23, below) use
the concepts automatization and de-
automatization to describe such phenomena. Compare also Klages's (382) and
T. T. Lessing's (448) anti-intellectualist
views in this connection. Note also that
while Bleuler does not consider "intuition" an autistic phenomenon, he does
consider its rationalizations to be such.
Though empathy and intuition certainly
are the archetype of our knowledge
about our fellow human beings, their
nature is still a closed book to us.

27. Here Bleuler touches upon the
various but as yet unclear roles of daydreaming. It seems evident that both
sexual and ambitious daydreams (Freud,
218) imply elements of planning. Day-

dreams following experiences of failure,
which have aroused guilt or anxiety, re-
plan and correct the experience in fantasy so as to lead to success and to allay
to some extent the guilt and anxiety.
There are, however, daydreams in which
the usual themes such as libidinous gratification, anxiety and guilt, and ambition
recede, while planning-like combinatory
activity is in the foreground. The dynamics and the possible disguise of more
primitive wishes employed by the latter
type of daydream have not yet been explored systematically. See Varendonck,
Chap. 22, note 30, below.

28. It is probable that much which
passes today for the science of psychology (academic and clinical) will be
looked upon—in times to come—as such
autistic thinking which broke ground
for scientific progress.

29. Cf. Bleuler, Chap. 20, note 17,
above.

ample, when the need to satisfy affects stands in the foreground, or when reality does not offer sufficient points of orientation for logical thinking. For the demands of everyday living, ordinary thinking suffices: we deal with our environment without committing major logical blunders; we can go through rather complicated considerations if they are not too unfamiliar to us. With our ordinary thinking we master certain areas quite well as, for example, does the average merchant in his business, which would be endangered if anything autistic were to slip in. When unschooled thinking is faced with unusual tasks, however, it usually fails, leaving the field open to autism or giving up. . . .

While from one point of view ordinary thinking is a mixture of autistic and realistic considerations, from another point of view it may be divided into *attentive and careless thinking*.[30] In the ordinary tasks of everyday life, this distinction is unimportant, since more or less everything occurs automatically and correctly; but as soon as a task becomes difficult and unusual, how much attention is paid and how much care is applied become very important. Experience teaches the laws of logic to everyone and the common concepts are clear enough for daily life. But as tasks grow difficult and unusual, there is an increased danger that ordinary thinking will become derailed and therefore there arises a greater need to counteract this danger by more intensive association-tension.[31]

Jung distinguishes between fantasying and dreaming on the one hand and "directed" thinking on the other.[32] This distinction is very similar to the one we have made between autistic and realistic thinking, but the expression is misleading. Though there is such a thing as undirected thinking, it plays a quite secondary role.[33] As soon as the logical needs are relaxed, affects and drives take

---

30. Cf. note 9, above. It is possible that while attentive thinking is on a higher cathectic level (cf. Chap. 15, pp. 324–25, above, and Chap. 23, note 20, below) than autistic thinking, careless thinking corresponds to fluctuations of attention-cathexes within the range permitted by this higher cathectic level.

31. Compare this formulation with my interpretation of "careless thinking" in notes 9 and 30, above. It shows similarity to Freud's cathectic theory of con-

sciousness, Chap. 16, note 14, above. See also Chap. 27, notes 10 and 16, below. By intensive association-tension Bleuler evidently means insistence on logically valid associative connections.

32. See Jung (364); cf. Bleuler, Chap. 20, pp. 399–400, above.

33. This apparently refers to Stransky's (719) experiments. Compare Freud's (209, pp. 484–85) views to the contrary.

charge of thinking so that in healthy people thinking is never really without direction. Autistic thinking is essentially even more goal-directed than ordinary or even realistic thinking. The latter often cannot reach its goal just because it takes into consideration every difficulty and obstacle and reckons only with reality.[34] The autistic thinking of religions promises us redeeming justice, eternal life, and the fulfillment of many other wishes of our hearts which realistic thinking denies or, at best, characterizes only as not impossible.

Ordinary thinking with its careless and autistic sidesteps is often contrasted with *scientific* thinking. I do not want to use this term, partly because it is so often misused, and partly because we see tightly built logical thinking outside of science too, as, for example, when the requirements of practical life demand it of businessmen, manufacturers, lawyers, and so on. Both careful and careless science make a claim of "scientific" thinking. Scientific thinking means not only strictly realistic-logical thinking, free of all detours and autisms, but also thinking in terms of a definite science conceived in the sense of certain "principles" and thought-formulas. Though from the point of view of science these "principles" are foolproof and may have a definite meaning for the student who has to master a certain area of knowledge, *their validity must be tested again and again whenever they are applied to a new area. . . .* Wherever definitions are important, as in law or in certain philosophical disciplines, we will find insufficient regard for scientific thinking. Good and telling definitions for correctly derived realistic concepts are at best few; the definitions of house, man, tree, a species, a psychological propensity, a sickness, must always remain incomplete; concepts which correspond to reality are derived from innumerable experiences which cannot be indicated in a few words, much less be circumscribed in a few sentences as to their common and differing constituents.[35]

[Passage omitted.]

Exact thinking is also a favorite requirement; some people will not recognize a science if it is not "exact." We cannot use this term either, because it seems quite indefensibly to imply a thinking only in terms of measurements and num-

---

34. Bleuler sees correctly that the goal-directedness of autistic (primary-process) thinking is more relentless than that of logical (secondary-process) thinking. Actually both are directed, but differently: the former to direct tension-discharge, the latter by detour.

The latter is often labeled ordered, goal-directed thinking, because its goal-direction is usually present in consciousness while the attempts to reach it are in progress. Cf. Ach, Chap. 1, above.

35. On concepts, cf. Bleuler, Chap. 26, VI, below.

bers. But this covers only a small portion of scientifically necessary thinking; by their very nature and complexity, qualitative differences are unreachable by quantitative treatment, and even many quantitative differences cannot be so measured with the means available at a given time or because of reasons of principle. . . .[36]

To limit the name "exact thinking" to the mathematical treatment of problems is justified only in the sense that the usual mathematical functions are unquestionably exact: 2×2 makes not approximately but quite exactly 4. . . . But mathematic exactitude has value only when the basis for the numbers is correspondingly exact, when the measure expressed by the numbers is just as exact as the numbers themselves. . . . *The real exactitude of thinking and of its results lies not merely in the application of mathematics but in their correct application: that is to say, the major emphasis is on the exactness of thinking.* . . .

. . . *In this sense "exact thinking"* [37] *does exist outside of mathematics.* It consists in correctly deriving concepts from exactly observed facts, testing their scope, constantly comparing them with reality, and never tolerating the same term for two different nuances or even for two different concepts, since this could lead to the error of substituting one for the other. It also demands that all presuppositions be sharply determined lest relevant ones be omitted or irrelevant ones included.

Therefore, we do not speak of scientific or exact but rather of *disciplined*

36. Cf. note 28, above. Note also the several attempts to introduce non-metric, yet exact methods into psychology: Lewin (468, 469), Heider (317), and Bavelas (38).

37. The issue of "exact thinking" again raises an epistemological question. In Kant's sense this question may be formulated as follows: Is "exact thinking" of empirical origin or is it rooted in the "categories of the pure mind and in the forms of apperception?" This problem pertains both to mathematical and non-mathematical exact thinking, that is, in Bleuler's terms to "disciplined thinking" in general. Clearly, the primary-process organizes experience according to rules inherent to human nature and not derived primarily from experience (even though these rules are later modified by experience). Are we to understand secondary-process thinking as derived from experience alone, as Bleuler would? (See note 4, above). Clearly we would have to make the reservation that even if it were so derived, it would stem from an experience first organized by the primary process. Cf. Rapaport (596). But there is some evidence that the outlines even of secondary-process mechanisms are inherent to the maturing organism. Cf. Hartmann, Chap. 19, IV.

thinking, a thinking educated to avoid the errors of other forms of thinking; to put it more positively, a thinking which tolerates only facts for its basis and draws conclusions from them only where clear analogies exist or, if it goes beyond that, labels the result as an assumption or hypothesis in need of verification. . . . It takes training to become adept in recognizing and avoiding all careless and autistic thinking. It is furthermore necessary to check and recheck the bases and results of our conclusions against the facts, whether by observation or experiment. Even apparently strictly logically, and indeed mathematically derived, conclusions may somewhere overlook a pertinent factor. . . .

To disciplined thinking belongs the ability to free oneself of mere opinions, no matter how widespread and old, of all biases, and of everything that is not based on observation; to it belongs the ability to form new logical combinations without becoming autistic.[38]

38. Cf. Windelband (773) on the epistemological problems of pre-Socratic Greek philosophers, particularly those of the Eleatics. Their philosophical problems are quite similar to the psychological ones raised here by Bleuler. The recrudescence of these problems in the thinking of the Sophists is also of considerable interest. See Bakewell's (3) collection of pre-Socratic Greek philosophy.

CHAPTER 22

THE PSYCHOLOGY OF DAYDREAMS [1]

By J. Varendonck

I. [PROCEDURE] [2]

IN RECALLING THE LINKS of the train of fantasies,[3] which my mind had been forging while it was wandering, I made use of a special and, in fact, a very simple method, which is familiar to every psychoanalyst. Professor Freud, who has invented it, describes it in his "Interpretation of Dreams" as follows:

. . . For the purpose of self-observation with concentrated attention, it is advantageous that the patient should occupy a restful position and close his eyes; he must be explicitly commanded to resign all criticism of the thought-formations which he perceives. He must be told further that the success of the psychoanalysis depends upon his noticing and telling everything that passes through his mind, and that he must not allow himself to suppress a single idea because it seems to him unimportant or irrelevant to the subject, or because it seems nonsensical. . . .[4]

1. Varendonck (740). A selection from this volume is included here, though it was published in English, because it is to my knowledge the only available collection and analysis of daydreams. The Belgian author wrote it in English which is often obscure, so that extensive omissions and insertions were necessary to make the meaning clear; even so the text leaves much to be desired.

The selection, only a fraction of the book, is taken from the first part, which reports and analyzes daydreams of his own. This part is divided into three sections: "The Genesis of Chains," "The Contents of Chains," and "The Termination of Chains." The present selection follows this structure. The second part of the book is theoretical. I include no selection from it because, first, it seemed almost impossible to disentangle it from the ill-defined concept of affect around which it is built (cf. Chap. 9, note 77); and secondly, the language difficulty is especially great in this part.

2. This selection is from (740, pp. 27–30).

3. The author means "daydreams," but he does not define what he means by either term. Actually, most of his material consists of hypnagogic-reveries; he is, however, unaware of Silberer's (Chaps. 8, 9, above) work on these. He fails to distinguish among the varieties of fantasy-thinking, such as hypnagogic and hypnopompic reverie, daydream, etc. He also seems unfamiliar with Freud's (218) study of daydreams.

4. Freud (209, p. 192). This is the "fundamental rule of psychoanalysis." Cf. Chap. 12, note 51, above.

The only noticeable difference in my use of this analytic method is that I try to retrace, step by step, all the ideas which have succeeded one another on the screen of my fore-consciousness,[5] but not at random. Usually I start from the last link (which I at once write down) and try to recapitulate the last but one, and so on, with the least possible attention and the greatest possible abandonment, until at a certain moment all the previous links of the concatenation come together. The whole process requires some practice, of course, especially in recovering the first idea which caused the mind to wander.[6]

During the process of analysis the distribution of energy over the different mental functions is . . . the same as . . . [in] actual daydreaming, as I shall

5. The usual psychoanalytic term is "preconscious." Varendonck appears to have been only superficially familiar with Freud's (209) theory of the pre-conscious, and not at all with its further development in "The Unconscious" (234). He speaks of daydreams as though they were "preconscious." This brings into sharp relief a point not usually discussed. Daydreams, fantasies, and rev-eries, once experienced, are *not* precon-scious, just as dreams are not uncon-scious, though they give us information as to the content and form of thought-organization prevalent in preconscious and unconscious ideation. The state of dream is not unconscious, nor is the state of daydream preconscious; but they do seem to be states of consciousness dif-ferent from that of usual waking. From the point of view of the theory of think-ing, the significance of dreams and day-dreams is precisely that they give infor-mation about forms of thought-organi-zation other than that prevailing in the normal waking state. Thus the latter be-comes relative, and thereby more easily amenable to understanding. Varendonck does not seem to have been aware of these considerations, nor of the fact that both the "unconscious" and the "precon-scious" are constructs: the one concep-

tualizes ideas which usually cannot be-come conscious without overcoming resistances; the other conceptualizes ideas which, though not conscious, are capable of becoming conscious any time. He reified the preconscious, and identi-fied it with the state of consciousness in which daydreams are experienced; thus he could say "the screen of my fore-conscious." Cf. also Chap. 23, II, par-ticularly notes 3, 11, and 20*, below.

6. In recording hypnagogic reveries and dreams, I too found that my records tended to begin with the end of the ex-perience. Efforts to begin at the begin-ning often result in losing or garbling part or all of the experience, or in slip-ping into new reveries. Somehow "re-cency" seems to have a great edge here over "primacy." It is quite possible that studies of this phenomenon may reveal the causal texture of "recency." For the moment, I should like to say only that an explanation in terms of cathectic dy-namics seems feasible.

My way of recording avoided the hunt for the "first idea": I recorded con-tinuously, interrupted only by dozing off. The new reverie or dream started where the record of the last broke off, and thus its beginning was easily estab-lished—provided it was legible.

prove later.[7] The slightest conscious reflection disturbs the process of remembering, and one writes almost automatically, without thinking. When I have to

7. Varendonck refers probably to the following passages (740, pp. 136–40):

. . . Writing . . . this book . . . I proceed in the following manner: . . . I have, lying beside me, my diaries . . . of over three years. . . . When I start the analysis of a new daydream I use a double sheet of foolscap paper, copying the fantasy sentence by sentence in a column on the . . . left, and afterwards assume the analyzing attitude while I ponder over every sentence, the direction of my musing being given by my wish to allow everything to rise to the surface that may come in useful for . . . detecting the mechanisms of fore-conscious thinking. These ideas . . . I scribble . . . down as quickly as possible, trying to write automatically, . . . to ensure that my consciousness shall not cast any reflection between two consecutive ideas, for this would produce a disturbing effect and cause me to abandon my fore-conscious mental attitude. . . . I reproduce as far as feasible the conditions of daydreaming with a consciously chosen purpose. . . . If in the end I were to read aloud all that is written from top to bottom . . . I should find the composition nonsensical. It would be full of abrupt deviations . . . comparable to the . . . apparently unconnected changes which we know in our dreams. . . .

In the next stage of my work I again rely mainly upon my fore-consciousness, but my aim has changed. I have gone over the jumble . . . and have retained the points that will enable me to develop a certain line of argument, as, for instance, in the present case: that fore-consciousness cannot correct the mistakes which it makes . . . because . . . reflection is denied to it, for it cannot swim upstream again; it knows only the forward movement of association.

If the order in which I want to present . . . my argumentation does not come forward at once fore-consciously, while I am reading them over, . . . I look after the fire, or play . . . the piano. . . . Provided I have been all this time in a half-dreamy state, the order of presentation is usually ready in my mind's eye without any apparent effort. (. . . Arrangements of this kind may occur to me wherever I am or whatever I am doing; but I always note them carefully, as I do my daydreams.)

But if I allowed my book to be printed as my fore-consciousness conceived it, it would be incomprehensible. . . . Therefore, my first work in the morning is to reread what I wrote almost spontaneously the day before; I complete, connect, rearrange, reserve points for later consideration, etc., until the whole produces a logical impression. . . . It has cost me very little conscious effort, and I owe it almost exclusively to my foreconscious self.

When I have come to the end of a section I cast a glance over my list of fore-conscious ideas, and I find that nearly all of them have automatically found their natural place in the text which my fore-consciousness has dictated. . . .

We are forced to conclude from this that among the reasons of the inferiority of our fore-conscious ideation the impossibility of halting at, and, worse still, of returning to, any given part of the preceding associations holds an important place. . . .

We know from our waking life how important it is to correct the verbal expression of our thoughts . . . but our inner self is incapable of . . . it. This activity is a privilege of consciousness.

. . . It is very probable that in directed thinking we commit as many mistakes as in fore-conscious thinking. . . . But in full awareness we can overlook the thoughts . . . with a critical intention.

translate visualized ideas into words, I invariably use several languages, writing the words in the language in which they come to the fore, because any attempt at translation would break the spell and disturb the train of recollection.[8]

II. [THE INCEPTION OF DAYDREAMS] [9]

"I was reading in bed Professor Ellwood's *Introduction to Social Psychology*, and when I dismissed all conscious activity I started automatically to compare certain definitions which I had just read with similar ones in Waxweiler's *Esquisse d'une Sociologie*. From this starting-point the chain went on: this volume is still at C. (the place where I lived before I came to the front). My only copy of my own book must still be there, too. Had I been able to show it to Principal T. during my interview with him, etc. . . . . until I find on awakening that I am thinking about the transport difficulties on the railroads in England." [10]

We condemn what is not to the point and retain what may come in useful. Let us suppose one has to write a letter . . . about a moral or material debt which one cannot pay. One thinks about the letter; and in one's mind it has already been composed over and over again before one writes it down; every argument that one can think of has been put forward and criticized, dropped or retained. . . . Numerous attempts . . . are forgotten by the waking self. This does not alter the fact that they have been judged by the critical faculties as not being to the point. . . . But whereas I have here retraced all my daydreams . . . in their spontaneous sequence, consciousness forgets all the preparatory work, retains only the correct solution. . . . Better still, the critical faculty has picked out from the rejected solutions the serviceable elements, and with these has composed the reply to the question. . . . If we could add up the total of all the suppositions offered before the conscious adoption of a solution . . . we should in all probability find in that total as many errors as in our fore-conscious chains of thought. . . .
The superiority of conscious thinking

lies in the possibility of recalling at will all the links of the association and of criticizing and correcting them with a conscious aim in view.

Particularly noteworthy is Varendonck's finding of the absence of reflective awareness and correction tendency in the state of consciousness of daydreams. Cf. Chap. 27, notes 25, 28, and 32, below. My observations corroborate this finding, but suggest that this is not an all-or-none affair and that qualitative variants of "awareness" seem to exist.

8. My experience corroborates this point.

9. This selection is from (740, pp. 35–53), and is part of the chapter "The Genesis of Chains." By "chains" Varendonck means the sequences of contents that make up daydreams.

10. Varendonck states that this and the following daydreams are quoted verbatim from his records. As to the sequence in this daydream cf. note 7, above.

In this example the concatenation started with the recollection of a day remnant (Ellwood's definitions) associated with older memories (Waxweiler's definitions). But a day remnant belongs to memory . . . as [does] a so-called remembrance; the only difference between the two is a question of time, the latter having been stored longer in our inner-self than the former.[11]

"It is eleven o'clock and I am trying hard to fall asleep. At a certain moment I become aware that the Germans are shelling the village. The explosion of a shell dropping a bit nearer than the others makes me think spontaneously of another shell, which six days ago dropped in the middle of our street and caused quite a number of casualties. Which way did it arrive and where did it come from? Did it come over the row of houses? Then it came from Mount Kemmel, etc. . . . until I am thinking of a schoolfellow of my youth who has become a specialist in ballistics, and of my days at the training college. At this moment the association is stopped and I become aware that 'I am off again.' "

In this instance the perception of the outer stimulus is indubitably followed by a recollection that entered my memory exactly six days before.

When I was collecting the material for this study and had often to interrupt my attempts to fall asleep in order to make notes, I soon observed that some kinds of fantasies kept me longer awake than others. But I first imagined that if I could start my associations with ideas that were not likely to stir any emotions . . . I should succeed in shortening my period of insomnia. Therefore I tried, and eventually succeeded in banishing from my mind any thought except the one I had voluntarily selected, and which I hoped . . . would not banish sleep. The end-result was not what I expected . . . for it is not the idea conceived at the outset that exercises a preponderant influence on the trend of the associations. The experiment proved simply to be an illustration of the proverb,

11. The usual term for what Varendonck calls the "day remnant" is "day-residue." The term does not seem fully justified here. Day-residues are unsettled experiences of the day which are used by the dream-wish in forming the manifest content of the dream. See Chap. 10, note 9, and Chap. 12, note 23, above. Varendonck uses it to designate the experience immediately preceding, and presumably setting off, the daydream.

At the end of this selection he states that these are "emotionally emphasized" —that is, in our terminology, connected with important strivings. In this respect they are similar to day-residues, but it must be kept in mind that the latter vary greatly in their drive-importance, and so in their relation to the dream-wish. It is possible that further study will show similar variants of the experience that sets off daydreams.

"All roads lead to Rome." [12] Here is part of a fantasy with a chosen genesis:

One night I was trying to think exclusively about the clever ways of a Brazilian thief operating in Paris, the account of which I had just read in the newspaper. When I returned to consciousness a short analysis brought to light the following chain:

"The Brazilian thief. . . . There is a branch of our International Society in San Paolo, too. The director once offered a brilliant post to my friend R. The branch in X. does splendid business (X. being in the country where I hoped at that time to get a chair) etc., all the rest centering round the same complex."

When I wrote above that "I was trying to think exclusively about," etc., I did not give a very exact description of my mental attitude: I certainly abandoned conscious thinking, for I did not concentrate, but as I knew that fore-conscious thoughts were bound to occupy the forum of my mind, I simply made an effort to avoid ideas about any other subject than the one I had chosen; I repressed part of my fore-conscious thoughts. . . . I cannot make out whether this mental attitude can be adopted without training, but I myself can assume it very readily.[13]

If we now summarize the different cases which we have examined, we may conclude [14] that fore-conscious chains which are formed *before sleep*, when the conscious Ego has been suspended, grow out of:

12. Varendonck's daydreams, as he indicates in his initial statement, display extensive preoccupation with his postwar plans: doctoral thesis and job-finding. Here he means that the "innocuous ideas" he started out with led to this preoccupation. We know that both hypnotically suggested dream-material and sensory-stimulation in sleep are used by the dream-wish just as the "innocuous idea" here is used by the consuming preoccupation. Cf. Chap. 10, note 9, above. Indeed, in problem-solving also, flexible people make use of all the feasible means available that can bring them closer to a solution. The difference may be described as one between the limitations of what is "feasible" for ordered problem-solving thinking, and the nearly limitless freedom of feasibility in dream and daydream. The daydream record which follows illustrates the point.

13. Varendonck is correct in his description that in the beginning of a reverie, one can dwell on a certain idea—though not just any—without discernible voluntary effort, until one begins to "drift." Whether *no* concentration or voluntary effort is involved is another unresolved question, unless "concentration" and "voluntariness" are used as descriptive terms rather than as concepts.

14. These conclusions may seem unimportant. But it must be remembered that what is now taken for granted was not thirty years ago; and whether or not Varendonck's conclusions are valid and important, we still have no others on daydreams as thought-processes.

a) The perception of an outer stimulus, of either a harmless or an exciting nature, which immediately associates with a recollection, and is soon lost to sight;

b) The coming to the surface of a day remnant, which may be indifferent or emotionally accentuated;

c) Ideas which are selected experimentally and may immediately link up with memories.

. . . The perception of an external stimulus . . . associates with a recollection of a day remnant that was waiting in the fore-consciousness, as it were, for the proper stimulus to form further associations and to progress. But the word or the idea which stimulates is interpreted in [the] sense imposed by the memorial elements; it is given a second meaning. . . . *These elements are always emotionally emphasized.*[15]

III. [THE CONTENTS OF DAYDREAMS] [16]

. . [The] daydreams [I presented] may have produced the impression that fore-conscious thinking is a concatenation of verbal expressions, that it thinks exclusively in words, like our conscious self. But I want the reader temporarily to suspend his judgment, for the case is not so simple. . . . Indeed, there are daydreams which are visual almost from beginning to end. . . .[17]

PRELIMINARY STATEMENT: At the beginning of the daydream there is a question of a medical certificate . . . : I had just returned to the front from an extra leave . . . [a telegram called me] to see my [sick] son. . . . As a proof of

15. The sum of these conclusions seems to be that daydreams start when a dynamically significant idea emerges, elicited either by unknown factors, or a thought, or an external stimulus. This idea—that is, the motivation which it represents—is in readiness, and seems to "wait" for an occasion to find expression. Varendonck also suggests that whatever elicits the idea is related to it and is interpreted accordingly. These relationships are quite familiar from observations of free-associations in psychoanalytic therapy, but about their workings much is still unknown.

16. This is a selection from (740, pp. 54–76), and is a part of the chapter, "The Contents of the Chains."

17. As the author notes in his final conclusions (Section V, 5, below), visualization becomes more prevalent as the reverie-state approximates the dream-state (that is, Varendonck's "unconscious" level). My experiences bear this out. Cf. Chap. 8, above, and Chap. 27, note 25, below. The next example in the text contains visualizations and elucidates their role.

the sincerity of the telegram . . . I . . . [submitted] a medical certificate, in which, however, something was not quite in order. But, as I had hoped, my superiors had not been aware of this.

The second part of the fantasy centers around an incident . . . the same day. An orderly from a Belgian Field Hospital had come into my office . . . and provoked my anger. He came with a request from Lady V., the head nurse, but spoke and behaved so impolitely that I flatly refused to grant it. He left the room threatening me with Lady V.'s vengeance. I immediately wrote a report on his behavior, demanding his punishment, and sent it to my commanding officer, Major H., as regulations prescribe. However, I had some doubts about . . . [how] Lady V. would regard the incident, for she was extremely influential, and I knew that the chief medical officer was practically at her mercy. . . .

DAYDREAM: "I have . . . [tried] to avoid obsessive thoughts . . . to fall quickly asleep. Therefore I have tried to think of nothing but . . . that I shall have an interview tomorrow with my commanding officer at Winnezeele. But I have soon forgotten my original purpose, and unawares I have associated with the chosen recollection the following ideas: my superior will not even mention the medical certificate I have sent him. Major H. also will have let it pass without looking at it. (Here I interrupt my concatenating with the reflection: I am thinking again! But never mind, the chain is of the indifferent sort.[18] Thereupon I resume unwittingly:) To whom will Major H. transmit my report? Either to the chief medical [or the administrative] officer; . . . not to Countess V. Still, the latter will have her say in the matter. What if I warned her so as to dispose her in my favor and arouse her feelings against the culprit? I begin to compose the letter which I intend to write to her with this purpose, but am interrupted by the idea: what if I enclosed my visiting-card (with my academic title)? What if I asked Captain Y. to send his corporal with the letter to the hospital? And I might add a copy of my report to it. But what a loss of

18. The meaning here seems to be: Varendonck notices that he is not daydreaming but thinking, and reproaches himself for this; he puts the reproach off by saying to himself: "No harm done; it is not an interesting daydream for the study." Some readers will undoubtedly raise the question: "Is this an objective scientific attitude?" It must be pointed out that this is a record of a reverie and reports what actually happened: in between the reverie and the state in which one records it, one finds all reasonable and unreasonable excuses to justify not making an effort to record.

time to copy that long report! Still, I might enclose my own copy and tear the sheet from my field notebook. However, I might still want that copy. I could ask her to return it to me after perusal. But what if I went to see her myself? I shall have to put on my best uniform. I'll send the orderly to ask her for an interview and tell him to give her my visiting-card. (Acting:) [19] I am talking to Lady V., and relate the events. Perhaps she will offer to send the man back to his regiment. I shall simply require a slight disciplinary measure. But what if she sides with him? One never knows. She might telephone to Major H. to thwart me.[20] Therefore I had better postpone calling on her till I myself have talked to him. I see myself already on the way to see Major H. But all at once I become aware that I am forging a fore-conscious chain of thoughts again, instead of sleeping. My first idea is to retrace it and write it down. But immediately I say to myself: 'No, it is not important enough.' But what if it were a case contradicting my theory, viz. that the association should be provoked by my emotion and not by a wish? But this supposition is wrong: in the present case the wish is a consequence of my emotion.[21] The wish inspiring the concatenation is . . . that the offender should not escape his punishment, and therefore I am trying to predispose Lady V. against him, thus depriving him of the assistance of the only person who is likely to take up his defense. Consequently the wish is a result of my emotion, and I am going to put the chain down in my diary.[22] I open my eyes and start writing."

. . . Previous analyses have made us already sufficiently familiar with the fore-conscious thought-processes, allowing us to perceive that my fore-conscious visualizing power [23] is fully active where I am talking to Lady V. From

19. This indicates that the experience is visualized: the author gives further information on this point below.

20. Cf. p. 465, below.

21. This passage refers to Varendonck's—to me quite unclear—attempt to construct a theoretical relation between affect and daydream similar to that Freud established between wish and dream.

22. Cf. note 18, above. Here it is difficult to decide which is more impressive, the honesty of the recording or the arbitrariness of the selection introduced

by self-observation. The methodological problems involved are still unsolved. But there is no way to study daydreams other than to study daydreams; the unreliability of self-observation must be taken into account, rather than discounted as a method. One way to reduce the unreliability is to record consecutive and complete periodic samples without selection, subsequently throwing out those periods which are known to be recorded incompletely.

23. Cf. Silberer (Chap. 9, pp. 225 ff., above), who shows that such visualizing

this point onwards the chain is comparable to a film in which I was, as said before, actor and spectator at the same time.[24] Making exception for a few reflections which we shall soon examine as a whole, every single sentence stands for
a whole acted scene. Some of these scenes I will presently describe.

As a matter of fact, the chain as it is written down here is absolutely similar
to the sketch of a film-play; the words simply express the part which I am acting in fancy. . . . Indeed, at a certain moment all the images stood before me
with the vividness of real dream pictures.

My superior will not even mention the medical certificate I have sent him:
this sentence represents a visualized recollection. . . . I see in my mind's eye
my commanding officer's office at the . . . moment when my certificate is
brought in by an orderly. He . . . is absent and his chair vacant. I see . . . my
colleague B., open the envelope, read my note, glance at the certificate and do
the necessary writing for its transmission to the general headquarters without
any suspicion that it is out of order.

Major H. also will have let it pass without looking at it. . . . The scene has
changed. Instead of . . . Winnezeele I am now in Cassel. As if no walls existed
for me, I see . . . my major's offices and . . . the filing of my certificate by a
secretary without my little fraud being detected. It is while my mind is closely
attentive to this well-known procedure in familiar surroundings that I "come
to," and my visualization is interrupted. . . . Afterwards it is resumed, and
even very distinctly, whilst I am composing my letter. Indeed, I notice very
distinctly the lines which I am supposed to be writing to Lady V., and see myself enclosing my visiting-card in the envelope.

With the next sentence, *"What if I asked Captain Y. to send his corporal with
the letter to the hospital?"* I am back in my own office again, which I share with
that officer. . . . I make my request to [him]. . . . He objects because of the
amount of work that still has to be done by his man. I suggest sending him
after office-hours. . . . [He] agrees.

But these visualizations call for one significant comment: they are not the

---

corresponds to a lowered "energy-level"
of psychic function.

24. This actor-spectator duality at
times produces—in reveries on levels
close to the state of consciousness of
dreams—experiences similar to those of

multiple personalities. This duality also
indicates that some *awareness* exists in
this state of consciousness, even though
it is not the reflective awareness with
which we are familiar in waking consciousness. Cf. Chap. 13, note 56, above.

recollections of scenes that have been perceived before; they are obviously composed by the admixture of images stored in memory: in the last instance the image of my own person moving in the memorial image of my office. This is what we call *thinking in pictures,* and . . . its verbal rendering is only a very incomplete translation of the actual happenings. . . . Every sentence stands for a whole acted scene, the words being like the legends of a film-play.

We notice also that my imagination suppresses the walls. . . . We shall come across more than one instance of this peculiarity. . . . [A] remark as to the similarity of day and nightdreams: I cannot doubt for a moment that I was really thinking fore-consciously at this point: "*If* I asked Captain Y.," etc., and yet the *if* is dropped at once, for I perform in fancy the act which is only introduced hypothetically in the text. "The dream ignores the supposition." My fore-consciousness does not ignore it, but at the same time acts as if it did not exist. This coexistence of hypothesis and reality is remarkable . . . and will give us . . . the key to understanding the above statement of Freud's.[25]

25. Freud (209, pp. 486–87) wrote:

The transformation to which the dream-thoughts are subjected because the expectation is put into the present tense is, perhaps, in this particular dream not so very striking. This is probably due to the special and really subsidiary role of the wishfulfilment in this dream. Let us take another dream, in which the dream-wish does not break away from the continuation of the waking thoughts in sleep; for example, the dream of Irma's injection. Here the dream-thought achieving representation is in the conditional: "If only Otto could be blamed for Irma's illness!" The dream suppresses the conditional, and replaces it by a simple present tense: "Yes, Otto is to blame for Irma's illness." This, then, is the first of the transformations which even the undistorted dream imposes on the dream-thoughts. . . . We dispose of it by a reference to the conscious fantasy, the daydream, which behaves in a similar fashion with its conceptual content.

We studied once a young man of 16 in a condition considered prodromal to schizophrenia whose description of his fantasies and daydreams, in which he was wholly absorbed, brought the here-discussed characteristics into sharp relief. In his daydreams he possessed three powers: that of immediate transportation, that of invisibility, and that of controlled strength. The first he described as "a very useful power because in a 14-minute rest-period, or during the last 14 minutes of a study-hour, I can transport myself from school to X. and back again." X. was the only town he felt happy in. *Invisibility* allowed him to observe while unobserved. By *controlled power* he meant that he had omnipotence, which he could direct or restrain from doing damage. It is noteworthy that this boy's (pathological) introspectiveness made him aware of basic characteristics of his fantasy-thinking. It is also noteworthy that the barriers between reality-thinking and daydream-thinking here crumble: he has powers in

. . . The same thing happens in the next scene, introduced by: *"But if I went to see her myself?"* Scarcely has this [been thought] . . . when I see myself making preparations for this call: I am . . . dressing. Immediately thereafter I am transported two miles away and find myself in the orderly-room of the hospital, asking a private to take my visiting-card to Lady V. And the next moment I am talking with her in her own private room. Still I had only thought that *I might call* upon her, and put it down as a hypothesis in my notes. The *if* is forgotten as soon as thought, and swifter than the wind I fancy myself in different places without any consideration of time or distance.[26]

Here I recall a previous remark: just as I lost sight of my colonel as quickly as I had evoked his spectre before me, I . . . forget [27] successively that I am in Winnezeele, then in Cassel, later in my own office, afterwards in my billet, to find myself finally back in Lady V.'s room.

The whole conversation . . . is summed up in a single sentence: "I am talking to Lady V. and relate what has occurred." I could easily fill a page with the description of the way in which she received me, of the satisfaction which I experienced at once again sitting comfortably in an easy-chair, conversing with a highly cultivated lady in the pleasant surroundings of her richly furnished boudoir. The reader's fancy will supplement the voluntary incompleteness of these comments, as they would lead us away from our main object.[28] Indeed, what has been written so far has sufficiently illustrated our first thesis, that verbal thinking is much briefer than thinking in images.[29]

---

daydream which he uses deliberately and must control; he speaks of them as "useful."

26. Cf. Freud (234, p. 120): *"Exemption from mutual contradiction, primary process* (motility of cathexis), *timelessness,* and *substitution of psychic for external reality*—these are the characteristics which we may expect to find in processes belonging to the system Ucs." Cf. also Freud (209, pp. 530–31). The coexistence of the conditional "if" with the disregard for it and for time is a coexistence of both secondary and primary modes of thought, characteristic of daydreams. Cf. Chap. 23, IV, below.

27. Varendonck refers to this "for-

getting"—both in his summary of this section, and in his conclusions at the end of this selection (Section V 6, below)— as essential in shaping the character of daydreams. The unidirectional character of daydreams, which Varendonck describes in note 7, above, and in his conclusions, is a more adequate interpretation of this characteristic than is "forgetting." Cf. Chap. 27, note 28, below.

28. "Selectiveness" of this type, without indication of whether a continuous record is extant and the sample presented is representative, seriously mars the value of Varendonck's volume.

29. My experience suggests that visual imagery in reveries is actually far terser

. . . At the end of the daydream the scenery has changed once more as I see myself *en route* to Major H.

. . . We again hark back to our analogy of a cinematographic film, and ask . . . how many sections we can distinguish. . . . Two entirely different preoccupations are discernible in the daydream: the first part . . . [to] the first interruption, is all about my medical certificate, which I hope will cause me no trouble; the second part tends toward the realization of my desire to revenge myself for the offense of the soldier sent to me by Lady V.[30]

---

than verbalization: it implies so much that verbal expression of it becomes most extensive. Inspection of Varendonck's material shows that the verbalization is terse only because of what it disregards. Indeed, verbal thinking is brief because of its selectiveness in terms of purpose. But even verbal thinking is usually rich in implication and connotation when its purpose is not merely description, but interpersonal communication.

30. The first part of the daydream brings about situations allaying the anxiety of the daydreamer lest his little fraud be detected. The second brings about situations which partly advance his revenge toward realization and partly allay his anxiety about Lady V.'s revenge. Cf. p. 465, below. This is not all: thought-representations of ego-attitudes —such as pride, social prejudice, "lick upward–kick downward" opportunism —also make their appearance.

This is the point where our general knowledge of daydreams, and Varendonck's analysis in particular, gives out. We do not know the specific relation between drives and these motivating factors of fantasy-thinking; we know only that they are derivatives of drives and defenses against them, and that their cathexes are neutralized in varying degrees. (See Kris, Chap. 23, IV, below). Further study of the nature of these motivations and of their role in daydreams is of the greatest importance for many reasons, among which one is outstanding. Daydreams often succeed in allaying, at least temporarily, the fears and urgings with which they deal. Their work of planning —by experimenting with possible solutions—seems to succeed at times in "binding" mobile cathexes (see Chap. 18, note 13, above). If this is actually the case, it seems an opportunity to study the little-understood process of "binding." The daydream then would not only deal with cathexes of various degrees of "binding," but would also "bind" them further. I have in mind the common observation that an "undigested" experience is slowly digested in the course of brooding over it.

Freud (238, p. 154) appears to refer to a similar process in describing the "work of mourning":

The task is now carried through bit by bit, under great expense of time and cathectic energy, while all the time the existence of the lost object is continued in the mind. Each single one of the memories and hopes which bound the libido to the object is brought up and hyper-cathected, and the detachment of the libido from it accomplished. Why this process of carrying out the behest of reality bit by bit, which is in the nature of a compromise, should be so extraordinarily painful is not at all easy to explain in terms of mental economics. It is worth noting that this pain seems natural to us. The fact is, however, that when

But if we do not take these two different purposes into account we can distinguish . . . five . . . sections: the first represents the reception of my certificate in my commanding officer's office. The second, the repetition of this scene in my major's office. The third episode . . . takes place in my own office, but in the beginning only my writing-paper is fully visualized; at the end, the whole room with its occupants is projected clearly on the screen while I am deliberating with Captain Y. The fourth part . . . represents my possible visit to Lady V. First I see myself . . . dressing (in my billet) . . . successively I find myself acting in the orderly-room of the hospital and in Lady V.'s boudoir. In the fifth . . . I am all of a sudden driving . . . to Major H.'s headquarters.

But the question arises: Why is the film interrupted four times? Fore-consciousness has realized in this fantasy two of the three . . . unities of the great French classical drama of the seventeenth century: unity of time and unity of action. But why not the third: unity of place? [31] Indeed, the scenery changes continually. In other words, why does not every single scene develop naturally with a slight transition out of the image immediately preceding it, exactly as in the verbal chain, where a link is observable between any pair of alternative ideas? For, strictly speaking, the link is missing between . . . [the] consecutive sections of the visual fantasy. . . .

I am perfectly aware that somebody might argue that some of the gaps which I have noticed in my visual imaginations did not exist in reality . . . but are due to my want of skill in observing. . . . [But] these sudden passages from one scene to another are familiar to everybody from our nocturnal dreams. Moreover, it would be impossible to explain how I could have lost sight of the scenes which I passed through . . . [in] transition between two successive parts, say, for example . . . from my office to my billet. Why should I have lost the remembrance of the visual representation, since I am able to fill up the gap each time with the proper verbal thought? . . . [32]

---

the work of mourning is completed the Ego becomes free and uninhibited again.

31. It is not usual for daydreams to observe the unity of time either.

32. It is quite possible that this is related to what Freud (209) describes as the "secondary elaboration" of the dream-content by the awakening consciousness (pp. 455 ff.). Indeed, Varendonck's Conclusion 5 (Section V, below), that "visualization is predominant when they [the chains] proceed closest to the unconscious level; in the reverse case verbal thoughts prevail" would lend indirect support to this assumption.

For reasons of method I ask permission to leave provisionally out of consideration . . . the two first sections of the fantasy. This procedure will allow us to discover that whenever a new part of the film is started we meet simultaneously with an *if* in the accompanying text.

Part III, in which I request Captain Y. to send his corporal with my letter . . . ends with the sentence: "I could ask Lady V. to return (my report after perusal)." And the next sentence is: "But *if* I went to see her myself?" This shows that I have all at once abandoned the idea of sending the corporal with a letter, for a new suggestion which has now arisen: that of calling . . . on Lady V. And immediately thereafter the scene has changed: I visualize my billet, in which I am dressing. . . . It looks as if the change of scene . . . were due to a new idea arising in . . . the mind.

When . . . we concentrate our attention upon the transition between Parts IV and V, we notice that something similar has happened: the film represents me in a boudoir talking to Lady V., when all at once I see myself driving in a car . . . to Cassel. If we look at the verbal rendering of the fantasy we get again the explanation of this sudden change of scene: during my discussion with the head nurse the idea has arisen that she might side with her orderly and telephone to Major H. to thwart my purpose. Immediately thereupon I conceive the idea of seeing this officer before I call upon her.[33] And as soon as I drop the idea of the interview with her the visualization is interrupted, and the hypothesis "*If* I went to talk to Major H. first" is at once represented.

The above discussion shows also that at the end of each visual part the mind has made an objection. (Between Parts III and IV it is [not] expressed explicitly. . . . "She might not return my report, which I may still want." Between Parts IV and V it is worded: "She might side with her orderly," etc.) It is . . . because of these objections that the pursuance of the idea, and consequently its visual representation, has been interrupted. This has necessitated on each occasion the search for another solution to the problem which occupies the fore-consciousness. The change of scene is . . . due to the objections that are successively raised, causing rejection and the introduction of a new hypothesis. *The visual elements are dependent upon the thought-process;* they form only a constituent part of it. . . . In each case the rejection is based on

33. Note the "reversibility" of time in the daydream: the visit to Major H. is inserted *before* the visit with Lady V., though the latter *had already* taken place.

the same reason: "Thus I shall not get the fellow punished." This is the main motive that sets my brain working, the touchstone for all the suppositions that are successively formulated; only the result of this . . . is not rendered each time in the verbal reproduction, although there is no doubt that the ultimate end was all the time present in the mind.[34]

When we . . . examine the . . . hypotheses . . . more closely, we notice that they are all introduced by the word "if." Our fore-consciousness visualizes the content of the supposition, but the hypothetic character of the phrase is not represented. Does that mean that our fore-consciousness ignores hypothesis? If it did, it could not object to it nor reject it. There cannot be any doubt that it sees the supposition, or what is the same, its image, but it is not the dupe of this actuality. It does not ignore that two ways are open to it: it may reject it or adopt it and associate upon it as a new basis. The point is that the possibility of this choice is not expressed in so many words; we have no awareness of it; still, it is present in the mind, and active at the required moment.[35]

34. In his Conclusion 5 (Section V, below), Varendonck indicates that the verbalizations arise when the daydream comes close to the state of consciousness of waking. He formulates these verbalizations here: "at the end of each visual part the mind made an objection."

With this in mind, we may reevaluate his assertion that "the visual elements are dependent upon the thought-process; they form only a constituent part of it." If this were a dream, then the wishful-filling primary process would bring about the experience of revenge. The visual elements would indeed be dependent upon the revenge-directed thought-process. But this is a daydream; critical consciousness awakens and interrupts the thought-process, whereupon it starts on a new track, either to be interrupted again or carried to fulfillment. Thus, if Varendonck meant that the visual elements are constituents of the *verbal* thought-process, he was incorrect; they are constituents of those wish-directed thought-processes which are interrupted by the realistic waking-thought, using verbalization.

Here the experimental character of some daydreams becomes clear, as does its dependence on the periodically intervening waking-thought. This is not always true, since many daydreams simply fulfill a wish, like dreams. Experimenting in thought always indicates the participation of the secondary process.

35. Cf. note 25, above. Imagery *cannot* express the conditional, and the unconscious has no "No." See also Freud (221, p. 184; 212, p. 70; 239, p. 559). Such patterns of thought as "if-then," "although," "nevertheless," "as," "consequently," "perhaps," "what if," are late products of mental development and appear to crystallize as quasi-stable anticipation-patterns; cf. Chap. 6, note 16, above, and Chap. 25, note 185, below; also Rapaport *et al.* (602, pp. 215–20).

It is probably incorrect to assert that "two ways are open" to the daydream process, that it does not ignore the "supposition," and makes "choices." Rather,

We gather from this discussion that when our thinking is preponderatingly visual, not all the elements of thought are represented by our mental images. Thus the latter are . . . the illustrations of our thoughts, just as when a certain number of isolated pictures accompany our [verbal] ideation in [waking]. . . . There is only one manner of rendering more or less completely, of taking into account all the relations between the elements of our intellections; that is, with the aid of conscious speech.[36] This does not alter the fact that our awareness is more impressed by the vivid pictures that accompany our mental processes than by the ideas that act in the background; we retain the former more easily. But it is precisely the role of psychoanalysis to explain the respective importance and action of the different factors that intervene in the ideation that goes on without the knowledge of consciousness. . . .[37]

The reader may not yet be convinced . . . that even in fore-conscious visualized thinking the visions do not constitute the principal mechanism of the process. Therefore . . . we will now reconstruct the visual images into a concatenation. If the picturesque part has played the leading role, not a single link should be missing. . . . But if there is a link missing, we shall only find its verbal correspondent somewhere in the verbal association, which forms a more perfect whole, as it gives an account of processes and relations of which the fore-consciousness is not aware.[38]

The third part of the film represents my conversation with Captain Y. in our office. In the fourth part I am . . . dressing in my own bedroom. All that has happened, or that in real life would have happened, in the interval between these two actions . . . is not represented. If in a cinema they projected two successive scenes like these on the screen without interpolating a short explanatory text, the spectators would be unable to follow the action. But we

it seems that many alternatives are present as potential drive-representations, but only one is hypercathected at a given moment; when critical consciousness, arising in the verbal form of a "supposition," halts the prevailing train of representations, the wish enforces hypercathecting another train on its way toward fulfillment. Concerning the nature of this hypercathexis, see Kris, Chap. 23, IV, below.

36. For reservations concerning the argument on both "illustrations" and "conscious speech," cf. notes 29 and 34, above.

37. Cf. note 5, above, on the quality of consciousness in daydreams.

38. The argument that the more "complete" element must be the "leading" one is unfounded; furthermore, the completeness of the verbal associations in this daydream is also questionable. Cf. note 34, above.

find the explanation of this lack of transition if we turn to our text: "I could ask Lady V. to return my report. But if I went to see her myself?" Here the absence of the missing thought (. . . "She might not return it". . .) does not strike us at all. In conscious life we are indeed used to omissions like the one in this sequence, and it . . . [is] easy to complete the short cut. Abbreviations of this kind are characteristic of realistic thinking. It may even be questioned whether our mind would have become the marvelous instrument that it is if we were not able to replace long-winded connections by short-cuts of this nature. Therefore, when I say: "I could ask Lady V. to return my report. What if I went to see her myself?" the missing link seems so natural that in our waking life we do not even become aware of its absence.[39]

But the same cannot be said about a missing transition in a film: in the last image of the third part I am discussing . . . with Captain Y. in our office, and in the first image of the fourth part, following immediately upon it, I am . . . dressing in my bedroom. As the two images succeed one another rapidly upon the screen, the mind does not seize this sudden change of conditions; . . . we are at a loss what to make of it. Moving pictures do not allow of any visual short cuts . . . the playwright . . . has recourse to a few sentences which he projects on the screen. Our fore-conscious visualizing ideation proceeds in a similar manner, only the thoughts . . . need not be projected, because they are present in the mind without any awareness, and only when our analysis retraces our processes do we translate them into words. The gap in the pictorial part is filled up by mental conditions which do not achieve expression in the fore-conscious state.[40]

39. In regard to the advantages of "elliptic" forms of communication, Varendonck is correct; cf. Hartmann's discussion of "automatization" and "formular abbreviation," Chap. 19, VIII, above. But his argument implies that visual imagery cannot use elliptic forms without impairing communication; and this not only is unconvincing, but distracts us from the real shortcomings of visual representation: (a) it is wanting in means to express relationships; (b) it is limited to either positing or not positing a content, and has only sparse means to qualify positing; (c) it lacks means to express abstractions; (d) it is "implicative," or condensing, a quality which defies ordered verbal communication. Cf. notes 29 and 35, above.

40. This appears to refer to the "implicative" character of visual imagery; the experience of visual imagery conveys many meanings in ways the subject cannot give an account of. For example: "In my dream I see my father, and I know that he approves of me now. But I do not know how I know that— he does not speak nor does he smile."

The same . . . holds . . . for the transition between the other parts of the fantasy: at the end of the fourth episode I am talking to Lady V. in her boudoir, and at the beginning of the fifth I am driving in a car far away, etc.

We are entitled to draw the conclusion that *the thought-associations*, which are rendered in words when we succeed in becoming conscious of our fancy, *are the principal part of the fantasy, the visual images only the illustrations. . . .*[41]

[Passage omitted.]

The field is now clear for the discussion of the verbal thought-process of this fantasy. We are now able to reproduce the text of the daydream—at least of that part which we considered before—in . . . [a] way, which makes it look like a problem which the fore-consciousness tries to solve by successive attempts. . . .

How shall I get the soldier punished?

What if I warned her (so as to dispose her in my favour and arouse her feelings against the culprit)?	I start composing the letter.
If I enclosed my visiting-card?	No reply (suggestion accepted).
If I asked Captain Y. to send his corporal with it?	He is too busy.
And if he went after office-hours?	No reply (suggestion accepted).
If I added a copy of my report?	A great waste of time to copy it.
If I tore my own report out of my notebook?	I might still want it.
If I asked her to return it?	(Understood: she might not do so.)
If I went to see her myself?	I shall put on my best uniform.
If I handed my card to an orderly and asked for an interview?	(Suggestion accepted and visualized, as well as the interview itself.)
If she offered to have the man sent back to his regiment?	I should only require a slight punishment.
But if she sided with him, telephoning to Major H. to thwart me?	Better not call upon her until I have seen Major H. myself.

41. Compare note 34, above, where an alternative explanation of the relation between visualization and verbalization is suggested. Indeed, it is hard to understand how Varendonck can reconcile his view here with his Conclusion 5, in Section V, below, or with Freud's theory of dreams which he consistently affirms.

. . . The analysis makes the whole dream appear as a concatenation of suppositions and objections, of questions and answers disposed in pairs, between which there do not seem to exist any very apparent transitions. And yet there is . . . a common tie, although it remains in the background. This common bond is the ever-recurring problem, after the objection has done away with the proposed hypnothesis: "Still, *I want the soldier punished!*" This ever-recurring expression of anxiety [42] might be inserted after each pair of questions and replies. . . .

This list of proposed solutions and refutations teaches us several things, among which one of the most apparent is that it brilliantly illustrates the truth of the popular saying that *the wish is father to the thought.* It is evident that the wish not to allow the disrespectful private to escape his punishment provokes every other thought, continually proposing new means of reaching its end, and is the incentive for the invention of the different proceedings. Therefore we might add that it illustrates another proverb: *Necessity is the mother of invention.*[43]

At the close of this chapter we may look back with some satisfaction . . . for we have discovered several data which will furnish the elements for an attempt to describe the mechanisms active in . . . fore-conscious thinking. . . . Our undirected trains of thought take the external form of a series of questions and answers, occasionally interrupted by memory-hallucinations, in which the recollections pass into the dynamic state: . . . internally the links are nothing but a continuous succession of remembrances; . . . forgetting plays as active and extensive a role as remembering; . . . the defects of this thought-process, as well as its superiorities, are mainly due to the capacity of the mind to forget as well as to remember, and to be distracted (and in a less degree to the use of external associations, although these are encountered more frequently than when we are conscious).

IV. [THE TERMINATION OF DAYDREAMS] [44]

Our analysis of daydreams will be completed when we have discovered how they terminate. In a few instances the conclusion seems obvious enough:

42. Cf. notes 30 and 34, above.

43. The implication is that a thought becomes an invention only when it cogwheels with reality; otherwise there is neither necessity, limitation, nor objection, but only drive-need and wishfulfilling thought.

44. This selection is from (740, pp. 154–60), and is a part of the chapter "The Termination of the Chains."

a) "I was (in bed) thinking about the stationery for which we had indented last Saturday, when the humming of aeroplanes awoke me."

b) "At 10:45 P.M. the buzz of the heavy motor of a car, which I had first taken for the sound of an aeroplane, awakes me from a reverie just as I am thinking of the torpedoed Sussex, in which my friend X. lost his life."

c) "I return to consciousness just as the clock strikes a quarter past ten. This concordance makes me think that there is a relation of cause and effect between the awaking and the striking; but this may be erroneous, for I often wake without any outer stimulus. . . . I was just musing about the means of passing my doctor's examination when my reverie was broken off."

This last observation, which I copy from my notes as I wrote it down in the early days of my investigation . . . is more profound than I thought at the time. . . . It is nevertheless true that the perception of external stimuli coincides as often with the abrupt conclusion of daydreams as with the genesis of others. At the same time, we note that the last link at which the association is broken off is in every instance a recollection.

[Passage omitted.]

. . . Fore-conscious satisfaction . . . often warns us intuitively that we are daydreaming. I copy from my notes: I was perusing Freud's *Psychopathology of Everyday Life*, Chapter IV, "Lapses in Reading and Writing," when on page 123 an idea arose to consciousness as I was rather distractedly reading the following lines: ". . . But I had to reflect for quite a while in order to discover what influence diverted me from my first attention without making itself known to my consciousness."

The thought that come to the surface was: "There is something going on in my fore-consciousness which is directly related to my subject. I ought to stop reading for a little while and let it rise to the surface." So I did indeed stop reading, and I was able to retrace a whole chain of ideation, which proved to be an inspiration and made me very happy.

[Passage omitted.]

From [these] examples we conclude that, whenever *we awake from a daydream*, we find that the last association was a memorial element. . . .

If we next inquire as to the cause of the awakening, we find external or internal stimuli. The internal stimuli are provoked most often in my own case by my wish for discovery; only seldom have I observed an awakening, either in the daytime or at night, in which no particular affect whatever could be traced.

Whosoever has once felt the joy that invades one when one has lit upon a new fact, unobserved before, will readily grant that it is really the emotion that is responsible for the interruption of our fantasies. . . .

We may conclude that the awakening from fore-conscious thought takes place at a moment of intellectual passivity under the impulse of an affect which may vary from a great intensity . . . [to one] only discernible through analysis; in the latter case the external stimulus may divert the recollecting in favour of the apperceiving process, with the result of bringing us back to the conscious state. . . . We conclude . . . that whenever fore-conscious wishes enter into a conflict, we are on the verge of becoming conscious again. . . .[45]

v. [CONCLUSION] [46]

In concluding this portion of our investigations we are able to describe our daydreams as follows:

1. A fore-conscious chain of thoughts is a succession of hypotheses and rejoinders, of questions and answers, occasionally interrupted by memory hallucinations.

2. These suppositions and criticisms look like a mental testing of memory elements [as to whether they are] adapted to meet a future situation.

3. The associative process is directed by one or several wishes, and is the more unsteady as the directive wishes are weaker.

4. Every chain originates with a remembrance that is, as a rule, emotionally accentuated and which is either brought forward on the occasion of an external stimulus or simply obtrudes itself upon our fore-conscious attention.

5. As the chains progress their depth varies continually; visualization is predominant when they proceed closest to the unconscious level; in the reverse case verbal thoughts prevail; but when the ideation proceeds in images, the re-

45. Thus Varendonck finds four "causes" for the termination of daydreams: (a) external stimuli; (b) internal stimuli due to a wish to awaken or to sleep; (c) elation accompanying inventions in daydream; (d) conflict with the critical faculty (as in the Lady V. daydream). The present selection does not represent these four varieties clearly, but neither does Varendonck: he rambles, illustrates only by referring back to daydreams previously quoted, and he does not summarize.

46. This is taken from (740, pp. 179–80).

lations between the visual representations are kept in mind without being represented, and only words can render them adequately when we decide to communicate these fantasies, which are not meant for communication.

6. They move only in a forward direction, which renders the later correction of their constitutive parts impossible except through the intervention of conscious functions. Another cause of errors is the mind's unlimited capacity for forgetting as well as for remembering.

7. These streams of thought are brought to an end (before or after their aim has been reached) at a moment of mental passivity under the influence of some affect which causes them to rise to the surface, or because memory is set in action in the service of apperception, following upon external stimuli. In both cases the result is a return to the conscious state.

CHAPTER 23

ON PRECONSCIOUS MENTAL PROCESSES [1]
By Ernst Kris

I. INTRODUCTION

[Section omitted.] [2]

II. PROBLEMS AND MAIN ASSUMPTIONS

ONE OF THE IMMEDIATE REASONS that may account for the fact that the discussion of preconscious mental processes has recently played a minor part in psychoanalytic writings may well lie in the history of psychoanalytic theory itself. Freud's thoughts were in a constant flux, his writings represent a sequence of reformulations; one might therefore well take the view that the systematic cohesion of psychoanalytic propositions is only or at least best accessible through their history. The clearest instance of such a reformulation was the gradual introduction of structural concepts. The introduction of these new concepts has never fully been integrated with the broad set of propositions developed earlier. Much of Freud's views on preconscious mental processes is contained in writings in which he discusses functions of the System Pcs,[3*]

1. Kris (429).

2. The Introduction, omitted for reasons of space, may be summarized as follows: (a) The concept of preconscious processes is frequently disregarded in recent psychoanalytic literature (Alexander, 16). (b) Actually, however, as psychoanalysts center their attention on ego-psychology they are studying it more carefully than ever before. This is due to the therapeutic rule "wait until what you wish to interpret is preconscious" (Freud, 257), to the necessity to pay as much attention to the ego as to the id, and superego, and reality in therapeutic work (A. Freud, 201), and to the interest in thought and fantasy in their relations to conflict and as parts of the "conflict-free sphere" (Hartmann, 305). (c) The term itself is neglected, but not the phenomena to which it refers; the study of the latter is prerequisite to an embracing psychoanalytic psychology. [Kris's own studies on various forms of art belong to the outstanding contributions on the role of preconscious processes. See particularly those on the psychotic art productions, 424, 422, 434; on caricature, 431; the comic, 423; laughter, 425; inspiration, 428; aesthetics, 430; and the psychology of art, 426, 421.]

3.* Freud (233, 234, 236).

[Freud (233) is the prolegomenon to

later attributed to the ego as a psychic organization.[4] In sharp contrast to these older formulations stand those of Freud's later days, when he considers "preconscious" merely as a "mental quality." [5*]

Freud (234), which contains Freud's major discussion of the preconscious processes. For an extract see Chap. 15, note 21, above. Freud (236) presents a simple restatement of the concept preconscious.

It may be helpful to the reader to know the historical background for Kris's formulation. Freud's first systematic discussion of the concept is in Chapter VII of "The Interpretation of Dreams" (209); see also Freud (225, pp. 25 and 27). For later discussion cf. Freud (243, pp. 21–88, and 241, pp. 15–20 and 41–42).

Freud in his schema of the mental apparatus (see Chap. 16, note 6, above), defines the preconscious as follows (209, p. 491):

The last of the systems at the motor end we call the *preconscious* (*Pcs*) to denote that the exciting processes in this system can reach consciousness without any further detention, provided certain other conditions are fulfilled, for example, the attainment of a definite degree of intensity, a certain apportionment of that function which we must call attention, etc. This is at the same time the system which holds the keys of voluntary motility. The system behind it we call the *unconscious* (*Ucs*), because it has no access to consciousness *except through the preconscious*, in the passage through which the excitation-process must submit to certain changes.

He also formulates (*ibid.*, p. 544):

The novel fact that we have learned from the analysis of psychopathological formations, and indeed from the first member of the group, from dreams, is that the uncon-

4. Though "The Interpretation of Dreams" (209) considers the preconscious as a psychic system, it contains discussions of consciousness, attention, and the process of hypercathecting, which clearly prepare the ground for treating "preconscious" as a "mental quality" (pp. 515, 529–30, 533–36). Cf. also Chap. 15, notes 19, 20, and 30, above.

5.* Freud (257, pp. 38–39).

[. . . we have attributed three qualities to mental processes: they are either conscious, preconscious, or unconscious. The division between the three classes of material which have these qualities is neither absolute nor permanent. What is preconscious becomes conscious, as we have seen, without any activity on our part; what is unconscious can, as a result of our efforts, be made conscious, though in the process we may have an impression that we are overcoming what are often very strong resistances.]

---

scious—and hence all that is psychic—occurs as a function of two separate systems, and that as such it occurs even in normal psychic life. There are consequently *two kinds of unconscious*, which have not as yet been distinguished by psychologists. Both are unconscious in the psychological sense; but in our sense the first, which we call *Ucs*, is likewise *incapable of consciousness;* whereas the second we call *Pcs* because its excitations, after the observance of certain rules, are capable of reaching consciousness; perhaps not before they have again undergone censorship, but nevertheless regardless of the *Ucs* *system.* . . . The system *Pcs* not only bars access to consciousness, but also controls the access to voluntary motility, and has control of the emission of a mobile cathec-

In defining the quality preconscious Freud follows Breuer; [6*] preconscious is what is "capable of becoming conscious," and he adds, "capable of becoming conscious easily and under conditions which frequently arise"; it is different with unconscious processes "in the case of which such a transformation is difficult, can only come about with considerable expenditure of energy or may never occur." [7*] However, this general differentiation is a somewhat simplified rendering of complex problems which Freud discusses in other of his writings. Three of these problems have here been selected for a brief discussion:

First, not all preconscious processes reach consciousness with equal ease.

---

tic energy, a portion of which is familiar to us as attention.

Freud considers the day-residues which the dream uses as preconscious. Cf. 209, pp. 501–2; see also Chap. 10, note 9 and Chap. 12, note 23, above. The conditions of the preconscious system during sleep are formulated by Freud (209, p. 501) as follows:

. . . we may assume with equal certainty that the state of sleep renders impossible the usual continuance of the process of excitation in the preconscious and its termination in becoming conscious. In so far as we can become conscious of our mental processes in the ordinary way, even during the night, to that extent we are simply not asleep. I cannot say what change is produced in the *Pcs* system by the state of sleep, but there is no doubt that the psychological characteristics of sleep are to be sought mainly in the cathectic changes occurring just in this system, which dominates, moreover, the approach to motility, paralyzed during sleep. On the other hand, I have found nothing in the psychology of dreams to warrant the assumption that sleep produces any but secondary changes in the conditions of the *Ucs* system. Hence, for the nocturnal excitations in the *Pcs* there remains no other path than that taken by the wish-excitations from the *Ucs;* they must seek reinforcement from the *Ucs,* and follow the detours of the unconscious excitations.

Furthermore (*ibid.*, pp. 515–16):

I must assume that the sensory surface of consciousness which is turned to the preconscious is rendered far more unexcitable by sleep than the surface turned toward the *Perception*-system. The giving up of interest in the nocturnal thought-process is, of course, an appropriate procedure. Nothing is to happen in thought; the preconscious wants to sleep. But once the dream becomes perception, it is capable of exciting consciousness through the qualities now gained. The sensory excitation performs what is in fact its function; namely, it directs a part of the cathectic energy available in the *Pcs* to the exciting cause in the form of attention. We must therefore admit that the dream always has a *waking* effect—that is, it calls into activity part of the quiescent energy of the *Pcs.* Under the influence of this energy, it now undergoes the process which we have described as secondary elaboration with a view to coherence and comprehensibility. This means that the dream is treated by this energy like any other perception-content; it is subjected to the same anticipatory ideas as far, at least, as the material allows. As far as this third part of the dream-process has any direction, this is once more progressive.]

6.* Breuer and Freud (259, pp. 166–67).

7.* Freud (255, pp. 100–101).

Some can only be recaptured with considerable effort. What differences exist between the former and the latter?

Second, preconscious mental processes are extremely different from each other both in content and in the kind of thought-processes used; they cover continua reaching from purposeful reflection to fantasy and from logical formulation to dream-like imagery. How can these differences be accounted for?

Third, when preconscious material reaches consciousness experiences can vary greatly. The process may not be noticed—the ordinary case if we use preconscious processes, as it were, as ready material—but reaching consciousness can be accompanied by strong emotional experiences. How can we account for these experiences in terms of our theory?

These three problems will here be taken up separately; at the end, however, we hope to establish a connecting link between them.

The essential theoretical assumptions made in order to differentiate between preconscious and unconscious mental processes have varied considerably. At a time when Freud still tried to characterize the preconscious as a functional system, he considered verbalization as one of its functions.[8*] Unconscious thoughts, he believed, had to pass through the stage of verbalization on their way to consciousness; feelings could reach consciousness "directly." [9*] Freud later avoided the obvious pitfalls of this assumption. "The presence of speech gives a safe clue to the preconscious nature of the process" but "the connection with a verbal memory trace cannot be considered as a prerequisite." [10*] The difference between preconscious and unconscious mental processes, however,

---

8.* See Nunberg (543), who treats the System Pcs and the Ego as parallel concepts.

9.* Freud (234, pp. 133–35, 109–12).

[Cf. also Freud (209, pp. 515 and 548), and Chap. 15, note 32, above. Freud (243, p. 26) wrote:

Actually the difference is that, whereas with Ucs *ideas* connecting-links must be forged before they can be brought into the Cs, with *feelings*, which are themselves transmitted directly, there is no necessity for this. In other words: the distinction between Cs and Pcs has no meaning where feelings are concerned; the Pcs here falls out of account, and feelings are either conscious or unconscious. Even when they are connected with verbal images, their becoming conscious is not due to that circumstance, but they become so directly.

The part played by verbal images now becomes perfectly clear. By their interposition internal thought-processes are made into perceptions. It is like a demonstration of the theorem that all knowledge has its origin in external perception. It may sometimes happen that a hyper-cathexis of the process of thinking takes place, in which case thoughts are *perceived* in the literal sense of the word—as if they came from without—and are consequently held to be true.]

10.* Freud (257, p. 42).

is explained by assumptions concerning the nature of psychic energy prevalent in either of them. Unconscious processes use mobile psychic energy, preconscious processes bound energy. The two degrees of mobility correspond to two types of discharge characterized as primary and secondary processes.[11] We are thus faced with the delimitation between the id and the ego. Let us briefly note that the two sets of characterizations here suggested by Freud (the types of energy, free and bound, and the types of discharge, primary and secondary process) account for the same events; the energy-formulation permits differentiations in degree, in shading; the process-formulation states extremes. Assumptions concerning transitions between extremes seem to myself, to Hartmann [12*] and possibly for other reasons to Rapaport [13*] preferable.[14*]

Assumptions concerning the ego's countercathexis directed against the id are essential to any study of preconscious mental processes, and so is the assumption that a preconscious process from which the ego withdraws cathexis becomes subject to cathexis with id energy, that is, with mobile energy, and will be drawn into the discharge by means of the primary process, an assumption which forms the basis of the psychoanalytic theory of dream-formation.[15] Conditions under which the reverse process occurs, namely under which unconscious

---

11. Freud (234, pp. 100–21) wrote:

The processes of the system Pcs display, no matter whether they are already conscious or only capable of becoming conscious, an inhibition of the tendency of cathected ideas towards discharge. When a process moves over from one idea to another, the first retains a part of its cathexis and only a small part undergoes displacement. Displacement and condensation after the mode of the primary process are excluded or very much restricted. This circumstance caused Breuer to assume the existence of two different stages of cathectic energy in mental life: one in which that energy is tonically "bound" and the other in which it moves freely and presses towards discharge. I think that this discrimination represents the deepest insight we have gained up to the present into the nature of nervous energy, and I do not see how we are to evade [it]. . . .

Further, it devolves upon the system Pcs to make communication possible between the different ideational contents so that they can influence one another, to give them a relation to time, to set up the censorship or censorships, and to establish the institution of "testing reality" and the reality-principle. Conscious memory, too, seems to depend wholly on the Pcs. . . .

Cf. also Freud (257, pp. 44–45).

12.* Hartmann (303).

13.* Rapaport (596).

14.* Freud himself was naturally aware of this problem. He explicitly states (236, pp. 261–62), that the primary process is unknown to preconscious thinking or *admissible rarely*.

15. Freud (209, pp. 529–31; and 257, pp. 47–48).

material becomes preconscious are equally familiar: id derivatives may be
cathexed with ego-energy and become part of preconscious mental processes
at a considerable distance from the original impulse; they may do so, if changes
in the distribution of countercathexis have taken place, for instance, if the level
of conflict has been reduced and the id-impulse has become more acceptable; [16]
they may enter preconscious mental processes sometimes at a considerable price
in terms of symptom formation.[17] The material may also reach consciousness
without ever becoming preconscious; metaphorically speaking, it may become
accessible to the ego not from its inside but from its outside; it then appears as
percept, acquiring as it were, at once the hypercathexis required for consciousness. We speak in this case of an abnormal (or rare) pathway to consciousness,
the pathway of hallucination.[18] In contrast we consider it as normal when preconscious material reaches consciousness by a further increase in cathexis, the
hypercathexis mediated by attention.[19] In some cases, however, this hypercathexis cannot become effective without considerable effort; this is the reason
why we assume the working of countercathectic energies at the passage into
consciousness; countercathectic energies that would prevent what is to some
extent ego-dystonic from entering full awareness.[20]*

16. Freud (233, pp. 87–88).

17. Freud (233, pp. 92 ff.).

18. On projection and regression in hallucinations, see Freud (237, pp. 146–49).

19. Cf. Freud, Chap. 15, note 21, above.

20.* Conditions constituting "ego-dystonicity" will be discussed in the following sections.

[It will be worthwhile to quote in detail Freud's rendering of this point because in it more clearly than elsewhere does he hint at a hierarchic conception of censorships, countercathectic systems, and levels of hypercathexes (234, pp. 125–26):

On the border of the Pcs the censorship thrusts back the Ucs, but its derivatives can circumvent this censorship, achieve a high degree of organization, and in the Pcs reach a certain intensity of cathexis;

when, however, this is exceeded and they try to force themselves into consciousness, they are recognized as derivatives of the Ucs, and are repressed afresh at the new frontier by the censorship between the Cs and the Pcs. Thus the former censorship is exercised against the Ucs itself, and the latter against its preconscious derivatives. We might suppose that in the course of individual development the censorship had been advanced a step. . . . The existence of the censorship between the Pcs and the Cs teaches us that becoming conscious is no mere act of perception, but is probably also a hypercathexis, a further advance in the mental organization.

Furthermore (*ibid.*, p. 124):

A very great part of preconscious material originates in the unconscious, has the characteristics of derivatives of the unconscious, and is subject to a censorship before it can pass into consciousness. Another part of the Pcs can become conscious

III. RECOGNITION, RECALL AND INTEGRATION

The conditions under which ego-dystonic preconscious material may reach consciousness have in psychoanalysis been studied in many contexts, mainly in relation to the slipping of memory in everyday life and in psychoanalytic observation when a dream, a thought, or a fantasy, are about to escape or have done so. It is well known that in these cases the voluntary effort, the concentration of attention not always leads to the recapture of the vanishing or vanished thought-process; but when this first attempt fails another method may prove successful. Self-observation may be turned onto the process itself, one ego-function may be pitted against another. Self-observation may achieve its end by re-establishing links that had been lost; the various stages of the preconscious thought-process are repeated, until, as we may say, the chain hangs firmly together again.[21] The recapitulation of stages of preconscious mental processes by self-observation can best be studied in situations in which the thought-process and the self-observation occur in distinct phases. . . .

[Passage omitted.] [22]

---

without any censorship. Here we light upon a contradiction of an earlier assumption: from the point of view of repression we were obliged to place the censorship which is decisive for consciousness between the systems Ucs and Pcs. Now it becomes probable to us that there is a censorship between the Pcs and the Cs. But we shall do well not to regard this complication as a difficulty, but to assume that to every transition from one system to that immediately above it (that is, every advance to a higher stage of mental organization) there corresponds a new censorship.]

21. It appears that this function of self-observation, which is here pitted against the function of censorship, though most important, is little understood as yet. Its relation to ego-ideal and superego have been clearly demonstrated, and Kris discusses it below in connection with the freedom from shame and guilt in daydreams. The ca-

thectic dynamics of self-observation as a phenomenon of consciousness are, however, still obscure. There is some evidence to suggest that just as ego-ideal and superego are "steps" in the ego, so is self-awareness an advance-step in consciousness: an additional hypercathectic organization. It may be that self-observation reestablishes lost links and thereby recaptures slipping memories by providing this additional hypercathexis.

22. In the omitted section the author quotes his report (432) of the interpretation by a psychoanalyzed person of her own doodling, illustrating by it the stages of recapturing of a preconscious process. He points out that the recapture is usually an indication that the ego's synthetic function has already succeeded in establishing "a unity of context or reestablishing control over a slipping area," though the help of the analyst's interpretation is often needed for reestablish-

The preconscious process that is under the control of the synthetic function of the ego is safe against withdrawal of preconscious cathexis and hence against repression; as a rule it has effortless access to consciousness.[23]

This assumption is not limited to the dynamics prevailing in what I here call the "slipping area"; it applies to the wider field of analytic observation and its dynamics. One aspect of the therapeutic situation in psychoanalysis can adequately be described if we focus on the patient's effort to recall the past:

(If) the interpretation has removed obstacles to recall, the forgotten memory can take its place within awareness. It is naturally not assumed that in such cases the interpretation produced recall; rather the situation existing previous to the interpretation, the one which suggested the interpretation, must be described as incomplete recall (and therefore, as in some measure similar to the situation in which the memory trace was laid down). Interpretation therefore acts here as a help in recall-completion. Incomplete recall had announced itself by a variety of signs in the individual's behavior,[24*]

which the interpretation uses in order to reconstruct the original event, from which the behavioral pattern was derived. The aim of such steps in interpretation can adequately be described by a term frequently used in the study of memory function: that term is recognition. When recall is not yet possible, recognition may already be accomplished. . . .[25]

In suggesting that the historical interpretation in analysis stimulates the memory-function of recognition leading to recall we are in tune with experimental findings, that tend to establish a similar relationship over and over again.[26*] They show how recognition improves recall or guarantees retention. The relationship between recognition and recall can be explained in terms of psychoanalytic theory: the synthetic function of the ego, the establishing of a context is, in the case of recognition, facilitated by the help of perception; in

---

ing such control. Kris refers here to the theory of free associations (Hartmann, 302, and Bernfeld, 55) and to the theory of the synthetic and organizing functions of the ego (Nunberg, 543, and Hartmann, 302, 305).

23. Concerning effortless access to consciousness cf. Rapaport *et al.* (602, I, 166–76), and Rapaport (597).

24.* Kris (427).

25. The omitted passage deals with the difficulty of reconstructing infantile experiences and refers to Freud's (239) most extensive report of such reconstructions.

26.* See for instance, recently Postman *et al.* (580). The unfortunate limitation of these investigations to nonsense syllables makes it difficult to establish closer links between the laboratory findings and psychoanalytic observations.

our example by the analyst's verbalization. Recall, then, fills a gap, fits into a pattern.[27]

If we examine the function of recognition in relation to mental qualities, a

27. Compare Bartlett's (37, pp. 195–96) strikingly similar conclusions arrived at by experimental investigation:

It is generally pointed out that remembering is a more complex process than recognizing. . . . But recall must differ from recognition not simply in complexity.

Remembering, like recognizing, involves:

(a) An original sensorial pattern;

(b) An original psychological orientation, or attitude;

(c) The persistence of this orientation or attitude in some setting which is different from the original at least in a temporal sense; and

(d) The organization, together with orientation or attitude, of psychological material.

But remembering, as distinct from recognizing, depends upon the possibility of exploiting the fourth of these factors much more fully. Material remembered usually has to be set in relation with other material, and in the most complete cases must be dated, placed and given some kind of personal mark. It is possible, and common, to recognize material which, even after it has been recognized, cannot be described in any detail, and indeed, whenever such description can be given, we invariably tend to regard the process as one of remembering rather than one of recognizing alone.

The immediate stimulus in the case of recognition is some sensory pattern. More often than not this is of the same mode as the original presentation. . . . But it appears that almost any factor that is capable of evoking a response at all may set up a process of remembering. . . . Remembering involves a greater degree of organization, both of psychological material

and of attitudes and interests, so that more bridges are built from one sensory mode to another, or from one interest to another. As we shall see, there is good reason to connect this with the growing importance of image and word functions; and, in fact, we find that both images and words play more prominent parts in remembering than they do in recognizing.

The essential difference between recognizing and remembering lies, however, not in an increase of complexity in the latter, but in a genuine difference in the way in which the necessary setting or scheme comes to play. In recognizing, the psychological material which persists "matches" some immediately present sensory pattern. In complex cases the "match" may be effected by means of image, comparison and judgment. But these are not necessary and, in fact, to the degree in which they occur, it seems that remembering is present as well. In remembering proper, the psychological material which persists is itself capable of being *described*. It does not merely help to produce a certain reaction, but its descriptive characteristics are utilized by the subject, and in the well-articulated cases its *mode* of organization is alleged to be known. Thus, taking any particular detail, a person who remembers can set it into relation with other detail, stating its setting in time and place. In recognizing, the scheme, or pattern, or setting, *uses* the organism, so to speak, to produce a differential reaction; in remembering, the subject uses the setting, or scheme, or pattern, and builds up its characteristics afresh to aid whatever response the needs of the moment may demand. In the former there is reaction *by means of* organized psychological material; in the latter there is *reaction to* organized psychological material. Clearly, if this is the case, there is a change, not of complexity

first formulation suggests itself. It states that what can be mobilized in recognition must have been preconscious. I should like to stress this formulation and to consider it as well established. And yet it might be advantageous not to take it too rigidly. We are familiar with cases in which a historical interpretation gradually—sometimes over long periods of treatment—opens the way to the recall of previously repressed material. . . .[28] It seems therefore reasonable to assume that the facilitation of the ego's integrative or synthetic function by recognition will be one of the factors operative in the dynamics leading to recall. . . .[29]

. . . The relation of recognition to recall of the repressed can be tentatively described in these terms: since the "original" situation has been recognized, previously not sufficiently invested id derivatives can be integrated into the pattern indicated by the reconstruction; this in turn strengthens the ego's position, permits a reduction of countercathexes and the gradual infiltration of further material . . . the full investment by the ego, the syntonicity of the event with superego and id strivings may then lead to the feeling of certainty, to the change from *I know of* to *I believe.* . . .[30]

IV. DISCHARGE AND REGRESSION

It is a strange fact that in spite of all varieties of clinical experience which throw light on preconscious mental processes the main source of reference for many of these processes should have remained for almost 30 years the book of

---

alone, but of the status of certain of the psychological factors present alike in recognizing and in recall.

Cf. also Chap. 3, notes 15 and 19, above.

28. The passage omitted indicates the dependence of recall on the state of the defenses and on the capacity of the ego to cope with conflict.

29. The passage omitted indicates that the recall of the repressed and the strengthening of the synthetic function of the ego are dependent variables related in terms of "circular causality."

30. In the omitted passage Kris—in contrast to B. D. Lewin's (457) view which links the certitude of recall in the course of psychoanalytic therapy to infantile omniscience—describes it as a "progress in the individual's mental organization." [Qualities of conscious experience, such as "believed," "assumed," "doubted," have been repeatedly discussed in my comments; cf. Chap. 3, note 31, and Chap. 17, note 18, above. Kris attributes these qualities to the relationship of the content of the experience to other contents and to the defenses and synthetic function of the ego and in final analysis to the underlying cathectic dynamics.]

the Belgian psychologist Varendonck which under the title *The Psychology of Daydreams* [31*] reports on a great variety of self-observed thought-processes. There are obvious and admitted gaps in Varendonck's reports. Upon closer inspection we discover a number of contradictions and suspect traits. . . .

The value of Varendonck's material consists in the fact that his reports cover a wide range of phenomena. We hear of deliberations on the question whom to choose as faculty reporter for his doctoral dissertation, of self-punitive fantasies, in which he loses both legs in the attempt to escape from military service, and of castles in Spain of a more conventional type. As divergent as the contents are the means of presentation. Many of Varendonck's fantasies are verbal only, others full of imagery and some replete with condensations and symbols that are to some degree reminiscent of dreams.

This variety of phenomena cannot be ascribed to the personal qualities of one observer. Material known from certain patients in psychoanalysis confirms that such a variety of phenomena exists in preconscious thinking. Recently conducted as yet unpublished experimental investigations [32*] show that, when asked to report their daydreams, college students record a variety of phenomena, that represent what we might call the "stream of their preconsciousness" in highly varied types of expressions dealing with highly varied contents. These are the impressions that justify my introductory remarks on the existence of two continua: one reaching from problem-solving to dream-like fantasy, and one reaching from logical cohesive verbal statements to dream-like imagery; both continua I claimed occur with some frequency in preconscious mental processes. [33]

The first and up to now only relevant critical evaluation of Varendonck's book from the point of view of psychoanalysis is contained in Freud's introduction to it. . . . [34*] In studying "the mode of thought activity to which one abandons oneself during the state of distraction and into which we readily pass before sleep and upon incomplete awakening" Varendonck has rendered a valuable service. While Freud appreciates confirmation found for his views on the psychology of dreams and "defective acts" he sharply opposes Varen-

31.* Varendonck (740). [Also Chap. 22, above.]

32.* Rudel (622).

33. On the interaction between the logical (goal-directed) verbal, and the dream-like (wishfulfilling) imagery aspects in daydreams, cf. Varendonck, Chap. 22, note 34, above.

34.* Varendonck (740).

donck's central thesis: Freud asserts that there is no difference between preconscious and conscious mental processes; what Varendonck calls daydreaming does not owe its peculiarities to "the circumstance that it proceeds mostly preconsciously." "For that reason I think it is advisable, when establishing a distinction between the different modes of thought-activity not to utilize the relation to consciousness in the first instance." Freud suggests to distinguish in the daydream as well as in the chain of thoughts studied by Varendonck *freely wandering fantastic thinking in opposition to intentionally directed reflection*, since it is known "that even strictly directed reflection may be achieved without the co-operation of consciousness." [35]

If we take this distinction as our starting point and remember that the economic and structural approach, the study of cathexes and ego-function has proved its value in discussing problems in the psychology of preconscious mental processes, we are easily led to one area of deliberations. The ego, we assume, has two kinds of bound energy at its disposal, neutralized energy, and libido and aggression in their not neutralized form.[36]* Fantastic, free wandering thought-processes tend to discharge more libido and aggression and less neutralized energy, purposeful reflection and problem-solving, more neutralized energy. In fantasy production the ego's thought-processes are largely in the service of the id,[37] but not only the id is involved, naturally the superego

35. Kris demonstrates here that Freud, as early as 1921, saw that preconsciousness is a quality and not a system; cf. notes 4 and 5, above. It appears also, that Freud criticized Varendonck's mistake of considering daydream experiences preconscious; for my discussion of this point, see Chap. 22, note 5, above.

Kris's quotes are from the English text of Freud's introduction, which was apparently translated by Varendonck. I have preferred the term "fantasy-thinking" to "fantastic thinking."

36.* Hartmann, Kris, and Lowenstein (311).

[See 311, pp. 20–25, and Hartmann, (303). Kris appears to distinguish here between "bound" and "neutralized" energies, since he speaks of bound but not neutralized drive-energies. I have throughout this volume assumed that it is the process of binding that neutralizes cathexes, and that there are various degrees of binding arising in a hierarchic order. Cf. Chap. 5, notes 61, 78 and 121, above.]

37. (Freud (234, p. 123) wrote:

Amongst the derivatives of the unconscious instinctual impulses, the character of which we have just described, there are some which unite in themselves opposite features. On the one hand, they are highly organized, exempt from self-contradictoriness, have made use of every acquisition of the system consciousness, and would hardly be distinguished by our ordinary judgment from the formations of that system. On the other hand, they are

and narcissistic strivings of the self [38] play their part. The content of the freely wandering fantasies is extended between the pleasure-unpleasure continuum, hence the probability that in this kind of processes, the discharge of non-neutralized libido and aggression will be maximized. In reflective thinking the contrary is likely to occur. Reflective thinking in the sense of Freud, problem-solving as we would prefer to say, serves to a higher degree the autonomous ego

---

unconscious and are incapable of becoming conscious. Thus they belong according to their qualities to the system Pcs, but in actual fact to the Ucs. Their origin remains decisive for the fate they will undergo. . . . Of such a nature are the *fantasy-formations* of normal persons as well as of neurotics, which we have recognized as preliminary phases in the formation both of dreams and of symptoms, and which, in spite of their high degree of organization, remain repressed and therefore cannot become conscious. They draw near to consciousness and remain undisturbed so long as they do not become strongly cathected, but as soon as a certain degree of this is exceeded they are thrust back. Substitute-formations are similar, more highly organized derivatives of the Ucs; but these succeed in breaking through into consciousness, thanks to some favourable relation, as, for example, when they coincide with a preconscious anti-cathexis.

38. The concept "self" has been little used in psychoanalytic literature until recently. It seems useful therefore to quote Hartmann's (303) discussion of the concept:

The definition of narcissism as libidinal cathexis of the ego was and still is widely used in psychoanalytic literature; but in some passages Freud also refers to it as cathexis of one's own person, of the body, of the self. In analysis a clear distinction between the terms ego, self, and personality is not always made. But a differentiation of these concepts appears necessary if we try to consistently look at the problems involved in the light of Freud's structural psychology. In using the term narcissism two actually different sets of opposites often seem to be fused into one. The one refers to the self (one's own person) in contradistinction to the object; the second to the ego (as a psychic system) in contradistinction to other substructures of personality. However, the opposite of object-cathexis is not ego cathexis, but cathexis of one's own person, that is self-cathexis; in speaking of self-cathexis we don't imply whether this cathexis is situated in the id, in the ego, or in the superego. This formulation takes into account that we actually do find "narcissism" in all three psychic systems; but in all of these cases there is opposition to (and reciprocity with) object-cathexis. It therefore will be clarifying if we define narcissism as the libidinal cathexis not of the ego but of the self. (Also it might be useful to apply the term self-representation as opposed to object-representation.) Often, in speaking of ego-libido, what we do mean is not that this form of energy is in the ego, but that it is directed toward one's own person rather than toward the object. Also in many cases where we are used to saying "libido has been withdrawn into the ego" or "object-cathexis has been replaced by ego-cathexis," what we actually should say is "withdrawal on the self" in the first, and "self-cathexis" in the second case. This difference is obviously important for the consideration of many aspects of structural psychology, and particularly of course for those of cathexes and their topography.

interests. Discharge of libido and aggression is therefore likely to be minimized and that of neutralized ego-energy to be of greater relevance.[39*]

We now turn to a brief discussion of the second continuum of preconscious thought-processes, that extended between logical verbalization and fantastic imagery; the hypnagogic fantasies to which Freud refers in the passage quoted above, some of the wandering fantasies of Varendonck's, and fantasies of some more fanciful patients in psychoanalysis designate the area of phenomena in question. We are clearly dealing with problems of ego-regression.[40]

The very fact that such phenomena of ego-regression are infinitely more frequent in fantasy than in deliberative preconscious process suggests the idea that in the former the discharge of libido and aggression may have constituted a general greater proximity to the id, to mobile energy discharges. The id as it were intrudes upon ego-functions.

But ego-regression in a topographical sense, primitivization of ego-functions, not only occurs under conditions of ego-weakness—in sleep, in falling asleep, in fantasy, in intoxication and in psychotic conditions—but also during many types of productive processes.[41] This suggested to me years ago the formula-

39.* Alternatively one might speak here of "degrees of neutralization" of the energy discharged; see Hartmann (303).

[Hartmann wrote (303, p. 20):

Aggressive as well as sexual energy may be neutralized, and in both cases this process of neutralization takes place through the ego (and probably already through its autonomous fore-stages too). Here I want to add that theoretical as well as clinical considerations speak in favor of assuming that there are gradations in the neutralization of those energies, that is, not all of them are "indifferent" in the same degree. We ought to distinguish them according to their greater or lesser closeness to drive-energy, which means according to whether and to what extent they still retain characteristics of sexuality (object-libidinal or narcissistic) or of aggression (object- or self-directed).

Kris's passage is the single most important contribution to the understanding of the difference between the primary and the secondary process since Freud's (209, 223) statement of these concepts: Kris maintains that corresponding to the degrees of neutralization of cathexes are the degrees to which thought is organized according to the primary or secondary process; the transition between these two forms of thought-organization is fluid.]

40. That is, conditions in which the ego's controlling mechanisms preventing id contents from entering consciousness, and the secondary-process mechanisms preventing primary-process mechanisms from operating on conscious material, are suspended.

41. Cf. Freud (234, p. 127):

Cooperation between a preconscious and an unconscious impulse, even when the latter is subject to very strong repression, may be established if the situation permits

tion that the ego may use the primary process and not only be overwhelmed by it.[42]* The idea was rooted in Freud's explanation of wit [43]* according to which a preconscious thought "is entrusted for a moment to unconscious elaboration" and seemed to account for a variety of phenomena during creation or other inventive processes.

However, the problem of ego-regression during creative processes represents only a special problem in a more general area: the general assumption says that under certain conditions the ego regulates its own capacity to regression, that the organizing functions of the ego include the function of voluntary and temporary withdrawal of cathexis, from one area or another, in order later to regain improved control.[44]* Our theory of the sleep is based upon the assumption of such a withdrawal of cathexis, sexual functions presuppose similar regressive

---

of the unconscious impulse operating in harmony with one of the controlling tendencies. The repression is removed for the occasion, the repressed activity being admitted as a reinforcement of the one intended by the Ego. In respect of this single constellation the unconscious becomes Ego-syntonic, falls into line with the Ego, without any change taking place in the repression otherwise. The effect of the Ucs in this cooperation is unmistakable; the reinforced tendencies reveal themselves as, in spite of all, different from the normal—they make possible achievements of special perfection, and they manifest a resistance in the face of opposition similar to that of obsessional symptoms.

Also (p. 119):

In the system Pcs the *secondary process* holds sway; where a primary process is allowed to take its course in connection with elements belonging to the system Pcs, it appears "comic" and excites laughter.

See also Freud (233, p. 89).
42.* Kris (431).

[A preconscious thought is committed *for a moment* to elaboration by the system Ucs. . . . Whereas in dreams, owing to the operation of the primary process, thoughts undergo distortion until they

become quite unrecognizable, the distortion in wit—and, we may add, in caricature—is only carried through by half, and is subject to the ego's control; a thought is disguised rather than distorted, its distortion goes only so far as is consistent with its remaining intelligible to the first comer (431, p. 294).

The clinical classification of these (inspirational) states is not always easy . . . (they are) not . . . limited to any one . . . clinical condition . . . (and) may be described as phenomena of regression . . . (that is,) withdrawal of ego control from many of the higher mental activities. . . . The coordination of motor activities is frequently affected . . . in states of inspiration speech becomes automatic. It is not the subject who speaks but a voice from out of him (428, pp. 378–79)].

43.* Freud (214) [pp. 745–61].
44.* Hartmann (305 and 306).
[See Chap. 19, II, above. Cf. also Kris (428, p. 389):

In ecstasy the process results in an emotional climax only, in states of inspiration it leads to active elaboration in creation. The process is dominated by the Ego and put to its own purposes—for sublimation in creative activity.]

patterns, and the inability to such suspension of ego-control constitutes one of the well-known symptoms of obsessional compulsive characters.

Further investigations seem to suggest some more detailed assumptions on the nature of the process which we describe, when we say that, specifically, the ego uses the primary process, or more generally that the organizing function of the ego includes the control of regression: the clinical observation of creators and the study of introspective reports on experiences during creative activity tends to show that we are faced with a shift in the cathexis of certain ego-functions. Thus a frequent distinction is being made between an inspirational and an "elaborational" phase in creation. The inspirational phase is characterized by the facility with which id-impulses or their closer derivatives are being received. One might say: countercathectic energies are withdrawn to some extent, and added to the speed, force or intensity with which the preconscious thoughts are formed. During the "elaborational" phase, the countercathectic barrier may be reinforced, work proceeds slowly, cathexis lies with other ego-functions, for instance, with reality-testing, with formulating, or generally speaking, with communication with the public. Alternations between the two phases may be rapid, oscillating or distributed over long stretches of time.[45]

45. In his studies of the work of psychotic artists Kris demonstrated that without the elaborative phase of creative work, art reverts from communication of experience to the magic from which it appears to have originated. The connection between the elaborative phase of creativity and communication is particularly important for the psychology of thinking. All thought has such elaborative phases and all these appear to be dependent on processes of communication. This relationship has, however, so far scarcely been studied.

On the relation of art and the art of psychotics, Kris and Pappenheim (434, p. 26) wrote:

The patient, identified with the creator God, omnipotent and omniscient, produces no works of art. His drawings do not serve the function of communication.

Freud has discussed this very problem in one of his most essential contributions to our understanding of art. In describing the literary work of art, and differentiating dream, daydream and novel, he said that only the novel reaches the level on which thought is communicated to others, the level where art exists; the dream is autistic, the daydream of no interest to others [Sachs, 628].

In his work the artist uses "inspiration": his unconscious produces thoughts which he permits to reach consciousness provided that they are presented in esthetic disguise [Sachs, 628].

This process can also be described in terms of ego-psychology. When the artist creates during inspiration he is subject to an ego-regression but it is a partial and temporary ego-regression, one controlled by the ego which retains the function of establishing contact with an audience. The artist identified himself with his public in

In describing regression under the control of the ego in terms of shifts in the cathexis of ego-functions, which can be related to or pitted against each other in various ways, we gain a frame of reference that might at the present tentative state of our deliberations in this area prove useful in various ways. One of the applications leads back to our central theme, the nature of preconscious mental processes. I refer to the shift of cathexis between the system Perception and preconscious thought. While we are immersed in preconscious thought we take less notice of the environment. If the thoughts are wandering fantasies . . . we speak of decrease of attention or, as Freud does, of being distracted by fantasy. If problem-solving or productive thinking takes place we speak of being concentrated on something.[46] At this point we seem to gain a further and improved understanding of one problem: We generally assume that preconscious thought-processes become conscious by hypercathexis. We now realize that there are various degrees of hypercathexis; if energy is turned from the perceiving function of the ego to fantasy production or thinking, this in itself may not lead to consciousness but simply to a higher investment of the precon-

---

order to invite their participation, a participation postulating their subsequent identification with him.

No such intention prevails in our patient. He does not produce in order to communicate with others any more than he converses with others. Basically his speech is soliloquy. His drawings have even less bearing on people around him. They are verdicts or statements bearing on the future which he creates.

Also (p. 28):

A comparison of the patient's creative process and of his work with that of normal artists seems to add clinical precision to Plato's distinction. The controlled and temporary ego-regression during inspirational creation was described by Plato as productive insanity and only the more permanent narcissistic regression of the psychotic is a pathological process.

Although the work of the psychotic is part of magic itself, that of the normal artist is not devoid of magic. He too attempts to control a world, and in his creation there is embodied some of the magic belief. But the difference is clear in two areas: first, the normal artist creates not to transform the outer world but to depict it for others he wishes to influence; second, the task of production has a definite realistic meaning. The artist proceeds through trial and error; he learns and his modes of expression change, or his style changes. The psychotic artist creates in order to transform the real world; he seeks no audience and his modes of expression remain unchanged once the psychotic process has reached a certain intensity.

46. "Being concentrated" means here apparently concentration of attention-cathexes. This usage, as becomes clear from Kris's subsequent passage, rightly stresses the continuity between "attention" and "concentration," concepts which have been dichotomously used by Rapaport *et al.* (602) and Rapaport (597).

scious thought itself; reaching consciousness would still be dependent on further conditions, which we shall discuss later.[47]

[Passage omitted.] [48]

V. REACTIONS TO THE REACHING OF CONSCIOUSNESS

[Passage omitted.] [49]

Let me return . . . to our central question: that of reactions to the reaching of awareness of preconscious thought-processes. We repeat that the normal case is characterized by absence of reactions. However, in many instances of both fantasy and creativity, discharge and satisfaction can be experienced; the mere feeling of relief is more manifest in the case of fantasy,[50] a mixture of relief and satisfaction more evident in the case of creativity and problem-

47. The stress here on various degrees of hypercathexis is a formulation new in psychoanalytic literature. It seems consonant with the view I expressed in commenting on the form of consciousness of daydreams (see Chap. 22, notes 5, 30, 34, above) as well as with the assumptions concerning varieties of states of consciousness which I have made in various contexts in this volume (for reference see note 30, above).

48. The omitted section discusses those preconscious automatic ego-functions which become conscious only in danger situations. It shows that preconscious performance can be more advantageous than conscious performance, and it stresses the extraordinary achievements of preconscious thought. Kris refers to Hartmann (Chap. 19, above) and to Delacroix (138).

49. The first part of the omitted section may be summarized as follows: (a) The individual reactions on becoming aware of preconscious fantasies support the cathectic theory of thinking. (b) Becoming conscious of fantasies is, as a rule, free from guilt and shame: there is a freedom from responsibility

for them. (c) This freedom from responsibility seems to be due to withdrawal of cathexes from the ego-ideal or from the punitive function of the superego. (d) Freedom from responsibility is more complete if the fantasy we follow is that created by the poet. (e) Problem-solving, like fantasy, provides relief and discharge, and so do other gratifications connected with mastery (Hartmann, 303) and creativity. (f) The latter forms of relief Kris links to Freud's (214) view that: "When our psychic apparatus does not actually act in search of some urgently needed gratification we let this apparatus itself work for pleasure gain." (g) Problem-solving implies preconscious work and matures slowly; solutions even once found are repeatedly lost, because of repression and insufficient integration by the synthetic function of the ego. Kris refers to Wertheimer's (763) study of Einstein, and to the fate of Freud's early discoveries (S. Freud, *Aus den Anfaengen der Psychoanalyse*, London, 1950).

50. Cf. Varendonck, Chap. 22, pp. 471–72, above.

solving.[51] But there are instances in which these very experiences appear in a special form, in which the feeling exists that awareness is produced by specific conditions: by its coming from outside. This is obviously the case of hallucination, but also that of revelation or inspiration.[52]* In revelation or inspiration a preconscious thought is attributed to an outside agent from which it is received passively. The literal and the attenuated meanings of the term form a continuum; we speak of inspiration also when a percept stimulates thought. This is the case of Newton's, who attributes the discovery of the law of gravity to the observation of the falling apple. The perception has here acted as a factor organizing previously prepared preconscious thoughts, thoughts in waiting for the stimulus. But why do creators of all kind tend to attribute their achievements with such preference to the influence of outside agents, to change, fate, or to the Divine itself? One of the reasons is obviously the escape from responsibility, the escape from the wrath and envy of the Gods; but there are other more significant and deeper motivations at work. The feeling of full control and tension discharge in the state of becoming aware of significant material mobilizes deep layers of the personality. Explanatory concepts are at hand. In the case of ecstatic revelation the hallucinatory character of the experience is manifest. We may then say that the process of becoming conscious of the preconsciously prepared thought is sexualized: hence the concomitant experiences in the case of revelation. Or we may say that id energies suddenly combine with ego energies to reach consciousness from the outside; mobile with bound and

51. Kris (421, p. 364):

In artistic production preconscious elaboration plays no less a part than in scientific thought; artists, too, are constantly in search of "problems" and their work consists of a sequence of problem-solutions. The uplift which may be felt when a preconsciously elaborated solution suddenly comes to consciousness is neither the only experience nor the experience most characteristic of artistic creation. More typical is a state of "semi-consciousness," which a tradition first formulated by Plato calls that of "productive madness."

52.* Kris (428).

[In the concept of inspiration, impulses, wishes and fantasies derived from the un-

conscious are attributed to a supernatural being and the process of their becoming conscious is experienced as an action of this being upon the subject, and thus *activity* is turned into passivity (p. 380).

. . . Through the idea of inspiration the communicant is relieved of the burden of responsibility . . . [which] is intimately linked up with anxiety and guilt. In speaking of archaic social conditions we may say that the tale the poet tells derives from or touches upon the forbidden sphere of wishes, desires, and impulses. Under the assumption of inspiration not he but the Divine is acting; he is not responsible, his feelings of guilt are relieved, and no anxiety need arise (p. 381).]

neutralized cathexis to produce the unique experience of inspiratory insemina-tion.[53] Unconscious fantasies at work in some of these conditions could be re-constructed and in a previous paper on the subject I tried to demonstrate the variety of experiences that are derived from the repressed fantasy of incorporat-ing the paternal phallus.[54*] It has since become plausible that other fantasies are involved: the feeling of triumph, of release of tension, seem to remind the individual of the situation in which passivity was preconditional of total grati-fication, and in which the hallucinated wishfulfilment had become true: the nursing situation. We here find another approach to the full intensity of be-lieving and its relation to infantile omniscience (Lewin) [55*] to which we re-ferred above; the analytic process and the insight it produces can be experi-enced in terms of an archaic wishfulfilment. Changes in the cathexis during the working of the psychic apparatus tend, I suggest, to be generally experienced in terms of such an archetype; the maturing of thought, the entry into aware-ness, from preconscious to consciousness, tend to be experienced as derived from outside, as passively received, not as actively produced. The tendency towards passive reception will take various shapes and forms, appear under the disguise of various modalities, but the subjective experience will remain that of reception. When after the completion of his theory of dreams Freud was urged to publish his theories of sexuality he answered to his urging friend: "If the theory of sexuality comes, I will listen to it."

Let me in conclusion say that this relation to passivity exemplifies once more one of the leading theses of this presentation: the organizing functions of the ego include that of self-regulated regression and permit to combine the most daring intellectual activity with the experience of receptiveness.

53. See Kris (421, pp. 365–66).   55.* Lewin, B. D. (457).
54.* Kris (428).

PATHOLOGY OF THINKING

PART SIX

PATHOLOGY OF THINKING

CHAPTER 24

ON THE DEVELOPMENT OF THOUGHTS [1]

By Paul Schilder

PROCESSES in which perceptual imagery is only a bridge by which a meaning is approached play an essential role in our psychic life.[2] I shall refer to these as thought-processes, and their goal I shall call thought. Images [3] are an aid to thought. We must investigate them with utmost care.

It is a recognized fact that images and thoughts pass through various (preparatory, transitory) stages before they appear in a clear [conscious] form. The case of Delbrueck's patient who was haunted by pseudo-memories of having been maltreated is a good illustration of this process. The patient's first "reminiscence" brought only the vaguest outlines of the event to his consciousness; the second "reminiscence" had the salient points in their correct relationships; and finally, the third "reminiscence" brought into consciousness the whole event with complete clarity and definiteness of detail.

According to G. E. Mueller,[4]* images show directly observable evolution from an indefinite state to one of increasing distinctness.[5] Because this develop-

---

1. Schilder (644). This translates *Gedankenentwicklung,* which refers not to the ontogenesis of thinking but rather to the process which always precedes the emergence of a specific thought in consciousness.

2. Schilder apparently refers to that role of the image in which it does not directly express the meaning which it carries, but rather is preparatory to and a signpost on the way toward the thought which does directly express the meaning. Some of the older academic writers, particularly Mueller-Freienfels (529), and some clinical writers, particularly psychoanalysts (Stekel, Chap. 14, above), were inclined to consider all imagery, as well as all verbalization, only as "bridges to" or "representatives of" meaning.

3. "Image" translates here *Vorstellung.* Schilder uses this term quite variously. He may mean by it image, idea, thought, or even generally, any mental presentation. The translation attempts to convey his meaning as judged by the context, and the term "presentation" will be used where Schilder seems to refer to mental content in general.

4.* Mueller (526).

5. The reference to G. E. Mueller is not entirely justified. The association psychologist Mueller could see development of ideas only in the *quantitative* terms of degree of clarity. Schilder's argument, as will become increasingly

ment often escapes observation, G. E. Mueller considered it an open question whether or not all images undergo such development. I consider his doubt unjustified. The observation of a quick and unobstructed psychological process is just as inaccurate as the observation of free-falling bodies without an Atwood-machine.[6]

Preliminary information concerning thought-development can be obtained by studying reproductive rather than productive thought.[7] But even then we must not use instances where recollection takes an unobstructed course.[8] Ex-

---

clear, refers to a *qualitative* development. Similar doubt may be raised even concerning the cogency of the example taken from Delbrueck.

6. The exploration of the processes preparatory to the emergence of thought in consciousness poses complex methodological problems. It is hard to follow Schilder's rejection of Mueller's reservations. Schilder apparently assumes that all thoughts are preceded by such preparatory processes as are observed in pathological conditions and in experiments in which the spontaneous flow of thought is obstructed. As long as no systematic proof of this generalization is offered, we are obliged to maintain Mueller's doubts, the more so since the phenomena of "automatism" described by Hartmann (Chap. 19, II and VIII, above) may support Mueller's point.

Nevertheless, the methodological principle implied by Schilder is valid and applies to the investigation of memory and thought-processes. The same principle was stated by Kurt Lewin (465) for the investigation of affect and action: "achievement concepts" do not give us an understanding of phenomena; we must study the processes that bring them about (Chap. 4, 3a, above). Consequently, Kurt Lewin and his pupils allotted to introspection a new place in

their studies. They used introspective records to elucidate behavior-records. Likewise, Schilder implies that the end results of recall experiments are not revealing of the thought-process without the direct study of the process itself. The reader will have noted the stress Schilder places on the assertion that while in the unobstructed thought-process only the results are observable, a thought-process which is interfered with reveals its preparatory phases.

7. This phrase and the subsequent treatment of recall show that Schilder conceived of the thought-process very broadly and considered memory but one aspect of an indivisible thought-process. For a similar treatment of memory, see Rapaport (591, pp. 6–8), and Rapaport, Gill, and Schafer (602, I, 385–89).

8. This is a principle of method which in recent clinical (and even academic) investigations has become broadly—if implicitly—accepted. Processes of perception, recollection, etc., are turned into projective techniques by interfering with or obstructing their usual course. The tachistoscopic presentation of structured material, presentation of unstructured material, dimming of illumination, decreasing acoustic clarity of presentation, delay of recall, etc., are the means of interference used. Schil-

perimental subjects of Nagel, when unable to find a syllable in the course of
reproducing a series of syllables, offered in quick sequence syllables obtained
by changing the vowels and consonants of a likely syllable until they felt they
had found the correct one. In other words, they ran through clang-associations
which lead to the sought-for syllable. Geissler attempted to facilitate the recall
of a certain word by saying words which seemed to be related to the one sought.
A series of such trials brought him progressively to the original word. The
individual trials were quite random. G. E. Mueller's experiments indicate that
the image sought appears in consciousness when the fragments of experience
presented are spatially or temporally contiguous with it.

I conclude that a presentation evolves through other presentations which are
associated with it by similarity and contiguity, primarily by clang and external
associations. According to the investigations of Pieron this process oscillates,
giving the impression that one is now nearer to, now again farther from, the
word sought.

It may be objected that the deflection onto associated presentations occurs
only when the presentation sought is not immediately found. The question
could then be raised: does the unobstructed development of a presentation also
pass through or activate this circuit? It is yet to be determined whether the
"intermediary presentations" have anything to do with the one aimed at, a
vague notion of which is extant from the inception of the thought-process.
These questions cannot be answered without taking the nature of thought into
consideration. For the time being let us hold on to our assumption: presentation-
development uses the same elements into which the presentation decomposes
in the course of the association experiment; [9] and the circuit of associations

---

der's references to Nagel illustrate the
point. Cf. also Chap. 27, note 80, below.

9. This assumption is the core of
Schilder's paper. Its scope is such that if
it were proven it would be one of the
cornerstones of the psychology of thinking. Despite the tendency in this paper
towards the sweeping generalizations
which make it seem to the reader that
Schilder regards this assumption as
proven, he indicates in places (cf. pp.

514–15, below) that the evidence offered may be regarded inconclusive.
The unsatisfactory aspects of the evidence and argument are outweighed by
the bold attempt to bring order into an
uncharted realm of phenomena by a
sweeping assumption. It should be also
kept in mind that over and above the evidence offered in this paper, the assumption arises from Schilder's vast clinical
experience. For further evidence bearing on the assumption, see Rapaport,

passed before the end product of the thought-process is obtained springs from the individual's life experience and yet coincides at certain points with the structure of reality.[10]

The development of an image is by no means limited to the realm of a single sense. Transpositions may take place from one sensory realm to another and may to some extent encroach upon the content. It is noteworthy that this process makes for an interpenetration of the various sensory realms; G. E. Mueller calls this a "partial fusion of contents." For instance, in an association experiment the stimulus word "penny" may elicit a copper-colored written image of the word penny. In other words, in the developmental process the presentation-material is pictured. In the recall of a series of visually presented vari-colored digits, Mueller's subject had images of the red digits which were not only more luminous but often larger, more in the foreground than the others. Frenkel's subjects presented with groups of letters, pictured the first of each group in letters larger than the rest, both on hearing and reciting the groups. In these examples we deal with an affective transformation of the reproduced material. Images which command special attention value (red digits and first letters) change their form.[11] Thus, we have found two new essential characteristics of the preparatory process of presentations: the associations (a) become fused; and (b) are rebuilt according to affective principles. It is noteworthy that in these last examples the affectively formed by-products per-

---

Schafer, and Gill (602, II, 15–37, particularly p. 23).

10. The resolution of this apparent paradox is one of the central goals of psychoanalytic ego-psychology. Thought, arising in the individual and directed toward reality, reconciles in the course of its development the requirements of intrapersonal dynamics and reality conditions. Cf. Chaps. 6 and 7, and particularly Chap. 15, note 6, above.

11. These statements involve the relation of affect and attention. The implied identity or parallelism of function could well be questioned. Cf. our comments on Bleuler's similar conception, Chap. 26, notes 137, 138, below. Though

it seems to be generally true that affect-toned material does command attention —unless it succumbs to repression—it is by no means obvious that all that commands attention is affect-toned. H. Hartmann's concept (Chap. 19, I, above) of the "conflict-free ego-sphere" seems to refer to contents and functions which command attention without being necessarily "affect-toned." On the relation of affect and attention see Jung and Silberer, Chap. 9, pp. 220 ff., above, and Rapaport, Gill, and Schafer (602, pp. 166–88).

For examples similar to those cited by Schilder, see Freud, "The Interpretation of Dreams" (209, pp. 530–31).

severe even after the development is completed.[12] These by-products too can escape introspection when the process is very rapid.

The affective transformation of presentations is closely related to symbolization. According to G. E. Mueller [13*] symbolization occurs when the perception of an object arouses the presentation in consciousness of another, the two being linked by similar impressions, feelings, or affective states.[14] It has been shown that in the course of learning and recall there emerge, besides the memories of the digits learned, symbolic complex-pictures which represent perceptually the value, "Praegnanz," and "closure" relationships of the elements making up the complex. For example, when in a complex of three elements the middle-element has significantly greater "Praegnanz" than the other two, the symbolic picture of that complex is $\triangle$.[15]

We have now reached certain conclusions concerning the development of presentations in normal individuals. Presentations develop through the progressive increase in clarity of originally indefinite and unclear images. A series of presentations, related by similarity and contiguity, follow each other in an oscillating fashion; in this process they condense and undergo affective transformation or symbolic translation. Various phases of this process may remain in consciousness even after the goal (that is, the final conscious form of the presentation) has been reached.

Two examples from the pathology of the visual sphere will elucidate this. Both are cases of optic agnosia. Stauffenberg [16*] obtained the following reac-

12. It is not quite clear what Schilder means. It is probable that he refers to the presence of these by-products in final recall.

13.* See Mueller (526).

14. For a parallel formulation, see Poetzl (574). Note, however, that Mueller's formulation defines symbolism as a specific case of association, that is, one in which the mediating link is affective. While this is true of symbolism as usually defined, it fails to take account of the fact that usually the symbolized content is unconscious.

15. "Praegnanz" translates *Eindringlichheit*, literally "intensity" or "impressiveness." "Closure" translates *Zu-*

sammenfassung, literally, "summation" or "cohesion." The use of these technical terms introduced by Gestalt-psychology is justified here, since Schilder was familiar with and felt close to its thinking.

It should be noted that Schilder uses here the term symbolism in Mueller's sense. Silberer's hypnagogic phenomena are also symbolic in a similar sense. His "material" and "functional" phenomena resemble Schilder's example. Though dream-work includes such phenomena, they are symbolism in a different sense from dream-symbolism proper. See Chap. 12, note 81, above.

16.* Stauffenberg (702).

tions to pictures presented to his patient: *a mouse* . . . "it isn't a cat"; *a bell* . . . "I know that one, it isn't a bottle"; *a snake* . . . "this one is more like a cat." Here we see in the field of perception that first only the sphere,[17] the general conceptual realm, comes to consciousness; then, recognition progresses within this sphere. According to Liepman [18*] patients afflicted with agnosia substitute conceptually related objects for each other. They may, for instance, call a pair of glasses a telescope (particularly in cases of agnosia of the Lissauer-type).

Poetzl's [19*] patient O was shown a bouquet of flowers in which an asparagus branch stood out conspicuously. Of the flowers he perceived only a red rose. After the bouquet was removed, he was asked to tell the color of the shoulder straps of an officer who was present. He said: "Like a green necktie pin." Here we clearly see the fusion of two spheres; this pathological mode of perceiving corresponds to what we called the "partial fusion of contents" in imagery.

After this detour, I shall now return to our theme. So far I have deliberately confined my discussion to perceptual experiences. It is beyond doubt that our thinking is not directed toward perceptual images. On the contrary, these are merely aids, and would become obstacles if they stayed with us too long. What we are after in most cases is not the image, but the thought, the knowledge. Kuelpe, Ach, Buehler, Messer, and others, demonstrated the existence of image-less experiences,[20] and even G. E. Mueller,[21] their sharpest opponent, agreed that only indistinct image-presentations permit easy and rapid function. This shows that the indistinct image cannot be the main ingredient of thinking;[22]

17. Schilder borrowed the concept "sphere" from Kuelpe (439) and enriched it. See the excerpt from Schilder (657) following this paper as an appendix. The referent of the concept "sphere" is in many respects the same as that of Freud's (209, Chap. VII) concept "primary process." The difference appears to lie in that Schilder observed mechanisms attributed to the primary process operating not only on material of the unconscious but also on material on the fringe of consciousness. Cf. James (353, I, 258). It seems that Bleuler's (68) concept "autistic thinking"

may also have had its origin in similar observations. The mechanisms of the primary process may not be as exclusive to the unconscious as has been thought. Cf. Freud (209, p. 536).

18.* Liepmann (474).

19.* Poetzl (573).

20. This is a reference to the celebrated issue of "imageless thought." See Ach, Chap. 1, and Buehler, Chap. 2, above; also Kuelpe (438), Messer (516).

21. Mueller (526).

22. Though this conclusion has the support of experience and systematic investigation, the argument does not seem

therefore, images must be conceived of as aids to "meaning," knowledge, and signification-experiences. Whether the stock of imageless knowledge be considered extensive, or only limited and circumscribed, it carries the brunt of the experiences of knowing and thinking. Buehler[23]* now maintains that "knowing that something is valid" is the main category of knowledge, and that from it "knowing that something exists" can be derived.[24] Lindworsky[25]* maintains that imageless apperceptions are somehow coordinated to primitive and most general schemata, which in turn are associatively linked to more specific schemata, which, in their turn, lead to the individual presentations: [26] thus he reduces the imageless component of thought to a minimum, namely to the apperception of relationships. Authors who assume the existence of imageless thought-components stress their essential role in thinking.

The next question is whether and to what extent the development of presentations here described obtains also in regard to "awareness" [27] and "meaning experiences." [28] The following is a random example from the work of a pioneer in this field. Buehler [29]* presented questions and his subjects were to answer "yes" or "no." Afterwards their subjective experiences were recorded. One of these records reads:

Question: "Do you understand this: And even if the worms disgust you, let it be, so that you may ascend one step further on your way?" The subject's experience: "After listening, there was an image of a stairway with somebody

---

logically watertight: Mueller's statement, if taken to support the importance of imageless thought, cannot be used to prove that images are an aid to thought, and vice versa.

23.* Buehler (106, particularly the footnote on pp. 372–73).

24. The point here is that since validity-experience is vague and general, while existence-experience is concrete, Buehler assumes the priority of the general, vague, and imageless.

25.* Lindworsky (467).

26. Lindworsky's conception is similar to that of Bartlett (37). See Chap. 3, note 19, and Chap. 23, note 27, above.

27. "Awareness" is a poor translation

of *Bewusstheit*. The German term refers to conscious contents *not otherwise* labeled or classified. See Ach, Chap. 1, above.

28. The experiences in question are of a more general nature than perceptions or apperceptions; their conscious content points—as it were—beyond itself; it "means" or "signifies" something. Those investigators who were concerned with such experiences often overlooked their fluid transition to more concrete experiences and postulated categorical differences between the two. See Buehler, Chap. 2, above.

29.* Buehler (111, I).

ascending, but there wasn't anybody to be seen, and this picture somehow im-plied understanding. 'Ascending' was conceived of in a very general way."

The example demonstrates that the apprehension of the meaning occurs through an image which is not adequate to the meaning; it is only an approxi-mate expression of the thought. Thus this thought develops through a symbolic image. To be sure, the question already implied part of the symbol. Yet it is striking that such a primitive and inadequate image suffices for the understand-ing of a complex thought. According to the report of the subject, there were neither verbal nor kinesthetic presentations; but even such would not clarify the experience of meaning-apprehension.

Two further examples:

Question: "Do you know how many steps there are to the main entrance stairway of the University?" . . . "No." "When I heard 'steps' I thought quickly of the steps of some philosophical systems and then I was aware that I didn't have the answer." [30]

It is quite certain that in this example, instead of the meaning- and significa-tion-experience proper, a symbolic presentation first emerges.

Question: "Do you know where our stopwatch is?" . . . "Yes." "I im-mediately had an image of the rooms at the Institute with the cabinet in the center. My glance wandered over it and I thought: 'presumably there' (spoken inwardly). The image appeared instantly, like an automatic reaction. Only with the 'presumably there' did thinking start. It was as if only that gave meaning to the image." [31]

Here we do not find a symbol or a symbol-like experience in the narrow sense.[32] But here too image and word fragments are only aids to the meaning, and I want to emphasize that the aids are related to the thought in the same way as is a symbol to what it symbolizes.[33]

These discussions give us insight into the process of the development of images. Actually, it is not the images which develop. It is the thought which develops with the aid of the images. Even in the examples of images we were concerned with thoughts; they were searched for and realized with the aid of images. The imageless (or rather, the relatively imageless) experience connects

30. Buehler (111, II, p. 4), also Chap. 2, above.

31. Buehler (111, II, p. 7), also Chap. 2, above.

32. It is questionable whether there are here symbols in any sense. But see note 15, above.

33. Cf. note 2, above.

isolated and partial phases of thought-development and finds its fulfillment in an "adequate" image, to the extent to which images can be adequate to a meaning. One could assume that imageless knowledge exists before thought-development begins and uses images merely as a garb.[34] The experience that first one has but an inkling of a thought, and only later the full thought, speaks against this assumption. Or one could perhaps assume that the thought emerges suddenly from the images. This, however, implies a development making this sudden emergence possible. It seems then that the relation of the image to the thought is not something extraneous, but that image and meaning are intrinsically related.[35] This justifies our having started out with an attempt to describe the development of presentations.

Let us examine Silberer's [36*] results concerning auto-symbolic phenomena. He showed that in hypnagogic states pictures emerge which, though they have no immediately recognizable relationship to the thoughts intended, can be considered symbols of those thoughts. Thus, for instance, the thought of improving a scientific paper was represented by working with a plane on a board.

The important conclusion is that thought-development passes through a phase of symbolic and symbol-like presentations.[37] These presentations are in part irrelevant to the thought concerned; fleeting and easily suppressed, they soon vanish, while what they lead to—the thought—remains.[38] Thus, from the point of view of thought, images are transitory stages. These images are very frequently symbolic. One might be inclined to consider even verbal images as transitory stages, since they too are only mediators of meaning.

34. Cf. also Mueller-Freienfels (529). Schilder implies that such a relation between image and thought would not be intrinsic.

35. "Intrinsic relationship" translates *Wesenszusammenhang*. The term implies that the relationship of thought and image is one in which: (a) neither can be considered to precede the other in existence; (b) neither can be considered as the "efficient cause" of the other; (c) the two must be considered as an integral unit. Actually, more recent psychological writing would probably prefer to characterize this by the phrase: "thought and image are merely two aspects of the same experience (or communication)."

36.* See Silberer [Chap. 8, above].

37. This argument, valid though it may be, has no sure footing in Silberer's material. Schilder goes beyond Silberer here by assuming that the symbolization of thought observed in the hypnagogic state is part of the usual preparatory process of normal thought. Cf., however, note 9, above.

38. Cf., however, pp. 500–501, and note 12, above.

We have yet further direct indications of thought-development.

Buehler [39] quotes the following statements of his subjects: "The memory of something from before (the thought!) came to me. But I didn't know at all what it was." "The direction toward it was there immediately, but I couldn't follow through."

Buehler's reference point is Kant's theory; the concept "dog" is a rule by which the power of imagination can put forth the form of a four-legged animal. There exists a general rule-consciousness, and thoughts are formed in accordance with it. [40]

It must be emphasized that here yet another psychological function is seen to be involved in the process of thought. One must add, however, that this rule-consciousness, this "direction," is very frequently linked with spatial schemes and diagrams. [41] Here, too, the quantitative relationship of the image to image-less thought is of no importance. It is the latter which is the main pillar of thought.

The objection may be raised that all the phenomena described so far are only isolated instances. Yet such observations impressed a great variety of workers, even in the course of investigations conducted for a quite different purpose—Michotte and Ransy, [42]* Buehler, [43]* G. E. Mueller, [44]* Lindworsky, [45]* Selz. [46]* Thus, it is beyond doubt that the occurrence of symbolic or symbol-like images in the course of the thought-process is not infrequent. The instances in which clear-cut formations of this sort appear are clues to the comprehension of the thought-process. Considering the wealth of allegories and metaphors in any language, one is inclined to assume that every thought that emerges in the psyche undergoes a process of development like the one described above. [47] In the final analysis, the general relationship between image and meaning is like that between the developmental phases of thought and their end product.

39. Buehler (111, II), also Chap. 2, above.

40. In modern psychology this problem is discussed under the heading of "concept formation." See Chap. 26, VI, below.

41. Cf. Selz (679) and Silberer, Chap. 8, above.

42.* Michotte and Ransy (520).
43.* Buehler (111).
44.* Mueller (526).
45.* Lindworsky (475).
46.* Selz (679).
47. This is another attempt to assert the ubiquity of "thought-development" by pointing to a new line of evidence.

To sum up: Images and thoughts have a development, a pre-history. What we know so far about this developmental process is:

a. Image and thought-development progress from the indefinite to the definite.

b. This process of development passes through associatively related realms. Anything which is associated with the presentation by either objective relationship or subjective experience may come into play.

c. Incompletely evolved thoughts contain presentation-fragments from various phases of development.

d. Incompletely evolved thoughts are particularly amenable to affective transformation, and

e. they frequently have a symbol-like character.

f. The image content of consciousness plays a less significant role in thinking than imageless thought-experiences, even though the latter are usually connected with presentation-fragments. The image-elements themselves are perhaps only symbols of meaning-experiences.

We want to stress that meaning-laden experiences carry relatively few and indistinct images. One of the essential characteristics of these experiences, which play a crucial role in thinking, is their poverty in sensory material.[48]

The basis of thought-development is always a unitary act of the will.[49] It is

48. By "meaning-laden" Schilder apparently means relatively abstract as against concrete experiences.

49. While the concept "will" played a great role in the thinking of some of the psychologists (for example, Lindworsky) on whose work Schilder leaned, it plays little systematic role in more recent psychologies. Rank (588) for whom "will" was an important concept, did not create a systematic psychological theory, and Rogers (617) in whose thinking "will" plays a considerable (at times covert) role has not yet done so. The upshot is that in modern psychology, only Lewin has a clear-cut definition of the will concept, which can be applied to the theory of thinking. Cf. Lewin, Chap. 5, II, 2, above. Lewin treated "will" as a phenotypical concept. It served him as an indicator of the presence of "needs," and was thus not the cause but merely a precursor of "intentions." These "intentions" set up "quasi-needs," specific "tension systems" derived from the tension system corresponding to the basic "need."

The main stream of psychoanalytic thinking also seems to have dealt with the "will" as an epiphenomenon, as an outcome of impulse dynamics. But see Knight (390) and Hartmann, Chap. 19, above. It is likely that the final word on "will" has not been said and that a psychoanalytic ego-psychology may develop a new concept of "will."

an intention. All developmental phases of a thought rise from the same affective ground and bear indications of this origin.[50] The development of thought originates in a unitary drive-orientation, in a uniformly directed intention of the individual.[51] We have found that affective transformation is a normal transitory phase of thought-development by which the various drive-orientations, determinations, and Gestalten are transformed into fleeting images which are in turn normally superseded by a pressure toward objectivity.[52] Clear conscious ideas are surrounded by an indefinite halo of obscure developmental forms. The color and richness of mental life derives from this penumbra. Here it is possible to remold that which would otherwise be rigid. This is the matrix from which, through continuous reformulations, our thoughts arise.

Were the original intention to penetrate, unobstructed and unchanged by intentions directed toward objectivity, the resulting thought could not do justice to the manifold conditions it has to meet. It appears that transitory phases of thought-development become manifest when various intentions related to reality meet, that is, when new reality-relationships enter the thought-process.[53] The value of thinking, however, lies in the utilization of these reality-relationships. According to this view, the images which indicate that an object-directed intention has been checked are essentials of fruitful thinking.[54] I am inclined to

---

Schilder's point is that thought-development is motivated just like any other psychological process. It is regrettable that Schilder's statement is blunted by the use of such an indefinite motivational concept as "will."

50. The term "intention" indicates that Schilder's will-concept is related to Lewin's. "Affective ground" apparently refers to the psychological stratum where intrapsychic needs and tensions prevail, rather than the logic of reality-adaptation. The term "affect" has been overused to designate everything that is intrapsychically determined. See note 11, above. Here Schilder more or less equates "will" and "affective ground."

51. This throws further light on Schilder's conception of "will." Cf. note 49.

52. According to Schilder, thought-development has two major determinants: (a) the affects and drives (will) which exert their transforming influence in the preparatory phase and (b) the striving toward objectivity (that is, for reality-adequacy) which gives thought its logical form. Point (a) refers to the "sphere" (see pp. 517–18, below). The parallel to Freud's "primary process" and "secondary process" is rather clear. The "pressure for objectivity" has a conceptually more solid counterpart in Freud's "reality-principle" (see Chap. 15, above).

53. This is a new assumption concerning the obstructions which slow down the thought-process and make its preparatory phases observable.

54. The term "check" seems to cor-

define thinking as an object-directed act checked by acts directed towards other objects. The checking effect becomes manifest in the form of images. The essence of productive thought-processes is that in spite of these checks they reach their goal, which is to gain insight into object-relations.[55*]

The development of thought can be interrupted before its completion by even a minor interference. Stransky [56*] found perseverations, contaminations, and clang-associations in the speech of subjects instructed to relax their attention.[57] According to the analysis presented here, these *formations* are also preparatory steps, that is, developmental phases of normal thought.

In schizophrenias and paraphrenias [58] preliminary phases of thought are abundant.[59*] I would like to give an example from a case of paraphrenia which, according to my rather extensive experience, is typical. Freud, Bleuler, and the Zurich school, have repeatedly demonstrated similar mechanisms.

The case is that of a chronically paraphrenic woman with an extensive delusional system based on pseudo-memories and perhaps on memories of hallucinations.[60] Her delusional system does not interfere with her everyday life. . . . The content of the system, in brief, is: a "molten" [61] man endows clover seeds with souls, whereupon these seeds get into the blood and there grow into worms.

---

respond to Freud's concept of representation of "delay." See Freud, Chap. 15, above. Freud's conception is that thought is a representation of an object which is to satisfy a need, in other words, the goal of a drive. Such a representation arises only when the discharge of the tension corresponding to the drive is *delayed*, that is, when the drive is checked. The concept of "delay" may well prove a cornerstone of the future theory of thinking.

55.* These are only preliminary formulations. In my paper, "On Identification" (657) I made an attempt to prove some of them more fully. I hope soon to be able to offer further proof. Poetzl's (573) paper quoted above contains factual material supporting these formulations.

56.* Stransky (719).

57. It may be questioned whether interfering with attention is only a minor interference with thinking. See Rapaport, Gill, and Schafer (602, I, 166 ff).

58. Paraphrenia is a term first used by Guislain early in the 19th century and reintroduced by Kraepelin. He applied it to paranoid disorders which are neither true paranoia nor paranoid schizophrenia. Today they are labeled "paranoid conditions." The term is often used synonymously with schizophrenia.

59.* I shall avoid here the discussion of dreams.

60. Schilder published the detailed material of this case in his *Selbstbewusstsein und Persoenlichkeitbewusstsein* (653).

61. "Molten" translates the word *zerlassen*, a neologism.

According to a plan that is marked out in the body, these worms build a "magnet child." For this, air must be blown in through the genitals. At birth "slava"-fire comes out of the genitals which burns everything into gold. With the magnet-child one can attract treasures to oneself. The slava-gold holds the earth to-gether. The patient had five magnet-children. Out of this anthropogony the patient created a peculiar cosmogony and an even more peculiar fairy-tale world. . . . The creations of her fantasy are closely related to her delusions. Worms and slava represent masculine and feminine and appear in many varia-tions.

The patient manifested various formal disturbances.[62] She showed condensa-tions of the widest variety: Many millions are deposited in the name of Vander-bilt (this is how she refers to her uncle's firm). The patient had to sign the peace-treaty after the Franco-Serbian War of 1893. All the bills were paid by her. At that time Vanderbilt money paid for everything. Fragments from various spheres of experience and knowledge are thus thrown together and fused, forming condensations. Since the nature of condensations is generally known, I shall now turn to my next point.

The patient related: "Her second son had a great bone-head; she wanted to cure her uncle with it. The child had a rubber suit on. It grew in the rubber suit. The limbs of a child thus grown can be used for curative purposes. Those who take such a cure say that they had a bath." The underlying series of images evidently pertain to the contraceptive-covered penis which is thereby protected from infection. This is apparently the point around which is developed the presentation of a bone-headed child whose limbs protect against sickness. In

62. "Formal" contrasts here with "content." Thus far Schilder has pre-sented only the content of the patient's fantasies and delusions. The interest in "formal characteristics" of thought and of their disturbances is currently re-awakening. Pre-psychoanalytic psy-chiatry showed considerable concern for these formal characteristics and dis-turbances of thought (Kraepelin, Bleu-ler). Freud himself paid much attention to them (Freud, 209, Chap. VII). Yet his work on content was fated to impress psychoanalysts, psychiatrists, and even psychologists more than did his work on formal characteristics, probably because the former seemed more immediately useful in treating patients. It is hard to say whether the day will come when contents can be dealt with by psychol-ogy in the way "secondary qualities" are treated by physics. It is clear, how-ever, that the formal characteristics of thought and Freud's contribution to their understanding are shifting closer to the center of attention than ever be-fore. The theory of projective and other tests has contributed a generous share to the reawakening of this interest.

my opinion, it would be incorrect to say that the child symbolizes the penis. But one could say that here symbol-like substitute-formations emerge in the thought-process. Special attention should be paid to the reversal brought about by the thought-process: the penis that is "to be protected" is changed into the child that "protects." [63] It can be demonstrated that at this stage of thought-development, acting and being acted upon are as yet hardly differentiated.

Let us now consider another formal disturbance. The slava (that slava is identical with the genitals is beyond doubt), the fire-gold resting under the earth must be served,[64]* and it must be served in the patient by a Czech. It must be served once a week. The Czech was with her and "served it." Slava, which is the spirit of the woman, sees the two people through the earth. Actually, it sees only the genital of the man and sees it as a whole man. The process lasts only a few seconds each time, but the slava is satisfied. When someone other than the Czech penetrated into the patient, the slava felt it as thorns.

It is noteworthy that intercourse appears to the patient in two different forms, one being in the "adequate" [65] and one in the symbolic sphere (serving the slava). Slava is the fire-gold coming from the genital and also the female genital in anthropomorphic form: it can see, it sees the male genital, perceiving it as an entire man. We can forego here the psychological analysis of the displacements, condensations, and playful repetitions which accompany the duplication of the event in the symbolic sphere.

I have already emphasized that the normal thought-process has a symbolic preparatory phase and that the preparatory forms do not necessarily disappear.[66] We have something analogous in this case history. While in normal people all relevant experience is compounded into a unitary meaning, here this does not occur.[67] The "duplication" of experience here described is not rare in

63. "Reversal" here translates *Vertauschung*, literally "exchange." The translation "reversal" was chosen to emphasize that Schilder deals here with the formal counterpart of the Freudian mechanism "reversal into the opposite." The "formal disturbances" discussed in this section are "symbol-like substitute formation" (the distinction of which from symbolism remains here unclear) and "reversal."

64.* The patient used the same expression for sexual intercourse.

65. "Adequate" translates *richtig*, literally "correct." See in this connection Silberer, Chap. 9, p. 217, above. The meaning of the sentence would be best conveyed by "both in realistic and symbolic form."

66. See note 12, above.

67. Schilder touches here on the cardinal differentiating characteristic of

psychopathology. It would be worthwhile to study the phenomenon of autoscopy [68] from this point of view. In autoscopy the individual's experience of his own body is redoubled and projected. It is noteworthy that the duplicate—in the cases I have seen—usually undergoes transformation according to affective principles. Thus, one of my patients, whose family life is a very unhappy one, saw herself in the distant past in the attire of a lady-knight.[69*] Bodily defects may also be projected as illusions or hallucinations without a loss of consciousness of these defects. In such projections the defect is usually exaggerated. For instance, a patient of mine with a crippled arm saw as crippled the leg as well as the arm of the person he encountered. This again corresponds to the psychological finding that the more important something is, the more we are inclined to exaggerate it.[70]

But let us return to our patient. She gives so many symbol-like pictures of fertilization and birth that the two processes seem to appear in her thinking as often as the picture of a candle in two mirrors at acute angles to each other.[71] Let us make this point clear. The scorpion, according to the patient, develops out of the semen of the man when it enters the woman (fertilization). Again, the poison of the scorpion is used to "melt" a man. It is easy to demonstrate that being "molten" is a symbol-like presentation of intercourse (fertiliza-

---

the primary and the secondary process. The claim is often made that ordered thinking (secondary process) is distinguished from the primary thought-process by unity of structure and absence of contradiction. This claim sounds sufficiently plausible and convincing, yet exact definitions for "unity" and "lack of contradiction" are lacking. If everyday conversation is to be considered a sample of ordered thought-processes, it has to be yet shown in what sense it fulfills these two criteria.

68. "Autoscopy," literally "self-seeing," usually refers to those hallucinations or illusions in which it seems to the patient that he meets himself. Schilder broadens the term to include aspects of the self.

69.* Schilder (656).

70. Compare pp. 500–501 and note 11, above.

71. This simile may have more to it than meets the eye. The infinite multiplication of an image in mirrors facing each other is also a good representation of a salient characteristic of awareness. Awareness is characterized by the fact that we are aware not only of our object, but also of our awareness of it, and can become aware of the awareness that we are aware of our object. There is some indication in my own material of self-recorded dreams and reveries that abortive effort directed at becoming aware of one's own state of consciousness may lead to a multiplication of symbol-like representations, either of one's subjective state or of the content of one's thought. Cf. Chap. 17, note 18, and Chap. 13, note 56, above.

tion): a "molten" man fertilizes the clover seeds (fertilization). The clover seeds get into the blood (fertilization), and there grow into worms. Also, a worm can penetrate the body in its own form (fertilization). A woman gets children through a "melting" of the abdominal wall. The slava-gold is being pumped into the body in the form of air (sex act). This is a long series of symbol-like presentations that represent a single process.

Another patient of mine does not at all differentiate among the presentations, thumb, snake, and worm. It is the concept of the phallus that underlies them.

These phenomena remind one of the fact that in normal thinking the search for meaning may invoke the aid of presentations of various kinds. One often observes while pondering a general subject, that instead of one illustrative image frequently a whole series appears.[72*]

Another thought-disorder of our patient, in a sense the counterpart of the one described, is the following: she does not distinguish between her mother's brother and her father's brother; the personality of the uncles, in turn, is identical with her father's. In her description their fate is identical too: namely, they have lost their heads. Finally, we are left with a picture which could be expressed as follows: father—uncle—man who has only his head left—old man. Here the final result of the process is treated as if it were the middle phase in the development of a completed thought.[73] The individual presentation substitutes for the general concept, necessarily resulting in a leveling of the individual presentation.[74]

I have considered only the most striking formal disturbances of the patient's thinking and have, I believe, demonstrated that they can all be understood as

72.* Child psychology has found that for children an object may have a great variety of names.

[Cf. Buehler, 106, p. 388.]

73. This point remains somewhat obscure. As I understand it, the final picture contradicts all that preceded it: the father and the uncles were one in that they lost their heads; now they are one in that they have nothing but their heads left. Schilder—I take it—has made an attempt to characterize the formal aspect of this state of affairs. He noted that the trend of this thought (up to the final point) is directed to a compounding of the figures, with the result that they become identically headless. This seemed to complete the thought-process. But then there is another, jump-like, completion that makes of the previous apparently completed thought only a transitory phase.

74. The presentation that substitutes for the general concept is the head. The "leveling" refers to the elimination of any distinction between the uncles and the father.

abortive formations produced in the course of the differentiation-process of thought.[75]

All these phenomena, which are neatly separated from each other in the presentations, hallucinations, and scenic [76] experiences of paranoid schizophrenias and paraphrenias, appear in condensed form in logorrheic verbigeration.[77] To demonstrate this, I want to quote a passage from Stransky's [78*] work on confusion of language:

It is characteristic of verbigerative expectorations that the same sentence-like groups of presentations appear over and over again. In these groups certain perseverating single presentations compete for the lead, gaining it alternatingly. It is as if they were swinging around an imaginary axis in kaleidoscopic, yet monotonous, fashion; within a continuously repeated sentence-like series of words, the same presentations keep recurring. The words of the series remain similar throughout, because heterogenous presentations tend to be contaminated by those recurring.[79*]

I feel that my analysis of the formal characteristics of schizophrenic thinking warrants the thesis that in many schizophrenic cases such formations, which normally would be only transitory phases in thought-development, appear as the end results of thought-processes. The point of view that these formations are abortive products of thought-development contributes considerably to their understanding.[80*]

75. This is the first time that Schilder refers to thought-development as a "differentiation process." The point is of import, since his discussion of the thought-process has thus far dwelt on aspects which make it appear an integration process. Passing through associated presentations in its preparatory phase, the thought-process gathers reality-relevant elements and integrates them into the final thought. The differentiation process begins with either a perception or a thought; then it "passes through associated presentations." Thereby the perception or thought differentiates into its associative connotations. The thought-process is probably a complex interweaving of simultaneous integration and differentiation. The nature and the governing rules of the differentiation aspect of the thought-process have only

been touched upon by Schilder. See in this connection, Rapaport, Schafer, Gill (602, II, 22–24), also Hartmann, Chap. 19, IV, above.

76. "Scenic" translates *scenisch*, and means, literally, "graphically expressed" or "theatrical." What it means here is unclear.

77. The "separation" of which Schilder speaks is that of the varieties of formal disorder of thought. In verbigeration all these varieties interpenetrate to such an extent that scarcely any specific formal disorder, or any meaning of thought is discernible.

78.* Stransky (719).

79.* I have unpublished notes of a detailed content analysis of such verbigerations.

80.* I have an extensive collection of data corroborating this point.

We need special investigations to establish which types of schizophrenia show such abortive thought-development and to what extent they do so.

The pathological alteration of the formal characteristics of thought is accompanied by typical thought-contents. Thinking gains its reality-orientation, its factual meaning, only in the last phase of its development. This, as we have seen, is preceded by a phase of affective transformations and symbolizations. When cognition is molded by these affective transformations and symbolizations the world seems governed by wishes. (Freud's "omnipotence of thought.") [81]* When wishes have such a direct effect on the development of thought it seems to the individual that every event is due to a wish and that nothing but wishes can bring about any event (the belief in magic). If it be true that development progresses from schematic to individual forms, then there must exist a phase in which only the general conception is important and the differentiation within its sphere negligible.[82] Thus, for example, the sphere, father-power-authority, will not be differentiated, but will remain a single affectively anchored global concept. Concepts like action, nature, and sexuality, will also be experienced as broad global unities; and since the effect of action will have to be identical,[83] matter will take on the character of a "wish-substance," the parts of which will be synonymous with the whole.[84] Consequently, each part sharing this propensity of matter will be infinitely divisible. Since this setting of sphere and schema [85] will be ruled by affectivity, all concepts will be divided by the ambivalence of affects [86] into the two great realms of Good and Bad. This ambiva-

---

81.* Freud (227).

82. The sphere in question is that of the general, global, and undifferentiated concept. See note 17, above.

Though Schilder speaks here of a "phase" of thought-development, his subsequent discussion makes it clear that he refers also to pathological conditions in which the thought-formations of this phase take the place of thought-products adapted to reality.

83. This is in keeping with the principle of "omnipotence of thought."

84. This consideration can be derived from the "participation" concept coined by Levy-Bruehl (455) and used extensively in ethnopsychology. See also H.

Werner (755, pp. 446–60). The relation of this concept to the logical fallacy and poetic form called "pars pro toto" needs no discussion. Leibnitz's "monads" are also an example in point.

85. The term "schema" has already been used by Schilder as a synonym for "general concept." He designates by it the vague, general, and undifferentiated matrix, which is part of the "sphere" and out of which concepts and thoughts arise. The rule of affects, schema, and sphere are here descriptive terms for different aspects of the same state of affairs.

86. The term "ambivalence" was coined by Bleuler (76, pp. 125–26):

lence, abetted by the tendency to spatial symbolization described by Lind-worsky [87*] and Selz,[88*] will coordinate such spatial relationships as right-left, far-near, and above-below to the two great realms of Good and Bad.[89] As a consequence of the equivalence of the individual presentations of the same realm of the sphere, the masculine may come to stand for good and right, the feminine for bad and left, etc.[90] Finally, the rule of drive-life, of affectivity,[91] brings assimilation and expulsion mechanisms, such as projection, identification, and appersonation,[92] to bear on the undeveloped thought material, causing affect-determined fluctuations [93*] in the possession relationship [94] between subject and object. All this is inferred from the results of "normal psychology" and verified by psychopathology. Therefore, the study of schizophrenia and paraphrenia is also of great significance for normal psychology.

I demonstrated in a previous publication,[95] more or less in agreement with Freud [96*] and Jung,[97*] that the characteristics of the content of abortive schizophrenic thought and the thought of primitive peoples are the same. In the de-

---

Even the normal individual feels, as it were, two souls in his breast; he fears an event and wishes it to come, as in the case of an operation, or the acceptance of a new position. Such a double feeling tone exists most frequently and is particularly drastic when it concerns persons whom one hates or fears and at the same time loves.

87.* Lindworsky (475).

88.* Selz (679).

89. See in this connection H. Werner (755, p. 171).

90. Schilder referred to this previously, using the phrase: "the leveling of individual presentations" (note 74, above). Psychoanalytic theory would refer to this as the equivalence of the various representations of an instinct or drive.

91. Here it again becomes quite clear that Schilder, like Bleuler, Jung, and Silberer, uses the concepts affect and affectivity in an extremely broad sense and interchangeably with the concepts

"drives," "drive-life," "drive-dynamics." For the historical roots and a critique of this usage, see note 11, above.

92. Appersonation is a term coined by Schilder to refer to a segment of the phenomena usually subsumed under the concept identification. See Schilder (657).

93.* See in this connection my publications (656, 657, 663).

94. "Possession relationship" apparently refers to the manner of evaluating objects. They may be experienced as external reality, as integral parts of the person, as thought, fantasy, obsession, etc. The expulsion and assimilation mechanisms to which Schilder refers do indeed determine in which of these ways the subject will experience the object. Cf. Freud (237).

95. Schilder (663).

96.* Freud (227).

97.* Jung (364).

velopment of thinking in the child we observe analogous phenomena. Thus the circle closes.

I have attempted to demonstrate that every thought is the product of a process of development. The steps of this development are traceable in the thinking of primitives, children, and schizophrenics. Even though our knowledge of this developmental process is still incomplete, what is already known justifies the assumption that every thought recapitulates the phylogenesis and ontogenesis of thinking.

We first think each thought in the fashion of our ancestors. This is *vita ipsa*. Every thought repeats the natural history of creation [98]* and in our thoughts we experience the development of the organic world.[99]

APPENDIX

[EXTRACT FROM THE PAPER "ON IDENTIFICATION"] [100]

I have shown [101]* that we are not justified in using the term symbol for many experiences the material of which comes from the sexual sphere,[102] and to which material from other spheres is assimilated.[103] We explained these experiences as the effects of will and "determining tendencies" and emphasized that the coincidence of these two drive-orientations [104] causes the "assimilation" to each other of material from different spheres. Thus the emergence of all images is determined by will-orientation. Therefore, we did not assume a categorical difference between the genesis of symbol-like images and of those not related to symbols.

98.* Schelling has already outlined these issues; Nietzsche and Weininger expressed similar ideas.

99. The sweep of Schilder's phrasing, totally unencumbered by caution, may be disquieting; however, his intuitive grasp and rich command of clinical material and literature will not—it is hoped —fail to impress and stimulate the reader.

100. Schilder (657).

101.* Schilder und Weidner (668).

102. See in this connection Silberer (Chap. 9, above) on sexuality and symbolism.

103. Assimilation is a concept of association psychology, the referent of which is subsumed by Freud in the concept condensation.

104. "Drive-orientations" is a phrase used by Schilder much the same way as the concept drive is used today: as a motivational concept implying a specific direction. Schilder subsumes here will-orientations under drive-orientations. The distinction is none too clear; see note 49, above.

There I left open the question of the form in which the "assimilated material" exists before "assimilation" takes place. Later on I developed the view that all past experience is represented psychologically as an unclear periphery or "fringe" of experience and that will- and drive-orientations create new formations out of this fringe.[105] It will require detailed investigation to determine the relationship and overlapping of the concepts, "fringe," state of consciousness, content of consciousness and sphere (in the sense of Kuelpe).[106]

The concept of the sphere is in need of elaboration. I can dwell on it only briefly. A sphere encompasses the totality of similar thought-formations. The sphere is the storage place of the experiences and drives of life. It is here that the various tendencies of will cross and the various forms of thought meet. It is a primeval form of psychic life. It is the unarticulated background of experiencing. It is unarticulated in the same sense as is the germ-plasm in comparison to the fully developed organism. If I were to give a general idea of the sphere, I would say that I do not conceive of it as something abstractly logical, but rather as of a realm [107] of similar and affectively equivalent experiences oriented in two directions: toward the objective world and toward that of the drives. The sphere serves both reality and drive-orientations; it is on the border-line of these two that symbol-like formations come about. The final impressions of experience, whether they be perceptions, presentations, verbalized thoughts, insight into facts, or feelings, all arise from transformations within the spheres. Anything so arising remains connected with its matrix. Therefore, we are left with the problems: what is really the relationship of meaning-experience to the sphere, and how do feelings connect the actual experience that is in the foreground with the background-experience pertaining to the sphere.[108]

105. For the concept "fringe" cf. James (353, I, 258, 281–82).

106. See Kuelpe (439).

107. Here it becomes clear that *the* sphere is a collection of spheres.

108. Cf. note 17. Here it becomes clear that since Schilder does not differentiate between a primary and a secondary process, he has to attribute both drive- and reality-syntonic functions to the sphere, and within it he has to *distinguish* reality and drive-orientations. Thus the dichotomy of the primary and secondary process reemerges *within* the sphere, that is, within the very concept that was to eliminate it.

CHAPTER 25

STUDIES CONCERNING THE PSYCHOLOGY AND SYMPTOMATOLOGY OF GENERAL PARESIS [1]

By Paul Schilder

I. A GENERAL PSYCHOLOGICAL INTRODUCTION

(a) Objects and Relationships

HUMAN BEINGS exist and act in a real world. This world has an articulation which they perceive.[2] The concept of perception, however, needs scrutiny. When speaking of perception we generally think of sense perception; indeed, we usually mean sensation. But—as I once showed [3]—sensation is an abstraction. Koffka [4] too has criticized the current concept of sensation, and rightly so. There is no constant correspondence between simple objects of the outside world, stimuli, and simplest experience.[5] The expression "sensation" should be used only for the subjective aspect [6] of the experience of perceiving. The experi-

---

1. Schilder (655).
2. Schilder's epistemological stand is indicated here. It is the articulation of the world which is given, not the "categories" of the "pure mind" (Kant). The point is of importance, since modern dynamic psychology has implications suggestive of solipsism. See, for example, Laforgue (441, pp. 57–59). The epistemological paradox of dynamic psychology is: how account for an adequate knowledge of reality when consciousness, the medium for gaining knowledge, is determined by intrapsychic laws? This paradox—implicit to the psychoanalytic concept of "reality-testing" and amenable to psychological solution—is rarely tackled. (See Freud, Chap. 15, note 6, and Hartmann on "fitting-in," Chap. 19, II, above.)

3. For a discussion of this point, see Schilder (649, pp. 3–6 and 172); see also Schilder (648, pp. 23–28).
4. See Koffka (406, pp. 103–5), and (404, pp. 147–49).
5. Schilder means that the concept sensation implies a quest for a simple psychological "element" (sensation) which would be elicited by a simple enough stimulus (reality-segment), if found. Here Schilder takes the point of view of Gestalt-psychology, and condemns as an idle dream the hope of finding a correspondence between isolated elements of reality and isolated elements of the psyche.
6. The concept "subjective aspect" reverberates with the influence of Meinong (511) and Brentano (90), and of Husserl's (346, 171) phenomenology.

ence of primitive percepts is by no means simpler than the experience of percepts of great complexity. It is, therefore, incorrect to say that perceptions are built of sensations. Actually, we are forever searching for the interrelations of our body, of our subjective sense-impressions, and of discrete parts of our percepts. We do this by means of complicated abstractions and experiments of our everyday life. When in this search we happen to hit upon units of subjective experience which seem in close correspondence with objects of simple structure, we call them sensations. Thus, sensations are by no means the natural units of psychic life, particularly not in the sense that psychic life is built of such simple sensations. There is a widespread opinion, more or less tacitly held, that only sensations are realities and that they become perception by being displaced into the outside world through projection. But starting with the sensations red, hard, round, it is impossible to arrive at the object, red billiard ball. Furthermore, red, hard, round, are by no means genuine primitive sensations. It is likely that in primitive sensation a great abundance of "elements" is interwoven; or more correctly, in primitive sensation elements would be altogether indistinguish-

---

Schilder—like Buehler (106), to whom he often refers—has been deeply influenced by these thinkers. Their influence is seen in Schilder's conception of all psychic life as consisting of "acts." Acts imply for him, just as for phenomenological philosophy, an object, turning of consciousness toward the object (intentionality), and the specific form the object takes in the act. See Schilder (648, p. 5), and (652, particularly the Introduction). Such phenomenological description of psychological happening is in harmony with the exploration by dynamic psychologies of the forms of conscious experience, and emphasizes one of their neglected aspects. For a discussion of "acts" and "intentionality," see Gurwitsch, in Farber (171, p. 65).

Gurwitsch writes:

The intentionality of consciousness may be defined as a relation which all, or at least certain, acts bear to an object. In this manner, Brentano introduced the notion into contemporary philosophy. Seeking to account for the difference between what he calls "physical phenomena" and what he calls "psychical phenomena," Brentano found, among other characteristics, that the latter are distinguished by a relation to, or a direction toward, an object. This directedness of psychical phenomena is interpreted by Brentano as their containing within themselves an "immanent" object-like entity. Although Husserl takes over Brentano's notion of intentionality, he raises some objections against this interpretation. His examination of Brentano's conception of intentionality finally leads him to abandon it completely; but he agrees with Brentano in acknowledging the existence of a highly important class of mental factors—for which Husserl reserves the title of acts—which have the peculiarity of presenting the subject with an object. Experiencing an act, the subject is aware of an object, so that the act may be characterized . . . as a *consciousness* of an object whether real or ideal, whether existent or imaginary.

able.[7] Actually, "sensation" indicates merely that while we are perceiving, something is going on in our body. I repeat: perception does not come about by projection. Rather it seems that every perception implies (a) that which is perceived, (b) my sensation, and (c) my act of turning toward the world.[8]

The world is not derived from my body or from my ego, but is just as genuine as they are. We are accustomed to separate perceiving an object, imaging it, and thinking it. It is a matter of dispute in psychology whether, besides perception-contents and image-contents, there are not imageless-contents also, such as thoughts (Buehler) [9] and awarenesses (Ach).[10] I do not believe that the existence of such imageless thoughts can be doubted, though it is an open question whether they can appear in isolation or require always the support of perceptual material; it is probable that fragments of perceptions and images are always present. Buehler also holds this view now. See also Willwoll.[11]* Fundamentally, perceptions, images, and thoughts always have a subjective and an objective aspect. What we call sensation is the subjective aspect of perception.[12] For the objective side of images and thoughts we have no term. Phenomenology has

7. The evidence for this assertion is the observed syncretic, global, diffuse, and undifferentiated character of primitive perception in infants, animals, the brain-injured, psychotics, etc. See in this respect, H. Werner (755, pp. 104 ff.).

8. In his sharp stand against attributing any role to projection in perception, Schilder leans on Brentano, Meinong, and Husserl. The assertion is directed against a frequent assumption of dynamic psychology: that the total mass of perceptual raw material obtained through the sense-organs becomes our "knowledge" of the outside world by being reorganized according to the principles of the individual's thought-organization, and then projected outward. It takes such a cumbersome explanation to account for our experiencing an *outside* world, when it is assumed that the organization of our percepts follows intrapsychic principles (note that the latter is held even by Gestalt-psychology). Schilder suggests that only part of the organization is intrapsychic (see note 2, above), and that in perception we need not assume a projection-mechanism because the very act of perceiving implies a *"turning toward the world."* While it is easy to go along with the first suggestion, the second (of phenomenological vintage) seems to beg the question; it gives a description only, not an explanation.

9. See Buehler, Chap. 2, above. "Thought" here translates *Gedanke*.

10. "Awareness" here translates *Bewusstheiten;* literal translation, "consciousnesses," meaning contents of consciousness which are neither percepts nor images. See Ach, Chap. 1, above.

11.* Willwoll (772).

12. Note the implication that the concept "perception" pertains to the "objective" aspect.

shown that a thought or an image always refers to an object, namely that one which is meant by the image or thought.[13] What finally emerges in image or thought is wholly analogous with the percept.[14] What is contained in the image or thought is closely related to what we call concept. But concepts are closely related to words; images and thoughts do not necessarily imply words. Our formulation is: concepts are the objective aspect of certain images and thoughts.

What is an object? . . .[15]

Talking about objects implies that the world is articulated into discrete parts. However, the expression "part" leaves it open whether or not there is an intrinsic relationship between the individual object and the world as the totality of objects. We shall take no stand on whether the world is the sum of individual objects or an organized whole.[16] At any rate, the fundamental implication of the concept "object" is that we can never experience the world as a uniform continuum. It remains, however, quite indefinite what is to be considered a single object: the chair or its back.[17] Wherever we may draw this dividing line, the fact remains that the world of our experience is discontinuous. I have shown elsewhere that we can hardly make the world as a whole the object of our actions.[18]

Only on very primitive levels of psychic life are there intentions [19] which come close to the wish to master the whole world as a single object. Objects are the units upon which we act. To enable us to act, the object must appear an unchanging unit. Phenomenology has correctly shown that the rigidity [20] of

13. In the phenomenological literature "meant by" often stands for "intended by."

14. That is, their "objective aspect," the object they "mean" or "intend."

15. The omitted part touches briefly on the problem of values.

16. The "sum" versus the "whole" is here the same as in Wertheimer's (762) distinction between "and-sum" and "Gestalt." For a concise definition see Katona (374, p. 27).

17. This is the problem of the hierarchy of Gestalts and sub-Gestalts. See Koffka (406, p. 718), on "sub-systems."

18. This use of action as a *criterion* reflects its central role in Schilder's

theory. It is similar to the role Freud assigns to action. See Schilder (652) and Freud (223).

19. Intention is used here in the sense of "directed will-activity preparatory to action," and not in the sense of Brentano's (90, p. 115) "intentionality."

20. Apparently what is meant here is "constancy." See Piaget, Chap. 6, above. The issue of constancy (color, size, etc.) is a major field of psychophysical experimentation. (See Koffka, 406, pp. 211–64.) Recently the problem of constancies and their relationship to personality organization and psychological economics has been reopened. (See, for example, George Klein, 387.)

objects is in sharp contrast to the rich variety of their form of appearance in our experience. The internal constancy of ego and objects belongs to the fundamentals of life, and comes to expression in the logical proposition a = a, which can never be proven by experience.[21] Apparently, stable objects are the prerequisite to action.

The world, however, does not consist of homogeneous isolated objects. The object shows as little uniformity as the Ego. It has propensities and parts. Thus, we have here two relationships: of the whole to its parts, and of the whole to its propensities. As I said, the partition of the world into objects is inevitable, but the limits of individual objects are set more or less arbitrarily. A part of an object could itself be considered an object. It is not always clear whether a thing is to be considered a whole or a sum of its parts.

Also there are relationships between wholes which are not necessarily summative.[22]

[Passage omitted.] [23]

There are static relationships, such as greater and smaller, surrounded, divided, inside, outside, near, far, harder, softer, lighter, darker. While our judgment of these may vary, the differences themselves belong to the essence of the world of objects. Then there are dynamic relationships: objects change, either their propensities are unstable or their spatial relations to other objects undergo a change.

It is in the nature of change that it occurs in time. Temporal relationships or changes are always of specific significance. Again, an object's change of propensities and change of place are frequently related to each other. Furthermore, there is a far-flung net of relationships between objects; it is evident that these too belong in the world of objects.[24] They belong to the world of perceptions

21. This assertion is an attempt at a psychological analysis of an axiom of logic. It is regrettable that no proof is offered. It is implied that, in spite of the protestations of logicians against what they call psychologism, all processes of thought, hence also logic, must be amenable to psychological analysis. This point is extensively discussed by Hermann (329, pp. 9–16). Neither Schilder's assertion, nor Hermann's derivation of the axiom of identity from the process of identification (see Hermann, 327, pp. 24–29), gives a satisfactorily documented psychological-genetic analysis.

22. In the sense of Gestalt-psychology, they do not form aggregates but are tied to each other by integrative forces.

23. The omitted section deals with the question of whether or not the world can be conceived of as a single Gestalt.

24. Even though this may seem "evident," philosophy debated this issue for

as well. The larger and smaller, here and there, movement and rest, thunder after lightning, pain after a blow, are all material of immediate perception. All that we label dynamic is included in this network of relationships. For example: a balcony is so built that it can support no more than five people. There is an object-relationship here. Insight into object-relations is the prerequisite of action. The better the insight into object-relations, the more favorable the conditions for purposive action.

Object-relations can be perceived directly: the greater and smaller are seen; the more and less loud or tasty are also perceived. Simple thought-processes may play a role here. Clearly, such processes of thought and imagery are already involved in a perception like that of the red billiard ball.

(b) Speech and Thinking

Word and speech play a significant role in grasping object-relations, particularly when complex. Whether there exists a thinking that involves few or no words is not the subject-matter of our discussion. Hoenigswald [25*] and Binswanger [26*] maintain that thinking always needs the support of words. . . . The word-sound becomes a word by acquiring a signification-function. Words are more than mere signs, they are the carriers of communication.[27] The realm of the general concept "horse" includes all horses; the word "horse" is the sign of the concept; and the content of the concept consists of all the characteristics

---

millennia. It has been argued that relationships are created by the perceiver. The objection that "operations" prove the objective "validity" of relationships was countered by the argument that they prove only the usefulness of man-made relationships. The argument implied that the object-reality of relations cannot be proven, and that our concepts of relationships are only tools for encompassing nature. It was then replied that there is no need for argument if operational definitions and evidence are the accepted criteria of object- and relationship-reality. The counterargument was that magic, mythos, and the other forms of primitive thought, as well as all philos-

ophy and art, were and are forms of relationship-assessment; implying that utility as the final criterion of knowledge, and operationalism as the means-criterion, are unacceptable.

25.* Hoenigswald (333).

26.* Binswanger (64).

27. The distinction between a "sign" and its function of "communication" is not clear here. An hysterical or any other neurotic symptom also has a communication function. One would have to go to symptoms of neurologic disorder, or to manifestations of physiologic function, to be reasonably sure of dealing only with "signs" and not "communications."

included in the concept "horse." The concept may designate either the "type" or all horses; but the word "horse" may also mean one certain horse, and then it is an individual-concept. The sign of a concept, that is to say the word-sound, has always a multiple meaning. In final analysis, the concept is an artificial unit. Propositions have primacy over concepts.[28]

Now, all this holds not only for concepts, but also for propositions. We speak of the realm of propositions, the content of propositions, and proposition-sounds.[29*] The content of the proposition is expressed in the proposition-sound.

Binswanger [30*] denies that a sound could be the image of an object; he attributes to it a mere signification-function. Buehler [31*] sharply distinguishes between the announcing, eliciting, and representing function of speech. The speaker announces what goes on in him, this elicits psychological processes in the listener, and thereby object-relationships are represented.

[Passage omitted.] [32]

It cannot be doubted that the primary forms of speech are expressions of strong needs. The most primitive words contain sounds like "pa," "ma," which are connected with the movements of biting, snapping, grabbing, and eating. The primitive speech-sounds are close relatives of expressive movements and expressive sounds. They are—to express it paradoxically—by-products of the function of feeding. Naturally, language must have other roots too. It can be surmised that each important biological function has a corresponding set of expressive movements and sounds,[33] and that the reaction [34] of the speech-

28. From the point of view of development, concepts as generic-abstract-conceptual terms are in a sense "artificial." Propositions, however, express or at least imply a belongingness and a subsumption, that is, conceptualization, even if not of an abstract order. Thus Schilder's thesis refers only to the highest levels of concept-development. See in this connection Reichard and Rapaport (605, particularly p. 99).

29.* I refer here to Gomperz's (286) treatment of the topic, and my own (652).

30.* Binswanger (64).

31.* Buehler (112).

32. The omitted section argues against Husserl's (346) and Klages's (382) dichotomy of "Natur" (nature) and "Geist" (spirit); the dichotomy refers to the clash of the "natural" and the "consciously human." This antithesis was one of the beloved hobbyhorses of metaphysical psychology.

33. This surmise implies Darwin's (136) theory of affect-expression, the evidence for which has been rather on the wane. For alternative views, see Vernon and Allport (26), and Federn (172).

34. Here "reaction" translates *Angriff*.

musculature yields as characteristic an expression of the function as the rest
of the body. In final analysis, one must surmise that biologically every reaction
has some relation to the function of feeding.[35] It is maintained that the biological function of sexuality also has a speech-expression. In this connection, the
great variety of sounds of animals in the breeding season comes to mind. It is
perhaps worth while to mention that all these primitive speech-functions have
strong rhythmic tendencies, as well as tone and timbre of their own. The
presence of rhythm and melody in the most primitive speech-products seems
to be related to their expressive function. It could be objected that expressive
movements do not mean anything, while words and sentences mean something,
and it is the essence of language to be the carrier of meaning.[36] But it is incorrect to assert that expressive movements mean nothing. The red face and
clenched fists of one in anger are at least a signal for other persons. Is the angry
person unaware of this? When the hungry dog snaps, or drips saliva, he communicates, knowingly or not, that he wants his share of the bones. Sexual excitement, too, has a communication character. It is incorrect to maintain that no
communication is intended: [37] though the decision to communicate by expression is not always fully conscious, the tendency to do so is always present,
even if only instinctively and with a low degree of awareness.[38]

35. The argument seems to be that since all parts of the body have expressive reactions, there is no reason to assume that the reactions of the speech-musculature should not be expressive. The logical weaknesses of the argument are obvious. The assumed relationship between all reactions and feeding is lacking in evidence.

36. The implication of this rhetorical objection may be made clearer by adding that "therefore expressive sounds cannot be the primordial form of language."

37. "Intended" is again a term of the phenomenological school of philosophy. Here it means "implied."

38. It is not explained here how this tendency to communicate becomes ever-present in expression. The formulation resembles the one assigning a reality im-plication to all percepts. See note 8, above. Both formulations convey that Schilder conceived of psychodynamics always in the context of an articulated object-world and of interpersonal relations implying communication. At present, this view has general acceptance. But there is some complacency in this acceptance: the theoretical framework is yet to be erected which would encompass human behavior as determined by drives, as determined by the perceiving of and adapting to a real world of objects, and as attuned to interpersonal relations and communication. To begin with, psychoanalysis centered mainly on drive-determined behavior; only in the last two decades, with the growth of ego-psychology, has it made strides towards the analysis of adaptation. The efforts of

It is true that people will carry out expressive movements, even when alone, but these, too, are aimed at an audience: an imaginary one. Whenever one has the opportunity to observe a major outbreak of desperation or violent affect, one cannot help noticing a communication tendency. In final analysis, every attack of affect is directed to an audience.[39] It is likely that our conception of instinct-manifestations exaggerates their instinctual character.[40] The expression of instincts does convey a message; expressive movements are not mere mechanical sequels of affects, but also real expressions and communications.[41] Thus, the connection between language and expressive movement is clear, and language may even be described as a differentiated expressive movement. Expressive movements, then, are more than signals. Darwin [42] saw it correctly: they are instrumental means and rudimentary forms of affect-directed actions. Expressive movements are a part of action, and so give some of that gratification which would be afforded by the action.[43] At primitive stages of develop-

---

Anna Freud (201), Hartmann (305), Bernfeld (55), and Sullivan (725) at encompassing interpersonal relationships and channels of communication, indicate the gaps that still exist in psychoanalytic theory in this respect. The solipsistic tendencies of dynamic psychology, and the concepts of transference, identification, and introjection as the only ones available for dealing with interpersonal relationships, indicate the difficulties facing us in this realm.

39. The developmental background and the theoretical implications of this state of affairs are not presented by Schilder. Clearly, a new genetic conception of affects is implied.

40. Schilder criticizes the inclination to conceive of instincts so mechanically (or biologically?) as to deny them any reference to an audience. Cf. Hartmann's similar view, Chap. 19, II and IV, particularly note 43, above.

In this paragraph "affect expression" is repeatedly equated with "expression of instinct." This equation, implying

probably both MacDougall's (493) theory and early psychoanalytic usage, is more than questionable; see, for example, Rapaport (591, pp. 28 ff.).

41. This is an insufficiently appreciated and explored point. Nonverbal communications between patient and therapist, and nonverbal communications involved in group contagion, have recently attracted the attention of investigators (Jurgen Ruesch, Fritz Redl).

42. Darwin (136).

43. For partially similar views, see MacCurdy (489, pp. 86–90) and Freud (234, p. 111). Freud conceives of affect as a discharge phenomenon: its energy-cathexis is the "charge of affect," that is, the quantitative aspect of the instinct-representation. This "charge of affect" is a small yet significant portion of the energy of the instinct which, when prevented from effecting action, gives rise to affect-discharge phenomena. See also Freud (209, p. 521). For a summary of various pertinent theories, see Rapaport (591, pp. 21–37).

ment, expressive movements are magic action effecting hallucinatory gratification.[44] Expressive movements may also be defined as action in the absence of
an object, or as fundamentally incomplete action. Primitive language is, therefore, partly expressive movement and partly magic action. The onomatopoetic
imitations in primitive language are magic passes: by making the sounds of an
object I become that object and thereby obtain power over it.[45] The beginnings of language clearly bear the marks of its need-character. Language does
not start with isolated words; C. and W. Stern [46*] have shown that the words
of children are one-word sentences. The one-word sentence, in turn, is the expression of a wanting-to-possess: of a need. Later this need-character is obscured and recedes into the background.[47] I therefore consider language a
partial action which appears when the action proper cannot be consummated.
In final analysis, action is more than a striving for an object; it is also of social
significance by virtue of its claim to the object. In the same way, language has
the character of communication, which becomes the more pronounced as
direct goal-attainment becomes less feasible.[48]

Thinking, too, has a direct relation to objects. We want to understand object-
structures [49] in order to cope with them through action. Our thinking constantly creates new relationships with a view to their potential usefulness for
action. It should be kept in mind that thinking and imagining do have an objective aspect,[50] even though the assumption that primordial thought and im-

44. Schilder refers here to the "omnipotence of thought." Cf. Freud (227,
pp. 873–77), and (223, p. 14). In Freud's
reconstruction (for which good though
indirect evidence is available), delay of
gratifying action results in the hallucinatory experience of the gratifying object and action, which in turn becomes
the predecessor of thought. Cf. Chap.
15, notes 12, 14, and 29, above.

45. The concept describing this process is "participation," coined by Levy-
Bruehl (455); compare H. Werner (755,
p. 352).

46.* C. and W. Stern (712).

47. All facets of action and thought
appear to share this fate. This need-
relatedness, obvious in the beginning,

recedes in the course of development to
a point of imperceptibility. As Freud
(209, p. 535) has put it, "all thought is a
detour on the path toward gratification." Cf. also Lewin, Chap. 5, pp. 129 ff.
and 142 ff., and Hartmann, Chap. 19,
VIII, above.

48. Note again the implied "intentionality." Cf. notes 6 and 8, above. The
social significance of action arises because of its claim on objects socially
shared.

49. "Object-structure" here translates
Sachstruktur. Judging by the context, it
stands for the organization of the world
of objects, not merely that of individual
objects.

50. See notes 8 and 44, above.

agery were hallucinatory forms is well-founded. Freud rightly asserts that thinking is experimental action using small quantities of energy.[51] A definition of "concept" which I once gave characterized it as "readiness for action" directed at a definite segment of reality.[52] This readiness for action is but incompletely consummated by words. Thus every verbal formulation contains in principle an unfulfilled residue. We always "intend" more than merely the word-sound, and I believe that the intended meaning-experience is closely related to the incomplete consummation which can be achieved by words. When the word and the sentence mean something, the force of the experience of this something is related to the fact that the word-sound as such can never bring complete consummation. It follows that there must exist thinking which needs no words or sentences.[53] There must also exist "readiness for action" which, in the absence of insight into object-relations, does not reach partial fulfillment.[54] Perception and visual imagery imply wordless thinking and "readiness for action." Primordial forms of action, such as the grasping action of the infant . . .[55] imply the percept or image directly. Where grasping is unfeasible, pointing develops. Where the object is not present, it is imagined. The presentation [56] of the object appears when the immediate intention towards it cannot

51. See Freud (209, pp. 533–34), and Chap. 15, above.

52. See Schilder (652, Chapter I). Compare the term "readiness for action" with those—"readiness to rhyme," "readiness to reverse," etc.—which Lewin (460) used to describe determiners of associations. These terms conceptualized his experimental results which disproved the contention of association psychology that associations are determined by spatial and temporal contiguity. His concepts of "readiness," and Ach's (Chap. 1, above) concept of "determining tendency," were the first dynamic ones in memory theory. Compare the concept of "readiness for action" with *Einstellung*, and with the concept of anticipation. See Rapaport, Schafer, and Gill (602, I, 385–89, and II, 22–24). Schilder implies (as do Rapaport, *et al.*) that all conceptual experi-

ences have an anticipation aspect. Cf. Buerger-Prinz and Kaila, Chap. 27, on attitudes and anticipations.

53. The logic of this argument is not clear. The point is actually a statement of the empirical findings of Ach and Buehler, to which Schilder subsequently refers.

54. See, for instance, Fenichel, Chap. 18, above.

55. The omitted section refers to the frequently simultaneous reemergence of grasping, snapping, and sucking reflexes as sequels to lesions of the frontal lobes, striatum, and pallidum.

56. "Presentation" here translates *Vorstellung*. In this monograph *Vorstellung* is generally translated as "image." Here, however, the context indicates that it may also refer to imageless memory or thought.

be realized. It seems that strong inhibition of intentions enhances imagery in thinking.[57*] Abundance of images always indicates that the goal is still distant. On approaching the goal of action, the images progressively recede; at last, immediate preparation for action is given in the form of concepts.[58] In this sense, words are images which correspond to brakes put on thinking.[59] In comparison with other "presentations," words are close to consummated action. That part of action which is not consummated by words is experienced as meaning, which in turn becomes the immediate predecessor of action.[60] Words are aids to thinking. Some insights into object relations need not be cast in words. Words and sentences are aids [61] to actions of a certain degree of complexity.

These considerations apply to the theory of aphasia. While early theories of aphasia assumed that speech and thought are identical, some more recent theories deny it. Pick [62*] speaks of a path from thought to speech. Against this, Hoenigswald, Kronfeld, and Sternberg, and Binswanger [63*] have recently asserted that, in final analysis, speechless-thought is no thought. . . .[64] While thought does have the tendency to manifest itself verbally, speechless-thought *is* thought, and speech is just an expressive movement. Some thoughts have more of a tendency to take verbal form than others. Moreover, the initial phases of a thought-process have a very different relationship to speech than the later

57.* Schilder (648, p. 245), and Martin (501).

58. This seems to imply that in the course of the thought-process, images indicating possible pathways to action crystallize into a unitary thought-form: the concept. Cf. Schilder Chap. 24, above, and Rapaport *et al.* (602, II, 22–24).

59. The phrase "correspond to" seems to imply a causal connection; "brakes put on" is a paraphrase for "inhibition" as used above. Whether, when images come about, the brakes are put on the impulse or on the thought, is a matter of relative emphasis. Image or thought arises when the impulse (drive) is inhibited. When in addition thought—that is, the motivational factor it imples—encounters diffi-

culty, we again fall back on images. Cf. pp. 508–9, above. For similar conceptions, see Muensterberg (532, pp. 193–94), Washburn (750), Spencer (699, pp. 452–59), Buehler (106, pp. 434 ff.).

60. Schilder has in mind a theory of meaning of his own, related to that of Husserl's philosophy of phenomenology. Compare also Ogden (549).

61. "Aid" translates *Stuetzpunkt*. The translation does not convey the "orientation-point" connotation of the German word.

62.* Pick (567) and (569).

63.* Honenigswald (333), Kronfeld and Sternberg (435), Binswanger (64).

64. The omitted section gives some details of Binswanger's argument.

ones.[65] To distinguish these I have coined the terms word-near and word-distant thought. It is certain that disorders of verbalization alone do not exist. Such isolated disorders were thinkable only while psychic life was considered a serial emergence of presentation- and perception-elements, and while these and the corresponding innervation-complexes were considered static.[66] Nowadays we conceive of presentation and perception as resultants of many superordinate and coordinate processes. The verbal image is likewise built of such psychological processes. Of these, I consider with Lindworsky [67*] the relationship-experiences to be the essentials of thinking. In the disorders of word-understanding, word-pronunciation, and word-finding, thinking is deprived of one of its essential supports, and thus finer differentiations in thinking are hampered.[68] Thus, speech-disorders and even perception-disorders in agnosia are to a certain extent disorders of thought. But we must not forget that while the aphasic disorder is word-near, that of dementia [69] is word- and perception-distant.

It will suffice to point out that the general behavior of motor-aphasics, even when their disorder is severe, shows considerable adaptation to reality. Goldstein and Gelb [70*] strove to demonstrate that amnesic-aphasia is not so much a disorder of word-finding as one of categorical behavior. In sorting colored skeins the patients showed a lack of any grouping principle: their choices always followed concrete experiences of similarity and coherence.[71] They manifested irrational, concrete-perceptual behavior, which may be called life-near and biologically primitive.[72] Yet we must emphasize that the patient afflicted with amnesic-aphasia deals in general quite purposively with objects he cannot name. If a thought-disorder is present, it can afflict only that small segment of think-

65. It is implied that early phases of thought are image-like and of a feeling character, while thought-development tends toward verbalized forms. See Schilder, Chap. 24, above.

66. This refers to the classical associationist conception: for example, G. E. Mueller's.

67.* Lindworsky (475).

68. Here words are considered the means of finer differentiation. Cf. Freud (209, p. 546), (243, p. 21), and (234, pp. 133–34). Cf. also Chap. 15, note 32 and

Chap. 23, II, particularly notes 9 and 10, above.

69. For the definition of dementia, see note 84, below, and p. 568, above.

70.* See Gelb and Goldstein (264, 265).

71. For descriptions of the procedure see Weigl (753), Goldstein and Scheerer (284).

72. Concrete-perceptual is contrasted here with abstract-conceptual. Concreteness is characterized as primitive, abstractness as remote from life.

ing which is closely connected with naming and word usage. We must, therefore, distinguish thought-functions of naming from other vital functions. Thus,
verbalization is merely a part of the thought-stream; yet the verbalized thought-
experience may decisively influence the course of the mainstream of thought.

(c) Judgment, Thought, and Action

Judgment may be considered the basic form of thinking. According to
Erdmann,[73*] the core of judgment is a predicative relationship. This formulation may be greatly influenced by the consideration of language. Russell [74*]
had correctly pointed to the existence of many other relationships. To each
fact corresponds a proposition [expressing a relationship]. . . .[75] The world
consists of many things, each of which has many propensities and relationships.

Clearly, in this sense judgment is based on a cognition, whether false or correct, of various relationships. Now the question arises: how do we arrive at
judgments?

In order to be able to arrive at a judgment, one must first of all be turned
toward the world, and be interested in objects. Thus, already perception implies an affective element. . . .[76] The memory- and apperception-material
which is the prerequisite of forming a percept becomes available only by means
of the affective experience. Petzold's [77*] formulation, emphasizing that every
percept implies a concept, becomes plausible.[78] Let us for the moment not talk

73.* See Erdmann (155).

74.* See Russell (625, 624).

75. In the omitted section Schilder
discusses examples of the symmetrical
and asymmetrical relationships treated
by Russell. Were Schilder's discussion of
Russell systematic and extensive, I
should not feel justified in omitting it.
The relationships treated in Russell's *Introduction* are a non-metric form of
mathematics which (in contrast to topology as applied by Lewin) have barely
been put to use by psychology. It seems
likely that in the psychology of interpersonal relationships and communications they will find exquisite usefulness.
See, for example, Heider (317).

76. The omitted section deals with

movements connected with all perception (for example, eye-movements) as
carriers of part of its affective element.
The term affective is used here as a
synonym of "intentional" and "motivational." Cf. note 79, below.

77.* See Petzold (533).

78. The term perception is used here
synonymously with apperception. The
latter obviously implies a conceptual integration of memory material. See p.
219, this volume; compare Rapaport,
et al. (602, I, 385–89). The distinction
here between memory-material and apperceptive material is unclear. For the
role of affective factors, see Schilder
(644), Chap. 24, this volume.

about the emotional factors in perception, but consider percepts as given and relatively static. In order to posit a relationship between two percepts, I must have an interest, a driving-force.[79] Positing a simple relationship between two objects is not a thought. Even relatively simple thought implies continuous movement, and its development requires the enrichment of its conceptual and propositional realm [80] by a continuous creation of new relationships. Observation of normal people shows that thought has a phasic development, that in its preparatory phases isolated and unrelated percepts, presentations, and thoughts [81] can stand side by side, and that its final formulation is achieved only at the end of the process. One may assert, therefore, that it must be driving-forces which, first, shape the material of perceptions and presentations; next, put it into relationships; and lastly, give the thought its final form. But this does not complete the role of driving-forces in thinking. Thoughts do not remain isolated; they get embedded into experience as a whole and become related to the goals of the personality. These considerations indicate the significance of driving-forces in thinking. The pathology of thinking provides ample proof. The driving-force of schizophrenics is often insufficient for tying together the

79. Affect, interest, and driving-force are apparently equated here, or at least used interchangeably. This is not just the conceptual nonchalance that so often accompanies Schilder's ingenuity. We find a similar looseness in Silberer on precisely these concepts. That thought is motivated, like all other human activity, is no longer doubted. But the character and mode of operation of the motivating forces in various forms of thinking have never been clarified. The analysis of the empirical material and the conclusions which I presented in 591, pp. 264–72, I no longer find adequate. Freud showed that the driving-forces of dream-thoughts—and primary-process thinking in general—are wishes, and their mode of operation is "imaging" by means of condensations, displacements, etc. By coining the concept "hypercathexis" (209, pp. 534, 536) he opened the way to a systematic treatment of the driving-

forces of goal-directed, ordered, secondary-process thinking. Note Silberer's treatment of the driving-forces of hypnogogic phenomena (Chap. 9, above), and Varendonck's (Chap. 22, above) attempt to establish the driving-forces of daydreams. A synoptic treatment of all these phenomena in terms of hypercathexes, however, is lacking. Cf. also Chap. 24, note 11, above.

80. See p. 563, particularly note 219, below.

81. "Thoughts" here means "isolated thoughts." Schilder asserts that thought-development integrates completed yet isolated thoughts, as well as images and presentations. The relativity of "wholeness" in objects, discussed earlier, seems to hold here too: what from one point of view is the product of a process of thought-development, from another is its subject-matter.

preparatory-phases of thought. In melancholics,[82] isolated thoughts may reach consummation, but the driving-force is insufficient for their further development.[83] In post-encephalitic cases, the thought-process is prone to get lost early because of a neurologically understandable insufficiency of driving-forces. In mania, completed individual thoughts do not undergo a higher integration because of an overabundance of driving-forces. In various forms of dementia,[84] the lack of driving-force prevents consummation of the thought-process.

An exact account of these problems requires a more detailed discussion of the thought-process. We shall again start with judgment. Judgment, as already stated, is either right or wrong. Psychologically, therefore, besides apperception of object-relations, judgments imply approval or negation.[85] The goal of judging is to achieve knowledge of a state of affairs. Since the goal of a thought-process is given in schematic form from its inception on, we reach it when our experience is that the schematic anticipation and the achieved thought match. This is easiest to demonstrate in thought-processes which reproduce experiences. G. E. Mueller investigated the factors which determine the occurrence and degree of experienced certainty [86*] in recall. According to Buehler's [87*] summary, the main determiners of certainty-experience are the clarity and wealth of recall-presentations. . . . Their manner of occurrence, such as their exclusiveness, rapidity, and stubbornness also plays an important role; so does recognition, that simple quality of familiarity of a presentation. . . . In recall-

---

82. At present "melancholia" is used as a synonym for "depressive psychosis," particularly in the sense of "manic-depressive, depressed."

83. Cf. note 81, above.

84. Hinsie and Shatsky (330):

Today dementia is defined as an absence or reduction of intellectual faculties, in consequence of known organic brain disease. . . . Many of the patients (for example, schizophrenic or dementia praecox) formerly described as demented are now described as regressed. . . .

Schilder more or less adhered to this definition.

85. See in this connection Freud, Chap. 15, p. 323, and Chap. 17, notes 12 and 18, above.

86.* G. E. Mueller (526).

["Experienced certainty" is the subject's confidence that his recall, knowledge, or recognition is "correct." Act-psychology of the Meinong-Brentano-Husserl vintage, as well as classical association psychology, paid considerable attention to such experiences; modern psychology, both behaviorist and dynamic, has neglected them, with the exception of Lewin and his collaborators. See Lewin (460) and Cartwright (124). A restudy of such experiences from the point of view of dynamic psychology should be rewarding. Cf. Chap. 17, note 18, above.]

87.* K. Buehler (106) [pp. 362 ff.].

ing a member of a learned series, recognition may refer either to its place-value or to its relation to another member.[88]

It is noteworthy that a fluent mechanical recall of a learned series, even while fulfilling the criteria of exclusiveness and rapidity, may lack the experience of certainty, and even be attended by an experience of incorrectness. This is usually explained by reference to a lack of recall-intentions.[89] The experience of varying degrees of certainty is most pronounced when preceded by doubting, checking, and questioning of certainty.

Experimental subjects use various methods in the search for criteria of certainty. "Subject N.G., when she could not name the color, in recalling a series of vari-colored digits and consonants, used the following method. She proceeded to image the item in each of the five colors used. If she imaged it easily in blue, but not in the other four colors, she reported that blue was correct." [90*] Critical thinking is replete with such "methods of search," which require the repeated intervention of thinking in the recall process. The search itself has characteristic intermediary and accompanying phases; for instance, ". . . but I doubted its correctness, went on searching, failed, and gave up this avenue as hopeless." [91*] The criteria, however, are not identical with the experience of certainty itself. Certainty (according to Buehler) [92*] is not an independent experience, but a contingent part of conscious events. An experience of certainty refers always to an object-relation which is conscious. I agree fully with Buehler's [93*] statement: "Doubt and certainty, goal-directed search for causal relationships—in other words, consideration and insight—belong to that arrangement of our psyche which centers around the knowledge of objects and object-relations." I want to reemphasize that certainty is always an experience of matching: analysis of the nature of action will lead us to a similar formulation.

It was not without purpose that I stressed the close relationship between thought and action. Every percept and image is connected with a movement

88. Concerning recognition, familiarity, and certainty, cf. Claparède, Chap. 3, and Kris, Chap. 23, III, above.

89. When attempting to remember a word which we have noted as similar to, say, our own name, we use a recall-intention previously formed. In reeling off mechanically a series of words, no such intentions are present to give an easy check on the correctness of recall. Cf. Hartmann, Chap. 19, VIII, above.

90.* G. E. Mueller (526) [III, 232].
91.* Buehler (106) [p. 366].
92.* Buehler (106) [pp. 371–72].
93.* Buehler (106) [p. 372].

and a change of tonus.[94] For infants, perceiving and grasping are fundamentally the same.[95]* Metzger's [96]* investigations show that even simple visual percepts involve a change of tonus. What is true for percepts is true in principle for imagery. I have repeatedly indicated that perception and imagery have the same psychological significance; Jaensch's well-known [97]* investigations have shown that eidetic images, lying between imagery and perception, follow in many ways the laws of perception. Attempts to isolate images and thoughts from motor-reactions to them are always artificial. It is often said that thinking and willing are closely related, and that remembering and thinking are voluntary [98] acts. It must be added that on primitive levels of development, thinking and imaging always have an immediate purpose, even if mainly in the realm of signs and magics.

After these preliminaries, we are ready for the analysis of action.

The goal of an action is given at the start, as for instance in the simple process of grasping. This goal may not always be fully conscious. In a simple action such as grasping an object, the goal is not the object alone, but also that my hand grasp it. Thus the goal implies the presentation: my hand surrounding the object. Again, it is incorrect to assume that the goal of this movement must be fully conscious. Mostly it is present in a germinal form. Nor is it enough that the goal of the movement be given: knowledge of one's own body must also be present.[99]* These considerations hold even if the goal of action is merely a change of body-position. The goal is reached when the germinal action-intention and the completed action match. This is the consummation experience. The parallel between judgment and action is obvious. If the goal of action is to be attained, the propensities of objects must be known; but as the theory of apraxia shows, not even then is attainment assured. Knowing has many varieties. A general intellectual knowing is not necessarily useful in action. Though the apraxia patient has a general knowledge of the object, he cannot use it in action. Evidence that cannot be discussed here makes it probable that

94. Compare, e.g., Washburn (750), Muensterberg (532), Jacobson (350).

95.* See Hoff and Schilder (334).

96.* Metzger (517).

97.* Jaensch (351). [See also 352, particularly p. 136.]

98. Dynamic psychology has no definition as yet for "will" and "voluntary."

See, however, Rank (588), and Knight (390); compare also Rapaport, et al. (602, I, 167–69). Remembering and thinking, though to some extent subservient to "will," are in the main involuntary automatic functions. Cf. Chap. 24, note 49, above.

99.* Schilder (646).

action-plans do not contain the details of methods of execution.[100] The purely kinetic melody of movement [101] becomes apparent only after the decision to act has been made.

In such melodies of motion something organic, of which the individual is not necessarily aware, expresses itself. The significant role of driving-forces in the initiation and execution of actions, and the analogy with thought-processes, has already been stressed. The close formal relationship between action, in our sense, and the reproduction of a content [102*] need not be further discussed.

(d) More about Thinking

ON KNOWLEDGE AND MEMORY. Stoerring [103*] has demonstrated experimentally that the awareness of finality lies in the after-thought, "I must think so." Incidentally, he has also shown that in the process of inference we form general ideas from which, as from perceptions, issue new object-relationships.[104] Selz [105*] presented to his experimental subjects stimulus-words with instructions on how to respond to them. He prevented thereby a response in keeping with a previous "Einstellung." [106] The instructions directed the subject to re-

100. The "action-plan" refers apparently to the "goal" and the "action-intention" given in the moment action begins. The interchangeability of means has since been studied, but it is possible that Schilder was among the first to point out that "means" are usually not included in action-plans.

101. See Schilder (648, pp. 79–85). This "kinetic melody" is, according to Schilder, the means of motor-action. While any of several "melodies" can be the means to achieve an end, an individual's choice is determined by his organic make and personality. Cf. Gerstmann and Schilder (268). With this conception, Schilder touches on the rarely treated problem of the psychology of motor-coordination and its control in action. Note, however, Freud's concept of the ego as controller of the sluices of motility; see Freud (223, p. 16); cf. also Rapaport, et al. (601, I, 249 ff.).

102.* G. E. Mueller (526) [pp. 230 ff.].

103.* Stoerring (714).

104. This is one of the almost countless instructive asides in Schilder's writing. Many were omitted here for lack of space or because they disrupted the argument. The present aside shows that certain object-relations can only be derived by inference. Where the process of inference is disturbed (as in paretics), knowledge and appraisal of object-relations are impaired.

105.* Selz (678, 679, 680).

106. Cf. Ach, Chap. 1, above. The German term is often made to imply anticipation. Actually, what Schilder calls Einstellung was called by Selz "anticipation." Schilder uses the term very generally; he speaks of "orientations" of drives, of will, of the total personality, etc. More recent usage limits attitudes and orientations to the realm of the ego.

act with words which would be coordinate, subordinate, and so on, to the stimulus-words. In some cases, the reactions were instant solutions without intervening experiences; in others, a knowledge-complex developed progressively which contained the solution. Where the material was familiar, a first unsuccessful search after a concept was suddenly followed by the correct solution. A repetition of the process several months later would first bring back the original reaction-word without any comprehension of the task, and only later the realization that it was correct. The explanation is that whole-relationships (like those created by the original response) have a high retention value; furthermore, the instant-solutions also must be considered actualizations of knowledge.[107] Selz also posits a law of complex-completion. A given fragment of a complex has the tendency to reproduce the whole complex in consciousness. Since awareness of object-relations implies knowledge of both the objects and their relationships, awareness of the task indirectly determines the solution by indicating the object-relationship in which it partakes. The stimulus-word itself does not directly cause the reaction; the search for the solution begins only after both stimulus-word and task are understood. . . . Arriving at the solution is accompanied by an experience of satisfaction. The method by which problems are solved is partly a search for, partly a determined reproduction of, the means of solution.[108] If no means can be found by reproduction, a favorable chance must be awaited. . . . These experiments of Selz clearly

---

Cf. Chap. 27, note 31, and Chap. 20, note 17, above.

107. In Schilder's terminology, "memories" are recalled, while "knowledge" passes from a state of potentiality into one of actuality. Schilder does not further define the difference between knowledge and memory. One possible definition is this: (a) Knowledge comes to consciousness by the same channels and according to the same laws as memory. (b) Knowledge, though derived from actual memories, has lost the spatial, temporal, personal, etc., earmarks which characterize memories (cf. Gillespie, 275). In this respect, the transition between knowledge and memory is quite fluid. (c) Knowledge includes potential awareness of the functions of the organism and of relationships between memories; this, in contrast to memories, is not learned material. (d) The relation of memory to knowledge may be described by the concept of automatization; see Hartmann, Chap. 19, VIII, above.

108. For the concept "determined reproduction," see Ach, Chap. 1, above. Schilder here implies that the search sets up "anticipations," or determining tendencies, which schematically forecast the means; the "determined reproductions" are defined by and fulfill the anticipations.

show that problems are not solved by a random or constellation-determined emergence of memory material.[109] Knowledge is organized into complexes and is brought to bear on problems by means of definite methods. Our knowledge is partly of object-relations, partly of pathways to them. In other words, the background of our experience [110] consists not of unformed but organized material. Indeed, complexes can be actually defined as organized material of memory and knowledge. G. E. Mueller [111]* also speaks of complexes, but these are merely associations of single elements. . . . The complexes of Selz are created by apperception in terms of knowledge, and by organization in terms of will.[112] I would add that this apperception in terms of [past] knowledge serves for insight into object-relations to be used in [future] action. This brings us to the fundamental problem of the relationship of knowledge and memory to intelligence. First, a few words concerning memory.

In pre-psychoanalytic times, it was believed that there is such a thing as using up memories or losing them. Everyday forgetting, the various forms of amnesia, forgetting in dementia and in the Korsakow syndrome, and finally in aphasia and agnosia, were all considered due to loss of memory pictures and were adduced as proofs thereof. Already Bergson [113]* had shown that one cannot speak of loss of memory pictures, since once imprinted they are never lost. In the meanwhile, psychoanalysis brought forth rich empirical material which unequivocally showed that what is once experienced can never be lost.[114] I have

109. This argument is directed in part against early, in part against later, association psychology. "Random emergence" refers to association due to contiguity. "Constellation" refers to the organization principle introduced by association psychology to account for associations contradicting the rule that the association which emerges is the one having the strongest bond to the idea in consciousness, and that the strength of the bond depends upon the frequency of contiguous occurrence. Later, association psychology assumed that all other existing bonds help determine which association will emerge. The aggregate of all pertinent bonds was termed "constellation." Note that a constellation is distinguished from a complex in that the latter has an affect-core around which the ideas are grouped.

110. Experience comes about when percepts are assimilated into the apperceptive mass, here referred to as "background."

111.* G. E. Mueller (526) [I, 253 ff.].

112. "Will" here refers apparently to interests, strivings, intentions, motivations, affects, etc. The duality of experience (memory) organization in terms of "knowledge" and "will" corresponds to that in terms of "schemata" (Bartlett, 37) and motivations (Freud, 209).

113.* Bergson (53).

114. See Freud (254, pp. 15–20).

myself demonstrated that even the so-called organic amnesia of epileptics and of people revived after asphyxiation can be lifted by hypnosis.[115] R. Stern [116*] confirmed the experience of White [117*] that alcoholic amnesias also can be lifted by means of hypnosis. Hartmann and I [118*] have demonstrated that the apparently forgotten material is available even in skull-fracture cases.

Individual differences in regard to forgetting are not due to destruction of memory-material in one person and absence of destruction in another, but to their comparative ease of utilization of memory-material. Hence, memory-disturbances are disturbances in utilization of memory-material. In fact, Brodmann,[119*] Gregor,[120*] Betlheim and Hartmann,[121*] have shown that residues of apparently forgotten experiences are demonstrable even in Korsakow patients. Hartmann [122*] eliminated by hypnosis even an amnesia following carbon-monoxide poisoning. . . .

The psychoanalytic study of forgetting shows that it subserves definite purposes, that it is repression. More generally, we forget what does not fit the present situation. Or, in a positive formulation, we remember only what we can and will use in the present situation. I once defined memory as the reawakening of the past in the service of the present.[123] This conception of memory does not isolate knowledge and memory from the live thought-process and its biological goals and needs. Surely, much material is communicated to every individual that has very little direct relation to action; much of school-knowledge belongs to this category. To keep him aware of this useless knowledge, the individual is pressed by threats of punishment, or by reference to a future usefulness of this knowledge. A measure of such useless knowledge is also considered the hallmark of certain social classes. The amount of such knowledge is therefore often out of proportion to intellectual ability; from this fact the inference has been drawn that memory, knowledge, and intelligence are not intrinsically related. Such discrepancies are more striking in pathological cases than in normals.[124]

115. For Schilder's pertinent work and reviews of earlier literature see Schilder (666 and 664). For his general view of the indestructibility of memory, see Schilder (659). For a further review of the literature, see Ruffin (623) and Rapaport (591, pp. 177–79).

116.* R. Stern (709).

117.* W. A. White and B. Sidis (769).

118.* Hartmann (308); Hartmann and Schilder (313).

119.* Brodmann (95).

120.* Gregor (289).

121.* Betlheim and Hartmann (58).

122.* Hartmann (308).

123. Schilder (659).

124. Note the high Vocabulary and Information scores on the intelligence

The literature contains many records of excellent memory achievements of imbeciles.[125] Their phenomenal achievements relate mostly to calendar dates. In these cases, having and reproducing memory-material is limited to one direction, and cannot be used for other purposes. Such unidirectional attitudes and memory are frequent among the poorly endowed. Memory implies not just a compulsory reproduction of series of items, but also the ability to break them down and put them to various uses. In this respect memory and intelligence are quite closely related.

Rueckle,[126*] the memory-man, succeeded in his number-memory feats because he had penetrated deeply into the nature of numbers. One of the prerequisites for this kind of memory-feat is a continuous preoccupation with the object, which in turn is not possible without an object-directed interest.[127] Such phenomena cannot be understood if good and poor memory are treated merely from the point of view of [mechanical] retention and reproduction. Besides the ability to remember, good memory implies the ability to turn to use what is remembered. When the task is the memory-achievement itself, usefulness consists in correct reproduction. This obtains for knowledge too, since it is but one aspect of memory. Real knowledge is the appropriate use of memories; the one-sided hypernormal memory found in some imbeciles is incapable of this.

[Passage omitted.] [128]

I have dealt in great detail with the relation of memory and knowledge to intelligence, for the reason that in my studies of paretic dementia the retelling of stories was the chief method of investigation.[129] Naturally I have used many other experimental methods, such as the routine procedures summarized by

---

tests of psychotic patients. See Rapaport, et al. (602, I, 79).

125. See Scheerer and Goldstein (637); and for a review of the material, Strohmayer (723).

126.* G. E. Mueller (526, I, 240–41).

127. The study of a master at playing chess blindfolded leads to similar conclusions. See K. A. Menninger (514). The continuous preoccupation with a subject-matter as the basis of phenomenal memory stresses the role of interest (intrapsychic need) in such achievements, but obscures their relation to gen-

eral intelligence. This chess-master's memory-achievement strikingly outdistanced his otherwise good general intelligence.

128. In the omitted section Schilder discusses the memory- and thought-disorder in Korsakow patients. For an extensive discussion of these, see Buerger-Prinz and Kaila, Chap. 27, below.

129. For other applications of this method, see Koeppen and Kutzinsky (402), Schilder (313), Bartlett (37), Despert (144).

Ziehen,[130]* the Binet-Simon-Bobertag [131] material, judgments of more and less complicated pictures and spatial structures, and tests involving the solving of more complex problems. Of all these, second only to free interviews, the retelling of stories proved most useful. The stories I used most frequently were:

Rabbi Moir, the great teacher, sat in the school on Sabbath instructing the people, while at his home his two sons died, struck by lightning.

The son of the minister Herbig, of Holzengel near Greussen, was swallowed by a shark. He was first officer of a Hamburg merchantman, and was washed overboard by a squall. Since rescue proved impossible, the unfortunate young man was caught, in front of the eyes of his terrified shipmates, by a shark which followed the steamer. He was dragged to the bottom of the ocean, leaving behind him a dark streak of blood.

II. THE PARETIC THOUGHT-DISORDER

(a) The Material and the Basic Findings

In summarizing their studies on the recall of brief stories by paretics, Koeppen and Kutzinski [132]* state:

In no case of paresis we have studied did we find a lack of differentiation between the self and the story, or the story and external impressions. But in far-gone cases we observed other forms of lack of differentiation: the organization and meaning of the story were lost, and on asking for the patients' judgment of the story we found them unable to carry out a longer series of differentiations and integrations. A construction once made persevered extraordinarily, and the mental mobility to create new combinations and to fill in gaps was minimal. Repetition did not improve achievement. Recall was at times badly impaired by poor language, due mainly to articulation difficulties." [133]

CASE NO. 1: M.S., 49 years. Hospitalized for the last two months; mentally changed, distracted, forgetful for 13 months; the year before, hospitalized at Steinhof; this time arrested on the street, running around naked. Spatial and temporal orientation only fair. After discharge from Steinhof, managed a factory of metal objects, with the help of a foreman. Doesn't know why she was hospitalized. Sings much and enjoys it. Is manicky yet composed, with moderate motor excitement. Calculates fairly well, making the common flighty mistakes of paretics.

130.* Ziehen (785).
131. The standard German version of the Simon-Binet. See Bobertag (79).

132.* Koeppen and Kutzinski (402) [p. 225].
133. Dysarthria is a common neurological symptom of general paresis.

Her reproduction of the Shark Story: "He went away and came back in a big river and went back again to where he came from. Did he get hurt?" After a second reading: "A shark has swallowed him long ago and then came Pope Herbert and everything floated away, and then he came back and brought everything. Brought me many things and the shark came and brought me everything, then he was gone again and Pope Herbert came. Then a great Shark came and swallowed me. Then a great casket came to the grave and I got sunk. Then I was dead. Then the fish came back again, shook my hand and gave me a kiss on the forehead."

After a third reading: [134] "I have been swallowed by a big animal and the minister Hebisch came to me and consoled me. The officer fell in the war and went down to the end where the lake begins, he went back and has chosen a little package and went again to the end of the lake and has gone through much till the end of the war. Then he had to fall.[135] They had waited till he recovered. Then he came up to the end of the lake. Then the shark swam away and swallowed me and I had to go down into the grave and was dead."

A week later she remembers [136] the story as follows: "About the shark, he was a shark, who swam in the water and got swallowed. (By whom?) [137] By a man. He had him in his mouth and devoured him. Then came Pope Heredi and made a check-up and kissed my hand and gave me a kiss on my forehead and pressed me so. Then the officer entered the war and fell and I nursed him for six months and he got well again, then he got the hemorrhage, then I had to nurse him again six months, and he recovered again and was well again and thanked ten times because I nursed him so long. Then I was very desperate and they had to cut open the stomach of the shark because he swallowed me, so that I can come out again."

At this time the patient was already in malarial treatment. Two days later, when asked what story we had told her, she answered, "About the grasshopper," and continued in a poetic way:

> The shark came and said then:
> It is for you I am waiting, since I swallow things

134. Apparently, after the recall Schilder reread the story to the patient, obtaining another.

135. "Fall" translates *gefallen*, implying death, and should be so understood throughout.

136. Apparently without repeated reading.

137. The interjections which appear in parentheses are evidently Schilder's, made in the course of the experiment.

And carry away everything, as long as I have a voice
One more word to say,
But I saw it didn't take long
What I have yet to say
In the quiet night I brought him
But I saw him again,
The Officer sang his songs.

She continued in childish rhymes. After two more days, following her third chill, she recalled the story as follows: [138] "The shark's stomach was again cut open, then I crawled out, he had me swallowed, then came the Pope Herbig and told me I should be real brave and then an officer fell in the war and I nursed him six months. He again helped me, I helped him, because he was so very sick. Then came the hemorrhage with blood. Then the officer recovered again and became well. Then he again once more got shot at. Then we nursed him again six months and he recovered again and they shot him dead twice and he had to die, now he reconsidered the matter again and he forgot himself, it was war and he had to enter again and he fell for the third time, he was in the army and he had the whole thing once more, then the third agony he had and he had to die. Now two went away already, the officer and the second officer, then the hemorrhage came again and he still recovered and the shark has still snuffled."

A day later she related the story about Rabbi Moir as follows: "There was a great teacher who was called Rabatz and had led the school, then he taught French and English and taught me gymnastics and singing and sang once more about the blue Danube and then he recovered again, he was once sick and had to enter the army and had to remain entered. Then the Pope Herbig came back again and put teachers again in the school and then two brothers were hit by lightning."

Nine days later, when the fever treatment had been discontinued, she recalled it thus: "There was a great teacher who taught French, English, Italian, Polish, Greek, etc., all languages, and we are in the morning in the school and in the afternoon in the gymnasium and they have made gymnastics on the bar and on the horse, and then the school was out and in the evening there was a great disaster and the lightning struck and killed the two Rabatt brothers."

138. Recall without rereading.

The recall of the Shark Story on the same day: [139] "The shark swam in the water, then he didn't come out for a long while, then the Pope Herbig came and told me a story, I should be brave, go to the church and confess at Eastertime, I should go and never on strange ways, rather to the theater and cinema. An officer fell, so we nursed him with the ladies and he became well again, a bullet hit him and the professor was so clever and tore it out again. Then a girl came and wanted to stop and then the shark came and swallowed me and they had to cut open his stomach and I crawled out like a rat."

The first recall of the Shark Story by this typical paretic patient shows that only a small part of the story was apperceived.[140] But even this small part reveals striking features.

The features of the recall-disorder may be summarized as follows:

(a) Substitution of general concepts for concrete.[141]
(b) Substitution of more familiar, coordinate concepts for those of the story.[142]
(c) Weakening and generalizing of affectively significant scenes into less significant ones.[143]
(d) Repetition of motifs.[144]
(e) Insufficient apprehension of the meaning of the whole, as well as of the details.[145]

After a second reading many more details appear, and the essence of the meaning is apprehended. Characteristically, the patient at first leaves it open

139. Both stories recalled without re-reading.

140. "Apperceived" here translates *auffassen*. The immediate context does not clarify the hierarchic position of this concept. Theoretically, failure in apperception may be caused by: (a) perceptual disorder, (b) attention-disturbance or distraction, (c) selectiveness of apperception due to over-valent strivings, wishes, etc., (d) apperceptive disorder. Each of these shades imperceptibly into the others, and may be merely an aspect of them. Judging from the broader context of the whole monograph, Schilder probably considered "auffassen" to refer to (b) and (c).

141. Substitution of "he" for "shark."

142. "Great river" for "sea"; "went away and came back" for "washed overboard."

143. A grisly death is minimized: "Did he get hurt?"

144. "Going away" and "coming back."

145. Nothing pertaining to the ship or officer is directly apprehended.

who was swallowed by the shark, and then has herself swallowed. This idea is instantly elaborated with many details; the most noteworthy is that the casket is made to come by itself to the grave. The unfamiliar setting of the sea is replaced by that of the land (the grave). The consequences of this change for the rest of the story are not drawn: the fish returns, shakes her hand, and gives her a kiss on the forehead. The inclination to a happy ending and the infantile-playful character of the narrative are obvious here. The replacement of minister Herbig by Pope Herbert is a matter partly of flighty apprehension, partly of the manic tendency to replace concepts by related ones of greater affective value. It is in accord with the wishes of our patient that the shark bring her something. The repetition of motifs plays a greater role in this second recall.

Thus the following features of the disordered recall are added to our list:

(a) The substitutions by coordinate concepts follow affective needs.[146]
(b) The patient takes the role of the hero of the story.[147]
(c) A motif once chanced upon is arbitrarily elaborated.[148]
(d) Painful ideas are canceled by their objective opposites.[149]
(e) Without regard for meaningfulness, primitive wishes are represented as fulfilled.[150]
(f) The infantile character of the reproduction.[151]

The third recall retains, in spite of the rereading, the notion that she has been swallowed by a big animal. Nevertheless, the Pope is now correctly replaced by the minister. Suddenly a new motif—an officer's fall in war—not contained in the story appears, probably as a result of the apprehension of the word "officer." [152] Again death is followed by new life. This motif, too, is thrice re-

146. "Pope Herbert" for "Minister Herbig."

147. It is she who is swallowed by the shark, comes to the officer's rescue, attends the school, etc.

148. First, Pope Herbert "brought everything"; then "the shark brought me everything," and later "shook my hand and gave me a kiss."

149. Being swallowed by the shark is followed by "the fish came back again, shook my hand and gave me a kiss on the forehead."

150. The shark brings her "everything" in contradiction to its role in the actual story.

151. Repetitive use of "and" and "then" to link sentences.

152. This assertion may be questioned: the motif seems to be a symbol-

peated. While in the previous recall the shark brought her something, now the officer chooses a little package. It is noteworthy that the patient renders her reports in terse, action-rich sentences.

The patient's next recall, given without further reading, has the following noteworthy features. Though she remembers that the story is about a shark, she is undisturbed by the nonsense that the shark is swallowed by a man, and even elaborates it. The Pope and the officer motifs recur, the latter in rhythmic repetition. The blood of the damaged victim in the story is recalled as a hemorrhage, noteworthy because absent in the earlier recalls.[153] That the patient ends her recall with the shark's stomach being cut open indicates that somehow she knows the correct story. The false self-reference is again striking.

The following characteristics of recall are added to our list:

(a) The original misapprehensions are retained in free recall.[154]
(b) Amidst misapprehensions, traces of a correct apprehension transpire.[155]
(c) Details absent in the immediate recall emerge several days later in free reproduction.[156]
(d) General carelessness, leaving contradictions and nonsense uncorrected, is again striking.[157]

[Passage omitted.] [158]

CASE NO. 2: A.M., age 54. Typical case of paretic dementia with retention disorder.

She retells the Shark Story on December 9, after three readings: "A steamer was swallowed by a shark of wood, a steamer of wood from the ship."

---

like restatement of the falling and death of the officer swept overboard by a squall.

153. This indicates that the disorder is not solely that of perception and/or retention, since the blood-motif had to be perceived and retained to be now recalled. It was not available, however, for use in the previous recall.

154. The Pope and the officer motifs.

155. Schilder's immediately preceding evaluation of "the shark's stomach being cut open.'

156. Hemorrhage.

157. Shark swallowed by man.

158. The omitted section further illustrates these recall features. Schilder adds rhyming and mixing the motifs of two different stories as features, and stresses the exaggeration of rhythmic motif-repetition.

On December 20, the story of Rabbi Moir is read to her. (In the interim she did not hear the Shark Story again.) "Rabbi Sabbat two sons with a teacher thrown into the sea. (Why thrown into the sea?) You are making fun of me, tell it to me again. Two sons have thrown the teacher into the sea. (What about the lightning?) The lightnings have struck him. (Whom?) The two teachers."

On January 2, she relates without repeated reading: "Two rabbis disappeared."

Now the story is reread to the patient by the repetition method.[159] Her recall: [160] "Two rabbis sat at the sea, there came a ship and dragged the two sons away." (She encourages the other patients to help her.) After a second reading: [160] "Two rabbis fell into the sea, in the meanwhile a storm came and both sons fell into the lake." When corrected, the patient says: "That's what I said."

On January 5, the patient reports: "Two teachers went to sea, there came a ship and swallowed the teachers. (Do ships swallow?) A fish."

On January 23, after one rereading: "Rabbi Moir, the great teacher, sat at the sea, there came a storm and dragged into it both sons." (Now she hears the story read six times to another patient, then recalls): "Rabbi Moir, the great teacher, fell into the water, in the meanwhile his sons struck by the storm fell into the water; (friendly, laughing) I have told this so often."

This very demented patient recalls the Shark Story, after three readings, incompletely and nonsensically: "A steamer was swallowed by a shark." In addition, she invents that the steamer is made of wood. Eleven days later the motifs of the Shark Story are woven into the incomplete recall of the Rabbi Moir Story. Words are interchanged: Rabbi Moir is called Rabbi Sabbat. The attributive phrase "the great teacher" is made into an independent figure, demonstrating piecemeal apprehension. When questioned, the patient varies the motif somewhat, mainly by replacing one of its elements by another: thus suddenly there are two [161] teachers who were thrown into the sea. Ten days later only two elements are left, namely "two" and "rabbi"; "died" is replaced by the more general concept "disappeared." It is noteworthy that in spite of rereading,

159. The repetition method apparently consists in reading the material phrase by phrase, having the patient repeat each. The method is used to minimize the effects of distraction on recall.

160. Apparently, these rereadings take place on January 2.

161. The change into "two teachers" apparently uses the element "two sons."

the misapprehensions are unerringly reproduced, a bit of the Shark Story originally not recalled now emerges,[162] and the main motif is redoubled.[163] Three
days later a part of the Shark Story originally not recalled emerges: the patient,
unconcerned about the nonsense, replaces ship by fish.[164] Eighteen days later,
after rereading, the first words of the Rabbi story are recalled correctly, but are
followed by a transposed piece of the Shark Story,[165] then by a detail of the
Rabbi Moir story previously not recalled.[166]

Hearing the story six times over at this point results merely in new variations
of interchanged elements. The stubborn clinging to misapprehensions and to
certain parts of the stories is noteworthy. The memory material, as such, sticks
surprisingly well, but its individual parts are treated quite arbitrarily. Similar
verbal formations, like ship and fish, are substituted for each other without regard for meaning. The indications are abundant that the patient does not regard
the story as a whole and picks out only individual parts of it. Though she is
satisfied with her achievements, the tendency to correct and improve is not
altogether absent, as when she says, "Say it again," protests that she is being
made fun of, or asks the other patients to help her.

The characteristics of recall of these two patients are easily demonstrable in
others. In my *Introduction to a Psychoanalytic Psychiatry*,[167]* I reported a
case dominated by false self-references. This patient always added to the stories
a few details from her personal life. Her incomplete recall lacked strong conviction;[168] for instance, she would often say that the story is not really about
her. Otherwise, however, she realized neither its meaning nor that it was a story:
she considered it true, or at least tested it for historical truth. This, however,
amounted to a fundamental misrecognition of the situation.

Our next example is a case of juvenile paresis [169] in which the technique of
learning is particularly noteworthy.

162. The ship-element.

163. The duplication of the motif
consists both in using *two* rabbis and
two sons, and in having both rabbis and
sons fall into the water.

164. Ship and fish in German: *Schiff*
and *Fisch*. The reversibility may have
facilitated the exchange.

165. "Fell into the water."

166. "Struck by storm."

167.* Schilder (647).

168. Cf. Betlheim and Hartmann,
Chap. 13, p. 302, particularly note 56,
above, and Buerger-Prinz and Kaila,
Chap. 27, pp. 663–67, below, on the experience of "conviction" and its relation
to the state of consciousness.

169. For material on juvenile paresis,
see W. C. Menninger (515).

CASE NO. 3, V.M., age 16. Hospitalized December 19 to February 9. The paresis began with fits. After malaria treatment the dementia, which was of considerable degree, improved greatly. The patient calculated rather well, judged situations fairly critically, but showed no affect.

On February 2, she gave a recall of the Rabbi Moir Story. First reading: "Rabbi sat. (Where?) I forgot. (What else happened?) Lightning." Second reading (repetition method): "Sabbath at the table, while of the two sons . . . sat at the table—while the lightning." (Stutters painfully.) Third reading (repetition method): "Rabbi, the great teacher, sat in the school (?) and meanwhile (!) lightning struck (!) the house. (And!) [170] Fourth reading: "Rabbi, teacher of the great teachings, sat in his room in the meanwhile." Fifth and sixth readings: "Rabbi Teacher sat in his room and taught the young, in the meanwhile the lightning struck (yes, and?) into the room and killed (what?) it (!)." Seventh reading: "Rabbi Teacher, the great teacher, sat in a room and taught the people. In the meanwhile died. (Who?)" Eighth reading: "Rabbi Moir, the great teacher, sat in his room and instructed the people, in the meanwhile lightning struck the room and killed the people." Ninth reading: "Rabbi Moir, the great teacher, stood in the school and instructed the people. In the meanwhile lightning struck the house. (And?)" Tenth reading: "Rabbi Moir, the teacher, sat in the room and taught the people, in the meanwhile . . ."

On February 6, the patient told the story rather readily: "Rabbi Moir, the great teacher, sat in the school on Sabbath and taught the people. In the meanwhile . . . (struck) [171] struck by lightning both his sons died." On February 9, she recalled the Shark Story as follows: "That the man travelled on the sea and that the shark dragged him to the sea-bottom, and a long streak of red blood visible."

The first notable thing here is that the patient learns piecemeal, picking up individual parts without surveying the whole. Registration is fairly faithful, yet words are interchanged: for example, Rabbi Teacher. Self-correction, though hampered, is feasible. In this case the intermission [172] facilitated learning. I have observed this type of learning in other juvenile paretics also, and even in pareses of grown-ups, though not in such clear form.

---

170. Exclamation and question marks signify the examiner's promptings.

171. Prompting by experimenter.
172. Between February 2 and 6.

I shall mention briefly a few other examples. Recall of the Shark Story by M.T., first reading: "I don't know anything." Second reading (in a low voice, full of significance): "Caught! (Who?) I, by a lion." The Ebbinghaus Story [173] she also relates to herself, saying "I was in my 'change' then and fell. But the hair was quite in order then, and I wrote a fiction, too, at that time: 'The First Mountain Tour.' " Apparently the reading of the Ebbinghaus Story awakens some important memory, fitting parts of which are assimilated to the story and the rest eliminated. Self-correction is still feasible.

The following is a similar example from a case reported in my *Introduction to a Psychoanalytic Psychiatry*.[174*] The patient's account ends with the words, "Frankly, there is not one true word in it." The recall of the Shark Story by the same patient: "You told me that he was something and that I was there, I was on that place, (?) that this man was on the ship and I was in the ship, I don't know the man at all." Second reading: "This son was caught by a ship and by the men, I don't know this story at all, you can summon this man for me, I never have been abroad, never have been in the countries." Here, too, the tendency to self-correction is apparent.

Now for another example of the improvement of memory-achievements following an intermission.

CASE NO. 4, M.M., age 27. Hospitalized from August 6 to October 6. General paresis with dementia. Shark Story, repetition method, first reading: "About a shark and a streak of blood, I don't know anything." Second reading: "About the shark which shipped itself overboard (?) dismembered itself (where?) the shark was dismembered because it fell into the water." Third reading: "About the whale, it fell into the water, sank into the sea-bottom and then came out again and was again gone." She believes she has told the story well. After a pause of a quarter of an hour without rereading: "A fish is swallowed in the sea-bottom and an officer is sunk too and I do not know any more." On August 13, she remembers that there was a story about a shark. "He was in the sea and spat (?) he has a bladder in his mouth." On August 15: "(?) About the whale, he was that big (indicates with her hands), he swam on the sea-bottom, he put out his tongue and splashed the water around." On October 3, the patient re-calls without rereading: "About the whale, there was the son of the minister,

173. See (785).   174.* Schilder (647).

he sunk into the sea and the ship, it sunk too, and was down on the sea-bottom and as he was down on the sea-bottom then he left a streak of blood behind, (?) because the waves are moving in the water. (?) The blood was that young man's, (?) he thus, because he sunk, I have bled today too from my nose, it is a pity for the young man."

It is fairly frequent that, without giving specific details, the patient passes a general judgment: "This is nice," "That is terrible," and so on. In the following illustrations the patient considers the story as a piece of history, and explains that she is unable to retell it "because I wasn't there!"

CASE NO. 5, H.S., general paresis with dementia, recalls the Shark Story as follows: "A man became unhappy. (How come?) From the shipwreck. (Which one?) That I do not know, because I wasn't there." After the second reading she says nothing whatever. Two months later, she recalls the Shark Story: "About the water it was something . . . we went over the water, one fell in! I don't know any more." The extreme generality of this patient's recall is notable: "The man became unhappy." . . .

CASE NO. 6, T.L., age 54, general paresis with dementia. Recall of the Shark Story: "An officer embarked with to . . . Then he came again to the land and then a lion devoured him. (A lion?) He was just searching for freedom." Five minutes later, her recall is about lions and bears: "They have devoured up and torn apart the man. (Where did that happen?) In Hamburg." Three days later, after rereading the Shark Story: "I wasn't there. The Europeans went out too and caught a young girl." Second reading: "Two companions shot themselves dead." Third reading: "I am so distracted I can't remember it, I got it in my head, can't get it out, about Hungary, the minister got locked up." Fourth reading: "A young officer, the enlisted men had him and he had himself here in Vienna at the city council, they have caught him there." Fifth reading: "A man had himself caught by a steamer, he just got him (?) the man. (Who caught the man?) The boy and threw him into the sea and he died."

With Austrians, who do not know the sea, the substitution of "lion" for "shark" is a relatively frequent mistake. However, our patient elaborates on her mistake and includes bears, too. The apparently senseless subsequent recalls are notable for several reasons. The catching of the young girl is reminiscent only generally of being caught by the shark; the phrase "two companions shot themselves dead" retains only the gruesome feeling-tone of the story. The re-reading derails the patient completely: though the "minister" motif reemerges, "caught" is later replaced by "locked up." The next rereading again results in an exchange of elements: "the boy threw him into the sea and he died." Active and passive roles are interchanged.[175]

A comparison of the recall of this very demented paretic with that of Case No. 1 is instructive. First of all, there is less spontaneity here. The manic features of the first case may partly account for this, yet it is certain that spontaneity decreases in high-grade dementia. So does attentiveness. Therefore, less material is registered,[176] and in many far-gone cases the patient is obviously so preoccupied with some idea that the story is altogether missed.

CASE NO. 7, J.T., age 61. Very demented general paretic, tells spontaneously of her experiences as a child of three when the Prussians were here and she brought them water.[177] "It is very nice that I have gotten this far, onto the throne, I hope I will remain healthy, the good Lord help me, all children should get well and remain well. Syphilis? That I got from someone who wanted to marry me; that's cured now." She pays no attention to the story she is told. "Our Henry has things, the music he has, he wrote it all . . . that, then he learned to sell music." Second reading: "About the child (?) who was poor and his parents died (?) there I have to speculate some more (?) about Henry." Third reading: "That I do not know." After the reading of the Shark Story she says: "I can't do that now anymore, my head is full of my child."

The registration-ability of such patients is particularly limited. They pick out mere parts and immediately transform them to fit a certain sense. A co-ordinate idea replaces the original one: shark—lion. There is a tendency to be derailed and multiply ideas: lions and bears have torn the man up. The trans-positions are more sweeping than in the first case: Hamburg—foreign country —Hungary. Finally, the story is taken here as a bit of history. Thus, in prin-

175. Cf. Schilder, Chap. 24, pp. 510-11, above.

176. "Register" here translates *aufnehmen*. The question is left open whether this is a perceptual or an apper-

ceptive disorder. The context suggests the former.

177. Apparently what follows is the first "recall" of the Rabbi Moir Story.

ciple the recall-disorder is the same as in less demented cases, only more exaggerated.

The dearth of driving-forces also [178] can be seen in the following examples.

CASE NO. 8, P.S., age 53. Hospitalized November 16 to February 10. At the time of admission she retells the Shark Story, after two readings: "A man he scratched and then he made a streak of blood." On November 29, she recalls: "Something about a fish in the Danube who rubbed a man and scratched bloody streaks on him."

Where the driving-force is weak, the correction tendencies are also weak.[179] Thus, they were weak in Case No. 1 also, but the setting there was different. That patient's attitude was playful, and though she obviously had little conviction of the reality of the story, she was not interested in testing its correctness. In such cases, the awareness of correctness is superficial and easily upset. . . .

The following case further illustrates awareness of correctness, correction tendencies, and the degree of conviction:

CASE NO. 8a, T.K., age 45. Hospitalized October 1 to November 12. Very demented, plays with her feces. She recalls the Rabbi Moir story as follows: "You told that he was struck by lightning. (Who?) I don't know." After rereading, she says, with demented laughter: "I don't know anything." Third reading: "Well, yes, you told that both sons were struck by lightning." The patient is dull and affectless: "(Did you have syphilis?) (Laughs) Nothing. (Do you have syphilis?) Nothing." When shown a newspaper clipping, she says: "Quite nice." She cannot recall, however, the content of the clipping. But when she is told that Mrs. T.K. yesterday took a walk to the Prater,[180] went to an inn and there drank a stein of beer, she says, "That's not true. (What have I told you?) You have told me so many things." Then she is told that Mrs. T.K. went to the Prater, met there a young man, and let him kiss her. (Vivid affect play, laughter). . . . (Is that true?) "Yes." Now the sentence is repeated with the addition that she then became pregnant. She recalls: "That I was in the Prater

178. This "also" apparently refers to the discussion on p. 553, above of lack of spontaneity and attention, which Schilder seems inclined to attribute to a dearth of driving-forces.

179. See note 168, above.

180. The amusement park of Vienna.

and met a man who kissed me. (What happened then?) Nothing." She omits the final passage, even after it is repeated to her: "That T.K. became pregnant? Oh no. (Have you been in the Prater?) All my life I haven't ever been in the Prater."

It is noteworthy that the patient accepts as reality the story made up about her as long as it does not clash with her interests. But her acceptance lacks real conviction.

(b) The Thought-Disorder

We will attempt now to give a general formulation of what we inferred from our patients' recall of brief stories. The first question is, does the disorder begin in apperception? [181] It is plausible to assume it does, since Gregor [182*] has unequivocally demonstrated the presence of apperception-disorder in paresis. This disorder of paretics is undoubtedly related to an inadequacy of the anticipations [183] formed by them. To put it another way, apperception-disorder is related to attention-disorder. Attention refers here to an active attitude, not merely to a clear percept which is its result. Attention, therefore, implies here articulation of the material, apprehension of it in whole or part, that is to say, an entirely active attitude.[184] Let us see what happens when normal people

181. Cf. note 140, above.

182.* Gregor (288).

183. See Chap. 27, IV, below.

184. This passage is important, since it comes close to defining the concepts "attention" and "anticipation."

Schilder's view may be summarized as follows: (a) Attention is not "clarity of percepts," that is, not a *state*, as often defined in the past, but an active attitude, that is, a *function*. For a similar view, see Koffka (406, p. 358). (b) Attention-disorder and inadequacy of anticipations are two aspects of the same process. (c) Attention as an active attitude accounts for the articulation of material in whole and part.

Though these points are cardinal for the understanding of the pathology of thought, each has loose ends: (a) Attention is defined as an active attitude, leaving no room for passive attention, an obvious and important psychological process. See, for example, the concept of "evenly hovering attention," Freud (226, p. 324); also Chap. 12, note 51, above. (b) The nature of the close relationship between attention and anticipation is not explicitly stated, nor is the difference between "Einstellung" (attitude) and "anticipation." Rapaport et al. (602, I, 385–89), consider attention, anticipation, and attitude all preparatory to the appearance of ideas in consciousness. (c) While articulation is a task of concentration (active, voluntary attention), percepts which are simple, or familiar, or of high inherent articulation,

listen to a story. At the beginning of each sentence they will make anticipations [185] as to how that sentence will end. These anticipations are probably quite general in the beginning, growing more definite and specific as the sentence progresses. In the meanwhile, a part of the anticipations is progressively rejected. After each sentence an anticipation is formed of the next sentence, or even of the whole story. In the absence of such anticipations, apprehension is piecemeal and without regard for the meaning of the whole. Case No. 3 is an example. Personal experience appears to play a crucial role even in the registration-process.[186] Jung [187]* demonstrated in his association-experiments that complexes determine the misapperception of stimuli that pertain to them. But by no means are the registration-disorders of our cases only complex-determined. When, for example, the patient (Case No. 1) recalls of the Shark Story only that "he went away," her lack of directedness [188] toward the material becomes obvious. This lack of directedness is closely related to a lack of interest.[189] Probably inadequate anticipations also have a share in the faulty and insufficient apperception.

---

are all apperceived even when passive attention prevails (602, I, 195–200). The transition between both forms of attention is fluid, much like that between objects of varying degrees of inherent articulation. Furthermore, where normal thought-organization finds inherent articulation, disordered thought-organization may not. Concerning attention, cf. Chap. 15, note 21, above; concerning anticipation, Chap. 27, notes 26 and 58, below.

185. Anticipations are at work in the process of both thought-production and perception. The anticipation is formed by the crosscurrents of those motivations (driving-forces) which are to find expression in the thought. To each motivation pertains a range of ideas which may represent it in consciousness. The interaction of simultaneous motivations narrows this range to ideas which can express at least the major motivations simultaneously. With the progression of

an idea, some motivations may be subdued or superseded, and new ones come into play. Hence the progressive discarding of some anticipations and the increasing specificity of the subsequent ones. Cf. Chap. 27, IV, below.

186. Here the concepts "apperception" and "registration" are apparently interchanged. The context suggests that Schilder meant "apperception." As the distinction is poorly defined, exact formulations can hardly be expected.

187.* Jung (365).

188. "Directedness" translates Zuwendung. Apparently Schilder means a lack of directedness in not recalling the rest of the story. In recalling "he went away" there seems to be an overdirectedness, a centering on, a spellbound-ness by, the idea of departure, death.

189. Cf. "lack of interest" with the point on "motivations," notes 79 and 112, above.

No doubt it is extremely difficult to distinguish insufficient apperception from insufficient reproduction. In cases No. 3 and 4, the patients' recall of the story improved considerably with a few days' intermission. . . .[190]* In normal psychology this is a well-known phenomenon.[191]* To understand it, we must keep in mind that registration is not immediately completed, and that perception is followed by elaboration. Registration and elaboration, however, are not distinguishable in principle. Once registered, the story is elaborated into a unified whole, of a definite feeling-tone. I have mentioned that many of our paretics register only a general impression of the story. After the whole has been grasped, intact thinking again and again falls back on detail. The course of the process of registration is: integration, anticipation, analysis.[192]

I want to stress that registration is not a passive process; it always implies elaboration. While a normal subject registers a story, many personal experiences enter his consciousness; but in his final elaboration of the story, this material is again pushed into the background. The correct reproduction of a story thus presupposes that what we usually call associations must be brushed aside.[193] This brings us to elaboration and reproduction.

In final analysis, elaboration is but the completion of registration by interchanging processes of integration and analysis, concurrent with those of correction.[194] Each of these processes is determined by affectivity, by general "Einstellung." [195] In reproduction the processes of selection and integration

---

190.* For similar evidence see Schilder (640) and Koeppen and Kutzinsky (402).

191.* See Herrmann (325).

192. Schilder's description of the registration-process is somewhat cryptic, and of necessity overlaps that of apperception. Integration refers here to the production of unified wholes. Anticipation refers to the expectancy regarding subsequent material, as determined by the preceding whole and by new motivations mobilized. Analysis refers to the falling back from the whole to details, to review them in the light of newly registered material, and consequently to arrive at a unified whole which includes this material.

193. Schilder suggests that the correct understanding (registration, apperception, apprehension) of a story requires a variety of anticipations to serve as selective principles, which in turn imply the mobilization of a wide range of associations. He further suggests that correct reproduction requires auxiliary anticipations to be progressively cast away during apperception, and dispensable associations progressively suppressed. Cf. note 185, above.

194. Cf. notes 168 and 193, above. The correction-process consists in the exclusion of auxiliary and irrelevant anticipations and associations.

195. *Einstellung* is here equated with "affectivity." Schilder's loose usage of

are the same as in registration. In the course of these, every concept is driven through all related conceptual spheres.[196] General affectivity and special complexes enter at each step. The concept in the foreground is steadily compared with the total theme anticipated. New correction processes keep arising.

That the gruesome motives of the story disappear altogether in the first recall of Case No. 1 is probably due to an affective tendency toward a happy ending. It is easy to demonstrate that many distortions in recall are complex-determined: for example, they often simply replace the unfamiliar by the familiar. For example, the shark is often replaced, in our cases, by a lion or a bear (Case No. 6).[197]

The summary of Case No. 1 describes the process of elaboration in detail. Only one point needs to be particularly stressed. Material of personal experience, more or less loosely related to the story, is considered and recalled as part of it. For instance, Case No. 2, drawing on knowledge, includes in the story that the steamer was made of wood. The tendency to merge two stories, even if presented on different days, also belongs here.[198*]

In advanced dementia, the inadequacy of verbalization is striking. It is difficult to decide how much of this is referable to the dementia itself, and how much to an inadequacy of verbal apperception as in sensory or amnesic aphasia. The interchange of the words "ship" and "fish," for instance, may well be related to an aphasic disorder.

It is striking how unconcernedly these patients accept as correct every

---

the term "affectivity" for any more or less central motivation has been stressed (for example, note 79, above). For his use of the term *Einstellung* (set, attitude, anticipation) to denote motivational direction or orientation, see note 106, above. Schilder's contribution here is (a) the consistent reduction of clinical observations on thought-disorders to a group of concepts; (b) the choice of motivational concepts: *Einstellung*, attention, driving-force (interest, affectivity). Its shortcomings are (a) the lack of sharp definitions of his concepts, with consequent overlapping; (b) their lack of hierarchic differentiation in terms of centrality.

196. The related conceptual spheres—that range of associations discussed in note 193, above—yield the various connotations of the concept. The reproduction process seeks the fitting connotation. Cf. Schilder, Chap. 24, note 75, above.

197. These distortions appear to be determined not by specific complexes, but rather by what Schilder calls "general affectivity." This term parallels what in these comments I have referred to as the "state of consciousness" and its corresponding thought-organization. Cf. Chap. 9, notes 78 and 93, above.

198.* Cf. Koeppen and Kutzinsky (402); see also p. 542, above.

presentation, memory, or thought that comes to mind. Gregor and Foerster [199*] have shown that the errors of paretics on the complicated questions of the Ebbinghaus test do not differ from intermediary steps which normals take in answering them. Normals transcend these steps, while paretics do not. . . .[200*] Correction tendencies are absent. This makes it understandable that general affective needs become easily operant. Adequate recall presupposes that corrections are continuously applied in both registration and reproduction. Anticipated schemata [201] must be completed, and everything that comes to mind must be tested for correctness. Our patients, lacking such correction-processes, are quite helpless against their own ideas. Herein lies the root of what clinical parlance calls "poor judgment," [202] an entity so hard to define. This lack of self-criticism is particularly striking in Case No. 1 who, disregarding logic and experience, revives the dead officer immediately. This example shows also the lack of a unifying tendency.

We do know [203] that insufficiency of unification and correction is characteristic of incomplete thoughts. Dreams and all those formations which belong to Freud's Ucs system,[204] to the sphere,[205] have similar characteristics; and we assume that in them the thought-process has terminated before its comple-

199.* See Foerster and Gregor (191).

200.* Cf. Schilder, Chap. 24, particularly p. 511, above.

201. This concept of schema originates with Selz (679); it has nothing to do with that of Head (314) and Bartlett (37), referred to in these pages. Schilder's description of Selz's experimental procedure and concepts appears in Section I, d, above. Selz noted that the responses he obtained were determined not by the strength of associative bonds, but by "anticipations" created by the task set. These "anticipations" appeared to be formal patterns, molds into which the correct responses would fit. These formal patterns he called schemata. His method and concepts earned Selz a place among the pioneers of the non-associationist theory of thinking, Koffka's (403) vehement and often justified criticism notwithstanding.

202. "Poor judgment" translates

Kritiklosigkeit. It is a standard clinical term for certain early symptoms of organic psychoses (paresis, senile psychoses, etc.). Cf. Buerger-Prinz and Kaila, Chap. 27, III and IV, particularly notes 28, 43 and 76, below.

203. "We do know" is too positive a phrase; it tends to obscure the fact that the statement itself is an explanatory working hypothesis, and that the subsequent statements refer to the observational material from which, and to explain which, the working hypothesis is derived. Cf. Chap. 24, note 67, above.

204. Before the introduction of the topographic organization (id, ego, superego) of the psychic apparatus (Freud, 243, p. 90), Freud (235, pp. 255–58) distinguished the *systems* Ucs (Unconscious), Pcs (Preconscious), and Cs (Conscious). Cf. Chap. 23, II, above.

205. Compare Schilder, Appendix to Chap. 24, above.

tion.[206] [We may assume, therefore, that] here [in paretic thought disorders], too, thought-processes come to a premature close.

All thought-processes end with awareness of the truth or falseness of the thought.[207] G. E. Mueller has stressed that the degree of truth-awareness varies greatly. We must distinguish, however, not only the degree but also the intensity of truth-awareness, which depends upon the amount of new experiences mastered.[208] Truth-awareness in our patients lacks intensity; their awareness of memory-certainty is weak: [consequently] they are quite suggestible.[209] I refer particularly to Case No. 8. Yet, as I indicated in reporting the case material, it would be wrong to assume that all correction-processes are absent in these patients.

A few peculiarities of primitive experience are particularly apparent in our patients. First of all, we see a tendency to iterate motifs. I refer again to Case No. 1. The affective transformation of the motif gives each reiteration its specific character.[210] This kind of motif-variation and repetition is familiar from the Ucs system.[211] [Secondly] we see a tendency to multiply figures in the story, and this too is reminiscent of the Ucs system. One is tempted to conclude that the regulations of the processes of the Unconscious are demonstrable in the paretic memory-disorder. [Thirdly] a striking feature of many paretics is their failure to see that they are dealing with stories whose historical reality is irrelevant. They excuse their inadequate reproduction by stating that they were not present. Often they will put themselves into the place of the hero and

206. See Freud (209, pp. 492 ff.).

207. This significant point is understated. Schilder succeeded here in conjoining the thinking of psychoanalysis (reality-testing), of associationism (G. E. Mueller: correctness), and of act-psychology (Brentano-Meinong: awareness).

208. Schilder seems to mean that, given a series of events, materials, and experiences, registration and apprehension proceed to mold them into a unified whole with past experiences. The success of this unification determines the degree of truth-awareness. The number of experiences so integrated determines the intensity (depth) of truth-awareness.

209. Cf. Buerger-Prinz and Kaila, Chap. 27, IV, below.

210. By "affective transformation" Schilder apparently means: (a) changes which retain the original affect (death, war, journey) but replace all verbal, situational, and meaning material; (b) changes which attenuate the original affect or substitute its opposite, and then assimilate the verbal, situational, and meaning material to the substitute affect —the motif so obtained may then again become subject to the transformations described under (a); (c) the "transformations" described in Chap. 24, pp. 500–501, above.

211. See Schilder, Chap. 24, above.

relate the events of the story as their own experiences.[212]* This, too, is a familiar tendency of the Unconscious. Emphasizing of one's self is apparently closely related to affective needs that lie close to the surface. Finally, if this kind of patient has once made a mistake he will cling most stubbornly to his creation, and rereading will hardly make a dent in it.[213]*

I believe I have covered the essential features of the [thought] disorder of our demented patients. I summarize: Inexpedient methods are applied in registration, elaboration, and reproduction. The necessary anticipations and the integration of parts into wholes do not take place. The whole-apperceptions that do come about are not sufficiently structured. In the process of apperception, concepts and situations are [freely] replaced by coordinate or superordinate concepts. The more far-gone the dementia, the more far-fetched the coordination. These misapperceptions are either complex-determined or related to the patient's personal life. The reproduction-processes meet the same obstacles. Since correction-processes are inadequate or absent, logically incompatible ideas remain juxtaposed. The driving-force to continue and complete the thought-process may be diminished, but an excess of driving-forces also may occur, resulting in overproduction dominated by rhythmic motif-repetition. Misapprehensions and misreproductions once created greatly resist change. Not only meaning is falsely apperceived and reproduced, but the situation is misunderstood in that the story is considered historical reality or even the patient's own experience. Truth-awareness is lacking in intensity, and does not initiate correction. The language is often extremely sloppy, with no tendency to correct it. . . .

The question is whether this description encompasses the essence of dementia. Obviously, none of the characteristics described above is specific to paretic dementia; they could well have been those of dream-processes or schizophrenic thought-disorders, and therefore must be somehow incomplete. Some characteristics have not yet been mentioned. The first of these is that the paretic's distortions in recall are altogether banal; the second, that in general the disorder is evenly distributed throughout the field of experience.[214] We may add that

212.* Koeppen and Kutzinsky (402) saw these phenomena in other organic psychoses. Chance selection of their comparatively small case material must be held responsible for their not having observed it in paretics.

213.* Koeppen and Kutzinsky (402) have also observed this.

214. That is, it occurs regardless of the thought-content, unlike repression phenomena. But this contrast is not strictly valid: repression, too, may gen-

in dreams and schizophrenia, just because of the selectivity of the "dementia," one gains the impression that the person could do better; but in paresis the disorder gives the impression of inevitability. . . . I have mentioned repeatedly that complex-material enters into the elaboration of these stories. Yet it is of a more or less superficial character. The wishes which come to expression are common, lacking in personal coloring. The salient feature of the disorder here described is the banality of its contents, which are those of the world of the bourgeois; the complexes are those of the superficies. The childishness so patent in Case No. 1 seems to contradict this; however, it is in many respects only playing at childishness, and is not a true regression to early stages of development.

I believe that now we have encompassed the essence of dementia. The concept of "deficit" is replaced by the dynamic concepts "changed attitude" and "inadequate technique of thinking." As the thought-processes come to a premature close, there is a dearth of correction-processes, and a full truth-awareness is never achieved. We must assume a lack of driving-forces, but then must distinguish between "internal" and "external" [215] driving-forces of thought. The "external" driving-force may remain normal. In Case No. 1 it is even excessive, though in most cases of far-gone dementia it is considerably decreased.

(c) On the Psychological Differential Diagnosis of Paretic Dementia

Attempting to characterize the nature of the concepts of schizophrenics, I once concluded that their major characteristic is the tremendous enlargement of the concept basis,[216] which came to include all of the patient's essential experience. For instance, for Case No. 1 in my book Seele und Leben [217*] the concept of death was far broader than its everyday meaning; along with it, the everyday concept also survived. In addition, in acute cases of schizophrenia the process of apprehension is not completed, and remains in steady flux.[218] A com-

---

eralize until it becomes an overriding characteristic of the state of consciousness.

215. The distinction between "internal" and "external" driving-forces of thought is not clear. It seems to be an *ad hoc* assumption made to account for the occurrence of both decreased and increased driving-forces in dementia. As far as I can see, the distinction has no ex-

planatory and little descriptive potency. Cf. Chap. 27, note 10, below.

216. See Schilder (652); cf. Rapaport, et al. (602, I, 254–57), and Kasanin (372).

217.* Schilder (652).

218. Schilder apparently refers to the fact that in acute schizophrenia a multitude of connotations of words tends to become simultaneously conscious, re-

parison of the concepts of our paretics with those of schizophrenics makes it obvious that the former do not differ very much from those of everyday. The meaning of officer, pope, shark, to the paretic is not very different from the normal. While the schizophrenic's concepts and propositions may be considered undeveloped, the paretic's concepts are those of everyday; only their application is disordered, in the manner described.

Naturally, the concepts of dementia patients are frequently incomplete and marked by a dearth of attributes. Yet we know that the concepts of imbeciles, for instance, are quite sharply defined by this very dearth. In studying imbeciles, one often gets the impression that the restructuring of the concept-basis,[219] which is continuous in normals, occurs most slowly or not at all. The all too literal learning of our juvenile paretic [220] illustrates this point.

Thus, the schizophrenic thought-disorder implies a farther-reaching conceptual disorder. The schizophrenic's thought-disorder encroaches on the concept "in statu nascendi," [221] while that of the paretic attacks a relatively developed concept. Each involves—so to speak—a different phase of the thought-process. In schizophrenia, affectivity and attitudes that bring about concepts are fundamentally altered; in dementia, the disorder affects the manner of utilization of relatively developed concepts. In other words: the schizophrenic's thought-disorder affects the core, the paretic's the periphery, of experience. Correspondingly, the schizophrenic's thought-disorder brings archaic,[222] the paretic's everyday, material to the fore. Schizophrenic thought-disorder pertains first of all to the basis of concepts and propositions,[223] and to their apperception in registration; paretic thought-disorder to elaboration. Schizophrenic thought-disorder affects the development of concepts and propositions, the paretic affects the developed concepts and propositions. In the background of and side by side with the schizophrenic's concepts, there still exists usually a correctly built conceptual world; [224] the two worlds stand not

sulting in doubt, perplexity, and confusion.

219. By "restructuring of the concept-basis" Schilder means apparently the process whereby the concept-basis and a new experience meet, the experience is assimilated to the concept-basis, and alters it. This process was observed and its paramount significance was cor-

rectly appraised by Head (314) and Bartlett (37).

220. Case No. 3, above.

221. In a nascent state.

222. For a characterization of archaic material, see Storch (716).

223. Cf. Kasanin (372).

224. Cf. Bleuler (71, pp. 4 ff.).

united. Within his disordered thought-organization the paretic still retains remnants of his pre-paretic system of relationships, only these cannot be brought to bear on experience as fully as those concepts of the schizophrenic which are adequate. This is why the dementia of the paretic seems irrevocable, while that of the schizophrenic reversible.

The formulation that the basic disorder of schizophrenia and paresis is essentially the same, but affects different subject-matter in each, is incomplete; the difference in subject-matter naturally changes the form of appearance of the basic disorder. Such comparisons are, moreover, always too general and schematic. Thus it is obvious that in paresis not only the layer of crystallized thought, but also the neighboring layers are disordered. This is well illustrated in far-gone paretics, in whom aphasic and agnosic disorders are hardly ever absent. Thorough studies of this aspect of other forms of dementia are not extant.[225*]

It will be necessary for our purpose to make an attempt here to clarify the nature of aphasic and agnosic disorders. Classical theory has considered aphasia a disorder of word-presentations,[226] that is, a disorder affecting verbalization. Recent theories of aphasia are inclined to consider it a thought-disorder. . . . It is certainly true that each of our presentations and words express something mental.[227] This makes it difficult to conceive of a disorder which affects only verbalization. . . . However, Binswanger [228*] is right: the thought which is put into words is not the same as the thought before it is verbalized; thus it would be incorrect to consider aphasia solely a thought-disorder. Nor is agnosia solely a thought-disorder, but also one of apperception.[229] The conception that amnesic aphasia is a disorder of categorical thinking (Goldstein and Gelb) [230*]

225.* The thorough study by Eliasberg and Feuchtwanger (153) of an unusual case of acquired dementia is an exception.

226. An alternative translation: "verbal images."

227. "Mental" translates *geistiges*, literally "spiritual." The implication is that presentations and words express something which reaches beyond them —that is, a meaning.

228.* L. Binswanger (64).

229. Since Schilder has so far treated apperception as a phase of the thought-process, the argument is somewhat hazy here. Verbalization also is such a phase. What is probably meant is that we must be specific, and distinguish between disorders of the thought-process in general and those of its specific phases. He also stresses that some general involvement of the thought-process is present in the disorder of any specific phase.

230.* Goldstein and Gelb (264).

[Compare also Goldstein's recent volume, 279.]

has its limitations. Verbal, visual, and acoustic presentations are not lost in aphasic disorders. The trouble in the so-called motor-aphasias lies rather in the inability to develop correct sequences of sounds. The sounds emerge in incorrect sequence. A sound, once found, will often not leave the aphasic: he keeps iterating it. A word available to the aphasic in one situation may not be at his disposal in another. That he can pronounce a certain letter may not mean that he can pronounce it in a word. A word available to him separately may not be at his disposal in a sentence. Contrariwise, a whole sentence successfully uttered does not mean success with its words and sounds taken separately. Moreover, the aphasic's achievements are subject to considerable fluctuation with the setting. This obtains for word-apprehension, too. Understanding the sentence as whole does not mean that its single words will be understood. Aphasic patients frequently replace sounds and words by others closely related. Single parts are often condensed or displaced. The patient clings to the misformations he creates. In final analysis, perseverations are closely related to such clinging to once-created forms. The problem of the speech-fragments of aphasics deserves reconsideration in this light. At any rate, aphasic and agnosic disorders affect a layer of the psyche which has little individual coloring and only a loose contact with personal experiences; it has a means [231] character, it is psychologically peripheral. Thus we encounter here the same basic disorder, again acting on a different material, and again taking on a new form of appearance.

A comparison of aphasic and paretic disorders shows that aphasia is psychologically even more peripheral than paretic disorder. Thinking may surely be regarded as a means of personality, yet it is undoubtedly a far more personal means than language. Still, it would be incorrect to assert that personal vicissitudes play no role in aphasia and agnosia. It is commonly observable that even in these disorders the selection of what will be retained and reproduced depends to a certain extent on personal inclinations and interests. This holds even though personal experience is far less decisive here than in the basic schizophrenic disorder. Consequently, these disorders are far more diffuse [232] than those of

231. "Means-character" here translates *werkzeugmaessig*. Schilder stresses that what is affected in aphasia is not motivation but the means by which it is carried out.

232. Here the antithesis of "diffuse"

is "selective." Thus, according to Schilder, in neuroses and schizophrenias personal motivation selectively determines the locus of the disorder, while in aphasias and agnosias this selectivity plays a lesser role: the disorder spreads

neuroses or schizophrenias. It is instructive to compare the slips of aphasics with the complex-determined slips of neurotics and normals. Aphasics, too, make slips more often when excited or when the topic touches on a complex; but in their slips, general factors like effort and fatigue rather than selectiveness are the major determiners. The overwhelming majority of the slips of neurotics and normals is complex-determined, even though the influence of such general factors as tiredness must not be underestimated.[233] . . . I stress these common features to show that fundamentally communication always exists between the various psychological layers.

At this point I want to advance the formulation that the disorders of means-layers [234] of the psyche are more diffuse than those of more central and personal layers. It needs no extensive proof that the asphasic-agnosic disorders are more peripheral and more diffuse than those of paretic dementia. By "diffuse" I do not mean, like Goldstein,[235*] that every aphasic or agnosic disorder implies a fundamental disorder of all that belongs to the means-layer of perception and language. Thus we know [236*] that optic agnosias pertain to a single, relatively isolated range of objects. For instance, in word-blindness other disturbances of optical apperception play only a minor role. Isakower and I [237*] have even observed relatively isolated agnosic disorders, not one of which involved a speech disorder. Therefore, I do not believe Goldstein is right in assuming that aphasic or agnosic disorder always involves all the realms of the psychological means-layer. One may say only that a disorder of one optic realm will involve

---

diffusely over the realms of speech and understanding. Here we encounter again the distinction between an isolated thought-disturbance or -formation, and a generalized, normal or pathological, thought-organization. Symbols versus the thought-organization of dreams, slips of tongue versus schizophrenic thought-organization, are other examples. Affect-or drive-influences, and states of consciousness, respectively, underlie these. Cf. Silberer, Chap. 9, particularly notes 55, 78, and 93; also Chap. 13, note 62, above.

233. Freud, in discussing thorough-going psychological determinism, attrib-

uted to the general factor merely a precipitating and not a determining role (210, p. 50). Schilder renders the distinction between causation and precipitation relative, by showing that in certain settings a precipitating factor becomes the major causal one. Such relativization of determining factors is actually a further extension of thoroughgoing psychological determinism.

234. See note 231, above.

235.* Goldstein (283).

236.* Poetzl (572) clearly demonstrated this.

237.* Isakower and Schilder (348).

other optic realms. The involvement will affect neighboring realms . . . but even these only to a small degree. . . .[238] In other words, the disordered psychic layer in aphasia and agnosia is articulated according to object realms, within any one of which the disorder is diffuse. . . .[239]

I should like to mention briefly that amentia [240] is again the same fundamental disorder manifesting itself in yet another layer of experience. The psychological layers affected are concerned with the immediate elaboration of the material of perception and imagery. Apparently the perceptual raw material must be organized into broader units before it can be usefully integrated into the total experience of the person. The apprehension of a situation is not purely the task of the thought-process; nor is it a very personal task, though in this phase of elaboration, individual experience and affective factors do play a greater role than in raw-perception.[241] Thus, the psychological layer involved in amentia is one situated between the perceptual and the affective. It is more ego-close than the layer of thought-organization disordered in paresis; however, it does

238. The omitted section discusses the concept of "neighboring," with respect both to objects and to brain-localization.

239. In the omitted section Schilder concludes that the ubiquity of aphasic and agnosic disorders in dementia suggests a yet unknown relationship in the cortical localization of the centers responsible for speech and cognition on the one hand, and thought-organization on the other. The section is problematic for two reasons: (a) Even if we acknowledge the relative autonomy of speech in particular, it would seem still necessary to subsume speech and cognition under the heading "thought-organization." (b) One wonders whether localization in this sense is still a bona fide working hypothesis, and whether accepting Schilder's arguments against Goldstein's clinical contentions invalidates the latter's (281) conclusions against localization in the older sense.

240. According to Meynert (518),

amentia is a psychosis the essential symptom of which is hallucinatory confusion —a phenomenon of functional loss, due to cerebral exhaustion. See however Freud (209, pp. 487 and 533), and (237, pp. 145 and 149); also Hartmann and Schilder (312).

241. As I understand it, Schilder assumes that the psychological apparatus is so adapted to its environment that certain of its layers function in a more "impersonal" and homogeneous manner, guaranteeing the basic commonality of the relation of individuals to the world. This is consonant both with Freud's conception of the development of the secondary process (Chaps. 15 and 17, above), and with Hartmann's conceptions of the "inborn ego-apparatuses" and "conflict-free ego-sphere" (Chap. 19, above). Bruner's (97, 100), Murphy's (533), and Klein's (387) experiments suggest a fluid transition between the central and peripheral, "personal," and "impersonal" layers.

not derive directly from that of thought-organization, but rather that of perception.[242] Later I shall proffer evidence that the essence of amentia is also a disorder of integration and differentiation.

We have reached the point where we may attempt to define dementia. First of all, it may be described as a disorder of thought and action, not referable to a defect of the perceptual apparatus or the organs of action, or unwillingness, or distraction, or even affect, but rather to inability. Secondly, it is rooted in a disorder of differentiation and integration in a layer of the psychological organization which does not belong to the individual-affective core of the personality, and which serves the conceptual elaboration of the experience-material already organized by perception and apperception.

Let us now compare this with the definitions collected in Fleck's [243]* survey. Kraepelin [244]* and Wundt [245]* are of the opinion that the concepts intelligence and intellectual function do not refer to unitary and well-delineated sets of facts; dementia is therefore only a link in a chain of disease-manifestations, and cannot be separated from the conditions preceding it. We must object that a psychological condition like the dementia of paretics must be psychologically understandable in itself, even though we should not expect it to correspond to the dementia of the feeble-minded. To determine the exact differences between the two would require detailed investigations. A cursory examination yields the following. The feeble-minded does not perceive the abundance of relationships among and propensities of objects; therefore his concept basis, and consequently his judgments, are meager and inadequate. His picture of the world will be analogous with those produced by sense organs which function inadequately or not at all. Since the essence of thinking is to posit relationships, not only will his concepts and concept bases be inadequate, but the relationships between them will not be apperceived. Therefore, he will be able neither to generalize the singular nor to apply the general. . . . However, these general inferences must be substantiated by special investigations. In this comparison, the dementia of the paretic would show richer and less definite concepts; the disorder of relationship-apperception would be common to both.[246]*

242. See Schilder (645). Note that his concept of thought-organization here is quite narrow, excluding such functions as perception, apperception, and verbalization.

243.* Fleck (190).
244.* Kraepelin (415, 417).
245.* Wundt (778).
246.* Compare Domarus (147a).

For Tuczek,[247]* dementia is a pathological poverty or impoverishment of knowledge and ability, a deficit in registration, in reproduction and mental elaboration of experiential material, and in its transformation into productive activity. This definition is only an incomplete description.

Jaspers [248]* distinguishes between store of knowledge and intelligence. This distinction is in agreement with the fact that reproduction of knowledge does not preclude the presence of dementia. Moreover, knowledge contains more than objects and object-relations, it contains judgments. If knowledge is not merely reproduction or reproducibility, but rather the utilization of what is reproduced, then loss of knowledge and dementia have just about the same meaning. Utilization of what is reproduced implies the ability to rearticulate latent or actual memory-material. For Jaspers, the force driving toward utilizing knowledge is part of intelligence. Fleck [249] considers this an overextension of the concepts intelligence and dementia. I believe I have demonstrated that anticipations and correction-tendencies are manifestations of an internal driving-force of thought. The external driving-forces of thought must also be taken into consideration. Haste will check correction-tendencies, while lack of driving-force will at least delay the articulation of the whole-impression and thereby hamper the internal articulation of thinking. I agree with Jaspers and not with Fleck: both internal and external driving-forces of thought play an essential role in intelligence and in dementia. Stockert,[250]* too, stresses the significance of driving-forces for intelligence (and dementia). Yet the possibility must be considered that insufficient insight into object-structure will bar appropriate interest and appropriate driving-force; therefore, besides a primary one, a secondary disorder of driving-forces must be expected in dementia. I believe that we should not conceive of psychological functions singly. Knowledge, thought-processes, memory, driving-forces, can hardly be conceived of in complete separation. All are various aspects of one fundamental process. The fact that we cannot think of these as absolutely distinct leads us to a new conception of intelligence and dementia. Eliasberg [251]*was right: research in dementia must learn to consider the individual as a whole, and to regard the relation of the individual to the community.

247.* Tuczek (736).
248.* Jaspers (357) and (356).
249. See note 243, above.

250.* Stockert (713).
251.* W. Eliasberg (152).

S. Fischer [252]* defines intelligence as the ability to make abstractions and apprehend object-relations in a correct and task-appropriate fashion, and to set itself such tasks independently. The core of this definition is certainly correct. I would stress only that all such tasks [253] imply affectivity and driving-force. The distinction between various psychic layers is not that some are affectless and some affect-connected. Every psychological process implies both object-reference and affect; there are no affectless object-experiences.[254] Affect and intellectual content are abstractions; [255] an affectless content can no more exist than redness without an object.[256] [Passage omitted.] [257]

Our discussion so far has traced the primary factors of dementia. It remains, however, fundamentally incomplete: the psychic layer of thought-organization described above communicates with other psychic layers. Pick,[258]* Isserlin,[259]* S. Fischer,[260]* and Benedek and I [261]* have shown that speech- and cognition-disorders exert an inhibiting effect on thinking and memory. . . . Here I have demonstrated similar phenomena in paresis. Disorders in the layer of gnosia and praxia do exert an inhibitory effect upon the memory-thought layer.

Moreover, everything that takes place in the affective central layers has an essential influence on thought-functions. We have seen this in dementia praecox, in hysteria, and in dreams. The picture of paretic dementia is also continuously modified by processes in the central layers.[262]* As I shall pursue this problem later on, here I point out only alterations of dementia due to the influence of other layers. I will not discuss here manic-depressive mood swings because they do not change the defects in dementia, but merely alter their course.

252.* S. Fischer (189).

253. Strictly speaking, it is not the task that implies affectivity and driving-force, but rather the setting of the task, apprehending it, and coping with it.

254. "Affect" throughout is meant as a motivational factor.

255. Cf. Rapaport (591, pp. 264 ff.); and Rapaport, et al. (602, I, 385 ff.).

256. Considering the varieties of color-experience other than object-colors, the comparison is none too fortunate. See D. Katz (375).

257. In the first part of the omitted section, Schilder takes issue with W. Stern's (711) concepts of practical and theoretical intelligence, and stresses that dementia is an inability to utilize existing knowledge. The second part deals with the role of Gestalt in thought-disorders, with emphasis on the processes that produce Gestalt.

258.* Pick (567).

259.* Isserlin (349).

260.* S. Fischer (189).

261.* Benedek and Schilder (42).

262.* My recent discussion of the relationship between pseudo-dementia and dementia pertains to this point.

[See Schilder, 648, pp. 233–36]

(d) The General Behavior of Paretics

(a) Rhythmic Phenomena. [Passage omitted.] [263] The case to be discussed is definitely one of general paresis. It is noteworthy that psychogenic factors played an important precipitating role. The unfavorable results of a spinal fluid examination, and the affair of her husband with her sister-in-law, shook and excited the patient greatly. She developed a delusional system centering around her husband. Her attitude toward him was most ambivalent: he was at once the devil and Christ nailed to the cross, who through the love of women finally became the emperor of Vienna. Simultaneously, the patient felt changed, first in her heart and then sex organs: something "came out down below" and she became a man.

Clinically she became conspicuous by asserting that she had been hospitalized repeatedly because of mental illness: at four, at twelve, and at nineteen years of age. She spoke much of her brother-in-law having poked her with his finger, tearing something in her abdomen. It transpired that this brother-in-law had died four years previously of a liver cancer, and the patient was inclined to assume that she too had this disease. . . . The examination of the patient showed that she identified her brother-in-law with her husband, both being extremely sensual. It made clear that her idea of having been hospitalized at the ages of five and twelve, and of having had paresis, was related to important experiences. When she was five years old, her father infected his finger and died of sepsis. This explains her assertion that the man who tried to seduce her at twelve had pricked his finger: she apparently identified him with her father. Her assertion that at nineteen she was hospitalized for paresis refers to an abortion she had at that time. Thus the patient seems to equate, (a) father, husband, and brother-in-law; (b) the liver cancer of her brother-in-law, . . . sexual infection, hurt finger, and the fatal finger-infection of the father. Moreover, any and all sickness is equated with paresis, as are venereal infection and change of sex. The patient's idea that she had repeatedly had paresis and been hospitalized were reduplications of her present experience, and proved to be fully determined by important erotic "Einstellungen." The patient's tendency to repress sexuality is expressed in her rejection of the sensuality of her brother-in-law and her

263. The omitted section contains the description of a case illustrative of the rhythmic phenomena to be discussed. Since the important features of the case are restated in the discussion, the description is omitted here.

husband; the repeated pareses and hospitalizations are punishments for sexual activities, even though these were not consummated. Thus the material yielded a nearly complete understanding of the psychological determination of this reduplicating paramnesia.

Pick [264*] was the first to describe this symptom. When the continuity of their everyday life was interrupted by an unusual event (for example, by a change of room), his patients began to have double-experiences; the [events] before and after [the interruption] appeared as independent, yet identical, experiences.[265] Westphal,[266*] in his review of the studies of reduplicating paramnesia by Rosenberg,[267*] Coriat,[268*] and Sittig,[269*] reported two additional cases and called attention to the psychogenic factors which probably underlay them. In one of Pick's cases, the reduplicating paramnesia led the patient to the assumption that there was not one hospital but several, two professors Pick, and three brothers instead of one. In one of Westphal's cases, the patient's husband and children were doubled. Another case, a paretic, experienced himself double. In a third case, the patient fabricated another person, endowing him with venereal disease and his own name.

In our case, we see a triplication of the torturing experience of paresis and hospitalization. It is not the experiences of the hospital which are doubled, but only that of hospitalization. Past and present experiences that imply the same complex become identical; this multiplies the experience in question, creating a rhythmic motif-formation. We can speak about this as the molding of past experiences according to their complex-content. Our patient had three catastrophic experiences, which now become identical. Thus, from the point of view of the Unconscious, it does make sense to assert that she had thrice been hospitalized for paresis. This is a misjudgment of the memory-material under the influence of certain "Einstellungen." . . . Mayer-Gross [270*] doubts whether this is a memory-disorder in the strict sense. He hypothesizes a primary inclination for reduplication and cites iteration-phenomena,[271] mentioning the psycho-motor system as their possible source but without giving his reasons. I

264.* Pick (568).

265. An event that took place *after* the interruption was experienced by the patient as having already occurred *before* the interruption.

266.* Westphal (766).

267.* Rosenberg (619).

268.* Coriat (134).

269.* Sittig (697).

270.* Mayer-Gross (508).

271. See Chapter 2, above.

find it easier to explain such phenomena in terms of the playful reduplications we have seen in the recall of the Shark Story in Case No. 1. It is noteworthy that the patient ascribes part of these experiences to herself.[272] The fundamental principle appears to be the same: a rhythmic function of memory, an iteration-principle. There seems to be no reason to separate it from memory-phenomena in general. The relationship of reduplicating paramnesia to *déjà vu* [273] has been pointed out by Rosenberg. *Déjà vu* is actually the experience of two matching events, one of which belongs to the sphere [274] and is thus undeveloped, while the other is completely developed.[275]* Thus Rosenberg is right when he considers it an abbreviated reduplicating paramnesia. . . .

A few general comments on the rhythmic principle. In the thought-formation of the paretic psychosis, as well as in the story recall of our patients, a motif is repeated over and over, with variations according to the situation and the affect-"Einstellung." [276] Examples like those in Case No. 1 are abundant. The tendency to multiply experiences appears often in the form of the substitution of several story-figures for one. The elaborations of these substituted figures may differ from each other, but the [affective] core of the motif remains the same. This is not an isolated phenomenon in psychopathology: in the delusional formations of schizophrenics the same principle obtains.[277]* . . . This repetition of motives is comparable to motif-variations in music. Often two versions of the delusional system are encountered in a patient, one very primitive and archaic, the other adapted to reality and rationalized. Yet, while each of these versions encompasses different aspects of the environment, the repetitive handling of the motif seems to be related to the same fundamental biological

272. We may consider this the re-evaluation of a past experience whose complex- or affect-content was identical with that of the story. This leads then to the story being experienced as a part of the patient's own past. See Chap. 27, 46, below.

273. Cf. Poetzl (574), Freud (230); and Claparède, Chap. 3, particularly note 9, above.

274. The sphere corresponds grossly to the "Unconscious" or the "primary process" (209, pp. 525 ff.). For their differences, see Chap. 24, Appendix, above.

The experience that belongs to the sphere is one of which only the affect-, mood-, or impulse-core is available to consciousness, but not its specific memory. The *déjà vu*, according to Schilder, is initiated by the fully developed experience, whose affect-, mood-, or impulse-content is identical with that of the undeveloped one; thus the two are experienced as identical, that is, matching.

275.* Compare Schilder (666) and (664).

276. See note 106, above.

277.* See Schilder (647) and (652).

tendencies, which are present—as we saw—in various psychological layers.[278] The same tendency is encountered in the play of children, in the motif repetitions of music, and in ornamenting [of architecture]. To use Lewin's [279] term, it is as though one performance cannot bring psychological satiation. It seems that the number of repetitions necessary for satiation decreases with age.

Freud spoke of repetition-compulsion [280] as a basic propensity of the psyche. He pointed to the return of traumata in dreams occurring in traumatic neuroses, to the repetitiveness of the play of young children, and to the return in transference [281] of infantile situations. In his view, [the driving-forces of] these phenomena are beyond the pleasure-principle, mainly in the ego-instincts,[282] but also in the sexual instincts. However, the manifestations of this rhythmic principle are still more widespread; we see them in the rhythmic character of primitive speech-sounds and repetitiousness of the infant's babbling, which has left its trace in the reduplications of our language. We encounter further instances of this rhythmic principle in the pathology of speech: in clonic stuttering, in the speech of post-encephalitics,[283]* and in the reduplications of motor-aphasia. The latter examples are important: they suggest that insufficient satiation may be one of the motivating agents of rhythmic repetition. The study of the motif-repetitions of our paretics and schizophrenics supports this suggestion. Studying the palilalia [284] of patients with lesions of the striatum, one gains the impression that in addition there is another, biologically deeper-rooted, rhythmic principle which is a propensity of the organic structure and the life process itself. . . .[285]

---

278. See Chap. 13, above.

279. See K. Lewin (467, pp. 254–57, 264 ff.) and Chap. 5, II, 1.c.1, above; see also A. Karsten (370). Lewin's psychology uses the explanatory construct "tension-system" to account for the dynamics of "needs." These "tension-systems" are hypothesized as the source of motivational energy of thought and action. When single action satisfies the need, the explanatory formulation is that the tension-system is *discharged*. When the action is continuous (for example, stringing beads), and the need satisfied, the explanatory formulation is that the tension system is *satiated*.

280. Freud (241, p. 19).

281. For the concept of transference, see Freud (235 and 224a).

282. For the concept "ego-instinct" see Freud (231). The concept became dated with the introduction of the topographic concepts of ego, id, and super-ego (Freud, 243). The assumption of a death-instinct corresponding to a repetition-compulsion has been rejected by many psychoanalysts. See, for example, Fenichel (176, pp. 59–61).

283.* See Leyser (472) and (473); Pollak and Schilder (576).

284. Pathological repetition of words.

285. In the omitted section, Schilder

(β) The Break-through of Affects [Section omitted] [286]

III. THE RELATIONSHIP OF SOME FORM-VARIANTS OF PARESIS TO DEMENTIA

[Sections omitted.] [287]

(d) *Confabulations*

This is an important group of phenomena. We saw in the recall of stories that paretics interweave their narratives with motives from their own lives. These motives, closely related to their immediate wishes and needs, correspond to the daydreams of adolescents and to the play of late childhood. All these memories, inventions, and fantasies emerge in our patients with a claim to reality-value; the conviction of correctness attached to them is, however, very shallow.[288*] Acts of asserting have little conviction-value in this kind of patient. This problem is encountered in confabulations and pseudologia fantastica.

We can assume that every play of fantasy, indeed every idea that comes to consciousness, has the tendency to be asserted as true.[289] Meinong [290*] maintained that this also holds for assumptions, only that they are "put into brackets"

---

makes an attempt to substantiate his assumption of this fundamental biological rhythmic principle. For this purpose he amasses examples of rhythmic organic processes, and then proceeds to relate all these to (a) their purposiveness in mastering reality, in that each repetition brings into play a new segment of reality in the new motif-variation; and (b) the lack of satiation by single performance. Finally, he dwells on perseveration as an example of motif-repetition, explaining it partly by Freud's stimulus-barrier concept (241, pp. 30–34), and partly by Lewin's satiation concept.

286. The omitted section contains a case history in which Schilder demonstrates that the paretic thought-disorder makes for an easy penetration of wishes into consciousness. He uses the case also to illustrate (a) the inability of the paretic patient to get away from ideas once formed; (b) the paretic patient's tend-

ency to be interrupted in his thought by any word conducive to serial verbigeration.

287. Since this chapter is not concerned with thought-organization, it is omitted here, except for the passage on confabulations. It deals with (a) the role of megalomanic ideas and numbers in manicky forms of paresis, (b) depressive form-variants of the paretic psychosis, (c) motor excitement and incoherence in paresis, (d) confabulations, (e) the defect-cured paretic, and (f) catatonic and hallucinatory form-variants of paresis.

288.* G. E. Mueller studied the degrees of this conviction of correctness. [See Section Ic, above.]

289. This is an implication of the concept "omnipotence of thought," which Schilder here suggests is present in germinal form in all normal thought.

290.* Meinong (513).

—as it were—and so kept pending. This bracketing is a specific psychological act. In fantasies and daydreams too, such acts of bracketing indicate that what is asserted is not reality.[291] In other words, the psychological acts of judging reality form a whole spectrum, ranging from those the truth of which is asserted, through those which are bracketed, to those accompanied by correction-tendencies.[292]

All these considerations are of fundamental significance for the Korsakow syndrome. Confabulations are closely related to a loss of correction-processes. . . . Now it is quite clear that "memory loss" and dementia, without driving-forces, are not sufficient to explain confabulation. Such driving-forces play a role even in the fantasies of normal people. It is noteworthy that the frequent memory-and orientation-disorders of brain-tumor cases, according to Pfeifer,[293]* are completely free of confabulations. It is difficult to give an exact psychological definition of driving-forces. One comes closest to it by tracing the psychological conditions of "daydreams." It is crucial to realize that the absence of bracketing and correcting may be due to various reasons. In pseudologia it is due to a strong affective need, in daydreams to a temporary recession of correction processes, in paresis and Korsakow to an inadequacy of the psychological systems responsible for bracketing and correcting.

[Passage omitted.] [294]

IV. CONCERNING THE VARIETIES OF PARETIC CONDITIONS DURING AND AFTER MALARIA-TREATMENT

[Chapter omitted.] [295]

V. CONTENTS AND RELATIONSHIPS IN THE EXPERIENCE OF PARETICS

[Chapter omitted.] [296]

291. Cf. Sartre (631).
292. Cf. Buerger-Prinz and Kaila, Chap. 27, IV, below.
293.* B. Pfeifer (554).
294. In the rest of the section, omitted here, Schilder demonstrates that confabulations represent early pre-psychotic interests, and that confabulating patients have had inclinations to daydreaming and fantasying before becoming paretic.

295. Though the material of this chapter much deserves translation, it is not directly related to the problem of thought-disorder and thought-organization.
296. This chapter deals with thought-organization and pathology of thought only peripherally. We shall briefly summarize it. Clinical psychiatry (for example, Jaspers, 356, and Bumke, 114) has not been interested in the personality of

VI. THE BASIC PLAN OF THE PSYCHE

[Section omitted.] [297]

We must realize that the primary processes of the Unconscious system are not limited to dreams. They are the basis of neurotic symptom-formation, and are manifest in the fully conscious thoughts of schizophrenics. Formations

---

the paretic. Its interest centered on the impaired achievements, and the personality of the paretic was regarded as an incoherent rudiment of a destroyed psyche. Schilder asserts that the psyche always remains a cohesive organization. He points out that the prodromal neurasthenic phase of general paresis is a reaction to the experience of incipient disability; that the depressive features and sad mood so frequent in paresis is a mourning over the experienced loss of functions; and finally, that the excuses so typical of paretics are but veiled admissions of inadequacy. Schilder expresses this state of affairs in psychoanalytic terms: dementia encroaches upon the ego (or what Schilder chooses to call the "perception- and thought-ego"), dealing severe blows at the ego-ideal, which still adheres to its usual criteria of objective thinking. Thereupon, the ego-ideal takes the role of a severe taskmaster, meting out punishment in the form of depression and hypochondriasis. Paretic mania and ideas of grandeur are, in turn, reaction-formations negating both insufficiency and super-ego accusations. In agreement with Ferenczi and Hollos (336), Schilder asserts that underneath the dementia, the mania, the grandiose ideas, the excuses, and the incoherence, the paretic remains aware of his syphilitic infection. Syphilis is experienced by the paretic as a punishment for sinful sexuality, mutual masturbation, incest, etc.,

297. In the omitted part, Schilder cites a dream of an anxiety-neurotic patient, to demonstrate the mechanisms of the Unconscious—that is, of the primary process—described by Freud. At the end of the preceding chapter, Schilder had summarized these mechanisms as follows: "(1) Distinction between internal and external reality is absent. (2) Experiences are timeless. (3) Displacements, condensations, and symbolizations take place. (4) The law of contradiction is suspended. (5) The cathexes are mobile and affect-quantities can be transferred completely from one idea to another."

---

and is symbolically equated by him with castration, dismemberment, and any and all diseases and catastrophes.

Schilder suggests that the form-varieties of the paretic psychosis depend upon the physiology of the syphilitic damage to the brain. For instance, he assumes that there is such a thing as a "manic-depressive brain-system" which, when affected by the syphilitic meningo-encephalitis, brings about manic-depressive forms of paresis. These suggestions remain vague and do not vitiate Schilder's argument as to the psychodynamics of the paretic psychosis, which he considers to be the superstructure of the physiological damage wrought by syphilitic meningo-encephalitis. [Cf. Kenyon, Rapaport and Lozoff, 381.]

clearly analogous to these primary processes are demonstrable, however, in aphasias and agnosias also. Optic agnosias are especially instructive in this respect. I quote from my *Medizinische Psychologie:* [298]*

(a) In optic agnosia there is a delay of apperception. (b) This delay makes the immaturity of thought apparent: what emerges in its course is not the percept but rather the general category [to which it belongs]. (c) Within these general categories what emerges is not the concept or percept sought, but one related to it; when the concept or percept sought does appear, it fails to take hold and is even rejected. (d) Delayed after-deliveries of the concept or percept sought will emerge, fused with objectively irrelevant impressions. (e) The placement within the spatial continuum is not correct. (f) Training makes it possible to veil this disorder. Patients are more prone to fail when faced with a task, than when allowed spontaneous activity.

We might add that memories and imagery often replace perception, and are then experienced as realities.

I have demonstrated that essentially the same process takes place in dementia. Paretics, for instance, are prone to put their wishes in the place of reality. Case No. 1 in retelling the Shark Story, reports that she was present, the officer was rescued, and so on. Contradictions do not exist for her: the officer is dead, but she continues as though he were alive. The affect pertaining to her own fate is transferred to the story. Concepts are replaced by coordinate and superordinate

---

Schilder takes issue with the contention of Ferenczi and Hollos that the paretic psychosis brings about a regression to archaic psychological material. He asserts that paretic dementia damages primarily the defense against preconscious rather than unconscious material; thus the content of the paretic psychosis is similar to adolescent fantasies and daydreams, rather than to the archaic unconscious material seen in schizophrenics. He quotes case-material to demonstrate that, in contrast to usual paretic psychoses, the hallucinatory psychoses of paretics which develop in the course of malarial fever-treatment do contain archaic material of the kind described by Ferenczi and Hollos. He argues that something else (for example, fever-delirium) must be added to paretic dementia in order to obtain regression to archaic material. The layer of thought-organization damaged by dementia normally performs the task of consummating drive-processes by asserting relationships and thereby controlling preconscious strivings. Dementia eliminates this controlling function and leads to suggestibility, distractibility, and gullibility. Hostility as a rule remains in abeyance, presumably because it is not simply preconscious; thus the whole demeanor usually has a friendly and kindly surface.

298.* Schilder (648, p. 44).

ones. One could even say that in paretics the mechanisms of the Unconscious system appear in the thought-material.[299]

I once attempted to show that a similar disorder is present in amentia, though the material affected is different. There the disordered layer of experience is the one which integrates the perceptual material into higher units. The apperception-disorder of amentia-patients varies from agnosia-like forms to those resembling complex-determined misapperceptions. The thought-contents of amentia-patients also are focused on the damage to the [psychological] apparatus; their ideational content is not so ego-distant as that of aphasias and agnosias, nor so ego-close as the material of schizophrenias. Those layers of perceiving and remembering which are disordered in amentia are mostly of an impersonal kind; at any rate, never as personal as the layers affected by the perception- and thought-disorders of schizophrenia.

Hartmann and I [300*] have described the apperception-disturbances of a case of amentia:

1. The part replaces the whole, the vague-general replaces the specific, and the dividing line between conceptually coordinate ideas is vague or nonexistent. 2. The disorder is not one of perception, like that in agnosia, but rather one of apperceptions of higher-order object-relations.

We encounter also similar disorders of imagery and thinking. It is noteworthy that here too, as in illusions and agnosias,[301*] there is a fading of the boundaries between subject and object.

We arrive at the following formulation: the raw material of perception is integrated by an unconscious synthetic function. This is the function whose disorder in aphasias and agnosias results in the agnosic parapraxes described, and often in similar disturbances of the process of imagery. [In the next phase of thought-development] the raw material of perception and imagery is integrated on a higher level, and implicit object-relationships are apperceived. This is the process which is disordered in amentia, leaving perceptions isolated. [In

299. Here we have an apparent contradiction. Earlier Schilder asserted that the material which comes to consciousness in the paretic is of "preconscious" origin; here he demonstrates mechanisms of the "Unconscious" in it. This contradiction is resolved if the arguments of Hartmann and Kris on the various degrees of neutralization of drives are considered. See Chap. 19 and 23, above.

300.* Hartmann and Schilder (312).

301.* See Stauffenberg (702).

the subsequent phase of thought-development] perceptions and presentations are integrated into higher units corresponding to objects, and are then conceptually evaluated. It is this process of elaboration, in terms of concepts and memories, which is disordered in dementia. Finally [in the completing phase of thought-development] all this perceptual raw material and organized perceptual material is put into relationship with the personality, with the personal wish directing the experience, with the attitudes of the person, that is to say, with the [central] drive-layer of the psyche. This is the process which is disordered in neurosis, schizophrenia, and the dream.

In all these layers, disorders lead to the same basic difficulties: the whole cannot be differentiated into its parts, the parts cannot be integrated into a whole. However, in each of the various disorders in question, this fundamental disturbance occurs in a different realm of the psyche. . . .[302]

302. The rest of this chapter deals with Schilder's conception of the psychological apparatus. For a presentation of these ideas, see Schilder (645) and (660). Schilder's summarizing chapter is omitted here.

CHAPTER 26

THE BASIC SYMPTOMS OF SCHIZOPHRENIA [1]

By Eugen Bleuler

THE BASIC SYMPTOMS [2] of schizophrenia are disorders of association and affect. They replace reality by fantasy and result in a withdrawal from reality (au-

1. From Bleuler's: *Dementia Praecox oder Gruppe der Schizophrenien* (71). The first section following here is the translation of pp. 10–31. Bleuler subdivides the symptoms of schizophrenia into basic and accessory. The present translation is taken from his discussion of the former group. He takes the psychological functions one by one and attempts to find which are altered and which are intact in the basic symptom-picture of schizophrenia. The discussion is divided into "simple" and "complex" functions. At this point we shall not discuss whether this division is justified.

The discussion of simple functions is subdivided into chapters on altered functions and intact functions. The altered functions are Associations, Affectivity, Ambivalence; of these we translated the discussion of the first of these only. The intact functions are Sensation and Perception, Orientation, Memory, Consciousness, Motility; we translated the material on Memory and Consciousness.

Bleuler devotes a section to each of the complex functions: Relationship to Reality and Autism, Attention, Will, The Person, "Schizophrenic Dementia," Action and Behavior. Of these we selected Attention, and the discussion of the pathology of concept-formation from the section on "Schizophrenic Dementia."

The principle of selection was *direct* pertinence to the pathology of thinking. Had we not rigidly applied this criterion, a great part of the bulky, meaty volume would have found its way into these pages. (An English translation by Joseph Zinkin was published by International Universities Press in 1950, after this was written.)

2. Today Bleuler's concept of "basic symptoms" may appear to some a commonplace, to others a misleading step in the development of psychiatric thinking. Disagreement with both views led us to include here these selections.

Those who view the concept as a commonplace would argue that it is commonly accepted that the symptoms of regression are the basic symptoms of schizophrenia (Fenichel 176, pp. 417 ff.), with restitution phenomena (Fenichel 176, pp. 424 ff.) playing an accessory role. However, when Bleuler's monograph was published this implication of Freud's investigations was not yet realized. Bleuler's thinking was influenced by Freud. His distinction between basic and accessory symptoms may be compared with Freud's formulation: "Delusion formation, which we take to be a pathological product, is in reality an attempt at recovery, a process of reconstruction" (224, p. 457).

The question of what is primary in schizophrenia if the obvious symptoms are of mere secondary significance has been variously answered. Jung (363) sought this "primary" disorder in the role of the "complexes," particularly in their contents, and regarded all thought-disorders as the result of "complex-thinking," without thoroughly investigating their specific *formal* characteristics as thought-processes. Abraham (8) also sought it in complexes and their contents, and explained the extreme effects of complexes in schizophrenic thinking by the regression of libido to "autoerotism" (p. 73). Though Bleuler also became absorbed (68, 70; see also Chaps. 20 and 21, above) with the content of thought in schizophrenia, he was the only one who searched systematically for the primary symptoms.

Those who would view Bleuler's concept of "primary symptoms" as sterile for the development of psychiatry, would point out that it assumes an organic etiology of schizophrenia, and it is based on a conception of psychological functions (see note 1, above) which is no longer tenable. The assumption of organic etiology is clearly stated by Bleuler (67) in his dispute with Jung (361) on schizophrenic negativism and reaches an extreme form in Bleuler's (74) last discussion of the topic two decades later. Though his first formulations are somewhat equivocal, Bleuler believed that *the* basic symptom of schizophrenia is *loosening of associations* based on an organic process, and is the prerequisite of the other basic and the accessory symptoms. But Bleuler was not alone in making the assumption of organic eti-

ology. Once the existence and crucial role of "complexes" had been proven in both schizophrenia and hysteria, Jung (363) hypothesized an "X metabolic toxin" (p. 89), and Abraham (8) a "specific psycho-sexual constitution" (p. 77), to distinguish between the two disorders. Furthermore, it must be remembered that all this happened in the huge shadow of Kraepelin's organically oriented psychiatry. Finally, it should be noted that the concept "organic" is ambiguous: in Bleuler's early writings (77, 67) it may not seem different from the physiological brain process which is the substratum of thought; in his late writings (74) it seems to mean something akin to gross anatomical change, like, for example, that produced by an encephalitis. The former has such modern protagonists as Schilder (643, 642) and Benjamin (43); for the latter, in spite of enormous efforts (see Lewis, 470; Bellak, 40; and Hoskins, 341), no real evidence has been found.

Though Bleuler did not recognize that there exists a direct relationship between the primary symptoms on the one hand, and drive dynamics and Freudian mechanisms on the other, his consistent effort to find the basic symptom in a disorder of thought is of lasting value. It has fallen into undeserved oblivion, though no comparable systematic attempt to study the schizophrenic thought-disorder has been made since, not even when interest in such studies was revived in the middle of the 1930's (see Kasanin, 372). Though his conception of psychological functions and their grouping is outdated, he highlights functions (attention, autism, consciousness, etc.) to which since then unduly little attention has been paid.

Bleuler's distinction between basic

tism).[3] The absence of symptoms which play an important role in other mental illnesses, such as primary perception-, orientation-, and memory-disorders, may also be counted among the basic symptoms.[4]

I. THE ASSOCIATIONS

[In schizophrenia] the associations lose their connections. This disorder may interrupt a few, many, or most of the thousands of threads which direct our thoughts. As a result, thought becomes unusual and often logically false.[5] Moreover, the associations follow new pathways, of which thus far the follow-

---

and accessory symptoms has become particularly fruitful in diagnostic psychological testing, where it gave rise to two fundamental questions: (a) can early symptoms of developing schizophrenia be found by testing procedures *before* the obvious secondary symptoms set in, that is, before the more or less overt break? (b) are there indicators in tests of schizophrenics which prognosticate a malignant course? (Cf. Rapaport *et al.*, 602, II, 329 ff.; Hanfmann and Kasanin, 299, pp. 66 ff.; Kasanin, 371, pp. 46–49; Benjamin, 43, pp. 66–70.) One of the disadvantageous aspects of the search for the basic symptom was the inclination to elevate a single feature of the schizophrenic thought-disorder to a unique position. Vigotsky (743) went so far in this direction as to consider disorders of concept-formation the basic symptom, if not the etiological agent, of schizophrenia. He contended that affect-disorder is a *consequence* of conceptual disorder (p. 1075). For further examples see the papers published by Kasanin (372). Bleuler himself avoided this pitfall. His clinical method and the variety of "functions" he studied, make Bleuler's book the richest single volume on the phenomena of schizophrenic thought-pathology.

3. Current theory reverses this sequence: withdrawal from reality into fantasy is considered the cause of the association- and affect-disorder. It would perhaps be more correct to say that association- and affect-disorder, autistic fantasy and withdrawal, are various aspects of the schizophrenic disorder. But even this is not quite precise; current conceptions demand a causal relationship between these various aspects of the disorder and drive-dynamics.

It should be noted that Bleuler's concept of *affect* is extremely broad and includes drives.

4. "Primary perception-, orientation-, and memory-disorders" apparently refer to those seen in organic cases.

5. For Bleuler, associations are the cornerstone of psychic life (73): their natural order emulates the natural order of objects and events. (At times Spinoza's "ordo et connectio idearum idem est vel ordo et connectio rerum" seems to reverberate in Bleuler's writing. Cf. Bleuler (71, p. 292, note). His "associative connections" are established by experience. His papers on autism show (Chaps. 20 and 21, above) that he was familiar with those associative connections which Freud labeled the "primary process"; but he could never regard these as "natural" and "lawful"; they were "arbitrary" and "false" in his eyes.

ing are known: two contiguous ideas are made into a thought, the logical form
of the connection being determined by the accident of their contiguity; clang
and indirect associations gain unusual significance; two or more ideas are condensed into one; [6] an inclination to stereotypy results in the train of thought
fastening onto an idea or returning to it again and again; there may be a general
paucity of ideas to the point of mono-ideism; often a random idea in the train
of thought becomes dominant in the form of "fascination," repetitive naming,
or echopraxia. Distractibility varies with the kind of schizophrenic condition
present. When the schizophrenic association-disorder becomes extreme, confusion results. In regard to the temporal course of associations there are only
two specifically schizophrenic disorders: *pressure of ideas*, that is to say a
pathologically increased flow of ideas, and *blocking*, which is particularly
characteristic.[7]

The following is a spontaneous production of a young schizophrenic who
first appeared paranoid or hebephrenic and in later years became severely
catatonic:

"The Blossoming-Time of Horticulture" [8]

"At the time of the new moon venuss stands in the Augustsky of Egypt and
lights up with its light rays the merchant-travel-harbors of Suez, Cairo, and
Alexandria. In this historically famous Caliphcity is the museum of Assyrian

6. These are obviously characteristic of the primary process. Cf. Freud (209, pp. 525 ff., particularly pp. 527 and 531; see also p. 484).

7. Stereotypy, mono-ideic paucity of ideas, "fascination" (*Bannung*), repetitive naming, echopraxia, distractibility, confusion, pressure of ideas, and block-ing, have no direct equivalents among the characteristics of the primary proc-ess.

8. Bleuler here proceeds to analyze selected spontaneous productions of schizophrenics to infer from them the nature of the schizophrenic association-disturbance. This procedure, though at present largely in disuse and fraught with methodological dangers, is the method *par excellence* of clinical re-search. Its inherent postulate is the fundamental lawfulness of the biological individual; its inherent danger lies in the difficulty of knowing the realm of ap-plicability of the inferences drawn from the sample chosen. This was the method used by Freud in his studies on dreams (209), parapraxes (210), wit (214), etc. Schilder used it in his *Seele und Leben* (652), *Wahn und Erkenntniss* (663), *Selbstbewusstsein und Persoenlichkeits-bewusstsein* (653). To my knowledge only Schilder (652) has directly dis-cussed the methodology of this proced-ure, though the more general discussions of Lewin (465) and Brenman and Gill (272) are also relevant. To eliminate

statues from Macedonia. Besides pisang, also corn, oats, clover, and barley grow there. Bananas, figs, lemons, oranges, and olives. Olive oil is an Arabian liqueur sauce which the Afghans, Blackamoors and Moslemites use for ostrich breeding. The pisang of India is the Whiyski of the Parsis and the Arabs. The Parsi or Caucasian has just as much power of influence over his elephant as the Blackamoor over his dromedary. The camel is the sport of the Jew and the hindu. In india barley, rice, and sugarcane that is artichoke grow excellently. The Brahmins live in castes on Beladschistan. The Tscherkess inhabit Manchuria of China. China is the Eldorado of the Pawnee."

A hebephrenic who has been ill for over 15 years but is still able to work . . . gave the following verbal reply to my question, "Who was Epaminondas?" [9]*

"Epaminondas was somebody powerful particularly on water and land. He led great fleet maneuvers and open sea battles against Pelopidas, but was hit over the head in the Second Punic War by the ship-wreck of an armored frigate. With ships he wandered from Athens to the grove of Mamre, brought there caledonic grapes and pomegranates and he subdued Beduoins. He besieged the Acropolis with gunboats and had the Persian garrison burned as living torches. The next Pope, Gregory VII—no, Nero—followed his example and because of him all people of Athens, all Romanic-Germanic-Celtic generations, who did not take a favorable stand to the priests, were burned by the Druids on Corpus-Christi-Day for the Sun-God Baal. This is the period of the Stone Age. Spearheads of bronze."

These products exhibit a moderate degree of schizophrenic association-disorder.[10] Though coming from patients of diametrically opposite behavior,

---

arbitrariness of the sample, Schilder (655; also Chap. 25, above), Koeppen and Kutzinsky (402), and others studied semi-spontaneous and controlled productions of patients. Most of the recent studies of the schizophrenic thought-disorder apply experimental methods or controlled conditions, both of which, however, usually restrict the wealth and cogency of the material and inferences (see, for example, Kasanin, 372; Rapaport *et al.*, 602). Cf. Chap. 27, note 80, below.

9.* The fact that the characteristics of a train of thought are identical in oral and written expression must be of an—as yet unrecognized—significance for the theory of associative thinking.

[In my clinical experience, well-organized schizophrenics display far less thought-disorder in writing than in speech. In general, spoken language is notoriously looser than the written composition. Cf. Vigotsky (742, pp. 45-46).]

10. The "moderate degree" is meant in relation to other hospitalized patients' productions. The manifestations of the schizophrenic thought-disorder

they are surprisingly similar: a goal-presentation, the most important determinant directing associations, is lacking in both.[11] The first patient wants to write about oriental gardens, a very strange idea for a clerk who never got beyond the borders of his little homeland and has been in a mental hospital for years; the second, though formally adhering to the question, does not actually talk about Epaminondas but about a much broader concept.[12]

Their ideas are held together not by a direction- or goal-presentation but rather by a sort of supraordinate concept. It is as though concepts of a certain category—in the first case the Orient, in the second ancient history—were thrown into a pot, mixed, then drawn out by sheer chance,[13] and connected by

---

are far more subtle in incipient schizophrenics, schizophrenic characters, ambulatory schizophrenics, and other chronic-schizophrenic adjustments, See Schafer (632), Rapaport *et al.* (602), and Benjamin (43).

11. Cf. Ach, Chap. 1, and Buehler, Chap. 2, above. Their concepts of task- and goal-presentation seem to coincide with Bleuler's. From the point of view of psychoanalysis, goal-presentation is the crucial characteristic of the secondary process. It plays a similar role in the secondary process as the object of the drive in the primary process. See Freud (209, pp. 535–36), and Chaps. 15 and 16, above.

12. The themes "oriental horticulture" and "Epaminondas" do recur in these narratives, indicating that a tendency toward a goal-presentation exists. This is probably why Bleuler refers to these as disorders of "moderate" degree. The initial idea of "Orient" overflows into the associated ideas of starry sky, Egypt, Macedonia, Assyria, and Caliphs; then the theme of agriculture returns, but the olive oil leads to Arabs and all their likely and unlikely associates; after a very brief return to pisang we are again with associated Oriental peoples, their

elephants, dromedaries, and camels; and the last return to agriculture leads to no better result than the Pawnee's Chinese Eldorado. As Schilder (Chap. 24, above) describes it: associated realms of ideas which are normally traversed and discarded in the preparatory phase of the development of thought come to consciousness in this disorder. The goal-presentation (or determining tendency) normally selects from among the many associations in readiness those which are appropriate to it. Here the determining tendency, though present in traces, is no longer effective: any of the associations in readiness may come to consciousness. Compare Cameron (120, p. 53):

. . . marked paucity of genuinely causal links (asyndesis), . . . a cluster of more or less related elements. . . . A normally syndetic, or linked together, topical organization would have automatically eliminated all but one or two such possibilities, and in this way have restricted the solution to something more *clean-cut* and precise. . . . We find all through *schizophrenic scattering* a lost ability to restrict, eliminate, and focus on the task at hand.

Cf. also Cameron (121).

13. This seems to suggest that Bleuler

grammatical forms and a few auxiliary ideas. Nevertheless, some adjacent concepts are still connected by somewhat closer common bonds; but even these are too loose to be logically useful (fleet maneuver—sea battle—armored frigate; Acropolis—Persian garrison—burning—living torch—Nero; priest—Druid—Easter—Sun-God Baal, and so on).

In analyzing association-disorders it is important to keep in mind those influences which in general direct our thoughts. Naturally, no fruitful train of thought can come of associations based merely on habit, similarity, subordination, causality, and so forth; it is the goal-presentation that shapes a series of concepts into thought. A goal-presentation is not an entity but rather an infinitely complex hierarchy of ideas. When we are working out a theme, our proximal goal is the formulation of the partial thought we are about to capture, and the sentence we are about to write is to be its symbol. The paragraph we are writing implies a more general goal, which in turn is subordinated to that of the section, and so on, and so on. In the thoughts of the farmer at work, his ultimate goal, to make his land as productive as possible, is never absent. It determines his associations even if at a given moment it is not in his consciousness, and if it were proven to him that what he is occupied with does not serve this ultimate goal, he would immediately stop the activity. There are many subsidiary purposes subordinate to the ultimate purpose: when the farmer sets aside a certain time for sowing, he has to reckon with interferences which may and will occur, such as time to eat and sleep, bad weather, and darkness. The single actions of which sowing is composed—preparation of the seed, going to the field, casting the seed—likewise have their own specific goals. These subsidiary goals as well as their connections, will also continuously influence the farmer's activities and primarily his associations.[14]

---

assumed that the schizophrenic's idea may be expressed by *any* of its associated ideas. Later Bleuler indicates (p. 597) that he does not literally mean "drawn by sheer chance." We know that no such chance conditions prevail in dreams, which also have an arbitrary appearance, but rather that day-residues, censorship, condensation, etc., overdetermine and thus select the actual form of representation. It is probable that similar overde-

termination is at work in schizophrenic productions. Indeed, Jung's (363) work showed the strict determination of schizophrenic productions.

14. At this point Bleuler rises far above the associationist theory which his thinking at times appears to imply (cf. note 5, above). This paragraph is a description in non-technical language of the hierarchy of goal-presentations and anticipations with a clarity which has

Not only the goal-presentations but even our commonly used and presumably simple concepts change with the context.[15] For example, the concept water varies greatly with its context, as in chemistry, physiology, shipping, landscape, flood, power supply, and so on. Every one of these special concepts is tied to our ideas by a different thread; no healthy person thinks of soda water when a flood is sweeping his house away, nor of buoyancy when he wants to quench his thirst.

Naturally, even the narrowest concept of water is compounded of many ideas, such as liquid, vaporizable, wet, cold, and colorless. In normal people only those ideas come to the foreground which fit the context; all the others exist only potentially, or at least they recede so far into the background that we cannot demonstrate their influence.

Thus the direction of our associations is determined not by single forces but by an almost infinite manifold of influences.

All the threads of association here described may, singly or in any combination, become ineffective in the thinking of the schizophrenic.[16]

---

perhaps been equaled but probably not exceeded in the literature.

When we have succeeded in translating this statement into terms of motivational concepts such as interests and strivings, and substantiating it both empirically and theoretically, the major battle for a dynamic theory of thought-organization will have been won. Ach's (Chap. 1, above) coordination of goal-presentation, *Einstellung* and determining tendency, and Lewin's (Chap. 5, above) coordination of need-, intention-, and valence, were steps in this direction.

15. The problem of concept-formation is discussed by Bleuler in greater detail in Section VI, below. Here we want to point out only the two most general factors which can interfere with those changes of the implications of a concept which make it appropriate to its context: (a) rigid concreteness (see H. Werner, 755, pp. 267–74), which prohibits the emergence of other than certain concrete

aspects of a concept ("narrowing of the concept basis"; see Rapaport *et al.* (602, I, 406); (b) fluid diffuseness (see H. Werner, 755, pp. 275–93), which brings too many aspects of the concept to consciousness ("enlargement of the concept basis"; see Rapaport *et al.*, 602, I, 405).

16. The threads of association here referred to all pertain to the secondary process. Cf. note 11, above. In the primary process the associative links connect only ideas related to the same drive (or wish), but connect them all whether or not they have logical, conceptual, and empirical connections in terms of ordered, realistic thinking (secondary process).

The development of the secondary process from the primary has been discussed in this volume (Chaps. 14–17, above) in relation to reality-testing and to identifications arising in the earliest interpersonal relationships. The failure of successful development of these two,

A few further examples:

"Dear Mother: Today I feel better than yesterday. Actually I don't feel like writing. Still I like to write to you. . . . I would have been very glad yesterday, on Sunday, if you and Louise and I would have been allowed to go to the park together. The view from the Stephansburg is very nice. It is actually very nice in Burghoelzli. Louise wrote Burghoelzli on the last two letters, I mean on —couverts, no envelopes, I received. I, however, wrote Burghoelzli where I put the date. There are patients in Burghoelzli who say Hoelzliburg. Others call it factory. It can also be considered a sanitarium.

"I am writing on paper. The pen I use for it is from a factory called Perry & Co. The factory is in England. I am assuming that. After the name Perry Co. the city of London is scratched in; but not the city. The city of London is in England. That I know from school.[17] There I have always liked geography. My last teacher of it was Professor August A. That is a man with black eyes.

---

accentuated by subsequent difficulties in the mastery of reality and in interpersonal relationships, appears to our present knowledge to be the etiological core of schizophrenia; the breakdown of the secondary process is its consequence in the realm of thought-organization. H. S. Sullivan was the investigator most concerned with the role of interpersonal relationships in the development and decomposition of the secondary process in schizophrenia. His concept "consensual validation" issued from his studies of schizophrenia. See Sullivan (726, pp. 4–15, particularly p. 13); and (725, pp. 124–27); cf. also Cameron (120, p. 51).

17. This example displays not only the association-disorder discussed by Bleuler but also a thought-disorder of the obsessional group, usually called circumstantiality and overmeticulousness. The drive-dynamics of this disorder in obsessional neuroses and obsessional characters is fairly well known under the heading "doubt" (see Fenichel (176, pp. 297 ff.). As a disorder of thought-organization it has not, to my knowledge, been specifically investigated and is an enticing field for exploration. The phenomenon of overmeticulous circumstantiality is characterized by too many associated ideas coming to consciousness because of too little selective suppression. Cf. note 12, above. The final effect, however, is not the unselected "expectoration" of these associations, but rather the subjective experience that the central idea has not been communicated until all of its facets have been conveyed. Thus many things that usually go without saying will be explicitly communicated, and certainly anything the omission of which could possibly give rise to the slightest misunderstanding. In this schizophrenic production it is carried to absurd length: the address was on the envelope, not on the letter; "London" on the pen was only the name, not the city itself, etc. In neurotics this uncertainty of the ability to communicate often takes the form of ostentatious honesty and precision. In schizophrenics such circumstantiality frequently survives together with other obsessional features.

I like black eyes, too. There are blue and grey eyes too and yet others. I have heard it said that snakes have green eyes. All people have eyes. There are those who are blind. The blind ones are led by the arm by a boy. It must be very terrible not to see anything. There are people who do not see anything and in addition those who do not hear anything. I know a few who hear too much. One can hear too much. One can even see too much. In Burghoelzli there are many sick people. They call them patients. One of them I liked. His name is E. S. He taught me: in Burghoelzli there are four kinds, patients, inmates, attendants.—Then there are those who aren't here at all.[18] All remarkable people. . . ."

Were the writer not schizophrenic, he would report on what in his environment influences his well-being, what touches him, pleasantly or unpleasantly, or what might be of interest to the person addressed. Here such a goal is lacking; what is common to all these ideas is that they are related to the environment of the patient, but not that they have a relationship to him. In this respect this train of thought is more disorganized than those on "Horticulture" and "Epaminondas." In its details however it is more ordered. While those show continuity only occasionally, and even then only for small groups of ideas, here we find no jumps.[19] In this respect the "laws of association" remain effective

18. The statement concerning the four kinds of people at Burghoelzli is conveyed here as a piece of information or knowledge ("he taught me"). Yet the distinction between patient and inmate, and the inclusion of those "who aren't here" strike us as humorous. The formal reason probably is partly the contrast of the air of imparting information with the "facts conveyed" and partly the unexpectedness of the "facts." We skirt here the problem of the relationship between the two forms of thought-organization: humor and schizophrenic thinking. (Cf. Freud, 214; Schiller, 670.)

19. It is not so much that the lack of a goal is more conspicuous here than in "Horticulture" or "Epaminondas," but that a far more concrete goal is expected in a composition on a theme than in a letter. The more general the task, the more clearly does it reveal the pathology. This is the principle underlying all projective testing (cf. Rapaport, 594). In the letter here quoted the general goal to write about things of interest to the writer or addressee brings to the fore the stimulus-boundness (see note 107, below; also Heilbrunner, 318; Sommer, 698; and Leupoldt, 449), the literalness (see Benjamin, 43, pp. 76 ff.), and the blending of the important and unimportant (see the section on memory, pp. 608–9, below; cf. also Bleuler, 76, p. 383), so characteristic of schizophrenic thinking.

The problem which this schizophrenic patient faced and failed to cope with in his letter becomes clearer if we consider the problems consciously faced by the normal person who is preparing a report on a rich set of data. The problem is to find a manner of organization which

here. In association-experiments which exclude goal-presentations, most of these associations would be acceptable: London—teaching of geography—geography teacher—his black eyes—grey eyes—green snake eyes—human eyes—blind—terrible fate, and so on. Though the ideas expressed are with few exceptions correct, the writing remains meaningless. The patient's goal was to write, but not to write *something*.[20]

A hebephrenic wants to sign her name to a letter as usual: "B. Graf." She writes "Gra" and then a word beginning with "gr" comes to her mind; she corrects the "a" to an "o" and adds a double "s," making "Gross," and then repeats this twice. Suddenly the whole mass of ideas behind the signature becomes ineffective except the letters "Gr." The patient thus loses himself in insignificant side associations with the result that no unitary train of thought develops. This symptom has been called *thinking-aside*.[21]

---

satisfies the following requirements: (a) it includes everything indispensable and excludes most of what is dispensable; (b) it includes sufficient supplementary material to make the indispensable data clear; (c) it so organizes the materials of (a) and (b) that the development toward the conclusion be as direct as possible. It goes without saying that the number of the *possible* implications of the data and that of their *possible* explanations is infinite, and that organizing is selecting. When writing an essay we consciously and deliberately select ideas over and above the unwitting selection of associations that occurs automatically in our thought-processes. At times we have to struggle against this automatic selection in order to find a "missing link." Cf. Chap. 23, III, above. Both deliberate and unwitting selection are more or less severely encroached upon in schizophrenia.

20. Compare Angyal (30, pp. 116–17):

Relations and systems differ from each other in various respects. A relationship involves only two members, (1) the *relata*

and (2) specific connections between them. Complex relationships can always be resolved into pairs of *relata*. Systems, on the other hand, may involve an indefinite number of constituents. . . . I wish to advance the hypothesis that *the thinking of the schizophrenic patient is not impaired so far as apprehending of relationships is concerned. The schizophrenic*—when he fails in the solution of an intellectual task—*fails in the apprehension of system connections*.

"System" here is the equivalent of Gestalt.

Put in another way: if sufficient material is available concerning the thought-product of a schizophrenic (or any thought-product bearing the hallmark of the primary process), the "relationships" within it will be understandable from the point of view of the psychological reality of the subject; but its "system connections" to the whole of his thinking and to his reality will be found inadequate.

21. That these side associations are insignificant and that the developing train of thought is not unitary is true only from the point of view of logic, of

To the question, "What was your father?" a patient answers, "John Frederick." He grasps that the question is about his father but that the query concerns his father's occupation has no influence on the answer; instead he answers a supposed query about his name. In studying such cases it is usually demonstrable that the patient understood the question but was unable to produce the corresponding ideas.[22]

---

reality. Similarly only those connections become ineffective which would express logical reality-relationships. This point is further developed in Freud's (209, p. 482) statement concerning free associations:

It can be shown that we can reject only those directing ideas which are known to us, and with the cessation of these the unknown—or, as we inexactly say, unconscious—directing ideas immediately exert their influence and henceforth determine the flow of the involuntary ideas.

In schizophrenic thinking such unknown directing ideas (or forces) often take the place of conscious ones. The two differ in their modes of operation. Often we are not in a position to discover these "unconscious forces" in schizophrenic thinking; but when we do discover them they turn out to be drives and defenses pitted against each other like those drives and defenses which determine the parapraxes. (See Freud's, 210, clinical analysis and Erickson's, 161, experimental demonstration of parapraxes.) Jung's (363), and Schilder's (652) studies contain massive evidence that this is the process by which the content of schizophrenic thinking is determined; the psychiatric and psychoanalytic literature is full of contributing evidence. For excellent examples see Nunberg (541, 542). The formal characteristics of this thinking, in contrast to its content, are however insufficiently

known. In Bleuler's example the intention to write "Graf" breaks down and we get "Gross." The unconscious determining idea is better served by the latter, becoming available to consciousness through the identity of the initial letters. While the memory-schemata (Bartlett, 37) or memory-frames of reference of ordered thinking (secondary process) group together only logical and reality-related ideas, the memory-organization of drive-thinking (primary process) groups together all ideas related to the drive (or its object), even if only by such arbitrary connections as clang-associations, alliterations (Graf-Gross), punning, rhyming, incidental contiguity, affect-tone, etc. We need to learn much more about the nature of these two kinds of memory-organization.

22. In intelligence tests, particularly those of information, similar answers are often obtained from even relatively well-preserved schizophrenics. As a rule the conceptual organization of memory-frame of reference is still operating in such cases but appears loosened, and the answer gives the impression of hitting just off the mark. It is as though touching such a loosened memory-schema does not give rise to anticipations, that is to a sifting of the associations according to the reality-context. As is seen in Bleuler's example, the question readies memories but does not touch off selective anticipation. Instead the selection is made by an

[Passage omitted.] [23]

When threads of peripheral associations are severed, the associations do not become completely nonsensical; rather do they appear *strange, bizarre,* and *misplaced,* though in the main correct. Thus when Brutus is called an "Italian," only the temporal relationship implied is incorrect; it is a strange designation in that the specific concept "Roman" is replaced by the more general "Italian." The author of "The Blossoming-Time of Horticulture" answered to "Where is Egypt?" with "Between Assyria and the State of Congo." This answer, the content of which is correct, appears strange because it defines the location by reference to an African and an Asiatic country, and moreover, to an ancient and a contemporary state. The usually present spatial and temporal components of concepts have here become ineffective.[24]

[Passage omitted.] [25]

In some cases all threads of the train of thought are torn asunder; if no new associative pathways are chosen, the result is *stupor* or *blocking.* But the patient may make a nonchalant transition of no discoverable associative connection

---

affect or impulse pushing to the fore the affectively most important memory-items. In a similar but more severe disorder, the question, "Who discovered the North Pole?" elicited the answer: *Napoleon.* In this case the memory-schema is still looser, and thus the memories readied are of the broad realm, *important names.* The selective principle operates here entirely as the *pars pro toto* mechanism of the primary process, according to which any part may stand for the whole. So does Napoleon stand for the important name sought. In many cases specific factors determine the choice from among the "important names." Another example from intelligence-testing material is on the order of Graf-*Gross*: "What is the *Apo*crypha?" —"An *apo*thecary." Here the memory-frame of reference chosen is determined by the word-sound without reference to its meaning; it is a clang-schema in which

similar sounding words are grouped. The abruptness of schizophrenic associations increases with the looseness of the frames of reference, until in the extreme case the organization of memories becomes purely that of drives.

23. The omitted section contains further examples.

24. The temporal and spatial determination of ideas may also be readily conceived in terms of memory-schemata (Bartlett, 37; cf. also Freud, 209, pp. 487 ff., and Chap. 16, note 6, above). Thus the connections Brutus-Italian, Assyria-Egypt-Congo, would be due to a loosening of the temporal and spatial memory frames-of-reference. Apparently this loosening is related to the loosening of the concept basis discussed in notes 15 and 22, above.

25. The omitted section contains further examples.

between the abandoned and the new ideas.[26] In the following fragment of an "autobiography" such leaps are marked by two slanted lines; some, but not all, can be explained by external distractions.

"One has to have gotten up at the right time, then one has the necessary 'appetite' for it. 'L'appetit vient en mangeant' says the French—//. In time and in years man becomes so comfortable in public life that he can't even write any more.—On such a sheet of paper one can put very many letters if one is very careful not to get over the edge by a 'square shoe.' // In such beautiful weather one should be able to walk in the forest. Naturally not alone but with Avec! [27*] // Always at the end of the year the books are closed.// Only now is the sun up in the sky and it is not yet more than 10:00 o'clock.—In Burghoelzli too?—That I do not know because I don't have a watch with me like I used to!—. Apres le manger 'On vap . . . !' There are entertainments good enough for people who do not belong and never belonged in this insane asylum. To do mischief with human flesh is not permitted in 'Switzerland!!' // La foi das Heu, l'herb the grass, morder = bite, etc., etc., etcetera, and so forth!— R. . . . K. . . .—At any rate enough 'material' from Zurich comes to the Burghoelzli, otherwise we wouldn't have to stay in bed until this one or that one

26. The problem of blocking is discussed by Bleuler below. In the example that follows, the train of thought is strikingly "torn asunder" and without "discoverable associative connection." This impression leads Bleuler to assume a "splitting" or "loosening" of associations as the primary and basic symptom of an organic process underlying schizophrenia. To answer Jung's (361) critique of his study on negativism Bleuler (67, pp. 477–78) wrote:

My conception of the psychological mechanisms that play a role [in schizophrenia] is essentially identical with Jung's, though, naturally, I did not emphasize this. The difference is only that I postulate a primary [organic] disorder. It is reflected in the association disorder and makes the extreme effects of complexes possible. In contrast to this, Jung believes that the pathological role of complexes [in schizophrenia] is due to the general disposition of the patient. Consequently in Jung's opinion the effect of complexes, in mine the [organic] primary disorder is what is specific to schizophrenia. According to Jung the cause and symptoms of schizophrenia are more or less fully explained by the effects of complexes; according to us, symptoms and complex-effects are all co-determined by a primary brain disorder.

That Bleuler did indeed consider his views on the "psychological mechanisms" to be essentially identical with Jung's will become clear in his argument below against blindly accepting that schizophrenic thinking is "torn asunder." See note 35, below.

27.* Avec, French for with; that is, with a girl (slang).

pleases to say *who is responsible that we can't go outdoors.* ○ ∧⋮∨ // *1000 tons* //
Appendages on acorns!!!!. . . ."

In the usual speech and writing [of schizophrenics] pure examples of this strange severance of the threads of association are rare since this severance usually occurs together with other disorders. In acute conditions this disturbance can be so far-reaching that only exceptionally can a thought be traced through several steps; in such cases we speak of *dissociative thinking* [28]* and *incoherence.* The condition itself is referred to as "confusion." [29] At times only the manner of expression is unclear, so that logical transitions may at least be surmised; it is then difficult to tell with certainty whether or not the train of thought underlying the deviant connection is completely disrupted.

[Passage omitted.] [30]

Thus for instance a rejoinder is often only formally an answer, and its content has nothing to do with the question.

A patient who is supposed to help in the housekeeping is asked why she doesn't work; her answer, "But I don't know French," has no logical relation either to the situation or to the question.

Sometimes the gaps are bridged by grammatical forms giving the illusion of a connection, that is, ideas which do not belong together are connected to make a sentence; the example, "But I do not know French" is an answer in its form but not in its content. Another example is the following answer to a greeting: "This is the watch of the little Jew as regards in Daniel." Or, let us take the above-mentioned autobiography: "At any rate enough material comes from Zurich to the Burghoelzli, otherwise we wouldn't have to stay in bed. . . ." A new idea, staying in bed, is put in a form that makes it appear a proof for what preceded it.[31]

28.* See Ziehen (786).

29. For a further discussion of "confusion" see Sections IV and V, below.

30. The omitted part contains two further examples.

31. The example, "But I don't know French," sheds light on the others. We do not know why this patient chose French for the grammatical object of her sentence, but there can be little doubt that she means to convey: "I haven't got what it takes," or more simply: "I can't." The anticipation that prepared the patient's answer is effective to some extent and is communicated to that extent. We do not know whether it is the selectiveness of the anticipation which is impaired, preventing its pene-

To summarize:

The innumerable actual and latent ideas which determine associations in normal trains of ideas may be rendered, singly or in any combination, ineffective in schizophrenia.[32] *In turn, ideas may come into play that have little or no connection to the main idea, and should have been excluded from the train of thought.*[33] *Thereby thinking is rendered incoherent, bizarre, incorrect, and*

---

tration to the reality-adequate one of all the "I can'ts" which are in readiness, or whether the loosening of the conceptual frame of reference from which the grammatical object has to be chosen is responsible for the reply. We need make no decision as between impairment of anticipation and loosening of frame of reference—the two are descriptions of the same phenomenon from different points of view. (Cf. Rapaport *et al.*, 602, I, 385–89, and II, 16–24.) In the second example, "otherwise we would not have to stay in bed," the anticipation is so ineffective that we see it only in a faint trace—the word "otherwise." The third example, "this is the watch . . ." shows no trace of the anticipation.

Thus Bleuler's assertion that the grammatical forms give only the "illusion of a connection" is not generally valid: they usually represent an anticipation. But the anticipations are not effectively expressed: the idea that would logically fulfill the anticipation is replaced by associated ideas of such tenuous connection that they impressed Bleuler as "torn asunder." Cf., with "distant reactions," Rapaport *et al.* (602, II, 28–31). If Jung, per contra, insisted that such thinking can be fully explained by "complex-effects," his insistence—though laudably motivated by enthusiasm for psychodynamics and thoroughgoing psychic determinism—was premature. Complex effects alone can explain only the con-

tent, for example, the relation of "French" to "I can't." The *formal characteristics* of the operation of these complexes in the thinking of schizophrenics, such as the role of anticipations and memory-frames of reference, is not explained by the demonstration that the content of this thinking is determined by complexes. Nor do such demonstrations give a causal explanation of the "torn asunder" character of schizophrenic associations which so impressed Bleuler. Actually, the major part of exploring the *how* of these complex-effects is yet to be accomplished.

32. These are probably the phenomena that impressed Goldstein as similar to those seen in organic cases. However, he did not account for all the other phenomena Bleuler discusses below. Goldstein's conception is that the adherence to concrete attitudes and inability to assume abstract attitudes are the fundament of both schizophrenic and organic psychopathology. (Goldstein, 280, pp. 23 ff.; also Bolles and Goldstein, 80; Goldstein, 282.) Benjamin's (43) concept "literalness" has a similar implication, though he also observed other aspects—even diametrically opposite ones—of schizophrenic thinking. Compare also the concepts "close reactions" (602, II, 24–28), and "narrowing of the concept basis" (602, I, 405–6), and "loss of distance" (602, II, 329 ff.).

33. These phenomena seem to be the

abrupt. At times all threads fail, and the train of thought is arrested; after such blocking, ideas lacking any recognizable connection to previous ones may emerge.

Only in certain cases of stupor does thinking cease altogether. . . .

The emergence of an idea totally unrelated to the train of thought or to an extraneous sensation is, despite Swoboda's [34]* contrary views, something so foreign to normal psychology that we are obliged to seek connecting associative pathways between even the ideas which appear to us most remote, from each other and the preceding thoughts or percepts. Though not always, such pathways are sufficiently often demonstrable to indicate some of the major directions such derailments take.[35]

---

same as those referred to by Cameron's concepts "overinclusion" (120, pp. 56–57; also Cameron, 119 and 122) and "ineffectual generalization" (120, pp. 58–59; and 122), Benjamin's "overabstraction" and "false abstraction" (43, p. 85), and Domarus's "identification of subjects from identity of predicables" (146, p. 112; and 147). Cf. also the concepts "loosening of the concept basis" (602, I, 405–6), and "increase of distance" (602, II, 329 ff.).

34.* Swoboda (727).

35. Here Bleuler indeed takes the point of view of Jung (cf. note 26, above), or rather that of psychoanalysis. Observation shows him that when the usual associations are absent, "associative pathways connecting even the ideas which appear to us most remote from each other" are often demonstrable. He even explores, below, the directions (formal characteristics) of these unusual associative pathways or, as he calls them, "derailments." But he does not concede that there are *always* such connections; for him organic severance of associations is a more acceptable working hypothesis than laws, yet to be found, by which the "torn asunder" character of schizo-

phrenic associations could be made psychologically comprehensible. From a heuristic point of view the two hypotheses are equally justified. The heuristic advantage of Bleuler's view was that it led to the search for the "basic symptom," and through it to the most extensive description of the phenomena of schizophrenic thought-disorder. Its shortcomings are shown by the following: (a) he did not succeed in bringing the phenomena he described into a unitary system of relationships; and (b) it has been shown by Ferenczi and Hollos (187) and by Schilder (641) that organic damage does not destroy the intrinsic unity and causal network of the psychic apparatus, does not "sever associations," but manifests itself in the reactions of the psychic apparatus to the damage. Against the psychoanalytic view the following arguments may be marshaled: (a) Jung's (363) and Abraham's (8) version of this view, according to which schizophrenic thinking is due to the effect of complexes, gave a necessary but not a sufficient explanation and failed to offer evidence against Bleuler's claim that complexes can explain only some of the content but not the fundamental causes

Even when only some of the association threads are severed, logical directives are replaced by influences which would be in abeyance under normal conditions. As far as we know, these influences are also responsible for the new connections made after thinking has been completely disrupted: incidental thoughts, condensations, clang associations, indirect associations, and perseverations (stereotypy). In the normal psyche such thought-connections, though not absent, are rare and unimportant; [36] but in schizophrenia they are exaggerated to the point of caricature and often completely dominate the train of thought.[37]

[*Contiguity.*] Frequently, *two ideas which have no internal connection will simultaneously occupy the patient and thus become connected.*[38] The logical

---

of schizophrenic thinking; (b) the Freudian version (see notes 6, 7, and 16, above) was not sufficiently specific to schizophrenia. The arguments in favor of the psychoanalytic view are these: (a) by insisting on thoroughgoing psychological determinism (particularly in Freud's version), it kept open heuristic avenues which Bleuler had closed; (b) it did come to a dynamic formulation of the etiology of schizophrenia (for a discussion of this see note 60, below); and (c) its concepts of "primary" and "secondary process" are good working concepts for the study of schizophrenic thinking, even if (and perhaps because) they are not specific to it.

36. Bleuler knew from experience and from Stransky's (719) experiment that the influences replacing logical directives in schizophrenia are not absent in the normal psyche; in his studies on autism (for example, Chap. 20, pp. 404–5, above) he called them "affective influences." Yet the different aspects of the schizophrenic thought-disorganization, autism, affect disorders, and association disorders remain independent factors in his conception. Bleuler was disinclined to settle the problem with one sharply

cast set of concepts; his concept of autism also shows this disinclination to a decisive conceptual formulation.

Freud, on the contrary, created a sharply cast dichotomous set of concepts to encompass influences which replace logical directives in schizophrenia, dreams, neuroses, etc.: primary and secondary process, pleasure- and reality-principle, conscious and unconscious, dream mechanisms and logic. We have only begun to appreciate the clarity, flexibility, and merits for all psychological research of this conceptual system.

37. In the following section Bleuler enumerates the major directions of "derailment," in other words, the influences replacing logical directives in schizophrenia. Some of these are obviously equivalents of dream-mechanisms or understandable in their terms, but some have not yet been explained and are not known to be explainable in terms of Freudian mechanisms.

38. Freud (209, pp. 531–32) describes how the dream uses loose superficial associations "disdained by serious thinking" and also tolerates contradictory thoughts "as though no contradiction existed between them." But he demon-

form of this connection will depend upon the prevailing circumstances: should he be asked something, the patient will give the idea just then in his mind as an answer; should he look for a cause he will simply link causally the ideas then in his mind. If his self-esteem is pathologically exaggerated, or if, on the contrary, he has feelings of inferiority, he will relate any new idea to himself in terms of these affect-toned complexes.[39]

Thus, for one patient a comb in a picture was "a wash-thing," because it appeared beside a wash basin; and a bug he called a "bug bird," because he had been shown a bird just before.[40]

---

strates that between these "obnoxious" associations there exists an essential though hidden relationship, in that both of the ideas connected by the superficial (for example, contiguous) association are representatives of the same striving, wish, or drive; an idea replaces another by virtue of such association when the new idea is less directly related to the wish and thus "conceals" it from censorship more effectively. He also shows that the wish can be reconstructed by means of free associations to the dream material. The demonstration of a similar state of affairs in schizophrenic thinking was the merit of Jung's (363) monograph.

39. This procedure of the patient may have three different roots: (a) the intention to answer or to find a cause is carried out, but the answer or cause given may not seem relevant because its *expression* is not in terms of secondary-process logic but in terms of a primary-process mechanism (for example, substitution, symbolism, etc.); (b) question and answer, cause and effect, do not have a logical *relationship*, but are connected by a link psychologically legitimate only in the primary process (for example, "post hoc propter hoc," "pars pro toto," etc.); (c) the "answer" or "cause" is relevant to a preceding intrapsychic ex-

perience and not to the question. In the latter two cases such pseudo-logical linkage plays a role similar to that of "secondary elaboration" in dreams, carried out by the awakening consciousness on the manifest dream-material.

40. Such examples as these cannot be understood solely as complex-effects (Jung) or effects of Freudian mechanisms. The formal characteristics of such thinking and the state of consciousness in which they occur, as well as the cathectic dynamics underlying these (cf. Chap. 9, notes 12, 32, 78, 93, above) will have to be taken into consideration if we are to understand them. This problem parallels that of symbolism, for which Jones found repression a sufficient explanation, while Silberer maintained that the prerequisite of symbolization is a state of consciousness characterized by apperceptive weakness—whether or not it results from affect or repression. The state of consciousness of schizophrenics and its underlying cathectic dynamics have scarcely been studied even by psychoanalysis, which otherwise made rich contributions to the understanding of the etiology and thought-content of schizophrenia. The state of consciousness of schizophrenics and the dynamics of attention-cathexes which this state im-

Why didn't you talk for such a long while? "I was angry." What about?
"One wants to go to the toilet, looks for paper, and has none." (Abraham.)
Here the first idea that comes along serves as the explanation. The wife of a
schizophrenic teacher lost a key; on the same day a Doctor N. visited the school;
therefore, Doctor N. has an affair with the teacher's wife.

It is quite common for patients to give an accidental idea as a reply. Therefore, if the question is put to them repeatedly they will contradict themselves
every time. Dawson's [41]* hebephrenic patient who had jumped into the water
explained his action variously as follows: he does not believe in the future and
does not expect to better himself; he belongs to the lower class of people and
must make place for the upper; he was poisoned; he did it because of religious
depression.[42]

At times both of the connected ideas derive from external circumstances or
directly from the current train of thought: How are you? "Bad" (laughs).
But you look well, you are all right (I tap the patient on the back). "No, I have
pains in my back." (Points to the place I tapped). Why do you laugh? "Be-

---

plies are a segment of ego-psychology.

Pre-analytic psychiatric investigators
of schizophrenia seem to have been
aware of the need to study the state of
consciousness and the function of attention in schizophrenics, but they lacked
the necessary concepts. E. Weigert
(752, p. 192) wrote about their efforts:

Among the psychiatrists too, we frequently find the failure of the "synthetic
functions" of the Ego mentioned in a descriptive sense as an essential factor in
dementia praecox: Wernicke speaks of a
"disintegration of the individuality," "insufficiency of the real personality"; Gross,
of a "disintegration of consciousness";
Vogt, of a "restriction of consciousness";
Janet, of "abaissement du niveau mental";
Minkowski, of "la perte du contact vital";
Berze, of "an insufficiency of psychical
activity" and "hypotonia of consciousness." These psychiatrists find the basic
disturbance (toxically or constitutionally
determined) that underlies schizophrenia

in an insufficiency of the actual, present-
day conscious personality, which should
comprise in a single integral entity the
whole of the realized potentialities of the
individual.

We might add from Jung's (363) summary that Sommer, Tschisch, Freusberg,
and Masselon spoke of a "diminution of
attention"; Kraepelin, Aschaffenburg,
and Ziehen of a "disturbance of attention."

41.* Dawson (137).

42. Bleuler describes here another important phenomenon of schizophrenic
thinking. His emphasis, however, is on
the manifest contradictions of the explanation and not on its "overdetermination." (See Freud, 205, p. 213; and 204,
p. 117.) To look into these "contradictions" would not obscure but rather help
to elucidate the motivation of the patient.
(Cf. Freud, 209, p. 330.)

cause you are emptying the chest of drawers." But you already laughed before that. "Because the things were still in it."

Most frequently, the connections refer to matters which affectively preoccupy the patient.[43]

It is an everyday occurrence that patients soil or tear their clothes "because they aren't allowed to go home." To the word *ship*, a patient associates: "The good Lord is the ship of the desert." The good Lord, who is often mentioned by him and who is the center of his pathological interest in religion, is put before the given word, and then the phrase is completed by words that belong to an entirely different train of thought. To the word *wood*, a girl associates: "That my cousin Max be alive again"; the patient uses the concept "wooden coffin," which played a role in her unhappy love affair, to connect the stimulus word with her complex.[44]

Clang-associations [45] are also frequent. . . . In *"ink"*—"fiddle" the clang quality is hardly noticeable to normals. . . . If, however, one gets the association *"but"*—"boots," and then *"battle"*—"that's beauty," the investigator who is familiar only with the associations of manics and normals will look for other connections of "boot" and "beauty" besides their mere assonance. Yet hundreds of such combinations have taught us that beyond doubt, the sameness, or mere similarity of single sounds, suffices to codetermine the direction of associations [in schizophrenics].

[Passage omitted.] [46]

Naturally, similarity of sound cannot alone determine an association. In the

43. Affectively motivated reactions are likely to belong to the variety of response discussed in note 39, above, under (c); but if the cue (for example, a question) already touches on the affect, the reaction may be of the varieties (a) or (b).

44. In this example Bleuler—apparently familiar with the patient's story—applies the method Jung and Freud used for the explanation of apparently disconnected associations. The linkage here is the familiar "pars pro toto" mechanism (a part representing the whole) of the primary process. There is no evidence that sufficient familiarity with any schizophrenic patient would yield a similar explanation of the content of *all* his thought-products. In regard to the theory and varieties of such disconnected associations, compare Rapaport et al. (602, II, 20–24, 28–31, 63–68, 229–66).

45. Freud (209, p. 531) wrote that in the primary process "assonances and punning associations are treated as equal in value to any other association." Cf. Rapaport et al. (602, II, 25, 41, 61–62).

46. The omitted section contains further examples of clang associations.

association "*but*"—"boots," and then "beauty," the assonance is but one of many determinants. There are hundreds of other words that begin with "b," so why just "beauty"?

In the case of "*ink*"—"fiddle," one of the determining circumstances was known: the patient had sexual thoughts which gained undisguised expression in some of his associations. In our dialect "fiddle" [47] is used mostly in the obscene sense rather than as a musical instrument. The same influence is demonstrable in other associations of the same patient as well as in those of other patients. Clang and sexuality as directives are so frequent in schizophrenics that inevitably they also appear in combination with each other. . . . The complex-determined mis-hearing of words is also very common, as for instance in delusions of persecution.

However, even these two influences do not completely determine an association. There certainly are many other words which have both a similar sound and a sexual meaning. The selection, then, must be determined by yet other factors which, in the main, elude us.[48]

[*Phrase-completion.*] Schizophrenics quite inappropriately complete sentences so as to make standard phrases. This kind of connection plays a role similar to that of clang-associations. A patient, about to tell of a walk she took with her family, began to enumerate the family members: "Father, Son," but she continued "and the Holy Ghost," and added even, "the Holy Virgin," showing that this familiar phrase threw her off completely.[49]

47. "Fiddle" translates *Geige;* the dialect in question is Swiss-German.

48. Here Bleuler takes overdetermination into consideration. Freud's view of these "other factors which elude us" is the following:

. . . with the abandonment of the conscious-directing ideas the control over the flow of ideas is transferred to the concealed directing ideas; . . . superficial associations are only a displacement substitute for suppressed and more profound ones (209, pp. 484–85).

49. These "phrase completions" are in principle associations by contiguity. Cf. Rapaport *et al.* (602, II, 25, 62–63).

A psychoanalytic explanation would assume that in the subject's mind there is a connection between "father, son," and "the Holy Ghost" other than their occurrence in the religious phrase. More concretely, it would be assumed that the meaning for the patient of "father, son" is of a character more consonant with "Holy Ghost" than with, say, "went for a walk."

However, when Bleuler says, "this familiar phrase threw her off completely," he seems to imply an hypothesis other than the above-stated psychoanalytic assumption, namely, that "perseveration" alone determines this associa-

Condensation, which is the fusion of many ideas into one, is not in principle different from association by chance connections.[50] This process was partly responsible for the thought "The Lord is the ship of the desert," in that it fused two things belonging to different complexes of ideas into one thought. A

tion: the patient cannot leave a phrase once started until it is completed. (Cf. Mueller and Pilzecker, 528.) But even extreme forms of such perseverations have been successfully interpreted psychoanalytically; complexes and affects have been shown to enforce phrase-completion or perseverative repetition of phrases (Jung, 363). Yet Bleuler implies that this is not always the case, that at times the content of the perseverating phrase is irrelevant, and that then the perseveration is due to the primary (organically caused) association-disorder. In fact, he assumes that even perseverations based on complex-effects could not come about without this primary disorder. (Cf. Bleuler, 67.) There is a cogent argument against this last point: such "perseverations" also occur in dreams and in waking states called "distractions" (cf. Stransky, 719). Thus Bleuler's argument could apply only to the explanation of the important role such "perseverations" play in schizophrenia, and particularly to those instances which cannot be shown to be complex-effects.

But even these phenomena can be explained otherwise than by the assumption of an organically caused primary association disorder. The psychological (non-organic) explanation of "perseveration" need not in every case be a specific complex, just as not every symbol needs to be explained by a repressed idea or drive. For certain states of consciousness (for example, hypnagogic) indirect pictorial representation is the character-

istic form of thought, a fact which facilitates the emergence of repressed ideas. Cf. note 40, above. There is evidence to support the assumption that the cathectic conditions in schizophrenia lead to an altered state of consciousness in which the formal characteristics of thought are those illustrated by Bleuler in these pages. Though these formal characteristics of schizophrenic thinking facilitate the expression of drives, affects, wishes, "complexes" in the content of thought, they are an aspect of schizophrenic thinking different from the drive-determination of its content.

Though all thinking arises ultimately from drive-dynamics, in conscious ordered thinking we recognize a new emergent organization with laws of its own. Similarly, the above-stated assumptions would recognize schizophrenic states of consciousness as emergent organization with new formal characteristics of thought. These states of consciousness would have a different relation to drive-dynamics than does normal waking consciousness; the forms of thought corresponding to them are known to show similarity to primary-process, primitive-, and dream-thought.

These assumptions may prove to be more fruitful working hypotheses in exploring schizophrenic thinking than those we have had so far.

50. See Freud's discussion of condensation (209, pp. 320-36; and 214, pp. 748-50). That condensation is not merely a matter of "association by chance connection" is indicated in

catatonic gave the reaction *"sail"*—"steamsail," a fusion of the two ideas "steam-boat" and "sailboat." Condensation plays an important role in the formation of delusions and symbols; it is also the basis of many neologisms: "sarrible" for "sad" and "terrible," and "waicillable" composed of waivering, vacillating, and unstable.

Indirect associations are surprisingly abundant in experimental investigations. I suspect that only the shortcomings of our observations prevent us from seeing them more often in the everyday thought-processes of patients. The above mentioned "wood"—(wood coffin)—"dead cousin" may be considered an indirect association. So are: *"heart"*—(heartwood)—"pinetree"; "shoe"—(shoe-horn)—"trumpet"; *"cook"*—(Cook Agency)—"travel," and so on.[51] Reis found indirect associations in reading experiments on the memory drum: in-

---

Freud's discussion of the cathectic dynamics of dreams (209, p. 467):

This product, the dream, has above all to be withdrawn from the censorship, and to this end the dream-work makes use of the *displacement of psychic intensities,* even to the transvaluation of all psychic values; thoughts must be exclusively or predominantly reproduced in the material of visual and acoustic memory-traces, and from this requirement there proceeds the *regard of the dream-work for representability,* which it satisfies by fresh displacements. Greater intensities have (probably) to be produced than are at the disposal of the night dream-thoughts, and this purpose is served by the extensive *condensation* to which the constituents of the dream-thoughts are subjected.

51. The Word Association Test studies by Schafer (634) and Rapaport *et al.* (602) suggest that the usual anticipation in standard Association Test situations is to react with a conceptually *coordinate* word (table-chair). Some obsessional cases consciously observe the process of arriving at such reactions and, if generalization from these cases is permissible, the process may be described as follows. A series of associations arise dissecting the concept, as it were, into its components (thus, to "table," leg, top, wood, iron, high, low) including functional as well as abstract components (to work on, to eat on, manufactured, furniture) and experiential connotations (my table, table as symbol of the family, examination table, work-table). Each of these components and connotations may branch out further; for instance, "work-table" into the ideas authority, slavery, livelihood, etc. Then in normals, at some point in the course of these associations the decomposition stops due to the anticipation of "a coordinate concept," and a synthesis of elements begins. The process may be short-circuited in the form of blocking, perseveration, or reaction by a concrete adjective ("close reaction") or may become rambling and never be finished, yielding an indirect association ("distant reaction"). The effectiveness of anticipations is in both cases impaired. If effective, the anticipation yields reactions which give the impression of "logical" acceptability. Cf. notes 32 and 33, above.

stead of "war," "quarrel," and instead of "beast," "horse" was read.[52] Here the primary perception does not even reach consciousness; yet it determines the new association.[53] Gross [54]* called attention to the fact that patients may react to a simple question with an idea that is an association to the answer.[55]

Inclination to stereotypy [56] is another frequent cause of derailment. The patient cannot get away from a realm of ideas, or certain words or phrases, or else keeps returning to these for no logical reason. Busch found in apperception experiments instances in which false reactions were the repetition of preceding stimuli.[57] In association experiments schizophrenic patients often hold on to the first stimulus- or reaction-word: *Star*—"That is the highest blessing"; *to stroke*—"That is perfection"; *magnificent*—"His will"; *child*—"of God"; *dark red*—"heaven and earth." The word "star" brings a religious idea to mind, which is then elaborated in the subsequent reactions with utter disregard for the further stimulus words. The first two reactions also show a stereotypy of form which is present in the majority of this patient's associations. . . .

Stereotypies may be stable over long periods. We have observed a few cases in which after a four-week interval 40 percent of the stimulus words elicited the same responses as before. Thus, one patient reacted to the word "so" with the incomprehensible "that is a canal." It turned out that originally she gave that reaction to the word "*sea*." [58] . . . In the pseudo-flight-of-ideas of acutely confused schizophrenics a constant return to what they previously said is quite common.

The inclination to stereotypy in connection with a lack of purpose in thinking may lead to "sticky thinking," *a sort of perseveration*, or to a general *paucity of thinking*. Thus some patients forever talk of one and the same theme (*mono-*

52. It may be questioned whether these are indirect associations in the same sense as the preceding examples.

53. Cf. Bruner (96, 97, 100), Poetzl (573), and Allers (21).

54.* Quoted by Stransky (719) [p. 1077].

55. Cf. note 39, above, particularly (a).

56. Bleuler indicates below that stereotypy shades into perseveration. What was said about perseveration holds for stereotypy (cf. note 49, above). Many stereotypes can be understood in terms of a compelling complex, affect, or drive; others may necessitate assuming a specific state of consciousness.

57. Cf. "close reactions" (602, II, 27–28, 67).

58. Cf. Rapaport *et al.* (602, II, 33–35), on the great stability and exactness of the reproduction of associative reactions.

ideism) and are unable to enter a conversation about anything else.[59] There may be a connection between this purposeless stereotypy and the fact that patients often reach a point where they do not think through anything completely, and senseless associating takes the place of thinking. A hebephrenic patient who could not get away from the concepts "love" and "have" spontaneously associated series like: "love, dove, shove, have, hove, love, dove, dame, shove, came back, came back, came back, have. . . ." In this fashion patients often fall into enumerations which again clearly reflect the schizophrenic association-disorder; for example, a patient wrote: "The heavens stand not only above the parson's house in Wil, but also over America, South Africa, Mexico, McKinley, Australia."

At times such associating sheds light on an idea from every possible angle: "I wish you then a good, happy, joyful, healthy, blessed and fruitful year, and many good wine-years to come, as well as a healthy and good apple-year, and sauerkraut and cabbage and squash and seed-year. A good egg-year and also a good cheese-year," and so forth. A patient wrote to her daughter who had embraced Catholicism that the rosary is a "*prayermultiplication* and that is *a multiplicationprayer*, which is nothing else than a *prayermill*, which again is a *millprayermachine*, which in turn is a *prayermachinemill*," and so on for two folio pages.[60]

59. Though the extreme form of this phenomenon is certainly characteristic of schizophrenics, its milder forms are rather commonly seen in so-called normal people. Its most common form is the "talk about the weather" among "polite people." "Shop talk" is a not much less common form. The one-sided emptiness of the conversation of rigid people also belongs to these phenomena. The paucity of ideas that besieges a great many people in a tense situation is probably also related. (The possible objection that in normal people—in contrast to schizophrenics—there are other thoughts present while these "safe" topics are repetitively discussed, is a matter of emphasis.) It seems probable that Sullivan's (725) theory of schizophrenia as a disorder of interpersonal relations has issued from such observations. It is also probable that the exploration of human inter-communication will shed considerable light on certain aspects of the schizophrenic thought-disorder.

60. This manner of dealing with words reaches its acme in neologisms. Some neologisms have been demonstrated to be condensations (for example, "woocide"; see 602, II, 42), while others have resisted such explanation. If we assume that these latter cannot be accounted for by Freudian mechanisms or by Bleuler's primary (organic) association-disorder, and ask ourselves what is known about the schizophrenic state of

In association experiments patients often react by calling the name of anything they see. Thus, they will react to most diverse stimuli with the names of the furniture in the room. Even if they understand thoroughly the nature of

consciousness that could account for this manner of handling words—our attention is attracted to Freud's observations and theorizing concerning the role of words in schizophrenia.

In order to clarify this point, it seems necessary to recall Freud's view of psychoses in general, and schizophrenia in particular.

Freud wrote:

Neurosis is a conflict between the Ego and its Id, whereas psychosis is the analogous outcome of a similar disturbance in the relation between the Ego and its environment (outer world) (pp. 250–51). . . . The pathogenic effect [of the conflict] depends on whether the Ego remains true in its allegiance to the outer world and endeavors to subjugate the Id [as in neurosis] or whether it allows itself to be overwhelmed by the Id and thus torn away from reality [as in psychosis] (p. 253).

The course of psychosis is described by him as follows (245, pp. 278–79):

Now one might expect that when a psychosis breaks out, something analogous to the process in a neurosis happens, though of course between different institutions in the mind; that is, two steps may be discernible in a psychosis also, the first of which tears the Ego away from reality, while the second tries to make good the damage done and reestablish the relation to reality at the expense of the Id. And something of the kind can really be observed in a psychosis; there are indeed two stages in it, the second of which bears the character of a reparation—but then the analogy gives way to a far more extensive similarity in the two processes. The second step in a psychosis is also an attempt to make good the loss of reality, not, however, at the expense of a restriction laid on the Id—but in another, a more lordly manner, by creating a new reality which is no longer open to objections like that which has been forsaken.

Freud (245, p. 280) in the same paper, and later Garma (263), Fenichel (176), and others recognized that reality is not entirely abandoned, the id is not completely victorious, and a psychosis is also a compromise, though of a different kind from neurosis.

Freud saw that some of the cardinal problems of psychosis, which as will be seen below, are of particular importance for schizophrenia, had not even been tackled (246, p. 254):

. . . what [is] that mechanism analogous to repression . . . by which the Ego severs itself from the outer world. This is not to be answered, in my opinion, without fresh investigations, but, like repression, the content of this mechanism must include a withdrawal of the cathexes emanating from the Ego.

The process of withdrawal from reality or loss of object-cathexis is described by Freud in his paper, "The Unconscious" (234). There he maintains that our ideas consist of two components: "the idea of the word" and "the idea of the thing." The former is the preconscious, the latter the unconscious idea (see Chap. 15, note 32, above). Becoming conscious depends upon a hypercathexis, joining the id-cathected unconscious idea with the preconscious idea (see Chap. 15, note 21, and Chap. 23, note 9*, 10*, above). Repression is due to the

the association experiment and are trying to get away from such reactions, they may not be able to do so.[61]

This symptom has a superficial, and occasionally also an intrinsic similarity to what Sommer calls *naming* and *touching*. In some patients, particularly those who are perplexed, the only recognizable associations to outside impressions consist in *naming* them, as "mirror," "table," or designating them by a sentence, as "that is a barometer," "that is a gas-pipe," "these are coats." [62*] Naming is not limited to visual impressions. For example, I take hold of a patient's hand,

---

withdrawal of this hypercathexis, and to its use as countercathexis (see Chap. 15, note 21, above) to insure that the unconscious idea will not become conscious. In schizophrenia the loss of object-cathexis consists in the withdrawal of id-cathexis from the unconscious "idea of the thing." At the same time the preconscious verbal ideas assume the role of objects. They obtain drive-cathexes and become subject to the mechanisms of the primary process. Freud suggests that this occurs as the first step of the restitution process, and writes (234, p. 136):

These endeavors [at restitution] are directed towards regaining the lost objects, and it may well be that to achieve this purpose their path to the object must be by way of the word belonging to it; they then have, however, to content themselves with words in the place of things.

Indeed schizophrenic neologisms and "theorizing" do give an impression corresponding to this Freudian conception. Yet we do not know whether this process is generally valid for schizophrenic thinking, or that it gives an exclusive explanation of its phenomena. On the one hand, schizophrenic hallucinatory and delusional reconstructions of the world use other means in addition to cathecting verbal ideas. On the other hand, obsessionals with their notorious "libidiniza-

tion" (drive-cathecting) of thinking do proceed in the manner Freud describes for schizophrenics. Yet without some such assumption the schizophrenic's use of words is beyond our understanding. Cf. Katan (373, pp. 355–56). Since consciousness is a function of cathectic dynamics, the above-described alteration of the cathectic dynamics in schizophrenia may offer a basis for assuming an altered state of consciousness in schizophrenics.

61. These reactions are equivalents of those associative reactions which repeat the stimulus-word, since in neither is a relevant thought-process initiated. (See note 51, above.) Thus both of these are "close reactions" par excellence. Compare Bleuler's following examples with "close reactions" of the "definition" variety (602, II, 25), and note that none of these "close reactions" are limited to schizophrenics. In general, experience with tests shows that the distribution of most association-disorders is rather continuous from normals, to neurotics, to psychotics, though it often reaches its maximum in schizophrenics.

62.* Some authors consider these motor anomalies; for example, Kleist (388, 389) calls them "short-circuit acts."

whereupon she says "la mano" (she is German). When asked to do something, she designates it with a cue-word: "in the garden," "undress." Similarly, patients' hallucinations will often name what they are doing: "now he sits down," "now he will write," "now he writes." [63] There is a fluid transition from this naming to the letters discussed above which simply enumerate things and events around the patient. The patient who reported what was written on the pen is not unlike those given to naming, nor is the one who saw a lantern and remarked: "I declare that that is a lantern." What these cases have in common is that in the absence of a goal-presentation they fasten on a sensory impression. Such patients grasp any internally or externally given idea and connect further ones to it. What these further ideas will be and in what direction they will lie is highly variable and chance-determined, as for example in the case of our letter-writing patient.

What Leupoldt describes as "touching" [64*] is quite similar: the patients move their fingers over the outlines of objects within their reach. Naming is here replaced by the gliding movement of the fingers. [65]

Sometimes the patient's only discoverable association to what he sees and

63. These phenomena, even though their formal similarity to "naming" is correctly stated by Bleuler, have been shown by Freud (231), Tausk (728), and Schilder (665), to be related to superego function in schizophrenics. Fenichel (176, p. 430), wrote:

The projection of the Superego is most clearly seen in ideas of reference and of being influenced. The patient feels that he is being controlled, observed, influenced, criticized, called upon to give an account of himself, and punished. The voices he hears utter criticisms of him. . . . Or the voices prove that they are observing the patient by commenting on what he is doing while he is doing it. "Now he is eating, now he is sitting down, now he is getting up."

Whether there is any intrinsic connection between the naming and the hallucinatory projection aspects of these examples we have yet to learn.

64.* Wernicke's (761) hyper-meta-morphotic movements.

65. Next Bleuler discusses "touching" and symptoms of "echopraxia" and "echolalia." There seems to be some evidence that these are "phenomena of restitution." (See Fenichel, 176, pp. 437–39.) The conception is that by tactually ascertaining the presence of the object and thus "introjecting" it (identifying with it) through imitation, the patient attempts to regain the world of objects from which he has withdrawn. Bleuler's grouping together of "naming" with these symptoms gains added significance if we remember that "naming" seems to be related to the schizophrenic's manner of dealing with words, which Freud considered also to be an attempt at restitution of the lost world of objects.

hears is imitation: "echopraxia" and "echolalia" (command-automatism). I am unable to separate, in principle, the phenomena of echopraxia and naming. All ideas have a motor component; this is clearly seen even in normals, in their ideas of both actions seen and words heard. When no other associations come into play, this motor component will of course not be suppressed. A pertinent example: a patient had knocked out a door panel; now another patient keeps crawling in and out the hole without any reason for doing so.[66]

[Passage omitted.] [67]

In most productions of severe cases of schizophrenia various characteristics of the schizophrenic train of thought coexist.

"I have never yet been in Hamburg, never yet in Luebeck, never yet in

66. An explanation of these symptoms either as restitution phenomena, or as the emergence of the motor component of ideas when other associations fail, seems incomplete from the point of view of a theory of thinking. "Naming," for example, cannot be completely explained by "content" and "purpose," but its understanding requires an assumption as to its cathectic dynamics. The psychology of motor processes is a field of such obscurity that Schilder (see Chap. 25, IId, above) was inclined to consider motor, iterative, and echopractic symptoms to be of organic (strio-pallidary) origin. A cue—even though vague—to the understanding of Bleuler's last example may be gained from those patients who explain this type of behavior by stating that they understood the event that initiated their repetitive behavior *to refer to themselves*. Thus the symptom can be described either as "objects easily obtain valence for the patient" (Lewin), or as "inclination to self-reference." Both formulations refer to the elimination of the normally sharp boundaries between the self and the outside world. It is likely that this change is connected with changes in cathectic dynamics, reality-testing and state of consciousness (see note 60, above).

The symptoms here discussed are related to the phenomena of "pattern coherence" (Rapaport *et al.*, 602, I, pp. 257 ff.) and "concrete behavior" (Goldstein, 280 and 282).

These, however, are merely tentative formulations. Even in normal motor behavior (expression of affect, symptomatic arts, habituated behavior), where the ego controls motility, there is much we do not understand. (Cf. Hartmann, Chap. 19, I, above; Rapaport *et al.*, 602, I, 249–53, 254–59, 271–75, 288–91.) The schizophrenic's control of motility is a virgin field for exploration.

67. The section here omitted pertains to attention; I have taken the liberty to transfer it to that section. Bleuler discussed attention here because according to him the "sticking," "perseverating" character of associations displays the diametrical opposite of impaired attention, namely, lack of distractibility. It is as though in these cases the cathectic charge of attention, once deployed, could not change its position.

Bern,[68*] I have never yet seen professor Hilty; I have never yet been at the University of Basel; I have never yet seen Luther, never yet had luetter,[69*] but I have already seen all the federal representatives; I am going to General Herzog, I shall show that ass. . . ."

Here the negation persists through seven thoughts. The naming of places is not systematic. There is a leap from Luebeck to Bern.[68*] The latter reminds the patient of a professor at the University of Bern; this mediates the transition to the "University of Basel." This university plays a role in the history of the Reformation, hence the association "Luther," followed by the quite senseless clang-association "luetter" which, however, is meant by the patient in the customary sense as the change of verb shows. The "federal representatives" are again connected with Bern; from these it is not entirely illogical, even if queer, to think of the long-dead General Herzog; and this in turn leads to the sense-less idea that the patient wants to see him. The concept "General" is connected with the idea of "power" or the like; hence the next senseless thought "I will show that ass . . ." indicating that the idea of "power" is associated, in the well-known manner of schizophrenics, to the patient himself who thus ap-pears to himself stronger than the general.

The train of ideas of the following letter is hardly amenable to such analysis: it seems to be incoherent, "confused" chatter. Knowledge of the patient's affect-toned complexes would no doubt help explain a great deal.

Burghoelzli, Nov. 20, 1905

Esteemed family Fridoeri and family Graf or Ears Schmidli.

Here in the Smith-house all isn't well. Here is no church, no parish house, not poorhouse but all year around there is noise, tumble, huckleberries-suns-rumbling heavens; some big and little farmer, humble-bee, Surbeck, Armtrunk, from Thalweil, Adlisweil, von Albis from Sulz, von Seen, von Rorbach, von Rorbas left his house, never came back, a butcherboy, Siegrist, farmer singers, and a farm-manager, Jakob the sacristan, old, younger Swiss soldiers, Ernest from Ernest, who cut off two of his fingers in the year 1900 month August, as

68.* Perhaps a clang-association to Bremen [which, in an enumeration, would usually follow the other two harbor cities].

69.* Colloquial for diarrhea.

his father Konrad and wife demised. Because the silk reel-men and women are tempted daily to murder visits, for they wait so long, till the patients scramble out, nor is there good milk, wattles, nurses are not different either fools capsuleresses who bore through one's heart, enough of the knitters of underskirts, underjackets, socks, of the day, must make unrest even at night to the heavens and earth-guests. . . .

Regards to all who are still alive.

Anna

[Passage omitted from the letter.]

Thus severe schizophrenic association-disorders lead to total *confusion.*

Confusion must not be considered a symptom *sui generis;* it is the result of various primary psychological disorders that become so overwhelming as to result in the loss of meaning-connections for the patient, or the observer, or both. Manic flight-of-ideas of high degree, which must be carefully distinguished from schizophrenic disorders of thought, also leads to confusion. Even inhibitions in depressions may result in confusion if slowness of thinking and inability to connect things make orientation in complex ideas and their mastery impossible. Hallucinations may also lead to confusion if they mix with percepts and thereby confound the picture of the world.

Thus, in schizophrenia confusion may be the result of various factors: decomposition of ideas, blocking coupled with emerging new ideas, suppression of single association-determinants coupled with the appearance of side-associations, "pressure of ideas" (see below), real flight of ideas, hallucinations, or even of several of these factors together.[70]

70. We know little about the quasi-stationary schizophrenic state of confusion. The natural avenue for its exploration leads through the study of those transitory confusional episodes, both momentary and more prolonged, so frequent in conditions prodromal to overt schizophrenic breaks. But there has been no systematic study of these either. Sporadic clinical reports indicate that it may be questioned whether "consciousness" in the usual sense is present in these states.

It is possible that confusion is an agglomeration and exacerbation of familiar schizophrenic thought-disorders. Traces of cohesiveness, that is, traces of the secondary process are as a rule still present in schizophrenic thought. The ability to reflect and the intent to communicate somehow persist even where the communication concerns the internal and not the external reality of the patient. In confusional states neither reflective consciousness nor intent to commu-

II. THE COURSE OF ASSOCIATIONS

We know next to nothing about the temporal aspect of the schizophrenic association-processes. It may well be that they are not characteristic. In intervening manic episodes we of course do see a "speed-up" as in flight of ideas, and in depressive episodes we do see a slowdown; we may assume that there is also a slowdown in those states of stupor which may be regarded as exacerbations of schizophrenic brain-processes. But these are episodes or complications, and not lasting states.

Even though it is rarely seen in "burned-out" cases, the *pressure of ideas* will often last for years. Some patients complain that they must think too much because the ideas chase each other in their minds. They speak of a "rush of ideas" because they cannot hold on to any idea, or of a "pressure of thought" because too much occurs to them at once. At times, however, the observer will gain the impression that while the patient complains of too many thoughts, actually he has too few.[71] Nevertheless it is a fact that some patients have a pathological pressure of thought. The patients experience this as a compulsion. Often they believe that someone makes them think in this fashion [72] and com-

---

nicate seem to remain. Thus, even though in the confusional state we recognize massed and exaggerated schizophrenic thought-disorders, we must also be prepared for the possibility of finding this state a *qualitatively* new condition, perhaps an altered state of consciousness.

71. From my experience both with patients and with normals I infer that in these conditions much goes through the mind, but not in the form of shaped "thoughts"; it is the stuff that may develop into thoughts. Here we deal with vague elusive formations which are hard to capture, even when they appear singly, and harder or impossible if they come in droves. It is as though one had lost the curtain that mercifully hides most internal happenings from observation. When this occurs in schizophrenia we gain the impression that conscious-

ness—which is the supraordinate sense-organ of perception and the sense-organ of internal perception—is no longer partitioned from the former and not shielded from the latter. Its ability to bend back upon itself is lost, its ability to separate wish from reality suffers, and it becomes a slave to external impressions. Now all external impressions relate to it, as though they were not its experiences but simply parts of it. It is similarly helpless against internal impulses, any of which can command its cathexis.

72. Such experiences appear to be variants of the normal and usual act of reflective self-observation (cf. note 128). In contrast to normal self-observation reflection here experiences its subject-matter as alien. It is only through such variants that we can hope to learn about

plain of the tiredness it causes. When pressure of thought is not experienced as a compulsion, it is accompanied by a sense of great accomplishment. Pressure of thought appears to be the opposite of blocking, of arrest of thought, which we will discuss below. Yet the two often occur together: one of our educated patients drew a line, indicating that to one side of it there was a "compulsive pressure of various thoughts" while to the other "simply nothing."

The content of such pressure of thought is like that of schizophrenic thinking in general. A "theologian" laughed all night long at "etymological jokes" that kept coming to his mind: "I am a joke—a hoax—a Hobbes."

This phenomenon was well described by an intelligent patient of Forel. Note that she observed the recurrence of ideas: "In my head ran a clockwork [73] of a compelling, tormenting, endless chain of ideas. They were of course not sharply formed or clearly worked out, but idea followed idea by the most amazing associations, and yet there was a connection between the parts. There was a system to it; for example, I had to distinguish constantly between the good and bad side of the things, people, acts, and expressions that came to mind. Oh, did I have a welter of ideas! What funny associations! I always came back to certain concepts and ideas, but I can hardly remember them all any more. For example, Droit de France! Tamins! Barbera! Rohan! They were stages, so to speak, in the thought-chase. I would quickly say the word, the slogan we might say, at which the breathless chase of thoughts had just arrived. I did this particularly at certain times of the day—as on entering the hall, when the door of my room was opened, at mealtime, when someone approached me, etc.—

---

the nature of introspection. These can also be observed in those states of consciousness which are transitions between waking- and dream-consciousness. They are characterized by the kind and extent of reflection possible and by the related extent of deliberate voluntary directing of ideas that can occur.

73. A patient I observed also described the experience of "pressure of thought" with the "clockwork" analogy, with the variation that "this clockwork has no controls; the spring has nothing to restrain it." Are these experiences related to an impairment of the "delay" function which is the prerequisite of reality-testing and ordered thought? See Chap. 15, note 29, above. Are they due to a failure of those selection-processes which, in the form of "sets" (*Einstellungen*) or "anticipations," suppress the preparatory associations that occur in the course of thought-development and make for the emergence of task- and goal- (*Aufgabe*) adequate ideas, that is, ordered logical thought? No definitive answer to these questions is as yet available. But these concepts at least permit the formulation of questions about these phenomena.

in order not to lose the thread, as it were, or to hold on to something in the mad rush of thoughts that closed in over my head." [74]

Blocking is the most striking formal characteristic of the schizophrenic thought-process. At times associations come to a sudden halt; when they are resumed, the new ideas are in no way, or only tenuously, connected with the preceding ones. One speaks to a patient; at first there seems to be nothing wrong with his train of thought; the give-and-take of the conversation is normal. Suddenly, in the midst of a sentence or at a transition to a new idea, the patient blocks and cannot go on. He may overcome the obstacle by a new try; or he may succeed only by shifting to a new direction of thought; but the blocking may also persist and then spread to the entire psyche, leaving the patient mute, motionless, and more or less devoid of thought.

Kraepelin's concept of "blocking" is of fundamental import for the symptomatology and recognition of schizophrenia. Blocking may occur in motility, action, memory, and even perception. It is in principle different from *inhibition*,[75] the latter being a common symptom in severe depressive mood-disorders. Inhibited thinking and action take place slowly, with difficulty, and with an unusually great expenditure of psychic energy. In inhibition, the psychological process moves like a viscous liquid in a system of tubes which is passable throughout; in blocking, an easy-moving liquid is suddenly stopped by the closing of a valve. Or, if we compare the psychic mechanism to a clockwork,

74. This description allows us a glimpse at one of the reasons why schizophrenic verbalization appears so utterly incomprehensible and "torn asunder." The occasion for verbalization is often merely a disturbance forcing the patient to verbalize in an attempt to hold on to the thread of his thoughts. It is comparable to the following situation: a bookkeeper is adding a long column of numbers; someone comes and speaks to him; he lifts his head and quickly says a number unrelated to the question and returns to his column. He was distracted and uttered his last sum to remember it and warn the disturber. We understand the bookkeeper because we see his figures. The schizophrenic's "ledger" is not before us, and we are prone not to take cognizance of his involvement, the more so since the schizophrenic's verbalization rarely explains his preoccupation to our satisfaction, and when he is asked about it the distraction is likely to make him "lose count." Normal people know this experience from the interruption of their musings and daydreams.

75. "Inhibition" translates *Hemmung*. Here Bleuler uses the term for what we now call "psychomotor retardation." The term "inhibition" is now most commonly used to denote the effects of repression. Cf. Freud (252). The mutual relationships of blocking, psychomotor retardation, inhibition, and repression, however, still need clarification.

inhibition corresponds to a high degree of friction, blocking to a sudden stop.[76] In the motor field, the difference is often easily demonstrable: when a patient who moves little or not at all and whose speech is slow and weak is asked to move his hands around each other as fast as he can or to count quickly up to ten, the inhibited patient will slowly turn and will count with great difficulty, while the blocked patient will do these things as fast as any normal—once the blocking is overcome.[77]

The patients themselves notice the blocking and describe it in various ways. Often, but not always, they find it unpleasant. An intelligent catatonic had to sit for hours "to find her thought again." Another could say only, "At times I can talk, at times I cannot." One patient "becomes dead" (Abraham),[78*] another has "obstacles" of thought, a third becomes "stiff in the head as if it were tightened up." One felt that "a rubber sack was suddenly pulled over him." A farmer's wife said, "It is shoved against me like a whole cart-load (making a gesture as if something advanced against her chest); it is as if one's mouth were held tight, as if one were told, 'shut up.' "[79] This example also describes the blocking of the motor speech-function, which a patient of Rust [80*] described as "my speech is being held fast." Patients frequently ascribe blocking to foreign influences. Thus, a patient is asked to sing; suddenly he cannot go on, and his voices tell him, "See, now you have forgotten it again"; he believes that those who spoke made him forget it.[81]

76. The actual state of affairs seems more complex than Bleuler's presentation would suggest, though he hints below, that the "sudden blocking" may be: (a) a genuine "deprivation" of thought subjectively experienced as a void: (b) inability to hold and communicate psychic contents because of pressure or indistinctness of thought; (c) a refusal or fear to communicate contents, resulting in their fading away.

77. Today we know that the state of affairs is also more complicated in the motor field. First of all, some forms of catatonic blocking bear the character of monotonous machine-like slowness. Secondly, as Escalona (166) has demonstrated, depressive retardation has at least two variants: action and decision retardation. The former uniformly slows down movement, while the latter prolongs its initial phases and may repeatedly interrupt it. Investigation in this area has hardly begun; it is a broad field for the application of the methods of decision-time studies. Cf. Cartwright (124) and (125).

78.* Abraham (10).

79. This seems to be an example of blocking due to overstimulation ("cart-load"). Perhaps this experience is comparable to that of normal people who find themselves speechless and blank upon realizing how much they would have to convey to someone to make real communication possible.

80.* Rust (627).

81. Cf. notes 63 and 72, above.

The best description of this was given by Jung's [82]* patient: he described it subjectively as "I am deprived of my thoughts." The phrase is so fitting that many schizophrenics understand it at once. If to the question, "Are you ever deprived of your thoughts?" the patient promptly answers in the affirmative or even describes the phenomenon, the diagnosis is fairly certainly schizophrenia. At least we have found no exception to this.[83] Even patients who use a different expression for blocking understand this phrase. Jung asked a patient whether he is ever deprived of thoughts and got the prompt answer: "So you call it being deprived of thoughts. I have always called it thought-constipation." One of Kraepelin's patients spoke of "being robbed of his thoughts."

Blocking seems extremely arbitrary, both to the observer and the patient. At one moment the patient can talk and move freely, but in the next he is blocked in speech *and* motility. On closer inspection, however, we usually find the reason for the blocking in the meaning which the blocked train of thought has for the patient. Conversely, in patients whom one does not know well one can infer from the blocking that an important complex has been touched upon.[84]

We are interviewing a girl. She gives a good chronology of her past. Suddenly she cannot go on. We keep asking what happened next but get nothing more. Much later, by way of a detour, she blurts out that she met her lover at that time. A teacher who had put all his energy into getting a salary raise was asked whether he got it. He answered: "What is a salary raise?" He could not understand the expression because the complex centering in salary was blocked.

82.* Jung (363).

83. Compare, however, the consistent presence of this experience in the dream-states Abraham (6) reports. This feature common to hysterical dream-states and schizophrenic blocking may be only apparent. Yet it suggests that the relationships of the states of consciousness of these two conditions to those of fugues, somnambulisms, amnesias, etc., need to be restudied, the more so since fugues (see Stengel, 708) and amnesias (see Geleerd *et al.*, 266) also occur in schizophrenic disorders. Cf. Rapaport (591, Chap. VII, "Psychopathology of Memory").

84. Bleuler here again takes a psychoanalytic, or Jungian, point of view, although his reservations are apparent in the "usually." Indeed, an explanation of blocking by the content is *not* always feasible. Actually we encounter cases where blocking is a quasi-stationary generalized characteristic of behavior and thinking and does not seem to be elicited by touching upon a specific complex. In such cases a stabilized state of consciousness with a salient characteristic of blocking would be a more plausible explanation than that of a massing of complex-effects.

Many patients ask to see the physician on an urgent matter, but when they come, they have nothing to say.

[Passage omitted.] [85]

Blocking is not always absolute and unconquerable; continued questioning and stimulation of various kinds,[86]* especially distraction, may often overcome or circumvent it.[87] Such procedures, however, may arouse negative reactions; one patient was actually frightened after having answered, as if she had done something wrong.

The patient's will, or at least his wish, may play a role in the blocking. A hebephrenic called the symptom-complex of blocking (connected with delusions and other pathological formations) "the post-marker"; he often switched it on when asked to do work he did not like. At such times he was "shut in" and nothing could be elicited from him. Of course, the gamut of transitions runs from behavior such as this, through conscious unwillingness, to all forms of simulation. Similarly, the boundary between blocking and *negativism* is vague, both theoretically and symptomatically.[88] The two phenomena may

---

85. The omitted section contains further examples.

86.* Sometimes alcohol will resolve blocking; therefore it can be used to facilitate examination.

87. The use of barbiturates and other drugs for this purpose is a commonplace in our days. Cf. Horsley (339), Berrington (56), Brenman and Gill (88), Grinker (293). Theoretical conclusions as to the nature of blocking have never been systematically inferred from the experience with these drugs; compare, however, Gill (271) on the synthetic function of the ego in spontaneous hypnotic regression, and Grinker (292) for some general orientation in this problem.

88. Bleuler (77) interprets negativism as follows:

In ordinary *external negativism*, which consists in the negation of external influence (for example, command) and of what one would normally expect the patient to do (for example, defecation in the bed instead of the toilet) the following causes are at work:

(a) The autistic withdrawal of the patient into his fantasies, which makes every influence acting from without an intolerable interruption. This appears to be the most important factor. In severe cases it is alone sufficient to produce negativism.

(b) The existence of a trauma (negative complex, unfulfilled wish) which must be protected from contacts.

(c) The misunderstanding of the surroundings and their purpose.

(d) Direct hostile relations to the surroundings.

(e) The pathological irritability of the schizophrenic.

(f) Pressure and other difficulties of action and thought, through which every reaction becomes painful.

(g) Sexuality, with its ambivalent feeling-tones, is also often one of the roots of negativistic reaction.

Inner negativism (contrary tendency opposed to the will, and intellectually opposed to the correct thoughts) is largely accounted for by ambitendency and am-

shade into each other, and passive negativism may even be explained by a combination of blockings.

The blocking of one patient was very similar to negativism: she gave slow, halting, and faint answers, and would even lose her voice, especially when closely questioned. This could be circumvented by addressing her indirectly. In some cases it is impossible to determine whether one deals with blocking or negativism, especially when the patient avoids the obstacle by giving answers that just miss the point. For example, one patient was asked in many different forms to give the date of her hospitalization. She answered variously as follows: in an ambulance, Sister L. brought me, I have been here three days and long nights, and so on (she had come the previous day).[89]

Partial blocking may come about in various ways. Speech may be blocked, but the thought can still be expressed by gestures. I have found that in these cases the thought-process stops when the patient resorts to pantomine to end the sentence. What one of Jung's patients called "fascination" is another kind of partial blocking. Some sense-impression blocks thinking completely, and then only this sense-impression remains in consciousness. Sommer's [90]* "optical fascination" probably refers in part to the same symptom.[91]

---

bivalency, which in view of the inner splitting of the thought explains the slight preference for the negativistic reaction. Very pronounced phenomena of inner negativism probably have other contributing causes, which at the present time we do not know.

In criticizing Bleuler's theory, Jung (361, p. 475) concludes:

Psychoanalysis demonstrates that the source of negativism is resistance originating in a specific course of sexual development, in schizophrenia as well as in other neuroses.

This conclusion is vague and non-specific.

Bleuler's paper (77) and rebuttal (67) are unsystematic, and though they display sympathy for some psychoanalytic ideas, they reveal fundamental lack of understanding of psychoanalysis. Yet, entirely devoid of doctrinaire axe-grinding and thus free to be unsystematic, they reflect richly the infinite complexity of the problem of schizophrenia. Jung (361) and Abraham (8)—but not Freud, see (237, p. 150, note)—preferred doctrinaire simplicity to facing this still insoluble problem.

89. This example is probably neither blocking nor negativism, but "loosened memory-frame of reference" (cf. notes 21, 22 and 31), as a result of which ideas associated with hospitalization come to consciousness, but the specific idea called for does not. This is not very different from what teachers observe in their pupils, and scientists in their colleagues' writings: an incompletely digested idea is hard to express and appears in an obscure form clouded by relevant and partially relevant associations.

90.* Sommer (698).

91. Partial blocking, "fascination,"

The experimental associations[92] in the chronic stages of mild cases are, as far as we know, often undisturbed. But we usually do find peculiarities which, though insufficient for a diagnosis, are suggestive of the disorder, such as:

1) Great irregularity of reaction times not explained by feeling-toned complexes. The reaction-time differences are far greater than in complexes of normals, and remarkable changes from very slow to very quick associations occur in the same experiment. One is tempted to ascribe these to fluctuations of cooperativeness, or at least to fluctuations of attention; but often no other indications of such fluctuations are to be found. In acute cases the reactions tend to slow down progressively in the course of the experiment.[93]

2) The tendency to return to earlier stimulus- or reaction-words is also striking. This effect of an earlier thought need not be uninterrupted: the patient may get away from the thought but return to it in a later association. . . . Sequences of perseverations are, however, more common.[94]

3) The after-effect of previous thoughts may also appear as a stereotypy of form or content: towards the end of the experiment some patients, especially those acutely ill, will answer only with few and quite senseless expressions, previously correctly used, such as "for eating," "for writing," "for thinking," and so on. Paucity of ideas will naturally favor such behavior.[95]

4) Sometimes the patient will hang onto the stimulus-word and repeat it as the reaction-word without associating to it another thought. This kind of *echolalia* occurs more in acute (perplexed) states than in chronic ones.[96]

5) Even where repetition of the stimulus is infrequent, a great paucity of ideas may become obvious. Though he does not perseverate with the stimulus-word, the patient will stick to similar and closely allied ideas.[97]

6) Schizophrenics have many individual reactions (Kent and Rosanoff).[98*] When the same stimulus words are represented after long intervals, the reac-

---

and the possibility of overcoming blocking by an indirect approach, indicate that blocking has many variants, the relationships of which are yet to be explored. Cf. note 84, above.

92. Cf. Jung (365).

93. Cf. Rapaport *et al.* (602, II, 17, 48, 51–57).

94. Cf. (602, II, 27–28, 41, 67).

95. Cf. "definitions" in (602, II, 40, 67, 69).

96. Cf. "repetition reaction" (602, II, 41, 61, 67, 69).

97. Cf. "close reaction" (602, II, 21, 24–28, 41, 59 ff., 67, 82).

98.* Kent and Rosanoff (380).

tions of schizophrenics vary more than those of normals [99] (Pfeffinger).[100*]

7) The most striking phenomenon is bizarre and seemingly or actually incoherent associations, in which the stimulus-word serves only as a signal for uttering any word.[101]

8) The search for connections between such associations is often fruitless, even when the patient cooperates. In these cases we usually, if not always, deal with the influence of a feeling-toned idea-complex which has been alerted. When I say "alerted" I do not mean "alerted in consciousness," since the patient is not aware of it. Thus, a still very intelligent patient with a quite well-ordered front reacted with the word "short" whenever a stimulus-word touched on his feelings. He did not know why, yet the explanation was simple: he was very short and the word "short" was an important part of his complexes.[102]

9) A strong tendency to give indirect associations is frequently observed.[103]

10) The indicators of feeling-toned complexes may become quite exaggerated. The reaction time on complex-connected stimulus-words may become extremely long or the reaction may fail to appear at all. All the other complex-indicators which Jung [104] found may become very pronounced: superficial associations with long reaction times, quotations, reactions in a foreign language, quick forgetting, and intellectual and affective influencing of subsequent associations. In some cases the complexes are so alerted that the patient will associate only to them. However, all these signs vary greatly, not only from patient to patient, but even in the same individual: they may change within a short time from a maximum to a minimum.

The need to appear intelligent (intelligence-complex) leads, as it does in imbeciles, to giving definitions, the bizarreness of which often bears the hallmark of schizophrenia: *eye*—"sightpoint," *grandmother*—"generation-share," *oven*—"warming item."

Diligent search failed to reveal indicators of *negativism* in experimental associations. Only in two patients did we find an inclination to associations by negation and contrast, but these two happened not to be negativistic patients.[105]

99. Cf. "reproduction disturbance" (602, II, 33–35, 42, 49, 70–75).

100.* Pfeffinger (555).

101. Cf. "distant reaction" (602, II, 28–31, 63–65).

102. Cf. (602, II, 15–16, 35).

103. See note 101, above.

104. Jung (365).

105. My experience shows (though I have no systematic data) that associa-

The association-disorders here described are characteristic of schizophrenia. Besides these, *other anomalies of the train of thought also occur*. Manic episodes in schizophrenia show a flight of ideas superimposed on the schizophrenic association-disorder. In depressive episodes we find thought-inhibition and association-disorders due to pathological reactions to affects: hysteric-like systematic repression often becomes dominant.[106] Obsessional thoughts are frequent.[107]

---

tions by negation and contrast are suggestive of relatively well-preserved paranoid cases. Such cases need not clinically show any obvious and striking negativistic symptoms.

106. This is true for symptoms of schizophrenia in general. Cf. (708) and (266) on schizophrenic amnesias and fugues. I have also seen major conversion symptoms (such as functional paralysis of the legs) in schizophrenic psychoses, apparently not described in the literature. It is possible that some of the major hysterias and hysterical psychoses of the past would today be diagnosed schizophrenia. For the characteristics of repressive, hysteric-like organization of thought, see Rapaport (591, Chap. VII).

107. We have already (note 17, above) pointed to one similarity between obsessional and schizophrenic thinking. The close relationship of the two becomes more obvious if one keeps in mind: the schizophrenics' way of handling words and objects (see note 60, above) and the relation of obsessions to magical thinking (see Freud, 227, pp. 865–83, on "Autism, Magic, and Omnipotence of Thought," particularly p. 874). The close similarity of these relationships to those described by Piaget (557) and Werner (755) indicates the genetic background of these pathological phenomena.

The close relationship between ob-

sessional and schizophrenic thinking is clarified in Freud's discussions quoted below. In both conditions there is a withdrawal of cathexis from objects; in obsessionals, thinking itself becomes drive-cathected, while in schizophrenics it appears that the drive-cathexes become attached to the verbal ideas. These two processes seem to shade into one another. It should be noted that the term "libidinization" in the first quotation is equivalent to "drive-cathecting," and that the dangers of philosophizing described in the second are inherent to all obsessional thinking.

Concerning obsessional thinking Freud (220, pp. 379–81) wrote:

The first kind of regression, that from acting to thinking, is facilitated by another factor concerned in the production of the neurosis. The histories of obsessional patients almost invariably reveal an early development and premature repression of the sexual instinct of looking and knowing (the scoptophilic and epistemophilic instinct). . . .

. . . Where the epistemophilic instinct is a preponderating feature in the constitution of an obsessional patient, brooding [ruminating] becomes the principal symptom of the neurosis. The thought-process itself becomes sexualized, for the sexual pleasure which is normally attached to the content of thought becomes shifted on to the act of thinking itself, and the gratification derived from reaching the conclusion of a line of thought is experienced as a *sexual* gratification. In the various forms of obsessional neurosis in which the epistemophilic instinct plays a part, its relation to thought-processes makes it particularly well adapted to attract the energy which is vainly endeavoring to make its way forward into action, and divert it into the sphere of thought, where there is a possibility of its obtaining pleasurable gratification of another sort. In this way, with the help of the epistemophilic instinct, the substitutive act may in its turn be replaced by preparatory acts of thought. But procrastination [delay] in action is soon replaced by dilatoriness in thought, and eventually the whole process, together with all its peculiarities, is transferred into the new sphere. . . .

. . . A thought-process is obsessive or compulsive when, in consequence of an inhibition (due to a conflict of opposing impulses) at the motor end of the psychical system, it is undertaken with an expenditure of energy which (as regards both quality and quantity) is normally reserved for actions alone; or, in other words, an *obsessive or compulsive thought is one whose function it is to represent an act regressively.* No one, I think, will question my assumption that processes of thought are ordinarily conducted (on grounds of economy) with smaller displacements of energy, probably at a higher level, than are acts intended to discharge an affect or to modify the external world.

Concerning schizophrenic thinking Freud (234, pp. 135-36) wrote:

If, in schizophrenia, this flight consists in withdrawal of instinctual cathexis from those points which represent the unconscious idea of the object, it may seem strange that that part of the same idea which belongs to the system Pcs—the verbal ideas corresponding to it—should, on the contrary, undergo a more intense cathexis. We might rather expect that the verbal idea, being the preconscious part,

would have to sustain the first impact of the repression and that it would be wholly insusceptible of cathexis after the repression had proceeded as far as the unconscious concrete ideas. This is certainly difficult to understand. The solution suggests itself that the cathexis of the verbal idea is not part of the act of repression, but represents the first of the attempts at recovery or cure which so conspicuously dominate the clinical picture of schizophrenia. These endeavors are directed toward regaining the lost objects, and it may well be that to achieve this purpose their path to the object must be by way of the word belonging to it; they then have, however, to content themselves with words in the place of things. . . . When we think in abstractions there is a danger that we may neglect the relations of words to unconscious concrete ideas, and it must be confessed that the expression and content of our philosophizing begins to acquire an unwelcome resemblance to the schizophrenic's way of thinking. We may, on the other hand, attempt a characterization of the schizophrenic's mode of thought by saying that he treats concrete things as though they were abstract.

Regrettably, there seems to be no systematic treatment of obsessional thinking available in the literature. The pertinent material is usually buried in clinical discussions (see for example, Straus, 720). Fenichel's (176) summary of our present understanding of obsessional thinking, derived from clinical observations, is instructive. He emphasizes the drive-cathecting of both thinking and words in obsessionals. We may compare this with Freud's emphasis on the cathexis of words in schizophrenia.

Fenichel wrote (176, pp. 295-96):

The regression toward anal sadism and the continuous conflict with the Superego influence the thinking processes of the compulsion neurotic in a characteristic way: they become permeated or replaced by their archaic forerunners.

In contrast to the visual daydream of the hysteric, the fantasies of the compulsion neurotic are verbalized and bring back the archaic attitudes that accompanied the first use of words.

The Ego's function of judgment by anticipation is immensely facilitated by the acquisition of *words*. The creation of this replica of the real world makes it possible to calculate and act out in advance in this "model world" before real action is taken. . . . The macrocosm of real things outside is reflected in the microcosm of thing representatives inside . . . [which] are "possessions"; that is, they are mastered by the Ego; they are an attempt to endow the things with "Ego quality" for the purpose of achieving mastery over them. He who knows a word for a thing, masters the thing. This is the core of the "magic of names" which plays an important part in magic in general. . . .

The compulsion neurotic, being afraid of his emotions, is afraid of the things that arouse them. He flees from the macrocosm of things to the microcosm of words. Being afraid of the world, he tries to repeat the process by which, as an infant, he learned to master the frightening aspects of the world. This time, however, under the pressure of warded-off impulses, the attempt fails. When he tries to flee from the emotion-arousing things to the sober words, what has been warded off comes back and the sober words do not remain "sober" but become emotionally overcathected; they acquire that emotional value which things have for other persons.

The first words acquired in infancy are magical and "omnipotent" because the microcosm is not yet differentiated enough from the macrocosm but still has its emotional value. Blessing and cursing are expressions of the still effective macrocosmic quality of words. . . . In compulsion neurosis, thinking and talking have become substitutes for the emotions connected with reality; they regain their original

qualities, become "sexualized" and lose their value for practical use. Words once more become powerful blessings or curses.

The characteristics of obsessional thinking thus far discussed in these pages are the following:

(a) Libidinization, that is, drive-cathecting of the thought and particularly the word, results in their taking on pleasure-function and omnipotence.

(b) The coming into consciousness of many associations related to an impulse or task, with concomitant difficulty and doubt in selecting the task-appropriate one, leading to vacillation, overmeticulous circumstantiality, and excessive partially relevant and irrelevant verbiage. Cf. this with Schilder, Chap. 25, I, c, and III, d, above, and Buerger-Prinz and Kaila, Chap. 27, IV, below, on "certainty experience."

(c) The tendency to operate with words and abstractions as if they were objects and not object-representations, resulting in losing touch with reality and submergence in speculation.

Obsessive thinking has several other salient features:

1) Isolation of thinking (see Freud, 252; A. Freud, 201; and Fenichel, 178) from impulses and affects results in a striving for a closed, objective, and cool logical system in all thinking, with the result that thinking becomes schematic, sterile, piecemeal, pedantic-overexact, and unproductive. These characteristics of obsessive-compulsive thought-organization are not necessarily pathological.

2) The isolation of affect and idea may result in the emergence of obsessional ideas. In this case the affect so isolated is either displaced or repressed, while the idea corresponding to it enters consciousness as an obsessional (overvalent) idea and is experienced as ego-

This description of association disturbances is incomplete in that the acute states are little considered. In these, however, no new qualitative characteristics, but only exaggerations of those described have so far been found.[108]

---

alien (involuntary, foreign, and compulsory). As long as the condition remains neurotic the obsessional idea is ego-alien, but it takes on a delusional, ego-syntonic form when the condition shades into psychosis. Thus, on the one hand, isolation of the irrational-affective element renders thinking devoid of its flexibility and productiveness; on the other hand, when this isolation produces obsessions, thinking becomes drive-cathected and omnipotent, that is, even more irrational than thinking not isolated from affects.

3) The process of isolation results in various degrees of loss of the distinction between the important and unimportant in the hierarchy of meaning; as a result, distinctions such as liked and disliked, interesting and uninteresting, significant and insignificant are blurred or eliminated. But these distinctions are essential guides and cues in learning and orientation.

By courtesy of Dr. H. P. Eddy I shall quote an obsessional patient he studied:

I couldn't take any short cuts in learning. I had to break each new item of information down into its most basic parts and compare each of the parts with all of the other basic pieces of information in my memory. Then I had to try variations. By the time the knowledge was actually assimilated I really knew it cold. I had sufficient capacity to do all this in a relatively short time during my early training, but as the things I learned became more complex and there was less class time allotted to discussion and the amount of previously learned material grew greater, it began taking longer and longer to complete my work, and I could not bear to part with my A plus, plus, plus, plus standards.

When this case was presented at the staff conference of the Riggs Foundation, the following comment was made:

There is no important or unimportant thing that stands out for this patient. Therefore, the only way he can learn something is to get a lot of relationships to clarify and anchor it. He has lost the process by which we do 99% of our learning. We don't, as a rule, learn by cramming or analyzing; we learn things because we are impressed by them. He wasn't; he had to break down everything into its elements and compare them with elements of other knowledge until everything fitted into a mosaic. When the material became complex this procedure was too cumbersome; he was no longer able to hold the mosaic together. At that point he had to give up. This is a consequence of a lack of hierarchic organization, which takes the form of a leveling of meaning, with the result that nothing stands out. . . .

4) Drive-cathecting of thinking may be either libidinous or aggressive. The consequences of this may be either: (a) excessive accumulation of information and "intellectualizing"; or, (b) secondarily, repressive defense measures may be applied, resulting in an inhibition of intellectual activity, learning and productivity (cf. E. G. Liss, 478, 479).

This is neither a systematic nor a complete coverage of the nature and form-varieties of obsessional thinking, which is a rich and relatively unexplored field of the pathology and organization of thinking.

108. This statement no longer holds. The acute and prodromal schizophrenic conditions show a rich variety of thought-disorders not considered by

I find it a serious shortcoming that we deduce most of our knowledge of these disorders from oral and written expressions of patients. Their complex acts are undoubtedly the outcome of the very thought-processes discussed so far.[109] All that we have done about these has been to question patients about the motives of their actions. Even less were we concerned with associations that direct the course of our routine actions. We do not determine these consciously; consciousness contains only the intention to do them, but little about the course of action.[110] When I write I think of the theme, but I do not know how I fetch the paper from my drawer, what movements I make, and so on. We have some support for the assumption that these extremely well-learned mechanisms are altered in schizophrenia, as seen, for example, in apraxia-like phenomena. But we do not know if these disturbances are due to a lack of the associations necessary for the specific activity. It is conceivable that [apraxia-like] clumsiness is due to negativism or perplexity.

III. MEMORY [111]

Memory as such does not suffer in this disorder. Patients reproduce experiences they had before and after the onset of the illness as well as any normal person.[112] In fact, often they recall the latter much better, since their minds register everything with the acuity of a camera, making no distinction between

---

Bleuler. Feelings of unreality, of depersonalization, of being influenced, of reading the mind of others, and of one's mind being read, are virgin and fruitful grounds for the psychopathology of thinking. The perceptual difficulties (for example, in space and time experiences) also offer many worthwhile opportunities for investigation.

109. Lewin's methods are eminently suited for such explorations, but have rarely been so used. Cf., however, Golant-Rattner (278), Krauss (418), Escalona (166), Dembo and Hanfmann (141).

110. Cf. Hartmann, Chap. 18, VIII, and Lewin, Chap. 5, pp. 141 ff., above; also Rapaport *et al.* (602, I, 249–53).

111. As will be seen below, Bleuler's

concept of memory refers to registration and retention. He subsumes the processes of organization and reproduction of memories under the concept of association, which for him, however, also covers thought-processes in general. This section is a translation of (71, pp. 48–50).

112. Schilder (659) and others showed that it is probable that nothing once experienced is lost to memory as long as the brain is intact (though it may become unavailable to recall). In this light the criterion of memory-disorder is not whether there is retention, but whether retained memories are available when necessary and appropriate. Bleuler evidently refers only to the memories that happen to be available.

the essential and unessential.[118] Thus they often remember more details than do normals. . . . They remember dates and similar extraneous matters amazingly well; this is especially striking in some paranoids who are able, for example, to give the dates of all the events they mention in their stacks of petitions. "I know of cases of paranoia where memory has undergone a peculiar change; it works—as it were—overtime (hypermnesia).[114]* These paranoids remember every smallest detail of things long past." [115]

113. This statement is vulnerable: (a) there is no evidence that such registration is necessarily followed by appropriate recall; (b) such registration is observed only in some schizophrenics and only in certain phases of their disorder (most frequently in obsessive and paranoid phases); there has been no systematic exploration of the conditions of appearance and the nature of this phenomenon.

114.* Berze (57), p. 443.

115. If the available fragmentary data and theory are brought to bear on this observation, several possible explanations appear, though they are all in need of empirical study and verification:

1) In some—but by no means all—cases of schizophrenia, wishes and strivings which are usually unconscious, and can, in neurotics, be discovered only by psychoanalysis or hypnosis, come directly to consciousness (*not* symbolically or in other indirect forms of representation). In these schizophrenics forgotten details of life-experience emerge in consciousness, together with these wishes and strivings. Anything that pertains to these wishes (and since they play a major role in consciousness, most of what is experienced will pertain to them) is vividly registered and reproduced. How widespread this "return of the repressed" in *direct* form is and how much of schizophrenic hypermnesia it accounts for can be decided only by empirical studies.

2) We have noted (note 17, above) that many schizophrenics show obsessive thinking. This may be accounted for by the fact that many schizophrenias come about as a decompensation of compulsive-obsessive adjustments. Therein lies another possible explanation of the hypermnesia. It is characteristic of obsessive-compulsives, as well as other "intellectualizing" clinical groups (see Rapaport et al., 602; and Rapaport, 597) that they accumulate and have available for use all kinds of information. This "knowledge" is a consequence of their defense method of isolation, as is the "ignorance" of hysteriform conditions a consequence of repression. (Cf. Rapaport et al., 602, I, 146.) This inclination to gather and use all possible factual information as a means of "being prepared" for the exigencies of instinctual and reality danger is coupled in these "intellectualizing" groups with hyperalertness (good concentration). (Cf. Rapaport et al., 602, I, 167–76, 214; also Rapaport, 597.) When this inclination persists after decompensation, it may play a role in schizophrenic hypermnesia.

3) Paranoids as a rule also belong to the intellectualizing nosological groups and their hyperalertness is particularly keen. In addition, their tendency to ex-

The usual fading of memory with the passage of time is present in our patients too; thus, for example, some school-acquisitions are lost. But considering all that normals forget, for instance, of their high school studies, it is astounding how much our patients do retain. Even bodily skills—which, according to the accepted view, would require the exercise of joints and muscles—are suddenly resumed after a pause of many years without showing any trace of disuse. A catatonic woman, who had not made a normal movement for thirty years and

---

perience everything as related to their fears and wishes (projection) is extreme. There are cases in which although prior to the paranoid break and in periods of remission hyperalertness is not present, nor are other intellectualizing characteristics very pronounced, when the break sets in these become sharply accentuated. I have observed several cases in which the Arithmetic and Picture Completion scores of the Bellevue Scale rose sharply in the acute phases of the disorder, only to drop in remissions. These considerations concerning paranoids are consonant with Bleuler's and Berze's (57) observations.

4) There is yet another possible explanation of schizophrenic hypermnesia, one which—as far as I can see—is least understood but most consonant with Bleuler's phrase, "their minds register everything like a camera." In our studies of "attention" Digit Span was the measuring rod. We found the following: (a) normally functioning attention is the condition for normal effortless accretion of memories (602, I, 129 ff.); (b) anxiety impairs effortless attention and gives rise to "temporary inefficiency" (slips) of memory; to make up for this, effortful concentration takes place which is conducive to an exaggerated accretion of memories, that is, "information" or "knowledge"; (c) in acute schizophrenic distress attention is impaired (lowering

of Digit Span score) by the turmoil and anxiety; (d) in bland schizophrenic cases, when "deterioration" does not prevent communication, the Digit Span score often exceeds that of all other subtests, and approximates the highest possible scores.

It is this last observation that may be related to hypermnesia. We attempted to explain this datum by the blandness, that is, the successful elimination of attention-disturbing anxiety by the schizophrenic process. (Cf. 602, I, 176–79, and particularly I, 186–87.) It is possible that in such "bland" cases we are dealing with a specific type of organization of consciousness characterized by a leveling of the hierarchic importance of meanings, excellence of involuntary attention, and hypermnesia. Another possible explanation (cf. note 60, above) would be the free availability of withdrawn object-cathexes for a new attempt at making contact with reality. This contact would be facilitated by encountering reality piecemeal, so as to guarantee that no relationships will be met which would arouse impulses and anxieties. It is noteworthy that recall of meaningful material fares very badly in these bland conditions (602, I, 323 ff., 345 ff.). Cf. also the success in visual-motor tasks at the price of impairment of "meaningful" organization (602, I, 257 ff., 269, 275, 326).

had not touched the piano for years, suddenly played a technically difficult piece correctly and with expression.[116]

Yet we hear every day in our anamneses that "forgetfulness" is the first, or one of the most important, symptoms of the illness, and the patients themselves complain about their memory.[117] Some observers also find that "memory" is weakened in dementia praecox; thus Masselon [118*] claims to have found that memory is poor for complex, but good for simple matters.[119]

Ziehen [120*] finds that memory is poor in all "defect conditions," though

116. A dynamic theory of memory (Bartlett, 37; Koffka, 406; Schilder, 666, 664; Rapaport, 591) would account for such fading of memories and their surprising revival by the absence and recurrence of the attitudes, interests, and strivings around which these memories were organized. Changes in these dynamic organizing factors of memory due to development and experience would be invoked to explain the normal "fading" of memories. Cf. Alper (28) on reminiscence.

117. This indeed is a common symptom of an impending schizophrenic break. I have observed cases in which although the break with reality had not yet occurred, the organization of cathexes available to the ego (see 602, I, 167 ff.) in the form of strivings, interests, etc., which regulate the effortless emergence of memories, was already crumbling. The struggle to maintain contact with reality was subjectively experienced as "I can't remember the simplest things." (A patient said, "My name confuses me," and had to look up his name and age on his driver's license.) Part of the crumbling takes the form of "blocking," which may or may not be the consequence of the evident last effort to repress wholesale everything that even remotely relates to the drives and impulses to be warded off. When this strug-

gle is over, memory does not function any better, certainly not at first, but the painful awareness of this fact is gone.

118.* Masselon (504).

119. To be conscious of a complex idea implies the grasping of its meaning and thus requires concentration, which is notoriously disturbed in the majority of schizophrenias. See note 115 (4), above; cf. also (602, I, 323 ff., 345 ff.).

120.* Ziehen (786). Though I have had considerable experience with idiocy and imbecility, I have not encountered the weakness of memory described by Ziehen and others. My concept of "memory" must differ from theirs. To me it seems natural that an idiot will not remember a speech or an event he did not understand, any more than I would a Chinese opera. There are, however, many imbeciles who retain details meaningless to them (the multiplication table, entire sermons) better than most normals, and who reproduce not-understood experiences which took place decades before with great plasticity, even though barely in command of the language. *I consider a memory test adequate only when it is as independent of other disorders as possible. Thus, in idiocy it must be independent of the lack of understanding, in schizophrenia of blocking, lack of interest, and inertia of thinking.*

generally it is less impaired than in such a "secondary dementia" [121] as paresis.

The apparent contradiction is easily eliminated. In schizophrenia registration of the material of experience and retention of the memory-image remain good, but reproduction of the experience may be disturbed at any given moment. This stands to reason if we consider that reproduction occurs by means of associations and is influenced by affectivity, the two functions particularly affected in schizophrenia.[122]

[Concerning the superior memory feats of mental defectives cf. Scheerer *et al.*, (637), and Chap. 25, pp. 541, 568, above. There is no decisive evidence available on the adequacy of memory-function in imbeciles. That in imbeciles comprehension difficulty commonly outstrips memory difficulty is true in so far as the two can be distinguished from each other. But, for theoretical reasons, such a distinction is not justified: the more we learn about the thought-process the more clearly it proves to be an integral and indivisible unity. Memory, attention, concept-formation, anticipation, etc.—which we deal with as though they were "functions" or components of thought-processes—appear to be merely convenient abstractions, that is, various ways human beings can use to look upon their thought-processes; objectively they are various *aspects* (cf. 602, I, 385 ff.) of the thought-process. Under different conditions different aspects of the thought-process predominate and become amenable to study; but always all aspects are at play. Thus Bleuler's requirements for comparing understanding and memory in imbeciles may be difficult to meet, while his demand for a memory test independent of all other disorders is theoretically impossible.]

121. "Defect conditions" is a term that subsumes all "dementias," that is, mental deficiency, psychotic deterioration (for example, that of *dementia praecox*) and organic deterioration (for example, that of general paresis). "Secondary dementia" refers to "dementia" other than mental deficiency, which is the primary.

122. This view implies a conception of registration and retention of memories which—as I have shown in *Emotions and Memory* (591)—is incompatible with a dynamic theory of memory and the known clinical facts of memory-pathology. In our preceding discussion of the tendency of schizophrenics "to just miss the point," some of the central concepts of a dynamic theory of memory— "schemata"—"memory-frames-of-reference"—have already been mentioned; see notes 21, 22, 31, above. The broad outlines of our present-day knowledge of memory-organization and -pathology may be stated as follows (cf., Bartlett, 37; Freud, 250, 223 and 248; Rapaport, 596):

a) Memories are originally organized around drives and arise in consciousness as representations of these drives when drive-tension rises (Freud, 223; Zeigarnik, 783; Lewin, 467).

b) Later on, as the pertinence of a memory to partial drives is established, this drive-organization (the primitive schema) yields to the conceptual schema (Bartlett, 37, pp. 212–13). This transition is parallel to, and an aspect of,

c) the emergence from drive sources of attitudes, interests, and strivings (All-

Blocking is frequent during psychiatric examination, interfering particularly with the recall of feeling-toned complexes. Derailment of associations brings forth many false answers; lack of interest and negativistic tendencies prevent correct thinking and facilitate the giving of answers entirely irrelevant or just missing the point. Thus it is natural that in examining schizophrenics we often receive false answers or none; *whether the answer would require remembering or thinking, the result is usually about the same; nor is it any better if the patient is to explain something concrete and actually at hand.* This indicates that what we are facing here is not a memory-disorder.[123] Naturally, complex or less habituated functions are more likely to be shipwrecked on these obstacles than simple and habituated ones. Thus in a sense Masselon is correct. However,

---

port, 24) as one of the implications of reality-testing and the reality-principle (Freud, 223). Attitudes, interests, etc., are cathectic processes derived from drive-cathexes; their regulation is structuralized as the reality-principle and as defensive ego-formations which arise when drive-demands meet reality-demands (Freud, 248).

d) The schemata are frames of reference determining the mode of apperception of new stimulations, in terms of both conceptual and attitudinal belongingness. In other words, the schemata organize perceptions both in terms of a reality-relevance (which includes social relevance; Sullivan, 725), and relevance to personal attitudes, in which drive- and reality-relevance merge. Remembering results from the activation of these schemata by attitudes and interests which are thus justified and rationalized (Bartlett, 37, p. 303).

Thus memory, that is, registration, retention, and reproduction, are dependent upon schemata, organized and activated by attitudes. Attitudes and schemata are two aspects of the same process. This is a generalization of the very

fragmentary insight expressed by Bleuler that "reproduction occurs by means of associations and is influenced by affectivity." It also sheds light on why in schizophrenia, where the structuralized integration of drive-demand and social reality-demand falls to pieces, remembering dependent on attitudes (which are structuralized integrations) suffers.

123. Cf. Bartlett (37, pp. 311 ff.), on the relation of memory, constructive imagination, and thinking. Bartlett holds that his experiments demonstrated thinking, imagination, and memory to be merely different modes of the attitude-schema dynamics. In "The Interpretation of Dreams" (209, Chap. VII), the "Two Principles" (223) and "The Mystic Writing Pad" (250), Freud came to a similar conclusion. These conclusions militate against Bleuler's distinction between thinking and memory from which he infers that there is no memory-disorder in schizophrenia. Thus in contrast to Bleuler, we must assert that there is a thought-disorder in schizophrenia which involves *all* aspects of thought-organization, including memory.

closer study shows that the simple psychological processes are also affected *by the pathology*. But the disorder is more frequently manifest in complex processes, much as the normal fading of memory impinges less upon the remembrance of the place where one went to school than upon the experiences of Alexander the Great.

As far as can be established by our present means of observation, memory is not disordered in common forms of schizophrenia. The associative recall of memory pictures is at times altered. This alteration obtains, however, only for certain psychological constellations and is a consequence of the general association- and affect-disorder.

Thus it can happen that patients appear forgetful, cannot recollect the simplest things, forget what they were about to do, or even—like senile patients—ask a question repeatedly in the same company without realizing it. It is important to note that patients at one moment know, and in the next "have forgotten" the same thing.

Naturally, the memory-function may be encroached upon by other psychological factors. Some patients give correct and lucid information about their life preceding the illness, while their description of the illness is unclear, rambling, and unintelligible. It may be that the experience of the illness cannot be described in the words of ordinary language. Another possible reason is that the experience of the illness has no logical connections for either patient or observer, so that even correct reproductions will appear confused.

IV. CONSCIOUSNESS [124]

Though the expression "disorder of consciousness" overlaps to some extent the old term "clouding of the sensorium," it does not correspond to any clear concept.[125]

124. This section is the translation of Bleuler (71, pp. 50–51).

125. In his *Textbook of Psychiatry*, Bleuler (76, p. 111) states this point more directly: ". . . 'disturbance of consciousness' and 'clouding of consciousness' . . . do not fit with the rest of our terminology, but . . . we have not yet found substitutes. . . ." Bleuler clearly felt that these descriptive terms, already old-fashioned in his day, were sterile, and that the academic psychological concept of consciousness, which he discusses in the immediately following footnote, was no better. The reasons for which Bleuler did not use or even mention the conception of consciousness which Freud advanced in the Chap. VII of "The Interpretation of Dreams" will not be conjectured here. Suffice it to say that

Orientation and memory are essential constituents of consciousness as understood here.[126] [Bleuler (71) p. 23: "Consciousness" means first of all that (not describable) propensity of psychological processes which distinguishes the sensible creature from the automaton.[127] Consciousness is generally not absent in psychotic conditions, except in stupor and deep syncope. There is no such disorder as a para-function of consciousness. We can conceive only of quantitive changes of consciousness, in that at any one time many or few processes can be conscious and in order to become that they must attain a certain degree of intensity.[128] This conception, however, cannot be applied consist-

---

Bleuler did not have an adequate conceptual framework by which to deal with disorders of consciousness. In his textbook (76, pp. 111 ff.) he mentions the following disorders of consciousness without attempting to treat them systematically: amentia (also p. 364), confusion (also p. 86), deliria (also p. 162), and twilight states (also p. 198). There are yet other schizophrenic symptoms involving disorders of consciousness not listed by Bleuler: depersonalization (cf. Schilder, 653), perplexity (cf. MacCurdy, 489, p. 393), and compulsive thoughts (cf. Schilder, 653, pp. 203 ff.).

It will be worth quoting MacCurdy's (489) definition of consciousness and his description of the clouding of consciousness:

Consciousness: (a) Simple awareness—awareness of self and awareness of environment; (b) The totality of mental processes associated with and involving awareness [p. 578]. Consciousness involves direction of attention outward, and this implies reaction to environmental stimuli, be it only in the maintenance of posture [p. 554]. *Clouding of consciousness:* A dulling of perception which results in a confusion about the environment, although mental processes of internal origin may be quite active. A dream-like state [p. 578].

126. This merely means that orienta-

tion and memory both suffer in states of "clouded sensorium." Bleuler's footnote that follows in the text shows that he did not use the term "constituent" in the sense in which we understand it today, and that he did not mean to assert that memory and orientation are *constituents* of consciousness. James (353) was justly praised by Sidis (687, p. 39) for having gotten rid of the spectre of a separately existing consciousness, whether indivisible or of many constituents. Consciousness, whatever its dynamics, and whether taken as a fact of subjective experience or as a construct, is an aspect of thought-processes.

127. Surely Bleuler did not mean to exclude animals from among "sensible creatures." We must assume that he did attribute consciousness to them, but not of the *kind* man has. Thus he involved himself in a contradiction when he stated below that "we can conceive only of quantitative changes in consciousness."

128. Bleuler seems to imply two kinds of quantitative variations of consciousness: those of extent and those of intensity. This is the classical fallacy of academic speculation concerning consciousness, which has been traced by Mueller-Freienfels (530) throughout the history of psychology. The more

ently: the "consciousness" of an idiot has often much less content than that of an intelligent epileptic or a dreamer in a twilight state, yet we consider the former normal and the latter clouded. As to intensity: minimal stimulation which may not have been noticed by the person in his normal condition may

"modern" way is to forget about consciousness altogether. Compare, for example, Hunter's (345) discussion of this point in his review of Boring, Langfeld, and Weld (84).

Since it is mainly a matter of introspection, the study of consciousness can easily lead to fallacies and equivocation, the most common of which is the postulation of consciousness as an irreducible and unknowable datum of subjective experience. Philosophers of the phenomenological school and clinicians followed accepted principles of science when they postulated that it is through its variants that the nature of an apparently intractable phenomenon becomes known to us.

Phenomenologists (346, 511), and in their wake Schilder, realized that consciousness of the self, consciousness of the psychological act, and consciousness of cognition as one of unreality, reality, supposition, perception, memory, etc., are all form-variants of consciousness, each of which may become affected in pathological conditions. They stressed the need for empirical investigation of each of these forms. See Schilder (653), Sartre (631, 630), and Rapaport's reviews of Sartre (598). Clinicians, particularly Silberer (693), Sidis (687), and others (cf. Chap. 17, note 18, above), realized that the normal waking state, hypnosis, dream, reverie, daydream, delirium, somnambulism, fugue, monoideism, epileptic twilight, stupor, confusional and perplexity states, are all form-variants of consciousness differing

from each other at least in the form of prevailing thought-organization, in the extent and quality of *voluntary* thought or action present, and in the kinds and qualities of reflection feasible. In addition, partial deviations from the usual state of consciousness were also noted, such as those present in automatisms, compulsions, isolated delusions, illusions, states in which post-hypnotic suggestions are carried out, etc. Sidis's (687) pertinent summary in his *Psychology of Suggestion* is an enlightening sample of the clinician's awareness of these problems:

I. *Desultory consciousness.* In this type of consciousness there is no connection, no association, between one moment of consciousness and another; there is certainly no synthesis of moments, and consequently no memory, no recognition, no self-consciousness, no personality. This type of consciousness may have its representatives in the psychic life of the lowest invertebrates.

II. *Synthetic consciousness.* In this type of consciousness there is synthesis of the preceding moments in each passing moment, but there is no recognition. Former experiences are reinstated in consciousness, but they are not recognized as such. Instinctive consciousness falls naturally under this type of mental activity. Memory is certainly present, but it is objective in its nature; it exists only for the observer, not for the individual consciousness itself. The subjective side of memory, the projection of the present experience into the subjective past of the present moment consciousness, is wanting; and, of course, it goes without saying that the synthetic con-

become conscious in a twilight state.[129] Internal stimuli are also usually quite conscious in twilight states, though we have no reason to ascribe to them special intensity.[130] We do not know anything about the dynamic conditions of psychological processes. The meaning of the word "consciousness" changes entirely if fragmentary orientation and insufficient rapport are labeled "disorders of consciousness." Some consider even delusions to be disorders of consciousness.[131] There were times when the ability to remember an experience

---

sciousness has no self-consciousness, no personality.

III. *Recognitive consciousness.* In this type of consciousness there is not only an objective synthesis of the preceding moments in each moment of consciousness, but there is also present a subjective synthesis. Former experiences are not only simply reinstated in consciousness, but they are also recognized as such. This type of mental activity may be represented by the consciousness of the higher vertebrate animals. There is here memory, there is the projection of the present into the subjective past, there is recognition, but there is no self-consciousness, no personality.

IV. *Desultory self-consciousness.* This type of self-conciousness has no synthesis in each present moment of the preceding past moments of self-consciousness. Such a form of consciousness may be regarded as a series of independent, instable personalities coming like bubbles to the surface of consciousness and bursting without leaving any marked trace behind them. It is evident that this type of personality, although it has a series of moments, has no memory of that series, nor has it any personal identity.

V. *Synthetic self-consciousness.* This form of self-consciousness has a series of moments, and all the moments in the series can be included in and owned by each present moment of self-consciousness. The moments in the series are intimately linked and intertwined. Each moment synthesizes, owns, knows, and controls the preceding ones. This type of consciousness possesses synthesis, reproduction, recogni-

tion, personality, personal identity, and is represented by man's mental activity.

This was written in 1897. We have advanced but little beyond it in our systematic empirical studies of consciousness, though we have learned how to criticize Sidis's schematic and arbitrary speculativeness.

129. This conclusion is the result of Bleuler's contradictions pointed out in note 127, above, and of his disregard for "para-functions of consciousness," that is, for the qualitative differences of forms of consciousness.

130. Note Freud (209, Chap. VII) and MacCurdy (489, pp. 511 ff.), to the contrary. Drives and impulses rise with the greatest intensity in twilight states. Cf. also Rapaport (591, Chap. VII).

131. The observers to whom Bleuler refers did not distinguish between a state of consciousness and its content. When they called delusions disorders of consciousness, they had in mind the content-disorder. But delusions, particularly when isolated, *are experienced* as occurring in a special state of consciousness. This is not clearly seen when the patient is diffusely deluded, since then his introspective report will be within the delusional frame of reference and will yield no comparison with other states of consciousness except by its content. Only when deludedness reaches the point of confusion and perplexity will the altera-

was considered the index of consciousness during that experience. It is clear that such a concept is altogether useless. The concept *consciousness of the self* is also clumsy and breeds confusion. Whoever is conscious will surely not confuse himself with the external world; he must therefore be conscious of the self in the psychologist's sense. If, however, the concept "consciousness of the self" refers to the apperception of one's personality, then it would be preferable to use this latter and clearer term.] [132*]

"Time and space consciousness" are but orientation in space and time. Nevertheless, because disorders of consciousness (clouding of the sensorium) usually involve a primary disorder, namely, the alteration of sensations and perceptions themselves, there is also a disturbance in the ordering of sensory time and space impressions. Many (never all) of the sensory stimuli are either not apprehended or else reinterpreted into illusions; out of these the psyche creates a world of its own, which is then projected outward. In such cases we speak of *twilight states*.[133]

Lucid schizophrenic conditions show no disorder of consciousness, if the latter is conceived of as implying a loss of sensory contact with the environment. Schizophrenics in general behave in this respect just like normal people.[134] However, there are many acute [schizophrenic] syndromes analogous to hysterical twilight-states and to confusional conditions of various origins.[135] Fur-

---

tion of the state of consciousness again become obvious, but this time to direct external observation.

132.* Janet wrote: "The word 'consciousness,' which we use continually in studies on the mental states of our patients, is an extremely vague word, which means many different things. When we use it in particular to designate the knowledge the subject has of himself, of his sensations and acts, it means a rather complicated psychological operation, and not an elementary and irreducible operation, as is generally believed" (p. 303).

[Cf. Claparède, Chap. 3, above.]

133. Cf. Rapaport (591, pp. 191–214), Gill and Rapaport (274), Abeles and Schilder (2).

134. In our comments above we have marshaled abundant evidence sharply contradicting this assertion.

135. Thus far, the only consistent theory of consciousness which leads to an explanation of the nature of these confusional twilight-states is that of Freud. It may be summarized as follows:

a) Consciousness is conceived of as a sense-organ.

b) Its function is twofold: to be the sense-organ of the perception of internal stimulation and the supraordinate sense-organ of external perception which apperceives the changes in the receptor organs.

c) It performs its function through regulating the distribution of attention-cathexis—that part of the energy freely

thermore, when autism is stable, it may, in a sense, be considered a disorder of consciousness.[136]

V. ATTENTION

Attention,[137] being an aspect of affectivity,[138] is encroached upon when affectivity is altered. To our present-day methods of observation attention [in schizophrenics] appears normal for matters of interest to the patient, that

available to the ego which is used in conscious thinking.

d) Normally this regulation is performed in terms of the reality-principle. Hypercathexis (attention-cathexis) is given to drive representations which are not countercathected, that is, repressed, and which have reached high intensity, and to external percepts in proportion to their relevance to the interests, strivings, etc., of the individual.

e) Part of the process of hypercathecting ideas is connecting them with preconscious verbal ideas, part of it the establishment of relationships to other ideas.

Cf. Chap. 16, note 14, and Chap. 23, note 11, above.

136. In keeping with our previous formulations we could argue that autism is a particular though vaguely defined form of thought-organization corresponding to certain altered states of consciousness. Cf. Chap. 20, notes 36, 45, and 17, above.

137. This section is the translation of Bleuler (71, pp. 56–57). Cf., Bleuler, *Textbook of Psychiatry* (76, p. 40): "Attention is a manifestation of affectivity. It consists in the fact that certain sensory perceptions and ideas which have aroused our interest are facilitated and all others inhibited." Compare also Bleuler, *Affectivity, Suggestibility, Paranoia* (66, p. 214 ff.), where it becomes clear

that this facilitation and inhibition are considered by him to be the only influences of affects on thought-processes, which he subsumes under the concept attention. Bleuler's concept of affect is coterminus with drives. The comparison of the two influences mentioned with the complexities of Freud's mechanisms of the unconscious shows the inadequacy of Bleuler's oversimple conception. Freud's theory of attention (see Chap. 15, note 21, above) considers it to be the distribution of cathectic energies at the disposal of the ego for use in ordered, logical thought-processes.

138. Bleuler (76, pp. 32–33), describes his view of affectivity as follows:

Every psychism can be divided into two sides, an intellectual and an affective. . . . Under the term affective we comprise the affects, the emotions, and the feelings of pleasure and displeasure. . . .

In (66, p. 14) he writes:

Hence the affects are connected not only with cognition but even more closely with volition. I might better say that *affectivity is the broader conception wherein volition and desire* [each] *represent only one side.* Affectivity, which is one with our instincts and impulses, determines the direction of our endeavors.

The catch-all vagueness of this concept of affectivity is obvious. For a critique of similar conceptions, see Rapaport (591).

is, in the milder cases for the majority of experiences, and in the more severe cases for affect-toned activities (for instance, plans to escape).[139] Where affect is lacking, the drive to follow internal and external processes and to direct one's senses and thoughts is also deficient: that is to say, active attention is impaired.[140]

The alteration of passive attention [141] is quite different: even though uninterested and autistically encapsulated patients pay little attention to the outside world, they register a remarkable number of events of no concern to them. The selection which attention exercises over normal sensory impressions may be reduced to zero, so that almost everything that meets the senses is registered. Thus both the facilitating and the inhibitory propensities of attention are disordered.[142]

The patient may reproduce every detail of an event that happened on the ward years before which was of no concern to him, or news items which he heard only in passing; yet at the time he may have appeared preoccupied with

139. This statement is circular: that which is of interest is affect-toned, but that which is affect-toned is attended to; thus the statement does not contain anything that is not implied in Bleuler's definition of attention.

140. Bleuler (76, p. 40) wrote:

If our attention is directed by the will, we designate it as *active;* if by external occurrences, we call it *passive.* Maximum attention will always be active while habitual attention may be either active or passive. The latter plays a special part in recording the daily happenings of one's environment.

This concept of active attention (borrowed from Wundt) corresponds grossly to the concept *concentration* of Rapaport *et al.* (602, I, 166 ff., 195 ff.), for whose studies in attention and concentration Bleuler's distinction between active and passive attention was one of the points of departure. Cf. also Diethelm and Jones (145).

Kraepelin observed the impairment of active attention and related it to impaired volition in schizophrenia. Jung's (363)

review of the literature shows that this impairment of attention was also observed by Tschisch, Binet, Masselon, and Jung. Rapaport *et al.* have shown that impaired active attention (concentration) is an often outstanding symptom of schizophrenia, but noted that in paranoid disorders it is frequently absent. They suggest an explanation of the presence as well as absence of this symptom in terms of the psychoanalytic theory of attention-cathexes.

141. Cf. Rapaport *et al.* (602, I, 166 ff., 176 ff.). The observation that passive attention is retained in certain schizophrenic conditions is one of Bleuler's real merits. For a discussion of this phenomenon see note 115, above.

142. Bleuler considers selective, facilitating, and inhibitory effects of attention to be affective—that is, according to him, instinctual—mechanisms. Rapaport *et al.* (602, I, 385 ff.) consider selective anticipation, attention, and concentration to be different aspects of the distribution of cathexes available to the ego.

himself or staring into a corner, so that it is hard to conceive how he learned about these. One of our catatonics, who for several months was preoccupied with making faces at the wall, after having improved, knew what had happened in the meanwhile in the Boer War; she must have picked up isolated comments from her altogether demented environment and retained them in an ordered fashion. . . .

The *tenacity* and *vigilance* [143] of attention may be altered independently of each other either in a positive or negative sense, but these disorders are not characteristic of schizophrenia. There are, however, specific disorders which result in hypo-vigilance, such as "being robbed of thoughts"; and when the train of thought gets lost in byways we cannot speak of tenacity.

The effectiveness of attention is quite varied.[144] It may be normal. However, patients often cannot concentrate even if they make a real effort because the *intensity of attention* is impaired. Usually its *extensity* suffers too: patients are unable to gather all the associations necessary for the task at hand. These disorders may be codetermined by as yet unknown primary obstructions of the psychic processes; beside the affects, the disorders of association have the greatest influence on the effectiveness of attention.[145] When the train of thought is derailed, a real thought is unattainable without abnormally great effort.

In some cases, a tendency to tire results in a rapid dissipation of attention; but chronic patients, if capable of active attention at all, show a normal and even hypernormal capacity to sustain attention.[146]

143. Bleuler (76, p. 40):

A distinction is also made between *tenacity* and *vigilance* of attention which are usually, but not always, antagonistic to each other. Tenacity is the ability to keep one's attention fixed on a certain subject continuously, and vigilance the capacity to direct one's attention to a new object, particularly to an external stimulus.

It is possible that we are dealing here merely with a specific application of active (tenacity) and passive (vigilance) attention.

144. Bleuler (76, p. 40):

. . . in attention the "interest" inhibits and facilitates the associations in the same way as is done by the affects. The more successfully this is done, the greater is the intensity or the *concentration*, and the greater the number of the useful associations put in operation, the greater the *extent* of attention.

This concept of concentration (similar to Wundt's) is different from that of Rapaport *et al.*

145. According to Bleuler attention, which is an aspect of affectivity, has a selective, facilitating or inhibiting, effect on associations. It is hard to see how attention so defined could be influenced by disorders of association.

146. Bleuler (71, pp. 19–20) wrote:

Preoccupation caused by complexes, blocking, or fascination often prevents the patient, momentarily or for a period of time, from following a definite train of thought or from thinking in a given direction. Thus some patients can follow a story or dramatic presentation only fragmentarily; others can retell them excellently, even if while listening they were in steady contact with their "voices"; thus *attention, too, may be split.* Like other functions, attention may also be *blocked:* in the midst of a conversation or some work the patients appear to have turned to another train of thought or to have completely stopped thinking. Remarkably enough, in either case they can later continue thinking with full knowledge of what passed during their inattention; thus they may belatedly answer an apparently unperceived question.

Some catatonics have a *compulsion* to direct their attention to certain external and internal processes, particularly the latter. Hallucinations especially succeed in enforcing continuous attention against the patient's will.

The condition of attention in perplexed, dreamlike, and hallucinatory states is not considered here, partly because it is difficult to describe and partly because it is self-explanatory.[147]

If "enslavement by optical impressions" is a pathological overemphasis of the sense-impressions, its opposite is that under other circumstances the patient ignores the outside world completely.

Between these two extremes all transitions are possible. . . . At the one extreme patients are easily distractible, seem to lack directives of their own and depend entirely on outer impressions; this is the case when the symptom of naming prevails; at the other extreme they are undistractible and even the strongest stimuli will fail to influence their train of ideas or arouse their attention.

In their daily life the majority of chronic cases shows little that is remarkable in this respect: they are at their work and attend to the new event in so far as it interests them. They can be interrupted in their talk. In more severe cases, however, the distractibility is diminished. Sommer proved this experimentally: he obtained the same arithmetic score from his patients with or without the interference of noises.

[Cf. Shakow, 681.] Affect, particularly anger, usually alters schizophrenic distractibility. Under its sway they will disregard objections or will understand them in terms of their own train of thought, so that the objection only adds fuel to their outburst. While excited, a change of the situation will influence them little. It is well-known that a railing schizophrenic is unconcerned whether anyone is present to hear his tirade.

Lack of distractibility may appear to spring from the patients' *lack of interest:* as they care about nothing, nothing can influence their behavior. But it can be shown that the same patients understand very well what goes on about them, even when they pay no active attention. In certain acute conditions distractibility is greatly reduced, often even to the vanishing point.

147. The fate of attention-cathexes in perplexity, confusion, twilight states, as well as in fugues, somnambulism, amnesias, multiple personalities, hypnotic

VI. CONCEPTS [148]

Concepts suffer under the decomposition of associations. In chronic schizophrenic conditions the majority of concepts is little less definite than in normals. The striking vagueness characteristic of concepts in epileptic dementia is rare, even though there is a tendency to use general concepts where concrete ones are called for: an iron tool may be called an "iron," a shovel a "household utensil." Such designations, more frequently observed on direct questioning than in spontaneous productions, are usually disorders of concept-formation and not merely of expression. I have never encountered a specific schizophrenic concept-impairment in which an aspect of a concept seemed actually to be lost; rather have I observed that *concepts are often thought of in a fashion disregarding some of their implications.*[149] However, these disturbances fluctuate from moment to moment. Consistent and enduring defects are seen only in concepts pertaining to delusions or to affect-toned complexes.[150]

---

regressions, etc., is one of the least understood though important problems of the theory of thought-processes.

148. This is the translation of a part of Bleuler's section on "Schizophrenic Dementia" (71, pp. 61–64). Cf. Bleuler (76, pp. 13–16). For a penetrating clinical analysis of concepts in schizophrenia, see Schilder, *Seele und Leben* (652, Chap. I, pp. 12–71). For the genetic and comparative aspects of concept-formation, see Werner (755, pp. 213–98). For a general treatment of the pathology of concept-formation, see Rapaport *et al.* (602, I, 385–484). For various approaches to the study of concept-formation in schizophrenia, see Kasanin (372). Cf. also notes 21, 22, 31, 32, and 33, above.

149. Thus we see that Bleuler had observed the outstanding features of the schizophrenics' use of concepts: they "use general concepts where concrete ones are called for" and "concepts are often thought of . . . disregarding

some of their implications"; that is, he notes the overgenerality and the concreteness of schizophrenic concept-formation. Compare the concepts "loosening" and "narrowing" in (602, I, 405–6, 455). Goldstein (280) describes only one side of this picture, while Cameron (120) and Benjamin (43) note both. See also notes 32 and 33, above.

150. Here Bleuler touches, but does not tackle, one of the essential issues of the schizophrenic disorder of concept-formation: delusions and affect-toned complexes play havoc with concepts under any condition, but over and above their effect there is a generalized disorder of concept-formation in schizophrenia. The fluctuations Bleuler observed are verifiable. My experience suggests that these fluctuations are due in considerable part to verbal conventions, which remain relatively refractory to impairment by the schizophrenic process. They may survive as empty shells, contrasting sharply with the otherwise

Wernicke's method of questioning patients about the differences between related concepts is therefore altogether unsatisfactory for the investigation of these disorders, though similarities and differences must occasionally be inadequate when concepts are not thought of with all their implications. . . .[151] I cannot believe that Wernicke's patient, who considered the attendant his sister Laura, had forgotten the memory-images of male and female clothing. As a rule chronic schizophrenics deal quite well with such concepts and memory-images.[152] Exceptions to this rule are: psychological constellations involving

---

obvious schizophrenic disorganization of concept-formation. Cf. Schilder, Chap. 25, II, c, above.

151. Bleuler's criticism of Wernicke is in part justified. "Similarities" is actually one of the tests most resistant to the destructive effects of the schizophrenic process (see 602, I, 146 ff.). It tests *verbal concept-formation* which is safeguarded by ingrained "verbal-coherence," that is, verbal convention. Yet the comparison of performance on "easy" and "difficult" items of "Similarities" and the analysis of the failures on the test are useful in detecting schizophrenic disorder.

152. Bleuler's argument is questionable. It is not necessary that an idea be forgotten for inadequate concepts to be formed. If it were forgotten Bleuler would speak of a primary memory-disorder and not of a concept-formation disorder.

We come closer to the understanding of the disordered concept-formation of Wernicke's patient, and of schizophrenics in general, if we consider primitive forms of concept-formation. We are indebted to H. Werner (755) for an admirable non-schematic and richly documented discussion of the genetic precursors and primitive parallels of concept-formation. His concept of "physiognomic perception" is of immediate interest here if it is kept in mind that perception always implies conceptualiza-

tion. Werner (755, p. 69) defines physiognomic perception as follows:

Such dynamization of things based on the fact that the objects are predominantly understood through the motor and affective attitude of the subject may lead to a particular type of perception. Things perceived in this way may appear "animate" and, even though actually lifeless, seem to express some inner form of life. All of us, at some time or other, have had this experience. A landscape, for instance, may be seen suddenly in immediacy as expressing a certain mood—it may be gay or melancholy or pensive. This mode of perception differs radically from the more everyday perception in which things are known according to their "geometrical-technical," matter-of-fact qualities, as it were. In our own sphere there is one field where objects are commonly perceived as directly expressing our inner life. This is in our perception of the faces and bodily movements of human beings and higher animals. Because the human physiognomy can be adequately perceived only in terms of its immediate expression, I have proposed the term *physiognomic perception* for this mode of cognition in general.

As examples we shall quote Werner (755) on a child's perception, on perception in mescalin intoxication, and on primitive language:

Neugebauer tells that his son at the age of two and one-half years called a towel-

complexes, distractedness, and probably also conditions of greater organic involvement. Thus, a hebephrenic associated *barrel*—"wheel," showing clearly that for him at that moment the concepts of hoop and wheel were more or less identical. Later, however, the same patient distinguished these two concepts quite well, though his condition was unchanged. Often, *when objects are mis-*

---

hook a "cruel" thing. When he was four and one-half years old he called the tripod of a camera a "proud" thing when it stood stiff and erect, and "sad" when it leaned at a precarious angle. At the age of three and one-half years he thought that one number 5 looked "mean" and another "cross." The number 4 appeared "soft" to him (p. 73).

It is also true that in certain states of intoxication (as when drugged by hashish or mescalin) in which the object-subject relation is less sharply articulated, the physiognomic and dynamic qualities of things stand out clearly. In a very real sense it appears that the optical field submits to a process of dynamization, and things continually change in form, size, and position. . . . One subject observed by Beringer says: "The crown of foliage on the laburnum which stands before my window seemed to me to be the image of something showering down, and that of the chestnut tree to be something striving upwards" (p. 80).

Things of equal affective value tend to come together. The "smallness" and "largeness" of objects or persons are not merely concrete, factual qualifications; they also represent affective evaluations. In the Bantu language there is a class of persons and also a class of things. But all persons who are in any way contemptible or unworthy are relegated to the class of things. The blind, the deaf, the crippled, and the idiot, all belong to this thing-like class. The language of the Algonquin Indians often puts small animals into the class of inanimate objects, whereas large plants are often placed in the class of animate things. In the Gola language of Liberia the prefix *o* denoting the human or animal class is substituted for the customary classification prefix when the object is to be emphasized as one that is especially large, valuable, or important. For instance, *ka-sie*, which means "oil palm," becomes "o-sie." This clearly shows the importance of the affective factor in concrete classification (pp. 232–33).

Werner's discussion and examples suggest that the "affective" (the term is here loosely used, as it is by Bleuler), "physiognomic" mode of experiencing is the primordial form of classification of objects and experiences. It is a primitive form of concept-formation. Werner also shows that this mode of classification is a special form of a more general characteristic of primitive experience. He quotes Koehler's experiments with chickens (755, pp. 216 ff.). When chickens trained to peck from the darker of two areas are put in a new setting in which the area they were trained to peck from is the lighter of the two, they will peck from the *now relatively* darker area and not the one to which they were previously accustomed. Werner calls this an "analogous process." The general significance of this experiment is that the primitive concept is not specific and stable but relative and shifting. This relative and shifting character comes to expression in physiognomic conceptualization, in contrast to the high stability and specificity of our abstract concepts. Wernicke's patient did not *forget* what male clothing was like; he was unim-

recognized only some of their characteristics are considered (though the others are not altogether "forgotten") and these are then freely completed to make another object. Thus for instance a picture on the wall in a deep frame is a spittoon; the fire-escape of the ward is "our barn ladder"; the director is Father F. (because he runs this place, like Father F. does the hospital); the cotton-mill where a patient works is a clothes factory.[153]

Condensation [154] congeals several concepts into a single one. Several people are often conceived of as one. A patient, for instance, is both father and mother to his children. . . . A female patient identified the history of young Moses

---

pressed by it. Something about the attendant (for example, friendliness or cruelty) led to his being physiognomically subsumed as "friendly" or "cruel" in the same relative category in which the patient's sister was an outstanding object. Normal adults, and particularly poets, also use such "physiognomic" concepts. The phenomenon of "déjà vu" (see Chap. 3, note 9, above) also operates by this process of subsuming experiences.

The concept of "physiognomic perception" is most useful in pulling together a broad range of phenomena of primitive conceptualization, but its limitation lies in the fact that it is non-specific and does not differentiate among the many phenomena it subsumes. Actually, it appears that all the phenomena it *describes* may be treated in terms of *explanatory concepts* of psychoanalysis: displacement, condensation, etc. It describes that form of "belongingness" which prevails in the "drive-organization of memories"; see notes 21, 22, and 31, above.

153. These examples also fall into the category of physiognomic perception. The fact that only some of the characteristics of objects are considered by schizophrenics should not be regarded as an indication of an inability to assume an abstract attitude (Goldstein, 280). On

the contrary, we are dealing here with overgeneralization which somehow partakes of the quality of abstraction (Cf. Cameron, 120, and Benjamin, 43.)

This form of conceptual disorder is not exclusive to schizophrenia. Gill and Rapaport (274) observed it in a case of "loss of personal identity," in which every percept was conceptualized in terms of a single, all-pervasive, and exclusive attitude of the patient in the period of his "loss of personal identity." He was obsessed with the idea that he was "out to find a job" and he perceived, conceptualized, and apperceived everything—the hospital, the beating noise of the heating plant, nurses, doctors—in terms of this all-pervasive preoccupation. It was as though his wish, drive, or attitude stamped a specific physiognomic character on everything he encountered. We have thus far no means of describing the difference between this conceptual disorder as it appears in such cases of amnesia and in cases of schizophrenia.

154. Cf. pp. 603 ff., particularly note 50, above; and Cameron's concept "interpenetration of themes" (120, pp. 55 ff.). Bleuler notes that condensation is a variety of concept-formation; indeed, it is usually overlooked that it is a primitive form of conceptualization.

with the murder of the children of Bethlehem. This alteration of concepts is often due to feeling-toned complexes.[155] A patient who expects something extraordinary of the future talks about her "future parents" as a matter of course. A paranoid patient who has great military ambitions sees himself pictured as a "General in French and Swiss uniform"; the mixing of the two armies does not bother him, and the objection that Switzerland has no generals he counters by "a colonel is a general too." In such cases it is easy to demonstrate that it is not only the manner of expression but also the concepts which are altered. A hebephrenic signs a letter to his mother with, "your hopeful nephew"; . . . he defends this nonsense by saying that his mother has a sister and he is her nephew; it is certain that the conception of family relationships has become unclear, at least for a few moments.[156] A catatonic patient is given a watch and she is very pleased; she is also pleased with her other possessions, for instance her jewelry; all these become a single concept for her, to which she refers as "presents." The vague expressions of hallucinations often hide extremely broadened concepts; a hebephrenic has "had pains twice, that is poison-murder."

The equating of two concepts on the basis of a common element often leads to *symbolism*, which in turn plays an outstanding role in delusions. A patient signs himself "the beginning and end of the world"; this expresses his delusion.

155. In many cases it can be demonstrated that condensation is a direct consequence of "feeling-toned complexes." But in schizophrenias this is just as often not demonstrable. The question is still open: Is condensation not a formal characteristic of the thought-processes feasible in one of the states of consciousness that occur in schizophrenia?

156. Von Domarus (146 and 147) has demonstrated that the issue in such cases is not "lack of clarity," but rather what he called paralogical thinking. The "Mode of Barbara" of logic: (a) "All men are mortal"; (b) "Socrates is a man"; (c) "Socrates is mortal" is used in paralogical thinking as follows: (a) "certain Indians are swift"; (b) "stags are swift"; (c) "certain Indians are stags." In Bleuler's example the mother and the aunt presumably share a characteristic in the way in which Indians and stags share swiftness. Domarus (146, p. 111) concludes: "Whereas the logician accepts identity only upon the basis of identical subjects, the paralogician accepts identity based upon identical predicates." We should like to add that in doing so the paralogician is led by conceptual frames of reference organized in terms of drives (affects) and corresponding physiognomic impressions which, in contrast to the conceptual frames of reference of the logician, are relative and unstable. In other words, Domarus overlooks that to the paralogician the predicate-subject relationship is fluid, and that the predicate is likely to be of great dynamic import. Cf. notes 21, 22, and 31, above.

Our patients readily accept symbols as realities; when "flames of a secret love burn them" they can see themselves burned, by real people and real flames.[157] The following conception is similar: a catatonic moves his eyebrows like Miss M. and asserts that he has had sexual intercourse with her; Miss M.'s gesture carried out on his own body is equivalent to Miss M. herself.[158]

The peculiarity of the alteration of concepts in schizophrenia is that simple concepts can become as disordered as complex and difficult ones. The decisive factor here is first of all the pertinence to a feeling-toned complex which may either facilitate or hinder concept-formation. But the disorder also fluctuates with the ups and downs of the illness sometimes engulfing most of thinking, at other times only some functions.

If concepts are incompletely developed clear thinking is naturally impossible.

157. For the role of symbolism in schizophrenia, see Jung (364), Abraham (5), and Storch (716); compare also the discussion of symbolism Chap. 12, note 81, above. Symbolization in schizophrenics raises some interesting questions. I am indebted to Dr. Bela Mittelmann for calling my attention to these. We usually assume that symbolization is a representation of something general or abstract by something concrete and pictorial, but this does not seem to be the case in many symbolizations of schizophrenics. While the case of "burned by real people and real flames" seems to fit the usual assumption, the case of "the beginning and the end of the world" does not. On closer scrutiny even common symbols pose some questions. For example, the snake is often a penis symbol; here something concrete seems to stand for another concrete thing. This difficulty is overcome if we note that the snake as a symbol usually includes various abstract connotations, such as a "dangerous penis." Religious symbols, for example, the invisible deity of the monotheist, are frequently very abstract, and certainly not pictorial. This is a difficulty much harder to overcome, but we do not actually deal here with a symbol in the technical sense. Yet such abstract "indirect representations" are frequent in schizophrenics. Clinically they are labeled as vague generalities, and subsumed under the "enlarged" concept-basis of schizophrenics. Symbolization is a specific form of the broader category "indirect representation," and the latter clearly belongs in the context of concept-formation. We have no clear solution of the problems touched on here; we can only point out that they seem to be related to the unique role of words in schizophrenic thinking (note 60, above).

158. This point is related to the magic of expressive movements, to the issue of "body language," and to the role of omnipotence. Cf. Werner (755, Chap. IX, "The Fundamental Ideas of Magic as an Expression of Primitive Conceptualization," pp. 337 ff.); Freud (227, Chap. III, "Animism, Magic and the Omnipotence of Thought," pp. 865 ff.); and Kris (424, "Ein Geisteskranker Bildhauer"). See Freud (234, pp. 129–33), and Nunberg (541, 542) on body-language in schizophrenia.

A long-inert patient finally works for a half hour. Now he believes that he is entitled to all kinds of possible and impossible rewards, and since he does not get them he again quits working. When he assumes that he should get a reward for his work his thinking is still correct; but he does not distinguish between continuous work and a half-hour's work, nor between small and large rewards; the bit of work means for him work at large, and reward means everything he then wants. His conceptions of work and reward are unclear; therefore, a correct quantitative relationship between the two is impossible. The vagueness of concept boundaries is conducive to nonsensical *generalizations*.[159]

In a paranoid patient the hallucinated sound of machines ceases, whereupon the whole institution ceases to exist for him. . . . A hebephrenic who was cross with his father believes that he must cleanse himself of this sin; before long he extends this cleansing to everything, and washes not only himself and the furniture, but puts his clothing on the roof to be cleansed by the rain. Delusional ideas proper often spread in the form of such generalizations.

159. This extreme recklessness of schizophrenic generalization is in some respects the opposite of the work of repression. Repression expels from consciousness not only the direct representative of the unacceptable drive, but everything that is even remotely connected with it (after-expulsion). A similar process took place in the history of the Jewish religion: the men of the Great Assembly held that, "A fence must be put around the law." The consequence was that since to work on the Sabbath was forbidden, anything that resembled work (for example, carrying a handkerchief) was forbidden, the touching of anything that *could* be a means of work was forbidden, and endless disputes began about "the egg the hen laid on the Sabbath." Freud (209, p. 473) wrote about repression in dreams:

If doubt is added to the indistinctness of an element of the dream-content, we may, *following this indication, recognize in this element a direct off-shoot of one of the* *outlawed dream-thoughts*. The state of affairs is like that obtaining after a great revolution in one of the republics of antiquity or the Renaissance. The once powerful, ruling families of the nobility are now banished; all high posts are filled by upstarts; in the city itself only the poorer and most powerless citizens, or the remoter followers of the vanquished party, are tolerated. Even the latter do not enjoy the full rights of citizenship. They are watched with suspicion. In our case, instead of suspicion we have doubt.

When repression is still successfully functioning, all these indirect representations of the drive remain in the unconscious where they have been elaborated. As a result of the search for a representation sufficiently remote from the drive to pass "censorship," this elaboration becomes a far-flung complex network. In the schizophrenic, when repression breaks down, any one of the remote connections in this network can come to consciousness, resulting in the reckless generalizations, clinically so striking.

Affect-disorder influences intelligence in various ways. On the one hand, where interest is lacking little is thought of, or at least little is *thought out;* but if the patient makes a real effort to achieve his goal he can produce sharp and complex deductions. On the other hand, some mild paranoids think incorrectly only concerning their complexes. Schreber effectively disputed the opinions presented at his sanity hearing, though at the same time he also defended his nonsensical delusional ideas.[160]

Intellectual achievements vary with affect-toned complexes, which sometimes suppress, and at other times use and facilitate thinking. (These fluctuations of function should not be mistaken for the fluctuations of the disease; at times patients appear more demented because the disease-process is more intensive.)

[In schizophrenics] affect disorder is the most important cause of the "loss of psychic value-signs." [161] Idiots and cases of organic disorder also fail to discriminate between the essential and unessential. Idiots fail because they cannot grasp complex ideas in their totality, organic cases for the same reason and also because their train of ideas is limited to what corresponds to the predominant affect. In schizophrenia this process is more complicated: ideas are thought of in quite irregular fragments, which at times include the far-fetched but omit the obvious. Here affects may inhibit or facilitate associations in an even more sweeping fashion than in organic cases and are in addition themselves changed, both qualitatively and quantitatively. When it is a matter of indifference to

160. The relative intactness and lack of fluidity of a great part of the conceptual frames of reference in even markedly paranoid cases, as distinguished from other schizophrenics, is a well-established clinical fact. In part, we can account for this by the fact that in such cases the defense-mechanism of intellectualization and rationalization plays a prominent role. Whether this is a *sufficient* explanation has not been established. For Schreber, see Freud (224).

161. Bleuler probably refers here to a loss of discrimination between the important and the unimportant, which is due in part to a general loss of apprecia-

tion of the hierarchic organization of concepts. E. Levy (471), discussing the schizophrenic's poor discrimination between the foreground and background of experience, points out correctly that this is not so much a loss as a change in foreground-background relationships, when intrapsychic, idiosyncratic forces gain in importance. Bychowsky (118) gives a striking example of such a loss of discrimination; when asked where her husband was, the patient said, "On the wedding picture." On the issue of the articulation of foreground and background, see also Angyal (30). Cf. note 107, above.

the patient whether he or his family be ruined, whether he remain locked up forever, whether or not he wallow in dirt, then these ideas, so important for others, can have no influence upon his thinking. When a patient has to choose between a whim and his position in life, he will decide against the latter without reflection, because only his whim is affect-toned. This is one of the most important aspects of schizophrenic dementia.

CHAPTER 27

ON THE STRUCTURE OF THE AMNESIC SYNDROME [1]

By Hans Buerger-Prinz and Martti Kaila

I. [INTRODUCTION]

WE INTEND TO DESCRIBE the structure of the amnesic syndrome,[2] by an intensive discussion of a few cases. Not every case shows all the disturbances in full clarity; the predominating elements differ from case to case and from time to time. Yet all cases show the same fundamental disorder. . . . The cases chosen show with particular clarity the various reactions and processes characteristic of this symptom-complex. Our task is to demonstrate the unitary structure of this syndrome, that is, the ubiquity of the basic patterns in various functions and under different conditions.[3*]

1. Buerger-Prinz and Kaila (117).

2. The "amnesic syndrome" or "amnesic symptom-complex" are alternative designations for what used to be called the "Korsakow psychosis." In Hinsie and Shatsky's (330) dictionary, as well as in the textbooks currently used, the old term and the old conception of this condition still persist. Cf. Henderson and Gillespie (320), Strecker (722), Noyes (539), W. A. White (768). Hinsie and Shatsky's description (330, pp. 312–13):

. . . [the] Korsakow psychosis . . . is characterized by mental and physical disorders. The outstanding physical symptom is polyneuritis. The organic mental syndrome is the result of a combination of attention and memory disorders. The memory disorder is of the nature of a lack of impressibility. The result of this combination is a special type of amnesia. There is defect in the recording of current events. The patient is usually disoriented, to some extent at least, and the things that have recently happened cannot be recalled. . . . The amnesic periods are generally filled in by confabulations. The Korsakow psychosis may be caused by a variety of agents —alcohol, metallic poisons, infections, or any of the encephalopathies.

Though the revision of our knowledge of the syndrome began with Brodmann's (95), Gregor's (288), and Roemer's (290) contributions in the first decade of the century, and was accelerated by Pick's (566) study published in 1915, Korsakow's (413) and Bonnhoeffer's (82) earlier conception is still with us. The present paper in a sense summarizes this process of revision.

3.* We present here only a small selection of our results, the minimum necessary to outline and document our views.

II. [THE INERTIA OF DRIVING-FORCES]

Patient *B* excelled in self-observation, the unusual sharpness of which facilitated the phenomenological analysis of his reactions and modes of experience.[4]

His general behavior was ordered and very quiet. He did not seek contact with the other patients; but when stimulated or talked to, he was attentive to the examiner. In conversation a common ground was immediately reached, without rapport difficulties. His mood oscillated between quiet indolence, bland indifference, and a mild but genuine depression which was particularly marked when in the course of testing he became aware of his defects.[5]

He complained: "Everything is so dead, I had more life before; nothing new comes and the old is gone. If I didn't know that I am older, I would think I am a child."

Meanwhile he noticed all the everyday happenings on the ward; he was interested in what happened to him and particularly in the tests he was given. But this interest endured only as long as the occasions lasted. Once these passed, they were settled for him and had no after-effects. "There is always something that occupies me, but it leaves no trace." [6] He showed the same indiffer-

---

We use only four cases, so as not to cloud the essentials by a mass of material. For the same reason we will forego an exhaustive review of the literature. The etiological factors in the four cases were carbon-dioxide poisoning, arteriosclerosis, skull-fracture, and strangulation. The case histories appear at the end of the paper.

4. The authors' emphasis on the importance of the patients' introspective reports for the understanding of their observed behavior is striking throughout this paper. Cf. Lewin's parallel systematic position, Chap. 4; see also Chap. 22, note 22, above.

5. The "organic" patient is prone to be unaware of his defect, and to react intensely when becoming aware of it. Cf. Goldstein (279, pp. 10–18, particularly p. 18). See also Ferenczi and Hollos (187); Schilder (655), and Chap. 25,

note 296, above, concerning regression in paretic cases as a protection against the damage to self-esteem implicit in awareness of defect. Their views are general and do not clearly differentiate the primary effects of organic damage from the secondary effects of defense against awareness of it. Cf. Rapaport, Kenyon, and Lozoff (381).

6. The authors demonstrate below that this phenomenon is not a primary memory-disorder. Earlier, Brodmann, Gregor, and Roemer had demonstrated experimentally that the apparent memory-disorder is one not of registration but rather of recollection. It seems probable that the exclusive impression, given by these patients to early investigators, of loss of registration-ability, antero-grade amnesia, and poor memory for current events, was rooted in phenomena like those seen here in Patient *B*. The

ence in relation to his wife and children. He liked them as before, he longed after them—"But then again I am indifferent, it doesn't affect me as it used to." He had sexual impulses, but "I am more indifferent than before, it doesn't mean as much to me." His interest in everything, even eating, seemed decreased. Though he could taste and smell it all, "The feeling for it is lacking, I cannot get satiated." For a while after his accident—so his wife told him—he ate inhuman quantities, until they put him on rations and schedule. This was still the case: "I can eat anytime, though I know I get enough to eat and it makes no sense to eat out of turn." [7]

Already the patient's general behavior indicates to us the first problems of the amnesic syndrome, warning the careful observer that the syndrome cannot be explained by a pure "memory theory," nor is the memory-disorder its most salient psychopathological characteristic. To the contrary: the entire structure of emotionality and drives is altered. All functions seem to be preserved, but the extent and depth of their effect upon the personality is wanting. [8*] Situation after situation appears momentarily, only to disappear without an after-effect. This is not a disorder of "retentive" or "elaborative" memory; [9*] it originates at a level which is a prerequisite of and preparatory to memory-function. Affective resonance exists only while the experience is present; all interests and strivings awaken only with the situation, but they do not bring it about. [10] The passive character of the general attitude, which has

---

question may be raised: What gave the impression that remote memory was less effected than recent? The latter are easier to observe, since the current events were known to the investigators and the forgetting of past events is frequently cloaked by confabulations in such cases. A more penetrating explanation will take into consideration the fact that past events have manifold anchorages in our experience. But these explanations are less than satisfactory, and the syndrome is still wide open for exploration. For instance, Stoerring's (715) case, which was reported to have had no loss of memory-material acquired prior to his carbon-monoxide poisoning, and to have

had a *complete* anterograde amnesia, would raise serious doubts as to the adequacy of these explanations.

7. This lack of "satiation" is considered by the authors one of the central features of the syndrome, and will be discussed repeatedly below.

8.* Schilder (648).

9.* W. Stern (710).

10. The authors assert that though a given situation does arouse affects, interests, and strivings, these do not arise spontaneously to create an internal situation in thought, nor an external one by action. The authors imply a passivity of motivating factors, and an organization of memory and thought by affects, inter-

been frequently stressed by previous investigators,[11*] means that the patient "lets the world approach him without actively encountering it." [12*] The entire dynamics of the personality are altered; strivings, drives, emotional impulses, are no longer driving-forces in quest—so to speak—of experiences.[13] This is not contradicted by the euphoria, loquaciousness, and distractibility of some patients. The essential point is that the patients lack spontaneity, must wait for external stimulation, and can do hardly anything on their own. Korsakow [14*] expressed this when he spoke of "apathetic" confusion. Later Bonhoeffer [15*] stressed that these patients, though attentive in conversation, lack interest and spontaneity when left alone. In encephalitics, external stimulation must supplement the internal, to give the last impetus to action, because the driving-forces appear to be dammed-up and awaiting an impetus to overcome the blocking; but here the driving-forces themselves appear to be stagnant, lie fallow, and in order to rise, need external stimulation. Indeed, they arise immediately with the total situation to which they pertain, and disappear with it, leaving no trace. The irritable cases of this syndrome do not contradict the observation. Irritability indicates only that affect-waves ride high, rise at every possible occasion, and are disproportionate to it; but it does not reveal anything about affect-dynamics and drive-life as such, nor about their role in the personality, its general life-situation, and its range of experience.[16]

------

ests, and strivings. The level of theorizing here lags far behind the sophistication and acuteness of observation and description: no specific mechanisms or processes characteristic of this organization are abstracted.

11.* Bonhoeffer (82), Steinthal (704).

12.* Buerger (113).

13. Compare this conception of the role of drives, strivings, and impulses, with Fenichel's (179) concept of "stimulus hunger" (Chap. 18, note 4, above). Lewin's tension-conception of needs is also similar to the one here implied: when the objects which have valence for the need are absent, they are sought out under the pressure of the need-tension. See Chap. 5, I, 2, above. It will be worth while to remind ourselves that we observe similar passivity also in psychopathology other than that of organic etiology; furthermore, we encounter individual variations of it in normal people, and most human beings have subjective states and/or objective situations in which they display it.

14.* Korsakow (413).

15.* Bonhoeffer (82).

16. At first glance, it is difficult to understand the authors' assertion that the euphoria, loquaciousness, irritability, and disproportionate affects are not revealing of the role of affect- and drive-dynamics in these patients' personalities. But those acquainted with these patients clinically will be reminded of the mask-

In this discussion of the emotional and drive-life of these patients, it is already evident that the very factors which are essential constituents of the personality are particularly altered and impaired. Considering the importance of this layer, it is obvious that its paralysis must rob the patient of the internal continuity of his personality. . . .

The generally observed bland indolence, and the uniform mild depression or euphoria, represent generalized emotional attitudes [*Einstellungen*] which do not preclude reacting to external stimulation. They are, however, the expression of the paralysis of feelings and strivings which make up the vital background for all those forces necessary to elaborate the experience-material

---

like, shallow, and volatile character of these manifestations, which give the impression of lacking anchorage in the dynamics of the personality. Unlike the affects of normals, neurotics, and psychotics, and often even the so-called "inappropriate affects" of schizophrenics, the affects of "organic" cases frequently elude empathy.

Since the theory of affects is still vague, and the exploration—and even description—of the affects of "organic" cases is in its very beginning, it is possible only to speculate about the dynamic conditions underlying this characteristic coexistence of inertia of motivations and volatility of affects. Let us take the psychoanalytic theory of affects as our point of departure. According to this theory (see Chap. 15, note 26, and Chap. 17, note 8, above), affects are indicators and safety valves of drive-tensions. They arise under usual conditions only when drive-tensions cannot be discharged and are pent up. The reasons for such a delay of discharge may be: (a) structural conditions, which demand either that drive-tension rise to a certain height before discharge occurs, or that discharge be held up until a specific drive-object is found; in Lewin's

terminology the first condition would correspond to "boundary-solidity," and the second to "fixation"; or (b) conflict, which prohibits discharge. To explain the conditions prevailing in cases of the amnesic syndrome, two conjectures might be made. First, that the boundaries of tension-systems of drives (Lewin) have no solidity, and thus continuous "leakage" of tension takes place. The lack of driving impetus on the one hand, and the volatile affects on the other, would then be the observable consequences of this "leakage." Krauss's (418) and Golant-Rattner's (278) studies lend some support to this conjecture. Secondly, that drive-tension is, quite apart from the leakage-effect, diminished. Schilder (647) in discussing this symptom of Korsakow patients made this assumption, attributing the decrease of tension to a damage of the striatum-pallidum. The two conjectures are not mutually exclusive. But assuming even that the processes implied by both are present, we still cannot easily account for the paradoxical coexistence of the lack of satiation by stimuli and the overready satiation of "meaning-experience." A discussion of these will be found below.

presented, and mobilize that which the person has stored up.[17] The lack of satiation and the unresponsive sexuality are particularly good indicators of the complete paralysis in the dynamic vital layers. That the patient is always able to eat is not explained by saying, for instance, that he forgot he had already eaten his lunch. But granted he did forget it, still he has no possibility of correcting himself by getting information from his own body, which unlike a normal organism does not indicate satiation by a certain general feeling-state.[18] Even these simple automatic processes—the primitive regulations which, for instance, steer the infant's life—are altered. This means that the retrenchment in the functions of the organism is not a regression to an earlier childish level.[19] Naturally, there occurs a "de-differentiation," [20] but the total state is not comparable to any phase of development.

Since this phenomenon aroused our attention, we have frequently observed, in cases of brain pathology, an absence of satiation-experiences in relation to other stimuli also. The bulimia of paretics is well known and has been frequently described. It is not a specific isolated symptom, but only the most impressive and obvious form of the lack of stimulus-barrier, the lack of satiation in regard to stimuli.[21]

At the time of this writing, we have under observation a patient (general paresis and lues cerebri) who shows a classic form of this total alteration of biological behavior toward the world of stimuli. Not only is he lacking inhibi-

---

17. Cf. note 10 above, on the theory of thought-organization implied here.

18. The only systematic experimental studies of satiation were conducted by Lewin's collaborators, Karsten (370) and Freund (261). The studies on pathological cases by Krauss and Golant-Rattner, mentioned above, used Lewin's method. Concerning satiation see also Lewin, pp. 124–25, above. The authors here seem to link "lack of correction," described first by Pick (566), to lack of satiation experience.

19. Cf. note 4, above, for reference to Schilder, and Ferenczi and Hollos, on regression. See also H. Werner (755, p. 34).

20. See Goldstein (279, pp. 3–8), and (281, pp. 131 ff.).

21. The "stimulus-barrier," as defined by Freud (Chap. 16, note 11, above), fends off undesirable stimuli and reduces to manageable size the intensity of desirable ones. In a sense its role is the opposite of that of "stimulus hunger"; cf. note 13 above. The connection between the two sets of phenomena referred to by "lack of stimulus-barrier" and "lack of satiation" is far from clear; this becomes particularly obvious if we consider that, in the authors' observations, they coexist. Cf. note 16, above.

tions toward food and drink, "gorging and gulping" like an animal everything he is offered; he will also stare for minutes at a brilliant light, unable to tear himself away from it; and though he complains of the pain and begs not to be pricked again, he will actively follow the needle shown to him. To a held-out hand, he reacts by incessantly reaching after it; and if a Barany-drum is put to his ear, he follows it, though his facial expressions shows displeasure.[22]

This is a totally altered biological behavior toward the environment, a being placed at the mercy of the world of stimuli, and a lack of that satiability by stimuli which usually protects the organism. For such behavior of brain-damage cases, Goldstein coined the term "lack of stimulus-barrier." [23]

III. [IMAGERY AND ATTITUDE-DISTURBANCE]

The information Patient G gives about his imagery is in agreement with that obtained from B. His images of everything, even of his children and wife, are vague; nothing is quite clear. When he tries to imagine his wife, her face is gone before he gets to her dress or figure. But even to imagine the face is difficult; he must rely on what comes by itself, his efforts do not help. Everything slips away, as though it had not been there at all.[24]

22. The schizophrenic symptoms of echolalia and echopraxia are similar to the phenomena described here. In them too, stimuli are experienced as compelling commands. Expressed in Lewin's terms, the valences are of commanding intensity, and are fixated to highly specific consummatory activities which are not modified by the situation, context, or setting. Cf. Lewin, Chap. 5, II, 1c, 3, above. The behavior resulting is therefore more like a reflex than common human behavior; in the latter, few if any valences (stimuli) have sufficient commanding intensity to disregard all controls, and hardly any valences are totally fixated, but rather modified usually by the external and internal situation, which is always multi-layered.

The disregard of the schizophrenic patient for the multi-layered meanings of the words and behavior he echoes, and the similar disregard of this organic patient for the multiple meanings of the stimuli he is attracted to, like a moth to flame, is as important a characteristic of either behavior as is "lack of satiation." It implies the impairment of the buffer which contextual thought offers against the direct impact of stimuli. Gruenthal recognized this, as we shall see below (note 28).

These considerations cast a sidelight on the hopelessness of explaining behavior by conditioning theories of any vintage.

23. In a personal communication Goldstein disclaims this assertion. The concept was coined by Freud (see note 21, above).

24. The importance of these authors' observations for the psychology, and not only the pathology, of thinking will be more clearly appraised if normal

This paleness of optical imagery has already struck many authors, including those who first described the syndrome. Yet optical imagery is only one example—the most easily studied—of the quality of these patients' imagery in general. It is certainly an independent disorder of a function. The theoretical significance of this alteration of imagery becomes clear only in relation to the disturbances of the "vital sphere" already mentioned, to the alterations of thought-function, and to the more physiological disturbances. In itself, this unclarity of imagery is not related to "drowsiness" or dream-like confusion, though the character of imagery in these conditions is perhaps analogous. The general state of consciousness [in our cases] need not be that of drowsiness, etc., which indicates that the character of imagery is only one of the necessary criteria for distinguishing states of consciousness in regard to their degree of clarity.[25]

While *B* was unable to change the paleness and vagueness of his images, he was able to make use of help given to him. "When I have a starting point, then it goes better, then I can follow." For instance, he was unable to describe the circumstances under which he was taken a prisoner of war. "Yes, the French caught us" was all at first. (Morning or evening?) "I think it was morning." (Did the sun shine?) "No, it was foggy." (In a village or out in the fields?) "It was a field and there were guns." (Was it in a depression or in the open?) "It was a hill, and they were on the other side. There were a few trees. Now I know how it was. The French came suddenly over the hill; we stood there, only

---

counterparts are recalled. It is well known, though no systematic studies prove it definitely, that there are great individual differences in vividness and stability of imagery. See Jaensch (352). Furthermore, the stability and clarity of imagery fluctuates greatly in the individual, depending on the situation, subjective state, and subject-matter. The figure of the craved-for beloved may appear to us in a sharp, stable, and even obsessionally persistent image; when love is flagging it may lose its sharpness. Yet even in the period of most intense love it may recede when we are fully engaged in work or overwhelmed by exhaustion. Under such conditions the experience is indeed one of something "slipping away" from us.

25. Indeed, Silberer's (Chap. 9, above) observations on drowsiness, and Hartmann and Schilder's (312) observations on amentia, show that these states of consciousness are actually conducive to vivid imagery. It does seem though that the vivid imagery has an extremely fleeting character, as thought also does in these states. Our comments on Betlheim and Hartmann's paper (Chap. 13, note 56, above) indicate some of the other criteria for distinguishing states of consciousness.

a few people, and they took us."—Or: (How did the school look to which you went?) "That I don't know any more. I don't know anything about that any more." (Big building, red, or like the other houses?) "Not like the others, red stones." (Where was the school yard?) "Around it." (Boys or girls?) "No, only boys; the girls were on the other side." (How did the classroom look? where did you sit?) "That I can't tell you any more." (Did you sit at the front?) "I don't think so." (Were there boys behind you?) "Yes, now I know; X sat behind me and in front of me my friend Y. Now I know even the name of the teacher." (How did he look?) "That doesn't come into my head now." (Big, slender, small, fat?) "Seems he was rather big, had pince-nez and a bald pate, a nice man. In the class there were landscapes on the wall and a bust of the Kaiser."

These examples show quite clearly how B uses help. One gives him a starting-point to hold on to, and narrows the number of possibilities by questions, centering him progressively. One directs him thus toward certain points, from which slowly the whole picture emerges. It is as though he were given fixed points to which to associate his memories. Even then the completion of the situation occurs only in a passive fashion, but the emerging images find solid reference-points. These images find their place and attain their proper positional value, not as random "diffuse reproductions," but rather by virtue of the definite direction given to the reproduction-tendencies.[26]* B's statement is revealing: "When one gets a hint, one can find it." It is this state of affairs

26.* Selz (679).
[This work, an off-shoot of the Wuerzburg school of Kuelpe, Marbe, and Ach, is frequently quoted by Pick (566), as well as the other investigators of the amnesic syndrome. See Chap. 25, I, d, above.

Selz delivered one of the important and devastating broadsides against the theory of thinking of association psychology. He demonstrated that thinking, far from being an outcome of association-complexes, is a directed function determined by *anticipations*. His experiments were justly criticized as limited in scope, area, and depth, and his

theory as purely intellectualistic. (See, for example, Koffka, 403.) Even his concept of *anticipation* was an extremely limited one, more or less identical with the narrowest conception of psychological "set." (See Gibson, 269, and Allport, 24.) Yet he was the first, to my knowledge, to stress explicitly the anticipation aspect of directional factors in thinking. The motivational character of these factors eluded his frame of reference.

The investigators who saw an attitude-disturbance in the amnesic syndrome found his concepts applicable to attitudes, which also imply expectation and readiness in a certain direction.]

Pick [27]* had in mind when he said that these patients lack "circumspection." According to Gruenthal,[28]* the patient's presentations "are determined only from one direction." We propose for this the term "isolation of presentations." The behavior of B shows quite clearly that presentations do not bring with themselves relationships and determinants, but are bare and lack relationships until the network of intentions—the system of fixed points [given the patient by the investigator] finally becomes sufficient; then suddenly the material appropriate to the situation segregates from the fluctuating mass of experience, and crystallizes around this network. Pick clearly recognized this nature of the process.[29]

27.* Pick (566).

[By "circumspection" Pick referred to Selz's (679) conception, according to which situations and stimuli actualize supporting, modifying, and contrary knowledge; the latter delineate, in the form of a schema, both the appropriate meaning of the stimulus and the adequate reaction. The schemata so arising he called anticipations.]

28.* Gruenthal (294):

[In a sense thinking becomes linear, without tributary sidestreams of collateral relationships, so that no new points of view, nor new material permitting comparisons, emerge. The presentations of the train of thought are determined only from *one* direction. Circumspection, which would arouse self-criticism and refer to corrective factors, is lacking (p. 127).]

29. Pick was the outstanding figure among the investigators who demonstrated that the amnesic syndrome is not specific to alcohol-psychoses, but is frequently found after any delirious condition of "organic" etiology. He also showed that the "attitude-disorder" is not specific to the amnesic syndrome, but often occurs after a severe clouding of consciousness has cleared up, for example, after hysterical twilight states and narcoses (566, pp. 380–81).

It seems justified to go even further than Pick. Experience in psychotherapy shows that neurotic patients, too, find it extraordinarily difficult to recollect crucial past experiences and their context. Often the therapist's role is to gather up for them scattered fragments of experience, amassing them and even interpreting them, until the patient has sufficient fixed points to be able to gather up and crystallize further relevant material. Concerning the psychological dynamics of this process, and particularly the role of the synthetic function of the ego in it, see Kris, Chap. 23, III, above.

Moreover, all of us observe similar processes in ourselves when learning entirely new material, and in others when we teach or examine students. Until there is a sufficient number of fixed points to give structure to the learned material, it is extremely difficult—if not impossible —to find those parts of it which are relevant to the situation. The experience in taking and giving examinations is of particular interest here, because even well-organized material seems to elude the anxiety-ridden examinee, and because the teacher with a few well-chosen hints can restore the student's ability to find it. Or as a little boy put it once, "Teacher, I

This is where the concept of attitude [*Einstellung*], which Gruenthal had put into the foreground of the theory of the amnesic syndrome, applies.[30]

IV. [THE CONCEPTS OF ATTITUDE AND ATTITUDE-DISTURBANCE]

We must digress here to discuss the concept of attitude [*Einstellung*] [31] in some detail, though we do not attribute a fundamental significance to this factor in the structure of the amnesic syndrome. We will attempt to reduce attitude as an explanatory principle to others which underlie attitude-disturbances in this disorder. . . .

---

knew it all the time, you just didn't ask the question that would fetch it."

These considerations are not intended to suggest that there is no difference between the examples discussed and the amnesic syndrome; but to show that such phenomena are not unique to pathology, and to suggest that organic damage, neurotic defense, examination anxiety, and reality difficulty in mastering new knowledge, all may use the same mechanisms, though differing in intensity and extent. There is here a broad area open to empirical investigation.

30. Gruenthal (294, p. 127) wrote:

At one moment, registration appears to have failed; at the next, the thought-material which seemingly was unregistered and unevocable, suddenly emerges. This is a matter of *attitude-disturbance:* whenever the disappeared material was followed up by questions arousing the pertinent attitudes, the knowledge immediately reappeared.

31. The term *Einstellung* may be rendered in English as "orientation," as "set" (as in postural-set), or as "attitude." It was one of the concepts which the Wuerzburg school introduced (see Ach, Chap. 1, above) to designate the non-associative, directional determiners of thought: task (*Aufgabe*), determin-ing tendency (*Determinierende Tendenz*), attitude (*Einstellung*).

The choice of translating *Einstellung* by "attitude" may be justified on two counts: (a) the present authors' use of *Einstellung* in the sense of a directional factor, one which is dependent on the "vital sphere of affects and drives," and yet seems to play a motivation-like role in thought- and behavior-organization; (b) both Allport's (24) and Chein's (129) conclusion that the concept of attitude subsumes instrumental as well as motivational factors. See Chap. 1, note 31, above. Cf. also Sherif and Cantril (686).

Though 15 years have passed since its publication, Allport's (24) paper is still the best statement of the nature and varieties of attitudes. It contains a particularly important discussion of their relation to and distinction from reflexes, conditioned reflexes, habits, instincts, needs, wishes, desires, vectors, quasi-needs, sentiments, motor sets, interests, subjective values, prejudices, stereotypes, concepts, opinions, and traits. Judging by the recent literature on attitudes, this important paper has not been carefully read. Concerning Bartlett's and Koffka's concepts of attitude, see our comments on Claparède, Chap. 3, notes 17 and 18, above.

Gruenthal describes attitude-disturbance as the difficulty or impossibility of leaving a realm of thought, and to connect with other thoughts outside it.[32] Actually, this definition is too narrow; it does not account for the possibility of "bringing the patient into the correct attitude," by questions which push him into the direction in which he can and should proceed.

Attitude, if overexpanded, becomes a dangerously meaningless, cover-all, general concept. However, to define it strictly, Gruenthal's criteria are insufficient; attitude-disturbance is embedded in many phenomenological givens, and it is necessary to describe more exactly what the concept should or should not imply.

Attitude is a directedness, but unlike intention it is not the direction of single acts. Attitude is both more and less: it is less, because it is not the direction toward a definite object; it is more, because it is a general orientation of the personality. It is not a matter of single acts, but rather a drive-, affect-, feeling-, and thought-supported bearing which the personality carries into every thought and action. Attitude then is not a matter of consciousness; it antecedes all conscious processes. This does not preclude its becoming conscious and known to self-observation. Normal psychology also uses the concept "attitude" in this "preconscious" sense.[33*] Attitude is the special mode in which a person approaches everything he encounters in his environment. . . .[34]

In order to determine what attitude-disturbances are, we must first ask what is to be expected of attitudes in normals.

32. Gruenthal (295, p. 255): The attitude-disorder of thinking has the following characteristic: partial or total inability to leave a train of thought once entered, and to make connections with ideas outside it. The result is a reproduction difficulty for contents which are distant from the momentary thought; this gives the impression of a loss of registration. The prevalent contents are related to customary life-situations or feeling-toned thoughts. These, since corrective comparison possibilities are absent, are taken to be real and present, even in the face of patent contradictions.

33.* For example, Marbe, Zirbel, and Klient.

[The authors refer again to the Wuerzburg school.]

34. The omitted section discusses von Kries's (420) concept of attitude, which is of the order of a "set" ("every total state of the apparatus effects the nature of the subsequent state"). The authors point out that this is a momentary attitude which may be limited to one sense or extremity, while Marbe's conception pertains to the entire organism and the entire life of the individual. They stress Gruenthal's failure to specify to what kind of attitude the disturbance of the amnesic syndrome pertains.

One presupposes of a normal person that he will follow freely and vividly the changes of situations, at least up to a certain point. However, he will never get away from a certain attitude, namely, that which is characteristic of him as a singular personality, and of his manner of apperceiving and assimilating the stimulus world.[35] Usually we do not even call this an attitude, but rather "the individuality." But past situations themselves always have after-effects, which may accumulate quite independently of the individuality, and may so perseverate as to falsify new experiences in terms of those past. It is justified to call these after-effects of experience, attitudes. It is clear that from this point there is a transition to sentiments [*Gesinnungen*] [36] which are unchanging, value-bearing trends of the personality . . . and to what are called "affective preconceptions." (For instance, I am irritated with a man and therefore take exception to everything about him.) Furthermore, there are transitions here to "moods." Naturally, "attitudes" arise in connection with all these. What is essential and form-giving in these phenomena is not the attitudes but their tangible background: the affect, the mood, the sentiment, and so on.[37]

35. This is, indeed, one of the most striking characteristics of thought-organization: the balance it strikes between *remaining* characteristically that of the individual, and *changing* appropriately with the situation. The characteristic is not limited to this aspect of thought: a continuous balance is struck between adherence to goal and utilization of means encountered. Gill, Schafer, and I (602) have pointed out that the function of concept-formation itself is also such a balance of inductive and deductive processes (p. 391). The integration which lends thought-organization the imprint of individuality is presumably one aspect of the "*synthetic function*" of the ego (Nunberg, 543; see also Chap. 21, notes 10 and 20, above); while those regulations which make the continuous adaptation to changing situations possible may be an aspect of the *differentiating function* of the ego (Hartmann, Chap. 19, IV, above).

The balance here discussed seems to be characteristic of the biological adaptation-process in general. Piaget's (556) derivation of intellectual function from that of biological adaptation (assimilation and accommodation) appears here in a new light. Cf. Chap. 7, above.

36. See McDougall (493), Cattell (128), and Eysenck (167).

37. Though the authors are inclined to regard attitudes proper rather as "sets," they clearly see how these accompany all directional and selective functions of the personality. The transitions between these various forms they see as clearly as Allport did, but unlike him, they do not face the issue of the motivating role of attitudes. We urgently need empirical studies to clarify further these relationships. The studies of Sanford and Brunswik (200, 199) on the relation of personality-structure and attitudes, though important, deal only with the general correlation, not with processes

In contrast to these, the concept of attitude covers something much more colorless, indefinite, and intangible, because in normal people it changes—at least in principle—from experience to experience. The absence of such changes may amount to an attitude-disturbance. The patient remains in a certain situation, perseverates in it. Pick stressed this factor of the amnesic syndrome, and in Gruenthal's definition it attained preeminence. The result of such a disturbance is that a patient cannot bring about relationships which lie outside of his momentary situation.[38] Conversely, this implies that he cannot shift his attitude himself, he cannot settle anything definitively. Either he cannot find his way to a new situation at all, or he interprets and falsifies it in terms of *his* attitude.[39]

Patient G displayed some excellent examples of such disturbances of attitude [*Einstellung*], which implied inability to shift attitudes [*Umstellung*].

---

which mediate it; studies of these would cast light on the development of the hierarchy of motivations, and on its actual mode of functioning.

38. Gruenthal (294, pp. 126–27) wrote:

The patient is unable to actualize all those experiences which are necessary to develop a correct, reality-adequate thought. Now only this experience, now only another, is actualized, and therefore the development of the train of thought proceeds on lopsided premises. The defect lies in the failure to bring existing images or thoughts into relation with the totality of experience, and in the inability to fit an externally or internally stimulated idea into the total situation that presents itself at the moment.

39. Goldstein's (279, 284) conception of the fundamental disorder in "organic" cases in general might also be considered one of "attitude-disturbance." He and his collaborators distinguish only two kinds of attitudes: abstract and concrete. They, too, consider the inability to shift attitudes one of the cardinal defects of "organic" cases (279, pp. 6 and 211).

Goldstein (280) has observed similar phenomena, however, in schizophrenics also.

Here again we deal with a phenomenon which has a normal counterpart and is multi-layered. When mathematicians persisted for 2,000 years in the attempt to prove Euclid's fifth postulate, was that not an inability to shift attitudes? The very form of the question which opened the road to non-Euclidian geometries— "What if the fifth postulate is *not* true?" —suggests that a shift in attitude has taken place. Prolonged periods of inability to shift an attitude is a commonly observed precursor of scientific discoveries, of problem-solving at large, and of mastering personal problems. The subjective experiences of elation and relief suggest that such shifts are shifts in cathectic balances. Kris (421) suggests they are of the kind Freud described in wit (214) and humor (253). If this be so, inability to shift may be linked to unavailability of the requisite cathexes. But the empirical evidence to substantiate this point is not yet available. See Kris, Chap. 23, V, above.

He offered the following interpretations for the pictures of Heilbronner's "Windmill" series: [40] a) a coffee-pot; b) a coffee-pot with two handles; c) the same, has an edge also; d) the same pot, only a line comes out of it on top; e) a pot too, only it is double at the bottom; f) this fits a pot too, it's the same; g) it's the same, here on top two lines are drawn; h) also the same, only there is something on the top; I don't know what you call these double lines(the sails of the windmill); i) a pot for coffee, but the handle is missing.—However, as soon as a tree, a carriage, a man, were sketched around the mill by a few lines, *G* knew immediately: "This is a windmill." [41]

Such processes we will consider more closely later on, in our discussion of thinking and perception. Here we are mainly interested in the fact that the patient sticks to an attitude once assumed and does not shift, though he recognizes and registers the objective changes from picture to picture. All changes appear to him as additions, and he does not create an intrinsic relation between them and the originally presented lines. This barrier is overcome only when the change becomes so great that a totally different, and by its very appearance overwhelming, situation arises.[42]

Similarly: . . . Patient *S* in the examination room: (Why are you here?)

40. The Minnesota Pre-school Test contains similar items. For instance: in a series of pictures, the first shows only a hardly recognizable line, subsequent ones show additional lines, until the final picture is the complete drawing of a shoe.

41. To my knowledge, the "normal" counterpart of this phenomenon, which seems to be important both for the theory of learning in particular and the theory of thought-organization in general, has not been studied systematically.

Some people are unable to master an abstract theory (for example, mathematics or physics), but as soon as its practical application is shown to them, they immediately master both theory and application. Even in solving single problems, people differ in the number of hints they need to see the solution. Furthermore, the same individual will require varying numbers of hints (fixed points), depending on his subjective state and the subject-matter. This is seen in the course of therapy, for instance, when the patient and therapist are struggling to gain a full view of a situation.

42. The objective changes were recognized by the patient, but were treated in an *additive* and not in a *synthetizing* fashion; the disorder may be described as an inability to form a Gestalt. If, as Koehler (400) maintains, Gestalts are isomorphic with electro-physiological brain-processes, one might conjecture that in these cases the energy-potentials involved are too low to overcome the resistance of the medium, and thus fail to lead to the Gestalt-experience. Only when further stimulations (and energy-sources) are added does Gestalt integration come about.

"I was looking for work." (Who am I?) "A son of the business." (What are the other men doing here?) "They sleep here." (Why?) "Because tiredness prevails." (What kind of a house is this?) "A bakery." (Are you not sick?) "Could be." (Why are you in the hospital?) "I broke my leg." [43] The patient apperceives the examining room as an office. On the ward he takes it for granted that he is in a hospital, but in the examining room it requires suggestive questions before he realizes the situation.

The doctor comes to the ward at prayer time. He asks *S:* "Who am I?" The patient answers, "The priest," which is quite natural in the context.

While in the laboratory, which is a strange environment for him, the patient is asked to name the occupation of the doctor. He answers: "A baker's apprentice." (But don't you see that this is not a bakery? He can't be a baker.) "No, he can't." (But why not?) The patient first looks around helplessly, then he takes it all for banter and says with a laugh: "He hasn't got the knack for it."

Here the attitude assumed completely falsifies the situation. In the first example it is the general attitude which effects it; in the second, a partial impression also (the white coat) facilitates it.

Similarly: Patient *G* is in bed. When asked where he is: "I am lying in the hospital, in the high school." (What are you doing here?) "It is war, I am a soldier." (What year is this?) "I think 1916."

This time it is the memory of a situation once experienced which makes him misrecognize his environment. Bonhoeffer [44*] has stressed that such phenomena are frequent. This last example is characteristic, in that the patient's inter-

---

43. This is an example of the confabulations so characteristic of the amnesic syndrome (see Williams and Rupp, 771). The German term applied to these is *Verlegenheits-Konfabulation*—"confabulations due to being at a loss"—that is, confabulations which fill in a gap resulting from the momentary unavailability of a memory. Pick (566) explained these by Bowden's principle: "The mind tends to order all the material presented to it, however disorganized, so as to make it meaningful." (This principle is in one sense identical with the Gestalt principle and in another with one aspect of the synthetic function of the ego.) Gruen-

thal (294, p. 124) gave the following explanation of confabulations:

Thinking [in these patients] is as a rule correct in its formal aspect, if viewed in the frame of reference of the direction it takes. It is free of perseverations, flight, or incoherence proper. The points of departure, assumptions, or premises of thinking, however, are often false. Therefore it is difficult or altogether impossible for the patient to distinguish between actualities and thoughts. But when there is no such conscious distinction, naturally there can be no need for correction either.

44.* Bonhoeffer (82).

pretation is based only on a few reference-points. Lying in bed and being sick suffice as the basis for an interpretation which satisfies him completely. Actually, it covers adequately the conditions under which it arose, and therefore the patient experiences not the slightest need to correct it.[45]* This disturbance arises when the patient's attitude results from an interpretation of the situation which is adequate for him, and according to which he assimilates all that he encounters.[46]

All these reactions have yet another important feature: the patients cannot themselves *assume an attitude;* they can only *be made to assume one.* However, if the situations are sufficiently rich in content, the total attitude of the patient may vary from experience to experience.

This is the case when *B*, who has just called the examiner "teacher," calls him "doctor" when asked about his illness, and "regimental surgeon" when asked about his war injuries.[47]

The attitude-disturbance . . . is one not only of the ability to shift, but also of the primary attitudes toward a part of the patient's life. This is the case, for instance, when *B* is unable to reproduce anything about the school he at-

45.* Pick (566) pointed out the general lack of need for self-correction in these patients. But the conditions under which it is lacking are as yet to be explored. They are certainly manifold, and we shall encounter some of them below.

46. This tendency to base interpretations on few reference-points is present also in *déjà vu* phenomena and dreams. In *déjà vu*, an identical affect, impulse, or defense, suffices to arouse the experience: "I have seen this before." In dreams, actions and persons may stand for each other by virtue of the slightest commonality. The differences are that the dream does not claim to be a communication, and disguises the common elements and the past event to which it refers; in *déjà vu*, the past event and the common underlying impulse are only indicated and remain outside consciousness; in this patient's "interpretation" the past becomes present and is communicated as reality. The direct symbolism of dream and delusion, and the subtle but uncanny indication of *déjà vu*, are absent in his "interpretation," and the scanty associative connections work unopposed in what would normally be ordered thinking. Schilder (644) would say that here a preparatory phase of thought occupies the place of thinking proper. Cf. also Chap. 3, note 9, above.

47. The implication is that these patients are in general so passive and sluggish that their attitudes do not arise, but must be aroused; but that certain meaning-laden situations arouse not single attitudes but total sets of them, such as being a soldier, a schoolboy, etc. The lack of balance between assimilation and accommodation may account for the coexistence of these extremes. Cf. note 35, above.

tended as a child, until he is given some points of departure. In such cases the attitude-disorder involves intentionality also.[48]

B expressed it himself: "Everything is so hazy. One does not know where to seek. When I want to look back, there is nothing, everything is empty."

This inability of the patient to set orientation-points for himself will be further discussed in relation to memory. Another obstacle in the way of establishing attitudes is that the memories toward which they would point are so fluctuating and unformed that neither goals nor orienting points can be found.[49]

Thus the patient's attitude-disturbances result from the haziness of goals, from the action-disturbance, and from the disturbances of the ability to shift and those of experience-consummation implied by it.[50] We want to emphasize again that we do not attribute a fundamental significance to the attitudes and attitude-disturbances in the understanding of the amnesic syndrome. We believe that these disturbances are results of those more fundamental changes which we have attempted to demonstrate. . . .[51]

48. "Intentionality," a concept introduced by Brentano and the phenomenological philosophers (Chap. 25, note 6. above), denotes the object-directedness which, according to them, inheres in all psychic acts. It is probable that the concept of intentionality was born from a general recognition of the goal-directedness of all psychic functions. The present authors seem to consider the inability of the patient to recall school-experiences as an inability to "intend" them, that is, to turn toward them mentally. This seems to them a disorder of the most fundamental and most general function of the psyche.

There is still little known about the relationship between drives and intentionality, and the insights of Brentano and the phenomenological philosophers have not been exploited so far by modern dynamic psychology. Of contemporary psychology, Gestalt alone was aware of the significance of these thinkers.

49. Here the argument may seem circular, but it is not necessarily so. Memories, and thus goals, were considered fluctuating because of the attitude-disturbance; in turn, their unformedness may contribute to exacerbate further the attention-disturbance.

50. The connection between the lack of satiation and the inability to shift has not been discussed. It may be conjectured that, according to the authors, satiation (consummation) of an activity is the prerequisite for a shift to another.

51. The omitted section may be summarized as follows: (a) It may be argued that the phenomena interpreted as attitude-disturbances lend themselves to explanation in terms of perseveration. (b) Ach's (15) experiments and Gruenthal's (295) observations are cited to argue that perseverations are a fundamental psychological process, not a secondary phenomenon (Heilbronner), and are not necessarily random "fillers" of a vacuum, but may have an "intended" and meaningful content. (c) The dif-

V. [PERCEPTION, APPERCEPTION AND "MEANING-FULFILLMENT"]

The apperception-disorder of these patients had been observed by the first investigators of the amnesic syndrome, and is an accepted fact. The paleness of imagery itself suggests that the perception and apperception process is altered. Bonhoeffer recognized the possibility that not only memory, but also apperception-processes, may be pathologically affected. Krauss [52*] succeeded in demonstrating this experimentally, on a case which was studied by Steinthal [53*] also. In accord with Gregor,[54*] Brodmann,[55*] and Krapelin,[56*] Krauss found that apperception works slowly and incompletely, and that the impressions, once come about, fade quickly. At this point it is necessary to keep apart the perception- and thought-processes involved in apperception; but this is possible only within limits, since perception itself involves thought. Testing these patients with pictures representing miniature situations, we frequently find that they are unable to apperceive the situations as whole Gestalts. They stick to details and fragment the whole. It is probably for this reason that Hartmann and Schilder [57*] linked this syndrome to the "parieto-occipital structures."

G is shown the Bobertag picture of the boy who broke the window: "The man is beating the other boy's head. He is holding him with the other hand. This one has a slate in his hand. There sits a boy. This is a woman, she is looking out the window." (His attention is called to the window.) "There is something black." (Whole or broken?) "Yes, it seems to be a window-pane, it is really broken." (What happened?) "There was a fight." (Nothing else happened and still the window is broken?) "Did this one break it?" (Points to the boy the man holds.)

G is shown Bobertag's "Blindman's-Buff" picture: "The girl's head is bandaged. Here somebody is pulling down the tablecloth. The cups are falling over. The father holds the girl. In the back there somebody has his hands up." (Why?) "I don't know why, either." (What is going on in the picture?)

---

ferences between attitude-disturbance and perseveration are listed: perseverations are automatic, while attitude-disturbances are accompanied by restlessness, effort, and disappointment; attitude-disturbances do not, while perseverations do, exclude the possibility of correct perception of changes.

52.* Krauss (418).
53.* Steinthal (704).
54.* Gregor (288).
55.* Brodmann (95).
56.* Kraepelin (416).
57.* Hartmann and Schilder (312).

"Well, perhaps it is a fight." (His voice is full of doubt, and he keeps looking at the picture.)

S is shown the picture representing a bride and bridegroom, and musicians playing for them. (What does this picture show?) "They are playing music." (What are they [the couple] doing here?) "They are playing music too." (But they do not have instruments!) "They have just put them away." (What about the carriage?) "The musicians travel on it." (How are these two clothed?) "Musically."

The third example comes closer to physiological perception-processes than the first and the second; the alteration and failure of visual perception-processes is clearer here.[58] The relationship to the "compression-disturbances" of Pick's occipital-lesion cases is obvious.[59] In the beginning of the second example, we

58. This point seems to be unclear. We may conjecture that the authors considered the patient's answers ("They are playing music too" and "Musically") to reflect physiological disturbances of perception. It seems that one could account for these by a simpler assumption, that they are confabulations directed by a persisting attitude from which no shift to a new attitude takes place.

It will be worth noting that the authors use the term attitude in the sense of both a momentary and an enduring propensity. This example of inability to shift attitudes may serve to illustrate that a concept of "anticipation," expressing the relation between the momentary and the enduring propensities, is useful in reconstructing how an attitude manifests itself in molding perceptual material. If we consider an attitude to be a more or less enduring general direction or motivation, we perceive that the musicians aroused one in the patient. We still must explain how the bridal pair and their clothing are not recognized, and become "musical." The persisting attitude alone does not explain it; the ideas and concepts it has put into readiness select, in the fashion of an anticipation, what can

and what cannot be apperceived. In this case the selective anticipation was: something connected with musicians. Concerning anticipations, cf. Rapaport *et al.* (602, I, 215–19; and II, 22–24).

It is possible that the distinction Allport has made between instrumental and motivational attitudes may eventually prove one between two phases of the process by which attitudes exert their effect. In other words, it is possible that one or more motivational attitudes underlie every instrumental attitude, and that any motivational attitude exerts its effect through instrumental attitudes. There appears to be a continuous transition between motivational and instrumental attitudes, the "anticipations" being the extreme form of the latter. It seems likely that many instrumental attitudes and many stereotyped anticipations are "automatized" or "ossified" forms of what was once a new-found mode of putting a motivational attitude into effect. Cf. Lewin, Chap. 5, pp. 141 ff., and Hartmann, Chap. 19, VIII, above.

59. "Compression-disturbances" apparently refers to the spread of the meaning "musician" to the other parts

see fragmentation and inability to reach a whole-apperception, and even the fragments are unclear: "The girl's head is bandaged; somebody has his hands up." But in the end an interpretation of the whole-situation is reached: "It is a fight." This example is more complex than the third: thought-processes also are at play, and they, too, show disorders. The following example shows that other factors besides perception are at work:

S is shown a picture of a train, together with the wedding-picture. (What do you see?) "Seems people are leaving. They are probably the musicians." (What is it?) "Well, some carriage, that I can see." (Pointing to the engine:— What is this?) "Somebody is pouring water in." (Pointing to the semaphore: —What is this?) "Semaphore." (What is the picture then?) "This is a train."

Here, also, the apperception-disorder implies thought- and attitudinal-processes.[60]

Two avenues are open for the exploration of this disorder: first, to analyze rigorously the course of sensory processes; second, to analyze thoroughly the thought-processes. Pick and Gruenthal followed the latter course. Naturally, the early investigators also noted thought-disorders in these patients; but at that time thinking was still too much regarded as a matter of intelligence and memory. We shall return to thought-processes later on, and now we will attempt to study the perception processes.

The testing of these patients by means of simple perception experiments— for instance, recognition of colors, or apperception and reproduction of simple figures, or recognition of letters—finds all these perception-processes intact. The findings are different when the experiments are changed in one of the following three directions:

a) in quantity, that is in the size or number of the elements to be apperceived;
b) in time, that is, when a color is presented for a long, rather than a brief, single period;
c) in Gestalt-relations, that is, surveyableness, appearance, and differentiation of the material to be apperceived; as when the internal coherence of the parts is altered and thereby the whole character is changed.[61]

---

of the picture, "compressing" all its elements into one meaning. Thus, "compression" would be related to the dream-mechanism of "condensation," and to what Levy-Bruehl (456) called "participation" in ethnopsychology.

60. It may be conjectured that the authors infer the attitude-disturbance from the fact that, once a sufficient number of fragments was apperceived, a comprehension of the whole picture emerged.

61. This method of introducing ex-

[Passage omitted.] [62]

An experiment using quantitative alteration: We put on a table, or on the floor, several sticks at random, but close enough to have a definite relation to each other, to be surveyable, and capable of being united into one total complex. The patient is first asked to fixate on this complex of sticks, then to close his eyes. The examiner takes a stick away and asks the patient to put it back into its place; or he takes all the sticks away and asks the patient to reassemble the original figure.

In this experiment a limit is soon reached, beyond which the patient is unable to retain the position of the sticks. One can begin with many sticks, and by progressively decreasing their number reach the limit at which the patient is able to reproduce their position. This limit is four with G, six with B, and three with S. The limit is higher if the sticks are placed close to the edge of the table, because then the patient has fixed orientating points which serve as aids. This also indicates that we are not dealing here with a simple test of registration.[63]

Similar reactions are given by the patient to the Rubin figure (two facing profiles, which can be perceived either separately as profiles, or together as a vase).

B was completely at a loss when presented with the figure in a 2 cm. size, failing to recognize the profile even when half of the picture was covered. When the figure was presented in a 10 cm. size, he recognized the faces im-

---

treme conditions, in order to analyze processes which otherwise would appear undisturbed, has become widespread in psychopathology and personality research.

62. The omitted section deals with the relation between quantitative change and alteration of Gestalt.

63. For a consideration of the conditions under which Gestalt-integration and Gestalt-fragmentation take place, see the discussion of the rationale of the W and Do scores on the Rorschach Test, in Rapaport et al. (602, II, 138–46, and 158–60).

It is worth noting, however, that on material like that of the Rorschach Test, "organic" cases respond by empty and vague generalization (Wv)—resembling the "musical" example—rather than by fragmentation. Thus the form of Gestalt-disturbance may depend on the type of material (task) used. Also of interest, in this connection, is Karsten's (370) finding that oversatiation may result in Gestalt-fragmentation (Gestalt-Zerfall). In the cases here discussed, however, lack of satiation coexists with fragmentation; cf. notes 16 and 21, above. The explanation may be that in the lack of satiability of these patients, as in oversatiation, the tension-level is extremely low: in oversatiation, because of the massed discharge-activities; in lack of satiability, because of "leakage" through "weak boundaries" of tension-systems.

mediately, but remained helpless about the smaller figure: "I can't say. I can't imagine anything. It is a drawing, but I can't imagine what it should mean." It is evident that here the enlargement of the size facilitates apperception, by making the figure more "human" and discernment of its halves easier.

Given the task to find a right-angle triangle in a group of stars, circles, and quadrangles made of cardboard, the patient always succeeded. But when any other triangles were present in the group, *G* became immediately helpless; *B* failed when there were three or more of these.

All the patients showed disturbances of color-naming when the colored surface was small. For instance, a red and a green paper of 20 sq. cm. were immediately named; but when the papers overlapped, so that only a small corner of the red showed, the "red" could no longer be named.

In this last experiment *the time-factor* plays a role, since the experiment must be repeated with several colored surfaces, of varied areas, before the naming-disturbance manifests itself. . . . We did not obtain unequivocal results, because the time intervals became so long that the effects of general tiredness obscured the findings.

The tests of skin-sensitivity yielded reliable results. Bonhoeffer thought that the attention-disturbance of these patients precluded reliable testing of the sensorium. It is justified to assume that he did observe sensory-disturbances, but did not accept them as objective facts since the great role of the time-factor in sensory perception was not yet known.[64]

It was just as customary to refer the disturbances of the sensorium to attention-fluctuations as to refer thought-disorders to disturbances of registration. Modern neurophysiology has, however, demonstrated that even the simplest perception implies the time-factor physiologically, and not only, by way of attention, psychologically. Clearly, psychology has been progressively abandoning the concept of attention, because it has proved more and more to explain everything and nothing. At any rate, attention no longer has its former ruling position in psychological considerations. Psychiatric research, which was dependent on these general psychological views, has also become more free of this concept. Henning's [65]* volume describes the present situation correctly:

64. The authors assume that Bonhoef-fer considered these as attention-disturb-ances *because* he was unaware of the role of the time-factor.

65.* Henning (324).

attention is a composite process, and merely an indicator of the total psychic state.[66] The same holds for fatigue, though it is often forgotten that local fatigue—that is, one limited to a certain process, such as attention—differs from general fatigue. The ability to get involved in new activities, even in a state of fatigue, shows that the organism is certainly not "generally" but only "specifically" fatigued.[67]

We were not in a position to subject the patients to rigorous laboratory procedures, such as the measurement of chronaxy. Nevertheless, the disturbances were demonstrable. When the same point of the skin was stimulated with a needle or stimulus-hair, from 3 to 10 times in sequence, the sensations immediately began to wane and then disappeared in all the patients, but most clearly in S and H.

S perceived sharp and dull, warm and cold, everywhere on his skin, but his sensorium was extremely fatigable. After 4–5 pinpricks he reported dull sensations; a few more pricks and he reported none. The same held for warm and cold.[68] . . . Experiments with graded stimulus-hairs and with chronaxy failed or gave unstable results. The Gestalt-perception of the skin was gone; the patient could not state what a figure drawn on his skin was, and could not even distinguish a curve from a broken line. But when told in advance that only numbers would be drawn on his skin, he recognized them rather consistently.[69] If, however, the numbers were drawn at the same place on the skin, he recognized only the 1 always, the 2 occasionally, and the 3 never. . . . In testing the localization of stimulation, an unexpected difficulty arose. He was blindfolded and asked which part of his body was pricked. He unfailingly reached with his hand to the stimulated point and said: "Here." He persisted in this even after explicit instructions against it. When his hands were tied, he became

66. Indeed, the Wundt or the Titchener conception of attention did outlive its usefulness, and has been progressively abandoned. Freud's cathectic concept of attention, however, permits of reopening the whole problem of attention-phenomena. It places attention as a dynamic concept in the very center of the theory of thought-organization and motivation of thought. See Freud, Chap. 15, note 21, above. Cf. also Rapaport (597).

67. The problem of "specific fatigue" is related to that of satiation. See Karsten (370).

68. The relationship of these observations to fatigue in general, to satiation- and extinction-phenomena in "organic" cases—see for instance Bender (41) and Reider (606)—is as yet unclear.

69. The anticipation aroused by the preparation is particularly clear in this instance.

restless at first and would not cooperate; when he calmed down, he was unable to name the stimulated part of his body.

The patient was unable to recognize by touch (eyes closed) any object, including those which he consistently recognized visually. He could not even state the use of the objects. He recognized—at least on single testing—the forms, texture, hardness, and occasionally the nature of the material, but could never capture by touch the total Gestalt of an object. . . . When a toothbrush was put into his hand he said: "Up to here it is a pen, and up to here it is a comb, but what it is, I don't know." . . .[70]

H's disorder of the sensorium was similar to that of *S.* . . . Only exceptionally did he recognize objects by touch, and of some of these he could not state the names, but only their use. He could identify only the form, but not the material, of those which he did not recognize.

Not in all cases are these disturbances of the sensorium as striking as in *S* and *H*. We are aware that these findings tell little about the essence or structure of these disturbances. . . .[71]

Of the experimental results described here . . . only the role of the time-factor is of real importance in the amnesic syndrome. . . . Disturbances of the sensorium were present over the whole surface of the body, without tangible neurological basis, and were dependent only on the duration of the stimulus within a certain time-span.

Now we turn . . . to the third method of altering the tests of perception, by changing the Gestalt-relations. Fragmentation, and inability to grasp visually whole-situations, have been already mentioned in connection with the test which used pictures of scenes. For the study of perception, as free of thought-processes as possible, this procedure is not simple enough. However, it is easy to create simpler experimental conditions.

If *G* was given first a drawing of the outline of a fish, and then a picture of the fish in colors true to life, he recognized the latter immediately, but interpreted the former as a "kind of bottle," "kind of a neck-bottle." Later on, after he recognized the drawing, the experiment was changed: the picture was pre-

70. The omitted section describes disturbances of deep-sensibility.

71. The omitted section states that no such data concerning *B* are available, since these methods were adopted after he was studied; in no amnesic-syndrome case studied were these disturbances absent; to verify these findings, it is necessary to study cases as introspective as *B*.

sented in the natural horizontal position, while the drawing was in the vertical. *G's* interpretation was, "A bottle with two handles," and he pointed to the fins as handles. A simple spatial reorientation sufficed to alter the "Gestalt" completely.[72]

On the "fish-picture" of Heilbronner, *G* performed as he had on the "windmill-picture." He stuck to his interpretation: "This must be a bottle"; "A bottle, with handles." Only after the water was indicated with a few pencil-strokes, did he get the correct designation immediately. . . .[73]

S and *B* reacted similarly. . . . Neither *S* nor *G* recognized simple figures (star, cross) formed by dots. *B*, who recognized them to begin with, failed when they appeared as red dots in a field of green dots.[74] [Passage omitted.] [75]

. . . When *B* was shown a triangle, and then a triangle with a dot beside it, he considered the dot meticulously and reported it. When two pictures of a hammer, each differently placed, were presented to him in succession, he would

---

72. This disturbance, or the inability to select a right-angle triangle when other triangles are also present, may seem extreme; yet it is on a continuum with similar difficulties which people not "organically" damaged experience. In the course of psychotherapy of neurotics, a relationship clearly recognized in one form of behavior may remain totally unrecognized by the patient in another. Here often an apparently slight change in the relation between the patient's behavior in question and his defenses will suffice to prevent recognition. Cf. Kris, Chap. 23, III, above. But we observe similar phenomena in so-called normal people, and even in situations where we may assume that no specific defenses are involved. In using newly acquired skills or ideas, the slightest alteration of the setting in which they were acquired may prevent, or make extremely laborious, recognition and application. But anxiety or general tiredness may have the same effect on familiar skills and ideas.

As long as we do not have definite proof that these parallels are merely apparent, it will be necessary to keep them in mind and explore them; their study will put pathology of thought into the general framework of the theory of thought.

73. The omitted section contains an example closely resembling the preceding one.

74. This experiment, like that using the Rubin picture, deals with the impairment of the figure-ground function. For the general theory of figure-ground perception, see Koffka (406, pp. 177–210). For a discussion of the role of figure-ground perception in pathology, see Goldstein (281, pp. 109–11). The most important recent experimental studies on disturbances of figure-ground perception are those of Werner (759, 756, 757), which used "endogenous" and "exogenous" feeble-minded children as subjects.

75. The omitted part contains another similar experiment with *B*.

state meticulously each time, "A hammer" and then "A hammer, but now the handle goes in the other direction." Or when the pictures were those of tables, one with a single drawer, the other with two, the patient would say, "A table with one (respectively, two) drawers." But if the pictures were simultaneously presented in pairs, the reaction was different. The dot was still reported with the triangle, but for the others: "A hammer and another one," "A table and another table."

In these simple experiments, one of the basic modes of reaction of these patients becomes clear. In successive presentation, each Gestalt is newly grasped and built up as a new content, and every detail is noted. In the simultaneous presentation of the triangles this is still the case; being so foreign to life, so devoid of live connotations, they must always be constructed anew. A triangle with a dot is no longer just a simple triangle. In contrast to this, the interpretation (naming) of the hammers and tables settles everything, clarifies the situation, fulfills the meaning, and completely satisfies the patient. He has no correction-need, because he did not undertake to clarify the situation completely, but only to the extent of his need for meaning-fulfillment. Therefore, to go further, he needs the examiner's question: "Are they quite alike?" Thus it is clear what here underlies the absence of need for correction: the patient's need for explanation is prematurely satiated.[76] The statement that the patients enter situations only to the point of attaining a meaning-fulfillment for themselves touches on the psychology of thinking and will be more generally discussed later. Here we want to state only that these perception-experiments make both

76. This formulation seems to be related to the one discussed in note 72, above. The "meaning-fulfillment" concept of the authors, though useful, appears to be partly on the level of phenomenological description, partly teleological. It is justifiable to ask: When more data of such behavior are available, will they support the formulation that the cathectic energy of attention available to these patients is of such a low level that it tends to "closure" and "meaning" via the "shortest path," that is, the least expenditure of energy? It might be objected that energy in any case tends to the shortest path and least expenditure. Though this is correct, it must be added that it tends towards *the least expenditure under the given conditions*. In meaning-apprehension these conditions are given in the details which must be taken into consideration to arrive at an adequate meaning; too much will cloud, too little will empty it. (Clinically, this problem is most striking in the thinking of obsessional patients. Cf. Bleuler, Chap. 26, note 17, above.) Thus there are many levels of meaning-apprehension; and the "least expenditure of energy feasible under the given condi-

the perceptual and the thought aspects of the disturbance palpable, and that the results clarify the fundamental modes of apperception and assimilation of these patients.

VI

[Section omitted.] [77]

VII. [MEMORY AND THOUGHT]

Now that we approach the discussion of thought and memory functions, the studies of Pick [78*] and Gruenthal,[79*] which laid the foundation for recent research in this field, should again be mentioned. Pick's method of verbatim recording of all questions and answers yielded significant insights into the thought-processes of the amnesic syndrome. We will attempt, as far as possible, to keep separate the patient's task-determined thinking and their thinking in simple conversation. This distinction is naturally relative. Every question is a task. Yet, in an experiment, where by deliberately chosen tasks he is tied to definite premises, the patient's thinking is different from his live thinking of everyday, where he is entirely within his own life-situation. In turn, the experiment has the advantage that it shows clearly the single steps and possibilities of thought, and permits segregation of definite single processes and performances. Naturally, the results of these two kinds of investigation must not contradict, but reflect, each other.[80]

---

tions" is not that which produces the shallow meaning, but the most adequate one, in terms of the energy available and the meaning sought. These considerations remain of necessity inconclusive: the nature and various levels of meaning, as well as their relation to states of consciousness and the cathectic energies of attention available in these for use, are some of the most obscure areas of the theory of thinking.

77. Section VI deals with disturbances of the body-image. It is omitted here because it bears only indirectly on the organization and pathology of thought. See Schilder (646), particularly p. 112, where he takes issue with the present authors' view of these body-image disturbances.

78.* Pick (566).

79.* Gruenthal (294).

80. The principle of method which the authors state here seems fundamental to clinical investigations, and perhaps even to all studies of personality and its disorders. In essence, the principle parallels Lewin's (Chap. 4, above). Further differences between experimental and observational procedures may be stated as follows: (a) Observation of everyday experience may overlook impairments and becloud processes, since the natural setting provides the patient with a rich variety of cues, and permits therefore

First we shall dwell on thinking free of definite tasks. Phenomenologically the thinking, like the imagery of these patients, has a fleeting character.

B said: "Now, I think of something. And now, it is gone. Then it is always as though there had been nothing there."

Subjectively, the patient's internal situations are not enduring.

"I cannot hold on to thoughts. When I think of something, what preceded it is completely gone." [81]

There is no contradiction between this and the fact that every conversation induces a complete change of life-situation in the patient. For instance, *G* when in bed becomes a soldier; when in the examination room he is a "private patient." Several factors interact here; first of all, what Pick labeled the lack of circumspection, and Gruenthal called the lack of relation to the totality of experience. To state this in a positive form, a few components of the situation presented are passively generalized into a total situation. This process is purely associative, and is identical with that which permits the crystallization

---

the vicarious or supplementary use of various functions in coping with the situations encountered. (b) On the other hand, the functional efficacy of the subject may be better judged in observing situations where natural cues are present. (c) Experimentally controlled conditions are prone to isolate a function for observation by controlling the available cues, and thereby also the possibilities of vicarious and supplementary functioning. But such procedure, used in a piecemeal fashion, is prone to give an exaggeratedly low estimate of the functional efficacy of the organism. Brunswik's (102) demand for systematic sampling of experimental design is aimed to cope with this very problem. (d) Experimental isolation of functions may yield, however, a spuriously positive picture of the functional efficacy of the organism. This may come about in various ways: for instance, when efficacy is dependent more on the coordination of the functions than on the single functions themselves, the former may be weak or impaired, while the experiment finds the latter intact (cf. p. 670, above); or the experimental setting may so expose the cue, normally hidden among others, that it centers the subject's attention on it and leads to a particularly successful performance. The latter consideration induced Halstead to map the "dynamic visual-field" instead of the usual perimetry.

81. Cf. note 72, above. Here again the pathological phenomenon has its normal counterparts. Silberer (Chap. 8, p. 196, above) records how, in a state of sleepiness, one abstract idea was gone as soon as he centered on another. These were abstract ideas he was otherwise in full command of and only the state of consciousness corresponding to sleepiness interfered with his "hold" on them. But in the struggle to master new facts or new abstractions, we have similar experiences without the interference of tiredness.

and tying-in of memories as soon as a fixed point is offered. But there is more to the patient's total situation than this: he is a soldier not only in thought, but also in his total momentary bearing. The situation is totalized not only in thought; the whole person becomes filled with its momentary content. This is the basis of the failure, which Pick stressed, to bring contrary knowledge to bear. There is no inclination to, nor any necessity for, correction—at least not in principle.[82]

B made this characteristic comment: "When I think or say something, I actually always believe that it is right. Recently I often doubt afterwards whether it is really that way."

The patient was at this time on the road to improvement, and we observe the attempt at self-correction. . . . As he improves, the impersonal quality of his experience abates, and the personal experience-structure manifests itself.[83] The following communication from B illustrates this:

"At first I knew nothing about myself.[84] Now I again have the feeling that I am older. Judging by my thoughts I should be young—I have so few. It must be because I know nothing any more about so many years. By my feeling, however, I am again older."

Here we reenter the issue touched on earlier in the discussion of drive- and feeling-life. In general these patients are only momentarily, situationally, what

82. The authors are concerned with the contradiction between two tendencies of these patients' thoughts, to be fleeting and to have an extraordinarily sweeping effect. They reconcile the two by referring to the commonly observed failure of thoughts and perceptions to arouse the totality of pertinent experiences; the consequences are both that whatever is present monopolizes consciousness, memory, and behavior, and that they vanish, lacking anchorage, as soon as a new generalization takes place.

This process of generalization is described as "purely associative." Pick (566) has stressed that such purely associative processes are never identical with thinking proper, and can never cope with the same tasks as thought. These patients lack the continuity so distinctive of ordered thought, and are in a sense a caricature of what thinking would be like if it were governed by the "laws" of association psychology.

83. Pick (566) had already observed that *need for correction* increases as the patient improves. All reports indicate the fluctuating character of these patients' attitude toward correcting, and believing in, their ideas. Compare Betlheim and Hartmann's observations, and our comment on the nature of fluctuating awareness (Chap. 13, particularly note 56, above).

84. Note the lack of reflective self-awareness which accompanies the state of consciousness of these patients.

they are. They consist of cross-sections, without the corresponding longitudinal continuity which is personal. This is in harmony with Gruenthal's observation, that these patients are unable to relate a content to their total life-experience. Their passivity is *one* of the factors which prevents the rise of even a need for this.[85] Pick and Gruenthal have realized that this implies the tendency to totalize situations, which in turn is related to the strongly associative character of their free thinking. If we do not take passivity merely for the opposite of activity proper, but also for—as indeed it is—the lying fallow of all drives and strivings, then these factors provide the broad outlines of the formal structure of the syndrome. . . .[86]

This view of the syndrome's structure clarifies some issues. Pick [87*] has questioned Bonhoeffer's [88*] assertion that these patients' "reasoning is intellectually correct" and their formal train of thought, as well as their combining-ability, good. He based his argument on factors we have already discussed here, such as the lack of need to correct, non-actualization of contrary knowledge, and coexistence of contradictory contents. Yet Bonhoeffer's view has a correct core, because the manifestations of the disturbance depend to a certain extent on the circumstances of the situation. *B*, for instance, in the course of a conversation about the war, cannot tell what machines he used to service; but he gives the correct information as soon as one engages him in a conversation about his occupation.

Actualization of memories and thoughts requires the aid of the situation; but when it is available, if associatively "prepared," the achievement is good.[89]

85. The term passivity is not fortunate here, since it is commonly used to describe a character-trait of normals and neurotics. Here it denotes the inertia and apathy of these patients.

86. We may outline the syndrome's structure thus: (a) Impulses, drives, and affects are inert. (b) Consequently, once one of these is aroused it lingers on without arousing others; therefore nothing else is regarded. Percepts, self-experience, and general bearing are assimilated to, falsified according to, and regulated by it. Existence becomes momentary and cross-sectional. (c) No satiation takes place; stimulus-hunger persists. Nevertheless, meaning-experience is shallow, that is, quickly satiated. (d) A new impulse sweeps away all previous thought, apparently because there is not energy available for both.

87.* Pick (566).

88.* Bonhoeffer (82).

89. Similarly, Fenichel (Chap. 18, above) describes boredom as a condition in which the "aid of the situation" is needed; and there are "normal" conditions also in which this holds. A few typical situations: (a) A friend comes to see me unexpectedly and wants to con-

Nevertheless, there is present in these cases a thought-disorder also, and it is more extensive even than Pick thought. This can be demonstrated by the experimental method, using varied techniques.

In the following we will first rediscuss part of the material presented above, and view it in other connections and new light.

"Fragmentation" as a disturbance of apperception has already been mentioned. The greater mobility and wealth of thinking in live situations, and its impoverishment in experiments which are not life-like, is analogous to the fact that fragmentation is more striking on abstract pictures, such as geometrical figures, than on live and perceptually rich experimental material. Material and situations which are not life-like are prone to bring the disturbances into sharper relief.[90]

We disregard here the disorders of registration which usually have been placed in the foreground of the psychopathology of this syndrome. Detailed experiments (Gregor and Roemer,[91*] Brodmann [92*]) demonstrated some time ago that these patients do have traces of past experiences. The concept of registration-disturbance describes therefore only a phenomenological characteristic of the syndrome. From the outside, the patients appear as though they forget everything. The concept does not contribute to the clarification of the structure of the syndrome. . . . It does not touch on the factors underlying the phenomenon of the registration-disturbance.[93]

---

tinue a discussion we had a while ago; I have to ask him to start it off, so as to get my bearings. (b) An obsessional or schizoid person begins to talk to me, taking it for granted—as such persons are wont to do—that his premises are as evident to me as to him. I have to wait patiently to find out the frame of reference within which his discourse moves. (c) I examine a student. He cannot answer my question until I convey to him, by general questions, its place in the scheme of things. Cf. note 29, above.

It is true that only in severe depressions, extremely inert and passive neurotics and some schizophrenics, do we find the extreme dependence on the "aid of the situation" that prevails in "organic cases" (see also Goldstein, 281, p. 154); but the dependence on such aid seems an intrinsic part of all thought-processes. The need for it is an expression of the delicate balance between the two basic characteristics of thought: internalization (see Hartmann, Chap. 19, above), and grasp on reality (see Freud, Chap. 15, above).

90. See note 80, above.

91.* Gregor and Roemer (290).

92.* Brodmann (95).

93. The authors' conception is that the apparent disturbance of registration is essentially one of attitudes (anticipa-

This is well demonstrated by the following experiment:

The patient is given a pack of cards with pictures on them. He is asked to take them *one by one* and to select, for instance, those which represent fruits and human occupations. Even B failed on this. He started out correctly, setting aside the pictures with animals, furniture, and tools on them, and separating the others. After having selected two pictures of fruits and one of a locksmith, he looked over the pictures aimlessly, picking out now and then an additional fruit picture. He was able to state correctly the task: "I should be looking for fruits." He looked at the pictures in indecision and added, "And perhaps occupations also?" But when all the pictures were spread out in front of him simultaneously, and he was again given the same task, he concentrated eagerly and selected the correct pictures.[94]

This experiment shows that in successive presentation the visual impressions at first become over-valent and absorb the patient completely, so that task-consciousness is lost and he is incapable of a thinking which would reach over and ahead of the visual impressions. But when the procedure is changed to simultaneous presentation, the situation becomes quite different. The pictures form a whole field, which the patient approaches with a definite ordering-principle. The single pictures then have a meaning for the patient only in relation to this schema of thought, and thus he can solve the task. . . .

These experiments demonstrate clearly the already mentioned factor, crucial in the structure of the syndrome, that successive impressions extinguish each other.[95]. . . Another simple experiment also demonstrates this well, though in it one must rely solely on the report of the patients, because no objective checks are feasible. . . .

When B was instructed to imagine a field, on it a tree, and finally on the tree a man, he always failed. Another task was: "What is the Sunday dress of your wife like? Imagine it. How does her face look? How does she look in her Sunday dress?" According to the lucid and unequivocal reports of B, he always

---

tion), rooted in a disorder of drive-, striving-, and affect-dynamics.

94. This behavior suggests not a lack of satiation, rather a premature satiation, like that in meaning-fulfillment. Cf. note 76, above.

95. Freud's cathectic theory of con-sciousness (Chap. 16, note 14, above) would suggest an explanation of these phenomena in terms of a dearth of available cathectic-energy of the ego. It seems, from the data, that in these patients there is a dearth of drive-energies as well.

had only one clear image: either the field or the tree, the dress or the face. As soon as he turned to the next image, the previous one disappeared.

This experiment—like the previous ones—indicates the background of what gives the impression of being a "disorder of synthesis."[96] The temporal sequence here plays an undoubtedly great role. If the predetermined ordering tendency implied in the task can be carried to the objects by a single act, then the patient succeeds, the pictures are divided and ordered in one move. If, however, the task deals with a series of objects appearing in time sequence, solving it necessitates "holding" the task and bringing each picture into relation with it. In this the patients do not succeed. The object-perceptions become too powerful and suppress task-consciousness. This is the case in the imagery-experiment also. A synthesis, a construction, fitting several elements together is impossible, because turning to a new one abolishes that which preceded it.[97]

These experiments must be altered in yet another direction in order to bring out a further characteristic, namely that these patients "cannot do several things simultaneously." . . . The task is to select [simultaneously] triangles of a certain type and circles from among other cardboard figures. B failed even when he had all the figures before him. He could not do both simultaneously, and did one or the other.

Naturally, this task is more difficult than that of selecting pictures, because it is less life-like. Therefore it shows clearly the limitations of these patients' thinking; that is, the narrow range of tasks which they can survey and pursue. A certain quantitative factor also plays a role here, though we cannot conceive of quantitative changes without corresponding changes in "Gestalt." This quantitative factor can be captured, as for instance in the recall of short stories.

96. The term "synthesis" is used here in a general sense, and not in the technical one of "the synthetic function of the ego."

97. Here again the authors describe a phenomenon common to all thought-disorders: one of the means overshadows the goal, the momentary displaces the long-range, and the continuity of thought is lost. Again, the phenomenon is observed in normal people wherever the task is difficult for the individual, or the thought is novel or of a high level of abstraction, or the individual's state of consciousness deviates from that of normal waking. If there are differences in this between normals, "functional" patients, and "organic" patients which are not quantitative—that is, do not consist in the extent of the disturbance, nor depend alone on the kind of task and its setting—but are qualitative, they have not so far been demonstrated.

Such an experiment has the further advantage that it demonstrates the process of finding and apperceiving meaning: the fragmentation and loss of the thread in the reproduction are manifest not only in the forgetting of material, but also in projections in the direction of the apperceived meaning.[98] [Passage omitted.] [99]

VIII

[Section omitted.] [100]

IX. [SUMMARY]

The structure of the amnesic syndrome appears to us very complex and richly articulated. Yet a few basic features can be discerned, which are present in all realms of these patients' psychic and psychophysical life. Certain disturbances and alterations in the modes of consummation underlie the characteristic features of the syndrome. Yet it should be stressed that its essence lies in the structural interrelations of all the specific disturbances we have demonstrated. In addition to the fundamental disturbance, there appear alterations and disturbances of specific psychic functions (for instance, thinking).

The most general background of the disorder seems to be the defect in the personal sphere, the passivity and paralysis of the vital layer. In addition, there is in all areas an alteration in the temporal course of processes, a decrease in the quantities which can be managed, a de-differentiation of and difficulty in Gestalt-construction.

98. By projections, the authors apparently mean alien material added to the story, in harmony with the patient's understanding of it.

99. The omitted part gives examples of story-recall, which demonstrate the perseveration-like inertia of positions once taken, the premature satiation of the need for meaning, the lack of need for correction, etc. It is not translated here, because (a) the authors fail to give the verbatim text of the original story, (b) the experiment leads to inferences identical with those of Schilder (Chap. 25, above) and the others reported in this paper.

100. This section first discusses Gam-per's (262) view, according to which the psychological character of these patients' behavior is similar to that of dream-experience, and draws the conclusion: "The fact that we find conditions of 'dreamlike confusion' in these patients, tells no more about the essence of [the amnesic syndrome] than the occurrence of stupors tells about schizophrenia in general." This is followed by a discussion of van der Horst's (340) theory of the syndrome, according to which its central disturbance is that of "temporalization." The authors argue that this cannot explain either the disorders of drive and affect, or of thought.

The altered vital-background and temporal course account for the patients' "cross-section-like" existence. The consequence in perception and appercep-tion, and generally where the sensorium is involved, is that the experiences which are present at the moment become over-valent and annihilate the preced-ing ones. The quantitative decrease of what can be mastered at the moment results in a limitation of thought-possibilities, in a sticking to once-assumed positions and interpretations, which cannot then be given up. The alteration of the Gestalt-function, abetted by the others discussed, results in the de-differen-tiation of Gestalt, in fragmentation into smaller complexes, in a vagueness of intentional goals; and amounts to a disturbance of synthesis in thinking and imaging. In thinking, the phenomenologically prevalent symptom is the prema-ture satiation of the need to find meaning.

In the various areas, there are additional specific disturbances. Fatigability is characteristic of all the more strictly psychophysical processes, such as percep-tion and body-image, and is also reflected in the alteration of the temporal course, described above. As for presentations, their image-content is consider-ably weakened. In thinking, the purely associative mode becomes prevalent. All these are consequences of changes in the vital layer.

The attitude- and registration-disturbances—the failure to actualize knowl-edge and the absence of correction-need—formerly considered the basic dis-turbances of the syndrome, prove phenomenal and derivable from the inter-action of the factors here described.

X

[Section omitted.] [101]

101. This section contains the four case histories. These may be summarized as follows:

B, age 35, machinist, victim of a car-bon-monoxide poisoning. Inconspicuous history, including war and war-prisoner experience between 24 and 29, and mar-riage at 34. Symptoms: apathy, and dis-orientation in space and time. Slow im-provement. After initially hyperactive reflexes, no neurological findings.

G, age 57, shoemaker, son of an alco-holic father. Always a quiet, religious, poetry-writing eccentric, who married at 26 and lived solely for his family. At 56 a sudden change in character: hypo-chondriasis, anxiety, depression, apathy, insomnia, self-accusations, and some sus-piciousness. Suicidal attempt by strangu-lation, unconscious when rescued. Initial pyramidal and extrapyramidal symptoms subsiding within three weeks, leaving a mild, flaccid akinesis and mildly mask-like facies. Initial clouding of conscious-ness, succeeded by apathy and lack of spontaneity, colored by a mild and steady euphoric mood. Disorientation in time and space, occasional confabulations and disturbance of registration. Progressive, slow improvement.

H, age 58, locomotive fireman, married for 27 years. Inconspicuous history. Skull-fracture in car accident, initial unconsciousness, weeks of somnolence and continued disorientation in time and space. Depressed and irritable, with suicidal ideas and threats against others. Amnesic aphasia. Reflexes intact, mild generalized ataxia, tendency to move-

ment-perseveration, poor general coordination.

S, age 47, baker. Nephritis at 31; at 35 apoplectic attack with confusion, restlessness, nausea, speech difficulty, all of which cleared up in three weeks. Since then irritable, drinks daily three bottles of wine. At 47 again minor apoplectic attack with aphasic but no motor difficulties, followed by forgetfulness. Neurological findings suggest arteriosclerotic etiology.

PART SEVEN

CONCLUSION

TOWARD A THEORY OF THINKING
By David Rapaport

I. INTRODUCTION

IN THIS SECTION I shall attempt to extract, without documenting, that conception of thought-processes which to me seems implicitly sketched in the foregoing papers. If one thinks of these papers as drawings, my comments have tried to emphasize and extend certain of their lines; and this section is an attempt to assemble these reinforced lines. This assembly is organized around the psychoanalytic theory of thinking.

I am not attempting to create a theory. Tested knowledge is too scant for that. I will merely try to integrate into a continuity the concepts and thought-patterns that have been used; integration into this continuity may render them amenable as hypotheses to empirical tests whereby the continuity itself may be recast. I am fully aware that much of what I propose to do, and have already done in my comments, does not meet the criteria of scientific rigor. Yet it seems to me that, in lack of anything better, it is the thing to do.

To minimize cumbersomeness I shall not cite references in this section. The italicized key words and the index may serve as substitutes.

II. THE PRIMARY MODEL OF ACTION

Let us assume that what we call the drive-needs of the organism are disequilibria in energy-distribution. Let us assume that the principles of physics hold here and such disequilibria tend toward reestablishment of equilibrium. It is characteristic of organisms that drives have drive-objects, needs have objects of valence. In organisms, reestablishment of equilibria is bound to the presence of specific objects.

Let us consider this sequence of infant behavior: *restlessness—appearance of and sucking action on the breast—subsidence of restlessness.* Taking this as our conceptual model, we may derive from it two sets of concepts: one in terms of common psychological usage, the other in terms of energy-dynamics. *Rest-*

lessness may be conceptualized as an indicator of "tension"; or as the extent of energy-disequilibrium, originated by the continuous supply of drive-energy. *The breast* may be conceptualized as the means of tension-reduction, or the drive-satisfying object; or as the necessary condition for the energy-discharge restoring energy-equilibrium. (It is taken for granted that we use the term "breast" here in a schematic sense; to the infant the breast is not a sharply defined, discrete percept but rather the nucleus of a diffuse global experience.) *Subsidence of restlessness* may be conceptualized as gratification of need; or as the equilibrium reestablished. This model implies a *direction*, which is conceptualized as the striving toward gratification, or the *pleasure-principle;* or as the tendency toward equilibrium.

Action, in this primary model, is a discharge-activity whose aim is to reestablish equilibrium. Since presence of the drive-object is the prerequisite of discharge, action is always object-directed.

III. THE PRIMARY MODEL OF THOUGHT

The study of dreams, of the fantasies and illusions of persons suffering dire deprivations, and of the hallucinations of cases of Meynert's amentia, suggest that when the need-tension mounts, and the need-satisfying object is absent, a hallucinatorily vivid image of it and/or of the gratification-experience arises. (The process by which the hallucinatory image of a memory thus arises is conceptualized as *projection*.) This implies that there exists a memory "trace" of these experiences, and that this trace, when cathected—charged with energy —by the drive, becomes conscious. Thus the primary model of thought is: *mounting drive-tension—absence of drive-object—hallucinatory image of it.*

A consideration of this model leads to the following conceptions. Because of the *delay* of gratification-discharge, the memory-traces of the gratification-experience are cathected to perceptual (hallucinatory) intensity. In this model, as in the primary model of action, a directedness is discernible; the cathexes are directed toward the memory-trace of gratification. This is conceptualized as *wishfulfillment;* or in terms of energy-dynamics, as an abortive attempt to reestablish equilibrium. The *delay*—of gratification-discharge by motor-action —becomes the cradle of "conscious experience." The quality, *consciousness of an experience*, is conceptualized as a matter of the cathecting of its memory-traces. The motivating force which propels an idea to consciousness is thus conceived of—in our primary model—as its drive-cathexis.

Ideas are thus indicators of drive-tension; and when they appear in hallucinatory form, they utilize and discharge a fraction of the drive-cathexis. Accordingly, ideas may be considered safety valves of drive-tension, even if they dispose only of relatively small amounts of cathexes.

IV. THE PRIMARY MODEL OF AFFECT

Above we conceptualized *restlessness* as an indicator of tension. It is customary, however, to conceptualize it also as affect-expression or affect-discharge. In harmony with the conflict theories of emotion, we may assume that affect-expression and -discharge come about when the gratification-discharge is hampered. Unlike the object-directed discharge in action, affect-discharge is a diffuse discharge into the motor and secretory systems, that is, into the interior of the body, without being directed toward an external object. Its observed manifestations are described as affective- or emotional-expression. Thus the primary model of affect is: *mounting drive-tension—delay—affect-discharge*.

Affect-discharge, however, rarely if ever eliminates the energy-disequilibrium. Let us formulate that affect-discharge is both an indicator and a safety valve of drive-tension, that is, of energy-disequilibrium. The energy so discharged is termed affect-charge, and is considered only a relatively small amount of the drive-cathexis which constitutes the energy-disequilibrium.

V. IDEAS AND AFFECT-CHARGE: THE BEGINNINGS OF STRUCTURE

In the last analysis ideas are drive-cathected memory-traces; affect-charge is that amount of drive-cathexis which is dischargeable into the motor and secretory system. Since both are indicators and safety valves of the drive-tension, they are called *drive-representations*. Ideas are referred to as the qualitative, affect-charge as the quantitative, aspect of the drive-representation. Each implies both quantity and quality: but the quantity of affect-charge is as a rule much the greater; while the quality, originally limited to the pleasure-pain continuum, is extended by ideas far more than by affects.

That ideas and affect-charge already presuppose "psychic structure," and cannot be derived alone from the cathectic dynamics, becomes clear from several considerations. (a) Both arise when the need-satisfying object, which by the very specificity of its relation to the drive suggests a structural anchorage, is absent. (b) Both refer to structural givens: the idea to the memory trace, the affect-charge to the segregation of those cathexes which are dischargeable into the somatic apparatus from those which are not. (c) Both are limited in their discharge capacity: neither can discharge more than a limited portion of the drive-tension.

With affects we shall not deal further, systematically. We wish to note only that when affective or emotional disorders are spoken of, the reference is to disorders of "psychological"—that is, "conflict"—origin. It is also worth noting that there are cases in which the cathectic energies of the affect-charge seem to determine (motivate) thought or action; but about these we know as yet almost nothing.

VI. THE PRIMARY PSYCHIC STRUCTURE

The apparatus which forms memory-traces; the threshold of tension tolerance, the exceeding of which by the tension of the drive-energy disequilibrium brings about affect-discharge and/or hallucinatory image; the specific discharge capacities of affect and idea; and the specific connection between the drive and its satisfying object—all appear to be structural givens, highly variable from individual to individual. There is also reason to believe that there are constitutionally given individual differences in the intensity of the drive and its temporal course—for example, rate of tension-rise and -discharge—both determining in part the tolerance for the delay of its discharge. It is likely that the channels of affect-discharge and its apparent intensity are also structural givens; that is, the distribution of the discharge between motility and secretory channels—and among their sub-organizations—is structurally determined to begin with. For instance, it is conceivable that the motor-apparatus has its own degree of excitability, which is independent of the affect-charge available for discharge, and codetermines the actual extent of discharge that occurs through it.

All these structural characteristics set the limit to cathectic discharge and thereby also to what can be treated and understood in terms of cathectic dynamics alone. Consequently there is always drive-tension present, which can never be fully discharged, since discharge is limited by structure. These structures, and others such as perception which play a similar role, are the prototypes for the controls which are formed later in the course of psychic development. They enter the formation of drive-controls autonomously. When the super-

organization of drive-controls (conceptualized as the *ego*) emerges, these structures are embodied in it, and provide the basis of its autonomy. In the course of
this development of the super-organization, attended by the extension of controls, a struggle arises which is conceptualized as *conflict*. Since these inborn
structures do not necessarily enter this conflict, they form the nucleus of what
is conceptualized as the *conflict-free ego-sphere*. These structures are also referred to as *ego-apparatuses*.

VII. THE DELAY AND ITS FIRST CONSEQUENCES

Delay of discharge may be due to structural as well as environmental conditions: either structural limitations or absence of the need-satisfying object may
bring it about. One consequence of delay is that experiences preceding, surrounding, and perhaps even following gratification, accumulate in the form
of memory-traces. The organization of these memory-traces is of primary interest for the theory of thinking. Evidence seems to be available to show that
such memories are organized around those drives, in the delay and/or discharge
of which they emerge first as hallucinatory images and later as ideas—that is,
around the drives of which they are representations. Evidence also shows that
these representations all carry drive-cathexes, which, however, are freely
shifted from any one to any other; when a representation is raised to hallucinatory vividness (as in dreams) it is either by a shifting (displacement) of drive-
cathexes to it, or by a compounding (condensation) of several representations
into one image.

Thus the primary organization of memories occurs around drives. All the
memories organized around a drive, and dependent for their emergence in
consciousness on drive-cathexis, are conceptualized as *drive-representations*. In
this drive-organization of memories the following hold: (a) Any representation may stand for the drive; that is, the memory of any segment or aspect of
experience accrued in the periods of delay, and around the gratification, may
emerge as an indicator of mounting drive-tension. (b) The characteristic of
energies which makes for this extreme freedom of representation, and allows
representations to be raised to hallucinatory vividness, is conceptualized as
"mobility" of cathexis. The cathectic energy in a drive-organization of memory
can freely move and center on any representation. (c) This free mobility is
inferred from the observations which are conceptualized as the mechanisms of

displacement, condensation, substitution, and so on. Conceptions like "participation," "omnipotence of thought," "pars pro toto," all express consequences of this "free mobility," and of its corollary, the complete interchangeability of the representations of a drive. This interchangeability is in turn the consequence of the fact that at this stage of memory-organization there do not yet exist discrete and well-delineated "objects" or "ideas," but only "diffuse" ones. In the language of developmental psychology: the concepts are syncretic. (d) The thought-process based on drive-organizations of memory, and using cathexes which are freely displaceable and strive towards discharge in terms of "wish-fulfillment," are conceptualized as the *"primary process."* The free displace-ability is a corollary of the unrestrained tendency toward full discharge by the shortest path (wishfulfillment), which is the characteristic of the "mobile" drive-energies.

VIII. THE DELAY AND ITS FURTHER CONSEQUENCES: PRIMAL REPRESSION

When the drive-tension mounts and the need-satisfying object is absent, the discharge into ideation and affect may not make the tension tolerable. The structural discharge-potentiality of ideation and affect may be too small; or the "structural tolerance for tension" may be low; or the drive-energies may be "constitutionally" excessive; or finally, the delay may be too long.

The fate of the drive-cathexes then may follow two major patterns: they may be repressed, or their freely mobile character may change to a *"bound"* form. The former is conceived as preventing the discharge of "mobile" ener-gies; the latter as converting them into a form analogous to that in which the energy providing the "tonus" of the musculature exists. The term "tonic bind-ing" or *"binding"* designates the process by which the "bound" cathexes come about. It is quite uncertain whether these two courses, which are not radically different from each other, are the only ones which undischarged drive-cathexes may take.

There are two basic means by which the organism deals in the beginning with external stimuli: *stimulus-barrier* and *withdrawal* (denial, flight). The stimulus-barrier scales down the intensity of external stimuli to a degree which the or-ganism can manage. It is usually assumed that no such barrier exists for internal stimuli, that is, for drive-tensions. The withdrawal is the removal of the sense-organ—for example, by reflex defenses—from the proximity or direction of the stimulus. Various intrapsychic defenses seem to be modeled on these two patterns.

In *primal repression*, analogously to withdrawal, the drive and its ideational representation are denied access to motility and consciousness. The affect-charge may or may not share the same fate, since it often remains the safety valve for the bottled-up tension, as in the affect-storms of hysterics. Yet in some cases the affect-charge succumbs to repression and the ideation does not. These cases show that the two aspects of the drive-representation may part ways and have differing fates. This fact is conceptualized as an aspect of the defense-mechanism of *isolation*. Repressed ideation is conceptualized as *unconscious:* the memory-trace cannot be so cathected as to become directly conscious. Originally, drive-cathexes could raise it to hallucinatory consciousness; now these cathexes are prevented from striving towards discharge. Affect-charge when repressed has no unconscious affect-quality, since it remains a cathexis hardly different (so far as we know) from the rest of the drive-cathexes; and the affect-discharge, with the concomitant of conscious feeling which lends it its distinctive character, is prevented by the repression from occurring.

How do we conceive of this repression? For reasons to be discussed in connection with *repression proper* (Section X, below) we must assume that, analogously to the stimulus barrier, an energy-charge is pitted against the drive-cathexis. This charge is conceptualized as *countercathexis*. The system of all such countercathexes is often conceptualized as *censorship*. Once such a system has been established, psychic structure-development is thereby advanced. One of the consequences of this structure-development is that not only the repressed but all drives are controlled by it. Drive-cathexis alone therefore no longer suffices to raise ideas to consciousness. The nature of consciousness is thus changed.

What are the sources of these countercathexes? The analogy of a river, which where it is slowed down builds up sand bars to slow it further, may help us to visualize what the evidence seems to suggest: the countercathexes seem to be derived from the drive which they repress. We may assume that in their genesis the structural limitations of discharge, discussed in Sections V and VI, play the role of initial obstruction. A "need is made into a virtue": the organization of the energy which is denied discharge so changes as to prevent future discharge.

The other fate of drive-cathexes—their transformation from a mobile into a bound state—is far less understood. We may assume that it is closely connected with the processes of "isolation" and "censorship." The system of countercathexes, although originating in the repression of specific drives, after it has emerged as a primitive structure comes to control and delay the discharge of *all* drive-cathexes. However, it allows for processes by which ideational representations of drives may emerge in consciousness as indicators of the drive-tensions; these processes may imply an isolation of the idea from the affect-charge, and this isolation may well be one of the mechanisms involved in "binding." To sketch what little more is known of binding, we have to consider first the changes which the drive-organization of memories undergoes in the establishment of the system of countercathexes.

IX. FROM THE DRIVE-ORGANIZATION TO THE CONCEPTUAL ORGANIZATION OF MEMORIES: BINDING

The drive-organization of memories abided by the law of wishfulfillment. Within it the cathexes strove toward reestablishment of equilibrium, that is, complete discharge. They were freely displaceable to any of the representations organized around the drive. The drive-cathexes of all those representations could be gathered on one of them, raising it to hallucinatory vividness. Several representations could be "condensed" achieving greater cathexis and thus access to perceptual consciousness.

In the course of accumulating experiences of delay, there arose a multitude of representations around the drive. In the same process, drives differentiated into partial-drives (Section XII, below), and single ideas came to represent several drives or partial-drives. Once this occurred, it was conceivable that cathectic displacements and ideational connections should take place not only among the representations of a single drive, but also between those of two or more drives. Ideas were then no longer bound to a single drive in order to attain cathexis for access to consciousness. Thus besides the drive-organization, dealing with objects perceived in a "diffuse" and "syncretic" fashion, there began to develop, superimposed on and cross-cutting it, an experiential connection-system of progressively more differentiated and discrete ideas. In this network, however, only minute amounts of cathexes could be displaced, and no longer to *any* other representation of the same drive, but only to those meaningfully connected in terms of experience.

The *short cut* by which formerly, in the absence of the need-satisfying object, any of its representations could be raised to consciousness as wishfulfillments, was replaced by a *detour:* now, through experientially meaningful connections of ideas, the need-satisfying object could be found in reality, or reality so changed as to result in finding it. The cathexes used now could no longer be concentrates of the cathexes of all other representations of a drive. Thus they remained minute in amount, with two results: (a) the traces which they cathected were experienced as memories rather than as hallucinatory reality; (b) the major drive-cathexes remained stored for action—that is, for alteration of reality, in finding and acting upon the need-satisfying object.

In this new organization of memory, the transition from one idea to another was no longer determined by a belongingness to the same drive, but rather by a *connectedness along the pathways in reality* toward the need-satisfying object. The connections began to take on the form of reality connections: space, time, contiguity, similarity. Such experiential connections, we learn from developmental psychology (Werner), evolve from syncretic ones and are at first "functional": objects become meaningful in terms of their relation to functions of the organism, that is, in terms of their "functional value." Developmental psychology designates these connections as *functional concepts,* though they do not meet our ideal of abstract conceptuality.

Thus the drive-organization of memories yielded to a conceptual-organization, even though the latter was still primitive. This yielding occurred not in the form of replacement but in that of a controlling system being superimposed. The pleasure-principle and wishfulfillment still remained effective but permitted of detours prescribed by a new principle—to be discussed soon—which works by means of the conceptual-organization of memory.

The cathexes operating within this new memory-organization, limited in displaceability and amount and not striving toward direct and complete discharge, were conceptualized as *bound cathexes.* As we shall see, this concept of binding is not as unequivocal as it may seem at first.

The new form of thought-processes is usually conceptualized as ordered or goal-directed thinking, or the *secondary process.*

X. COUNTERCATHECTIC ENERGY-DISTRIBUTIONS: REPRESSION PROPER

Clinical observation shows that if thoughts become even remotely connected with repressed drives, they may themselves be repressed. This process is conceptualized as *after-expulsion* or *repression proper*. It appears that once a system of countercathexes has been established, removal of the countercathexis will not suffice to make a memory conscious: its drive-cathexis cannot make it so, and it must obtain an additional cathexis, about which more below. Repression proper consists in the withdrawal of this additional cathexis and the application of countercathexis. The study of repression suggests that when the countercathexes, initially established to repress specific drives, are integrated into a controlling system of energy distributions, a saving in cathectic energy is thereby achieved. The prevailing conditions may be conceived as analogous to the establishment, in a war, of a unified front instead of a series of isolated posts: holding garrisons replace the full manning of the posts, and the surplus thus released forms a reserve to reinforce these as needed. Likewise, the integration of countercathexes results in a system which has at its disposal cathectic energies of its own. It is customary to conceptualize such conditions thus: the structure in question has a certain *autonomy*.

XI. ATTENTION-CATHEXES: CONSCIOUSNESS

The additional cathexis, which a drive-cathected idea must obtain to become conscious, is conceptualized as *hypercathexis* or *attention-cathexis*. Ideas which otherwise have access to consciousness, but at a given moment are not conscious are described as *preconscious*—that is, not countercathected, but without hypercathexis. It has been assumed that attainment of attention-cathexis amounts to establishing connection with verbal traces. This is indeed often the case. However, it seems safer to assume that full consciousness of an idea entails only its hypercathecting and the availability of its relationships to all relevant psychic content; among these, its relationship to the verbal-trace may or may not play a role. By contrast, a drive-cathected idea (such as a hallucinatory image, an obsessional or delusional thought, or a dream-picture) usually entails perceptual memories, but may entail verbal memories also, or even verbal memories alone; but its relationships are restricted to those of the drive-organization of memories; its form, unlike that of a hypercathected idea, may be distorted or symbolically disguised by these relationships. What a drive-cathected idea does not entail is its *relations* to reality by which its "unreality" —or in other words its mere "intrapsychic reality"—may be assessed.

Consciousness therefore is now conceptualized as a matter of the distribution of attention-cathexes, which are available only in a certain quantity. Evidence seems to suggest that these attention-cathexes are identical with those used in countercathecting, and when excessive energies are required for the latter it limits those available for the former.

Countercathectic organizations come about in the establishment of, and are used in, all defense-processes—not only in repression, as here described. Whatever the defense-process in which a given countercathectic organization originates, it is probable that a role is played in its inception by those preexisting structures discussed in connection with delay (Sections V and VI, above). Therefore, the same would hold for attention-cathexes also.

XII. AFFECTS, CONTROLLING ENERGY-DISTRIBUTIONS, AND DRIVE-DERIVATIVES

Delay of drive-discharge apparently results in a differentiation of the drive-cathexes. The cathexes differentiate into (a) those dischargeable only when the need-satisfying object is present, that is, only in the form of gratification-discharge; (b) affect-charge dischargeable in the form of affect-expression; (c) cathexes which appear as drive-cathexes of memory-traces. We have seen that there is reason to assume that this differentiation is based on structural givens of the organism, and that it eventually results in the establishment of a counter-cathectic energy-distribution which controls the original drive-energy distribution. We will now see that it results in further differentiations, usually conceptualized as *drive-derivatives*.

There seems to be evidence to indicate that the drives differentiate into *partial-drives* also, dependent upon maturational conditions and the corresponding somatic and external experiences. As they mature, the somatic apparatuses —both those which come into play as motor and secretory channels of discharge (for example, oral, anal) and those which play a role in perceiving the stimuli of the external world—provide systems of memory-traces which seem so uniquely integrated as to suggest the inference that the drive itself had differentiated into partial-drives. (For instance, as sphincter control is established, a system of ideas is organized in the wake of the experiences surrounding it. It is patterned on expulsion-retention, compliance-defiance, cleanliness-dirt; and it becomes so extended as to involve even interpersonal relationships, thus suggesting that an anal partial-drive had come about.) The complexities of one or several original drives, their character, their "fusion" and "defusion" in the course of development, need not be discussed here; however, for ego-psychology at large they are of great importance, even though proper to the theory of the id.

How do drive-derivatives arise? Of this we can form a picture if we consider the dynamics of affects, keeping in mind that affects are not drive-derivatives in the sense here discussed, and are mentioned here only as an analogy. It appears that affects do not arise in any rich variety if the countercathectic controlling organization is either weak—with drive-discharge more or less instantaneously possible—or rigid and overstrong. The optimal conditions are modulated and varied controlling energy-distributions, which, while delaying all drive-discharges deal with them differentially; thus the affect-discharge expresses differentially, in subjective experience, the intensity and quality of the tension and control of the drive.

How are we then to conceive of drive-derivatives? Once we assume that countercathectic energy-distributions arose in relation to single drives or partial-drives, we may infer that all such distributions sooner or later are integrated into a single energy-distribution, which controls the discharge even of drives other than those for whose control it was erected. If this countercathecting organization is extremely rigid, then it will repress all drives to a greater or lesser degree. If it is flexible, it will come to terms with those which it controls but does not actually repress: it alters their character and drive-derivatives arise.

The conditions arising from the establishment of a generalized system of countercathectic energy-distribution may be described as follows: (a) The various countercathecting energy-distributions, no matter how they arose, tend to generalize and thus to control all drive-discharges. (b) These controlling energy-distributions are usually conceptualized as *defenses*. (c) The drives which are not repressed are altered in their rhythm, discharge-conditions, and discharge-form. The so altered drive is more attuned to reality-demands, being on the one hand more amenable to delay, and on the other more flexible as to the conditions of discharge, in that a greater variety of objects and activities will serve as its gratifiers. These altered drives are conceptualized as *drive-derivatives*. The term is at times used to denote only their ideational representations. There seems to be a continuous transition from these drive-derivatives to the motivations conceptualized as ego-interests, to be discussed below. (d) The very existence of this new controlling energy-distribution gives rise to new forces, some of which are the drive-derivatives. Others arise from the defensive controlling energy-distribution itself. Of these we may note that, theoretically, every energy-distribution is expected to manifest itself as forces; empirically, defenses do come to our attention as motivations of observed behavior. For example, the defense of reaction-formation against aggression may manifest itself in the form of "altruistic" motivation. Whether these two kinds represent all the forces arising from drives defended against is uncertain; but there seems to be no sharp dividing line between these drives and those which give rise to drive-derivatives.

We may add from earlier considerations the following: (e) Such emergent energy-distributions have an autonomy, and have energy of their own at their disposal. (f) Considering the drive-derivatives, the forces (motivations) arising from the defenses themselves, and the energies used in counter- and hyper-cathecting which seem to be at the disposal of the system, we may say that here there are energies which are divested of the hallmarks of their drive-origin, that is, "bound" in various degrees. This is conceptualized as degrees of *neutralization* of cathexes. We might add that much about personality-organization in general, and thought-organization in particular, cannot be understood unless we assume that the process here described repeats itself in a hierarchic series, controlling organizations thus being layered over each other.

XIII. THE ROLE OF THOUGHT-ORGANIZATION IN REALITY-TESTING AND DRIVE-MASTERY

Delay, by establishing countercathecting energy-distributions, becomes a potent factor in the development of the all-over organization of controls which is conceptualized as the ego. This, when fully developed, performs many functions other than that of control; among others, it integrates those arising as consequences of delay, such as regulation of attention-cathexes, consciousness, and secondary-process thought as internalized experimental action.

Secondary-process thought has at its disposal and can cathect all memories, excepting those repressed; it is therefore—unlike primary-process thought, which cathects only drive-representations—a potent tool of reality-appraisal. It does not accept or reject according to immediate pleasure or pain, but seeks the pleasurable object—that is, the tension relieving, the gratifying—by detours. This search by detours is conceptualized as *reality-testing*. It may be hypothesized to have consisted originally in the motor-action of withdrawal. That which the organism could withdraw from by motor-action was external; that which it could not, was internal. Thought refined such testing of reality immeasurably. It showed the safest way to tension-release; it established relative independence from pain and pleasure signals but, in final analysis, sustained the goal of the pleasure-principle; reached it not on the path of least resistance, but on that of greatest advantage.

In this reality-testing function, consciousness—that is the distribution of attention-cathexes—reached a remarkable refinement, much of which is still little understood theoretically. We can experience an object in many ways, such as present, absent, in the past, in the future, in dream, and in wish; facts also we can experience variously, such as true, believed, denied, doubted, assumed, and certain. The immense importance of these variants of conscious experience for reality-testing and judgment is well known, but little studied; and their cathectic dynamics remain unexplored. The "poor judgment" of organic cases, the suggestibility of certain character-types, and the belief in their own lies shown by cases of pseudologia phantastica, show the significance of these variations of conscious experience in reality-testing.

Not only in regard to external reality but in intrapsychic economy also the secondary process is one of the salient functions of the ego. To clarify its role in intrapsychic dynamics, we must first consider its relation to the autonomy of the ego. Its development was intertwined with the organization of the energies which the ego has at its disposal in so far as it is autonomous. The meaning of autonomy has already been discussed: (a) the ego arises not only from the drives, but also from the preexisting apparatuses; (b) its emergence is a structuralization of new regulations, of which we are familiar with secondary-process thought, bound cathexes, and reality-testing; (c) it has energies at its disposal besides the drive-energies which it controls; (d) consequently it appears as a partly independent factor in the struggle of drive-demands and reality-demands, and not merely as a buffer or expression of their momentary balance.

In the ego's defensive maneuvers, these energies and secondary-process thought are used in the struggle with the drives, the totality of which is conceptualized as the *id*. The specifically intensive development of the secondary-process thought, conceptualized as *intellectualization*, is capable of binding and neutralizing great amounts of drive-energy, and is thus one of the main contributors to the autonomy of the ego in its relation to the drives. We shall turn below to the little we know about this process of intellectualization. Secondary-process thought provides also a means for an often effective compromise between the drives and the ego, wherein prohibited drive-goals are permitted and even pursued in the guise of more or less realistic goal-pursuits. This process is conceptualized as *rationalization*. The distinction between *intellectualization* and *rationalization* is quite fluid. Whether a thought-process is one or the other depends on how much the purposive thought has actually bound the drive-cathexes and is their master, or on how much the drive-cathexes merely use the guise of the purposive thought and remain "mobile." In the first case, the intellectual activity is neither compulsive nor impulsive-spasmodic; in the second, either no thought develops at all, or it only follows action, or if it precedes action it is "out of hand" and compellingly over-valent.

The thought-organization of the secondary process, like the ego, crystallizes in the conflict between reality- and drive-demands. But as a part of the ego it is built also on constitutional equipments, such as memory-capacity, perceptual systems, stimulus-barriers, and general endowment. By apperceiving external and internal stimuli, it subserves the ego's internalizing of the conflict between reality and drives. To begin with, reality clashed with drives whenever it denied them discharge-opportunity. The establishment of countercathexes internalized this clash. The result of this internalization is conceptualized as the *intrapsychic conflict* of ego and id. By this conflict and the attendant defenses the thought-organization may either suffer as in repressive forms, or be enhanced, as in intellectualizing forms: thus it attains its specific individual cast. The development of the ego's motivational and defensive dynamics shapes the development of thought-organization. We have assumed that the organization of cathectic energies is a hierarchy in which the forces of the basic energy-distribution are controlled by a superimposed one arising from it, which in turn gives rise to another set of forces which are then similarly controlled, and so on; we assume that thought-organization also follows this hierarchic layering. It should be noted, however, that these controls are by no means a one-way affair. The "controlled" motivations closer to the base of the hierarchy are still at work, and may trigger and activate the "controlling" motivations. Thus the control is mutual, and no total autonomy exists.

This is also true of thought-organization. We know empirically that it may be repressive, that is, tend to exclude memories and relationships, thus keeping energy-distributions at an equilibrium; or it may be intellectualizing, that is, acquisitive, thus keeping an equilibrium by overextending itself in binding cathectic-energies. We also know that the symbols, displacements, and condensations in dreams are forms of thought-organization corresponding to drive-motivations; though ego-motivations also may be represented, particularly in the secondary elaboration of the manifest dream-content. In other forms of thought-organization (hypnagogic states, daydreams, drug-states, amnesias, brain injuries) we may observe motivations from other levels of the hierarchy, with correspondingly different qualities of consciousness, and different "mechanisms" and formal characteristics of thought.

XIV. MOTIVATIONS OF THOUGHT

Lewin's experiments on and theory of quasi-needs show that we can think even when no fundamental need motivates us: by acts of intending, we make use of existing (but at the moment not compelling) needs to create others (quasi-needs) to motivate us in thought and action. In other terms, by acts of intending we can endow objects with cathexes (valences), and thereby change them from means to a valent goal into subsidiary goals. Thus means assume transitorily a goal character; they may also assume it permanently if the activity becomes automatized and retains cathexes as an autonomous organization. Such quasi-needs may obtain their cathexes from a genuine need, or from the "reservoir of attention-cathexes," if such exists. The development of the motivational hierarchy transformed the drives, periodic in nature, into a system of continuously acting motivations. It is thus that we can think even when no immediate drive-needs motivate us. This is one aspect of the autonomy of both ego and secondary process.

The process of quasi-need formation implies, as a prerequisite, reflective and forward-looking consciousness. Without the cathexes of consciousness, which presumably are drawn upon in the acts of intending, the quasi-needs could not be derived, even from genuine-needs; since without reflection no necessity, and without forward-looking no possibility, of intending could arise.

Quasi-needs, attitudes, wishes, strivings, values are all either regulators of drive-motivations, or autonomous motivations of both thought-processes and actions. Some or all of these are conceptualized as *ego-interests*. It is characteristic of the flexible, normal ego that: (a) it has energies at its disposal which it can autonomously mobilize (as in rote learning); (b) it has strivings of its own —that is, organized directed cathexes—which, though arising from drives and defenses as derivatives, are nevertheless autonomous; (c) it can permit such strivings to serve as instruments of drives, in thought and action; (d) it can suspend control of consciousness and motility, and afford drives access to them.

But this does not seem to be merely a matter of id- versus ego-motivations. Motivations seem to be hierarchically layered, some working more like "mobile," others more like "bound" cathexes, with a continuous transition between. Each motivational layer is both controlled by the one above it and may use it as its instrument. This combination of autonomy, dependence and interpenetration seems to be characteristic of the motivational hierarchy.

Thus it is that, though thinking operates by a set of autonomous rules, hunch and inspiration can play a role even in abstract scientific and creative thought. The allegedly ordered, logical, secondary-process thinking of the every-day is shot through with wishful thinking as content and with formal errors of thinking—such as *pars pro toto* and *post hoc propter hoc*—which are proper to more basic and archaic forms of thought-organization.

XV. STATES OF CONSCIOUSNESS

The normal state of consciousness is characterized by having contents and being capable of awareness of having them. Furthermore, it is capable of becoming aware of itself. These awarenesses and the implied varieties of reflectiveness are presumably forms of appearance which specific distributions of attention-cathexes take. But about these we know woefully little. The experiences discussed (in Section XIII) attended by a consciousness of belief, doubt, and so on, belong to those about which we have rudimentary information. Since the days of purely philosophical psychologies, more attention has been paid to these experiences by act-psychology (Brentano, Meinong, and particularly Buehler), phenomenological philosophy (Husserl), and Claparède, than by any other modern psychology.

We also know about variants of consciousness from states—such as those of drugging, extreme tiredness, hypnosis, and dreams—in which reflective awareness is either absent or limited. Such experiences as the "uncanny," "déjà vu," and boredom, also give information. In some psychiatric conditions of "organic" etiology, such as amnesic, agnosic, and aphasic syndromes, striking losses of reflective awareness are observed. In the major neuroses, impaired reflective awareness is indicated by lack of insight, the inability to conceive of a change of one's state, and special phenomena, such as states of depersonalization, multiple personalities, loss of personal identity, and amnesia. In major psychoses it is indicated impressively by lack of awareness of the illness, hallucinations, delusions, and kindred phenomena.

How are we to conceive of the distributions of attention-cathexes which account for reflective awareness? We are again forced to an analogy. Experience shows that in studying any science, a set of abstractions is always built up with considerable difficulty. Meanwhile we are prone at every step to fall back upon the concrete facts to which the abstract constructs refer. Once such a set of abstractions is conquered and we can operate with it, considerable relief is experienced—a saving in cathectic expenditure; but as soon as unusual difficulty is encountered, we again fall back upon the concrete material to aid us in applying our abstract constructs to the difficult new case. It is as though every set of abstractions amounts to a hypercathectic organization in which, at lesser expenditure of cathectic energy but presumably on a higher level of potential, a broad system of objects or relationships is integrated. (The conception of "lower intensity—higher potential" was formed by Breuer and Freud, as analogous to the familiar electrodynamic conception, in order to represent relationships, such as the one here discussed, not previously conceptualized.) Indeed, such sets of abstract-constructs mirror concrete facts; we can think and talk about these in such abstract terms, including them without being particularly concerned with them and yet without disregarding them. In the realm of discourse of such abstract terms, it is possible to become aware of the concrete facts in a reflective fashion, but it is not possible more than dimly to perceive abstractions in the concrete material before we have conceptualized them. It goes without saying that every set of abstractions may serve as the "concrete material" for higher-order abstractions, and this repeats itself in a hierarchical series.

We may assume that a similar pattern of hierarchic progression of hyper-cathectic organizations is experienced in the varieties of reflective awareness. The lower orders of reflective awareness are mirrored in the higher. Like higher-order abstractions, reflective awareness also suffers when tiredness or other normal or pathological conditions sap the available amount of hyper-cathexis. Again like abstractions, reflective self-awareness, too, may become charged with drive-cathexes (libidinized) and thus take on the aspect of symptom: pathological generalizing on the one hand, and pathologically distorted or exaggerated reflectiveness on the other, arise.

This formulation of self-reflective awareness only by-passes, but does not disregard, the role in reflectiveness played by "ego-ideal," "superego," and "identifications." These are discussed below in Section XXIII, "Socialization of Thinking."

From the point of view of the theory of thinking, reflective awareness is important because, among other things, it is involved in keeping thinking within a given "realm of discourse": this is characteristic of ordered thinking, and its absence is striking in the shifts of conceptual level common, for instance, in schizophrenic thinking. Those states of consciousness in which thought-forma-tions of the primary-process type abound are as a rule characterized by a limi-tation or absence of reflective awareness. Drive-action, and drive-cathected ideas (hallucinations, delusions), usually occur unaccompanied by reflective awareness; however, in borderline schizophrenic conditions, delusions may be accompanied by some such awareness, and it can be present even in dreams: "This is just a dream." On the other end of the continuum, there are dreams which are experienced as full reality. The average run of dream, however, has neither of these qualities clearly, and is characterized by a playfully unexplicit awareness, singularly the dream's own. The so-called "normal" waking state of consciousness is dependent upon the available attention-cathexes; to it cor-responds the thought-organization of the secondary process.

We may discern the following groups of variants of the state of conscious-ness: (a) a continuum of normal states of consciousness, ranging from the wak-ing to the dream; (b) special states of normal consciousness, such as absorption, hypnosis, boredom; (c) developmental states of consciousness, such as those of children of various ages, and of preliterates; and (d) pathological states of consciousness.

Each of these appears to be characterized by: (a) a specific form of thought-organization; (b) specific forms—including absence—of reflective awareness; (c) specific limitations of voluntary effort and/or spontaneity; and (d) underlying the others, a specific quality (degree of binding), quantity, and organization of available cathexes.

XVI. CONCEPTS

In the framework of a theory of thinking, concepts and the process of concept-formation appear not as independent entities, but as aspects of the thought-process. That is to say, concept-formation is one of the points of view from which the thought-process can be studied; and it seems so general an aspect that almost any facet of the thought-process may be profitably approached from it. It is noteworthy that certain forms of the thought-process appear to be altogether monopolized by it (for instance that of finding a common element in a set of phenomena). This fact is responsible for our inclination to reify concept-formation and treat it as a quasi-independent function; and indeed, on high levels of thought-integration it appears to have its own rules and autonomy. These characteristics are not unique to concept-formation; other aspects of thought-organization, such as anticipation and memory, share them.

We have seen that concept-formation is intimately linked with memory-organization (Section IX), as well as with that of attention-cathexes (Section XV).

The fundamental question which concept-formation answers is: What does an idea belong with? Where the primary process and the drive-organization of memories hold sway, ideas belong with a drive and all of its representations. As a result everything belongs with everything that shares an attribute of it (conceptualized as "participation"); ideas merge with each other and with percepts in disregard of the rule of the "excluded third" (conceptualized as "syncretism"); reasoning does not move inductively from the parts to the whole, or deductively from the whole to its parts, but from part to part with the assumption that the step will hold for the whole (conceptualized as "transduction"). Conception in this phase is "physiognomic," and correspondingly the world is animated and ideas have omnipotence (H. Werner). The mobile cathexis of the ideational representation, bent on full discharge, effects this.

As the secondary process, reality-testing, and the new memory-organization emerge, belongingness, too, changes its character. As Piaget puts it, "invariants of displacement-groups" are formed which safeguard the continuous existence of discrete objects. Later this spreads to temporal and spatial sequences, both those leading and those not leading to gratification. Thus memory frames of reference, which correspond to reality relationships, crystallize; their complexity surpasses imagination. The experience is assimilated to a manifold of concept-systems in terms of every sensory and every already existing abstract quality; but particularly in terms of time, space, matter, weight, and so on. The gain from such organization is that apparently the single idea need not be kept cathected, or only on a low level of intensity; and it is the built-up conceptual frames of reference which are cathected and highly responsive, as a whole.

It must not be forgotten that, underneath this conceptual-organization, there still operates the drive-organization of memories, implying the more archaic forms of concept-formation, such as those we encounter in schizophrenias, and in the symbols and mechanisms of dreams. Furthermore, there is no sharp dichotomy between either form of memory-organization, or either kind of concept-formation; there is rather a continuous transition, since strivings, attitudes, ego-interests—that is, all drive-derivatives—also create around themselves a memory-organization, one which is akin to the drive-organization of memories. These drive-derivatives, however, are products also of organic maturation and experience, and thus their cathexes are in some degree bound; their memory-organization is therefore akin to the conceptual framework of memory-organization also. If we assume that the higher the order of the drive-derivatives the more "tamed" to reality they can be considered, then their corresponding memory-organizations may be assumed to approximate asymptotically the conceptual-organization of memory. Actually, however, this extreme is only an ideal, and the conceptual-organization also incorporates organizations of memories around strivings, attitudes, and interest. The operations of cathectic dynamics in the conceptual-organization of memory do not use solely the completely neutralized attention-cathexes—if there are such—but also directed cathexes of ego-interests and drive-derivatives as well. Thinking is never a purely "cold" process.

XVII. MEMORY

Memory, too, is an aspect of thought-organization. But the impressive fact of retention, demonstrably built on an inborn apparatus, is conducive to considering it an independent function; and it has indeed a certain degree of autonomy. This, however, is often grossly overestimated. Certain memory impairments, such as the amnesic syndrome, which in the past have been considered relatively isolated phenomena—that is, occurring without other psychic disturbances—are now known to be connected with other disorders. This demonstration has dealt a telling blow to the assumption of total autonomy. Manifestations of the drive-organization of memory—such as slips of tongue, dream-work, forgetting due to repression, expression in symptoms of repressed memories, hypnotic and drug-hypnotic recovery of memories, and symbol-translations of hypnotically suggested tabooed material—certainly cast extreme doubt on the conception of complete autonomy of memory-function.

It has been difficult to reconcile these findings making memory dependent on the general laws of drive-organization and on the specific dynamics of the individual personality, with the seemingly inter-individually valid theories of association, conditioning, law of effect, and others which apparently support the conception of an autonomous memory-function. With the exception of Stern's personalistic theory and a few fragmentary others, these theories left room only for quantitative individual differences, and even these have been investigated rarely and unsystematically. The attempts to study repression—a phenomenon which apparently contradicts autonomy—within the framework of these theories, using materials of pleasant and unpleasant feeling-tones, in general paid attention to neither drive- nor personality-specificity, and brought inconclusive and contradictory results. These then seemed to cast doubt on the validity of the repression concept, and implicitly to confirm autonomy. The Gestalt experiments on meaningful learning and "intelligent" use of memory further bespoke autonomy, and contradicted drive- and personality-determination.

The Freudian distinction between primary and secondary process remained for long without body and recognition. Yet so far only the theory of development of the conceptual-organization of memory out of its drive-organization can reconcile the contradictory evidence for and against autonomy. The more recent ego-psychological developments in psychoanalysis have given body to this theory.

Thus memory-function may be conceived as built on an autonomous inborn apparatus, which in the course of maturation plays a double role. On the one hand, it is built into the drive-organization of memory; on the other, by registering reality-sequences of events it becomes the foundation of the later maturing conceptual-organization of memory and reality-testing. We have already discussed the relationship of structure and cathectic dynamics in this process. The conceptual-organization itself becomes progressively autonomous: that is, it consists of a hierarchic layering of organizations, in which the laws of drive-organization and the laws of realistic-logical organization are balanced against each other; this balance progressively shifts, with the rising levels of hierarchy, toward preponderance of the laws of realistic-logical organization. An ideal purity of these, however, is never achieved. The balance achieved between the two memory-organizations is an internalized expression of the balance between the needs of the organism and the potentialities of the environment. It is also the balance between neutralized cathexes and cathexes of partial or no neutralization.

That learning experiments, particularly the Gestalt, suggest that complete autonomy and logical-realistic organization is achieved, and that other learning experiments suggest other sorts of autonomy, may mean only that the restrictions of the experimental setup prevent manifestation of other aspects of the memory-organization. (I by-pass here the complexities of Hull's theory; it would require extensive discussion to demonstrate that his concept of drive is different from the concept here used, and that his theory, though extensively developed, cannot meet the complexities of the observations collated in this volume.) Bartlett's non-restrictive experiments showed abundantly the role of affects, strivings, interests, and attitudes in memory-organizations other than drive-organizations.

The continuous transition from the drive-organization to the conceptual-organization of memory was well demonstrated by the Lewin-Zeigarnik experiments and the host of those that followed. The original Zeigarnik experiment demonstrated the dependence of memory on quasi-needs, in defiance of the laws of frequency and recency. The related experiments of Rosenzweig and others showed the dependence of the quasi-need effect on self-esteem, anxiety, and other ego-dynamic conditions; those of Block and Alper showed the dependence of memory upon interests labeled as ego-involvement and task-involvement. Test-studies in "Information" and "Association," by Rapaport *et al*. seemed to indicate the process by which pathology results in a reversal from the conceptual- to the drive-organization of memories.

XVIII. ANTICIPATION

That tasks determine our thoughts by "setting" us, by eliciting "attitudes" (*Einstellungen*) in us, was demonstrated by the Wuerzburg school. Selz demonstrated that tasks create "abstract" schemata or patterns, delimiting the ideas which will solve the task to those which fit these patterns. That in this sense every situation to be responded to by thought is a "task" is, however, often overlooked. An example: when in a conversation one utters the word "although," he thereby prepares the other for—that is, makes him anticipate—two coordinate antithetic phrases. The significance of fixed expectations (anticipations) for misunderstandings and misinterpretations of facts and communications is well known in everyday life and is indeed a major subject-matter in the exchanges between therapist and patient. Jokes which ostensibly prepare for a certain anticipation, while they hide subtly the preparations for another, and finally fulfill the hidden one are good demonstrations of the dynamic effect of anticipations. The import of these observations for the theory of thinking has not been explored.

In a sense, the primary models of action and thought already imply anticipations: it is a specific object which permits gratification-discharge, and it is a specific set of ideas (drive-representations) the cathecting of which constitutes wishfulfillment. Thus, in this sense, drives "anticipate" their real or ideational objects—though this sense is not very different from that in which ears "anticipate" sounds and eyes lightwaves. In animals these "anticipations" appear to have a great degree of rigidity, but are not rigidly fixated in most animals nor in all of their instinctive behavior. This is true of human drives in general; and, where such rigidity is observed, it is conceptualized as *fixation* of the drive on its object. It appears that, just as drives anticipate their objects, so, on every level of the motivational hierarchy, motivations anticipate theirs. With ascending levels of hierarchy, the variability of satisfying objects tends to increase and the frequency of fixations to decrease. Yet as Lewin has conclusively shown, on all levels we encounter completely fixated anticipations also. This difference in fixation and variability is not the only one between drive-anticipations and those of a higher level. We shall now discuss three others.

First, the higher-level anticipations do not usually depend on a single motivating force, but rather on an interaction of a great variety of motivational forces, the intermeshing of which determines the anticipation-niche by which we expect and understand events, as well as prepare and execute actions. These interacting forces may arise even from varying levels of the motivational hierarchy: such are drive-needs, self-esteem, realistic-purposiveness, and regard for others. It is as though any single motivational force has a whole retinue of possible satisfiers, but the interaction of forces eliminates them except for those which simultaneously satisfy all, or at least the decisive, forces involved. Indeed, we do seem to experience consciously such anticipations in complex and critical situations; and in the ruminations of obsessional patients there is rich opportunity to observe them. Yet neither this type of anticipation nor the more or less fixated drive-anticipation is the major form we encounter every day.

Second, the higher the hierarchic order of anticipations, the more they tend to lose their idiosyncratic-individual character and to become socially shared. The anticipation aroused by saying "although" is an example of those so shared. The overwhelming frequency of popular reaction-words in Word Association Tests, and the existence of popular responses even on a relatively unstructured test like the Rorschach Ink-Blots, are also examples in point. F. Allport's J-curve hypothesis refers to related phenomena. The more the cathexes used are bound, the more the anticipations tend to be socially agreed ones; this development is related to the increased possibility, on higher hierarchic levels, of creating quasi-needs to cope with "objectively necessary" tasks for which genuine-needs are not extant. It is further related to the automatization and becoming autonomous of certain quasi-need systems, so that they need not be newly set up every time, but are available in an "ossified" form without special acts of intending being performed or specific genuine-needs being present. These autonomous and automatized quasi-need systems, described by Lewin, have their own anticipation-patterns, which are correspondingly automatized; this automatization, arising from the permanence of objective necessity, is the basis of their socially shared character. These appear to be the commonest kind of anticipations, and least noticed (the "although" example). They amount to quasi-stable thought-patterns which seem to underlie not only everyday but strict logic and thinking also. Yet these anticipation- and thought-patterns have been little studied as such, and syntax is more familiar with them than psychology. Compare however Tolman on field-anticipations.

Third and finally, such quasi-stable thought-patterns are not restricted to motivations and strivings of socially agreed character. The anticipations of the more fundamental drive- and drive-derivative motivations also ossify, and thus crystallize such quasi-stable thought-patterns. These however are often repressed, together with the corresponding motivations, or fall into disuse, or are overlain by others in the course of development and become barely recognizable. It seems that they play a crucial role in creative thinking; in the creation of philosophical systems, in the "tough-" and "tender-minded" dichotomies, and in adolescent struggles over choice of "philosophy," such patterns of thought do become obvious. The "reconciler of contradictions," the "tough materialist," the "purer-than-thou idealist," the "dialectician," each experiences and expresses a set of fundamental anticipations—that is, quasi-stable thought-patterns.

The thought-process is predicated upon the interaction of the anticipation-patterns of various hierarchic levels.

XIX. ATTENTION AND CONCENTRATION

We have seen that, in order to become conscious, both internal and external perceptions must attain hypercathexes, that is, attention-cathexes. There seems to be evidence that different degrees of hypercathecting, combined with countercathecting are at work in and determine the character of selective apperception.

Ego-syntonic ideas as a rule immediately find conscious expression: either they correspond to ego-interests—that is, directed motivations whose energies are to some degree neutralized; or they immediately attract attention-cathexes —that is, neutralized ego-energies. Which of these two assumptions is the more parsimonious, or what relationships obtain between them if both should prove necessary, cannot at present be conjectured. If an incoming *stimulus* has valence for an ego-syntonic motivation, the conditions are usually not different from those just described for ideas. If there is no such motivation present, attention-cathexis may be available to make the stimulus conscious. It is not clear whether, when no genuine-need is present, the process must include something like the creation of quasi-needs, or can draw directly on a reservoir of attention-cathexes. In all these cases the experience is involuntary, spontaneous, effortless; it is free of an impulsive or compulsive "must," and of effort of will. Those forms of conscious experience which are involuntary, effortless, without "musts," and ego-syntonic are conceptualized as *attention-dependent*.

In Digit Span tests, where no long-range retention enforces effort and the material has no specific relevance to ego-interests, performance is usually dependent upon the ready availability of attention-cathexes. Thus, such performances appear to reflect the amount and/or availability of attention-cathexes. It should be noted, however, that individuals vary greatly in regard to "effortlessness"; the irrelevance of the material to ego-interests does not preclude a relevance of success in performance. For these reasons we can say only that Digit Span reflects effortless attention better than other tests.

The conditions are quite different when there are external or internal interferences with "attending." Some of the major possible interferences are: (a) a reinforcement of repressed impulses, which requires a reinforcement of countercathexes, and thereby depletes the available amount of attention-cathexes: this occurs in states of tenseness, restlessness and boredom, or in anxiety-states in which even the reinforced countercathexes are insufficient and the threatening break-through of repressed drives continually produces signals of anxiety; (b) a reinforcement of repressed drives and/or drive-derivatives, so that they break through in such forms as obsessional, over-valent ideas or "distracting" fantasies; (c) an external stimulation claiming part or all of the available attention-cathexis: this occurs when a conversation, or simply the presence of an important person in the room, or strong noises, changing lights, or other intense competing sensory-stimuli "distract" us from what we "attend" to; (d) a condition such as tiredness, sleepiness, or drugging, which depletes the available amount of attention-cathexis; (e) the complexity of the subject-matter to which we attend, which changes the effortless-involuntary character of attention. (We shall postpone the discussion of this last point.)

Under the five major conditions described, "attending" either becomes impossible, or appears in snatches, or loses its effortless-involuntary character. The cathectic theory of consciousness and attention seems to account easily for the first two of these alternatives; the third needs further scrutiny. Here attending changes into a voluntary, effortful pursuit, conceptualized as *concentration*. The nature of the process of concentration is not clear, though we have some information about it. First, it appears as though a quasi-need has been created which gathers the still available attention-cathexes—and perhaps also available, not fully neutralized, cathexes corresponding to ego-interests. Lewin's theory of will suggests that the difference between the free availability of cathexes and their mobilization by the creation of a quasi-need corresponds to the difference between the subjective experience of involuntary-effortlessness and of voluntary-effortfulness. Second, there is some evidence to suggest that in tense, over-alert people, as well as in many of those for whom intellectualization is characteristic as a personality trait of defense, involuntary-effortless attending is usually supplanted by voluntary-effortful concentrating. Possibly, in such people the function of attending itself is hypercathected and built into a continuously acting quasi-need system which may become automatized in varying degrees. Such at least seems to be the case in projective overalert people with regard to interpersonal relationships, and generally in intellectualizing people with regard to facts and relationships. Third, the preceding point is supported, though in a somewhat obscure way, by the fact that effortless attending, though it may become aware of itself, is not usually so; when it attempts to become so, particularly if continuously, it changes into effortful-voluntary concentration. Concentration, however, is usually aware of itself; it is as though it were continuously prodding itself by being so. We have seen before that such reflective awareness can be conceptualized as a hierarchic superimposition over each other of hypercathectic organizations.

At this point we may return to the nature of the subject-matter to be attended to, the fifth of those major factors that may alter the process of attending. When the subject-matter is new, requiring *organization* of material or building of *abstractions*, the subjective experience usually changes to that of voluntary effortful concentration. This usually implies a reflective "bending back upon" the concrete data taken in, so as to unite them into a meaning. It appears that these organizing processes usually create new quasi-stable thought-patterns, of the sort discussed above in connection with anticipations.

Formulating this more broadly: the creation of new thought-patterns and meanings, thereby extending the scope of the thought-process, appears to require always a voluntary-effortful concentration. Once such new patterns have been created and stabilized, and are in continuous use, their employment may become involuntary and effortless; this suggests that here the voluntary effort has created an autonomous, automatized pattern. But when such patterns fall into disuse, or when the material to be apperceived is complex and hides rather than reveals them, *meaning-discernment* then becomes a matter of voluntary-effortful concentration. The difference between the two forms of meaning-discernment may be illustrated by that between reading a mystery story and reading Kant. The individual differences, however, are worth noting. For some people, the reading of a mystery story and of Thomas Mann's *Faustus* will be a contrast of attending and concentrating; for others, it may not. For a mathematician, the contrast in this respect between *Faustus* and a mathematical text may not be very great; for non-mathematicians, it is. These differences involve not only individual differences in intellectual endowment, which may be taken for granted: they involve also individual personality dynamics, experiential determination—surely dependent on those dynamics—and general "types" of personality-organization, with corresponding "types" of thought-organization.

For instance, proficiency in simple arithmetic in the adult of our civilization is based on such automatized thought-patterns. In the child these patterns do not yet exist, and the process of learning and application is usually effortful. We observe that addition becomes effortless while division is still effortful. As a rule, the four basic calculations later become attention-dependent functions, while the more complex ones, such as direct and inverse proportions, remain concentration-dependent. Surely such is not the case for people who are steadily concerned with numbers and their relationships, but this is not merely a matter of experience: it takes certain personality-structures to acquire that experience. The balance between attention- and concentration-dependent functions is fairly well reflected in the proficiency on Arithmetic Tests (Rapaport *et al.*)

The difference between effortless-involuntary and effortful-voluntary thought-processes may be illustrated also by the experience of understanding and producing. A mathematical proof effortlessly understood may require great voluntary effort to produce or even only to reproduce. The difference is similar between enjoying a written product and attempting to create one. This does not imply that creating is always or mainly an effortful-voluntary process; the conditions of creativity are more complex, and we shall touch on them briefly below.

XX. DAYDREAMING AND PRECONSCIOUS MENTAL PROCESSES

Daydreams—reveries, fantasies—are not a homogeneous group of phenomena, though all share the involuntary-effortless character and a form in which imagery, visual and acoustic, predominates. They range from planning to wish-fulfillment, from the realistic to the fantastic, and the usual laws of logic may or may not hold in them. Preconscious thinking also includes all these variants, as evidenced in preconscious fantasies of patients brought to daylight by psychoanalysis, and by thoughts and problem-solutions that arise ready-made in our minds. Even most complex, ordered thought-processes take place without the participation of consciousness. Though there are obvious differences between their extremes, there is no sharp dividing-line between daydreams and ordered thinking.

Daydreams and preconscious thought-processes thus use both neutralized cathexes and drive-cathexes of various degrees of neutralization. That such processes are not always conscious shows the need of an additional "attention-cathexis"—hypercathexis—to become so. The fact that daydreams though "conscious" do not take the same form as conscious thought appears to indicate that they occur in a state of consciousness different from that of normal waking; and we may assume that the hypercathexis lending consciousness in that state is of a different intensity and/or subject to different regulations. Different degrees of difficulty are encountered in making various daydreams conscious, and in holding on to them once they are conscious; this indicates that a countercathectic energy-distribution controls the transition from preconscious to conscious processes.

Various forms of thought described as "autistic" phenomena arise where preconscious thought has easy access to consciousness. Such is certainly the case with daydreams. Whether the child's and the preliterate's "autistic" thinking should be viewed in terms of such easy access is uncertain; the hypercathecting energy-organization may not be established in them in the same fashion as in the adult of our civilization. Clearly, in pathological autisms the countercathectic energy-distributions have been weakened, probably both those which counteract unconscious drive-representations and those which control access to consciousness. But it is likely that we deal here not with only two but with a whole hierarchy of such controlling energy-distributions. At any rate, it seems that consciousness is not an all-or-none proposition; rather there exists a continuous series of its forms. These are dependent on the solidity of counter-cathectic energy-distributions preventing inroads, and on the hypercathexes available.

The significance of preconscious thought-processes for ordered thinking can hardly be overstated. Not only do they provide us with the right memories and relationships at the right time in our everyday work and discourse, without which every minute of life would grow into an insolubly complex problem; they also provide complex ideas to the good speaker, the teacher, the participants in involved discussions. Preconscious automatism is a better guarantee of many adaptive performances than any consciously willed and planned process.

The automatic sorting-out and organizing of experiences and knowledge by the preconscious thought-processes is indeed amazing, as we see when returning to a complex problem after a period of relaxation. Yet the great individual variability in the degree to which people can make use of these processes, and probably in which they have them, is one of the important areas of thought-organization, and its role in personality dynamics, to be explored. For example, some can make use of these processes only in the absence of any pressure, others only in the presence of maximal pressure.

XXI. CREATIVE THINKING

Insight, invention, and inspiration are the terms used to describe creative thinking. From the point of view of the theory of thinking, it is of only peripheral interest that the contents of creative thought, particularly in literature, have been demonstrated to be often ideational-representations of repressed drives. It is only somewhat less peripheral that these "insights" into repressed drives—that is, their penetration into consciousness—have been shown to become possible when their emergence subserves the defense against a still more forbidden striving. The cathectic dynamics involved here—the liberation of the energies used formerly as countercathexes against those drives which now come to consciousness, and the application of part of them to reinforce the countercathexes of other drives—are of interest. These experiences are accompanied by relief, elation, exultation, and so forth, corresponding to the liberation of countercathexes; in this they are similar to the experiences attending another form of thought-organization, namely, wit and humor.

Of more central interest to the theory of thinking, however, are two other aspects of creative thought.

First, when an unconscious idea rises to consciousness, the ego suspends its "censoring" function momentarily, only to resume it again. This formal characteristic of creative activity has been stressed by Kris. In terms of energy-dynamics: the countercathectic energy-distributions become momentarily ineffective, and part of their energy is probably used to hypercathect the arising repressed idea. This is the "inventive" phase of creative thinking, which abides by the rules of the primary-process. The idea so arising in consciousness may take various forms—a vague general "feel," a sense of relationship, a schematic pattern, a verbal or visual fragment, and so on. In any case, it is characterized by a paucity of relationships to other contents of consciousness: repression and other defenses deprive drive-representations of these relationships, the presence of which gives full consciousness to a thought. The "elaborative" phase of creative thinking establishes these relationships, and turns the idiosyncratic "inventive" product of the individual into the social communication of art or science. The unconscious idea which rises to consciousness because of pathological conditions is usually not so elaborated. One reason for this is touched on below. The elaborative phase, in contrast to the inventive, is effortful and operates by the rules of the secondary process.

The significance of these aspects of creative thought for the theory of thinking is rooted in the fact that much productive and ordered thinking also has a biphasic character, most of it being preconsciously prepared. Perhaps in creative thinking the "invention" originates from deeper and more idiosyncratic levels of the hierarchy of motivations and thought-organization, and is therefore more perceptible and even startling, and its elaboration bound to more stringent conditions, than that of productive and ordered thought. Notwithstanding, there seems to be an unbroken continuity between these forms, and the more striking creative ones spotlight the nature of the thought-process.

Second, among the forms which inventions may take once they reach consciousness we mentioned *schematic patterns of thought*. These patterns were discussed earlier as the quasi-stable forms of anticipations, pertaining to motivations of various hierarchic levels. Those pertaining to repressed motivations appear to play a specific role in creative thinking. Alone, neither the repressed drive nor its ideational representations yield creative thought upon reaching consciousness: nor can either or both capture relationships which cogwheel into nature to coin natural laws, or into interpersonal relations to mold that form of communication which is art. To do either, these impulses and ideas must carry with them quasi-stable thought-patterns, which correspond both to them and to a segment of nature, and by means of which they can translate themselves into scientific or artistic expressions. It is not infrequent that such patterns, once having emerged, stay conscious in a vague way for long periods before the arduous work of elaboration provides them with the "relationships," "know-how," or "facts," which make them communicable.

In creative thinking also, therefore, energy-dynamics alone provide no complete explanation, and structural factors must be taken into account. Here the structural factors are the ego's ability to renounce control (countercathexis) momentarily, and the existence of quasi-stable thought-patterns derived from anticipations pertaining to repressed drives.

XXII. THE POSSIBILITY OF KNOWLEDGE

The fundamental problem of epistemology is, How can the mind form knowledge of the world of objects? The 2,500 years of struggle of Western epistemology with this problem testify that the grasp of thinking on objective reality was most puzzling to man. The importance of this problem can be gauged from the fact that it stood in the center of the systems of most great Western philosophers, from Parmenides and Heraclitus to Kant and Husserl. A study of the various solutions offered—the Sophists' denial of the possibility of knowing, the solipsistic solutions from the Eleatics to Berkeley, the idealistic ones of Plato and Aristotle, English empiricism, Descartes' dualism, Spinoza's monism, Geulincx and Malebranche's occasionalism, and Leibnitz's prestabilized harmony, Kant's solution in terms of integration by the categories of pure reason—might add an important chapter to the theory of thought-processes.

When at the end of the last and the beginning of the present century, attempts were made to wrest this epistemological problem from philosophy and offer a psychological solution (for example, Leisegang), these attempts were discredited not so much by philosophical a priori criticism as by attacks upon their factual relevance. The growth of psychological knowledge brought us closer to the possibility of a more satisfactory answer. I shall avoid here the philosophical question of whether psychology—itself based on fundamental assumptions of the sort epistemology studies—can claim competence to answer epistemological problems. From the point of view of science, this is not a philosophical problem, but one of methodological theory and empirical findings.

In his developmental studies, Piaget has demonstrated that the possibility of knowing is rooted in the organic adaptation-relationship of man to his environment. He has shown how, from this basic root, a hierarchic series of thought-organizations arises, in the course of maturation and development, culminating in reality-adequate thinking. The functional categories which he found to exist on all levels of this hierarchy led him to specific epistemological conclusions closely similar to Kant's. The relatedness of Kant's epistemology to the assumptions underlying dynamic psychology seems to be more than apparent or accidental.

We may now outline the possibility of knowledge in terms of the concepts in which thought-processes have been discussed in these pages. (a) A naive formulation of the problem would read: If thinking is part of human nature, how can it reflect accurately facts other than those of human nature? (b) One speculative answer might be that it is artificial to divide human nature from the rest of nature; the two constitute an indivisible unity. Indeed, this answer is not basically different from Spinoza's pantheistic or Leibnitz's monad theory. Modern "holistic" theories flirt with similar answers. (c) If we were familiar only with the primary process and the corresponding ideation, we should formulate the problem thus: How can ideation which represents only need-satisfying objects acquire knowledge of the world of objects at large? In this frame of reference the question would have to remain unanswered. Only "knowledge" of drive-objects would exist, as indeed is the case to some extent in the world of animals (Uexkuell). (d) Our understanding of the process by which the reality-principle arose from the pleasure-principle, the conceptual-organization of memories from their drive-organization, the secondary process from the primary, points the way toward a solution. The rise of the ego-organization of thinking from its id-organization freed us from the confinement of a limited number of drives, a limited number of drive-objects, a limited world and limited knowledge. Derivative motivations broadened the range of objects of interest. These derivatives arose in interaction with the environment; thus, the original drive-determination of ideation became overlaid by thought-formations which were no longer regulated solely by the wish to reach the gratification-experience by the shortest route, if necessary by hallucination; it was regulated also by the striving to reach it in reality, if necessary by detours. As a result, thinking and action still serve drive-gratification, in final analysis, but at the same time have an independence, autonomy. It is this relative autonomy which guarantees that valid knowledge of reality can be acquired by thought. Yet because this autonomy is relative, knowledge is limited and never infallible; thus every advance in knowledge is won by effort and struggle. Man's knowledge of the world is therefore attained by progressive approximation and objectivation. But however powerful knowledge may grow, and autonomy of thought be extended, the fact remains that one of the ancestors of human knowledge *is* the idea of the need-satisfying object. Knowledge therefore is and will be used directly for the purpose of discharge of drive-cathexes, and not only for experimental action to find the most adaptive path toward gratification.

XXIII. SOCIALIZATION OF THINKING

In the course of individual development, ideation changes into thought. This change is marked not only by the shift from the pleasure-principle to the reality-principle; nor only by the turn, from the short-circuit of reaching the goal in fantasy, to the detour to it in reality; nor only by the superimposition of a conceptual-organization on the drive-organization of thought-processes. There is also a crucial change from the idiosyncratic character of ideation to the socially shared character of thinking. Ideation was syntonic only with the drive-need of the individual and with the regulations of discharge—"safety valves," "tension-thresholds," "discharge-capacities"—characteristic of the individual organism. *Thinking* tends to be syntonic with society. Indeed, the very motivations of ordered thought are, in varying degree, socially shared (Section XIV, above). But at this point caution raises its finger: empirical data show that *ideation*, however idiosyncratic in general, shows some inter-individual commonality; and *ordered thinking*, however socialized, is syntonic with the individual's organization—that is, with the thinker's personality.

How can we conceive of the development of socialized thought?

We know from Piaget's studies that the transition from "egocentric" thinking and its naive absolute realism, to a higher level of thinking which recognizes the relativity of qualities, is dependent upon the discovery of the relativity of the "me." Motility, by drawing a line between the excitations from which we can withdraw by motor action and those we cannot, draws the line between the "me" and "not-me"; but the self-awareness so achieved is quite incomplete. Self-awareness depends not only upon the distinction between external and internal stimulation, nor only upon the implicit reactions of others to the "me"; it depends also upon their explicit communication. Only the implicit reactions and explicit communications of a variety of other "me"s can free the "me" from its solipsism (autism), by providing mirrors to reflect various sides of the "me." The experience of these variations replaces the autistic *naive realism* of the sensory-motor "me," by a relativism of self-awareness. This is prerequisite to that process by which thinking and knowledge of the world is freed of artless subjective realism, and even of that brand of relativism which is itself conceived as something absolute. It is the establishment of such self-awareness which expels subjectivity from "knowledge," and ushers in the possibility of objectivity.

Though Piaget's conclusions link the socialization of thinking to *reflective awareness* (Section XV, above) his findings concerning this process are limited, and our understanding of them in terms of a cathectic theory is scant.

Psychoanalytic findings help us a step further. We have assumed here that the predecessor of thought and knowledge is the idea of the drive-object. The first "social relationships" of the developing individual are those with persons who are his drive-objects (conceptualized as *love-objects*). When reality obliges him to give up these objects, they are not given up intrapsychically: in fact, their intrapsychic existence only then really begins, since their memory-trace instead of their perception is then drive-cathected (Section III, above). This process is conceptualized as *introjection*. Such introjected objects constitute major sub-organizations within the developing memory-organization. Psychoanalytic observations show that they also become major organizations of the ego—that is, of the super-organization of drive-controls—which grows on the renunciation of drive-objects necessitated by the environment, maturation, and development. These organizations which arise in the ego in the wake of an introjection are conceptualized as *identifications*. Indeed, from certain vantage points, the ego is the precipitate of abandoned drive-objects, that is, of *identifications* (Freud). On the one hand, these introjected objects become integrated, lose their independence, and give rise to a homogeneous ego, whose strength is greatly dependent on the completeness of their integration; on the other hand, they give rise to the ego-ideal and the superego, which permit the individual to see himself with the eyes of others, and thus to make himself and his thoughts the object of his observation. Introjection and identification thus enable us to take over, as our own, the feelings and reactions of other people, and later their thoughts also—both those directed specifically towards us and those more general. The ego-ideal and superego also appear to be specific cathectic organizations, like those which give rise to reflective awareness (Section XV, above).

Such is our picture of the cathectic dynamics which lay the foundation for socially shared thinking. Its key-concepts are *introjection* and *identification*. This development is not independent from that of reality-testing and secondary process; it is but a different aspect of the indivisible process of individual maturation and development.

Introjection and identification not only lay the foundations of socially shared thought; they seem to partake in building it also, by recurring on the various levels of the hierarchy of motivations and thought-organization. In so recurring, they fulfill a definite role, among others, in the cathectic economy of "learning." Instead of a separate cathecting of each behavior-form, reaction, and thought, introjecting an "object" makes possible a cathecting of systems of behavior-forms and reactions, and thereby a saving of cathectic energies. At first, such introjected systems may stand apart from the rest of the ego. Later they become integrated with it, at a further saving of cathexes.

Even in purposeful high-level learning processes we discern this economy. In studying a science, to have assimilated a theory, as against "holding" isolated facts and relationships, permits a saving in cathexes. The very process of an individual's development in a field of study seems molded on a pattern similar to that of introjection, identification, and integration into the unity of the ego. Knowledge, when first acquired, remains fragments from various textbooks. It is only later that the local memories of the textbooks and of their dividing-lines recede. This recession is accompanied by a progress in the applicability of the knowledge to instances and relationships other than those given in the texts. The result of this process is that the knowledge, originally learned as this or that teacher's or text's, becomes *our own*. When needed, it is spontaneously available and does not require the self-questioning: "What does Woodworth say about it?" or "How does Koffka regard this?"

At this point many observations of interest for the psychology of thinking are met with, of which only two will be mentioned. (a) When difficult problems are encountered, such self-questioning again arises, even though the general integration of knowledge is not thereby reversed. (b) In certain types of personality-organization, despite the fact that knowledge is assimilated and integrated, its original sources remain easily available; such personalities unite high integration and articulation.

From this integration of knowledge, there leads a further process of integration by which the knowledge is permeated by the organizing principles of the individual personality, and in turn influence his life-style and behavior-forms. Finding a form of thought-organization which can provide a synthesis of knowledge assimilated, motivations at work, and reality-opportunities available, is part of this process. The fortunate development of such a synthesis is the guarantee of occupational gratification and creativeness. At this point, the realms of the *psychology of thinking*, of *adaptation*, and of *creativity* border on each other. It becomes clear how complex are the requirements for such fortunate solutions, and why the range of creative productivity is narrow.

We have only begun to understand the process of socialization of thought. On the one hand, the dynamic and economic role of introjection and identification, particularly in their reemergence on higher hierarchic levels of motivation, and on the other hand, the development of reality-testing, secondary process, and the corresponding motivational hierarchy, promise to provide a basis on which to build further understanding.

XXIV. COMMUNICATION

Communications range from those which are grasped only by empathy and intuition, through those emotional expressions which are apprehended in part intuitively and in part by understanding amenable to verbalization, to those which are directly verbalized and understood. Verbalized communications range from intimate exchanges of profound personal significance, through shop-talk of well-defined interest, to talk "about the weather."

It should be noted that the referents of the terms empathy and intuition are ill-defined. Until proved otherwise, the possibility must be kept open that unrecognized channels of communication may exist. For the present, let us assume that empathy and intuition refer to communications which are minute, or are momentarily unrecognized because of other preoccupations of the perceiver, or are so distributed in space or time that the cues are no longer consciously integrated: thus, a preconscious perception and/or integration of these apparently takes place, the results of which are experienced as empathy and intuition.

To envisage the role of communication in psychic life, it must be remembered that ideation and thought arise when memory-traces are cathected, and that the major condition of forgetting is repression—that is, the withdrawal of cathexes from memory-traces. We must also keep in mind that the differentiation of drives into drive-derivatives is closely linked with the establishment and cathecting of memory-traces, which are instrumental in bringing about new hierarchic levels of motivation. Furthermore, in safeguarding repression, there is a tendency to repress ideas often even remotely connected with a drive-representation, and only ideas of sufficiently remote connection can become conscious; therefore, exposure to a wealth and variety of experiences counteracts the tendency of repression to narrow in the extreme the volume of conscious thought. Finally, it will be useful to envisage that, on the one hand, interpersonal communication brings us the broadest and most condensed form of external experiences and, on the other, forces and enables us to observe our internal experiences in preparation for, and in, our reactions. These facts would lend communication a unique role in psychic life, even if contact with human beings did not in itself play the exceptional role in psychic development discussed under "Socialization of Thinking."

These considerations suggest that the role of communication in psychic life may have been underestimated, or at least given too little systematic scientific attention.

It seems justifiable to make these formulations: (1) Communication enriches the store of experiences and thereby counteracts ego-limitation. (2) Psychic life is not a one-way avenue in which defenses limit communications: communications may also combat the deleterious effects of defenses. Though defenses operate in perception also, they are less effective in recognition of percepts than in recall of memories; it is this differential which communications appear to utilize in combating defenses. (3) The enrichment by experiences—originating, in the course of communication, in external perceptions and introspective observations—furthers the differentiation of ego-interests (strivings, feelings, attitudes, and other such motivations) and thereby contributes to the process of "binding" drive-energies. (4) This increased variability of ego-motivations renders memories more easily cathected, and thus more available for use in solving problems and reaching gratification. (5) All defenses—though we know this definitely only about repression—tend to encroach upon the thought-content at its weakest point. On the one hand, disuse of memories and relationships, and on the other, a lack of relation to other ideas and relationships, provide such weak points. Communication, by creating ever-new relations between ideas and casting light on relationships between relationships, combats the spread of ego-limiting defenses. (6) It provides new percepts and resuscitates old ones; thus it also makes for an integration of isolated experiences, and further integration into broader or new units. In this process considerable cathectic saving is usually achieved, accompanied by relief, insight, or discovery. Communication enhances the "synthetic function of the ego."

To avoid misunderstanding: it is not implied here that the possibilities for communication are not themselves determined by intrapsychic dynamics; nor that where communication is prevented by such dynamics, forcing it is of any use; nor that communication itself may not have deleterious psychological effects, in the sense of precipitating pathological processes. It is implied, however, that as long as all or part of that segment of the psychic apparatus which subserves communication is in the "conflict-free ego-sphere," it seems to exert the influences here discussed.

The study of communication may require many new concepts and avenues. So far four major avenues of study are known: (a) *non-verbal, empathic* communication (Redl); (b) the individual's *channels of communication*, both those open in general and those open to specific situations or persons (Bernfeld); (c) the nature of communication as crystallized and reflected in the language, particularly in that segment of it which refers to interpersonal relations (Heider); the geometric-topological nature of communication-networks (Bavelas).

XXV. PATHOLOGY OF THINKING

The pathology of thinking in schizophrenia, in general paresis, and in the amnesic syndrome has been discussed in detail in this volume. The comments tried to indicate how the various forms of thought-pathology imply and relate to the vague outlines of a theory, a synopsis of which has been attempted in this chapter.

In addition to these three types of thought-disorder, others touched on were those of hysteria, obsession, amentia, agnosia, aphasia, pseudologia, amnesia, multiple personality, mania, depression, and paranoia; reference was made also to forms of thought-organization characteristic of personalities with certain dominant traits, such as compulsive, dependent, intellectualizing, and inhibited.

Withal, the material on pathology gathered in this volume is scant and fragmentary. I believe it to be a shortcoming not solely of this volume: the literature itself seems fragmentary, and not ripe for a synopsis of the sort that can be given here. A synopsis reaching beyond that which the footnotes attempted would have to deal with the differential specificity of thought-disorders in various conditions; but the available material is fragmentary and would require much speculative reconstruction. This does not mean, however, that it is not amenable to systematization.

However, a few general points concerning the pathology of thought do emerge from the material presented. *First*, Schilder's bold reconstruction suggesting that pathology brings to the fore thought-formations which normally are merely the preparatory phases of developing thought. *Second*, Schilder's general finding that thought-pathology varies in its character according to the degree in which the apparatuses involved are central to the personality. *Third*, Hartmann's thesis that both the de-automatization of what is usually automatic, and the automatization of what is usually flexible, can be a form taken by thought-disorder. *Fourth*, the presentations of Bleuler and of Buerger-Prinz and Kaila suggesting that when derivative motivations—for instance, attitudes —lose their dynamic effectiveness, the result is not only that more fundamental and primitive motivations come to the fore (they may or may not), but also that the anticipations corresponding to the derivative motivations, and with them the persistent and variable goal-directed thinking, tend to disappear. That is, a process like remembering is as dependent on the freedom from disorder of such attitudes and anticipations as on freedom from repressive disorder. *Fifth*, the presentations of Bleuler and of Betlheim and Hartmann, and the experiments in dream-symbolism, suggesting that to each form of state of consciousness, pathological and normal, there corresponds a specific form of thought-organization; in thought-disorders both the state of consciousness and the thought-organization may fluctuate. They also suggest that thought-pathology may consist either in the disruption by drives and their derivatives of a thought-organization corresponding to a given state of consciousness, or in its replacement by a different state of consciousness and corresponding thought-organization. *Sixth*, Freud's formulations, to the effect that thought-disorder may take the form either of a lack of the cathexes necessary to operate with abstractions, or of hypercathecting or drive-cathecting abstractions. Thus the formula "abstract attitude vs. concrete attitude" is entirely too narrow a framework to cover the phenomena of thought-pathology. *Seventh*, the evidence advanced by Buerger-Prinz and Kaila, Bleuler, and Schilder, suggests that thought-pathology always involves all aspects of the thought-process, even though it may temporarily seem—as with the Korsakow syndrome—to involve mainly one aspect. *Eighth*, psychoanalytic observations and theorizing, suggesting that all these characteristics of thought-disorders, and others not discussed here, depend on the dynamics of drive-cathexes and their relation to those of cathexes at the disposal of the ego. They also suggest that dynamics alone, without corresponding structural considerations, cannot explain either thought-organization or its pathology.

Thus a complex picture of thought-disorders emerges, which cannot be reduced to any single factor. Not even the powerful conception of regression to earlier phases of thought-development—which certainly is one aspect of most thought-disorders—can account by itself for these complex phenomena: much of what is automatized and autonomous remains unreversed by regression, and some may be irreversible in principle. It would seem that, after the many attempts to explain thought-disorders by a simple theory have proved partial or irrelevant, this complex phenomenon will finally exact a complex explanation.

BIBLIOGRAPHY

1. Abel, K. Ueber den Gegensinn der Urworte. Leipzig, W. Friedrich, 1884.
2. Abeles, M., and P. Schilder. "Psychogenetic Loss of Personal Identity: Amnesia." *Arch. Neurol. Psychiat.*, 34 (1935), 587–604.
3. Abraham, K. "Character-Formation on the Genital Level of the Libido." In *Selected Papers of Karl Abraham* (London, Hogarth, 1927), pp. 407–417.
4. Abraham, K. "Contributions to the Theory of the Anal Character." In *Selected Papers of Karl Abraham* (London, Hogarth, 1927), pp. 370–392.
5. Abraham, K. Dreams and Myths. New York, Nerv. and Ment. Dis. Publ., 1913.
6. Abraham, K. "Hysterical Dream-States." In *Selected Papers of Karl Abraham* (London, Hogarth, 1927), pp. 90–124.
7. Abraham, K. "The Influence of Oral Erotism on Character-Formation." In *Selected Papers of Karl Abraham* (London, Hogarth, 1927), pp. 393–406.
8. Abraham, K. "The Psychosexual Differences between Hysteria and Dementia Praecox." In *Selected Papers of Karl Abraham* (London, Hogarth, 1927), pp. 64–79.
9. Abraham, K. Traum und Mythus. Leipzig, Deuticke, 1909.
10. Abraham, K. "Ueber die Bedeutung sexueller Jugendtraeumen fuer die Symptomatologie der Dementia Praecox." *Zentralblatt f. Nervenk. u. Psychiat.*, 18 (1907), 409–415.
11. Abramowski, E. "La Resistance de l'oublie et les sentiments génériques." *J. Psychol. Norm. et Path.*, 7 (1910), 301–331.
12. Ach, N. Ueber die Begriffsbildung. Hamburg, Buchner, 1921.
13. Ach, N. "Ueber die geistige Leistungsfaehigkeit im Zustande des eingeengten Bewusstseins." *Z. Hypnot.*, 9 (1899), 1–84.
14. Ach, N. Ueber den Willensakt und das Temperament. Leipzig, Quelle and Meyer, 1910.
15. Ach, N. Ueber die Willenstaetigkeit und das Denken. Goettingen, Vandenhoeck und Ruprecht, 1905.
16. Alexander, F. Fundamentals of Psychoanalysis. New York, Norton, 1948.
17. Alexander, F. "Metapsychologische Betrachtungen." *Int. Z. Psa.*, 7 (1921), 270–285.
18. Alexander, F. "Metapsychologische Darstellung des Heilungsvorganges." *Int. Z. Psa.*, 11 (1925), 157–178.

19. Allers, R. Psychologie des Geschlechtslebens. Handbuch der vergleichenden Psychologie. Ed. Gustav Kofka. 3 vols. Munich, Reinhardt, 1922.

20. Allers, R. "Ueber Psychoanalyse." *Abh. Neur. Psychiat. Psychol. u. Grenzgeb.*, Heft 16, Berlin, Karger, 1922.

21. Allers, R., and I. Teller. "Ueber die Verwertung unbemerkter Eindruecke bei Assoziationen." Z. *Neurol. Psychiat.*, 89 (1924), 492–513.

22. Allesch, G. von. "Die aesthetische Erscheinungsweise der Farben." *Psychol. Forsch.*, 6 (1925), 1–91.

23. Allesch, G. von. "Bericht ueber die drei ersten Lebensmonate eines Schimpansen." Preussische Akademie der Wissenschaften, Sitzungsberichte, 1921, pp. 672–685.

24. Allport, G. "Attitudes." In *A Handbook of Social Psychology*, ed. Carl Murchison (Worcester, Mass., Clark Univ. Press, 1935), pp. 798–844.

25. Allport, G. Personality. New York, Holt, 1937.

26. Allport, G., and P. Vernon. Studies in Expressive Movement. New York, Macmillan, 1933.

27. Alper, T. "Memory for Completed and Incompleted Tasks as a Function of Personality: an Analysis of Group Data." *J. Abn. Soc. Psychol.*, 41 (1946), 403–420.

28. Alper, T. "Task-Orientation and Ego-Orientation as Factors in Reminiscence." *J. Exp. Psychol.*, 38 (1948), 224–238.

29. Alper, T. "Task-Orientation vs. Ego-Orientation in Learning and Retention." *Amer. J. Psychol.*, 59 (1946), 236–248.

30. Angyal, A. "Disturbances of Thinking in Schizophrenia." In *Language and Thought in Schizophrenia*, collected papers, ed. J. S. Kasanin (Berkeley, Univ. of Calif. Press, 1944), pp. 115–123.

31. Aristotle. "Categories." In *The Basic Works of Aristotle* (New York, Random House, 1941), pp. 7–37.

32. Atkinson, J. and D. McClelland. "The Projective Expression of Needs, II: The Effect of Different Intensities of the Hunger Drive on Thematic Apperception." *J. Exp. Psychol.*, 38 (1948), 643–658.

33. Bacon, F. Novum Organon. Ed. T. Fowler. Oxford, Clarendon Press, 1889.

34. Bakewell, C. Source Book in Ancient Philosophy. New York, Scribner, 1907.

35. Bally, G. "Die fruehkindliche Motorik im Vergleich mit der Motorik der Tiere." *Imago*, 19 (1937), 339–366.

36. Barker, R., T. Dembo, and K. Lewin. Frustration and Regression: an Experiment with Young Children. Univ. Iowa Studies, Child Welfare, 18, No. 2, 1941.

37. Bartlett, F. C. Remembering: a Study in Experimental and Social Psychology. Cambridge, England, Cambridge Univ. Press, 1932.

38. Bavelas, A. "A Mathematical Model for Group Structures." *Appl. Anthrop.*, 7 (1948), 16–30.

39. Beach, F. Hormones and Behavior. New York, Hoeber, 1948.

40. Bellak, L. Dementia Praecox. New York, Grune & Stratton, 1947.

41. Bender, M. B. "Extinction and Precipitation of Cutaneous Sensations." *Arch. Neurol. Psychiat.*, 54 (1945), 1–9.

42. Benedek, L., and P. Schilder. "Ueber Nachsprechen von Testworten bei einer in Rueckbildung begriffenen motorischen Aphasie." *Allg. Z. Psychiat.*, 81 (1925), 79–87.

43. Benjamin, J. "A Method for Distinguishing and Evaluating Formal Thinking Disorders in Schizophrenia." In *Language and Thought in Schizophrenia*, collected papers, ed. J. S. Kasanin (Berkeley, Univ. of Calif. Press, 1944), pp. 65–90.

44. Benussi, V. "Zur experimentellen Grundlegung hypnosuggestiver Methoden psychischer Analyse." *Psychol. Forsch.*, 9 (1927), 197–274.

45. Bergler, E. The Basic Neurosis. New York, Grune & Stratton, 1949.

46. Bergler, E. "A Clinical Approach to the Psychoanalysis of Writers." *Psa. Rev.*, 31 (1944), 40–70.

47. Bergler, E. "A Contribution to the Psychoanalysis of Déjà Vue." *Psa. Quart.*, 11 (1942), 165–170.

48. Bergler, E. "An Inquiry into the 'Material Phenomenon.'" *Int. J. Psa.*, 16 (1935), 203–218.

49. Bergler, E. "On a Five-Layer Structure in Sublimation." *Psa. Quart.*, 14 (1945), 76–97.

50. Bergman, M. Contribution à l'étude de la psychose de Korsakow (aperçu clinique et recherches sur la mémoire). Thèse de Médecine No. 150, Geneva, 1907.

51. Bergman, P. "The Germinal Cell of Freud's Psychoanalytic Psychology and Therapy." *Psychiatry*, 12 (1949), 265–278.

52. Bergman, P., and S. Escalona. "Unusual Sensitivities in Very Young Children." In *The Psychoanalytic Study of the Child*, Vol. III/IV (New York, Int. Univ. Press, 1949), pp. 333–352.

53. Bergson, H. Matter and Memory. New York, Macmillan, 1911.

54. Bernfeld, S. "The Facts of Observation in Psychoanalysis." *J. Psychol.*, 12 (1941), 289–305.

55. Bernfeld, S. "Die Gestalttheorie." *Imago*, 20 (1934), 32–77.

56. Berrington, W. "A Psycho-Pharmacological Study of Schizophrenia, with Particular Reference to the Mode of Action of Cardiasol, Sodium Amytal and Alcohol in Schizophrenic Stupor." *J. Ment. Sci.*, 85 (1939), 406–488.

57. Berze, J. "Das Primaersymptom der Paranoia." *Z. Nervenk. Psychiat.*, 17 (1906), 432–448.

58. Betlheim, S., and H. Hartmann. "Ueber Fehlreaktionen bei der Korsakow-schen Psychose." *Arch. Psychiat. Nervenk.*, 72 (1924), 275–286.

59. Bettelheim, B. "The Dynamism of Anti-Semitism in Gentile and Jew." *J. Abn. Soc. Psychol.*, 42 (1947), 153–168.

60. Bettelheim, B. "Individual and Mass Behavior in Extreme Situations." *J. Abn. Soc. Psychol.*, 38 (1943), 1–28.

61. Bibring, E. "The Development and Problems of the Theory of the Instincts." *Int. J. Psa.*, 22 (1941), 102–131.

62. Binet, A. Étude expérimental de l'intelligence. Paris, Schleicher, 1903.

63. Binswanger, L. Ausgewaehlte Vortraege und Aufsaetze. Bern, Francke, 1947. Vol. I: Zur phaenomenologischen Anthropologie.

64. Binswanger, L. "Zum Problem von Sprechen und Denken." *Schweiz. Arch. Psychiat. Neurol.*, 18 (1926), 247–283.

65. Birenbaum, G. "Das Vergessen einer Vornahme. Isolierte seelische Systeme und dynamische Gesamtbereiche." *Psychol. Forsch.*, 13 (1930), 218–284.

66. Bleuler, E. Affectivity, Suggestibility, Paranoia. Utica, N.Y., State Hosp. Press, 1912. Also: *State Hosp. Bull.*, 4 (1912), 481–601.

67. Bleuler, E. "Antwort auf die Bemerkungen Jungs zur Theorie des Negativismus." *Jhb. Psa. Psychopath. Forsch.*, 3 (1912), 475–478.

68. Bleuler, E. "Das autistische Denken." *Jhb. Psa. Psychopath. Forsch.*, 4 (1912), 1–39.

69. Bleuler, E. "Autistic Thinking." *Amer. J. Insanity*, 69 (1913), 873–886.

70. Bleuler, E. Das Autistisch-Undisziplinierte Denken. Berlin, Springer, 1922.

71. Bleuler, E. Dementia Praecox oder Gruppe der Schizophrenien. Leipzig, Deuticke, 1911. Translated into English as: Dementia Praecox or the Group of Schizophrenias. New York, Internat. Univ. Press, 1950.

72. Bleuler, E. "Freudsche Mechanismen in der Symptomatologie von Psychosen." *Psychiat. Neurol. Wochenschrift*, 8 (1906–7), 316–338.

73. Bleuler, E. Naturgeschichte der Seele und ihres Bewusstwerdens. Berlin, Springer, 1932.

74. Bleuler, E. "Primaere und sekundaere Symptome der Schizophrenie." *Z. Neurol. Psychiat.*, 124 (1930), 607–646.

75. Bleuler, E. "Die Psychoanalyse Freud's." *Jhb. Psa. Psychopath. Forsch.*, 2 (1910), 623–730.

76. Bleuler, E. Textbook of Psychiatry. New York, Macmillan, 1924.

77. Bleuler, E. The Theory of Schizophrenic Negativism. New York, Nerv. and Ment. Dis. Pub., 1912.

78. Blumenfeld, W. "Das Suchen von Zahlen im begrenzten ebenen Felde und das Problem der Abstraktion." *Z. angew. Psychol.*, 26 (1925), 58–107.

79. Bobertag, O. "Binets Arbeiten ueber die intellektuelle Entwicklung des Schulkindes." *Z. angew. Psychol.*, 3 (1909), 230–259.

80. Bolles, M., and K. Goldstein. "A Study of the Impairment of 'Abstract Behavior' in Schizophrenic Patients." *Psychiat. Quart.*, 12 (1938), 733–737.

81. Bonaparte, M. "Time and the Unconscious." *Int. J. Psa.*, 21 (1940), 427–468.

82. Bonhoeffer, K. Die akuten Geisteskrankheiten der Gewohnheitstrinker. Jena, Fischer, 1901.

83. Boring, E. A History of Experimental Psychology. New York, Appleton-Century, 1950.

84. Boring, E., H. Langfeld, and H. Weld. Foundations of Psychology. New York, Wiley, 1948.

85. Boumann, L. "Experimentelle Untersuchungen ueber den Willen bei Normalen und Psychopathen." *Psychiat. Neurol. Bladen*, 23 (1919), 237–319.

86. Brenman, M. "Dreams and Hypnosis." *Psa. Quart.*, 18 (1949), 455–465.

87. Brenman, M. "Experiments in the Hypnotic Production of Anti-Social and Self-Injurious Behavior." *Psychiatry*, 5 (1942), 49–61.

88. Brenman, M., and M. Gill. Hypnotherapy. Menninger Monogr. Series No. 5, New York, Int. Univ. Press, 1947.

89. Brenman, M., and M. Gill. "Research in Psychotherapy" (Round Table, 1947). *Amer. J. Orthopsychiat.*, 18 (1948), 92–118.

90. Brentano, F. Psychologie vom empirischen Standpunkt. Leipzig, Dunker and Humbolt, 1874.

91. Breuer, J., and S. Freud. Studies in Hysteria. New York, Nerv. and Ment. Dis. Pub., 1937.

92. Brierley, M. "Affects in Theory and Practice." *Int. J. Psa.*, 18 (1937), 256–268.

93. Brierley, M. "Specific Determinants in Feminine Development." *Int. J. Psa.*, 17 (1936), 163–180.

94. Brillouin, L. "Life, Thermodynamics and Cybernetics." *Amer. Sci.*, 37 (1949), 554–568.

95. Brodmann, K. "Experimentelle und klinische Beitraege zur Psychopathologie der polyneuritischen Psychose." *J. Psychol. Neurol.*, 1 (1902), 225–246 and 3 (1904), 1–48.

96. Bruner, J., and C. Goodman. "Value and Need as Organizing Factors in Perception." *J. Abn. Soc. Psychol.*, 42 (1947), 33–44.

97. Bruner, J., and L. Postman. "Emotional Selectivity in Perception and Reaction." *J. Personality*, 16 (1947), 69–77.

98. Bruner, J., and L. Postman. "Symbolic Value as an Organizing Factor in Perception." *J. Soc. Psychol.*, 27 (1948), 203–208.

99. Bruner, J., and L. Postman. "Tension and Tension Release as Organizing Factors in Perception." *J. Personality*, 15 (1947), 300–308.

100. Bruner, J., L. Postman, and E. McGinnies. "Personal Values as Selective Factors in Perception." *J. Abn. Soc. Psychol.*, 43 (1948), 142–154.

101. Brunschvicg, L. L'Expérience humaine et la causalité physique. Paris, Alcan, 1922.

102. Brunswik, E. Systematic and Representative Design of Psychological Experiments. Berkeley, Univ. of Calif. Press, 1947.

103. Buehler, C. Das Seelenleben des Jugendlichen. Jena, Fischer, 1922.

104. Buehler, K. "Antwort auf die von W. Wundt erhobenen Einwaende gegen die Methode der Selbstbeobachtung an experimentell erzeugten Erlebnissen." *Arch. Psychol.*, 12 (1908), 93–122.

105. Buehler, K. Ausdruckstheorie. Jena, Fischer, 1933.

106. Buehler, K. Die geistige Entwicklung des Kindes. 6th ed. Jena, Fischer, 1930.

107. Buehler, K. Die Instinkte des Menschen. In *Bericht ueber den IX. Kongress fuer experimentelle Psychologie* (Munich, Barth, 1926).

108. Buehler, K. Die Krise der Psychologie. Jena, Fischer, 1929.

109. Buehler, K. The Mental Development of the Child. New York, Harcourt, 1930.

110. Buehler, K. Sprachtheorie. Jena, Fischer, 1934.

111. Buehler, K. "Tatsachen und Probleme zu einer Psychologie der Denkvorgaenge, I: Ueber Gedanken," *Arch. Psychol.*, 9 (1907), 297–365. "II: Ueber Gedankenzusammenhaenge," *ibid.*, 12 (1908), 1–23. "III: Ueber Gedankenerinnerungen," *ibid.*, 12 (1908), 24–92.

112. Buehler, K. "Ueber das Sprachverstaendnis vom Standpunkt der Normalpsychologie aus." In *Bericht ueber den III. Kongress fur experimentelle Psychologie*, Munich, Barth, 1909.

113. Buerger, H. "Zur Psychologie des amnestischen Symptomenkomplexes." *Arch. Psychiat. Nervenk.*, 81 (1927), 348–352.

114. Bumke, O. Die Diagnose der Geisteskrankheiten. Wiesbaden, Bergmann, 1919.

115. Busch, A. "Auffassungs-und Merkfaehigkeit bei Dementia Praecox." *Psychol. Arb.*, 5 (1908), 293–337.

116. Buxton, C. "The Status of Research in Reminiscence." *Psychol. Bull.*, 40 (1943), 313–340.

117. Buerger-Prinz, H., and M. Kaila. "Ueber die Struktur des amnestischen Symptomenkomplexes." *Z. Neurol. Psychiat.*, 124 (1930), 553–595.

118. Bychowski, G. "Physiology of Schizophrenic Thinking." *J. Nerv. Ment. Dis.*, 98 (1943), 368–386.

119. Cameron, N. "Deterioration and Regression in Schizophrenic Thinking." *J. Abn. Soc. Psychol.*, 34 (1939), 265–270.

120. Cameron, N. "Experimental Analysis of Schizophrenic Thinking." In *Language and Thought in Schizophrenia*, collected papers, ed. J. S. Kasanin (Berkeley and Los Angeles, Univ. of Calif. Press, 1944), pp. 50–64.

121. Cameron, N. Reasoning, Regression and Communication in Schizophrenics. Psychol. Monog. Soc., Washington, 1938.

122. Cameron, N. "Schizophrenic Thinking in a Problem-Solving Situation." *J. Ment. Sci.*, 85 (1939), 1012–1035.

123. Cantril, H., A. Ames, A. Hastorf, and W. Ittelson. "Psychology and Scientific Research, I: The Nature of Scientific Inquiry," *Sci.*, 110 (1949), 461–464. "II: Scientific Inquiry and Scientific Method," *ibid.*, 491–497. "III: The Transitional View in Psychological Research," *ibid.*, 517–522.

124. Cartwright, D. "Decision-Time in Relation to the Differentiation of the Phenomenal Field." *Psychol. Rev.*, 48 (1941), 425–442.

125. Cartwright, D. "Relation of Decision-Time to the Categories of Response." *Amer. J. Psychol.*, 54 (1941), 175–196.

126. Cassirer, E. Philosophie der symbolischen Formen. Berlin, Cassirer, 1925.

127. Cassirer, E. Substance and Function and Einstein's Theory of Relativity. Chicago, Open Court, 1923.

128. Cattell, R. "Sentiment or Attitude." *Character and Personality*, 9 (1940), 6–17.

129. Chein, I. "Behavior Theory and the Behavior of Attitudes: Some Critical Comments." *Psychol. Rev.*, 55 (1948), 175–188.

130. Claparède, E. "Does the Will Express the Entire Personality?" In *Problems of Personality*, ed. C. McF. Campbell (London, Kegan Paul, 1925), pp. 37–43.

131. Claparède, E. Comments in the "Scèance du 28, 2. 1907 Société Médicale du Genève," *Revue médical de la Suisse romande.* 27 (1907), 301–303.

132. Claparède, E., and W. Baade. "Recherches expérimentales sur quelques procèsses psychiques simples dans un cas d'hypnose." *Arch. de Psychol.*, 8 (1909), 297–394.

133. Claparède, E. "Recognition et moïté." *Arch. de Psychol.*, 11 (1911), 79–90.

134. Coriat, I. "Reduplicative paramnesia." *J. Nerv. Ment. Dis.*, 31 (1904), 577–587, 639–659.

135. Cubberly, A. "How the Normal Dream Is Effected by Tension on the Body Surface." In *The World of Dreams*, ed. Ralph Woods (New York, Random House, 1947), pp. 819–827.

136. Darwin, C. Expression of the Emotions. London, Murray, 1904.

137. Dawson, W. "A Case of Hebephrenia." *J. Ment. Sci.*, 49 (1903), 303–311.

138. Delacroix, H. "L'Invention et le genie." In *Nouveau Traité de Psychologie*, ed. G. Dumas, Vol. VI, Part 4 (Paris, Alcan, 1939), pp. 447–539.

139. Delacroix, H. Le Langage et la pensée. Paris, Alcan, 1930.

140. Dembo, T. "Der Aerger als dynamisches Problem." *Psychol. Forsch.*, 15 (1931), 1–144.

141. Dembo, T., and E. Hanfmann. "The Patient's Psychological Situation upon Admission to a Mental Institution." *Amer. J. Psychol.*, 47 (1935), 381–408.

142. Descartes, R. "Meditations." In *The Method, Meditations and Selections from the Principles* (Edinburgh and London, Blackwood & Sons, 1887), pp. 76–169.

143. Descartes, R. Discourse de la methode. Passions de l'âme. Paris, Gallimard, 1932.

144. Despert, J. Emotional Problems in Children. Utica, N.Y., State Hosp. Press, 1938.

145. Diethelm, O., and M. Jones. "Influence of Anxiety on Attention, Learning, Retention and Thinking." *Arch. Neurol. Psychiat.*, 58 (1947), 325–336.

146. Domarus, E. von. "The Specific Laws of Logic in Schizophrenia." In *Language and Thought in Schizophrenia*, collected papers, ed. J. S. Kasanin (Berkeley and Los Angeles, Univ. of Calif. Press, 1944), pp. 104–114.

147. Domarus, E. von. "Zur Theorie des schizophrenen Denkens." Z. *Neurol. Psychiat.*, 108 (1927), 703–714.

147a. Domarus, E. von. "Zur Charakteristik des schwachsinnigen Denkens." Z. *Neurol. Psychiat.*, 111 (1927), 511–515.

148. Dooley, L. "The Concept of Time in Defence of Ego Integrity." *Psychiatry*, 4 (1941), 13–23.

149. Dostoevski, F. The Possessed. New York, Dutton, 1931.

150. Duerr, E. Erkenntnistheorie. Leipzig, Quelle and Meyer, 1910.

151. Duncker, K. On Problem-Solving. Psychol. Monog. 58, No. 5, Washington, D.C., Amer. Psychol. Assn., 1945.

152. Eliasberg, W. "Die Schwierigkeiten intellektueller Vorgaenge und ihre Beziehung zur Intelligenzpruefung." *Schweiz. Arch. Psychiat. Neurol.*, 12 (1923), 136–143.

153. Eliasberg, W., and E. Feuchtwanger. "Zur psychologischen und psychopathologischen Untersuchung und Theorie des erworbenen Schwachsinns. Dargestellt an einem Fall von fortschreitender Demenz nach Hirnverletzung." Z. *Neurol. Psychiat.*, 75 (1922), 516–596.

154. Ellis, W. Sourcebook of Gestalt Psychology. New York, Harcourt, Brace, 1938.

155. Erdmann, B. Logik. Halle, Niemeyer, 1907.

156. Erikson, E. "Childhood and Tradition in Two American Indian Tribes." In *The Psychoanalytic Study of the Child*, Vol. I (New York, Int. Univ. Press, 1945), pp. 319–351.

157. Erikson, E. "Ego Development and Historical Change." In *The Psychoanalytic Study of the Child*, Vol. II (New York, Int. Univ. Press, 1947), pp. 359–396.

158. Erikson, E. "Hitler's Imagery and German Youth." *Psychiatry*, 5 (1942), 475–493.

159. Erikson, E. "Observations on Sioux Education." *J. Psychol.*, 7 (1939), 101–156.

160. Erikson, E. "Observations on the Yurok: Childhood and World Image." *Amer. Archeol. and Ethnol.*, 35 (1943), 257–301.

161. Erickson, M. "Experimental Demonstration of the Psychopathology of Everyday Life." *Psa. Quart.*, 8 (1939), 338–353.

162. Erickson, M. "An Experimental Investigation of the Possible Anti-Social Use of Hypnosis." *Psychiatry*, 2 (1939), 391–414.

163. Erickson, M., and E. Erickson. "Concerning the Nature and Character of Post-Hypnotic Behavior." *J. Gen. Psychol.*, 24 (1941), 95–133.

164. Erickson, M., and L. Kubie. "The Permanent Relief of an Obsessional Phobia by Means of Communications with an Unsuspected Dual Personality." *Psa. Quart.*, 8 (1939), 471–509.

165. Erickson, M., and L. Kubie. "The Translation of the Cryptic Automatic Writing of One Hypnotic Subject by Another in a Trance-like Dissociated State." *Psa. Quart.*, 9 (1940), 51–63.

166. Escalona, S. "The Effect of Success and Failure on the Level of Aspiration in Manic-Depressive Psychoses." *Univ. Iowa Studies Child Welfare*, 16 (1940), 199–302.

166a. Escalona, S. An Application of the Level of Aspiration Experiment to the Study of Personality. New York, Teachers College, Columbia Univ., 1948.

167. Eysenck, H. Review of *The Psychology of Ego-Involvements* by M. Sherif and H. Cantril (New York, Wiley, 1947). *J. Soc. Psychol.*, 28 (1948), 301–305.

168. Fabre, J. Souvenirs entomologiques. Paris, Delagrave, 1923.

169. Fairbanks, K. "Note sur un phenomène de prévision immédiate." *Arch. de Psychol.*, 1 (1902), 95–98.

170. Farber, L., and C. Fisher. "An Experimental Approach to Dream Psychology through the Use of Hypnosis." *Psa. Quart.*, 12 (1943), 202–216.

171. Farber, M. Philosophical Essays in Memory of Edmund Husserl. Harvard Univ. Press, 1940.

172. Federn, P. "Die Ichbesetzung bei den Fehlleistungen." *Imago*, 19 (1933), 312–338, 433–453.

173. Federn, P., ed. "Spielen und Spiele." Z. *psa. Paedagogik*, special issue, 6 (1932), 173–264.

174. Fenichel, O. "The Counter-Phobic Attitude." *Int. J. Psa.*, 20 (1939), 263–274.

175. Fenichel, O. Outline of Clinical Psychoanalysis. New York, Psa. Quart. Press, and Norton, 1934.

176. Fenichel, O. The Psychoanalytic Theory of Neurosis. New York, Norton, 1945.

177. Fenichel, O. "Ueber organlibidinoese Begleiterscheinungen der Triebabwehr." *Int. Z. Psa.*, 14 (1928), 45–64.

178. Fenichel, O. "Zur Isolierung." *Int. Z. Psa.*, 14 (1928), 243–248.

179. Fenichel, O. "Zur Psychologie der Langeweile." *Imago*, 20 (1934), 270–281.

180. Ferenczi, S. "Stages in the Development of the Sense of Reality." In *Sex in Psycho-analysis* (Boston, Badger, 1916), pp. 213–239.

181. Ferenczi, S. Further Contributions to the Theory and Technique of Psycho-analysis. New York, Boni and Liveright, 1927.

182. Ferenczi, S. "The Ontogenesis of Symbols." In *Sex in Psycho-analysis* (Boston, Badger, 1916), pp. 276–281.

183. Ferenczi, S. "The Problem of Acceptance of Unpleasant Ideas." In *Further Contributions to the Theory and Technique of Psycho-analysis* (New York, Boni and Liveright, 1927), pp. 366–379.

184. Ferenczi, S. "The Psyche as an Inhibiting Organ." In *Further Contributions to the Theory and Technique of Psycho-analysis* (New York, Boni and Liveright, 1927), pp. 379–383.

185. Ferenczi, S. "Sunday Neuroses." In *Further Contributions to the Theory and Technique of Psycho-analysis* (New York, Boni and Liveright, 1927), pp. 174–177.

186. Ferenczi, S. "Thinking and Muscle Innervation." In *Further Contributions to the Theory and Technique of Psycho-analysis* (New York, Boni and Liveright, 1927), pp. 230–232.

187. Ferenczi, S., and S. Hollos. Psychoanalysis and the Psychic Disorder of General Paresis. New York, Nerv. and Ment. Dis. Pub., 1925.

188. Fervers, C. "Analyse in Hypnose." *Der Nervenarzt*, 11 (1938), 25–30.

189. Fischer, S. "Die Intelligenz und ihre Pruefung bei leichten Schwachsinnformen." *Z. Neurol. Psychiat.*, 97 (1925), 53–106.

190. Fleck, U. "Der klinische Begriff der Demenz." *Klin. Wochenschr.*, 5 (1926), 1401–1404.

191. Foerster, R., and Gregor, A. "Ueber die Zusammenhaenge von psychischen Funktionen bei progressiven Paralyse." *Monatschr. Psychiat. Neurol.*, 26 (1909), 42–86.

192. Forel, A. Der Hypnotismus oder die Suggestion und die Psychotherapie. Stuttgart, Enke, 1921.

193. Frank, L. Projective Methods. Springfield, Thomas, 1948.

194. Frank, L. "Projective Methods for the Study of Personality." *J. Psychol.*, 8 (1939), 389–413.

195. Frank, L. ed. "Teleological Mechanisms." *Annals New York Acad. Sci.*, 50 (1948), 189–196.

196. Freeman, H. and E. Rodnick. "Autonomic and Respiratory Responses of Schizophrenic and Normal Subjects to Changes of Intra-Pulmonary Atmosphere." *Psychosom. Med.*, 2 (1940), 101.

197. French, T. "Interrelations between Psychoanalysis and the Experimental Work of Pavlov." *Amer. J. Psychiat.*, 12 (1933), 1165–1203.

198. French, T. "Reality and the Unconscious." *Psa. Quart.*, 6 (1937), 23–61.

199. Frenkel-Brunswik, E. "Dynamic and Cognitive Categorization of Qualitative Material, I: General Problems and the Thematic Apperception Test," *J. Psychol.*, 25 (1948), 253–260. "II. Application to Interviews with the Ethnically Prejudiced," *ibid.*, 261–277.

200. Frenkel-Brunswik, E. "A Study of Prejudice in Children." *Human Relations*, 1 (1948), 295–306.

201. Freud, A. The Ego and the Mechanisms of Defence. New York, Int. Univ. Press, 1946.

202. Freud, S. (1894). "The Defence Neuro-Psychoses." In *Collected Papers*, Vol. I (London, Hogarth, 1924), pp. 59–75.

203. Freud, S. (1895). "The Justification for Detaching from Neurasthenia a Particular Syndrome: The Anxiety-Neurosis." In *Collected Papers*, Vol. I (London, Hogarth, 1946), pp. 76–106.

204. Freud, S. (1895). "A Reply to Criticisms on the Anxiety-Neurosis." In *Collected Papers*, Vol. I (London, Hogarth, 1946), pp. 97–127.

205. Freud, S. (1896). "The Aetiology of Hysteria." In *Collected Papers*, Vol. I (London, Hogarth, 1946), pp. 183–219.

206. Freud, S. (1896). "Further Remarks on the Defence Neuro-Psychoses." In *Collected Papers*, Vol. I (London, Hogarth, 1946), pp. 155–182.

207. Freud, S. (1898). "Sexuality in the Aetiology of the Neuroses." In *Collected Papers*, Vol. I (London, Hogarth, 1946), pp. 220–248.

207a. Freud, S. (1899). Aus den Anfaengen der Psychoanalyse. Briefe an Wilhelm Fliess. Abhandlungen und Notizen aus den Jahren (1887–1902). London, Imago Publ. Co., 1950.

208. Freud, S. (1900). Die Traumdeutung. Vienna, Deuticke, 1921.

209. Freud, S. (1900). "The Interpretation of Dreams." In *The Basic Writings* (New York, Modern Library, 1938), pp. 179–548.

210. Freud, S. (1904). "Psychopathology of Everyday Life." In *The Basic Writings* (New York, Modern Library, 1938), pp. 33–178.

211. Freud, S. (1905–1910). "Case Histories." In *Collected Papers*, Vol. III (London, Hogarth, 1948).

212. Freud, S. (1905). "Fragment of an Analysis of a Case of Hysteria." In *Collected Papers*, Vol. III (London, Hogarth, 1946), pp. 13–146.

213. Freud, S. (1905). "Three Contributions to the Theory of Sex." In *The Basic Writings* (New York, Modern Library, 1938), pp. 553–629.

214. Freud, S. (1905). "Wit and Its Relation to the Unconscious." In *The Basic Writings* (New York, Modern Library, 1938), pp. 633–761.

215. Freud, S. (1908). "Character and Anal Erotism." In *Collected Papers*, Vol. II (London, Hogarth, 1946), pp. 45–50.

216. Freud, S. (1908). " 'Civilized' Sexuality Morality and Modern Nervousness." In *Collected Papers*, Vol. II (London, Hogarth, 1946), pp. 76–99.

217. Freud, S. (1908). "Hysterical Phantasies and Their Relation to Bisexuality." In *Collected Papers*, Vol. II (London, Hogarth, 1946), pp. 51–58.

218. Freud, S. (1908). "The Relation of the Poet to Day-Dreaming." In *Collected Papers*, Vol. IV (London, Hogarth, 1946), pp. 173–183.

219. Freud, S. (1909). "General Remarks on Hysterical Attacks." In *Collected Papers*, Vol. II (London, Hogarth, 1946), pp. 100–104.

220. Freud, S. (1909). "Notes upon a Case of Obsessional Neurosis." In *Collected Papers*, Vol. III (London, Hogarth, 1946), pp. 293–383.

221. Freud, S. (1910). "The Antithetical Sense of Primal Words." In *Collected Papers*, Vol. IV (London, Hogarth, 1946), pp. 184–191.

222. Freud, S. (1911). "Formulierungen ueber die zwei Prinzipien des psychischen Geschehens." In *Gesammelte Werke*, Vol. VIII (London, Imago, 1943), pp. 230–238.

223. Freud, S. (1911). "Formulations Regarding the Two Principles in Mental Functioning." In *Collected Papers*, Vol. IV (London, Hogarth, 1946), pp. 13–21.

224. Freud, S. (1911). "Psychoanalytic Notes upon an Autobiographical Account of a case of Paranoia (Dementia Paranoides)." In *Collected Papers*, Vol. III (London, Hogarth, 1946), pp. 387–470.

224a. Freud, S. (1912). "The Dynamics of the Transference." In *Collected Papers*, Vol. II (London, Hogarth, 1946), pp. 312–322.

225. Freud, S. (1912). "A Note on the Unconscious in Psycho-Analysis." In *Collected Papers*, Vol. IV (London, Hogarth, 1948), pp. 22–29.

226. Freud, S. (1912). "Recommendations for Physicians on the Psychoanalytic Method of Treatment." In *Collected Papers*, Vol. II (London, Hogarth, 1924), pp. 323–333.

227. Freud, S. (1912). "Totem and Taboo." In *The Basic Writings* (New York, Modern Library, 1938), pp. 807–883.

228. Freud, S. (1913). "The Predisposition to Obsessional Neurosis." In *Collected Papers*, Vol. II (London, Hogarth, 1946), pp. 122–132.

229. Freud, S. (1913). "The Theme of the Three Caskets." In *Collected Papers*, Vol. IV (London, Hogarth, 1946), pp. 244–256.

230. Freud, S. (1914). "Fausse Reconnaissance ('Déjà Raconté') in Psychoanalytic Treatment." In *Collected Papers*, Vol. II (London, Hogarth, 1925), pp. 334–341.

231. Freud, S. (1914). "On Narcissism: an Introduction." In *Collected Papers*, Vol. IV (London, Hogarth, 1946), pp. 30–59.

232. Freud, S. (1915). "Instincts and Their Vicissitudes." In *Collected Papers*, Vol. IV (London, Hogarth, 1946), pp. 60–83.

233. Freud, S. (1915). "Repression." In *Collected Papers*, Vol. IV (London, Hogarth, 1946), pp. 84–97.

234. Freud, S. (1915). "The Unconscious." In *Collected Papers*, Vol. IV (London, Hogarth, 1946), pp. 98–136.

235. Freud, S. (1917). A General Introduction to Psychoanalysis. New York, Boni & Liveright, 1920.

236. Freud, S. (1917). Introductory Lectures on Psychoanalysis. London, Allen & Unwin, 1922.

237. Freud, S. (1917). "Metapsychological Supplement to the Theory of Dreams." In *Collected Papers*, Vol. IV (London, Hogarth, 1925), pp. 137–151.

238. Freud, S. (1917). "Mourning and Melancholia." In *Collected Papers*, Vol. IV (London, Hogarth, 1946), pp. 152–170.

239. Freud, S. (1918). "From the History of an Infantile Neurosis." In *Collected Papers*, Vol. III (London, Hogarth, 1925), pp. 473–605.

240. Freud, S. (1919). "Turning in the Ways of Psychoanalytic Therapy." In *Collected Papers*, Vol. II (London, Hogarth, 1946), pp. 392–402.

241. Freud, S. (1920). Beyond the Pleasure Principle. London, Int. Psa. Press, 1922.

242. Freud, S. (1921). Group Psychology and the Analysis of the Ego. London, Hogarth, 1948.

243. Freud, S. (1923). The Ego and the Id. London, Hogarth, 1927.

244. Freud, S. (1924). "The Economic Problem in Masochism." In *Collected Papers*, Vol. II (London, Hogarth, 1946), pp. 255–268.

245. Freud, S. (1924). "The Loss of Reality in Neurosis and Psychosis." In *Collected Papers*, Vol. II (London, Hogarth, 1946), pp. 277–282.

246. Freud, S. (1924). "Neurosis and Psychosis." In *Collected Papers*, Vol. II (London, Hogarth, 1946), pp. 250–254.

247. Freud, S. (1925). "Die Verneinung." In *Gesammelte Werke*, Vol. XIV (London, Imago, 1948), pp. 11–15.

248. Freud, S. (1925). "Negation." In *Collected Papers*, Vol. V (London, Hogarth, 1950), pp. 181–185.

249. Freud, S. (1925). "Notiz ueber den Wunderblock." In *Gesammelte Werke*, Vol. XIV (London, Imago, 1948), pp. 3–8.

250. Freud, S. (1925). "A Note upon the 'Mystic Writing-Pad.'" In *Collected Papers*, Vol. V (London, Hogarth, 1950), pp. 175–180.

251. Freud, S. (1924). "Hemmung, Symptom und Angst." In *Gesammelte Schriften*, Vol. XI (Vienna, Psa. Verlag, 1928), pp. 21–115.

252. Freud, S. (1926). The Problem of Anxiety. New York, Psa. Quart. Press, 1936.

253. Freud, S. (1928). "Humor." In *Collected Papers*, Vol. V (London, Hogarth, 1950), pp. 215–221.

254. Freud, S. (1930). Civilization and Its Discontents. New York, Cape, 1930.

255. Freud, S. (1932). New Introductory Lectures on Psychoanalysis. New York, Norton, 1933.

256. Freud, S. (1937). "Analysis Terminable and Interminable." *Int. J. Psa.*, 18 (1938), 373–405.

257. Freud, S. (1938). An Outline of Psychoanalysis. New York, Norton, 1949.

258. Freud, S. (1939). Moses and Monotheism. New York, Knopf, 1939.

259. Freud, S., and J. Breuer (1895). Studies in Hysteria. New York, Nerv. and Ment. Dis. Pub., 1936.

260. Freud, S., S. Ferenczi, K. Abraham, E. Simmel, and E. Jones (1919). Psycho-Analysis and the War Neuroses, London, Int. Psa. Press, 1921.

261. Freund, A. "Die psychische Saettigung im Menstruum und Intermenstruum." *Psychol. Forsch.*, 13 (1930), 198–217.

262. Gamper, E. "Schlaf, Delirium Tremens—Korsakowsches Syndrom." *Zentralblatt Neur. Psychiat.*, 51 (1928), 236–238.

263. Garma, A. "Die Realitaet und das Es in der Schizophrenie." *Int. Z. Psa.*, 18 (1932), 183–200.

264. Gelb, A., and K. Goldstein. "Psychologische Analysen hirnpathologischer Faelle." *Psychol. Forsch.*, 6 (1925), 126–186.

265. Goldstein, K. "Das Wesen der amnestischen Aphasie." *Deutsche Z. Nervenk.*, 83 (1925), 327–339.

266. Geleerd, E., F. Hacker, and D. Rapaport. "Contribution to the Study of Amnesia and Allied Conditions." *Psa. Quart.*, 14 (1945), 199–220.

267. Gerard-Varet, L. "Le Jeu dans l'animal et dans l'homme." *Revue Sci.*, 17 (1902), 485–491.

268. Gerstmann, J., and P. Schilder. "Studien ueber Bewegungsstoerungen, I: Eigenartige Formen extrapyramidaler Motilitaetsstoerung," *Z. Neurol. Psychiat.*, 58 (1920), 266–275. "II: Ein eigenartiger Typus motorischer Reizerscheinungen," *ibid.*, pp. 276–279. "III [by P. Schilder]: Ueber die motorischen Symptome der chronischen Chorea und ueber Stoerungen des Bewegungsbeginnes," *ibid.*, 61 (1920), 203–218. "IV: Zur Frage der Katalepsie," *Med. Klin.*, 17 (1921), 197–198. "V: Ueber die Typen extrapyramidaler Spannungen und ueber die extrapyramidale Pseudobulbaer-paralyse (akinetisch-hypertonisches Bulbaersyndrom)," *Z. Neurol. Psychiat.*, 70 (1921), 35–54. "VI: Unterbrechung von Bewegungsfolgen (Bewegungsluecken) nebst Bemerkungen ueber Mangel an Antrieb," *ibid.*, 85 (1923), 32–43. "VII: Das Fallen der Spaetencephalitiker," *ibid.*, pp. 44–51. "VIII: Ueber Wesen und Art des durch stria-pallidaere Laesion bedingten Bewegungs-uebermasses," *ibid.*, 87 (1923), 570–582.

269. Gibson, J. "A Critical Review of the Concept of Set in Contemporary Experimental Psychology." *Psychol. Bull.*, 38 (1941), 781–817.

270. Giese, F. Handbuch psychotechnischer Eignungspruefungen. 2d ed. Halle, Marhold, 1925.

271. Gill, M. "Spontaneous Regression in Hypnosis." *Bull. Menninger Clin.*, 12 (1948), 41–48.

272. Gill, M., and M. Brenman. "Problems in Clinical Research" (Round Table, 1946). *Amer. J. Orthopsychiat.*, 17 (1947), 196–230.

273. Gill, M., and M. Brenman. "Treatment of a Case of Anxiety Hysteria by an Hypnotic Technique Employing Psychoanalytic Principles." *Bull. Menninger Clin.*, 7 (1943), 163–171.

274. Gill, M., and D. Rapaport. "A Case of Loss of Personal Identity and Its Bearing on the Theory of Memory." *Character and Personality*, 11 (1942), 166–172.

275. Gillespie, R. "Amnesia." *Arch. Neurol. Psychiat.*, 37 (1937), 748–764.

276. Glover, E. "Medico-Psychological Aspects of Normality." *Brit. J. Psychol.*, 23 (1932), 152–166.

277. Goethe, J. W. von. Faust: a Tragedy. London, G. Bell and Sons, 1883.

278. Golant-Rattner, R., and T. Menteschaschwili. "Zur Frage der Stoerungen des Behaltens (Gedaechtnisstoerungen) bei progressiver Paralyse." *Monatschr. Psychiat. Neurol.*, 85 (1933), 222–242.

279. Goldstein. K. Language and Language Disturbances. New York, Grune & Stratton, 1948.

280. Goldstein, K. "Methodological Approach to the Study of Schizophrenic Thought Disorder." In *Language and Thought in Schizophrenia*, ed. J. S. Kasanin (Berkeley, Univ. of Calif. Press, 1944), pp. 17–40.

281. Goldstein, K. The Organism. New York, American Book, 1939.

282. Goldstein, K. "The Significance of Psychological Research in Schizophrenia." *J. Nerv. Ment. Dis.*, 97 (1943), 261–279.

283. Goldstein, K. "Ueber Aphasie." *Schweiz. Arch. Neurol. Psychiat.*, 19 (1926), 3–39.

284. Goldstein, K., and M. Scheerer. Abstract and Concrete Behavior; an Experimental Study with Special Tests. Psychol. Monog. 53, No. 2, Washington, D.C., Amer. Psychological Assn., 1941.

285. Gomperz, H. Psychologische Beobachtungen an griechischen Philosophen. Leipzig, Int. Psa. Verlag, 1924.

286. Gomperz, H. Weltanschauungslehre. Jena, Diederichs, 1905.

287. Gregor, A., and H. Roemer. "Beitraege zur Kenntnis der Gedaechtnisstoerung bei der Korsakowschen Psychose." *Monatschr. Psychiat. Neurol.*, 21 (1907), 19–45; 148–166.

288. Gregor, A. "Beitraege zur Psychopathologie des Gedaechtnisses." *Monatschr. Psychiat. Neurol.*, 25 (1909), 218–225, 339–386.

289. Gregor, A. Experimentelle Leitfaeden der Psychopathologie. Berlin, Karger, 1910.

290. Gregor, A., and Roemer, H. "Zur Kenntnis der Auffassung einfacher optischer Sinneseindruecke bei alkoholischen Geistesstoerungen, insbesondere bei der Korsakowschen Psychose." *Neurol. Zentralblatt*, 25 (1906), 339–351.

291. Greisinger, W. Pathologie und Therapie der psychischen Krankheiten. Braunschweig, Wreden, 1871.

292. Grinker, R., and J. Spiegel. Men under Stress. Philadelphia, Blakiston, 1945.

293. Grinker, R., and J. Spiegel. War Neuroses in North Africa. The Tunisian Campaign, January–May, 1943. New York, Jos. Macy Fdn., 1943.

294. Gruenthal, E. "Zur Kenntnis der Psychopathologie des Korsakowschen Symptomenkomplexes." *Monatschr. Psychiat. Neurol.*, 53 (1923), 89–132.

295. Gruenthal, E. "Ueber das Symptom der Einstellungsstoerung bei exogener. Psychosen." Z. *Neurol. Psychiat.*, 92 (1924), 255–266.

296. Hacker, F. "The Concept of Normality and Its Practical Significance." *Amer. J. Orthopsychiat.*, 15 (1945), 47–64.

297. Hacker, I. "Systematische Traumbeobachtungen mit besonderer Beruecksichtigung der Gedanken." *Arch. Psychol.*, 21 (1911), 1-131.

298. Hadamard, J. The Psychology of Invention in the Mathematical Field. Princeton, Princeton Univ. Press, 1945.

299. Hanfmann, E., and J. S. Kasanin. Conceptual Thinking in Schizophrenia. New York, Nerv. and Ment. Dis. Pub., 1942.

300. Harnik, F. "Die triebhaft-affektiven Momente im Zeitgefuehl." *Int. Z. Psa.*, 11 (1925), 32–58.

301. Hartmann, H. "Comments on the Psychoanalytic Theory of Instinctual Drives." *Psa. Quart.*, 17 (1948), 368–388.

302. Hartmann, H. Die Grundlagen der Psychoanalyse. Leipzig, Thieme, 1927.

303. Hartmann, H. "Ego Psychology." *Psa. Quart.*, 20 (in press, 1951).

304. Hartmann, H. "Gedaechtnis und Lustprinzip. Untersuchungen an Korsakow Kranken." Z. *Neurol. Psychiat.*, 126 (1930), 496–519.

305. Hartmann, H. "Ich-Psychologie und Anpassungsproblem." *Int. Z. Psa. Imago*, 24 (1939), 62–135.

306. Hartmann, H. "On Rational and Irrational Action." In *Psychoanalysis and the Social Sciences*, Vol. I, ed. Geza Roheim (New York, Int. Univ. Press, 1947), pp. 359–392.

307. Hartmann, H. "Psychoanalysis and the Concept of Health." *Int. J. Psa.*, 20 (1939), 308–321.

308. Hartmann, H. "Zur Frage organischer Amnesie und Hypnose." *Wiener Klin. Wochenschr.*, 40 (1927), 1507–1508.

309. Hartmann, H., and E. Kris. "The Genetic Approach in Psychoanalysis." In *The Psychoanalytic Study of the Child*, Vol. I (New York, Int. Univ. Press, 1945), pp. 11–29.

310. Hartmann, H., E. Kris, and R. Loewenstein. "Comments on the Formation of Psychic Structure." In *The Psychoanalytic Study of the Child*, Vol. II (New York, Int. Univ. Press, 1946), pp. 11–38.

311. Hartmann, H., E. Kris, and R. Loewenstein. "Notes on the Theory of Aggression." In *The Psychoanalytic Study of the Child*, Vols. III–IV (New York, Int. Univ. Press, 1949), pp. 9–36.

312. Hartmann, H., and P. Schilder. "Zur Klinik und Psychologie der Amentia." *Monatschr. Psychiat. Neurol.*, 55 (1923), 321–326.

313. Hartmann, H., and P. Schilder. "Zur Psychologie Schaedelverletzter." *Arch. Psychiat.*, 75 (1925), 287–301.

314. Head, H. Studies in Neurology. London, Frowde, 1920. Vols. I and II.

315. Hegel, G. Phenomenologie des Geistes. Leipzig, Duerr, 1907.

316. Heidbreder, E. "The Attainment of Concepts, I: Terminology and Methodology," *J. Gen. Psychol.*, 35 (1946), 173–189. "II: The Problem," *ibid.*, 191–223. "III: The Process," *J. Psychol.*, 24 (1947), 93–138. "IV [by Heidbreder *et al.*]: Regularities and Levels," *ibid.*, 25 (1948), 279–329. "V: Critical Features and Contexts," *ibid.*, 26 (1948), 45–69. "VI: Exploratory Experiments on Conceptualization at Perceptual Levels," *ibid.*, 193–216. "VII: Conceptual Achievements during Card-Sorting," *ibid.*, 27 (1949), 3–39. "VIII. The Conceptualization of Verbally Indicated Instances," *ibid.*, 263–309.

317. Heider, F. "Attitudes and Cognitive Organization." *J. Psychol.*, 21 (1946), 107–112.

318. Heilbronner, K. "Ueber Haftenbleiben und Stereotypie." *Monatschr. Psychiat. Neurol.* (Suppl. issue), 18 (1905), 293–371.

319. Heilbronner, K. "Zur klinisch-psychologischen Untersuchungstechnik." *Monatschr. Psychiat. Neurol.*, 17 (1905), 115–132.

320. Henderson, D., and R. Gillespie. A Text-Book of Psychiatry: for Students and Practitioners. 6th ed. London, Oxford Univ. Press, 1947.

321. Hendrick, I. "Ego Development and Certain Character Problems." *Psa. Quart.*, 3 (1936), 320–346.

322. Hendrick, I. "Instinct and the Ego during Infancy." *Psa. Quart.*, 11 (1942), 33–58.

323. Hendrick, I. "Work and the Pleasure Principle." *Psa. Quart.*, 12 (1943), 311–329.

324. Henning, H. Die Aufmerksamkeit. Berlin and Vienna, Urban and Schwarzenberg, 1925.

325. Herrmann, A. "Ueber die Faehigkeit zu selbstaendigem Lernen und die natuerlichen Lernweisen zur Zeit der Volksschulreife." *Z. Psychol.*, 109–110 (1929), 116–190.

326. Hermann, I. "Intelligenz und tiefer Gedanke." *Int. Z. Psa.*, 6 (1920), 193–201.

327. Hermann, I. Das Ich und das Denken. Vienna, Int. Psa. Verlag, 1929.

328. Hermann, I. "Das System Bw." *Imago*, 12 (1926), 203–210.

329. Hermann, I. Psychoanalyse und Logik. Vienna, Int. Psa. Verlag, 1924.

330. Hinsie, L., and J. Shatsky. Psychiatric Dictionary. New York and London, Oxford Univ. Press, 1940.

331. Hobbes, T. "De Homine." In *The English Works of Thomas Hobbes of Malmesbury*, coll. and ed. W. Molesworth, London, J. Bohn, 1845.

332. Hoeffding, H. Der menschliche Gedanke, seine Formen und seine Aufgaben. Leipzig, Reisland, 1911.

333. Hoenigswald, R. Die Grundlagen der Denkpsychologie: Studien und Analysen. 2d ed. Leipzig, Teubner, 1925.

334. Hoff, H., and P. Schilder. Die Lagereflexe des Menschen. Vienna, Springer, 1927.

335. Hollos, S. "Ueber das Zeitgefuehl." *Int. Z. Psa.*, 8 (1922), 421–439.

336. Hollos, S., and S. Ferenczi. Psychoanalysis and the Psychic Disorder of General Paresis. New York, Nerv. and Ment. Dis. Pub., 1925.

337. Hoppe, F. "Erfolg und Misserfolg." *Psychol. Forsch.*, 14 (1931), 1–62.

338. Hornbostel, E. von, and M. Wertheimer. "Ueber die Wahrnehmung der Schallrichtung." *Berliner Berichte*, 20 (1920), 388–396.

339. Horsley, J. Narco-Analysis. London, Oxford Univ. Press, 1943.

340. Horst, N. van der, "Ueber die Psychologie des Korsakowsyndroms." *Monatschr. Psychiat. Neurol.*, 83 (1932), 65–84.

341. Hoskins, R. The Biology of Schizophrenia. New York, Norton, 1946.

342. Housman, A. The Name and Nature of Poetry. New York, Macmillan, 1944.

343. Hume, D. Inquiry Concerning the Human Understanding. Oxford, Clarendon Press, 1894.

344. Humphrey, G. Directed Thinking. New York, Dodd, Mead, 1948.

345. Hunter, W. Review of *Foundations of Psychology*, ed. Boring, Langfeld, and Weld (New York, Wiley, 1948). *Psychol. Bull.*, 46 (1949), 54–57.

346. Husserl, E. Logische Untersuchungen. 2 vols. Halle, Niemeyer, 1921. Vol. I: Prolegomena zur reinen Logik. Vol. II: Untersuchungen zur Phaenomenologie und Theorie der Erkenntnis.

347. Isakower, O. "A Contribution to the Pathopsychology of Phenomena Associated with Falling Asleep." *Int. J. Psa.*, 19 (1938), 331–345.

348. Isakower, O., and P. Schilder. "Optisch-raeumliche Agnosie und Agraphie." *Z. Neurol. Psychiat.*, 113 (1928), 102–142.

349. Isserlin, M. "Ueber Agrammatismus." *Z. Neurol. Psychiat.*, 75 (1922), 332–411.

350. Jacobson, E. Progressive Relaxation. Chicago, Univ. Chicago Press, 1929.

351. Jaensch, E. Die Eidetik und die typologische Forschungsmethode. Leipzig, Quelle and Meyer, 1925.

352. Jaensch, E. Eidetic Imagery. London, Paul, Trench, Truebner; New York, Harcourt, Brace, 1930.

353. James, W. The Principles of Psychology. New York, Holt, 1890. Vols. I and II.

354. James, W. Psychology. New York, Holt, 1892.

355. Janet, P. Nevroses et Idées fixes. 2d ed. Paris, Alcan, 1904.

356. Jaspers, K. Allgemeine Psychopathologie. Berlin, Springer, 1948.

357. Jaspers, K. "Die Methoden der Intelligenzpruefung und der Begriff der Demenz." Z. *Neurol. Psychiat.*, Ref. Band I (1910), 401–452.

358. Jelliffe, S., and W. A. White. Diseases of the Nervous System. 6th ed. Philadelphia, Lea & Febiger, 1935.

359. Jones, E. "The Concept of a Normal Mind." *Int. J. Psa.*, 23 (1942), 1–8.

360. Jones, E. "The Theory of Symbolism." In *Papers on Psychoanalysis*, 5th ed. (Baltimore, Williams & Wilkins, 1948), pp. 87–144.

361. Jung, C. "Kritik ueber E. Bleuler: Zur Theorie des schizophrenen Negativismus." *Jhb. Psa. Psychopath. Forsch.*, 3 (1911–1912), 469–474.

362. Jung, C. Psychological Types. London, Routledge, 1923.

363. Jung, C. The Psychology of Dementia Praecox. New York, Nerv. and Ment. Dis. Pub., 3, 1944.

364. Jung, C. Psychology of the Unconscious. New York, Dodd, Mead, 1927.

365. Jung, C. Studies in Word Association. New York, Moffatt, Yard, 1919.

366. Kanner, L. "Early Infantile Autism." *J. Pediatrics*, 25 (1944), 211–217.

367. Kant, I. Critique of Pure Reason. 2d ed., rev. New York, Macmillan, 1902.

368. Kant, I. Prolegomena to All Future Metaphysics. London, Macmillan, 1889.

369. Kardiner, A. The Traumatic Neuroses of War. Psychosomatic Med. Monog. II–III, Washington, D.C., Nat. Research Coun., 1941.

370. Karsten, A. "Psychische Saettigung." *Psychol. Forsch.*, 10 (1928), 142–254.

371. Kasanin, J. S. "The Disturbance of Conceptual Thinking in Schizophrenia." In *Language and Thought in Schizophrenia* ed. J. S. Kasanin (Berkeley, Univ. of Calif. Press, 1944), pp. 41–49.

372. Kasanin, J. S., ed. *Language and Thought in Schizophrenia*. Collected Papers. Berkeley, Univ. of Calif. Press, 1944.

373. Katan, M. "A Contribution to the Understanding of Schizophrenic Speech." *Int. J. Psa.*, 20 (1939), 353–362.

374. Katona, G. Organizing and Memorizing: Studies in the Psychology of Learning and Teaching. New York, Columbia Univ. Press, 1940.

375. Katz, D. "Die Erscheinungsweisen der Farben und ihre Beeinflussung durch die individuelle Erfahrung." *Z. Psychol.* (Suppl. vol. 7), Leipzig, Barth, 1911.

376. Katz, D. Hunger und Appetit. Leipzig, Barth, 1932. Also *Kong. Ber., exper. Psychol.,* 13 (1932), 255–279.

377. Katz, D., and A. Toll. "Die Messung von Charakter und Begabungsunterschieden bei Tieren." *Z. Psychol.,* 93 (1923), 287–311.

378. Katzaroff, D. "Contribution a l'ètude de la récognition." *Arch. de Psychol.,* 11 (1911), pp. 2–78.

379. Kaywin, L., D. Hilger, and W. Finzer. "Interpretation of Dreams of Others by Subjects in Hypnosis." Unpublished manuscript, 1948.

380. Kent, G., and A. Rosanoff. "A Study of Association in Insanity." *Amer. J. Insanity,* 67 (1910), 317–377.

381. Kenyon, V., M. Lozoff, and D. Rapaport. "Metrazol Convulsions in the Treatment of the Psychosis of Dementia Paralytica." *Arch. Neurol. Psychiat.,* 46 (1941), 884–896.

382. Klages, L. Der Geist als Widersacher der Seele. 3 vols. Leipzig, Barth, 1929–1932.

383. Klages, L. The Science of Character. Cambridge, Mass., Sci-Art, 1932.

384. Klein, D. "The Experimental Production of Dreams during Hypnosis." In *The World of Dreams,* ed. R. L. Woods (New York, Random House, 1947), pp. 828–841.

385. Klein, F. Elementary Mathematics from an Advanced Standpoint. 2 vols. New York, Dover, 1939. Vol. II: Geometry.

386. Klein, G. "Adaptive Properties of Sensory Functioning: Some Postulates and Hypotheses." *Bull. Menninger Clin.,* 13 (1949), 16–23.

387. Klein, G., and H. Schlesinger. "Where Is the Perceiver in Perceptual Theory?" *J. Personal.,* 18 (1949), 32–47.

388. Kleist, K. Untersuchungen zur Kenntnis der psychomotorischen Bewegungsstoerungen bei Geisteskranken. Leipzig, Klinkhardt, 1908.

389. Kleist, K. Weitere Untersuchungen an Geisteskranken mit psychomotorischen Stoerungen. Leipzig, Klinkhardt, 1909.

390. Knight, R. P. "Determinism, 'Freedom' and Psychotherapy." *Psychiatry,* 9 (1946), 251–262.

391. Knight, R. P. "Practical and Theoretical Considerations in the Analysis of a Minister." *Psychoanal. Review,* 24 (1937), 350–364.

392. Knight, R. P. "Psychotherapy in Acute Paranoid Schizophrenia with Successful Outcome: a Case Report." *Bull. Menninger Clin.,* 3 (1939), 97–105.

393. Knight, R. P. "The Relationship of Latent Homosexuality to the Mechanism of Paranoid Delusions." *Bull. Menninger Clin.,* 4 (1940), 149–159.

394. Koehler, P. "Beitraege zur systematischen Traumbeobachtung." *Arch. Psychol.,* 23 (1912), 415–483.

395. Koehler, W. "Die Farben der Sehdinge beim Schimpansen und beim Haushuhn." Z. *Psychol.*, 77 (1917), 248–255.

396. Koehler, W. "Gestaltprobleme und Anfaenge einer Gestalttheorie." *Jhb. Physiol.*, 3 (1922), 512.

397. Koehler, W. Gestalt Psychology. New York, Liveright, 1929.

398. Koehler, W. Intelligenzpruefungen an Anthropoiden. Berlin, Abh. Preuss. Akad. Wiss., 1917.

399. Koehler, W. Die physische Gestalten in Ruhe und im stationaeren Zustand. Erlangen, Philosoph. Akad., 1920.

400. Koehler, W. "Zur Theorie des Sukzessivvergleichs und der Zeitfehler." *Psychol. Forsch.*, 4 (1923), 115–175.

401. Koehler, W., and H. von Restorff. "Ueber die Wirkung von Bereichsbildung im Spurenfeld." *Psychol. Forsch.*, 18 (1933), 299–342.

402. Koeppen, M., and Z. Kutzinsky. Systematische Beobachtungen ueber die Wiedergabe kleiner Erzaehlungen durch Geisteskranke. Berlin, Karger, 1910.

403. Koffka, K. "Bemerkungen zur Denk-Psychologie." *Psychol. Forsch.*, 9 (1927), 163–182.

404. Koffka, K. The Growth of the Mind. New York, Harcourt, Brace, 1924.

405. Koffka, K. "On the Structure of the Unconscious." In *The Unconscious: a Symposium*, ed. E. Dummer (New York, Knopf, 1927), pp. 43–68.

406. Koffka, K. Principles of Gestalt Psychology. New York, Harcourt, Brace, 1935.

407. Koffka, K. "Psychologie." In *Lehrbuch der Philosophie: Die Philosophie in ihren Einzelgebieten*, ed. M. Dessoir (Berlin, Ullstein, 1925), pp. 497–602.

408. Koffka, K. Zur Analyse der Vostellungen und ihrer Gesetze. Leipzig, Quelle & Meyer, 1912.

409. Kogerer, H. "Beitrag zur Psychologie der Gedaechtnisstoerungen." *Allg. Z. Psychiat.*, 76 (1920), 774–790.

410. Kohnstamm, O. "Ueber das Krankheitsbild der retro-anterograden Amnesie und die Unterscheidung des spontanen und des lernenden Merkens." *Monatschr. Psychiat. Neurol.*, 41 (1917), 373–382.

411. Koerner, G. "Zur Psychopathologie des amnestischen Syndroms." *Monatschr. Psychiat. Neurol.*, 90 (1934), 177–216.

412. Korsakoff, S. "Erinnerungstaeuschungen (Pseudoreminiszenzen) bei polyneuritischer Psychose." *Allg. Z. Psychiat. Neurol.*, 47 (1891), 390–410.

413. Korsakoff, S. "Ueber eine besondere Form psychischer Stoerung." *Arch. Psychiat.*, 21 (1890), 669–704.

414. Kounin, J. "The Comparative Rigidity of Different Chronological Age Groups with Equal Mental Ages." *Psychol. Bull.*, 36 (1939), 628.

415. Kraepelin, E. Psychiatrie. Leipzig, Barth, 1909–1913

416. Kraepelin, E. "Ueber die Merkfaehigkeit." *Monatschr. Psychiat. Neurol.*, 8 (1900), 245–250.

417. Kraepelin, E. "Ueber psychische Schwaeche." *Arch. Psychiat. Nervenkr.*, 13 (1882), 382–426.

418. Krauss, S. "Untersuchungen ueber Aufbau und Stoerung der menschlichen Handlung." *Arch. Psychol.*, 77 (1930), 649–692.

419. Kretschmer, E. Medizinische Psychologie. Leipzig, Thieme, 1922.

420. Kries, J. von. Allgemeine Sinnesphysiologie. Leipzig, Vogel, 1923.

421. Kris, E. "Approaches to Art." In *Psychoanalysis Today*, ed. S. Lorand (New York, Int. Univ. Press, 1944), pp. 354–370.

422. Kris, E. "Art and Regression." *Trans. New York Acad. Sci.*, 6 (1944), 236–250.

423. Kris, E. "Ego Development and the Comic." *Int. J. Psa.*, 19 (1938), 77–90.

424. Kris, E. "Ein geisteskranker Bildhauer." *Imago*, 19 (1933), 384–411.

425. Kris, E. "Das Lachen als Mimischer Vorgang; Beitraege zur Psychoanalyse der Mimik." *Int. Z. Psa. & Imago*, 24 (1939), 146–148.

426. Kris, E., and O. Kurz. Die Legende vom Kuenstler. Vienna, Krystall Verlag, 1934.

427. Kris, E. "The Nature of Psychoanalytic Propositions and Their Validation." In *Freedom and Experience* (Ithaca, N.Y., Cornell Univ. Press, 1947), pp. 239–259.

428. Kris, E. "On Inspiration." *Int. J. Psa.*, 20 (1939), 377–389.

429. Kris, E. "On Preconscious Mental Processes." *Psa. Quart.*, 19 (1950), 540–560.

430. Kris, E. "Probleme der Asthetik." *Int. Z. Psa. und Imago*, 26 (1941), 142–178.

431. Kris, E. "The Psychology of Caricature." *Int. J. Psa.*, 17 (1936), 285–303.

432. Kris, E. "Bemerkungen zur Bildnerei der Geisteskranken." *Imago*, 22 (1936), 339–370.

433. Kris, E., and N. Leites. "Trends in Twentieth Century Propaganda." In *Psychoanalysis and the Social Sciences*, ed. Geza Roheim. New York, Int. Univ. Press. 1 (1947), 393–409.

434. Kris, E., and E. Pappenheim. "The Function of Drawings and the Meaning of the 'Creative Spell' in a Schizophrenic Artist." *Psa. Quart.*, 15 (1946), 6–31.

435. Kronfeld, A., and E. Sternberg. "Der gedankliche Aufbau der klassischen Aphasieforschung im Lichte der Sprachlehre." *Psychol. Med.*, 2 (1927), 254–295.

436. Krueger, F. Der Strukturbegriff in der Psychologie. In *Bericht ueber den VIII Kongress fuer experimentelle Psychologie*, Jena, Fischer, 1924.

437. Kubie, L. "A Critical Analysis of the Concept of a Repetition Compulsion." *Int. J. Psa.*, 20 (1939), 390–402.

438. Kuelpe, O. "Ueber die moderne Psychologie des Denkens." *Int. Monatschr. Wiss.*, 6 (1912), 1069–1110.

439. Kuelpe, O. Vorlesungen ueber Psychologie. 2d ed. Leipzig, Hirzel, 1922.

440. Ladd, G. "Contribution to the Psychology of Visual Dreams." *Mind*, 2 (1892), 299–304.

441. Laforgue, R. The Relativity of Reality. New York, Nerv. and Ment. Dis. Pub., 1940.

442. Landauer, K. "Affects, Passions and Temperament." *Int. J. Psa.*, 19 (1938), 388–415.

443. Landauer, K. "Automatismen, Zwangsneurose und Paranoia." *Int. Z. Psa.*, 13 (1927), 10–19.

444. Lashley, K. "Experimental Analysis of Instinctive Behavior." *Psychol. Rev.*, 45 (1938), 445–471.

445. Lau, E. Beitraege zur Psychologie der Jugendlichen in Pubertaetszeit. 2d ed. Langensalza, Belz, 1924.

446. Leibnitz, G. "New Essays on the Human Understanding." In *Monadology and Other Philosophical Writings*, Oxford, Clarendon Press, 1898.

447. Leitch, M. "Perception in Early Infancy." Unpublished report to the U.S.P.H.S. Council on Mental Health, 1949, pp. 1–10.

448. Lessing, T. T. Untergang der Erde am Geist (Europa und Asien). Hannover, Adam, 1924.

449. Leupoldt, J. Zur Symptomatologie der Katatonie. Halle, Sommers Klinik, 1906.

450. Levey, H. "Description of the Free Artist as a Character Type and in Terms of His Unconscious Mental Processes." *Psychiatry*, 3 (1940), 278–293.

451. Levey, H. "Poetry Production as a Supplemental Emergency Defense against Anxiety." *Psa. Quart.*, 7 (1938), 232–242.

452. Levey, H. "A Critique of the Theory of Sublimation." *Psychiatry*, 2 (1939), 239–270.

453. Levine, J., and G. Murphy. "The Learning and Forgetting of Controversial Material." *J. Abn. Soc. Psychol.*, 38 (1943), 507–517.

454. Levine, R., I. Chein, and G. Murphy. "The Relation of the Intensity of a Need to the Amount of Perceptual Distortion: a Preliminary Report." *J. Psychol.*, 13 (1942), 283–293.

455. Levy-Bruehl, L. Primitive Mentality. London, Allen and Unwin, 1923.

456. Levy-Bruehl, L. The "Soul" of the Primitive. London, Allen and Unwin, 1928.

457. Lewin, B. D. "Some Observations on Knowledge, Belief and the Impulse to Know." *Int. J. Psa.*, 20 (1939), 426–431.

458. Lewin, K. "Die psychische Taetigkeit bei der Hemmung von Willensvor-

gaengen und das Grundgesetz der Assoziation." Z. *Psychol.*, 77 (1916), 212–247.

459. Lewin, K. "Kriegslandschaft." Z. *Psychol.*, 12 (1917), 440–447.

460. Lewin, K. "Das Problem der Willensmessung und der Assoziation." *Psychol. Forsch.*, 1 (1922), 191–302, 2 (1922), 65–140.

461. Lewin, K. "Ueber die Umkehrung der Raumlage auf dem Kopf stehender Worte und Figuren in der Wahrnehmung." *Psychol. Forsch.*, 4 (1923), 210–261.

462. Lewin, K. "Idee und Aufgabe der vergleichenden Wissenschaftslehre." *Symposion*, 1 (1925), 61–94.

463. Lewin, K. "Vorbemerkungen ueber die psychischen Kraefte und Energien und ueber die Struktur der Seele." *Psychol. Forsch.*, 7 (1926), 294–329.

464. Lewin, K. "Vorsatz, Wille und Beduerfnis." *Psychol. Forsch.*, 7 (1926), 330–385.

465. Lewin, K. "Gesetz und Experiment in der Psychologie." *Symposion*, 1 (1927), 375–421.

466. Lewin, K. Der Begriff der Genese in Physik, Biologie und Entwicklungsgeschichte. Berlin, Springer, 1922.

467. Lewin, K. A Dynamic Theory of Personality. New York, McGraw-Hill, 1935.

468. Lewin, K. Principles of Topological Psychology. New York, McGraw-Hill, 1936.

469. Lewin, K. The Conceptual Representation and the Measurement of Psychological Forces. Durham, N.C., Duke Univ. Press, 1938. Vol. I, No. 4, Serial 4 (reprint, 1948).

470. Lewis, N. Research in Dementia Praecox. New York, Nat. Comm. for Ment. Hygiene, 1936.

471. Levy, E. "Some Aspects of the Schizophrenic Formal Disturbance of Thought." *Psychiatry*, 6 (1943), 55–69.

472. Leyser, E. "Ueber einige Formen von dysarthrischen Sprachstoerungen bei organischen Erkrankungen des Zentralnervensystems." Z. *Neurol. Psychiat.*, 88 (1924), 383–420.

473. Leyser, E. "Zum Problem der Iteration." *Monatschr. Psychiat. Neurol.*, 55 (1923–1924), 175–206.

474. Liepmann, H. Ueber Stoerungen des Handelns bei Gehirnkranken. Berlin, Karger, 1905.

475. Lindworsky, L. "Das schlussfolgende Denken." *Stimme der Zeit*, Suppl. issue, ser. 2, No. 1, Freiburg, Herder, 1916.

476. Lindworsky, J. Der Wille, Leipzig, Barth, 1919.

477. Lipps, T. Leitfaden der Psychologie. Leipzig. Engelmann, 1903.

478. Liss, E. "Learning: Its Sadistic and Masochistic Manifestations." *Amer. J. Orthopsychiat.*, 10 (1940), 123–129.

479. Liss, E. "Libidinal Fixations as Pedagogic Determinations." *Amer. J. Orthopsychiat.*, 5 (1935), 126–131.

480. Lissner, K. "Die Entspannung von Bedeurfnissen durch Ersatzhandlungen." *Psychol. Forsch.*, 18 (1933), 218–250.

481. Locke, J. "An Essay Concerning Human Understanding." In *Philosophical Works of J. Locke*, ed. J. A. St. John (London, G. Bell, 1877).

482. Loewenstein, R. "The Vital or Somatic Instincts." *Int. J. Psa.*, 21 (1940), 377–400.

483. Loewy, M. "Versuch einer motorischen Psychologie mit Ausblicken auf die Charakterologie." *Jhb. Characterologie*, 5 (1928), 335–374.

484. Lorenz, K. "Der Kumpan in der Umwelt des Vogels. Der Artgenosse als ausloesendes Moment sozialer Verhaltungsweisen." *J. Ornith.*, 83 (1935), 137–213.

485. Lowes, J. The Road to Xanadu. New York, Houghton Mifflin, 1927.

486. Lucerna, C. 'Das Maerchen,' Goethes Naturphilosophie als Kunstwerk. Leipzig, Eckardt, 1910.

487. Luria, A. "Die Methode der abbildenden Motorik bei Kommunikation der Systeme und ihre Anwendung auf die Affektpsychologie." *Psychol. Forsch.*, 12 (1929), 127–179.

488. MacCurdy, J. T. Common Principles in Psychology and Physiology. Cambridge, Mass., Harvard Univ. Press, 1928.

489. MacCurdy, J. T. The Psychology of Emotion, Morbid and Normal. New York, Harcourt, Brace, 1925.

490. McClelland, D., J. Atkinson, and R. Clark. "The Projective Expression of Needs, I: The Effect of Different Intensities of the Hunger Drive on Perception," *J. Psychol.*, 25 (1948), 205–222. "II: The Effect of Different Intensities of the Hunger Drive on Thematic Apperception," *ibid.*, 38 (1948), 643–658. "III: The Effect of Ego-Involvement, Success, and Failure on Perception," *ibid.*, 27 (1949), 311–330.

491. McCord, F. "Report of Hypnotically Induced Dreams and Conflicts." *J. Personality*, 14 (1946), 268–280.

492. McDougall, W. The Energies of Men: a Study of the Fundamentals of Dynamic Psychology. New York, Scribner, 1933.

493. McDougall, W. An Introduction to Social Psychology. Boston, Luce, 1921.

494. McDougall, W. Outline of Abnormal Psychology. New York, Scribner, 1926.

495. McDowell, M. "An Abrupt Cessation of Major Neurotic Symptoms Follow-

ing an Hypnotically Induced Artificial Conflict." *Bull. Menninger Clin.*, 12 (1948), 168–177.

496. Mach, E. Die Mechanik in ihrer Entwicklung. Leipzig, Brockhaus, 1921.

497. Mahler, W. "Ersatzhandlungen verschiedener Realitaetsgrade." *Psychol. Forsch.*, 18 (1933), 27–89.

498. Maier, N. "Reasoning in humans, I: On Direction," *J. Comp. Psychol.*, 10 (1930), 115–143. "II: The Solution of a Problem and Its Appearance in Consciousness," *ibid.*, 12 (1931), 181–194. "III: The Mechanisms of Equivalent Stimuli and of Reasoning," *J. Exp. Psychol.*, 35 (1945), 349–360.

499. Marbe, K. Experimental-psychologische Untersuchungen ueber das Urteil. Leipzig, Engelmann, 1901.

500. Markuszewicz, R. "Beitrag zum autistischen Denken bei Kindern." *Int. Z. Psa.*, 6 (1920), 248–252.

501. Martin, L. "Zur Lehre von den Bewegungsvorstellungen," *Z. Psychol.*, 56 (1910), 401–447. "Die Projektionsmethode und die Lokalisation visueller und anderer Vorstellungsbilder," *ibid.*, 61 (1912), 321–546. "Quantitative Untersuchungen ueber das Verhaeltnis anschaulicher und unanschaulicher Bewusstseinsinhalte," *ibid.*, 65 (1913), 417–490.

502. Maslow, A. "Preface to Motivation Theory." *Psychosom. Med.*, 5 (1943), 85–92.

503. Maslow, A. "A Theory of Human Motivation." *Psychol. Rev.*, 50 (1943), 370–396.

504. Masselon, R. Psychologie des Dementia Precox. Paris, Boyer, 1902.

505. Maury, A. "De certains faits observés dans les rêves et dans l'ètat intermédiaire entre le sommeil et la veille." *Annales Medico-Psychol.*, 3 (1857) 157–176.

506. Maury, A. "Nouvelles observations sur les analogies des phenomènes du rêve et de l'aliénation mentale." *Annales Medico-Psychol.*, 5 (1853), 404–544.

507. Maury, A. Le Sommeil et les rêves. 3d ed. Paris, Didier, 1865.

508. Mayer-Gross, W. "Nachwort zu der Arbeit von Kurt Westphal." *Z. Neurol. Psychiat.*, 110 (1927), 607–611.

509. Mayman, M., R. Schafer, and D. Rapaport. "Projective Methods of the Wechsler-Bellevue Scale." 1950. To be published in Anderson's *Clinical Testing Methods*. In press.

510. Mead, G. Mind, Self and Society. Chicago, Univ. Chicago Press, 1934.

511. Meinong, A. Gesammelte Abhandlungen, I: Abhandlungen zur Psychologie. Leipzig, Barth, 1914.

512. Meinong, A. Hume-Studien. Vol. I: Zur Geschichte und Kritik des modernen Nominalismus. Vol. II: Zur Relationstheorie. In *Sitzungsberichte der Koenigl. Akademie der Wissenschaften*. Vienna, Gerold's Sohn, 1877, 1882.

513. Meinong, A. "Ueber Annahmen." *Z. Psychol.*, (Suppl. Vol. 2), Leipzig, Barth, 1902.

514. Menninger, K. Unpublished paper and personal communication.

515. Menninger, W. C. Juvenile Paresis. Baltimore, Williams and Wilkins, 1936.

516. Messer, K. "Experimentell-psychologische Untersuchungen ueber das Denken." *Arch. Psychol.*, 8 (1906), 1–224.

517. Metzger, M. "Ueber das physiologische Substrat der optisch-motorischen Erlebniseinheit." *Klin. Wochenschr.*, 4 (1925), 2179.

518. Meynert, T. "Amentia, die Verwirrtheit." *Jhb. Psychiat.*, 9 (1889–1890), 1–112.

519. Michotte, A., and E. Pruem. "Étude expérimentale sur le choix volontaire et ses antécédents immédiats." *Arch. de Psychol.*, 10 (1910), 117–299.

520. Michotte, A., and C. Ransy. Contribution à l'étude de la mémoire logique. *Annales Louvain, Inst. sup. de philos.*, 1 (1912), 3–95.

521. Miller, N., and J. Dollard. Social Learning and Imitation. New Haven, Conn., Yale Univ. Press, 1941.

522. Moenckemoeller, O. "Casuistischer Beitrag zur sogenannten polyneuritischen Psychose." *Allg. Z. Psychiat.*, 84 (1898), 806–874.

523. Moll, A. Hypnotism. New York, Scribner, 1890.

524. Montessori, M. The Montessori Method. New York, Stokes, 1912.

525. Mowrer, O. H., and C. Kluckhohn. "Dynamic Theory of Personality." In *Personality and the Behavior Disorders*, ed. J. M. Hunt. Vol. I (New York, Ronald, 1944), pp. 69–135.

526. Mueller, G. "Zur Analyse der Gedaechtnistaetigkeit und des Vorstellungsverlaufes." *Z. Psychol.*, Suppl. Vol. 5, 1911; Suppl. Vol. 8, 1913; Suppl. Vol. 9, 1917, Leipzig, Barth.

527. Mueller, G., and A. Pilzecker. "Experimentelle Beitraege zur Lehre vom Gedaechtnis." *Z. Psychol.* (Suppl. Vol. 1), Leipzig, Barth, 1900.

528. Mueller, G., and A. Pilzecker. Die Lehre von der sinnlichen Aufmerksamkeit. Inaugural dissertation, Goettingen, 1889.

529. Mueller-Freienfels, R. "Der Einfluss der Gefuehle und motorischen Faktoren auf Assoziation und Denken." *Arch. Psychol.*, 27 (1913), 381–430.

530. Mueller-Freienfels, R. The Evolution of Modern Psychology. New Haven, Conn., Yale Univ. Press, 1935.

531. Muensterberg, H. Beitraege zur experimentellen Psychologie. Freiburg, Mohr, 1889.

532. Muensterberg, H. Psychology, General and Applied. New York, Appleton, 1914.

533. Murphy, G. Personality: a Biosocial Approach to Origins and Structure. New York, Harper, 1947.

534. Murray, H. "The Effect of Fear upon Estimates of the Maliciousness of Other Personalities." *J. Soc. Psychol.*, 4 (1933), 310–329.

535. Myers, C. "The Comparative Study of Instincts." *Brit. J. Psychol.*, 36 (1945), 1–9.

536. Nachmansohn, M. "Zur Erklaerung der durch Inspiration entstandenen Bewusstseinserlebnisse." *Arch. Psychol.*, 36 (1916), 255–279.

537. Nachmansohn, M. "Ueber experimentell erzeugte Traeume nebst kritischen Bemerkungen ueber die psychoanalytische Methodik." *Z. Neurol. Psychiat.*, 98 (1925), 556–586.

538. Nietzsche, F. "Menschliches, Allzumenschliches." In *Nietzsche Werke*, 2 vols. (Stuttgart, Kroener, 1930), Vol. I, pp. 109–264.

539. Noyes, A. Modern Clinical Psychiatry. Philadelphia, Saunders, 1948.

540. Nunberg, H. "Beitraege zur Theorie der Therapie." *Int. J. Psa.*, 23 (1937), 60–67.

541. Nunberg, H. "On the Catatonic Attack." In *Practice and Theory of Psychoanalysis* (New York, Nerv. and Ment. Dis. Pub., 1948), pp. 3–23.

542. Nunberg, H. "The Course of the Libidinal Conflict in a Case of Schizophrenia." In *Practice and Theory of Psychoanalysis* (New York, Nerv. and Ment. Dis. Pub., 1948), pp. 24–59.

543. Nunberg, H. "The Synthetic Function of the Ego." In *Practice and Theory of Psychoanalysis* (New York, Nerv. and Ment. Dis. Pub., 1948), pp. 120–136.

544. Oberndorf, C. "Cases Allied to Manic-Depressive Insanity." N.Y. State Hosp. Bull., ser. 2, 5 (1912), 393–405.

545. Oberndorf, C. "Depersonalization in Relation to Erotization of Thought." *Int. J. Psa.*, 15 (1934), 271–295.

546. Oberndorf, C. "The Genesis of the Feeling of Unreality." *Int. J. Psa.*, 16 (1935), 296–306.

547. Oberndorf, C. "On Retaining the Sense of Reality in States of Depersonalization." *Int. J. Psa.*, 20 (1939), 137–147.

548. Oberndorf, C. "A Theory of Depersonalization." *Trans. Amer. Neurol. Assn*, 59 (1933), 150–151.

549. Ogden, C. The Meaning of Meaning. New York and London, Harper, 1926.

550. Ovsiankina, M. "Die Wiederaufnahme unterbrochener Handlungen." *Psychol. Forsch.*, 11 (1928), 302–379.

551. Parr, E. Adaptiogenese und Phylogenese. Berlin, Springer, 1926.

552. Peters, W. "Begabungsprobleme." *Z. Psychol.*, 26 (1925), 12–13.

553. Petzold, V. "Komplex und Begriff." *Z. Psychol.*, 99 (1926), 74–104.

554. Pfeifer, B. "Ueber psychische Stoerungen bei Hirntumoren." *Arch. Psychiat.*, 47 (1910), 558–739.

555. Pfenninger, W. "Untersuchungen ueber die Konstanz und den Wechsel der psychologischen Konstellation bei Normalen und Fruehdementen (Schizophrenen)." *Jhb. Psa. Psychopath. Forsch.*, 3 (1911), 481–524.

556. Piaget, J. "Le Problème biologique de l'intelligence." In *La Naissance de l'intelligence* (Neuchâtel and Paris, Delachaux and Niestlé, 1936), pp. 9–28.

557. Piaget, J. "Children's Philosophies." In *A Handbook of Child Psychology* (Worcester, Mass., Clark Univ. Press, 1931), pp. 377–391.

558. Piaget, J. The Child's Conception of Physical Causality. London, Kegan, 1930.

559. Piaget, J. The Child's Conception of the World. New York, Harcourt, Brace, 1929.

560. Piaget, J. Judgment and Reasoning in the Child. New York, Harcourt, Brace, 1928.

561. Piaget, J. The Language and Thought of the Child. 2d ed. London, Routledge, 1932.

562. Piaget, J. The Moral Judgment of the Child. Glencoe, Ill., Free Press, 1948.

563. Piaget, J. La Naissance de l'Intelligence. Neuchâtel and Paris, Delachaux and Niestlé, 1936.

564. Piaget, J. "Principal Factors Determining Intellectual Evolution from Childhood to Adult Life." In *Factors Determining Human Behavior*, Harvard Tercentenary Publ. (Cambridge, Mass., Harvard Univ. Press, 1937), pp. 32–48.

565. Pick, A. Die agrammatischen Sprachstoerungen. Berlin, Springer, 1913.

566. Pick, A. "Beitraege zur Pathologie des Denkverlaufes beim Korsakoff." *Z. Neurol. Psychiat.*, 28 (1915), 344–383.

567. Pick, A. "Ueber Beeinflussung des Denkens und Handelns durch das Sprechen." *Z. Neurol. Psychiat.*, 38 (1917), 331–370.

568. Pick, A. "Ueber eine neuartige Form von Paramnesie." *J. Psychol. Neurol.*, 20 (1901), 1–35.

569. Pick, A. Ueber das Sprachverstaendnis. Leipzig, Barth, 1909.

570. Plato. "Meno." In *The Dialogues of Plato*, tr. B. Jowett (New York, Random House, 1937), Vol. I, pp. 349–382.

571. Plato. "Theaetetus." In *The Dialogues of Plato*, tr. B. Jowett (New York, Random House, 1937), Vol. II, pp. 143–220.

572. Poetzl, O. "Die Aphasielehre vom Standpunkte der klinischen Psychiatrie: die optisch-agnostischen Stoerungen." In *Handbuch der Psychiatrie*, ed. G. Aschaffenburg, Leipzig, Deuticke, 1928.

573. Poetzl, O. "Experimentell erregte Traumbilder in ihren Beziehungen zum indirekten Sehen." *Z. Neurol. Psychiat.*, 37 (1917), 278–349.

574. Poetzl, O. "Zur Metapsychologie des *déjà vue*." *Imago*, 12 (1926), 393–402.

575. Poincare, H. The Foundations of Science. New York, Science Press, 1913.

576. Pollak, E., and P. Schilder. "Zur Lehre von den Sprachantrieben." Z. *Neurol. Psychiat.*, 104 (1926), 480–502.

577. Postman, L., and J. Bruner. "Perception under Stress." *Psychol. Rev.*, 55 (1948), 314–323.

578. Postman, L., J. Bruner, and E. McGinnies. "Personal Values as Selective Factors in Perception." *J. Abn. Soc. Psychol.*, 43 (1948), 142–154.

579. Postman, L., and W. Jenkins. "An Experimental Analysis of Set in Rote Learning: the Interaction of Learning Instruction and Retention Performance." *J. Exp. Psychol.*, 38 (1948), 683–689.

580. Postman, L., W. Jenkins, and D. Postman. "An Experimental Comparison of Active Recall and Recognition." *Amer. J. Psychol.*, 61 (1948), 511–519.

581. Postman, L., and G. Murphy. "The Factor of Attitude in Associative Memory." *J. Exp. Psychol.*, 33 (1943), 228–238.

582. Postman, L., and V. Senders. "Incidental Learning and Generality of Set." *J. Exp. Psychol.*, 36 (1946), 153–165.

583. Prince, M. "Can Emotion Be Regarded as Energy?" In *Feelings and Emotions, The Wittenberg Symposium*, ed. M. Reymert (Worcester, Mass., Clark Univ. Press, 1928), pp. 161–169.

584. Prince, M. The Unconscious. 2d ed., rev. New York, Macmillan, 1921.

585. Proshansky, H., and G. Murphy. "The Effects of Reward and Punishment on Perception." *J. Psychol.*, 13 (1942), 295–305.

586. Rado, S. "Die psychischen Wirkungen der Rauschgifte, Versuch einer psychoanalytischen Theorie der Suchte." *Int. Z. Psa.*, 12 (1926), 540–556.

587. Rank, O. The Myth of the Birth of the Hero. New York, Nerv. and Ment. Dis. Pub., 1914.

588. Rank, O. Will Therapy and Truth and Reality. New York, Knopf, 1945.

589. Rank, O., and H. Sachs. The Significance of Psychoanalysis for the Mental Sciences. New York, Nerv. and Ment. Dis. Pub., 1916.

590. Rapaport, D. "Concerning a Clinically Meaningful Theory of Memory." Unpublished paper.

591. Rapaport, D. Emotions and Memory. Baltimore, Williams and Wilkins, 1942.

592. Rapaport, D. "The New Army Individual Test of General Mental Ability." *Bull. Menninger Clin.*, 9 (1945), 107–110.

593. Rapaport, D. "Principles Underlying Non-Projective Tests of Personality." *Annals New York Acad. Sci.*, 66 (1946), 643–652.

594. Rapaport, D. "Principles Underlying Projective Techniques." *Character and Personality*, 10 (1942), 213–219.

595. Rapaport, D. "Psychoanalysis as a Psychology." Unpublished manuscript.

596. Rapaport, D. "On the Psycho-analytic Theory of Thinking." *Int. J. Psa.*, 31 (1950), 1–10.

597. Rapaport, D. "Psychological Testing, Its Practical and Its Heuristic Significance." *Samiksa* (Journal of the Indian Psychoanalytical Society), 1 (1947), 245–262.

598. Rapaport, D. Review of Sartre's *The Psychology of Imagination* (New York, Philosophical Library, 1948). *Psa. Quart.*, 18 (1949), 389–390.

599. Rapaport, D. "Technological Growth and the Psychology of Man." *Psychiatry*, 10 (1947), 253–259.

600. Rapaport, D. "The Theoretical Implications of Diagnostic Testing Procedures." In: *Rapports, Congrès International de Psychiatrie*, Vol. II (Paris, Hermann & Cie, 1950), pp. 241–271.

601. Rapaport, D., and J. Frank. "A Review and Preliminary Remarks on the Problems of the Psychology of Research." Unpublished manuscript.

602. Rapaport, D., M. Gill, and R. Schafer. Diagnostic Psychological Testing. 2 vols. Chicago, Year Book Publishers, 1945–1946.

603. Rapaport, D., and E. Lewy. "The Psychoanalytic Concept of Memory and Its Relation to Recent Memory Theories." *Psa. Quart.*, 13 (1944), 16–42.

604. Reich, W. Charakteranalyse. Vienna, Selbstverlag des Verfassers, 1933.

605. Reichard, S., and D. Rapaport. "The Role of Testing Concept Formation in Clinical Psychological Work." *Bull. Menninger Clin.*, 7 (1943), 99–105.

606. Reider, N. "Phenomena of Sensory Suppression." *Arch. Neurol. Psychiat.*, 55 (1946), 583–590.

607. Reik, T. The Psychological Problems of Religion, I: Ritual. New York, Farrar, 1946.

608. Ribot, T. Diseases of Memory. London, Kegan, 1906.

609. Ribot, T. Essay on the Creative Imagination. Chicago, Open Court Publ. Co., 1906.

610. Rich, J. "Goals and Trends of Research in Geology and Geography." *Sci.*, 107 (1948), 581–584.

611. Richter, C. "Biology of Drives." *J. Comp. Physiol. Psychol.*, 40 (1947), 129–134.

612. Riklin, F. Wunscherfuellung und Symbolik im Maerchen. Leipzig, Deuticke, 1908.

613. Rivers, W., A. Tansley, A. Shand, T. Pear, B. Hart, and C. Myers. "The Relations of Complex and Sentiment: a Symposium." *Brit. J. Psychol.*, 13 (1922), 107–148.

614. Roffenstein, G. "Experimentelle Symboltraeume: ein Beitrag zur Diskussion ueber Psychoanalyse." *Z. Neurol. Psychiat.*, 87 (1924), 362–372.

615. Roffenstein, G. "Ueber Psychoanalyse," in "Ueber Psychoanalyse," ed.

R. Allers. *Abh. a. d. Neurol. Psychiat. Psychol. u. Grenzgeb.*, 16 (Berlin, 1922), 1–119.

616. Roffenstein, G. "Zum Problem des Unbewussten." *Z. Neurol. Psychiat.*, 80 (1923), 75–95.

617. Rogers, C. Counseling and Psychotherapy. New York, Houghton Mifflin, 1942.

618. Rorschach, H. Psychodiagnostics: a Diagnostic Test Based on Perception. Bern, Hans Huber; New York, Grune & Stratton, 1942.

619. Rosenberg, M. "Die Erinnerungstaeuschungen der reduplizierenden Paramnesie." *Z. Pathopsychol.*, 1 (1912), 561–602.

620. Rosenzweig, S. "The Experimental Study of Repression." In *Explorations in Personality*, ed. H. A. Murray (New York, Oxford, 1938), pp. 472–490.

621. Rosenzweig, S., and G. Mason. "An Experimental Study of Memory in Relation to the Theory of Repression." *Brit. J. Psychol.*, 24 (1934), 247–265.

622. Rudel, R. "The Function of the Daydream." Master thesis (directed by M. Scheerer) at the New School for Social Research, New York, 1949.

623. Ruffin, H. "Ueber die Gewinnung von Erlebnisinhalten des epileptischen Anfalls und Ausnahmezustands mit Hilfe von Wachsuggestion und Hypnose." *Deutsche Z. Nervenk.*, 107 (1909), 271–315.

624. Russell, B. Introduction to Mathematical Philosophy. New York, Macmillan, 1919.

625. Russell, B. Our Knowledge of the Outside World as a Field for Scientific Method in Philosophy. Chicago, Open Court, 1914.

626. Russell, B., and A. Whitehead. Principia Mathematica. Cambridge, England, Cambridge Univ. Press, 1910–1913.

627. Rust, Georg. Ueber die Katatonie oder das Spannungs-Irresein. Goerlitz, 1879.

628. Sachs, H. The Creative Unconscious: Studies in the Psychoanalysis of Art. Cambridge, Mass., Sci-Art, 1942.

629. Sander, F. "Experimentelle Ergebnisse der Gestaltpsychologie." *Ber. Kong. exper. Psychol.*, 10 (1928), 23–87.

630. Sartre, J. The Emotions. New York, Philosophical Library, 1948.

631. Sartre, J. The Psychology of Imagination. New York, Philosophical Library, 1948.

632. Schafer, R. The Clinical Application of Psychological Tests. Menninger Monog. 6, New York, Int. Univ. Press, 1948.

633. Schafer, R. "Psychological Tests in Clinical Research." *J. Consulting Psychol.*, 13 (1949), 328–334.

634. Schafer, R. "A Study of Thought-Processes in a Word Association Test." *Character and Personality*, 13 (1945), 212–227.

635. Schafer, R., and G. Murphy. "The Role of Autism in a Visual Figure-Ground Relationship." *J. Exp. Psychol.*, 32 (1943), 335–345.

636. Schafer, R., and D. Rapaport. "The Scatter in Diagnostic Intelligence Testing." *Character and Personality*, 12 (1944), 275–284.

637. Scheerer, M., E. Rothman, and K. Goldstein. A Case of "Idiot Savant": an Experimental Study of Personality Organization. Psychol. Monog., Vol. 58, No. 4, Washington, D.C., Amer. Psychol. Assn., 1945.

638. Schelling, F. "Ueber Mythen, historische Sagen und Philosopheme der aeltesten Welt." In *The Complete Works of Schelling, Cotta* (Stuttgart and Augsburg, 1856–1861), Vol. I, pp. 72 ff.

639. Scherner, R. Das Leben des Traumes. Berlin, Schindler, 1861.

640. Schilder, P. "Der Begriff der Demenz." *Wiener Med. Wochenschr.*, 78 (1929), 936–938.

641. Schilder, P. "Bemerkungen ueber die Psychologie des paralytischen Groessenwahns." Z. *Neurol. Psychiat.*, 74 (1922), 1–14.

642. Schilder, P. Brain and Personality. New York, Nerv. and Ment. Dis. Pub., 1931.

643. Schilder, P. "Einige Bemerkungen zu der Problemsphaere: Cortex, Stammganglien–Psyche, Neurose." Z. *Neurol. Psychiat.*, 74 (1922), 454–481.

644. Schilder, P. "Ueber Gedankenentwicklung." Z. *Neurol. Psychiat.*, 59 (1920), 250–263.

645. Schilder, P. "Der Ichkreis (ein Phaenomenologischer Versuch)." Z. *Neurol. Psychiat.*, 92 (1924), 644–654.

646. Schilder, P. The Image and Appearance of the Human Body. London, Kegan, 1935.

647. Schilder, P. Introduction to a Psychoanalytic Psychiatry. New York, Nerv. Ment. Dis. Pub., 1928.

648. Schilder, P. Medizinische Psychologie fuer Aerzte und Psychologen. Berlin, Springer, 1924.

649. Schilder, P. Mind: Perception and Thought in Their Constructive Aspects. New York, Columbia Univ. Press, 1942.

650. Schilder, P. "Psychische Symptome bei Mittel- und Zwischenhirnerkrankung." *Wiener Klin. Wochenschr.*, 40 (1927), 1147–1148.

651. Schilder, P. "Psychology and Psychopathology of Time." In *Mind: Perception and Thought* (New York, Columbia Univ. Press, 1942), pp. 213–232.

652. Schilder, P. Seele und Leben. Berlin, Springer, 1923.

653. Schilder, P. Selbstbewusstsein und Persoenlichkeitsbewusstsein. Berlin, Springer, 1914.

654. Schilder, P. "Studien ueber den Gleichgewichtsapparat." *Wiener Klin. Wochenschr.*, 31 (1918), 1350.

655. Schilder, P. Studien zur Psychologie und Symptomatologie der progressiven Paralyse. Berlin, Karger, 1930.

656. Schilder, P. "Ueber Halluzinationen." *Z. Neurol. Psychiat.*, 53 (1920), 169–178.

657. Schilder, P. "Ueber Identifizierung, auf Grund der Analyse eines Falles von Homosexualitaet." *Z. Neurol. Psychiat.*, 59 (1920), 217–249.

658. Schilder, P. "Zur Kenntnis der Psychosen bei chronischer Encephalitis epidemica." *Z. Neurol. Psychiat.*, 118 (1929), 327–345.

659. Schilder, P. Ueber das Wesen der Hypnose. Berlin, Springer, 1922.

660. Schilder, P. "Das Unbewusste." *Z. Neurol. Psychiat.*, 80 (1922), 96–116.

661. Schilder, P. "The Vestibular Apparatus in Neurosis and Psychosis." *J. Nerv. Ment. Dis.*, 78 (1933), 1–137.

662. Schilder, P. "Westibulo-Optik und Koerperschema in der Alkoholhalluzinose." *Z. Neurol. Psychiat.*, 128 (1930), 784–791.

663. Schilder, P. Wahn und Erkenntnis. Berlin, Springer, 1918.

664. Schilder, P. "Zur Lehre von den Amnesien Epileptischer, von der Schlafmittelhypnose und vom Gedaechtnis." *Arch. Psychiat. Nervenk.*, 72 (1924), 323–325.

665. Schilder, P. "Zur Pathologie des Ichideals." *Int. Z. Psa.*, 8 (1922), 322–325.

666. Schilder, P. "Zur Psychologie epileptischer Ausnahmezusteande (mit besonderen Beruecksichtigung des Gedaechtnisses)." *Allg. Z. Psychiat.*, 80 (1924), 33–39.

667. Schilder, P., and C. Kauders. Hypnosis. New York, Nerv. and Ment. Dis. Pub., 1927.

668. Schilder, P. "Zur Kenntnis symbolaehnlicher Bildungen im Rahmen der Schizophrenie." *Z. Neurol. Psychiat.*, 26 (1914), 201–244.

669. Schiller, F. "Das verschleierte Bild zu Sais." In *Saemtliche Werke* (Stuttgart, Cotta, 1847).

670. Schiller, P. "A Configurational Theory of Puzzles and Jokes." *J. Gen. Psychol.*, 18 (1928), 217–234.

671. Schmideberg, M. "On Motoring and Walking." *Int. J. Psa.*, 18 (1937), 42–53.

672. Schneirla, A. "Army-Ant Life and Behavior under Dry-Season Conditions with Special Reference to Reproductive Functions, II." *Zoologica*, 33 (1948), 89–112.

673. Schroedinger, E. What Is Life? New York, Macmillan, 1947.

674. Schroetter, K. "Experimentelle Traeume." *Zentralblatt f. Psa.*, 2 (1911), 638–648.

675. Schwartz, G. "Ueber Rueckfaelligkeit bei Umgewohnung, I: Ruckfalltendenz und Verwechslungsgefahr," *Psychol. Forsch.*, 9 (1927), 86–158.

"II: Ueber Handlungsganzheiten und ihre Bedeutung fuer die Ruckfaelligkeit," *ibid.*, 16 (1934), 143–190.

676. Sears, R. Survey of Objective Studies of Psychoanalytic Concepts. New York, Soc. Sci. Research Council, Bull. 51, 1943.

677. Seeleman, V. The Influence of Attitude upon the Remembering of Pictorial Material. New York, *Arch. Psychol.* No. 258, 1940.

678. Selz, O. "Die Gesetze der produktiven Taetigkeit." *Arch. Psychol.*, 27 (1913), 367–380.

679. Selz, O. Ueber die Gesetze des geordneten Denkverlaufs. Bonn, Cohen, 1913.

680. Selz, O. Zur Psychologie des produktiven Denkens: eine experimentelle Untersuchung. Bonn, Cohen, 1922.

681. Shakow, D. The Nature of Deterioration in Schizophrenic Conditions. New York, Nerv. and Ment. Dis. Pub., 1947.

682. Sharpe, E. Dream Analysis. London, Hogarth, 1949.

683. Sharpe, E. "Similar and Divergent Unconscious Determinants Underlying the Sublimations of Pure Art and Pure Science." *Int. J. Psa.*, 16 (1935), 186–202.

684. Sherif, M. A Study of Some Social Factors in Perception. New York, *Arch. Psychol.*, No. 187, 1935.

685. Sherif, M., and H. Cantril. "The Psychology of 'Attitudes.'" *Psychol. Rev.*, 52 (1945), 295–315; 53 (1946), 1–21.

686. Sherif, M., and H. Cantril. The Psychology of Ego-Involvements. London, Chapman & Hall; New York, Wiley, 1947.

687. Sidis, B. The Psychology of Suggestion. New York, Appleton, 1907.

688. Sigmar, J. "Ueber die Hemmungen bei der Realisation eines Willensaktes." *Arch. Psychol.*, 52 (1925), 91–176.

689. Silberer, H. "Bericht ueber eine Methode, gewisse symbolische Halluzinations-Erscheinungen hervorzurufen und zu beobachten." *Jhb. Psa. Psychopath. Forsch.*, 1 (1909), 513–525.

690. Silberer, H. "Phantasie und Mythos." *Jhb. Psa. Psychopath. Forsch.*, 1 (1910), 541–603.

691. Silberer, H. "Symbolik des Erwachens und Schwellensymbolik ueberhaupt." *Jhb. Psa. Psychopath. Forsch.*, 3 (1912), 621–660.

692. Silberer, H. Der Traum: Einfuehrung in die Traumpsychologie. Stuttgart, Enke, 1919.

693. Silberer, H. Zur Symbolbildung. *Jhb. Psa. Psychopath. Forsch.*, 4 (1912), 607–683.

694. Silberer, H. Ueber die Symbolbildung. *Jhb. Psa. Psychopath. Forsch.*, 3 (1912), 661–723.

695. Simpson, G. The Meaning of Evolution. New Haven, Conn., Yale Univ. Press, 1939.

696. Simpson, G. "The Problem of Plan and Purpose in Nature." *Sci. Monthly*, 44 (1947), 481–495.

697. Sittig, O. "Beitrag zur Kasuistik und psychologischen Analyse der reduplizierender Paremnesie." Z. *Pathopsychol.*, 2 (1914), 162–180.

698. Sommer, W. "Zur Lehre von der 'Hemmung' geistiger Vorgaenge." *Allg. Z. Psychiat.*, 50 (1894), 234–257.

699. Spencer, H. Principles of Psychology. New York, Appleton, 1871. Vol. I.

700. Spielrein, S. "Die Zeit im unterschwelligen Seelenleben." *Imago*, 9 (1923), 300–317.

701. Spranger, E. Psychologie des Jugendalters. Leipzig, Quelle and Meyer, 1924.

702. Stauffenberg, J. von. "Klinische und anatomische Beitraege zur Kenntnis der aphasischen, agnostischen und apraktischen Symptome." Z. *Neurol. Psychiat.*, 39 (1918), 71–213.

703. Stein, M., and Buerger-Prinz, H. "Ueber die veraenderte Erregbarkeit bei zentralen optischen Stoerungen." *Arch. Psychiat.*, 86 (1929), 322.

704. Steinthal, E. "Ein eigenartiger Fall Korsakowscher Psychose." Z. *Neurol. Psychiat.*, 67 (1921), 287–310.

705. Stekel, W. "In Memoriam Herbert Silberer." *Fortschr. Sexualwiss. und Psa.*, 1 (1924), 408–420.

706. Stekel, W. "Polyphonie des Denkens." *Fortschr. Sexualwiss. und Psa.*, 1 (1924), 1–16.

707. Stekel, W. Die Sprache des Traumes. Wiesbaden, Bergman, 1911.

708. Stengel, E. "On the Aetiology of the Fugue States." *J. Ment. Sci.*, 87 (1941), 572–599.

709. Stern, R. "Ueber die Aufhellung von Amnesien bei pathologischen Rauschzustaenden." Z. *Neurol. Psychiat.*, 108 (1927), 601–624.

710. Stern, W. General Psychology from the Personalistic Standpoint. New York, Macmillan, 1938.

711. Stern, W. Psychology of Early Childhood up to the Sixth Year of Age. New York, Holt, 1930.

712. Stern, C., and W. Stern. Monographien ueber die seelische Entwicklung des Kindes, I: Die Kindersprache (Leipzig, 1907), Barth. II: Erinnerung, Aussage und Luege in der ersten Kindheit. (Leipzig, Barth, 1909).

713. Stockert, F. Ueber Umbau und Abbau der Sprache bei Geistesstoerung. Berlin, Karger, 1929.

714. Stoerring, F. "Experimentelle und psychopathologische Untersuchungen ueber das Bewusstsein der Gueltigkeit." *Arch. Psychol.*, 14 (1909), 1–42.

715. Stoerring, G. "Ueber den ersten reinen Fall eines Menschen mit voelligem isoliertem Verlust der Merkfaehigkeit." *Arch. Psychol.*, 81 (1931), 257–284.

716. Storch, A. The Primitive Archaic Forms of Inner Experience and Thought in Schizophrenia. New York, Nerv. and Ment. Dis. Pub., 1924.

717. Straecke, J. "Neue Traumexperimente im Zusammenhang mit aelteren und neueren Traumtheorien." *Jhrb. Psa. Psychopath. Forsch.*, 5 (1913), 233-306.

718. Staercke, A. "Die Rolle der analen und oralen Quantitaeten im Verfolgungswahn und in analogen Systemgedanken." *Int. Z. Psa.*, 21 (1935), 5-22.

719. Stransky, E. Ueber Sprachverwirrtheit. Halle, Marhold, 1905.

720. Straus, E. On Obsession. New York, Nerv. and Ment. Dis. Pub., 1948.

721. Straus, E. Vom Sinn der Sinne, ein Beitrag zur Grundlegung der Psychologie. Berlin, Springer, 1935.

722. Strecker, E. Fundamentals of Psychiatry. 2d ed. Philadelphia, Lippincott, 1944.

723. Strohmayer, W. "Angeborene und im fruehen Kindesalter erworbene Schwachsinnszustaende." In Bumke's *Handbuch der Geisteskrankheiten*, X (1928), 1-192.

724. Stumpf, C. Erscheinungen und psychische Funktionen. Berlin, Reimer, 1907.

725. Sullivan, H. Conceptions of Modern Psychiatry. Reprinted from *Psychiatry*, Vol. III, No. 1, 1940, and Vol. VIII, No. 2, 1945.

726. Sullivan, H. "The Language of Schizophrenia." In *Language and Thought in Schizophrenia*, collected papers ed. J. S. Kasanin (Berkeley, Univ. of Calif. Press, 1944), pp. 4-16.

727. Swoboda, H. Studien zur Grundlegung der Psychologie. Leipzig, Deuticke, 1905.

728. Tausk, V. "On the Origin of the 'Influencing Machine' in Schizophrenia." *Psa. Quart.*, 2 (1933), 519-556.

729. Thorpe, W. "The Modern Concept of Instinctive Behavior." *Bull. Animal Behaviour*, 7 (1948), 12.

730a. Titchener, E. Lectures on the Experimental Psychology of the Thought-Processes. New York, Macmillan, 1909.

730b. Titchener, E. Lectures on the Elementary Psychology of Feeling and Attention. New York, Macmillan, 1908.

731. Tolman, E. "Behaviorism and Purpose." *J. Phil.*, 22 (1925), 36-42.

732. Tolman, E. Purposive Behavior in Animals and Men. Berkeley, Univ. of Calif. Press, 1932.

733. Tolman, E. "There Is More than One Kind of Learning." *Psychol. Rev.*, 56 (1949), 144-156.

734. Tresselt, M., and B. Levy. "Recognition for Ego-Involved Materials." *J. Psychol.*, 27 (1949), 73-78.

735. Troemner, E. Hypnotismus und Suggestion. Leipzig and Berlin, Teubner, 1913.

736. Tuczek, F. "Ueber Begriff und Bedeutung der Demenz." *Monatschr. Psychiat. Neurol.*, 14 (1903), 1-16.

737. Uexkuell, J. Theoretical Biology. New York, Harcourt, Brace, 1926.

738. Uexkuell, J., and G. Kriszat. Streifzuege durch die Umwelten von Tieren und Menschen. Berlin, Springer, 1934.

739. Varendonck, J. Ueber das vorbewusste phantasierende Denken. Vienna, Int. Psa. Verlag, 1922.

740. Varendonck, J. The Psychology of Daydreams. New York, Macmillan, 1921.

741. Vaschide, N. "Les Recherches expérimentelles sur les rêves." *Rev. Psychiat.*, 5 (1902), 145–164.

742. Vigotsky, L. "Thought and Speech." *Psychiatry*, 2 (1939), 29–54.

743. Vigotsky, L. "Thought in Schizophrenia." *Arch. Neurol. Psychiat.*, 31 (1934), 1063–1077.

744. Vold, J. "Einige Experimente ueber Gesichtsbilder im Traume." *Z. Psychol.*, 13 (1896), 66–74.

745. Waelder, R. "The Principle of Multiple Function: Observations on Over-Determination." *Psa. Quart.*, 5 (1936), 45–62.

746. Waelder, R. "The Problem of Freedom in Psychoanalysis and the Problem of Reality-Testing." *Int. J. Psa.*, 17 (1936), 89–108.

747. Waelder, R. "Ueber schizophrenes und schoepferisches Denken." *Int. Z. Psa.*, 12 (1926), 298–308.

748. Wagner-Jauregg, J. "Ueber einige Erscheinungen im Bereiche des Zentral-nervensystems, welche nach Wiederbelebung Erhaengter beobachtet werden." *Jhb. Psychiat. Neurol.*, 8 (1889), 313–332.

749. Wallas, G. The Art of Thought. New York, Harcourt, Brace, 1926.

750. Washburn, M. Movement and Mental Imagery. Boston and New York, Houghton Mifflin, 1916.

751. Watt, H. "Experimentelle Beitraege zu einer Theorie des Denkens." *Arch. Psychol.*, 4 (1905), 289–436.

752. Weigert-Vowinckel, E. "A Contribution to the Theory of Schizophrenia." *Int. J. Psa.*, 17 (1936), 190–201.

753. Weigl, E. "On the Psychology of So-called Processes of Abstraction." *J. Abn. Soc. Psychol.*, 36 (1941), 3–33.

754. Weininger, O. Sex and Character. New York, Putnam, 1914.

755. Werner, H. Comparative Psychology of Mental Development. New York, Harper, 1940.

756. Werner, H. "Development of Visuo-Motor Performance on the Marble Board Test in Mentally Retarded Children." *J. Gen. Psychol.*, 64 (1944), 269–279.

757. Werner, H. "Perceptual Behavior of Brain-Injured Children." Gen. Psychol. Monog., No. 31 (1945), pp. 51–110.

758. Werner, H. "Studien ueber Strukturgesetze, I: Ueber das Problem der motorischen Gestaltung." Z. Psychol., 94 (1924), 265.

759. Werner, H. "Thought Disturbance with Reference to Figure-Background Impairment in Brain-Injured Children." Confinia Neurologica, 9 (1949), 255–263.

760. Werner, H., and E. Lagercrantz. "Experimentell-psychologische Studien ueber die Struktur des Wortes." Z. Psychol., 95 (1924), 316–363.

761. Wernicke, C. Grundriss der Psychiatrie. Leipzig, Barth, 1900.

762. Wertheimer, M. "Gestalt Theory." Soc. Research, 11 (1944), 78–99.

763. Wertheimer, M. Productive Thinking. New York, Harper, 1945.

764. Wertheimer, M. "Untersuchungen zur Lehre von der Gestalt, II." Psychol. Forsch., 4 (1923), 301–350.

765. Westphal, K. "Haupt-und Nebenaufgaben bei Reaktionsversuchen." Arch. Psychol., 21 (1911), 219–434.

766. Westphal, K. "Ueber reduplizierende Paramnesie (Pick) und verwandte Symptome bei progressiver Paralyse." Z. Neurol. Psychiat., 110 (1927), 585–607.

767. White, R. "A Preface to the Theory of Hypnotism." J. Abn. Soc. Psychol., 36 (1941), 477–505.

768. White, W. A. Outlines of Psychiatry. New York, Nerv. and Ment. Dis. Pub., 1935.

769. White, W. A., and B. Sidis. Mental Dissociation in Alcoholic Psychosis. Stacket, 1902.

770. Wiener, N. Cybernetics. New York, Wiley, 1949.

771. Williams, H., and C. Rupp. "Observations on Confabulation." Amer. J. Psychiat., 95 (1938), 395–405.

772. Willwoll, A. "Begriffsbildung: eine psychologische Untersuchung." Psychologische Monog., No. 1 (1926), pp. 4–144.

773. Windelband, W. A History of Philosophy. 2d ed., rev. New York, Macmillan, 1901.

774. Winterstein, A. "Angst vor dem Neuen, Neugier und Langeweile." Psa. Bewegung, 2 (1930), 540–554.

775. Wolberg, L. Hypnoanalysis. New York, Grune & Stratton, 1945.

776. Wolberg, L. Medical Hypnosis. 2 vols. Vol. I, The Principles of Hypnotherapy. Vol. II, The Practice of Hypnotherapy. New York, Grune & Stratton, 1948.

777. Woodrow, H. The Measurement of Attention by Reactions to a Change in Intensity. Psychol. Monog., Vol. 17, No. 76, Princeton, N.J., Psychological Review Co., 1914.

778. Wundt, W. Principles of Physiological Psychology. New York, Macmillan, 1904.

779. Wundt, W. "Ueber Ausfrageexperimente und ueber die Methoden zur Psychologie des Denkens." *Psychol. Studien*, 3 (1907), 301–360.

780. Young, P. "Experimental Hypnotism: a Review." *Psychol. Bull.*, 38 (1941), 92–104.

781. Young, P. Emotion in Man and Animal. New York, Wiley, 1943.

782. Young, P. "Food-Seeking Drive, Affective Process, and Learning." *Psychol. Rev.*, 56 (1949), 98–121.

783. Zeigarnik, B. "Ueber das Behalten von erledigten und unerledigten Handlungen." *Psychol. Forsch.*, 9 (1927), 1–85.

784. Zeller, E. History of Greek Philosophy. London, Longmans, Green, 1881.

785. Ziehen, T. Prinzipien und Methoden der Intelligenzpruefung. Berlin, Karger, 1908.

786. Ziehen, T. "Ueber Stoerungen des Vorstellungsablaufes bei Paranoia." *Arch. Psychiat. Nervenk.*, 24 (1892), 112–154.

787. Ziehen, T. Das Verhaeltnis der Herbartschen Psychologie zur physiologisch-experimentellen Psychologie. Berlin, Reuther and Reichard, 1900.

NAME INDEX

SUBJECT INDEX